The Development of European Private Law in a Multilevel Legal Order

Esther
van Schagen

The Development of European Private Law in a Multilevel Legal Order

intersentia

METRO

Intersentia Ltd
Sheraton House | Castle Park
Cambridge | CB3 0AX | United Kingdom
Tel.: +44 1223 370 170 | Fax: +44 1223 370 169
Email: mail@intersentia.co.uk
www.intersentia.com | www.intersentia.co.uk

Distribution for the UK and Ireland:
NBN International
Airport Business Centre, 10 Thornbury Road
Plymouth, PL6 7 PP
United Kingdom
Tel.: +44 1752 202 301 | Fax: +44 1752 202 331
Email: orders@nbninternational.com

Distribution for Europe and all other countries:
Intersentia Publishing nv
Groenstraat 31
2640 Mortsel
Belgium
Tel.: +32 3 680 15 50 | Fax: +32 3 658 71 21
Email: mail@intersentia.be

Distribution for the USA and Canada:
International Specialized Book Services
920 NE 58th Ave. Suite 300
Portland, OR 97213
USA
Tel.: +1 800 944 6190 (toll free) | Fax: +1 503 280 8832
Email: info@isbs.com

The Development of European Private Law in a Multilevel Legal Order

ISBN 978-1-78068-367-6
D/2016/7849/8
NUR 822

British Library Cataloguing in Publication Data. A catalogue record for this book is available from the British Library.

CONTENTS

Chapter 1

INTRODUCTION

1.1. Introduction

As transnational trade has developed, national legislators and courts can exercise less control over the conduct of legal persons trading beyond their territory. National legislators and courts may also not be familiar with the needs and preferences of international actors. These developments necessitate the creation of transnational rules. Consequently, more actors[1] have become involved in the development of private law in the European Union, i.e. the area of material[2] law[3] that stipulates transactions between

1 The actors considered in this book can be divided into state actors, including national legislators and courts, as well as the European legislator, the CJEU, international organisations, and non-state actors, including stakeholder groups, academics and private parties (contract parties and other parties relying on private law). "Private parties" is a large, diverse group that consists of parties who are directly or indirectly involved in entering into transactions through private law. Private parties are an extensive group, including contracting parties, tortfeasors and their victims, owners, tenants, employers and employees, but also third parties whose rights are affected by other parties' transactions. Private parties realistically include legal practitioners advising and representing them. In addition, private parties may also be represented by stakeholder associations. Typically, these stakeholder groups enable private parties to inform themselves of ongoing developments and organise themselves, trying to influence the development of private law by legislators.

2 The focus of this book is not on 'procedural' law. See for a definition L. Del Duca, 'Developing global transnational harmonisation procedures for the twenty-first century: the accelerating pace of common and civil law convergence', 42 *Texas International Law Journal* 2006–2007, p. 658.

3 Law includes both hard law and other rules, referred to as alternative regulation (comp. I. Giesen, 'Alternatieve regelgeving in privaatrechtelijke verhoudingen', in: *Alternatieve regelgeving, Handelingen Nederlandse Juristen Vereniging* 2007-I, p. 73: all rules that are not normal rules, i.e. rules that are established by the legislator. Accordingly, alternative regulation includes soft law (norms without legally binding force which may affect parties' behaviour: Comp. L. Senden, *Soft law in European Community Law*, Portland: Hart 2004, p. 111–112), co-regulation, which involves both the cooperation between public and private actors in the making of new rules, and the reinforcement of rules negotiated by stakeholders with hard law, while these forms cannot be characterised as traditional legislation from the state. (Comp. also for a definition of co-regulation Ph. Eijlander, 'Possibilities and constraints in the use of self-regulation and co-regulation in legislative policy: Experiences in The Netherlands – Lessons to be learned for the EU?' *EJCL* 2005, p. 3.) Alternative regulation further incudes self-regulation, which can be understood as the making of rules and norms by both by contract parties or a group of persons or bodies binding contract parties or this

legal persons.[4] Accordingly, the European legislator[5] has increasingly harmonised parts of private law.

Thus, the development of private law in the European Union entails the involvement of multiple actors, and increasingly complex processes through which private law is developed. This may be beneficial for private law for various reasons. It has been argued that Europeanisation enables Member States, the Union and other actors to learn from one another.[6] Similarly, the development of regulatory competition, which should provide states with an additional incentive to develop rules that are attractive to foreign investors, has been defended.[7] Yet problems may also develop as actors maintain a nationalist approach towards the development of private law. This approach, criticised as methodological nationalism,[8] is visible also at the European level. However, the use of codification-like instruments such as the DCFR is hardly uncontroversial.[9] The shortcomings in the debate[10] preceding the development of the DCFR and other European measures that develop a horizontal approach, such as the since withdrawn proposal for a Common European Sales Law[11] (hereafter: 'CESL') and Directive 2011/83 on consumer rights, have not helped to decrease controversy. These potential benefits and problems give rise to the main question in this book: is the involvement of multiple actors in the development of European private law problematic, or can it also be beneficial for European private law?

The answer this question this book will rely on theories that have taken the coexistence of actors in the European Union as a starting point, most prominently multilevel

group, and often, but not necessarily, other private actors that choose to be bound by the rules made through self-regulation. In German debate, the term 'alternative regulation' has not been used in this context. Instead, authors have considered 'privatised lawmaking' ('*privatisierte Rechtssetzung*'), 'civil rule-making' ('*zivile Regelsetzung*') and private governance, see J. Köndgen, 'Privatisierung des Rechts', *AcP* 2006, p. 481, or G. Bachmann, *Private Ordnung. Grundlagen ziviler Regelsetzung*, Tübingen: Mohr Siebeck 2006, p. 4 who refers to both 'private governance' and self-regulation when discussing privately developed rules.

4 This definition does not mean this thesis is limited to contract law. Parties may also enter into transactions when a tortfeasor is paying damages to a victim. Also, private law may impose restrictions on the freedom of parties to enter into transactions; mandatory law may be in accordance with society's legal views on justice, for example when restrictions are imposed because one party is not capable of sufficiently protecting his interests. See further on society's legal views on justice par. 2.5.1. European private law, or private law in the European Union, refers to law developed at international, European and national level. The book focuses particularly on private law in the Dutch and German legal order, including relevant European law and treaties.

5 This book will focus on the coexistence of European and national state and non-state actors involved in the development of European private law. See more on this limitation, par. 1.8.

6 O. Gerstenberg, 'Private law and the new European constitutional settlement', *ELJ* 2004, p. 786. Comp. N. Walker, 'The idea of constitutional pluralism', *MLR* 2002, p. 358–359.

7 G. Rühl, 'Regulatory competition in contract law: Empirical evidence and normative implications', *ERCL* 2013, p. 61.

8 See further on this par. 1.5.

9 See for example R. Zimmerman, N. Jansen, '"A European Civil Code in all but name": Discussing the nature and purposes of the Draft Common Frame of Reference', *CLJ* 2010, p. 98.

10 W. Doralt, 'Strukturelle Schwäche in der Europäisierung des Privatrechts', *RabelsZ* 2011, p. 260.

11 COM (2011) 635 final.

governance, discussed in paragraph 1.2 and legal pluralism, discussed in paragraph 1.3. Paragraph 1.4. will compare multilevel governance and pluralism perspectives. Paragraph 1.5. will set out how multilevel governance theories can provide an answer to the question whether the coexistence of actors is detrimental for European private law. Paragraph 1.6. will sketch how pluralism insights may provide an answer to the question whether the coexistence of actors is beneficial for European private law. Paragraph 1.7. will defend interaction in the form of deliberation. Paragraph 1.8. will sum up the limitations in this book, and paragraph 1.9. will sketch the outlook for the book, before turning to the methodology in paragraph 1.10.

1.2. Multilevel governance

Multilevel governance perspectives analyse the European legal order in a descriptive manner. In political science, the debate on multilevel governance has emphasised the coexistence of actors, and the interaction and interdependence between actors, as becomes clear from the well-established definition of multilevel governance by Marks:[12]

12 G. Marks, 'Structural policy and multilevel governance in the EC', in: A. Cafruny, G. Rosenthal (eds.), *The state of the European Community Vol. 2: The Maastricht debates and beyond*, Boulder: Rienner 1993, p. 392. This analysis has been developed specifically for the European legal order and is better suited to analyse the development of European private law than other concepts, which this book will not focus on. Some of these concepts focus on the international level. Accordingly, multi-perspectival governance, see for example J.G. Ruggie, 'Territoriality and Beyond: Problematizing Modernity in International Relations', *International Organization* 1993, p. 139, focusses on the development of the EU from the perspective of international relations. The concept of 'fragmegration' (also: 'spheres of authority'), from J. Rosenau, *Along the domestic-foreign frontier. Exploring governance in a turbulent world*, Cambridge: CUP 1997, p. 38, also describes simultaneous integration and fragmentation, where the distinction between domestic and foreign problems have become less clear-cut, highlighting the disaggregation of global governance. Other concepts have been developed in a different context. For example, "polycentric governance" has been developed to analyse U.S. metropolitan decision-making. Already in 1961, empirical studies led V. Ostrom, C.M. Tiebout, R. Warren, 'The organization of government in metropolitan areas: A theoretical inquiry', *American Political Science Review* 1961, p. 831 to develop this concept, which they defined as follows: 'many centers of decision-making which are formally independent of each other. Whether they actually function independently, or instead constitute an inter-dependent system of relations, is an empirical question in particular cases. To the extent that they take each other into account in competitive relationships, enter into various contractual and cooperative undertakings or have recourse to central mechanisms to resolve conflicts, the various political jurisdictions in a metropolitan area may function in a coherent manner with consistent and predictable patterns of interacting behaviour. To the extent that this is so, they may be said to function as a "system." Another perspectives that is not considered in depth is the concept of "Functional, Overlapping, and Competing Jurisdictions', developed by B.S. Frey, R. Eichenberger, *The New Democratic Federalism for Europe. Functional, Overlapping, and Competing Jurisdictions*, Cheltenham: Elgar 1999. This perspective adopts a functional approach, arguing for new institutional arrangements, according to which various units are constituted to perform a specific task. It is difficult to imagine how this could be applied to the development of general national private law, which is not particularly problem-oriented. Such a perspective, if applied consistently to the development of private law, would likely necessitate rigorous changes at the national level, which falls beyond the scope of this book. The main focus of this book is on analysing the development of European private law, and while the book (see further chapter 10) does study techniques to be used in addition to or instead of currently used "techniques" (on the definition of which see further

'a system of continuous negotiation among nested governments at several territorial tiers – supranational, national, regional, and local – as the result of a broad process of institutional creation and decisional reallocation that has pulled some previously centralized functions of the state up to the supranational level.'

According to this description, the authority of the state has been fragmented: upwards, especially to the European Union,[13] as well as international actors, downwards, to sub-national actors, and sideways, to non-governmental actors.[14] Multilevel governance thus emphasises developments in which the roles of governments across levels change and become interdependent.

According to the discourse on multilevel governance, this multilevel legal order is characterised by interdependence and interaction. Scott[15] has analysed the interdependence between state actors and between state and non-state actors from the perspective of key resources, such as financial resources, expertise, organisational capacities and even legal competence, that have been fragmented between these actors. Interdependence is particularly visible in cases where the Union and its Member States undermine one another. According to Scharpf,[16] Member States and the Union will be motivated to undermine one another especially when their interests diverge.[17]

The increasing interdependence between actors necessitates interaction between actors,[18] which for example becomes visible in the prejudicial procedure under article 267 TFEU, where the CJEU and national courts need to interact with one another to ensure the correct interpretation of the *acquis*. Similarly, the interdependence between state actors and non-state actors leads to more interaction, as becomes visible in the interaction between non-state actors and the European legislator in the development and review of Directives.[19]

par. 1.5.), this does not include suggesting techniques that could be used to replace codifications, blanket clauses or general principles that currently play a prominent role in the development of European private law. Changing these techniques is not only politically unfeasible, it is also problematic from a constitutional point of view, at least for the Dutch legal order.

13 This book focuses on the European legal order, which refers to the competences of and relations between Member States and the Union, as well as international organisations and non-state actors, based on national constitutions, the TFEU and the TEU, treaties, and the law, in particular European private law, established in accordance with these constitutions and Treaties.

14 L. Hooghe, G. Marks, 'Unravelling the central state, but how? Types of multi-level governance', *American Political Science Review* 2003, p. 233. This book focuses on the reallocation of competences to the European level and to non-state actors rather than the allocation of competences to sub-national actors, see further par. 1.8.

15 C. Scott, 'Analysing regulatory space: fragmented resources and institutional design', *PL* 2001, p. 329.

16 F.W. Scharpf, *Governing in Europe: Effective and democratic?*, Oxford: OUP 1999, p. 191.

17 Comp. L.A.J. Senden, 'De lidstaten en de kwaliteit van Europese wetgeving: geen consumenten, maar co-actoren', *SEW* 2006, p. 47.

18 Comp. J. Neyer, 'Discourse and order in the EU: A deliberative approach to multi-level governance', *JCMS* 2003, p. 689, who points to the interdependence between the European institutions as well as the interdependence between Member States seeking to affect European Union policies.

19 For example the involvement of the ISDA and its 2000 report on collateral arrangements in the European financial market, available at www.isda.org/c_and_a/pdf/NeedLawReform.pdf, in the drafting of Directive 2002/47 on financial collateral arrangements.

The increased role of non-state actors is also visible in the development of co-regulation and self-regulation at the European level.[20] The development of co-regulation, self-regulation and other "soft" alternatives to law are sometimes characterised as "governance", in contrast to "government", the development of hard law.[21] However, this contrast has been criticised[22] and there is wide disagreement on the definition of governance.[23] In this book, "governance" can be defined as 'rules, procedures and behaviour that affect the way in which powers are exercised'.[24]

1.3. Pluralism

In European private law, both European and national actors, as well as non-state actors, develop rules that claim authority and guide individuals' behaviour. Accordingly, pluralist accounts of European private law have been defended. Legal pluralism recognises that within the same space, various actors that claim some form of authority have developed rules that may overlap.[25] Pluralism can take many forms: "strong" or "radical" pluralism emphasises heterarchy rather than hierarchy, which may also imply the absence of an overarching framework. "Weak" or "moderate" pluralism does recognise the coexistence of actors, but within a framework, for example, different actors operating within a legal order.[26] Defenses of legal pluralism can range from weak to strong pluralism.[27]

20 For example in the involvement of the IASB in the development of international accounting standards under Regulation 1606/2002, see further par. 7.4.1.1.

21 J. Scott, D. Trubek, 'Mind the gap: Law and new approaches to governance', *ELJ* 2002, p. 1.

22 Ch. Möllers, 'European governance, meaning and value of a concept', *CMLR* 2006, p. 313.

23 See on the potential meanings of governance F. Möslein, K. Riesenhuber, 'Contract governance – a draft research agenda', *ERCL* 2009, p. 251, with further references.

24 Comp. European Commission, *European governance, a white paper*, COM (2001) 428 final.

25 Comp. the definition of L. Miller, *The emergence of EU contract law: Exploring Europeanization*, Oxford: OUP 2011, p. 166: 'the co-existence of different bodies of norms within the same social space'. J.M. Smits, 'A radical view of legal pluralism', in: L. Niglia (ed.), *Pluralism in Europe*, Oxford: Hart 2013, p. 161, has referred to pluralism as 'different equally valid claims to legal authority have come to exist, leading to different bodies of law that partly overlap and conflict with each other in governing the same acts and actors'. In accordance with the focus of this book on the development of multiple actors involved in the development of European private law, the definition of pluralism in this book focusses on the coexistence of actors, which typically, but not necessarily, leads to the coexistence of overlapping sets of rules.

26 See for a discussion on the various forms of pluralism N. Krisch, *Beyond constitutionalism: The pluralist structure of postnational law*, Oxford: OUP 2010, p. 71 et seq, who distinguishes between "strong" and "weak", or "radical" "moderate" forms of pluralism. See for a discussion on constitutional pluralism M. Avbelj, J. Komárek (eds.), *Four visions of constitutional pluralism*, EUI Working Paper 2008/21, with further references.

27 This paragraph points out which arguments have generally been defended by pluralists, rather than distinguishing whether these arguments are in accordance with "weak" or "strong" pluralism, or which authors have defended which arguments. Under pluralism, many, even contrary arguments, can be defended, and the views described here are accordingly not defended by all 'pluralist' authors, who freely disagree with one another on various topics.

Pluralism theories have adopted a normative perspective,[28] defending that the coexistence of actors is beneficial for the following reasons.

Firstly, it has been argued that the multilevel legal order, where various actors coexist, is better suited to develop rules responsively to divergent preferences.

On the one hand, it has been argued that the coexistence of actors at different levels is beneficial. Krisch[29] finds that the development of "checks and balances" where actors can challenge one another's decision-making is beneficial. According to his argument, transnational actors are better placed to develop rules in accordance with transnational preferences and practice, but national actors are situated more closely to their constituency. According to Cohen and Sabel,[30] reallocating decision-making to various levels and between various actors at similar levels, combined with strict constitutional limits, can be beneficial as such reallocation limits the power of national and European state actors.

The reallocation of competences to the European level and the development of checks and balances may in addition enhance the responsiveness of national law. Specifically, actors at the European level may prevent that national decision-makers displace costs and disadvantages of their decisions to actors who are not able to influence these decisions, which motivates these national actors not to weigh costs and benefits evenly in their decision-making. Joerges[31] has found that European law obliges Member States to also take into account the interests of foreign interested parties that do not have a say in national democratic processes.

On the other hand, it has been argued that the coexistence of national actors developing divergent laws may be beneficial. In European private law, it has been defended that the coexistence of national actors developing divergent private laws is beneficial as the differences reflect various legal views on social justice.[32] This perspective stresses that harmonised law is also closely intertwined with general contract law. Consequently, it has been doubted whether harmonisation will be successful even if it is attempted.[33]

28 P.S. Berman, 'Global legal pluralism', *Southern California Law Review* 2007, p. 1159, L. Miller, *The emergence of EU contract law: Exploring Europeanization*, Oxford: OUP 2011, p. 193.

29 N. Krisch, *Beyond constitutionalism: The pluralist structure of postnational law*, Oxford: OUP 2010, p. 70.

30 J. Cohen, Ch. Sabel, 'Directly-deliberative polyarchy', *ELJ* 1997, p. 314. Comp. similarly B.R. Weingast, 'The economic role of political institutions: Market preserving federalism and economic development', *Journal of Law, Economics and Organization* 1995, p. 6. Comp. N. Walker, 'The idea of constitutional pluralism', *MLR* 2002, p. 337, who notes that pluralism is associated with a normative claim based on mutual respect and recognition between national and supranational actors.

31 Ch. Joerges, 'On the legitimacy of Europeanising private law: Considerations on a justice-making law for the EU multi-level system', *Electronic Journal of Comparative Law* 2003, par. III.1.2., available at www.ejcl.org/ejcl/73/art73-3.html. Comp. B.S. Frey, R. Eichenberger, *The New Democratic Federalism for Europe. Functional, Overlapping, and Competing Jurisdictions*, Cheltenham: Elgar 1999, p. 10–11 who defend the development of overlapping, functionally oriented jurisdictions that also overlap (hereafter: 'FOCJ'). In FOCJs, all costs are not necessarily internalised, but Frey and Eichenberger point out this is also not the case in "traditional" jurisdictions.

32 For example R. Sefton-Green 'Social justice and the European identity in European contract law', *ERCL* 2006, p. 275.

33 P.S. Berman, 'Global legal pluralism', *Southern California Law Review* 2007, p. 1164.

Secondly, multiple actors provide one another with opportunities to learn from one another's experiences Gerstenberg[34] has pointed to the potential for mutual learning and experimentation as one of the advantages of the multilevel structure of European private law. Miller[35] notes that from this perspective, interaction becomes attractive in itself rather than a necessity, as a source of 'experimentation' and 'mutual learning'. These opportunities for learning within the European Union are lost, or severely limited, if private law is fully harmonised.

Thirdly, regulatory competition is also an often defended benefit of the coexistence of multiple actors. Accordingly, actors should competitively improve their laws, in accordance with private actors' preferences. Ribstein and O'Hara[36] have outlined the potential for a law market, and some Member States accordingly "advertise" their laws.[37] Esty and Geradin[38] have criticised the concept of regulatory competition and instead defended regulatory co-opetition, a combination of competition and cooperation between state actors within and across Member States and supranational state actors, as well as non-state actors. In this view, promoting cooperation within Member States, between levels and between state and non-state actors is more likely to produce innovative rules than competition between states.

Other authors have rejected the idea of regulatory competition outright, stating that it will lead to a "race to the bottom".[39] In European private law, such a race to the bottom for example could imply that Member States competitively lower standards of contractual employee protection to become more attractive jurisdictions for employers. This is implicitly recognised in articles 6 and 8 Regulation 593/2008 (hereafter: 'Rome I') that limits parties' choice of applicable law in contracts involving "weaker" parties, such as consumers or employees.

Notably, the argument for regulatory competition does not put as much emphasis on the continuing opportunities for learning,[40] as, theoretically, a 'law market' may eventually lead to the survival of an optimal set of rules.

Yet pluralism acknowledges that the coexistence of actors may also be problematic: it is detrimental for stability[41] and it may unfairly benefit already powerful actors.[42] If the law is developed in accordance with the preferences of "strong" actors, the law may

34 O. Gerstenberg, 'Private law and the new European constitutional settlement', *ELJ* 2004, p. 786. Comp. N. Walker, 'The idea of constitutional pluralism', *MLR* 2002, p. 358–359.

35 L. Miller, *The emergence of EU contract law: Exploring Europeanization*, Oxford: OUP 2011, p. 195.

36 L.E. Ribstein, E. O'Hara, *The law market*, Oxford: OUP 2009, comp. also H. Eidenmüller, 'Recht als Produkt', *JZ* 2009, p. 641.

37 For example the German initiative, at www.lawmadeingermany.de/.

38 D.C. Esty, D. Geradin, 'Regulatory co-opetition', *Journal of International Economic Law* 2000, p. 238.

39 J.W. Rutgers, 'An optional instrument and social dumping', *ERCL* 2006, p. 199.

40 L. Miller, *The emergence of EU contract law: Exploring Europeanization*, Oxford: OUP 2011, p. 195, O. Gerstenberg, 'Private law and the new European constitutional settlement', *ELJ* 2004, p. 766, 786.

41 Comp. arguments against "too much" pluralism for which coordination is needed, see for example A. Torres Perez, *Conflict of rights in the European Union, A theory of supranational adjudication*, Oxford: OUP 2009, p. 67.

42 N. Krisch, *Beyond constitutionalism: The pluralist structure of postnational law*, Oxford: OUP 2010, p. 255.

fail to sufficiently protect weak parties. Especially the lack of stability may sound familiar to private lawyers confronted with the ongoing revision and development of the private law *acquis*.[43] The argument that pluralism favours already strong actors also does not sound completely new for academics studying, for example, the development of the DCFR.[44]

1.4. Multilevel governance and pluralist perspectives compared

This book asks whether the coexistence of actors developing European private law is beneficial or problematic. Both multilevel governance and pluralists perspectives provide starting points for answering the question whether coexistence is problematic or beneficial. Pluralism perspectives and multilevel governance, while different, do not exclude one another. Various similarities can be found:

Firstly, both pluralism and multilevel governance demonstrate that the European multilevel legal order cannot be adequately characterised by formalist analyses that portray the legal system, as 'a single, unified and exclusive hierarchical normative ordering'[45] in which the state plays a central role, simply because of states' de facto power.[46] Both pluralist perspectives[47] and multilevel governance perspectives[48] recognise interdependence.

Secondly, in both the debate on multilevel governance and pluralism, it has been recognised that a sharp distinction between the European legal order and national legal orders is problematic. Van Gerven and Lierman[49] have rightly held that there is no sharp distinction between the international, European, and national legal orders; they overlap and may conflict with one another, or inspire one another. Accordingly, a clear contrast between "traditional" state law and typical "multilevel" private law is not justified. Typically, "multilevel" areas of law consist of both harmonised law and traditional national law. Accordingly, the private law *acquis* expressly leaves room for national

43 The revision of the *acquis* can be traced to COM (2001) 398 final. Almost fifteen years later, important measures – including Directive 99/44 on consumer sales, Directives 93/13 on unfair contract terms and Directive 90/314 on package travel – still need to be revised. It is not clear if and when these measures will be revised.

44 Comp. M.W. Hesselink, 'Who has a stake in European contract law?', *ERCL* 2005, p. 295–296.

45 As portrayed by J. Griffiths, 'What is legal pluralism?', *Journal of Legal Pluralism* 1986, p. 3.

46 Comp. also J.M. Smits, 'Democracy and (European) private law – A functional approach', in: M. Faure, A. van der Walt (eds.), *Globalization and private law: The way forward*, Cheltenham: Elgar 2010, p. 26, who describes private law as independent of the state, with its own rationality.

47 For example M. Delmas-Marty, *Ordering pluralism, A conceptual framework for understanding the transnational world*, Oxford: Hart 2009, p. 13, as well as N. Walker, 'The idea of constitutional pluralism', *MLR* 2002, p. 355–356.

48 For example Study Group on Social Justice in European Private Law, 'Social justice in European contract law: A manifesto', *ELJ* 2004, p. 670.

49 W. van Gerven, S. Lierman, *Algemeen Deel, Veertig jaar later*, Mechelen: Kluwer 2010, p. 33–39, similarly, L. Miller, *The emergence of EU contract law: Exploring Europeanization*, Oxford: OUP 2011, p. 155 and B. de Sousa Santos, 'Law: A map of misreading. Toward a postmodern conception of law', *Journal of Law and Society* 1987, p. 298, N. MacCormick,' Democracy, Subsidiarity, and Citizenship in the 'European Commonwealth', *Law and Philosophy* 1997, p. 336.

general contract law, national property law and national civil procedure law, in accordance with the procedural autonomy of Member States.[50]

Thirdly, both multilevel governance and pluralism recognise the development of new governance. Multilevel governance emphasise the interdependence between national and European state and non-state actors, which is reflected in new forms of governance. Pluralism criticises state-centred views and stresses the potential for interaction through new forms of governance.[51]

The pluralist perspective can however also be contrasted with multilevel governance[52] in various ways.

Firstly, pluralist perspectives emphasise that both interdependence and interaction are beneficial in and of themselves. It follows that pluralism emphasises the benefits of the coexistence of actors rather than potential problems. Any overall conclusion that coexistence of actors developing European private law is beneficial is rather generalist as it does not distinguish between areas of private law. At first sight, this argument also does not appear very appealing to private lawyers,[53] especially those who have witnessed the implementation of Directives into national codes,[54] or who have observed the European legislative process,[55] even though the advantages of comparative law are widely recognised.

In contrast, multilevel governance concludes that interaction is a necessity, considering the increasing interdependence between actors – and not necessarily, therefore, an advantage in itself. Multilevel governance also does not recognise interdependence and the corresponding need for interaction as problematic as such.[56]

50 CJEU 16 December 1976 (Rewe-Zentralfinanz eG et Rewe-Zentral AG v Landwirtschaftskammer für das Saarland), Case 33/76, [1976] ECR, p. 1989. H.-W. Micklitz, 'Monistic ideology versus pluralistic reality', in: L. Niglia (ed.), *Pluralism and European private law*, Oxford: Hart 2013, p. 47, characterises this development as "hybridization" and suggests instead the development of regulatory private law, 'reconstructing' traditional private law within the framework of nation states to a regulatory European private law as developed within the European market state. Potential for hybrisation is especially visible in the area of remedies, in which European law imposes restrictions on the procedural autonomy of Member States.

51 Comp. P.S. Berman, 'Global legal pluralism', *Southern California Law Review* 2007, p. 1196, who refers to "procedural mechanisms, institutional designs and cursive practices', which may overlap with "new" forms of governance, such as mutual recognition.

52 See however N. Reich, 'Pluralism and private law in the Union: Some thoughts on the impact of the non-discrimination principle on private autonomy', in: L. Niglia (ed.), *Pluralism and European private law*, Oxford: Hart 2013, p. 74, who finds that '[v]ertical pluralism of private law is a more specific aspect of EU law as a multilevel system of governance'. Some authors have defended both multilevel governance and pluralist perspectives, see for example Ch. Joerges, 'On the legitimacy of Europeanising private law: Considerations on a justice-making law for the EU multi-level system', *Electronic Journal of Comparative Law* 2003.

53 L. Miller, *The emergence of EU contract law: Exploring Europeanization*, Oxford: OUP 2011 does welcome pluralist insights, see for further references R. Michaels, 'Why we have no theory of European private law pluralism', in L. Niglia (ed.), *Pluralism and European private law*, Oxford: Hart 2013, p. 139.

54 For example, prominently W.H. Roth, 'Transposing pointillist EC guidelines into national systematic codes – Problems and consequences', *ERPL* 2002, p.761.

55 For example W. Doralt, 'Strukturelle Schwäche in der Europäisierung des Privatrechts', *RabelsZ* 2011, p. 260.

56 The question arises whether the detriments recognised by pluralists, i.e. the potential lack of stable and predictable development of the law and the favourism for powerful actors, can be linked to

Secondly, pluralism has criticised state-centered law.[57] In European private law, this idea has been voiced by Caruso[58] who finds that private law has furthered the 'decline of the state' as private law typically focusses on relations between equal actors. At the national level, the "state-centered" paradigm has also been criticised. Accordingly, Akkermans[59] argues that creating a new paradigm is necessary. Rather than considering law as being developed by the legislator and the courts, a new paradigm should be more in accordance with the large diversity of groups that contribute to private law and interact with one another. The development of private law in the traditional sense, through the legislator and the judiciary on the one hand, and the development of private law through self-regulation on the other hand should no longer be a primary distinction. The idea that European private law should be developed more through regulatory competition, thereby diminishing the influence of the state, has also been defended.[60]

Accounts of pluralism that argue against a "state-centered" view of law, including private law, may not be easily recognisable for traditional private lawyers. The prominent role of codifications and case law in European private law generally do give the impression that state actors retain an essential role, notwithstanding a prominent role of non-state actors and interdependence between national and European actors. After all, many forms of self-regulation are developed within the framework provided by hard law, either from a national or a European origin.[61]

The criticism of state-centered law is not reflected as such in the debate on multilevel governance. Although multilevel governance perspectives recognise that the role of state

interdependence between state and non-state actors at the national and European level, and to a lack of interaction between these interdependent actors. Possibly, some 'pluralist' arguments also benefit stronger parties. For example, the idea of a "law market" may be especially beneficial to parties with at least some expertise of foreign laws, which will usually be strong parties. This question will however not be considered separately in this book.

57 Especially J. Griffiths, 'What is legal pluralism?', *Journal of Legal Pluralism* 1986, p. 1, as well as G. Teubner, 'Rethinking legal pluralism', *Cardozo Law Review* 1992, p. 1448. See however B. de Sousa Santos, 'Law – A map of misreading. Toward a postmodern conception of law', *Journal of Law and Society* 1987, p. 298 who finds that 'the centrality of state law (...) is still a decisive political factor'.

58 D. Caruso, 'Private law in the age of state-making and globalization', *New York Journal of International Law and Politics* 2006, p. 3.

59 A.J. Akkermans, 'Beter recht door herziening van ons beeld van de herkomst van rechtsnormen', *NTBR* 2011, 72. Similar arguments can be found in the German legal order, comp. U. Di Fabio, *Das Recht offener Staaten*, Tübingen: Mohr Siebeck 1998.

60 J.M. Smits, 'A radical view of legal pluralism', in: L. Niglia (ed.), *Pluralism and European private law*, Oxford: Hart 2013, p. 161.

61 This is especially visible as German law distinguishes between self-regulation on the basis of contracts and on the basis of associations, but Dutch law does not. Diverging notions on hetero-determination, or *Fremdbestimmung* (on which see further par. 4.5.1. and 7.2.2.) and different ideas about the binding force of one-sided juridical acts (see further par. 7.5.3. and 8.5.3.) may explain these differences. Moreover, this book will argue that the development of German and Dutch alternative regulation should take place in accordance with the principle of private autonomy and concerns of hetero-determination ('*Fremdbestimmung*'), see further par. 7.2. and 8.2.

is subject to change, states retain an important role.[62] Multilevel governance does however emphasise that in the harmonisation of private law, actors depend on one another and therefore need to interact.

Thirdly, pluralist views may support the conclusion that harmonisation means that there will be less opportunities to learn from diverse national laws.[63] In contrast, multilevel governance does not, as such, take a stance on either the question whether private law could or should be harmonised or whether the state should play a central role in the development of private law.

Perspectives on multilevel governance and pluralism converge with regard to the existence of interdependence and a need for interaction, as the distinction between national, European and international layers become less sharp. Yet importantly, multilevel governance adopts a more neutral approach than pluralism. Particularly, multilevel governance does not see interdependence and interaction as beneficial in itself, nor does it necessarily regard "state-centered" law as problematic.

1.5. Detrimental coexistence: Multilevel governance, interdependence and methodological nationalism

Multilevel governance perspectives provide starting points for answering the question whether the coexistence of interdependent actors in the development of European private law is problematic. This paragraph will explain how interdependence becomes visible in the development of European private law, in accordance with the debate on multilevel governance, which necessitates interaction. If interaction does not develop, actors may not take into account that they have become interdependent, which increases the chance that they undermine one another's actions. If this is the case, problems might develop.

In the Dutch and German legal order, large parts of European private law are developed through national techniques:[64] codifications,[65] blanket clauses and general principles.

62 G. Marks, L. Hooghe, 'Contrasting visions of multi-level governance', in: I. Bache, M. Flinders (eds.), *Multi-level governance*, Oxford: OUP 2004, p. 19. Similarly N. Walker, 'The idea of constitutional pluralism', *MLR* 2002, p. 334: 'the state – however modified and however diminished –continues to be a player in the emerging multi-dimensional, multi-level order.'

63 Comp. L. Miller, *The emergence of EU contract law: Exploring Europeanization*, Oxford: OUP 2011, p. 195.

64 Techniques is a broad, collective term for codifications, blanket clauses, soft law, general principles and other means through which private law may be developed.

65 This book will consider the use of codifications in the multilevel legal order, which refers to traditional codifications such as the BW and the BGB. Codifications, in this sense, may appear more prone to problems when multiple actors develop private law, but of course it is also possible to codify the law through revising and replacing various statutes by one statute on a particular part of private law. These codifications may seek to describe the law at a specific point in time, but they may also seek to initiate changes in the law. Codifications in this sense are similarly less capable of providing a consistent and predictable set of rules if the European legislator subsequently introduces harmonisation, and the use of blanket clauses in these statutes may similarly be affected. Therefore, the questions considered in this book should also be of interest for codifications in this sense.

These techniques are national because their use – also beyond the national level – is modelled on the assumption of characteristics typical of the nation state.[66] Codifications presuppose a central legislator, who develops private law as a coherent, consistent whole. Similarly, blanket clauses typically require the existence of a hierarchical, well-developed judicial system that consistently interprets these blanket clauses, as well as an adequate system of enforcement. Also, general principles play an important part in the development of coherent national private law, especially if national private law is codified. In codified systems, general principles serve to order private law. Moreover, the development of private law based on general ideas on justice, reflected in general principles, presupposes some measure of agreement on those ideas. Such agreement may be difficult to find at the European level.[67]

The use of national techniques in the development of private law is closely intertwined with benchmarks of predictability, consistency and accessibility – which contribute to the more general benchmark of legal certainty – and responsiveness to society's legal views on justice and to practice.[68] This book will refer to the comprehensibility of European private law to denote compliance with these benchmarks. Accordingly, if European private law is predictable, accessible and consistent, it will be easier to comprehend. If private law is responsive to society's legal views on justice, it will be more easily understood and accepted by private parties. If private law is aware of the needs of businesses, it might be less complicated to make a translation from the law in the books to practice. On the contrary, if European private law is not predictable, consistent or accessible, or if it does not develop in accordance with the needs of practice and legal views on justice, parties will have more difficulty relying upon private law as it will be difficult to comprehend private law. Notably, complying with these benchmarks is a matter of degree rather than a binary matter.

Techniques have been considered in the light of their suitability to develop private law in accordance with these benchmarks.[69] Accordingly, legislators designing Civil Codes may seek to develop private law consistently and accessibly, by ensuring that private parties may easily identify relevant sources of law and the rules that apply to their situation.

66 This does not refer to a historically-correct picture of a particular traditional nation state but rather to an idea that implicitly underpins the development of European private law. See N. Jansen, Legal pluralism in Europe', in: L. Niglia (ed.), *Pluralism in Europe*, Oxford: Hart 2013, as well as P. Oestmann, 'Rechtsvielfalt', in: N. Jansen, P. Oestmann (eds.), *Gewohnheit, Gebot, Gesetz*, Tübingen: Mohr Siebeck 2011, p. 99 et seq. This has also been argued for the Dutch legal order comp. W.J. Zwalve, 'Regelgeving in het vermogensrecht', *RM Themis* 2009, p. 20.

67 As exemplified in M.W. Hesselink, 'If you don't like our principles, we have others', in: R. Brownsword et al. (eds.), *The foundations of European private law*, Oxford: Hart 2011, p. 59, also L. Niglia, 'The double life of pluralism in Europe: Between constitutionalism and private law – Arguments for a post-formalism paradigm', in: L. Niglia (ed.), *Pluralism and European private law*, Oxford: Hart 2013, p. 17–18.

68 See further on these benchmarks chapter 2. See further on the choice for these benchmarks rather than legitimacy par. 1.8.

69 Comp. for a historical-political perspective P.A.J. van den Berg, *Codificatie en staatsvorming. De politieke en politiek-theoretische actergronden van de codificatie van het privaatrecht in Pruisen, de Donaumonarchie, Frankrijk en Nederland, 1450–1811*, Groningen: Wolters-Noordhoff 1996, p. 33.

Bentham[70] defended codification for this very reason. The use of blanket clauses[71] and general principles[72] has been defended as they allow the law to develop consistently, and in accordance with ideas of fairness. They also allow for flexibility in the development of the law – thus preventing that private law becomes outdated and unresponsive, i.e. not in accordance with modern practice. There is no clear hierarchy of these benchmarks within and between Member States and European actors and benchmarks do not exclude one another: it is possible to simultaneously pursue, for example, predictability and responsiveness to society's legal ideas on justice.

Typically, national techniques are modelled on the characteristics of nation states rather than the European multilevel legal order, where legislative competence in various areas of European private law is shared between the Member States and the European Union under article 114 TFEU. In accordance with this shared competence, interdependence has developed.[73] Interdependence between national and European state actors becomes clearly visible when studying the extent to which national techniques

70 J. Bentham, *Principles of the civil code*, Chapter XIVV, available at http://oll.libertyfund.org/index.php?option=com_staticxt&staticfile=show.php?person=172&Itemid=99999999. Comp. later on the accessibility of the law A. Diamond, 'Codification of the law of contract', *MLR* 1968, p. 861. The English Law Commission also lists as one of its aims in consolidating the law, to increase the clarity and accessibility of the law, see http://www.lawcom.gov.uk/consolidation/.

71 E.M. Meijers, *De taak der rechtswetenschap ten aanzien der vrijen rechtspraak* (inaugural address Leiden), Haarlem: Tjeenk Willink 1910, p. 9–10, T. Koopmans, 'Lof der onbestemdheid', *RM Themis* 1991, p. 209, A.S. Hartkamp, 'Judicial discretion under the New Civil Code of The Netherlands', *American Journal of Comparative Law* 1992, p. 569, W.-H. Roth, 'Generalklauseln im Europäischen Privatrecht', in: J. Basedow, K.J. Hopt, H. Kötz (eds.), *Festschrift für Ulrich Drobnig zum siebzigsten Geburtstag*, Tübingen: Mohr Siebeck 1998, p. 140.

72 W. Wilburg, *The development of a flexible system in the area of private law* (inaugural address Graz, 1950), Vienna: Manzsches Verlag- und Universitätsbuchhandlung 2000, (translation from H. Hausmaninger), p. 8–9 emphasises the flexible development of law based on the interplay between legal principles. Comp. for Dutch law prominently J.H. Nieuwenhuis, *Drie beginselen van contractenrecht*, Deventer: Kluwer p. 4–5. K.P. Berger, *The creeping codification of the lex mercatoria*, Alphen aan den Rijn: KLI 2010, p. 124, states that 'blanket clauses leave room for the application of general principles of law' and increase the flexibility of the law.

73 More generally, interdependence has also been recognised by the Study Group on Social Justice in European Private Law, 'Social justice in European contract law: A manifesto', *ELJ* 2004, p. 670: 'Law production in the European Union's multilevel system results from the continuous interaction between semi-autonomous actors comprising legislators, the judiciary, and non-governmental organisations, at different levels – European, national, and regional. Law making can neither be monopolised nor achieved in isolation by just one branch of government or a single institution.' See also on European private law and multilevel governance E.A.G. van Schagen, 'The draft common frame of reference and multilevel governance', *Edinburgh Student Law Review* 2010, p. 74. L. Miller, *The emergence of EU contract law: Exploring Europeanization*, Oxford: OUP 2011, p. 155 refers to the interdependence of the European and national level in addressing problems – in this case the development of European private law – calling for continuous negotiation between actors at the European and national level. Comp. differently K. Lenaerts, 'Constitutionalism and the many faces of federalism', *American Journal of Comparative Law* 1990, p. 205–206, characterizing the European legal order as a federation, particularly 'a constitutional order that strives at unity in diversity among previously independent or confederally related component entities', with characteristics of a confederation.

are still able to safeguard the development of European private law predictably, consistently, accessibly, and responsively.

Firstly, decreased independence is visible in the decreased ability of national legislators to comprehensively develop private law through codifications such as the Dutch *Nieuw Burgerlijk Wetboek* (BW) or the German *Bürgerliches Gesetzbuch* (BGB), as the private law *acquis* continues to develop. The need to maintain the predictable and accessible development of private law through codifications should prompt national legislators to develop a consistent strategy towards implementing the *acquis* within or outside of codifications. The need to safeguard the predictability of private law through these codes should prompt national actors to attempt to foresee which areas of private law are to be harmonised. In turn, the European legislator and the CJEU[74] should leave Member States sufficient room for implementing the *acquis* within their codes in a manner that does not undermine the consistency and the responsiveness of private law. More generally, the extent to which national legislators safeguard the quality of private law in codifications should give the European legislator pause in intervening with these codes.

Secondly, the extent to which blanket clauses facilitate the consistent and responsive development of law may become compromised as European actors have started to develop blanket clauses that have been inspired by national blanket clauses.[75] Yet European actors who seek to contribute to responsiveness to national legal views on justice and national practice through blanket clauses may not have sufficient insight in these views and practices. Consequently, they have to rely on Member States' insights.

Alternatively, if European blanket clauses in the *acquis* set harmonised standards, aimed at providing access to markets for foreign and international actors,[76] this limits the extent to which these clauses may simultaneously contribute to the consistency of national private law and the responsiveness of private law to national legal views on justice and national practice.

Thirdly, European actors necessarily adopt a more instrumentalist approach to the development of European private law, which also entails a different approach to general ideas on justice. Tamanaha[77] has pointed out that '[a] pragmatist cannot argue, in other than instrumental terms, that one set of moral terms is evil and another is good, only that it has good or bad consequences'. Consequently, if European actors develop the law in accordance with general ideas on justice, they do so in a manner that diverges from the way in which national actors would. However, European measures will still influence

74 This research will refer to the CJEU, which, before the TFEU was known as the ECJ, for the sake of consistency.

75 See further par. 9.4.1.

76 H.-W. Micklitz, 'Monolistic ideology or pluralistic reality', in L. Niglia (ed.), *Pluralism and European private law*, Oxford: Hart 2013, p. 38–39. see further below par. 4.5.2.

77 B. Tamanaha, *The perils of pervasive legal instrumentalism*, Nijmegen: Wolf Legal Publishers 2006, p. 26. Comp. H.-W. Micklitz, 'Monolistic ideology versus pluralist reality', in L. Niglia (ed.), *Pluralism and European private law*, Oxford: Hart 2013, p. 38, who distinguishes traditional national private law, underpinned by principles, from private law at the European level, which he describes as regulatory private law, noting that the Union 'was never concerned with the underpinnings of national private law, such as private autonomy or freedom of contract'.

national law and possibly also the ideas underpinning the law. Arguably, this may compromise the development of national rules that reflect these principles.

Interdependence between state and non-state actors in developing private law predictably, accessibly, consistently and responsively also becomes visible. When state actors promote the development of alternative regulation, they should take into account relevant non-state actors and their initiatives. Likewise, both European and national state actors increasingly need to address non-state actors. If state actors ignore input from expert non-state actors, or if consultations do not adequately identify stakeholders, this will decrease the chance that private law develops in accordance with practice. As problems become more complex – for example, because of Europeanisation – the role of non-state actors may also become more prominent because of the increasing need for non-state actors' expertise and their organisational and financial resources.

Accordingly, it has been argued that the multilevel legal order may have far-reaching consequences for the use of techniques in the development of private law throughout the Union.[78] However, at the national, European or international level, the development of private law takes place in a "nationalist" manner. Accordingly, authors have criticised this "methodological nationalism."[79] Methodological nationalism is visible, for example, in efforts to transpose successful national techniques to the European level, especially in soft law instruments.[80] Arguably, methodological nationalism implies that actors do not amend the use of national techniques: they are either not aware of increasing interdependence, or, if they do, they are unwilling to adapt the use of techniques.

Thus, in accordance with multilevel governance, theoretically, problems may arise if actors, in accordance with methodological nationalism, do not recognise interdependence and do not sufficiently interact with other actors who might undermine the predictable,

78 W. van Gerven, S. Lierman, *Algemeen Deel. Veertig jaar later*, Mechelen: Kluwer 2010. Although their argument applies to the Belgian legal order, their reasoning may be applied to other Member States as well – even though the multi-layered legal order in Belgium seems particularly complicated. Comp. for an introduction to the constitutional reform in Belgium H. Vuye, 'België: Een staat in hervorming of in ontbinding', *AA* 2008, p. 719, and with regard to future reforms H. Vuye, 'Communautaire pacificatie in België: is de grens bereikt?' *AA* 2008, p. 797. See similarly H. Collins, 'Governance implications for the European Union of the changing character of private law', in: F. Cafaggi, H. Muir-Watt (eds.), *Making European private law: Governance design*, Cheltenham: Elgar 2008, p. 270, as well as the introduction of F. Cafaggi and H. Muir-Watt in the same book at p. 9. Also J.M. Smits, 'A radical view of legal pluralism', in: L. Niglia (ed.), *Pluralism in European, private law*, Oxford: Hart, p. 166–167. Interestingly, M. Storme, 'There is nothing like European private law twenty years later', *ERPL* 2012, p. 1–2, points out that the state of European private law is increasingly similar to the state of private law in the 16th century, where multiple sources of private law coexisted.

79 L. Miller, *The emergence of EU contract law: Exploring Europeanization*, Oxford: OUP 2011, p. 167, J.M. Smits, 'The Draft-Common Frame of Reference, methodological nationalism and the way forward', *ERCL* 2008, p. 270. Comp. also H.-W. Micklitz, 'Monolistic ideology versus pluralistic reality', in: L. Niglia (ed.), *Pluralism and European private law*, Oxford: Hart 2013, p. 29.

80 Accordingly, soft laws such as the PECL and the DCFR will be considered as national techniques, as they are typically based on models of national legislation, containing black letter rules and providing extensive rules in the area of private law. Often, these sets of soft law are based on national codes and seek to provide a model for a European code. See for example R. Michaels, 'Umdenken für die UNIDROIT-Prinzipien. Vom Rechtswahlstatut zum Allgemeinen Teil des Transnationalen Vertragsrechts', *RabelsZ* 2009, p. 873–874. See further on this point par. 9.3.1.

consistent, accessible and responsive development of private law through national techniques. Accordingly, the case studies and subsequent chapters will consider whether problems are likely to arise because of a lack of sufficient interaction between interdependent actors.

1.6. Beneficial coexistence: Pluralist perspectives

Pluralist perspectives provide starting points for answering the question whether the coexistence of interdependent actors in the development of European private law is beneficial. This paragraph will explain why interdependence and the need for interaction may benefit the predictability, accessibility, consistency, and responsiveness of private law.

In accordance with pluralist perspectives, coexistence can be beneficial for various reasons.

Firstly, the reallocation of national competences to the European level under article 114 TFEU may lead to the creation of checks and balances in both the European and national legislative process. Theoretically, this should prevent that national and European actors develop private law in a manner that is unpredictable, inconsistent, inaccessible or unresponsive. In accordance with this reasoning, national actors should resist the development of incomprehensible European law, while national law that is not predictable, accessible, consistent and responsive justifies harmonisation. The development of checks and balances may also prompt national actors to pay more attention to the interests of foreign parties affected by national laws.

Alternatively, national law may be closely intertwined with national legal views on justice. If this is the case, coexistence of national laws is beneficial for the responsiveness of the law to national legal views on justice and Member States might resist harmonisation.

Secondly, the involvement of multiple actors in the development of European private law might also be beneficial if it provides actors with opportunities for mutual learning. For example, actors take into account insights from comparative and international law in the drafting of codifications or the interpretation of law.[81] General principles may also play an important role in providing starting points for debate in the form of general ideas on justice, as reflected in more specific rules.[82]

81 See for example H. Kötz, 'Der Bundesgerichtshof und die Rechtsvergleichung', in: C.-W. Canaris et al. (eds.), *50 Jahre Bundesgerichtshof. Festgabe aus der Wissenschaft, II*, München: Beck 2000, p. 825. Comp. R. Zimmerman. 'Schuldrechtsmodernisierung?' in: W. Ernst, R. Zimmerman (eds.), *Zivilrechtswissenschaft und Schuldrechtsreform*, Tübingen: Mohr Siebeck 2001, p. 22 who notes that if legislators want their legislation to play a role in the discussion in other states, or beyond the national level, they should take into account foreign law and international discussion. Previously, similarly, E.M. Meijers, 'Wijzigingen en aanvullingen van het Burgerlijk Wetboek na 1838', in: P. Scholten, E.M. Meijers (eds.), *Gedenkboek Burgerlijk Wetboek 1838–1938*, Zwolle: Tjeenk Willink 1938, p. 61.

82 In this sense V. Mak, 'A shift of focus: systematisation in European private law through EU law', *ELJ* 2011, p. 417: '[Principles] are anchor points, able to ensure the observance of fundamental values and a coherent development of the legal system, while leaving room for further development according to the needs of society.' Similarly V. Trstenjak, E. Beysen, 'European consumer protection law: *Curia simper dabit remedium*?' *CMLR* 2011, p. 116.

Thirdly, regulatory competition may motivate actors to develop the law in a manner that is attractive to foreign parties, which in turn should benefit the predictability, consistency, accessibility and responsiveness of the law. Law in accordance with these benchmarks is more attractive to parties than laws that are not.

Thus, benefits are considered in terms of the benchmarks elaborated above.[83] Theoretically, benefits may become apparent directly because actors are interdependent, or because actors interact. In accordance with pluralist debate, theoretically, interaction is beneficial, also if interdependence has not developed. Accordingly, the case studies and subsequent chapters will consider whether benefits have developed in accordance with pluralist arguments.

1.7. The need for deliberation

Multilevel governance and pluralist perspectives similarly emphasise the need for interaction. According to the debate on multilevel governance, if hardly any interdependence has developed, there is little need for interaction. Somewhat differently, pluralist perspectives emphasise that interaction is beneficial in itself, even if no interdependence has developed. Yet what is meant with "interaction"?

'Interaction' may entail many forms of contact between actors, but mere contact will generally not suffice to prevent problems or generate advantages. Instead, the quality of interaction should be sufficient, in order to enable actors to profit from one another's insights. Therefore, this volume will refer to the concept of deliberation.[84] Deliberation in this book is defined as discourse that takes place in a society where groups and subcultures – and in the European Union, groups and subcultures in different states – have different backgrounds, in terms of, for example, religion, on which they base their convictions about right and wrong, while disputes between those groups may arise on an increasing number of issues. Deliberation takes place between actors that have to be able to put themselves in the position of other actors, who are trying to reach consensus, based on as many rational arguments as possible. Neyer[85] argues that deliberation is superior to other modes of negotiation when it comes to problem-solving. Although deliberation may not necessarily achieve consensus on future action – i.e. the way in which European private law should be developed – deliberation generally limits the number of options for future action, and also contributes to the quality of those options. These options can subsequently be taken as a starting point in decision-making and facilitate political compromise. Moreover,

83 See previously par. 1.5. and see further on these benchmarks chapter 2.

84 J. Habermas, *Between facts and norms*, Cambridge, Mass.: MIT 1996. Comp. the translator's introduction: 'As understood by participants engaged in interaction and discourse, truth claims are claims about the objective world that all human beings share, and moral claims have to do with norms for interpersonal relationships that any autonomous adult should find rationally acceptable from the standpoint of justice and respect for persons', p. xv.

85 J. Neyer, 'Discourse and order in the EU: A deliberative approach to multi-level governance', *JMCS* 2003, p. 697–698.

deliberation can affect the preferences of participants in the debate.[86] If actors pursue different aims, deliberation can prompt them to reconsider their preferences, which may lead actors to amend their preferences.[87] In other words, through deliberative processes, actors can align their preferences.

Debate should also meet the following requirements:

1) Representativeness

A deliberative process should include a representative number of stakeholders, state actors, and experts.[88] Interestingly, Van Gerven and Lierman[89] have suggested that actors who are well placed to represent the interests of stakeholders, and who are well placed to gather information in a transparent and professional manner, should have a prominent place in deliberative discourse.

2) Inclusiveness

A deliberative process should include all relevant actors. Relevant actors are actors whose rights are affected by the development of European private law. This also entails that parties should have the possibility to participate in the drafting of private law in other Member States if private law affects the rights and duties of these parties.

Inclusiveness may also mean that the differences in the availability of financial and organisational resources, as well as expertise, should be neutralised as far as possible. Meuwese[90] points out that the necessary equality presupposes a number of circumstances, including the ability of actors to place themselves in the position of other actors participating in debate.

3) Openness and transparency

Debate should be open and transparent, which forces actors to account for their choices and give insight in the arguments used to justify such choices. Ideally, in the development of European private law, transparent debate may give more insight into the arguments considered in the development of European private law. Such insight may '[sharpen] our focus on the weight of

86 Ch.F. Sabel, J. Zeitlin, 'Learning from difference: The new architecture of experimentalist governance in the EU', *ELJ* 2008, p. 272.

87 Comp. Ch.F. Sabel, J. Zeitlin, 'Experimentalist governance in the European Union', in: J. Zeitlin, Ch.F. Sabel (eds.), *Experimentalist governance in the European Union: Towards a new architecture*, Oxford: OUP 2010, p. 2.

88 Comp. J. Neyer, 'Discourse and order in the EU: A deliberative approach to multi-level governance', *JMCS* 2003, p. 694, who notes that wide participation involves and connects important actors, and also increases responsiveness.

89 W. van Gerven, S. Lierman, *Algemeen Deel, Veertig jaar later*, Mechelen: Kluwer 2010, p. 287: 'voorrang zou [kunnen] worden gegeven aan organisaties die dusdanig gestructureerd zijn dat zij specifieke en algemene belangen van burgers naar buiten toe kunnen vertegenwoordigen, en bij machte zijn om informatie op een transparante en deskundige wijze te verzamelen, haar intern af te toetsen, en degene te verspreiden die nuttig is voor het nemen van beleidsbeslissingen'.

90 A.C.M. Meuwese, *Impact assessment in EU lawmaking*, Zutphen: Wöhrmann Print Service 2008, p. 42.

competing considerations. And it reminds us that the law is part of the world of competing ideas markedly influenced by cultural differences'.[91]

4) Actors should be able to gain an overview of debate

Deliberation should not lead to a 'cacophony of viewpoints',[92] or a 'noisy dialogue of the deaf'.[93] To avoid too much cacophony, deliberation should take place in a coordinated manner, for example, within the framework of the European Law Institute.[94]

5) Actors should not use debate primarily to pursue their own interests

Actors participating in the debate must be willing and able to reflect on the arguments by other parties, instead of seeking to further their own interests. Currently, that may not always be the case. Hirsch Ballin[95] states that '[m]any Member States representatives participating in the decision-making are driven by the desire to derive the greatest possible benefit and the least possible inconvenience.'

Interaction between actors should serve to make actors aware of interdependence, and adjust the use of their techniques accordingly.[96]

However, is deliberation, often considered as tied to the nation state, and the existence of a *demos*,[97] realistic?

Deliberation has been defended in relation to European decision-making. Cohen and Sabel, in their defence of directly deliberative polyarchy,[98] recognise that decision-making in the European legal order – and thus the development of European private law – is subject to change. Cohen's and Sabel's ideal of 'directly-deliberative polyarchy' accommodates these changes by allowing for the direct participation of interested parties, depending on the issue at hand, on the basis of rational decision-making, tailored to divergent preferences, in which local insights are shared and in which there is sufficient

91 *McFarlane v Tayside Health Board* [2000] 2 AC 59 (HL), 81, *per* Lord Steyn.

92 H.-W. Micklitz, 'The visible hand of European regulatory private law. The transformation of European private law from autonomy to functionalism in competition and regulation', *EUI Working Paper* 2008, p. 29.

93 J. Neyer, 'Discourse and order in the EU: A deliberative approach to multi-level governance', *JMCS* 2003, p. 695.

94 Possibly, making use of techniques such as networks and databases may also contribute to structuring the debate; see further par. 10.2.3. and 10.2.4.

95 E.M.H. Hirsch Ballin, 'Reflections on co-actorship', in: E.M.H. Hirsch Ballin, L.A.J. Senden (eds.), *Co-actorship in the development of European law-making*', The Hague: TMC Asser Press 2005, p. 14.

96 See on the use of techniques further below chapter 9 and 10.

97 This argument is set out clearly by N. MacCormick, ' Democracy, subsidiarity, and citizenship in the 'European Commonwealth'', *Law and Philosophy* 1997, p. 339–340.

98 J. Cohen, Ch. Sabel, 'Directly-deliberative polyarchy', *ELJ* 1997, p. 314. The term polyarchy rather than democracy does not denote a fundamentally different meaning from "democracy". Cohen and Sabel, at p. 317–318, describe polyarchy as 'political systems in which virtually all adults have rights of suffrage, political expression, association, and office-holding, as well as access to diverse sources of information; in which elected officials control public policy; and citizens choose those officials through free and fair elections.'

coordination for decision-makers to learn from one another's solutions.[99] Directly-deliberative polyarchy takes place both within state actors' and within non-state actors' organisations, and it may also exist when state actors and non-state actors cooperate. Cohen and Sabel[100] find that directly-deliberative polyarchy is particularly well suited for areas where current political institutions and private actors fail. Eventually, in a directly-deliberative polyarchy, the roles of legislatures shift towards accommodating private actors' decision-making, rather than acting to solve particular problems.[101] The functional approach in new governance approaches is also in accordance with the sector-specific approach that has been detected in European private law.[102] It has been argued that new modes of governance can foster deliberation. Neyer[103] and Joerges[104] have defended deliberation especially in comitology,[105] which has also been proposed in article 40 of the proposal for a consumer rights Directive with regard to black and grey lists of unfair terms.

Unfortunately, directly-deliberative polyarchy may allow for inequal opportunities for parties to exercise influence in decisions, as participation in debate presupposes a specific level of expertise.[106] Thus, problems may arise in terms of inclusiveness and representativeness.[107]

99 Ch.F. Sabel, J. Zeitlin, 'Learning from difference: The new architecture of experimentalist governance in the EU', *ELJ* 2008, p. 276–277 defend a similar concept, 'experimentalist governance'.

100 J. Cohen, Ch. Sabel, 'Directly-deliberative polyarchy', *ELJ* 1997, p. 331.

101 O. Gerstenberg, 'Law's polyarchy', *ELJ* 1997, p. 346–348 finds that directly-deliberative polyarchy makes clear that democratic decision-making in the European legal order is possible. He criticises the distinction between the traditional national democratic state and the development of European law that adopts a functional rather than a democratic approach as false. Gerstenberg argues that democracy is not necessarily tied to the nation state, especially not if decisions are made through directly-deliberative processes in a functional approach.

102 M.W. Hesselink, 'The structure of the new European private law', in: M.W. Hesselink, *The new European private law*, KLI: The Hague 2002, p. 227, also H.-W. Micklitz, 'Monistic ideology versus pluralistic reality', in: L. Niglia (ed.), *Pluralism and European private law*, Oxford: Hart 2013, p. 29. B.S. Frey. R. Eichenberger, *The new democratic federalism in Europe. Functional, Overlapping and Competing Jurisdictions*, Cheltenham: Elgar 1999, adopt a similarly functional approach.

103 J. Neyer, 'Discourse and order in the EU: a deliberative approach to multi-level governance', *JMCS* 2003, p. 690–691.

104 Ch. Joerges, 'On the legitimacy of Europeanising private law: considerations on a justice-making law for the EU multi-level system', vol 7.3 *EJCL*. Comp. Ch.F. Sabel, J. Zeitlin, 'Learning from difference: The new architecture of experimentalist governance in the EU', *ELJ* 2008, p. 272, who find that decision-making in the EU 'is at least in part deliberative'.

105 Comitology entails that the European legislator, under articles 290 et seq TFEU, delegates further decisions on technical matters to expert committees, see further par. 7.4.1.1.

106 C. de la Porte, P. Nanz, 'The OMC – a deliberative-democratic mode of governance? The cases of employment and pensions', *JEPP* 2004, p. 270–271 distinguish the argument of Joerges and Neyer for deliberative supranationalism from deliberative democracy defended by Habermas. They argue that Joerges and Neyer focus on comitology, where experts participate in evidence-based deliberative discourse. Notably, deliberative discourse ideally takes place within a limited circle of people with sufficient expertise, as is the case in comitology.

107 Comp. N. Walker, 'The idea of constitutional pluralism', *MLR* 2002, p. 353, on the tension between on the one hand general democratic discourse and on the other hand decision-making in specialist discourse where expertise, in accordance with functional decision-making, has an influential voice.

Notwithstanding these shortcomings in deliberative discourse, measures that adopt a horizontal approach, such as Directive 2005/29 on unfair commercial practices or Directive 2011/83 on consumer rights will likely continue to be developed, and it is therefore necessary to consider how the development of these broad measures can be improved. Accordingly, the debate preceding measures pursuing this broad approach in European private law, should be developed gradually, as it becomes clear how Directives in the private law *acquis* are implemented and how they relate to each other and to national private law. In accordance with Walker's[108] argument that a polity and a constitution are mutually constitutive, it is submitted that as the European legal order and with it, European private law develops further, the development of debate that is more in accordance with deliberation should also start developing. Yet as more actors are involved in the development of European private law, it may take more effort to identify relevant state and non-state actors and keep track of their initiatives. Possibly, interaction between actors from different levels and different legal orders may not be as well-organised as interaction within nation states.

At the national level, abandoning the use of codifications and other national techniques is not feasible or desirable. Yet at the European level, using techniques in addition to the legislative process or instead of legislation should be more elaborately considered than is currently the case. Notwithstanding the potential of additional and alternative techniques, and the weaknesses in some of these techniques, their use has rarely been discussed.[109] This is unfortunate as it increases the chance that techniques that are well suited to improve debate or compensate for weaknesses of currently used techniques are overlooked.

Therefore, the case studies and subsequent chapters will consider the use of techniques in addition to or instead of currently used techniques. Are these techniques likely to enhance deliberation and support the comprehensibility of European private law?

108 N. Walker, 'The idea of constitutional pluralism', *MLR* 2002, p. 341–342.

109 Especially by L. Miller, *The emergence of EU contract law: Exploring Europeanization*, Oxford: OUP 2011. Contributions in F. Cafaggi, H. Muir Watt (eds.), *Making European Private Law: Governance Design*, Cheltenham: Elgar 2008 focus on governance of European private law and take into account the multi-level structure of European private law. F. Cafaggi (ed.), *The institutional framework of European private law*, Oxford: OUP 2006, also focusses on the multilevel structure of the European legal order in which private law is developed, especially the institutional background.
K. Gutman, *The constitutionality of European contract law*, Leuven 2010, and C.M.D.S. Pavillon, *Open normen in het Europees consumentenrecht. De oneerlijkheidsnorm in vergelijkend perspectief*, Deventer: Kluwer 2011, are exceptions to this general trend. However, both Gutman and Pavillon do not consider new governance in the light of interdependence, multilevel governance or pluralism perspectives, but in the light of their suitability to further harmonise private law. Generally, literature on soft law, such as the DCFR, does not consider the DCFR in the light of interdependence and multilevel governance, on which see further par. 9.3. See further on the need for more research on governance F. Möslein, K. Riesenhuber, 'Contract governance – a draft research agenda', *ERCL* 2009, p. 248.

1.8. Limitations

The question discussed in this book is very broad, and therefore some limitations are necessary.

Firstly, this book takes benchmarks of predictability, consistency, accessibility and responsiveness as a starting point. This book was defended as a PhD thesis. Accordingly, it was necessary to make explicit to which benchmarks I referred when I sought to answer the main question in this book, whether the coexistence of actors was beneficial or detrimental for European private law. Chapter 2 has been written from this perspective. While writing, however, the idea developed that benchmarks are often implied in European private law debate and not made explicit. Accordingly, the book tries to make benchmarks explicit, and hopefully thereby contributes to debate.

Arguably, benchmarks of predictability, consistency, accessibility and responsiveness, which are also in accordance with standards of good law-making,[110] ensure that private parties may unproblematically rely on private law when entering into transactions with one another.[111]

Authors defending pluralist and multilevel governance perspectives have frequently emphasised legal certainty and responsiveness, noting that, on the one hand, it is more difficult to develop the law in accordance with these benchmarks, while on the other hand, the coexistence of actors should enable the law to respond better to divergent preferences.[112] Criticism of private law as such frequently focusses on the quality of private law in terms such as predictability, accessibility and consistency,[113] and on

110 Originally developed by F. Bacon, *Treatise on universal justice or the foundations of equity*, by aphorisms, from: *The works of Francis Bacon*, 1889, Yale, aphorism 8 and L.L. Fuller, *The morality of law*, London: Yale University Press 1973, 9th ed, p. 33 et seq. See further below, par. 2.2.

111 Comp. W.J. Witteveen, 'Laws of lawmaking', in: W.J. Witteveen, W. van der Burg (eds.), *Rediscovering Fuller*, Amsterdam: Amsterdam University Press 1999, p. 321: 'Practices of lawmaking are infused with social expectations about what "good" laws are supposed to be and to achieve.'

112 B. Fauvarque-Cosson, 'EU contract law through and beyond pluralism', in: L. Niglia (ed.), *Pluralism and European private law*, Oxford: Hart 2013, p. 95, refers to consistency. M. Delmas-Marty, *Ordering pluralism, A conceptual framework for understanding the transnational world*, Oxford: Hart 2009, p. 13–14 recognises the need for predictability and consistency, and pinpoints, at p. 17, that unpredictability and inconsistency as problems typically arising from globalisation. Similarly, K.-H. Ladeur, 'Methodology and European law – Can methodology change so as to cope with the multiplicity of the law?', in: M. van Hoecke (ed.), *Epistemology and methodology of law*, Oxford: Hart 2004, p. 96 notes the 'decline of unity in law'. L.E. Ribstein, E. O'Hara, *The law market*, Oxford: OUP 2009, p. 9 also refer to predictability. Arguments that private law is – and should be – developed in accordance with society's legal views on (social) justice can be found in H. Collins, *The European Civil Code. The way forward*, Cambridge: CUP 2008, as well as and J. Cohen, Ch. Sabel, 'Directly-deliberative polyarchy', *ELJ* 1997, p. 319.

113 Authors criticising or praising private law on the basis of these benchmarks include, for example, C.M.D.S. Pavillon, *Open normen in het Europees consumentenrecht*, Deventer: Kluwer 2011, J.M. Smits, 'European private law: a plea for a spontaneous legal order', in: D.M. Curtin et al (eds.), *European integration and law*, Antwerp: Intersentia 2006, p. 57, H.-W. Micklitz, N. Reich, 'Der Kommissionsvorschlag vom 8. 10. 2008 für eine Richtlinie über „Rechte der Verbraucher", oder: „der Beginn des Endes einer Ära ...", *EUzW* 2009, p. 279, W.H. Roth, 'Transposing pointillist EC guidelines into national systematic codes – Problems and consequences', *ERPL* 2002, p. 761. Comp. S. Vogenauer,

private law's responsiveness to society's legal views on justice and to everyday practice.[114]

Although legitimacy, legal equality, coherence and justice are expressly not used for benchmarks in this book, this book does not mean to argue law should not be just, coherent, or legitimate, or that it should not respect legal equality. Rather, it will be defended that legal certainty and responsiveness allow for evaluating the existence of either problems or benefits more palpably, while it will be defended that there is (hopefully) considerable overlap between the benchmarks defended in this book and justice, legitimacy, coherence and legal equality.

Secondly, to be able to sketch the role of actors in some detail, this book chooses to focus on two states in particular: Germany and The Netherlands. In subsequent chapters, a comparison between Germany and The Netherlands will take place. In the German legal order, a constitutional framework has been developed that also provides indications for the development of private law through legislation or alternative regulation. Possible objections to the development of alternative regulation become visible in this framework, which may provide insight in the possible objections to the development of alternative regulation in other Member States and by EU actors.

Thirdly, this volume should be seen in the light of the debate in European private law that portrays state legislatures and judiciaries as primary actors in private law. European and national actors are the most prominent actors who develop binding private law, while the reallocation of legislative competences to the European level is likely to continue. Therefore, the research will focus on the interdependence between European and national actors. This also entails that the book will not pursue an in-depth analysis of the reallocation of competences to sub-national actors.

Fourthly, the book will focus on the use of national techniques, because these techniques currently still play, and will continue to play, a primary role in the development of private law in many civil law jurisdictions. Accordingly, in the Dutch and German legal order, the development of private law takes place primarily through these top-down techniques. At the national level, the development of private law does not seem likely to change – the use of codifications may even be constitutionally required, for example in article 107 Dutch constitution ('*Grondwet*', hereafter: 'Gw').

Fifthly, this book will study the development of private law in the Dutch and German legal order, and consider the initiatives from European actors where relevant. The overviews will show that European initiatives are increasingly relevant, but the primary

'Common Frame of Reference and UNIDROIT Principles of International Commercial Contracts: Coexistence, competition, or overkill of soft law?', *ERCL* 2010, p. 143–183 and comp. the criticism of R. Zimmerman, 'The current state of European private law', *American Journal of Comparative Law* 2009, p. 479. The report of M.W. Hesselink, 'An optional instrument on European contract law: could it increase legal certainty and foster cross-border trade?', in: M.W. Hesselink et al. (eds.), *Het Groenboek Europees contractenrecht: Naar een optioneel instrument?*, The Hague: BJU 2011, p. 9–23, makes clear that the European legislator is especially interested in legal certainty. German authors have typically stressed *Folgerichtigkeit*, for example M. Schmidt, *Konkretisierung von Generalklauseln im Europäischen Privatrecht*, Berlin: De Gruyter 2010.

114 Comp. prominently W. Wilburg, *A flexible system for the area of private law* (inaugural address Graz, 1950), Manzsches Verlag und Universitätsbuchhandlung: Vienna 2000, p. 3.

level where private law is developed remains the national level. That does not mean that this might not change – but it is not yet sufficiently likely that the role of European actors, notwithstanding a considerable amount of new initiatives and proposals for further harmonisation, will increase to the extent that the European level will become the central level where private law is developed. Essential parts of national private law, for example property law, remain applicable.

1.9. Outlook

The main research question asks: to what extent is the development of European private law by multiple actors problematic or beneficial for the quality of European private law? The book will answer this question as follows:

Before turning to the case studies, it is, logically, necessary to debate the benchmarks that will be used to evaluate whether the coexistence of actors is beneficial or problematic. Therefore, chapter 2 will turn to benchmarks of legal certainty and responsiveness.

Chapter 3 will introduce the case studies, focussing on the coexistence of actors in the development of the law on STCs. Multilevel governance theories and pluralist insights imply that because of the coexistence of actors, problems and benefits may arise for European private law. Chapters 4 and 5 will analyse whether this is the case for respectively German and Dutch law on STCs.

Chapter 6 will ask whether the findings of the case study can be generalised to the development of European private law and sketch the approach of the following chapters.

The case studies have focussed on the development of the law on STCs through national techniques, which implies a prominent role of state actors. Chapter 7 and 8 will ask more generally what actors play a role in the development of European private law in respectively the German and Dutch legal order. Do state actors retain a central role and can that be justified?

Chapter 9 will study the development of European private law through codifications, soft laws, blanket clauses and general principles in the light of the case studies. Do national and European actors more generally deliberate and how has that affected the extent to which national techniques safeguard the comprehensibility of the law, in accordance with multilevel governance perspectives? Have benefits developed, in accordance with pluralist debate?

Chapter 10 will consider the development of European private law through techniques in addition to or instead of currently used techniques.[115] Theoretically, techniques supporting or encouraging deliberation should be beneficial if, in accordance with multilevel governance insights, they enhance debate between interdependent actors. According to pluralist insights, if these techniques will enable better debate or deliberation, they will allow for more opportunities for mutual learning, or they may prompt national actors to consider the interests of actors not involved in national democratic processes. More debate will make actors more aware of divergent preferences, and develop the law in a responsive manner.

[115] The distinction between additional and alternative techniques is not meant as a sharp distinction. See further par. 4.7 and par. 5.7, and more generally chapter 10.

Is the use of additional and alternative techniques more generally likely to foster deliberation and mutual learning? In addition, if techniques have already been widely used, can their improved use strengthen deliberation, mutual learning, and the predictability, consistency, accessibility and responsiveness of European private law? Which techniques could potentially also strengthen European private law, considering their strengths and weaknesses?

Chapter 11 will draw conclusions and answer the main research question: is the coexistence of actors beneficial or detrimental for European private law?

1.10. Methodology

This book started out from a traditional, national perspective on private law and it primarily uses the traditional legal research methods by researching legislation, case law and legal literature, as well as other relevant documents.

However, political science, specifically the discourse on multilevel governance, adds an important insight to the development of European private law. Multilevel governance stresses the coexistence of actors in the European multilevel legal order and draws attention to the interdependence between actors and the need for interaction, a perspective that has generally not been considered in the debate on European private law.

The answer to the question of whether the coexistence of actors in the development of European private law is problematic or beneficial, depends on the definition of the quality of European private law, as well as the question of what interaction is necessary to safeguard the quality of private law. Insights from jurisprudence, or legal theory, prove especially valuable in three respects. Insights from jurisprudence are useful for determining the benchmarks for the quality of European private law that are in accordance with views on benchmarks for European private law by private lawyers. Also, jurisprudence provides insights on the interaction that is required in decision-making, thereby providing further clarification on the need for interaction between actors in accordance with the discourse on multilevel governance. Legal theory may also be beneficial for the discussion on legal pluralism.

This volume also contains comparative legal research. The volume does not directly compare legal rules as such, but instead aims to analyse and compare the roles of actors in the Dutch and German legal order. However, some comparative remarks have been made in chapter 6 and comparative insights have served as interesting alternative or additional perspectives in chapters 8, 9 and 10 as well.

Chapters 4 and 5 also contain an analysis of the German and Dutch law on STCs. This part of the book does not, however, aim to compare the differences and similarities between German and Dutch law, but rather, the way in which these rules have been developed, in particular, the interaction between actors involved in the development of these rules. For both chapters 4 and 5 and chapters 7 and 8, this volume has made extensive use of European, German and Dutch legislation, case law, parliamentary history, sources of alternative regulation, international materials, and legal literature.

Chapter 2

PREDICTABILITY, CONSISTENCY, ACCESSIBILITY AND RESPONSIVENESS

2.1. Introduction

Even though the development of European private law has become more complex, European private law still has to be developed in accordance with benchmarks of predictability, consistency, accessibility and responsiveness, because private parties need to be able to rely on private law when entering into transactions with one another. This chapter will make explicit what benchmarks will be used in this book to assess whether the coexistence of actors in the development of European private law is problematic or beneficial. This has necessitated a limitation of benchmarks. Particularly, justice, legitimacy, coherence and legal equality will not serve as benchmarks in this book, although evidently, law should generally be developed in accordance with these ideas.

This chapter however pursues an additional aim, beyond making benchmarks for European private law in this book explicit. While these benchmarks have partially been deduced from debate in European private law,[116] debate in European private law has so far rarely critically questioned which benchmarks should be met, how these benchmarks should be defined, and how they relate to one another. In addition, it will be submitted that developing European private law in conformity with the benchmarks used in this book should contribute to justice, legitimacy, coherence and legal equality more generally.

Accordingly, this book aims to consider what requirements of predictability, accessibility, consistency and responsiveness entail, and, in doing so, defends not only the idea that these benchmarks are especially suitable for the multilevel legal order, but also emphasises the importance of all these benchmarks. Notably, in developing the law, actors often seek to develop the law as much as possible with benchmarks defended in this chapter, which renders developing a hierarchical order between these benchmarks problematic.

The approach of this chapter will be as follows. Paragraph 2.2 will discuss benchmarks for good law more generally and paragraph 2.3. will turn to benchmarks for good European private law. Paragraph 2.4. will consider the benchmarks predictability, accessibility and consistency. The paragraph will argue that these benchmarks can be

[116] See previously par 1.8. See for an exception A.J. Verheij, ' Wie is verantwoordelijk voor hanteerbaar privaatrecht?' in A.L.M. Keirse et al. (eds.), *Beter Burgerlijk Recht*, Deventer: Kluwer 2012, p. 179.

seen as requirements of the more general benchmark of legal certainty. Paragraph 2.5 will address the responsiveness of private law to society's legal views on justice and to the needs and preferences of legal practice. Paragraph 2.6 will discuss why justice, coherence and legal equality are not considered as (separate) benchmarks in this book. Paragraph 2.7 will draw conclusions.

2.2. Benchmarks for good law

This chapter will look at well-known requirements that become apparent when looking at national private law and emphasise the perspective of private parties as a starting point. This book builds upon general benchmarks of good lawmaking that can be traced to Bacon.[117] His benchmarks coincide with the requirements developed by Fuller:[118]

1) The generality of laws
2) The public promulgation of laws
3) Laws should not be developed or applied retroactively if possible
4) The comprehensibility of laws
5) The consistency of laws
6) The enforceability of laws that should not prescribe impossible results
7) The stability of laws
8) Convergence between laws as they are announced and applied.

In Fuller's view, rules have to comply with these requirements in order to qualify as law. Further, the parable of King Rex outlines that legislation that does not meet these benchmarks is not likely to affect behaviour.

Other authors, who criticised Fuller, in particular Hart,[119] have not rejected these requirements outright. Bentham,[120] to whom Hart[121] referred, developed conditions that legislation – in particular codifications – had to meet in order to achieve the aims that were pursued. Bentham emphasises that legislation needs to be developed in accordance with utility, but also refers to more generally accepted criteria, such as the public availability of laws and their consistency.

117 F. Bacon, *Treatise on universal justice or the foundations of equity*, by aphorisms, from: *The works of Francis Bacon*, 1889, Yale, aphorism 8, who held that '[c]ertainty is so essential to law, that the law cannot even be just without it.' See further on the similarities between Bacon and Fuller W.J. Witteveen, 'Laws of lawmaking', in: W.J. Witteveen, W. van der Burg (eds.) *Rediscovering Fuller*, Amsterdam: Amsterdam University Press 1999, p. 328.

118 L.L. Fuller, *The morality of law*, London: Yale University Press 1973, 9th ed, p. 33 et seq.

119 See further on this argument J. Waldon, 'Positivism and legality: Hart's equivocal response to Fuller', *New York University Law Review* 2008, p. 1135.

120 J. Bentham, *Principles of the civil code*, in: J. Bowring (ed.), *The Works of Jeremy Bentham, vol. 1 (Principles of Morals and Legislation, Fragment on Government, Civil Code, Penal Law)*, Chapter XIVV, available at http://oll.libertyfund.org/index.php?option=com_staticxt&staticfile=show.php?person=172&Itemid=99999999.

121 H.L.A. Hart, 'Positivism and the separation of law and morals', *Harvard Law Review* 1958, p. 594.

2.3. Benchmarks for European private law

The benchmarks of good law-making have been considered in recent discussions on the quality of European private law.[122] Yet this book seeks to build upon requirements of good lawmaking and offer benchmarks more specifically tailored to European private law. The benchmarks of good law-making as discussed above have not been developed for private law, but more generally for law. Therefore, characteristics of private law, in particular the discussion on whether private law does or should pursue particular aims, and the suitability of private law for effectively influencing behaviour, have not been considered. Although for private parties, the enforceability of rules remains important, a lack of enforceability may also be traced to parties' lack of knowledge,[123] which is especially prominent in private law where parties have traditionally played a key role in the enforcement of rules. This requirement does not stand in the way of vague provisions that leave room for discretion for the judiciary to enforce the law in accordance with the needs of legal practice and legal views on justice. These provisions have, moreover, evidently not stood in the way of the development of a considerable amount of case law, as becomes visible in both the Dutch and the German legal order. Furthermore, the definition of European private law in this research is broader than the understanding of law that becomes apparent from Fuller. Whereas the benchmarks and allegories from Fuller focus on legislation, this research also includes rules other than legislation, developed through self-regulation and co-regulation. Moreover, Fuller[124] has developed benchmarks for a good system of law, not for the quality of a particular area of material law.

2.4. Legal certainty

For private parties, the importance of legal certainty has often been emphasised. Popelier[125] has considered Fuller's requirements of Fuller in the light of legal certainty, which, in turn, she traces to principles of the *Rechtsstaat* that require that subjects should be able to determine their legal position.[126] These benchmarks largely coincide with the following requirements:

122 Comp. prominently W. van Gerven, S. Lierman, *Beginselen van Belgisch privaatrecht. Algemeen deel, veertig jaar later*, Mechelen: Kluwer 2010, p. 176, as well as M. Safjan, *Why a European Law Institute?*, Speech held at the ELI Founding Congress, Paris 1 June 2011, text available at www.europeanlawinstitute.eu/fileadmin/user_upload/p_eli/_17__Marek_Safjan.pdf, and S. Worthington, 'The unique charm of the common law', *ERPL* 2011, p. 348, who finds that '[a] legal system is regarded as just only if its rules are reasonable, general, equal, predictable, and certain.'

123 W. van Gerven, S. Lierman, *Beginselen van Belgisch privaatrecht. Algemeen deel, veertig jaar later*, Mechelen: Kluwer 2010, p. 180 point out that requiring that people factually know the law is not realistic. See further below par. 2.3. on accessibility.

124 L.L. Fuller, *The morality of law*, New Haven: Yale University Press 1969, revised edition, p. 43.

125 P. Popelier, *Rechtszekerheid als beginsel voor behoorlijke regelgeving*, Antwerp: Intersentia 1997, p. 7.

126 M.W. Hesselink, 'An optional instrument on European contract law: could it increase legal certainty and foster cross-border trade?', in: M.W. Hesselink et al. (eds.), *Het Groenboek Europees contractenrecht: Naar een optioneel instrument?*, The Hague: BJU 2011, p. 20 points out that legal certainty also has a psychological

i) Predictable
In turn, this benchmark entails that private law is not retroactively developed (in accordance with requirement 3), as well as the stability of laws (requirement 7). In addition, for private law, the reliability of private law and the clear wording of the law will be discussed.

ii) Accessible
In turn, this benchmark requires that private law is publicly promulgated (requirement 1). The accessibility of private law is specifically concerned with the parties' ability to identify relevant sources of law, which may be particularly complicated if it concerns unwritten law or unpublished binding alternative regulation. In particular, accessibility of private law requires that parties – or rather their lawyers – can understand laws (requirement 4), which is essential for the enforcement of private law. This further entails the convergence between the wording and the application of the law (requirement 8) that is also important for the predictability of law.

iii) Consistent
This benchmark is in accordance with the consistency of law (requirement 5). Also, the generality of law (requirement 1) diminishes the chance that laws develop in isolation from one another, which in turn decreases the chance that inconsistencies develop.

Thus, the requirements of legal certainty may roughly be divided into benchmarks of predictability, accessibility and consistency. These benchmarks may well overlap, and they may also influence and be influenced by benchmarks of responsiveness discussed in paragraph 2.5.

The subsequent paragraphs will discuss the requirements important for legal certainty. Paragraph 2.4.1 will discuss predictability, paragraph 2.4.2 will turn to accessibility and paragraph 2.4.3 will consider consistency. Paragraph 2.4.4 will consider the overlaps between these benchmarks.

2.4.1. Predictability

Predictability requires that parties can use private law as guidance in determining their own behaviour and avoiding conflicts, which entails that European private law needs to meet the requirements of (1) clarity, (2) reliability, and (3) stable development.[127] Codifications contribute to the clarity of private law by providing clear, abstract rules.

aspect, referring to how secure, or certain, parties are about rules. This psychological notion will not be assessed in this book. P. Popelier, *Rechtszekerheid als beginsel voor behoorlijke regelgeving*, Antwerp: Intersentia 1997, p. 8, also considers legal certainty in the context of the influence of the law on peoples' behaviour.

127 Similarly W. van Gerven, S. Lierman, *Beginselen van Belgisch privaatrecht. Algemeen deel, veertig jaar later*, Mechelen: Kluwer 2010, p. 180–182.

The abstraction in Civil Codes in turn also contributes to the stable development of the law, as it prevents that law becomes obsolete, necessitating legislative intervention.[128]

Firstly, private law should preferably contain key concepts and rules with a clear, predictable meaning. In trade, it is important to be able to assess one's risks and act upon that assessment; private law is important for this assessment as it allows parties to assess, for example, what duties arise out of a contract, or whether an exclusion clause is valid. This idea is recognised for instance, in the DCFR, where Von Bar[129] notes that the predictable outcome of a case in some areas is more important than the substance of the rules under which the case is determined. Dutch law,[130] German law,[131] and English law[132] have similarly recognised the need for clarity. Hondius[133] has pointed out that in several states, clarity can be a constitutional requirement of law. At a European level, the ECHR[134] has held that article 6 ECHR implies that citizens must be able 'to foresee, to a degree that is reasonable in the circumstances, the consequences which a given action may entail'.

This does not mean that rules have to be very precise[135] – a blanket clause in statutory law may also contribute to the predictability of private law, depending on its interpretation.

Secondly, predictability entails that if parties have justifiably relied on the statement of behaviour of another party, and acted upon their reliance, in accordance with the law, their reliance should not be disappointed.[136] Predictability may,

128 Comp. W.B. Schünemann, 'Wandlungen des Vertragsrechts', *NJW* 1982, p. 2033. Comp. for the Dutch recodification C.J. van Zeben, W.G. Belinfante, O.W. van Ewijk, *Parlementaire geschiedenis van het nieuwe burgerlijk wetboek : parlementaire stukken systematisch gerangschikt en van noten voorzien. Algemeen deel, Voorgeschiedenis en algemene inleiding*, Deventer: Kluwer 1962, p. 7. Hereafter, this book will refer to the parliamentary history of the BW in the following manner: Parl. Gesch. NBW, Boek 7, p. 7, where the legislator recognises the need to provide general provisions, rather than individual, divergent decisions, on complex societal developments. R. Zimmerman, 'Codification: history and present significance of an idea', *ERPL* 1995, p. 114, refers to W. Lorenz, 'On the "calling" of our time for civil legislation', in: A. Harmathy, A. Nemeth (eds.), *Questions of civil law codification*, Budapest: Hungarian Academy of Sciences 1990, p. 128, who states: 'The reason why in Countries with old Civil Codes the courts are still able to find their way lies in the fact that legislators did not attempt too much.' Similarly P.S. Atiyah, 'Common law and statute law', *MLR* 1985, p. 5.

129 Ch. Von Bar et al (eds), *Principles, definitions and model rules of European private law. Draft Common Frame of Reference, Outline Edition*, München: Sellier 2009, p. 83.

130 For example L.D. Pels Rijcken, 'Rechtszekerheid, Assepoester van rechtsvindingstheorieën', in: P. Abas et al (eds.), *Non sine causa*, Zwolle: Tjeenk Willink 1979, p. 310.

131 H. Wiedemann, 'Rechtssicherheit – ein absoluter Wert?' in: G. Paulus, U. Diederichsen, C.-W. Canaris (eds.), *Festschrift für Karl Larenz zum 70. Geburtstag*, München: Beck 1973, p. 199–215. Comp. for Belgian law L.J. Wintgens, 'Zeker weten? Enkele rechtsfilosofische en rechtstheoretische opmerkingen over rechtszekerheid', *RW* 1993–1994, p. 1077.

132 *Black-Clawson International Ltd v Papierwerke Waldhof-Aschaffenberg AG* [1975] AC 591, 638, more generally Lord Bingham of Cornhill, 'The rule of law', Sir David Williams Lecture, Cambridge 2006, p. 6.

133 E.H. Hondius, *Sense and nonsense in the law. Towards clarity and plain meaning* (inaugural address Utrecht) 2007, p.19.

134 ECHR 26 April 1979 (Sunday Times v United Kingdom), application number 6538/74, par. 49.

135 As argued by J.M. Barendrecht, *Recht als model voor rechtvaardigheid*, Deventer: Kluwer 1992, and J.de Mot, G. de Geest, 'De toekomst van het Europees privaatrecht na het Groenboek', *NJB* 2002, 18, pleading for an extremely detailed European Civil Code.

136 C. von Bar et al. (eds.) *Principles, definitions and model rules of European private law. Draft Common Frame of Reference, Outline Edition*, München: Sellier 2009, par. 73. For Dutch law, see prominently

therefore, mean giving an enforceable claim to the person who justifiably relied on someone's behaviour; for example, if a party has relied on an offer and his reliance was reasonable, this may entail that an offer is held to be irrevocable, under article 2:202 PECL.

Thirdly, predictability requires that private law is developed and applied predictably. Arbitrarily amending private law decreases the predictable development of private law,[137] as well as continuously amending private law. Also, changes should not take effect retroactively, as this may make it considerably more difficult for parties to assess their future legal position to determine their actions.[138]

2.4.2. *Accessibility*

Accessibility requires that parties have sufficient access to private law, in order to determine their legal position. This entails, in particular, access to sources that impose binding rules on these parties.[139]

The accessibility of sources of private law does not only mean that they should be publicly accessible. Parties should also be able to identify relevant sources, and rules should not be unintelligible.[140]

This was already recognised by Bentham,[141] who emphasised the "cognoscibility" of private law in a codification. Codifications significantly enhance the access to private law by providing private parties with one source of private law in which private law is systematically ordered, especially compared to private law that can be deduced by various coexisting statutes, case law, or unwritten law.[142] Similarly, a weakness of local usages or self-regulation is that they are often not sufficiently publicly available to parties that are inexperienced in trade or that contract across borders.[143] Van Caenegem,[144] who also refers to cognoscibility, points out that this does not mean that private law

J.B.M. Vranken, 'Vertrouwen en rechtszekerheid in het overeenkomstenrecht', in: *Vertrouwensbeginsel en rechtszekerheid in Nederland*, Deventer: Tjeenk Willink 1997, par. 3.

137 Comp. for example J.M. Smits, 'European private law: a plea for a spontaneous legal order', in: D.M. Curtin et al (eds.), *European integration and law*, Antwerp: Intersentia 2006, par. 6.

138 Comp. CJEU 22 January 1997 (Opel Austria GmbH v Council of the European Union), T-115/94, [1997] ECR, p. II-39, par. 124.

139 Comp. ECHR 26 April 1979 (Sunday Times v United Kingdom), application number 6538/74, par. 49.

140 W. van Gerven, S. Lierman, *Beginselen van Belgisch privaatrecht. Algemeen deel, veertig jaar later*, Mechelen: Kluwer 2010, p. 179–180.

141 J. Bentham, *Principles of the civil code*, Chapter XIVV, available at http://oll.libertyfund.org/index.php?option=com_staticxt&staticfile=show.php?person=172&Itemid=99999999.

142 This was also a motivation to reform the BGB, see J. Schmidt-Räntsch, 'Reintegration der Verbraucherschutzgesetze durch den Entwurf eines Schuldrechtsmodernisierungsgesetzes', in: R. Schulze, H. Schulte-Nölke (eds.), *Die Schuldrechtsreform vor dem Hintergrund des Gemeinschaftsrechts*, Tübingen: Mohr Siebeck 2001, p. 169, and a motivation for the Dutch recodification, see *Parl. Gesch. NBW*, Boek 7, p. 7, 9, comp. also A.S. Hartkamp, *Aard en opzet van het nieuw vermogensrecht*, Deventer: Kluwer 2010, p. 8.

143 V. Mak, 'According to custom ...? The role of 'Trade Usage' in the proposed Common European Sales Law (CESL)', *ERCL* 2014, p. 84, refers to accessibility or 'knowability'.

144 R. van Caenegem, *Judges, legislators, and professors*, Cambridge: CUP 1987, p. 161.

cannot be accessible if it is not codified. It is very well possible to simultaneously support the accessibility of private law and reject codification; for example, the accessibility of private law may be increased by overviews and handbooks.[145]

Even if parties manage to discover the relevant sources, they will still be confronted with specialised legal terms. Accordingly, it has been suggested that plain language should be used in the drafting of legislation.[146] It is submitted that efforts to make provisions in, for example, Civil Codes, more intelligible for private parties themselves may not necessarily lead to clearer or more predictable private law; even if, for example, very simple rules are formulated, these simple rules will subsequently also have to be applied to complex cases.[147] Furthermore, plain language in legislation should not be used when that would lead to inconsistencies with, for example, case law. The use of plain language can also be compromised by the need for political compromise. At the European level, the use of plain language is made more difficult by the need to cope with different languages and the arguments against using a concept that, at first sight, may have a clear meaning, but that already has a meaning in national private laws.[148] Further, when arguing that legislation should be comprehensible to laymen, it should be noted that the layman may not necessarily always read legislation relevant for assessing his legal position – possibly, he may instead rely on advice from lawyers, or advice from organisations providing free legal advice.[149] For these reasons, plain language should not be the sole criterion for assessing the accessibility of private law. Instead, law should not be unintelligible.

2.4.3. Consistency

Inconsistency is problematic because it is irreconcilable with the rational character of the law: how can the law logically decide that behaviour is both lawful as well as giving rise to damages for tort? As law establishes order and gives commands, it cannot be contradictory: orders that contradict each other cancel each other out, and law that contradicts itself does not create order but the opposite. Accordingly, consistency has been widely recognised as a benchmark throughout the Union: in English law,[150] as well as in Dutch

145 Comp. Lord Goff, 'The search for principle', *Maccabean lecture on jurisprudence, proceedings of the British Academy* 1984, p. 174.

146 In The Netherlands, this has for example led to the project in which the Dutch Constitution is 'translated' in plain language: L. van Almelo (ed.), *Onze Grondwet: de rechtsstaat en de grondrechten verklaard voor nieuwe Nederlandse burgers*, The Hague: VNG 2003. See for the English plain language movement www.languageandlaw.org/PLAINENGLISH.HTM.

147 Comp. for the Dutch debate J.B.M. Vranken, 'Niets in het recht is blijvend, behalve verandering', *WPNR* 6560 (2004), note 17.

148 See G. Danneman, S. Ferreri, M. Graziadei, 'Language and terminology', in: Ch. Twigg-Flessner (ed.), *Cambridge companion to European Union private law*, Cambridge: CUP 2010, p. 70.

149 Such as, for example, in The Netherlands, the *Consuwijzer*, at www.consuwijzer.nl/, or in England Community Legal Advice, see www.legalservices.gov.uk/public/community_legal_advice.asp.

150 N. MacCormick, *Rhetoric and the rule of law*, Oxford: OUP 2005, p. 2: 'Law is institutional normative order.'

law[151] and German law.[152] At the European level, consistency is similarly recognised.[153] Codifications should contribute to consistency as various areas of law are stipulated in one piece of abstract legislation, systematically ordered, which ought to clarify the relations between the different areas of private law.[154] The development of private law on the basis of general principles, as reflected in blanket clauses in general parts of codifications – such as article 3:12 BW[155] or article 242 BGB should help consistency as well.[156]

Consistency requires that rules do not contradict one another. Yet that does not mean that provisions may not provide rules for different situations, and these rules may, at first sight, contradict one another. Rather, consistency implies that the arguments upon which obligations are based coincide with one another and within the legal order.[157] Arguably, consistency should also not necessarily be equated with convergence, even though at the European level, consistency has been connoted with convergence or harmonisation.[158]

Inconsistencies become problematic once parties are obliged to comply with conflicting, contradictory rules, which undermine legal certainty.

Thus, inconsistency becomes problematic if it leads to contradictory rules that are simultaneously applicable. Inconsistency can arise if legislation contains provisions that contradict themselves, but alternative regulation, which may similarly impose duties on private parties, may also contradict itself. Notably, alternative regulation is not developed by one legislator but by multiple actors who do not necessarily have similar aims, which increases the chance that provisions in multiple sets of alternative regulation that are

151 P. Scholten, *Mr. C. Asser's Handleiding tot de beoefening van het Nederlands burgerlijk recht. Algemeen deel. Deel I*, Zwolle: Tjeenk Willink 1974. Hereafter, this volume will refer to this book as: Asser/Scholten 1974.

152 K. Larenz, *Methodenlehre der Rechtswissenschaft*, Berlin: Springer 1991, 6th ed., p. 450. Comp. K. Riesenhuber, *System und Prinzipien des Europäischen Privatrechts*, Berlin: De Gruyter 2003, p. 9 who points out the importance of '*Folgerichtigkeit*'.

153 Comp. COM (2003) 68 final.

154 Comp. the praise in H. Schmoeckel, '100 Jahre BGB: Erbe und Aufgabe', *NJW* 1996, p. 1697, with further references. Asser/Scholten 1974, nr. 12, p. 45 refers to the unity of law, which is closely intertwined with the codification of private law. Scholten notes, in chapter 5, that because of the amendments and special laws adopted alongside the civil code, the unity of private law had decreased. See also A.S. Hartkamp, *Aard en opzet van het nieuwe vermogensrecht*, Deventer: Kluwer 2010, p. 7.

155 Comp. critically P.T.J. Wolters, 'De strikken van de redelijkheid en billijkheid', *WPNR* (7045) 2015, who finds that the Dutch Civil Code does not use consistent terminology to ensure consistency. Wolters states that a recodification should help make the law clearer and more consistent.

156 Comp. Staudinger Komm zum BGB/Honsell (2013), introduction to the BGB, nr. 70–71.

157 W. van Gerven, S. Lierman, *Beginselen van Belgisch privaatrecht. Algemeen deel, veertig jaar later*, Mechelen: Kluwer 2010, p. 186.

158 See for example W. van Gerven, S. Lierman, *Beginselen van Belgisch privaatrecht. Algemeen deel, veertig jaar later*, Mechelen: Kluwer 2010, p. 24–25, who defend increasing convergence. They find that approximisation of laws ('*nader tot elkaar brengen*') – which need not necessarily lead to uniformity – has become a paradigm of EU law. Comp. also C.M.D.S. Pavillon, *Open normen in het Europees consumentenrecht*, Deventer: Kluwer 2011. The question whether and by whom blanket clauses in the *acquis* should be interpreted autonomously is analysed in depth by M. Schillig, *Konkretisierungskompetenz and Konkretisierungsmethoden im Europäischen Privatrecht*, Berlin: De Gruyter 2009.

simultaneously applicable may not be in accordance with one another. However, the scope of alternative regulation is smaller than legislation and the binding effect of alternative regulation is limited to particular sectors or to parties who have subjected themselves to rules developed through alternative regulation; and collective labour agreements, standard contract terms, or model contracts will not be very successful if they impose conflicting duties on parties or contradict themselves.

The development of the private law *acquis* and the incorrect implementation of the *acquis* may also give rise to inconsistencies. Yet if private parties rely on implemented provisions, whilst not challenging the implementation of a particular Directive, inconsistency between a Directive and national implementation law is not necessarily directly problematic for private parties. Directives themselves are typically not directly applicable between parties, which leads to the conclusion that inconsistencies between a Directive and the national law are not inconsistencies between simultaneously applicable rules. However, this inconsistency may be problematic for another reason: the incorrect implementation of European law may be more likely to be amended or reformed, especially if Member States are held liable by the CJEU, which reduces the reliability of incorrectly implemented rules.

2.4.4. *Overlaps between predictability, consistency and accessibility*

Thus, predictability, consistency and accessibility can be established as benchmarks for European private law. Notably, predictability, accessibility and consistency show significant overlap, and consequently, complying with one requirement may facilitate compliance with another requirement. For example, increasing consistency may well improve predictability, and improving predictability may well improve the accessibility of private law. Similarly, a clear overview of relevant sources may well increase some parties' ability to adequately determine their legal position. Also, accessibility of private law may in turn facilitate the understanding of private law, which enables a more rational debate on the development of private law, and a stable development of private law.

In contrast, if private law is not in accordance with one requirement, this also negatively affects the other requirements. For example, inconsistencies in private law also seriously undermine the predictability and accessibility of private law. Likewise, inaccessibility makes it more difficult for parties to adequately determine their legal position, and retroactive or continuous amendments will undermine the accessibility of private law.

2.5. Responsiveness

Whilst legal certainty is important for private parties, more benchmarks should be set for private law. Parties require more from private law than merely predictability, accessibility, and consistency. Private law should not develop in isolation to its surroundings. Rather, private law should be responsive to society's legal views on justice[159] and business practices.[160]

Notably, private law does not merely provide neutral rules, although that may happen; law provides normative rules, especially through mandatory law. Accordingly, if private parties make an agreement that enables them to exploit a third party, or if parties agree on something distinctly immoral, private law should not facilitate these endeavours. Consequently, these normative rules are imposed on private parties and should, therefore, be in accordance with ideas of justice, which has been recognised more generally.

For example, if the legislature establishes that murderers can inherit the property of their victims, because this exception is in accordance with the principle of *ne bis in idem*, society may consider this unacceptable, for example, because murderers are being rewarded with the property of their victims. This rule could be avoided in several ways. Firstly, the people will try to prompt the legislator to reconsider the exception. Secondly, people could change their wills, providing, insofar as that is permitted by national law, that whomsoever murders them shall not inherit their property. If that clause is not permitted by the law, it is not unthinkable that testators would try to avoid having to apply that particular piece of law, for example by a choice of law, or in whatever other way they could. Thirdly, the scope of the rule could be limited by the judiciary. Fourthly, if individual cases in which murderers are allowed to inherit lead to public outrage, this could re-prompt the legislator to amend the law.

Furthermore, private parties, in particular businesses entering into contracts with one another, also want private law to take into account their practices. Everyday practice develops continuously, and private law should be able to cope with existing and developing practices.[161] If private parties establish a new business, or start using a new technology, or construct their business in a new manner, it is important that private law allows parties to determine their legal position, even if the law was not designed with the new practice or the technology in mind. If private law is not in accordance with legal practice, this may also inhibit the parties' ability to rely on private law. Arguably, if private law is easily outdated, it is likely to become obsolete. If private law cannot adequately accommodate the transactions that they have entered into, this may complicate rather than facilitate entering into transactions. Outdated law may also increase parties' ability to circumvent national law.

159 Justice in itself is problematic as a benchmark, see further below par. 2.6.1.

160 Comp. W. Wilburg, *A flexible system in the area of private law* (inaugural address Graz, 1950), translated by H. Hausmaninger, Vienna: Manzsches Verlag und Universitätsbuchhandlung, 2000, p. 3: 'One cannot deny that in many cases the legal order fails to satisfy the needs of everyday life and society's sense of justice' and who accordingly argues for a flexible system of private law. E.M.M. Meijer, *De taak der rechtswetenschap ten aanzien der vrijen rechtspraak* (inaugural address Leiden), Haarlem: Tjeenk Willink 1910, p. 21, emphasises that legal academics should not isolate themselves from society but should place themselves within it, in order to serve justice. Comp. A. Watson, *Legal transplants*, Edinburgh: Scottish Academic Press 1974, p. 21, who notes that while ' a people's law can be regarded as being special to it', this does not stand in the way of legal transplants, or borrowing. Different convictions may however result in divergent laws.

161 See further par. 2.5.2.

Thus, private parties do not want private law to develop in isolation; rather, private law should be responsive to ideas on justice and the needs of parties entering into transactions with another.[162] In other words, the law should be responsive.

Nonet and Selznick[163] distinguish responsive law from authoritarian or repressive law[164] and autonomous law.[165] They define responsive law as law that has 'a capacity for responsible, and hence discriminate and selective, adaptation'.[166] Without following all of society's views on justice, responsive law perceives social pressures as sources of knowledge and opportunities for self-correction. Thus, a theory for legal change is developed that recognises societal pressures as an external factor that may affect change,[167] emphasising participation and a purpose for changing the law. Witteveen[168] notes that the idea of responsive law is likely to be in accordance with Fuller's ideas on the inner morality of law, as it emphasises the development of the law in accordance with ethical principles closely interrelated to the development of rules, rather than focusing on the origin of rules. More generally, Fuller, in developing his criteria, recognises that law is developed in a social context, and his criteria are in accordance with the idea that if law is to be complied with, interaction between the legislator and the citizens on what the law is to achieve, is necessary. Interaction of this sort is more generally important if private law is to facilitate transactions between private parties. Arguably, the question of whether private law is of good quality also depends on what parties expects of private law. In turn, the answer to this question is closely interrelated with normative ideas on justice as well as practical requirements. The need for interaction is particularly important in pluralistic legal orders and responsive law accordingly pays attention to the need to involve different views on the development of private law.[169] Similarly, the importance of developing private laws in accordance with society's views on justice and developing private law in accordance with the needs and preferences of practice has been emphasised.

Accordingly, paragraph 2.5.1 will consider the responsiveness of private law to society's legal views on justice, and paragraph 2.5.2 will discuss the responsiveness of private law to practice. Paragraph 2.5.3 will discuss the connection between

162 Comp. G. Teubner, 'The two faces of Janus: Rethinking legal pluralism', *Cardozo Law Review* 1992, p. 1448 who also refers to responsiveness.

163 P. Nonet, P. Selznick, *Law & Society in transition : towards responsive law*, New Brunswick: Transaction Publishers 2001, p. 16, 17-18, 29, 53.

164 See J. Austin, *The providence of jurisprudence determined*, London: Murray 1861, p. 15–25.

165 Comp. M. Rheinstein (ed.), *Max Weber on law in economy and society*, London: OUP 1969, 3rd print, p. 336, on domination based on 'rational rules'.

166 P. Nonet, P. Selznick, *Law & society in transition: towards responsive law*, New Brunswick: Transaction Publishers 2001, p. 77.

167 Comp. also P. Selznick, *Law, society, and industrial justice*, New York: Russell Sage Foundation 1969, p. 33, tracing development in strict liability law to technical developments, and emphasising "principles of legality" if law is developed by 'special-purpose organisations'.

168 W.J. Witteveen, 'Laws of lawmaking', in: W.J. Witteveen, W.J. van den Burg (ed.), *Rediscovering Fuller*, Amsterdam: AUP 1999, p. 343.

169 Comp. R.A. Kagan, 'On "responsive law"', in: R.A. Kagan, M. Krygier. K. Winston (eds.), *Legality and community, on the intellectual legacy of Philip Selznick*, Berkeley: Rowman & Littlefield/Berkeley Public Policy Press 2002, p. 86.

responsiveness to society's legal views on justice and legal practice, and the overlap with requirements facilitating legal certainty.

2.5.1. *Private law should be responsive to society's legal views on justice*

The relationship between private law and normative views in society has been characterised as continuously interactive: on the one hand, views on just and appropriate behaviour continuously develop in society, and eventually find their way into private law. On the other hand, private law provides a framework for transactions between private parties and affects society's views.[170] Accordingly, blanket clauses in private law refer to views held in society, for example, article 3:12, article 6:162 BW, par. 151 BGB or, in the case of the current UK Supreme Court, to the views of commuters on the Underground.[171] A lack of responsiveness may also be an incentive to revise codifications, in order to systematically clarify upon which legal principles private law is built.[172]

Do ideas on justice converge between the Member States, and consequently, do common ideas on justice underpin European private law?[173] At an abstract level, the ideas on justice may well converge – consider, for example, respect for human rights or principles such as freedom of contract. According to Dworkin[174] general principles, such as '*pacta sunt servanda*', or 'legal equality' do not by themselves decide the outcome in a specific case, and a choice for a solution that is in accordance with principle A rather than principle

170 See on Dutch private law P. Memelink, *De verkeersopvatting*, The Hague: BJU 2009, p. 24–27. Comp. for German law MunchKomm zum BGB/Busche (2012), article 157, nr 16 et seq. Comp. also S.E. Merry, ' Legal pluralism', *Law and Society Review* 1988, p. 883–886. Comp. also the aims of the French proposal to revise the law, C.M.D.S. Pavillon, 'Een nieuw contractenrecht voor Frankrijk', *NTBR* 2015, 11, who considers the reformulation of article 1134 Cc in the light of concerns on "social justice". She however points out that "reasonableness", ('*redelijkheid en billijkheid*') in the sense of article 6:2 and 248 BW, or society's legal views on justice ('*verkeersopvattingen*') in the sense of article 3:12 BW does not form a central theme in the *Code Civil*.

171 See, for example, *McFarlane v Tayside Health Board* [2000] AC 82–83 *per* Lord Steyn. O.A. Haazen, 'Precedent in The Netherlands', in: E.H. Hondius (ed.), *Precedent and the law*, Brussels: Bruylant 2007, p. 250 argues that the case law of the Hoge Raad also shows that the Hoge Raad looks to the 'popular support' of a rule when deciding to overrule or conform to previous case law. Comp. on German law A. Röthel, *Normkonkretisierung im Privatrecht*, Tübingen: Mohr Siebeck 2004, p. 28–29 on '*wertausfüllungsbedurftigen Begriffen*', or '*Wertbegriffen*'.

172 E.M. Meijers, 'Voor- en nadelen van het samenstellen van een nieuw burgerlijk wetboek', in: E.M. Meijers, *Verzamelde privaatrechtelijke opstellen, I*, Leiden: Universitaire Pers Leiden, p. 173.

173 As defended by G. Alpa, 'European Community resolutions and the codification of "private law"', *ERPL* 2000, p. 328.

174 R. Dworkin, *Taking rights seriously*, London: Duckworth 1977, p. 35–36. Comp. for German law. J. Esser, *Grundsatz und Norm in der richterlichen Fortbildung des Privatrechts*, Tübingen: Mohr Siebeck 1956, reprinted 1990, p. 221–223, who, referring to the stable development of German private law before and after the adoption of the BGB, finds that principles enable the judiciary to decide more transparently, whilst also taking into account previous decisions and the wording of the law. In this view, principles are not only derived from the system of the BGB, and their use is necessary, but recourse to legal principles may present a problem of legitimacy, see J. Köndgen, 'Josef Esser – Methodologie zwischen Theorie und Praxis', *JZ* 2001, p. 808. Comp. N. Reich, *General principles of EU civil law*, Antwerp: Intersentia 2014, p. 3–4.

B does not mean that principle B is not a recognised principle underpinning private law anymore. Rather, general principles may give weight to a particular argument. In the absence of a hierarchy of principles or a permanent choice between principles, legal opinion on how individual cases should be decided may well differ.

For example, in wrongful birth cases, the Hoge Raad indicated that damages for wrongful birth included the costs of raising the child, and could also include compensation for loss of income of the mother.[175] In contrast, the House of Lords in *MacFarlane v Tayside Health Board*[176] decided that the mother should be compensated for general damages that included the pain and suffering of pregnancy and birth, while the claim for compensation for the costs of upbringing was rejected. Lord Steyn stated that it would not be in accordance with generally-held views that parents should be able to claim compensation for the upbringing of a healthy child, considering the amount of couples not able to have children or caring for disabled children, and the possibility that parents would have to argue in court that the unwanted child 'is more trouble than it is worth'. Accordingly, the House of Lords held that awarding pure economic loss in this case would not be 'fair, just, and reasonable'.

These different outcomes do not mean that one of the solutions is unjust. In other words, the outcome of one case cannot serve as a requirement that should be applied in other jurisdictions, as that would overlook the necessity of responsiveness to the different views on justice in the different societies.

However, these differences do raise the question whether this requirement can also be made of law developed at the European level – if these legal views do not exist, how can European law be developed in accordance with these views? The answer should be sought in the developing character of the European legal order. Walker[177] convincingly notes that the constitutions and their polities are mutually reinforcing. Accordingly, the European legal order is still developing, whereas national polities are much further developed and coherent. As legal views on justice develop, the European polity will develop as well, and vice versa.[178] Yet national private laws are based more clearly and systematically on legal views on justice. In the light of these differences, values at the European level[179] are expressed in abstract terms and should provide starting points for deliberation between actors.[180] As deliberation develops, legal views on justice

175 HR 21 February 1997, *NJ* 1999, 145, par. 3.7 and 3.13.

176 *McFarlance v Tayside Health Board* [2000] 2 AC 59, 81–83, *per* Lord Steyn.

177 N. Walker, 'The idea of constitutional pluralism', *MLR* 2002, p.341–342.

178 Comp. in this sense also the argument that further harmonisation will foster the EU polities. Comp. on the one hand M.W. Hesselink, 'The case for a common European Sales Law in an age of rising nationalism', *ERCL* 2012, p. 342, and on the other hand E.A. Posner, 'The questionable basis of the Common European Sales Law: The role of an optional instrument in jurisdictional competition'' *CMLRev* 2013, p. 272–275.

179 Comp. for example article 2 TEU that considers 'respect for human dignity, freedom, democracy, equality, the rule of law and respect for human rights' in a pluralist society and the Union's aim to stimulate these values, under article 3 TEU, while article 6 TEU notes that the rights, freedoms and principles recognised in the EU charter shall have the same legal value as the Treaties. Similarly W. van Gerven, S. Lierman, *Beginselen van Belgisch privaatrecht. Algemeen Deel, veertig jaar later*, Mechelen: Kluwer 2010, p. 33, also noting that the EU legal order is based on the legal orders of its Member States.

180 See further on this idea below par. 9.5.1.

could solidify and become more concrete, which in turn should facilitate deliberation.[181]

That however does not mean that deliberation will develop quickly – even within Member States, differences between societal groups may increase, which makes deliberation more difficult. The argument also need not entail that the European legal order will gradually develop into a "super-state", or that in time, there will be sufficient convergence to develop a European Civil Code. This argument overlooks that European law does not, as such, develop on the basis of principles. Instead, European law is oriented towards building the internal market.[182] However, even if European law does not develop in a manner similar to national law, it affects national private laws and can therefore hardly be seen apart from legal views on justice.

By referring to views in society, private law imparts society's ideas on what is just. These views concern basic ideas about justice, such as compliance with human rights and the rule of law, as well as more controversial political points of view, such as allowing surrogate motherhood. Arguably, the support of those ideas by a democratic majority does not ensure, in itself, that private law is just, only that it is in accordance with views held in society. Unfortunately, such views can be unjust.[183] In other words, the responsiveness of private law does not ensure that private law itself is just, nor is it just because it converges with societal views and developments.[184] Accordingly, in the Dutch Civil Code, the legislator did not want blanket clauses such as article 3:12 BW to be interpreted too subjectively; this article refers not to 'opinion' but '*legal* opinion' ('*rechtsovertuiging*')[185] which is not determined by a democratic majority.[186] Typically, the influence of the majority's views on what is just is mitigated as national constitutions and treaties may also reflect society's views on what is just and appropriate. Private law cannot go against these laws, and, therefore, private law should not be able to facilitate manifest injustice. Consequently, judges are not obliged to undertake a survey of the actual views on a matter

181 Comp. in this respect H.-W. Micklitz, N. Reich, 'The Court and the Sleeping Beauty: The revival of the unfair contract terms Directve', *CMLRev* 2014, p. 806, who note that in protecting consumers against unfair clauses, consumers appear to consider the CJEU as a court of last instance, which offers consumers protection where national actors do not. In this respect, Micklitz and Reich note that '[i]t looks as if the ECJ is in fact developing hand in hand with the consumers and citizens what has been called "a European civil society"'.

182 H.-W. Micklitz, 'Monolistic ideology or pluralistic reality', in L. Niglia (ed.), *Pluralism and European private law*, Oxford: Hart 2013, p. 38–39. Comp. however W. van Gerven, 'Codifying European private law? Yes, if …!', *ELR* 2002, p. 174, who notes that provisions in a European Civil Code – or in the DCFR – are often derived from national provisions.

183 M.W. Hesselink, *De redelijkheid en billijkheid in het Europese privaatrecht*, Deventer: Kluwer 1999, p. 32, points to the use of blanket clauses by the Nazi regime. Simultaneously, abstract notions of justice can be used to set aside democratic polities, as argued by A.J. Menéndez, 'Whose justice? Which Europe?', in: D. Kochenov, G. de Búrca, A. Williams (eds.), *Europe's justice deficit?*, Oxford: Hart 2015, p. 137.

184 J.H. Nieuwenhuis, *Confrontatie & compromis*, Deventer: Kluwer 2007, 7–10.

185 J.H. Nieuwenhuis, *Confrontatie & compromis*, Deventer: Kluwer 2007, 57–58.

186 Comp. the opinion of A.G. Kist before HR 17 November 1970, *NJ* 1971, 373: 'Dit betekent dat het bij de beoordeling van de aanstotelijkheid [van de eerbaarheid] niet zozeer aankomt op de opvattingen van de zuiver numerieke meerderheid van de bevolking'. Comp. for German law K. Larenz, *Methodenlehre der Rechtswissenschaft*, Berlin: Springer 1991, 6th ed., p. 291–292.

held in some parts of society. Rather, the judge must determine whether society will tolerate his interpretation of that view or whether it will reject that view as manifestly unjust.

Thus, while the responsiveness of private law in itself does not ensure that private law is just, responsiveness does ensure that private law takes into account the legal views of the people bound by it, which is just.

What ideas might society's views consist of, and where can these ideas be found? Firstly, the constitutional ideas of a legal order, such as respect for human rights, can be seen as society's legal views on justice.[187] Secondly, arguably, ideas on justice relevant to private law can not only be found in national constitutions, but also in treaties, or other areas of law, such as administrative law. Thirdly, it is submitted that general principles as recognised by Dworkin,[188] such as the idea that nobody may profit from his own wrongdoing,[189] as well as more general ideas on party autonomy and freedom of contract, also constitute ideas on justice recognised in private law.[190] Fourthly, ideas on justice can be found in unwritten law. In Dutch law, liability for tort can also be established if an act is contrary to society's views ('*verkeersopvatting*') in accordance with unwritten law, as stipulated in article 6:162 par. 3 BW. Similarly, in German law, blanket clauses such as article 242 BGB are closely intertwined with society's legal views on justice.[191] According to Meijers,[192] legal academics may provide support for legal views on justice. Finally, those views may also be found in political discourse.[193] Accordingly, views on distributive justice can be seen as underlying choices made in private law.[194] The ideas found in these sources may well overlap – for example, the principle of legal equality can both be guaranteed in national constitutions and be recognised as a principle in private law.[195]

This volume asks whether a particular solution is responsive, focusing on the reasoning used to decide especially controversial cases.

187 Comp. S. Grundmann (ed.) *Constitutional values in private law*, Alphen aan den Rijn: KLI 2008.

188 R. Dworkin, *Taking rights seriously*, London: Duckworth 1977, p. 40: 'the origin of (...) legal principles lies not in a particular decision of some legislature or court, but in a sense of appropriateness developed in the profession and the public over time.'

189 Lord Wright, 'Precedents', *Cambridge Law Journal* 1944, p. 133, considers this a matter of public policy.

190 Comp. on possible new ideas on justice in Dutch private law the special issue of the *WPNR* on justice in private law ('*Rechtvaardigheid in het privaatrecht*'), *WPNR* 6843 (2010).

191 Staudinger Komm zum BGB/Honsell (2013), introduction to the BGB, nr. 71.

192 E.M. Meijers, *De taak der rechtswetenschap ten aanzien der vrijen rechtspraak* (inaugural address Leiden), Haarlem: Tjeenk Willink 1910, p. 27. Comp. Ch. Joerges, 'The Europeanisation process of private law as a rationalization process and as a contest of disciplines – an analysis of the Directive on unfair terms in consumer contracts', *ERPL* 1995, p. 184 who, rather than referring to an abstract notion of justice, points to the context within which notions of justice develop, i.e. the interplay between legal academia, case law, and public interested in the normative quality of decisions.

193 See particularly for empirical research on political discourse and private law in the Dutch legal order, W.H. van Boom, S.D. Lindenbergh (eds.), *Politiek privaatrecht*, The Hague: BJU 2013.

194 A. Kronman, 'Contract law and distributive justice', *Yale Law Journal* 1980, p. 472.

195 Comp. C.-W. Canaris, *Systemdenken und Systembegriff in Jurisprudenz*, Berlin: Duncker & Humblot 1983, 2nd ed., p. 16–17 who has pointed out that the systematic unity introduced by Civil Codes is based on legal equality as legal equality requires consistency and coherence.

2.5.2. *Private law should be responsive to practice*

If parties enter into a transaction with one another, private law should be adequately aware of everyday practice. The practicality (*'hanteerbaarheid'*) of private law has been emphasised for Dutch private law.[196] Traditionally, the need for pragmatic private law has been widely recognised. Especially in English law, pragmatism has been emphasised.[197] Similarly, Dutch[198] and German[199] law have sought to pragmatically respond to business practices. European law has also sought to take into account trade practices in article 67 draft CESL,[200] reflecting article II. -1:104 DCFR.[201] According to defences of regulatory European private law,[202] European law, oriented on building the internal market, is focussed on facilitating the access to domestic markets throughout the Union, which should be in line with the interests of parties in cross-border trade. On an international level, the need to develop the law in accordance with trade practice has been recognised in article 9 CISG and article 1.9 UNIDROIT Principles.[203]

Wiarda[204] has argued that the increasing use of blanket clauses can be traced to the decreased ability of the legislator to foresee specific situations. Specifically, the legislator provides more ambiguous provisions which leave sufficient room for the courts to

196 A.J. Verheij, ' Wie is verantwoordelijk voor hanteerbaar privaatrecht?' in A.L.M. Keirse et al. (eds.), *Beter Burgerlijk Recht*, Deventer: Kluwer 2012, p. 179, with further references.

197 See, for example, P.S. Atiyah, 'Pragmatism and theory in English law', *Hamlyn Lectures* 1987, Lord Goff, 'The search for principle', *Maccabean Lectures on Jurisprudence, Proceedings of the British Academy* 1984, p. 186: 'Pragmatism must be the watchword.' S. Whittaker, K. Riesenhuber, 'Conceptions of contract', in: G. Danneman, S. Vogenauer (eds.), *The Common European Sales Law in context*, Oxford: OUP 2013, p. 123 refer to the widely considered commercial approach of English contract law. Comp. also H. Collins, 'European private law and the cultural identity of states', *ERPL* 1995, p. 361, who stresses that private law is based on social practices. W. van Gerven, 'Codifying European private law? Yes, if ...!', *ELR* 2002, p. 174 also reiterates the need to develop rules within a legal environment. He finds that if a European Civil Code would be adopted, a new legal environment should be created, to ensure the stable development of law.

198 Particularly prominently in Dutch law Asser/Scholten 1974, p. 98.

199 Staudinger Komm zum BGB/Honsell (2013), introduction to the BGB, nr. 70, H.A. Engelhard, 'Zu den Aufgaben einer Kommission für die Überarbeitung des Schuldrechts', *NJW* 1984, p. 1202. Comp. also A. Röthel, *Normkonkretisierung im Privatrecht*, Tübingen: Mohr Siebeck 2004, p. 89–90.

200 Critically on this provision V. Mak, 'According to custom ...? The role of 'Trade Usage' in the Proposed Common European Sales Law (CESL)', *ERCL* 2014, p.64 and L. Bernstein, 'An (un)common frame of reference: An American perspective on the jurisprudence of the CESL', *CMLRev* 2013, p. 169, who also finds that the proposed CESL presupposes the existence of 'usage of trade, good commercial practices, the practices of the parties and other elements of the contracting context to give meaning to contracts and content to its many standard-like default rules'.

201 Comp. also N. Jansen, *The making of legal authority*, Oxford: OUP, 2010, p. 43: the "abstract authority of a text giving expression to a legal norm consists in the legal profession accepting it as an ultimate source of the law".

202 H.-W. Micklitz, 'Monolistic ideology or pluralistic reality', in L. Niglia (ed.), *Pluralism and European private law*, Oxford: Hart 2013, p. 38–39.

203 In addition, par. 1 – 303, sub c UCC also refers to 'usage of trade'.

204 G.J. Wiarda, *3 typen van rechtsvinding*, (comments from T. Koopmans), Deventer: Tjeenk Willink 1999, 4th ed., p. 92.

develop the law in accordance with new developments. Fikentscher[205] refers to the '*Rationalisierungsfunktion*' of blanket clauses: legislators seek to provide an abstract rule for an enormous amount of individual cases.

If private law is to provide an efficient framework for private parties, it should take an adequate starting point and not close its eyes to existing business practices or technological developments.[206] If private law is responsive, this will contribute to the efficiency of private law.[207] The need for responsiveness to legal practice has increased as private law has been used as an instrument to further policy aims at a European level and, in some cases, also at a national level, in accordance with questions from the European legislator.[208] Notably, if the private law *acquis* is to *effectively* enhance the internal market, it arguably needs to adequately assess existing and developing practices in order to correctly identify problems and barriers to the internal market.

2.5.3. Relations between responsiveness and legal certainty

This paragraph will consider the connection between the responsiveness of private law to society's legal views on justice and legal practice, and secondly, consider possible conflicts.

Firstly, the connection between responsiveness to society's legal views on justice and responsiveness to practice has been sketched especially clearly by the Dutch Professor Nieuwenhuis,[209] who sketches how requirements of legal practice ('*realia*') and ideas on justice ('*idealia*') both influence private law and, in turn, are influenced by private law; there is interaction between the demands of legal practice, ideas on justice and private law, in the following ways:

205 W. Fikentscher, *Methoden des Rechts in vergleichenden Darstellung, Teil IV: Dogmatischer Teil, Anhang*, Tübingen: Mohr Siebeck 1977, p. 308, Staudinger Komm zum BGB/Honsell (2013), introduction to the BGB, nr. 70.

206 Comp. K.-H. Ladeur, 'Methodology and European law – Can methodology change so as to cope with the multiplicity of law', in: M. van Hoecke (ed.), *Epistemology and methodology of comparative law*, Oxford: Hart 2004, p. 93–94 who stresses that law is pressured to adapt to continuously evolving social practices, which may entail that private actors who drive these developments and have superior knowledge become closely involved in the development of the law.

207 A.D.M. Forte, 'If it ain't broke, don't fix it: On not codifying commercial law', in: H.L. MacQueen (ed.), *Scots law into the 21st century*, Edinburgh: Sweet & Maxwell 1996, p. 93–94.

208 See, for example, European Commission, *Communication from the Commission to the Council and the European Parliament on European contract law*, COM (2001) 398 final, stating: 'The European Commission is interested (…) in gathering information on the need for farther-reaching EC action in the area of contract law' (par. 10) or 'The Commission would like to find out if the co-existence of national contract laws in the Member states directly or indirectly obstructs to the functioning of the internal market.' [sic] (par. 23).

209 J.H. Nieuwenhuis, *Drie beginselen van contractenrecht*, Deventer: Kluwer 1977, p. 41–42. See for further references to the Dutch debate preceding the new Dutch Civil Code C. Sieburgh, *Tertium datur. De niet uitgesloten derde in het burgerlijk recht* (inaugural address Nijmegen), Deventer: Kluwer 2004, p. 11. See also in this sense H. Collins, 'European private law and the cultural identity of states', *ERPL* 1995, p. 362.

Firstly, rules may be accepted in private law because practice demands that acceptance. Secondly, ideas on justice are not neutral; they prescribe certain behaviour. If ideas on justice grow prominent enough, they can be reflected in rules of private law or they can influence the interpretation of blanket clauses. As Nieuwenhuis rightly points out, there is interaction between on the one hand, the demands of practice, and on the other hand, ideas on justice. If ideas on justice are unattainable, this will lessen their chance of acceptance in private law, and conversely, if demands of legal practice lead to injustice, they will not be accepted.

The requirements of responsiveness and legal certainty may in some cases not be easily reconciled. This possible conflict has been widely debated. In particular, Radbruch[210] has argued that requirements of legal certainty may contradict principles of justice, especially if the law prescribes injustice in a predictable, consistent and accessible manner.[211] Requirements of responsiveness to society's legal views on justice and requirements of predictability may also overlap. Even Radbruch,[212] pointing to the possible conflict between legal certainty and justice, simultaneously recognised that legal certainty and justice cannot also be seen separately from one another. Arguably, the requirements of predictability, accessibility and consistency are also in accordance with the idea of justice: if private law is binding on private parties, private law should comply with the requirements that facilitate legal certainty. It is unfair to hold a private party liable for failure to comply with one of multiple contradictory rules, as he cannot comply with both rules, or to expect parties to comply with rules that they cannot have been aware of, because these rules have gone into effect retroactively or were not publicly accessible. Also, the convergence between private law and views in society plays an important role in the ability of private parties to know what the law is, without possessing specific expertise on private law. Lack of clarity, inconsistencies, and inaccessibility affect some parties more than others: when bringing a successful claim becomes more difficult, especially actors with little expertise and financial resources may be discouraged from bringing a claim. In this way, weak parties protected by the legislator can be denied their protection, which will generally be considered unfair.

Also, responsiveness may require that private law is predictable. Chalmers[213] already indicated that the common law has developed predictably, because English commercial practice expressed the need for predictability. In Dutch law, some authors have even understood legal certainty and practicality as synonyms.[214]

The need for responsiveness to practice and the need for legal certainty may also clash. Responsiveness to practice may undermine legal certainty if it means that the law

210 G. Radbruch, *Rechtsphilosophie, Gestamtausgabe Band 2* (ed. and rev. A. Kaufmann), Heidelberg: Müller 1993, p. 169.

211 See in more detail G. Radbruch, 'Statutory lawlessness and *supra*-statutory law (1946)', *OJLS* 2006, p. 1.

212 G. Radbruch, *Rechtsphilosophie, Gesamtausgabe Band 2* (ed. and rev. A. Kaufmann), Heidelberg: Müller 1993, p. 170.

213 M.D. Chalmers, 'Codification of mercantile law', *LQR* 1903, p. 14.

214 For example H. Drion, 'Het rechtszekerheidsargument', in: H. Drion et al. (eds.), *De hanteerbaarheid van het recht*, Zwolle: Tjeenk Willink 1981, p. 1–13. The Hoge Raad has mentioned these benchmarks separately, see relatively recently HR 8 July 2011, *NJ* 2011, 309.

develops too rapidly or if, for example, the binding force of contracts is made subject to (too) many exceptions.[215] Actors seeking to develop European private law in accordance with the requirements of predictability, accessibility and consistency will generally exercise restraint when adapting, introducing or revoking parts of private law, rather than opportunistically or randomly. Nonet and Selznick[216] find that in order to avoid opportunistic change, the law must have a specific purpose. Theoretically, the aim of the private law *acquis* – to improve the internal market and to protect consumers – should inhibit the unstable development of the private law *acquis*.[217] Possibly, however, one could argue that the ambiguity of this aim does not help to limit the unpredictable development of the *acquis*. Alternatively, although national private laws need not necessarily pursue a specific objective, the coherence of private law imposes some restraint on actors developing the law. The ideas underlying private law serve as starting points for amending the law.[218]

2.6. Justice, legitimacy, coherence, and legal equality

Concepts of justice, legitimacy, coherence and legal equality are necessary qualities of law more generally,[219] and the development of private law through national techniques should be closely intertwined with these notions.

It would be difficult to defend that the law should be unjust, or illegitimate. Similarly, arguments against the coherent development of law are often directed against the systematisation of law through "rigid codes", rather than some degree of normative coordination between related areas of private law that allow one to 'make sense of the law'. Equally, arguments based on legal equality – vehemently – disagree on the question whether legal equality should be expressed in separate private law provisions, or which cases are sufficiently equal, rather than rejecting the idea of legal equality itself. Yet even though European private law should clearly be just, legitimate, coherent and respect legal quality, they will not serve as separate "benchmarks" in this book, as explained below. Paragraph 2.6.1 will consider justice, and paragraph 2.6.2 will discuss legitimacy. Subsequently, paragraph 2.6.3 will turn to coherence and paragraph 2.6.4. will consider legal equality. Paragraph 2.6.5. will end with a conclusion discussing the relation between

215 Comp. in this respect critically on the proposed revision of the French law of obligations C.M.D.S. Pavillon, 'Een nieuw contractenrecht voor Frankrijk', *NTBR* 2015, 11, who finds that the aims of the legislator to promote the attractiveness of French law for international trade and the aim to develop the law in accordance with ideas on social justice undermine one another.

216 P. Nonet, P. Selznick, *Law & society in transition: towards responsive law*, New Brunswick: Transaction Publishers 2001, p. 77.

217 Comp. for example the criticism in H. Eidenmuller et al, 'Towards a revision of the consumer-*acquis*', *CMLR* 2011, p. 1077.

218 Comp. P.S. Atiyah, 'Pragmatism and theory in English law', *Hamlyn Lectures* 1987, p. 101–103 on the disadvantages of amending the law without a sound theoretical basis.

219 It has been argued that if law is not just, it should not be called law. Comp. also more generally, with regard to justice, J. Rawls, *A theory of justice*, Cambridge, Mass.: Harvard University Press 1999, p. 3: 'laws (…) no matter how efficient and well-arranged must be reformed or abolished if they are unjust.'

justice, legitimacy, coherence and legal equality, and explain why they will not serve as separate benchmarks in this book.

2.6.1. *Justice*

The criticism of Hart[220] on the "inner morality" defended by Fuller indicates that Fuller's requirements overlook an essential benchmark of law. Hart found that referring to the inner morality of law was confusing, and argued that similar requirements could also, for example, justify the inner morality of poisoning. In other words, the development of private law in accordance with Fuller's criteria does not necessarily mean that the law is also moral.[221]

The need for just law is poignant at the European level. Kochenov[222] has pointed out that so far, despite the incorporation of justice in articles 2 and 3 TEU, it remains unclear what role justice should play in the development of European Union law. Accordingly, although the drafters of the DCFR have indicated that justice is one of the fundamental principles underlying European private law,[223] the Commission, in developing the private law *acquis*, is bound to the competences conferred upon it and seems to have therefore sought to develop the private law *acquis* as a means to advance the internal market, rather than justice.

According to the definition of "just" in the Oxford English dictionary, law is well-founded, upright and impartial, or in accordance with principles of fairness. These definitions arguably do not exclude one another. Under this definition, the development of a just private law entails the development of material law that is morally right. Views on justice are *normative* views on both the content of the law and the outcome of individual cases in accordance with the law. Moreover, these are not individual views; as Dworkin[224] points out, they are views shared by the community – which perhaps is a reason why there is disagreement on the question of whether the rules in the private law *acquis* should be the result of considerations of justice, given the different views between Member States. As the law purports to say something about wrong and right, its views are subjected to the question of whether this view of the law on wrong and right is correct.

It has been defended that private law is especially concerned with questions of corrective justice, rather than distributive justice.[225] Private law, in this view, is concerned

220 H.L.A. Hart, 'Book review', *Harvard Law Review* 1964–1965, p. 1286. Comp. also H.L.A. Hart, *The concept of law*, Oxford: OUP 1961, p. 157: 'Indeed, there is no absurdity in conceding that unjust law forbidding the access of coloured persons to the parks has been justly administered, in that only persons genuinely guilty of breaking the law were punished for it and then only after a fair trial.'

221 B. Bix, *Jurisprudence: theory and context*, Durham: Carolina Academic Press 2006, 4th ed., p. 103 notes that justice is a 'subset' of morality.

222 D. Kochenov, 'The ought of justice', in: D. Kochenov, G. de Búrca, A. Williams (eds.), *Europe's justice deficit?*, Oxford: Hart 2015, p. 22.

223 Comp. Ch. Von Bar et al (eds.), *Principles, Definitions and Model Rules of European Private Law. Draft Common Frame of Reference, Outline Edition, Volume I*, München : Sellier 2009, p. 84.

224 R. Dworkin, *Law's empire*, Cambridge, Mass.: Harvard University Press 1986, p. 211.

225 Aristotle, *Nichomean Ethics*, through http://classics.mit.edu/Aristotle/nicomachaen.html, Book V, 6. See for this argument J. Gordley, *Foundations of private law*, Oxford: OUP 2006.

with corrective justice as it protects the status quo and provides remedies for breaches of that status, such as tort, for breach of the status quo (good X belongs to Y). However, as the distinction between public and private law becomes less clear, the distinction between private law as a means for corrective justice also become less convincing. This view is reflected in arguments for social justice that private law should compensate for unequal positions between parties and provide protection to weak parties such as consumers.[226] Thus, questions whether private law is just do not only concern corrective justice but also distributive justice.

Nevertheless, justice as a benchmark is problematic because it is difficult to determine in which cases private law is in accordance with justice. Of course one can hardly argue that the content of law, including private law, should be just, but the question, what justice is, and what it requires, is not so easily answered. Are there absolute requirements of justice and if so, how can we know them? And how would an absolute requirement be applied in specific cases? Arguably, justice, or a just solution in a particular case, also depends upon the circumstances specific to that case, and the meaning of justice becomes clear in those specific situations.[227] Alternatively, the view of what is just may also vary with the perspective that one takes: justice from the perspective of consumers, businesses, international organisations, philosophers? Views on what is just may already differ within states; in the European Union, these views are divided even more. Is it then possible to formulate requirements of justice with which the contents of private law have to comply, which could be imposed on private laws? It seems not really in accordance with the idea of, for example, the right to influence the rules that one is subjected to, in accordance with the idea of democracy, to impose such absolute requirements on private laws. In contrast, if justice does not provide an absolute requirement, how can it serve as an objective requirement?

2.6.2. *Legitimacy*

Theories on deliberation and pluralist perspectives emphasise the legitimacy of European private law.[228] Legitimacy is an abstract concept. In the Oxford English dictionary, "legitimacy" denotes 'conformity to rule or principle', or 'lawfulness'. When applied to law, legitimacy may arguably refer to multiple things: to the existence of sufficient popular support for the law,[229] which may be related to both the efficiency of the law[230]

226 Study Group on Social Justice in European Private Law, 'Social Justice in European Contract Law: a Manifesto', *ELJ* 2004, p. 653.

227 Comp. C.J.H. Brunner, *De normen van het privaatrecht*, Deventer: Kluwer 1996, p. 8.

228 For example N. Walker, 'The idea of constitutional pluralism', *MLR* 2002, p. 317, Ch. Joerges, 'On the legitimacy of Europeanising private law: Considerations on a justice-making law for the EU multi-level system', *Electronic Journal of Comparative Law* 2003, available at www.ejcl.org/ejcl/73/art73 3.html, L. Niglia, 'The double life of pluralism in Europe', in: L. Niglia, (ed.), *Pluralism and European private law*, Oxford: Hart 2013, p. 15.

229 C.H. Sieburgh, 'Legitimiteit van de confrontatie van Europees recht en burgerlijk recht van nationale origine', in: W.J.M. Voermans, M.J. Borgers, C.H. Sieburgh, *Controverses rondom legitimiteit en legitimatie, Preadvies Nederlandse Juristen Vereniging*, Deventer: Kluwer 2011, p. 190.

230 Comp. below the argument on "output" legitimacy.

or the development of law in accordance within the democratic procedure,[231] or higher principles that reflect ideas on corrective or distributive justice.[232] Legitimacy also denotes the development of law in accordance with procedural principles (or 'rules of recognition'), which can be associated with arguments for democratically developed law. These requirements, which may overlap but, as will be argued, may also contradict one another, can be seen in the necessity for decision-makers to justify the binding force of rules in the development and enforcement of the law, rather than only the right of the strongest.[233] At the European level, debate on legitimacy has developed. Especially the democratic legitimacy of European law, or the lack thereof, has been criticised. Majone[234] has defended the "democratic deficit" as long as European decision-making remains a-political. At first sight, European decisions in private law accordingly adopt an a-political approach.[235] Yet this approach is misleading and has rightly been criticised.[236] Yet, the debate on European private law has more drastically denied the suitability of the standard of democratic legitimacy, because private law traditionally has not been primarily developed throughout the legislative process, but rather is "found" by practitioners, scholars and judges.[237] The development of the law on the basis of general principles is in conformity with this argument.[238] Similarly, if private law is also

231 Comp. M.W. Hesselink, 'Democratic contract law', *ERCL* 2015, p. 81.

232 Comp. par. 2.6.1.

233 Comp. M.W. Hesselink, 'Democratic contract law', *ERCL* 2012, p. 88, who traces the need for democratic legitimacy to its binding force: 'It is for the citizens to decide collectively on the conditions under which State officials are allowed to use force against its citizens and others.'

234 G. Majone, 'Europe's "democratic deficit": A question of standards', *ELJ* 1998, p. 5.

235 R. Michaels, 'Why we have no theory of European private law pluralism', in: L. Niglia (ed.), *Pluralism and European private law*, Oxford: Hart 2013, notes that German history may support the conclusion that the development of technical private law is well suited for a pluralistic society.

236 See prominently Study Group on Social Justice in European Private Law, 'Social justice in European contract law: A manifesto', *ELJ* 2004, p. 670. Comp. B. van Zelst, *The politics of European Sales Law*, Alphen aan den Rijn: KLI 2008, on the political choices involved with European Sales Law – if private law is developed on the basis of political choices, this entails the involvement of democratically legitimated actors.

237 For European private law, this has been argued by J.M. Smits, 'Democracy and (European) private law; A functional approach', in: M. Faure, A. van der Walt (eds.), *Globalization and private law: The way forward*, Cheltenham: Elgar 2010, p. 26. Comp. Asser/Scholten 1974, p. 12, stating that the law exists, but must be found. This has historically also been defended, for example by Sir John Davies, in his preface to *Le Pimer Report des Cases en Ireland*, 1615, who finds that customary law is superior to statutes as it has been tried and tested, and statutes may be `in effect` reversed so that well-established customs can be accommodated. See also R. Zimmerman, 'Das Römisch-Kanonische Ius commune als Grundlage europäischer Rechtseinheit, *JZ* 1992, p. 8 who links European private law to the *ius commune europaeum*. C.H. Sieburgh, 'Legitimiteit van de confrontatie van Europees recht en burgerlijk recht van nationale origine', in: W.J.M. Voermans, M.J. Borgers, C.H. Sieburgh, *Controverses rondom legitimiteit en legitimatie, Preadvies Nederlandse Juristen Vereniging*, Deventer: Kluwer 2011, p. 190 notes that in Dutch debate, the question about the legitimacy of the effect of European law on national private law has received little attention. While recognising the development of private law by the judiciary, as well as the thorough argumentation from judges and shortcomings in legislative procedures, M.W. Hesselink, 'Democratic contract law', *ERCL* 2015, p. 113 still prefers democratic procedures over judicial or expert lawmaking.

238 See further below par. 9.5.

increasingly developed by non-state actors who do not produce binding rules, it may be doubted whether standards of democratic legitimacy are suitable standards.

Scharpf[239] has argued that the deficits in "input" democratic legitimacy have been supplemented or replaced with "output" legitimacy, i.e. *'government for the people'*, focussing on problem-solving. Accordingly, many "new" forms of governance that take place beyond the democratic process focus on problem-solving.[240] When considering European private law, "output" legitimacy at first sight appears problematic as the effectiveness of especially the *acquis* requires empirical research well beyond the scope of one thesis. At the national level, it is difficult to measure output as national private law does not necessarily pursue a clear aim.

Because of these difficulties, this book will not focus on legitimacy as a separate benchmark for European private law. That does not mean, however, that this book argues that European private law should not be legitimate.

2.6.3. *Coherence*

Coherence has been defined divergently in the debate on European private law. On one end of the spectrum, the Commission[241] implies that private law is coherent if it is not inconsistent, and on the other end of the debate, coherence implies systematisation: 'a completely self-referential, systematic, abstract and comprehensive body of law'.[242]

Arguably, this book does not adopt either definition but emphasises that if private law is coherent, it can be derived from general ideas on justice, and these underlying ideas and principles 'allow one to make sense of the law'.[243] It follows that coherence goes beyond the consistency that merely requires that the law does not contradict itself. Specifically, if private law consists of a collection of detailed provisions that do not contradict one another, it is consistent. Yet if private law is consistent but incoherent, it is not clear why a statute or regulation contains this collection of provisions and not others.

239 F.W. Scharpf, *Governing in Europe: Effective and democratic?*, Oxford: OUP 1999, p. 188.

240 Potential problems of these new forms of governance, which also touch upon democratic legitimacy, will be discussed in chapter 10.

241 European Commission, *A more coherent European contract law. An Action Plan*, COM (2003) 68 final.

242 L. Miller, *The emergence of EU contract law: Exploring Europeanization*, Oxford: OUP 2011, p. 177, noting, at p. 174 that this definition is based on the nation state. Miller, at p. 176, finds that coherence is often left undefined and instead serves as a way to resist harmonisation. This is however not always the case, see for example W. van Gerven, S. Lierman, *Beginselen van Belgisch privaatrecht. Algemeen deel, veertig jaar later*, Mechelen: Kluwer 2010, p. 186, who also distinguish between consistency and coherence, and find that the law is coherent if it is a systematic whole.

243 N. MacCormick, *Rhetoric and the rule of law*, Oxford: OUP 2005, p. 201, p. 190. Ch. von Bar et al., 'Introduction', in: Ch. von Bar et al. (eds.) *Principles, definitions and model rules of European private law. Draft Common Frame of Reference, Outline Edition*, München: Sellier 2009, par. 11, "fundamental" principles are equated with "basically abstract values", which may provide a basis for private law and its further development. However, these values (freedom, security, justice and efficiency) differ from the principles of justice that underpin the law that Dworkin refers to, for example "no one should profit from his own wrong".

Coherence is not a *factual* characteristic of private law. According to Moral Soriano,[244] '[t]he legal system is made up of precedents and legislative acts which share neither a single author, nor the same socio-political (and moral) context. Moreover, its values and principles are in a state of continuous tension.'

Improving coherence need not necessarily mean codification or placing all of (an area of) private law in a rigid system, although the assumption that private law should be coherent lies at the basis of efforts for systematisation. Instead, coherence may be improved in many ways and in many degrees. For example, actors may make private law more coherent by reforming the law, but coherence may also be improved by establishing academic overviews of (areas of) private law.

The coherent development of law depends on the sufficient relation between the areas of law.[245] The question of whether there is a sufficient relation between the areas of law depends on one's perspective; thus, actors taking a functional approach to the development of law may find that areas of public law and private law should be developed coherently, whereas state actors emphasise the coherent development of (areas of) private law. It follows that degrees of coherence are not necessarily tied to the national legal system, but arguments for coherence are often based on methodological nationalism,[246] particularly if proponents assume that various areas of private law should be developed coherently. In addition, if law is coherent as one can make sense of the law, as rules are based on common principles, ideas, or aims, this arguably presupposes, firstly, that agreement on these ideas exists, and secondly, that principles, ideas and aims, could and should play a role, while in reality, even common ideas at the European level, but especially the translation of these ideas or aims in specific rules, is problematic. Admittedly, however, the difficulty in agreeing on common ideas need not necessarily mean that actors should not at least try to reach agreement on these ideas. However, coherence will not serve as a separate benchmark in this book. Frequently, however, actors developing private law coherently do so because they find this is in accordance with developing private law in accordance with the requirement of responsiveness. If private law consists of an arbitrary collection of rules, it is hard to imagine how that would respond to societal views on justice. If private law should take into account those views, how can it be arbitrary? Views on justice may change over time, and they may not be absolute, but as private law takes these views into account, it ceases to be arbitrary and starts to make sense – there are reasons for the underlying choices made in private law.[247]

244 L. Moral Soriano, 'A modest notion of coherence in legal reasoning. A model for the European Court of Justice', *Ratio Juris* 2003, p. 302.

245 Comp. W. van Gerven, S. Lierman, *Algemeen deel. Veertig jaar later*, Mechelen: Kluwer 2010, p. 190 and C.-W. Canaris, *Systemdenken und Systembegriff in Jurisprudenz*, Berlin: Duncker & Humblot 1983, 2nd ed., p. 13.

246 See L. Miller, *The emergence of EU contract law: Exploring Europeanization*, Oxford : OUP 2011, p. 174.

247 Comp. also the definition of the Study Group on Social Justice in European Private Law, 'Social justice in European contract law: A manifesto', *ELJ* 2004, p. 656: 'any system of contract law expresses a set of values, which strives to be coherent, and which is regarded as fundamental to the political morality of each country.'

As the law starts making sense, this will in turn enhance the accessibility of private law.[248]

Zimmerman[249] finds that the coherence of private law, reflected by the systematic unity of private law in a codification, enables private parties to consider the normative context in which their case can be seen, to avoid inconsistencies and to reach solutions that fit in with solutions for other problems. Actors may also pursue the coherent development of law in order to ensure the stable development of private law. Accordingly, this book recognises that techniques that emphasise the coherent development of private law, in particular codification, are a well-established and widely recognised manner of developing the law in accordance with the requirements of accessibility, predictability, consistency and responsiveness and may effectively contribute to those requirements.

2.6.4. Legal equality

Legal equality firstly requires that private law is developed in such a way that equal cases are decided equally, and secondly that it prohibits discrimination.[250]

Legal equality is an important principle that reflects a basic notion of justice. It has, however, also been considered as a controversial principle, as it raises the question in which respects are parties equal and should be treated equally. Aristotle[251] particularly distinguished between these views on equality:

> 'it is thought that justice is equality, and so it is, though not for everybody but only for those who are equals; and it is thought that inequality is just, for so indeed it is, though not for everybody, but for those who are unequal.'

Therefore, equality does not mean that private law should provide the same rules for all private parties. Rather, equality demands that private law provides rules that adequately distinguish between private parties. The grounds for distinguishing between private parties, and the consequences for distinctions in private law, may vary throughout the Union.

Legal equality has affected the development of private law in two respects.

Firstly, Canaris[252] has pointed out that the systematic unity introduced by Civil Codes is based on legal equality, as legal equality requires consistency and coherence.

248 See N. MacCormick, *Rhetoric and the rule of law*, Oxford: OUP 2005, p. 201, p. 190.

249 R. Zimmerman, 'Codification: History and present significance of an idea', *ERPL* 1995, p. 110. Comp. also W. van Gerven, S. Lierman, *Beginselen van Belgisch privaatrecht. Algemeen deel, veertig jaar later*, Mechelen: Kluwer 2010, p. 180.

250 Comp. D. Schiek, 'Freedom of contract and a non-discrimination principle – irreconcilable antonyms?' in: T. Loene, P.R. Rodrigues (eds.), *Non-discrimination law: comparative perspectives*, The Hague: KLI 1999, p. 86.

251 Aristotle, *Politics*, Book 3, section 1280a, available at www.perseus.tufts.edu.

252 C.-W. Canaris, *Systemdenken und Systembegriff in Jurisprudenz*, Berlin: Duncker & Humblot 1983, 2nd ed., p. 16–17, also H.A. Engelhard, 'Zu den Aufgaben einer Kommission für die Überarbeitung des Schuldrechts, *NJW* 1984, p. 1203.

This idea has also been recognised in the Dutch legal order.[253] In the English legal order, the isolated development of specialised fields of private law has similarly been held to frustrate legal equality.[254] More generally, the principle of *stare decisis* emphasises the importance of deciding equal cases equally. Legal equality has similarly been recognised at the European level, and harmonised law especially seeks to promote equality between parties from different legal orders.

Secondly, the prohibition on discrimination has increasingly invaded private law, which has become particularly apparent, as provisions in Civil Codes, for example 7:646 BW directly emphasise equal treatment. Notably, article 7:646 BW is an implementation of Directive 2000/78, which considers in its preamble[255] that the European Union is founded upon respect for human rights and the rule of law. Additionally, predictability, accessibility and consistency can be severely undermined if rules are applied differently for groups of people on the basis of characteristics often falling within the sphere of human rights.

However, legal equality should not serve as a separate requirement. Firstly, legal equality already follows from developing European private law in accordance with society's legal views on justice. This becomes particularly apparent when considering article 7:646 BW. This provision does not establish a new norm, but it specifies the requirements of legal equality in labour contracts and gives private parties a direct claim when an employer makes a distinction that violates article 7:646 BW.[256] Thus, women who, for example, enjoy fewer fringe benefits than their male colleagues, can base their claim on this specific article and do not have to base their claim on blanket clauses or unwritten law.[257] The increasing referral to legal equality, as legislators develop rules compensating for unequal bargaining positions, may similarly be sought in the changing views on which groups are equal and the insight that the inequality between parties in some cases necessitates unequal treatment.[258] This tendency could also be defended on the basis of fairness: as private law addresses private parties as equal, they should be treated equally, and as groups of people, for example consumers, employees or tenants, are found to be in a weaker position than their counterparties, they should not be treated equally.

Secondly, legal equality is as such also an unsuitable benchmark as it is too abstract. What treatment is 'equal'? This becomes clear when asking for what cases equal treatment would be established. Considering the infinite amount of differences between individual

253 A.R. Bloembergen, 'De eenheid van het recht', in: A.R. Bloembergen, *Bloembergens werk*, Deventer: Kluwer 1992, p. 559.

254 [1981] AC 675, 701. See similarly P. Birks, 'The need for the Institutes in England', *Zeitschrift der Savigny-Stiftung für Rechtsgeschichte, Romanistische Abteilung* 1991, p. 711.

255 Consideration 1, 4, 11–12, preamble to Directive 2000/78.

256 J.M. Smits, 'Constitutionalisering van het vermogensrecht', in: J.M. Smits, P.H.M. Gerver, D.A. Lubach, *Preadviezen uitgebracht door de Nederlandse Vereniging van Rechtsvergelijking*, Deventer: Kluwer 2003, par. 7, 23.

257 Comp. for the Dutch legal order HR 8 April 1994, *NJ* 1994, 704, par. 3.5.

258 H. Collins, 'Transaction costs and subsidiarity in European contract law', in: S. Grundmann, J. Stuyck (eds.), *An academic Green Paper on European contract law*, The Hague: KLI 2002, p. 269–282. For the German legal order see recently D. Looschelders, 'Diskriminierung und Schutz vor Diskriminierung im Privatrecht', *JZ* 2012, p. 105.

cases, absolute equality would be difficult to achieve – and moreover, the law tends to differentiate between groups of people (such as businesses and consumers) who should be considered equal. Also, determining whether private parties are treated equally may well be a politically sensitive issue – for example, the question of whether the equal treatment of same-sex couples and heterosexual couples requires that states allow same-sex couples to marry is a political one, and the views of Member States differ widely on this and other questions. Even within Member States, these questions may be controversial, and there are different views on whether and how legal equality affects private law, and different approaches are visible in Member States.[259] The lack of agreement on this topic among states, as well as ongoing societal, ethic, and scientific developments have led the European Court of Human Rights to consider that states have a wide margin of appreciation on this topic.[260] From this perspective, different treatment is not necessarily to be unequal treatment. Consequently, imposing one's views on legal orders that do or do not recognise same-sex marriage may entail that private law is no longer developed in accordance with society's legal views on justice, which is clearly undesirable.

For these reasons, this book will not use legal equality as a separate requirement.

2.6.5. *Just, legitimate, coherent and equal European private law?*

There is a clear interrelation between justice, coherence, legal equality and legitimacy. This is especially clear between justice and legal equality as, arguably, legal equality can be seen as a legal principle reflecting basic ideas on justice. It has also been argued that just law has to be developed democratically, not only as notions of justice require sufficient agreement that is achieved through the democratic process, between people that form a *demos*, but also as subsequently enforcing these ideas requires democratic legitimation.[261] Coherence is clearly also interrelated with ideas of justice and equality. Canaris[262] finds that the idea of justice – in particular legal equality – requires generalisation to the point that specific rules can be seen as specifications from general ideas on justice. This view is not specific to the German legal order. For Dutch private law, Scholten[263] has similarly held that coherence, for private law, can be considered as the internal systemic unity of private law in which rules of private law are tuned in to one another, as they can be deduced from a limited number of general principles, while the development of new law can also be based on those general principles. In turn, as the law is developed coherently in accordance with these ideas, this should increase the legitimacy of private law.

More generally, legitimacy is often associated with the extent to which private law is in accordance with notions of justice. This may be a rather narrow, procedural

259 See for a comparison C. Mak, *Fundamental rights in European contract law*, Alphen aan den Rijn: KLI 2008.

260 ECHR 20 March 1997 (X, Y, and Z v United Kingdom), appl. no. 21830/93, *NJ* 1998, 235, par. 44.

261 Comp. previously for the idea of European legal views on justice and a European polity par. 2.5.1.

262 C.-W. Canaris, *Systemdenken und Systembegriff in der Jurisprudenz*, Berlin: Duncker & Humblot 1983, p. 12, p. 16–17.

263 Asser/Scholten 1974, p. 45.

understanding of justice as corrective justice, or a narrow understanding of justice as 'a right to justification' of one's freedom. Neyer[264] has defended justice rather than democracy as a basis for the legitimacy of the European Union. Alternatively, it has been argued that if law is developed through democratic discourse, it is likely just and therefore legitimate. Hesselink[265] has defended a pluralist, procedural theory of contract law that emphasises the process in which private law is developed. If, accordingly, all relevant arguments have been discussed by diverse groups who have had a fair and equal chance to participate in the development of law, 'the outcome may be hard to challenge on the basis of (…) justice'. While both of these perspectives stress the importance of deliberative discourse, the latter view seems to leave more room for a broader concept of justice, which is not identical to either democracy or legitimacy.[266] More generally, the relation between these notions does not mean that they are identical. If actors develop a coherent set of rules, for example through clearly structured statutes, this need not increase legitimacy or justice if those rules are inefficient, or if actors completely ignore matters of justice in developing statutes.

There are more similarities between notions of justice, legitimacy, coherence and legal equality: they are all rather abstract concepts, which makes it difficult to determine whether, for example, European private law becomes more or less just or legitimate. In addition, the coexistence of multiple actors in the development of European private law and the extent to which European private law is just, legitimate, and respects legal equality is not necessarily related, depending on one's definition of these concepts. More specific concepts, such as predictability, seem to provide a clearer answer to the question in this book. Similarly, the idea that private law should be just is also expressed in the idea that private law should be in accordance with society's legal views on justice. This benchmark also avoids the difficulties involved in specifying what justice requires in individual cases, while recognising the relevance of normative ideas and underlining that private law cannot isolate itself from legal views on what is just. The idea of responsive law offers a more workable alternative to determine whether problems or benefits develop because of the involvement of multiple actors in the development of European private law. The reference to 'society's legal views' makes clear in what respect coexistence can be problematic or beneficial: as EU actors influence national private law, could and should that involvement leave less room for the law to develop in accordance with national legal views on justice? Conversely, if national actors are involved in the development of European and international level, what attention should be paid to transnational notions of justice? That does however not mean that this book argues that more generally, European private law should only meet benchmarks of legal certainty and responsiveness.

Moreover, fortunately, developing European private law in accordance with benchmarks of legal certainty and responsiveness should hopefully also foster justice,

264 J. Neyer, 'Justice, not democracy: The legitimacy of the European Union', *CMLS* 2010, p. 908.

265 M.W. Hesslink, 'Democratic contract law', *ERCL* 2015, p. 83.

266 See further also D. Kochenov, 'The ought of justice', in: D. Kochenov, G. de Búrca, A. Williams (eds.), *Europe's justice deficit?*, Oxford: Hart 2015, p. 21.

legitimacy, coherence and legal equality.[267] Importantly, that does not mean that these concepts are identical or that they will never contradict one another.[268]

Therefore, in this book, deliberation is not considered from the perspective of legitimacy – although deliberation should improve legitimacy – but from the perspectives of predictability, consistency, accessibility and responsiveness. Similarly, deliberation should decrease injustice as it arguably lessens the chance that individuals become bound by rules they have not been able to influence, which has been described as *Fremdbestimmung*,[269] or hetero-determination, in accordance with the normative framework defended in chapter 7. Theoretically, this could lend support to the argument that deliberation should be valued, but, arguably, not as a value in itself, but as a principle of justice. More generally, optimizing private autonomy and decreasing chances of hetero-determination, which may develop especially in the multilevel legal order as an increasing amount of especially non-state actors develop binding rules that are not consistently accessible, is also in accordance with more general views on justice. These more general legal views on justice may however differ throughout the Union, as will become visible in chapter 8.[270] Simultaneously, this book does not defend a concept of justice *solely* as a right to justification, although deliberation ideally should prompt actors to critically examine their own arguments and where necessary, alter them, in accordance with pluralist arguments.

Instead, deliberation between interdependent actors is considered as a necessity to develop European private law, in accordance with the discourse on multilevel governance. Particularly, deliberation is necessary if national and European state and non-state actors are not able to independently develop private law in accordance with benchmarks of legal certainty and responsiveness through national techniques. Deliberation also should allow actors to benefit from the involvement of other actors in the development of European private law, by enhancing responsiveness, through mutual learning and regulatory competition. In other words, while this book does defend deliberation, it does not focus on democratic legitimacy, but rather considers deliberation in the light of the legal certainty and responsiveness of European private law.

267 Firstly, the overlap between legal certainty and coherence is most clearly visible in the overlap between consistency and coherence, as coherence has been reduced to a mere lack of internal inconsistency, although, as argued above, in this book, coherence entails more than a lack of inconsistencies, on which see further previously, par. 2.6.2. Secondly, there is a clear overlap between responsiveness to legal views on justice, legal equality, and justice. See further on the overlap between responsiveness to legal views on justice previously par. 2.6.2. Generally, developing European private law through deliberative discourse, in accordance with benchmarks of legal certainty and responsiveness, should strengthen both input and output legitimacy. In particular, developing the law in accordance with practice should increase output legitimacy. Thirdly, there is a less clear link between legal certainty and legal equality: if equal cases are decided equally, this should enhance the predictability, consistency, and accessibility of the law.

268 That is most clearly the case for output legitimacy. Arguably, developing the law responsively, predictably, consistently, and accessibly does not guarantee that private law will effectively, for example, foster the internal market, nor has it been established that private law should be seen exclusively in the light of aims it pursues.

269 See further on this concept par. 7.1.

270 See particularly the comparison in par. 8.6.1.

2.7. Conclusion

In this book, predictability, accessibility, consistency, responsiveness towards society's legal views on justice and responsiveness to the needs and preferences of practice will be used as benchmarks, or requirements, to evaluate the quality of European private law. These requirements have been widely recognised, both at the national level and at the European level, although they are rarely critically considered or made explicit.

Benchmarks of predictability, accessibility, consistency and responsiveness should not be seen in isolation. Instead, they should be mutually reinforcing. In some cases, however, conflicts between responsiveness to society's legal views on justice and legal certainty have become visible. Importantly, no clear hierarchy in these requirements has been recognised.

Ribstein and O'Hara[271] have noted that debate has not focused on the question what benchmarks law has to meet in order to be of good quality, as there is profound disagreement on the aims that legislators should pursue. This book also does not defend a specific hierarchy between benchmarks. The benchmarks do not prescribe the development of the law in a particular direction or manner. Accordingly, they do not indicate, as such, a high or a low level of consumer protection, nor do they prescribe the reallocation of competences to the national or European level. This book also does not argue that actors developing private law should pursue particular policy aims. Equally, this volume does not defend which ideas on justice private law should pursue or reflect. However, the book will evaluate whether the law is in accordance with society's legal views on justice – regardless of what those ideas are – and in accordance with everyday practices. It follows that in this book, the development of private law is not a purely technical, a-political exercise.

271 E.A. O'Hara, L.E. Ribstein, *The law market*, Oxford: OUP 2009, p. 19.

Chapter 3

STUDYING INTERDEPENDENCE IN THE LAW ON STCS

3.1. Introduction

As multiple actors have become involved in the development of European private law, interdependence has developed. Multilevel governance theories and pluralist insights imply that the coexistence of actors may lead to both problems and benefits for European private law.

Case studies of one specific area of law should make these perspectives more specific. Thus, the case studies in subsequent chapters 4 and 5 will ask whether a lack of deliberation between interdependent actors is reflected in the extent to which a specific area of law complies with benchmarks of predictability, accessibility, consistency and responsiveness or whether actors have benefited from one another's involvement.

In the choice of an area of law for a case study, several dilemmas have arisen. Choosing a national area of law, such as property law, may not make apparent whether the involvement of multiple actors is problematic. Yet opting for hybrid areas that develop functionally, such as labour law or company law, may be problematic because the development of law in these functional areas could be considered atypical for areas of traditional private law. Alternatively, in highly Europeanised areas of law, many actors coexist, which may lead to arguments that this area is similarly atypical and that the conclusions with regard to this area are not relevant for other, more traditional areas.

Arguably, choosing an area of European private law where many actors coexist provides an opportunity to look at the simultaneous development of European private law by different actors. Furthermore, the number of actors involved in the development of European private law is not likely to become smaller over time. Accordingly, European initiatives have started developing in traditional areas of private law.[272] Eventually, mandatory rules in traditional areas such as property law may also be difficult to reconcile with the right to free movement within the European Union and they may become harmonised.[273] Thus, national areas of private law can also look to the development of other areas of private law if and when increased international trade

[272] Comp. Directive 2014/17 on credit agreements relating to residential property.

[273] See further on the compatibility of property law and European law B. Akkermans, E. Ramaekers, 'Free movement of goods and property law', *ELJ* 2013, p. 237.

necessitates the development of, for example, European initiatives on the registration of immovable property in national registers.

These considerations led to the choice to study the law on STCs in the German and Dutch legal order. The German law on STCs has generally been recognised as a success story,[274] and it has served as an example to both the Dutch and European legislator. However, Dutch law on STCs does show weaknesses.[275] Can the comprehensibility of German law, and the shortcomings of Dutch law be explained in the light of multilevel governance and pluralism perspectives?

Studying this area of law may prove interesting as STCs are used widely, both in B2B contracts and B2C contracts. STCs are important for both national and international trade and they have even been described as principles of European contract law, more so than the PECL, because of their central importance to legal practice. The European legislator agrees[276] and has accordingly been involved in the development of this area of law, while national actors have retained an important role as national contract law continues to play a central role for the inclusion and interpretation of STCs.[277] Private actors have also been involved; the law on STCs has been characterised as the *lex mercatoria extraordinaire*.[278] Thus, the law on STCs is a good example of an area of law that has been developed in a multilevel context, by multiple state and non-state actors and studying this area may provide insight in the problems and benefits that may arise from the involvement of multiple actors. It is also an area where parties may have to deal with mandatory law provisions while other parties largely decide for themselves which STCs to include. It is further an area where relevant previous comparative law research already exists,[279] which facilitates a comparative case study.

Paragraph 3.2 will discuss which actors coexist in the German and Dutch legal order, and paragraph 3.3. will turn to multilevel governance perspectives and paragraph 3.4

274 See for example P. Ulmer, 'Zehn Jahre AGB-Gesetz – Rückblick und Ausblick', in: H. Heinrichs, W. Löwe, P. Ulmer (eds.), *Zehn Jahre AGB-Gesetz*, Köln: Kommunikationsforum Recht 1987, p. 5, see further par. 4.2.

275 See for example C.E. Drion, 'Een pamflet voor het fundamenteel op de schop nemen van onze regelgeving over algemene voorwaarden', *Contracteren* 2007, p. 3, see further par. 5.2.

276 Communication from the Commission to the European Parliament and the Council, *A more coherent European contract law: An action plan*, COM (2003) 68 final, p. 21 et seq.

277 Looking at STCs themselves may reveal that the validity of STCs may not only depend on contract laws, but also on, for example, national property laws, or civil procedure laws. Although it makes clear that the different areas of law should not be seen in isolation from one another, these areas of law are not included in the case study. Notably, this case study concentrates on the use of techniques in the development of the law on STCs rather than the cross-border effectiveness of STCs themselves. This case study will also not separately consider private law that may be relevant for negotiations such as the rules on liability for breaking off negotiations.

278 H. Großmann-Doerth, 'Selbstgeschaffenes Recht der Wirtschaft und staatliches Recht', reprinted in U. Blaurock, N. Goldschmidt, A. Hollerbach (eds.), *Das selbstgeschaffene Recht der Wirtschaft. Zum Gedenken an Hans Großmann-Doerth (1894–1944)*, Tübingen: Mohr Siebeck 2005, p. 77.

279 For the Dutch legal order prominently E.H. Hondius, *Standaardvoorwaarden. Rechtsvergelijkende beschouwingen over de standaardisering van kontraktsbedingen en overheidstoezicht daarop*, Deventer: Kluwer 1978 and more recently R.H.C. Jongeneel, *Algemene voorwaarden en het AGB-Gesetz*, Deventer: Kluwer 1991. Comparative information on the implementation of Directive 93/13 can be found in the EC Consumer Law Compendium (the CLABB-database is no longer available).

will address pluralist perspectives. Paragraph 3.5 will end with a conclusion and sketch the approach in the case studies.

3.2. Coexistence of actors developing the law on STCs

The law on STCs has been developed by various actors:

1) The German and Dutch legislator have developed general contract law as well as specific provisions for STCs.

2) The European legislator has developed various measures on the law of STCs.

These measures are Directive 93/13 on unfair contract terms, as well as other Directives that may affect the content and judicial evaluation of STCs. Thus, article 7 Directive 2011/7 on late payment stipulates that the terms on the date or period of payment, interest, or recovery costs that are grossly unfair to the creditor shall either be unenforceable or give rise to damages. Article 7 provides a number of criteria to establish whether a term is grossly unfair. Also, article 4 par. 4 Directive 90/314 on package travel limits the possibility of changing the price of package travel when the contract has already been concluded. In addition, Directive 2008/48 on consumer creditor and Directive 2007/64 on payment services have affected STCs in contracts between German banks and other creditors and consumers.[280] Other Directives that do not directly stipulate the unfairness of contract terms may in addition be relevant for assessing whether a term is fair or unfair, for example by guaranteeing an intellectual property right.[281] Furthermore, Annex A to Directive 2003/55 contains provisions on consumer contract law and the CJEU[282] has ruled that Directive 87/344 does not allow an insurer to stipulate that its employees will provide legal counsel, and that the costs for an attorney, elected by the policyholder, will only be compensated if the insurer decides that external legal aid is necessary.

Article 3 par. 1 Directive 86/653 on self-employed commercial agents and article 3 par. 2 Directive 2002/65 on distance contracts for financial services also contain blanket clauses referring to good faith, although this does not mean that article 3 Directive 93/13 has to be interpreted consistently with these clauses. Unfair terms may also constitute an unfair commercial practice under Directive 2005/29 on unfair commercial practices.

Other Directives may also be applicable for consumer contracts containing unfair terms: Directive 2000/31 on e-commerce, Directive 2011/83 on consumer rights, as well as timeshare contracts falling under Directive 2008/122 or credit contracts falling within the scope of Directive 2008/48. Alternatively, contracts may fall under all of these Directives, if a timeshare contract linked with a credit agreement is entered into from a distance.

The European legislator has also developed rules on the jurisdiction, applicable law and the execution of foreign decisions relating to STCs in Regulation 44/2001 (Brussels I) and Regulation 593/2008 (Rome I).

280 See in more detail Ulmer/Brandner/Hensen/AGB-Recht/Fuchs, Specific STCs, Banks, nr 1–2.

281 OLG Stuttgart 3 November 2011, *BeckRS* 2012, 5352.

282 CJEU 7 November 2013 (Sneller v DAS), C-442/12, [2013] ECR p. I-o.

For cases falling within the scope of Rome I, the competence to determine whether German or Dutch law on STCs – or other law – is applicable has been reallocated to the European level. For B2C contracts, in addition to article 6 par. 2 Rome I, and similarly to various Directives in the private law *acquis*, article 6 par. 2 Directive 93/13 stipulates that a choice of law may not deprive the consumer of the rights conferred upon him by the Directive.

For cases falling within the scope of Brussels I, the competence to determine which judge will be competent to hear a dispute has been reallocated to the European level. The CJEU[283] has made it clear that the validity of a clause making a choice of jurisdiction can only be evaluated by the standards of article 23 Brussels I. This means that article 23 Regulation precedes article 305 BGB, and articles 6:233 sub b and 6:234 BW for determining whether a clause indicating a choice of jurisdiction has been validly entered into and has become part of the contract, as well as the criteria in article 307 BGB and article 6:233 sub a BW on the fairness of these clauses. Yet in some cases, provisions in the private law *acquis* may precede questions of private international law. Accordingly, in *Océano*,[284] and subsequent case law,[285] Directive 93/13 stood in the way of jurisdiction clauses in B2C contracts, and in Ingmar/Eaton,[286] the applicability of Directive 86/653 preceded a valid choice of law.

3) The UN has adopted the CISG.

The CISG is applicable if parties have not opted out of it. If parties have made a choice for Dutch or German law, article 1 par. 1 sub b CISG entails that this does not exclude the applicability of the CISG.[287] The CISG may precede national law.[288] Articles 14–24 CISG have precedence over articles 305 pars. 2 and 3 BGB as well as articles 6:233 sub b and 6:234 BW on the valid inclusion of STCs, depending on the wording of a choice of law.[289]

The CISG may coincide with Rome I. Should the question which law is applicable in international B2B contracts be decided under article 1 CISG or under Rome I? It has been argued that if both contract parties are settled in a contracting state that has not made reservations under article 95 CISG, the CISG should, in those cases, determine the question of applicable law.[290] If that is not the case, the CISG can become applicable if private international law indicates the application of the law of a contracting state. Article 25 Rome I explicitly recognises the precedence of multilateral treaties concluded between Member States such as the CISG. Accordingly, questions of applicable law are decided under the CISG rather than Rome I.

283 CJEU 16 March 1999 (Trasporti Castelletti Spedizioni Internazionali SpA v Hugo Trumpy SpA), C-159/97, [1999] ECR, p. I-1597.

284 CJEU 27 June 2000 (Océano Grupo Editorial SA v Quintero and others), Joined cases C-240/98 to C-244/98, [2000] ECR, p. I-4941.

285 CJEU 4 June 2009 (Pannon GSM Zrt v Győrfi), C-243/08, [2009] ECR p. I-4713.

286 CJEU 9 November 2000 (Ingmar/Eaton), [2000] ECR p. I-9305.

287 Ferrari/Kieninger/Mankowski et al/ Internationales Vertragsrecht/Saenger (2011) article 6 CISG, nr 4, who points out that if parties agree that the BGB is applicable, this entails that parties have opted out of the CISG. See for Dutch law Rb. Arnhem 29 July 2009, *LJN* BJ4645, Rb Zwolle 22 January 2003, *LJN* AF3345.

288 In the German legal order, the CISG has been implemented into national law. Thus, the statute implementing the CISG sets aside other national laws.

289 Ferrari/Kieninger/Mankowski et al/ Internationales Vertragsrecht/Saenger (2011) article 4 CISG nr 23.

290 Ferrari/Kieninger/Mankowski et al/ Internationales Vertragsrecht/Saenger (2011) article 1 CISG nr 14, comp. for Dutch law also Hof 's-Hertogenbosch, 13 November 2007, *RCR* 2008, 18.

If the CISG is applicable despite the choice for German or Dutch law, German or Dutch law may be applied to fill gaps.[291] In accordance with article 4 sub a CISG, the evaluation of STCs in contracts applying the CISG is subjected to article 307 BGB and article 6:248 BW, although the evaluation has to take into account the standards established in the CISG. If the ineffectiveness of STCs gives rise to gaps, these are to be filled in accordance with article 306 par. 2 BGB, as well as article 7 CISG.[292]

4) Other international organisations have also established treaties relevant for the law on STCs.

Contracts may also be concluded under other international regimes, especially in the area of transport.[293] Important regimes in this area include the CMR as well as the Montreal Convention, ratified by the EU through Regulation 889/2002. Further, treaties have been established for specific clauses, in particular the Benelux Convention on Penalty Clauses. The 2005 Hague Convention on the choice of court clauses may become relevant once it enters into force.

The CJEU[294] has held that if the rights of third states are not involved, Member States may not rely on treaties to limit the freedoms provided by the Treaty. Consequently, if European measures and treaties collide, the question should not be whether the treaty provides an exclusive regime, but whether the treaty provides sufficient predictability and does not limit cross-border trade. It is unclear how this should be determined.

The CMR and the Montreal Convention may well overlap with European measures. The CMR may show overlap with Brussels I. The CJEU[295] has held that article 71 Brussels I may not entail that treaties falling within the scope of the Regulation may provide for less beneficial effects than provided for by the Regulation. The rules in treaties may be applied if they provide a high degree of predictability, facilitate the administration of justice and limit the risk of parallel procedures.

5) International non-state actors such as the ICC have developed alternative regulation that may reflect customary law or that may indicate well-established business practices.

6) Non-state actors at the European level have developed alternative regulation.

Alternative regulation has also been established by the Economic Commission for Europe (ECE) that provided standard forms of contracts and general conditions of sale to facilitate international commercial contracting.[296]

291 Ferrari/Kieninger/Mankowski et al/ Internationales Vertragsrecht/Saenger (2011) article 6 CISG nr 4.
292 Ulmer/Brandner/Hensen/AGB-Recht/Schmidt (2011) annex to article 305, nr 10.
293 See further Baumbach/Hopt/Handelsgesetzbuch/Hopt (2012) introduction before article 1, nr 27.
294 CJEU 22 September 1988 (Ministère Public/Deserbais), case 286/86, [1988] ECR, p. 4907.
295 CJEU 4 May 2010 (TNT/Axa Versicherung), C-533/08, [2010] ECR, p. I- 4107.
296 UNCITRAL Report of the Secretary-General, 23 September 1966, Sixth Committee, doc.no. A/6396, par. 67, referring to the ECE General Conditions of Sale and Standard Forms of Contract.

7) Academic groups have developed soft laws that parties may choose to incorporate into their contracts.

Thus, various actors have developed the law on STCs. Although the national and the European legislator play an important role, actors at the international level may also play a role.

3.3. Multilevel governance perspectives

The law on STCs is an area of law where multiple actors have become involved in law-making, and interdependence between national and European actors has generally been recognised.[297] Specifically, interdependence is visible in the development of the law on STCs in accordance with benchmarks of predictability, accessibility, consistency and responsiveness through codifications, blanket clauses and general principles.

Firstly, national legislators and courts are less able to guarantee the predictable, accessible and consistent development of private law through codifications.

Harmonisation in this area means that both the German and Dutch legislator need to implement and take into account the possible reform of Directive 93/13. National actors may participate in the drafting process of a new Directive, but it is possible that the Directive is reformed in a manner contrary to the preferences of both Member States. Consequently, the national legislator's ability to revise the law in order to preserve the consistency and the accessibility of the law through codifications has decreased. More generally, codifications need not limit overenthusiastic reform of the law at the European level. Therefore, the extent to which a codification may preserve the predictable development of law has diminished. Implementation may also compromise the structure of codifications. As harmonisation develops, moreover, sources alongside codifications, particularly Regulations, may develop, which undermines the extent to which a codification safeguards the accessibility of the law on STCs.

Simultaneously, the European legislator needs sufficient support of national state actors to pursue harmonisation.[298] National legislators may be motivated to resist harmonisation that undermines their codifications.

Secondly, as harmonisation develops, the extent to which national blanket clauses curb national reform has become limited. In addition, the extent to which national blanket clauses safeguard responsiveness and consistency may theoretically become compromised

297 Ch. Joerges, 'On the legitimacy of Europeanising private law: Considerations on a justice-making law for the EU multi-level system', *Electronic Journal of Comparative Law* 2003, available at www.ejcl.org/ejcl/73/art73-3.html, (par. III.1.1.) described the development of "diagonal conflicts": 'activities oriented towards the solution of economic and social problems will often have to involve both Community and Member State powers. The resulting overlaps compel the Community and Member States de facto to complex coordination of their activities: each can block the other, but neither can arrive at solutions when acting alone'.

298 Comp. H Collins, 'Governance implications for the European Union of the changing character of private law', in: F. Cafaggi, H. Muir-Watt (eds.), *Making European private law: Governance implications*, Cheltenham: Elgar 2008, p. 272.

as blanket clauses such as article 3 Directive 93/13 harmonise national blanket clauses, such as articles 307 BGB and 6:233 sub a BW. National courts should interpret these blanket clauses in accordance with harmonised law. Arguably, harmonised interpretation may not be aimed at preserving the consistency and responsiveness of national law.

Simultaneously, national courts may not be inclined to interpret or apply harmonised law in a manner that undermines the predictability, consistency or responsiveness. Instead, national courts may exercise restraint when referring questions on the interpretation of harmonised law to the CJEU, particularly if the interpretation touches upon the interpretation of central blanket clauses such as article 242 BGB.

Thirdly, the development of the law on STCs on the basis of general principles may be compromised if the European legislator develops the law differently – not on the basis of general principles, or not on the basis of the same principles. Arguably, differences may also limit the extent to which general principles can serve as a starting point for interaction between courts or legislators.

Fourthly, interdependence has developed between state actors and non-state actors. As state actors become less able to control the behaviour of actors beyond their territory, and as private parties are increasingly able to choose the applicability of state actors' laws, state actors should take into account decisions and initiatives from foreign and international actors. It follows that German and Dutch state actors may take note of foreign and transnational developments to develop and apply the law in accordance with transnational actors' preferences. Is interdependence between state and non-state actors also reflected in the use of codifications, blanket clauses and general principles?

Because interdependence in the development of comprehensible European private law has developed between European and national state and non-state actors, these actors should deliberate. If there is a lack of deliberation, is this visible in problems for the law on STCs, or has deliberation prevented that actors undermine the extent to other actors promote the development of the law on STCs, in accordance with benchmarks of predictability, consistency, accessibility, and responsiveness?

In addition, as actors are less able to develop the law comprehensibly through national techniques, the use of techniques in addition to or instead of national techniques becomes necessary. Which techniques are likely to enhance the law on STCs and which techniques are problematic?

3.4. Pluralist perspectives

In accordance with pluralist perspectives, benefits may arise from the coexistence of national, European and state and non-state actors.

Firstly, it has been argued that the coexistence of actors at different levels can lead to the development of a system of checks and balances, and lead to the development of rules more in line with transnational needs and preferences, as they are developed by a transnational actor who is better informed of these needs or as the existence of a transnational actors prompts national actors to take these interests into account.[299]

[299] N. Krisch, *Beyond constitutionalism: The pluralist structure of postnational law*, Oxford: OUP 2010, p. 70.

Accordingly, is the European legislator better placed to take into account the interests of transnational parties, especially those that do businesses across borders but who are not involved in the development of national rules? Can the development of Directive 93/13 be seen in this light? On the one hand, article 1 par. 2 makes clear that clauses reflecting default or mandatory provisions of national law or international conventions that the Member States or the Union are party to, shall not be subjected to evaluation under the Directive. This rule is in accordance with article 307 BGB, and it has been argued that if foreign law is applicable to the contract – for consumer cases, in accordance with article 6 Rome I Regulation – the provisions reflecting foreign law should not be subject to evaluation.[300] In addition, Micklitz[301] has defended that the standard of 'fairness', Directive 93/13, in combination with the model list, has harmonised the conditions under which businesses have access to domestic markets. In this view, the European legislator has defended the interests of businesses trading with consumers living in different Member States. On the other hand, the Directive aims to protect consumers. Thus, consumers who enter into cross-border transactions, while not involved in the development of rules abroad, are ensured of a minimum level of protection. Minimum harmonisation is in accordance with this aim, but less so with the idea of guaranteeing equal market access throughout the Union.

Alternatively, harmonisation, and the possibility of further harmonisation, may prompt national actors to take into account the interests of foreign and international actors who are not included in the national democratic process. Is this the case for the law on STCs?

On the other hand, it has been argued that the coexistence of national actors developing divergent laws may be beneficial to responsiveness and because law is intertwined with national legal views on justice, unification is unlikely.[302] This may also be reflected in the integration, or lack thereof, of legal transplants as legal concepts inserted into a legal system that are either integrated in national law or repulsed by national law. The concept of legal transplants has been defended by Watson,[303] who has argued that legal transplants should not be problematic, even if they come from systems that are radically different from the host system. Watson traces the lack of difficulties to the relatively small effect that legal rules have on individuals.

The development of legal transplants should also be visible in the development of Dutch law. Notably, the Dutch legislator was inspired by German law. Does this mean that German law has been transplanted into Dutch law, and if so, have German concepts retained their meaning or have "transplanted" concepts been given a meaning that diverges from German law?

Similarly, the development of Directive 93/13 has prompted arguments that because law is intertwined with, in this case, German and Dutch legal traditions, harmonisation

300 J. Maidl, *Auslandische AGB im deutschen Recht*, München: Beck 2000, p. 187-188.

301 H.-W. Micklitz, 'The concept of competitive contract law', *Penn State International Law Review* 2005, p. 572.

302 See previously par. 1.3.

303 A. Watson, *Legal transplants*, Edinburgh: Scottish Academic Press 1974, p. 95–96.

will not result in practical uniformity.[304] Yet harmonisation is not a "typical" transplant as legislators transposing Directives into national law need not amend national law, or amendments remain minor. This was also the case in the implementation of Directive 93/13 in German[305] and Dutch[306] law. Possibly, this approach, combined with the implementation of Directives within codifications, increases the chance that harmonised law will continue to be interpreted in a national manner.[307] In addition, whereas the idea of legal transplants leaves some room for remaining divergences between legal systems,[308] European law may not do so. European law may be an atypical "transplant" because decisions from the CJEU should help to ensure that harmonised concepts are interpreted autonomously and consistently throughout the Union. CJEU decisions also make clear that harmonisation is not limited to the transplantation of rules, but may also affect, for example, the interpretation methods used by courts.[309]

The idea of legal transplants has been criticised prominently and fiercely by Teubner,[310] who describes the notion of good faith in article 3 Directive as a "legal irritant": a foreign concept, imposed on national law, that will trigger further developments in national law, until the national system has reconstructed the meaning of the foreign concept, without however 'domesticating' this concept. However, these arguments should not overlook that the 1993 Directive in fact expressly leaves room for differences. Therefore, divergences may both be traced to the domestic context within which the Directive has been implemented and the minimum harmonisation clause.

Benefits may also arise if regulatory competition develops.[311] However, harmonisation limits the scope left for regulatory competition. The emergence of regulatory competition, and its beneficial effects, have also been doubted.[312] Esty and Geradin[313] have recognised

304 H. Collins, 'European private law and the cultural identity of states', *ERPL* 1995, p. 356, comp. also Ch. Joerges, 'The Europeanisation process of private law as a rationalization process and as a contest of disciplines – an analysis of the Directive on unfair terms in consumer contracts', *ERPL* 1995, p. 184.

305 See further on the implementation of the Directive in German law below par. 4.3.2.

306 See further on the implementation of the Directive in Dutch law below par. 5.3.3.2.

307 For example the Dutch legislator in *Handelingen I*, 2004/05, 28 874, nr. 17, p. 760, similarly H. Rösler, 'Europeanisation of private law through Directives – determining factors and modalities of implementation', *European Journal of Law Reform* 2010, p. 317.

308 Comp. A. Watson, *Legal transplants*, Edinburgh: Scottish Academic Press 1974, p. 27 as well as A. Watson, 'Legal Transplants and European Private Law', *Electronic Journal of Comparative Law* 2000, available at www.ejcl.org/ejcl/44/44-2.html, par. I.

309 See further for Dutch law prominently M.H. Wissink, *Richtlijnconforme interpretatie van burgerlijk recht*, Deventer: Kluwer 2001.

310 G. Teubner, 'Legal Irritants: Good faith in British law or how unifying law ends up in new divergencies', *MLR* 1998, p. 11.

311 Particularly G. Rühl, 'Regulatory competition in contract law: Empirical evidence and normative implications', *ERCL* 2013, p. 61.

312 S. Vogenauer, 'Regulatory Competition through choice of contract Law and choice of forum in Europe: Theory and evidence', *ERPL* 2013, p. 20 who points out that even if businesses do not prefer the German law on STCs, they may prefer German law for other reasons, and parties can often not adequately predict which law will ultimately serve their interests best.

313 D.C. Esty, D. Geradin, 'Regulatory co-opetition', *Journal of International Economic Law* 2000, p. 255.

the need for simultaneous cooperation and competition in their defence of regulatory co-opetition.

If regulatory competition or regulatory co-opetition does not develop, the coexistence of European state and non-state actors may still offer opportunities for mutual learning. Walker[314] sketches how the coexistence of actors who claim authority and who require that actors justify their actions may improve debate and provide opportunities for learning. Similarly, Krisch[315] has argued that actors may be pushed towards arguing. Accordingly, harmonisation or comparative law may spur legislators or judges to amend, for example, outdated law.[316] Is this the case for the law on STCs?

It has been argued that new governance is well suited to further improve interaction. Accordingly, Miller[317] has advocated a framework of coordination and refers to the Open Method of Coordination (hereafter: 'OMC'), the DCFR, the European Law Institute and networks to facilitate judicial dialogue in a more structural manner. Similarly, Sabel and Zeitlin[318] have defended the concept of "experimentalist governance", and emphasise the structure of decision-making where European actors, in cooperation with Member States, set and evaluate frameworks and policy aims and national and subnational actors tailor these frameworks to regional circumstances. These characteristics can be found in new forms of governance such as the OMC. Joerges[319] has defended that deliberation can take place within comitology, and he has further pointed to collective bargaining.[320]

Have benefits, in accordance with pluralist perspective, developed for respectively the German or Dutch law on STCs? Methodological nationalism implies that these new forms of governance are currently overlooked. If this is the case, which techniques in addition to or instead of the legislative process – new governance – would be beneficial for the law on STCs?

3.5. Conclusion and outlook

The case studies will focus on the questions that have been raised in paragraph 3.3 and paragraph 3.4.

Accordingly, chapter 4 will look at the development of the law on STCs in the German legal order. The chapter will take the high quality of German law as a starting point, and ask whether the absence of direct problems can be attributed to the extent to which

314 N. Walker, 'The idea of constitutional pluralism', *MLR* 2002, p. 358.

315 Comp. N. Krisch, *Beyond constitutionalism: The pluralist structure of postnational law*, Oxford: OUP 2010, p. 234.

316 T. Wilhelmsson, 'Private law in Europe: harmonised or fragmented Europeanisation?', *ERPL* 2002, p. 91.

317 L. Miller, *The emergence of EU contract law: Exploring Europeanization*, Oxford: OUP 2011, p. 202 et seq, see similarly with regard to the OMC F. Cafaggi, 'Introduction' in F. Cafaggi (ed), *The Institutional Framework of European Private Law*, Oxford: OUP 2006, p. 16–17.

318 Ch.F. Sabel, J. Zeitlin, 'Learning from difference: The new architecture of experimentalist governance in the EU', *ELJ* 2008, p. 276–277.

319 Ch. Joerges, 'On the legitimacy of Europeanising private law: considerations on a justice-making law for the EU multi-level system', vol 7.3 *EJCL*.

320 Ch. Joerges, 'The Europeanisation of private law as a rationalization process and as a contest of disciplines – an analysis of the Directive on unfair terms in consumer contracts', *ERPL* 1995, p. 182.

deliberation has taken place, in accordance with the degree of interdependence between actors, or whether the coexistence of actors has contributed to the high quality of German law, in accordance with pluralist arguments.

Chapter 5 will consider the question whether the lesser quality of the Dutch law on STCs can be traced to a lack of deliberation between interdependent actors, or whether the coexistence of actors has prevented further problems, in accordance with pluralist arguments.

Chapter 6 will summarise the findings of the case studies in the light of multilevel governance and pluralist perspectives and ask whether these conclusions can be generalised.

The case studies will focus on the reasoning visible in the development of respectively the German and the Dutch law on STCs. This allows for answering the question whether actors have adequately recognised other actors' initiatives in the development of this area of law, and interacted accordingly, in line with multilevel governance perspectives. This focus simultaneously allows an answer to the question whether actors have benefited from the coexistence of actors, in accordance with pluralist insights.

Some limitations have been set to the case studies. The case studies will focus on the use of national techniques, but they will also consider additional and alternative techniques. This does not include all possible techniques. Accordingly, the case studies will not study the Lamfalussy procedure, the use of which seems confined to financial law. A further "technique" that will not be discussed is education. This is not to deny the benefits of wider education that make lawyers more aware of foreign and European developments, nor does this book deny the role that education plays in facilitating interaction between actors in nation states. However, the effects of education are long term and hard to assess, and it is wrong to simply consider education as a means to an end rather than an end in itself. In addition, academic research and scholarly writing may support the development of private law. Although academic research and scholarly writing may fulfil an important role, it is difficult to pinpoint how academic research in general supports the comprehensibility of private law, especially as academic research need not necessarily lead to developments and the effects of scholarly writing may be visible only in the long term. Moreover, the question arises whether describing research as a technique is accurate, while it may also coincide with the development of soft laws and the development of networks and databases. Therefore, academic research will not be considered separately. Other techniques may have been overlooked; however, the possible alternative techniques that could be used in the development of private law seem a fruitful subject for further research.

Further, the case study will not seek to provide a comprehensive overview of abundantly available case law, but rather consider relatively recent decisions in order to determine whether the courts take into account the development of law by other actors. The case studies will both look at decisions in which initiatives from other actors are clearly taken into account, as well as decisions where the initiatives from other actors seem to have been ignored.

Both the German and the Dutch case studies will include the DCFR. However, the DCFR is not part of positive law that can be invoked before the courts. Therefore, the extent to which German and Dutch law on STCs is comprehensible to private parties cannot be found by studying the relevant provisions in the DCFR. Despite its lack of binding force, the DCFR may play an important role in the development of the private law *acquis*, and, as a toolbox, possibly, in the interpretation and reform of the private law *acquis*. Accordingly, the DCFR will be studied as a technique in addition to the *acquis* and national laws. If actors, in the development of the DCFR, have adequately taken into account relevant initiatives from other actors, is it likely to contribute to the quality of the law on STCs? Notably, studying the rules of the DCFR on unfair contract terms may make it clear whether the DCFR, as an additional set of rules, provides a clear additional value.

Furthermore, some differences between the German and Dutch legal orders should be noted beforehand. In the German case study, BGH case law plays a role, while the Dutch case study pays more attention to the decisions from lower courts and ADR decisions. The Dutch chapter considers lower courts' decisions more extensively, because less case law from the Hoge Raad has developed. Also, the German ADR system is a decentralised system, and the various ADR schemes do not necessarily result in binding decisions and decisions are also not consistently published.[321] In addition, European developments that have been considered in chapter 4 will be considered in less detail in chapter 5, to prevent unnecessary repetition.

321 See the comparative oversight of the Study on the Use of Alternative Dispute Resolution of Civil Consulting of the Consumer Policy Evaluation Consortium, available at www.civic-consulting.de/reports/adr_study.pdf, p. 200 et seq.

Chapter 4

THE DEVELOPMENT OF THE LAW ON *ALLGEMEINE GESCHÄFTSBEDINGUNGEN*

4.1. Introduction

The German law on STCs has been recognised for its high quality.[322] In accordance with the debate on multilevel governance, this should be reflected in German actors' recognition of other actors' initiatives and deliberation between these actors. Can the high quality of the German law on STCs also be attributed to the coexistence of actors? According to pluralist arguments, this is the case if the coexistence of actors is beneficial to responsiveness, if it has enabled mutual learning or resulted in regulatory competition or regulatory co-opetition.

The approach of this case study in answering the questions raised in the previous chapter is as follows. Paragraph 4.2. will consider the high quality of the German law on STCs. Subsequently, paragraphs 4.3–4.5 will analyse the use of codifications, blanket clauses and general principles respectively. Paragraph 4.6. will draw a conclusion on the use of national techniques. Paragraph 4.7. will consider the use of techniques in addition to or instead of currently used techniques. Paragraph 4.8. will end with a conclusion.

4.2. The law on *Allgemeine Geschäftsbedingungen*

Since 1976, the German legislator stipulated the law on STCs, outside the BGB, through *Sonderprivatrecht*, in the *Gesetz zur Regelung des Rechts der Allgemeinen Geschäftsbedingungen* (AGB-Gesetz, hereafter: 'AGBG'), established in 1976. The AGBG has been amended only slightly for the implementation of Directive 93/13, and it was incorporated in the BGB in the *Schuldrechtsreform*. The revision of the law on STCs was not considered during the *Schuldrechtsreform*, which took place under considerable time pressure that decreased the chances that the law on STCs would be critically reconsidered. The most controversial question seems to have been whether the AGBG should be incorporated in

322 See further below par. 4.2.

the BGB.[323] Thus, the AGBG, and later articles 305–310 BGB, have provided a stable framework for the development of the law on STCs.

Although unpredictability and inconsistency may be difficult to avoid with the introduction of more judicial control through blanket clauses, the extent to which this was the case was limited, as preceding case law already evaluated STCs.[324] The introduction of the AGBG served to establish a more consistent standard for evaluating clauses as inconsistencies in case law became apparent.[325] Since its introduction, the BGH has provided clear guidelines on the assessment of the fairness of clauses[326] that have made article 307 BGB one of the most prominent blanket clauses in the BGB.[327]

Thus, the room left to the judiciary under the AGBG and later articles 305–310 BGB, has not resulted in unpredictability or inconsistency.[328] Ulmer[329] finds that the AGBG has contributed significantly to the quality of STCs and the transparency in trade.

However, the regime has also been criticised.[330] Private initiatives to reform the law have been developed. These initiatives do not concern the quality of the law in terms of predictability, consistency or accessibility, but argue that the law hinders trade because clauses in business contracts are subjected to judicial evaluation[331] and because the requirement that clauses have not been individually negotiated is interpreted too strictly.[332]

Thus, generally, the quality of the regime is excellent. Can this success be traced to the sufficient recognition of interdependence and corresponding interaction between relevant actors, or the coexistence of actors, in accordance with pluralist arguments?

323 Comp. Th. Pfeiffer, 'Die Reichweite der Inhaltskontrolle nach Art. 4 Abs. 2 RL 93/13/EWG und §8 AGBG im Kontext der "Schuldrechtsmodernisierung"', *VuR* 2001, p. 95, 99 who criticises the haste of the process, which he explains by pointing to the need to make use of political support for the reform of law while it lasted. He questions whether rushing the incorporation of an important subject such as STCs is convincing.

324 BGH 27 November 1974, *NJW* 1975, 163.

325 H. Kötz, *Welche gesetzgeberischen Massnahmen empfehlen sich zum Schutze des Endverbrauchers gegenüber Allgemeine Geschäftsbedingungen und Formularverträgen: dargestellt an Beispielen aus dem Kaufs- und Werkvertrags- sowie dem Maklerrecht, Gutachten für den 50. Deutschen Juristentag*, München: Beck 1974, Volume I, A, p. 52–53.

326 M. Wolf, 'Vertragsfreiheit und Vertragsrecht im Lichte der AGB-Rechtsprechung des BGH', in: C.-W. Canaris, A. Heldrich, (eds.), *50 Jahre Bundesgerichtshof. Festgabe aus der Wissenschaft, I*, München: Beck 2000, p. 113.

327 MunchKomm zum BGB/Basedow (2012), introduction to articles 305 et seq BGB, nr 15.

328 P. Ulmer, 'Zehn Jahre AGB-Gesetz – Rückblick und Ausblick', in: H. Heinrichs, W. Löwe, P. Ulmer (eds.), *Zehn Jahre AGB-Gesetz*, Köln: Kommunikationsforum Recht 1987, p. 5.

329 P. Ulmer, 'Zehn Jahre AGB-Gesetz – Rückblick und Ausblick', in: H. Heinrichs, W. Löwe, P. Ulmer (eds.), *Zehn Jahre AGB-Gesetz*, Köln: Kommunikationsforum Recht 1987, p. 17–18.

330 Comp. prominently Staudinger Komm zum BGB/Schlosser (2006), Introduction to articles 305 et seq, nr 24, also K.P. Berger, 'Abschied von Privatautonomie im unternehmerischen Geschäftsverkehr?' *ZIP* 2006, p. 2149.

331 See further below par. 4.3.3.1.2.

332 See, for example, E. Gottschalck, 'Neues zur Abgrenzung zwischen AGB und Individualabrede', *NJW* 2005, p. 2493. See on both points of criticism convincingly F. Graf von Westphalen, '30 Jahre AGB-Recht – Eine Erfolgsbilanz', *ZIP* 2007, p. 149.

4.3. The development of the law on STCs through the BGB

As the private law *acquis* develops, the extent to which the BGB can contribute to the predictability, accessibility, consistency and responsiveness of private law decreases. Therefore, deliberation between German state actors and European state actors has become necessary. This paragraph asks whether German state actors have taken into account that EU actors also develop private law, and interacted with these actors accordingly, and how this has affected the predictability, consistency, accessibility and responsiveness of private law. Moreover, have benefits, defended by pluralists, benefited the development of the German law on STCs?

Paragraph 4.3.1 will consider the choice of the legislator between the development of the law on STCs through *Sonderprivatrecht* or through the BGB. Paragraph 4.3.2 will consider the implementation of Directive 93/13 by the German legislator and judiciary. Paragraph 4.3.3 will consider the German law on STCs and international trade and paragraph 4.3.4 will end with a conclusion.

4.3.1. Codification or Sonderprivatrecht?

This paragraph will ask whether the German legislator, in the development of the law on STCs, has adequately taken into account that other actors also develop private law, which may inhibit the extent to which the BGB can contribute to benchmarks of predictability, accessibility, consistency and responsiveness. Has the German legislator adequately deliberated with European actors and how has this affected the predictability, consistency, accessibility and responsiveness of the law on STCs? Do benefits become visible, in accordance with pluralist arguments?

Paragraph 4.3.1.1 will consider the initial choice for *Sonderprivatrecht*. Paragraph 4.3.1.2 will turn to the 1980s initiatives for the reform of the law of obligations. Paragraph 4.3.1.3 will turn to the *Schuldrechtsmodernisierung* and paragraph 4.3.1.4 will end with a conclusion.

4.3.1.1. A national choice for *Sonderprivatrecht*

Why did the German legislator initially opt for *Sonderprivatrecht*, and did the German legislator sufficiently recognise interdependence between actors developing the law on STCs?

Importantly, when the AGBG was drafted, the role of the EU was much smaller than it is today. As competence had not yet been reallocated to the European level, or to a much smaller extent, there was less interdependence between actors. Consequently, there was less need to develop a strategy to deal with the ongoing development of private law at a European level. However, generally, the added value of comparative research in the drafting of legislation had been recognised. Also, the use of codifications in a pluralistic modern industrial society had been criticised, as reaching consensus became more difficult while the legislator also needed to deal with social and economical issues, frequently through *Sonderprivatrecht*.[333] In the 1970s, the EU had published an outline for a Directive on unfair terms, in accordance with its pursuit to establish a consumer protection policy.[334] The European developments did not, however, inhibit Germany to develop the law in this area.[335] What were the reasons for developing the law on STCs outside the BGB?

1) As the AGBG pursued a social aim, it did not belong in the BGB that took private autonomy and freedom of contract as a starting point.[336]

The drafting of the AGBG should be seen against the background of the 1971 statement of the *Bundesregierung* on establishing a consumer policy.[337] Accordingly, the first draft of the working group on the AGBG emphasised that the freedom of contract, which in normal cases effected a balance of contract parties' rights and duties, was, in reality, used to the advantage of one contract party with a better bargaining position who drafted STCs.[338] In particular, the proposal emphasised that a retreat of the legislator from the law on STCs, also characterised as the self-created law of trade ('*selbstgeschaffenes Recht der Wirtschaft*') was irreconcilable with the constitutional task of the legislator to establish a social state, and the proposal accordingly sought to establish a social contract law.[339] This emphasis was not in accordance with the general principles of the contractual freedom of the BGB. Accordingly, article 24 AGBG stipulated that, although some of its provisions were not applicable in cases where STCs were used against businesses or legal persons under public law, some provisions – including the blanket clause in article 9 AGBG – were applicable.

In its advice before Parliament, the committee argued that the AGBG is necessary to protect consumers from the one-sided drafting of STCs by sellers, to their detriment. The scope of the AGBG is not limited to B2C contracts, as the committee noted that in the long term, protection of businesses is to the benefit of consumers as well, as the extra costs caused by unfair STCs are likely to be at least partially passed on to consumers.[340]

The choice for *Sonderprivatrecht* because of the social character of the AGBG may be criticised on the following grounds:

333 J. Esser, 'Gesetzesrationalität im Kodifikationszeitalter und heute', in: H.-J. Vogel, J. Esser, *Recht und Staat im Geschichte und Gegenwart, 100 Jahre oberste deutsche Justizbehörde*, Tübingen: Mohr Siebeck 1977, p. 13, comp. also F. Wieacker, 'Aufstieg, Blüte und Krisis der Kodifikationsidee', in: G. Boehmer (ed.), *Festschrift für Gustav Boehmer*, Bonn: Roerscheid 1954, p. 48–49.

334 Comp. the Preliminary programm of the European Economic Community for a consumer protection and information policy, OJ C 92/2, 25.4.1975.

335 See for a comparative overview HKK/Hofer (2007), articles 305–310, nr 30.

336 Comp. N. Reich, 'Zivilrechtstheorie, Sozialwissenschaften und Verbraucherschutz', *ZRP* 1974, p. 187.

337 Arbeitsgruppe zur Verbesserung des Verbraucherschutzes gegenüber Allgemeine Geschäftsbedingungen, *Vorschläge zur Verbesserung des Schutzes der Verbraucher gegenüber Allgemeine Geschäftsbedingungen, Erster Teilbericht*, Bonn: Referat für Presse und Öffentlichkeit 1974, p. 18–20.

338 *Erster Teilbericht*, Bonn: Referat für Presse und Öffentlichkeit 1974, p. 13.

339 *Erster Teilbericht*, Bonn: Referat für Presse und Öffentlichkeit 1974, p. 35.

340 Bericht des Rechtsausschusses, 23 June 1976, Drucksache 7/5422, p. 1, 4, available at http://dipbt.bundestag.de/dip21/btd/07/054/0705422.pdf.

i) The AGBG did not exclusively aim to increase consumer protection, but was extended to protect businesses subjected to STCs as well. Should the AGBG therefore not have been incorporated in the BGB?[341]
ii) The BGB is, as such, not completely unfamiliar with the protection of a contract party who is in a less advantageous bargaining position than its counterparty. Despite the focus of the BGB on private autonomy, the BGB, before the incorporation of the AGBG, already provided for compensation of unequal bargaining positions.[342]

Notwithstanding these objections, the distinction between general private law and *Sonderprivatrecht* is still defended.[343]

2) The initial choice to develop rules outside the BGB was in accordance with the choice to develop *Sonderprivatrecht* outside of the BGB to safeguard the stable development of the BGB as well as the flexibility of laws outside the BGB. Accordingly, the committee recognised the possibility that the AGBG would need to be amended.[344]

3) The inclusion of provisions on civil procedure law indicated the development of *Sonderprivatrecht* in the AGBG.

4) If the AGBG had been incorporated in the BGB, this would have been part of a more general reform of the law of obligations, which would probably have postponed the introduction of the AGBG. The drafting of the AGBG did give rise to arguments for reform.

These arguments for *Sonderprivatrecht* are not based on foreign experiences or European initiatives.[345] Although the first draft pointed to comparative research on the judicial evaluation of STCs,[346] the draft proposal focused on a national level and did not mention the debate that had also started at a European level, and it does not evaluate foreign solutions. Therefore, arguably, the successful draft of the AGBG cannot be traced to mutual learning or regulatory competition, in accordance with pluralist arguments. Consequently, the choice to establish separate legislation cannot really be seen as an argument against the incorporation of the private law *acquis* into the BGB.

341 U. Preis, 'Persönlicher Anwendungsbereich der Sonderprivatrechte', *ZHR* 1994, p. 603.

342 Comp. M. Lieb, 'Sonderprivatrecht für Ungleichgewichtslagen?' *AcP* 1978, p. 197 who has argued that the AGBG only partially codified the law on the judicial evaluation of contracts on the basis of article 242 BGB, which went beyond the evaluation of STCs.

343 J. Stürner, 'Der hundertste Geburtstag des BGB – nationale Kodifikation im Greisenalter?', *JZ* 1996, p. 742.

344 Bericht des Rechtsausschusses, 23 June 1976, Drucksache 7/5422, p .1, 4, available at http://dipbt.bundestag.de/dip21/btd/07/054/0705422.pdf.

345 See critically W. Tilman, 'Das AGB-Gesetz und die Einheit des Privatrechts', *ZHR* 1978, p. 54, who argues that in the drafting of the AGBG, too little attention was paid to alternative possibilities, in particular, the alternative to include the AGBG in the BGB.

346 See for an overview H.E. Brandner, 'Wege und Zielvorstellungen auf dem Gebiet der Allgemeinen Geschäftsbedingungen', *JZ* 1973, p. 613.

However, the reasons to develop *Sonderprivatrecht* rather than incorporate special rules into the BGB should be considered in the implementation of the *acquis*. Are these arguments still considered or are there reasons for the German legislator to change its approach, as *Sonderprivatrecht*, both at the national and the European level, continues to develop?

4.3.1.2. Comparative law and the continued existence of *Sonderprivatrecht*

The development of *Sonderprivatrecht* alongside the BGB, especially the AGBG, gave rise to the question as to whether this was a desirable development, whether these subjects should really be stipulated outside the BGB, or whether the BGB should be reformed.[347] Consequently, only a few years after the AGBG was established, initiatives to reform the BGB were developed. The government organised the drafting of preliminary reports (*Vorschläge und Gutachten*).'[348]

A separate report on comparative law should enable the German legislator to benefit from experiences in other legal orders on the inclusion of separate laws into a codification.[349] This preliminary report on comparative law[350] concluded that in prominent legal orders – especially with similar codifications, in Switzerland and the Netherlands – the development of separate legislation alongside codifications had been regarded with suspicion, while other legal orders, especially France, had chosen separate legislation. The reasoning for incorporation or *Sonderprivatrecht* differed. While Italy and the Netherlands, at the time, had both already chosen to incorporate the law on STCs into the codification, this was more difficult for legal orders with older codifications such as France, who had chosen separate legislation. Austria opted for a middle road by establishing a separate law for consumer protection (*Konsumentenschutzgesetz*), which was, however, criticised as having little relevance for German law. The comparative law report paid limited attention to Member States – such as the United Kingdom and Sweden – that used techniques that differed too much from the German experiences.[351] Thus, the experience in these legal orders with the coexistence of separate laws without a codification was not an object of inspiration, even though the experience with the

347 See further A. Wolf, 'Die Überarbeitung des Schuldrechts', *AcP* 1982, p. 80.

348 Bundesminister der Justiz, 'Einleitung', in: Bundesminister der Justiz (ed.), *Vorschläge und Gutachten zur Überarbeitung des Schuldrecht*, Vol. I, Köln: Bundesanzeiger 1981, p. XI.

349 Bundesminister der Justiz, 'Einleitung', in: Bundesminister der Justiz (ed.), *Vorschlage und Gutachten zur Uberarbeitung des Schuldrecht*, Vol. I, Köln: Bundesanzeiger 1981, p. XI. H.-G. Landfernmann, 'Überarbeitung des deutschen Schuldrechts', *RabelsZ* 1981, p. 127 also notes that comparative law may give an insight in the strategies adopted by other states in the development of private law within or outside the civil code.

350 Max Planck Institut für ausländisches und internationales Privatrecht, 'Rechtsvergleichung', in: Bundesminister der Justiz (ed.), *Vorschläge und Gutachten zur Überarbeitung des Schuldrecht*, Vol. I, Köln: Bundesanzeiger 1981, p. 67–68.

351 Max Planck Institut für ausländisches und internationales Privatrecht, 'Rechtsvergleichung', in: Bundesminister der Justiz (ed.), *Vorschlage und Gutachten zur Uberarbeitung des Schuldrecht*, Vol. I, Köln: Bundesanzeiger 1981, p. 68.

development of particular legislation was a reason to include these states in the comparative law report.[352]

The report merely listed the strategies adopted in other legal orders without specifically arguing for a course of action. The other reports were also not unequivocal. Interestingly, Westermann,[353] noted that the Austrian *Konsumentenschutzgesetz* could serve as a source of inspiration for the legal order as it provided an alternative between *Sonderprivatrecht* and incorporation. However, he considered the development of a separate code for consumer contracts unattractive, as it could give rise to demarcation difficulties.

The assignment to the commission on the reform of the law of obligations aimed at revising parts of the law of obligations and prescription that were in need of reform,[354] especially against the background of initiatives for harmonisation in this area and comparative research.[355] Even though the development of consumer protection legislation alongside the BGB prompted the legislator to consider revision,[356] and the inclusion of *Sondergesetze* into the BGB had been subject to debate,[357] the revision aimed to incorporate the experiences of legal practice since the establishment of the BGB, thereby maintaining the methodology and the principles underlying the BGB. Drafts for Directives in the area of revision were not a reason to postpone the revision.[358]

According to Ulmer,[359] incorporating the AGBG into the BGB was not subject to debate, while it was also not in need of revision. Dörner[360] notes that the development of *Sonderprivatrecht* avoided amendments of the BGB. Consequently, the 1992 proposal for the *Schuldrechtsreform* aimed to preserve the AGBG, and limit amendments to this law to those that had become necessary by the *Schuldrechtsreform*.[361] However, after the 1994 *Deutscher Juristentag*, despite a positive reception, the draft did not result in the reform

352 Max Planck Institut für ausländisches und internationales Privatrecht, 'Rechtsvergleichung', in: Bundesminister der Justiz (ed.), *Vorschlage und Gutachten zur Uberarbeitung des Schuldrecht*, Vol. I, Köln: Bundesanzeiger 1981, p. 9.

353 H.P. Westermann, 'Verbraucherschutz', in: Bundesminister der Justiz (ed.), *Gutachten und Vorschläge zur Überarbeitung des Schuldrechts*, Vol. III, Köln: Bundesanzeiger 1983, p. 74.

354 H.A. Engelhard, 'Zu den Aufgaben einer Kommission für die Überarbeitung des Schuldrechts', *NJW* 1984, p. 1201.

355 R. Stürner, 'Empfiehlt sich die von der Schuldrechtskommission vorgeschlagene Neuregelung des allgemeinen Leistungsstörungsrechts, der Mängelhaftung bei Kauf- und Werkvertrag und des Rechts der Verjährung? – Versuch einer Themenpräsentation', *NJW*-Beil 1994, p. 2.

356 A. Wolf, 'Überarbeitung des Schuldrechts", *AcP* 1982, p. 80.

357 Comp. the discussion sketched in R. Damm, 'Verbraucherrechtliche Sondergesetzgebung und Privatrechtssystem', *JZ* 1978, p. 175–176.

358 A. Wolf, 'Die Überarbeitung des Schuldrechts', *AcP* 1982, p. 87.

359 P. Ulmer, 'Zehn Jahre AGB-Gesetz – Rückblick und Ausblick', in: H. Heinrichs, W. Löwe, P. Ulmer (eds.), *Zehn Jahre AGB-Gesetz*, Köln: Verlag Kommunikationsform 1987, p. 6, 16.

360 H. Dörner, 'Die Integration des Verbraucherrechts in das BGB', in: R. Schulze, H. Schulte-Nölke (eds.), *Die Schuldrechtsreform vor dem Hintergrund des Gemeinschaftsrechts*, Tübingen: Mohr Siebeck 2001, p. 178.

361 Abschlussbericht der Kommission zur Überarbeitung des Schuldrechts, 1992, p. 278. Comp. however, critically W. Ernst, 'Zum Kommissionsentwurf für eine Schuldrechtsreform', *NJW* 1994, p. 2179 who finds that the draft does not sufficiently take into account consumer protection law, including the AGBG.

of the BGB until 2000, when the draft for the *Schuldrechtmodernisierungsgesetz* was published.[362]

It may be concluded that the incorporation of the AGBG was not a subject of thorough discussion during the drafting of both the AGBG and the 1981 initiative for the *Schuldrechtsreform*, despite comparative research on this point and the comparative preliminary report. The choice to maintain the development of *Sonderprivatrecht* was not based on foreign experiences. Despite the potential for mutual learning, the choice for either the development of *Sonderprivatrecht* or codification was not based on the experiences of foreign actors. Arguably, opportunities for mutual learning are limited and bound to existing law; seriously considering the coexistence of various laws instead of the codification would require drastic chances and does not seem realistic.

The German legislator also did not anticipate the ongoing development of the private law *acquis* and did not reconsider its reasoning for codification or postpone the revision of the law of obligations in the light of draft Directives.

4.3.1.3. The *Schuldrechtsreform* and the choice for incorporation

Interdependence had hardly developed during the drafting of the AGBG and the 1981 and 1983 preliminary reports, but it had developed at the time of the *Schuldrechtsmodernisierung*. The development of the Directive on consumer sales prompted the German legislator to reform the law of obligations and, in contrast to the 1992 draft, the discussion draft in 2000 incorporated large parts of the AGBG in the BGB. This, however, did not entail drastic changes to the AGBG as such.[363] Did the German legislator recognise that the development of the *acquis* could eventually inhibit the extent to which the BGB ensures the predictability, accessibility, consistency and responsiveness of private law?

In the discussion draft, various reasons for incorporating the AGBG into the BGB are considered:

1) The codification principle, according to which private law should be contained within a uniform, theoretical and dogmatically-sound code that shows no gaps. In turn, this furthers the accessibility[364] and coherence[365] of private law.[366] Moreover, as the law on STCs concerns a central area of contract law, the development of *Sonderprivatrecht*

362 See further R. Zimmerman, 'Schuldrechtsreform?' in W. Ernst, R. Zimmerman (eds.), *Zivilrechtswissenschaft und Schuldrechtsreform*, Tübingen: Mohr Siebeck 2001, p. 15–16.

363 However, some changes in the evaluation of STCs may be visible. These changes may be attributed to the more general reform of the law of obligations and prescription, as this may affect the fairness of STCs as default law is taken as a starting point to assess the fairness of these terms under article 306 BGB.

364 See especially J. Schmidt-Räntsch, 'Reintegration der Verbraucherschutzgesetze durch den Entwurf eines Schuldrechtsmodernisierungsgesetzes', in: R. Schulze, H. Schulte-Nölke (eds.), *Die Schuldrechtsreform vor dem Hintergrund des Gemeinschaftsrechts*, Tübingen: Mohr Siebeck 2001, p. 169.

365 See for example Th. Pfeiffer, B. Schinkels, 'Schuldrechtsmodernisierung und AGB-Gesetz', in: H.-W. Micklitz et al. (eds.), *Schuldrechtsreform und Verbraucherschutz*, Baden Baden: Nomos 2001, p. 140.

366 BGB-Diskussionentwurf, available at www.dnoti.de/DOC/2001/eschurmo.pdf, p. 164.

would undermine the central role of the BGB, while incorporation helps to ensure the central role of the BGB.[367]

2) The close relation between the BGB and the law on STCs.

The incorporation of the AGBG in the BGB also benefits consistency. Graf von Westphalen[368] points to the clearer relation between articles 305–310 BGB and more general contract law provisions in the BGB. Importantly, this reasoning does not imply the incorporation of all *Sonderprivatrechte* into the BGB.[369] Accordingly, laws less intertwined with the BGB, in particular the law on product liability, remained outside the BGB.[370] Insofar as separate laws have developed that should not be considered a part of general private law, the development of private law alongside the codification would, in this view, still be possible – and desirable.

This reasoning implies a change from the earlier approach of the German legislator, because the close relation between the AGBG and the BGB was previously not considered a reason for integration.[371] The AGBG was already closely intertwined with the BGB. Not only had the AGBG developed on the basis of article 242 BGB, it took default law in the BGB as a starting point to decide which contractual provisions could be considered fair, and requirements for the inclusion of STCs were in accordance with principles underlying contractual rules for the conclusion of contacts.[372] Before the AGBG was included in the BGB, the close relation between the BGB and the AGBG was clearly indicated, and problems of inconsistency do not seem to have arisen. Arguably, this lack of problems may draw into doubt the necessity of inclusion.[373] Why, therefore, did the close relation later become an important argument for incorporation?

3) The predictable development was less convincing as a reason against incorporation.

In 2000, the AGBG had proven itself stable enough that incorporation would not render the BGB vulnerable to regular amendments, which would undermine the predictable development of the law on STCs.

The experiences with the AGBG raise questions with regard to the need to codify areas of private law, even central areas of private law, to ensure consistency and predictability. The lack of unpredictability and inconsistency after the introduction of the AGBG,

367 J. Schmidt-Räntsch, 'Reintegration der Verbraucherschutzgesetze durch den Entwurf eines Schuldrechtsmodernisierungsgesetzes', in: R. Schulze, H. Schulte-Nölke (eds.), *Die Schuldrechtsreform vor dem Hintergrund des Gemeinschaftsrechts*, Tübingen: Mohr Siebeck 2001, p. 171.

368 F. Graf von Westphalen, 'AGB-Recht ins BGB – Eine erste "Bestandsaufnahme"', *NJW* 2002, p. 18–19, who also states that this change will increase the relevance of case law.

369 M. Lieb, 'Grundfragen einer Schuldrechtsreform', *AcP* 1983, p. 331.

370 Critically A. Staudinger, 'Zur Novellierung des Produkthaftungsgesetzes', *NJW* 2001, p. 275.

371 P. Ulmer, 'Das AGB-Gesetz: Ein eigenständiges Kodifikationswerk', *JZ* 2001, p. 492.

372 Th. Pfeiffer, B. Schinkels, 'Schuldrechtsmodernisierung und AGB-Gesetz', in: H.-W. Micklitz et al. (eds.), *Schuldrechtsreform und Verbraucherschutz*, Baden Baden: Nomos 2001, p. 139.

373 Th. Pfeiffer, 'Die Integration von Nebengesetzen in das BGB', in: W. Ernst, R. Zimmerman (eds.), *Zivilrechtswissenschaft und Schuldrechtsreform – Zum Diskussionsentwurf des Bundesministeriums der Justiz*, Tübingen: Mohr Siebeck p. 501, also M. Lieb, 'Grundfragen einer Schuldrechtsreform', *AcP* 1983, p. 331.

alongside the BGB, may even indicate that the implementation of Directives alongside the BGB more generally need not be problematic.

→ **Did the German legislator adequately recognise interdependence in its reasoning?** Various instances of interdependence have been overlooked:

i) Developing a coherent system is not as feasible as originally envisaged, because private law is also developed by the European legislator, who pursues aims that may well differ from the aims pursued by the German legislator.

ii) The extent to which the German legislator is able to maintain a dogmatically sound system may diminish as the private law *acquis* develops.

Articles 305–310 BGB have been criticised for this reason. If the system established by the BGB was followed, articles 305–310 BGB should have been implemented in the general part of the BGB.[374] Pfeiffer and Schinkel[375] argue that implementing the AGBG in the general part of the BGB would facilitate the protective aim of these provisions, in accordance with Directive 93/13. Notably, placing the provisions on STCs within the law of obligations may imply that outside the law of obligations, in binding one-sided juridical acts or juridical acts stipulated outside the BGB, the regime on STCs is not applicable.

Article 310 par. 4 BGB provides that for employment contracts, specific characteristics of employment law should be taken into account, Article 310 par. 4 BGB exempts contracts under company law, and contracts in the area of family law and succession from evaluation under articles 305 et seq BGB. This provision has similarly been criticised, as these exceptions are not in accordance with the system of the BGB.[376]

Yet implementation that follows the system of the BGB means scattering the provisions implementing the Directive over the BGB: provisions on the fairness of contract terms would be implemented near article 242 BGB, provisions on ineffectiveness would be implemented near article 138 BGB, and provisions on the *contra legem* interpretation and the requirement of transparency would be situated in yet another part of the BGB. This strategy would result in multiple European islands within the codification, and would perhaps not meet the requirements of clarity on the implementation of Directives that confer rights on consumers; it is not likely that such implementation would make consumers sufficiently aware of their rights.

However, the approach to implement Directives in a group of provisions, rather than in separate provisions, may, in turn, be undermined as Directives also affecting the law on STCs develop. Thus, the proposal for the implementation of Directive 2011/7[377] makes clear that article 7 is not implemented in articles 305–310 BGB.

374 Interestingly, this approach would be in accordance with the solution in the PECL and the UNIDROIT principles.

375 Th. Pfeiffer, B. Schinkels, 'Schuldrechtsmodernisierung und AGB-Gesetz', in: H.-W. Micklitz et al. (eds.), *Schuldrechtsreform und Verbraucherschutz*,Baden Baden: Nomos 2001, p. 146.

376 Grabitz/Hilf/Das Recht der Europäische Union/Pfeiffer (2009), article 1 nr 17–19.

377 BT-Drucks. 17/10491.

iii) The German legislator is less able to independently maintain the central role of the BGB, as this also depends on the development of the private law *acquis* and the case law of the CJEU.[378]

Particularly, the development of Regulations and the development of Directives that should be implemented as *Sonderprivatrecht* may undermine the central role of the BGB.

iv) Despite the emphasis on the codification principle and the distinction between general private law and *Sonderprivatrecht*, the question whether Directives are *Sonderprivatrecht* has not been debated, nor have the reasons to keep *Sonderprivatrecht* out of the BGB expressly been considered in the implementation of the *acquis*. It follows that the distinction, therefore, does not currently provide a sound basis for a predictable approach to the implementation of the private law *acquis*.

v) Arguably, in its reasoning under (2), the German legislator has overlooked that there is no close relation between the provisions in Directives and general private law. Instead, Directives typically seek to advance the internal market.

vi) The reasoning in (3) overlooks the fact that articles 305–310 BGB also implement Directive 93/13. The question whether the predictable development of the BGB is sufficiently guaranteed also depends on the further development of the *acquis*, in particular, the future reform of this Directive, and the interpretation of the Directive by the CJEU. More generally, the extent to which the BGB can contribute to the predictable development by limiting the need for legislative reform may be limited as the European legislator still perceives a need for harmonisation. If harmonisation takes place through Directives, this in turn initiates national reform to implement Directives.

→ Thus, the arguments for incorporation in the *Schuldrechtsreform* have overlooked the fact that as the private law *acquis* develops, the capability of the BGB to contribute to the predictability, accessibility, consistency and responsiveness of private law becomes subject to limitations.

Arguably, the reasons for developing *Sonderprivatrecht* offer an interesting starting point for discussions on the implementation of the *acquis* that may provide a starting point for a more predictable and consistent implementation of the *acquis*. Yet the debate on the question whether the rules on STCs can be characterised as *Sonderprivatrecht* indicates the need for clearer standards for classifying rules as *Sonderprivatrecht* or *Generalprivatrecht*. Moreover, it should not be overlooked that even though Directives may cover a large part of contract law, Directives are more likely to pursue a specific aim and their development may also be less predictable than overlapping national law.

378 Th. Pfeiffer, 'Die Integration von Nebengesetzen in das BGB', in: W. Ernst, R. Zimmerman (eds.), *Zivilrechtswissenschaft und Schuldrechtsreform – Zum Diskussionsentwurf des Bundesministeriums der Justiz*, Tübingen: Mohr Siebeck 2001 p. 485–486.

4.3.1.4. Conclusion on the choice for codification

The German legislator did not consider the role of European actors in safeguarding the development of the law on STCs in a predictable, consistent, accessible and responsive manner. It follows that interaction between German, European and foreign actors has not served to adjust the development of the law on STCs through the BGB, in accordance with methodological nationalism.[379] The German regime was also not based on inspiration from successful foreign, European or international laws. Instead, the careful drafting process of the AGBG and its success has contributed to the continued, unaltered use of codification.

However, it does not become apparent that this lack of attention for interdependence also undermines the predictability, consistency, and the accessibility of private law. Even though the German legislator overlooked that it cannot independently further the coherence of private law through codification, it has not become apparent that the German legislator pursued coherence in order to resist further harmonisation initiatives. Arguments for coherence should therefore not only be seen in this light,[380] but also in the light of the need to preserve the comprehensibility of national law. To the contrary, the AGBG, and later articles 305–310 BGB, have been considered as success stories. The law on STCs is not as such in need of revision.

Yet as the private law *acquis* continues to develop, the extent to which the BGB contributes to predictability, accessibility and consistency diminishes further. Regrettably, a more general strategy for coping with the ongoing development on the law of STCs by the European legislator and in different areas of law has not been generally considered, despite interesting starting points in the distinction between general private law and *Sonderprivatrecht*.

The arguments for incorporation during the *Schuldrechtsreform*, also reflected in article 307 par. 3 BGB and articles 308–309 BGB, make clear that a close relationship between the law on STCs and national law exists. This close relationship supports Collin's[381] claim that despite harmonisation, and despite attempts for maximum harmonisation in this area, the practical application of the law on STCs has continued and will continue to differ throughout the Union. Possibly, the close relationship between the law on STCs, general contract law, and corresponding legal views on justice, may also limit the extent to which regulatory competition will develop. In accordance with this argument, the law on STCs will likely develop in accordance with default law, which reflects German legal views on justice, which may differ from other national views on justice. Thus, at first sight, the coexistence of national actors and resulting divergences in this area can be beneficial as it enables the law to develop responsively to national legal views on justice.

379 L. Miller, *The emergence of EU contract law: Exploring Europeanization*, Oxford: OUP 2011, p. 168.

380 Comp. L. Miller, *The emergence of EU contract law: Exploring Europeanization*, Oxford: OUP 2011, p. 173.

381 H. Collins, 'European private law and the cultural identity of states', *ERPL* 1995, p. 356.

4.3.2. *The existence of well-developed legislation and harmonisation*

The approach of German actors towards harmonisation is twofold: in the drafting of Directive 93/13, German actors have actively interacted with European actors, which has benefited the consistent and predictable development of German law. In contrast, in the implementation of the Directive, German actors have not adequately interacted with European actors. In the short term, this may benefit predictability, consistency and responsiveness, but the lack of interaction may inhibit the predictable, consistent and responsive development of the *acquis* in the long term.

Paragraph 4.3.2.1 will consider the development of the Directive 93/13 and paragraph 4.3.2.2 will turn to the subsequent approach of the legislator to the implementation of this Directive. Paragraph 4.3.2.3 will turn to the application of the Directive by the courts and paragraph 4.3.2.4 will discuss the attempted reform of the Directive. Paragraph 4.3.2.5 will end with a conclusion.

4.3.2.1. The debate in the development of the Directive

The drafting of Directive 93/13 was preceded by extensive comparative research as well as the 1975 resolution from the European Council[382] and the 1984 consultation from the European Parliament.[383] Eventually, this led to the 1990 proposal for a Directive on unfair terms in consumer contracts.[384]

The consultation in the German legal order was held after Directive 93/13 had been established. Nevertheless, German experts criticised the 1990 draft for a Directive,[385] and the federal government rejected the 1990 draft. The decision of the *Bundesrat*[386] mainly takes German law, as well as the position of German businesses, as a starting point, arguing for a European regime that is more in accordance with German law. This approach is in accordance with the view that national actors adopt a nationalist perspective towards EU concepts.[387] German academia did not pay much attention to the European initiative, especially not when compared to the drafting of the AGBG.

German law was one of the first and one of the best-developed laws on STCs in the Union, and the European legislator took note of German insights. The 1990 draft for a Directive was amended, largely in accordance with German criticism. Thus, the late consultation on Directive 93/13 did not withhold the German legislator and German experts from participating in the European discussion. However, the comments on the draft Directive were hardly based on comparative research, which was available in

382 OJ No C 92, 25.4.1975.

383 Supplement 1/84, Bulletin of the European Communities.

384 COM (90) 322 final.

385 Among others, see especially the criticism of H.E. Brandner, P. Ulmer, 'EG-Richtlinie über mißbräuchliche Klauseln in Verbraucherverträgen. Kritische Bemerkungen zum Vorschlag der EG-Kommission', *BB* 1991, p. 701.

386 Decision of the Bundesrat 1 March 1991, BR-Drucks. 611/90, as well as the recommendation of the committees of 1 March 1991, BR-Drucks. 611/90.

387 L. Miller, *The emergence of EU contract law: Exploring Europeanization*, Oxford: OUP 2011, p. 169.

abundance.[388] Thus, opportunities to draft the best possible law – notwithstanding the high quality of German law – may have been missed.

The way in which the discussion was conducted, and the way in which German interests were defended at the European level, demonstrates that the proposal did not prompt the German legislator to consider the perspectives of foreign actors with an interest in German law, as argued more generally by Joerges.[389] Also, it is not apparent that European actors initiated harmonisation to protect the interests of businesses and consumers in cross-border trade, as considered in the preamble to the Directive. Accordingly, the competitiveness and employment statement, in the Annex[390] to the proposal, makes clear that harmonisation was not undertaken to serve the interests of businesses engaged in cross-border contracts, although the European legislator was optimistic about the effects of the draft Directive in this respect. Instead, the statement found that the responses of industry consulted over this proposal were 'antagonistic', and failed to 'perceive the true significance for them of the proposal'. The statement went even further in stating that the proposal was not detrimental to their interests and existing legislation was not detrimental to small- to medium-sized businesses.

Thus, debate preceding the drafting of the Directive was limited, it but did not limit the discussion to such an extent that the German legislator and academics did not contribute to the discussion in the drafting process on the Directive. In turn, the participation of German actors benefited the stable and consistent development of the German law on STCs, which is beneficial for practice. Harmonisation was not prompted by concerns for the interests of transnational actors, nor did it prompt such concerns at the national level.

4.3.2.2. The implementation of the Directive

After the Directive had been established, two models for implementation were considered: on the one hand, amendment of the AGBG, and on the other hand, new legislation alongside the AGBG and the BGB. However, establishing a separate law alongside the BGB and the AGBG would be undesirable because of potential problems with consistency and predictability.[391] The expert draft ('*Referententwurf*')[392] did not refer to comparative law, and assumed that the Directive already largely resembled the AGBG, arguing that the law should be amended as little as possible. This draft was subsequently criticised on

388 See the overview from H.E. Brandner, 'Wege und Zielvorstellungen auf dem Gebiet der Allgemeinen Geschäftsbedingungen', *JZ* 1973, p. 613 and the preliminary report on comparative law discussed in par. 4.3.1.2.

389 Ch. Joerges, 'On the legitimacy of Europeanising private law: Considerations on a justice-making law for the EU multi-level system', *Electronic Journal of Comparative Law* 2003, available at www.ejcl.org/ejcl/73/art73-3.html.

390 In response to the question 'Have both sides of industry been consulted?'

391 K. Baier, *Europaische Verbrauchervertrage und missbrauchliche Klauseln, die Umsetzung der Richtlinie 93/13/EWG uber missbrauchliche Klauseln in Verbrauchervertragen in Deutschland, Italien, England und Frankreich*, Hamburg: Kovač 2004, p. 50.

392 Referententwurf, *BB* 1995, p. 110.

various points. The draft implementation law (*'Regierungsentwurf'*) partially took into account the criticism on the expert draft.

Accordingly, the definition of STCs as terms that are drafted for multiple contracts in the BGB has been adapted to the definition in the Directive which does not require multiple contracts. Article 310 par. 3 sub 2 BGB stipulates that terms in contracts with consumers will also be considered STCs if they have been drafted for one contract. The emphasis on the requirement that STCs need not be included in a contract in order to fall under the scope of the contract, but merely been 'set' (*'gestellt'*) by the user of the STCs is in accordance with the Court's decision in Invitel.[393]

After the Directive had been established, attention was paid to the duties of Member States to implement the Directive. For example, Heinrichs[394] extensively discusses the duties to implement the Directive under European law and argues that parts of the Directive can be implemented through the interpretation of national law in accordance with the Directive; an argument that has later been superseded by the CJEU decision in *Commission v The Netherlands*.[395]

However, other, more critical comments were not followed. In particular, the criticism from Schmidt-Salzer[396] is convincing in the light of later BGH case law on the Directive.[397] Schmidt-Salzer pointed out that the approach to maintain the AGBG as much as possible, increased the risk that the underlying changes would be insufficiently clear. Schmidt-Salzer[398] also pointed out that, from the view of foreign observers, differences between the AGBG and the Directive are apparent, making the assumption that the AGBG and the Directive are already largely in conformity with the Directive less convincing towards other Member States and the EU. Therefore, the participation of foreign and international actors in the debate on the implementation of the Directive could have provided useful insights for German actors. In addition, foreign observers might have alerted national actors to the interests of foreign actors, in accordance with Joerges'[399] argument. At least, such participation could have made the needs and preferences of international and foreign actors clearer, enabling German actors, if they so choose, to develop the law in accordance with these needs and preferences. The insights of foreign actors could,

393 CJEU 26 April 2012 (Hatóság v Invitel Távközlési Zrt), C-472/10, [2012] ECR p. I-0, par. 37.

394 H. Heinrichs, 'Umsetzung der EG-Richtlinie über mißbräuchliche Klauseln in Verbraucherverträgen durch Auslegung Erweiterung des Anwendungsbereichs der Inhaltskontrolle', *NJW* 1995, p. 153.

395 CJEU 10 May 2001 (Commission of the European Communities v Kingdom of the Netherlands), C-144/99, [2001] ECR p. I-3541.

396 J. Schmidt-Salzer, 'Transformation der EG-Richtlinie über mißbräuchliche Klauseln in Verbraucherverträgen in deutsches Recht und AGB-Gesetz', *BB* 1995, p. 735.

397 See further below par. 10.3.2.3. and 10.4.1.2. J. Schmidt-Salzer, 'Transformation der EG-Richtlinie über mißbräuchliche Klauseln in Verbraucherverträgen in deutsches Recht und AGB-Gesetz', *BB* 1995, p. 736–737 moreover, notes that the interpretation of STCs also differed from the interpretation foreseen in the Directive.

398 J. Schmidt-Salzer, 'Transformation der EG-Richtlinie über mißbräuchliche Klauseln in Verbraucherverträgen in deutsches Recht und AGB-Gesetz', *BB* 1995, p. 739.

399 Ch. Joerges, 'On the legitimacy of Europeanising private law: Considerations on a justice-making law for the EU multi-level system', *Electronic Journal of Comparative Law* 2003, available at www.ejcl.org/ejcl/73/art73-3.html.

therefore, have prompted a more critical approach to the AGBG and led to a more critical evaluation as to whether the AGBG was in accordance with Directive 93/13.

The Directive does not provide a specific rule on surprising clauses similar to article 305c par. 1 BGB. Basedow[400] notes that the BGB is more precise than the Directive. In particular, the question arises of whether the further indication in article 307 par. 2 BGB (in which cases a term can be unfair), is in conformity with the autonomous interpretation established by the Directive, especially article 4 which relates that the unfairness of a term shall be assessed taking into account the nature of the goods or services on which parties are contracted, and by referring to all relevant circumstances at the time of the conclusion of the contract as well as the other terms of the contract.[401] Article 307 par. 2 BGB would have become problematic if the CJEU had ruled that default rules in the DCFR, which may well contradict national default law,[402] were relevant for determining whether clauses are unfair under the Directive. The CJEU has however not adopted such an approach.[403] Arguably, the divergences between article 307 par. 2 BGB and article 4 Directive are not problematic as the Directive aims for minimum harmonisation. Therefore, despite the divergence in the wording of the Directive and the AGBG – and currently article 307 BGB – the legislator assumed that the BGB was in accordance with the Directive and would be interpreted in conformity with the Directive.[404] Furthermore, it has been argued that the Directive may be indirectly applied for contracts between public bodies and consumers, as article 1 Directive speaks of contracts between suppliers and sellers and consumers, which, under article 2 par. 3 Directive, are defined as either publicly or privately owned.[405] However, these contracts may be determined by mandatory law that leaves no room for the evaluation of STCs under articles 305 et seq BGB.[406]

The opportunities to learn from foreign implementation practices were limited. Little information seems to have been available on the implementation practices in other Member States that were also slow in implementing the Directive. However, even if the German legislator had taken into account the approaches of foreign legislators, it does not necessarily follow that this would have prompted a more active approach to the implementation of the Directive. Various Member States adopted restraint in the implementation of the Directive[407] – and if the German legislator had, for example, been

400 MunchKomm zum BGB/Basedow (2012), introduction to articles 305–310, nr 24.

401 Somewhat confusingly, Grabitz/Hilf/Das Recht der Europäische Union/Pfeiffer (2009), article 4 nr 2 notes that article 4 par. 1 is not intended as a realisation of article 3 but rather as noting which objects are subject to interpretation. J. Schmidt-Salzer, 'Transformation der EG-Richtlinie über mißbräuchliche Klauseln in Verbraucherverträgen in deutsches Recht und AGB-Gesetz', *BB* 1995, p. 734 notes that referral to all circumstances during the time of contracting differed radically from case law and literature on the judicial evaluation and the interpretation of STCs on the objective ('*generallen*') control and interpretation.

402 See further E.-M. Kieninger, 'Vollharmonisierung des Rechts der AGB', *RabelsZ* 2009, p. 793.

403 CJEU 15 March 2012 (Pereničová and Perenič v SOS financ spol), C-453/10, [2012] ECR, p. I-0, par. 30.

404 MunchKomm zum BGB/Basedow (2012), article 307, nr 4.

405 MunchKomm zum BGB/Basedow (2012) introduction to articles 305–310 BGB, nr 26, similarly Grabitz/Hilf/Das Recht der Europäische Union/Pfeiffer (2009), article 2 Directive 93/13, nr 23.

406 See for example Hessisches LSG 9 June 2011, *BeckRS* 2011, 76272, with references to further case law, on contracts with health care insurers that fall under the SGB.

407 COM (2000) 248 final.

inspired by the approach of the Dutch legislator, this might have resulted in even more restraint in amending the AGBG. Thus, even where opportunities for learning developed, using these would hardly have been practical or beneficial.

In the implementation of Directive 93/13, the German legislator, in accordance with the general restraint exercised in the amendment of private law, beneficial for the stable development of the law and advantageous for practice, did not affect drastic changes to the successful AGBG.[408]

Despite this restraint and the apparent similarity between the Directive and the BGB, the implementation of the Directive into German law was late.[409] Moreover, the decision in *Commission v The Netherlands*[410] indicated that the assumption that the BGB was already in accordance with the Directive was incorrect with regard to the *contra preferentem* interpretation of clauses.[411] This decision demonstrates that it is not without risk to assume that current law already meets the requirements set out by the Directive. However, the view of the German legislator was based on previous CJEU case law that emphasised the discretion of national legislators in the implementation of Directives.[412] More interaction with the CJEU would likely not have made national actors aware of further going obligations.

Thus, foreign observations on compliance with the Directive would have been welcome, especially in the light of *Commission v The Netherlands*. However, more interaction with foreign legislators to gain insight on foreign implementation strategies would not have been useful, and more interaction with European actors would also not necessarily have added useful insights, unless such interaction would have revealed further going duties of implementation.

408 P. Ulmer, 'Der AGB-Gesetz nach der Umsetzung der EG-Richtlinie über mißbräuchliche Klauseln in Verbraucherverträgen', in: P. Ulmer, U. Hübner, *Das Recht der Allgemeinen Geschäftsbedingungen nach der Umsetzung der EG-Richtlinie über mißbräuchliche Klauseln in Verbraucherverträgen, Karlsruher Forum 1997*, Karlsruhe: Versicherungswirtschaft 1998, p. 9. According to K. Baier, *Europäische Verbraucherverträge und missbräuchliche Klauseln, die Umsetzung der Richtlinie 93 /13 /EWG über missbräuchliche Klauseln in Verbraucherverträgen in Deutschland, Italien, England und Frankreich*, Hamburg: Kovač 2004, p. 49, the Directive was also influenced by the AGBG, which may have contributed to this assumption.

409 The BGH has, however, interpreted German law in accordance with the Directive before it was implemented; comp. BGH 24 May 1995, *NJW* 1995, 2034.

410 CJEU 10 May 2011 (Commission of the European Communities v Kingdom of the Netherlands), C-144/99, [2001] ECR, p. I-3541.

411 This has since been corrected, despite objections that expressly including the *contra preferentem* rule would be difficult to reconcile with the system in the BGB, where the requirement of transparency was implied and could be realised through different ways, comp. P. Ulmer, 'Zur Anpassung des AGB-Gesetzes über mißbräuchliche Klauseln', *EuZW* 1993, p. 344. K. Baier, *Europaische Verbrauchervertrage und missbrauchliche Klauseln, die Umsetzung der Richtlinie 93 /13 /EWG uber missbrauchliche Klauseln in Verbrauchervertragen in Deutschland, Italien, England und Frankreich*, Hamburg: Kovač 2004, p. 72, moreover, points out that the *contra legem* interpretation may stand in the way of subsequent judicial control that takes the interpretation to the detriment of the consumer – or other party – as a starting point in its evaluation.

412 CJEU 9 April 1987 (Commission v Italy), Case 363/85, ECR [1987], p. 1733, par. 7, CJEU 23 May 1985, (Commission v Germany), Case 29/84, ECR 1985, p. 1661, par. 23.

4.3.2.3. The application of the Directive by the courts

Do courts in the interpretation of articles 305–310 BGB take into account Directive 93/13, CJEU case law, and foreign decisions to ensure the harmonised interpretation of the Directive?

In various national cases falling within the scope of the Directive, both higher courts[413] and lower courts[414] do not refer to the Directive or foreign case law, but rather to previous case law and literature. The decisions demonstrate that courts frequently rely on national default law to determine whether a clause is unfair. Thus, national courts also adopt a national perspective on European law.[415] However, in other cases, a more active approach towards the Directive is visible.[416]

Furthermore, in cases where the Directive has been considered, both the lower courts[417] and the BGH[418] leave open the possibility that questions could, and for the BGH should have been referred to the CJEU.

413 See for example BGH 8 February 2012, *NJW* 2012, 1431, BGH 11 June 2010, *NJW* 2010, 2873, BGH 13 April 2010, *NJW* 2010, 1742, BGH 30 March 2010, *NJW* 2010, 2041, BGH 28 January 2010, *NJW* 2010, 2046, BGH 9 November 2008, *NJW* 2009, 912, BGH 5 July 2009, *NJW* 2009, 3506, BGH 13 October 2006, *NJW-RR* 2007, 962.

414 See for example OLG München 9 June 2011, *NJW-RR* 2011, 1359, LG Bonn 23 February 2011, *BeckRS* 2011, 22639, LG Münster 22 February 2011, *BeckRS* 2011, 05151, OLG Hamburg 17 February 2010, *BeckRS* 2010, 12863, OLG München 17 January 2008, *NJW-RR* 2008, 1233; comp. also LG Heilbronn, 12 March 2009, *BeckRS* 2009, 8141.

415 As argued by L. Miller, *The emergence of EU contract law: Exploring Europeanization*, Oxford: OUP 2011, p. 169. T. Pfeiffer, 'Europäisch-autonome Auslegung der Klauselrichtlinie am Beispiel der Hauptleistungsklauseln', *NJW* 2014, p. 3069–3070 convincingly considers the existence of well-established legislation and case law, as well as the interpretation of the decision in *Freiburger Kommunalbauten* (on which see below par. 4.4.1.2.) as possible reasons for this restraint.

416 See for example OLG Stuttgart 18 January 2006, *BWNotZ* 2007, 16, which however concerned a contract between a municipality and a business. The court questioned the privileged position of contracts used by notaries under the Directive and subjected them to judicial review.

417 See, for example, OLG Brandenburg 21 June 2006, *BeckRS* 2006, 8091, considering that the Directive is not applicable as it has not been established that the clause has been drafted in advance, while article 3 par. 2 Directive that states that 'a term shall *always* be regarded as not individually negotiated where it has been drafted in advance and the consumer has, therefore, not been able to influence the substance of the term', which also allows for the conclusion that consumers may not have been able to influence terms even if they have not been preformulated. This decision is, however, in conformity with a later BGH decision, BGH 15 April 2008, *BeckRS* 2008, 12098. In the light of the aim of the Directive, particularly the CJEU decision in Océano, the question arises whether the OLG Brandenburg should have established this matter of its own motion, particularly as it concerned a clause enabling the supplier to alter the price, falling within the scope of sub j of the annex to the Directive. J. Basedow, 'Der Europäische Gerichtshof und die verweigerte Dialog', in: G. Müller et al (eds.), *Festschrift für Günter Hirsch zum 65. Geburtstag*, München: Beck 2008, p. 62 notes that cases concerning clauses on the annex to the Directive should be referred to the CJEU.

418 See, for example, BGH 15 April 2008, *BeckRS* 2008, 12098, in which it was held that consumers should prove that they did not have an opportunity to affect the terms in the meaning of article 310 par. 3 sub 2 BGB. However, this arguably concerns the interpretation of standard terms in the sense of article 3 Directive, which defines standard terms as not individually negotiated, while stipulating in par. 2 that terms have not been negotiated when terms have been preformulated. The second sentence expressly states that the circumstance that other terms have been negotiated does not entail that other terms will be considered negotiated as well. In contrast, the BGH considers that as the consumer negotiated other

Notably, this does not necessarily mean that the cases in which courts do not refer to the Directive or foreign materials but rather to national materials have been decided incorrectly – rather, it is not *harmonised* interpretation. One of the reasons for the lack of harmonised interpretation may be the lack of clarity on courts' obligation to do so - after all, Directive 93/13 pursues minimum harmonisation and allows for divergences between national laws. Even if such an obligation exists, lower courts in particular, who do not have to refer to the CJEU, are insufficiently able to interpret articles 305–310 BGB in accordance with the Directive and foreign decisions, especially because foreign decisions may not be sufficiently available – although the database in the EC Consumer Law Compendium provides a starting point.[419]

Basedow[420] rightly points out that considering the divergence of laws in this area prior to harmonisation, national courts cannot achieve harmonised interpretation independently, without the harmonising role of the CJEU. The CJEU has unfortunately not provided much clarity on the unified interpretation of central provisions in the Directive. However, the ability of the CJEU to do this depends upon the amount of questions referred to it by lower courts.

The relatively small number of cases before the CJEU – certainly small if compared to the number of cases before German courts – may arguably also be traced to various circumstances:

i) Concerns over lengthy procedures in relatively straightforward cases.
ii) The restraint of the CJEU in providing consistent guidelines in the interpretation of Directives,[421] especially as article 307 BGB plays an important role in the BGB.
iii) The practice of minimum harmonisation and the view that questions on the interpretation of provisions offering more protection than the Directive need not be interpreted in accordance with the Directive, and referral to the CJEU need not be

parts of the terms, he will have to prove that he did not have the chance to influence the other terms. Arguably, as it concerned the interpretation of article 3 Directive, the BGH could, and perhaps, should have referred this question to the CJEU. Comp. also BGH 19 November 2002, *BeckRS* 2003, 736 on the requirement of transparency, both in article 5 Directive 93/13 and in article 4 par. 4 Directive 90/314, that obliges the users of STCs to draft clauses amending the price in such a way that it enables contract parties subjected to STCs to calculate the price. Otherwise, contract parties are unreasonably disadvantaged. CJEU 30 April 2014 (Kásler and Káslerné Rábai v OTP Jelzálogbank Zrt), C-36/13, [2014] ECR p. I-0, par. 58–59 makes clear that this interpretation is in accordance with the Directive Interestingly, the BGH emphasises the protection of parties subjected to STCs, notwithstanding conflicting requirements set by default law that implemented Directive 90/314 on package travel. Similarly, BGH 22 November 2012, *NJW* 2013, 995 briefly, in accordance with settled case law, considers the question whether clauses that impose additional fees and charges on consumers are exempt from evaluation in accordance with article 307 par. 3 BGB. CJEU 26 April 2012 (Hatóság v Invitel Távközlési Zrt), C-472/10, [2012] ECR p. I-0, makes clear that is also in conformity with the Directive, although the BGH does not refer to this decision. Yet its later decision, BGH 13 May 2014, *NJW* 2014, 2420, extensively considers contradictory decisions and discussion in literature.

419 See www.eu-consumer-law.org/index_en.cfm. The CLABB-database is no longer available.

420 J. Basedow, 'Der Europäische Gerichtshof und die verweigerte Dialog', in: G. Müller et al (eds.), *Festschrift fur Gunter Hirsch zum 65. Geburtstag*, München: Beck 2008, p. 58

421 See on the interpretation of article 3 Directive by the CJEU further below, par. 4.4.1.1.

made.[422] However, decisions of the BGH[423] indicate that the BGH does not support this view.

It can be doubted whether the apparent restraint of German courts in referring questions to the CJEU is in conformity with the wider duty of conform interpretation, according to which all provisions of national law need to be interpreted in accordance with European law.[424] It can also be doubted whether this restraint is consistent with the CJEU's decision to accept competence over cases which fall beyond the scope of harmonising measures, but which fall under the implemented law that extends the scope of the harmonised regime in the interest of consistency.[425]

Thus, in the application of the Directive, courts have not interacted much with European actors or foreign actors. This may have undermined the harmonised interpretation of the Directive throughout the Union, but it has not undermined the quality of the law on STCs. To the contrary, the restraint of lower courts especially may benefit the predictability of the law for private parties, as parties do not have to rely on decisions from foreign courts that they are not familiar with, and as decisions do not suffer much delay. Also, the restraint of courts ensures that decisions are consistent with national law. Although the restraint of courts may be problematic as it may limit the awareness of consumers of their rights under the Directive, German law already provides consumers with protection. Therefore, the lack of referral to the CJEU is not directly problematic for consumer. Thus, contrary to pluralist arguments, while mutual learning sounds beneficial, forgoing opportunities to do so may also be beneficial.

However, the lack of interaction may eventually affect the revision of Directive 93/13 as problems in national practice do not become visible at the European level, and the CJEU has little opportunity to provide clarity on the interpretation of concepts in the Directive. Similarly, the question of how competences are allocated between the CJEU and national courts, in particular whether minimum harmonisation allows for more discretion for national courts, is also not likely to be considered in the future reform of the Directive. In the long term, the lack of interaction may thus stand in the way of a more predictable development of the private law *acquis*. Therefore, even though opportunities for mutual learning may be detrimental for contract parties in terms of predictability, consistency and accessibility, it is beneficial for the responsive development of the law on STCs through the Directive.

It may be concluded that opportunities for learning have been missed, which may hinder the long-term development of the Directive. However, creating such opportunities might not have been beneficial for private parties and would have come at considerable costs, for relatively simple cases.

422 Comp. H. Heinrichs, 'Das Gesetz zur Änderung des AGB-Gesetzes Umsetzung der EG-Richtlinie über mißbräuchliche Klauseln in Verbraucherverträgen durch den Bundesgesetzgeber', *NJW* 1996, p. 2196.

423 BGH 14 April 2010, *NJW* 2010, 2122 and BGH 15 April 2010, *NJW* 2010, 2942. In these cases, the BGH has upheld clauses falling under the European model list.

424 CJEU 13 November 1990 (Marleasing), C-106/89 [1990] ECR p. I-4135.

425 MunchKomm zum BGB/Basedow (2012) introduction to article 305, nr 34.

4.3.2.4. The discussion on the revision of Directive 93/13

This paragraph will ask whether actors in the attempted reform of Directive 93/13 have sufficiently recognised interdependence and interacted accordingly. How has this affected the accessibility, predictability, consistency or the responsiveness of the law on STCs?

The proposal for a Directive on consumer rights was preceded by a more general consultation on the reform of the consumer *acquis*.[426] This 2007 consultation launched in February 2007 and closed in May 2007, followed previous consultations to cope with problems in the consumer *acquis*, in particular problems of fragmentation. To increase the quality of the consumer *acquis*, the consultation suggested a horizontal approach rather than a vertical approach. The consultation can be criticised for steering and narrowing the debate, as it set out a limited number of options.[427] The consultation further consisted of more detailed questions that presupposed the preference for a horizontal instrument. The proposal for a Directive on consumer rights[428] was published in October 2008.

The proposal was accompanied by an impact assessment report.[429] Although the report recognises, in passing, the relevance of enforcement mechanisms and self-regulation for the level of consumer protection in Member States,[430] it identifies the minimum harmonisation clauses as the main source of fragmentation,[431] which it uncritically considers as the source of problems for the internal market. The impact assessment has assessed more options than originally envisaged in the 2007 consultation.[432] However, the suggestions to use self-regulation in addition to the preferred policy options and the suggestion to raise awareness have not been followed in the Directive.[433] The responses to the consultation[434] are not based on the impact assessment report and do not focus on the various policy options presented in the report, nor are suggestions made with regard to additional measures that the report recognised as useful.

Consequently, the extent to which the impact assessment contributed to evidence-based decision making was limited. It also did not draw attention to the optimal use of techniques in the revision of the Directive. Moreover, the unconvincing assertion that fragmentation can be resolved by abandoning minimum harmonisation completely overlooks the relation between the Directive and national law, as well as the possibility of national legislators and courts to develop the law in accordance with diverging legal views on justice.

426 COM (2006) 744 final.
427 See more generally below par. 10.2.1.2.
428 COM (2008) 614 final.
429 SEC (2008) 2544.
430 SEC (2008) 2544, p. 12, note 11.
431 SEC (2008) 2544, p. 8.
432 COM (2008) 614 final, p. 5–6.
433 SEC (2008) 2544, p. 21.
434 See http://ec.europa.eu/consumers/cons_int/safe_shop/acquis/responses_green_paper_acquis_en.htm.

The 2008 proposal for Directive 2011/83 on consumer rights, which initially also included the revision of Directive 93/13, was not accompanied by a separate German consultation. It has, nevertheless, been discussed both in legal journals[435] as well as newspapers.[436] The lack of a separate consultation also does not mean that the German legislator did not take a position in the debate. In its 2009 decision, the *Bundesrat*[437] indicated various problematic points in the proposal that also came back in its response to the European consultation:[438]

a) The maximum harmonisation approach, which would lead to a *de facto* European consumer contract law would make national law largely obsolete, which would in turn lead to legal uncertainty that would hinder rather than help cross-border trade.
b) The binding model list was not in accordance with dogmatically developed concepts ('*Zivilrechtsdogmatik*') and German practices. The BMJ also pointed to the discussion preceding Directive 93/13
c) The subjection of individual negotiations to judicial control, as this question was also an important point in negotiations preceding Directive 93/13
d) The extension of the scope of the Directive to the main terms of the contract, which seems particularly difficult to reconcile with the national contract law doctrines.[439]

Interestingly, many business associations take a position similar to the Bundesrat.[440] Some business stakeholders support a black list or a grey and black list in the interest of predictability, although it remains unclear how such a list would relate to articles 308 and 309 BGB.[441] Interestingly, the Bundesverband Direcktvertrieb Deutschland[442] also refers to the drafting process of Directive 93/13 in rejecting the extension of judicial control of unfair clauses, while supporting a black list. In contrast, consumer organisations[443] do not advocate a binding black list under a Directive pursuing maximum harmonisation, as this would lower the level of consumer protection in the German legal order and necessitate the adaptation of a successful system. Consumer organisations further point out that national default law serves as a standard for assessing

435 See for example K. Tonner, M. Tamm, 'Der Vorschlag einer Richtlinie über die Rechte der Verbraucher', *JZ* 2009, p. 277.

436 See especially S. Lorenz, 'Der geplante Verbraucherschutz in Europa ist trügerisch', *FAZ* 14 July 2009.

437 BR-Druck. 765/08, p. 3, 6. The legislator, at par. 3, also notes that proposal is not in accordance with better legislation programme.

438 Response of the BMJ to the Green Paper on the review of the consumer *acquis*, COM (2006) 744, p. 4, 16, 17, 18, in accordance with the previously agreed position in the Bundesrat, BR-Drucks. 112/07. Responses to the consultation are available at http://ec.europa.eu/consumers/cons_int/safe_shop/acquis/responses/ms_bundesministerium.pdf.

439 In particular the *Richtigkeitsgewähr*, on which see further below, par. 4.5.1. and par. 7.5.1.1.

440 See the responses of the BDWi, Deutscher Notarverein, and Deutsche ReiseVerband, the HDE, BAG and bvh, and the VDMA, as well as the Wettbewerbszentrale.

441 See the responses of the Bundesverband deutscher Banken, the German Bar Association, the Deutsche Bank, the Deutschen Versicherer, the Markenverband, the ZVEI, the Bundesrechtsanwaltskammer, and the ZGE, p. 4.

442 See the response of the Bundesverband Direcktvertrieb Deutschland, p. 6.

443 See the responses of the Verbraucherzentrale Bundesverbandes, p. 13–14, and the ECC Germany, p. 7.

the fairness of a clause, while they also do not object to extending judicial control, criticising the idea of negotiations and emphasising the weak position of consumers in negotiations.[444] Thus, stakeholders, occasionally also criticising the European consultation procedure,[445] seem to take positions in accordance with the interests of their members, with business stakeholders supporting maximum harmonisation,[446] and with consumer organisations arguing for minimum harmonisation.[447]

However, many of the responses of stakeholders are brief, which limits their value in the debate.[448] Further, it can be doubted whether the debate included all relevant German stakeholders – especially if compared to the debate preceding the AGBG, in which around 150 stakeholders were consulted.[449] Unfortunately, the responses from some international stakeholders that could otherwise have provided valuable input were rather brief and remained general.[450] The responses of stakeholders also seem to have been drafted in cooperation, considering the close resemblance between the wording of the responses from different stakeholders.[451] Including more actors, especially actors such as the *Verbraucherschutzverein*, with its experience in the enforcement of the Directive, would have widened the debate and helped to ensure that the debate did not overlook relevant insights.

444 See the responses of the Verbraucherzentrale Bundesverbandes, p. 15–16, VerbraucherKommission Baden-Württemberg p. 11, pointing out that various Member States have extended judicial control, ADAC p. 4–5.

445 See for example the responses of the Bundesnotarkammer, p. 2, particularly sharply the Deutscher Notarverein, p. 1–2, as well as the Bundesverband Direcktvertrieb Deutschland, p.7, as well as the response from B. Heiderhoff and M. Kenny, p. 1.

446 See for example the responses of the Deutsche Reiseverband, p. 1, the Deutschen Versicherer, p. 5, the HDE, BAG, and bvh, p. 3, the Markenverband, p. 3, the ZVEI, p. 2, the ZGE, p. 4, the Wettbewerbszentrale, p. 3, more cautiously the Bundesverband Direcktvertrieb Deutschland, p. 4, as well as the Deutsche Bank, p. 3, and Vorwerk, p. 3, differently the responses of BDWi, p. 2, as well as the VDMA, p. 3.

447 See the elaborate responses of the Verbraucherzentrale Bundesverbands, p. 5–9, and the Verbraucherskommission Baden-Württemberg, also extensively, p. 3–7, as well as the ECC Germany, p. 5, and the ADAC, p. 1.

448 Some responses are an exception, such as the response of the Bundesverband Direktvertrieb Deutschland that draws attention to the inclusion of subjects that had not been harmonised previously in the 2008 draft, stating that this course was considered unattractive not only by Member States but also by businesses, because Member States with a history of superogatory implementation – like Germany – would likely also extend the scope of provisions in the draft, which would inhibit the freedom of contract for businesses in cross-border contracts. Various responses from national stakeholders may also be interesting, such as the reaction from the Deutscher Notarverein and the Deutschen Versicherer, as well as the VerbraucherKommission Baden-Württemberg that explicitly refers to implementation practices in other Member States.

449 H.-D. Hensen, 'Zur Entstehung des AGB Gesetzes', in: A. Heldrich, P. Schlechtriem, E. Schmidt (eds.), *Recht im Spannungsfeld von Theorie und Praxis, Festschrift für Helmut Heinrichs zum 70. Geburtstag*, München: Beck 1998, p. 76.

450 Especially the views from the ICC, but the views from Visa Europe might also have been interesting.

451 Particularly the responses of the Bundesverband Direktvertrieb Deutschland, the Federation of German Industries, the Association of German Chambers of Industries and Commerce, the National association of German commercial agencies and distribution, and the German Confederation of skilled crafts and small businesses.

The focus of the German legislator logically is a national one, which should not, however, deter it from taking into account the approaches of foreign legislators to implementation, or their views in the debate, or the needs and preferences of international trade. This is unfortunately not the case.

In the discussion, references to comparative law have been few. Occasionally, reference to comparative law have been made in academic responses to the consultation,[452] and in some stakeholders' responses.[453] Similarly, the response of the Ministry refers to comparative analysis on the implementation of eight Directives,[454] but not to the regimes of other Member States, nor to CJEU case law. More attention to comparative law research might provide valuable insight on existing implementation practices and obstacles and possible objections to harmonisation.[455] Comparative research on the implementation of the Directive is available in the EC consumer law compendium.[456]

Both the European and the German legislator have adopted a narrow view on the reform of the Directive. The European legislator sought to limit the fragmented approach in the private law *acquis*. The German legislator wished to ensure that the Directive would be in accordance with national law and national principles. The European legislator has unfortunately narrowed and steered the debate without sufficiently considering the potential options. In contrast, the German approach is directed at the status quo, and does not consider how the Directive has functioned and what improvements are possible.

This preference for the status quo is particularly visible in the rejection of the suggestion that the model list in the Annex to the Directive should become binding. After all, notwithstanding previous negotiations, the developments since the Directive has been established may merit a reconsideration of the indicative character of the EU model list, especially considering the very limited role of the EU model list in the German legal order.

Thus, the shortcomings in the interaction between actors have limited the debate in the reform of the Directive. The attempts to streamline the debate have not resulted in actual reform and it is not clear whether and how the 1993 Directive will be reformed. Actors with relevant insights have not been consulted or have only provided brief responses, which may increase the chance that a reformed Directive will overlook relevant insights, which may undermine the responsiveness of a reformed Directive.

452 Comp. the responses of Heiderhoff and Kenny, while the response of Micklitz and Reich involves European law and CJEU case law.

453 Comp. the response of Vorwerk, which, however, does not refer to the questions of the consultation on the control of unfair clauses.

454 Response of the BMJ, p. 4, 17.

455 N. Jansen, 'Klauselkontrolle im Europäischen Privatrecht. Ein Beitrag zur Revision des Verbraucheracquis', *ZeuP* 2010, p. 69.

456 Available at www.eu-consumer-law.org/index_en.cfm as well as comparative research on implementation, see especially K. Baier, *Europaische Verbrauchervertrage und missbrauchliche Klauseln, die Umsetzung der Richtlinie 93/13/EWG uber missbrauchliche Klauseln in Verbrauchervertragen in Deutschland, Italien, England und Frankreich*, Hamburg: Kovač 2004, and the special issue of the *ERPL* in 1997.

The approach of both European and German state actors is defensive and the multilevel structure has not sparked competition between national and European actors on this point.[457] Debate has in addition not prompted either actor to justify their actions or consider one another's interests. Yet the approach of actors is not one of "strident fundamentalism".[458] Rather, actors bargain to maintain or expand their influence and do not seem inclined to engage with one another if that does not directly serve their interest.

This form of interaction also does not enable regulatory co-opetition between European and national state actors. State actors do not sufficiently compete with one another in improving the law, nor do they sufficiently cooperate.

4.3.2.5. Conclusion on the development of German law on STCs and harmonisation

Interdependence in the development of Directive 93/13 and its reform has become clearly visible. Have German actors, in the implementation of Directive 93/13, adequately taken into account interdependence in ensuring the predictability, accessibility, consistency and responsiveness of the law and have they interacted accordingly?

In the implementation of Directive 93/13, German state actors have adopted restraint, which may have benefited predictability, consistency and responsiveness for private parties. Eventually, however, the restraint in the interaction between German and European actors may leave questions on the interpretation of the *acquis* and the allocation of competences between courts and legislator at the national and European level unresolved, which, in turn, undermines the extent to which the private law *acquis* develops in accordance with the benchmarks of predictability, accessibility, consistency and responsiveness.

The development of Directive 93/13 did not prompt the German legislator to reconsider the AGBG or its choice for *Sonderprivatrecht* and later recodification. However, the active participation of German actors at the European level increases the chance that the *acquis* will develop in accordance with German law, which limits the extent to which the *acquis* will undermine the BGB's ability to contribute to the benchmarks of predictability and consistency. Thus, the development of Directive 93/13 indicates that the development of consumer protection beyond the national level need not necessarily be attributed to pro-consumer groups, but also to states wishing to retain existing legislation and minimising potentially disturbing effects of EU legislation.[459] Comparing the participation of business and consumer stakeholders in the process preceding Directive 2011/83[460] further makes clear that business stakeholder are better represented at the EU level than consumer organisations, which also makes it less likely

[457] Comp. D.C. Esty, D. Geradin, 'Regulatory co-opetition', *Journal of International Economic Law* 2000, p. 245, who describe federalism as "inherently competitive", as visible in the U.S.

[458] In accordance with the two possible developments sketched by N. Walker, 'The idea of constitutional pluralism', *MLR* 2002, p. 358.

[459] As argued by E.A. O'Hara, L.E. Ribstein, *The law market*, Oxford: OUP 2009, p.134.

[460] See above, par. 4.3.2.4.

that a high level of protection can be attributed to consumer organisations at the European level.

Moreover, the incorporation of the law in STCs in the BGB underlines the close relation between the law on STCs and national law. Because of this close relation, the extent to which further harmonisation and regulatory competition may develop and lead to convergence may be limited.

The development of Directive 93/13, its subsequent implementation and attempts to reform the Directive make clear that harmonisation has not prompted the German legislator to consider the interests of foreign and international parties not participating in the German legislative process, either at the national or European level. In accordance with criticism on methodological nationalism, German actors have adopted a German approach to European concepts. Opportunities for learning have developed, and while these opportunities seem to have been explored by European actors, they have not prompted critical reflection of German actors. However, using these opportunities for mutual learning might also have entailed detriments. If the German legislator would have taken into account foreign experiences with implementation, this would have delayed implementation. Additionally, experiences with implementation in other Member States would hardly have prompted the German legislator to look critically at its own efforts. To the contrary, the approach of other legislators, particularly the Dutch legislator,[461] could have prompted the German legislator to adopt more restraint in implementing the Directive, which, in turn, would have been problematic in the light of the later decision *Commission v The Netherlands*.[462] Thus, opportunities for mutual learning need not always be beneficial.

4.3.3. German law on STCs and international trade

The development of treaties and international trade may prompt state actors to interact with foreign actors and non-state actors. The approach of German actors is not uniform: the German legislator has rejected regulatory competition, but has taken into account insights from practice to help ensure the responsiveness of the law. The rejection of regulatory competition is compensated by courts that are more inclined to interact with foreign, European, and international state and non-state actors in cases decided under German law, which has benefited the responsiveness of German law to international practice. The private initiative for regulatory competition has rightly not prompted the German legislator to change this approach.

Paragraph 4.3.3.1 will consider whether internationalisation has induced the German legislator to take into account the views of foreign legislators and non-state actors. Paragraph 4.3.3.2 will ask whether courts have interacted with foreign courts and non-state actors in the interpretation of STCs in international contracts. Paragraph 4.3.3.3 will end with a conclusion.

461 See below, par. 5.3.3.2.

462 CJEU 10 May 2001 (Commission v The Netherlands), C-144/99, [2001] ECR, p. I-3541.

4.3.3.1. Regulatory competition

This paragraph will ask whether the German legislator, in the development of the law on STCs, has taken into account the development of the law by foreign legislators and how this has affected the predictability, consistency, accessibility and responsiveness of the law on STCs.

Paragraph 4.3.3.1.1 will consider the interaction with foreign legislators and paragraph 4.3.3.1.2 will consider the interaction with non-state actors in the drafting of the AGBG. Paragraph 4.3.3.1.3 will consider the interaction with non-state actors who drafted a private initiative to enhance regulatory competition. Paragraph 4.3.3.1.4 will end with a conclusion.

4.3.3.1.1. Regulatory competition: undesirable in the law on STCs

The German legislator originally did not consider regulatory competition as a challenge to improve the law. This does not mean that the German legislator could not take into account insights from comparative law; the draft AGBG was preceded by extensive comparative research.[463] The idea of amending the law contradicts the typical restraint of the legislator in amending private law in the interest of a stable, predictable development of private law.[464] Accordingly, the AGBG effectively provided a stable framework for the development of law.[465]

Until 1986, the AGBG included choice of law clauses in its grey list. Specifically, choice of law clauses were likely to be unfair if the choice of law was not based on a justifiable interest. This provision was amended after Germany ratified the Rome Convention. However, in the draft implementation of the Directive, proposed article 12 did not only, in accordance with article 6 par. 2 Directive, prohibit a choice of the law of non-Member States, but more generally prohibited the choice of law. Reich[466] doubts whether this extension would have been covered by article 8 Directive. Notably, an extension of this article to business contracts would breach the freedom of the choice of law in international business contracts in article 3 Rome I Regulation.

Thus, the choice of law was considered as an escape route from domestic mandatory law that should be blocked. This approach is in accordance with the idea that regulatory competition can lead to a race to the bottom, which can also be deduced from the German response to the 2006 consultation on the review of the consumer *acquis*. Particularly, the *Bundesrat*[467] welcomed the decision to harmonise the law in this area,

463 See especially the Gesellschaft für Rechtsvergleichung, *Richterliche Kontrolle von AGB*, Frankfurt am Main: Metzner 1968.

464 P. Ulmer, 'Zur Anpassung des AGB-Gesetzes über mißbräuchliche Klauseln in Verbraucherverträgen', *EuZW* 1993, p. 339.

465 J. Schmidt-Salzer, 'Transformation der EG-Richtlinie über mißbräuchliche Klauseln in Verbraucherverträgen in deutsches Recht und AGB-Gesetz', *BB* 1995, p. 735.

466 N. Reich, 'The implementation of Directive 93/13/EEC on unfair terms in consumer contracts in Germany', *ERPL* 1997, p. 168.

467 Decision of the Bundesrat of 1 March 1991, BR-Drucks. 611/90, p. 1.

stating that the harmonisation of the law on STCs would benefit German businesses which were at a disadvantage because of the high level of protection of consumers in German law.

Thus, regulatory competition is not associated with improving the law, but regulatory competition or harmonisation that results in the application of German law is not rejected.

4.3.3.1.2. Interaction with non-state actors

If the legislator does not seek to compete with other legislators in the development of the law, it is also possible to draft an attractive regime by taking into account the needs and preferences of transnational legal practice.

The drafting of the AGBG was primarily directed at the codification of case law that would also make the law more accessible and consistent for contract parties. In the drafting of the AGBG, over 150 stakeholders (both business and consumer representatives), have been consulted on the draft AGBG.[468]

The amended draft extends the scope of clauses subject to judicial control while limiting judicial control for clauses converging with default law. The draft also refers to individually negotiated clauses that are not subject to judicial control, while the reference to written contracts was dropped. Also, some clauses under articles 10 and 11 ABGB were nuanced. Article 13, which became article 24 AGBG, stipulated that business contracts were also subject to judicial control, while also referring to business practices.[469]

Thus, the German legislator has sought to draft the law in such a way as to make it a regime that develops consistently and predictably, which has prompted other states to consider the AGBG and German experiences,[470] especially as the German regime on STCs was one of the first regimes to be established. Also, German criticism on the 1990 draft Directive led to important amendments in the Directive, which had, in accordance with the French regime, pursued a more general control over clauses in consumer contracts.

Not all of the amendments can be traced to the consultation of stakeholders; thus, the extension of judicial control to business contracts had also been discussed at the *Deutschen Juristentag*.

Although these discussions have primarily focused on national legal practice, the German judiciary does seem to take into account international legal practice. Brandner[471] already noted that, although BGH case law is not always unequivocal, it seemed to evaluate clauses in business contracts in most branches less strictly than clauses in consumer contracts, depending on the interest protected by the judicial control of clauses.

468 BR-Drucks. 360/75, 30.5.1975.

469 The amended draft was not published. See in more detail H.-D. Hensen, 'Zur Entstehung des AGB-Gesetzes', in: A. Heldrich, P. Schlechtriem, E. Schmidt (eds.), *Recht im Spannungsfeld von Theorie und Praxis, Festschrift fur Helmut Heinrichs zum 70. Geburtstag*, München: Beck 1998, p. 351-352.

470 For example the Dutch legislator, see further chapter 5.

471 H.E. Brandner, 'Die Rechtsprechung der BGH-Senate zum AGB-Gesetz', in: H. Heinrichs, W. Löwe, P. Ulmer (eds.), *Zehn Jahre AGB-Gesetz*, Köln: Kommunikationsforum Recht 1987, p. 50.

4.3.3.1.3. The private initiative for regulatory competition

The careful preparation of the AGBG may also be a reason to continue to exercise restraint in the face of later proposals for reform in accordance with regulatory competition. While the idea of regulatory competition has been criticised because non-state actors need not be homogenous or clearly established,[472] the German private initiative for reform indicates that groups of actors with thorough experience in this system have tried to pressure the legislator to revise the law in accordance with their interests. These non-state actors have advocated regulatory competition,[473] and have proposed reform[474] that explicitly refers to the initiative of 'Law – made in Germany'.[475]

The private initiative was developed by the Industrie- und Handelskammer Frankfurt am Main.[476] This draft has been discussed,[477] and an amended draft has been published by the German Bar Association, which emphasises that it does not seek to represent stakeholders' interests through this draft.[478] The draft is accompanied by examples that should support the arguments for revising the law.[479]

The proposal from the German Bar Association targets the judicial control of STCs in business contracts, in particular, the judicial evaluation of business contracts under article 307 BGB and the indirect effect of articles 308 and 309 BGB. The draft emphasises that STCs that have been negotiated, even if no changes result from negotiation, should not be considered STCs in the sense of article 305 BGB, in contrast to current BGH case law.[480] Moreover, the draft suggests a more lenient evaluation of STCs in business contracts by stipulating that clauses are not unreasonable depending on the content of the contract, the circumstances of the conclusion of the contract, and business practices. Interestingly, the draft from the German Bar Association explicitly states that the law with regard to the inclusion of STCs is not in need of amendment.

The draft stresses that the protective aim of legislators towards businesses is undermined in cases of transnational trade. In transnational cases, a choice of law to the detriment of German businesses is permitted, while foreign businesses may subject clauses to judicial control under articles 305–310 BGB. Thus, as the law in this area fails to adequately cope with international practice, in particular, by imposing national standards on international trade, it might just as well facilitate the preferences of international trade. In turn, if businesses in international trade are subject to no or less intense judicial control, the question arises as to whether a similar standard should not also be applied for domestic contracts.

472 S. Vogenauer, 'Regulatory competition through choice of contract law and choice of forum in Europe: Theory and evidence', *ERPL* 2013, p. 26.

473 Comp. D.C. Esty, D. Geradin, 'Regulatory co-opetition', *Journal of International Economic Law* 2000, p. 247 who state that non-state actors may more generally generate competitive pressure.

474 See www.frankfurt-main.ihk.de/recht/themen/vertragsrecht/agb_recht_initiative/.

475 Critically B. Dauner-Lieb, C. Axer, 'Quo vadis AGB-Kontrolle im unternehmerischen Geschäftsverkehr?' *ZIP* 2010, p. 309, who note that advertising with German law while simultaneously arguing it is in need of reform, is not convincing.

476 See www.frankfurt-main.ihk.de/recht/themen/vertragsrecht/agb_recht_initiative/.

477 See for an overview www.frankfurt-main.ihk.de/recht/themen/vertragsrecht/agb_recht_initiative/.

478 Available at http://anwaltverein.de/downloads/Stellungnahmen-11/DAV-SN-23-2012.pdf.

479 See www.frankfurt-main.ihk.de/imperia/md/content/pdf/recht/AGB_b2b_Fallbeispiele_aus_der_Praxis.pdf.

480 BGH 19 May 2005, *NJW* 2005, 2543.

Moreover, revision of the law in the light of regulatory competition is in line with the objectives of the EU to establish an internal market, if the revision facilitates the use of STCs in cross-border contracts. If the revision leads to the convergence of national laws in this area, it, if going far enough, would take away the need for harmonisation.

Should the limited ability to maintain protective standards prompt the German legislator to take more note of the preferences of international trade and national stakeholders?

So far,[481] there has been no official reaction from the German legislator towards the proposals. Constitutional constraints may arise, as article 33 par. 4 GG stands in the way of a blanket approval of the proposal by the German legislator without substantive, critical democratic debate in Parliament. The current proposal should not lead to reform because of the following shortcomings:

1) The draft from stakeholders is contradictory.

The list of examples accompanying the proposal[482] claims that German users of STCs may not opt out of German law entirely, and as a result, their clauses are subjected to the strict German judicial evaluation under article 307 BGB. In contrast, the draft claims that currently, German businesses tend to opt out of German law, especially opting for Swiss law and English law.[483] The list of examples goes on to claim that in cases where a German business is subjected to a clause that would be considered unfair in German law, it will not be able to pass on this clause to a German subcontractor, opting instead for a foreign subcontractor to whom this potentially objectionable clause will be passed on.

2) The examples accompanying the proposal do not sufficiently take into account that the BGH is more lenient in its evaluation of clauses in international cases.

This becomes particularly clear from example 12 that argues that a clause requiring a surety to be available upon request will generally be held ineffective. Even though the BGH[484] has held these clauses ineffective in domestic cases, international cases may be judged differently. The OLG Stuttgart[485] upheld a clause described in this example, denying that parties – big businesses – in this case were hardly in need of protection. The OLG upheld the decision from the LG Stuttgart,[486] which distinguished between previous cases on sureties that concerned domestic cases and international cases.

481 May 2015.

482 Available at www.frankfurt-main.ihk.de/imperia/md/content/pdf/recht/AGB_b2b_Fallbeispiele_aus_der_Praxis.pdf, examples 2, 5 and 8.

483 S. Vogenauer, 'Regulatory competition through choice of contract Law and choice of forum in Europe: Theory and Evidence', *ERPL* 2013, p. 36, with further references, also points out that while it is difficult to assess how often this happens, there are concerns that large firms opt for Swiss law, in combination with an arbitration clause, to circumvent strict evaluation of their STCs under German law.

484 BGH 18 April 2002, *NJW* 2002, 2388.

485 OLG Stuttgart 1 December 2010, *BeckRS* 2011, 2432.

486 LG Stuttgart 3 May 2010, *BeckRS* 2010, 19376.

3) Both the original proposal and the amended proposal do not make sufficiently clear how small businesses would be protected under articles 305–310 BGB, and how these cases would be delineated from cases where small businesses have agreed to STCs while not hindered by a weaker bargaining position.

Possibly, however, the approach defended in Dutch law could be taken as a starting point: where a business is in a bargaining position similar to a consumer's bargaining position, and it concerns a contract not different from normal consumer contracts, businesses may invoke the indirect effect of articles 308 and 309 BGB. Notably, however, Dutch law on this point has hardly developed. Regardless, the draft does not consider this possibility.

4) The draft overlooks the normative view underpinning articles 305–310 BGB, instead emphasising law as a product.

The argument that the legislator should not even attempt to pursue a normative system because it is not able to do so independently, is not particularly appealing. Even if the aim of the German legislator is undermined, this does not make the question of how the legislator should cope with this development in a manner that preserves the normative values underlying the law irrelevant, especially as the law might increasingly develop inconsistently and less in accordance with society's views on justice.

5) The attractiveness of German law might also be inhibited by other factors.

Berger[487] argues that case law on the interpretation of international and foreign clauses is limited, and has developed through cases on consumer contracts and relatively simple contracts. Consequently, it is not a law developed for (international) businesses contracts.

6) Contrary to the idea of regulatory competition, the draft has paid limited attention to developments from other legislators.

The draft from the German Bar Association[488] explicitly refers to the proposal for a Regulation on a draft CESL, and notes that if the draft takes the negotiation (*'verhandlen'*) of STCs as a starting point, this will distinguish it from the proposal that takes the joint negotiations (*'aushandeln'*) as a starting point. Although the draft recognises that especially English and Swiss law are a favourite choice of contract parties, it does not look at English or Swiss law to establish what is so attractive about these laws. The draft does not ask how the reform may make German law a competitive law within the Union that will be elected by both foreign and German parties. Rather, the draft aims to make German law less unattractive for German parties.

As comparative contract law is readily available, the inaccessibility of relevant materials should not be an obstacle to more attention to comparative law. Moreover, the draft, until now, has especially been circulated between German parties. Since the proposal has been drafted in the context of regulatory competition, it would not be illogical to contact foreign parties, especially

487 K.P. Berger, 'Für eine Reform des AGB-Rechts im Unternehmerverkehr', *NJW* 2010, p. 466.

488 See the draft at www.frankfurt-main.ihk.de/imperia/md/content/pdf/recht/AGB_b2b_Fallbeispiele_aus_der_Praxis.pdf, p. 16.

parties in Member States that are important trade partners of Germany, to establish whether they find German law exceptionally unattractive, and if so, why.

7) The draft does not sufficiently consider other options that may facilitate cross-border trade.

The draft does not address the extent to which prominently used STCs in international contracts are evaluated, and does not consider the possibility to encourage, for example, the development of guidelines for the interpretation of clauses in international contracts. Also, the draft leaves open the possibility that parties may circumvent the evaluation of clauses by opting for ADR or foreign law,[489] or, as Kaufhold[490] points out, the possibility that parties, by reconsidering and documenting their negotiations, prevent that clauses are considered STCs in the sense of article 305 BGB. The use of collective negotiations, which may be a reason for the judiciary to evaluate STCs less strictly, is also not considered.

4.3.3.1.4. Conclusion on regulatory competition

The German legislator has rejected the idea of regulatory competition in this area of mandatory law where weaker parties are protected. The German legislator has not expressly recognised interdependence in this area, but at the European level it has actively advocated for a high level of consumer protection, which may prevent that harmonisation or regulatory competition in this area undermines the high level of consumer protection in German law. Eventually, however, the German legislator does not have a decisive say in the reform of Directive 93/13, and it is possible that reform may oblige the German legislator to lower the level of consumer protection. If this is the case, German actors will have to consider alternative ways to preserve the responsive development of private law.

More generally, the legislator has recognised the added value of comparative insights, in the drafting of the AGBG.[491] At first sight, also, the German legislator has recognised the potential of regulatory competition in the more general initiative for 'Law – made in Germany'.[492] The restraint of the German legislator in amending the law benefits predictability, and the attention for national stakeholders benefits the responsiveness of the law to business practices and preferences. The restraint of the German legislator has, moreover, not stopped foreign legislators and the European legislator from turning to German law as a source of inspiration.

The private initiative for regulatory competition demonstrates that the preference of businesses should not override the development of the law in accordance with legal views on justice. The initiative particularly highlights concerns of "regulatory capture" that may arise if too much interdependence develops between state and non-state actors. This

489 F. Kästle, 'M & A – Verträge unterliegen nicht der AGB-Kontrolle', *NZG* 2014, p. 295.
490 S. Kaufhold, 'AGB-Anschein trotz Verhandlungsbestätigung – Ist der Individualvertrag im Unternehmerverkehr noch zu retten?', *NJW* 2014, p. 3491–3492.
491 See above par. 4.3.1.2.
492 See www.lawmadeingermany.de/.

is however not the case for the present initiative, if only because the legislator has not showed much inclination to amend the law. Geradin and Esty[493] find the participation of various, representative stakeholders in decision-making processes will generate competition between stakeholder groups. Accordingly, medium-sized businesses have argued to preserve the law on STCs.[494] The initiative has been made public, and any approval of the legislator would necessitate further debate in parliament and between more stakeholders, also in the light of article 33 par. 4 GG that stipulates that the execution of legislative competences should be left to public services.[495]

The private initiative raises questions on the ability of the legislator to ensure that the law develops in accordance with legal views on justice. The decreasing independence of the legislator and courts to do so is in accordance with the analysis of multilevel governance that points to the changing role of national state actors. The initiative makes clear that private actors attempt to develop rules themselves rather than simply complying with law, and they have the resources to do so.[496] The initiative further makes clear that if they contract with foreign parties, non-state actors may be able to circumvent national mandatory law and create their own transnational legal space, particularly if they opt for ADR. Yet contrary to theories about regulatory competition, businesses have pressured for law reform rather than not opting for German law. As Vogenauer[497] points out, German businesses have a competitive advantage (‘*Standortvorteil*’) over their contract parties if they opt for German law, which explains why they would rather convince the legislator to amend the law to their advantage than opting for foreign law. Yet this interest need not withhold German actors from circumventing German law.

Interestingly, business actors focus on the law and not alternatives to law reform, for example facilitating ADR. Thus, a state-centered perspective remains visible, despite a potentially prominent role for non-state actors. Accordingly, competition between state and non-state actors in providing rules for the behaviour of contract parties does not seem to have developed. The presence of the European legislator and the increased ability of actors to circumvent German law has also not prompted the German legislator to consider the initiative for regulatory competition favourably. Likewise, the debate on the reform of the law on STCs remains nationally oriented – so far, foreign or international actors have not indicated their views on German law. The amendment is not aimed at taking into account the interest of foreign or international actors – quite the reverse, the proposal can be seen in the light of the interests of a limited group of German businesses. Interestingly, these actors have not made use of comparative law insights, and opportunities for mutual learning have not been realised.

493 D.C. Esty, D. Geradin, ‘Regulatory co-opetition’, *Journal of International Economic Law* 2000, p. 255.

494 See www.markenverband.de/presse/pm/pmverbaendeinitiativeagb_recht/pm_agb_recht_anlage.

495 See J. Krüper, ′Lawfirm – legibus solutus?′, *JZ* 2010, p. 655.

496 R. Michaels, ‘Umdenken für die UNIDROIT-Prinzipien. Vom Rechtswahlstatut zum Allgemeinen Teil des Transnationalen Vertragsrechts’, *RabelsZ* 2009, p. 868.

497 S. Vogenauer, ‘Regulatory competition through choice of contract law and choice of forum in Europe: Theory and evidence’, *ERPL* 2013, p. 53.

4.3.3.2. The interpretation of international contracts

As international trade develops, German courts are faced with more international cases.[498] The approach of the German courts differs depending on the question whether a case is decided under German, European or international law. The approach to international and European state and non-state actors in cases decided under German law may increase responsiveness. In contrast, the restraint of courts in cases decided under international or European law may inhibit responsiveness, as well as the consistent and predictable interpretation of clauses under treaties and European law, especially for foreign parties who are accustomed to courts taking international and European sources into account.

Paragraph 4.3.3.2.1 will consider the decisions of courts on the criteria whether clauses have been individually negotiated. Paragraph 4.3.3.2.2 will consider the valid inclusion of STCs. Paragraph 4.3.3.2.3 will turn to the adequate availability of STCs and paragraph 4.3.3.2.4 will address the interpretation of clauses. Paragraph 4.3.3.2.5 will end with a conclusion.

The paragraph distinguishes between these questions as different sources of law may be applicable per question. The paragraph will not only look at international cases, but compare decisions in international cases to decisions in domestic cases, to determine whether courts adopt a different approach to domestic decisions, which may also be relevant for the consistent development of the law on STCs.

4.3.3.2.1. Negotiating STCs

Article 305 BGB requires that STCs have been presented ('*gestellt*'), and not negotiated ('*ausgehandelt*').[499] Notably, in some international cases, the question whether a clause has been presented or not in the sense of article 305 BGB is not addressed as European law or international law may precede article 305 BGB, and the question whether clauses have been negotiated is not similarly emphasised under European or international regimes.[500] Interestingly, the ICC[501] has held that clauses that parties have negotiated on, but that have not been altered can be considered as negotiated in the sense of article 305 BGB. The ICC extensively refers to BGH case law and goes on to follow criticism of the requirement of *aushandeln*, and the distinction between STCs and individually negotiated clauses as this distinction overlooks the possibility that parties will often not be interested in negotiating on STCs, which later will provide them with an opportunity to challenge those terms.[502]

498 The evaluation of STCs article 307 BGB is not considered in this paragraph, but below in par. 4.4.3.

499 Similarly, article 449 HGB refers to *aushandeln*, which has been interpreted in conformity with article 305 BGB, see BGH 1 December 2005, *BeckRS* 2006, 3324.

500 Comp. for example, relatively recently OLG Brandenburg 26 June 2012, *BeckRS* 2012, 15696, with further references.

501 ICC 29 January 2001, *SchiedsVZ* 2005, 108.

502 Graf von Westphalen/Vertragsrecht und AGB-Klauselwerke/Schöne (30. Ergänzungslieferung 2012), Stromlieferungsverträge, nr 48.

The ICC decision will likely not be followed by German courts that consider the unequal bargaining power between parties when one party has set his STCs to be either accepted or rejected by his counterparty. The BVerfG[503] has emphasised the need to prevent *Fremdbestimmung*[504] in the use of STCs, including model contracts. Accordingly, the OLG München[505] rejected the individual negotiation of clauses in international cases, referring to BGH decisions in domestic cases.[506]

The BGH may, however, be more lenient for clauses in international business contracts.[507] In rare cases, the BGH[508] has referred to foreign courts. The BGH may also evaluate clauses more leniently when STCs have been drafted by a relatively neutral institute in which interests from all relevant contract parties have been represented.[509]

The line in domestic cases is considerably stricter, as the BGH[510] has distinguished between *aushandeln* (jointly negotiating) and *verhandeln* (considered). *Verhandeln* does not meet the requirements for individual negotiations in article 305 BGB, which accordingly also speaks of *aushandeln*. This requires that the user of STCs has to seriously make the content of his STCs subject to negotiation, enabling his potential contract party to defend his own interests. This means that the contract party must have been able to influence the content of the STCs, which in turn presupposes that the contract party has adequately understood the STCs. This may require that he is educated on the content of STCs.

Thus, German courts take a stricter approach in deciding whether STCs have been negotiated – and therefore do not fall within article 305 BGB – in domestic cases that are developed in line with the law on B2C contracts. In international cases, German courts

503 BVerfG 7 September 2010, *NJW* 2011, 1339.

504 *Fremdbestimmung* is the opposite of private autonomy and it arises if one is bound by rules one has not been able to influence. See further on this concept par. 7.1.

505 OLG München 7 March 1986, *BeckRS* 2010, 25740.

506 BGH 3 July 1985, *NJW-RR* 1986, 54.

507 BGH 15 February 2007, *NJW* 2007, 2036 held that a clause appointing the shipowner as transporter was individually negotiated as the clause was printed in bold on the front of the bill of lading. Wolf/Lindacher/Pfeiffer/AGB-recht/Hau (2009), AGB im internationalen Geschäftsverkehr, nr 4 argue that the BGH may accept that clauses have been drafted taking into account various interests, which may lead to less intense judicial evaluation. Comp. also BGH 17 February 2010, *NJW* 2010, 1131, a domestic case between two private parties, where the BGH held that the question whether STCs had been presented depended on the question which party had introduced the STCs – drafted by third parties – in the negotiations and required the use of these STCs. The BGH pointed out that the assumption that STCs had been presented by the seller was not applicable beyond B2C contracts. BGH 14 May 1992, *NJW* 1992, 2160 also points to contracts in which the interests of parties have been adequately balanced.

508 BGH 15 February 2007, *NJW* 2007, 2036.

509 Wolf/Lindacher/Pfeiffer/AGB-Recht/Hau (2009), AGB im internationalen Geschäftsverkehr, nr 57, see for example BGH 26 June 1997, *NJW-RR* 1997, 1253, although this seems not to have been considered in BGH 28 June 2001, *NJW-RR* 2002, 536.

510 BGH 20 March 2014, *NJW* 2014,1725, BGH 22 November 2012, *NJW* 2013, 856, BGH 19 May 2005, *NJW* 2005, 2543, confirming previous decisions in domestic cases in BGH 18 April 2002, *NJW* 2002, 2388, and BGH 3 November 1999, *NJW* 2000, 1110. See critically of this standard S. Kaufhold, 'AGB-Anschein trotz Verhandlungsbestätigung – Ist der Individualvertrag im Unternehmerverkehr noch zu retten?', *NJW* 2014, p. 3488, who rightly points out that the BGH seems to adopt a more lenient approach in BGH 17 February 2010, *NJW* 2010, 1131.

are more likely to take into account the role of neutral organisations and in rare cases, decisions from foreign courts.

4.3.3.2.2. The valid inclusion of STCs

The question of whether STCs have been included in international contracts may be answered under different regimes that do not always leave room for the additional applicability of article 305 BGB. Moreover, in addition to article 305 BGB, other provisions may also be applicable, especially article 312g BGB, implementing Directive 2000/31 on e-commerce, and article 246 EGBGB.[511] This paragraph will turn to international cases decided under respectively the CMR, CISG, Regulation Brussels I, or the Lugano Convention,[512] and German law, and contrast these decisions with domestic cases.

In cases under the CMR, German courts have expected foreign contract parties to be familiar with the use of prominently used terms in transport contracts ('*Allgemeine Deutsche Spediteurbedingungen*', 'ADSp'). As the CMR does not aim to establish a comprehensive regime for transport contracts, insights from German law or other applicable law may also be relevant.[513] The BGH[514] has taken into account foreign laws and foreign decisions. In previous cases, the ADSp have similarly been held applicable on the basis of silent agreement,[515] while courts expressly held that this was not contrary to articles 31 and 41 CMR. These decisions were in accordance with BGH case law in domestic cases.

In cases falling under the CISG, the BGH[516] has not referred to foreign materials, instead addressing diverging opinions in German literature. German lower courts[517] have followed the BGH and only rarely refer to foreign courts.[518]

For the valid inclusion of jurisdiction clauses, article 23 Brussels I or article 17 Lugano Convention plays a central role. The BGH[519] has accordingly referred to CJEU case law, and interpreted the requirements of article 17 Convention strictly. However, it accepted

511 Article 22 Directive 2006/123 also contains information duties and may be relevant too, but it has not been implemented in the BGB; see further BT-Drucks. 16/10493. Notably, however, article 312g BGB is limited to contracts for the delivery of goods or services, although the Directive is not limited to these contracts, while the limitation to merchants in the sense of article 14 BGB may also diverge from service providers in the Directive, see MunchKomm zum BGB/Wendehorst (2012) article 312g, nr 9–10.

512 Regulation Brussels I replaces the European Execution Treaty and is almost identical to the Lugano Convention between Member States of the European Free Trade Organisation.

513 Ferrari/Kieninger/Mankowski u.a., Internationales Vertragsrecht/Ferrari (2011), article 1 CMR, nr 3.

514 BGH 26 March 2009, *NJW-RR* 2010, 247.

515 OLG Schleswig, 25 May 1987, *NJW-RR* 1988, 283 and LG Gießen 31 July 2008, BeckRS 2009, 395.

516 BGH 31 October 2001, *NJW* 2002, 370. See subsequently BGH 9 January 2002, *NJW* 2002, 1651, followed by OLG Koblenz 1 March 2010, 2 U 816/09, www.globalsaleslaw.com/content/api/cisg/urteile/2126.pdf. See for an overview Kröll/Mistelis/Viscasillas, UN-Convention on the International Sales of Goods (CISG)/Ferrari (2011), article 19, nr 14–17.

517 OLG Frankfurt am Main 26 June 2006, 26 Sch 28/05, www.cisg-online.ch/cisg/urteile/1385.pdf, OLG Jena 10 November 2011, *BeckRS* 2011, 3846, and OLG Celle 24 July 2009, *NJW-RR* 2010, 136.

518 OLG Düsseldorf 23 March 2011, *BeckRS* 2011, 17832 similarly followed BGH case law but referred primarily to article 8 CISG as well as a decision from the Hoge Raad, published in a German journal.

519 BGH 9 March 1994, *NJW* 1994, 2699, confirmed in BGH 25 February 2004, *NJW-RR* 2004, 1292.

an agreement on relative competence ('*Zuständigkeitsvereinbarung*') holding that the Regulation did not provide rules for the valid establishment of such an agreement, which had to be determined in accordance with applicable (English) law. Nevertheless, it held that the requirements in article 23 Brussels I had been met. The LG München[520] similarly referred to the Convention and CJEU case law, but also to German case law and literature.

In international cases decided under German law, the BGH[521] has taken business practices and foreign – Dutch – law into account. Notably, the knowledge and experience of international contract parties is often estimated to be higher than in domestic cases.[522] The decision of the OLG Karlsruhe[523] indicates that these BGH decisions may not always have been followed.

In contrast, in domestic cases, the BGH[524] has adopted a much stricter approach. The inclusion of STCs in the contract under article 305 BGB, while not requiring explicit confirmation, does require agreement on the inclusion of STCs, either silently or explicitly. Even though handing over the text of STCs is not required as such, the user of STCs needs to refer unequivocally to the STCs he wishes to use in such a way that contract parties cannot doubt their application while also being able to read them. This is similarly true if it concerns often-used clauses. In cases of battle of forms, businesses asserting the application of their standard terms cannot assume that their contract party agrees with this application, in particular if the other party's terms contain a clause rejecting the applicability of other parties' terms and conditions.[525] However, if parties have done business with each other for a considerable time, the inclusion of STCs can be made silently.[526] In these cases, only converging clauses will be applicable.[527]

In international cases decided under German and European law, the BGH has frequently taken into account foreign judgments, CJEU case law and international business practices, while it adopts a stricter approach in domestic cases. German courts have taken into account sources that allow them to develop the law responsively, in accordance with transnational and foreign practices. Thus, interests of foreign and international actors that have not as such been considered in the legislative process are still recognised, regardless of the question whether competences are shared between the European or national level.

520 LG München 29 May 1995, *NJW* 1996, 401.

521 BGH 4 March 2004, *BeckRS* 2004, 3238, previously also BGH 18 June 1971, *NJW* 1971, 2126 and BGH 6 December 1990, *NJW-RR* 1991, 570.

522 K.P. Berger, 'Die Einbeziehung von AGB in internationale Kaufverträge', in: K.P. Berger, N. Horn (eds.), *Zivil- und Wirtschaftsrecht im europäischen und globalen Kontext, Festschrift für Norbert Horn zum 70. Geburtstag*, Berlin: De Gruyter 2006, p. 4.

523 OLG Karlsruhe, 19 October 1992, *NJW RR* 199, 567.

524 BGH 3 December 1987, *NJW* 1988, 1210, followed in BGH 12 February 1992, *NJW* 1992, 1232, confirming earlier decisions in domestic cases, BGH 20 March 1985, *NJW* 1985, 1838, as well as BGH 7 June 1978, *NJW* 1978, 2243 with further references, confirmed in BGH 15 January 2014, NJW 2014, 1296.

525 BGH 20 March 1985, *NJW* 1985, 1838, as well as BGH 24 October 2000, *NJW-RR* 2001, 484.

526 Rejecting this option BGH 5 May 1982, *NJW* 1982, 1751 referring to previous case law.

527 BGH 28 June 1990, *NJW-RR* 1991, 357.

4.3.3.2.3. Adequately making STCs available

The question whether STCs have been made sufficiently available may be decided under various regimes. This paragraph will consider decisions under Brussels I or the Lugano Convention, as well as the CISG and German law, and compare these decisions with decisions in domestic cases.

Under article 17 Lugano Convention, the BGH[528] has interpreted the requirements for the availability of STCs strictly, in accordance with CJEU case law.[529] However, the BGH is also bound to take into account mandatory national law. In this case, the declaration in the form that the clauses had been read and understood constituted an unfair clause under article 11 par. 15 AGBG (as well as the Annex to Directive 93/13 under q) as it altered the burden of proof. However, this was not relevant for the question as to whether a choice of jurisdiction had been validly established.

In this case, the question arises as to whether additional national law that is in accordance with a non-binding part of a Directive may be taken into account in answering the question of whether a clause has been validly established under the Regulation. While the BGH extensively refers to CJEU case law and its own previous decisions, it does not refer to foreign decisions that support its conclusions on this point. Other decisions similarly raise questions with regard to simultaneously applicable sources of private law. The OLG Köln[530] upheld a clause for arbitration under article 23 Regulation 44/2001, noting that colliding clauses similarly opted for arbitration, referring to the rules on colliding clauses in the CISG that was applicable in this case, and leaving the question as to which clause had been validly included in the contract. The LG Aachen[531] followed previous BGH decisions and the decision of the OLG Köln, and held that a choice for jurisdiction had not been validly established.

However, questions on the simultaneous application of European measures and international measures should preferably be resolved by the CJEU, which is well-placed to do this because of its competence and because of its ability to prevent national courts coming to diverging decisions throughout the Union. More generally, it is desirable that the CJEU develops a clear line on the relation between European measures on private international law and the material private law *acquis*.

Under the CISG, the BGH[532] has expressly pointed to diverging practices and clauses that may be usual within branches, which may make it more difficult for the offeree to gain access to these clauses. In turn, this may entail that an offeror should send the text of the STCs used by him to the offeree, or make the text otherwise available, which is in accordance with the duties of cooperation of potential contract parties and which may

528 BGH 28 March 1996, *NJW* 1996, 1819, also BGH 22 February 2001, *NJW* 2001, 1731.

529 CJEU 14 December 1976 (Colzani/Rüwa), Case 24-76, [1976] ECR, p. 1831 (referred to the CJEU by the BGH).

530 OLG Köln 24 May 2006, 16 W 25/06, www.cisg-online.ch/cisg/urteile/1232.pdf.

531 LG Aachen 22 June 2010, *BeckRS* 2010, 15502.

532 BGH 31 October 2001, *NJW* 2002, 370. Accordingly, OLG Koblenz 1 March 2010, 2 U 816/09, www.globalsaleslaw.com/content/api/cisg/urteile/2126.pdf.

also prevent undue delay in transactions. Schmidt-Kessel[533] has criticised this decision. He finds that the BGH has consciously set stricter standards for making available the text of STCs than is the case under German law, that in relation to businesses merely requires the possibility to inform oneself of the STCs. He also disapproves of the attempt of the BGH to develop the law in accordance with consumer protection law, even though the BGH did not, as such, refer to Directive 93/13. Yet the BGH did find that in the interest of the responsiveness of the law to practice, as well as preventing detriments to contract parties not acting in a professional capacity, it was necessary to ensure that similar principles underline the law with regard to the inclusion of STCs. In this view, similar principles should underline the CISG as well as articles 305–310 BGB. The CISG is not part of the *acquis* and has not been developed to improve consumer protection – article 2 CISG expressly excludes contracts with consumers from its scope, and it is hardly self-evident that the CISG should be interpreted in accordance with national consumer protection law.

Moreover, developing the law implementing Directive 93/13 in accordance with the CISG should be left to the CJEU, as it concerns overlaps between the *acquis* and a treaty. Additionally, as Schmidt-Kessel[534] points out, the BGH interpretation has not taken into account diverging foreign case law and it is difficult to reconcile with the use of well-established international model contracts and clauses.

The desirability of paying more attention to foreign case law and international materials may become clearer from a previous decision of the LG Düsseldorf,[535] where a Danish buyer had acquired a generator from a German seller that had included a choice for German law in its STCs. Without asking whether the case fell within the scope of the Directive – which had not been implemented yet but entered into force on 1 January 1995 – the LG held that the clause did not exclude the application of the CISG, although article 2 CISG clearly excludes the sale of goods for personal use from the CISG. Referring this case to the CJEU could have provided insight on the delineation of the CISG and the Directive.

The BGH has been lenient on the valid inclusion of clauses in international contracts under German law. Under German law, requirements to make STCs available are less strict for business contracts than for consumer contracts, and article 310 par. 1 BGB makes clear that the requirements in article 305 par. 2 and 3 BGB are not applicable to business contracts.

The BGH has referred to parties′ intentions and business practices in determining whether clauses have validly been included. In 1971, the BGH[536] already held that referral to STCs sufficed as it made clear that the users of STCs wished to include them in the

533 M. Schmidt-Kessel, 'Einbeziehung von Allgemeinen Geschäftsbedingungen unter UN-Kaufrecht', *NJW* 2002, p. 3445.

534 M. Schmidt-Kessel, 'Einbeziehung von Allgemeinen Geschäftsbedingungen unter UN-Kaufrecht', *NJW* 2002, p. 3445–3446.

535 LG Düsseldorf 11 October 1995, 2 O 506/94, at www.unilex.info/case.cfm?id=234. The OLG Düsseldorf 25 February 2004, I-15 U 88/03, at www.cisg-online.ch/cisg/urteile/915.pdf expressly followed the 2001 decision of the BGH, extensively citing its previous decision of 15 February 2001, 6 U 86/00, upheld by the BGH.

536 BGH 18 June 1971, *NJW* 1971, 2126.

contract. The question of whether it was usual to send the text of STCs to business partners was considered irrelevant, as the contract involved a service that the German bank's STCs were clearly designed to cover. In a later case the BGH[537] decided that STCs that had been drafted in such small print as to be practically illegible were not validly included in the contract, even though similar clauses were often used in that particular branch, on which the BGH expressly elaborated. This was because the user of STCs could not reasonably expect that by taking notice of hardly legible clauses his contract party had agreed upon these terms.

Similarly, the LG Gießen[538] upheld the inclusion of the Dutch FENEX-clauses by referral to these clauses in an email, as well as the referral to ADR in accordance with BGH case law in domestic cases. However, the court did not refer to the applicable Directive 2000/31 on e-commerce.

Article 10 par. 3 Directive e-commerce sets standards for making STCs sufficiently available. However, article 312g BGB implementing these requirements was not considered. Should the court have applied the Directive of its own motion? This seems contrary to the needs of practice and may also lead to surprises for contract parties that have relied on the applicability of STCs. Also, in accordance with article 10 par. 1 Directive, article 312g par. 5 BGB stipulates that businesses contracting with one another may agree otherwise. It is, however, unclear whether parties can agree otherwise implicitly by accepting mere referral to a website, or whether they have to expressly agree that referral to well-established STCs is sufficient. The latter seems undesirable, as this could entail the establishment of a Directive meant to further online trade inhibiting trade and posing requirements contrary to the needs of trade.

In contrast, in domestic cases the BGH[539] has adopted a stricter approach. Mere referral to STCs does not suffice, as inclusion requires explicit or implicit agreement.

It may be concluded that the BGH frequently takes into account relevant decisions from the CJEU. Courts deciding cases under German law also seek to take into account the needs of international practice by taking a lenient approach to the requirements of making STCs sufficiently available. In contrast, the BGH has adopted a stricter approach for determining this under international regimes, which may lead to inconsistencies with the decisions of foreign courts and could be difficult to reconcile with the use of international model STCs. Additionally, its restraint in referring questions on the overlap between European measures to the CJEU may undermine consistency throughout the Union, despite existing CJEU case law. In turn, this may diminish predictability, as the expectations of private parties relying on CJEU case law may be undermined.

Thus, the existence of the Directive and the reallocation of competences from the national to the European level has not prompted German courts to justify their decisions or interact more with foreign or international actors, especially when courts decide cases under the CISG, even though courts are clearly aware of opportunities to do so, and of

537 BGH 30 May 1983, *NJW* 1983, 2772. Similarly, OLG Hamm 20 November 1987, *NJW-RR* 1988, 944, in a domestic case, held that STCs should be legible.

538 LG Gießen 31 July 2008, *BeckRS* 2009, 395.

539 BGH 12 February 1992, *NJW* 1992, 1232, previously also BGH 3 July 1981, *BeckRS* 1981, 31065460.

the advantages of such an approach. Thus, the coexistence of actors need not necessarily lead to more responsiveness.

The conclusion that the BGH has evaluated the inclusion of clauses more strictly under the CISG than under German law is convincing and the question arises whether this approach can be traced to regulatory competition. If so, regulatory competition can pose a decided disadvantage for international regimes.

4.3.3.2.4. The interpretation of clauses in international contracts

Typically, the interpretation of international contracts takes place in accordance with the applicable regime. Thus, the question of applicable law precedes the interpretation of STCs. However, if a clause has a well-established meaning in international legal practice – which will especially be the case for clauses often-used in international practice – the courts may take that international meaning as a starting point.[540] In the interpretation of clauses in international contracts, courts may accordingly refer to international sources.

Already in 1967 the BGH[541] had held that the insurance conditions agreed upon by parties had a distinct meaning in international trade and should be interpreted accordingly. The BGH went on to consider that the meaning of these clauses in international law differed from German law and referred to English law. Similarly, a 1984 decision of the BGH[542] referred to the usual meaning of cash on delivery clauses, referring to its own previous case law in domestic cases as well as international materials. In a 1986 decision, the BGH[543] likewise held that the interpretation of an English clause required that the court evaluated the meaning of the clause for contract parties taking into account practices established in international trade. Also, in a 1991 case, the BGH[544] held that generally, an indemnity clause was to be interpreted in accordance with English law, even though the circumstances did not indicate that English law was applicable.

Recently, the BGH[545] held that the interpretation of a term drafted by the ICC should be interpreted in accordance with the directions from the ICC, in accordance with article 8 CISG. This was because the term had a well-established meaning that parties were likely to be familiar with when entering into the contracts. The BGH referred both to foreign and European decisions on this point.

The BGH has also taken into account parties' intentions. Accordingly, the BGH[546] has held that the use of the clause referring to *deadfreight* did not stand in the way of the applicability of article 588 HGB as parties had obviously intended this, although *deadfreight* usually had a different meaning than *Fautfracht* in articles 580 et seq HGB.

540 J. Maidl, *Ausländische AGB im deutschen Recht*, München: Beck 2000, p. 150.
541 BGH 13 November 1967, *BeckRS* 1967, 3037507.
542 BGH 19 September 1984, *NJW* 1985, 550, comp. also BGH 2 July 1984, *NJW* 1985, 550.
543 BGH 16 October 1986, *NJW* 1987, 591.
544 BGH 2 December 1991, *NJW-RR* 1992, 423.
545 BGH 7 November 2012, *BeckRS* 2012, 24430, comp. also BGH 22 April 2009, *NJW* 2009, 2606.
546 BGH 4 December 1989, *NJW* 1990, 2257.

Lower courts have followed the BGH's referral to international and foreign materials.[547] Earlier, the OLG München[548] had already explicitly referred to Incoterms in its interpretation of the terms agreed upon between parties. The OLG Hamm[549] upheld a clause stipulating that all additional agreements to the contract should be written under articles 29 par. 2 CISG. The OLG Hamm[550] also held that the place of delivery should be determined in accordance with applicable European law as well as the directions from the ICC the clauses of which were applied to the contract.

Interestingly, the approach towards the interpretation of English clauses differs from the interpretation of these clauses in international contracts by the English judiciary that adopts a more neutral approach to the interpretation of clauses in foreign languages.[551] Dutch judges have also adopted a different approach, and interpret clauses in accordance with Dutch concepts.[552] Triebel and Balthasar[553] have pointed out that this course towards the interpretation of clauses in foreign languages is difficult to reconcile with articles 133 and 157 BGB. Parties unfamiliar with English law will generally not intend to refer to a concept as it has been developed in English law, while the use of English in the drafting of the contract does not necessarily amount to a choice of English law.

The BGH[554] has distinguished between international and domestic contracts in the interpretation of clauses, and rejected referral to international guidelines to determine whether an exclusion clause in a domestic contract was acceptable, while distinguishing the duties of banks in international and domestic contracts. In the interpretation of domestic contracts, the courts have taken the objective interpretation of STCs as a starting point. Thus, STCs are interpreted in accordance with the intentions of rational and reasonable contract parties, taking into account the interests typically involved in transactions where the STCs are applied.[555] Individual circumstances are not taken as a starting point.[556]

German courts have frequently interacted with foreign courts and the CJEU in the interpretation of clauses in international contracts, which increases the chance that these clauses will be interpreted consistently in different states, which may also benefit

547 See however Amtsgericht Duisburg 13 April 2000, 49 C 502/00, www.unilex.info/case.cfm?id=715 that is more in line with national law. In an international case decided under the CISG, the court held that two deliveries did not constitute established business practices between parties within the meaning of article 9 CISG, which is reminiscent of BGH 12 February 1992, *NJW* 1992, 1232, a domestic decision.

548 OLG München 19 December 1957, *NJW* 1958, 426.

549 OLG Hamm 31 November 2010, I-19 U 147/09, www.globalsaleslaw.org/content/api/cisg/urteile/2291.pdf.

550 OLG Hamm 9 September 2011, *BeckRS* 2012, 1173.

551 V. Triebel, S. Balthasar, 'Auslegung englischer Vertragstexte unter deutschem Vertragsstatut – Fallstricke des Art. 32 I Nr. 1 EGBGB', *NJW* 2004, p. 2193.

552 Rb. Haarlem 11 May 1993, *NJ* 1993, 71.

553 V. Triebel, S. Balthasar, 'Auslegung englischer Vertragstexte unter deutschem Vertragsstatut – Fallstricke des Art. 32 I Nr. 1 EGBGB', *NJW* 2004, p. 2193-2194.

554 BGH 26 September 1989, *NJW* 1990, 225. Comp. however BGH 6 July 1995, *NJW* 1995, 2991 where the BGH extensively referred to case law and held that applying an exclusion clause to the employee of the user of the STCs was customary – and therefore not unduly surprising – also in international regimes.

555 BGH 19 January 2005, *NJW* 2005, 1183.

556 BGH 10 July 1990, *NJW* 1990, 2383.

accessibility and predictability. Moreover, the approach of German courts also takes into account well-established clauses drafted by non-state actors as well as the intention of parties. This increases the chance that German decisions are in accordance with the needs and preferences of international practice. It may be concluded that courts have used opportunities to learn about the needs and preferences of international and foreign parties in a way that the German legislator has not done. Thus, despite the lack of participation of international and foreign parties in the drafting of the AGBG and the implementation of Directive 93/13, their needs and preferences may be taken into account.

It is not clear whether German courts have considered the potential for regulatory competition in their approach. If this is the case, it can be considered as a clear benefit of regulatory competition.

4.3.3.2.5. Conclusion on the interpretation of international contracts

The approach of German courts to international cases differs depending on the question whether it concerns a case under German law or international law. Courts are more inclined to refer to foreign materials and international business practices in cases falling under German law. The interaction between courts and foreign and international actors contributes to the responsiveness of German law to international practice. The active approach of the courts may compensate for the restraint of the German legislator with regard to regulatory competition. The approach of the courts is in accordance with the idea of regulatory co-opetition: regulatory competition does not only depend on the willingness of national legislators, but also on the approach of the courts. However, as case law is less visible in international trade than legislation, the extent to which courts may compensate for the legislator's restraint remains limited. The interest of national non-state actors may also support or weaken initiatives pursuing regulatory competition. However, competition remains focussed on legislation and non-state actors have not sought to facilitate ADR or choices of law or alternative means which would allow them to include possibly unfair clauses in their contracts. Therefore, the state-centered view of the law on STCs, to some extent at least, seems to be shared by non-state actors.

Since the courts clearly recognise the added value of international and foreign materials in cases decided under German law, it is surprising that the courts have simultaneously adopted restraint in referring to foreign and international materials in cases falling under international regimes. In these cases, there are more, rather than fewer, reasons for referring to these materials. Particularly, the lack of referral to foreign and international materials may diminish the consistent and predictable interpretation of treaties. Especially if treaties indicate that they should be interpreted uniformly, the lack of referral to international materials and foreign decisions may be contrary to especially foreign parties' expectations. German courts have also adopted restraint with referring to the CJEU, which may be problematic if treaties and European measures overlap. Inconsistency and inaccessibility may remain as the relation between the different measures remains undecided by the CJEU. The inclination of German courts to refer to German materials may in addition inhibit accessibility for foreign parties as these parties may not have access to German materials.

Simultaneously, German courts have adopted a more lenient approach in international cases than in domestic cases, which may be in accordance with the needs and preferences of parties in international trade. Yet this development also increases the chance that the law on international B2B contracts is developed differently from domestic B2B and B2C contracts, which may increase the chance of inconsistencies despite the implementation of the Directive within the BGB.

4.3.3.3. Conclusion on the development of German law and international trade

Have German actors interacted adequately with international actors, European actors and non-state actors in the development of the law on STCs in an international context? How has this affected the predictability, accessibility, consistency and responsiveness of the law on STCs?

The German legislator has shown restraint in interacting with international actors, particularly with regard to regulatory competition, German courts have considered initiatives and preferences from international actors in cases decided under German law. More generally, the private initiative demonstrates that regulatory competition need not motivate actors to select the best part of foreign or international laws and develop an optimal set of rules. Similarly, regulatory competition has not motivated German non-state actors to consider input from foreign or international actors, nor has it been a reason to invite or enable these actors to participate in German debate so far.

Simultaneously, courts have not sufficiently considered foreign, EU and international materials in deciding cases under international regimes. The consistent lack of interaction between German courts and the CJEU, especially with regard to cases on the overlap between European measures, German law and international law, may leave room for inconsistency and unpredictability. The division of competences between the European level and the national level has not prompted German actors to justify that they decide on these cases, nor have they considered foreign cases. Thus, the division of competences has not furthered the responsiveness of international regimes.

Notwithstanding the explicit choice against regulatory competition, German actors could have encouraged international and foreign actors to participate more in debate, which could have enhanced responsiveness to international practices.

4.3.4. Conclusion on the development of the law on STCs through the BGB

Have German actors adequately taken into account interdependence in the development of the law on STCs, and interacted accordingly? How has this affected the predictability, consistency, accessibility and responsiveness of the law developed through the BGB?

In accordance with insights from multilevel governance, interdependence has developed. However, the use of codification, and previously the choice to develop *Sonderprivatrecht*, was not based on foreign experiences or European initiatives and has not been reconsidered as the *acquis* developed. The German legislator has not recognised interdependence in ensuring predictability, accessibility, consistency and responsiveness through the BGB. Yet this lack of recognition seems not to have detrimentally affected the quality of German law.

Possibly, this can be traced to the carefully drafted, successful AGBG and the subsequent active approach of German actors towards European initiatives. Notwithstanding the national approach towards harmonised law, German actors have actively interacted with European actors in the development of the *acquis*, which limits the extent to which the *acquis* disturbs the BGB. Further, German law has likely been developed responsively to international regimes insofar as German courts have taken into account foreign and international materials and practices.

However, some detriments may become visible over the long term. National actors have not strategically recognised interdependence in the development of the BGB, and this may undermine the predictability of the future implementation of European measures. Furthermore, the lack of interaction in the implementation and application in the *acquis* may eventually undermine the responsiveness of the law.

Generally, the coexistence of European and national actors has not resulted in benefits defended by pluralists.

Firstly, general arguments that the coexistence of actors may be beneficial seem to be recognised by German and European actors. The European legislator may for example well have benefited from German experiences. Yet although comparative law research was available, German law was not developed based on these comparative insights. In addition, the 'minimum implementation' approach of German actors, and the narrow approach of European actors make it less likely that European law will continue to benefit from experiences at the national level.

Secondly, the division of competences has not resulted in "checks and balances". National actors have not motivated European actors to improve the law. German law in this area developed successfully when competences had not yet been reallocated to the European level. European actors have not stimulated the improvement of German law. Rather than considering the quality of national law, the European legislator seems to screen for divergences, which in turn justify harmonisation. European actors do not seem interested in exploring reasons for fragmentation, reasons to maintain national diversity or national experiences. Yet the need and the incentive for further harmonisation is not apparent for national actors. Similarly, the division of competences has not prompted the German legislator to take into account the interests of foreign or international actors, who generally do not participate in the German democratic process.

Thirdly, the high quality of German law cannot be traced to regulatory competition.

In accordance with pluralist insights, however, there are opportunities for mutual learning. Mutual learning may take place if European actors can take into account national experiences with Directive 93/13. Likewise, the participation of foreign and European actors in national processes could be valuable. Moreover, in accordance with pluralist insights, the close relationship between the law on STCs and general contract law reflecting German legal views on justice supports the view that coexistence of national actors developing national regimes on STCs is beneficial as it contributes to responsiveness. This may in addition contribute to the rejection of regulatory competition, and it may be a reason against full harmonisation.

4.4. Blanket clauses

Overlapping blanket clauses coexist, notably article 3 Directive, implemented by article 307 BGB, which nevertheless diverges slightly from article 3 par. 1 Directive,[557] as well as article 242 BGB. Have actors taken into account the fact that other actors also develop private law and that the extent to which actors may ensure the predictable, consistent, accessible and responsive development of the law through blanket clauses may accordingly be diminished? Have actors interacted with other actors accordingly and how has this affected the predictability, consistency, accessibility and the responsiveness of private law in this area? Has the coexistence of national and European actors benefited the law on STCs, in accordance with pluralist arguments?

Paragraph 4.4.1 will ask whether German and European courts have recognised the competence of courts at the European and national level to interpret article 307 BGB and interacted accordingly. Paragraph 4.4.2 will turn to model lists and paragraph 4.4.3 will consider the evaluation of clauses in international contracts. Paragraph 4.4.4 will end with a conclusion.

4.4.1. *Competence to interpret blanket clauses*

It is not clear how the competence to interpret article 3 Directive 93/13 is divided between the CJEU and national courts. Paragraph 4.4.1.1 will consider CJEU case law on this question and paragraph 4.4.1.2 will contrast these decisions with BGH case law. Paragraph 4.4.1.3 will end with a conclusion.

4.4.1.1. The CJEU on the competence to interpret article 3 Directive 93/13

The CJEU is competent to interpret European law under article 267 TFEU. National courts do not have to refer to the CJEU if it concerns an *acte éclairé*, if the interpretation of a blanket clause is so obvious that it does not have to be referred to the CJEU.[558] However, this concerns the uniform interpretation of European law. Is article 3 Directive also meant to be interpreted uniformly? In *Freiburger Kommunalbauten*,[559] the CJEU ruled that:

> 'the Court may interpret general criteria used by the Community legislature in order to define the concept of unfair terms. However, it should not rule on the application of these general criteria to a particular term, which must be considered in the light of the particular circumstances of the case in question'

The CJEU expressly refers to the conclusion of A.G. Geelhoed,[560] who finds that although the CJEU is competent to interpret article 3 Directive, the CJEU is not competent to interpret

557 MunchKomm zum BGB/Wurmnest (2012) article 307 nr 24.

558 CJEU 6 October 1982 (CILFIT v Ministry of Health), Case 283/81, [1982] ECR, p. 3415.

559 CJEU 1 April 2004 (Freiburger Kommunalbauten v Hofstetter), C- 237/02, [2004], ECR, p. I-3403.

560 Opinion of A.G. Geelhoed of 25 September 2003) before case C-237/02, (ECR [2004] 3403, pars. 25 et seq.

contractual terms and assess the circumstances relevant for deciding whether a clause is, in fact, unfair. He goes on to defend that article 3 is not intended to be interpreted uniformly. Although the CJEU does not refer to that particular part of his conclusions, this conclusion does not seem irreconcilable with the wording of article 1 Directive that states that it is the aim of the Directive to approximate – not unify – the law of Member States on this point.

However, later case law may draw this conclusion into doubt. In *Océano*,[561] the CJEU did not restrain from deciding that a jurisdiction clause in a consumer contract was unfair. A.G. Trstenjak, in her conclusion before *Pénzügyi Lízing*,[562] explicitly refers to the conclusion of A.G. Geelhoed in this matter, finding that subsequent case law supported A.G. Geelhoed's view that the judicial evaluation of clauses in consumer contacts should be decentralised. She specifically points to the relevance of national law and individual circumstances to determine the fairness of a clause, and she concludes that:

> 'the guidelines on assessment given in those judgments cannot in any way be regarded as definitive. They are just some of the 'general criteria' within the meaning of the case-law which the Court can provide to the national court under its monopoly on the interpretation of Community law. The specification of what constitutes unfairness under Article 3(1) of the Directive at the level of Community law must ultimately be construed as an ongoing process the end point of which it is for the Court to determine. It must be the task of the Court gradually to give specific expression to the abstract criteria for reviewing whether a term may be classified as unfair and, with increasing experience, to establish a profile for reviewing the unfairness of terms at the level of Community law.'

The wording of the decision in *Freiburger Kommunalbauten* leaves open the possibility that the CJEU ruled that it is competent to provide abstract criteria to interpret article 3, while it was left to national judges to determine whether a clause was, *in fact*, unfair. In other words: a *factual* decision.[563]

This view is supported by the wording in more recent case law, where the CJEU[564] has held that '[i]t is thus clear that the Court of Justice must limit itself, in its response, to providing the referring court with the indications which the latter must take into account in order to assess whether the term at issue is unfair'. Accordingly, the CJEU refers to the Annex to the Directive, and the reasons for and methods of including a term that is

561 CJEU 27 June 2000 (Océano Grupo v Quintero), joined cases C-240/98 to C-244/98, [2000] ECR, p. I-4941.

562 Conclusion of A.G. Trstenjak of 6 July 2010 before case C-137/08 (VB Pénzügyi Lízing/ Schneider), [2010] ECR p. I-0, pars. 96–97, 99.

563 Also in this sense H.-W. Micklitz, N. Reich, 'The Court and the Sleeping Beauty: The revival of the unfair contract terms Directive', *CMLR* 2014, p. 780, J. Hijma, *Algemene voorwaarden*, Deventer: Kluwer 2010, p. 25–26. Comp. L. Miller, *The emergence of EU contract law: Exploring Europeanization*, Oxford: OUP 2011, p. 158 who considers the distinction between interpretation and application 'perilously thin'.

564 CJEU 26 April 2012 (Hatóság/Invitel), C-472/10, ECR [2012], p. I-0, par. 22, similarly CJEU 9 November 2010, (VB Pénzügyi Lízing/ Schneider), C-137/08, [2010] ECR p. I-0, par. 44, CJEU 26 April 2012 (Hatóság v Invitel Távközlési Zrt), C-472/10, [2012] ECR p. I-0, par. 22, CJEU 10 September 2014 (Kušionová v SMART Capital, a.s.), C-34/13, [2014] ECR p. I-0, par. 71.

potentially unfair, as well as the clarity of that term. In *Aziz v Catalunyacaixa*[565] and *Constructora Principado SA v Menéndez Álvarez*,[566] the CJEU repeated that it establishes general criteria that national courts must or may consider in the factual assessment of clauses. The CJEU pointed to the relevance of national law that would have been applicable in the absence of the agreement, to compare the position of the consumer under the clause with the position of the consumer under national law. If the position of the consumer is decidedly less advantageous, this is an indication that the clause is to the detriment of the consumer. Whether this is unfairly so may be another question, answered in line with the criteria of article 4 Directive 93/13. The CJEU also considered the nature of the goods or services of the contract.[567]

In other cases, the CJEU has also provided further guidelines relevant for the assessment of the fairness of clauses. Accordingly, in *Pereničová and Perenič v SOS financ spol. s r.o.*,[568] the CJEU held that the unfairness of a commercial practice could be a relevant circumstance for the interpretation of unfairness under article 4 Directive. In *Morcillo and García v Banco Bilbao Vizcaya Argentaria SA*,[569] the Court referred to the Charter. In *Pohotovosť s.r.o. v Korčkovská*,[570] *Hatóság v Invitel Távközlési Zrt*,[571] *Sebestyén*,[572] and *Matei v SC Volksbank România SA*,[573] the CJEU pointed to the Annex to the Directive and the consequences of clauses under the applicable law. Further, in *Van Hove v CNP Assurances SA*[574] the Court referred to the question whether a term would be understood by 'an average consumer, who is reasonably well informed and reasonably observant and circumspect', and emphasised the importance of transparency in the Directive, also in the assessment of the fairness of terms. In *Kásler and Káslerné Rábai v OTP Jelzálogbank Zrt*[575] and *Matei v SC Volksbank România SA*,[576] the Court considered the promotional material and information provided to the consumer in that respect. In *Pannon v Győrfi*,[577] the CJEU decided that it is for the national court to assess

565 CJEU 14 March 2013 (Aziz v Caixa d'Estalvis de Catalunya, Tarragona i Manresa (Catalunyacaixa)), C-415/11, [2013] ECR, p. I-0.

566 CJEU 26 January 2014 (Constructora Principado SA v Menéndez Álvarez), C-226/12, [2014] ECR p. I-0, par. 21.

567 As confirmed in CJEU 15 January 2015 (Šiba v Devėnas), C-537/13, [2015] ECR p. I-0, par. 33–34. The Court also held that the national court should take into account the services for which the consumer had contracted in considering whether terms are plain and intelligible in the sense of article 5 Directive.

568 CJEU 15 March 2012 (Pereničová and Perenič v SOS financ spol. s r.o.), C-453/10, [2012] ECR, p. I-0, par. 43.

569 CJEU 17 July 2014 (Morcillo and García v Banco Bilbao Vizcaya Argentaria SA), C-169/14, [2014] ECR p. I-0.

570 CJEU 16 November 2010 (Pohotovosť s.r.o. v Korčkovská), C-76/10, [2010] ECR, p. I-0, par. 58, 60.

571 CJEU 26 April 2012 (Hatóság v Invitel Távközlési Zrt), C-472/10, [2012] ECR p. I-0, par. 26.

572 CJEU 4 April 2014 (Sebestyén v Zsolt Csaba Kővári and Others), C-342/12, [2014] ECR p. I-0, par. 66.

573 CJEU 26 February 2015 (Matei v SC Volksbank România SA), C-143/13, [2015] ECR p. I-0, par. 59–60.

574 CJEU 23 April 2015 (Van Hove v CNP Assurances SA), C-par. 47, 27. CJEU 15 February 2015 (Šiba v Devėnas), C-537/13, [2015] ECR p. I-0, par. 33 can also be read in this light.

575 CJEU 30 April 2014 (Kásler and Káslerné Rábai v OTP Jelzálogbank Zrt), C-26/13, [2014] ECR p. I-0, par. 74.

576 CJEU 26 February 2015, (Matei v SC Volksbank România SA), C-143/13, [2015] ECR p. I-0, par. 75.

577 CJEU 4 June 2009, (Pannon v Győrfi), C-243/08, ECR [2009], p. I-4713, par. 44.

the fairness of a clause in fact, taking into account that a term conferring exclusive jurisdiction to the court in the place of residence of the seller (a clause that was found to be unfair in *Océano*[578]) 'may be considered to be unfair', and in *Sebestyén*,[579] the Court provided general guidelines to determine the possible unfairness of arbitration clauses in consumer contracts. In addition, general principles may also play a role in the interpretation of blanket clauses by the CJEU.[580]

The European view on the allocation between the CJEU and the national courts in the interpretation of article 307 BGB leaves room for unclarity. Although initially the CJEU seemed to leave considerable room to national courts, later CJEU case law may indicate a more active role for the CJEU in the interpretation of article 3 Directive. Thus, the question whether the CJEU is competent to provide guidelines for the interpretation of provisions implementing article 3 Directive 93/13 and how that affects the competence of national courts has not been clearly decided by the CJEU. This question is therefore not an *acte éclairé*.[581] The question of whether the CJEU is competent to interpret or provide guidelines on article 3 Directive has not as such been asked before; the question in *Freiburger Kommunalbauten* was whether a specific clause was unfair in the meaning of the Directive. As the Directive indicates that this requires an individual rather than an abstract evaluation of the fairness of a clause, the factual evaluation remains with national courts. National courts accordingly have to refer questions on the allocation of competence in the interpretation of blanket clauses.

This does not mean that the CJEU will necessarily declare itself competent. National courts may well have decided cases in which they interpreted and applied article 307 BGB correctly. The problem is that this question has not yet been decided by the CJEU.

Quite another question is whether it is desirable for the CJEU to have competence to provide guidelines for the interpretation of article 307 BGB. Guidelines have already been well established at the national level, and CJEU guidelines may be different, which could undermine the consistency of the law. Moreover, the CJEU does not provide consistent guidelines for the development of the *acquis*; the allocation of competences and the guidelines may differ depending on the Directive.

4.4.1.2. The BGH and the interpretation of article 307 BGB

Initially, the BGH[582] seemed to followed the view that in accordance with the minimum harmonisation character of the Directive article 307 BGB goes beyond the standard of article 3 par. 1 Directive. Consequently national courts are competent and referral is not

578 CJEU 7 June 2000 (Océano v Quintero), joined cases C-240/98 to C-244/98, [2000] ECR, p. I-4941.

579 CJEU 4 April 2014 (Sebestyén v Zsolt Csaba Kővári and Others), C-342/12, [2014] ECR p. I-0.

580 See previously already MunchKomm zum BGB/Basedow (2012) article 307 nr 26. Comp. CJEU 17 July 2014 (Morcillo and María del Carmen Abril García v Banco Bilbao Vizcaya Argentaria SA), C-169/14, [2014] ECR p. I-0, par. 49 where the Court referred to the principle of audi alteram partem in evaluating whether national procedural law was in accordance with the Directive.

581 CJEU 26 March 1963 (Da Costa v Netherlands Inland Revenue Administration), Joined cases 28 to 30–62, [1963] ECR, p. 31.

582 BGH 7 July 1998, *BeckRS* 1998, 30018428.

necessary.[583] The BGH ruled that it would not refer to the CJEU the question whether clauses are fair or unfair within the meaning of articles 9–11 AGBG, as this is a matter for the German judiciary that the CJEU is not competent to determine. In contrast, the BGH later referred questions on the interpretation of article 307 BGB to the CJEU in *Freiburger Kommunalbauten*,[584] concerning a clause in a building contract that provided the respondents with a surety, in accordance with article 7 of the Regulation on real estate agents and builders (*'Makler- und Bauträgerverordnung'*). The BGH considered that it was doubtful whether the clause was unfair, as it was compensated by another clause to the benefit of the consumers. However, as the clause could be considered unfair in different legal orders, it was referred to the CJEU. This decision is in accordance with the view that although article 307 BGB provides more protection to the consumer than article 3 Directive, referral need not be made when clauses are found to be unfair. In contrast, in cases where a clause is upheld, the case should be referred to the CJEU, as the minimum standard should be complied with, which may become relevant in these cases.[585]

The BGH[586] subsequently cited *Freiburger Kommunalbauten*[587] to confirm its own competence to interpret article 307 BGB and evaluate the fairness of clauses under article 307 BGB in cases falling within the scope of the Directive. Accordingly, since *Freiburger Kommunalbauten*, the BGH has interpreted article 307 BGB and evaluated clauses under this provision without referring questions to the CJEU, taking into account CJEU case law, Directive 93/13, or foreign case law.[588] However, the CJEU has not

583 Comp. H. Heinrichs, 'Das Gesetz zur Änderung des AGB-Gesetzes Umsetzung der EG-Richtlinie über mißbräuchliche Klauseln in Verbraucherverträgen durch den Bundesgesetzgeber', *NJW* 1996, p. 2196, more refined MunchKomm zum BGB/Basedow (2012) introduction to articles 305–310 BGB, nr 34, considering the autonomous interpretation of article 3 Directive and the definitions that determine the scope of the Directive, and more recently, comp. T. Kuhn, 'Überschießende Umsetzung bei mindest- or vollharmonisierenden Richtlinien: Einheitliche oder gespaltene Anwendung?', *EuR* 2015, p. 226.

584 BGH 2 May 2002, *NZM* 2002, 764. The annotation of G. Basty to the decision under *DnotZ* 1999, 482 further explains the practical relevance of these clauses.

585 P. Ulmer, 'Der AGB-Gesetz nach der Umsetzung der EG-Richtlinie über mißbräuchliche Klauseln in Verbraucherverträgen', in: P. Ulmer, U. Hübner, *Das Recht der Allgemeinen Geschaftsbedingungen nach der Umsetzung der EG-Richtlinie uber misbrauchliche Klauseln in Verbrauchervertragen, Karlsruher Forum 1997*, Karlsruhe: Versicherungswirtschaft 1998, p.38.

586 BGH 14 July 2004, *BeckRS* 2004, 07903, par. II, 3, see similarly, with an overview of case law, F. Graf von Westphalen, 'AGB-Recht im Jahre 2004', *NJW* 2005, p. 1987.

587 CJEU 1 April 2004 (Freiburger Kommunalbauten v Hofstetter), C- 237/02, [2004], ECR, p. I-3403.

588 See for example recently BGH 29 April 2015, *BeckRS* 2015, 9079, on the understanding of the average consumer of clauses, or BGH 5 February 2015, *BeckRS* 2015, 6518 on the possibility to weigh the economic consequences of clauses when clauses are challenged by consumer organisations. See earlier BGH 22 May 2012, BeckRS 2012, 15087, referring however, to Directive 2007/65 on payment services and its predecessor, BGH 8 May 2012, BeckRS 2012, 14567 and BGH 8 May 2012, *NJW* 2012, 2337 (two similar decisions, also referring to the *contra preferentem* interpretation of terms and the interpretation to the detriment of the consumer that is the starting point for the evaluation of the clause under article 307–309 BGB), BGH 17 April 2012, *BeckRS* 2012, 11675, BGH 20 March 2012, *BeckRS* 2012, 10736, BGH 14 March 2012, *BeckRS* 2012, 8786, BGH 9 December 2010, *NJW* 2011, 1347, as well as BGH 5 December 2006, *NJW* 2007, 997, on the question whether a clause that need in itself not be unfair is unfair in combination with other clauses, or earlier, BGH 13 February 2001, *NJW* 2001, 1419, in which the BGH emphasised the main duties of contract parties and the inadmissibility of charging an extra fee for those duties.

provided a conclusive answer and it therefore does not concern an *acte éclairé*. The controversy of this question in German debate[589] also indicates that it is hardly a settled question that can easily be deduced from existing CJEU case law. Lower courts largely follow BGH case law, although some lower courts have referred to the Directive in the interpretation of article 307 BGB.[590]

However, in a 2011 decision the BGH[591] did consider the competence of the CJEU to interpret the Directive, specifically article 1 par. 2 Directive, implemented in article 307 par. 3 BGB. The BGH asked the CJEU whether a term for the unilateral amendment of prices in contracts for the supply of gas should be evaluated under the Directive, as the terms reflected legislative provisions applicable to similar contracts for the supply of gas. The CJEU[592] held that if the legislature has chosen to exempt particular contracts from legislation that would otherwise prevent the evaluation of clauses in accordance with article 307 par. 3 BGB, parties cannot circumvent evaluation under article 307 BGB by reflecting the provisions of law that are not applicable. To determine the fairness of the term, the question of whether consumers could foresee changes when they entered into the contract and realistically terminate the contract, was important.

Interestingly, the change of the approach of the BGH in this matter was preceded by a prejudicial question from the OLG Oldenburg.[593] The terms reserving the right for the suppliers of gas to unilaterally amend their prices were increasingly challenged by consumers.[594] The CJEU decision renders previous BGH decisions on this point uncertain.[595]

589 MünchKomm zum BGB/Basedow (2012) article 307 nr 25, with further references.

590 OLG München 9 October 2003, *NJW-RR* 2004, 212 (the decision has not become binding) noted that in the evaluation of clauses, the court should take into account surrounding clauses, as stipulated in article 4 Directive. OLG Stuttgart 3 December 2009, *BeckRS* 2009, 88415 upheld a clause that stipulated a tariff that was owed to the bank when the credit contract (*Bausparvertrag*) was concluded constituted a clause on the price that fell under the main terms of the contract, referring to the preamble of the Directive. However, the clause endured judicial evaluation under article 307 BGB, and followed BGH case law. OLG Frankfurt 15 April 2010, *BeckRS* 2010, 14553 held that a clause that limited the validity of tickets did not cause a significant imbalance in parties' rights and obligations in the sense of article 3 Directive, as implemented by article 307 BGB, and upheld the clause accordingly.

591 BGH 9 February 2011, *NJW* 2011, 1392.

592 CJEU 31 March 2013 (RWE Vertrieb AG v Verbraucherzentrale Nordrhein-Westfalen), C-92/11, [2013] ECR, p. I-0. In CJEU 30 April 2014 (Barclays Bank SA v García and Barrera), C-280/13, [2014] ECR p. I-0, par. 41, the Court declined to assess the compatibility of national legislation with Directive 93/13 and general principles underlying the Directive as it did not concern an unfair term between a business and a consumer.

593 OLG Oldenburg 14 December 2010, *BeckRS* 2011, 8627.

594 Comp. BGH 2 December 2014, *BeckRS* 2014, 23529 criticising the decision to refer questions to the CJEU as it concerns a contract between businesses that therefore does not fall within the scope of the Directive.

595 L. Zabel, 'Die Anforderungen an Preisanpassungsklauseln in Gas- und Fernwärmelieferverträgen', *KommJur* 2011, p. 269, as well as K. Uffmann, 'Informationspflichten und ergänzende Auslegung bei Preisanpassung in Energielieferverträgen', *NJW* 2015, p. 1216, who finds that the previous approach of the BGH with regard to amendment clauses for contracts for the supply of gas and energy is not convincing.

This does not mean that German decisions are not in accordance with the Directive,[596] but it does mean that the interpretation of article 307 BGB is currently oriented at national law,[597] which may differ from the standard established in article 3 Directive in several respects:

1) In extreme cases, constitutional law may theoretically become relevant in the assessment of the fairness of terms.[598] It can be doubted, despite the existence of the Charter, whether this will similarly be the case for the assessment of terms under the Directive, which has been considered in the light of consumer protection rather than private autonomy or freedom of profession.[599]
2) The BGH evaluates clauses in a more objective manner than indicated in the Directive and in CJEU case law.[600]
3) The BGH[601] may show less restraint in evaluating the main terms or the prices in contracts than the CJEU.[602]

The interdependence between European and national courts in correctly interpreting and applying the *acquis* has been considered as a reason to refine the notion of supremacy of European law.[603] Further, the unclarity regarding the division of competences between the CJEU and national courts does not, in fact, mean that the CJEU will conclude, if a

596 Comp. OLG Bamberg 19 October 2011, *BeckRS* 2011, 28303 that held a clause that was contrary to the duties following from Directive 2007/64 as ineffective under article 307 BGB, holding that previous case law of the BGH was outdated. OLG München 17 January 2008, *NJW-RR* 2008, 1233 held that a clause that limited the validity of a gift coupon to a year was ineffective under article 307 BGB, referring to national law and case law of the BGH and lower courts. OLG Bamberg 26 June 2012, *NJW* 2012, 2282 holding a clause that sought to affect consumers' choice for a lawyer ineffective, recognising the need for competition and the constitutional free choice of a lawyer, is very likely also in accordance with the Directive. OLG Koblenz 13 June 2012, *BeckRS* 2012, 12430, holding that a clause that excluded the consumer's right to assignment would be ineffective under article 307 BGB is in accordance with the Annex to the Directive that includes clauses that inappropriately limit consumers' rights towards the supplier who has breached the contract under sub b. OLG Stuttgart 24 May 2012, *BeckRS* 2012, 11663 rejecting a clause that enabled an English insurer to limit the value of the claim of the policy holder that had terminated the contract is likely also in accordance with the Directive, as the clause may fall under either sub d or sub e of the Annex. Despite the abundance of case law on this topic, very few cases that may be problematic under the Directive become apparent.

597 In accordance with L. Miller, *The emergence of EU contract law: Exploring Europeanization*, Oxford: OUP 2011, p. 169. The standard used in the evaluation of STCs under article 307 BGB can be traced to BGH 11 June 1979, *NJW* 1979, 1886.

598 Comp. BverfG 25 October 2004, *NJW* 2005, 1036, BverfG 23 November 2006, *NJW* 2007, 286.

599 CJEU 27 February 2014 (Pohotovosť s. r. o. v Miroslav Vašuta), C-470/12, [2014] ECR p. I-0, par. 52, CJEU 10 September 2014 (Kušionová v SMART Capital), C-34/13, [2014] ECR p. I-0, par. 47.

600 K. Baier, *Europaische Verbrauchervertrage und missbrauchliche Klauseln, die Umsetzung der Richtlinie 93/13/EWG uber missbrauchliche Klauseln in Verbrauchervertragen in Deutschland, Italien, England und Frankreich*, Hamburg: Kovač 2004, p. 86–87.

601 Comp. BGH 25 March 2015, *BeckRS* 2015, 8621, where the BGH expressly considered the "market price" of gas supply. This case however concerned a business contract.

602 CJEU 30 April 2014 (Kásler and Hajnalka Káslerné Rábai v OTP Jelzálogbank Zrt), C-26/13, par. 49, 55.

603 L. Miller, *The emergence of EU contract law: Exploring Europeanization*, Oxford: OUP 2011, p. 158.

question is referred, that it is competent to interpret article 3 Directive. The minimum harmonisation character of the Directive may be a reason for the CJEU to allow for discretion at the national level.

Additionally, it is not desirable that courts would have to start referring all their cases to the CJEU. The need to refer frequently to the CJEU would undermine the protection offered by national courts, and increase the amount of time necessary to decide a case, as referral to the CJEU may considerably extend the length of the procedure. This will not benefit consumer protection.[604] Moreover, article 307 BGB is closely connected with good faith, a fundamental principle in the German legal order.[605] Reallocating competence to interpret central principles to the European level could drastically affect the consistent and coherent development of German private law. In these cases, the question arises whether a reformed article 3 Directive 93/13 could become a legal irritant, in the sense that it disturbs surrounding law and necessitates adaptation of wider law to maintain consistency.

Therefore, the decision to reallocate competences on the interpretation of good faith should be subject to critical democratic debate. Regrettably, the lack of interaction on this question decreases the chance that the allocation of competences between the CJEU and national courts will be discussed in the reform of Directive 93/13, as also became visible in the attempt to reform the Directive.[606]

4.4.1.3. Conclusion on the competence to interpret blanket clauses

Courts at the national and European level have insufficiently recognised interdependence between courts in interpreting blanket clauses, and have therefore not adequately interacted. At first sight, the lack of interaction has not directly led to problems for private parties, as German courts have ensured the predictable, consistent and responsive development of the law through article 307 BGB. However, unclarities have remained, particularly with regard to the allocation of competences between courts, and because of the lack of interaction, this question has remained invisible in the European debate on the reform of the Directive. This is unfortunate, as such a reallocation of competences to the European level should be addressed in the legislative process. Such a change may inhibit consistency as well as responsiveness, as national courts are better placed to interpret blanket clauses in accordance with national legal views on justice and national practice.

The close relation between article 307 BGB and fundamental principles of German law confirms the close relationship between the law on STCs and may raise questions on the desirability to initiate further harmonisation as well as regulatory competition.

604 P. Ulmer, 'Der AGB-Gesetz nach der Umsetzung der EG-Richtlinie über mißbräuchliche Klauseln in Verbraucherverträgen', in: P. Ulmer, U. Hübner, *Das Recht der Allgemeinen Geschaftsbedingungen nach der Umsetzung der EG-Richtlinie uber misbrauchliche Klauseln in Verbrauchervertragen, Karlsruher Forum 1997*, Karlsruhe: Versicherungswirtschaft 1998, p.38, 39.

605 B. Heiderhoff, 'Die berücksichtigung des Art. 3 Klauselrichtlinie bei der AGB-Kontrolle', *WM* 2003, p. 510.

606 See further above par. 4.3.2.4.

4.4.2. *Model lists*

Model lists have been established both by the European and the German legislator. Neither the German[607] nor the European model list[608] provides an exhaustive list of unfair clauses. Thus, clauses that do not fall within the scope of either list may still be unfair. Generally, model lists should clarify how blanket clauses should be interpreted, thereby contributing to consistency and predictability. The European list may also be used to increase the accessibility of private law for especially foreign parties, who can more easily get an oversight of clauses that are not considered acceptable.[609]

Does the simultaneous use of model lists undermine or strengthen the predictability, consistency and accessibility of one or both of these lists? Alternatively, does the existence of actors producing overlapping model lists foster responsiveness, create opportunities for regulatory competition or mutual learning?

Paragraph 4.4.2.1 will consider the development of the German and European model lists and paragraph 4.4.2.2 will discuss the implementation of the European model list. Paragraph 4.4.2.3 will turn to the application of the model lists by the courts and paragraph 4.4.2.4 will end with a conclusion.

4.4.2.1. The development of the German and European model lists

The German legislator was one of the first legislators to establish a regime, including black and grey lists, while harmonisation had not yet developed. Consequently, the German legislator had less opportunity to draw from the experiences from other legislators in the European Union with regard to the use of black and grey lists. In other words, there were limited opportunities for mutual learning. However, international initiatives had developed. Especially the Warsaw Contention was relevant and should have been taken into account.

The German black and grey lists are inspired by standing case law on unfair terms that were developed for businesses. They are relevant both for business and consumer contracts.[610] Ulmer and Habersack[611] note that the judicial evaluation under article 307 BGB has been sharpened as the effect of the model lists on article 307 BGB have become visible, and as article 307 BGB has been used to fill up gaps in the model lists. In a later stage the Dutch legislator has looked to the German regime for inspiration.[612]

Notably, the German legislator initially objected to the use of the model list at a European level,[613] and the indicative nature of the list in the Annex is attributed to

[607] BGH 24 September 1980, *NJW* 1981, 118.

[608] CJEU 7 May 2002 (Commission v Sweden), C-478/99, [2002] ECR p. I-4147.

[609] Wolf/Lindacher/Pfeiffer/AGB-Recht/Damman (2009), introduction to articles 308–309, nr 1 however, notes that the list, with the exception of article 309 par. 11 BGB, aims to protect consumers, not users of STCs.

[610] W. Tilman, 'Das AGB-Gesetz und die Einheit des Privatrechts', *ZHR* 1978, p. 58.

[611] Ulmer/Brandner/Hensen/AGB-Recht/Ulmer/.Habersack (2012) introduction, nr 71.

[612] See par. 5.3.

[613] BR-Drucks. 611/90, p. 1.

German criticism.[614] Because of the correlation between model lists and general default law, the use of binding model lists has also been rejected because it could be a back door to a European contract law.[615] Thus, the European initiative did not lead the German legislator to critically reflect on the accessibility of the law for foreign and international actors.

Originally, the 1990 version of the model list to the Directive was not considered to be of much added value, as it did not provide clear guidance on how to balance parties' rights in determining whether a term was unfair. That does not mean that the model list as such was considered of little value, as it was simultaneously considered that in an amended version the list could contribute to predictability.[616]

Thus, the active participation of German actors limited the obligation of the German legislator to amend existing model lists.

4.4.2.2. The implementation of the European model list

Because of the indicative character of the European model list, it was not clear how far the obligation of the German legislator to implement the model list went. Preamble 17 to the Directive, referring to its minimum character, allows Member States to alter the wording of the annex depending on their national law. Preamble 17 also seems to allow for more restrictive drafting.[617] Yet the non-binding nature of the European list does not mean that Member States are free to ignore the model list, as this may undermine the extent to which the European model list contributes to the predictability of article 3 Directive. The decision of the CJEU in *Commission v Sweden*[618] made it clear that the model list should be a source of information both for legislators, judiciaries, and contract parties, and consequently, Member States must implement the list in a way 'that offer[s] a sufficient guarantee that the public can obtain knowledge of it'.

Moreover, in *Grimaldi*,[619] the Court more generally held that even if measures are not binding, this does not mean that they have no legal effect at all, and they should be taken into account by national judiciaries in their decisions. Since then, the Court[620] has

614 P. Ulmer, 'Der AGB-Gesetz nach der Umsetzung der EG-Richtlinie über mißbräuchliche Klauseln in Verbraucherverträgen', in: P. Ulmer, U. Hübner, *Das Recht der Allgemeinen Geschaftsbedingungen nach der Umsetzung der EG-Richtlinie uber misbrauchliche Klauseln in Verbrauchervertragen, Karlsruher Forum 1997*, Karlsruhe: Versicherungswirtschaft 1998, p. 31, 33–34.

615 N. Jansen, 'Klauselkontrolle im Europäischen Privatrecht. Ein Beitrag zur Revision des Verbraucher-acquis', *ZeuP* 2010, p. 82.

616 See for example H.E. Brandner, P. Ulmer, 'EG-Richtlinie über mißbräuchliche Klauseln in Verbraucherverträgen. Kritische Bemerkungen zum Vorschlag der EG-Kommission', *BB* 1991, p. 706.

617 Grabitz/Hilf/Das Recht der Europäischen Union/Pfeiffer (2012), article 3, nr 89, similarly MunchKomm zum BGB/Wurmnest (2012) article 308, nr 10.

618 CJEU 7 May 2002 (Commission v Sweden), C-478/99, [2002] ECR p. I-4147, par. 22.

619 CJEU 13 December 1989 (Grimaldi v Fonds des maladies professionnelles), C-322/88, [1989] ECR, p. I-4407, par. 18.

620 CJEU 26 April 2012 (Hatóság v Invitel Távközlési Zrt), C-472/10, [2012] ECR p. I-0, par. 26, where the Court held that the Annex 'is (…) an essential element on which the competent court may base its assessment as to the unfair nature of that term'. CJEU 26 February 2015 (Matei v SC Volksbank România SA), C-143/13, [2015] ECR p. I-0, par. 59–60.

made clear that the Annex may be relevant for not only assessing the fairness of clauses, but also in the interpretation of article 4 par. 2 Directive. Accordingly, Wolf,[621] considering the role of the Annex in the clarification of article 3 Directive, has held that divergences from the Annex should be based on good reasons. Graf von Westphalen[622] finds that the implementation of the model list in German law is insufficient, as the present implementation is neither publicly accessible, nor publicly known. Similarly, Baier[623] has held that implementation in German law does not suffice because, differing from the Swedish legislator, the German legislator has not made the Annex available for the consumer: '*Für den deutschen Verbraucher existiert die Liste gewissermaßen gar nicht.*'

In these views, implementation apparently requires that the model list in the Annex is made separately available to consumers. However, this would undermine accessibility, as it may be confusing that two apparently largely similar model lists would be available to indicate whether a clause is unfair. In this respect, the opportunity for mutual learning is limited.

However, that does not mean that the German legislator did not critically consider the need to amend the law in accordance with the model list. In the implementation of the model list, the German legislator amended articles 308 and 309 BGB, but these provisions do not completely reflect the European model list.

- Some clauses have been inserted after the Directive was established.

Thus, article 309 par. 7 sub a was extended to prohibit the exclusion of damages for death or injury to consumers caused by a fault or omission of the user of STCs.

- Some differences have remained.

In particular, articles 308–309 BGB do not include arbitration clauses, included under 1 sub q in the Annex. Article 309 par. 8 sub b BGB is formulated more narrowly, prohibiting exclusion clauses with regard to the sale of new goods, while the Annex, under 1 sub b, prohibits all exclusion clauses. According to Wurmnest,[624] this more narrow interpretation should be seen against the trade in secondhand goods that may often show small defects but that are sold for a lower price than new goods. Additionally, articles 308 and 309 BGB do not include an express prohibition on clauses falling under the Annex par. 1 sub d, although these clauses can be held ineffective under articles 308 par. 7, and 309 pars. 5 and 6 BGB. Similarly, articles 308–309 do not expressly prohibit clauses falling under the Annex par. 1 sub f, although these clauses can be challenged under articles 308 pars. 3 and 7, and 309 pars. 5 and 6 BGB. Also, articles 308 and 309 do not directly bar clauses falling under the Annex par. 1 sub g. Moreover, although clauses in the Annex under par.

621 Wolf/Lindacher/Pfeiffer/AGB-Recht/Wolf (2009) Annex to the Directive, nr 1.

622 F. Graf von Westphalen, 'Das Verbot von Nr. 1b des Anhangs zur EG-Klauselrichtlinie 93/13/EWG', *ZGS* 2004, p. 467.

623 K. Baier, *Europaische Verbrauchervertrage und missbrauchliche Klauseln, die Umsetzung der Richtlinie 93/13/EWG uber missbrauchliche Klauseln in Verbrauchervertragen in Deutschland, Italien, England und Frankreich*, Hamburg: Kovač 2004, p. 77.

624 MunchKomm zum BGB/Wurmnest (2012), article 308, nr 11.

1 sub m are not expressly prohibited under articles 308 and 309, they will generally affect the right of the consumer to performance, and will fall under article 309 par. 7 BGB. Additionally, articles 308–309 do not expressly prohibit clauses falling under the Annex par. 1 sub q, although these clauses may be challenged under articles 309 nrs 5 and 12, while clauses limiting consumers' right to a fair process will generally be held ineffective under article 307 BGB.

– Furthermore, provisions in the BGB may prohibit clauses under the Annex.[625]

Notably, some clauses under the Annex may diverge from default law and can therefore be considered unfair. For example, clauses under Annex par. 1 sub n, which diverges from article 164 BGB and that may also fall under article 309 par. 11 BGB can be unfair. Choice of jurisdiction clauses between a business and a consumer are contrary to article 38 par. 1 ZPO, and therefore void.

These divergences do not have to lead to the incorrect implementation of the Directive, but it may be doubted whether the model list has been implemented in such a way that the European model list serves as a source of information.

Pfeiffer and Schinkels[626] note that the legislator decided not to copy-paste the grey list in the Annex to the Directive. The legislator followed this course despite arguments for implementing the list in the Annex to the Directive, especially with regard to clauses in the black and grey list that are stricter than German law, because the CJEU would likely use the black and grey list in its interpretation of article 3 Directive.[627]

The decision of the German legislator not to implement the Annex to the Directive in German law may be seen against the background of the general restraint of the German legislator in restricting amendments to the AGBG and the BGB to absolutely necessary amendments.[628] Moreover, it was not clear whether the German legislator was bound to amend the law for the implementation of the model list in the Annex to the Directive, while articles 308 and 309 BGB already largely reflected the clauses in the Annex. The correlation between national default law and the model list may have played a role in the legislator's unwillingness to amend the law as well.

Thus, interdependence has not clearly developed, but it is possible that the German legislator has not sufficiently recognised the potential importance of the European model list. Opportunities for learning seem limited, as the overlapping model lists seem confusing rather than a source of learning. Although the legislator did amend German law, this does not seem to have been aimed at foreign or international actors.

625 Clauses falling under the Annex par. 1 sub i will generally not be valid as they are in breach of article 305 BGB. Also, clauses falling under par. 1 sub f in rent contracts are prohibited by article 547 par. 2 BGB, while article 551 BGB limits the possibility to stipulate a security for future rent.

626 Th. Pfeiffer, B. Schinkels, 'Schuldrechtsmodernisierung und AGB-Gesetz', in: H.-W. Micklitz et al. (eds.), *Schuldrechtsreform und Verbraucherschutz*, Baden Baden: Nomos 2001, p. 171.

627 K. Frey, 'Wie ändert sich das AGB-Gesetz?' *ZIP* 1993, p. 579.

628 BT-Drucks. 13/4699 and 13/2713.

4.4.2.3. The application of the European model list by the German courts

How have German courts approached the evaluation of clauses that may fall in the scope of the model list in the Annex to the Directive?

Paragraph 4.4.2.3.1 will consider the approach of the BGH, and paragraph 4.4.2.3.2 will turn to the decisions from the lower courts. Paragraph 4.4.2.3.3 will end with a conclusion.

4.4.2.3.1. The approach of the BGH towards the European model list

The BGH has not developed a clear approach towards the European model list and has not interacted with the CJEU on the status of this list.

The BGH[629] has emphasised the CJEU decision in *Commission v Sweden*[630] where the CJEU ruled on the indicative and illustrative character of the model list in the Annex to the Directive.

The decision of the BGH to uphold an arbitration clause in this case can be seen against the background of a well-established arbitration system that complies with civil procedure law, and the undesirability to overturn a well-established practice on the basis of a non-binding model list that, moreover, refers to arbitration not covered by legal provisions. Notably, these are sufficient reasons to uphold these clauses, and the decision is likely not to be contrary to the Directive. Nevertheless, the conclusion that the Annex need not be implemented can hardly be deduced from *Commission v Sweden*. Arguably, it does also not follow from *Hatosag v Invitel Tavkozlesi Zrt*,[631] where the CJEU held that '[i]f the content of the annex does not suffice in itself to establish automatically the unfair nature of a contested term, it is nevertheless an essential element on which the competent court may base its assessment as to the unfair nature of that term'.

Further decisions of the BGH do not reveal a consistent approach. In the majority of cases, the BGH does not refer to the Directive. Nevertheless, some decisions have referred to the Directive, while other decisions uphold clauses falling under the European list without referring to the Directive.

The majority of cases do not refer to the Directive or the model list, which does not necessarily mean that these decisions are contrary to the Directive.

These decisions include the decision of the BGH in a case on a clause limiting the possibility of interim cancellation to cancellation with a doctor's declaration specifying which health problems prevented clients from attending a sports studio.[632] The decisions also concern a clause that was interpreted as a penalty clause under article 309 par. 5 BGB,[633] a clause providing that the offer of the seller of a house

629 BGH 13 January 2005, *NJW* 2005, 1125.

630 CJEU 7 May 2002 (Commission v Sweden), C-478/99, [2002] ECR, p. I-4147.

631 CJEU 26 April 2012 (Hatóság v Invitel Távközlési Zrt), C-472/10, [2012] p. I-0, par. 26.

632 BGH 8 February 2012, *NJW* 2012, 1431.

633 BGH 18 February 2015, *BeckRS* 2015, 4832.

would be valid for four months and three weeks,[634] as well as a clause limiting the prescription period for actions of the buyer for breach of contract and compensation thereof.[635] Similarly, a clause for amending the contract, which also falls under Annex under 1 sub j, was held to be ineffective under article 308 par. 4 BGB. It was insufficiently clear to allow the consumer to calculate future interests.[636] A clause concerning a fictive declaration of inclusion, also falling under the Annex under 1 sub i, was held ineffective under article 308 par. 5 BGB.[637]

Cases in which the BGH has referred to the Directive and the Annex include a 2012 decision for the evaluation of a penalty clause[638] and a 2013 decision on clauses for adapting prices.[639]

The BGH ruled that the all-in exclusion of strict liability is contrary to the principle of good faith in article 3 Directive, because it causes a significant imbalance in parties' rights and obligations. A clause that stipulates a disproportionate long period for the user of STCs to perform the contract, thereby excluding the consumers' rights to damages for delay in performing the contract, or the right of the consumer to withdraw from the contract, is similarly unfair. The application of article 4 UWG – implementing Directive 2005/29 – is in accordance with the Directive.

Arguably, this decision of the BGH may indicate that the BGH considers itself competent to provide guidelines for the interpretation of the Directive. If that is the case, the question arises as to whether this decision adequately takes into account the possible competence of the CJEU to provide such guidelines.

Although the reasoning of the BGH is convincing and probably correct, the interpretation of the BGH is less likely to be followed by foreign courts than the interpretation of the CJEU, not only because the case law from the BGH is less easily accessible for foreign courts, but also because foreign courts may consider penalty clauses less objectionable, or may attach more weight to civil procedure law that stands in the way of the evaluation of clauses.[640]

In a 2013 case, the BGH ruled on a clause for adapting the price in a contract for the supply of gas. Referring first to domestic law and its own case law, and secondly to CJEU case law, the BGH found that replacing the clause with a provision of national default law was permissible, as this does not undermine the deterrent effect of the Directive. In this respect, the BGH distinguishes replacing a clause with national clause ('*ergänzende Auslegung*'), which serves to fill a gap in the contract, to an interpretation that converses an unfair clause to un unfair clause ('*geltungserhaltende*

634 BGH 11 June 2010, *NJW* 2010, 2873.

635 BGH 15 November 2006, *NJW* 2007, 674.

636 BGH 13 April 2010, *NJW* 2010, 1742. This decision is in line with later CJEU decisions on similar clauses, see, with further references, CJEU 26 February 2015 (Matei v SC Volksbank România SA), C-143/13, [2015] p. I-0.

637 BGH 11 November 2009, *NJW* 2010, 864.

638 BGH 31 May 2012, *GRUR* 2012, 949.

639 BGH 23 January 2013, *NJW* 2013, 991.

640 For example HR 22 June 2007, *NJ* 2007, 344. However this decision should be seen against the background of Dutch law that holds that clauses are avoidable rather than invalid, which entailed that judges did not *ex officio* evaluate clauses.

Reduktion') which is not permitted.[641] In addition, the BGH explains that the extensive interpretation is based on good faith, and, in accordance with BVerfG case law, can only be applied under strict conditions, in rare cases.

As Pfeiffer[642] points out, this question has not been settled by the CJEU and should therefore have been referred. Particularly, notwithstanding the reasons for adapting the clause, the decision may be difficult to reconcile with CJEU case law.[643] The later decision in *Unicaja Banco SA v Rueda and Others*[644] makes clear that while a clause can be replaced by a supplementary provision of national law, this should be in accordance with the requirement that the provision aims to achieve a real balance between parties. Moreover, courts may only do this in cases where the invalidity of the unfair term would require the court to annul the contract in its entirety, which would lead to disadvantageous consequences for the consumer.

Therefore, the existence of European rules may prompt the BGH to explain why German rules are in accordance with European law. This may be interesting for European actors, but the advantages of this approach are not immediately apparent, as German law does not become more accessible. In the long term, however, critically reconsidering German law may make clear if revision is necessary, but the restraint in referring to the CJEU decreases the chance that revision will be prompted by CJEU decisions. It is unfortunate that this case has not been referred to the CJEU, and that no clear course has been developed.

In other cases, the BGH has upheld clauses falling under the European model list, in contrast with the view that cases upholding clauses should be referred to the CJEU as these decisions may go below the minimum standard set by the Directive.[645]

The BGH[646] upheld a clause fixing the amount of damages ('*Schadenspauschalierungsklausel*') under article 309 par. 5 sub b BGB. The BGH considered that the clause did not exclude the possibility for the consumer to dispute that there were no damages, in which case the clause would be ineffective – and it would also fall under the Annex under 1 sub q.

In another case, the BGH[647] also upheld a clause setting a period for termination that exceeded the duration of the contract, which was challenged on the basis of articles 307 and 309 under 9 sub b BGB, also falling under the Annex under 1 sub h.

641 K. Uffmann, 'Informationspflichten und ergänzende Auslegung bei Preisanpassung in Energielieferverträgen', *NJW* 2015, p. 1218, criticises the restraint of the BGH in replacing an unfair amendment clause with an effective one, which would entail *geltungserhaltende Reduktion*, which is prohibited.

642 T. Pfeiffer, 'Europäisch-autonome Auslegung der Klauselrichtlinie am Beispiel der Hauptleistungsklauseln', *NJW* 2014, p. 3072.

643 Particularly CJEU 14 November 2013 (Banco Español de Crédito SA v Camino), C-168/10, [2013] ECR p. I-0.

644 CJEU 21 January 2015 (Unicaja Banco SA v Rueda and Others), joined cases C-482/13, C-484/13, C-485/13, C-487/13, [2015] ECR p. I-0, par. 33.

645 Grabitz/Hilf/Das Recht der Europäischen Union/Pfeiffer (2012), article 3, nr 84.

646 BGH 14 April 2010, *NJW* 2010, 2122.

647 BGH 15 April 2010, *NJW* 2010, 2942.

Arguably, the BGH decisions, and the lack of a consistent approach, are in line with the emphasis on the indicative nature of the list, which may be criticised because:

i) The emphasis on the non-binding status of the list overlooks that the non-binding character of the model list does not mean that state actors are free to ignore the model list if they choose.
ii) The approach of the BGH leaves room for a similarly inconsistent approach of lower courts, which may be detrimental for the consistent and predictable use of model lists, and it may limit the extent to which the European model list may contribute to the predictable and consistent interpretation of article 307 BGB.

The inclusion of clauses under the model list should be a reason to critically consider the fairness of these clauses. Notably, however, the BGH does take into account national practice and national legal views on justice that become apparent from default law. Arguably, it is desirable that the CJEU makes clear that the need to evaluate clauses in a manner consistent with practice or legal views on justice, may justify diverging from the European model list.

However, because of the lack of interaction between the BGH and the CJEU, questions on the obligation of national legislators and courts to implement and apply the list in the Annex to the Directive may remain subject to doubt, which may eventually undermine the predictable development of the private law *acquis*.

4.4.2.3.2. The approach of lower courts: referring to the Directive

Lower courts have not referred questions on Directive 93/13 to the CJEU, perhaps because this may considerably lengthen the duration of the procedure, while other relevant materials to decide the case are available. Thus, opportunities for learning exist, but using them may not be beneficial for private parties. Lower courts especially refer to BGH case law, as well as decisions from other lower courts. Courts have not developed a consistent approach to referring to the Directive and the list in the Annex to the Directive, but referral to the Directive is not decisive: some decisions referring to the Directive or other relevant Directives are in line with Directive 93/13, while other decisions not referring to the Directive may also be in line with the Directive. In rare cases, both decisions referring to the Directive and not referring to the Directive are not in accordance with Directive 93/13.

– Many decisions referring to the Directive are in line with Directive 93/13.

Accordingly, the OLG München[648] held a clause that allowed the drafter to amend the contract ineffective. The clause was contrary to article 308 par. 4 BGB, in accordance with established case law of the BGH that underlines that clauses that allow for amending the contract limit the extent to which parties can determine their future rights and obligations under the contract. The decision

648 OLG München 21 September 2009, *BeckRS* 2006, 11928.

also referred, in passing, to the Annex to the Directive. The OLG Brandenburg[649] held a clause excluding liability, including liability for damages that fell under article 309 par. 7 BGB, caused by reckless or intentional wrongful behaviour, ineffective. Referring to the duty of national courts to interpret national law in accordance with the Directive, it held that articles 307 et seq BGB were also applicable in this case.

– Some decisions, moreover, refer to other relevant Directives.

LG Frankfurt[650] held that a clause that stipulated that statements of accounts would be sent to the consumer for payment, unless he rejected this within 30 days was ineffective. The court, following the case law of the BGH, did not refer to the Directive, but held that article 248 EGBGB imposed information duties on the bank, as well as article 675d BGB, which should, respectively, be seen against the background of a treaty and a the Directive on payment services. The LG Hamburg[651] held that a clause that required the consumer to inform the seller of defects was contrary to article 5 par. 2 Directive 1999/44 on consumer sales, and was contrary to article 309 par. 5 sub b. The OLG Düsseldorf,[652] in a case that also fell under Directive 85/577, held a clause that declared that the consumer had negotiated prior to the visit of the salesman and agreed with the offer unfair under article 309 par. 12 BGB, referring to BGH case law as well as a previous decision from a lower court. Alternatively, the OLG München,[653] although not referring to the Directive, held clauses imposing costs on the consumer for reminders for payment that exceeded 1,20 Euros per reminder were ineffective under article 309 par. 5 BGB, but the referral to Directive 2011/7 and its predecessor was rejected as this Directive concerned the late payment by businesses, not consumers. KG Berlin[654] referred to Directive 1995/46 in holding several clauses used by Facebook ineffective.

– Decisions not referring to Directive 93/13 may equally be in line with the Directive.

Courts have held that a clause imposing interest on the consumer for late payment that went beyond the legally set interest was ineffective.[655] The OLG Frankfurt[656] similarly rejected a clause that excluded the consumer's possibilities to prove that there was an additional agreement under article 309 par. 12 BGB. The consumer would therefore be given the opportunity to prove the existence of additional agreements. In reality, proving this point may be rather difficult. The OLG Hamburg[657] accepted the possibility for setoff, holding in passing that any clause that excluded this right was contrary to article 309 par. 3 BGB, especially setoffs with regard to claims immediately due. The LG Hamburg[658] held that a clause that enabled the supplier to cancel the contract when a host family could not be found was ineffective. Although the possibility to cancel was based on sufficient justification, the clause did not, in accordance with article 308 par. 8 BGB,

649 OLG Brandenburg 17 November 2010, *BeckRS* 2010, 30461.
650 LG Frankfurt 8 April 2011, *BeckRS* 2011, 8796.
651 LG Hamburg 5 September 2003, *MMR* 2004, 190 (without legal force).
652 OLG Düsseldorf 26 February 2009, *BeckRS* 2009, 27333.
653 OLG München 28 July 2011, *BeckRS* 2011, 16062.
654 KG Berlin 24 January 2014, *BeckRS* 2014, 3648.
655 OLG Brandenburg 7 July 2012, *BeckRS* 2012, 15697.
656 OLG Frankfurt 30 November 2011, *BeckRS* 2012, 7451.
657 OLG Hamburg 30 March 2011, *NJW* 2011, 3524.
658 LG Hamburg 20 October 2009, *BeckRS* 2010, 14188.

oblige the supplier to inform the consumer as soon as possible and to return payments that had already been made. OLG Düsseldorf,[659] following the BGH, held a clauses imposing extra clauses ineffective under article 308 par. 6 BGB. The LG Köln,[660] referring to BGH case law, held a clause that stipulated that a sum would be owed to the bank if orders for payments were made while the account contained insufficient funds was unfair and contrary to article 309 par. 5 BGB.

- In rare cases, both decisions that refer explicitly to the Directive and CJEU case law and decisions that do not refer to the Directive but follow BGH case law may not be in accordance with the Directive, or could have led to interesting questions to the CJEU.

Accordingly, the KG Berlin,[661] later repealed by the BGH,[662] held that the evaluation of clauses is a matter for national courts, and did not subject the VOB/B to judicial evaluation, in accordance with article 310 par. 1 BGB. Although the court distinguishes between providing general criteria for the interpretation of article 3 Directive and the factual question of whether a clause is unfair in individual cases, it goes on to characterise the question whether the VOB/B are subject to judicial evaluation as a purely factual one. However, this question may arguably also entail, firstly, whether clauses that have been drafted in cooperation between stakeholders and state actors may be exempt from judicial control as such, as is the case under article 310 BGB. Secondly, the question may arise whether the implementation of the Directive obliges the judiciary to evaluate clauses in the VOB/B, despite the exemption in article 310 BGB. Thirdly, if clauses in the VOB/B are subject to judicial evaluation, it may be asked whether the circumstance that these clauses typically have not been drafted solely by the user to improve the position of the user of STCs should be decisive in the judicial evaluation of clauses under article 3 Directive. These are all questions that are not purely factual questions, while the response of the CJEU to these questions would have provided an insight into the admissibility of collectively negotiated STCs, which may in turn be interesting for the use of STCs in transnational cases if they have been collectively-negotiated and have been sanctioned by democratically elected actors. The court considers the question of whether the VOB/B should be exempt at some length and refers to CJEU case law, European law, and national debate, but eventually upholds the VOB/B, in accordance with article 310 BGB established BGH case law.

A case that could similarly have provided interesting questions for the CJEU is the decision of LG Bamberg[663] that decided that a clause in a contract falling under Directive 90/314 for package travel that stipulated that 40% of the contract price would be due within a week after the confirmation by the travel agency, was not necessarily ineffective considering the case law of the BGH, which it however recognised as not uncontroversial. This decision seems to be inconsistent with later decisions that have held these clauses ineffective.[664] The court rejected the respondents' call for interpretation in accordance with the Directive, as the Directive on package travel did not stipulate the amount of the sum to be paid by the consumer. Notably, the decision is not necessarily contrary to the Directive, and the court was not obliged to refer questions to the CJEU. Yet possibly, a question to the CJEU could have provided insight in the overlap between the Directive

659 OLG Düsseldorf 29 January 2015, *NJOZ* 2015, 604.

660 LG Köln 11 June 2003, *BeckRS* 2004, 3151 (without legal force).

661 KG Berlin 15 February 2007, *BeckRS* 2007, 6334.

662 BGH 24 July 2008 – VII ZR 55/07, *BeckRS* 2008, 15864.

663 LG Bamberg 12 April 2011, *BeckRS* 2011, 21455.

664 OLG Dresden 21 June 2012, *BeckRS* 2012, 14828 with references to other decisions.

on unfair terms and the Directive on package travel. This would, however, have likely led to a delay in the procedure which is hardly to the advantage of the consumer.

Similarly, the OLG Frankfurt[665] upheld a clause limiting the consumer's right to withdraw from the package travel contract. The court considered domestic law, and extensively referred to not only Directive 93/13 but also, at some length, Regulation 261/2004 and IATA recommendations and the underlying practical considerations for the clause. Various aspects of the decision could have provided interesting questions for the CJEU: the consideration of the court to the standard under article 307 and article 3 Directive, the relation between the fairness of clauses and the rights of consumers under simultaneously applicable measures, in particular Regulation 261/2004, and its referral to BGH case law on the fairness of clauses recommended by IATA.

A problematic decision that followed BGH case law rather than the Directive is the decision of the OLG Brandenburg.[666] The court upheld a clause that required the consumer to declare that he was of age and competent to enter into juridical acts, stating that this does not constitute a clause under article 309 par. 12 BGB that reallocates the burden of proof to the detriment of the consumer.

The OLG Hamm[667] followed the BGH in upholding a clause silently extending a contract for 24 months for another year. Interestingly, these clauses are more critically evaluated in the Dutch legal order, especially after the recent reform of Dutch law, also inspired by experiences in the French, Belgian, English and Austrian legal order.[668] These practices are also in accordance with the Annex to the Directive that includes clauses silently extending contracts if the deadline for the consumer to terminate is unreasonably early.

The decision of the OLG Koblenz[669] that upheld a clause that stipulated that the consumer was to pay 25% of the price if the consumer wanted to cancel the contract, referring to BGH case law, may similarly be questioned. The court held that this was not contrary to article 309 par. 5 BGB as it had not been established that the seller had suffered remarkably less damages. This decision may be difficult to reconcile with previous decisions of the OLG München[670] that held a clause that imposed costs for reminders ineffective under article 309 par. 5 BGB. The question arises whether the court should have taken into account the possibility that this decision could go below the minimum level of protection under the Directive.

Because lower courts generally follow BGH case law and decisions from other lower courts, a clear approach on the status of the model lists can also not be found in these decisions. Opportunities for mutual learning have not been used. Although this would have resulted in delay for contract parties, questions might have provided European legislators with more insight in national practice. More consideration for comparative law might also have prompted German courts to consider some clauses differently. However, without interaction, the status of the European model list is not going to be resolved at the European level. Instead, decisions will continue to be made at the national level, but these decisions may be undermined if courts in other Member States ask

665 OLG Frankfurt 4 September 2014, *BeckRS* 2014, 19112.

666 OLG Brandenburg 11 January 2006, *BeckRS* 2006, 869. Comp. similarly OLG Hamm 24 May 2012, *BeckRS* 2012, 13246.

667 OLG Hamm 8 April 2010, *BeckRS* 2010, 20831.

668 See further par. 5.3.3.5.

669 OLG Koblenz 13 October 2011, *BeckRS* 2012, 8719, comp. also AG München 31 August 2007, *BeckRS* 2007, 18278.

670 OLG München 28 July 2011, *BeckRS* 2012, 16062.

questions on the status of the model list, which would necessitate a different approach from German courts. Such a change would undermine predictability.

4.4.2.3.3. Conclusion on the application of the European model list by German courts

The BGH has not adopted a consistent approach to the European model list, nor has it recognised the potential competence of the CJEU to determine what status the list in the Annex to the Directive should have in the adjudication of disputes. Lower courts have followed this approach. Thus, the status of the model list has not been clarified by the CJEU. As a result, also, opportunities for mutual learning have not been realised.

Furthermore, the development of the Directive has not contributed to the development of a system of checks and balances, either for the CJEU or for German courts. A system of checks and balances may be helped by a clearer division of competences.

Although the lack of interaction need not be problematic for private parties, as German courts generally decide cases predictably, consistently and responsively, and, in line with the Directive, except in rare cases, problems have arisen in the long term. Because of the lack of interaction, the obligations of national legislators and courts in the implementation and application of the European model list has remained unclear, and the extent to which the European list fosters accessibility is also undermined.

4.4.2.4. Conclusion on the development of the law on STCs through model lists

This paragraph has asked whether actors have interacted in the use of model lists and how that has affected the predictability, consistency, accessibility and responsiveness of the law on STCs.

Whereas the German legislator could not make much use of comparative insights, the drafting of model lists was focused on national practice and consequently overlooked relevant treaties. Foreign legislators and the European legislator have turned to German law for inspiration, and the German legislator has participated actively in the development of the model list in the Annex to the Directive, thereby limiting the effect it has on national law. Because of the active approach of the German legislator, the interdependence between national and European actors in ensuring the predictability, consistency, and accessibility of private law through model lists has not become outspoken. Nevertheless, the ability of the national legislator to ensure the predictability, consistency, accessibility and the responsiveness of the law through model lists may become limited as international sources of law indicate that clauses falling under national model lists should be upheld.

Because of the indicative nature of the model list, unclarity has arisen in relation to the obligation of Member States to implement the list. The German legislator has not separately implemented the European model list. The restraint of the legislator is reinforced by the courts that have not developed a consistent approach to the European model list – it does not have a specific status, nor does the inclusion of clauses under the European model list necessarily form an indication that a clause should be held ineffective. Because of the strict approach of courts to unfair clauses, however, cases are only rarely decided contrary to the Directive.

German actors have shown restraint in interaction with relevant European actors on the obligation for national state actors in the implementation of the model list. However, this restraint of German state actors does not directly lead to problems for private parties, as the restraint serves to maintain consistency, predictability, accessibility and responsiveness for private parties. The resistance of German actors to binding model lists also limits problems of accessibility and consistency that may arise if the European list would become binding.

Yet eventually, the lack of interaction may lead to persistent unclarity on the status of the European model list, a question that has remained invisible in the attempted reform of Directive 93/13. The added value of the European model list is undermined as it does not play a clear role in national legal practice.

Benefits, in accordance with pluralist insights, have not been realised. The development of a European model list has not motivated the German legislator to consider foreign and international actors' interests, despite the amendment of articles 308–309 BGB. In addition, harmonisation has not led to a system of checks and balances. The unclear status of the European list does not contribute to its suitability to provide an adequate system of checks and balances for German law which is generally not perceived as problematic. Similarly, the German legislator and German courts are focussed on national law and are not compelled to improve the non-binding European model list. In addition, opportunities for mutual learning have not been realised.

4.4.3. *The evaluation of clauses in international contracts*

Have the courts sufficiently taken into account foreign, European and international state and non-state actors, and how has this approach affected the predictability, consistency, accessibility, and responsiveness of the law on STCs in international contracts? Has interaction led to more responsiveness, regulatory competition, or mutual learning?

Paragraph 4.4.3.1 will consider the evaluation of international business contracts under article 307 BGB and treaties, and paragraph 4.4.3.2 will discuss the evaluation of clauses in international consumer contracts. Paragraph 4.4.3.3 will turn to the evaluation of domestic business contracts. Paragraph 4.4.3.4 will end with a conclusion.

4.4.3.1. The evaluation of international business contracts

In the evaluation of clauses in international business contracts, courts have generally not referred to foreign materials. Referral to international materials differs, depending on the applicable regime. Under German law, courts have frequently referred to international sources and taken into account international practice, which should benefit responsiveness. In contrast, in the evaluation of clauses under international regimes, courts have referred to applicable international regimes, but they have not referred to other materials or international practice, which may undermine the responsiveness of international law to international practice.

Paragraph 4.4.3.1.1 will consider some preliminary questions, and paragraph 4.4.3.1.2 will discuss the evaluation of clauses in international contracts under the Montreal

Convention that has been ratified by the EU[671] and implemented through Regulation 889/2002. Paragraph 4.4.3.1.3 will turn to the evaluation of clauses in international contracts under the CMR. Paragraph 4.4.3.1.4 will analyse the evaluation of clauses under the CISG and German law and paragraph 4.4.3.1.4 will end with a conclusion.

4.4.3.1.1. Preliminary questions: comprehensive international regimes?

The intensity of judicial evaluation depends on the question of whether international law aims to provide a comprehensive regime to parties.[672] If a regime is comprehensive, the regime provided by international law is referred to as a standard.[673] This is, for example, the case for the Montréal convention, where national rules are only applicable insofar as the Convention does not aim to provide rules – for example, civil procedure law.[674] The CMR in some areas also aims to provide a comprehensive regime.[675]

Accordingly, if international regimes do not leave room for the application of article 307 BGB, it will not be applied. It is not uncontroversial whether article 307 BGB is a provision of *ordre public* in the sense of article 9 Rome I.[676] However, this does not seem to be the case. For example, in the decision of the OLG Hamburg,[677] in a case on an international contract falling under the CISG, the OLG did not apply article 307 of its own motion as a matter of *ordre public*, even though penalty clauses fall under article 309 par. 6 BGB – penalty clauses are not necessarily unfair in business contracts. The lack of clarity on the question whether the law on STCs can be characterised as *ordre public* has been criticised by Ribstein and O'Hara[678] who point out that clarity on this question makes clear what limits have been set to regulatory competition.

Not all treaties aim for a comprehensive regime: article 4 par. 2 CISG makes clear that the CISG does not aim to provide a comprehensive regime, which means that article 307 BGB will be applicable.[679] If German law is applicable, clauses are subject to judicial evaluation under article 307 BGB.

671 Council Decision 2001/539/EC of 5 April 2001.

672 Wolf/Lindacher/Pfeiffer/AGB-Recht/Hau (2009), AGB im internationalen Geschäftsverkehr, nr 52–55, also J. Maidl, *Auslandische AGB im deutschen Recht*, München: Beck 2000, p. 225.

673 Thus, clauses in contracts for transport contracts ('*Allgemeine Deutsche Spediteurbedingungen*') falling under the Montréal Convention would not be subject to judicial evaluation under article 307 BGB, while clauses in contracts under, for example, the CMR, would be subject to judicial evaluation; comp. F. Graf von Westphalen, Vertragsrecht und AGB-Klauselwerke/Vogt (30. Ergänzungslieferung 2012), Transportrecht, nr 203. See critically on the interpretation of these clauses K.U. Bahnsen, 'AGB-Kontrolle bei den Allgemeinen Deutschen Spediteurbedingungen', *Transportrecht* 2010, p. 19.

674 BGH 22 July 2010, *BeckRS* 2011, 721, accordingly, denying the applicability of the Convention, OLG Düsseldorf 12 March 2008, *BeckRS* 2008, 9758.

675 See for the areas in which the CMR does not aim to provide a comprehensive regime Ferrari/Kieninger/Mankowski et al., Internationales Vertragsrecht/Ferrari (2011), article 1 CMR, nr 3.

676 MunchKomm zum HGB (2009), introduction to articles 343 et seq, nr 39. See further Ferrari/Kieninger/Mankowski u.a., Internationales Vertragsrecht/Staudinger (2011), article 9 Rome I, nrs 5 et seq.

677 OLG Hamburg, 25 January 2008, 12 U 39/00, www.unilex.info/case.cfm?id=1352.

678 E.A. O'Hara, L.E. Ribstein, *The law market*, Oxford: OUP 2009, p. 138.

679 Ulmer/Brander/Hensen/AGB-Recht/Schmidt (2011), annex to article 305 BGB, nr 33.

If parties have made a choice of law other than German law, the question has arisen whether foreign default law, instead of default national law, should be taken as a starting point for the evaluation of clauses based on foreign clauses. The applicability of foreign default law would mean that clauses in conformity with foreign default law are not subject to judicial control in accordance with article 307 par. 3 BGB.[680] Clauses that are in accordance with European law are also not subject to judicial review.[681] A different view would mean that the German judiciary *de facto* evaluates the default regime of other states, which seems undesirable. However, if clauses violate mandatory, *ordre public* provisions, the German judiciary will have to evaluate them of its own motion.

Under German law, individually negotiated clauses in international contracts will not be evaluated under articles 305–310 BGB. This will, for example, be the case for some well-established clauses that are more likely to be considered to have been initiated by both parties.[682] Further, if clauses reflect practices in the sense of article 346 HGB, or in the sense of article 9 CISG, they will not be subject to judicial control. This exception is in accordance with article 307 par. 3 BGB that stipulates that terms that reflect provisions from mandatory or default national or international private law, are not subject to judicial evaluation. Although this will not often be the case,[683] this exception corresponds with the need in business practice to speedily deal with these matters, while they also have more experience with the use of STCs. Maidl[684] finds that FOB clauses from the ICC (A.5) often converge with international practice, although they do not establish international practice as such.[685] Pilz[686] finds that referring to Incoterms is a practice in the sense of article 9 CISG, while the terms cannot be characterised as individually negotiated terms. However, Hopt[687] notes that the applicability of Incoterms does not exclude the applicability of the CISG, and they may be subjected to judicial evaluation of article 307 BGB.

4.4.3.1.2. The evaluation of clauses under the Montréal Convention

The Montréal Convention provides a comprehensive regime and does not leave room for any additional evaluation of clauses under article 307 BGB.

680 J. Maidl, *Auslandische AGB im deutschen Recht*, München: Beck 2000, p. 187–188.

681 BGH 3 February 1993, *NJW-RR* 1993, p. 691.

682 See previously par. 4.3.3.2.1.

683 Baumbach/Hopt/Handelsgesetzbuch/Hopt (2012) article 346 nr 10.

684 J. Maidl, *Auslandische AGB im deutschen Recht*, München: Beck 2000, p. 112–113. Accordingly OLG München 19 December 1957, *NJW* 1958, 426. Comp. for domestic trade, for the inclusion of the ADSp, BGH 10 May 1984, *NJW* 1985, 2411.

685 Ulmer/Brandner/Hensen/AGB-Recht/Ulmer/Habersack (2011) article 305 nr 172.

686 B. Pilz, 'Incoterms und UN-, Kaufrecht', in: K.-H. Thume (ed.), *Transport- und Vertriebsrecht 2000, Festschrift fur Prof. Dr. Rolf Herber*, Luchterhand: Neuwied 2000, p. 21. Accordingly LG Hamburg, 26 September 1990, 5 0 543/88, www.unilex.info/case.cfm?id=7.

687 Baumbach/Hopt/ Handelsgesetzbuch/Hopt (2012), introduction to Incoterms.

- Initially, the BGH emphasised the uniform interpretation of the Convention.

The BGH[688] expressly indicated the methods of interpretation for a uniform interpretation. In particular, it held that an international interpretation entailed a grammatical interpretation. Especially if the legislative history of the international instrument was unclear, the aim of the instrument was to be taken into account, as well as the internal coherence of the instrument, while referral to national concepts was to be avoided.

- Despite this emphasis, the BGH has not interacted with foreign actors, and although the courts take into account the CMR, other international sources are not considered. Courts have typically evaluated clauses in accordance with German law.

The tendency to decide in accordance with German law is clearly visible in a decision where the BGH[689] held that, although an air operator had excluded liability in accordance with the Montréal Convention (at that time still the Warsaw Convention), German law on breach of contract was additionally applicable. The BGH held that the convention only stipulated compensation for property arising from air traffic, which includes delay. However, damages arising from breach of contract because the air operator had overbooked a flight did not constitute a delay, while it was also not a risk inherent to air traffic. Rather, overbooking is the result of organisational procedures that are under the control of the air operator. As the damages did not fall within the scope of the convention, the convention was not applied on this point. It followed that the clause excluding damages arising from delay was also not applicable to cases where damages arose because a flight had been overbooked.

In a later decision, the BGH[690] solely referred to German sources.

- This approach is also followed by lower courts.

This BGH decision was followed by the OLG Köln[691] that similarly applied national law on breach of contract. Although the court extensively referred to previous German case law, as well as German commentaries to the Convention, it did not take into account foreign decisions. The A.G. Hamburg[692] ruled that the applicability of the Convention would lead to a similar result reached in German law.

→ Although the BGH recognised the need for uniform interpretation, this did not entail referring to foreign sources or overlooking national mandatory law. Instead, courts have maintained a consistent interpretation of the Convention within the German legal order.

688 BGH 19 March 1976, *NJW* 1976, 1583, followed by the OLG Frankfurt 23 December 1992, *NJW-RR* 1993, 809, however, without referral to foreign sources.

689 BGH 28 September 1978, *NJW* 1979, 495.

690 BGH 21 September 2000, *NJW-RR* 2001, 396.

691 OLG Köln 2 December 2003, *BeckRS* 2004, 3006.

692 AG Hamburg 4 April 2007, *BeckRS* 2007, 15103.

4.4.3.1.3. The evaluation of clauses under the CMR

The CMR provides a regime that does not leave room for additional evaluation under article 307 BGB, but it does not provide a comprehensive regime in all respects.

- Initially, the BGH[693] referred to the Incoterms to determine parties' rights and obligations.

The BGH held that all clauses on prescription were to be judged exclusively by the CMR that aimed to provide a comprehensive regime in matters of prescription. The court further referred to the Incoterms for establishing the rights and duties of parties towards one another. The court held that the case did not have to be evaluated under the *Kraftverkehrsordnung*.

This decision was followed by the OLG Frankfurt[694] that held a clause on prescription from the *Allgemeine Deutsche Spediteurbedingungen* (ADSp) was ineffective as it was incompatible with article 32 CMR

- Since this decision, however, the BGH has generally not referred to international sources other than the CMR, or foreign decisions, but rather to its own previous decisions, while national mandatory law played a more prominent role in the evaluation of clauses.

In a 1983 decision, the BGH[695] held that a clause, forming part of the ADSp that excluded setoff and counterclaims was irreconcilable with article 41 CMR. In addition, it held that the clauses also contradicted complementary mandatory national law, in particular the law on goods transport ('*Güterkraftverkehrsgesetz*') as well as the regulation on goods transport (*Kraftverkehrsordnung*), and civil procedure law.

In a 1984 decision, the BGH[696] held that a clause in an insurance contract under the CMR, excluding article 6 Law on insurance contracts ('*Versicherungsvertragsgesetz*'), was ineffective under article 9 AGBG. The clause unfairly excluded the duty of the insurer in all cases where the insured was negligent, however minimal that negligence was, and regardless of whether the negligent behaviour affected the position of the insurer.

→ In the evaluation of clauses under the CMR, the BGH has taken into account the CMR, but only very rarely international sources and generally not foreign decisions. Instead, clauses are evaluated in accordance with national law, and German courts have maintained the consistent evaluation of clauses under the CMR.

693 BGH 18 February 1972, *NJW* 1972, 1003.
694 OLG Frankfurt, 14 July 1980, *NJW* 1981, 1911.
695 BGH 20 January 1983, *NJW* 1983, 1266.
696 BGH 9 May 1984, *NJW* 1985, 559.

4.4.3.1.4. The evaluation of clauses under the CISG and German law

If the CISG is applicable, clauses are subject to evaluation under article 307 BGB. Have clauses in cases falling under the CISG been evaluated differently than clauses in cases falling under German law?

- Courts have held clauses under the CISG ineffective under the AGBG and article 307 BGB, without referring to foreign materials or other international sources. Instead, clauses have been evaluated in accordance with national law, in particular articles 10–11 AGBG and later articles 308–309 BGB.[697]

LG Heilbronn[698] held that in an international contract between businesses falling under the CISG, an exclusion clause was invalid under article 9 AGBG, expressly referring to previous case law in its statement that these articles were also applicable in business contracts. The court, moreover, held that as judicial evaluation was not established in international law, the standard of article 9 AGBG had to be applied. Nevertheless, the court also referred to default rules in the CISG, in particular, article 74 CISG, as a standard.

OLG Braunschweig[699] held a clause fixing the amount of damages ineffective, referring to article 11 AGBG, and for the applicability of German law, German literature, holding that the CISG did not provide rules that entailed a different conclusion. The court, furthermore, held that the decision would be similar under German law.

- In the evaluation of clauses in cases under German law, surrounding national law plays a role.

Accordingly, the BGH held that the exclusion of liability in the ADSp included in a transport contract was ineffective under article 9 AGBG as it diverged from articles 475 HGB and 278 BGB.[700]

- However, clauses may also be upheld despite conflict with national law if they are in accordance with international business practices. In these cases, considerably more referral is made to international materials.

In a sea transport case where a clause of the ADSp excluded liability, contrary to article 606 HGB, the BGH[701] ruled that this clause was not ineffective under article 9 AGBG considering the well-established business practice to establish these clauses, as reflected in the International Convention for the unification of certain rules of law relating to bills of lading (Hague Rules).

The BGH, has moreover, ruled that clauses are ineffective if they aim to circumvent mandatory rules on liability in the Hague Rules, which is contrary to article 662 HGB,[702] although it also held

697 Also Baumbach/Hopt/ Handelsgesetzbuch/Hopt (2012), introduction to Incoterms, nr.
698 LG Heilbronn, 15 September 1997, 3 KFH O 653/93, www.unilex.info/case.cfm?id=439, par. 4.3.
699 OLG Braunschweig, 28 October 1999, 2 U 27/1999, www.unilex.info/case.cfm?id=444, par. 3 hh and b.
700 BGH 15 September 2005, *BeckRS* 2005, 14476.
701 BGH 26 June 1997, *NJW-RR* 1997, 1253.
702 BGH 30 May 1983, *NJW* 1983, 2772.

that even if this is the case, forum clauses may still be acceptable if the Hague Rules are incorporated in the contract.[703]

In another case for sea transport, the BGH[704] held that exclusion clauses drafted by the Baltic and International Maritime Conference (BIMCO) were contrary to good faith under article 9 AGBG, but pointed to the necessity of adequately establishing whether the claimant had not suggested the use of clauses.

In another international contract for sea transport, the BGH[705] expressly did not consider penalty clauses unfair, and referred to various international model contracts containing such clauses, including BIMCO clauses, while also considering the justification for the use of such clauses in sea transport. Interestingly, however, the BGH did mention article 11 AGBG in passing.

The BGH[706] held an exclusion clause of a shipbuilding yard to be effective as it did not, in this case, constitute an exclusion of the main obligations in the contract, which would undermine the aim of the contract. The court also pointed to the generally usual and widely established practice with no known exceptions to insure the ship owner for damages to the ship, on which the shipyard could reasonably rely. Simultaneously, however, the court held that article 11 AGBG, although not applicable in business contracts, could indicate that a clause is unfair under article 9 AGBG.

- This approach has been followed by lower courts, who have also taken into account international business contracts.

The OLG Stuttgart,[707] in holding a model-like declaration for surety effective, expressly held that these clauses are not unusual in international trade and particularly in international trade, there was a justifiable need for these sureties, while parties to the agreement were hardly in need of protection. Also, the OLG Saarbrücken[708] upheld a clause in an insurance contract that imposed a duty of care on the transporter and stipulated that the damages would not be refunded if this duty had been breached. The court referred not only extensively to previous BGH case law but also to international materials, and held that this duty of care is well-established in transport law, upholding the clause. The court further expressly referred to the CMR and held that upholding the clause was also consistent with the CMR.

→ In the evaluation of clauses under the CISG, the courts have adopted more restraint in the referral to international sources than is the case if clauses are evaluated under German law. Thus, the courts do recognise the added value of international sources, and it is likely that the evaluation of clauses under German law is more responsive to international practice.

703 BGH 21 December 1971, *NJW* 1971, 325.
704 BGH 28 February 1983, *BeckRS* 1983, 30386936.
705 BGH 28 September 1978, *NJW* 1979,105.
706 BGH 3 March 1988, *NJW* 1988, 1785.
707 OLG Stuttgart 1 December 2010, *BeckRS* 2011, 2432.
708 OLG Saarbrücken 18 June 2003, *BeckRS* 2003, 30321130.

4.4.3.1.5. Conclusion on the evaluation of clauses in international business contracts

The referral to international materials in cases decided under German law promotes the responsiveness of German law to international practice, while the restraint of courts in cases decided under international regimes may undermine responsiveness. Even though German courts have consistently evaluated clauses under international treaties, this may not be as accessible to foreign parties. Moreover, in decisions on the CISG, courts have not referred to easily available foreign decisions. This approach lends support to the conclusion that German courts do not only adopt a national view towards European law – the national approach is also visible under international law. The nationalist view diminishes the chance that international law prompts German actors to critically reflect on German law. Further, opportunities for mutual learning have not been realised. Decisions from foreign courts have also not been considered as a means to ensure the consistency of decisions under international regimes.

So why have courts adopted more restraint in the evaluation of clauses, especially considering the easy availability of foreign decisions under the CISG? The emphasis on interpretation in accordance with national law suggests that the consistent evaluation of clauses within the German legal order has a higher priority. Does the different approach to cases under international regimes and cases under German law contribute to the beneficial position of German law over international sources? If this is the case, regulatory competition has not prompted German courts to consider the accessibility of international law decided in accordance with German case law. This approach likely will not contribute to the attractiveness of German courts as adjudicators.

The legislator's rejection of regulatory competition in this area may perhaps be compensated by the courts, even though the approach of courts is not as visible to foreign parties as legislative intervention. However, the active approach of courts combined with restraint for the legislator facilitates the consistent development of the law on STCs within a clear framework, which also benefits predictability.

4.4.3.2. The evaluation of clauses in international consumer contracts

In the evaluation of clauses in international consumer contracts, the BGH has interpreted clauses in accordance with national mandatory law despite contradictory international or foreign law, and exercised restraint with referring questions to the CJEU. This has undermined accessibility and predictability though it may benefit responsiveness to society's legal views on justice.

- Initially, the BGH took international regimes into account in the evaluation of clauses in international consumer contracts.

In a 1978 decision, the BGH[709] upheld a clause limiting the liability of the airline operator in accordance with article 22 Warsaw Convention, stating that article 22 also concerned the loss of

709 BGH 28 November 1978, *NJW* 1979, 496.

valuables that were handed to the crew as the plane had to make an emergency landing. In this decision, the BGH emphasised that the Convention should be interpreted uniformly, referring to its earlier decisions where this had similarly been emphasised. The BGH did not, however, refer to foreign decisions that would have contributed to a uniform interpretation, although one of these previous decisions[710] expressly relied on French and U.S. materials for the interpretation of the Convention.

- In later cases, the BGH has held clauses to be ineffective despite relevant international and foreign law and article 1 par. 2 Directive 93/13 that stipulates that clauses reflecting national law or international law are not subject to judicial evaluation under the Directive.

In a 1983 decision, the BGH[711] held that a clause that stipulated that times of arrival were merely estimates and did not bind airline operators, which excluded compensation for damages caused by delay, was ineffective, even though this clause reflected the recommendation of the International Air Transport Association (IATA) and was in accordance with the Warsaw Treaty, and article 22 of the Montréal Convention. Similarly, a clause giving the airline operator the right to amend the contract was held ineffective. Interestingly, this decision was cited by the European Commission in its 1990 proposal for a Directive on unfair contract terms, to demonstrate the ineffectiveness of internationally used clauses in contracts with consumers in Germany, as a reason for harmonisation.

In a 2005 case,[712] the BGH also held that a clause in an international bus transport contract with a consumer was ineffective as it limited the basic performances of the contract to the extent that the purpose of the contract was undermined, which, under article 307 par. 2 BGB, leads to the ineffectiveness of the clause. The strict approach of the BGH is also visible in a later case, where the BGH[713] held that a clause limiting the liability of the airline operator for damages to luggage, and stipulating that airline operators had a right to refuse vulnerable or perishable goods in the luggage, was contrary to article 17 of the Convention. The BGH held that if a clause diverging from article 17 limits the liability of the airline operator, this results in an unfair detriment to the consumer that is ineffective under article 307 BGB. The BGH rightly does not consider the recommendation of international organisations or often-used model clauses in consumer contracts as decisive. Especially if these clauses fall under the Annex to Directive 93/13, they should be adapted.

OLG Frankfurt[714] later followed this decision, finding that the mere fact that these clauses are often used in contracts does not mean they cannot be unfair. However, the court extensively considered the IATA recommendations, as well as Regulation 261/2004 and the reasons for including the clause, and accordingly upheld the clause.

The German judiciary also adopted a strict approach with regard to international contracts that have been validly concluded under English law and have made a valid choice of jurisdiction

710 For example BGH 23 March 1976, *NJW* 1976, 1587, as well as BGH 24 June 1969, *NJW* 1969, 2008.

711 BGH 20 January 1983, *NJW* 1983, 1322. Comp. also BGH 24 September 1985, *NJW* 1986, 1610 where an exclusion clause from an international association contrary to article 11 par. 6 AGBG was held ineffective.

712 BGH 1 February 2005, *NJW* 2005, 1774, comp. also KG Berlin 12 December 2007, *BeckRS* 2009, 24853.

713 BGH 5 December 2006, *NJW* 2007, 997.

714 OLG Frankfurt 4 September 2014, *BeckRS* 2014, 19112.

for English courts, as becomes apparent from the decision of the OLG Frankfurt.[715] In this case it was held that the clauses should be evaluated under the AGBG as the contracts showed a close connection with Germany, while it was also not sufficiently established that the clauses would not be applied in consumer contracts. Even if this was not the case, the clauses had to be evaluated under German law as a different decision left open the possibility that the outcome of cases would be irreconcilable with the AGBG. Despite harmonisation in this area, the court held that it was unclear whether English law provided sufficient protection to consumers as the Unfair Contract Terms Act 1977 was not applicable to credit contracts, and it was unclear whether the Unfair Terms in Contracts Regulations 1994 would be applicable to the contracts in this case. The court, however, proceeded to uphold the clauses.

Thus, German courts have steadfastedly refused to recognise the ability of international or European actors to limit national mandatory law. Accordingly, interdependence has not been recognised and interaction with European, foreign and international actors has remained limited. A system of checks and balances, for example to ensure international and foreign parties' access to the German market, has not developed. German actors have also not critically reconsidered German law in the light of international agreements.

This refusal for interaction need not be problematic for consumers, who can rely on national law, but it may undermine predictability for international or foreign actors who rely on treaties and European law. Moreover, questions about the relation between the Montréal Convention and Directive 93/13 have remained unresolved at the European level, which undermines consistency and accessibility.

Both European and national legislators who have ratified the Convention should reconsider either article 22 of the Convention or make an exception for the Convention in the Directive. Also, this change should be clearly implemented in national legislation in order to ensure that this change is sufficiently followed by the courts.

Moreover, the question arises whether article 8 Directive justifies the conclusion that Member States can evaluate clauses that are in conformity with treaties that have been ratified in and by the Union. This question also seems relevant for the aim of the Directive to further the internal market, especially as allowing judicial evaluation of clauses in conformity with international law undermines the use of clauses under international regimes in the internal market under article 1 par. 2 Directive. As it concerns the interpretation of a Directive, the CJEU is competent.

What is more, the question arises German courts are competent to set aside mandatory national law, especially as international law, implemented in national law, does not have priority over other national law. This question should be resolved if clauses in accordance with future European measures may similarly undermine national mandatory law, which may lead to further inconsistencies.

These questions indicate that mutual recognition may be problematic in areas where foreign law is contrary to national mandatory law, especially if the competences of courts to set aside mandatory rules and the question which mandatory rules are part of

715 OLG Frankfurt 1 November 2006, *BeckRS* 2007, 1589.

ordre public have not been sufficiently resolved. Thus, mutual recognition need not necessarily start dialogue between the CJEU and national courts.[716] Because of the lack of interaction between German courts and the CJEU, these questions have not been addressed and it can be doubted whether such questions will be addressed in the revision of the Directive.

4.4.3.3. The evaluation of clauses in domestic business contracts

The approach of the BGH to the evaluation of clauses used in international trade is more lenient than the evaluation of clauses used in national trade. The standard applied in the judicial evaluation of clauses in business contracts under article 307 BGB is largely similar to the standard of evaluation for consumer contracts under articles 307–309 BGB.[717]

- This becomes especially apparent from the indirect applicability of article 309 BGB in business contracts. Clauses falling under article 309 BGB are unfair.

The BGH[718] held a clause limiting the period of prescription ineffective, noting that business practices did not indicate otherwise, as businesses were disadvantaged by these clauses in a way similar to consumers, while they were not inherently better placed to discover deficiencies in goods that inherently became visible only after some years.

Similarly, the BGH[719] considered a comprehensive exclusion clause as ineffective. Generally, exclusion clauses are, in accordance with article 11 par. 7 AGBG and article 309 par. 7 under b BGB, not necessarily prohibited, but they are held ineffective if they concern a main obligation of the contract which undermines the aim of the contract.[720]

Additionally, the BGH[721] has ruled that clauses with regard to the burden of proof that fall under article 309 par. 12 sub a BGB are unfair in business contracts as rules on the burden of proof are closely correlated with ideas on justice. Although article 436 BGB, implementing Directive 1999/44, allows that the burden of proof is shifted to the detriment of the seller, this should be seen against the background of consumer protection. In this case, the user of STCs does not have a weak position similar to a consumer, and STCs that shift the burden of proof to the advantage of the user of the STCs are accordingly ineffective.

716 P.S. Berman, 'Global legal pluralism', *Southern California Law Review* 2007, p. 1224.

717 R. Koch, 'Das AGB-Recht im unternehmerischen Verkehr: Zu viel des Guten oder Bewegung in die richtige Richtung?' *BB* 2010, p. 1813, who also finds that the rarity of cases where clauses are upheld because of business practices is difficult to reconcile with the wording of article 310 BGB. See however BGH 17 September 2014, *NJW* 2014, 3508, where the BGH expressly held that price amendment clauses that would have been invalid in consumer contracts, were acceptable for business contracts.

718 BGH 8 March 1984, *NJW* 1984, 1750.

719 BGH 19 September 2007, *NJW* 2007, 3774.

720 Comp. for example also BGH 24 October 2001, *NJW* 2002, 673, BGH 11 November 1992, *NJW* 1995, 335.

721 BGH 5 October 2005, *NJW* 2006, 47.

- Business practices are only rarely accepted as a reason to hold clauses effective.

Examples of such an exception are penalty clauses in building contracts.[722] In contrast, clauses may be ineffective despite the recommendation of stakeholder organisations.[723]

Thus, courts have adopted a considerably more lenient approach to clauses in international contracts, which may benefit the responsiveness of the law on STCs to the preferences of parties with sufficient expertise in international trade. Hau[724] finds that the diverging approach can be traced to the assumption that parties engaged in international trade are in less need of protection than parties in national trade, with the apparent exception of consumers engaged in international trade.

4.4.3.4. Conclusion on the evaluation of clauses in international contracts

The interaction between courts with international actors differs depending on the question whether it concerns a business contract or a consumer contract, as well as the regime under which clauses are evaluated. Clauses in international consumer contracts and domestic business contracts are strictly evaluated, despite the relevance of international and European law in international consumer contracts. Although this restraint is not directly detrimental to consumers, it diminishes predictability, especially for foreign or international businesses. Questions on the relation between European measures and on the competence of German courts have been left unanswered, which may undermine the predictable, accessible, and consistent development of the *acquis*.

The difference between the evaluation of clauses in international contracts, especially under German law, and the evaluation of clauses in domestic contracts reinforces the impression that the strictness of German law and the rejection of regulatory competition by the German legislator is compensated by the approach of the courts. Even though German law is strict, it is not similarly applied in international cases. This approach allows the German legislator to maintain the development of the law in accordance with national legal views on justice while not diminishing the responsiveness of the law on STCs to international practice, something that is overlooked by the concerns for the attractiveness of German law[725] as well as the private initiative for regulatory competition

722 BGH 12 October 1978, *NJW* 1979, 212. Comp. also OLG Köln 3 April 1992, *NJW-RR* 1992, 1448.

723 BGH 25 October 1995, *NJW* 1996, 389. Comp. BGH 10 September 2014, *NJW* 2014, 3722, where the BGH held a clause invalid as it breached the requirement of transparency in article 307 BGB, finding that violations against transparency were not in accordance with business practices in the sense of article 310 par. 1 BGB.

724 Wolf/Lindacher/Pfeiffer/AGB-Recht/Hau (2009), AGB im internationalen Geschäftsverkehr, nr 57. Comp. for a separate standard for international trade M. Wolf, 'Auslegung und Inhaltskontrolle von AGB im internationalen kaufmännischen Verkehr', *ZHR* 1989, p. 312.

725 Bundesregierung, *Entwurf eines Gesetzes zur Modernisierung des Schuldrechts*, BT-Drucks. 14/6857, p. 17.

in this area[726] Arguments that German law poses barriers to the internal market should similarly be reconsidered insofar as it concerns business contracts.[727]

4.4.4. Conclusion on the development of the law on STCs through blanket clauses

Have actors taken into account the fact that other actors also develop private law, which may limit the extent to which blanket clauses contribute to the predictability, consistency, accessibility and responsiveness of law, and how has that affected these benchmarks?

CJEU case law makes clear that German courts are not exclusively competent to develop the law under article 307 BGB, which is however not clearly reflected in German decisions. Further, German courts have not adopted a clear, consistent course on the European model list.

The lack of direct problems gives the impression that even between interdependent actors, a lack of deliberation need not immediately lead to problems, as argued in the debate on multilevel governance. Yet the lack of problems can arguably be traced to the active approach of the legislator in the debate at the European level preceding harmonisation and its subsequent restraint in implementation. In some cases, the lack of interaction has more clearly undermined comprehensibility. Particularly, the restraint of German actors in international cases may be detrimental to some private parties in terms of predictability and accessibility, as well as responsiveness. Further, generally, the lack of interaction may eventually severely undermine the predictable, consistent, accessible and responsive development of the *acquis*.

Has the coexistence of actors developing overlapping blanket clauses led to benefits?

Responsiveness to the needs and preferences of international and foreign actors has not increased because of the coexistence of actors. The lack of clarity on the allocation of competences between European and national actors stands in the way of the development of a system of check and balances, in which European and national actors motivate one another to develop better law.

The coexistence of national actors may however be beneficial in terms of responsiveness. The close relation between article 307 BGB and more general contract law has however not resulted in legal irritants. Good faith was not a foreign concept to German law at all and article 3 Directive shows similarities with German law, possibly because of German criticism.[728] Thus, article 3 may be a legal transplant, which in turn has been transplanted into other legal systems. As a result, the transposition into German law did not necessitate any changes, but it can be doubted whether this is a good example of a legal transplant imposed by European law.

726 Differently M. Günes, T. Ackermann, 'Die Indizwirkung der §§308 und 309 BGB im unternehmerischen Geschäftsverkehr', *ZGS* 2010, p. 400, 402, with further references, who argue that the judicial control of clauses in business contracts makes it nearly impossible for the German legislator to present German law as an attractive product for international contract parties.

727 Also K.P. Berger, 'Für eine Reform des AGB-Rechts im Unternehmerverkehr', *NJW* 2010, p. 467.

728 See further below par. 4.5.3.

It does however stand in the way of regulatory competition and of further harmonisation. So far, regulatory competition has not motivated the legislator to improve the law, which has already of high quality. Additionally, although the European legislator[729] and the Dutch legislator[730] have benefited from German experiences, the German regime has not been built on comparative law or international law. The approach of the courts to the evaluation of clauses under article 307 BGB as well as international regimes confirms the national approach to European and international concepts. This may make it unlikely that European and international initiatives are considered as sources for learning.

4.5. Principles

European actors necessarily adopt a more instrumentalist approach to the development of European private law, which also entails a different approach to general ideas on justice. Accordingly, what principles have played a role in the development of German and European law on STCs, can different principles be discerned and has the extent to which national law develops on the basis of general principles been compromised? How has that affected the extent to which principles have contributed to the predictability, accessibility, consistency and responsiveness of the law on STCs? Alternatively, have principles served as a starting point for interaction and have they facilitated mutual learning?

This paragraph will in particular consider three principles that have played an important role in the development of the law on STCs:

1) Good faith
   The development of German law on STCs was based on article 242 BGB on good faith, and since the AGBG and its later inclusion in the BGB, good faith in article 307 BGB remains a central concept in the judicial evaluation of standard contract terms. At a European level, good faith has similarly been included.
2) Consumer protection
   The development of the AGBG was initiated against the background of a consumer protection policy, and Directive 93/13 similarly takes consumer protection as a starting point.
3) Freedom of contract and the *Richtigkeitsgewähr.*
   The *Richtigkeitsgewähr* will also be considered, as this principle is often referred to as underlying articles 305–310 BGB, which raises the question whether it converges with consumer protection underlying the Directive. At the European level, Directives, including Directive 93/13, have been considered in the light of freedom of contract.

Paragraph 4.5.1 will consider the development of German law on the basis of these principles, and paragraph 4.5.2 will consider the development of European law on the basis of consumer protection and good faith. Paragraph 4.5.3 will consider similarities in

729 See further above par. 4.3.2.1. and below par. 4.5.2.
730 See further below par. 5.3.

the development of the law on STCs by German and European actors and paragraph 4.5.4 will turn to divergences. Paragraph 4.5.5 will end with a conclusion.

4.5.1. *The development of the German law on STCs*

The development of the German law on STCs can be seen against the background of three principles: consumer protection, good faith, and the *Richtigkeitsgewähr.*

The AGBG was developed against the background of German consumer policies.[731] The AGBG aimed to provide more clarity for contract parties and especially consumers as case law provided insufficient predictability, which withheld consumers from challenging unfair STCs before the courts, while the limited effect of case law enabled practitioners to successfully enforce slightly different forms of clauses that had been prohibited.[732]

In the development of the law on STCs, the principle of good faith has played an important role. The Erster Teilbericht[733] stated that draft article 6 AGBG – eventually article 9 AGBG – would enable sufficient protection for consumers, without leaving gaps, and it would make the principles underlying the new regime clear. In particular, the draft held that a judicial evaluation of STCs was needed as the user of STCs usually drafted STCs to his own advantage, limiting the contractual freedom of his contract party to the choice to accept or decline the STCs. Good faith obliged the person drafting STCs to take into account the interests of his contract parties. Thus, parties may use STCs as long as a balance between contract parties' rights and obligations was effected. The principle of good faith, in addition, looks at the relation between parties in general, and does not limit itself to isolated facts and clauses. In addition, article 9 AGBG established a more accessible and consistent standard than had previously been established in case law based on article 242 BGB.[734]

Kötz[735] pointed to the necessity to establish a blanket clause that clearly indicated which principles underpinned the legislative measure, and added that although case law had developed on this basis, a legislative provision was desirable, as the standard in case law differed and accessibility decreased as the amount of case law using slightly different criteria as a starting point developed. Kötz does not expressly refer to good faith. Instead, he takes the *Richtigkeitsgewähr*, an important principle underpinning general contract

[731] Comp. Bericht der Bundesregierung zur Verbraucherpolitik, 18 October 1971, BT-Drucks. VI/2724 (reprinted in E. von Hippel, *Verbraucherschutz*, Tübingen: Mohr Siebeck 1986, p. 295.

[732] Arbeitsgruppe zur Verbesserung des Verbraucherschutzes gegenüber Allgemeine Geschäftsbedingungen, *Vorschlage zur Verbesserung des Schutzes der Verbraucher gegenuber Allgemeine Geschaftsbedingungen, Erster Teilbericht*, Referat für Presse und Öffentlichkeit: Bonn 1974, p. 18.

[733] Arbeitsgruppe zur Verbesserung des Verbraucherschutzes gegenüber Allgemeine Geschäftsbedingungen, *Vorschlage zur Verbesserung des Schutzes der Verbraucher gegenuber Allgemeine Geschaftsbedingungen, Erster Teilbericht*, Referat für Presse und Öffentlichkeit: Bonn 1974, p. 52.

[734] Arbeitsgruppe zur Verbesserung des Verbraucherschutzes gegenüber Allgemeine Geschäftsbedingungen, *Vorschlage zur Verbesserung des Schutzes der Verbraucher gegenuber Allgemeine Geschaftsbedingungen, Erster Teilbericht*, Referat für Presse und Öffentlichkeit: Bonn 1974.

[735] H. Kötz, Welche gesetzgeberischen Massnahmen empfehlen sich zum Schutze des Endverbrauchers gegenuber Allgemeine Geschaftsbedingungen und Formularvertragen: dargestellt an Beispielen aus dem Kaufs- und Werkvertrags- sowie dem Maklerrecht, Gutachten fur den 50. Deutschen Juristentag, München: Beck 1974, Volume I, A, p. 52-53.

law.[736] This principle underlines the importance of contract parties' bargaining for accepting the binding force of contracts.[737] In the use of STCs, the *Richtigkeitsgewähr* is absent – it is usually assumed that STCs have not been negotiated by parties. Accordingly, the development of the law on AGBG has also been based on the *Richtigkeitsgewähr.*[738] The use of STCs as a legal problem that gave one party too much opportunity to impose his own rules on weaker parties, and which led to a separate private order beside the law, had already been identified in 1933.[739] The importance of the *Richtigkeitsgewähr* and private autonomy is also visible in BGH case law.

In its 1956 decision in which the BGH[740] evaluated a clause in the STCs with the standard of article 242 BGB, it explicitly referred to scholarly work[741] establishing the problems arising from the use of STCs. Particularly the BGH considered the weak justification of STCs by private autonomy, although it did not explicitly refer to the idea of *Richtigkeitsgewähr.* In 1974, the BGH[742] emphasised as standing case law that parties using STCs, claiming the amount of contractual freedom allowed within the legislative framework to their own advantage, must take the interests of future contract parties into account.

Since these decisions, the development of the law on STCs and the need for a judicial evaluation of STCs but not of individual contracts, can be seen in the light of the *Richtigkeitsgewähr.*[743] Thus, academics have succeeded in providing a convincing explanation for the control over STCs that more generally underpins the BGB and is correlated to important legal principles such as self-determination ('*Selbstbestimmung*') und hetero-determination ('*Fremdbestimmung*'), the opposite of private autonomy, which develops if parties are bound by terms they have not been able to influence,[744] and that may serve to provide guidelines for the stable development of the law on STCs.

Notably, the principles of consumer protection, good faith and *Richtigkeitsgewahr* show considerable overlap; as *Richtigkeitsgewähr* is absent in cases where parties have not

736 W. Schmidt-Rimpler, 'Grundfragen einer Erneuerung des Vertragsrechts', *AcP* 1941, p. 156. This concept has, as such, not been studied in the Dutch legal order and also does not seem to have been studied in common law jurisdictions despite the emphasis on "contract as bargain". The concept may be more familiar in legal orders more influenced by the German legal order such as the Austrian legal order.

737 See further on this concept par. 7.5.1.1.

738 See for example F. Becker, 'Die Reichweite der AGB-Inhaltskontrolle im unternehmerischen Geschäftsverkehr', *JZ* 2010, p. 1098.

739 H. Großmann-Doerth, 'Selbstgeschaffenes Recht der Wirtschaft und staatliches Recht', reprinted in U. Blaurock, N. Goldschmidt, A. Hollerbach (eds.), *Das selbstgeschaffene Recht der Wirtschaft. Zum Gedenken an Hans Großmann-Doerth (1894–1944)*, Tübingen: Mohr Siebeck 2005, p. 77.

740 BGH 29 October 1956, *NJW* 1957, 17.

741 This included the prominent work of L. Raiser, *Das Recht der Allgemeinen Geschäftsbedingungen*, Hamburg: Hanseat. 1935, p. 277 et seq who subsequently disagreed with the *Richtigkeitsgewähr* defended by W. Schmidt-Rimpler, 'Grundfragen einer Erneuerung des Vertragsrechts', *AcP* 1941, p. 130, see L. Raiser, 'Vertragsfunktion und Vertragsfreiheit', in: E. von Caemmerer, E. Friesenhahn, R. Lange (eds.), *Hundert Jahre deutsches Rechtsleben, Festschrift zum hundertjährigen Bestehen des Deutschen Juristentages, I*, Karlsruhe: Muller 1960, p. 118.

742 BGH 27 November 1974, *NJW* 1975, 163.

743 Ulmer/Brandner/Hensen/AGB-Recht/Fuchs (2011) article 307 nr 3.

744 See further on this concept par. 7.1.

negotiated contractual terms, the general duty of good faith imposes on the user of STCs an obligation to take into account the reasonable interests and the legitimate expectations of his counterparty, in particular if that counterparty is in a weaker bargaining position.

However, the principle of *Richtigkeitsgewähr* and the principle of consumer protection do not necessarily coincide. Consumer protection emphasises that the capacity of one contract party as a consumer is a reason for judicial evaluation. However, this is not always the case. The capacity of one party as the consumer need not necessarily exclude the *Richtigkeitsgewähr*, for instance if legal professionals acting as consumers negotiate with small businesses.

This became clear in a case in which the BGH[745] held that a consumer who had negotiated on part of the STCs should prove that the STCs had been presented. This decision can be contrasted with the wording of article 3 par. 2 Directive 93/13, which stipulates that any seller or supplier who claims that a clause has been individually negotiated, should prove this claim. This article further provides that the circumstance that part of a contract has been individually negotiated, shall not exempt the STCs from judicial control whether 'an overall assessment of the contract indicates that it is nevertheless a pre-formulated standard contract'.

Thus, principles of consumer protection, but especially good faith and the *Richtigkeitsgewähr* continue to play an important role in the development of the law on STCs. This may stand in the way of regulatory competition and it raises the question whether harmonisation is likely to be successful. Possibly, success may depend on the convergence of principles underlying the Directive. If principles converge, this may also facilitate deliberation and mutual learning.

4.5.2. The development of the European law on the basis of principles?

Has Directive 93/13 similarly been developed on the basis of principles of consumer protection, good faith and the *Richtigkeitsgewähr*?

It is controversial whether the 1993 Directive has been developed on the basis of general ideas on justice, which may in turn provide a basis for the further development of the law. For the European legal order, the development of the law has been based on article 114 TFEU to advance the internal market as well as consumer protection. Micklitz[746] emphasises that the Union has not developed private law on the basis of general ideas on justice in the way national private law has been developed, but rather centred on market-building. Similarly, Joerges[747] finds that harmonisation is a rationalization process – it does not take

[745] BGH 15 April 2008, *BeckRS* 2008, 12098.

[746] H.-W. Micklitz, 'Monolistic ideology or pluralistic reality', in L. Niglia (ed.), *Pluralism and European private law*, Oxford: Hart 2013, p. 38–39.

[747] Ch. Joerges, 'The Europeanisation process of private law as a rationalization process and as a contest of disciplines – an analysis of the Directive on unfair terms in consumer contracts', *ERPL* 1995, p. 181–182.

place in the context of national traditions. Instead, harmonisation reflects a compromise between the aim to foster the internal market and Member States' regulatory policies.

Accordingly, rather than basing its initiatives on abstract ideas of fairness, the European legislator has intervened in areas that it considers important for the internal market. The internal market presupposes the freedom of contract,[748] as recognised by the CJEU has referring to article 16 EU Charter.[749] In the area of unfair terms, the CJEU[750] has however not referred to article 16 EU Charter but to article 38 Charter on consumer protection in interpreting the Directive.

Limitations to businesses' and consumers' freedom to agree on STCs have been defended in the light of market or economic failures[751] that can be remedied through information requirements.[752] At first sight, however, it is difficult to see Directive 93/13 in this light, as it does not impose an obligation upon professionals to inform consumers of their STCs. However, this obligation can be found in other Directives,[753] and the preamble to the Directive[754] does find that consumers should be given an opportunity to examine STCs, which should be drafted in plain, intelligible language, as reflected in article 5. Accordingly, further, article 4 par. 2 exempts the main terms from evaluation, but only insofar as they are clearly worded, and article 5 stipulates that if terms are not worded clearly, the interpretation most favourable to the consumer should prevail. The CJEU[755] has since stressed the importance of the principle of transparency, considering not only the clear wording of terms, but also the opportunity to study terms, in order to decide whether to enter into the contract, which is consistent with the reasonably circumspect consumer.

748 N. Reich, *General principles of EU civil law*, Antwerp: Intersentia p. 21–24.

749 CJEU 18 July 2013 (Alemo-Herron and Others v Parkwood Leisure Ltd), C-426/11, [2013] ECR, p. I-0.

750 CJEU 27 February 2014 (Pohotovosť s. r. o. v Miroslav Vašuta), C-470/12, [2014] ECR p. I-0, par. 52, CJEU 10 September 2014 (Kušionová v SMART Capital), C-34/13, [2014] ECR p. I-0, par. 47.

751 J. Basedow, 'Freedom of contract in the European Union', *ERPL* 2008, p. 904–905, 916.

752 CJEU 7 March 1990 (GB-INNO-BM v Confédération du commerce luxembourgeois), C-362/88,[1990] p. 667, par. 18 recognises information requirements as a primary method of consumer protection. Comp. CJEU 20 November 1972 (Rewe-Zentral AG v Bundesmonopolverwaltung für Branntwein), case 120/78 [1979] ECR p. 649, par. 13 which held that limitation of free movement is not justified as protection against unfair commercial practices if protection could sufficiently be guaranteed by information requirements.

753 See for example article 22 Directive 2006/123 on services, imposing information requirements on service providers. According to consideration 2 in the preamble, the Directive aims to give consumer more choice by increasing transparency and information. Likewise, article 4 par. 2 sub b Directive 90/314 on package travel stipulates that the tour operator should provide consumers with the standard terms applicable to the contract.

754 Consideration 20 in the preamble to Directive 93/13.

755 CJEU 23 April 2015 (Van Hove v CNP Assurances SA), C-96/14, [2015] ECR p. I-0, par. 40–41, with further references.

Alternatively, the protection of consumers is justified with reference to social justice,[756] the protection of weak parties.[757] The unequal bargaining position of parties can in addition be defended in the light of controlling *Fremdbestimmung*, the opposite of private autonomy, which arises if parties are bound by terms they have not been able to influence.[758] The Court[759] has emphasised that Directive 93/13 is based on the idea of the unequal bargaining position between consumers and professional sellers and suppliers, which may result in the consumer's agreement to pre-drafted clauses that he is not able to influence. The ineffectiveness of unfair terms restores the balance between contract parties, thus preventing that the stronger party imposes his terms on the weaker party. In this way, the development of Directive 93/13 can be seen in the light of promoting substantial freedom of contract.[760]

The emphasis on the unequal bargaining position between parties and the protection of consumer protection is in line with the development of Directive 93/13 against the background of development in the national laws on STCs as well as the calls for a development of a European consumer policy at the European level.[761] Accordingly, the preamble to the Directive refers to a consumer protection and information policy and notes that buyers should be protected against abuse of powers from sellers or suppliers, and the CJEU has referred to the principle of consumer protection in article 38 Charter.[762]

In the Directive, the principle of good faith is also clearly visible in article 3. Yet does a European principle exist or not, and if so, is it a principle confined to this particular Directive or is it a general principle that has been recognised, to a different extent, throughout the Union? Geelhoed[763] has argued that article 3 Directive need not be interpreted uniformly, but subsequent CJEU case law appears prepared to provide

756 Study Group on social justice in European contract law, 'Social justice in European contract law: A manifesto', *ELJ* 2004, p. 656, refers to a balance between 'private autonomy as expressed in the freedom of contract' and principles which respect other equally important demands for social solidarity, which prohibit individuals from taking advantage of superior economic strength or from ignoring the claims of justified reliance upon others'. O.O. Cherednychenko, *Fundamental rights, contract law and the protection of the weaker party: a comparative analysis of the constitutionalisation of contract Law, with emphasis on risky financial transactions*, München: Sellier 2007, links the protection of weak parties, which she contrasts to party autonomy and freedom of contract, to the constitutionalisation of contract law.

757 E.H. Hondius, 'The protection of the weak party in a harmonised European contract law', *JCP* 2004, p. 245.

758 See further on this concept par. 7.1.

759 CJEU 27 June 2000 (Océano Grupo Editorial SA v Murciano Quintero and Salvat Editores SA v Sánchez Alcón Prades and others), joined cases C-240–244/98 [2000] ECR p. I-4941, par. 25, CJEU 26 October 2006 (Mostaza Claro v Centro Móvil Milenium SL), C-168/05, [2006] ECR p. I-10421, par. 25, CJEU 9 November 2010 (VB Pénzügyi Lízing Zrt. v Schneider), C-137/08, [2010] ECR, p. I-10847, par. 46.

760 F. Cafaggi, 'Self-regulation in European contract law', *EJLS* 2007, 1 accordingly considers the harmonisation of especially mandatory contract law in the light of consumers' freedom of contract.

761 Comp. resolution 543 (1973) of the consultative assembly of the European council on a consumer protection charter. The OECD similarly promoted consumer protection, comp. its 1972 report on consumer policy in member countries.

762 CJEU 27 February 2014 (Pohotovosť s. r. o. v Miroslav Vašuta), C-470/12, [2014] ECR p. I-0, par. 52, CJEU 10 September 2014 (Kušionová v SMART Capital), C-34/13, [2014] ECR p. I-0, par. 47.

763 CJEU 1 April 2004 (Freiburger Kommunalbauten v Hofstetter), C- 237/02, [2004], ECR, p. I-3403, par. 30.

general guidelines for the interpretation of national law implementing article 3 Directive. Notably, article 3 Directive also refers to the balance of parties' rights and obligations.[764] The 1990 draft of the Directive was also influenced by German criticism.[765]

The recognition of freedom of contract, good faith, consumer protection and to some extent even *Fremdbestimmung*, does however not mean that these principles have played a similar role in the development of the Directive. This national emphasis on principles indicates that even if general principles do not underpin the *acquis* in the same way that general principles underpin national private law,[766] ideas on justice did prompt the inclusion of good faith in Directive 93/13. Though based on the predecessor of article 114 TFEU, the 1993 Directive addresses a topic at the heart of general contract law, and seeks to transpose general principles to the European level. Nevertheless, the CJEU has stressed the aim of the Directive, particularly consumer protection, rather than a general principles of good faith or *Richtigkeitsgewähr.*[767] Accordingly, Collins[768] considers the Directive in the light of enhancing consumer confidence, correcting market failures and social protection.

Alternatively, Micklitz[769] argues that the standard of 'fairness', Directive 93/13, in combination with the model list, has harmonised the conditions under which businesses have access to the market. The mutual recognition clause in article 1 par. 2 Directive can also be seen in this light.

764 Comp. H.-W. Micklitz, 'The concept of competitive contract law', *Penn State International Law Review* 2005, p. 583 who finds that the CJEU, in *Freiburger Kommunalbauten*, allocated the task to evaluate clauses to a fairness to national courts. If the CJEU nevertheless considers itself competent to provide guidelines for the interpretation of article 3,the CJEU has an even stronger role in "market clearance", under article 3 Directive 93/13, in accordance with Micklitz' conclusion.

765 H.E. Brandner, P. Ulmer, 'EG-Richtlinie über mißbräuchliche Klauseln in Verbraucherverträgen. Kritische Bemerkungen zum Vorschlag der EG-Kommission', *BB* 1991, p. 706.

766 Comp. H.-W. Micklitz, 'The concept of competitive contract law', *Penn State International Law Review* 2005, p. 554 notes that the European legislator 'cannot take over the "protective" outlook consumer law bears in national legal orders, although it often pretends to do so.'

767 CJEU 1 April 2004 (Freiburger Kommunalbauten v Hofstetter), C-237/02, [2004] ECR, p. I-3403, par. 19: the Court emphasised that '[a]rticle 3 of the Directive merely defines in a general way the factors that render unfair a contractual term that has not been individually negotiated', and did not refer to principles common to the Member States. See more recently also CJEU 26 April 2012 (Hatóság v Invitel),C-472/10, [2012] ECR, p. I-0.

768 H. Collins, 'The alchemy of deriving general principles of contract Law from European legislation: In search of the philosopher's stone', *ERCL* 2006, p. 217. Interestingly, Collins, at p. 219, argues that regulation targets the effects of a rule on the market – in accordance with the aim of the Directive – whereas private law concentrates on individual cases. In that light, it is interesting that whereas article 4 Directive prescribes the evaluation of clauses in accordance with individual circumstances, German law adopts a more objective approach to the evaluation of clauses, K. Baier, *Europaische Verbrauchervertrage und missbrauchliche Klauseln, die Umsetzung der Richtlinie 93/13/EWG uber missbrauchliche Klauseln in Verbrauchervertragen in Deutschland, Italien, England und Frankreich*, Kovač: Hamburg 2004, p. 86–87.

769 H.-W. Micklitz, 'The concept of competitive contract law', *Penn State International Law Review* 2005, p. 572. O. Gerstenberg, 'Private law and the new European constitutional settlement', *ELJ* 2004, p.785, interprets the decision in CJEU 27 June 2000 (Océano Grupo), C-244/98, [2002] ECR, p. I-4941, in the light of market citizens' economic rights.

Yet BGH case law[770] does not support the conclusion that the model list in the Annex to the Directive has contributed much to the predictable and consistent interpretation of article 307 BGB that implements article 3 Directive. Similarly, clauses in international consumer contracts have not been interpreted in a way that facilitates businesses' access to the German market.[771] Furthermore, the extent to which model lists contribute to accessibility is limited as clauses that do not fall within the scope of either national or European lists may still be unfair. Consequently, businesses in cross-border trade can hardly rely on these model lists to ensure that their clauses will be upheld throughout the Union. Likewise, Joerges[772] holds that the Directive is not in accordance with the European rationalization process that focusses on building the internal market. Unlike other measures, the Directive does not provide for clarifying ambiguous concepts in the Directive, which would facilitate market access. Further, the CJEU[773] has not interpreted article 1 par. 2 as widely as possible, instead allowing German courts to evaluate clauses that reflected legal provisions that were not applicable. The CJEU[774] has similarly refused to evaluate whether national procedural law was in accordance with Directive 93/13 under general principles underlying this Directive, finding that the EU legislator presumes that national legislators have struck a balance in national legislation, in accordance with article 1 par. 2 Directive.

Michaels[775] has analysed these different ideas as "rationalities": a juristic rationality, reflected in German law, in which the law is based on principles, and an instrumentalist rationality, in which the law serves as a means to an end. The principles underlying the Directive illustrate that these views coexist and that one view has not proven victorious, but rather interact. However, the juristic rationality, currently predominant at the national level, may not be beneficial for the effectiveness of the Directive.

Although German ideas on justice underpinning the AGBG have influenced German criticism that subsequently led to amendments of the 1990 draft Directive, they did not form a starting point for interaction between German or European actors, nor did these principles serve to establish common ground in the European debate. Nevertheless, the Directive may indirectly be based on abstract ideas of substantive freedom of contract, consumer protection, and good faith. The reasoning of the CJEU on the substantive freedom of contract shows some similarities with the *Richtigkeitsgewähr*, specifically with regard to the stronger party that imposes its terms on a weaker party.

770 BGH 13 January 2005, *NJW* 2005, 1125.

771 BGH 5 December 2006, *NJW* 2007, 997.

772 Ch. Joerges, 'The Europeanisation process of private law as a rationalization process and as a contest of disciplines – an analysis of the Directive on unfair terms in consumer contracts', *ERPL* 1995, p. 181–182.

773 CJEU 31 March 2013 (RWE Vertrieb AG v Verbraucherszentrale Nordrhein-Westphalen), C-92/11, [2013] ECR, p. I-0.

774 CJEU 30 April 2014 (Barclays Bank SA v Sara Sánchez García and Alejandro Chacón Barrera), C-280/13, par. 39–44.

775 R. Michaels, 'Of islands and the ocean', in: R. Brownsword et al. (eds.), *The foundations of European private law*, Oxford: Hart 2011, p. 142–143.

4.5.3. *Principles underlying the development of the law on STCs: similarities*

Various similarities with regard to the principles of good faith and consumer protection become visible in German law and the Directive.

1) Both the AGBG and the Directive have been developed against the background of consumer protection policies.

In the German legal order, this principle follows from the protection of contract parties that are in a weaker bargaining position than their counterparties that, in turn, may undermine the bargaining process. The Directive was similarly developed against the background of the development of a consumer protection policy. A common development on the law of STCs and, more generally, a common development of consumer protection, has been visible throughout the Union.[776]

2) Both the AGBG and the Directive consider the effect on trade.

The Directive expressly considers consumer protection in the context of the internal market, stating that divergences in consumer protection lead to unpredictability in cross-border contracts, and distortion of competition.[777] In the German legal order, the increasing role of STCs in national trade, their effectiveness in stipulating one's legal relations with a multitude of parties, and the need to ensure that contract parties would not inherently distrust STCs, played a role in the drafting of the AGBG.

3) Good faith plays a central role in evaluating parties' contractual rights and obligations.

It has been argued that the inclusion of good faith in articles 307 BGB and article 3 Directive is in line with a common principle of good faith underlying European private law.[778] If this is the case, does the interpretation of this principle depend upon the national interpretation of that principle? Brandner and Ulmer,[779] criticising the 1990 draft Directive, found that good faith provided sufficient guidance to decide which clauses were unfair, as it was clear that the Directive aimed for an overall assessment of the terms of the contract, especially with regard to the rights and obligations of the consumer and seller towards each other. It is, however, unclear in what way practitioners could derive guidance on the question when rights and obligations would be deemed to be sufficiently balanced. Possibly, this denotes the well-established interpretation of a principle that is assumed to be common to the Union and its Member States, the interpretation of which is further developed at a national level. This seems especially plausible considering that

776 Comp. the conclusion of A.G. Trstenjak of 29 October 2009 before Caja de Ahorros, case C-484/08, [2010] ECR, p. I-4785, par. 64.

777 Similarly B. Dauner-Lieb, C. Axer, 'Quo vadis AGB-Kontrolle im unternehmerischen Geschäftsverkehr?' *ZIP* 2010, p. 310.

778 Th. Pfeiffer, B. Schinkels, 'Schuldrechtsmodernisierung und AGB-Gesetz', in: H.-W. Micklitz et al. (eds.), *Schuldrechtsreform und Verbraucherschutz*, Baden Baden: Nomos 2001, p. 175–176.

779 See for example H.E. Brandner, P. Ulmer, 'EG-Richtlinie über mißbräuchliche Klauseln in Verbraucherverträgen. Kritische Bemerkungen zum Vorschlag der EG-Kommission', *BB* 1991, p. 706.

article 3 Directive was based on similar blanket clauses that had been developed throughout the Union.[780]

If article 3 Directive 93/13 may, accordingly, be interpreted in a decentralised manner, one may wonder whether article 3 would serve as a basis for the development of case law, similar to the way article 242 BGB has served as a basis for the development of German law on STCs. How can this possibility be reconciled with the aim of Directive 93/13 to harmonise national laws to advance the internal market?

4) Substantive freedom of contract

Both German and European law consider substantive rather than formal freedom of contract. In other words, limitations of parties' freedom to contract through mandatory law have been considered in the light of consumers' unequal bargaining position and the lack of freedom resulting from the inequality between consumers and professionals.

Notably, however, the existence of a common principle does not necessarily have to lead to unification. Instead, it may be a reason for the CJEU to leave discretion to national courts to assess the fairness of clauses in accordance with the general principle of good faith. This enables courts to evaluate clauses responsively as well as consistently with national law.

4.5.4. *Principles underlying the development of the law on STCs: divergences*

Some differences in principles underlying the development of the law on STCs by German and European actors also become apparent. Generally, the deduction of legal principles from the *acquis* is much more controversial than deduction of principles from national laws that may, moreover, lend itself more easily for generalisation than the *acquis* with its functional, fragmented approach.

In addition, EU law may develop inconsistently, even if common underlying principles have been recognised. In *Schulz v Technische Werke Schussental GmbH und Co. KG*,[781] the Court expressly recognised the inapplicability of Directive 93/13, and did not consider the principle of transparency as a reason to develop the law on information obligations coherently and consistently. Despite its previous decision in *RWE Vertrieb*,[782] where the Court decided that consumers had to be informed of their rights before the conclusion of the contract, in this later case, the Court ruled that consumers had to be informed with 'adequate notice, before that adjustment [of main terms] takes effect', stressing notions of consumer protection underlying Directive 2003/55, in connection with the liberalisation of the markets and a stable electricity and gas supply

[780] See further E. Von Hippel, 'Der Schutz des Verbrauchers vor unlauteren Allgemeinen Geschäftsbedingungen in den EG-Staaten', *RabelsZ* 1977, p. 244–245.

[781] CJEU 23 October 2014 (Schulz v Technische Werke Schussental GmbH und Co. KG and Egbringhoff v Stadtwerke Ahaus GmbH), joined cases C-359/11 and C-400/11, [2014] ECR p. I-0, par. 47–52.

[782] CJEU 21 March 2013 (RWE Vertrieb AG v Verbraucherzentrale Nordrhein-Westfalen eV), C-92/11, 2013] ECR p. I-0, par. 52.

1) It can be doubted whether a more general principle of the protection of weaker parties can be deduced from the Directive, to prompt and steer the development of EU contract law more generally.

This becomes especially clear in *Barclays v Sánchez García and Chacón Barrera*,[783] which concerned mortgage agreements, even though the national court had not considered the fairness of a particular clause in the contract. Instead, the national court asked whether national law was in accordance with Directive 93/13 and general principles of EU contract law on the balance between contract parties. The Court instead emphasised Directive 93/13 as a *lex specialis*, for cases in which the imbalance between contract parties becomes apparent. If that *lex specialis* expressly excludes a dispute from its scope, the Court, remarkably, held 'the underlying general principles are also inapplicable'. Possibly, this ruling can also be seen in the light of article 52 par. 5 EU Charter, which refer to principles in the context of implementing legislative acts, stressing the role of principles in the interpretation of those acts. The Explanation to the Charter similarly distinguishes between rights and principles, finding that principles 'become significant for the Courts only when such acts are interpreted or reviewed', and reiterating that principles do not give rise to direct claims for positive action from the EU or Member State.

More worryingly, it can be seen in the light of *Alemo-Herron*,[784] which emphasises freedom of contract at the expense of weaker parties. Weatherill[785] points out that this decision, which does not concern Directive 93/13 or the consumer protection *acquis* more generally, diverges radically from existing CJEU case law that emphasises the freedom of contract of weaker parties, and deserves to be forgotten.

In addition, Frey[786] points out that the aim of the Directive is not unequivocal as it also aims to further the internal market, and seeks to protect consumers because of their importance to the internal market, a view that has since frequently been returned in other Directives in the private law *acquis*.

2) The *Richtigkeitsgewähr* can probably not be deduced from the *acquis*.

Notwithstanding CJEU case law[787] on the substantive freedom of contract of consumers faced with unfair clauses, the Directive does not consider the use of STCs *as such* problematic, and

783 CJEU 30 April 2014 (Barclays v Sánchez García and Chacón Barrera), C-280/13, [2014] ECR, p. I-0, par. 44.

784 CJEU 18 July 2013 (Alemo-Herron and others v Parkwood Leisure Ltd), C-426/11, [2013] ECR, p. I-0.

785 S. Weatherill, 'Use and abuse of the EU Charter of Fundamental Rights: on the improper veneration of "freedom of contract"', *ERCL* 2014, p. 167.

786 K. Frey, 'Wie ändert sich das AGB-Gesetz?' *ZIP* 1993, p. 572.

787 CJEU 27 June 2000 (Océano Grupo Editorial SA v Murciano Quintero and Salvat Editores SA v Sánchez Alcón Prades and others), joined cases C-240–244/98 [2000] ECR p. I-4941, par. 25, CJEU 26 October 2006 (Mostaza Claro v Centro Móvil Milenium SL), C-168/05, [2006] ECR p. I-10421, par. 25, CJEU 6 October 2009 (Asturcom Telecomunicaciones SLv Rodríguez Nogueira), C-40/08, [2009] ECR p. I-9579, par. 29, CJEU 3 June 2010 (Caja de Ahorros), C-484/08, [2010] ECR, p. I-4785, par. 27, CJEU 9 November 2010 (VB Pénzügyi Lízing Zrt. v Schneider), C-137/08, [2010] ECR, p. I-10847, par. 46, CJEU 27 February 2014 (Pohotovost's r.o. v Vašuta), C-470/12, [2014] ECR p. I-0, par. 39, CJEU 30 April 2014 (Kásler and Rábai v OTP Jelzálogbank Zrt), C-26/13, [2014] ECR, p. I-0, par. 39, CJEU 10 September 2014 (Kušionová v SMART Capital, a.s) C-34/13, [2014] ECR p. I-0, par. 48, CJEU 15 January 2015 (Šiba v Devėnas), C-537/13, [2015]ECR p. I-0, par. 22–23 (specifically on contracts between clients and lawyers), CJEU 26 February 2015 (Matei v SC Volksbank România SA), C-143/13, [2015] ECR p. I-0, par. 51, CJEU 23 April 2015 (Van Hove v CNP Assurances SA), C-96/14, [2015] ECR p. I-0, par. 26.

neither does it stand in the way of the use of international model contracts. On the contrary, the EU has recognised the importance of STCs and sought to promote the use of EU-wide STCs. Although article 3 par. 1 limits itself to clauses that have not been individually negotiated, the Directive focuses on contracts between businesses and consumers and emphasises the unequal position of these parties, which may lead to unfair contract terms. Even if it is true that unfair contract terms may also be concluded between businesses, the reasoning in Directive 93/13 remains that businesses are in an equal position, and thus do not merit special protection if one contract party is faced with STCs to his detriment.

The different approach towards STCs can also be illustrated by the 1990 proposal for a Directive that aimed to protect consumers in all contracts, also with regard to the central terms of the contract. These suggestions met with widespread protest.[788] Accordingly, article 4 par. 2 Directive excepts the main contract terms from the judicial evaluation under the Directive, which seems in accordance with the idea of *Richtigkeitsgewähr*, under which these main terms will fall as they have typically been individually negotiated. However, in *Caja de Ahorros*, the CJEU[789] held that article 4 par. 2 did not limit the scope of the Directive, and Member States were accordingly free to provide stricter protection to consumers by extending judicial control to the main terms of the contract. A.G. Trstenjak[790] notes that it cannot be deduced from the legislative history of the Directive that the EU legislator wished to exempt these terms from judicial control, as the main terms of the contract may well be unfair if they have been negotiated by parties in an unequal position. Trstenjak does however refer to German literature[791] in explaining the limitation in article 4 par. 2 Directive in the light of both parties' freedom of contract as well as 'the interest of a functioning market based on competition in respect of price and efficiency'. Trstenjak construes the evaluation of standard terms as an exception to the freedom of contract. In contrast, it has been defended that the *Richtigkeitsgewähr* is not based on parties' wills, but the process of negotiation,[792] and Micklitz and Reich[793] convincingly point out that the protection developed in CJEU case law will help contribute to consumers' de facto autonomy.

Despite this emphasis on the free will of both parties, in *Kàsler*,[794] the Court rejected that individually negotiated terms should be considered the main terms of the contract excluded from judicial evaluation under article 4 par. 2: 'The fact that a term has been negotiated by the co-contracting parties, in the context of their contractual freedom and of market conditions, cannot constitute a criterion making it possible to assess whether that term falls within the 'main subject-matter of the contract' within the meaning of Article 4(2) of Directive 93/13.' Instead, the Court held that the Directive was not applicable to terms that are individually negotiated.

[788] See especially P. Hommelhoff, 'Zivilrecht unter dem Einfluß europäischer Rechtsangleichung', *AcP* 1992, p. 90–93.

[789] CJEU 3 June 2010 (Caja de Ahorros), C-484/08, [2010] ECR, p. I-4785, par. 42–44.

[790] Comp. the conclusion of A.G. Trstenjak before Caja de Ahorros of 29 October 2009, case C-484/08, [2010] ECR, p. I-4785, par. 65.

[791] Comp. particularly R. Damm, 'Europäisches Verbrauchersvertragsrecht und AGB-Recht', *JZ* 1994, p. 162, who considers that the subject of the draft Directive addresses central concerns of private law which justifies reflection on central principles including private autonomy, also at the European level.

[792] W. Schmidt-Rimpler, 'Grundfragen einer Erneuerung des Vertragsrechts', *AcP* 1941, p. 157, 170–172 as well as W. Schmidt-Rimpler, 'Zum Problem der Geschäftsgrundlage', in: R. Dietz (ed.), *Festschrift für Hans Carl Nipperdey zum 60. Geburtstag*, München: Beck 1955, p. 8.

[793] H.-W. Micklitz, N. Reich, 'The Court and the Sleeping Beauty: The revival of the unfair contract terms Directive', *CMLRev* 2014, p. 804.

[794] CJEU 30 April 2014 (Kásler and Káslerné Rábai v OTP Jelzálogbank Zrt), C-26/13, [2014] ECR p. I-0, par. 47–49.

Subsequently, in *Matei v SC Volksbank România SA*, the Court[795] emphasised that the main terms of the contract 'define the very essence of the contractual relationship', limited more particularly to the price in relation to the services or goods paid for, as there is no legal scale or criterion for such a review. Interestingly, the Court does not refer to freedom of contract in this respect. Instead, the Court referred to the aim of the Directive, and, notably, held that the main terms of the contract should not be interpreted by referring to article 3(g) Directive 2008/48 on consumer credit, which refers to the total cost of credit to the consumer. The Court particularly focussed on the extensive interpretation of article 3(g) Directive 208/48, in the light of transparency pursued by that Directive, and the narrow interpretation of article 4 par. 2 Directive 93/13, in the light of consumer protection. The latter narrow interpretation does not include terms that may influence the price a consumer pays focus on previous negotiations between parties, and terms that have been individually negotiated may not fall within this definition. Confusingly, however, in *Van Hove v CNP Assurances SA*,[796] the Court did refer to terms that were not individually negotiated.

The exclusion of STCs in accordance with national, EU or international law can similarly be interpreted differently. Whereas the exclusion of article 307 BGB can be explained in the light of legislators' consideration of the balance of interests of parties, the Directive is also concerned with promoting international trade, which may be a reason for a restrictive interpretation of these terms.[797] Particularly, terms that have been drafted on the basis of legislation may still fall within the scope of the Directive, even though these rules presumably reflect a fair balance of interests between parties. Possibly, this narrow interpretation limits the scope for exceptions, which in turn limits the chances for Member States to create exceptions for national traders that international or foreign actors are unfamiliar with, or to restrict transnational trade in some other way. However, in *RWE*,[798] the Court considered the limited scope of article 1 par. 2 Directive in the light of consumer protection, and the necessity to circumvent evaluation by reflecting provisions in contracts that were designed with specific parties and specific contracts in mind.

Moreover, the difference in views may also explain the difference in the interpretation of these clauses. The objective interpretation of STCs in the German legal order is in accordance with the scope of terms that will often transcend individual contracts. In contrast, the Directive focuses on individual circumstances at the time of the conclusion of the contract, as the focus is on the protection of one party that may have been subjected to unfair terms because of his weak bargaining position, whereas German case law does not take into account the weak position of the consumer in assessing the fairness of a clause.[799]

795 CJEU 26 February 2015 (Matei v SC Volksbank România SA), C-143/13, [2015] ECR p. I-0, par. 54–57.

796 CJEU 23 April 2015 (Van Hove v CNP Assurances SA), C-96/14, [2015] ECR p. I-0, par. 27. For insurance contracts, the Court considered on the one hand, the premium paid, and on the other hand, the risk assured, as the main terms of the contract, including terms that rule out the cases where a consumer will receive compensation in accordance with the insurance policy.

797 The emphasis on promoting international trade is also visible in the since withdrawn proposal for a CESL, COM (2011) 635 final. H. Schulte-Nölke, 'No market for lemons', *ERPL* 2015, p. 195, construes the test of fairness for clauses in business contracts (in addition to other motives) in the light of ensuring that both businesses and consumers do not have to analyse STCs before entering into a contract, which would be ineffective. This perspective, especially for STCs in consumer contracts, is however difficult to reconcile with the CJEU's emphasis on transparency.

798 CJEU 21 March 2013 (RWE Vertrieb AG v Verbraucherzentrale Nordrhein-Westfalen eV), C-92/11, [2013] ECR p. I-0, par. 28–30.

799 P. Hommelhoff, K.-U. Wiedenmann, 'Allgemeine Geschäftsbedinungen gegenüber Kaufleuten und unausgehandelte Klauseln in Verbraucherverträgen', *ZIP* 1993, p. 568.

Furthermore, the *Richtigkeitsgewähr* can be seen in correlation with ideas of private autonomy, also protected within the sphere of article 2 GG, and the idea that private parties, acting in their own interests, should not be able to impose their terms onto other private parties. Even if the idea of *Richtigkeitsgewähr* can be accepted at the European level – quod non – it has not been associated with article 16 Charter, nor does it have a similar connotation at a European level. Notably, the CJEU does not have a constitutional task to intervene to protect contract parties' general right to private autonomy, as also evidenced by the leeway it leaves to national courts, rather than deciding for itself that a term is unfair. The CJEU instead is competent to interpret EU law, and it may be doubted whether the value of the negotiating process is a leading concept in the development of the *acquis* or whether it is considered a useful concept that should be taken into account in the development of the internal market.

Thus, differences can be detected with regard to the possible deduction of general principles, but also with regard to ideas underpinning national private law and European law, most clearly with regard to consumer protection and the *Richtigkeitsgewähr*. However, these differences do not mean that the principles of the protection of weaker parties or the *Richtigkeitsgewähr* cannot provide starting points for debate. Moreover, as the *Richtigkeitsgewähr*, good faith and consumer protection partially overlap, the relevance of one principle need not mean that other principles may not play a role anymore in the development of the law.

4.5.5. Conclusion on principles underlying the law on STCs

The development of Directive 93/13 is not directly based on general principles, but because of the active approach of German actors, German ideas on justice have clearly influenced the Directive. Yet Directive 93/13 is not based on the *Richtigkeitsgewähr*, which may be especially problematic in cases where the *Richtigkeitsgewähr* and consumer protection do not indicate a similar outcome, and the level of protection in the Directive is undermined. Yet the principle of good faith is inextricably connected with *Richtigkeitsgewähr*, which arguably offers a convincing analysis for subjecting STCs to judicial evaluation more generally.

Even though courts have not interacted much with one another, problems for private parties have not directly developed. Thus, at first sight, it appears that a lack of interaction is not directly problematic, in contrast to multilevel governance insights.

Yet a clear approach of both the CJEU and of German courts would benefit predictability and accessibility, as foreign and international parties may not have much insight in these principles. However, even if courts develop a more consistent approach, this need not necessarily indicate in which direction the law will develop. The way in which good faith and consumer protection are weighed against one another and the rules developed on the basis of these principles may differ.

Further, it may be asked whether a future revision of the Directive will take place in accordance with an instrumentalist rationality that focusses on facilitating access to domestic markets throughout the Union. The suggestion of comitology to ensure the flexible development of binding European black and grey lists lends support to this possibility.

Have benefits developed, in accordance with pluralist arguments? In accordance with criticism of methodological nationalism,[800] the idea that the development of European law is based on principles, in a manner similar to national law, is visible in debate on the systematisation of European law.[801] The question whether a common European principle can be discovered upon which European law could further be developed has also been criticised.[802]

Opportunities for learning can be detected, even if general principles such as the *Richtigkeitsgewähr* cannot be deduced from the *acquis*, and even where European law restricts the development of rules. In these cases, general principles continue to provide a basis for the development of national law and they may still form starting points for debate. Currently, general principles have not served as starting points for debate. Good faith, in particular, can become a general principle that leaves room for national courts to evaluate clauses in a manner that is responsive to national legal views on justice, national practice and consistent with national law. The idea of *Richtigkeitsgewähr* could form a starting point for interaction. European and foreign legislators should seek to benefit from the well-developed ideas and the abundant amount of case law and research in the German legal order, without uncritically copying these ideas.

4.6. Conclusion on the development of the law on STCs through national techniques

The German law on STCs is generally considered a success story. An important part of the law on STCs has been developed through national techniques. Paragraph 4.6.1. will ask whether, in accordance with insights from multilevel governance, that means that actors have recognised that interdependence has developed and interacted accordingly? Paragraph 4.6.2. will ask whether benefits recognised by pluralists have become visible. Paragraph 4.6.3. will consider improving interaction and the absence of deliberation.

4.6.1. *The development of the law on STCs and insights from multilevel governance*

Generally, the ability of German actors to independently safeguard benchmarks of predictability, accessibility, consistency and responsiveness through the BGB and articles 307 and 242 BGB has been diminished as European actors also develop private law. In addition, European law may indicate more protection of consumers, even if they have negotiated clauses, which seems difficult to reconcile with the *Richtigkeitsgewähr*.

800 L. Miller, *The emergence of EU contract law: Exploring Europeanization*, Oxford: OUP 2011, p. 168.

801 Com. K. Riesenhuber, *System und Prinzipien des Europäischen Vertragsrechts*, Berlin: De Gruyter 2003, p. 2–3. Comp. H. Collins, 'The alchemy of deriving general principles of contract Law from European legislation: In search of the philosopher's stone', *ERCL* 2006, p. 219–220 who notes the differences between the regulatory perspective and the general contract law perspective. Obviously, this does not mean that general principles cannot be used in the development of European law; see N. Reich, *General principles of EU civil law*, Antwerp: Intersentia 2014, p. 12–13.

802 O. Gerstenberg, 'Private law and the new European constitutional settlement', *ELJ* 2004, p. 767.

Further, revised European law may stand in the way of developing stricter measures of consumer protection. National law may be a source of inspiration for European measures, which may diminish the extent to which national law has to be amended to implement European law. Yet once the law has been harmonised, the CJEU becomes competent and its case law may be difficult to predict, hard to reconcile with surrounding national law and driven by other Member States.

More generally, this case study has made clear that the extent to which the BGB can act as a filter for overenthusiastic European legislation is curtailed. So far, German actors have resisted the revision of Directive 93/13 in a manner that would be inconsistent with German law. Additionally, to ensure that the German law on STCs is in accordance with the needs of international trade, interaction between the German legislator and foreign legislators as well as non-state actors is necessary. Interaction between German courts, foreign courts, European actors and international actors is also necessary to ensure that international regimes develop consistently in different jurisdictions.

Collins[803] has stressed the dependence of European actors on national actors. National actors also develop harmonised law in accordance with their own legal traditions. The restraint of national courts, visible in decisions on international cases between business and consumers,[804] have also cut across the regulatory approach of the European legislator, as outlined by Micklitz.[805] There are exceptions to this resistance, for example when the OLG Oldenburg[806] apparently prompted the BGH to refer to the CJEU,[807] which allowed German courts to evaluate clauses if they did not in fact fall under legislation exempting clauses from such evaluation. Regulatory private law however implies a wider interpretation of clauses falling under article 1 par. 2 Directive 93/13.

The case study indicates that the aims of European actors and national actors do not converge. The national legislator and national courts have attempted to develop the law on STCs comprehensibly. From this perspective, it is beneficial if European law does not necessitate substantial amendments. Logically, no such focus can be detected at the European level. Similarly, the failed revision of the Directive clearly shows that the European legislator does not share the aims of the German legislator. Consequently, the interdependence between German and European actors is likely to become more rather than less visible.

803 H. Collins, 'Governance implications for the European Union of the changing character of private law', in: F. Cafaggi, H. Muir-Watt (eds.), *Making European private law: Governance implications*, Cheltenham: Elgar 2008, p. 272.

804 BGH 1 February 2005, *NJW* 2005, 1774, comp. also KG Berlin 12 December 2007, *BeckRS* 2009, 24853, BGH 5 December 2006, *NJW* 2007, 997, and OLG Frankfurt 1 November 2006, *BeckRS* 2007, 1589.

805 H.-W. Micklitz, 'Monistic ideology versus pluralistic reality', in: L. Niglia (ed.), *Pluralism and European private law*, Oxford: Hart 2013, p. 29, who, at p. 46, refers to German case law on litigation on gas prices, in which the BGH has eventually referred a question to the CJEU, see BGH 9 February 2011, *NJW* 2011, 1392.

806 OLG Oldenburg 14 December 2010, *BeckRS* 2011, 8627. This referral does not mean that the BGH will from now on consistently refer more actively to the CJEU. In the absence of further active referral to the CJEU, that assumption seems unlikely.

807 CJEU 31 March 2013 (RWE Vertrieb AG v Verbraucherzentrale Nordrhein-Westfalen), C-92/11, [2013] ECR, p. I-0.

In addition, in international cases decided under German law, courts have recognised the added value of international materials and business practices, and to a lesser extent, foreign decisions. This approach to international cases contributes to the responsiveness of German law to international practice, and it indicates that even actors in states where the law is developed within a "strict system" still take into account international and foreign perspectives.[808] The approach of the courts to international cases under German law enables the German legislator to maintain a predictable, consistent regime that is in accordance with national legal views on justice for national cases, but that is applied more leniently in international cases. Thus, in developing the law responsively in an international context, the dependence between the national legislator and the courts should not be overlooked.

Has a lack of interaction between interdependent actors led to problems, in accordance with insights from multilevel governance? Although German actors have not strategically recognised their decreased ability to safeguard the quality of the law, the legislator has developed an active approach to European initiatives. This active approach, combined with restraint in implementing the Directive, has ensured that Directive 93/13 is similar to German law. Thus, interaction has contributed to the consistent and predictable development of the law on STCs, and it has prevented that successful law that adequately handled national practice and was in accordance with national legal views on justice had to be adapted after harmonisation. This approach has been reinforced by the restraint of German state actors in the implementation and interpretation of the Directive. It is not clear whether the German legislator has similarly actively participated in the drafting of treaties that it has entered into and ratified, but it does not seem likely that the active approach has suddenly been abandoned. Nonetheless, German courts have adopted restraint in interacting with international and foreign actors in the interpretation of treaties. Reasons for this restraint may be the predictability and accessibility of the law. Moreover, the consistent referral to German materials has contributed to the consistent application of treaties within the German legal order.

As a result, notwithstanding the restraint of German actors, problems have not become directly apparent for private actors, in contrast with insights from multilevel governance.

Thus, the lack of interaction in the implementation and application of the *acquis* has maintained, rather than undermined, the quality of the law on STCs. However, in the long term, the lack of interaction means that relevant questions have been overlooked in the attempted reform of Directive 93/13 and will likely continue to be overlooked. Arguably, problems will develop in the following respects:

i) Predictability may be compromised as the implementation of Directives may take place in the BGB or in separate statutes, as became clear from the choices to develop the law on STCs through *Sonderprivatrecht* or through codification. The reasons for the development of *Sonderprivatrecht* offer interesting starting points for debate and a more predictable, consistent approach to the implementation of the *acquis* would be beneficial.

[808] Comp. somewhat differently T. Wilhelmsson, 'Private law in Europe: Harmonised or fragmented Europeanisation?', *ERPL* 2002, p. 93.

ii) Questions remain on the allocation of competences between the CJEU and national courts in the interpretation of blanket clauses. The restraint of the BGH is undermined as foreign courts increasingly refer questions to the CJEU. If the CJEU considers itself competent, this may not be only be problematic for predictability, but, if insufficient room is left to national courts, also for the responsiveness of the law on STCs.
iii) Questions remain on the obligation of national state actors to implement the model list in the Annex to Directive 93/13.

Similarly, more interaction could contribute to the quality of the law on STCs in an international context:

i) More referral to international and foreign materials in international cases under international regimes could increase the responsiveness and the accessibility of international regimes to the needs of international actors.
ii) The overlap between European measures or European measures and treaties could be clarified.
iii) The competence of German courts to set aside national mandatory law if it conflicts with international law could be made clearer.
iv) A clear choice for an optional instrument such as the withdrawn CESL should more clearly permit parties to include clauses in accordance with the optional instrument, even if clauses are contrary to national law, including consumer protection law. This would benefit predictability, and it may be in line with businesses' preferences. However, inconsistency may arise between other instruments that do allow judges to apply national mandatory law, such as the Directive. If national mandatory law reflects legal views on justice, such a choice would also undermine responsiveness to these views.

These oversights mainly undermine the consistent, predictable and responsive development of Directive 93/13 and the law on STCs in an international context. Missed chances to improve the Directive are unfortunate, as it makes little sense to maintain unpredictability and inconsistency.

The lack of interaction may eventually lead to a circle: because of the lack of interaction, the reform of the Directive overlooks questions that are relevant for improving the Directive, and because of these oversights, the Directive is not improved. Consequently, national actors continue to exercise restraint in the implementation and application of the Directive. And so on, and so forth.

4.6.2. The development of the law on STCs and pluralist insights

Has the coexistence of actors developing the law on STCs led to benefits, in accordance with pluralist insights?

Generally, the division of competences between the Union and its Member States have not been advantageous for the comprehensibility of the law of STCs. Also, contrary to arguments that in the U.S., federalism has helped ensure that actors at lower levels function effectively,[809] the existence of the European legislator and the CJEU has not

[809] D.C. Esty, D. Geradin, 'Regulatory co-opetition', *Journal of International Economic Law* 2000, p. 252, comp. N. Krisch, *Beyond constitutionalism: The pluralist structure of postnational law*, Oxford: OUP 2010, p. 85 et seq.

done so – although German law does not seem in immediate need for "checks". The lack of clarity on the division of competences between the CJEU and national courts may further stand in the way of the development of a system of checks and balances as the roles of actors in such a system is not clear, and not calculated to balance or compensate one another. BGH case law[810] also indicates that CJEU decisions establishing further competence for the CJEU has not been taken into account at a national level. The development of a system of checks and balances may also be undermined as it is not clear why the European decision-maker is better situated than the national legislator to deal with the evaluation of clauses in domestic disputes.

Harmonisation has also not increased the responsiveness of national law to the needs and preferences of transnational actors. On the one hand, the drafting of Directive 93/13 demonstrates that the European legislator was not prompted by the concerns of transnational actors with insufficient access to domestic markets, and the Directive has been substantially affected by German criticism. On the other hand, harmonisation has not prompted national actors to take more note of the needs and preferences of foreign and transnational actors. Foreign, European and international actors have not participated in debate on implementation at the national level, although they could have offered a valuable outsider's perspective, especially on the implementation of a future revised Directive. At the European level, the contributions of these actors were brief. Possibly, a revised Directive could more clearly adopt a regulatory approach. Especially a Directive pursuing full harmonisation, supported by a comitology committee, could theoretically facilitate access to the German market for foreign and international actors. Yet suggestions for comitology and full harmonisation have been clearly rejected by German actors. Similarly, German decisions under international regimes refer to German materials rather than easily available foreign materials. Yet in cases where no harmonisation has taken place, in the adjudication of international cases, German actors have taken into account foreign and international materials.

A close relationship exists between the law on STCs and German legal views on justice. Thus, the coexistence of a German regime, alongside other national regimes reflecting different views, should be beneficial to responsiveness. The relation between the law on STCs and legal views on justice may also stand in the way of further, full, harmonisation in a manner contrary to German law,[811] as visible in the failed attempt to reform the 1993 Directive.

Generally, the German legislator has also rejected regulatory competition. Possibly, the lack of regulatory competition may also be attributed to the close relationship between the law on STCs and German legal views on justice. The question arises, however, if German law is such a success story, why is it not more of a success story internationally? The private initiative and academic criticism gives the impression that the strict evaluation of clauses under German law has diminished the attractiveness of

810 See previously par. 4.4.1.2.

811 Comp. for example H. Collins, 'Governance implications for the European Union of the changing character of private law', in: F. Cafaggi, H. Muir-Watt (eds.), *Making European private law: Governance implications*, Cheltenham: Elgar 2008, p. 272 and more generally M. Delmas-Marty, *Ordering pluralism, A conceptual framework for understanding the transnational world*, Oxford: Hart 2009, p. 21.

German law. Possibly, the importance of German case law, which is not easily accessible to private parties, has not helped the attractiveness of German law. Yet that has not withheld the European legislator from adopting a regime largely in line with German law. The rejection of choice of law and the active approach towards harmonisation indicates that neither the German legislator nor the European legislator are convinced that, at least for consumer contracts, choice of law is superior to harmonisation.[812]

In some cases, opportunities for learning from other actors' experiences have been realised. The European legislator has relied on German law as a source of inspiration. The CJEU has considered that default law should play a role in assessing the fairness of clauses, as consumers' position under STCs should be compared to the legal position of a consumer under default law, in the absence of these clauses. Yet even though EU law is inspired by German law, it does not similarly meet benchmarks of predictability, consistency and responsiveness. Further, in the adjudication of international disputes under German law, German courts have contributed to the responsiveness and accessibility of the law by taking into account foreign and international materials.

In other cases, opportunities for mutual learning have not been realised. In accordance with criticism of methodological nationalism, German actors have adopted a national approach towards European law. It appears, therefore, that methodological nationalism can be detected not only with regard to methods, but more generally towards the content of Directives, which is interpreted in accordance with national law. This is visible in the *Schuldrechtsmodernisierung*, the implementation of the Directive, and in the drafting of 1993 Directive. As a result, German actors have largely, and successfully, focussed on maintaining the comprehensibility of German law. Even though German actors have recognised the value of comparative law research, German law is not based on such research.

The European legislator is not overly interested in further opportunities for learning, for example through minimum harmonisation. Minimum harmonisation, while harmonising the law, leaves room for mutual learning. However, the European legislator seems not interested in learning from the use national legislators have made from the possibility to protect consumers under article 8 Directive, even though, in the reasoning of the European legislator,[813] these experiences could be valuable to enhance consumer confidence. Instead, the European legislator seeks to leave no more room for national legislators and finds that minimum harmonisation is the cause for the fragmentation more widely visible in the private law *acquis*. It follows that, future review will likely target minimum harmonisation as a source of fragmentation rather than a source of inspiration.

Further opportunities for mutual learning should be realised. The BGH could take into account comparative law insights in evaluating clauses, especially if foreign actors consider clauses unfair. Further, studying the concept of the *Richtigkeitsgewähr* as a source for the binding force of contracts more generally would be interesting. Additionally,

812 See further for this argument E.A. O'Hara, L.E. Ribstein, *The law market*, Oxford: OUP 2009, p. 223.

813 Notably, preambles to Directives state that increasing consumer protection will help enhance consumer confidence, see for example consideration 8 in the preamble to Directive 2008/48 on consumer credit, or consideration 5 to Directive 99/44 on consumer sales.

national experiences in developing the law on STCs further should be a source of learning for the European legislator in revising Directive 93/13.

Opportunities for learning may simultaneously lessen the responsibility of European private law. Especially if lower courts frequently decide in accordance with foreign law or repeatedly refer questions to the CJEU, this may diminish the predictability and accessibility of decisions in relatively straightforward cases. Foreign decisions could also be in accordance with foreign default law, which may diverge from German default law, which may be detrimental for consistency and responsiveness to national legal views on justice. Further, referral to the CJEU is a lengthy process and CJEU decisions are not always easy to predict and usually are not attuned to surrounding national private laws.

It can be concluded that the coexistence of European and national actors has not increased responsiveness to the needs and preferences of foreign and international actors. The coexistence of regimes may be beneficial in terms of responsiveness, but the relation between the German law on STCs and German legal views on justice likely stand in the way of unification and regulatory competition. Opportunities for mutual learning have not consistently been realised and benefits could arise if more opportunities for mutual learning are created and realised. However, potential disadvantages of mutual learning may withhold actors from realising these opportunities. The benefits of regulatory competition and a system of checks and balances have not become apparent.

4.6.3. *Facilitating deliberation?*

Debate can be improved if the interaction between actors is adjusted, which may entail that more opportunities for learning are realised.

Interaction between actors should serve to improve the quality of the law on STCs. Thus, interaction should make European actors aware of national experiences with Directive 93/13. In turn, interaction should make German actors more aware of the use of techniques. More interaction between German, European and foreign actors, as well as academics should also draw more attention to the increasing number of Directives providing rules on STCs.[814] There should in addition be more attention for possible conflicts between simultaneously applicable sources – such as the CISG and national law implementing the Directive[815] as well as the Montréal Convention and Directive,[816] as well as the CISG, national law and Directive 2000/31.[817] This may prompt actors to consider how these sources should be coordinated, which may help to resolve current conflicts. Closer coordination, in turn, should contribute to the consistent and accessible development of European private law. If the legislator seeks to maintain the central role for the BGB, the question in what ways the legislator can best cope with the development of the *acquis* should be considered more carefully. Interaction between national, European and international state and non-state actors should make German actors more

814 See previously par. 3.2.

815 Especially LG Düsseldorf 11 October 1995, 2 O 506/94, at www.unilex.info/case.cfm?id=234.

816 Comp. BGH 1 February 2005, *NJW* 2005, 1774.

817 Comp. LG Gießen 31 July 2008, *BeckRS* 2009, 395.

aware of the possibility to make the German legal order a more attractive forum for the adjudication of disputes under international law, not necessarily by amending the law, but for example by making case law more accessible.

These possible starting points for improving the comprehensibility of European private law may well reinforce one another. Future CJEU decisions on the cases in which the Montréal Convention and the Directive overlap should be considered in the future reform of the Directive, which in turn may provide useful insights for the development of a future initiatives.

However, more interaction need not necessarily lead to deliberation if the approach of German and European actors does not change. European and national actors clearly pursue different aims, and actors have not aligned their preferences.

National state actors very clearly prioritise safeguarding the predictability, accessibility, consistency and responsiveness of the law on STCs, despite the development of harmonisation and cross-border trade, which should be taken into account by criticism of "state-centric" accounts of the law.[818] Because of the problems in the quality of the private law *acquis*, and because of the well-established, successful AGBG, as later integrated in the BGB, national state actors may be even more inclined to take a defensive approach in which they limit interaction with other actors, especially if that might undermine the quality of the law on STCs. In contrast, European decision-makers seem focussed on furthering harmonisation. Interestingly, EU decision-makers appear to circumvent debate – for example, the terminology used for the "Draft Common Frame of Reference", or the proposal for the "Common European Sales Law", which is an optional instrument rather than an optional code of sales contract law, and possibly a blueprint for further harmonisation in this area.

If national actors are mainly focused on national laws, and European actors are not focused on national laws, they pay less attention or even neglect the insights provided by comparative law as well as the European view, which may stand in the way of deliberation in the revision of Directive 93/13. The revision of the *acquis*, in accordance with benchmarks of predictability, consistency, accessibility and responsiveness, has not served as a common aim that facilitates interaction.

Therefore, a change of perspective at both the national and European level is desirable: national actors could and should take into account the interests of foreign parties in drafting national law.[819] This has as an added benefit that foreign and international parties can offer a critical perspective on the obligation to implement Directives and they can inform legislators and courts of international business practices. In turn, the European legislator should pay more attention to the close relation between the law on STCs and national law. This could and should prompt the European legislator to reconsider the idea that maximum harmonisation is possible, or desirable, as the law is

818 Yet the role of state actors may change over time, and a less prominent role of state actors may be justified if state actors become less capable of safeguarding predictability, consistency, accessibility and responsiveness.

819 Ch. Joerges, 'On the legitimacy of Europeanising private law: Considerations on a justice-making law for the EU multi-level system', *Electronic Journal of Comparative Law* 2003, par. III.1.2., available at www.ejcl.org/ejcl/73/art73-3.html.

closely intertwined with and should reflect national legal views on justice and national practices.[820] Possibly, as the role of non-state actors increases, a more prominent role for non-state actors in debate may be indicated. Conversely, a less prominent role of state actors may be justified if state actors become less capable of safeguarding predictability, consistency, accessibility and responsiveness.

Importantly, if a future reform of the 1993 Directive were to take place in accordance with these suggestions, the legislative process might have to be considerably lengthened. Processes at the European and the national level should be carefully coordinated to prevent unnecessary delays. Arguably, some delay is preferable over future problems that may arise if a future Directive does not sufficiently take into account the needs and preferences of legal practice or national legal views on justice. Such oversights may entail that the law will be more quickly outdated, necessitating further reform, which is arguably also detrimental to the stable and consistent development of the law.

4.7. The use of additional or alternative techniques

Actors have typically not recognised interdependence as such, and have, therefore, not consciously sought to mitigate the decreased extent to which national techniques may ensure the comprehensibility of law through the use of additional or alternative techniques. Usually, techniques are used in combination with one another, and additional and alternative techniques may well contribute to benchmarks of predictability, consistency, accessibility and responsiveness. These techniques could also be valuable in improving debate, in accordance with the ideal of deliberation. In turn, this could enhance the law on STCs. Therefore, this paragraph will ask what techniques could be used in addition to, or instead of currently used techniques.

This paragraph will consider the use of techniques especially at the European level. Notably, at the national level, some room for experimentation may exist, but the main parts of the law on STCs will continue to be developed through national techniques. Thus, while European private law should not be developed following this national blueprint, as also argued by Miller,[821] national techniques will continue to play an important part in the development of European private law.

The narrow approach of both German and European state actors also increases the chance that actors will reject suggestions for the use of additional or alternative techniques that is not in accordance with their interests. Therefore, techniques will only be considered insofar as they are not likely to be rejected outright.[822] Accordingly, this chapter will not consider suggestions for the use of Regulations, which would likely meet with resistance from national actors that wish to retain the central role of the BGB. Additionally, the use of the OMC may not be considered favourably by German actors if

820 H. Collins, 'European private law and the cultural identity of states', *ERPL* 1995, p. 356.

821 L. Miller, *The emergence of EU contract law: Exploring Europeanization*, Oxford: OUP 2011, p. 166–167.

822 The strengths and weaknesses of additional and alternative techniques more generally will be considered in chapter 10.

it aims to improve regulatory competition in this area.[823] The success of the OMC depends on the willingness of actors to participate in it, which should not be assumed, while the weaknesses of the OMC may reinforce the shortcomings apparent in the debate on the reform of the *acquis*, including Directive 93/13. Other techniques that are likely to be rejected include the use of techniques that may lead to hetero-determination, or *Fremdbestimmung*,[824] especially comitology, which has already been rejected by German actors.[825] The development of Guidance by the European Commission can similarly be rejected although this does not stop European actors from exploring the possibilities. It is however highly unlikely to be considered by national courts. Although the use of alternative regulation for the interpretation of blanket clauses may be problematic as it might lead to *Fremdbestimmung*, this possibility will, nevertheless, be considered. Courts have recognised the added value of alternative regulation that may reflect business practices,[826] as has also become visible in international cases[827] as well as domestic cases.[828] Taking into account well-established self-regulation – which is abundantly available in the German legal order[829] – will contribute to the responsiveness of German law to national practices. German actors may also not be very receptive to suggestions for the study of STCs to identify barriers to the internal market, as this may reinforce the functional, fragmented approach of the *acquis*, which makes it considerably more difficult to maintain the predictable, consistent and accessible development of private law within the BGB. However, these initiatives may also serve to make the law more accessible to foreign actors. As German law has provided a successful set of rules, making German law more available may well be a way to increase the attractiveness of German law. Further, if the study leads to harmonisation, albeit fragmented, this may lead to more convincing initiatives and support for harmonisation and improve the quality of the *acquis*.

Conversely, European actors are also likely to reject some suggestions. Particularly, European actors are likely to object to the use of techniques inspired by in the U.S. legal order, instead of currently used European measures, such as model laws. Additionally, it is unlikely that model laws will contribute to the comprehensibility of the law on STCs as UNCITRAL has not established model laws or legislative guides for the laws on STCs. It can be doubted whether a model law could be developed sufficiently quickly to be taken into account in the reform of Directive 93/13. However, this chapter will discuss the potential added value of the DCFR that has been characterised as a Restatrment.

823 This is for example the case in company law, see further par. 10.5. The use of the OMC in European private law may also, more generally, entail that the Union encourages Member States to coordinate their policies, in the interest of the internal market or the freedoms established in the Treaties.

824 *Fremdbestimmung* is the opposite of private autonomy and it arises if one is bound by rules one has not been able to influence. See further on this concept par. 7.1.

825 Comitology entails that the European legislator, under articles 290 et seq TFEU, delegates further decisions on technical matters to expert committees. It will be discussed in more detail in par. 5.7.3.1. as Dutch actors have not rejected this option.

826 BVerfG 9. 5. 1972, *NJW* 1972, 1504, C 2.

827 See further previously par. 4.5.3.1.4.

828 In particular in the area of insolvency administration, see further below par. 7.5.2.3.

829 Especially in the area of consumer sales law, see further below par. 7.5.3.4.

Some suggestions that may meet with objections will nevertheless be discussed. The development of collective bargaining between a limited number of Member States is likely to meet with European objections, as this may lead to a two-tier Europe. In addition, the success of collective bargaining depends on the willingness of actors to participate, and this willingness should not be overestimated. However, German actors have considerable experience in collective bargaining and parties may be interested to engage in it if this would motivate the judiciary to evaluate STCs less strictly. Moreover, the chances that a two-tier Europe is created may decrease as agreements are limited.

This paragraph will start by considering the least disruptive additional techniques and end with techniques that may be more disruptive, if they are adopted.[830] Accordingly, paragraph 4.7.1. will consider additional techniques that are typically used to support the legislative process. Paragraph 4.7.2. will focus on the development of the DCFR and paragraph 4.7.3. will turn to techniques in addition to blanket clauses to support predictability, consistency and responsiveness. Subsequently, the paragraph will turn to alternative techniques. Paragraph 4.7.4 will consider whether studying the use of STCs in cross-border trade will enhance the comprehensibility of the law on STCs. Paragraph 4.7.5 will consider the development of optional regimes, paragraph 4.7.6 will turn to the introduction of collective bargaining and paragraph 4.7.7 will end with a conclusion.

4.7.1. Techniques to support the legislative process

Typically, debate in the legislative process is generated and facilitated through consultations.[831] At the European level, the use of impact assessments has also been recognised as an important way to improve decision-making.[832] Databases strengthen debate by providing actors with (more) opportunities to inform themselves. Networks can improve the inclusiveness of debate by helping to identify representative or expert actors. However, the extent to which these additional techniques are used to support the legislative process could strengthen interaction in the revision of the 1993 Directive is limited.

Impact assessments at the national level could draw more attention to the use of techniques and provide a valuable impetus for reconsidering the use of techniques. Respondents may also be prompted to consider impact assessments if comments based on the impacts of future initiatives are likely to be taken into account. However, German actors are not familiar with impact assessments for private law. Moreover, impact assessments presuppose that a (proposed) measure pursues a policy aim. The debate on the question whether articles 305–310 BGB that implement Directive 93/13 constitute

830 This order will also be adopted paragraph 5.7. and in chapter 10. The distinction between additional and alternative techniques is not meant as a sharp distinction.

831 COM (2002) 704.

832 COM (2012) 746 final, p. 5. The added value of impact assessments have also been recognised at the national level, for example in the UK legal order, see https://www.gov.uk/government/collections/impact-assessments-guidance-for-government-departments. Impact assessments for private law in the German or Dutch legal order are however not commonly used.

general or special private law, shows that the idea that these provisions aim to improve the internal market and consumer protection may be controversial.

Even though German actors have not representatively participated in consultations at the European level, this has not inhibited German actors from successfully participating in debate. Instead, publications in journals and newspapers have prompted participation. However, participation of actors at the European level could still be improved. European or national actors should make more use of well-established networks, targeting parties with valuable expertise and experience and encourage them to participate, or participate more extensively, in European debate.

It is not likely that actors will increasingly refer to databases on foreign law implementing Directive 93/13. Currently, courts do not refer to foreign materials in the implementation of the *acquis*. Foreign decisions are likewise not taken into account in the adjudication of disputes under international regimes, and are hardly used despite the existence of easily accessible databases. Perhaps, however, if German actors are more aware that this restraint may inhibit the attractiveness of Germany as a forum to adjudicate disputes, this restraint might be reconsidered. However, even if the added value of foreign decisions is more consistently recognised, restraint may continue to be exercised because of the abundant amount of domestic materials and because of potential problems with predictability, accessibility, consistency and responsiveness.

Interestingly, however, the improved use of databases may encourage mutual learning. Possibly, the increased accessibility of German case law could increase knowledge of German practice and provide an insight into a well-developed legal system that could inspire foreign legislators and judges, who do not, apparently, realise that recent BGH case law is already freely accessible.[833] For example, Dutch judges, in decisions under the CISG, have consistently referred to one decision from the BGH, while surely, there are also other relevant decisions.[834] Thus, merely making available case law may not suffice, as case law may prove less accessible than legislative provisions or commentaries. Perhaps, the accessibility of databases for oreign actors can be enhanced. For example, BGH decisions on the CISG, or BGH decisions on article 307 BGB could be made available in groups, accompanied, perhaps, by a short introduction. Importantly, foreign and European actors should be sufficiently aware of these initiatives in order to benefit from them.

Thus, the improved use of consultations and impact assessments may strengthen the legislative process. Particularly, targeting representative parties may be helpful. More attention for impact assessment would however require a less narrow view at the national level. The use of accessible databases may facilitate mutual learning.

833 See http://juris.bundesgerichtshof.de/cgi-bin/rechtsprechung/list.py?Gericht=bgh&Art=en&sid=ce31dc208856bd2b345fbc3471f1e593.

834 See par. 5.3.4.2.2.

4.7.2. The development of the DCFR

Currently, the DCFR does not sufficiently take into account parts of the *acquis* and national experiences, which may limit the extent to which the DCFR will contribute to the predictability, consistency, accessibility and responsiveness of the law on STCs. The DCFR does provide a clear added value to the PECL and the UNIDROIT Principles.

Paragraph 4.7.2.1 will consider the DCFR and the private law *acquis*, and paragraph 4.7.2.2 will discuss the DCFR and national practice. Paragraph 4.7.2.3 will turn to other sets of soft laws and paragraph 4.7.2.4 will end with a conclusion.

4.7.2.1. The DCFR and the private law *acquis*

The drafters of the DCFR have diverged from relevant European initiatives without sufficient explanation. In particular, drafters have diverged from Directive 93/13, which has undermined the extent to which the DCFR can contribute to predictability, consistency, accessibility and responsiveness in the form of a toolbox.

In some cases, the rules in the DCFR expressly take into account the *acquis*. Accordingly, article II – 9:102 et seq DCFR provides rules for pre-contractual statements that can be regarded as a contract term, in accordance with CJEU case law.[835] The DCFR expressly refers to various national laws as well as Directive 1999/44 on consumer sales as well as article 434 BGB. The rule in the DCFR is, in an amended form, mirrored in article 69 of the since withdrawn CESL.

However, the DCFR also diverges from the *acquis* in various respects:

i) The definition of STCs differs from the definition in Directive 93/13. Proposed article 30 of the consumer rights Directive did not follow the definition of the DCFR, but the CESL does reflect the definition of the DCFR.

The PECL, the UNIDROIT Principles and the DCFR similarly provide rules on general contract law and STCs. Interestingly, both articles II – 1:109 DCFR and 2.1.19 UNIDROIT Principles refer to standard terms as terms that are prepared in advance for repeated use and that are not individually negotiated with other parties. Interestingly, the DCFR expressly refers to Directive 93/13, but does not refer to German law.[836] The DCFR, moreover, diverges from 2:209 par. 3 PECL that refers to terms that have not been individually negotiated and that have been formulated in advance for an indefinite number of contracts, which it rightly considers as too strict.[837]

In addition, Directive 93/13 does not require that terms have been drafted for multiple contracts, and the German legislator, accordingly, amended article 310 par. 3 BGB to ensure that STCs that were only used once in consumer contracts would also be subject to judicial evaluation.[838] Interestingly, article 30 of the proposal for a Directive on consumer rights referred to terms

835 CJEU 26 April 2012 (Hatóság v Invitel Távközlési Zrt), C-472/10, [2012] ECR p. I-0, par. 37.

836 Ch. Von Bar et al (eds.), *Principles, Definitions and Model Rules of European Private Law. Draft Common Frame of Reference, Outline Edition*, Volume I, München: Sellier 2009, p. 164.

837 Ch. Von Bar et al (eds), *Principles, Definitions and Model Rules of European Private Law. Draft Common Frame of Reference, Outline Edition*, Volume I, München: Sellier 2009, p. 160.

838 MuchKomm/Basedow (2012), article 310, nr 67.

'drafted in advance by the trader or a third party, which the consumer agreed to without having the possibility of influencing their content'. Although this definition does emphasise drafting terms in advance, it also does not require that terms are drafted for multiple contracts. Yet article 2 sub d of the since withdrawn Regulation for a CESL defines STCs as 'contract terms which have been drafted in advance for several transactions involving different parties, and which have not been individually negotiated by the parties within the meaning of Article 7 of the Common European Sales Law'. Accordingly, article 7 of the proposed CESL also provided that contract terms are not individually negotiated 'if it has been supplied by one party and the other party has not been able to influence its content'.

The DCFR does not expressly exempt the main terms of the contract from the definition of standard contract terms. The debate preceding Directive 2011/83, however, shows that this distinction is important for German actors.[839] Unfortunately, article 7 of the proposed Regulation also does not make this distinction.

ii) The test of unfairness in the DCFR differs from Directive 93/13.

Article II – 9: 403 DCFR stipulates that a clause in a consumer contract is unfair if it significantly disadvantages the consumer, contrary to good faith. According to the comments,[840] this wording implies that the test should not be extended to the main contract terms, which, however, could have been remedied by exempting the main terms of the contract from judicial evaluation. It is, moreover, not necessary, as article II – 9: 406 par. 2 DCFR provides that the main terms of the contract are exempt from the unfairness test. A similar exception would also have been desirable for article 9:405 that defines unfair terms in business contracts, which, as such, is controversial enough as it is. Accordingly, article 83 of the withdrawn CESL does not provide for a similarly strict unfairness test.

Simultaneously, however, the unfairness test is in accordance with later CJEU decisions,[841] insofar as article II-9:407 DCFR refers to the real opportunity of the consumer to become acquainted with the terms of the contract.

The differences between the DCFR and the *acquis* may stand in the way of the potential use of the DCFR as a toolbox, as the differences between the DCFR and the *acquis* may lead to confusion.[842]

Further, the suitability of the DCFR is compromised as it does not resolve inconsistencies visible in the private law *acquis*. For example, article II – 9: 103 DCFR stipulates that parties must have taken reasonable steps to make the other party aware of the provisions, and if a contract is concluded electronically, STCs made available in textual form, which, according to the comments, includes the 'presentation of terms on

839 See previously par. 4.3.2.4.

840 Ch. Von Bar et al (eds), *Principles, Definitions and Model Rules of European Private Law. Draft Common Frame of Reference, Outline Edition*, Volume I, München: Sellier 2009, p. 634–635.

841 CJEU 26 April 2012 (Hatóság v Invitel Távközlési Zrt), C-472/10, [2012] ECR p. I-0, par. 28, CJEU 30 April 2014 (Kásler and Káslerné Rábai v OTP Jelzálogbank Zrt), C-26/13, [204] ECR p. I-0, par. 73–74, CJEU 26 February 2015 (Matei v SC Volksbank România SA), C-143/13, [2015] ECR p. I-0, par. 74–75.

842 Comp. R. Michaels, 'Privatautonomie und Privatkodifikation', *RabelsZ* 1998, p. 622, who observes that even if soft law exactly describes existing law, it need not induce private parties to adopt it as a model law.

an internet site in such a way that they can be downloaded, stored and printed by the other party'. This rule is in accordance with CJEU case law[843] stressing the importance of transparency, particularly the opportunity for consumers to become aware of the terms and conditions under which he is to contract with the trader. Article 10 par. 3 Directive 2000/31, to which the DCFR accordingly refers, as well as article 23 Regulation Brussels I, more clearly set out the strict requirements for the inclusion of jurisdiction clauses.[844] Unfortunately, however, the DCFR does not consider article 22 par. 1 sub f and par. 2 Directive 2006/123 that, in contrast, stipulates that STCs may be provided in various ways, depending on the preference of the provider.[845]

Similarly, the DCFR could have been of use in the distinction between "individually negotiated terms", the main terms, STCs and terms that are characteristics of the contract. Like the Directive, article II-9:406 par. 2 DCFR exempts main terms from evaluation in article II-9:403 and 404 DCFR, without however holding that the main terms are also necessarily individually negotiated. The comments to the DCFR[846] make clear that main terms have been excepted because 'such control would require an application of legal criteria which do not exist', and that the main terms of the contract are the obligations that are characteristic of the contract.

The Court[847] has referred to terms that have not been individually negotiated. The Court has made clear that if terms are individually negotiated, they do not fall within the scope of the Directive. It is not clear when terms have been individually negotiated, but neither the Court nor A.G. Wahl refer to the to the DCFR that appears to set a relatively high standard in their reasoning,[848] in accordance with article 3 par. 2 Directive.[849] Previously, A.G. Trstenjak,[850] who has shown a clear interest the DCFR, had also not

843 CJEU 26 April 2012 (Hatóság v Invitel Távközlési Zrt), C-472/10, [2012] ECR p. I-0, par. 28, CJEU 30 April 2014 (Kásler and Káslerné Rábai v OTP Jelzálogbank Zrt), C-26/13, [204] ECR p. I-0, par. 73–74, CJEU 26 February 2015 (Matei v SC Volksbank România SA), C-143/13, [2015] ECR p. I-0, par. 74–75.

844 However, the comments and notes to article II – 9:409, Ch. Von Bar et al (eds.), *Principles, Definitions and Model Rules of European Private Law. Draft Common Frame of Reference, Outline Edition*, Volume I, München: Sellier 2009, p. 660–661 do expressly consider CJEU decisions.

845 These ways include the possibility for the provider to provide the information on his own initiative, making the information easily available in places where the contract is concluded, by making the text of the STCs easily available online, or by including the STCs in general information documents provided by the seller.

846 Ch. Von Bar et al (eds.), *Principles, Definitions and Model Rules of European Private Law. Draft Common Frame of Reference, Full edition* 2008, available at http://ec.europa.eu/justice/contract/files/european-private-law_en.pdf, p. 675–676.

847 CJEU 23 April 2015 (Van Hove v CNP Assurances SA), C-96/14, [2015] ECR p. I-0, par. 27, as well as CJEU 3 June 2010 (Caja de Ahorros y Monte de Piedad de Madrid v Asociación de Usuarios de Servicios Bancarios (Ausbanc)), C-484/08, [2010] ECR p. I-4824, par. 34 where the Court seems to consider individually negotiated terms as the main terms, which has since however been addressed in CJEU 30 April 2014 (Kásler and Káslerné Rábai v OTP Jelzálogbank Zrt), C-26/13 [2014] ERCR p. I-0.

848 Comp. CJEU 30 April 2014 (Kásler and Káslerné Rábai v OTP Jelzálogbank Zrt), C-26/13, par. 47, which merely refers to parties' negotiations in the context of freedom of contract and market conditions.

849 CJEU 30 April 2014 (Sebestyén v Zsolt Csaba Kővári and Others), C-342/13, [2014] ECR p. I-0, par. 24.

850 V. Trstenjak, 'Die Auslegung privatrechtlicher Richtlinien durch den EuGH: Ein Rechtsprechungsbericht under Berücksichtigung des Common Frame of Reference', *ZEuP* 2007, p. 145.

considered the DCFR in her opinion before *Caja de Ahorros*,[851] that was followed by the Court. In *Kásler and Káslerné Rábai v OTP Jelzálogbank Zrt*[852] refers to the lack of legal standards.

The standard in both the DCFR and the CJEU's decision are in accordance with article 4 par. 2 Rome I, that refers to the 'characteristic performance of the contract' although this provision does not concern the law applicable to consumer contracts. Notably, article 4 par. 2 does not provide a clearly defined concept and it does not aim to protect consumers. Rather it aims to find a starting point for determining the applicable law by considering which one of the parties performs the obligation characteristic of the contract, for example the characteristics of specific consumer contracts that sets them apart from other sorts of consumer contracts. The main terms of the contract may therefore be interpreted differently, and less narrowly, than article 4 par. 2. This abstract standard may not be easy to reconcile with the subjective test prescribed in article 3 Directive 93/13, and it may entail that the non-monetary obligation is considered as the characteristic obligation of the contract, which may not be beneficial for the consumer.[853] The Court refers to the opinion of A-G Wahl who in turn refers to Schillig,[854] who considers the lack of a legal standard to assess the price/quality ratio of contracts, and the terms that define parties' main obligations under the contract, in the light of German criticism and German law. The DCFR however does not consider the possible differences between article 4 par. 2 Rome I and article 4 par. 2 Directive 93/13, or the suitability of this standard for the interpretation of the Directive.

Notably, if the DCFR is to act as a toolbox, it could be of clearly added value to draw attention to inconsistencies such as this, which unfortunately is not the case. Interestingly, article 6 par. 8 Directive 2011/83, however, stipulates that the requirements in the Directive should complete the requirements in Directive 2006/123 and Directive 2000/31, while Member States should retain the possibility to impose additional requirements on service providers. However, if the provisions conflict with the requirements of the Directive, the provisions in the Directive prevail. Article 6 does not expressly include STCs, but terms often included in STCs, such as clauses on the extension of the contract as well as conditions and rights with regard to after-sale services and out-of-court redress.

Other rules and comments in the DCFR have also not been followed. The comments to article II – 9:103 DCFR[855] expressly refer to usages that may entail that parties are bound to terms not made available to them directly, but are made available generally by

[851] Opinion of A.G. Trstenjak of 29 October 2009 before Caja de Ahorros y Monte de Piedad de Madrid v Asociación de Usuarios de Servicios Bancarios (Ausbanc) C-484/08, [2010] ECR p. I-4785, par. 61–66.

[852] CJEU 30 April 2014 (Kásler and Hajnalka Káslerné Rábai v OTP Jelzálogbank Zrt),), C-26/13, par. 49, 55, comp. also CJEU 3 June 2010 (Caja de Ahorros y Monte de Piedad de Madrid v Asociación de Usuarios de Servicios Bancarios (Ausbanc)), C-484/08, [2010] ECR p. I-4824, par. 34 where the Court considers the main terms as the essential obligations of the contract.

[853] Ferrari/Kieninger/Mankowski u.a., Internationales Vertragsrecht/Ferarri/2011/Regulation Rome I, article 4, par. 62–64.

[854] M. Schillig, 'Directive 93/13 and the "price term exemption": a comparative analysis in the light of the "market for lemons" rationale', *ICLQ* 2011, p. 947.

[855] Ch. Von Bar et al (eds), *Principles, Definitions and Model Rules of European Private Law. Draft Common Frame of Reference, Part I*, München: Sellier 2009, p. 591.

stakeholder or international organisations. This referral seems at odds with the BGH decision with regard to the obligation of users of STCs to make their STCs sufficiently available, but is in accordance with the decisions of the BGH under German law in which the use of terms was found to be well established, and parties should assume that their contract party wanted to include these clauses in their contracts.[856] Oddly, these rules have not been reflected in the withdrawn CESL that does not appear to provide separate rules for making STCs adequately available to one's counterparty. Arguably, this is an important gap that should be dealt with.

In some respects, the DCFR may provide a clearly added value. It may be of added value to existing soft laws because of the specific rules on unfair terms in articles II – 9:401 et seq DCFR, as the UNIDROIT Principles and the PECL do not provide specific rules on unfair terms. Also, the comparative overview provided by the DCFR[857] could be helpful for the future reform of the 1993 Directive. According to the comments, these rules are modelled on Directive 93/13 and may go beyond the protection conferred on consumers by the Directives. Accordingly, article II – 9: 402 par. 2 DCFR provides that a term in a consumer contract that is not transparent, may be unfair for that reason alone, which was not followed in article 83 of the withdrawn CESL.

Thus, in various important respects, the DCFR diverges from the *acquis*, and in some cases, the DCFR has – rightly so – not been followed. In some cases, the DCFR should be followed, in particular with regard to business practices and the sufficient availability of STCs. In other cases, such as the definition of STCs, following the DCFR is problematic and should be reconsidered.

4.7.2.2. The DCFR and national practice

The drafters of the DCFR have not adequately taken into account questions arising in national practice, which has undermined the added value of the DCFR for national and European actors. Contrary to expectations,[858] the DCFR has not played a role in German judicial reasoning.

Unfortunately, the DCFR does not address the question of whether clauses can be upheld if judges interpret them leniently,[859] or whether model contracts should fall within the scope of the Directive.[860] Moreover, compliance with article 1 par. 2 Directive that exempts clauses in accordance with applicable national default law or international law, has been problematic in the German legal order.[861]

856 See above par. 4.3.3.2.2.

857 For example with regard to the implementation of the Directive, Ch. Von Bar et al (eds), *Principles, Definitions and Model Rules of European Private Law. Draft Common Frame of Reference, Outline Edition, Volume I,* München: Sellier 2009, p. 637–638.

858 L. Miller, *The emergence of EU contract law: Exploring Europeanization*, Oxford: OUP 2011, p. 206.

859 MunchKomm zum BGB/Basedow (2012), article 306 nr 28–29.

860 This is the case in German law, see MunchKomm/Basedow (2012), article 305, nr 13, 18–19, 21, while this has been debated in Dutch law, on which see further par. 5.2.

861 See previously par. 4.4.3.2.

Notably, the comments to article II – 9:406 DCFR,[862] although they expressly refer to the exemption of clauses in accordance with the Warsaw and subsequent Montréal Convention, do not refer to BGH decisions that contradict these decisions, even though these decisions may indicate problems for optional regimes such as the withdrawn CESL.[863] Neither the comments nor the notes to the DCFR,[864] in discussing unfairness in article II – 9:403 DCFR pay attention to the question which court should be competent to interpret the DCFR. Yet this question has been debated,[865] and the BGH[866] does not seem particularly inclined to consider the question whether the CJEU is competent to provide guidelines for the interpretation of national law implementing article 3 Directive. The notes, though referring to the principle of good faith in German law, do not discuss the *Richtigkeitsgewähr*. Admittedly, the *Richtigkeitsgewähr* has been criticised[867] and shows considerable overlap with good faith,[868] but it still provides an interesting notion for justifying the binding force of contracts and it may, therefore, also be interesting for foreign and European state actors and academics.

4.7.2.3. The DCFR and other soft laws

The DCFR provides specific rules on STCs that are not reflected in other soft laws, and it might have been valuable for the development of the since withdrawn CESL and the revision of Directive 93/13. Yet in cases where other soft laws have also developed rules for STCs, divergences from and between the different sets of soft laws have not been adequately discussed.

In some cases, the rules in the DCFR largely converge with other soft laws, such as article II – 4: 209 DCFR that closely resembles article 2:209 pars. 1 and 2 PECL and article 2.1.22 UNIDROIT Principles. Yet although the comments note that the DCFR has followed the UNIDROIT principles in this respect, it is not mentioned that differently from the UNIDROIT Principles, the DCFR – as well as the PECL – stipulates that no contract is formed if a party has indicated in advance that it does not intend to be bound, not by way of standard terms.

862 Ch. Von Bar et al (eds.), *Principles, Definitions and Model Rules of European Private Law. Draft Common Frame of Reference, Outline Edition, Volume I,* München: Sellier 2009, p. 647.

863 BGH 1 February 2005, *NJW* 2005, 1774. See further previously par. 4.4.3.2.

864 Ch. Von Bar et al (eds.), *Principles, Definitions and Model Rules of European Private Law. Draft Common Frame of Reference, Outline Edition, Volume I,* München: Sellier 2009, . 634 et seq.

865 See Staudinger Kommentar zum BGB/Coester (2006), article 307, par. 70–71.

866 Comp. BGH 14 July 2004, *BeckRS* 2004, 7903, see further previously par. 4.4.1.2.

867 See prominently L. Raiser, 'Vertragsfunktion und Vertragsfreiheit', in: E. von Caemmerer, E. Friesenhahn, R. Lange (eds.), *Hundert Jahre deutsches Rechtsleben, Festschrift zum hundertjährigen Bestehen des Deutschen Juristentages, I,* Karlsruhe: Muller 1960, p. 118.

868 Notably, the *Richtigkeitsgewähr* is absent for STCs as they have not been negotiated, which gives the user of STCs the opportunity to improve his legal position to the detriment of his counterparty. This may, however, be contrary to good faith, which requires the user of STCs to take into account the legitimate interests and expectations of his counterparty. See further previously, par. 4.5.1.

Various differences between the DCFR, the PECL and the UNIDROIT Principles deserve further explanation:

i) The different rules on formation of contract and the inclusion of clauses in contracts if one party's clauses reject the applicability of the other party's clauses.

According to the comments, experience has shown that parties that include clauses in their contract that stipulate there is no contract unless their own terms apply, subsequently act in accordance with the contract. Thus, the comments find that, to uphold these clauses while parties perform the contract, 'would erode the rule'. The present rule in the DCFR, followed in article 39 withdrawn CESL, leaves open the possibility that both parties have included these clauses in their contract and subsequently performed the contract, for which situation the solution preferred by the DCFR does not become apparent. The DCFR also refers to the CISG. Articles 18 and 19 CISG similarly provide that parties need to object orally or by sending notice, which implies that objection cannot take place through STCs. As the DCFR in this respect follows the CISG rather than the PECL or the UNIDROIT Principles, reasoning that indicates why the CISG provides the better rule would have been welcome.[869] It would also have been interesting to consider the question of whether clauses in battle of forms cases can, nevertheless, be included because the use of these clauses represents well established commercial practices, for example, with regard to the retention of title clauses.

Moreover, differently from the PECL and the UNIDROIT principles, article II – 4: 209 DCFR, followed in article 39 withdrawn CESL, requires that parties inform the users of STCs about their lack of willingness to be bound with undue delay, which is reminiscent of article 19 par. 2 CISG. The DCFR does not elaborate on this additional requirement, which may, however, leave additional room for arguments. If the notes had more extensively referred to CISG case law, more clarity could have been provided.

ii) Different rules on individually negotiated and standard merger clauses

Article II – 4:104 DCFR distinguishes between individually negotiated merger clauses and merger clauses that have not been individually negotiated. A similar rule can be found in article 2:105 PECL. Although the DCFR, according to the comments, follows article 2.1.17 UNIDROIT Principles, this provision does not make a similar distinction, nor does the usefulness of this distinction become convincingly apparent. Although the DCFR points out that merger clauses that have not been individually negotiated are unfair in consumer contracts, according to the indicative European model list, this does not mean that such a distinction is useful for merger clauses. The necessity for this distinction is further not clear because clauses that are individually negotiated should not be subject to judicial evaluation under article II –1:109 DCFR.

The distinction in the DCFR is also not followed in article 72 of the withdrawn CESL, which has instead opted to provide more protection to consumers by simply stipulating that in a B2C contract, a consumer is not bound to a merger clause. However, the comparative overview in the note may provide valuable information for the further development of the withdrawn CESL.

869 See critically on the rule provided by the CISG P. Schlechtriem, 'Battle of forms in international contract law, evaluation of approaches in German law, UNIDROIT Principles, European principles, CISG; UCC approaches under consideration', www.cisg.law.pace.edu/cisg/biblio/schlechtriem5.html.

iii) Different rules on clauses for form requirements

Article II – 4:105 DCFR stipulates that clauses imposing form requirements on a modification or termination of the agreement only result in a presumption, in accordance with article 2:106 PECL, but contrary to article 2.1.18 UNIDROIT Principles. According to the DCFR, this rule is in accordance with most of the laws of the Member States, but it has not been reflected in the withdrawn CESL.

Arguably, diverging from other sets of soft law is not, as such, problematic, but more explanation on the differences could have made clear why the DCFR differs from the PECL and the UNIDROIT Principles, which would have improved accessibility and provided an explanation for actors looking to the different set of soft laws for inspiration in the drafting of legislation or the adjudication of disputes.

4.7.2.4. Conclusion on the DCFR as an additional technique

The divergences between the *acquis* and the DCFR limit the extent to which the DCFR contributes to a more predictable development of the *acquis*, as well as the consistent implementation of the *acquis*.

The lack of attention for national experiences in the implementation of the *acquis* limits the extent to which the DCFR adequately responds to problems or lack of clarities that have become visible in practice.

Notwithstanding the clearly-added value of specific rules on STCs in the DCFR, the lack of attention for divergences between the DCFR and other soft laws has lessened the degree to which the DCFR improves the accessibility of European private law.

Arguably, the added value of the DCFR should not be sought primarily in black-letter rules. The experience with the implementation of the Directive indicates that despite harmonisation, the law on STCs is still developed in a national manner.[870] Instead, the added value of the may be sought especially in discussing national experiences and the divergences from the *acquis* and other sets of soft law, as these discussions may provide legislators and courts with more in-depth arguments for preferring or not preferring a particular set of rules, which would have improved the accessibility of European private law.

Nevertheless, the DCFR, if it takes national and European experiences into account, could not be a valuable source for mutual learning.

4.7.3. Techniques in addition to blanket clauses

The use of alternative regulation may contribute to the responsive interpretation of blanket clauses, which will be considered in paragraph 4.7.3.1. Moreover, the development of the German law on STCs reveals that lower regulation may also play a role in the

[870] Similarly L. Miller, *The emergence of EU contract law: Exploring Europeanization*, Oxford: OUP 2011, p. 168 who considers the use of black letter rules in the light of 'methodological nationalism'.

interpretation of the law. This will be discussed in paragraph 4.7.3.2. Paragraph 4.7.3.3 will end with a conclusion.

4.7.3.1. The use of self-regulation

Well-established self-regulation in the area of consumer sales[871] may contribute to the predictable and consistent interpretation of blanket clauses. Taking into account these rules expressly recognised by users of STCs may also be in accordance with consumers' expectations.

Several difficulties may diminish the extent to which self-regulation may enhance the predictable and accessible interpretation of blankert clauses. The success of this option depends upon the existence of well-established self-regulation. Notably, even successful self-regulation may not always be accessible to foreign and international parties. Further, German actors may have objections against the use of self-regulation in the interpretation of blanket clauses, especially if parties are subjected to rules developed through self-regulation that they have not agreed to. Such problems of *Fremdbestimmung* can however be avoided if successful self-regulation on consumer sales is considered in cases where both contract parties have recognised self-regulation. If self-regulation provides clear rules of conduct that have subsequently been breached by the seller, it seems consistent to consider these rules. Nevertheless, courts have rarely considered self-regulation.[872] Arguably, taking into account codes of conduct and other self-regulation may in addition be in accordance with article 6 Directive 2005/29 that stipulates that non-compliance with codes providing clear rules of conduct that the seller has expressly complied with, may constitute a misleading commercial practice.

4.7.3.2. The use of lower regulation

The extent to which lower regulation may contribute to predictability, consistency, accessibility and responsiveness may be limited.

Possibly, the choice of the legislator to implement Directives into the BGB could be combined with a choice to implement more detailed provisions outside the BGB, in lower regulation.[873] This option may be particularly interesting if Directives that do not provide rules for private law as such, do contain rules affecting the interpretation of STCs. As a result, provisions on information duties and withdrawal periods would be stipulated outside the BGB, which will facilitate maintaining the abstract approach of the BGB. In

871 This concerns the trustmark '*Geprüfter online shop – Bundesverband des Deutschen versandhandlers*' (see further www.bvh.info/bvh/leistungen/guetesiegel/?no_cache=1&sword_list[0]=g%C3%BCtesiegel, as well as the s@fer shopping trustmark for online shopping (see www.safer-shopping.de/qualitaetskriterien.html.) and the Trusted Shops trustmarks (see www.trustedshops.de/guetesiegel/kaeuferschutz.html). See further below par. 7.5.3.4.

872 Comp. LG Düsseldorf 22 June 1995, *BeckRS* 2011, 7145, a case on the appraisal of a company to be sold where the court in passing referred to professional rules of conduct.

873 Similarly P. Hommelhoff, 'Zivilrecht unter dem Einfluß europäischer Rechtsangleichung', *AcP* 1992, p. 86.

addition, concepts that are not easily reconcilable with principles underlying the BGB – especially withdrawal periods – do not have to be inserted within the BGB, which may help to preserve the logical structure of the BGB. In addition, placing these provisions outside the BGB would make the European background of these provisions more apparent.

Accordingly, the use of lower regulation was used in the implementation of Directive 2000/31 on e-commerce. Article 241 EGBGB initially enabled the Ministry for Justice to establish a regulation on the information duties of several Directives, which led to the *BGB-Informationspflichten-Verordnung*. Although the regulation still contains provisions on the information duties of tour operators, article 3 of the regulation implementing article 10 par. 3 Directive has since been revised, and currently this article has been implemented in articles 246 par. 3 EGBG and article 312g BGB.

After the revision of Directive 87/102 on consumer credit, the German legislator[874] reconsidered its course as it found that lower regulation failed to provide sufficient predictability to contract parties and left too much discretion to the courts to undermine the use of models for information duties of the seller.[875] Yet detailed provisions on information duties should also not be included into the BGB, as this would be difficult to reconcile with the abstract approach of the BGB. Consequently, article 246 par. 3 EGBGB now implements the detailed provisions, alongside other detailed information provisions from other Directives, in addition to article 312g BGB and article 675a BGB.

Consequently, it is unlikely that the German legislator will use lower regulation to provide models that enable sellers or suppliers to meet information requirements.

Several other objections may also arise:

1) The use of lower regulations leads to the development of a large amount of regulations alongside the BGB, which may undermine accessibility and consistency.

The development of these rules outside the BGB should be kept to a minimum, to prevent that, in cases where multiple Directives are simultaneously applicable, provisions in the BGB as well as provisions in several regulations are applicable, which may undermine accessibility and consistency. Keeping the amount of lower regulations to a minimum may, however, not be an easy task as the *acquis* continues to develop.

Also, especially if provisions in lower regulations concern important parts of private law, the effort to maintain the central role of the BGB is undermined.

874 BT-Drucks. 16/11643, p. 66, 69. Notably, article 246 par. 3 EGBGB is only indirectly applicable, if article 312g BGB refers to it.

875 See for example LG Koblenz 20 December 2006, *BeckRS* 2007, 34 which held that information provided in accordance with the model provided by the regulation was not in accordance with article 312 BGB and therefore invalid.

2) The development of lower regulation may make the reform of law considerably more complicated.

The revision of a Directive would necessitate not only the amendment of the BGB but also surrounding, simultaneously applicable regulations. Currently, the additional implementation of Directives in the EGBGB depends on the application of provisions in the BGB, while it also allows for a more ordered implementation of information duties. However, the additional implementation of Directives into the EGBGB is also a complicated system that is not easy to comprehend, especially for consumers seeking to enforce their rights.

3) Questions whether the use of lower regulation sufficiently implements Directives may also arise.[876]

→ The use of lower regulation will hinder rather than help accessibility, while it is not likely to contribute to the predictable and consistent interpretation of blanket clauses. These problems may be difficult for the German legislator to compensate as the *acquis* continues to develop.

4.7.3.3. Conclusion on the use of techniques in addition to blanket clauses

Well-established self-regulation may contribute to the predictable, consistent and responsive interpretation of article 307 BGB. However, courts have rarely considered self-regulation. Similarly, courts have disregarded lower regulation. Despite this lack of attention, however, the use of self-regulation and lower regulation is still interesting for other legal orders where courts are less likely to ignore lower regulation, such as the Dutch legal order.

4.7.4. Studying the use of STCs

The study of the use of STCs could focus on the use of STCs in international trade, the comparison of the interpretation of these clauses, and the comparison of model lists throughout the Union. These initiatives may contribute to the responsiveness of the *acquis* and may make national laws more accessible and predictable to foreign parties. Improvements are possible in the following ways:

1) Comparative research on clauses converging with national default or mandatory law could draw attention to generally accepted or rejected clauses and point to possible differences between clauses in different Member States. In turn, this information could be useful in the revision of Directive 93/13, in particular, article 1 par. 2 Directive.

[876] CJEU 19 October 1987 (Commission v The Netherlands), case 236/85, [1987] ECR, p. 3989, par. 4.5.2.6.

2) Comparing the approach to the interpretation of contracts, model lists, and the evaluation of clauses in contracts may provide more insight in the question of whether, and if so which divergences in private laws may constitute barriers to cross-border trade and may improve the accessibility and predictability of national law for foreign parties.

Differences and similarities in model lists throughout the Union could form a starting point for discussion about the interpretation of article 3 Directive. Thus, the different approach towards clauses silently extending consumer contracts for a considerable length of time could be discussed.[877]

Possibly, comparison might make the added value of the use of national default law in the evaluation of clauses more apparent, and indicate which provisions are merely established to provide order rather than provide a normative viewpoint, which, in turn, would make clear from which default provisions parties can diverge without further problems. Comparing model lists may also include comparing the influence of these model lists on clauses in business contracts.

→ The study of the use of STCs may increase the responsiveness of the *acquis* and the accessibility and predictability of the law for parties engaged in cross-border trade, provided that information resulting from these studies is clearly organised and does not lead to information overload, while parties should also be aware of these initiatives.

4.7.5. *Optional regimes*

In accordance with pluralist arguments,[878] the development of optional regimes may provide opportunities for mutual learning, and it may stimulate the development of regulatory competition. Yet it is not clear whether optional regimes such as the withdrawn CESL may contribute to the predictability, consistency, accessibility and responsiveness of the law on STCs.

The extent to which the withdrawn proposal would have contributed to these benchmarks would have depended on its success. More generally, the success of optional regimes depends on the question of whether it provides more predictability and consistency than well-established national regimes, while questions with regard to possible overlaps should also be addressed. The support for optional regimes in the area of consumer contract law will also depend on the level of consumer protection.

A starting point for the level of protection could be the level of protection offered in the consumer *acquis*. Yet what if the level of consumer protection makes it unattractive for businesses to opt for optionally harmonised rules? Of course, it might be possible that businesses do not oppose a high level of consumer protection if that would mean they could apply one level of consumer protection throughout the Union when doing business with consumers.[879] Interestingly, the reactions to

[877] The case law on the silent extension of contracts concerns established BGH case law, see already BGH 29 April 1987, *NJW* 1987, 1012, followed by OLG Hamm 8 April 2010, *BeckRS* 2010, 2083110.

[878] L. Miller, *The emergence of EU contract law: Exploring Europeanization*, Oxford: OUP 2011, p. 171.

[879] K. Riesenhuber, 'A competitive approach to EU contract law', *ERCL* 2011, p. 129.

other recent measures, such as the consumer rights Directive[880] from stakeholder organisations,[881] show that businesses may not necessarily plead for the highest level of consumer protection, but, instead, advocate a maximum harmonisation approach that will, in their view, ensure predictability and consistency. Therefore, it would be interesting to know whether businesses throughout the Union would be willing to accept a high level of consumer protection.

In contrast, a low level of consumer protection may be problematic. Possibly, this may entail that an optional instrument in this area of law would allow for circumventing mandatory law to the detriment of the consumer. Whittaker[882] has argued that a lower level of consumer protection than provided in national laws may give rise to questions as to whether STCs applying the Optional Instrument to business-to-consumer contracts could be an unfair term in the meaning of Directive 93/13, or an unfair commercial practice in the meaning of Directive 2005/29. A lower level of consumer protection could in addition prompt consumers to consider sellers who abide by national, higher standards.[883] In that case, the choice for an optional instrument by businesses might even inhibit cross-border trade.

Problems of predictability, consistency and accessibility may, however, arise as the BGH has refused to uphold clauses contrary to articles 305–310 BGB, even if they are in conformity with, for example, the Montréal Convention.[884] Predictability may be undermined if it is not clear what sources may be used in the interpretation and evaluation of STCs under an optional regime.

In addition, the withdrawn proposal for a Regulation establishing a CESL,[885] frequently used concepts that needed additional interpretation. For example, what did the duty to negotiate in good faith (article 8) mean? What duties could have been imposed on parties on the basis of this rule? How would courts have interpreted contracts if article 56 withdrawn CESL distracted that a contract is to be interpreted in accordance with parties' common intentions? What if parties are accustomed to relying upon the wording of the contract, having negotiated carefully on that wording? If parties can be bound by usages and practices, as stipulated in article 65, how would it have been established that such a general usage exists? Especially when an optional instrument is

880 COM (2008) 614 final.

881 Available at http://ec.europa.eu/consumers/rights/responses_green_paper_acquis_en.htm#stakeholders. See, for example, the response from the British Retail Consortium that supports a fully harmonised and horizontal approach, stating that the review 'should not aim to extend the Acquis at the highest possible level' (p. 2). Similarly, Direct Selling Europe opposes the extension of consumer protection in the *acquis* and argues for consistency and predictability. eBay also pleads for full harmonisation, and abandoning minimum harmonisation which in the view of eBay has led to legal uncertainty. Similar responses have been made by other organisations, such as Platform Detailhandel Nederland, Retail Ireland, and the German Retail Federation. Comp. also the argument of J.W. Rutgers, 'An Optional Instrument and social dumping revisited', *ERCL* 2011, p. 350.

882 S. Whittaker, 'The Optional Instrument of European contract law and freedom of contract', *ERCL* 2011, p. 387–389.

883 M.B.M. Loos, 'Scope and application of the Optional instrument', in: D. Voinot, J. Sénéchal (eds.), *Vers un droit européen des contrats spéciaux/Towards a European Law of Specific Contracts*, Gent: Larcier 2011, p. 128.

884 BGH 20 January 1983, *NJW* 1983, 1322. Despite harmonisation, a similar strict approach is visible in BGH 1 February 2005, *NJW* 2005, 1774.

885 COM (2011) 635 final.

just adopted, there will be no CJEU case law on the interpretation of these terms and rules that private parties and their advisors could turn to.[886] Neither would there be an extensive amount of academic debate, as is the case in national jurisdictions. This might arguably set an optional instrument at a competitive disadvantage. The extent to which an optional instrument contributes to the responsiveness of the law on STCs may be severely diminished because judges, in the evaluation and interpretation of clauses in contracts falling under an optional instrument, may not refer to already developed case law.

Theoretically, the development of an optional instrument might prompt the CJEU to develop clear guidelines on the interpretation and evaluation of clauses under that optional instrument. This could contribute to the consistent and, therefore, more predictable interpretation and evaluation of clauses throughout the Union, provided that the methods indicated by the CJEU are acceptable for national legislators and judiciaries.

Thus, it is difficult to predict the extent to which an optional instrument will contribute to predictability, accessibility, consistency and responsiveness.

4.7.6. Collectively negotiating STCs for cross-border trade

It is not clear to what extent encouraging collective negotiations for cross-border trade will be beneficial for the predictability, consistency, accessibility and responsiveness of the law on STCs.

Possibly, collective bargaining can be accommodated in the *acquis*. Revised Directives could enable parties to diverge from mandatory law through collectively negotiated STCs, creating so-called three-quarter mandatory law at a European level.

An important condition for collective bargaining is that criteria of representativeness, transparency and inclusiveness are met. As national actors are better placed to assess the representativeness of stakeholder groups involved in collective bargaining, sufficient discretion should be left to national actors to ensure that these criteria are met.

Moreover, negotiations should take place between well-established parties with equal bargaining positions. The role of national actors in evaluating whether parties are sufficiently representative should prevent collective negotiations taking place between carefully selected repeat players at the European level rather than relevant stakeholders, which may also be problematic as these negotiations may well result in contract parties submitted to alternative regulation that falls beyond national democratic control that they also did not agree to – in other words, *Fremdbestimmung* will develop.

Agreements negotiated in collective negotiations in accordance with these criteria may, subsequently, be collected in a database. The participation of representative actors, as well as networks and possibly publications in well-established journals and newspapers could increase accessibility and actors' awareness of these possibilities.

Possibly, inserting three-quarter mandatory law in a revised Directive 93/13, or a revised Directive 99/44 would allow for the development of the law in accordance with

[886] W. Doralt, 'The Optional European Contract law and why success or failure may depend on scope rather than substance', *Max Planck Private Law Research Paper* 2011, p. 20–21.

the needs and preferences of legal practice in a manner that does not breach consumer protection. Such initiatives may also be in accordance with the prominent role of parties in some legal orders. Furthermore, the possibility to diverge from provisions may encourage users of STCs to enter into negotiations in which STCs may be negotiated in accordance with consumers' preferences as well, which may reduce the amount of one-sided STCs more generally.

The development of collective bargaining also has disadvantages. Generally, the introduction of three-quarter mandatory law may further complicate the development of the private law *acquis*. The success of these initiatives depends on the willingness of actors to enter into negotiations. If collectively negotiated STCs are subjected to less intense judicial control, parties may have more incentives to engage in cross-border negotiations. Particularly in legal orders where collective negotiations have already been established, actors may be interested.

Thus, although successful collective negotiations may well contribute to the comprehensibility of the law on STCs, this depends on the acceptability of this option for European and German actors and the willingness of actors to participate.

4.7.7. *Conclusion on the use of additional and alternative techniques*

Which techniques, in addition to or instead of currently used techniques, are likely to contribute to the predictability, accessibility, consistency and responsiveness of the law on STCs?

Techniques that may be successful are the study of STCs in cross-border trade. In addition, the development of databases to make actors more familiar with foreign law may support debate. Further, despite the lack of attention for well-established codes of conduct, the use of alternative regulation may strengthen the responsive interpretation of blanket clauses. This may be stimulated by developments at the European level, where the use of codes of conduct has already been encouraged.

In contrast, it is difficult to predict to what extent the development of optional regimes and the introduction of collective negotiations will improve the comprehensibility of the law on STCs.

To what extent do techniques compensate for the shortcomings of currently used techniques, and do techniques strengthen debate?

In line with pluralist arguments, allowing for more self-regulation and developing optional regimes would facilitate mutual learning. However, one may ask whether national actors will be receptive for opportunities for mutual learning, considering the national approach of these actors towards EU initiatives.

The question may also arise whether initiatives such as the withdrawn CESL would have been developed in accordance with German law, in a manner reminiscent to the Directive. Instead, the approach of actors in the case study indicates that courts may adopt restraint in referring questions to the CJEU, and in referring to foreign materials.

The narrow view of actors in the European debate may similarly affect the use of additional techniques. Arguably, because of the interest-based approach of actors towards the debate, actors are less receptive to suggestions for the study of STCs to identify barriers to the internal market. National actors may especially reject these options if they increase the chance that the *acquis* develops differently than national law. European actors are less likely to object to that approach. European actors could initiate further research in this area, despite Member States' concerns. Theoretically, such studies could also support the use of impact assessments as a targeted study, in accordance with the functional approach more generally. Studies need not necessarily lead to harmonisation; they could also be a valuable source for mutual learning which should benefit the law on STCs.

Unfortunately, the limited view of actors means that actors are less open to insights from databases and comparative research, even though these techniques may respectively provide much-needed support for the quality of the *acquis*, and the responsive interpretation of international law.

Additional techniques, in particular, are often bottom-up techniques. Initiatives for these techniques are sufficiently available. It is not clear to what extent these techniques will actually benefit the law on STCs as the willingness of actors to participate in these initiatives is difficult to estimate.

These suggestions for additional and alternative techniques may well overlap and reinforce one another: the study of the use of STCs may support the development of an optional instrument or the introduction of collective bargaining on STCs in cross-border trade.

4.8. Conclusion

The German law on STCs is often considered a success story. Arguably, the success of the law on STCs can be contributed to several factors, not least the careful drafting process of the AGBG and the careful way in which courts have developed the law in this area, without, however, interacting extensively with international or European actors.

At first sight, the success of German law cannot be traced to German actors' awareness of interdependence and sufficient interaction, in accordance with multilevel governance. Yet interdependence has clearly developed in this area. National actors are less able to develop the law on STCs comprehensibly through national techniques and European actors also depend on national actors. Does this mean that despite interdependence, interaction is not needed?

This is not the case. On closer inspection, it becomes clear that the stable development of the law on STCs may also be attributed to the active participation of German actors in the European legislative process and subsequent restraint in the implementation and application of the Directive. Because of this approach, at first sight, the ability of blanket clauses to contribute to consistency and responsiveness have not been diminished.

However, because of the lack of interaction, problems may develop in the long term. Particularly, a predictable strategy towards the implementation of the private law *acquis* has not been developed. The ongoing development of the *acquis* increases the chance that multiple and possibly inconsistent Directives will develop that will affect the law on STCs. Eventually, despite the BGB, private law may be developed less predictably, consistently, and accessibly. The lack of interaction may also undermine the responsive development of Directive 93/13, and a circle of "non-interaction" may develop. Equally, cases decided under international regimes are not decided in accordance with foreign decisions, which undermines consistency throughout the Union. Not taking into account international and foreign materials that may reflect business practices and the needs and preferences of foreign and international actors also diminishes responsiveness.

It has been argued that the extent to which national law is developed on the basis of general principles can be affected by the more regulatory approach of European actors. However, good faith and the *Richtigkeitsgewähr* remain central ideas underpinning the German law on STCs. This may also be due to the German influence on the drafting of the Directive.

Similarly, the high quality of the law cannot be attributed to the development of a system of checks and balances between the European legislator, the CJEU, and the national legislator and courts. Harmonisation has not prompted German actors to consider the interests of foreign and international actors. The coexistence of national regimes, if they are closely intertwined with legal views on justice, are beneficial in terms of responsiveness.

The close relationship between the law on STCs and national legal views on justice however stands in the way of further harmonisation and regulatory competition. Accordingly, the quality of the German law on STCs is not the result of regulatory competition. German law in this area is also not based on mutual learning. Although the European legislator has benefited from German experiences, it has not benefited from national experiences in the failed attempt to revise Directive 93/13.

A defensive, nationalist approach towards Directive 93/13 can be detected at the national level. The success of the law on STCs may have further limited the German legislator's willingness to critically reflect on the law on STCs or to (re)consider the use of techniques. German actors may participate less actively in debate in areas where German law is less well-developed or successful. If German actors may have less interesting insights to offer in European debate, it is not unlikely that the *acquis* will be developed differently from German law. In these cases, the *acquis* may well necessitate amendments of the BGB, or separate statutes, which eventually may diminish the stable and consistent development of the law through the BGB.

However, it may be doubted whether an approach aimed at maintaining the development of the Directive in a manner similar to national laws before the introduction of Directive 93/13, as well as other Directives, will, in the long term, safeguard comprehensibility. Maintaining a defensive approach may overlook future difficulties and possibilities to improve the law on STCs. The European legislator will likely suggest the revision of Directive 93/13 in a manner that differs from German law.

Thus, improvements are possible in accordance with pluralist insights. Currently, because the German legislator does not recognise the diminished ability of national techniques to contribute to predictability, accessibility, consistency and responsiveness, the weaknesses of these techniques will logically not likely be compensated by the use of additional techniques. Studying STCs in a transnational context could be a valuable source of mutual learning. Similarly, if the DCFR took into account national experiences, it could serve as a source of learning for European actors. More generally, German principles such as the *Richtigkeitsgewähr* could also be studied in the development of the law on STCs. Encouraging national practitioners, experts and judges to participate at the European level is promising, as these actors are more aware of the needs and preferences of national practice. More and better debate at the European level also increases the chance that important decisions on the competence of courts to interpret blanket clauses are the outcome of extensive debate. Involving European and foreign actors in the debate at the national level may enable German actors to take into account the interests of these actors.

Interesting techniques for the European legislator will likely meet with resistance at the national level, but this need not withhold European actors from exploring the possibilities. More generally, the European legislator should consider the use of techniques more critically. However, the limited view of both German and European actors makes it unlikely that drastic changes will be affected in the use of techniques in the short term.

The changes suggested in this chapter are long term and do not imply an immediate change of the law, although a reform of the 1993 Directive on unfair contract terms likely will eventually be forthcoming. Rather, the changes include recognising interdependence, overcoming potential problems that may arise from interdependence, and where possible, benefiting from the insights from other actors involved in the development of the law on STCs.

Chapter 5

THE DEVELOPMENT OF THE LAW ON *ALGEMENE VOORWAARDEN*

5.1. Introduction

Unlike German law, the Dutch law on STCs has not been celebrated as a success story. Instead, weaknesses have been detected. Accordingly, can weaknesses in Dutch law be traced to a lack of interaction between interdependent actors, in line with insights from multilevel governance?

In accordance with pluralist arguments, has the coexistence of actors contributed to the strong points of Dutch law, or could the coexistence of actors also help to improve Dutch law? Has the coexistence of national and European actors strengthened the responsiveness of the law to foreign and international actors or have Dutch actors recognised the benefits of mutual learning and regulatory competition?

Paragraph 5.2 will introduce the law on STCs and discuss the strengths and especially the weaknesses. Paragraphs 5.3–5.5 will analyse the use of codifications, blanket clauses and general principles. Paragraph 5.6. will draw a conclusion on the use of national techniques. Paragraph 5.7. will consider the use of techniques in addition to or instead of currently used techniques. Paragraph 5.8. will end with a conclusion, debating whether the coexistence of actors is beneficial or detrimental for the Dutch law on STCs, in accordance with multilevel governance and pluralist perspectives.

5.2. The law on *algemene voorwaarden*

The Dutch law on STCs can be found in articles 6:231 et seq BW. The blanket clause, article 6:233 sub a BW, which bans the use of unfair contract terms has led to the development of a lot of case law, especially from lower courts.

The BW is commonly considered as a successful codification. Articles 6:231 et seq BW are, however, relatively new and at some points, it has developed differently than the legislator had expected.[887] In some respects, the regime is a success: it has enabled, and encouraged, collective negotiations on STCs.[888]

887 E.H. Hondius, 'Tien jaar Nieuw Burgerlijk Wetboek: De regeling van de algemene voorwaarden', *WPNR* 6472 (2002).

888 See further below par. 8.5.1.2.

The Dutch regime has, however, been severely criticised on the following points:[889]

1) The rules on the availability of clauses

The strict interpretation of the duty to make STCs available under article 6:234 BW[890] has been criticised as it wrongly presupposes that clauses are read prior to the contract.[891]After the implementation of Directive 2006/123 in articles 6:230a-c BW, possible overlap with article 6:234 BW, which imposes a stricter duty on parties, remains. Schelhaas[892] prefers a rule that is in accordance with article 6:230a et seq BW that provides a more lenient rule.

2) Articles 6:235 and 247 BW stipulate that (parts of) the regime does not apply in contracts with or between, respectively, big businesses and international parties.

The distinction in article 6:235 BW was introduced by lack of a better benchmark and has been criticised as arbitrary.[893] Loos[894] finds that the distinction is unnecessary, as article 6:233 sub a BW enables the judge to take the capacity of businesses challenging the fairness of clauses into account, and it is, also, not in accordance with the needs of (some) large businesses that are not in a position to negotiate on STCs. Article 6:235 BW is further problematic as it limits the scope of article 6:234 BW that implements Directive 2000/31. The exemption of article 6:247 BW for international contracts leads to a lacuna: in international cases, it is not clear whether there is a duty for parties to make STCs sufficiently available, also for electronic contracts, despite Directive 2000/31. Schelhaas[895] notes that the distinctions in article 6:235 and 247 BW have led to different regimes for different contract parties, and should be simplified.

3) Article 6:232 BW aims to further predictability by ensuring that STCs are applicable even if the user knew or should have known that the party subjected to the terms did not know the terms.

The question whether clauses have been validly included in the contract is answered under articles 3:33 and 35 and 6:217 BW. Article 6:232 BW merely stipulates that if parties have justifiably relied on the inclusion of STCs, that reliance includes the whole set of clauses rather than some.[896] The Hoge Raad has, however, made an exception for unduly surprising clauses,[897] but it will decide similarly under the BW.[898] Compared to article 305 BGB, under which claus es that are not

889 See for example C.E. Drion, 'Een pamflet voor het fundamenteel op de schop nemen van onze regelgeving over algemene voorwaarden', *Contracteren* 2007, p. 3.

890 HR 6 April 2001, *NJ* 2002, 385.

891 See for an overview J. Hijma, *Algemene voorwaarden*, Deventer: Kluwer 2010, p. 58.

892 H.N. Schelhaas, *Algemene voorwaarden in handelstransacties*, Deventer: Kluwer 2011, p. 41.

893 J. Hijma, *Algemene voorwaarden*, Deventer: Kluwer 2010, p. 81–82.

894 M.B.M. Loos, *Algemene voorwaarden*, The Hague: BJU 2001, p. 25–26.

895 H.N. Schelhaas, *Algemene voorwaarden in handelstransacties*, Deventer: Kluwer 2011, p. 39.

896 T.H.M. van Wechem, *De toepasselijkheid van algemene voorwaarden*, Deventer: Kluwer 2007, p. 24–25.

897 HR 20 November 1981, *NJ* 1982, 517.

898 A.S. Hartkamp & C.H. Sieburgh, *Mr. C. Asser's Handleiding tot de beoefening van het Nederlands burgerlijk recht. 6. Verbintenissenrecht. Deel III*. Algemeen overeenkomstenrecht*, Deventer: Kluwer 2010, nr. 473. Hereafter, this volume will refer to this book in the following manner: Asser/Hartkamp & Sieburgh 2010.

made sufficiently available have not become part of the contract, this construction creates an unnecessary extra step. It is not clear to what extent this provision has, in fact, contributed to predictability – German practice manages quite well without a similar rule.[899]

Article 6:232 BW has, moreover, had some unexpected results. Loos[900] points out that article 6:232 BW entails that large parties are quickly bound to clauses without being able to invoke the avoidability of clauses on the basis of articles 6:233 and 234 BW. Jongeneel[901] also notes that because the main terms of the contract do not fall under article 6:231 sub a BW, the valid inclusion of these terms will have to be assessed under article 3:33 and 35 BW rather than article 6:232 BW, which can hardly have been intended by the legislator. There is also debate on the question whether article 6:232 BW is applicable on clauses referring to other sets of STCs.[902]

4) The blanket clause in article 6:233 sub a BW has given rise to unpredictability and inconsistency

Barendrecht[903] noted that case law on exclusion clauses does not provide sufficient starting points to determine the fairness of clauses, which may be a reason for the courts to pay little attention to one another's decisions on blanket clauses. After the introduction of article 6: 233 sub a BW, Hondius,[904] however, found that indications on the fairness and unfairness of clauses can sufficiently be deduced from case law and a lack of predictability seems limited. Yet Pavillion[905] points out that article 6:233 sub a BW imposes a considerable burden of proof on consumers who consequently fail to successfully challenge unfair terms, and inconsistency has developed.[906]

5) Battle of forms

Debate has arisen on battle of forms, as the rule in article 6:225 par. 3 BW leaves room for unpredictability and does not correspond with business practices.[907]

899 Comp. MunchKomm zum BGB/Basedow, Introduction, nr 15, as well as the draft for reform of the law on STCs of the German Bar Association, at http://anwaltverein.de/downloads/Stellungnahmen-11/DAV-SN-23-2012.pdf, that states that the law with regard to the inclusion of STCs is not in need of amendment.

900 M.B.M. Loos, *Algemene voorwaarden*, The Hague: BJU 2001, p. 21.

901 R.H.C. Jongeneel, *Algemene voorwaarden en het AGB-Gesetz*, Deventer: Kluwer 1991, nr. 158.

902 See on this question T.H.M. van Wechem, *De toepasselijkheid van algemene voorwaarden*, Deventer: Kluwer 2007, p. 37–39, who extensively considers the views of other authors.

903 J.M. Barendrecht, *Recht als model van rechtvaardigheid*, Deventer: Kluwer 1992, p. 11.

904 E.H. Hondius, 'Tien jaar Nieuw Burgerlijk Wetboek: De regeling van de algemene voorwaarden', *WPNR* 6472 (2002).

905 C.M.D.S. Pavillon, 'Beter consumentenrecht: Naar een scherpere consumentvriendelijke onredelijk bezwarend-norm', *NTBR* 2011, 63. In this sense much earlier also G.J. Rijken, 'De Wet algemene voorwaarden na één jaar: een trieste tussenbalans', *NJB* 1994, p. 643.

906 See also below par. 5.4.1.2.

907 H.N. Schelhaas, *Algemene voorwaarden in handelstransacties*, Deventer: Kluwer 2011, p. 15, M.B.M. Loos, *Algemene voorwaarden*, The Hague: BJU 2001, p. 14. Comp. T.H.M. van Wechem, *De toepasselijkheid van algemene voorwaarden*, Deventer: Kluwer 2007, p. 198 who notes that although it is commonly assumed that a first-shot rule has developed, in the light of the wording of article 6:225 par. 3 BW, the knock-out rule is preferable and can be included in article 6:215 par 3 and 6:231 sub a BW.

6) Article 6:214 BW on standard regimes has remained a dead letter.[908]

7) Article 6:239 BW that enables the legislator to amend the law through lower regulation has similarly remained a dead letter – the legislator has, instead, amended article 6:237 BW through the normal legislative procedure.[909]

In addition, at some points, the law leaves room for questions:

1) The definition of STCs in article 6:231 BW

It is not clear whether model contracts or clauses drafted by lawyers and notaries in standard contracts also fall under the definition of article 6:231 sub a BW.[910]

2) The indirect effect of articles 6:236 and 237 BW on clauses in business contracts.

Case law on this matter does not make clear whether these provisions have an indirect effect in business contracts. Hijma[911] suggests several perspectives that can be relevant for assuming the indirect effect of the Dutch model lists.

→ In some cases, criticism can partially be traced to disagreement with the legislator's choice, for example, to exclude big businesses from articles 6:233 and 234 BW, but the majority of criticism can be traced to problems with predictability, consistency, and responsiveness.

Can these weaknesses be traced to the lack of recognition of interdependence and corresponding lack of interaction between relevant actors, and missed opportunities to improve the law?

5.3. The development of the law on STCs through the BW

Have actors adequately considered interdependence in the development of the law on STCs through the BW, and how that has affected the predictability, consistency, accessibility, and responsiveness of the law on STCs? Moreover, has the coexistence of actors benefited the development of the law on STCs?

Paragraph 5.3.1 will consider the choice to codify the law on STCs. Paragraph 5.3.2 will discuss the attitude of the drafters of the BW towards self-regulation. Paragraph 5.3.3 will turn to the drafting and implementation of Directive 93/13, as well as attempts to reform the Directive and national law implementing the Directive. Paragraph 5.3.4 will discuss the law on STCs and international trade and paragraph 5.3.5 will end with a conclusion.

908 See further on this provision below, par. 5.3.2.

909 See further on these amendments below, par. 5.3.3.5.

910 J.H.M. van Erp, 'De NVM-koopakte: géén algemene voorwaarden', *WPNR* 6037 (1992) rejects this option, while R.H.C. Jongeneel, 'Reactie', *WPNR* 6217 (1996) defends it.

911 J. Hijma, *Algemene voorwaarden*, Deventer: Kluwer 2010, p. 46–48.

5.3.1. The choice for codification

When the choice for a recodification in the form of the BW was made, interdependence had not yet developed. However, academics drafting the BW extensively considered comparative law, which has benefited the quality of the code. Later initiatives for harmonisation prompted the legislator to consider the development of separate laws, but this would have undermined the consistency and predictability of the law on STCs.

In 1961, when the first draft for the BW was published,[912] interdependence, as such, was not an issue in debate. On the contrary, the idea of a new civil code implicitly and necessarily assumes that the legislator is capable of safeguarding the consistent and accessible development of private law. As private law had developed alongside the old Civil Code, especially in case law, Prof. Meijers[913] pleaded for a renewed codification of private law, and was, accordingly, assigned with the drafting of the new civil code. In his efforts, Prof. Meijers was inspired by comparative law, except in matters that were considered innovative from a social or legal point of view.[914]

Interestingly, the 1961 draft initially did not consider STCs such a subject.[915] However, during the seventies, the interest in this subject increased, and in 1979, two preliminary reports on standard contract terms were published, pleading for more extensive rules on STCs. Previously, one of the authors had published his PhD thesis on STCs, which included extensive comparative law research.[916] After the draft containing the first two articles was passed in 1980,[917] the second part of the draft was submitted, which was based on the advice of the Committee on Consumer Affairs ('*Commissie Consumentenaangelegenheden*', hereafter CCA).[918] The 1980 draft took into account German, Austrian, French, and English developments, as well as the 1976 resolution

912 The first draft for book 6 of the BW contained two articles with regard to STCs: article 6.5.1.2, which later became article 6:214 BW, and article 6.5.1.3 that stipulated that parties who had accepted the application of STCs was bound to those STCs, but, according to par. 2, a clause would be avoidable if the user, at the conclusion of the contract, knew or should have known that if the party subjecting to his STCs would have been aware of their content, he would not have entered into the contract. See E.M. Meijers, *Ontwerp voor een Nieuw Burgerlijk Wetboek, Boek 6*, completed by J. Drion, G. de Grooth, and F.J. de Jong, The Hague: Staatsdrukkerij 1961.

913 E.M. Meijers, 'Het feillooze deel van ons Burgerlijk Wetboek', in: E.M. Meijers, *Verzamelde privaatrechtelijke opstellen, Eerste deel*, Leiden: University Press Leiden 1954, p. 98.

914 V.J.A. Süto, *Nieuw vermogensrecht en rechtsvergelijking – reconstructie van een wetgevingsproces (1947–1961)*, The Hague: BJU 2004, p. 28.

915 C.J. van Zeben, W.H.M. Reehuis, E.E. Slob, *Parlementaire geschiedenis van het nieuwe burgerlijk wetboek: parlementaire stukken systematisch gerangschikt en van noten voorzien. Invoering boeken 3, 5 en 6. Boek 6, Algemeen gedeelte van het verbintenissenrecht*, Deventer: Kluwer 1990, p. 839. Hereafter, the parliamentary history of this book of the BW will be referred to in the following manner: Parl. Gesch. NBW, Boek 6 (Inv. 3, 5 en 6).

916 E.H. Hondius, *Standaardvoorwaarden*, Deventer: Kluwer 1978.

917 Stbl. 1980, 432.

918 Comp. CCA, *Advies inzake het vraagstuk van de toepassing van standaardvoorwaarden bij transacties met de consument*, The Hague: SER 1978, which in annex 4 provides an overview of the development of the law in this area in other states.

from the Council of Europe. The draft was passed in 1987[919] and became law upon the introduction of the BW on 1 January 1992.

The new law on STCs was strongly influenced by German law. As a result, Dutch law resembles German law in the following respects.

Dutch law resembles German law in the following respects. The definition of STCs in article 6:230 sub a BW refers to preformulated clauses designed for use in multiple contracts. The standard for evaluation of clauses is '*onredelijke bezwarendheid*', clauses that are unfairly to the detriment of the consumer. This standard has been derived from the concept of good faith more generally, in articles 6:2 and 6:248 BW, which also refers to the position of parties under (default) law.[920] Dutch law also provides a black and a grey list under articles 6:236 and 237 BW.

However, even if the Dutch legislator had not been inspired by German law, one may ask whether the Directive would not have resulted in a further similarities. Yet although Dutch law was inspired by German law, Dutch law differs from German law.

Articles 6:230 et seq BW differ from articles 305 et seq BGB in various respects: The definition of STCs in article 6:230 sub a BW differs from the definition of article 305 BGB, as it does not refer to clauses that have not been individually negotiated. It is not clear whether this definition includes model contracts. Dutch law also differs from the Directive in this respect, but the CJEU[921] has since made clear that individually negotiated clauses do not fall within the scope of the Directive, and the individual negotiation of clauses does not mean that clauses are main terms in the sense of article 4 par. 2 Directive. Article 6:230 sub a BW accordingly makes an exception for clauses that concern the main subject matter of the contract. The BGB also does not have an equivalent of article 6:232 BW; instead, article 305 BGB requires that STCs have been made available to the contract party. If this is not the case, STCs have not been validly included into the contract. Thus, German law does not stipulate that STCs that have not been made sufficiently available are avoidable, as is the case under Dutch law under article 6: 233 sub b, article 6:234 and 6:230c BW. Instead, under German law, unfair clauses are invalid. The BGB also does not have an equivalent of article 6:235 BW; articles 305 –310 BGB are also applicable to big businesses. The BGB also does not enable amending the law on STCs through royal degrees ('*Algemene Maatregelen van Bestuur*') as Dutch law does under article 6:239 BW. Unlike German law, Dutch law is not applicable to international business contracts, in accordance with article 6:247 BW.[922] The Dutch draft did not codify case law on STCs. Although problems arising from the use of STCs had been

919 Stbl 1987, 327.

920 See further on the evaluation of clauses under article 6:233 sub a BW below par. 5.4.

921 CJEU 30 April 2014 (*Kásler and Hajnalka Káslerné Rábai v OTP Jelzálogbank Zrt*), C-26/12, [2015] ECR p. I-0, par. 47-49.

922 See critically with regard to articles 6:235 and 244 BW R.H.C. Jongeneel, *De Wet algemene voorwaarden en het AGB-Gesetz*, Deventer: Kluwer 1991, p. 292.

signalled prior to the design of the BW[923], the explanatory memorandum makes clear that judges exercised considerable restraint towards the judicial evaluation of STCs.[924] Although the Minister pointed out that the judiciary already anticipated the BW, and that businesses would likely similarly anticipate the BW by adapting their STCs[925], the legislator rejected the idea of leaving the development of the law on STCs to case law. Decisions from the Hoge Raad indicated that the judiciary would not develop case law, which would leave a gap in the law.[926] Moreover, as the draft introduced the judicial evaluation of STCs, this created a potential for unpredictability, which required that the draft carefully considered – and remedied – this potential shortcoming. Therefore, problems would arise if STCs were not dealt with through legislation.

These differences indicate that German law was clearly not transplanted into Dutch law. Accordingly, the legislator noted that 'although comparative law provides interesting material, it only seldom provides the legislator with a ready-made answer'.[927] Logically, the Dutch legislator wished to ensure that the new regime fitted well within the BW, and that it reflected needs and preferences of practice. These wishes, as well as the relation between the regime on STCs and more general contract law, limits the possibility for legal transplants.

The influence of German law can hardly be traced to interdependence – rather, the interest of Prof. Meijers in comparative law emphasised that comparative law may invite one to regard well-settled concepts in a more critical light.[928] In accordance with pluralist arguments, the coexisting regimes in the European Union offered a source of inspiration and mutual learning. This does not mean, however, that later problems may not arise.

By the time the draft was passed, initiatives for harmonisation had developed. In its advice to the government on the law on STCs, the Committee on Consumer Affairs[929] already took notice of these initiatives, but did not consider them as an obstacle to codification. However, these initiatives did prompt Parliament to briefly consider separate legislation implementing the *acquis*. During the discussion in Parliament, the introduction of the law on doorstep selling, an implementation of Directive 85/577 on doorstep selling, was discussed, and the introduction of a separate law was considered, because the BW might not be implemented before 1990.[930] The introduction of separate

923 See for an overview of the most important publications Jongeneel 1991, p. 11, note 14.

924 Parl. Gesch. NBW, Boek 6 (Inv 3, 5, and 6), p. 1649, p. 1518. E.H. Hondius, 'Het Nieuw Burgerlijk Wetboek en de gewone burger: de algemene voorwaarden', *Rechtshulp* 1991, p. 4, points out that the standard in article 6:233 sub a BW had been previously developed by the *Hoge Raad*.

925 Parl. Gesch. NBW, Boek 6 (Inv 3, 5, and 6), p. 1506.

926 Parl. Gesch. NBW, Boek 6 (Inv 3, 5, and 6), p. 1497. See in favour CCA 1978, p. 41 referring to legislation in surrounding states as well as the EU to support the need for consumer protection.

927 Parl. Gesch. NBW, Boek 6 (Inv. 3, 5 en 6), p. 1455. At p. 1467 and 1505 it is, however, remarked that the AGBG has served as a direct example.

928 V.J.A. Süto, *Nieuw Vermogensrecht en rechtsvergelijking – reconstructie van een wetgevingsproces (1947-1961)*, The Hague: BJU 2004, p. 29.

929 CCA, *Advies inzake het vraagstuk van de toepassing van standaardvoorwaarden bij transacties met de consument*, The Hague: SER 1978,p. 3.

930 Parl. Gesch. NBW, Boek 6 (Inv. 3, 5 en 6), p. 1472–1473.

laws was, however, rejected as this might delay the introduction of the BW even further.[931] Other objections included the possible tension between old Dutch law and the BW, which also made a separate introduction of a new law on STCs more difficult.[932]

Thus, the defence of codification by Prof. Meijers may sit somewhat uneasily with the increasing interdependence of actors developing private law. Notably, codification was defended for reasons of predictability, accessibility, consistency and responsiveness, as well as coherence, without considering the possibility of interdependence.

However, the important role of comparative law in the drafting of the BW ensured that the law of STCs was the result of critical consideration of foreign law. In accordance with pluralist arguments, the Dutch legislator made ample use of opportunities for learning. This approach was however not prompted by European law that not only invites, but demands such a critical view.

Further, while especially German law provided inspiration, it was not a legal transplant. The need to develop the new regime consistently with the needs and preferences of practice, with surrounding law and in accordance with society's legal views on justice limits the possibility for legal transplants and possibly, harmonisation. In addition, the timing and the drafting of the Dutch law on STCs and Directive 93/13 meant that critically reflecting on Dutch law or the codification, which had not even entered into force yet, was problematic.

5.3.2. Replacing self-regulation through the BW

In the drafting of article 6:214 BW, which provides for a regime where the legislator and stakeholder parties can draft binding standard rules, the legislator did not sufficiently take into account that later initiatives increased the role of private parties, reflecting a different view on the role of private parties. Thus, this provision was not responsive to national practice or to national legal views on the role of private parties, and has, accordingly, been reduced to a dead letter. The wording of this provision gives a different impression, thus undermining the accessibility of the law for parties not familiar with Dutch practice.

At first sight, the impression arises that the legislator expressly provided a role for private parties through article 6:214 BW. This provision provides that standard rules ('*standaardregeling*') can be drafted for a particular branch or profession, to be designated by royal decision ('*koninklijk besluit*'). Standard rules are designed by a committee to be appointed to the Ministry of Justice, the composition of which is to be determined by law.[933] The standard rules enter into effect upon the approval of the Ministry, as officially published. Standard rules can diverge from default law, and parties may, in turn, diverge from standard rules, which may, however, be made subject to the requirements of form. Standard rules would be applicable to business contracts.

Article 6:214 BW, was drafted because it was recognised that STCs were often drafted one-sidedly, without taking into account the public interest. The involvement of the state

[931] Parl. Gesch. NBW, Boek 6 (Inv. 3, 5 en 6), p. 1490.

[932] Parl. Gesch. NBW, Boek 6 (Inv. 3, 5 en 6), p. 1506.

[933] Notably, the law on standard rules committees ('*Wet commissies standaardregelingen*').

in drafting STCs, and, preferably, the inclusion of all relevant parties would remedy these defects and would, moreover, be in line with a tendency to involve the state in the recognition of collective contracts.[934]

Did this regime enable private parties, by creating a possibility for co-regulation, or did it, in contrast, limit the role of contract parties? The regime did not take away contract parties' ability to draft STCs, nor did it force them to enter into negotiations on standard rules or even to comply with them. However, if article 6:214 BW had been successful, this would have limited the role of contract parties in independently drafting STCs. This limitation was considered desirable because of contract parties' limited perspective and the disadvantages associated with the use of STCs. This point of view has been traced to the critical attitude of Prof. Meijers and others to self-regulation.[935] The requirements set for drafting standard rules, in accordance with a critical view of private parties' role, have not facilitated a successful use of this possibility, even though the increased use of this regime has been debated in Parliament[936] and in literature.[937]

The subsequent draft took a less restrictive role towards the role of non-state actors and explicitly aimed to increase negotiations between stakeholder groups.[938] The CCA[939] expected that designing private law specifically for STCs would induce businesses to enter into negotiations with organisations representing consumers, for which it had developed a pilot project on which it extensively reported. Collective negotiations on consumer contracts have, subsequently, developed in the framework of the CCA. The success of these collective negotiations for consumer contracts has severely limited the success of the standard rules. Also, the judicial control developed by the 1981 draft may have contributed to the quality of STCs, which may further undermine parties' motivation to draft standard rules.

The standard regime, logically, does not take into account interdependence between European and national actors that subsequently developed. Standard rules may, at first sight conflict with international model contracts, for example, from the ICC.[940] Yet on closer inspection, conflict need not arise. Prof. Meijers[941] emphasised that standard rules

[934] C.J. van Zeben, W.J. du Pon (eds.), with cooperation from M.M. Olthof, *Parlementaire geschiedenis van het nieuwe Burgerlijk Wetboek, Boek 6, Algemeen gedeelte van het verbintenissenrecht*, Deventer: Kluwer 1981, p. 839. Hereafter, this book will refer to the parliamentary history of this book of the BW in the following manner: Parl. Gesch. NBW, Boek 6.

[935] J.B.M. Vranken, *Mr. C. Asser's Handleiding tot de beoefening van het Nederlands burgerlijk recht. Algemeen deel. Een vervolg. Deel III*, Deventer: Kluwer 2005, nr. 78. Hereafter, this volume will refer to this book in the following manner: Asser/Vranken 2005.

[936] *Kamerstukken II*, 2006–2007, 29279, nr 41, p. 18.

[937] E.H. Hondius, 'Standaardregelingen in de bouw', in: E.H. Hondius, A.G.J. van Wassenaer, *Van standaardvoorwaarden naar standaardregeling?, Preadviezen voor de Vereniging van Bouwrecht*, Deventer: Kluwer 1993, p. 10–11. The procedure had already been criticised by CCA, *Advies inzake het vraagstuk van de toepassing van standaardvoorwaarden bij transacties met de consument*, The Hague: SER 1978, p. 13.

[938] Parl. Gesch. NBW, Boek 6 (Inv. 3, 5 en 6), p. 1455.

[939] CCA, *Advies inzake het vraagstuk van de toepassing van standaardvoorwaarden bij transacties met de consument*, The Hague: SER, 1978, p. 8-9, the report on the pilot project can be found in annex 3.

[940] Parl. Gesch. NBW, Boek 6, p. 850.

[941] Parl. Gesch. NBW, Boek 6, p. 851.

would be devised for areas in which the quality of STCs showed severe shortcomings. In contrast, if STCs were the result of collective negotiations, standard rules would merely sanction existing rules. Prof. Meijers found that if international model contracts functioned effectively, additional rules should not be developed.

Also, relevant Directives will stand in the way of the possibility to mitigate the consequences of mandatory consumer protection law through drafting standard rules.[942] In areas falling outside the scope of these Directives this need not be problematic.[943] Further, the question arises whether standard regimes fall under the exception in article 1 par. 2 Directive 93/13, as standard rules are not incorporated into the contract, but they are additional law applicable to the contract.[944] If this is the case, the development of standard rules could, theoretically, circumvent the minimum level of protection established in the Directive. In the unlikely scenario that standard rules are developed, European actors should be consulted beforehand, to see whether standard rules for consumer contracts fall within the scope of Directive 93/13. It is detrimental for the predictability of law to develop a practice that may later be challenged before the courts and, eventually, the CJEU.

In accordance with the debate on multilevel governance, interdependence between state and non-state actors has developed. Arguably, the lack of the success of article 6:214 BW indicates that other initiatives that also overlook the prominent role of private parties in this area will be similarly unsuccessful. This article does not respond to practice and it diminishes accessibility. Article 6:214 BW should be reconsidered, both because its lack of importance in legal practice as well as possible difficulties with Directive 93/13.

The reasoning of the legislator shows compelling reasons to limit contract parties' freedom. State actors may be well-placed to provide rules that take the interests of parties subjected to STCs into account – as it is less likely that users of STCs will independently do so. Although the law on STCs had not been subject to harmonisation, the legislator took into account the likely interests of foreign and international actors that likely did not include being subjected to a national regime. Simultaneously, the products of these actors were not considered as sources of inspiration. The reasoning of the legislator indicates that the legislator did not blindly consider all possible sources of learning.

5.3.3. *The development of Dutch law and harmonisation*

Have Dutch actors, in the drafting and implementation of Directive 93/13 and other relevant Directives, adequately taken into account that the development of harmonisation necessitates interaction with European actors, and if so, how has that affected the predictability, accessibility, consistency and responsiveness of the law on STCs? Has the

942 Asser/Hartkamp & Sieburgh 2010, nr. 513.

943 For example in contracts for the sale of houses, article 7:2 par. 4 BW, which fall outside the scope of Directive 1999/44.

944 Asser/Hartkamp & Sieburgh 2010, nr. 513, who also note that diverging from standard rules will make it more likely that they are unfair under article 6:233 BW.

coexistence of Dutch and European actors led to benefits for the law on STCs, in accordance with pluralist arguments?

Paragraph 5.3.3.1 will consider the development of Directive 93/13 and paragraph 5.3.3.2 will discuss the implementation of the Directive. Paragraph 5.3.3.3 will consider the application of the Directive by the courts. Paragraph 5.3.3.4 will consider the attempted revision of Directive 93/13 and paragraph 5.3.3.5 will discuss legislative reform at the national level. Paragraph 5.3.3.6 will end with a conclusion.

5.3.3.1. The drafting of Directive 93/13

The reports of the Dutch legislator reflected an active participation in the European debate that also served to prevent drastic amendments to new articles 6:231 et seq BW.

Before the Directive was established, the Dutch legislator consulted the CCA[945] that had also advised on the drafting on articles 6:231 et seq BW.

The CCA was divided on the need for a Directive, but it approved the limitation of the Directive to consumer contracts. The CCA did draw attention to the definition of 'consumer' that should be interpreted narrowly, in accordance with CJEU case law, as well as the exemption of the main terms of the contract from the scope of the Directive. The CCA proposed limiting the scope of the Directive to written clauses, and argued for the inclusion of an information duty for businesses in the Directive. With regard to future article 3, the CCA held that technically, the inclusion of a blanket clause or ambiguous provisions were necessary, and a blanket clause should enable judges to take into account the way in which a clause had been drafted. The CCA also indicated that more clarity on the status of the model list in the Annex to the Directive would be desirable. The CCA found that the model list could reflect clauses that were ineffective in all Member States, although this would be a short list. The CCA emphasised that clauses needed to be drafted in a manner that would avoid unpredictability and opposed a European grey list for the same reason. The question of whether this would be a limitative list depended on the question of whether the Directive would pursue minimum or maximum harmonisation.

Further debate on the points raised by the CCA hardly developed, although, with the benefit of hindsight, this would have been beneficial.

The criticism of Bakker and Jongeneel[946] is an exception. Bakker and Jongeneel, who also refer to the advice from the European Consumer Law Group and the advice of the Economic and Social Committee, as well as German criticism, similarly refer to the definition of consumer and also find that the Directive should be limited to consumer contracts. They likewise note that the Directive should not cover the main terms of the contract. They also join the request that the status of the model list in the Annex to the Directive should be clarified, and add that the collection of clauses in the 1990 draft seems arbitrary, and apparently does not contribute to the interpretation of the proposed blanket clause. Bakker and Jongeneel, however, draw into doubt the added value of an information duty, although they support the inclusion of a rule similar to the German duty

945 CCA, *Oneerlijke bedingen in consumentenovereenkomsten*, advice 91/11, 30 May 1991, p. 12, 16.
946 H.J. Bakker, R.H.C. Jongeneel, 'Een rechtlijnige richtlijn', *TvC* 1992, p. 7.

of transparency, the *Transparanzgebot*, and consider the inclusion of future article 3, the wording of which they criticise.

The CCA advice provided a good starting point for the position of the Dutch legislator,[947] who briefly discussed the discussion on the proposal for a Directive on unfair contract terms and the advice of the CCA on the draft in Parliament, from which it diverged in several points.

While the Dutch government agreed with the importance of self-regulation, and restraint with harmonisation initiatives, it supported the proposal for a Directive on unfair terms, and did not discuss the need for the Directive.

The Dutch government[948] reported to Parliament that the debate in the European Council focused on the scope of the Directive, the question of whether the main terms of the contract should be subjected to judicial evaluation, and stated that a Dutch compromise would form the basis for further discussions in the council. The Dutch government[949] subsequently reported that the amendments to the proposal were in accordance with Dutch objections, and Dutch law, accordingly, did not have to be amended. Interestingly, in the German legal order, the amendments to the 1990 drafts are attributed to German criticism. As Dutch law took German law as an important starting point, German and Dutch criticism may well have coincided. The rather brief and general statement of the government on the CCA advice, without further debate, did not make Parliament aware of differences between the CCA advice and this seems not to have been debated in Parliament who earlier, and more generally, criticised the incomplete and late information it received on proposals for Directives.[950]

Thus, the active participation of the Dutch legislator may have prevented Directive 93/13 necessitating drastic amendments to newly drafted law that had yet to become effective.

Opportunities for learning were available but Dutch law has not benefited from them. In contrast to German debate, Dutch debate was not very extensive, but it did include insights from foreign and European actors, which provided a more critical perspective on Dutch law. This perspective was not adopted by the Dutch legislator, who had an interest in not amending the newly introduced BW. As a result, mutual opportunities for learning were available within the Dutch legal order, but these opportunities were not used in subsequent political debate. Because of the timing of the Directive, the Dutch legislator likely was not particularly inclined to consider the needs and preferences of foreign and international actors, despite harmonisation, if it had not already done so.

947 *Kamerstukken II*, 1992–1993, 23162, nr 1, p. 5.
948 *Kamerstukken II*, 1991–1992, 21501–15, nr 4, p. 2.
949 *Kamerstukken II*, 1991–1992, 21501–15, nr 6, p. 1–2.
950 *Kamerstukken II*, 1991–1992, 21209, nr 47, p. 10–11.

5.3.3.2. The implementation of Directives affecting the law on STCs

The interaction between Dutch, European and foreign actors in the implementation of Directive 93/13 and other relevant Directives has been limited, and problems of predictability, consistency and accessibility have, accordingly, arisen.

Because the Dutch legislator considered that Dutch law was already in accordance with the Directive, the law on STCs was not amended, and a consultation was also not initiated.[951]

Accordingly, some differences between the Directive and Dutch law remained. Thus, articles 6:231 et seq BW initially did not include a rule on *contra preferentem* interpretation, while it was also limited to written clauses. Initially, it seemed as if the Hoge Raad limited this rule,[952] and it was argued that the codification of this rule was necessary.[953]

Furthermore, article 6:231 BW did initially not provide that the main terms of the contract would be subject to judicial evaluation if they are not clearly formulated. Article 6: 231 BW defines STCs as clauses that have been drafted to be used in multiple contracts. Interestingly, the German legislator amended article 310 par. 3 sub 1 BGB as it was considered that maintaining a similar requirement for consumer contracts was contrary to the Directive.[954] Notably, however, the Commission did not single out this definition, which raises the question whether the German legislator unnecessarily amended its law. Clarifying this question should be reserved to the CJEU.

Additionally, it has been debated whether unfair terms invalid rather than avoidable, especially after CJEU decisions that clauses are to be evaluated *ex officio*.[955] Maintaining the avoidability rather than the invalidity of unfair clauses may be problematic as avoidability cannot be considered by the judge *ex officio*. The sanction of avoidability is in accordance with the general rule in article 3:40 par 2 BW that if a provision aims to protect one of the contract parties, this leads to avoidability, unless the provisions entails otherwise. In this view, sanctioning unfair clauses with invalidity is not necessary, also because article 3:40 par. 2 BW does not exclude the possibility that the judge sets aside clauses contrary to provisions aiming to protect the consumer. Article 3:40 par. 2 BW expressly allows for divergences from this general rule by stipulating that provisions are avoidable unless the provisions entails otherwise. Consequently, provisions that implement Directives more generally justify invalidity rather than avoidability in this sense.[956] However, this

951 *Kamerstukken II*, 1991–1992, 21501–15, nr 6, p. 1–2, similarly R.H.C. Jongeneel, 'Een richtlijn die weinig schade aanricht', *TvC* 1993, p. 118.

952 HR 28 April 1989, *NJ* 1990, 583, which, however, included a contract between businesses. In HR 24 September 1993, *NJ* 1993, 760, in an international consumer contract, it was, however, held that interpretation *contra preferentem* was merely one point of view between other views.

953 E.H. Hondius, 'Non-implementation of the Directive on unfair contract terms: The Dutch case', *ERPL* 1997, p. 195, similarly A.G. Tizzano in his conclusion before C-199/44 (Commission v Netherlands), par. 23.

954 See previously par. 4.3.2.2.

955 CJEU 27 June 2000 (Océano Grupo Editorial SA v Murciano Quintero and others), joined cases C-240/98 to C-244/98, [2000], ECR, p. I-4941.

956 N. Frenk, 'Ambtshalve toetsing van dwingend Europees consumentenrecht: gevolgen van het arrest van het Europese Hof van Justitie van 27 juni 2000 voor het Burgerlijk Wetboek', *WPNR* 6431 (2001), p. 74–75.

argument suggests that avoidability in article 3:40 par. 2 BW would have different implications depending on the context.[957]

The Dutch position was not based on discussion but rather on the previous advice of the CCA and the drafting process, and the position did not change after criticism that the Dutch regime was not in accordance with the Directive. Especially Hondius[958] pointed to differences between the Directive and Dutch law, and held that Dutch law should be amended. Hijma[959] also found that while the differences between Dutch law and the Directive were superficial and would probably be covered by an active approach of the judiciary towards the implementation of the Directive, the restraint adopted by the Dutch legislator should be reconsidered, even if the amendments to Dutch law would only be introduced for politeness' sake.

However, the later decision of the CJEU has learned that the Dutch legislator should be more careful in its approach. *Commission v Netherlands*[960] makes clear that the possibilities for the Dutch legislator to maintain a stable development of the law are limited once Directives have been established.

Would more debate, however, have led to a different approach of the legislator? Possibly, a more elaborate discussion in Parliament, or observations from foreign parties, could have prompted the Dutch government to reconsider its approach. However, more attention for CJEU case law would not have prompted a different approach. Like the German legislator, the Dutch legislator mistakenly relied on CJEU case law[961] reiterating the discretion of the legislator in the implementation of Directives. However, the interaction with the European Commission indicated that the implementation of Directive 93/13 was insufficient.[962]

The Commission accepted that the case law of the Hoge Raad already exempted the main terms of the contract from judicial control, but, nevertheless, advised that these provisions of the Directive were implemented in the BW rather than case law.[963] Although the legislator had started the procedure to amend the law accordingly, it did not make amends within two months, as requested by the Commission, which consequently started a procedure to demand correct implementation. The CJEU,[964] accordingly, held that articles 4 par. 2 and 5 Directive should be implemented in the BW, as relying on case law was insufficient implementation.

957 C. Cauffman, M. Faure, T. Hartlief, *Harmonisatie van het contractenrecht in Europa: consequenties voor Nederland*, Advice 26 March 2009, The Hague: WODC 2009, p. 269.

958 E.H. Hondius, 'Non-implementation of the Directive on Unfair Contract Terms: the Dutch case', *ERPL* 1997, p. 193.

959 J. Hijma, Richtlijn 93/13/EEG betreffende oneerlijke bedingen in consumentenovereenkomsten', in: S.C.J.J. Kortmann et al. (eds.), *Onderneming en 5 jaar Nieuw Burgerlijk Recht*, Deventer: Tjeenk Willink 1997, p. 425.

960 CJEU 10 May 2001 (Commission v The Netherlands), C-144/99, [2001] ECR, p. I-3541.

961 Particularly, CJEU 9 April 1987 (Commission v Italy), Case 363/85, ECR [1987], p. 1733, par. 7, CJEU 23 May 1985, (Commission v Germany), Case 29/84, ECR 1985, p. 1661, par. 23, see previously par. 4.3.2.2.

962 *Kamerstukken II*, 1998–1999, 26470, nr. 5, p. 2.

963 *Kamerstukken II*, 1998–1999, 26470, nr. 3, referring to HR 19 September 1997, *NJ* 1998, 6, that does, however, not refer to *contra legem* interpretation.

964 CJEU 10 May 2001 (Commission v The Netherlands), C-144/99, [2001] ECR, p. I-3541.

After the CJEU decision in *Commission v The Netherlands*, article 6:238 par. 2 BW was inserted, codifying *contra preferentem* interpretation, and article 6:231 BW was amended so as to exempt the main terms of the contract, provided that they were sufficiently clear, from judicial control. That does, however, not mean that the Dutch legislator could not have chosen to go beyond the level of protection in the Directive, provided that it had done so through legislation, as became apparent after the decision of the CJEU in *Caja de Ahorros*.[965]

The subsequent amendments of articles 6:231 et seq BW further demonstrate the decreased ability of the national legislator to maintain the predictable development of the law on STCs, in particular, by exercising restraint in amending the law.

In 2004, article 6:234 BW was amended to implement article 10 par. 3 Directive 2000/31 on e-commerce. This provision imposes information obligations on businesses that businesses can diverge from. Notably, however, article 6:235 BW stipulates that article 6:234 BW is not applicable to large businesses in the sense of article 6:235 par. 1 BW. In 2009, article 6:234 BW was amended for the implementation of Directive 2006/123, stipulating that if STCs fell under article 230c par. 6, the user can make the STCs available in the ways prescribed under article 6:230c BW. Article 6:230c BW stipulates that the information is made available on the initiative from the provider of services, is easily accessible for the consumer at the place where the service is provided or the contract is concluded, is easily available at an internet address made available by the provider, or is included in all documents provided by the provider of services that describe the services in detail. Unsurprisingly, this amendment led to criticism that the law was unclear on the way in which STCs should be made available. A 2010 amendment[966] revised article 6:234 BW and left out the referral to 6:230c BW, which enabled sellers to make STCs available on their website. The Dutch government recognised the need to compensate this amendment,[967] and, accordingly, amended article 6:234 BW.[968] In these cases, the simultaneous implementation of various Directives in one part of the code has clearly given rise to inconsistency and inaccessibility, and inhibited the stable development of the law.

Thus, the interaction in the development of the law on STCs and the interaction in the European debate, as well as the timing of the Directive 93/13 limited the willingness of the Dutch legislator to amend the law. Although the Dutch legislator, like the German legislator, has exercised restraint in the implementation of Directives, this approach was not similarly successful. It can be questioned whether, in accordance with multilevel governance perspectives, those problems have developed because of a lack of interaction between Dutch and European actors, as European law was not clear on the obligations of Member States. However, encouraging more debate could have prompted the Dutch legislator to make some small amendments, despite the introduction of the BW, which could have prevented further problems.

965 CJEU 3 June 2010 (Caja de Ahorros v Ausbanc), C-484/08, [2010] ECR, p. I-4785.
966 Stbl. 2010, 222.
967 *Kamerstukken I*, 2010–2011, 31358, G.
968 Stbl. 2011, 500.

Simultaneously, restraint in amending the law has not become visible in the amendments of articles 6:230c and 6:234 BW, and predictability, consistency and accessibility have been diminished. Possibly, more careful debate in he implementation of Directive 2006/123 could have limited the amendments needed to implement the *acquis*. In hindsight, the question arises whether an active approach of the Dutch legislator in the drafting of Directive 2006/123 could have contributed to the need to amend Dutch law.

The Dutch legislator has not benefited from the involvement of other actors in the development of the law on STCs, in accordance with pluralist insights. The Dutch legislator did not consider opportunities for learning in the implementation of the Directive. Instead, a national approach to the Directive has been adopted, and the Dutch legislator did not encourage debate. Notably, opportunities to learn from the implementation of the Directives in other Member States may be limited because of time constraints.

The debate between the Commission and the Dutch government prior to *Commission v The Netherlands* and the subsequent 2001 CJEU decision makes clear that the reallocation of competences to the European level entails more control on Member States transposing Directives. Yet despite this control, and the subsequent insertion of article 6:238 par. 2 BW on *contra preferentem* interpretation, the Hoge Raad has maintained its case law on *contra preferentem* interpretation.[969] Arguably, even after the CJEU ruling, the Hoge Raad has rejected the transplant in the Directive, which was subsequently transposed into national law.[970] The European legislator and the CJEU have also not prompted the Dutch legislator to more carefully implement Directives. The development of this control has not benefited the law on STCs, as becomes visible in the repeated amendments to articles 6:230c and 234 BW. As ongoing, uncoordinated revision of the *acquis* also takes place at the European level,[971] one may ask whether a system of checks and balances, in accordance with pluralist arguments, is going to be very effective in preventing inconsistency or unpredictability at the national level. It may also be doubted whether such a system would be well received. A control system to enhance the implementation of the *acquis* more generally would require more expertise of national law than European actors possess. Further, exercising control over the implementation practices in 27 Member States requires much effort and time, which may not be

969 Comp. also HR 14 October 2002, *NJ* 2003, 258.

970 Comp. A. Watson, Legal transplants, Scottish Academic Press: Edinburgh 1974, p. 27.

971 Particularly, since the Communication on European contract law, COM (2001) 398 final, Directive 2011/83 on consumer rights revises and repeals Directive 85/577 on doorstep selling and Directive 97/7 on distance selling. The Directive does not repeal Directive 93/13 on unfair contract terms and Directive 1999/44 on consumer sales, although the proposal for a consumer rights Directive did intend to. These Directive are still to be revised, as is Directive 90/314 on package travel. Meanwhile, Directive 2008/122 revised Directive 94/47 on timeshare and Directive 2008/48 revised Directive 87/107 on consumer credit. Alongside these projects, the DCFR has been developed. It has served as a starting point for the withdrawn CESL, COM (2011) 635. A proposal for an optional insurance contract laws also developed, see the report of the Expert Group at http://ec.europa.eu/justice/contract/insurance/expert-group/index_en.htm. In addition, Directives that overlap have been adopted, apart from the revision of the *acquis*, in particular Directive 2014/17 on mortgage credit.

sufficiently present at the European level. Despite the control at the European level, the drafting of Directives 93/13 and 2006/123 has not motivated the Dutch legislator to reflect more on the needs and preferences of foreign and transnational actors who want easier access to the Dutch market.

5.3.3.3. The application of Directives by the courts

In the application of national law implementing Directives, the restraint of the legislator in interacting with European, foreign and national actors has been echoed by the courts, which has further lessened the predictability, consistency, accessibility and responsiveness of the law on STCs.

- Initially, restraint did not become apparent, as the Hoge Raad had anticipated on the draft for articles 6:231 et seq BW.[972]
- Further decisions of the Hoge Raad, however, show that national law implementing Directive 93/13 is interpreted in accordance with Dutch law and the preferences of the Dutch legislator.

A 1997 decision of the Hoge Raad,[973] as well as the conclusion of A.G. Vranken, refers to Parliamentary history on the drafting of articles 6:231 et seq Directive, and although the exception in article 6:231 sub a BW for main contract terms was included on the instigation of the Commission, the Hoge Raad does not refer the question how main contract terms in the sense of article 4 par. 2 Directive are to be interpreted to the CJEU. In its 2003 decision, the Hoge Raad[974] confirmed this decision, without referring to the Directive at all, similar to the conclusion of the A.G. A less wide interpretation of the main terms of the contract in the meaning of article 4 par. 2 Directive seems in accordance with the aim of the consumer protection of the Directive and need not necessarily be problematic, as the CJEU decision in *Caja de Ahorros* made clear that national actors may choose to extend judicial evaluation.

The CJEU has since ruled that the concept of "main terms" should be interpreted narrowly, in accordance with the considerations of the Hoge Raad and the Dutch legislator. In *Van Hove v CNP Assurances SA*,[975] the Court emphasised 'individually negotiated terms' that stipulate the essential obligations of the contract, in contrast to ancillary obligations. Previously, the Court stressed the 'essential obligations' covered by main terms, that characterise the contract.[976] The question arises whether this standard coincides with the Hoge Raad's standard that it concerns terms without which the contract would not have been entered into, or without which it would be impossible to

972 HR 25 April 1986, *NJ* 1986, 714 (with a critical note of W. van der Grinten), repeated in HR 16 January 1987, *NJ* 1987, 553. The question whether clauses are in accordance with good faith, is a question of law, not of fact.

973 HR 19 September 1997, *NJ* 1998, 6.

974 HR 21 February 2003, *NJ* 2004, 567.

975 CJEU 23 April 2015 (Van Hove v CNP Assurances SA), C-96/14, [2015] ECR p. I-0, par. 30–31.

976 CJEU 26 February 2015 (Matei v SC Volksbank România SA), C-143/13, [2015] ECR p. I-0, par. 54–55, as well as CJEU 30 April 2014 (Kásler and Káslerné Rábai), C-26/13, [2015] ECR, p. I-0, par. 49–50. CJEU 26 April 2012 (Hatóság v Invitel Távközlési Zrt), C-472/10, [2012] ECR p. I-0, par. 23 did not extensively consider terms falling under article 4 par. 2 Directive.

speak of true agreement between parties, measured objectively. The CJEU ruled that in the case of insurance contracts, the main terms concerned the premium paid. With this definition, it becomes clear that the distinction in article 4 par. 2 Directive that refers to the main subject matter of the contract or the adequacy of the price and remuneration is not a sharp one.

It is, however, not a harmonised interpretation of the term used in the Directive, and the Dutch interpretation, accordingly, differs from the German interpretation.[977]

- In addition, in some cases, the Hoge Raad has maintained its own case law rather than interpreting a case in accordance with Directive 93/13.

Accordingly, the Hoge Raad[978] referred to its own case law, maintaining that *contra preferentem* interpretation was merely a relevant point of view among other points, and did not anticipate the inclusion of article 6:238 par. 2 BW.

The extension of the scope of the regime on STCs also does not entail that cases involving business contracts are decided in accordance with the Directive. Before the Directive went into effect, the Hoge Raad did not anticipate the Directive in the way it had done with articles 6:231 et seq BW,[979] and after the Directive went into effect, decisions have not referred to the Directive either.[980]

Lower courts,[981] in the interpretation of articles 6:231 et seq BW in consumer cases, have similarly not referred to either Directive 93/13 or foreign decisions that could be relevant for the consistent interpretation of the Directive throughout the Union. Some decisions are clearly in contrast with Directive 93/13.[982] However, other lower courts[983] have expressly referred to the Directive and CJEU case law.

A national approach to the Directive is also visible in the interpretation methods of the Hoge Raad, as well as some lower courts, which may not be in line with European law. Particularly, the emphasis on legislative history may be difficult to reconcile with the decision from the CJEU in *Björnekulla Fruktindustrier*,[984] where the CJEU ruled that national courts need to interpret national law in the light of the wording of Directives, despite contrary interpretation that may follow from the *travaux préparatoires*. That

977 Comp. BGH 14 October 1996, *NJW* 1998, 383.

978 Comp. also HR 14 October 2002, *NJ* 2003, 258.

979 HR 9 September 1994, *NJ* 1995, 285.

980 For example HR 12 July 2002, *NJ* 2002, 542, Hof Amsterdam 26 June 1996, *NJ* 1997, 264.

981 Ktr. Heerlen, 8 April 2009, *Prg.* 2009, 73, Ktr. Venlo, 1 July 2009, *WR* 2010, 17, referring to article 7:219 BW for a clause holding that a contract for accommodation would be terminated if the tenant breached articles 2 or 3 on the forbidden substances act (*Opiumwet*), Rb. Utrecht 23 July 2008, *Prg.* 2009, 9, Hof 's-Hertogenbosch 29 May 2009, *NJF* 2009, 336.

982 Especially Ktr. Haarlem 22 January 2003, *Prg.* 2003, 6031, refusing to evaluate STCs in a consumer contract of its own motion as the consumer had invoked the unreasonableness of the STCs, and similarly Rb. Utrecht 4 January 2006, *NJF* 2006, 152. Comp. also Hof 's-Gravenhage 10 September 2004, *Prg.* 2005, 13, upholding a clause in a consumer contract excluding liability falling under article 6:237 BW.

983 See for example Rb. Arnhem 14 April 2010, *NJF* 2010, 209, Ktr. Amsterdam 15 January 2010, *RVR* 2010, 50, Ktr. Haarlem 13 May 2009, *Prg.* 2009, 105, Ktr. Rotterdam 17 July 2008, *Prg.* 2008, 163.

984 CJEU 29 April 2004 (Björnekulla Fruktindustrier v Procordia Food), C-371/02, [2004] ECR, p. I-5791, par. 13.

does not mean that courts may not rely on parliamentary history. In *Commission v Sweden*, the CJEU[985] accepted that parliamentary history is an important source for interpreting (implemented) law in some Member States, and upheld the inclusion of the list in the Annex to the Directive in parliamentary history. Accordingly, Dutch courts frequently assume that the legislator aims to implement a Directive and, therefore, national law is in accordance with, or should be interpreted in accordance with, a Directive.[986] However, *Björnekulla Fruktindustrier* indicates that if legislative history is contrary to the wording of the Directive, legislative history does not justify interpretation contrary to the wording of the Directive. Relying primarily on parliamentary history in the interpretation of articles 6:231 et seq BW may be problematic because the legislative history that the courts refer to regards the introduction of the BW and not the implementation of Directives. Therefore, assuming that the Dutch legislator meant to implement the Directive, and referring to parliamentary history, may not be correct.

- The courts have similarly adopted restraint in the interpretation of national law implementing Directives 2006/123 or Directive 2000/31, which decreases the chance that the courts will remedy the careless implementation of these Directives by the Dutch legislator.

A 2007 decision from the Hoge Raad[987] was also decided in line with national law. The Hoge Raad distinguishes between the question of whether parties have included STCs in their contract, a question that should be decided under article 3:33 et seq BW, and the question of whether STCs have been made available in practice in accordance with article 6:233 and 234 BW, upholding the decision of the court of appeal that the terms had been made available under article 6:234 par. 1 BW.

A 2011 decision[988] similarly shows restraint. The Hoge Raad decided on the question of whether STCs had been made reasonably available and could be found online with a search engine. As the party subjected to the STCs had not expressly agreed with taking note of the STCs electronically, the Hoge Raad held that the STCs had not been made reasonably available, and that interpretation responsive to legal practice did not entail that, if STCs may be made available online, the user of STCs merely has to ensure that STCs may be found online after an online search.

The Hoge Raad does not refer to either of the Directives. A.G. Wissink refers to Directive 2006/123 on services, but not to Directive 2000/31 on e-commerce, and he does not consider that parties who are not consumers, as in this case, may diverge from article 10 par. 3 Directive 2000/31. It is unclear whether parties may also agree on this silently. This possibility, which is not included in article 6:234 BW, is left open, as this had not been argued before the court. Also, questions with regard to the simultaneous applicability of the Directives and questions of priority arise from this

985 CJEU 7 May 2002 (Commission v Sweden), C-478/99, [2002] ECR, p. I-4147.

986 M.H. Wissink, *Richtlijnconforme interpretatie*, Deventer: Kluwer 2001, p. 154.

987 HR 21 September 2007, *NJ* 2009, 50. The conclusion of A.G. Spier under pars. 3.23 and 3.38 however, does refer to CJEU case law on jurisdiction clauses under article 17 Lugano Convention, Directive 93/13 and soft law.

988 HR 11 February 2011, *NJ* 2011, 571, comp. pars. 2.2 et seq in the conclusion of A.G. Wissink.

case. A CJEU decision clarifying the potential overlap between these Directives would have been welcome.

The approach of lower courts differs. Decisions from some lower courts[989] do not refer to either the Directive or foreign decisions. Some lower courts explicitly follow the course adopted by the Hoge Raad.[990] Other lower courts[991] have diverged from the course adopted by the Hoge Raad and the decisions from other lower courts,[992] as well as the explanation of the Minister of Justice in the amendment of article 6:234 BW that merely referring to STCs on a website did not suffice to make STCs available.[993]

The decision of the court of appeal Arnhem[994] is one of the few decisions that has taken into account Directive 2006/123. The court upheld STCs that were made available to the counterparty at the office of the user of STCs, expressly referring to article 6:230c and Directive 2006/123, apparently diverging from the Hoge Raad.

- However, in a 2013 decision the *ex officio* obligation of the courts to evaluate the fairness of clauses, the Hoge Raad[995] did not similarly adopt restraint.

The Hoge Raad referred to CJEU case law and explained the consequences within national civil procedure law. The Hoge Raad stressed that judges must *ex officio* evaluate the unfairness of clauses in consumer contracts. This includes judges in appeal cases, even if parties have not submitted complaints on this point, as the judge would do for other law that falls under public policy. However the Hoge Raad simultaneously holds that the judge should not go beyond the dispute brought by parties. That means that if parties have not challenged a claim, the judge may not be competent to examine the fairness of clauses. Yet if the judge suspects that a contract contains an unfair clause, he needs to examine further into this possibility, even if this is not the basis of parties' claim, whilst however respecting the limits of the dispute as brought by parties. The Hoge Raad went on to consider the obligation of the judge to order parties to provide further information and the obligation of the judge to hear both parties' arguments on the fairness of clause. The Hoge Raad in passing considered judges' obligations to evaluate clauses in cases of default of one of the parties, under article 139 Civil Procedure Code. This decision touches on various essential principles of Dutch civil procedure law and is bound to lead to further questions.

989 See for example Ktr. Roermond 11 August 2008, *NJF* 2009, 378, Rb. Utrecht 23 July 2008, *NJF* 2008, 436. Ktr. Alkmaar 2 May 2007, *Prg.* 2008, 9 refers to case law from the Hoge Raad.

990 Rb. Zwolle 14 January 2009, *LJN* BI3429.

991 See for example Hof 's-Hertogenbosch 13 October 2009, *LJN* BL1921, deciding that a clause that the user of STCs had referred to in an email, referring to the address of a website on which the STCs could be downloaded, had been validly included in the contract, Ktr. Haarlem, 29 August 2007, *NJF* 2008, 42, finding that referral to the website, on the offer that was in writing, sufficed for inclusion under article 6:234 BW. Both decisions did not refer to Directive 2000/31. Rb. Oost-Brabant 18 March 2015, ECLI:NL:RBOBR:2015:1538 considered that the user of STCs had not given his contract party sufficient opportunity to inform himself of the STCs as the user could not prove that his STCs were clearly accessible via his website. The court does not refer to either Directive 2000/31 or Directive 2006/123.

992 Rb. Maastricht 20 January 2010, *NJF* 2010, 253. Rb. Zutphen 19 August 2009, *NJF* 2009, 463 refers to legislative history.

993 *Kamerstukken II*, 2007–2008, 31358, nr. 3, p. 9–10.

994 Hof Arnhem 11 December 2012, *NJF* 2013, 115.

995 HR 13 September 2013, *NJ* 2014, 274.

This decision has since been followed by lower courts.[996] Other lower courts however continue to refer to the CJEU.[997]

The question arises whether this decision marks a more general change of approach of the Hoge Raad, which could be followed by Dutch courts. Arguably the decision of the Hoge Raad should be considered against the background of an increasing number of Dutch lower courts' decisions following the CJEU while ignoring the Hoge Raad.[998] The decision of the Hoge Raad should stop this practice. It remains to be seen whether the Hoge Raad will more generally adopt an active approach. This is not likely if it interferes with the obligation of the Hoge Raad to ensure the uniform and consistent interpretation of Dutch law.

→ The restraint adopted by the courts diminishes the chance that shortcomings in the implementation of relevant Directives are compensated. This is detrimental to private parties as the lack of predictability, accessibility and inconsistency resulting from articles 6:234 and 6:230c BW are not remedied. Also, the lack of interaction between courts has led to inconsistency and unpredictability for private parties and has entailed that law that is more lenient to business parties has been overlooked, which may diminish the responsiveness of private law to practice. Because of the restraint of courts in referring questions to the CJEU, unpredictability, inconsistencies and a lack of responsiveness remain.

The restraint of courts in referring to the CJEU also is detrimental for the development of the *acquis* in the long term, as it decreases the chance that inconsistencies and problems in the implementation of Directives are brought to the attention of European actors, which increases the chance that problems in the *acquis* will not be remedied.

Presently, it does not seem as if the coexistence of actors has resulted in much benefits for the law on STCs. It is not apparent that the Hoge Raad or lower courts will more frequently refer to the CJEU, or that the national approach to the Directive or even the *acquis* will more generally be considered.

5.3.3.4. The attempted reform of Directive 93/13

Dutch actors have shown restraint in interacting with European actors and national non-state actors, which entails that the attempted reform did not deal with problems currently visible in the law on STCs. Consequently, the responsive development of the Directive is undermined.

996 Ktr. Amsterdam 12 December 2013, *RVR* 2014, 31, comp. Ktr. Eindhoven 20 March 2014, *NJF* 2014, 219 that refers to the Directive but not to the Hoge Raad or the CJEU.

997 Ktr. Rotterdam 28 February 2014, *NJF* 2014, 199, as well as Ktr. Amsterdam 10 March 2014, *Prg.* 2014, 142.

998 See further below par. 5.4.

Although the Dutch legislator did not initiate a separate consultation on the proposed reform of the 1993 Directive, it did refer to the CCA for advice on the draft,[999] and included stakeholders preceding the advice. The WODC also provided a report.

The evaluation of the Directives was not finished when the draft Directive was published, and the reports are, therefore, not based on the experiences with the Directive.

The advice of the CCA,[1000] after criticising the positions of the European Commission and the impact analysis, extensively considers the potential consequences of maximum harmonisation. It does not reject maximum harmonisation outright and finds that maximum harmonisation may still leave some room for Member States in matters falling outside the scope of the Directive. However, the CCA doubts claims that maximum harmonisation will increase cross-border trade and warns of a lower level of consumer protection.

The CCA[1001] also criticised the wording of the proposed EU model list that left room for discussion as to whether clauses fell under the list. Interestingly, the CCA noted that the question of whether a model list should be precisely worded or not depends on the question of what aim these model lists pursue. The national model list was strictly enforced in Germany, but the clauses in the Dutch legal order left more discretion to the courts. The CCA – incorrectly – held that clauses falling under the black list also allowed for some discretion, and convincingly stated that the list should be specified for points where discussion in practice was likely to arise.

The CCA held that it would benefit consumers if the list was more closely related to special regimes that were of interest to the consumer, such as the regime on consumer sales in book 7 BW. The CCA, furthermore, provided an overview of clauses in articles 6:236 and 237 BW that are used often against consumers, and wondered at the absence of these clauses in the proposal. In addition, the CCA pointed to clauses contrary to mandatory law, clauses diverging from default law, and unduly surprising clauses, noting that these should be included in the draft Directive and Annex.

Although the CCA[1002] noted the suggestion to include the possibility to amend binding EU model lists by committees of experts, through the comitology procedure under article 290 TFEU, the CCA rejected the possibility to amend the EU model lists in this manner, because it concerned an issue too important for practice. Therefore, the CCA preferred a democratic procedure that takes into account the views of stakeholders.

The WODC report[1003] that was published prior to the advice of the CCA, also contributed to the discussion and provided information for the Dutch legislator in the European debate. Differing from the CCA, the report[1004] suggested replacing articles 6:236 and 237 BW by the EU model list, considering that the comparison of the Dutch and the European list would be 'too complicated'

999 See the letter of the Minister, 10 December 2008, at www.ser.nl/~/media/DB_Adviezen/2000_2009/2009/b27871.ashx.

1000 CCA, *Consumentenrechten in de interne markt*, advice 09/05, 17 June 2009, available at www.ser.nl/~/media/DB_Adviezen/2000_2009/2009/b27871.ashx, p. 15, 21–26.

1001 CCA, *Consumentenrechten in de interne markt*, advice 09/05, 17 June 2009, available at www.ser.nl/~/media/DB_Adviezen/2000_2009/2009/b27871.ashx, p. 68-74.

1002 CCA, *Consumentenrechten in de interne markt*, advice 09/05, 17 June 2009, available at www.ser.nl/~/media/DB_Adviezen/2000_2009/2009/b27871.ashx, p. 74.

1003 C. Cauffman, M. Faure, T. Hartlief, *Harmonisatie van het contractenrecht in Europa: consequenties voor Nederland*, Advice 26 March 2009, WODC.

1004 C. Cauffman, M. Faure, T. Hartlief, *Harmonisatie van het contractenrecht in Europa: consequenties voor Nederland*, Advice 26 March 2009, WODC, p. 142-143.

– and it may be doubted whether articles 6:236 and 237 BW could be maintained under a Directive pursuing maximum harmonisation. The report went on to critically evaluate to what extent articles 6:236 and 237 BW could be maintained, and which clauses would have to be removed, moved to the grey list – clauses on the grey list are, interestingly, not moved to the black list – and which clauses would be introduced. The report[1005] further recommended that the sanction of avoidability, which seemed in accordance with article 3:40 par. 2 BW, should be amended, so that it stipulates that clauses will not be binding on the consumer.

In addition, in the WODC report,[1006] the amendments of Dutch law in accordance with the proposed Directive also prompt a reconsideration of the information duties under article 6:233 sub b and 6:234 BW. Amending article 6:231 sub a BW, so that it would include the notion of STCs as not individually negotiated terms would ensure the correct implementation of the Directive. Also, the debate on the question of whether the avoidability of unfair clauses sufficiently implements the Directive, could have prompted the Dutch legislator to reconsider article 3:40 BW, which has more generally been described as a failure.[1007]

The WODC report[1008] notes that the proposal will lead to a lower level of consumer protection, and recognises the dilemma of legislators in either exercising restraint in the implementation of Directives or a more active approach. On the one hand, exercising restraint is beneficial for the consistency and predictability of law, but it may undermine the correct implementation of Directives. On the other hand, a more active approach contributes to the correct implementation of the Directive, but it may weaken the consistency and predictability of the law.

However, the Dutch experience in the implementation of Directives shows that despite restraint, problems of predictability, accessibility and consistency may still arise.

In Parliament, the Dutch government[1009] stressed that maintaining a high level of consumer protection was important.[1010] The Dutch government further stated that national law would form a starting point in the negotiation process at the European level, although it simultaneously indicated that it supported the idea of maximum harmonisation.[1011] This statement is in accordance with criticism of nationalism, not only with regard to methods, but also with regard to national law. In a later stage of the drafting process of the Directive, the Dutch government reported that it supported limiting the scope of the proposal as governments could not reach agreement on the regime on STCs.

1005 C. Cauffman, M. Faure, T. Hartlief, *Harmonisatie van het contractenrecht in Europa: consequenties voor Nederland*, Advice 26 March 2009, WODC, p. 156-157.

1006 C. Cauffman, M. Faure, T. Hartlief, *Harmonisatie van het contractenrecht in Europa: consequenties voor Nederland*, Advice 26 March 2009, WODC, p. 264-270.

1007 A.S. Hartkamp, 'Het nieuwe BW – ontwikkelingen sinds 1992', *AA* 2012, p. 50.

1008 C. Cauffman, M. Faure, T. Hartlief, *Harmonisatie van het contractenrecht in Europa: consequenties voor Nederland*, Advice 26 March 2009, WODC, p. 251, 252.

1009 *Kamerstukken II*,2008–2009, 22112, 742, p. 7, 8.

1010 *Kamerstukken II*, 2010–2011, 21501–30, nr 246, p. 8.

1011 *Kamerstukken I*, 2009–2010, 30520, nr D, p. 1. The Dutch response to the previous consultation, available at http://ec.europa.eu/consumers/cons_int/safe_shop/acquis/responses_green_paper_acquis_en.htm, p. 14–16 adopted a more nuanced approach to maximum harmonisation, stating that the question whether maximum harmonisation is desirable may be answered differently for different Directives, and should be based on a thorough assessment.

At the European level, the Dutch reaction[1012] followed the advice from the CCA and the WODC and criticised the lack of empirical evidence of the claims of the Commission. It considered, with regard to the suggestion to include clauses, that it is unfamiliar with cases that would justify subjecting individually negotiated clauses to judicial control. The Dutch response further favoured a combination of a black and grey list at a European level, emphasising that this approach functions well in the Dutch legal order. In its response, the Dutch government also stressed the importance of maintaining the current level of consumer protection. The option to extend the judicial control to clauses on the main terms of the contract is rejected as this would entail giving the judiciary the competence to completely evaluate contracts. Interestingly, the Dutch response does not focus on previous negotiations, and emphasises experiences that may be useful for the European legal order.

Unfortunately, however, the response does not address the suggestion of comitology, although the CCA clearly rejected that option. Interestingly, article 6:239 BW provides for the amendment of articles 6:237, sub a to n BW, through delegated law-making, without requiring a full legislative procedure. Article 6:239 par. 2 BW, in addition, enables the legislator to consult representative organisations. The legislator[1013] emphasised that this provision enabled the legislator to adequately deal with developing practices, but the procedure has not been used since and amendments have been made through the normal legislative process.

The existence of article 6:239 BW draws into doubt whether the Dutch legislator would support the argument that article 6:237 BW should be amended only in a full legislative process. Notably, however, comitology would mean that national Parliament loses control over these amendments. In addition, whereas the WODC report[1014] rejected the fear of a race to the bottom as not convincing, the Dutch legislator does not take a clear position on regulatory competition.

Although the Dutch government did not initiate a separate consultation, the proposal sparked some debate in Dutch literature.[1015] The responses from other Dutch actors in the European consultation show a diverse approach to the reform of the 1993 Directive. In particular, the response from Hondius[1016] extensively considers the approaches towards the implementation of Directives in various Member States. However, the participation of other relevant actors, including Dutch consumers' organisations,[1017] has been limited to the closed consultation prior to the CCA advice.

1012 Dutch response, p. 7, 18–19, 19–20.

1013 Parl. Gesch. NBW, Boek 6 (Inv. 3, 5 en 6), p. 1756.

1014 C. Cauffman, M. Faure, T. Hartlief, Harmonisatie van het contractenrecht in Europa: consequenties voor Nederland, Advice 26 March 2009, WODC, p. 256.

1015 See for an overview of Dutch literature M.B.M. Loos, J.A. Luzak, 'Ontwikkelingen betreffende het voorstel voor een Richtlijn consumentenrechten: de positie van de Raad en het Europees Parlement', *NTER* 2011, p. 168.

1016 Reaction from E.H. Hondius, p. 1–3,7–9.

1017 However, the ECC Netherlands has participated. However, its contribution seems to be limited to publishing its response to the questionnaire from the Commission on the review of the consumer *acquis*. The response is available at http://ec.europa.eu/consumers/cons_int/safe_shop/acquis/responses/ecc_Netherlands.pdf.

The amount of businesses participating in the European consultation also seems rather limited. The responses of businesses are in accordance with their interests. The employers' organisation VNO-NWC[1018] remarked that Directives that have not been included in review, such as Directive 2000/31 on e-commerce, may be relevant and should have been included, and argued that a sufficient, rather than a high, level of consumer protection should be established under maximum harmonisation Directives, if harmonisation was necessary. VNO-NWC further pointed out that the availability of evaluation reports of the Directives under review would have been beneficial. Also, VNO-NWC expressly rejected the suggestion for comitology, extending the scope of the Directive to individually negotiated clauses or the main terms of the contract. It considered, however, the possibility that maintaining a black list only would be beneficial for predictability. The Platform Detailhandel Nederland,[1019] the other business organisation that responded to the consultation, similarly supported the maximum harmonisation of the current level of consumer protection. However, the Platform rejected a clause for mutual recognition as this would entail applying stricter provisions in cross-border contracts, which would complicate cross-border trade. The Platform further supported a black list only, and rejected the suggestion that the scope of the Directive should be extended to the main terms of the contract or individually negotiated clauses.

The limited participation of Dutch stakeholders is in contrast to the contribution of stakeholders from other legal orders – for example, Germany – and does not compare favourably to the contribution of businesses to national amendments.[1020] Also, the lack of participation from Dutch consumers' organisations does little to prevent or mitigate the uneven representation of actors participating in the drafting process that has already been criticised.[1021]

Because of the limited interaction between Dutch and European state and non-state actors, experiences in the implementation of Directive 93/13 were not addressed, which limits the extent to which a future reformed Directive could have responded to these experiences. Also, the lack of an additional consultation has undermined the inclusiveness and representativeness of actors in the European debate.

Although the Dutch government took Dutch law as a starting point in its participation in the European consultation, its intention in negotiations was not necessarily maintaining the status quo. Although the Dutch legislator seems open to possibilities of reform, it does not use the draft Directive as an opportunity to reconsider the law on STCs in accordance with the recommendations of the WODC report. Considering the future reform of the 1993 Directive,[1022] the restraint of the Dutch legislator may also

1018 VNO NWC, p. 1–3.

1019 Platform Detailhandel Nederland, p. 2.

1020 For example, the contributions of stakeholders to amendments to articles 6:236 and 237 BW, see further par. 11.3.3.5.

1021 M.W. Hesselink, 'Who has a stake in European contract law?' *ERCL* 2005, p. 295.

1022 Comp. preamble 62 to Directive 2011/83 that stipulates that in the evaluation of the Directive, the Commission will pay particular attention to the minimum harmonisation approach in Directives 93/13 and 99/44.

have been motivated by the wish to avoid multiple successive amendments of the law – however, Dutch law has meanwhile been amended.

Thus, more and better interaction could have increased the chance that the national legislator raised questions and considered solutions for problems in the implementation of Directives. Consequently, the lack of interaction may undermine the responsive development of the *acquis.*

Nationalism is visible with regard to the content of law, in the statement that Dutch law would form a starting point for negotiations – rather than debate – for the Dutch legislator. Methodological nationalism it is also visible in the assumption that because model lists work well at the national level, they can be transposed to the European level. Although comparative law insights were available, the Dutch legislator did not consider these insights in European debate. This limited view undermines the possibility that the Dutch legislator will be inspired by other actors, or that it will use the revision of law at the European level to critically consider weaknesses in national law, not even if advice highlights the need to address these weaknesses.

5.3.3.5. The revision of the law on STCs at a national level

In the revision of articles 6:236 and 237 BW, the approach of the Dutch legislator to interact with other actors varies. With regard to subscription contracts, the Dutch legislator has carefully interacted with foreign and European actors, which has enabled the legislator to benefit from insights from these actors. This is much less the case with regard to the supply of gas, warmth and electricity, which may increase the chance that the law will have to be amended if relevant Directives are revised. For arbitration clauses, the legislator has taken more note of Directive 93/13 and the needs and preferences of international actors.

Articles 6:236 and 237 BW fall within the scope of the Directive, although they do not, as such, implement the model list in the Annex to Directive 93/13. However, these provisions may entail that clauses falling under article 6:233 sub a BW, which implements article 3 Directive 93/13, are considered unfair, or likely unfair. Thus, these provisions cannot be seen in isolation from the Directive.

The legislator has amended the law in three instances:

1) The amendment of articles 6:236 and 237 BW on the termination of subscriptions and similar contracts

Article 6:236 BW was amended to stipulate, in sub o, that clauses that limit or exclude the possibility for consumer to terminate electronically, orally, or in writing contracts that have been concluded electronically, orally, or in writing are unfair. Also, sub p prohibits clauses in contracts for subscriptions on newspapers and journals that silently extend or renew the contract for a period of more than three months, if the consumer cannot terminate the contract at the end of the contract that is renewed with a termination period of, at most, a month. Additionally, article 6:236 sub q prohibits clauses in contracts for subscriptions on journals or newspaper that silently extend the subscription indefinitely, if the consumer cannot terminate the contract at all times with a termination period of, at most, a month or three months, depending on the frequency of the newspaper or journal. Article 2:36 BW was also amended, stipulating that, unless the articles of association decide otherwise, members can terminate their membership at the end of the financial year, with a termination period of four weeks. Termination that diverges from par. 1 end the membership at the earliest possible time, if the member would have terminated in accordance with article 2:36 par. 1 BW. Articles 3 and 4 provide exceptions and stipulate that members can terminate their membership immediately if decisions within a month after a decision limiting his rights or increasing his obligations, unless the articles of association specifically describe the duties and rights concerned. Members may also terminate immediately after a decision of merger, division, or conversion of the legal form of the association. The proposal made clear that associations are to clearly provide information on the possibilities to terminate.[1023]

Article 6:237 BW has recently been amended to include, in sub k, that clauses that set the period of contracts stipulated in article 6:236 subs j, p or q (mostly subscription contracts) are presumed to be unreasonable, unless the consumer has the possibility, after a year, to terminate the contract, with a termination period of, at most, a month. The amendment also amended sub l in article 237, stipulating that clauses are presumed to be unfair if they stipulate that consumers are bound to a period of termination that exceeds the period of termination that the user of STCs has to take into account.

In amending the law, the Dutch legislator[1024] considered the solutions in other Member States – notably, surrounding Member States such as England, France and Belgium, as well as Austria – that also set limits to the silent extension of contracts, or that have proposed to do so, but especially focused on undesirable national practices.

Interestingly, neither the proposal nor the comments on the proposal initially refer to the Directive.[1025] During the negotiations on the draft Directive on consumer rights, however, the question arose whether the Dutch legislator would take the amendment into account in these negotiations, and it was noted that the Dutch government had directed its attention to the differences between the European and Dutch model lists, also taking into account the amendment. It was also noted that if the clause was not included in the Directive, it would have to be removed if the Directive aimed for maximum harmonisation.[1026]

In the absence of maximum harmonisation, it can be doubted whether the Directive stands in the way of the amendments, as the amendments aim to increase the level of consumer protection in accordance with the minimum harmonisation character of the Directive. Interestingly, the amendments are in accordance with the Annex to the Directive, that in par. 1 sub h expressly refers to clauses that automatically extend a contract of fixed duration where the consumer does not indicate otherwise, when the deadline fixed for the consumer is unreasonably early.

1023 *Kamerstukken II*, 2008–2009, 30520, nr 8, p. 21.

1024 *Kamerstukken II*, 2005–2006, 30520, nr. 3, p. 3.

1025 For example G.P.J. de Vries, 'Paal en perk aan bedingen ter stilzwijgende verlenging van consumentenovereenkomsten, maar hoe?' *TvC* 2007, p. 122.

1026 *Kamerstukken I*, 2009–2010, 30520, nr D.

The amendment is also in accordance with case law from lower courts that held clauses that silently extended contracts ineffective,[1027] although they did not refer to the EU model list.[1028] However, other decisions have upheld these clauses.[1029] The proposal does not aim to clarify the EU model list and correctly assumes that problems arise in practice and, therefore, a transitional period has been introduced to allow business to amend their contracts. However, courts[1030] have anticipated the amendment, which does not seem especially problematic considering previous decisions and the EU model list. Thus, the amendment provides more clarity for consumers as well as businesses and may eradicate inconsistent decisions of lower courts.

2) Amendments for contracts on the supply of gas, electricity, and warmth

The amendments to the legislation on the supply of gas and energy sought to extend the effect of articles 6:236 and 237 BW to contracts between businesses, particularly small to medium enterprises. Simultaneously, it was suggested to limit the character of clauses in the black list to grey clauses that were assumed to be unfair, also for contracts with consumers.[1031] The proposed amendment overlooked previous advice from the Raad van State, to remove a previous article of the same effect,[1032] and stated that the extension of articles 6:236 and 237 BW would enable parties contracting with suppliers of gas and electricity to negotiate. At first sight, the extension of article 6:236 or article 237 BW hardly increases businesses' room to negotiate – rather, it imposes mandatory law on parties generally considered capable of negotiating on clauses and disadvantages the users of STCs who supply gas and energy compared to other users whose STCs in business contracts are not subject to articles 6:236 and 237 BW. However, the extension limits the possibility of users to impose clauses on the other party, thereby providing other parties with more room to negotiate on clauses. This restriction may further be justified by the monopolist position of suppliers of energy and gas.[1033] Simultaneously, limiting the effect of article 6:236 BW as a grey list in consumer contracts may give rise to questions with regard to the Directive, as this seems a measure that may lower consumer protection.

The amendment has been criticised as contrary to the regime in articles 6:231 et seq BW.[1034] In particular, articles 6:236 and 237 BW were drafted for contracts between consumers and businesses. Parties other than consumers were assumed to be in a position in which they could negotiate on clauses, which required less mandatory rules. This restriction also becomes apparent from article 6:235 BW that excludes big businesses

1027 Ktr. Hoorn 10 April 2006, *NJF* 2007, 252, as well as Ktr. Eindhoven 9 March 2006, *Prg.* 2006, 95, Ktr. Eindhoven 10 November 2005, *Prg.* 2006, 9, Rb. Limburg 2 October 2013, *Prg.* 2014, 5.

1028 The decision in Ktr. Rotterdam 2 August 2007, *Prg.* 2008, 37 seems an exception that was not followed in later decisions, see below par. 11.4.2.2.

1029 Ktr. Tiel 15 June 2005, *Prg.* 2005, 143.

1030 In particular Ktr. Haarlem 12 January 2012, *NJF* 2012, 94.

1031 *Kamerstukken II*, 2001–2002, 28174, nr 39.

1032 *Kamerstukken II*, 2001–2002, 28190, nr 3, p. 12.

1033 I.S.J. Houben, 'Sectorspecifieke wetgeving en algemene voorwaarden', *NbBW* 2004, p. 107–108 remarks that the market for energy and gas is new, there may be market failures, and parties contracting for the supply of energy and gas are typically dependant on the supply of these utilities.

1034 S.C.J.J. Kortmann, N.E.D. Faber, 'Het moet niet veel gekker worden!', *WPNR* 6531 (2003).

from the scope of articles 6:233 and 234 BW.[1035] Subsequently, questions were raised in Parliament.[1036] The state secretary,[1037] after agreeing with the negative advice from the Raad van State, subsequently found that the advice of the Raad van State has been elaborately discussed in Parliament, which has resulted in current article 14 Gas Act (*Gaswet*) and article 26a Electricity Act (*Elektriciteitswet*) that have maintained the extension and limitation of articles 6:236 and 237 BW.[1038] The state secretary concluded that these articles are not contrary to articles 6:231 et seq BW.

The secretary[1039] further found that the limitation of black clauses to grey clauses does not materially alter the position of the consumer, because it is highly unlikely that businesses will succeed in proving that these are fair, as these clauses are found unfair throughout this sector. Thus, the amendment is in accordance with Directive 93/13 or article 3 par. 3 Directive 2003/55 that stipulates that states will ensure a high level of consumer protection.[1040] These amendments have since been extended to contracts for the delivery of warmth falling under the Warmth Act (*Warmtewet*) that in proposed article 5 par. 9 provides for similar divergences from articles 6:236 and 237 BW .[1041]

Criticism that the amendment is contrary to Directive 93/13 may be debated after *RWE Vertrieb AG v Verbraucherzentrale Nordrhein-Westfalen eV*.[1042] The CJEU held that clauses falling under the scope of national legislation are, in accordance with article 1 par. 2 Directive 93/13, not subjected to an evaluation of fairness, as the legislator has specifically considered a balance of the rights and obligations of contract parties in these cases.

3) The amendment of article 6:236 for arbitration clauses

This amendment was part of the revision of arbitration law more generally, prompted by Prof. Van den Berg, discussed in the 2013 special edition of the journal for arbitration, which also referred to international arbitration and the revision of Belgian law.[1043] The revision intended to modernise arbitration law after 25 years, and to improve The Netherlands as an attractive forum for dispute resolution through arbitration.[1044] Accordingly, the legislator took into account the UNCITRAL

1035 Advice from the Raad van State of 19 September 2000, nr W10.00.0327/II.

1036 *Kamerstukken II*, 2002–2003, 28174, nr 110a, p. 8–9.

1037 *Kamerstukken II*, 2002–2003, 28174, nr 110b, p. 11–12.

1038 *Kamerstukken II*, 2002–2003, 28174, nr 110d, p. 3.

1039 *Kamerstukken II*, 2002–2003, 28174, nr. 110d, p. 3.

1040 Specifically, the article provides a high level of consumer protection 'particularly with respect to transparency regarding general contractual terms and conditions, general information and dispute settlement mechanisms. Member States shall ensure that the eligible customer is effectively able to switch to a new supplier.' The article further refers to Annex A to the Directive that establishes that provides more specific rules for contracts between consumers and gas suppliers.

1041 As discussed in *Kamerstukken I*, 2008–2009, 29048, nr 51, p. 7–9.

1042 CJEU 21 March 2013 (RWE Vertrieb AG v Verbraucherzentrale Nordrhein-Westfalen eV), C-92/11, [2013] ECR, p. I-0.

1043 *Tijdschrift voor Arbitrage* 2013, volume 3 (special edition), with a general comparison by H.J. Snijders, 'Algemene beschouwingen bij het Wetsvoorstel Modernisering Arbitragerecht', *Tijdschrift voor Arbitrage* 2013, 31.

1044 *Kamerstukken II*, 2012–2013, 33611, 3.

Model Law on International Commercial Arbitration[1045] as well as the views of international actors during consultations.[1046]

This approach is in accordance with regulatory competition, but the approach towards arbitration clauses in consumer contracts has not been motivated by regulatory competition. The particular revision of article 6:236 BW can also be seen against the background of the Hoge Raad's[1047] decision that arbitration clauses were not as such unreasonable as they were not included in the black list.[1048] The amendment was widely supported by Dutch stakeholder groups and experts,[1049] though it can be doubted to what extent this will increase consumers' confidence in arbitration, as considered by the Dutch legislator.[1050]

At first sight, it appears that this amendment is in accordance with Directive, as it allows for more protection for consumers, as well as the Annex. The legislator carefully considered the Directive, as well as the Annex and relevant CJEU decisions, but does not consider comparative law.[1051] However, the adoption of Directive 2013/11 on consumer ADR may require adjustments, as article 10 stipulates that Member States shall ensure that ADR clauses that have been concluded before the dispute has materialised shall not be binding on the consumer, while par. 2 makes clear that clauses that entail recourse to ADR should be "specifically agreed upon" by the consumer.[1052] However, article 6:236 sub n BW does allow for ADR clauses provided that they allow the consumer at least a month to opt for adjudication. In the implementation of Directive 2013/11, the Dutch legislator[1053] has expressly chosen to not re-amend article 6:236 BW. Instead, article 9 of the law on extra-judicial dispute resolution ('*Implementatiewet Butiengerechtelijke geschillenbeslechting consumenten*') specifically stipulates that clauses that have been concluded before the materialisation of the dispute cannot be held binding against the consumer. According to the legislator, this entails avoidability of the clause, which should normally be invoked by the consumer. The wording of Directive 2013/11 is however identical to the wording of article 6 Directive 93/13, which may imply an obligation of courts to examine the fairness

1045 F. de Ly, 'Het wetsvoorstel Modernisering van het arbitragerecht en de internationale arbitrage', *TvA* 2013, 38 points out that the legislator took into account the 1986 model law rather than the 2006 revised version, although only various states have adapted their laws in accordance with the 2006 model law. He also finds that the new law may not be very accessible to foreign parties.

1046 Particularly, the Permanent Court for Arbitration and the International Chamber of Commerce.

1047 HR 21 September 2012, *NJ* 2013, 431. This decision was preceded by inconsistent decisions from appeal courts Hof Leeuwarden 17 March 2009, ECLI:NL:GHSHE:2009:BH6958, and Hof Leeuwarden 5 July 2011, *NJF* 2011, 382, quashed by the Hoge Raad in its decision under *NJ* 2013, 431.

1048 *Kamerstukken II*, 2012–2013, 33611, nr 3, p. 7.

1049 *Kamerstukken II*, 2012–2013, 33611, nr 3, p. 5.

1050 See for example critically C.J.M. Klaassen, 'Verzekeringsgeschillen en ADR. Enkele observaties over geschilbeslechting in "een kleine wereld"', *AV & S* 2014, 22.

1051 *Kamerstukken II*, 2012–2013, 33611, nr 3, p. 7. Comp. particularly CJEU 6 October 2009 (Asturcom Telecomunicaciones SL v Rodríguez Nogueira), C-40/08, [2009] ECR p. I-9579 and article 1064a Dutch Civil Procedure Code stipulating that parties have three months to challenge the arbitral award.

1052 See further on the possible meaning of this provision N. Reich, 'A "Trojan Horse" in the access to justice – Party autonomy and consumer arbitration in conflict in the ADR-Directive 20133/11/EU?', *ERCL* 2014, p. 272–274.

1053 *Kamerstukken II*, 2013–2014, 33982, nr. 3.

of clauses of their own motion.[1054] Typically, however, Dutch courts will not consider questions which may result in avoidability of their own motion, as these are generally not matters of public policy. The legislator's choice may therefore create confusion, notwithstanding the Hoge Raad's 2013 decision[1055] on the *ex officio* evaluation of unfair clauses.

→ Thus, although the Dutch legislator recognises the added value of foreign and European law, as well as national legal practice, it has not developed a predictable, consistent approach to amending the law. The Dutch legislator had not strategically made use of opportunities for learning, which may also be detrimental: If amendments are not uncontroversial or if they precede law reform at the European level, the Dutch legislator may be forced to amend the law repeatedly, which does not strengthen predictability or accessibility.

5.3.3.6. Conclusion on the development of Dutch law and harmonisation

Interdependence in the development of Directive 93/13 and its reform has become clearly visible. Have Dutch actors, in the implementation of Directive 93/13, adequately recognised interdependence and have they interacted accordingly? How has that affected the comprehensibility of the law on STCs?

The approach of the Dutch legislator is reminiscent of the German legislator who actively participates in debate and, subsequently, exercises restraint in the implementation of the law on STCs. However, the approach of the Dutch legislator has not been nearly as successful as the German approach. Possibly, this lack of success, despite a similar strategy, can be traced to the recent introduction of Dutch law that had not even entered into force when the Directive was drafted, whereas German law was well-developed.

As a result, the *acquis* has more visibly limited the extent to which the BW can safeguard the predictability, consistency, accessibility and responsiveness of Dutch law. This has however not prompted the Dutch legislator to reconsider the choice for codification, or the development of separate laws alongside the new code, which would more directly undermine the comprehensibility of the law.

The timing of Directive 93/13 also entailed that it was especially unattractive for the Dutch legislator to amend the law. As the restraint of the Dutch legislator went further than the restraint of other legislators, it drew the attention of European actors. The ability of national actors to exercise restraint in the implementation of European measures, which also benefited the predictable development of the law, was curtailed.

The extent to which the BW facilitates the stable development of the law is further undermined as the Dutch legislator has exercised less restraint in amending the law than the German legislator. Both German and Dutch courts have followed the restraint of legislators in implementing the *acquis*. However, in the Dutch legal order, this was more problematic as the law on STCs showed more shortcomings that were not compensated

1054 N. Reich, 'A "Trojan Horse" in the access to justice – Party autonomy and consumer arbitration in conflict in the ADR-Directive 20133/11/EU?', *ERCL* 2014, p. 272.

1055 HR 13 September 2013, *NJ* 2014, 274.

by an active approach of the courts. Dutch lower courts have also not adopted a consistent approach. As a result, despite recodification, unpredictability and inconsistency have developed.

Dutch actors have not adequately recognised interdependence in ensuring the predictability, consistency, accessibility, and responsiveness of the law on STCs. Consequently, Dutch actors have not consistently interacted with European, foreign and international state and non-state actors, which has aggravated unpredictability and inconsistency that may arise from the introduction of new legislation more generally.

The coexistence of actors has not benefited the predictability, consistency, accessibility or responsiveness of the law on STCs.

Notably, the development of European control mechanisms to ensure the proper implementation has not caused Dutch actors to develop the law more in accordance with benchmarks of predictability, accessibility, consistency and responsiveness. The narrow perspective of Dutch actors makes it unlikely that harmonisation will prompt Dutch actors to take into account the interests of foreign or international actors. Presently, with rare exceptions, these actors generally do not participate in the legislative approach, but even if they did, it remains to be seen whether their perspectives will be considered by the Dutch legislator.

While the Dutch legislator has recognised the benefits of comparative law, the Dutch legislator has failed to take opportunities for learning, which would have improved the law, into account. This failure can more generally be attributed to a national approach of Dutch actors. Particularly, the Dutch legislator seemed convinced of the quality of the Dutch regime, despite criticism and advice. Similarly, resistance can be found in courts decisions rejecting European legal transplants, particularly with regard to article 6:238 par. 2 BW. Even though Dutch law was relatively recently adopted, that did not make it more open to EU influences. Possibly, the narrow perspective decreases the likelihood that Dutch law will in turn be a donor for other systems.[1056] Interestingly, the German private initiative for regulatory competition, though suggesting a delineation between "big" contract parties and other contract parties still protected by the German regime, did not consider article 6:235 BW – or other foreign law, for that matter.[1057]

5.3.4. *Dutch law on STCs and international trade*

The development of treaties and international trade should motivate state actors to interact with European, international, and foreign actors and non-state actors. Is this also the case for the Dutch legislator and courts, and how has that affected the predictability, consistency, accessibility and responsiveness of the law on STCs? Has the coexistence of actors increased the quality of the law on STCs, in accordance with pluralist insights?

1056 A. Watson, *Legal transplants*, Edinburgh: Scottish Academic Press 1974, p. 99.
1057 See previously above par. 4.3.

Paragraph 5.3.4.1 will consider regulatory competition in the drafting of articles 6:231 et seq BW and paragraph 5.3.4.2 will turn to the approach of the courts to the interpretation of clauses in international contracts. Paragraph 5.3.4.3 will end with a conclusion.

5.3.4.1. Regulatory competition

Has the Dutch legislator taken into account insights from foreign, European and international actors in developing the law on STCs? Has regulatory competition increased the comprehensibility of the law on STCs?

The Dutch legislator has recognised the added value of regulatory competition in the law on STCs. In accordance with the idea of regulatory competition, the drafting of the BW relied extensively on comparative law, which enables the drafters of legislation to decide on the most convincing argument for and against the development of the law in a particular direction.[1058] Notably, however, the inclusion of comparative law did not focus on foreign regimes with the lowest possible evaluation of clauses in business contracts, as criticised by Spier.[1059]

In addition, in the drafting of articles 6: 231 et seq BW, the views of relevant actors in practice were carefully considered. For example, the legislator consulted the Dutch association for the judiciary (*'Nederlandse Vereniging voor rechtspraak'*)[1060] on questions of transitional provisions, which should limit unpredictability arising from the introduction of new legislation that confers a relatively new task on the judiciary. Furthermore, the legislator clearly stated the importance of the advice from the CCA[1061] and business stakeholders.[1062] This attention for national stakeholders increases the chance that Dutch law will reflect the needs of businesses and is, therefore, an attractive regime for these businesses that are less likely to opt out of Dutch law.

The support of regulatory competition becomes particularly visible for international business contracts. In the drafting process, the Dutch legislator argued that subjecting international business contracts to the Dutch regime might be problematic, and might jeopardise the Dutch position in international trade.[1063] Accordingly, the Dutch legislator has chosen not to subject international business contracts to judicial evaluation by the insertion of article 6:247 par. 1 BW, stating that doing so would hinder international trade.[1064] The Dutch legislator further states that it should not be made unattractive for Dutch contract parties to opt for international trade.[1065]

1058 See previously par. 4.3.1.
1059 J. Spier, 'Nogmaals het wetsontwerp algemene voorwaarden', *Kwartaalbericht Nieuw BW* 1985, p. 7–8.
1060 Parl. Gesch. NBW, Boek 6 (Inv 3, 5, and 6), p. 1463.
1061 Parl. Gesch. NBW, Boek 6 (Inv. 3, 5 en 6), p. 1451, 1456–1457.
1062 Parl. Gesch. NBW, Boek 6 (Inv. 3, 5 en 6), p. 1453, 1472.
1063 J. Spier, 'Het wetsontwerp algemene voorwaarden: voor de praktijk funest', *Kwartaalbericht Nieuw BW* 1984, p. 130–131.
1064 Parl. Gesch. NBW, Boek 6 (Inv. 3, 5 en 6), p. 1815.
1065 Parl. Gesch. NBW, Boek 6 (Inv. 3, 5 en 6), p. 1816, see also with regard to article 6:232 p. 1486.

However, this view is limited to international business contracts, which was subsequently criticised by Spier,[1066] who argued that in chains of contracts, the regime would not be applicable to a part of the contractual chain, if the contract would be concluded between a Dutch and a foreign business. This limits the mobility of national parties, which is a requirement for full regulatory competition. However, the subsequent link of the chain – a contract between Dutch businesses – would be subjected to this regime. The Dutch legislator apparently did not consider this argument, which would provide domestic businesses with a possibility to circumvent the regime, particularly persuasive.[1067]

At first sight, the approach of the Dutch legislator may have implicitly have recognised the limited territorial scope of Dutch law and the increasing relevance of the preference of non-state actors in international trade. Accordingly, the legislator sought to develop an attractive system for these actors, inspired by the English regime.[1068] It was supposed that the lenient approach of the law in this area should be in accordance with foreign and international actors' preference. Unfortunately, this assumption was not tested by consulting these actors. Thus, the question arises whether the Dutch legislator recognises the decreased ability of national actors to develop the law in accordance with the needs and preferences of transnational, rather than national actors. This perspective from multilevel governance appears to have been overlooked.

The legislator has sought to pursue regulatory competition, which may have enhanced the responsiveness of the law as the legislator carefully considered comparative law. The course of the legislator contradicts case studies that showed that legislators did not take a competitive approach in the development the law in this area.[1069] Notwithstanding the emphasis of the Dutch legislator on regulatory competition, areas of the law in this field – in particular, the battle of forms – are in need of reform.[1070] The approach of the Dutch legislator shows that the legislator does not fear a 'race to the bottom', but the legislator does limit regulatory competition to international business contracts. Thus, regulatory competition is not promoted in areas where a race to the bottom, leading to low standards of consumer protection, will develop, which would also not be permitted under Directive 93/13 or Regulations Rome I or Brussels I. Accordingly, considerations of regulatory competition are not apparent in recent reforms for consumer contracts. These amendments focus on national practices. However, regulatory competition did not prompt the Dutch legislator to include foreign or international actors in the drafting of Dutch law.[1071]

1066 J. Spier, 'Nogmaals het wetsontwerp algemene voorwaarden', *Kwartaalbericht Nieuw BW* 1985, p. 7, similarly J.E. Vollebregt, 'Wetsonwerp algemene voorwaarden', *NJB* 1984, p. 813–814.

1067 Comp. the reaction of the Minister, Parl. Gesch. NBW, Boek 6 (Inv. 3, 5, and 6), p. 1484 with regard to the discussion (in an international context see p. 1478, and 1482) whether the regime would be detrimental to businesses, as argued by Vollebregt 1984, p. 809. Comp. also HR 26 May 1989, *NJ* 1992, 105 where the Hoge Raad limited the ability of parties in domestic contracts to exclude national mandatory law by opting for an international regime that aims to provide a comprehensive regime on some points, such as the CMR.

1068 Parl. Gesch. NBW, Boek 6 (Inv. 3, 5 en 6), p. 1807.

1069 S. Vogenauer, 'Regulatory competition through choice of contract Law and choice of forum in Europe: Theory and evidence', *ERPL*2013, p. 76.

1070 C.P.B. Mahé, 'Pleidooi voor de herziening van de Nederlandse battle of forms-regeling', *VrA* 2006, p. 5.

1071 Ch. Joerges, 'On the legitimacy of Europeanising private law: Considerations on a justice-making law for the EU multi-level system', *Electronic Journal of Comparative Law* 2003, par. III.1.2., available at www.ejcl.org/ejcl/73/art73-3.html.

5.3.4.2. The interpretation of international contracts

Has the judiciary, in the interpretation of STCs in international contracts, recognised interdependence as international trade develops and have courts interacted accordingly with international, European and foreign state and non-state actors? How has that affected the predictability, consistency, accessibility and responsiveness of the law on STCs? Has the coexistence of actors enhanced the comprehensibility of the law on STCs?

Paragraph 5.3.4.2.1 will consider decisions on the inclusion of STCs and paragraph 5.3.4.2.2 will consider the decisions on the question of whether STCs have been made adequately available. Paragraph 5.3.4.2.3 will consider the interpretation of STCs. Paragraph 5.3.4.2.4 will end with a conclusion.

5.3.4.2.1. The valid inclusion of STCs

Courts have not consistently and adequately interacted with national, European, foreign and international state and non-state actors in the inclusion of STCs in cases falling under respectively the CISG, the CMR, article 23 Brussels I, and Dutch law, which has severely undermined predictability and consistency.

- In cases falling under the CISG, the Hoge Raad has decided in accordance with the CISG, without referring to foreign law or international materials, but the conclusion of the A.G. does refer to international materials.

In a 2005 decision under the CISG, the Hoge Raad[1072] held that the question of whether STCs had been validly included in the contract was to be decided under article 7 par. 2 CISG, in accordance with the general principles underlying the CISG, and in the absence of such principles, in accordance with applicable law, as the CISG includes rules on the conclusion of contracts, including the question whether parties have agreed with the application of STCs. Neither the Hoge Raad nor the A.G. refers to foreign decisions on the inclusion of STCs, but A.G. Strikwerda does refer to literature on the CISG and UNCITRAL. Van Wechem, Spanjaard and Kruisinga[1073] however point out that opinion 13 of the CISG advisory council on the inclusion of standard contract terms[1074] makes clear that the question whether STCs have been validly included should be considered under article 8 rather than article 7 CISG.

- A consistent approach does not become apparent in the approach of lower courts.

Decisions from lower instances prior to the 2005 decision had referred to foreign law, although foreign law was not considered extensively, but merely mentioned.[1075] Lower courts[1076] have since

1072 HR 28 January 2005, *NJ* 2006, 517, see the conclusion of the A.G. Strikwerda under pars. 8 and 9.

1073 T.H.M. van Wechem, J.H.M. Spanjaard, S.A. Kruisinga, 'Een bespreking van CISG Advisory Council opinion no 13 inclusion of standard contract terms under the CISG', *NTHR* 2013, p. 267.

1074 Available at www.cisg.law.pace.edu/cisg/CISG-AC-op13.html.

1075 For example Rb. Arnhem 17 March 2004, *NJF* 2004, 497, also Rb. Zwolle 22 January 2003, *LJN* AF3345, referring to applicable Dutch law as well as German law, as well as Hof 's-Hertogenbosch 16 October 2002, *LJN* BA7248, referring to the PECL and UNIDROIT, as well as (briefly) to Dutch and French law.

1076 For example Rb. Rotterdam 20 March 2013, *NJF* 2013, 217, Hof 's-Hertogenbosch 17 December 2013, *RCR* 2014, 21, Rb. Rotterdam 1 October 2014, *NJF* 2014, 499, Hof 's-Hertogenbosch 2 January 2007, *LJN* AZ6352, not referring to foreign law.

followed the decision of the Hoge Raad. The court Gelderland[1077] did not refer to the Hoge Raad decision, but instead referred to a decision from the OLG Düsseldorf and the CISG Opinion, finding that the user of STCs should not assume that the other party would understand the STCs that were composed in Dutch, even though the negotiations had been conducted in German and English. The court further held it could not be expected that the other party would translate the STCs on his own.[1078] The court Overijssel[1079] similarly referred to the CISG advisory opinion. Other decisions from lower courts have not decided the question of whether STCs had been validly included in the contract under article 7 CISG. For example, the district court Amsterdam[1080] decided the question of whether a choice of law clause had been validly included under article 3 Rome Convention.

- In cases falling under the CMR, the Hoge Raad has referred to both international and foreign materials.

The Hoge Raad[1081] held that in order to decide whether the validity of the jurisdiction clause under article 31 CMR should be determined under the CMR or not, it should first be established that the CMR was applicable to the case, which concerned transport through multiple means. The Hoge Raad considered the scope of the CMR, referring to the provisions and agreement of states parties to the CMR to negotiate on treaties for transport through other means, and considered that it followed that the CMR is not applicable to these contracts. In its decision, the Hoge Raad addressed English and German case law that the court of appeal of appeal had relied on, and followed the BGH decision, stating that it did not follow from the reasoning of the English decision that the CMR should be applicable. Consequently, the Hoge Raad upheld the jurisdiction clause as not invalid because of article 31 CMR.

- The approach of lower courts varies. Whereas some lower courts have decided cases accordingly and also refer to foreign materials,[1082] or the CMR, Brussels I, and CJEU case law,[1083] other courts have decided cases under Dutch law.[1084]

1077 Rb. Gelderland 6 November 2013, *RCR* 2014, 13.

1078 The court differed from HR 2 February 2001, *NJ* 2001, 200 that was decided under Dutch law, where the court held that it should be expected of the other contract party to enquire after the STCs, considering the customary use of STCs in international trade.

1079 Rb. Overijssel 3 December 2014, *RCR* 2015, 34.

1080 Rb. Amsterdam 20 April 2011, *RCR* 2011, 69. S. Kruisinga, 'De battle of forms in internationaal perspectief: een eerlijke strijd?' *Contracteren* 2005, p. 5 refers to decisions in which courts held that questions on battle of forms should be determined under article 6:225 par. 3 BW.

1081 HR 1 June 2012, *NJ* 2012, 516.

1082 Comp. Hof 's-Gravenhage 28 November 2007, *LJN* BB9150 that upheld the applicability of the CMR, also noting that the STCs of parties expressly noted that the CMR could be applicable. The court also referred to German literature on the CMR.

1083 Rb. Rotterdam 20 August 2014, *S & S* 2015, 43. Interestingly, the court first considered whether the clause met the requirements of article 31 CMR and then considered whether the clause was in accordance with article 23 Brussels I, which was not the case.

1084 Rb. Rotterdam 17 September 2008, *LJN* BF1813 held that it was insufficiently established that the STCs, recognising the applicability of the CMR and containing a clause for arbitration, had been included in the contract under Dutch law.

- Some cases may, however, be problematic, even though they refer to foreign and international sources as well as soft laws.

The district court Rotterdam[1085] considered Rome I, Brussels I, the CMR and Dutch law.

The court rejected the claimant's referral to the applicability of the CMR because this constitutes changing the legal basis of one's claim in the sense of article 130 Civil Procedure Code, which is not permissible in the preliminary procedure on competence.

However, the court overlooks that article 31 CMR provides that parties may agree on a competent court in contracting states, while, in addition, the competent court is the court where the defendant ordinarily resides or has his principal place of business, or the branch or agency through which the contract of carriage was made is competent, or the court of the place where the goods were taken over by the carrier or the place designated for delivery is situated, which in this case would entail that the court in The Hague is competent.

Thereby, this decision overlooks previous CJEU[1086] case law providing that in accordance with article 71 Brussels I, this provision precedes article 23 Brussels I, provided that it is 'highly predictable, facilitate[s] the sound administration of justice and enable[s] the risk of concurrent proceedings to be minimised and that they ensure, under conditions at least as favourable as those provided for by the regulation, the free movement of judgments in civil and commercial matters and mutual trust in the administration of justice in the European Union', while application of the CMR may also not lead to a result less favourable than the result reached under the Regulation.

If this is not the case – which the court does not explain further – then the question of whether a jurisdiction clause has been validly included in the contract is to be determined under article 23 Brussels I. Although the court refers to article 23 Brussels I, the question of whether STCs have validly been included in the contract is decided under Dutch law, as the court apparently confuses a choice of law with a choice of jurisdiction. Holding that the STCs of the respondent have been validly included in the contract, which contains a jurisdiction clause for an Italian court, the court declares itself incompetent, without, however, evaluating whether this choice has validly been made under article 23 Brussels I. This decision contradicts CJEU case law.[1087]

- In cases on jurisdiction clauses in accordance with article 23 Brussels I, lower courts have decided in line with the Regulation, but they only rarely[1088] refer to international and European materials.

The court of appeal in 's-Hertogenbosch[1089] held that a clause, although in writing, had not been given a prominent place in the STCs, but the court upheld the clause as jurisdiction clauses were not unusual in international trade, while the party challenging the clause had also included a jurisdiction clause in its own STCs. Parties had entered into multiple contracts that they had also

1085 Rb. Rotterdam 28 January 2009, *LJN* BH1797.

1086 CJEU 4 May 2010 (TNT v Axa Versicherung), C-533/08, [2010] ECR, p. I- 4107.

1087 CJEU 16 March 1999 (Trasporti Castelletti Spedizioni Internazionali SpA v Hugo Trumpy SpA), C-159/97, [1999] ECR, p. I-1597.

1088 See Hof Amsterdam 27 November 2007, *RCR* 2008, 44 that found that a jurisdiction clause did not meet the requirements of article 23 Brussels I, expressly following the CJEU, as well as Rb. Rotterdam 10 July 2013, ECLI:NL:RBROT:2013:6001. Rb. Rotterdam 17 December 2014, *S & S* 2015, 65 only refers to article 23 Brussels I, without further reference to CJEU case law.

1089 Hof 's-Hertogenbosch 4 September 1997, *NJ* 1998, 578.

begun to perform, in which the jurisdiction clause was also deemed to have been validly included under article 17 Lugano Convention. The court did not refer to European or foreign decisions.

The district court Dordrecht[1090] upheld a jurisdiction clause, firstly considering that STCs had been validly included in the contract as the confirmation of the commission referred to the STCs, which were printed on the back of the confirmation, in English, and the user of STCs had, therefore, justifiably assumed that the counterparty accepted its STCs, in accordance with Hoge Raad case law. The court, subsequently, held that as no further objections had arisen to the jurisdiction clause, and the STCs had been validly included in the contract, on which parties commercial practice was based, the jurisdiction clause had been validly included in the contract, in accordance with article 23 Brussels I. The court did not expressly refer to the CJEU or to foreign or international materials.

The court of appeal Arnhem-Leeuwarden[1091] extensively referred to both CJEU and Hoge Raad decisions, as well as, briefly, German law in upholding a jurisdiction clause.

The district court Rotterdam[1092] referred to article 23 Brussels I in a case concerning a jurisdiction clause, but first turned to the interpretation of the clause and, subsequently, held that as the jurisdiction clause met the requirements under article 23 Brussels I and other objections had not arisen, it was valid. In later cases, the same court,[1093] referring to article 23 Brussels I, and, in one decision, 'settled CJEU case law' held that jurisdiction clauses had not been agreed upon by parties.

- Some decisions referring to international, foreign and national decisions, as well as soft law, are nevertheless problematic.

The district court Amsterdam[1094] decided on the inclusion of a jurisdiction clause under the CISG, and referred to both the decision of the Hoge Raad on the valid inclusion of STCs under the CISG as well as the BGH and the PECL, ruling that STCs had not been validly included in the contract as it had not been established that the users of STCs had made the text available to their contract party, noting that a general duty to inform after the STCs have been included cannot be accepted, while merely referring to one's STCs is not sufficient and does not indicate agreement or a well-established practice between parties.

The district court 's-Hertogenbosch[1095] similarly incorrectly decided on the applicability of a jurisdiction clause under the CISG, referring to article 23 Brussels I, but subsequently stating that this Regulation does not provide rules for the valid inclusion of STCs. The court then considered this question, and, referring to BGH case law as well as an Austrian decision, held that this had not been the case, which also meant that the jurisdiction clause did not meet the requirements of article 23 Brussels I. Although the outcome of the case is unproblematic, the reasoning of the

1090 Rb. Dordrecht 16 January 2008, *RCR* 2008, 50.

1091 Hof Arnhem-Leeuwarden 24 December 2013, ECLI:NL:GHARL:2013:9841.

1092 Rb. Rotterdam 1 August 2007, *LJN* BB6035.

1093 Rb. Rotterdam 20 February 2014, ECLI:NL:RBROT:2014:1327, Rb. Rotterdam 1 October 2014, ECLI:NL:RBROT:2014:8057.

1094 Rb. Amsterdam 3 June 2009, *LJN* BK0976. Comp. also Rb. Zutphen 14 January 2009, *NJF* 2009, 244, referring to both the Hoge Raad and the BGH.

1095 Rb. 's-Hertogenbosch 26 January 2011, *RCR* 2011, 52. Similarly, the Hof 's-Hertogenbosch 22 June 2012, *RCR* 2010, 66 also decided the question whether STCs – including a jurisdiction clause – had been validly included in the contract under the CISG rather than article 23 Brussels I.

court is contrary to CJEU case law[1096] establishing that the validity of a jurisdiction clause is to be established solely under article 23 Brussels I.

- In international cases decided under Dutch law, the Hoge Raad has not referred to international or foreign materials.

In a 1977 international case decided under Dutch law, the Hoge Raad[1097] rejected the view that because the Dutch seller, in a contract drafted in English, had referred to his STCs, printed on his stationary, in Dutch, these STCs had become applicable, unless the party subjected to these terms proved otherwise. In this decision, the Hoge Raad, nor the diverging conclusion from the A.G., refer to foreign or international decisions.

In a 1985 decision, the Hoge Raad,[1098] however, decided that a retention of title clause that had not been included in the confirmation of an assignment between parties but that had been included in the STCs in the stationary of the seller, had not been validly included in the contract, notwithstanding the long business relation between contract parties, as the buyer did not reasonably have to expect a clause that had not been included in his confirmation, and the seller could not reasonably expect the buyer to have become aware of this clause.

In a 2001 case,[1099] for a contract concluded before the CISG had been ratified by the Dutch legislator, the Hoge Raad upheld a decision from the court of appeal ruling that an arbitration clause had been validly included in a contract. The Hoge Raad held that the German contract party should have asked for clarification on the Dutch pre-printed text sent by the Dutch party upon request of the German party to send his STCs. The German party, as a business operating in international trade, should been alert to this way of referring to STCs that is also used by German contract parties. A.-G Strikwerda notes that this conclusion is in line with previous case law on domestic contracts. Neither the Hoge Raad nor the A.-G refer to German law.

→ As the Hoge Raad has adopted a different approach for contracts concluded under the CISG, it is unclear whether this decision should be followed for international sales contracts – it may, however, still be relevant for international contracts where the CISG has been excluded or for international contracts not falling under the CISG, such as mixed contracts.

- Decisions in national cases only rarely refer to foreign materials[1100] and they differ from decisions in international cases.

In national cases, the question whether STCs have been validly included under the contract should be answered under articles 3:33 and 35 BW. Although these rules at first sight seem more

1096 CJEU 16 March 1999 (Trasporti Castelletti Spedizioni Internazionali SpA v Hugo Trumpy SpA), C-159/97, [1999] ECR, p. I-1597.

1097 HR 9 December 1977, *NJ* 1978, 187.

1098 HR 18 October 1985, *NJ* 1987, 189.

1099 HR 2 February 2001, *NJ* 2001, 200 see the conclusion of A.G. Strikwerda, par. 10. Comp. also Rb. Rotterdam 28 November 2012, *NJF* 2013, 79, on the silent acceptance of terms, as well as Rb. Rotterdam 26 June 2013, *S & S* 2014, 18.

1100 Comp. however, the conclusion of A.G. A.G. Biegman-Hartogh before HR 6 November 1992, *NJ* 1993, 27.

lenient than international regimes, some confusion has arisen with regard to clauses that are particularly disadvantageous for the contract party subjecting to the STCs.

In a 1981 decision, the Hoge Raad[1101] had held that for the valid inclusion of STCs, there were no additional requirements beyond the normal requirements usual in business practices for concluding a contract. The Hoge Raad, however, also held that the agreement cannot supposed to be aimed at clauses that were especially disadvantageous, which it repeated in a later decision.[1102] Although the Hoge Raad in this domestic contract unsurprisingly does not refer to comparative or foreign sources, the converging conclusion does refer to research that includes comparative research and takes note of European decisions on jurisdiction clauses. The Hoge Raad[1103] repeated that notwithstanding the applicability of STCs, the silent agreement of the subjecting party with terms, the content of which he is not completely familiar with, may not be assumed for clauses on far-going exclusion clauses that the court of appeal had deemed applicable because of their widespread use in that particular branch of business. Even if such clauses are widespread, the Hoge Raad maintained that the agreement should not be assumed. Rather, this question should be decided by interpreting the contract.

It can be doubted whether these decisions under old Dutch law are reconcilable with article 6:232 BW. In later decisions, the Hoge Raad[1104] maintained the applicability of articles 3:33 and 35 BW in deciding whether STCs had validly been included in the contract, without, however, confirming the idea that counterparties cannot be held to have agreed with surprising or unusual clauses.

In its 2015 decision, the Hoge Raad[1105] ruled on a case where the user of STCs had referred to two sets of contradictory STCs. The Hoge Raad noticed that there was sufficient agreement on the inclusion of the clauses, also considering the long business relationship between parties, and the contradiction between the different sets of clauses was not a reason to hold both sets applicable, referring to a 2003 decision[1106] where the valid inclusion of either set was successfully disputed.

→ Thus, courts have not developed a consistent approach to international and foreign materials in international cases. In some cases, referral to multiple sources does not indicate a carefully reasoned-out decision. Courts have not been inspired by international, European and foreign materials, but rather confused. More interaction between Dutch courts could have prevented the development of inconsistent, unpredictable, or incorrect decisions and may enable mutual learning in a more structured manner.

1101 HR 20 November 1981, *NJ* 1982, 517.

1102 HR 6 November 1992, *NJ* 1993, 27.

1103 HR 1 July 1993, *NJ* 1993, 688.

1104 HR 10 June 1994, *NJ* 1994, 611, HR 28 November 1997, *NJ* 1998, 705, as well as HR 2 December 2011, *NJ* 2011, 574, as well as Hof 's-Hertogenbosch 1 November 2001, *NJ* 2002, 507.

1105 HR 24 April 2015, ECLI: NL:HR:2015:1125.

1106 HR 13 juni 2003, *NJ* 2003, 506. The situation in the 2015 case also seems to differ from the CISG Advisory opinion, par. 3.4. that finds that if there are several sets of terms and it is not clear which set applies, neither set will be applicable, as it should not be left to one party to guess which set of terms if applicable.

5.3.4.2.2. Making STCs adequately available

The approach of courts to international and foreign materials in decisions on the availability of STCs differs, which has undermined the predictability, consistency and responsiveness of the law on STCs.

- Various decisions of lower courts[1107] on the availability of STCs in international cases under the CISG refer to a decision from the BGH.[1108]

These decisions include the district court Rotterdam[1109] that referred to the BGH while stating that a 2001 decision from the Hoge Raad could not serve as a starting point in its decision, as the Hoge Raad decision concerned a case in which the CISG was not (yet) applicable.[1110] The district court Utrecht[1111] also referred to the BGH decision, and, moreover, distinguished between the inclusion of STCs in international contracts and domestic contracts. Unfortunately, however, some comments and case law on the BGH decision seem to be referring to the wrong publication.[1112]

- Other decisions from lower courts do not refer to the BGH.

Accordingly, the district court Rotterdam,[1113] in multiple decisions, does not refer to the BGH but instead refers to the 2005 decision of the Hoge Raad on the valid inclusion of STCs, as well as the

1107 As there are no relevant decisions of the Hoge Raad on the availability of STCs, this paragraph will mainly consider lower courts decisions. However, the importance of uniform interpretation had been emphasised for the predecessor of the CISG, see HR 13 September 1991, *NJ* 1992 110.

1108 BGH 31 October 2001, *NJW* 2002, 1651. See critically T.H.M. van Wechem, J.H.M. Spanjaard, 'De toepasselijkheid van algemene voorwaarden onder het Weens Koopverdrag: Nieuwe trend in de Nederlandse (lagere) rechtspraak?' *Contracteren* 2010, p. 35, 38, who find this decision incorrect – inconsistent with foreign decisions, and too much oriented on national law. In contrast, S.A. Kruisinga, 'Reactie op T.H.M. van Wechem en H.J.M. Spanjaard', *Contracteren* 2010, p. 110, does find the 2001 BGH decision persuasive, especially the reasoning of the BGH and the outcome of the case. She also argues that the BGH has not oriented itself on German law that she finds considerably less strict. German criticism of this decision has come to the same conclusion, see previously par. 4.3.3.2.3.

1109 Rb. Rotterdam 25 February 2005, *LJN* BH6416.

1110 HR 3 May 2013, *RvdW* 2013, 669 does not provide a further rule but is rejected on the basis of article 81 RO.

1111 Rb. Utrecht 21 January 2009, *NJF* 2009, 148.

1112 Curiously, BGH 31 October 2001, *NJW* 2002, 1651 concerned a question on article 19 and 7 CISG on battle of forms. It was not a decision on the question whether the STCs had been made adequately available. A decision on the same date under article 8 CISG, on the question whether STCs had been made adequately available, was BGH 31 October 2001, *NJW* 2002, 370. Kruisinga does refer to this decision. Comp. Rb. Arnhem 23 May 2012, *LJN* BW7459, referring to case of 31 October 2001, VIII ZR 60/01, *NJW* 2002, 1651. The case number, VIII ZR 60/01, however, refers to the decision published under *NJW* 2002, 370. For similar references see Rb. 's-Hertogenbosch 28 March 2012, *LJN* BW0028. In a later decision, Rb. 's-Hertogenbosch 1 August 2012, *RCR* 2012, 78, cites from the decision of the BGH under *NJW* 2002, 370, but does not refer expressly to the *NJW* anymore. Hof 's-Hertogenbosch 17 December 2013, *RCR* 2014, 21 also refers – in passing – to this BGH decision, without referring to the *NJW*, stating however that as STCs have not been validly included under the CISG, this question will not be addressed.

1113 Rb. Rotterdam 29 December 2010, *LJN* BP1037, Rb. Rotterdam 31 March 2010, *LJN* BN2112.

district court Arnhem.[1114] In a previous case, the district court Arnhem[1115] did not refer to either the decision of the Hoge Raad or the BGH. Instead, the district court decided the inclusion of STCs under article 7 par. 2 CISG, stating that a contract party cannot merely refer to the STCs without making the text of STCs available, while it can generally not be required of contract parties to inform after the content of STCs. This approach was also adopted in a later decision of the appeal court Arnhem.[1116]

Similarly, the district court Zwolle[1117] held that it has not been sufficiently proven that the text of STCs was made available to the German counterparty, without referring either to the Hoge Raad or the BGH. Additionally, the district court Breda,[1118] though recognising the need for a harmonised interpretation of the CISG, did not refer to either the decision of the BGH or the Hoge Raad, and concluded, under articles 8 and 9 CISG, that STCs were validly included in the contract, as the party subjected to the STCs should have realised that in international as well as national trade, the use of STCs is widespread. As the STCs had been printed on the back of the stationary of the user, and the counterparty had not protested against these STCs and had started to perform the contracts, the user was allowed to assume that the STCs had been accepted. Thus, the silence of the counterparty did not stand in the way of assuming the applicability of STCs under article 18 CISG.

Alternatively, courts have started referring to international materials. The district court Amsterdam,[1119] the court Overijssel,[1120] the court of appeal The Hague[1121] and the court of appeal 's-Hertogenbosch[1122] accordingly followed the CISG Advisory Council Opinion no 13 Inclusion of standard terms under the CISG. This opinion[1123] expressly notes that the interpretation of 2001 BGH decision, as meaning that the requirement that 'the terms themselves should be handed over or sent to the offeree at the time of contracting' is too stringent.

A decision made in arbitration,[1124] although referring to the PECL, does not refer to either the Hoge Raad or the BGH but holds that as the party subjecting to STCs had not protested the application of STCs, while the intention of the user was sufficiently clear and a reasonable person acting in international trade would have understood that the seller meant to apply his STCs, and the text of the STCs had been mailed by regular mail, the buyer had accepted the STCs, although this did not apply for the initial contract, concluded by fax, on which the text of STCs was not printed.

1114 Rb. Arnhem 10 February 2010, *LJN* BL4484, similarly Rb. Arnhem 17 January 2007, *LJN* 9279.

1115 Rb. Arnhem 16 December 2009, *LJN* BK8904.

1116 Hof Arnhem-Leeuwarden 27 May 2013, ECLI:NL:GHARL:2013:CA3329.

1117 Rb. Zwolle 9 December 2009, *LJN* BL0104.

1118 Rb. Breda 27 February 2008, *LJN* BC6704.

1119 Rb. Amsterdam 8 January 2014, *RCR* 2014, 36.

1120 Rb. Overijssel 3 December 2014, *RCR* 2015, 34.

1121 Hof 's-Gravenhage 22 April 2014, ECLI:NL:GHDHA:2014:1341. The court further cites the 2001 BGH decision at some length, critically comparing it to the decision of various other foreign courts and the CISG advisory opinion.

1122 Hof 's-Hertogenbosch 24 February 2015, *NJF* 2015, 194.

1123 CISG-AC Opinion No. 13, Inclusion of Standard Terms under the CISG, available at www.cisg.law.pace.edu/cisg/CISG-AC-op13.html#35, par. 2.5.

1124 NAI 10 February 2005, http://cisgw3.law.pace.edu/cases/050210n1.html.

- In cases under Dutch law, article 6:247 BW makes clear that articles 6:233 sub b and article 6:234 are not applicable. Thus, for international cases, a lacunae has developed.

A 2012 decision of the Hoge Raad, which did not refer to foreign or international materials, did not provide clarity on this point.[1125] The conclusion of A.G. Wissink before the case that elaborately considers the answer to this question by soft law, the CISG, and BGH case law, also does not provide an unequivocal answer and, moreover, fails to consider Directive 2000/31.

- In domestic cases, the Hoge Raad has generally not referred to European, foreign or international materials, but recognised the relevance of business practices. It does not become apparent that the courts have consistently decided these cases more strictly than international cases, even though article 6:247 BW clearly distinguishes between national and international cases.

The Hoge Raad has decided that article 6:234 BW should be interpreted in a limited manner, which entailed that the user of STCs can only refer to the availability of STCs at the registry of the court or the possibility to send the text of the STCs upon request, if there are no other options to make the STCs available. However, the Hoge Raad[1126] held that an interpretation in accordance with the needs of practice entails that the party subjecting to the STCs may not invoke the avoidability if, at the time of the conclusion of the contract, he was familiar with the content of the STCs or should have been familiar, which would, for example, be the case if STCs have been included in multiple contracts between parties, the text of which has been handed to the party subjecting to STCs, while it is also possible that invoking the avoidability of STCs is irreconcilable with good faith under article 6:248 BW.

In a subsequent case, the Hoge Raad[1127] accepted that in accordance with civil procedure law, the court had apparently assumed that STCs had been made available in accordance with article 6:234 BW.

In a 2011 decision, the Hoge Raad[1128] held that by merely making the STCs available online, where they could be found through a Google search, was not sufficient.

However, the thought that business parties in international trade ought to be aware of the widespread use of STCs[1129] has also been reflected in some domestic cases.[1130]

→ Neither lower courts nor the Hoge Raad has developed a consistent approach in referring to international, European or foreign materials in international cases, nor do lower courts consistently take into account one another's decisions. This has undermined the predictability and consistency of the law on STCs. Moreover, the responsiveness of the law on STCs to international practice is lessened as lacunaes become visible that are not remedied by the courts.

1125 HR 11 May 2012, *NJ* 2012, 318, comp. the conclusion of A.G. Wissink under pars. 3.8.2–3.8.5.

1126 HR 1 October 1999, *NJ* 2000, 207, HR 6 April 2001, *NJ* 2002, 385.

1127 HR 21 September 2007, *NJ* 2009, 50, comp. previously also HR 11 July 2008, *NJ* 2008, 416.

1128 HR 11 February 2011, *NJ* 2011, 571.

1129 Expressed for example in HR 16 February 1996, *NJ* 1996, 394.

1130 HR 19 December 1986, *NJ* 1987, 947.

5.3.4.2.3. The interpretation of clauses

Courts have not distinguished between the interpretation of clauses in domestic or international contracts, nor have they especially taken into account foreign or international materials in interpreting clauses in these contracts. In other words, foreign or international materials do not take a special place in the interpretation of international clauses. A consistent approach to the place of foreign and international materials in the interpretation of clauses in international contracts would, however, benefit predictability, accessibility consistency and responsiveness.

– International contracts are interpreted in line with domestic case law.

The Hoge Raad[1131] in the interpretation of an entire agreement clause in an international contract, held that the court of appeal had rightly interpreted the contract in accordance with a leading domestic case of the Hoge Raad,[1132] according to which a contract is to be interpreted in accordance with the reasonable expectations of parties. The court of appeal had taken a linguistic interpretation as a starting point, holding that this contract had been carefully negotiated and drafted, and, moreover, included an entire agreement clause. In the interpretation of the contract, the court also referred to the negotiation process of the contract.

The Hoge Raad does not refer to foreign or English law, in which this clause is well-known, and A.G. Timmerman only briefly refers to English law. In his note to the decision, Wissink[1133] finds that the entire agreement clause does not prescribe how the terms in the contract are to be interpreted, nor does he find it in accordance with Dutch law, as well as the PECL and the UNIDROIT principles, to bar the negotiation process from circumstances relevant for the interpretation of the wording of the contract.

In a 2013 domestic case, the Hoge Raad[1134] did recognise the function of entire agreement clauses under English law, but maintained that such clauses do not have special meaning under Dutch law.

In a case involving foreign parties, the Hoge Raad[1135] similarly referred to guidelines established in domestic case law.[1136]

1131 HR 19 January 2007, *NJ* 2007, 575, see later also HR 19 October 2007, *NJ* 2007, 565, where the Hoge Raad held that parties should take the legitimate interests of counterparties into account, as well as HR 4 June 2010, *NJ* 2010, 312, where the Hoge Raad emphasised the capacity of professional parties, and HR 5 April 2013, *NJ* 2013, 214, where the Hoge Raad held that the linguistic interpretation provided a starting point for judges in interpreting the contract, but other circumstances can entail that another meaning than the linguistic meaning of the contract can be decisive.

1132 HR 13 March 1981, *NJ* 1981, 635.

1133 Note to HR 29 June 2007, *NJ* 2007, 576, par. 8.

1134 HR 5 April 2013, *NJ* 2013, 214, see also the conclusion of A.G. Timmerman under 3.13, followed by Hof Leeuwarden 21 May 2013, *NJF* 2013, 298.

1135 HR 29 June 2007, *NJ* 2005, 576.

1136 HR 20 February 2004, *NJ* 2005, 493. More recently, in a domestic case, the Hoge Raad also considered the interpretation of contradictory clauses that were both applicable, HR 24 April 2015, ECLI:NL:HR:2015:1125.

- However, this line also permits courts to take into account parties' expectations, in which case foreign or international materials might become relevant.

The Hoge Raad[1137] expressly considered that the expectations from parties, when established, could justify an interpretation that took these expectations rather than the wording of the contract into account.

Accordingly, the Hoge Raad[1138] also upheld a decision from the court of appeal that emphasised the importance of the English wording of an initial public offering, as most parties participating in the agreement were assisted by professionals, and were situated in England or the US and the agreement was the result of extensive negotiations. In a subsequent decision,[1139] an interpretation based on the wording was difficult as the wording ('net proceed') allowed for multiple meanings. The Hoge Raad upheld the decision from the court of appeal that took into account the relevant circumstances of the case, including the drafting of the clause, the wording of the clause and parties' intentions.

In other cases, however, the Hoge Raad[1140] held that the court of appeal should also consider the argument that in shipping, the expression "as agents" had a particular meaning diverging from the meaning established by the court. Thus, parties' expectations and definitions generally recognised in trade may well be relevant.

- Lower courts similarly interpret international cases in accordance with domestic law.

The district court Rotterdam[1141] followed the line set out by the Hoge Raad, expressly referring to parties' reasonable expectations. The decision of court of appeal Arnhem[1142] makes clear that international guidelines may influence parties' expectations. The decision of the court Northern Holland[1143] allows for an arbitration clause under Dutch law, in accordance with article II New York Convention that allows for the application of more lenient, national law.

The district court Haarlem,[1144] deciding a case under Dutch law, held that the term 'negligence' should be interpreted in a way that is in accordance with Dutch law, and as comparative law showed that negligence converged with the Dutch unlawfulness in article 6:162 BW, negligence would be interpreted in accordance with this article.

→ The guidelines established by the Hoge Raad allow judges to take into account the capacity of international parties, and, possibly, their expectations as based on international materials, which leaves room for a responsive interpretation. However, applying a domestic standard to international transactions may not be in accordance with the international character of that transaction, which might undermine responsiveness. For foreign parties, moreover, the decisions from the Hoge Raad are not easily accessible and the lack of a consistent approach may give rise to unpredictability for international parties.

1137 HR 19 November 2010, *NJ* 2010, 623.

1138 HR 9 April 2010, *JOR* 2010, 179.

1139 HR 18 November 2011, *RvdW* 2011, 1422.

1140 HR 26 October 2001, *JOR* 2001, 275.

1141 Rb. Rotterdam 4 February 2009, *RCR* 2009, 42.

1142 Comp. Hof Arnhem 9 Marc 2010, *LJN* BL7399, that referred to the CISG Advisory Council Opinion nr 2.

1143 Rb. Noord Holland 25 June 2014, *RCR* 2015, 42.

1144 Rb. Haarlem 11 May 1993, *NJ* 1993, 71.

So far, however, referring to foreign law or international materials has been the exception rather than the rule. Taking into account that foreign and international materials might form a starting point for developing a separate approach to the interpretation of clauses in international clauses, that might benefit responsiveness to international trade.

5.3.4.2.4. Conclusion on the interpretation of international contracts

In accordance with multilevel governance perspectives, the lack of interaction between interdependent actors has undermined the comprehensibility of the law on STCs. Interdependence become visible most clearly between domestic courts as some courts do not have a clear overview of overlapping sources, which may decrease the accessibility of the law. Thus, courts should take more note of one another's decisions, and especially decisions from the Hoge Raad that may provide guidelines for consistent and more accessible decisions in international cases. Instead, the lack of interaction between Dutch courts has led to inconsistencies and unpredictability. Yet the lack of attention of some courts for the decisions of the Hoge Raad raises the question whether more or clearer guidelines from the Hoge Raad would be followed.

Although the law clearly distinguishes between international and national contracts, concerns of regulatory competition have not motivated courts to more consistently refer to international and foreign materials. In the absence of such an approach, a lack of responsiveness, as well as unpredictability for parties may develop. The referral to domestic decisions also lessens the accessibility of Dutch law for foreign contract parties.

Courts have not developed a consistent approach to international, European and foreign materials. Interestingly, whereas German courts do not generally refer to soft law, Dutch courts have referred to both the PECL and UNIDROIT. This has not visibly contributed to the comprehensibility of the law. Thus, even if courts use opportunities for learning, this need not be beneficial.

5.3.4.3. Conclusion on the development of Dutch law and international trade

In accordance with multilevel governance perspectives, in the development of the law on STCs in an international context, interdependence has become visible, especially between courts. Lower courts need more support in gaining an overview of overlapping sources. The Hoge Raad should provide more guidance on the obligations of contract parties to adequately make STCs available in international cases and on the valid inclusion of STCs in international cases. Lower courts should consistently follow such guidelines and they should refer to one another's decisions. Dutch courts have also not sought to compensate for shortcomings visible in Dutch law and lacunae have developed as a result. The inconsistency and unpredictability arising from case law outlines the interdependence between the legislator and the courts in the context of regulatory competition.

Furthermore, if legislators seek to make their laws attractive for foreign and international actors, they should involve these actors in the development of the law in order to learn more about their needs and preferences. Possibly, the Dutch legislator assumed that, because of the thorough drafting process of articles 6:231 et seq BW and the general success of the BW, the law on STCs was successful and did not need to be critically reconsidered. These practices likely diminish the attractiveness of Dutch law in international trade, despite the Dutch legislator's support of regulatory competition. The interests of international and foreign actors likely include the stable development of the law, which should be a reason for the legislator to adopt restraint in amending the law.

Because of these problems, potential benefits of the coexistence of actors emphasised in the pluralist view have not been realised. Regulatory competition prompted Dutch actors to take into account the likely interests of actors not involved in the national legislative process, but it has not benefited the comprehensibility of the law. Dutch actors have not critically considered the predictability, consistency, accessibility and responsiveness of Dutch law. Unclarities and a potential lack of responsiveness have therefore not been addressed.

Opportunities for mutual learning have also not been used. The problems in Dutch case law may instead serve to illustrate the risks of a pluralist approach[1145] that requires courts to consider a variety of potentially relevant 'normative communities'. The pluralist approach may be problematic because the coexistence of sources is confusing and judges make errors in interpreting and applying rules from diverging sources that seem simultaneously applicable. If domestic contract parties are moreover permitted to make choices of law, including choices for non-state law, this will likely lead to more, not less confusion. Thus, a pluralist course necessitates a stronger highest court and lower courts need to systematically take into account lower case law. Accordingly, opportunities for learning could be facilitated if the Hoge Raad provides guidelines for the use of foreign, European or international materials.

5.3.5. *Conclusion on the development of the law on STCs through the BW*

In the recodification of the law, the Dutch legislator has not strategically recognised the diminished ability of the BW to independently ensure the predictability, accessibility, consistency, and responsiveness of the law on STCs. However, the adoption of Directive 93/13, which coincided with the introduction of the BW, made interdependence in ensuring the stable development of the law clear. Since then, the legislator has had to amend the law repeatedly. Additionally, lower courts did not consistently follow the decisions of the Hoge Raad, with some courts opting to follow the CJEU instead. As a result, inconsistency and unpredictability developed despite recent recodification.

In the law on STCs, the interdependence between the legislator and the courts has become clear both in the implementation of Directive 93/13 and in the pursuit of regulatory competition. As a result, in accordance with insights from multilevel governance, the legislator and the courts should interact with one another, and a failure to do so has undermined the predictability, consistency, accessibility, and responsiveness. The interdependence between courts similarly necessitates an active approach of courts in interacting with one another.

1145 P.S. Berman, 'Global legal pluralism', *Southern California Law Review* 2007, p. 1231-1232.

The coexistence of actors has been beneficial insofar as it has inspired the Dutch legislator in the drafting of articles 6:231 et seq BW and in the subsequent amendment of articles 6:236 and 237 BW. However, German and other laws have hardly been transplanted into Dutch law. Although similarities can be explained by the role of German law in the drafting process, they can also be explained by Directive 93/13. The adoption of this Directive has however not caused a change in Dutch law. The Hoge Raad has maintained its case law on *contra preferentem* decisions and only after well-established CJEU case law and inconsistency in lower courts decisions has it accepted the *ex officio* obligation of courts to consider the evaluation of clauses. This EU transplant will continue to be integrated in Dutch law, as further questions will arise on the interplay with harmonised law and national civil procedure law. More generally, it can however be doubted whether the Hoge Raad will start to actively refer questions to the CJEU, as it remains focussed on maintaining the unity of national law. It also remains to be seen whether lower courts will follow the Hoge Raad rather than the CJEU.

Clearly, the development of harmonisation in this area has not led to the development of a system of checks and balances, despite the control of the CJEU. Arguably, the lack of clarity with regard to national actors' obligations initially stood in the way of checks and balances. However, even when more clarity was established, the problems of Dutch law make clear that the control introduced by harmonisation is limited – European actors need to be aware of problems before they can intervene. Even if they are aware of problems arising in domestic disputes, the CJEU cannot intervene if questions are not referred to it, and even the control of the Hoge Raad to ensure consistency and unity in national law seems compromised.

The development of harmonisation in this area has also not prompted national actors to consider the interests of international actors, as visible in the introduction of article 6:247 BW. However, involving foreign and international actors in national debates may prove an interesting starting point for considering their needs and preferences. These actors may also provide a more critical perspective on Dutch law.

The Dutch legislator has recognised the added value of regulatory competition but this has not prompted the inclusion of foreign and international stakeholders in the drafting of the BW. Like the German legislator, the Dutch legislator participated actively in European debate on harmonisation measures. At first sight, the Dutch legislator also adopts a less narrow view than German actors, as the Dutch legislator does not reject maximum harmonisation or comitology outright, which should be beneficial for debate. Yet on closer inspection, it becomes clear that the legislator considers the process in terms of "negotiation", and national law forms a starting point in the negotiations. It follows that neither harmonisation nor regulatory competition has prompted Dutch actors to include foreign or international actors or refer consistently to international materials.

The coexistence of actors does provide for opportunities for mutual learning. The coexistence of actors of various starting points for improving the law on STCs. Wilhelmsson[1146] has argued that coexistence may 'break up petrified structures of national law that are hampering the development of the law', for example, article 6:214 or

[1146] T. Wilhelmsson, 'Private law in the EU: Harmonised or fragmented Europeanisation?', *ERPL* 2002, p. 91–92.

239 BW, dead letters that however do not hinder the development of law as such. Similarly, the link between the law on STCs, the model lists and default law could have been considered. Unfortunately, this was not the case for Dutch law.

However, the limits of mutual learning should also be considered. The timing of the adoption of the Directive meant that the use of opportunities for learning would jeopardise the stable development of newly adopted law – in addition to potential unpredictability that may arise from the introduction of a new code.

5.4. Blanket clauses

This paragraph will consider whether actors have recognised interdependence and interacted accordingly, and if so, how this has affected the extent to which blanket clauses – article 3 Directive 93/13, article 6:233 sub a BW and article 6:248 BW[1147] – contribute to the predictability, consistency, accessibility and responsiveness of the law on STCs. Has a lack of interaction between interdependent actors led to problems or has the coexistence of actors strengthened the comprehensibility of the law?

Paragraph 5.4.1 will turn to the development of the law through article 6:233 sub a BW and paragraph 5.4.2 will discuss model lists. Paragraph 5.4.3 will turn to the evaluation of clauses under in international cases. Paragraph 5.4.4 will end with a conclusion.

5.4.1. *The development of the law through article 6:233 sub a BW*

Have actors recognised that other actors may also develop the law through blanket clauses, and interacted with these actors accordingly? How has that affected the extent to which article 6:233 sub a BW may contribute to the predictability, accessibility, consistency and responsiveness of the law on STCs?

Paragraph 5.4.1.1 will discuss the drafting of article 6:233 sub a BW and paragraph 5.4.1.2 will consider the interpretation of this provision by the courts. Paragraph 5.4.1.3 will end with a conclusion.

5.4.1.1. The drafting of article 6:233 sub a BW

The Dutch legislator has taken into account especially German experiences with the successful AGBG, which increased the chance that Dutch law would also function well in practice.

The introduction of article 6:233 BW followed the recommendation of the CCA,[1148] inspired by the AGBG, to introduce a blanket clause that could be used for the evaluation of diverging STCs throughout different branches and in individual relations that may

[1147] HR 14 June 2002, *NJ* 2003, 112 decided that article 6:233 BW does not exclude the simultaneous applicability of article 6:248 BW.

[1148] CCA, *Advies inzake het vraagstuk van de toepassing van standaardvoorwaarden bij transacties met de consument*, The Hague: SER, 1978, p. 21, 32-35.

differ considerably from one another. Therefore, a blanket clause would allow the law on STCs to be developed through case law.[1149] The CCA advice was approved by the preliminary report of Prof. Hondius,[1150] who, after comparing the various methods that had been developed in other legal orders to control the use of STCs, argued for the use of a blanket clause, in combination with a model list, referring to the AGBG. Parliament considered the creation of a new regime desirable. Although German law had largely developed on the basis of article 242 BGB, and later article 9 AGBG, the Dutch judiciary showed more restraint in developing the law, and a new regime would also contribute to predictability.[1151]

If the legislator has taken other legal orders as inspiration in the drafting of article 6:233 BW, this was not made explicit. However, the legislator[1152] has indicated that the resolution adopted by the Council of Europe was taken into account, which, in turn, was preceded by the 1984 consultation that discussed various means to control the use of STCs, including the use of blanket clauses.

Yet the German regime has not served as a legal transplant. The legislator[1153] has explicitly referred to the relation between articles 6:233 and 6:248 BW, noting that the avoidability in article 6:233 BW concerns clauses that diverge from the consequences that the contract of parties would have had, in accordance with article 6:248 BW that stipulates that contracts do not only have the consequences which parties have contracted for, but also consequences following from the law – especially default law, which according to the legislator 'strives for justice rather than predictability' – customs and good faith. The legislator[1154] later abandoned including the comparison with default law in article 6:233 sub a BW. It was held that this perspective would overlook the possibility that good faith stood in the way of invoking a rule from default law.

The coexistence of other actors has also been beneficial. Hartkamp[1155] notes that initially the courts did not take an active approach to the interpretation of articles 6:231 et seq BW; this developed after CJEU case law on the Directive. That does however not mean that the Directive or CJEU decisions have consistently been integrated in Dutch law. Specifically, CJEU decisions[1156] makes clear that default law can play a role in the evaluation of clauses.[1157] Initially, the comparison with default law in the evaluation of

1149 Parl. Gesch. NBW, Boek 6 (Inv. 3, 5 en 6), p. 1457.

1150 E.H. Hondius, 'Naar een wettelijke regeling van algemene voorwaarden', in: *Handelingen der Nederlandse Juristen-Vereniging*, volume 109, issue 1, Zwolle: Tjeenk Willink 1979, p. 150, 169-171.

1151 Parl. Gesch. NBW, Boek 6 (Inv. 3, 5 en 6), p. 1586–1587.

1152 Parl. Gesch. NBW, Boek 6 (Inv. 3, 5 en 6), p. 1455.

1153 Parl. Gesch. NBW, Boek 6 (Inv. 3, 5 en 6), p. 1579–1580.

1154 Parl. Gesch. NBW, Boek 6 (Inv. 3, 5 en 6), p. 1599.

1155 A.S. Hartkamp, 'Het nieuwe BW – ontwikkelingen sinds 1992', *AA* 2012, p. 53.

1156 See prominently CJEU 14 March 2013 (Aziz v Caixa d'Estalvis de Catalunya, Tarragona i Manresa (Catalunyacaixa)), C-415/11, [2013] ECR, p. I-0. See previously on this decision par. 4.5.

1157 Comp. A.G.F. Ancery, 'Toetsing van oneerlijke bedingen: de fictieve toetsing op de kaart?', *MvV* 2014, 104 who asks whether this points towards a more abstract evaluation of clauses. On the one hand, this should help judges determine whether they should *ex officio* evaluate clauses, in accordance with HR 13 September 2013, *NJ* 2014, 274, even though the Hoge Raad has rejected this approach in HR 21 September 2012, *NJ* 2013, 431.

clauses played no role in practice.[1158] However, recently, some lower courts[1159] have started to refer to default law in the evaluation of clauses.

Thus, convergence between Dutch and German law can be traced to the role of German law in the drafting of Dutch law, but also to the Directive. Clear differences between German and Dutch law remain, for example with regard to the role of default law. Although the Directive should have been integrated in Dutch law, this may not consistently be the case. Nevertheless, the CJEU has stimulated the development of the law under article 6:233 sub a BW.

5.4.1.2. Interaction between the judiciary in the interpretation of article 6:233 sub a BW

The Hoge Raad has not developed a consistent approach to the Directive but it has generally exercised restraint in referring to the Directive and the CJEU. The Hoge Raad has sought to decide cases in accordance with national law. This restraint is not directly detrimental to private parties, but as it is difficult to reconcile with European decisions, the extent to which these Hoge Raad decisions provide guidance to lower courts is limited.

- Initially, the Hoge Raad decided cases in accordance with Directive 93/13, although it exercised restraint in referring questions to the CJEU.

The Hoge Raad held, in accordance with the aim of Directive 93/13 to increase consumer protection, that the main terms of the contracts should be interpreted in a limited manner.[1160] However, as it concerns a term used in the Directive, it should be interpreted autonomously, as confirmed by the CJEU,[1161] that has however since interpreted article 4 par. 2 Directive in a narrow manner as well.[1162]

- Since this decision, the Hoge Raad has adopted restraint in referring cases to the CJEU.

In a decision[1163] on an exclusion clause for personal injuries of the consumer, the consumer had invoked the avoidability of this clause under article 6:233 BW. However, he had only done so after the statement of grounds of appeal ('*memorie van grieven*'), without making clear that he had already invoked the avoidability of this clause in an earlier letter. The Hoge Raad held that,

1158 C.M.D.S. Pavillon, *Open normen in het Europees consumentenrecht*, Deventer: Kluwer 2011, p. 85.

1159 Rb. Rotterdam 22 February 2014, ECLI:NL:RBROT:2014:944, Rb. Amsterdam 4 March 2014, ECLI:NL:RBAMS:2014:1965, Hof 's-Hertogenbosch 3 February 2015, ECLI:NL:GHDHA:2015:66, Rb. Midden-Nederland, 1 April 2015, ECLI:NL:RBMNE:2015:2116.

1160 HR 19 September 1997, *NJ* 1998, 6.

1161 CJEU 26 February 2015 (Matei v SC Volksbank Romania SA), C-143/13, [2015] ECR p. I-0, par. 50.

1162 CJEU 23 April 2015 (Van Hove v CNP Assurances SA), C-96/14, [2015] ECR p. I-0, par. 33, with further references.

1163 HR 22 June 2007, *NJ* 2007, 344. Comp. also the decision in Hof Amsterdam 24 January 2012, *RF* 2012, 42, in which the avoidability of a clause (in a contract with a CEO acting as a consumer) that had been invoked in first instance is not assessed.

although the claimant was allowed to widen the scope of his complaint in appeal, he needed to do before the statement of appeal, in order to concentrate the dispute in appeal. Consequently, invoking the avoidability of the clause went beyond the limits of the dispute ('*grenzen van de rechtsstrijd*'). Invoking article 6:233 sub a BW constituted a new ground of appeal that was not allowed in this stage of the dispute as the counterparty needs to be able to assess against which claims he should defend himself.

Reading this decision may give one the impression that neither the Hoge Raad nor the A.G. is aware of the existence of the Directive, or the obligation of the judiciary to assess the unfairness of clauses *ex officio* as established by the CJEU.

This is particularly apparent from the CJEU decision in *Banif Plus Bank v Csipai*,[1164] where the CJEU held that the court is bound to assess of its own motion, on the basis of facts and law at its disposal, or the facts that were available to the court as answers to the inquiries of the court raised of its own motion. If the court, subsequently, finds that a term is unfair, it needs to enable parties to react to this decision.[1165] However, the active role of the courts does not mean that parties invoking the unfairness of a clause do not need to prove why this clause is unfair, unless the clause falls under articles 6:236 and 237 BW, which was the case.

A later decision of the CJEU is even more difficult to reconcile with the Hoge Raad decision. The CJEU[1166] evaluated whether national law limiting parties' possibility to argue on the basis of new facts relevant for the fairness of a clause, severely hindered the application of Union law or rendered it impossible, considering the obligation of the court to assess this question of its own motion.

Arguably, the Hoge Raad did not consider it self-evident whether civil procedure law would allow for the *ex officio* evaluation of the clause, and the CJEU decision in *Van Schijndel*[1167] may support this conclusion. However, the answer to this question is not easy to deduce from CJEU case law and should, therefore, not be considered as an *acte éclairé*,[1168] and the later decision of the CJEU[1169] indicates a radically different approach that is contrary to the decision of the Hoge Raad. Therefore, this question should have been referred to the CJEU.

- In subsequent decisions, the Hoge Raad also exercised restraint and emphasised national legislative history rather than the Directive.

In a 2010 decision on an exclusion clause in a contract between an insurer and the insured, who had raped his wife, the insured, subsequently, claimed payment for damages inflicted by rape. The

1164 CJEU 21 February 2013 (Banif Plus Bank v Csipai), C-472/11, [2013] ECR, p. I-0.

1165 A.G.F. Ancery, *Ambtshalve toepassing van EU recht*, Deventer: Kluwer 2012,p. 199–200 points out that courts are only bound to do so if parties, without such interference, are not able to invoke rights derived from European law, which is generally considered to be the case in cases falling within the scope of Directive 93/13.

1166 CJEU 30 May 2013 (Aegon Magyarország Hitel Zrt v Jörös), C-397/11, [2013] ECR, p. I-0.

1167 CJEU 14 December 1995 (Van Schijndel), Joined cases C-430/93 and C-431/93, [1995] ECR, p. I-4705.

1168 See previously par. 4.4.1.1.

1169 CJEU 30 May 2013 (Aegon Magyarország Hitel Zrt v Jörös), C-397/11, [2013] ECR, p. I-0.

Hoge Raad[1170] maintained that European law – in this case competition law – does not oblige the judge to evaluate clauses of its own motion. Moreover, A.G. Rank-Berenschot, whose conclusion was followed by the Hoge Raad, held that the clause is exempt from evaluation as it concerns one of the main terms of the contract. Rather than referring to the Directive, the A.G. considered the *travaux préparatoires* to the BW that defend a less strict regime for insurance contracts, as decisive. Possibly, the restraint of the Hoge Raad in the *ex officio* interpretation of an exclusion clause may be traced to questions regarding the limits of the judiciary to evaluate a clause *ex officio*.[1171]

In a 2012 decision, the Hoge Raad[1172] considered that the court of appeal had incorrectly evaluated the fairness of an arbitration clause by an abstract standard, insufficiently considering the individual circumstances of the case. Therefore, its decision implied that arbitration clauses should be generally considered unfair in consumer contracts, which need not be the case as the clause did not fall within the scope of articles 6:236 and 237 BW. Since then, article 6:236 sub n has however been amended to include arbitration clauses. The Hoge Raad's emphasis on the individual circumstances of the case, is nevertheless convincing, in line with the Directive, and previous and subsequent CJEU case law.[1173] The amendment of Dutch law places ADR clauses on the black list, unless it concerns clauses that provide the consumer with a term of at least a month after the user has invoked the clause in writing against the consumer, to choose to turn to traditional adjudication. This time limit is considerably shorter than the time limit in *Asturcom*,[1174] where national law provided the consumer with a time limit to contest the arbitration award of 60 days, starting from the day of the notification of the award. The Court held this time limit was not problematic as such. Because the time limit started on the day of the notification, there was no chance that the consumer would find herself in the situation that the limitation period had expired before she was even aware of the effects of the arbitration clause. Therefore, it was likely to make the exercise of rights granted under Directive 93/13 impossible. One may ask whether Dutch law provides sufficient guarantees for the consumer in that respect. The Hoge Raad did however not consider this question, or refer a question to the CJEU.

Subsequent considerations of the Hoge Raad are more problematic. Referring to *Freiburger Kommunalbauten*,[1175] rather than *Mostaza Claro*,[1176] the Hoge Raad holds that the CJEU has left the assessment of the fairness of clauses to national courts. Interestingly, however, the Hoge Raad does not refer to subsequent CJEU case law, which may be especially problematic in the light of the guidelines provided by the CJEU for the interpretation of article 3 Directive 93/13.[1177]

1170 HR 23 April 2010, *NJ* 2010, 454, see the conclusion of the A.G. under par. 3.20–3.21.

1171 C.M.D.S. Pavillon, 'De wisselende betekenis van de Richtlijn oneerlijke bedingen in de Nederlandse rechtspraak: een overzicht', *VrA* 2006, p. 43.

1172 HR 21 September 2012, *NJ* 2013, 431. See further on the *ex officio* application of European law A.G.F. Ancéry, *Ambtshalve toepassing van EU recht*, Deventer: Kluwer 2012.

1173 CJEU 26 October 2006 (Mostaza Claro v Centro Movil Milenium SL), C-168/05, [2006] ECR p. I-10421, CJEU 6 October 2009 (Asturcom Telecommunicaciones CL v Rodriguez Nogueira), C-40/08 [2009] ECR p. I-9579, CJEU 27 February 2014 (Pohotovost s.r.o. v Vasuta), C-470/12, [2014] ECR p. I-0.

1174 CJEU 6 October 2009 (Asturcom Telecommunicaciones CL v Rodriguez Nogueira), C-40/08 [2009] ECR p. I-9579, par. 43–46.

1175 CJEU 1 April 2004 (Freiburger Kommunalbauten v Hofstetter), C- 237/02, [2004], ECR, p. I-3403.

1176 CJEU 26 October 2006 (Mostaza Claro v Centro Movil Milenium SL), C 168/05, [2006] ECR p. I-10421. The conclusion of A.G. Spier, under 3.8.1. does however consider this decision.

1177 CJEU 26 April 2012 (Hatóság v Invitel), C-472/10, ECR [2012], p. I-0, par. 22, similarly CJEU 9 November 2010, (VB Pénzügyi Lízing v Schneider), C-137/08, [2010] ECR p. I-0, par. 44, CJEU 15 March 2012 (Pereničová and Perenič v SOS financ spol. s r.o.), C-453/10, [2012] ECR, p. I-0, par. 43, CJEU 16 November 2010 (Pohotovosť s.r.o. v Korčkovská), C-76/10, [2010] ECR, p. I-0, par. 58, 60, as discussed previously in chapter 4.

- In 2013, the Hoge Raad[1178] adopted a different approach that may offer more guidance for lower courts, which should help consistency.

In contrast to its 2007 decision,[1179] the Hoge Raad upheld the *ex officio* obligation of the court of appeal to evaluate the fairness of a penalty clause in a consumer contract. After considering CJEU case law on the *ex officio* obligation of courts, the Hoge Raad turned to the limits of the dispute that, in 2007, limited the possibility for the consumer to invoke the avoidability of the clause. In its 2013 decision, the Hoge Raad continued to reiterate the ambits of the dispute, adding that the court of appeal should *ex officio* evaluate the fairness of clauses, including cases where the grounds of appeal did not refer to the fairness of clauses. Thus, in its 2013 decision, the Hoge Raad stressed the role of the courts in actively turning to clauses that can potentially be unfair. The court may however not do so if the party has not challenged the allowance of the claim that was based on an unfair clause. Thus, the 2013 limits the cases in which the court is not obliged to examine the fairness of clauses.

The decision of the Hoge Raad need not necessarily indicate that it has abandoned restraint and will start to actively refer questions to the CJEU. This is visible in the conclusion of A.G. Wissink,[1180] who noted that various cases were pending before the courts. The A-G. accordingly recommended that the Hoge Raad adjourned its decision until the CJEU decide, and possibly, referred it own questions to the CJEU. The Hoge Raad has accordingly decided after the CJEU ruled in *Banif Plus Bank*,[1181] *Jörös*[1182] and *Asbeek Brusse v De Man Garabito and Jahani*.[1183]

The Hoge Raad referred to *Banif Plus Bank* and *Asbeek Brusse*, but not to *Jörös*, which concerned the duty of the court to consider rules of public policy, more particularly Directive 93/13, and the principle of equivalence. The CJEU also ruled, with regard to the principle of effectiveness, that Hungarian procedural rules did not make the protection of the rights which Directive 93/13 confers on the consumer impossible or excessively difficult in this case.

The decisions of the Hoge Raad are likely in line with CJEU decisions. However, the restraint of the Hoge Raad is still visible.

→ Thus, the decisions from the Hoge Raad do not show a consistent approach to the Directive, although restraint has generally been visible, notwithstanding its 2013 decision. Generally, not referring to the CJEU need not mean that cases are decided contrary to the Directive and it may not have been directly problematic for private parties, especially not as the restraint in *ex officio* evaluation of clauses benefits the predictability of the law. Moreover, decisions in line with national law are advantageous for consistency.[1184] However, the decisions of the Hoge Raad prior to 2013 seem difficult to reconcile with CJEU case law, and lower courts differ, which has led to inconsistencies.

1178 HR 13 September 2013, *NJ* 2014, 274.
1179 HR 22 June 2007, *NJ* 2007, 344.
1180 Conclusion of A.G. Wissink before HR 13 September 2013, *NJ* 2014, 274, par. 3.40.
1181 CJEU 21 February 2013 (Banif Plus Bank Zrt v Csipai), C-472/11, [2013] ECR, p. I-0.
1182 CJEU 30 May 2013 (Jöros v Aegon Magyarország Hitel Zrt), C-397/11, [2013], p. I-0.
1183 CJEU 30 May 2013 (Asbeek Brusse and De Man Garabito v Jahani), C-488/11, [2013], p. I-0.
1184 For consumers, however, restraint towards the *ex officio* obligations of the judge may entail that clauses are not evaluated, to their detriment.

- Notably, some lower courts have decided in accordance with surrounding national law and decisions from the Hoge Raad.

The court Arnhem[1185] followed the Hoge Raad's decision that an arbitration clause is not necessarily unfair, and accordingly upheld the clause. The court The Hague[1186] similarly followed the Hoge Raad, upholding the clause in the light of the restraint generally adopted in the evaluation of arbitral awards, and as the claim for avoiding the clause had expired under article 3:52 BW.

The cantonial court Venlo,[1187] in a clause for termination because of criminal offences in a contract for accommodation, also did not refer to the Directive but rather article 7:213 BW which stipulates that tenants should behave in accordance with good faith, as well as a decision from the Hoge Raad.

The district court 's-Gravenhage,[1188] deciding on a case in which a jurisdiction clause for the cantonial sector was included in the STCs, did not refer to CJEU case law, but rather to article 96 Civil Procedure Act that held such a clause for invalid.

In line with the CJEU's later decision in *Šiba v Devėnas*,[1189] the cantonial court Assen[1190] held a clause between a consumer and her lawyer which resulted in an increase of costs for the consumer as being ineffective, and referred to the guidelines established by the Dutch Bar that prescribe that lawyers discuss the possibility that costs are raised with a consumer.

The cantonial court Rotterdam held that a provider of electricity could not effectively invoke the clause that excluded liability for malfunctions, except for damages caused with intent or by considerable negligence, and held that the clause was ineffective as the provider had not made the facts of the case available in such a way that the consumer was able to defend that intent or negligence caused the defect, referring to article 6:75 BW. The decision is also in line with article 21 Civil Procedure Code that obliges parties to bring forward all facts that are relevant for the decision, which the provider in the opinion of the court had not done. The court does not refer to a previous decision from the Hoge Raad.[1191]

The court of appeal 's-Gravenhage[1192] upheld a clause stipulating that the consumer would pay at the time of delivery as this clause reflects article 7:26 BW, while it is also not part of the STCs, but a main term of the contract. The court Mid-Netherlands[1193] held a clause that obliged the consumer to the full price pay in advance, in a distance sale, for unfair as it contradicted default law. The district court Amsterdam[1194] upheld a clause resulted in a more advantageous position for the consumer than was the case in applicable default law, while the district court Rotterdam[1195] held a clause that disadvantaged the consumer in comparison to the consumer's position under default law, for unfair.

1185 Rb. Arnhem 10 April 2013, ECLI:NL:RBGEL:2013:CA0523.

1186 Rb. 's-Gravenhage 29 May 2013, *NJF* 2013, 332.

1187 Ktr. Venlo 1 July 2009, *WR* 2010, 17.

1188 Rb. 's-Gravenhage 11 February 2009, *Prg.* 2009, 155.

1189 CJEU 15 January 2015 (Šiba v Devėnas), C-537/13, [2015] ECR p. I-0.

1190 Ktr. Assen 11 September 2007, *Prg.* 2008, 3. Comp. also Hof 's-Hertogenbosch 25 March 2014, *NJF* 2014, 216 where the court upheld a clause, referring to the obligations of a lawyer in accordance with professional rules.

1191 HR 16 May 1997, *NJ* 2000, 1.

1192 Hof 's-Hertogenbosch 3 February 2015, ECLI:NL:GHDHA:2015:66.

1193 Rb. Midden-Nederland, 1 April 2015, ECLI:NL:RBMNE:2015:2116.

1194 Rb. Amsterdam 4 March 2014, ECLI:NL:RBAMS:2014:1965.

1195 Rb. Rotterdam 22 February 2014, ECLI:NL:RBROT:2014:944.

The court of appeal 's-Hertogenbosch[1196] held that a clause that held the consumer who had rented a trailer liable in cases of loss or theft, was contrary to societal views on justice, as established by the Hoge Raad,[1197] and considered whether clauses that diverged from this view were, nevertheless, an established practice. The court was not convinced by the other sets of STCs that the lettor had provided and considered that the consumer was not able to insure himself against damages arising from the loss or theft of a rented trailer. For these reasons, the court held the clause was ineffective.

The cantonial court 's-Gravenhage[1198] held that the use of a similar clause was not unfair, considering that this clause was included in STCs that had been negotiated collectively between consumers' organisations and electricity providers.

→ In these decisions, the minimum character of Directive 93/13 and the shape of the measure allow courts to decide in accordance with national law and practice, which benefits the consistent and responsive development of the law on STCs.

- Some decisions are in accordance with surrounding Directives.

The district court Utrecht,[1199] in a case in which a health insurer sought to amend its policy on the basis of a clause that allowed it to amend its STCs, did not assess the fairness of this term. Instead, the court judged that the way in which the insurer exercised its right to amend its STCs was contrary to good faith under articles 6:2 and 6:248 BW, which falls outside the scope of the Directive. However, the insurer, by amending its clauses may have acted contrary to Directive 2005/29 on unfair commercial practices – which had not yet entered into effect at the time of the decision – as well as misleading advertising, as it had used its wide policy specifically to attract new consumers. The court Noord-Holland[1200] more directly held clauses for invalid as they undermined the claim that consumers would rent fully insured motorbikes, without deductibles ('*eigen risico*'), referring to article 6:193 BW that implements Directive 2005/29.

The court of appeal 's-Hertogenbosch[1201] held a dissolution clause that obliged the consumer to complain within 8 days, after which the rights of the consumer would be dissoluted, as unfair as it feel under sub b of the Annex, and it limited the right of the consumer to complain, contrary to articles 7:6 and 23, which implement Directive 1999/44 on consumer sales.

[1196] Hof 's-Hertogenbosch 9 January 2007, *LJN* AZ5893, followed by Ktr. Sneek 9 May 2012, *Prg.* 2012, 218. Comp. also Hof Amsterdam 12 August 2014, *Prg.* 2014, 245 upholding the lower court's reference to the code of conduct on mortgage credit.

[1197] HR 24 October 1997, *NJ* 1998, 69, comp. the conclusion of A.G. Vranken under par. 15–16.

[1198] Ktr. 's-Gravenhage 5 August 2008, *NJF* 2009, 460. Some decisions in accordance with national practice may however, be more problematic, for example the decision of the Board of 29 September 2009, nr 31530, at www.degeschillencommissie.nl/klacht-indienen/eerdere-uitspraken/31530/afwezigheid-van-7-maanden that invoking article 6:233 sub a BW is not possible as it concerns STCs that have been negotiated with the Dutch consumers' organisation.

[1199] Rb. Utrecht 8 June 2007, *NJF* 2007, 359. Comp. also Ktr. Rotterdam 17 July 2008, *Prg.* 2008, 184, stating that good faith stands in the way of invoking the STCs against the consumer, considering the small breach of the consumer.

[1200] Rb. Noord-Holland 17 September 2014, *NJF* 2014, 498.

[1201] Hof 's-Hertogenbosch 11 March 2014, ECLI:NL:GHSHE:2014:677.

A decision of the cantonial court Utrecht[1202] showed similar overlap. The court held a contract, that did not provide the consumer with a possibility to cancel the contract, was unfair, especially because the consumer concluded the contract in the studio of the offeror and signed the contract without adequately considering the costs and benefits of the contract, because she was overwhelmed by the provider who had promised a free and noncommittal intake interview. This situation seems to fall under Directive 85/577 on doorstep selling, since revised by Directive 2011/83 on consumer rights. The decision of the court under article 6:233 sub a BW seems surprising as the main complaint seems to be that the provider did not include a term that allowed the consumer to cancel the contract, which is a requirement for the applicability of article 6:233 BW. The decision does not refer to either Directive or CJEU case law.

→ These decisions demonstrate that decisions in accordance with the *acquis* may also be in accordance with national legal views on justice, as reflected in articles 6:2 and 248 BW as well as national law.

- Problems, however, become apparent in areas where the decisions of the Hoge Raad are difficult to reconcile with CJEU decisions with regard to the definition of the main terms of the contract and the obligation of courts to examine clauses of their own motion. Some courts have expressly followed the Hoge Raad.

Accordingly, the court of appeal Amsterdam[1203] upheld a clause in an insurance contract that limited the coverage in case the consumer terminated the contract, holding that this term fell under the main terms of an insurance contract. Although the court does not directly refer to the Directive itself, it does refer extensively to legislative history as well as a previous decision from the Hoge Raad,[1204] which Hartkamp[1205] characterises as an example of indirect effect, to determine the meaning of 'main terms of the contract' in the meaning of article 6:231 BW.

In another case, concerning a consumer in Germany and an insurer, the court of appeal 's-Hertogenbosch[1206] held that a clause limiting the coverage of the policy was a main term, exempt from judicial evaluation, and referred to previous decisions from the Hoge Raad in business contract that did not fall within the scope of the Directive. However, the decision is also in line with the 2010 decision of the Hoge Raad on an exclusion clause in a consumer contract. The decision of the court of appeal, finding that a term that directly affects the scope of the policy is not an STC in the sense of article 6:233 sub a BW, may be contrary to the CJEU's decision in *Van Hove v CNP Assurances SA*[1207] as it overlooks the question whether these terms are formulated transparently.

In its 2014 decisions the court of appeal Amsterdam[1208] also did not consider at length whether terms were main terms, ruling that this was clearly not the case because it did not concern a clause

1202 Ktr. Utrecht 5 July 2006, *Prg.* 143.

1203 Hof Amsterdam 30 September 2008, *LJN* BG2107.

1204 HR 19 September 1997, *NJ* 1998, 6.

1205 A.S. Hartkamp, *Mr. C. Asser's Handleiding tot de beoefening van het Nederlands burgerlijk recht. 3. Vermogensrecht algemeen. Deel I* Europees recht en Nederlands vermogensrecht*, Deventer: Kluwer 2011. Hereafter, this volume will refer to this book in the following manner: Asser/Hartkamp 2011.

1206 Hof 's-Hertogenbosch 22 March 2011, *LJN* BP9625.

1207 CJEU 23 April 2015 (Van Hove v CNP Assurances SA), C-96/14, [2015] ECR p. I-0.

1208 Hof Amsterdam 12 August 2014, *Prg.* 2014, 245, Hof Amsterdam 12 August 2014, *Prg.* 2014, 246, Hof Amsterdam 12 August 2014, *Prg.* 2014, 247, considering that 'het hier niet gaat om een beding zonder hetwelk de overeenkomst van geldlening, bij gebreke van voldoende bepaalbaarheid van de

without which the contract for credit would not be concluded because parties did not reach sufficient agreement. The court of appeal The Hague[1209] may be more problematic, as it summarily considers that the clause is a standard clause as it has not been individually negotiated.

- However, other, previous decisions contradict these decisions, which leads to inconsistency and unpredictability.

Interestingly, the court of appeal 's-Hertogenbosch[1210] did not similarly hold that a term on the coverage of an insurance policy was a main term of the contract. The court held instead that even if the clause in the insurance contract with the consumer was a main term, it was irreconcilable with standards of fairness, and the clause should, therefore, not be upheld.

- Decisions on other issues similarly show inconsistencies. Thus, some lower courts, in line with the Hoge Raad's earlier case law, have refused to evaluate clauses *ex officio.*

Thus, the court of appeal Arnhem[1211] assessed of its own motion a clause that stipulated that in the case of cancellation, the consumer was obliged to pay 30% of the price, or, in cases that the consumer is aware that the contract can be performed, 50% of the price. The court of appeal referred to CJEU case law and stated that it would assess the terms of its own motion as the consumer was unable to pay for legal advice. It may, however, be doubted whether courts may only assess clauses of their own motion when consumers are not able to substantiate why a clause is unfair.

Nevertheless this view was subsequently adopted by the district court Haarlem[1212] that refused to assess terms of its motion as the consumer had invoked the unfairness of the clause while it was not established that the consumer was unable to pay for legal advice.

Similarly, the district court Utrecht,[1213] referring to CJEU case law, refused to assess a term of its own motion, holding that the claimant – a consumer organisation – was aware of the protection conferred upon the consumer, as demonstrated by its request to the court to apply article 6:236 BW of its own motion, while the consumer organisation was not a weak party in need of protection. The court, also, found that the organisation had not sufficiently established that the disputed clause fell within the scope of article 6:236 BW. This reasoning seems contrary to the idea of applying the provision of its own motion. The ability of the judge to do so can, however, be limited if the judge has insufficient information on the clause, but it does not become apparent whether the judge has allowed the organisation sufficient opportunity to establish that the clause fell under article 6:236 BW. The decision, further, does not seem to be in line with the reasoning of the legislator when this article was established. Notably, the black list under article 6:236 BW was drafted narrowly to facilitate the predictable interpretation of article 6:233 BW.

verbintenissen, niet geacht kan worden tot stand te zijn gekomen' referring to HR 19 September 1997, *NJ* 1998, 6 and HR 21 February 2003, *NJ* 2004, 567. Comp. less expressly Court of appeal Amsterdam 3 March 2015, ECLI:NL:GHAMS:2015:602.

1209 Hof 's-Gravenhage 28 October 2014, *Prg.* 2015, 96.

1210 Hof 's-Hertogenbosch 26 May 2009, *NJF* 2009, 336.

1211 Hof Arnhem 5 June 2001, *NJ* 2001, 622.

1212 Ktr. Haarlem 22 January 2003, *Prg.* 2003, 6031.

1213 Rb. Utrecht 4 January 2006, *NJF* 2006, 152.

Since its 2013 decision, however, various lower courts[1214] evaluating clauses *ex officio* have done so while following the Hoge Raad.

- Other courts have, however, decided differently and evaluated clauses of their own motion.

The cantonial court Eindhoven[1215] held that a clause in a contract between a consumer and a library, insofar as it aimed to exclude the duty of the library to mitigate its own damages, was ineffective of its own motion, referring to CJEU case law.[1216]

The cantonial court Assen,[1217] after referring to CJEU decisions in *Océano*[1218] and *Mostazo Claro*,[1219] allowed parties to argue whether the clauses in a consumer contract were unfair or not. The court, subsequently, decided that the penalty clause was unfair as there was no limit to the penalty. Similarly, the cantonial court Breda,[1220] also referring to the CJEU decision in *Pannon*,[1221] raised the fairness of clauses of its own motion and rejected the claim for compensation as based on these clauses.

After the 2013 decision of the Hoge Raad, these decisions are still visible. Accordingly, the cantonial court Rotterdam[1222] held that it was bound to raise the fairness of STCs of its own motion, in accordance with CJEU case law, and held a penalty clause could not be held partially ineffective under article 3:41 BW, as became apparent from the CJEU decision in *Unicaja Banco*.[1223] The court Gelderland[1224] held a clause unfair, following the CJEU's decision in *Asbeek Brusse*.[1225] The court of appeal Arnhem-Leeuwarden[1226] similarly referred to *Asbeek Brusse*.

In addition, The Netherlands has a well-established system of ADR by the *Geschillencommissie* (the Board[1227]) that has resolved disputes in a large amount of cases.[1228] The alternative character

1214 Hof 's-Hertogenbosch 5 November 2013, *RCR* 2014, 11, Hof Arnhem-Leeuwarden 10 December 2013, *Prg.* 2014, 54, Rb. Amsterdam 10 March 2014, *Vermogensrecht* 2014, 185, also following CJEU case law, Hof 's-Hertogenbosch 8 April 2014, *NJF* 2014, 237, Hof 's-Hertogenbosch 9 September 2014, *NJF* 2014, 433. The court eventually upheld the clause, considering, among other things, it had been collectively negotiated.

1215 Ktr. Eindhoven 22 My 2008, *Prg.* 2008, 151. Comp. without express referral to either CJEU or Hoge Raad case law Hof Amsterdam 12 August 2014, *Prg.* 2014, 245.

1216 Ktr. Rotterdam 4 May 2012, *NJF* 2012, 398 while upholding a clause that enabled the provider to suspend its obligations, held that invoking the clause was unreasonable under article 6:248 BW, stating that the provider would otherwise circumvent consumer protection standards described in a report on the *ex officio* application of European consumer law.

1217 Ktr. Assen 14 February 2008, *LJN* BC4373.

1218 CJEU 27 June 2000 (Océano), joined cases C-240/98 to C-244/98, [2000], ECR, p. I-4941.

1219 CJEU 26 October 2006 (Mostaza Claro), C-168/05, [2006] ECR, p. I-10421.

1220 Ktr. Breda 3 February 2010, *LJN* BL2804.

1221 CJEU 4 June 2009 (Pannon), C-243/08, [2009] ECR, p. I4713.

1222 Ktr. Rotterdam 5 October 2012, *LJN* BY5236.

1223 CJEU 21 January 2015 (Unicaja Banco SA v José Hidalgo Rueda and Others), joined cases C-482/13, C-484/13, C-485/13, C-487/13, [2015] ECR p. I-0, par. 28–31 with further references.

1224 Rb. Gelderland 17 April 2–15, ECLI:NL:RBGEL:2015:2636.

1225 CJEU 30 May 2013 (Asbeek Brusse and De Man Garabito v Jahani BV), C-488/11, [2013] ECR p. I-0.

1226 Hof Arnhem-Leeuwarden 11 February 2014, *NJF* 2013, 439.

1227 The decisions of the different committees are hereafter indicated as decisions from the Board.

1228 Although parties are not provided with an enforceable title in ADR cases, both consumers and businesses have indicated that compliance with binding advice is generally high, see A. Klapwijk, M. ter Voert, *Evaluatie De geschillencommissie 2009*, available at www.wodc.nl.

of dispute resolution by the Board entails a more active approach,[1229] which may mitigate possible problems with regard to the duties of courts to evaluate unfair clauses *ex officio*. The active approach of the Board, however, depends on the code of the different committees. Accordingly, in some cases, the approach of the Board seems more in accordance with the Directive than the approach of some courts. In a case where a seller invoked the disclaimer on his webpage, the Board[1230] held that this clause fell under article 6:236 BW and was ineffective. Interestingly, the consumer appears not to have invoked the avoidability of the clause in so many words. The Board apparently did not consider this an obstacle. However, the reasoning of the Board in this case may be problematic, as the Board incorrectly held that the disclaimer did not fall under the definition of STCs in article 6:231 sub a BW, but it similarly held that article 6:236 applied by analogy.

- The lack of guidance of the Hoge Raad is also visible in the referral of questions to the CJEU by lower courts, notwithstanding case law from the Hoge Raad.

Thus, the court of appeal Arnhem[1231] has referred questions to the CJEU whether Directive 1999/44 obliges the court to examine the capacity of the buyer of it own motion, in particular, whether the buyer is a consumer in the sense of the Directive.

→ The decisions from lower courts exercising restraint with regard to the *ex officio* obligation prove incorrect after the 2013 decision. Possibly, the chance that the CJEU will decide a case in such a way that forces the Hoge Raad to alter its approach increases as lower courts, rather than referring to the Hoge Raad, directly refer cases to the CJEU.

- In other cases, the question whether the decision is line with the Directive despite referral to the Directive remains open.

For example, the decision of the court of appeal Amsterdam,[1232] which upheld clauses in a contract of settlement that limited the legal rights of claimants on the basis of previous contracts on the lease of securities, were held to constitute the main terms of the contract. The court referred to the Directive, stating that the Directive did not justify a different conclusion. Arguably, considering the nature of the contract, and the circumstance that the offer constituted an improvement to the consumers' rights under the contract, it can be doubted whether this decision is contrary to the Directive. This would be especially true if the consumers had entered into the contract after legal advice. It may also be argued that a different conclusion would limit the predictability that parties pursue by entering into a settlement contract. Nevertheless, it would have been interesting to see how the question of whether clauses included on the black list of the annex to the Directive or national lists, may constitute the main terms of the contract[1233] – which will often be contrary to mandatory law – and if this is the case, how the question of whether they are exempt from control if they are the main terms of the contract, would have been answered by the CJEU.

1229 HR 17 November 1995, *NJ* 1996, 143.

1230 Decision of 2 March 2009, nr 33773, at www.degeschillencommissie.nl/klacht-indienen/eerdere-uitspraken/33773/disclaimer-is-onredelijk-bezwarend-beding-in-de.

1231 Hof Arnhem 9 April 2013, *LJN* BZ6346.

1232 Hof Amsterdam 14 October 2008, *NJF* 2008, 481.

1233 This is doubted in the conclusion of A.G. Hartkamp before HR 16 May 1997, *NJ* 2000, 1.

→ Thus, the restraint of the Hoge Raad and lower courts in referring questions to the CJEU may, at first sight, not be problematic for private parties, especially not if it benefits the consistent and predictable development of the law. Nevertheless, questions on the interpretation of the Directive have remained. The restraint of the courts does therefore not strengthen the predictable development of the law on STCs in the long term.

5.4.1.3. Conclusion on the development of the law through article 6:233 sub a BW

The diminished ability of article 6:233 BW to safeguard the comprehensibility of the law has not strategically been recognised by legislator or by the courts. Interdependence between lower courts, between lower courts and the Hoge Raad, and between the Hoge Raad and the CJEU has become visible. Notably, the role of the Hoge Raad is undermined in cases where contradictory CJEU decisions are available that have activated national courts. The 2013 decision of the Hoge Raad may perhaps also be seen in the light of the decreased ability of the Hoge Raad's to ensure the consistent interpretation of Dutch law where contradictory CJEU decisions exist. Hopefully, the Hoge Raad has contributed to more consistency and predictability in lower courts' decisions. In addition, the restraint of Dutch courts can be undermined if foreign courts actively refer questions to the CJEU.

Because courts have not sufficiently recognised interdependence, they have not sufficiently interacted with one another and with the CJEU, which has undermined predictability, consistency and accessibility, and which is also not likely to be in accordance with the needs and preferences of contract parties or with legal views on justice.

Simultaneously, the coexistence of actors has been advantageous to the law on STCs, in accordance with pluralist insights. Particularly, comparative law inspired the drafting of the Dutch regime and the active approach of the CJEU inspired an active approach of national courts.

In other cases, however, the coexistence of actors has not strengthened the law on STCs. Harmonisation has not prompted more consideration for the interests of foreign and international actors who have not been involved in the national legislative process. In addition, one may ask if harmonisation leads to a system of checks and balances, why European actors are well-placed to exercise control, if it does not concern transnational cases. After all, the competence of the European legislator does not empower it to evaluate the quality of the law in domestic cases in accordance with benchmarks of predictability, consistency, accessibility and responsiveness. Presently, the reaction of national actors has not been consistent: some actors rejected EU legal transplants, and some have followed CJEU decisions.

The coexistence of state and non-state adjudicators is also not unequivocally advantageous. There are clear indications to limit the role of non-state actors such as the Board, notwithstanding criticism of the state-centric view. Particularly, the lack of accessibility and predictability of decisions, as well as potential inconsistency with decisions of national courts and the CJEU should be remedied.

5.4.2. Model lists

Have actors, in the development of model lists, recognised interdependence and interacted accordingly, and how has that affected the predictability, consistency, accessibility and the responsiveness of the law? Has a lack of interaction resulted in problems, in accordance with multilevel governance perspectives, or has the coexistence of actors strengthened the law, in accordance with pluralist insights?

Paragraph 5.4.2.1 will turn to the development of articles 6:236 and 237 BW and paragraph 5.4.2.2 will turn to the interpretation of these provisions. Paragraph 5.4.2.3 will end with a conclusion.

5.4.2.1. The drafting of model lists

Dutch actors, in the drafting of articles 6:236 and 237 BW, have benefited from the insights of comparative law, but exercised restraint in amending the law to implement Directive 93/13, which has increased consistency and predictability.

Hartkamp[1234] notes that the inclusion of articles 6:237 and 238 BW was based on comparative law, in particular, the 1979 preliminary report on STCs. The legislator[1235] noted that model lists had different functions in different legal orders – while in some legal orders, model lists aim to restrict the use of clauses that are considered particularly undesirable, model clauses in other legal orders seemed to provide guidance for the interpretation of corresponding blanket clauses. The legislator preferred the latter approach.

The Dutch legislator,[1236] in particular, held that it wanted to mitigate any potential unpredictability that could arise from the introduction of the judicial evaluation of STCs, while also alleviating the workload of the judiciary that was bound to increase given the use of blanket clauses in the BW. Parliamentary history[1237] further makes clear that the list is oriented on national case law, practice and literature. The Dutch legislator,[1238] referring to German and Austrian law, did not think that limiting the applicability of articles 6:236 and 237 BW would lead to unpredictability. Notably, the legislator also argued that it was important that the lists would not petrify practice.[1239]

Interdependence and a corresponding need for interaction has not become as visible in the drafting of model lists as the status of the EU list is not clear. It is not clear whether

1234 Asser/Hartkamp & Sieburgh 2010, nr. 492.
1235 Parl. Gesch. NBW, Boek 6 (Inv. 3, 5 en 6), p. 1648–1649.
1236 Parl. Gesch. NBW, Boek 6 (Inv. 3, 5 en 6), p. 1651.
1237 Parl. Gesch. NBW, Boek 6 (Inv. 3, 5 en 6), p. 1686 et seq.
1238 Parl. Gesch. NBW, Boek 6 (Inv. 3, 5 en 6), p. 1656.
1239 Parl. Gesch. NBW, Boek 6 (Inv. 3, 5 en 6), p. 1488.

the list, which is after all non-binding, should be implemented.[1240] Van Erp[1241] states that he has no idea what the 'indicative list' means, and points to the need for clarification by the CJEU. The CJEU has accordingly referred to the annex of the Directive in the interpretation of article 3, and ruled, in *Sweden v Commission*,[1242] that Member States did not have to include the model list in legislation, as long as the list is sufficiently available for consumers as a source of information. Nevertheless, the existence of a European lists that may show overlaps with articles 6:236 and 237 BW may diminish accessibility.

Accordingly, after the implementation of the Directive, the legislator has maintained the lists in article 6:236 and 237 BW. The restraint of the Dutch legislator may have been motivated by the extent to which the Dutch model lists could support predictability and consistency. Jongeneel[1243] has objected to amending the model lists in accordance with the EU list as this may stand in the way of the development of practice on these lists. Possibly, amending articles 6:236 and 237 BW would have undermined the aim of these provisions, to add to the predictable and consistent interpretation of article 6:233 BW. Also, revising the list may have been problematic as this could have entailed revising corresponding default rules in the BW that was still to be introduced. Nevertheless, Jongeneel recognises the possibility that national lists will have to be amended. While interdependence does not become visible in the drafting of article 6:236 and 237 BW, it has become visible in the failed attempt to revise Directive 93/13. If the 1993 Directive is revised and the European model list becomes binding, this may severely undermine the aim of the Dutch model lists, which has not been considered by the Dutch legislator, who did not oppose a binding model list as such.[1244]

Thus, in the drafting of articles 6:236 and 237 BW, the Dutch legislator benefited from the experiences and insights from other legal orders. However, the Dutch legislator did not amend these lists in accordance with the model list in the Annex to Directive 93/13. This may not have strengthened accessibility, but it preserved predictability and consistency.

5.4.2.2. The interpretation of articles 6:236 and 237 BW

Dutch courts have insufficiently recognised interdependence and problems have developed as a result. Actors have exercised restraint in referring cases to the CJEU and other Dutch courts in the evaluation of clauses falling under articles 6:236 and 237 BW,

1240 Comp. for example J. Hijma, 'Richtlijn 93/13/EEG betreffende oneerlijke bedingen in consumentenovereenkomsten', in: S.C.J.J. Kortmann et al. (eds.), *Onderneming en 5 jaar nieuw burgerlijk recht*, Deventer: Tjeenk Willink 1997, p. 424 finds that the model list does not oblige Member States or judges to implement it, although he considers that the judiciary might refer to the list and in this way give weight to the list.

1241 J.H.M. van Erp, 'Van onredelijk bezwarend naar oneerlijk, of: van Nederzwart en Nedergrijs naar Euroblauw', *WPNR* 6079 (1993), p. 82.

1242 CJEU 7 May 2002 (Commission v Sweden), C-478/99, [2002] ECR p. I-4147, par. 22.

1243 R.H.C. Jongeneel, 'Een richtlijn die weinig schade aanricht', *TvC* 1993, p. 125.

1244 See the Dutch response to the Green Paper on the review of the consumer acquis, available at http://ec.europa.eu/consumers/cons_int/safe_shop/acquis/responses/ms_netherlands.pdf, par. 4.5.

which has undermined consistency and predictability. Moreover, the restraint has decreased the chance that in the reform of Directive 93/13, questions that have become apparent in these cases are not considered, which inhibits the responsive development of the Directive.

- The Hoge Raad has generally considered the status of the model list in the Annex to Directive 93/13.

The Hoge Raad[1245] notes that the inclusion of a clause in this list is an indication that a clause may be unfair. Whether the clause is unfair depends upon the circumstances of the case. The Hoge Raad follows the conclusion of AG Wesselink-Van Gent, who refers expressly to the Directive. The AG takes the indirect effect as a starting point to determine to what extent the model list is relevant to the assessment of the fairness of clauses and expressly refers to *Commission v Sweden*, arguing that this decision justifies the conclusion that the inclusion of a clause in the European list is a point of view, and not decisive.

Thus, the European list stays behind articles 6:236 and 237 BW: if a clause falls under the Dutch grey list, the user of this clause has to prove that considering the circumstances of the case, the clause is not unfair. In contrast, if a clause falls under the Annex to the Directive, but not the Dutch black or grey list, the consumer still has to prove that a clause is unfair. At most, the judge will have to allow the consumer to prove that the clause if unfair under article 6:233 sub a BW, and the circumstance that the clause is included in the Annex to the Directive is merely one viewpoint among several relevant points of view.

Referring this case to the CJEU would have provided more insight in the status of the European model lists, which, in turn, could have provided more insight in the approach that judges – and possibly, legislators – have to adopt towards this list, in particular, whether the judiciary has to assess of its own motion, and whether a clause falling under the Annex is unfair. As it is, one may ask whether the Hoge Raad's decision is easily reconcilable with, particularly, *Hatóság v Invitel Távközlési Zrt*,[1246] where the CJEU held that '[i]f the content of the annex does not suffice in itself to establish automatically the unfair nature of a contested term, it is nevertheless an essential element on which the competent court may base its assessment as to the unfair nature of that term'.

The Hoge Raad's decision is problematic in another respect: it finds that judges should, in the evaluation of the fairness of a penalty clause, take into account the mitigation of the penalty under article 6:94 BW. Later CJEU decisions[1247] make clear that this course undermines the preventive effect of the Directive.

This decision does, however, not mean that courts are obliged to take the European model list into account, which also follows from subsequent decisions from the Hoge Raad[1248] in which it does not pay attention to the European model list as such.

1245 HR 24 March 2006, *NJ* 2007, 115, see the conclusion of A.G. Wesseling-van Gent pars. 2.50–2.53, comp. also HR 17 December 2004, *NJ* 2005, 271.

1246 CJEU 26 April 2012 (Hatóság v Invitel Távközlési Zrt), C-472/10, [2012] p. I-0, par. 26.

1247 CJEU 21 January 2015 (Unicaja Banco SA v José Hidalgo Rueda and Others) joined cases C-482/13, C-484/13, C-485/13, C-487/13, par. 28–31, with further references.

1248 HR 16 May 1997, *NJ* 2000, 1 held the users of STCs had not sufficiently established that an exclusion clause, which fell under the grey list in article 6:237 BW, was not unfair. The conclusion of A.G.

The Hoge Raad has not often referred cases to the CJEU.[1249] That does not mean that these cases have been decided incorrectly. However, arguably, the Hoge Raad's decisions touch upon the interpretation of article 3 Directive 93/13 and may, moreover, entail that Dutch law goes below the level of protection established by the Directive. In addition, the CJEU is competent to establish the allocation of tasks between the CJEU and national courts. Therefore, these questions should have been referred to the CJEU.[1250]

The restraint need not be directly problematic for private parties as the restraint may well may be motivated by the wish to maintain the consistent, predictable and responsive development of the law on STCs. Regrettably, however, the restraint of the Hoge Raad entails that questions that could be relevant for the reform of Directive 93/13 may not become visible at the European level, which undermines the responsive development of this Directive.

However, notwithstanding this restraint, the Hoge Raad has provided some guidance to lower courts on the status of the European model list. As the decision does not conflict with CJEU decisions, the role of the Hoge Raad should not be undermined, but the decision itself, in fact, does not oblige courts to take a particular approach, as it merely provides that the indicative list can have such a status; this does not mean that the European model list must be consistently taken into account.

However, in rare cases, the inclusion of a clause under the European model list has prompted courts to presume that clauses are unfair unless the user of that clause can prove otherwise.[1251]

Hartkamp that was followed by the Hoge Raad referred to Dutch law and parliamentary history, and to German law. Neither the decision of the Hoge Raad nor the A.G. refers to Directive 93/13, but that does not mean that the decision, which emphasises the aim of the Dutch regime – that coincides with the European regime – is contrary to the Directive. HR 24 March 2006, *NJ* 2007, 115 decided that the discretion of the judge to mitigate a penalty clause under article 6:94 BW was relevant for assessing whether the penalty clause was unfair. With this decision, the Hoge Raad also diverges from case law in which it has emphasised restraint that should generally be adopted in the mitigation of penalty clauses, see HR 27 April 2007, *NJ* 2007, 262, HR 13 July 2012, *NJ* 2012, 459. See the conclusion of A.G. Hartkamp under pars. 10–12.

1249 Comp. B. Wessels, 'Collectief actierecht komt moeizaam tot bloei', *WPNR* 6249 (1996), p. 885, who found that the Hoge Raad might well have referred the decision in HR 16 May 1997, *NJ* 2000, 1. Particularly, a question to the CJEU would provide more insight in relevant circumstances to be taken into account in the evaluation of the fairness of clauses.

1250 See previously par. 4.4.1.1.

1251 Ktr. Maastricht 16 July 2008, *NJF* 2008, 397 held that a clause that stipulated that the consumer was obliged to pay for the entire subscription period, even though the contract had been terminated, fell under sub e in the list in the Annex to the Directive. Therefore, this clause would be presumed to be unfair, unless the user could prove that the clause was fair. With this decision, the court seems to diverge from the approach from the Hoge Raad, attaching more weight to the Annex, and evaluating the clause of its own motion, without referring whether the clause falls under articles 6:236 or 237 BW. Comp. also Hof Amsterdam 12 August 2014, *Prg.* 2014, 245, Hof Amsterdam 12 August 2014, *Prg.* 2014, 246, Hof Amsterdam 12 August 2014, *Prg.* 2014, 247, where the court allowed parties to argue whether a clause that fell under sub j in the Annex, even though it did not concern a clause under article 6:236 sub a BW. Comp. further Rb. Amsterdam 10 March 2014, *Vermogensrecht* 2014/185, holding a clause unfair as it fell under the Annex.

– Some lower courts have followed the decisions from the Hoge Raad.

Accordingly, with regard to a penalty clause in a contract for accommodation, the cantonial court Amsterdam[1252] upheld the claim of the user to mitigate the penalty clause to an extent that it would not constitute an unfair term under article 6:233 BW. The judge explicitly referred to the Directive and CJEU case law, but not to foreign decisions.[1253]

Similarly, the court of appeal Amsterdam[1254] upheld a clause in an accommodation contract that imposed a fine on the tenant in cases of illegal subletting. The court held that damages arising from illegal subletting is difficult to determine, which entails that it will not be evaluated whether the clause obliges the consumer to pay a disproportional amount of damages, as defined in the Annex to the Directive. Moreover, as the clause aims to prevent illegal subletting, it should be sufficiently high to have a preventive effect, which entailed that the mitigation imposed by the cantonial court was reversed.

The decisions in *Banco Español de Crédito v Calderón Camino*[1255] and *Asbeek Brusse*[1256] indicate that these decisions are contrary to the Directive. The CJEU held that the discretion of the judge to mitigate penalty clauses under national law was contrary to the wording of article 6 Directive and the overall objective of the Directive. The court of appeal 's-Gravenhage[1257] has followed *Asbeek Brusse*, finding that clauses that have been held unfair may not be applied, not even if the seller mitigates his claim.

The Court[1258] has in addition considered that replacing a term with a provision of supplementary national law – in Dutch law, in the sense of article 6:248 par. 1 BW – is permissible, provided that this does not compromise consumer protection in accordance with article 6 Directive and insofar as it achieves a true balance between the rights and obligations of contract parties. Holding clauses ineffective should also not adversely affect consumers.

– Other decisions do not follow the Hoge Raad and inconsistency has developed.

For example, the cantonial court Haarlem[1259] held a penalty clause unfair as the provider of a credit card had not limited the amount of the penalty in the contract. Article 6:94 BW was not invoked. The decision of the court refers to CJEU case law, but not to the decision of the Hoge Raad.

Similarly, the court of appeal 's-Gravenhage[1260] held that a clause obliging the consumer to pay 50% of the invoice by way of compensation for cancellation was unfair. The court considered

1252 Ktr. Amsterdam 15 January 2010, *RVR* 2010, 50.

1253 German law would have provided a more critical perspective, as converting an unacceptable clause to an acceptable clause is much more controversial in German law, as this would indirectly reward the use of unfair STCs. See MuchKomm BGB/Basedow (2012), article 306, nr 12, 28.

1254 Hof Amsterdam 21 February 2012, *BR* 2012, 89.

1255 CJEU 14 June 2012 (Banco Español de Crédito v Calderón Camino), C-618/10, [2012] ECR p. I-0, par. 65, 69–70.

1256 CJEU 30 May 2013 (Asbeek Brusse and De Man Garabito v Jahani), C-488/11, [2013] ECR, p. I-0.

1257 Hof 's-Gravenhage 28 October 2014, *Prg.* 2015, 96.

1258 CJEU 30 April 2014 (Kásler and Hajnalka Káslerné Rábai v OTP Jelzálogbank Zrt), C-26/13, [2014] ECR p. I-0, par. 79–83 and CJEU 21 January 2015 (Unicaja Banco SA v José Hidalgo Rueda and Others), joined cases C-482/13, C-484/13, C-485/13 and C-487/13, [2015] ECR p. I-0, par. 31–34.

1259 Ktr. Haarlem 13 May 2009, *Prg.* 2009, 105.

1260 Hof 's-Gravenhage 12 February 2008, *NJF* 2008, 158.

that the clause was a penalty clause in the sense of article 6:91 BW that was included in the list in the Annex to Directive 93/13, while it was not apparent that the seller had alerted the consumer on the possibility that 50% of the invoice would be charged if the consumer cancelled the contract. Notably, the court does not refer to the previous decision of the Hoge Raad, nor does it follow the approach set out by the Hoge Raad by limiting the amount of the fine to an amount that is considered reasonable under article 6:94 BW.

This line is also visible in ADR decisions. Thus, the Board,[1261] with regard to a clause that fixed the costs of the consumer on 15% of the contract price, did not hold the contract ineffective, but mitigated the clause. This decision is in contrast to previous case law,[1262] although the mitigation of the amount that is to be paid to the consumer may be in accordance with the case law from the Hoge Raad, which has however proven to be contrary to the Directive.

- Generally, however, a consistent approach does not become visible. Some cases seem particularly problematic.

A particularly problematic decision is the decision of the court of appeal 's-Gravenhage[1263] that upheld an exclusion clause that fell under article 6:237 BW, holding that the clause excluding the liability of the landlord for damages arising from a leakage in the flat over the flat of the tenant was a clause that was often used in contracts for accommodation. Arguably, this evaluation is reminiscent of the evaluation under article 6:233 sub a BW that takes as a starting point the mutual apparent interests of parties at the time of the conclusion of the contract. However, the court explicitly – and incorrectly – holds that this article (which it curiously indicates as article 7A:233 BW) is not yet applicable, even though it considers article 6:237 BW to be applicable. The court subsequently finds that the argument of the landlord that tenants can easily insure themselves against the damage, as well as the fact of common knowledge that tenants frequently insure themselves, sufficiently rebuts the assumption that the clause is unfair. However, a correct evaluation under article 6: 237 sub h BW arguably would have taken the question of whether the tenant had, in fact, insured himself for this damage because he was aware that the landlord had excluded liability in order, for example, to maintain a low rent, as a starting point, which is not the case. It can be doubted whether this decision is in accordance with the Directive.

The decision of the district court Almelo[1264] and the district court Amsterdam[1265] are also problematic in the light of the Directive. The court upheld the declaration that acceptance of this form entailed that the consumer has received the STCs as it constituted a private act ('*onderhandse akte*') in the sense of article 157 Civil Procedure Code. Later decisions have not followed these decisions, and characterised similar clauses as clauses falling within the scope of article 6:236 sub k BW that were considered unfair.[1266] With regard to the dissolution clause, according to which

[1261] Decision of 2 March 2009, nr 33813, at www.degeschillencommissie.nl/klacht-indienen/eerdere-uitspraken/33813/15-annuleringskosten-is-een-eenzijdig-beding-in, comp. also the decision of 29 January 2009, nr 33289, at www.degeschillencommissie.nl/klacht-indienen/eerdere-uitspraken/33289/annulering-door-consument-wegens-overmacht-niet, also the decision of 24 November 2011,nr 34411, at www.degeschillencommissie.nl/klacht-indienen/eerdere-uitspraken/34411/annulering-na-aanvang-volledig-kosten.

[1262] Hof Arnhem 1 August 2000, *NJ* 2001, 71.

[1263] Hof 's-Gravenhage 10 September 2004, *Prg.* 2005, 13.

[1264] Rb. Almelo 6 September 2006, *NJF* 2006, 536.

[1265] Rb. Amsterdam 2 July 2014, *TvC* 2015, p. 24.

[1266] Ktr. Oud Beijerland 17 September 2007, *Prg.* 2008, 4, Ktr. Heerlen 8 October 2008, *NJF* 2009, 9, Rb. Utrecht 2 September 2009, *NJF* 2010, 33.

the rights of consumer were dissolved unless he brought a complaint within a specific period – which the consumer had not done – the district court Almelo, moreover, held that the clause was negotiated between travel organisations and a consumers' organisation, while the consumer had insufficiently established that the mutual apparent interests of parties brought about that the clause was unfair. The court does not consider article 6:237 BW, although the clause may well fall within the scope of article 6:237 sub h BW. This oversight is unfortunate, because if the clause would have fallen within the scope of this article, the travel organisation would have had to prove that the clause was fair.

– These decisions are, in addition, contradicted by other decisions from lower courts

The district court Amsterdam,[1267] referring to CJEU case law, rejected a clause that declared that the consumer had received the STCs of its own motion, holding that the clause fell under article 6:236 sub k BW.

The cantonial court Oud Beijerland[1268] likewise held that a clause that stated that the consumer had received text of clauses did not, in fact, prove this, in accordance with article 157 Civil Procedure Code, as it concerned a clause that fell under article 6:236 sub k BW. The consumer had challenged the statement of the provider that he had received the STCs, but had not, in so many words, challenged the clause that stipulated that he had received the STCs.

The cantonial court Heerlen[1269] similarly rejected this clause as it concerned a clause that fell under article 6:236 sub k BW. Notably, the consumer in this case had expressly challenged the fairness of this clause.

The district court Utrecht[1270] held a similar declaration invalid on the same grounds.

– Equally problematic decisions also become visible.

The cantonial court Tiel[1271] upheld a clause automatically renewing a subscription trial. The court decided that article 6:236 sub j BW stipulated that clauses renewing a contract for more than one year were unfair, and article 6:237 sub l BW indicated that clauses stipulating a termination period of more than three months were presumed unfair. As the clause did not have this effect, it was upheld.

The judge interpreted articles 6:236 and 237 BW *a contrario*, holding that clauses that do not fall under these articles are not unfair. It can be doubted whether this interpretation is in accordance with article 6:233 sub a BW and the aim of these rules to increase consumer protection.[1272] The court of appeal 's-Hertogenbosch[1273] seems to take a similar approach, upholding clauses that do not fall under article 6:236 sub j BW, as the clause predated this provision, without referring to article 6:233 BW.

1267 Rb. Amsterdam 12 November 2003, *NJF* 2003, 71.
1268 Ktr. Oud Beijerland 17 September 2007, *Prg.* 2008, 4.
1269 Ktr. Heerlen 8 October 2008, *NJF* 2009, 9.
1270 Rb. Utrecht 2 September 2009, *NJF* 2010, 33.
1271 Ktr. Tiel 15 June 2005, *Prg.* 2005, 143.
1272 Comp. C.M.D.S. Pavillon, 'Private standards of fairness in European contract law', *ERCL* 2014, p. 105–106 who points out that Dutch lower courts also refer to trade practices to evaluate fairness, unlike French and English courts.
1273 Hof 's-Hertogenbosch 25 March 2014, *NJF* 2014, 227.

- These decisions are in contrast with other decisions.

Other decisions already held the automatic extension of contracts was unfair under article 6:233 sub a BW prior to the amendment of the law.[1274] Accordingly, lower courts,[1275] expressly referring to the Annex to the Directive, held that a clause automatically extending a test subscription, which had only been used during the first week, was ineffective. Interestingly, the user of STCs indicated that the effects of the clause automatically renewing the contract may have been unfair towards the consumer in this case.

- In other cases, courts apparently do not find sufficient guidance in the decisions from the Hoge Raad.

The court of appeal Amsterdam[1276] recognises that Directive 93/13 may be applicable and, accordingly, has referred questions to the CJEU. In response to these questions, the CJEU[1277] has held that the contract in this case fell within the scope of the Directive. The CJEU further emphasised the *ex officio* obligation of courts to assess unfair terms of their own motion, and, subsequently, considered the procedural autonomy of Member States, the principle of equality and the effectiveness of Union law. Particularly, the CJEU decided that the Directive consists of mandatory law, and according to the CJEU, it is of fundamental importance to the improvement of the standard of living within the Union. Consequently, national law implementing the Directive should be considered as rules of public policy. Thus, if national courts are bound to apply provisions of public policy of their own motion, national judges should also apply law implementing the Directive of their own motion. Further, Directive 93/13 has not enabled judges to mitigate clauses rather than hold these clauses ineffective.

The decision from the court of appeal Amsterdam shows considerable similarities with a 2012 decision in which it upheld a penalty clause in a contract for accommodation,[1278] In its 2012 decision, the court of appeal Amsterdam has, unfortunately, not waited for the response from the CJEU, which arguably increases the chance that the decisions are not consistent with the answers provided by the CJEU.

→ The restraint of the Hoge Raad has diminished predictability as various CJEU decisions have made clear that previous decisions of the Hoge Raad should be reconsidered. Further, the lack of guidance of the Hoge Raad has left room for courts to develop diverging approaches that may undermine predictability and consistency. The lack of guidance may also have decreased the extent that smaller courts follow the Hoge Raad,

1274 See further par. 5.3.3.5.

1275 Ktr. Rotterdam 2 August 2007, *Prg.* 2008, 37. Comp. also Ktr. Maastricht 16 July 2008, *NJF* 2008, 397, Ktr. Hoorn 10 April 2006, *NJF* 2007, 252 and Ktr. Zaandam 31 July 2008, *Prg.* 2008, 192 on a contract for a duration of two years. The court assumed that the consumer had meant to challenge the fairness of the clause that required the contract, entered into by phone, with a mentally handicapped man would have to be cancelled in writing – which the consumer, a mentally handicapped man, was not capable of – could not be cancelled prematurely. The court decided this clause was unfair under article 6:237 sub k BW.

1276 Hof Amsterdam 8 March 2011, *NJF* 2011, 242, as well as Hof Amsterdam 13 September 2011, *NJF* 2011, 421.

1277 CJEU 30 May 2013 (Brusse and Garabito v Jahani BV), C-488/11, [2013] ECR, p. I-0.

1278 Hof Amsterdam 21 February 2012, *BR* 2012, 89.

as visible in cases where lower courts have not followed the Hoge Raad, without referring to CJEU decisions.

Although the lack of interaction between the Hoge Raad and the CJEU as such may not directly be problematic for private parties, it may undermine consistency if CJEU decisions and Hoge Raad decisions are not easily reconcilable and lower courts do not consistently follow the CJEU[1279] or the Hoge Raad.

5.4.2.3. Conclusion on model lists

Although the legislator benefited from the use of comparative insights in the development of model lists, courts have not. Interdependence has become especially visible between the Hoge Raad and the CJEU. The role of the Hoge Raad may be diminished as its decisions are difficult to reconcile with CJEU decisions. Possibly, as not many consumer cases come before the Hoge Raad, the extent to which the Hoge Raad can develop a consistent line in these cases may be limited. Even if this were the case, the current amount of cases diverging from the Hoge Raad may give rise to doubts whether a more active approach from the Hoge Raad will suffice.

Arguably, more interaction between the Hoge Raad and the CJEU, between domestic courts, and between the Board and courts would improve consistency and predictability.

The coexistence of actors has not led to a system of checks and balances. Currently, the restraint of national courts, especially the Hoge Raad, and the lack of binding status stands in the way of the further development of a system of checks and balances. Further opportunities for learning could be realised if more cases would be referred to the CJEU. Similarly, experiences of the Board should be considered more consistently by national state actors and at the European level. More referrals should help to develop the Directive in accordance with national experiences, but CJEU decisions are not easy to predict and the CJEU may not decide in a manner consistent with surrounding national law, especially if it is insufficiently aware of relevant provisions. The CJEU is also not best placed to decide in accordance with national legal views on justice.

5.4.3. The evaluation of clauses in international and domestic business contracts

This paragraph will consider whether actors, in the evaluation of clauses in international business contracts, have recognised that the initiatives of other actors may also be relevant for the evaluation of clauses and interacted with these actors accordingly. How has this affected the extent to which blanket clauses strengthen the predictability, consistency, accessibility and responsiveness of the law of STCs for international business contracts? Have detriments developed because of a lack of interaction or has the law on STCs benefited from the coexistence of actors?

1279 For example CJEU 14 June 2012 (Banco Español de Crédito v Calderón Camino), C-618/10, [2012] ECR, p. I-0.

Paragraph 5.4.3.1 will consider preliminary questions on the applicability of international regimes or Dutch law on STCs in international contracts. Paragraph 5.4.3.2 will turn to the evaluation of clauses under the Montréal Convention (previously the Warsaw Convention) and paragraph 5.4.3.3 will address the evaluation of clauses under the CMR. Paragraph 5.4.3.4 will consider the evaluation of CISG and Dutch law. Paragraph 5.4.3.5 will compare decisions in international cases to the evaluation of clauses in domestic business contracts. Paragraph 5.4.3.6 will end with a conclusion.

5.4.3.1. Applicable regimes

Which regime can be applicable to international contracts? Possible applicable regimes include the Montréal Convention, the CMR, the CISG as well as Dutch law.

If Dutch law is applicable, article 6:247 BW stipulates that articles 6:231 et seq are not applicable for cases in which one of the parties is situated abroad, even if they have opted for Dutch law, which has recently been confirmed by the Hoge Raad.[1280] The Dutch legislator[1281] aimed to prevent unpredictability and inconsistency by imposing the mandatory regime of articles 6:231 et seq BW on international contracts that were already subject to the regime of other legislators, and also sought to facilitate international trade. This decision from the Dutch legislator was inspired by the English Unfair Contract Terms Act 1977. Consequently, international contracts are not evaluated under article 6:233 or 236 and 237 BW. The debate in Parliament especially considered the necessity of article 6:247 BW against the background of Rome I, and decided to provide an exception for contracts with consumers in article 6:247 par. 4 BW. Notably, this rule diverges from article 6 Rome I, but it goes beyond article 6 par. 2 Directive 93/13 that stipulates that Member States shall ensure that consumers will not lose the protection conferred upon them through a choice of law for non-Member States. Therefore, article 6:247 par. 4 BW is permissible under article 8 Directive. Thus, the European legislator, by inserting provisions on private international law in consumer contract law Directives, has provided Member States with possibilities to diverge from Regulation Rome I, in accordance with national legal views on justice, which however diminishes the extent to which the Regulation increases the accessibility of law.

As international contracts are not evaluated under article 6:231 et seq BW, the question whether an international regime that provides an exhaustive regime that allows for the additional application of national provisions becomes less urgent. However, the question arises as to whether article 6:248 BW may still be applicable for the evaluation of international contracts. According to Hartkamp,[1282] this article can be applied by the judge of his own motion, which would indicate that it is a provision of public policy.

However, the suggestion that this provision is a provision of public policy is contradicted by decisions of the Hoge Raad that article 6:248 par. 2 BW is not applicable

1280 HR 11 May 2012, *NJ* 2012, 318. This can be an unpleasant surprise for German contract parties, as was the case in Hof Arnhem-Leeuwarden 7 October 2014, *NJF* 2014, 147. The court however incorrectly found that STCs were applicable on the basis of article 6:232 BW.

1281 Parl. Gesch. NBW, Boek 6 (Inv. 3, 5 en 6), p. 1807.

1282 Asser/Hartkamp & Sieburgh 2010, nr. 395.

in addition to the Warsaw Convention[1283] and the Hague Visby Rules as well as the IMCO International Convention Relating to the Limitation of the Liability of Owners of Seagoing Ships.[1284]

Article 6:248 BW will be applicable if international regimes expressly leave room for the additional application of national law, as is the case for the CISG. Article 4 sub a CISG expressly provides that the validity of contracts, or any provisions, is not a matter decided under the CISG, which entails that clauses in contracts falling under the CISG can be evaluated under article 6:248 BW.[1285]

The Hoge Raad[1286] has emphasised that the question of whether a clause is contrary to article 6:248 par. 2 BW goes beyond the question of whether invoking this clause is in accordance with good faith. Instead, the court should indicate why good faith entails that invoking a clause is unacceptable in these circumstances.

5.4.3.2. The evaluation of clauses under the Montréal Convention

The Montréal Convention aims to provide a comprehensive regime. Very few decisions of the Hoge Raad are available and it is therefore difficult to deduce a consistent approach from its case law of the Hoge Raad. The Hoge Raad[1287] has, however, held a clause that held limited liability ineffective under the Warsaw Convention. The Hoge Raad referred to the legislative history of the Treaty and held that this clause was void as it was contrary to article 26 of the Convention. The conclusion of the A.G. expressly considered international materials as well as comparative law.

5.4.3.3. The evaluation of clauses under the CMR

The Hoge Raad has recognised the needs and preference of businesses. It has interpreted the law in accordance with especially national preferences and views, but less with international preferences.

The Hoge Raad[1288] has evaluated clauses opting for the CMR leniently, despite the wording of article 8:1102 par. 1 BW that aimed to prevent that parties would be surprised

1283 HR 12 February 1982, *NJ* 1982, 589, HR 24 April 1992, *NJ* 1992, 688.

1284 Respectively HR 11 February 2008, *NJ* 2008, 505 and HR 4 November 1994, *NJ* 1996, 534. Comp. also Rb. Midden-Nederland 15 April 2015, ECLI:NL:RBMNE:2015:2526, which evaluated a clause under article 305, 305c and 307 BGB. Unfortunately, the court limited itself to evaluating the transparency of the clause and not the fairness of the clause.

1285 Comp. Rb. Arnhem 29 July 2009, *RCR* 2009, 69 where the court held that the lien of goods was irreconcilable with standards of fairness. Comp. also Rb. Rotterdam 31 March 2010, *LJN* BN2112.

1286 HR 15 October 2004, *NJ* 2005, 141. HR 27 April 2007, *NJ* 2007, 262 that concerned a penalty clause in a domestic business contract, emphasised a similarly restrictive approach towards article 6:94 BW. Comp. also the conclusion of A.G. Wuisman before HR 18 February 2011, *RvdW* 2011, 288. Comp. however Hof Arnhem-Leeuwarden 17 December 2013, *Prg* 2014, 64 that considered both article 6:233 sub a and 6:248 BW, finding that that a clause that was acceptable under article 6:231 sub a may still be unfair under article 6:248 BW.

1287 HR 12 February 1982, *NJ* 1982, 589, comp. the conclusion of A.G. Franx under par. 6.

1288 HR 10 August 2012, *NJ* 2012, 652, similarly HR 29 May 2009, *NJ* 2009, 245, and HR 5 January 2001, *NJ* 2001, 391, see the conclusion of A.G. Strikwerda in pars. 16–17.

by the applicability of the CMR.[1289] This lenience is likely in accordance with the preferences of businesses. Especially professional parties that have expressly referred to the CMR and that have done business with one another for various years, should be assumed to be aware of the differences, and they should, therefore, not be required to copy out the reference to the CMR. The Hoge Raad has also interpreted the concept of wilful misconduct strictly,[1290] in accordance with article 8:1108 BW, but also in accordance with national practice.[1291] However, Dutch law diverges from the CMR with regard to the limitation of liability that can be imposed despite wilful misconduct. The carrier might, therefore, well prefer the application of Dutch law rather than the CMR.

The Hoge Raad has not consistently referred to international materials. Haak[1292] has noted that the line of the Hoge Raad has changed. Different from previous decisions, in which international materials were carefully considered (in the conclusions of the AGs),[1293] it now suffices with referring to article 29 CMR.[1294]

However, in more recent decisions, the conclusions of the A.G., in some cases explicitly followed by the Hoge Raad, have expressly referred both to different linguistic versions and foreign decisions and literature.[1295]

Thus, although the Hoge Raad recognises the added value of foreign materials, this approach need not necessarily be continued in future decisions, which may limit the responsiveness of the law to the needs of international practice as well as predictability.

5.4.3.4. The evaluation of clauses in international contracts under Dutch law

The Hoge Raad's decisions show an increasing tendency to limit the effect of article 6:248 BW in international commercial contracts,[1296] which may strengthen the predictability of the law on STCs, in accordance with the preference of experienced parties in international trade. The restraint of the Hoge Raad is also in accordance with the view that good faith should play a limited role in cases where experienced parties in an equal bargaining position have been assisted by legal counsel.

1289 M.H. Claringbould, *Parlementaire geschiedenis van het nieuw burgerlijk wetboek: Parlementaire stukken systematisch gerangschikt en van noten voorzien. Invoering boeken 3, 5 en 6. Boek 8, Verkeersmiddelen en vervoer*, Deventer: Kluwer 1992, p. 1052.

1290 Thus, leaving containers unattended near the public road during the weekend did not constitute wilful misconduct in this sense.

1291 Note to HR 5 January 2001, *NJ* 2001, 391.

1292 Note to HR 5 January 2001, *NJ* 2001, 392.

1293 Comp. HR 29 June 1990, *NJ* 1990, 106, and HR 14 June 1996, *NJ* 1997, 703, where the Hoge Raad considered the different linguistic versions as well as relevant international materials, encouraged by A.G. Haak, as well as HR 16 November 1990, *NJ* 1992, 107, where it refers to the conclusion that expressly considers German law.

1294 Comp. in particular also HR 29 May 2009, *NJ* 2009, 245.

1295 Comp. the conclusion of. A.G. Timmermans to HR 10 August 2012, *NJ* 2012, 652, HR 14 July 2006, *NJ* 2006, 599, as well as HR 19 November 1998, *NJ* 1999, 175.

1296 H. Schelhaas, 'Pacta sunt servanda bij commerciële contracten', *NTBR* 2008, 21.

Accordingly, the Hoge Raad[1297] upheld an exclusion clause that also excluded liability for serious breaches of contract by a shipyard, caused by contractors in the sense of article 6:170 BW. It concerned a clause between two branches regularly doing business with one another that is usual and not contrary to good faith.

Similarly, the Hoge Raad[1298] upheld an expiration clause in an international contract between a bank and a business. The Hoge Raad took article 6:140 par. 2 BW as a starting point for its decision and considered that the clause was not unfair, because article 6:236 sub g BW should be seen in correlation with this article. Although article 6:236 sub g BW is not applicable in international contracts, it was relevant as the Dutch bank had apparently taken this article as a starting point in the drafting of its STCs.

Furthermore, the Hoge Raad[1299] established that an insurer is free to limit the terms of his policy, referring to a previous decision[1300] in an international case where an insurer had also limited the possibility to recover damages under the policy, which was, however, decided with reference to domestic case law.[1301]

Interestingly, the Hoge Raad, though referring to business practices between parties[1302] that may also be affected by foreign views[1303] did not consistently refer to international or foreign materials in international cases, but decided the cases largely in line with domestic case law.

In rare cases, clauses have been held ineffective.

The Hoge Raad[1304] held that invoking an expiration clause in an international contract was unacceptable, because the parties invoking this clause had suffered a small amount of damage, which justified a proportional limitation of the claim. In his conclusion before the case, A.G. Spier referred expressly to common law decisions that have also held that a complete dissolution of a contract party's claim if parties neglect any incidents because of an expiration clause is rather drastic. For insurers, this option is also rather unpractical, as cautious policy holders might report each and every small incident, which imposes a considerable workload on insurers.

Thus, the Hoge Raad has taken into account business practices and foreign views, but decided cases in accordance with national law. The emphasis on business practices, however, entails that decisions are likely to be in accordance with business practices even if the Hoge Raad does not refer to international materials.

1297 HR 31 December 1993, *NJ* 1995, 389. In his note to the case, Brunner finds that for the evaluation of contracts in accordance with good faith, the nature of the contract, and the societal position and relation between the parties are decisive. See for similar restraint Rb. Rotterdam 30 April 2014, *S & S* 2014, 131. Hof 's-Hertogenbosch 8 July 2014 ECLI:NL:GHSHE:2014:2069 expressly followed HR 14 juni 2002, *NJ* 2003, 112, a decision in a domestic case, on the relevant circumstances in applying article 6:248 BW.

1298 HR 23 February 2001, *NJ* 2001, 277. Comp. HR 14 May 2004, *NJ* 2006, 188, where invoking a clause on the dissolution of rights was held irreconcilable with standards of fairness as it was contrary to Dutch legal views on justice in the sense of article 3:12 BW.

1299 HR 16 May 2008, *NJ* 2008, 284.

1300 HR 9 June 2006, *NJ* 2006, 326.

1301 HR 27 October 2000, *NJ* 2001, 200.

1302 Comp. HR 31 December 1993, *NJ* 1995, 389.

1303 Comp. HR 17 February 2006, *NJ* 2006, 378.

1304 HR 17 February 2006, *NJ* 2006, 378, comp. the conclusion of A.G. Spier under par. 4.41.

5.4.3.5. The evaluation of domestic "black" and "grey" clauses under Dutch law

Good faith is invoked in a considerable amount of business contracts,[1305] but the Hoge Raad exercises restraint in holding clauses ineffective under article 6:233 sub a BW.

The Hoge Raad[1306] may refer to article 3:12 BW that refers to legal views in society to establish whether a clause is contrary to good faith under article 6:248 par. 2 BW. The Hoge Raad may also refer to surrounding law, such as the principles of good administration, in this case in the evaluation of a contract between a business and a municipality.

Similarly, the Hoge Raad[1307] held that a clause that stipulates that rights to compensation of the insured expire after a year is contrary to good faith under article 6:248 BW if the insurer does not warn the insured that he will invoke the expiration of the claim. The Hoge Raad also refers to article 3:12 BW and refers to the council that handles dispute resolution for the Dutch Association of Insurers to determine these views. The Hoge Raad finds that if this council considers a practice to be detrimental to the reputation of insurance, that practice is likely to also be contrary to good faith.

In some cases, the Hoge Raad[1308] has upheld the decision that invoking an exclusion clause was contrary to article 6:248 par. 2 BW, pointing to the extensive factual circumstances that the court of appeal had considered in its decisions. Wessels[1309] has criticised decisions of the Hoge Raad that held that invoking clauses that undermined the main terms of the contract were contrary to good faith.

For domestic business contracts, articles 6:236 and 237 BW are not applicable. The decision of the legislator to exempt domestic business contracts from these clauses was based on experiences by foreign legislators – excluding the German legislator –that had also opted to exempt clauses in business contracts from evaluation under black or grey lists.[1310] Article 6:235 BW further limits possibilities for some business to invoke the avoidability of STCs under article 6:233 sub a BW.

Generally, the Hoge Raad has shown restraint in allowing articles 6:236 and 6:237 BW to influence the evaluation of clauses in domestic business contracts under article 6:233 sub a BW.

Thus, the Hoge Raad[1311] showed restraint in a case where the court of appeal had referred to article 6:236 BW in its decision that invoking these clauses was contrary to good faith. The Hoge Raad[1312] also showed restraint in a case where the court of appeal held that an exclusion clause was contrary to good faith, referring to article 6:237 BW. Lower courts[1313] seem, on occasion, to adopt

1305 See further A.S. Hartkamp, 'Het nieuwe BW – ontwikkelingen sinds 1992', *AA* 2012, p. 52.

1306 HR 9 January 1998, *NJ* 1998, 363.

1307 HR 24 May 2004, *NJ* 2006, 188, following HR 12 January 1996, *NJ* 1996, 683.

1308 HR 5 September 2008, *NJ* 2008, 480.

1309 B. Wessels, 'Drie vuistregels voor de uitleg van algemene voorwaarden', *WPNR* 6239 (1996), p. 720–721.

1310 Parl. Gesch. NBW, Boek 6 (Inv. 3, 5 en 6), p. 1661.

1311 HR 15 October 2004, *NJ* 2005, 141.

1312 HR 18 June 2004, *NJ* 2004, 585.

1313 Comp. B. Wessels, 'Reflexies bij reflexwerking'. *WPNR* 6240 (1996), p. 725, who signalled that courts had started to apply these articles. Indirect effect of these articles is visible in, for example, Ktr. Leiden 26 August 2009, *RCR* 2009, 79, Rb. 's-Gravenhage 28 May 2014, *NJF* 2014, 339 and Hof 's-Hertogenbosch

somewhat less restraint towards the indirect effect of articles 6:236 and 237 BW, although this does not mean that they decide cases in accordance with the Directive.[1314] The indirect effect of articles 6:236 and 237 BW depends on the contract party invoking the avoidability. It has been argued that indirect effect should be allowed if legal persons invoking it are in a bargaining position that is similar to the consumer, while the contract should not be different from regular consumer contracts.[1315] It has also been argued that some degree of protection through civil procedure law could be extended to small business, for example through redefining "consumer".[1316]

Interestingly, the approach of the BGH on this matter is well developed, but the Hoge Raad has not referred to German developments.

Thus, the Hoge Raad has referred to business practices and non-state actors initiatives in evaluating whether a clause is unfair, which will not often be the case. In turn, this benefits the predictability of the law. The restraint of the Hoge Raad may enhance the ability of contract parties to negotiate on STCs and rely upon these clauses, in accordance with predictability.

5.4.3.6. Conclusion on the evaluation of clauses in international contracts

Have Dutch actors recognised that the initiatives of other actors may also be relevant for the evaluation of clauses and interacted with these actors accordingly? Have detriments developed because of a lack of interaction or has the coexistence of actors led to benefits?

The Dutch legislator and Dutch courts have recognised the increased relevance of international contract parties' needs and preferences as international trade develops. The Hoge Raad has recognised the added value of foreign insights and international materials to determine parties' expectations and business practice, both in cases decided under international regimes and under Dutch law, which benefits responsiveness.

That does not mean that the Hoge Raad consistently refers to these materials, and the use of these materials may be difficult to predict. Further, the Hoge Raad has decided international cases in accordance with national law. On the one hand, this may benefit the consistency as well as the responsiveness of the law to national practice and national legal views on justice. On the other hand, if national law differs from international law, this may diminish the consistency of the law on STCs more generally.

9 December 2014, *Prg* 2015, 32. Comp. also, implicitly, Ktr. Zaandam 9 August 2001, *Prg.* 2001, 5756. See earlier also Ktr. Middelburg 23 November 1998, *Prg.* 1999, 5130, Ktr. 's-Gravenhage 18 February 1998, *Prg.* 1998, 4961, and Rb. Zwolle 14 August 1996, *Prg.* 1996, 4635. Comp. however Rb. 's-Gravenhage 12 January 2011, *RAV* 2012, 29, rejecting a claim based on article 6:236 BW, finding that the Parliamentary history clearly shows that the legislator did not intend a clause as challenged in this case to be unreasonable under article 6:236 BW. Indirect effect has also been rejected, see for example Rb. Amsterdam 5 March 2014, ECLI:NL:RBAMS:2014:1165, Hof Amsterdam 28 January 2014, ECLI:NL:GHAMS:2014:304, and Hof Arnhem-Leeuwarden 17 February 2015, ECLI:NL:GHARL:2015:1180.

1314 This has been rejected in Rb. 's-Hertogenbosch 18 April 2012, *NJF* 2012, 343.

1315 J. Hijma, *Algemene voorwaarden*, Deventer: Kluwer 2010.

1316 AG F. Ancery, C.M.D.S. Pavillon, 'Processuele aspecten van reflexwerking van consumentenrecht', *WPNR* (7026) 2014.

Has Dutch law benefited from the coexistence of actors, in accordance with pluralist insights? In accordance with the idea of regulatory competition, the Dutch legislator has taken into account the approach of the English legislator that has sought to develop an attractive regime for international parties. However, the Dutch legislator has limited the possibility for parties to opt out of Dutch law, as consumer contracts remain subject to the Dutch regime. The exemptions in articles 6:235 and 247 BW reveal that the Dutch legislator and Dutch courts do not consider businesses as parties that are in need of active protection. Therefore, introducing regulatory competition is not necessarily problematic in this area. Simultaneously, the law on STCs, especially with regard to consumer contracts, is closely intertwined with national legal views on justice. This close relationship may stand in the way of regulatory competition for these contracts. Thus, the coexistence of national regimes may be beneficial for the responsiveness of the law to national legal views on justice and to national practice. Although the Dutch legislator has not opposed full harmonisation in this area, it has emphasised that national law formed a starting point for negotiations.[1317] The coexistence of national regimes also offers opportunities for mutual learning. Accordingly, the Hoge Raad has taken into account foreign and international materials. Opportunities for learning for Dutch courts could become more consistent if the Hoge Raad would indicate a more consistent and predictable approach to foreign and international materials.

5.4.4. *Conclusion on blanket clauses*

Interdependence between Dutch and European actors has not been recognised as such, as the drafting of article 6:233 sub a BW preceded the Directive, and the Dutch legislator asserted that Dutch law was already in accordance with the Directive. If European actors gain more competence to draft, amend or interpret blanket clauses, the extent to which national blanket clauses contribute to the responsiveness of the law to national legal views on justice diminishes. The extent to which model lists support the predictable and consistent interpretation of blanket clauses, as well as the accessibility of the law, may also diminish as overlapping lists develop.

The interdependence between the CJEU and the Hoge Raad has also not adequately been recognised. The restraint of the Hoge Raad in referring questions to the CJEU has likely remained, notwithstanding the 2013 decision of the Hoge Raad. The inconsistency of Dutch decisions on penalty clauses with CJEU decisions demonstrates that the role of the Hoge Raad has been undermined, which, in turn, has aggravated the development of inconsistent and unpredictable case law from lower courts. These difficulties have not been addressed in the revision of Directive 93/13. Questions that have become visible in the German legal order, in particular the allocation of competences between courts in the interpretation of harmonised law, and the obligation of legislators to implement the model list in the Annex to the Directive, have also not been considered in the Dutch legal order. Thus, the lack of interaction between national and European actors may decrease the responsive development of Directive 93/13.

1317 See previously par. 5.3.

Generally, the interdependence between state and non-state actors has likewise not been recognised. The success of the Board seems to have contributed to the relatively low number of cases before the courts. Arguably, the prominent role of the Board, combined with the lack of interaction with the courts, may undermine the extent to which article 6:233 sub a BW contributes to the consistent, accessible, and predictable development of the law. Specifically, decisions may contradict courts decisions, and decisions of the Board are not consistently published.

Thus, because interdependence has not generally been recognised, a lack of interaction between courts and between courts and the Board has undermined the comprehensibility of Dutch law, in accordance with multilevel governance insights.

Has the coexistence of actors enhanced the predictability, consistency, accessibility and responsiveness of the law on STCs?

Harmonisation has not prompted the Dutch legislator to consider the interests of foreign actors interested in access to the Dutch market. The restraint of courts has also stood in the way of the development of a system of checks and balances. It can be doubted, also, whether such a system, once developed, would consider the development of the law in terms of predictability, consistency, accessibility and responsiveness. The competence of European actors is limited, especially in domestic cases, and targeted at European policy aims rather than the quality of law more generally.

Courts adopt a considerably more active approach to the evaluation of clauses under articles 6:233 than the evaluation under 248 BW. Can this difference be traced to the influence of Directive 93/13, in accordance with Watson's[1318] argument that the influence of donor systems remains visible in legal transplants? Arguably, especially the decisions of the CJEU have helped to ensure the active approach of courts. Arguably, this cannot be traced to the influence of German law, notwithstanding the active approach of the German courts. In this case, in accordance with pluralist arguments,[1319] the CJEU may have diminished restraint that could have stood in the way to the further development of the law on STCs.

However, the inconsistent decisions on article 6:233, 236 and 237 BW demonstrate that legal transplants have hardly been fully integrated and that the distinction between the possible reactions to legal transplants – integration or rejection – may not be clear-cut. Possibly, the lack of consistent decisions can be a sign of rejection or a lack of integration. Or can this development be attributed as one of the risks of introducing a new blanket clause in national law more generally? The development of inconsistent and unpredictable case law may further be attributed to the lack of interaction between Dutch courts that is not visible in the German legal order. The lack of consistent decisions also raises questions with regard to the relation between the law on STCs and legal views on justice. However, the rejection of regulatory competition for consumer contracts and the distinction between international, business and consumer contracts, as well as the decisions in consumer cases in line with surrounding national law

1318 A. Watson, *Legal transplants*, Edinburgh: Scottish Academic Press 1974.

1319 T. Wilhelmsson, 'Private law in the EU: Harmonised or fragmented Europeanisation?', *ERPL* 2002, p. 91–92.

indicate that the law on STCs does reflect developing Dutch legal views on justice. From that perspective, the coexistence of national actors is beneficial in terms of responsiveness.

Regulatory competition has prompted the Dutch legislator to exempt international contracts from evaluation under article 6:233 sub a BW. Article 6:248 BW is applicable, but courts have exercised restraint in holding clauses ineffective under this provision. Dutch courts have also considered foreign and international materials, in the evaluation of blanket clauses, which should enhance the law's responsiveness to the need of foreign and international actors, which should strengthen the position of Dutch law in regulatory competition. However, the use of blanket clauses is not advantageous from the perspective of regulatory competition, because it entails that case law plays an important role in the development of the law. Dutch case law may not be especially accessible to foreign and international actors. The insertion of article 3 Directive similarly entails that national case law plays an important role, which may not be accessible, and it is also inconsistent. In this respect, harmonisation may not have facilitated access to the Dutch market.

Notwithstanding the use of comparative law by the legislator, neither the Hoge Raad nor lower courts take into account foreign decisions in the evaluation of clauses under articles 6:233 sub a BW or article 6:236 and 237 BW. However, lower courts and the Hoge Raad have recognised the added value of foreign materials in decisions under international regimes.

The differences in the approach in the evaluation of clauses under international business contracts and consumer contracts may in some cases, such as international contacts falling under the CISG be explained by the easier availability of foreign decisions. More often, especially for decisions in lower courts in consumer contracts, the relative straightforwardness of cases that do not require referral to the CJEU or to foreign materials may be a reason for less referral. Further, the evaluation of clauses under articles 6:231 et seq BW concerns the interpretation of national law, and referral to foreign cases may lessen the consistent development of the law on STCs by national law, as well as the development of the law in accordance with national practice and national legal views on justice. The use of foreign materials may also lessen the predictability of law if there is no consistent approach to foreign materials and if parties are not familiar with foreign cases.

In the approach of the Dutch legislator and the courts, a national approach to the development of the law remains visible. Although the CJEU has prompted the Hoge Raad to reconsider its decisions with regard to *ex officio* obligations, further restraint is still visible, and the Hoge Raad logically remains focussed on national law. This may stand in the way of opportunities for learning. However, simultaneously, some Dutch courts do refer to the CJEU. Further opportunities for learning could be facilitated if the Hoge Raad or the CJEU more clearly indicate when considering foreign, European and international materials is warranted.

5.5. Principles

What principles have played a role in the development of Dutch and European law on STCs, can different principles be discerned and has the extent to which national law develops on the basis of general principles been compromised? How has that affected the extent to which principles have contributed to the predictability, accessibility, consistency and responsiveness of the law on STCs? Alternatively, have principles served as a starting point for interaction and have they facilitated mutual learning?

In particular, this paragraph will consider three principles that have played an important role in the development of the law on STCs:

1) The principle of good faith, or fairness, visible in article 6:233 sub a BW
2) The principle of consumer protection
3) The principle of party autonomy, which, in Dutch reasoning, shows remarkable similarities with the *Richtigkeitsgewähr.*

Paragraph 5.5.1 will consider principles underlying Dutch law[1320] and paragraph 5.5.2 will point out in which ways the development of Dutch law converges with the development of Directive 93/13. Paragraph 5.5.3 will ask in which ways the development of Dutch law diverges from the development of Directive 93/13. Paragraph 5.5.4 will end with conclusions.

5.5.1. The development of the Dutch law on STCs on the basis of principles

The development of articles 6:231 et seq BW was based on principles of good faith, consumer protection and party autonomy.

Nieuwenhuis[1321] finds that because the unequal position of contract parties and the resulting prevalence of one party, good faith obliges the party drafting STCs to take into account the legitimate interests of its counter parties. Accordingly, in the evaluation of STCs, the position of parties plays a role. This was already decided by the Hoge Raad[1322] in a judgment preceding the BW. The legislator[1323] remarked that the draft article 6:233 sub a BW did not aim to provide different criteria, and noted that German law had developed efficient control on the basis of good faith in article 242 BGB. Article 6:233 sub a BW, therefore, alludes to the way clauses have been drafted, the mutual recognisable interests of parties as well as other relevant circumstances, which include the capacity of parties.[1324]

1320 The development of Directive 93/13 and principles have been discussed previously in par. 4.5.2. and will therefore not be discussed separately.
1321 J.H. Nieuwenhuis, *Drie beginselen van contractenrecht*, Deventer: Kluwer 1977, p. 145.
1322 HR 19 May 1967, *NJ* 1967, 261.
1323 Parl. Gesch. NBW, Boek 6 (Inv. 3, 5 en 6), p. 1586–1587.
1324 See for example HR 15 December 1995, *NJ* 1996, 318.

In addition, consumer protection has played a role in the development of articles 6:231 et seq BW that were developed against the background of consumer protection policies. However, the protection of STCs is not limited to consumers but instead takes the position of the party subjected to STCs as a starting point.

Notably, Nieuwenhuis[1325] finds that the unequal position of contract parties with regard to STCs is situated in the occupation of private autonomy by one contract party – and therefore, the other party is subjected to these terms without having the possibility to influence them. This reasoning shows remarkable similarities with the principle of hetero-determination ('*Fremdbestimmung*'), the opposite of private autonomy, which develops if parties are bound by terms they have not been able to influence.[1326] Accordingly, in the discussion in Parliament, one of the underlying ideas was that parties subjected to STCs should be protected, as parties will only exceptionally have the possibility to influence the content of STCs and generally are unfamiliar with the content of STCs. This meant that not only consumers could be subjected to unfair terms – businesses, depending on their bargaining position, could also be exposed.[1327]

Negotiations on STCs may indicate that a clause is not unfair, as recognised in article 6:233 sub a BW that stipulates that one of the circumstances relevant for the evaluation under this article is the way in which a clause has been drafted. This is in accordance with the idea of *Richtigkeitsgewähr*, the principle which underlines the importance of contract parties' bargaining for accepting the binding force of contracts in German law.[1328] However, the Hoge Raad[1329] has since ruled that this limitation aimed to prevent the introduction of the *iustum pretium* doctrine that would oblige judges to evaluate whether the main terms of the contract were sufficiently balanced.

Clearly, the principles may show significant overlap. Accordingly, businesses dealing with parties in weak bargaining positions, especially consumers, may not impose their conditions on these parties but should take their interests into account, in accordance with the principle of good faith. Parties in stronger positions, especially international businesses, are not illogically considered to be in less need of protection than consumers. Theoretically, the idea that strong consumers are not protected as the court may take into account that a consumer had a realistic opportunity to influence the STCs is possible, although the legislator considered this possibility as rather unlikely: even if a consumer is in a strong bargaining position, he will generally contract over a matter only once, while the user of STCs is typically a repeat player, who may also simply choose to contract on the basis of his STCs or not at all, regardless of the resources and expertise of the consumer.[1330]

Thus, these principles have played an important role in the development of the law on STCs.

[1325] J.H. Nieuwenhuis, *Drie beginselen van contractenrecht*, Deventer: Kluwer 1977, p. 145.

[1326] See further on this concept par. 7.1.

[1327] Parl. Gesch. NBW, Boek 6 (Inv. 3, 5 en 6), p. 1452–1453, 1455.

[1328] See further previously par. 5.4.1.

[1329] HR 19 September 1997, *NJ* 1998, 6.

[1330] Parl. Gesch. NBW, Boek 6 (Inv. 3, 5 en 6), p. 1496.

5.5.2. *Principles underlying the law on STCs: similarities*

Various similarities with regard to the principles of good faith and consumer protection become visible the law on STCs at the national and European level.

1) Both at the national and European level, good faith plays a central role in the assessment of clauses.

Like the Dutch and German legislator, the European legislator takes good faith as a starting point that enables an overall evaluation of the interests involved in the contract, although it is not uncontroversial whether this concept should be interpreted uniformly.

2) Dutch and European law has developed against the background of consumer protection.

Although article 6:233 sub a BW is also applicable more broadly, it has become especially relevant for the evaluation of clauses in consumer contracts. Interestingly, despite the weaker position of consumers, the European legislator has also recognised the added value of negotiations between stakeholder groups and may, therefore, also consider the possibilities for collective negotiations on STCs in consumer contracts.[1331] Both the Dutch and the European approaches are more lenient towards STCs in business contracts.

3) Both the Dutch and European legislator has recognised the added value of the use of STCs.

Thus, these basic principles underpin national law and have played a role in the development of Directive 93/13.

5.5.3. *Principles underlying the law on STCs: divergences*

Differences between the development of the law on STCs at the national level and have played a role in the development of the European level also exist:

1) The principle of consumer protection does not justify the conclusion that the development of the *acquis* is based on the principle of protection of weaker parties.

2) The principle of private autonomy is also recognised at the European level, but the European legislator has not referred to the *iustum pretium* doctrine. Instead, the European legislator held that the protective aim of the Directive allows for extending judicial evaluation of STCs to the main contract terms.[1332]

[1331] See further below, par.7.5.2.1.
[1332] CJEU 3 June 2010 Caja de Ahorros), C-484/08, [2010] ECR, p. I-4785.

However, these differences do not mean that these principles cannot form a starting point for more interaction between actors.

5.5.4. *Conclusion on principles underlying the law on STCs*

Principles of good faith and party autonomy, which shows similarities with the *Richtigkeitsgewähr*, remain important concepts underpinning Dutch law. Harmonisation has not visibly limited the development of Dutch rules on the basis of principles. Whereas, in the German legal order, the idea of *Richtigkeitsgewähr* may be a reason for upholding clauses that the consumer negotiated over, this is less likely to happen in Dutch law. Although the Dutch legislator recognised this situation as a possibility, it was held a rather unlikely outcome, and Dutch law appears to attach more weight to the idea of consumer protection than German law, as becomes visible in the limited scope of articles 6:236 and 237 BW and the unclarity over the indirect effect of these lists in business contracts.

Principles may form a starting point for interaction between actors. The differences between principles underlying the law, or the different weight that is attached to these principles, or the different role that principles play in the development of the law, need not stand in the way of interaction or common developments on the law of STCs throughout Europe. Therefore, principles may facilitate mutual learning: they facilitate mutual understanding and they may inspire actors in developing the law, although that does not mean that these laws will develop similarly.

However, although principles can form a starting point for interaction, they have not visibly improved the quality of the law on STCs. The question arises whether more attention for principles at the national level would lead to more consistent decisions of Dutch courts. In this respect, the Hoge Raad is well placed to provide further guidance.

5.6. Conclusion on the development of the law on STCs through national techniques

The Dutch law on STCs is successful in some respects. Dutch law less strictly scrutinizes whether clauses have been individually negotiated and therefore do not fall under the regime of articles 6:231 et seq BW, which may provide contract parties with more incentives to negotiate, both individually and collectively. Further, the legislator has developed the Dutch regime on STCs consistently with surrounding national law. Dutch law however also shows shortcomings. There is uncertainty with regard to the definition of clauses and article 6:232 BW. A lack of clarity is visible with regard to the obligation of parties to make STCs adequately available, and the distinction between parties not in need of protection may lead to inconsistency and leaves gaps. Articles 6:214 and 239 BW have become dead letters.

An important part of the law on STCs has been developed through national techniques. Paragraph 5.6.1. will ask whether, in accordance with insights from multilevel governance, actors have recognised that interdependence has developed and interacted accordingly. Paragraph 5.6.2. will ask whether benefits recognised by pluralists have developed. Paragraph 5.6.3. will consider improving interaction and the absence of deliberation.

5.6.1. The development of the law on STCs and multilevel governance insights

In the law on STCs, interdependence has clearly developed, which means that the extent to which actors can ensure the comprehensiveness of the law on STCs through the use of national techniques has become limited.

Because of the timing of the adoption of the Directive and the introduction of the BW, the decreased independence of the national legislator and the courts to ensure the predictable development of the law becomes clear, even though drastic amendments were not needed. European law was insufficiently clear with regard to the obligations of Member States in this respect. Arguably, European actors should more clearly indicate what obligations are imposed on Member States, but it is also desirable that national actors more actively examine the extent of their obligations.

Lower courts' problems with overlapping, simultaneously applicable sources, and their failure to sufficiently interact with one another, have likewise become visible. This is unfortunate, because the legislator clearly depends on courts to actively develop the law through blanket clauses, which limits the need for the legislator to amend the law within the code. Notably, the approach of the Dutch judiciary has limited the extent to which article 6:233 sub a BW reduces the need for legal reform.

Moreover, the multilevel legal order, in particular the active role of the CJEU and of active lower courts, especially in consumer cases that do not often come before the Hoge Raad, require that the Hoge Raad adopts a more active approach towards the development of the law. The inconsistency that has developed in Dutch law as lower courts do not only not refer to decisions of other lower courts but also overlook relevant decisions from the Hoge Raad indicates that the role of the highest court is undermined if it does not actively provide guidance for lower courts. The Hoge Raad should also ensure that its decisions are in line with CJEU decisions, as inconsistencies between CJEU and Hoge Raad cases leave room for lower courts to follow the CJEU rather than the Hoge Raad.

Simultaneously, the case study underlines the dependence of the CJEU and the European legislator on national actors. If national courts do not refer questions to the CJEU, and if they do not sufficiently and representatively participate in the European legislative debate, the extent to which European actors can revise and develop the Directive in accordance with national practice, is limited. The focus of European actors on further harmonisation may however lead one to doubt whether European actors are particularly interested in developing the law in accordance with *national* practice.

Interdependence has also become visible between courts and The Board. Because of the amount of cases decided before the Board, less cases have come before the courts, and there is less clarity about how these cases are decided. In addition, if the legislator provides for self-regulation, the success of this approach depends on the willingness of non-state actors, which may not be particularly high if these actors have other, easier alternatives to develop STCs.

Interdependence is also clear in an international context. The restraint of national courts, which obliges foreign and international actors to examine domestic case law, as well as inconsistent and unpredictable decisions make Dutch law less attractive for foreign and international actors, undermining the efforts of the legislator to participate in regulatory competition.

The case study shows that the aims of Dutch and European actors, at first sight, do not seem to diverge as clearly as the aims of German actors, concerned with maintaining the comprehensibility of the law and European actors, focussed on achieving EU policy aims. The Dutch legislator is less inclined to reject the revision of the Directive in a manner that may limit the ability of national techniques to ensure the comprehensibility of the law. However, upon closer inspection, the Dutch legislator is concerned with maintaining the stable development of Dutch law and accordingly has adopted a minimum implementation approach towards Directive 93/13, like the German legislator. The relatively abrupt introduction of the law on STCs however made it considerably more difficult to defend that the *acquis* should develop in accordance with national law. The minimum harmonisation approach also went beyond other legislators' restraint and attracted the attention of European actors. Fortunately, however, the German legislator did have a prominent role in the European debate and Dutch law was inspired by German law. Further, especially the Hoge Raad is focused on preserving the unity of national law. Lower courts are focused on effectively and quickly resolving disputes, which may involve referring to the CJEU, referring to the Hoge Raad, or both. Because of these differences, interdependence is likely to become more rather than less visible.

In accordance with insights from multilevel governance, weaknesses in the law on STCs and shortcomings in the interaction between actors have reinforced one another. Particularly, the debate on the implementation of the Directive was limited and Dutch non-state actors barely participated in the European debate preceding Directive 93/13 and Directive 2011/83. This limits the extent to which Dutch actors can influence the development of Directives. After Directives have been established, the debate on implementation also remains limited. This has aggravated the following problems:

i) Dutch courts have taken a much less active approach in the development of the law on STCs than German courts, which has resulted in inconsistency and unpredictability in consumer cases.

The different approach of German and Dutch courts may be traced to the development of the law on STCs by German courts on the basis of article 242 BGB, which simultaneously makes it less likely that lower courts will change their approach and start referring to the CJEU. Perhaps, the interaction between courts may also be traced to the initial judicial development of the German law on STCs. The prominent role of the courts in the development of the law on STCs may have instilled a habit in German lower courts to pay more attention to other lower courts and the BGH. In addition, the lack of consistent interaction between courts can also be attributed to fewer decisions of the Hoge Raad that provide less guidance to lower courts to distinguish and apply potentially overlapping international and European regimes. Inaccessibility and inconsistency have developed as a result.

However, it is also possible that German lower courts simply adopt a more thorough approach. In other areas where Dutch courts have played an active approach in the development of the law, Dutch lower courts refer to the Hoge Raad rather than decisions from other lower courts.

In contrast, Dutch courts show less restraint in referring questions to the CJEU. An explanation for this difference may be that Dutch courts were prompted by the CJEU that clearly and directly imposes obligations while guidance from the Hoge Raad was less available.

ii) Inconsistency and gaps remain with regard to the duty of international actors to make STCs sufficiently available under Dutch law and with regard to battle of forms.

iii) Inaccessibility has developed as courts do not consistently and correctly apply European and international law.

Although Dutch courts show less restraint than German courts in referring to international and foreign materials when deciding cases under international regimes, as well as soft laws, in cases under international regimes, this does not happen consistently and predictably. In some cases, confusion has become visible.

In the long term, the lack of interaction may entail that relevant points are not addressed in the reform of Directives.

i) The allocation of competences between the CJEU and national courts to interpret blanket clauses.
   Both the BGH and the Hoge Raad have cited *Freiburger Kommunalbauten* to underpin national courts' competence to assess the fairness of contract terms and have not regarded subsequent CJEU case law.
   However, even if the reform of Directive 93/13 leads to more clarity, this does not mean that a similar allocation of tasks can be assumed for the interpretation of blanket clauses in other Directives – for example, the allocation of tasks may differ depending on the degree of harmonisation pursued by a Directive.
ii) The implementation of Directive 2000/31 and Directive 2006/123.
iii) The obligation of the legislator to implement the model list in the Annex to Directive 93/13.
   The Hoge Raad has provided more clarity on the status of the model list in the Annex to Directive 93/13 than the BGH. It would be interesting to see whether the view of the Hoge Raad is shared by the CJEU or by European actors in the reform of Directive 93/13.

The restraint of especially the Hoge Raad in referring to foreign cases entails that questions that have been raised in the German legal order and that may affect the role of actors and the development of the law on STCs, are completely overlooked. Particularly, it would have been interesting for Dutch actors to discuss the idea of the *Richtigkeitsgewähr*.

Consequently, the lack of interaction between national and European actors may lead to a circle: because of a lack of interaction, reformed Directives do not adequately respond to national experiences, which increases the chances that legislators and courts will adopt restraint in implementing and applying national law implementing Directive, and so on.

5.6.2. The development of the law on STCs and pluralist insights

The coexistence of actors developing the law on STCs has led to the development of a system of checks and balances. Regulatory competition has developed, and opportunities for mutual learning have been realised. However, generally, these developments have not increased the comprehensibility of the law.

Responsiveness has not been increased as the European legislator has harmonised the law on STCs. While the drafting of Directive 93/13 was not prompted by the concerns of transnational actors, this is less clear with regard to Directive 2006/123 on services, which aims to make domestic markets more accessible to foreign service providers. However, these regimes are also applicable to domestic contracts. Directive 2006/123 also applies to domestic contracts, in addition to national regimes, which may create confusion. It is not clear why European actors would be better placed to develop rules in accordance with the preferences of actors engaged in domestic trade, or actors not interested in cross-border trade.

In addition, the Dutch case study makes clearer than the German study that checks and balances have developed, as made clear by the incorrect implementation of Directive 93/13, the impulse to the evaluation of clauses in lower courts from the CJEU, and the changed position of the Hoge Raad with regard to the obligation of the courts to evaluate clauses of their own motion. However, these checks and balances currently do not contribute to comprehensibility of the law on STCs. Weaknesses in the law on STCs were also not improved by harmonisation. The implementation of Directives 93/13, 2000/31 and 2006/123 did not prompt the Dutch legislator to critically reconsider its laws after harmonisation had been established. When the 1993 Directive was passed, insufficient time had passed to allow for a critical evaluation of national law. The development and the difficult implementation of subsequent Directives, as well as the suggestions for the reform of Directive 93/13 also did not prompt reconsideration, despite suggestions to amend national law.

European actors have a limited ability to develop a system of checks and balances, in particular because of the limited competences of European actors in this respect, which are generally not oriented towards the quality of the law, especially not the law in domestic disputes. The national approach towards the development of European private law entailed that clear opportunities to critically reflect on national law were not used. This approach may also help explain that the checks and balances, insofar as they have developed, have not served to improve the law.

The Dutch regime on consumer contracts appears closely interrelated with surrounding law and national practice. As a result, the coexistence of national regimes may benefit responsiveness. Theoretically, this may stand in the way of further harmonisation. However, this has not prompted the Dutch legislator from supporting further harmonisation – in accordance with Dutch law. In this matter, the Dutch legislator underestimates the possibility that once harmonised, the CJEU, driven by references from other Member States' courts, decides in a manner that is difficult to predict and hard to reconcile with surrounding national law.

The question arises whether the relation between the law on STCs for consumer cases has lessened the extent to which legal transplants have become integrated in Dutch law.

Notwithstanding the role of German law in the drafting of the Dutch regime, German law has not been transplanted to the Dutch legal order. Even if such a transplant would have taken place, Dutch law would have had to be amended after the adoption of Directive 93/13. Interestingly, the points where Dutch law is most complicated and least accessible are the points where Dutch law has not followed German law – in particular, article 6:232 BW, the availability of STCs, and the rules on unduly surprising or unfair clauses.

Article 6:232 BW was adopted for sake of predictability, but it is not clear how it has contributed to predictability. Instead, the emphasis on the applicability and subsequent avoidability of clauses has led to tensions with European law and inconsistent case law. If clauses that have not been made sufficiently available do not become part of a contract, would this not mitigate these problems? Following the German rules on unduly surprising clauses in article 305c BGB would already add to clarity. German experiences demonstrate that it is well possible to maintain predictability if clauses are simply not included in contracts.

Moreover, article 6:214 BW would have been better placed in the German legal order, considering the exemption for VOBs in article 310 BGB, but it remains a dead letter in the Dutch legal order and should be reconsidered. Article 6:239 BW has similarly been reduced to a dead letter and should be rethought.

Unfortunately, the Dutch legislator has also not been inspired by the restraint of the German legislator in amending the law on STCs.

However, at some points, Dutch law has not followed German law, and should continue to diverge.

In particular, the definition of STCs and the emphasis on clauses that have not been individually negotiated may have disadvantages in German law as it may motivate businesses to not negotiate on clauses. Also, Dutch law on the battle of forms have not proven less or more successful than German law, where a specific rule has consciously not been established.

Further, the existence of article 6:235 BW and the absence of an equivalent provision in the German legal order reflect different legal views on justice that are further reflected in German and Dutch case law and the German emphasis on the *Richtigkeitsgewähr* rather than consumer protection. Even if the role of article 6:235 BW is not very visible, and the extent to which it contributes to predictability is not clear, it should, therefore, be maintained. However, the gaps it leaves should be remedied.

The Dutch and German legislator and courts have adopted different approaches with regard to the evaluation of clauses in international business contracts under article 6:248 BW and article 307 BGB. German courts have adopted a relatively lenient approach towards the evaluation of clauses in international contracts decided under German law; the strict and well-developed standard in article 307 BGB requires express motivation for upholding clauses, for example, in the form of international materials. This approach, for whatever reason, is, however, not reflected in German courts' evaluation of clauses under the CISG. In contrast, Dutch courts require justification for limiting the effect of clauses under article 6:248 par. 2 BW, for example, through international or foreign materials or business practices. Thus, both German and Dutch courts recognise foreign and international materials as sources that may be used – among other materials – to underpin decisions requiring extensive motivation.

The existence of a legal transplant is more visible after the adoption of Directive 93/13. However, Dutch courts have simultaneously decided cases contrary to the Directive and followed the CJEU. It is not clear whether the Directive has been rejected, integrated, or both.

The relation between the law on STCs and Dutch legal views has not hindered the pursuit of regulatory competition in the law on STCs with regard to business contracts. The Dutch legislator has sought to develop an internationally attractive regime, but that has not prompted Dutch actors to critically consider their regime from the perspective of international or foreign actors, or to clarify rules of public policy that apply regardless of a choice of law. The refusal of the Dutch legislator to reconsider the law on STCs may have undermined the attractiveness of Dutch law in international trade. This is unfortunate, as amending Dutch law on the availability of STCs would benefit predictability and accessibility, as well as responsiveness. Particularly, reconsidering article 6:232 BW and the applicability of STCs, and the relationship between articles 3:33 and 35 BW, would be beneficial. German law could provide a source of inspiration in this respect. Possibly, drawing from German law may be more attractive as Dutch law is already inspired by German law.

In the absence of an active approach towards the comprehensible development of the law, Dutch courts have undermined the legislator's efforts at regulatory competition. The approach of Dutch courts can be contrasted to the approach of German courts that have exercised restraint in cases decided under international regimes, but that have more actively referred to international and foreign materials in cases decided under German law.

As regulatory competition has not prompted Dutch actors to critically reflect on Dutch law, regulatory competition has not boosted innovation.[1333] Currently, regulatory competition is limited to business contracts. In contrast, for consumer contracts, more concerns arise with regard to a "race to the bottom". In these cases, harmonisation and limitations on choices of law – typically used by stronger parties – may well be justified.[1334] For choice of law, European actors are better placed to develop restrictions. However, European law does not do so consistently and predictably. The restraint of Dutch courts and the emphasis of the Dutch legislator on consulting non-state actors, even though they were not international or foreign parties, underlines that the success of regulatory competition also depends on the cooperation between various state actors and between state and non-state actors, in line with the idea of regulatory co-opetition.[1335]

However, the coexistence of actors has been beneficial as it has resulted in mutual learning. Dutch actors were inspired by German law, which has likely contributed to the comprehensibility of the law on STCs. German and European actors have similarly recognised the added value of comparative law. Yet simultaneously, processes using opportunities for mutual learning are extensive. As a result, the expertise and time invested in the development of codifications may lead to lengthy drafting processes that

1333 E.A. O'Hara, L.E. Ribstein, *The law market*, Oxford: OUP 2009, p. 224.

1334 E.A. O'Hara, L.E. Ribstein, *The law market*, Oxford: OUP 2009, p. 223.

1335 D.C. Esty, D. Geradin, 'Regulatory co-opetition', *Journal of International Economic Law* 2000, p. 238.

diminish the willingness of national legislators to subsequently accommodate the development of a system of checks and balances or critically revise the law resulting from this process, prompted by opportunities for mutual learning. Notably, the European legislator has a different perspective, as legal comparison is also a way to discover divergences that stand in the way of the proper functioning of the internal market. In the development of the law on STCs, Dutch actors have also recognised the need to take into account the preferences of international actors.

Unfortunately, possibilities for further learning are unlikely to be used for critically revising the law as Dutch actors, after having drawn on comparative law, have adopted a national approach towards European law. In some instances, referral to foreign decisions could have prompted courts to consider the evaluation of clauses more critically.

In particular, the Hoge Raad[1336] upheld a decision from the court of appeal, stating that the discretion of the judge to mitigate a penalty clause under article 6:94 BW was relevant for assessing whether a penalty clause was unfair. This approach can be contrasted with the German controversy on *Geltungserhaltende Reduktion* that emphasises that changing STCs that are unfair to STCs that are barely allowed, rewards users of STCs that are encouraged to remain using unfair terms in contracts that shall be adapted by the judiciary until they are acceptable.[1337] It can moreover be contrasted with CJEU[1338] decisions emphasising that the deterrent effect of the Directive is undermined if judges amend the content of unfair clauses rather than holding them ineffective.

A national approach is visible in international cases. Even though courts recognise the added value of comparative law and international materials, the courts have decided cases in accordance with domestic cases, despite the legislator's distinction between domestic and international cases in article 6:247 BW.

Some pluralists have criticised the state-centric approach towards the development of law. The Dutch case study demonstrates the important role of non-state actors, also in the development of the law through national techniques. Interaction may also become more important, even though actors are not obliged to interact. Accordingly, Dutch lower courts should refer more to other lower courts, but they are not bound to do so. Instead lower courts may emphasise the lack of binding force of the decisions of other lower courts and parties – especially parties who lack expertise – do not refer to these decisions in their arguments, and the need to quickly and efficiently decide cases where a limited financial interest is at stake may outweigh the need for extensive further research. The criticism on state actors' central roles may also be questioned in the light of the role of the Board. While the Board undoubtedly provides an accessible manner of dispute resolution, problems and the need for further control on the decisions of the

1336 HR 24 March 2006, *NJ* 2007, 115. See before this case, similarly, Ktr. Amsterdam 1 March 1996, *Prg.* 1996, 4601.

1337 MunchKomm zum BGB/Basedow (2012), article 306, nr 12, 28.

1338 CJEU 14 June 2012 (Banco Español de Crédito v Calderón Camino), C-168/10, [2012] ECR p. I-0, par. 65, 69, CJEU 30 May 2013 (Asbeek Brusse and de Man Garabito v Jahani BV), C-488/11, [2013] ECR p. I-0, par. 58. CJEU 30 April 2014 (Kásler and Káslerné Rábai v OTP Jelzálogbank Zrt), C-26/13, [2014] CR p. I-0, par. 79, CJEU 21 January 2015 (Unicaja Banco SA v José Hidalgo Rueda and Others), joined cases C-482/13, C-484/13, C-485/13 and C-487/13, [2015] ECR p. I-0, par. 31–32.

Board, for example in the form of consistency and review on the consistency of decisions with courts' decisions, have also become apparent.

5.6.3. *Facilitating deliberation?*

Debate can be improved if opportunities for learning are realised more. Also, arguably, the interaction between actors should be adjusted.

Interaction between actors should serve to improve the quality of the law on STCs. Particularly, Dutch actors need to become aware of interdependence and pay more attention to the use of techniques at the European level and the influence of the use of techniques on the development of private law at the national level.

Interaction between national actors should be enhanced. Giesen and Schelhaas[1339] have suggested more cooperation between the legislator, judiciary and other relevant actors. Increased cooperation between the legislator and the judiciary will contribute to the development of better law more generally, ensuring that relevant experiences and insights are taken into account in the legislative process. More cooperation between the legislator, the Hoge Raad, lower courts and the Board, as well as academics, and possibly, European and foreign actors should make actors more aware of relevant developments and problems arising in practice. This suggestion has also been inspired by the English Law Commission that contains members from legal practice, the judiciary, as well as academics. Theoretically, more cooperation with organisations that are to facilitate the enforcement of consumer law may prompt more enforcement of articles 6:231 et seq BW through collective redress, which enables the court, possibly the Hoge Raad, to set clearer guidelines. Decisions in collective redress may draw more attention and compliance from lower courts.

Courts' decisions need to be better coordinated. A more consistent approach could be prompted by the Hoge Raad. Accordingly, clearer guidance on the use of international and foreign materials from the Hoge Raad should be beneficial. The Hoge Raad should also expressly refer to principles underpinning national law to further consistency and responsiveness. Experiences in the German legal order indicate that commentaries may also be a source of inspiration for courts. However, especially Dutch lower courts have rarely referred to commentaries.

The debate at the European level should also be improved. The Dutch government is well-placed to contact representative national actors, to encourage them to participate. A further opportunity for further leaning can be found in article 74 Judicial Organisation Act provides that the Hoge Raad provides information to the government upon request. The government should make use of this possibility in discussing the revision and the implementation of Directives.

Also, national practices should be considered in the light of European initiatives, and national actors should play a more active role in alerting European actors to relevant or interesting practices.

[1339] I. Giesen, H.N. Schelhaas, 'Samenwerking bij rechtsvorming', *AA* 2006, p. 159.

In particular, Dutch ADR practices in consumer cases on STCs should be carefully considered. Currently, ADR decisions on consumer cases may contradict articles 6:231 et seq BW[1340] and diverge from the decisions of lower courts. Consistent publication of these decisions should be seriously considered, because the lack of publicity may limit parties' ability to predict the outcome of a dispute and lead to inconsistent development of consumer law in these areas with general national private law.[1341] A lack of publicity is likely to disadvantage parties with little experience more than repeat players. Publicity may in this respect also serve as a control mechanism.[1342] The lack of publicity may also mean that a large amount of cases does not contribute to the development of the law on STCs, and the experiences of the Board and problematic cases remain invisible before they come before the courts.

Other features of current ADR practices should also be reconsidered: Loos[1343] convincingly argues that the restraint adopted under article 7:902 BW towards the evaluation of ADR decisions[1344] is outdated and might lead to a breach of the obligation of national actors to correctly implement the Directive 93/13. His objections seem particularly convincing in the light of the Court's decisions in *Asturcom*[1345] and *Pohotovost*[1346] that national courts should assess possible unfair terms between parties, in the same manner in which courts, under national civil procedure law, would have to assess whether the arbitral award is in accordance with matters of public policy. Further, Snijders[1347] has convincingly argued that changing the binding advice procedure into an arbitral procedure may offer more legal guarantees with regard to the appointment and challenging of arbitrators.[1348] In addition, the possibility to turn to ADR in cross-border cases is limited as the

1340 For example Decision of 29 September 2009, nr 31530, at www.degeschillencommissie.nl/klacht-indienen/eerdere-uitspraken/31530/afwezigheid-van-7-maanden., as well as Decision of 26 July 2006, nr 32021, at www.degeschillencommissie.nl/klacht-indienen/eerdere-uitspraken/32021/artikel-6–237-onder-k-bw-niet-van-toepassing. and Decision of 24 August 2011, nr 34376, at www.degeschillencommissie.nl/klacht-indienen/eerdere-uitspraken/34376/ovk-aangegaan-voor-24-mnd-beeindigen-na-12-mnd. J.H. Wansink, 'Het KIFID en vervalbedingen: Verval van recht of recht in verval?' *AV & S* 2011, 17 has criticised the decisions of the committee on the resolution of disputes between consumers and providers of financial services, as inconsistent with case law on intentional deceit by consumers. See equally critically of the decisions of the Board with regard to information duties the note of D.P.C.H. Hellegers under Geschillencommissie Financiële Dienstverlening 11 April 2011, *TvC* 2011, p. 160. Similarly, Ch.E. Bethlem, 'Beslechting van consumentengeschillen: hoe alternatief zijn de alternatieven?' *TvC* 2006, p. 1 pointed out that inconsistencies between the decisions of ADR committees and judicial decisions are visible, as well as inconsistencies between the judicial decisions within the same court and between different courts. Also in this sense W.A. Jacobs, *ADR en consument, Een rechtsvergelijkende studie naar de mogelijkheden van alternatieve geschiloplossing*, Deventer: Kluwer 1998, p. 189.

1341 M.B.M. Loos, 'Individuele handhaving van het consumentenrecht', in: M.B.M. Loos, W.H. van Boom (eds.), *Handhaving van het consumentenrecht, preadviezen uitgebracht voor de Vereniging voor Burgerlijk Recht* 2009, Deventer: Kluwer 2010, p. 105–106. Similarly E. Bauw, 'Ruim baan voor de consument. Achtergronden en gevolgen van de verhoging van de competentiegrens van de kantonrechter', *TvC* 2010, p. 256.

1342 W.A. Jacobs, *ADR en consument*, Deventer: Kluwer 1998, p. 187–188.

1343 M.B.M. Loos, 'Verboden exoneraties in energieleveringsovereenkomsten en vernietiging van met de wet strijdige bindende adviezen', *TvC* 2006, p. 4–5.

1344 Comp. HR 24 March 1994, *NJ* 1995, 23.

1345 CJEU 6 October 2009 (Asturcom Telecomunicaciones SL v Cristina Rodríguez Nogueira), C-40/08, [2009] ECR p. I-0, par. 53.

1346 CJEU 27 February 2014 (Pohotovosť s. r. o. v Vašuta), C-470/12, [2014] ECR p. I-0, par. 42.

1347 H.J. Snijders, 'Arbitrage en/of bindend advies bij de SGC', *TvC* 2011, p. 3.

1348 Notably, the evaluation of the Committee, A. Klapwijk, M. ter Voert, *Evaluatie De geschillencommissie 2009*, available at www.wodc.nl, p. 12, shows that only 46% of consumers and 55% of businesses in a

business to a contract has to be a member of the branch affiliated with the committee, and the consumer has to choose to turn to the committee.[1349]

Fortunately, Directive 2013/11 on ADR for consumer disputes obliges Member States to make several of these adjustments. In particular, the Directive imposes some requirements on the independence of individuals handling disputes as well as the transparency of ADR systems, most of which seem to be already met by the Board. In addition, by allowing Member States to retain existing ADR systems, the European legislator prevents that an additional ADR system is established that is, subsequently, hardly used.

However, the Directive does not require decisions to be published,[1350] and article 17 par. 4 Directive stipulates that the duty of cooperation between authorities is without prejudice to provisions on commercial and professional secrecy. Also, the Directive does not require that the procedure takes the form of arbitration procedures, which may affect the cross-border enforcement of decisions, nor does the Directive consider the evaluation of ADR decisions by the courts.

Interestingly, the proposed Directive, as well as proposed Regulation 524/2013, though partially based on Dutch practice, prompted the Dutch Senate to submit a complaint on subsidiarity,[1351] which also considered the content of the draft Directive and Regulation.

The Dutch legislator has adopted a defensive approach in maintaining the law on STCs, assuming that it was of good quality. Although the Hoge Raad has prioritised maintaining the consistency of the law,[1352] its role has been undermined by the CJEU and active lower courts. The Dutch legislator has not exercised restraint in amending the BW, and Dutch courts have not carefully maintained the quality of the law on STCs by carefully following the Hoge Raad and one another's decisions. Rather, the approach of some courts seems directed at consumer protection, while other courts seem stubbornly opposed to ruling in favour of consumers. Perhaps because of these differences in lower courts case law, the approach of Dutch actors in the development of Directives is not as visibly aimed at safeguarding the quality of the law on STCs as German actors. The obligations between European and national actors therefore seem less oddly divided than is the case in the German legal order. However, differently than European actors, Dutch actors logically do not primarily aim to further harmonisation. This makes facilitating deliberation in order to enhance predictability, consistency, accessibility and responsiveness more difficult.

dispute in the framework of the *Geschillencommissie* considers the committee hearing their claim as independent.

1349 M.B.M. Loos, 'Individuele handhaving van het consumentenrecht', in: M.B.M. Loos, W.H. van Boom (eds.), *Handhaving van het consumentenrecht, preadviezen uitgebracht voor de Vereniging voor Burgerlijk Recht* 2009, Deventer: Kluwer 2010, p. 103.

1350 Unfortunately, problems with the consistent publication of ADR decisions seem more widespread, see C.M.D.S. Pavillon, 'Private standards of fairness in European contract law', *ERCL* 2014, p. 101.

1351 *Kamerstukken I*, 2011–2012, A. The senate doubted the need for an online platform and complained about the reallocation of costs, but also maintained that it was not convinced of the need to establish a competent entity on ADR through legislation, as the successful Dutch system was based on self-regulation rather than legislation. The Senate also criticised aspects of international private law, or the lack thereof, in the proposed Directive. See for the answer of the European Commission *Kamerstukken I*, 2011–2012, D.

1352 Especially after the report of Commissie normstellende rol van de Hoge Raad, *Versterking van de cassatierechtspraak*, 2009, available at www.minjus.nl. See further par. 8.3.1.

Interaction between actors will not improve if the approach of Dutch and European actors is not changed, even though the view of Dutch actors is less narrow than the view of German actors. The current approach of both Dutch and European actors falls short of deliberation. Rather than considering debate as something that should be won, and national political goals such as maintaining the level of consumer protection, or promoting maximum harmonisation, the aim of interaction should be to develop the law in a manner that is predictable, consistent, accessible and responsive.

Although this may entail that the legislative procedure at the European level is considerably lengthened, more and better debate between all relevant actors that are sufficiently representative is desirable. Arguably, more and better interaction may prevent that the application and the effect of Directives in practice remains invisible in the debate, or that the *acquis* will need to be readjusted shortly after it is developed.

5.7. Additional and alternative techniques

As Dutch actors have not generally recognised interdependence, they have not interacted to mitigate problems that can arise from interdependence. Although the use of techniques has not been considered in the context of the multilevel legal order and increasing interdependence between actors, new techniques have been developed. Interaction may be significantly improved through instances of new governance. Usually, techniques are used in combination with one another, and additional and alternative techniques may well contribute to benchmarks of predictability, consistency, accessibility and responsiveness. Therefore, this paragraph will ask what techniques could be used in addition to, or instead of currently used techniques. These techniques could be valuable in either improving debate, in accordance with the ideal of deliberation. In turn, this could enhance the law on STCs. The use of techniques in addition could compensate for the weaknesses of currently used techniques, for example by compensating for the top-down approach at the European level.[1353]

This paragraph will not separately reconsider additional and alternative techniques at the European level that have already been considered in detail in the previous chapter, in particular, the development of optional regimes and comparative research on STCs. The development of collective bargaining will be considered as actors in the Dutch legal order are familiar with the use of collectively bargaining STCs and raise less objections to this possibility than German actors. This paragraph will also not consider techniques that are not likely to contribute to the comprehensibility of European private law, such as the use of Regulations rather than Directives.[1354] In addition, this paragraph will not

1353 The characteristics of additional and alternative techniques more generally will be considered in chapter 10.

1354 See previously par. 4.7. Not only may the introduction of Regulations be problematic politically, the question also arises whether a Regulation would provide more clarity on the obligation of judges to address unfair terms *ex officio* and whether judges would be able to rely on previous case law or other sources in order to ensure that they decide cases in a consistent and predictable manner. Possibly, existing national case law already concerns the interpretation of harmonised law, but a Regulation may make clearer that it concerns European law rather than national law, which may prompt the judiciary

consider the use of the OMC, a technique that emphasises cooperation between actors to align their preferences.[1355] Arguably, the use of the OMC is not necessarily successful because of the weaknesses that have become apparent in the use of the OMC, in particular, the limited circle of debate.[1356] A lack of inclusiveness is already visible in Dutch debate. Rather than limiting debate, the debate should be widened.

The view of Dutch actors is not as narrow as the view of German actors that have stressed the *status quo*. The wider view is also visible in the participation of Dutch actors in the European debate. Because of this wider view, fewer suggestions for additional or alternative techniques have been excluded beforehand. Accordingly, maximum harmonisation has not been rejected, despite the emphasis on the need for a high level of consumer protection, and suggestions for comitology have not been immediately turned down. The wider view of Dutch actors can be traced to two characteristics: Dutch actors seem less opposed the alternative regulation.[1357] Consequently, there is more room for experimentation. Dutch actors are also less focused on maintaining the *status quo* as a way to ensure that the quality of the law on STCs remains high. Accordingly, this paragraph will consider techniques that may be more controversial in the German legal order:

i) The use of comitology
ii) The use of alternative regulation in the interpretation of blanket clauses
iii) The introduction of a prejudicial procedure
   An equivalent of the prejudicial procedure will not be found in the German legal order, as the amount of case law in the German legal order makes such a procedure quite unnecessary.
iv) The development of Guidance
   The development of Guidance has been suggested at the national level and considering current problems of inconsistency and unpredictability, these suggestions should at least be considered.

Paragraph 5.7.1 will focus on techniques to support the legislative process. Paragraph 5.7.2 will consider the DCFR and paragraph 5.7.3 will focus on techniques to support the extent to which blanket clauses can contribute to comprehensibility. Paragraph 5.7.4 will turn to the introduction of collective bargaining and paragraph 5.7.5 will end with a conclusion.

5.7.1. *Techniques supporting the European legislative process*

The use of consultations and impact assessments may well contribute to more and better debate on the development of the law on STCs, which, in turn, may prompt actors to critically reconsider the law on STCs and improve the law where necessary.

to reconsider relying on the legislative history of articles 6:231 et seq BW in the interpretation of these provisions. Theoretically, a Regulation may prompt the Hoge Raad to adopt a more active approach towards the harmonised interpretation of the law, especially if sufficient information on foreign decisions is available.

1355 See further par. 10.5.

1356 See prominently V. Hatzopoulos, 'Why the Open Method of Coordination is bad for you: A letter to the EU', *ELJ*, p. 325. See further par. 10.5.3.

1357 See previously par. 5.3.2. and below, par. 8.5.5.

A more consistent use of wider and more open consultations on European proposals, as well as the implementation of Directives once proposals have been accepted, could increase the participation of Dutch actors in the debate. More participation is beneficial as especially few Dutch stakeholders have directly participated in the debate at the European level. The participation of these actors may increase the chance that relevant insights are not overlooked in the debate at the European level, which should contribute to the responsiveness of the law.

Notably, this does require that parties do not provide brief responses, but participate in debate and respond to one another's comments, which currently does not seem to be the case in the European democratic process. Wider consultations may also contribute to the accessibility of the law.

The use of consultations may be supported by the improved use of impact assessments from the European level. In particular, the improved use of impact assessments entails that proposals from the Commission would be critically considered, asking whether there is a need for harmonisation and reform, whether the measure suggested is the most suitable way of dealing with problems for the internal market or consumer protection, as well as other European policy aims, or whether other techniques are available that should be used in addition to or instead of proposed measures. The improved use of impact assessments may also lead to more carefully considered choices for a particular combination of techniques.

Further, the use of impact assessments at the national level, possibly based on European consultations and impact assessments, would be consistent with Dutch calls for more empirical support for European measures.[1358] The Dutch legal order is not unfamiliar with empirical legal research that supports or criticises a proposal discussed in Parliament.[1359] The development of national impact assessments may also draw more attention to the use of techniques and the effect of the use of techniques at the European level on the development of national private law. Notably, however, the Commission need not necessarily take additional impact assessments into account.

The improved use of networks and databases may further support more thorough debate, by establishing more contacts between actors from different legal orders and between actors from different levels.[1360] This may encourage European actors to take note of discussions in national law. It may likewise encourage national actors to participate in European debate.

Rather than developing additional networks, European actors should make use of well-established national networks and databases, as these networks and databases

1358 See particularly the Dutch response to the Green Paper on the review of the consumer *acquis*, COM (2006) 744, available at http://ec.europa.eu/consumers/cons_int/safe_shop/acquis/responses, p. 4, 16, 17, 18.

1359 Legal sociological research on STCs includes F. Gras, *De sociale werkelijkheid van het standaardkontrakt: een rechtssociologisch onderzoek*, Amsterdam: Kobra 1979.

1360 Currently, for example, the Dutch Consumentenautoriteit is already involved in the International Consumer Protection and Enforcement Network (ICPEN), which in turn participates in the European Justice Forum (see http://europeanjusticeforum.org/faq/key-players/international-consumer-protection-and-enforcement-network.html), and cooperates with the OECD (see www.icpen.org/about.htm).

already contain a considerable pool of expertise and experience and developing additional networks may make it more difficult to keep track of relevant initiatives and contacts.

The improved use of databases, and the increased availability of foreign law decisions and relevant international materials might be interesting for Dutch actors, especially because of the shortcomings in Dutch law. The confusion of lower courts in international cases, however, demonstrates an increased need for guidance and direction. Therefore, networks and databases should not unlimitedly make new materials available – rather, databases should structure information on foreign and international developments and make relevant decisions more easily available.

The improved use of databases could be strengthened by a more consistent approach of the Hoge Raad to the use of foreign, European and international materials and a more active approach in developing guidelines to lower courts.

Dutch actors should seek to make their legal system more accessible to foreign actors through the improved use of databases.[1361] Especially for legal orders that use a language that is not easily accessible to all foreign actors, such as the Dutch legal order, this may contribute to accessibility and it would be in line with the Dutch legislator's focus on regulatory competition.

If Dutch actors do not provide comparative insights in their legal system, pessimistically, this may limit the accessibility of Dutch law to foreign parties to the Belgian and optimistically some German, Swiss, and Austrian actors. Generally, however, potential inaccessibility may also be mitigated by the Centre of International Legal Cooperation (CILC), a Dutch non-profit organisation supported by Dutch legal experts and practitioners that cooperates with foreign states in the development of private law.[1362]

In conclusion, the improved use of consultations, impact assessments, networks and databases may contribute to more and better interaction between Dutch, European, foreign and international actors.

5.7.2. *The development of the DCFR*

The previous chapter has argued that the DCFR diverges from the private law *acquis* and other soft laws in various respects, without clear or convincing justification for these divergences. This chapter will briefly discuss the differences of the DCFR from the *acquis* and other soft laws in paragraph 5.7.2.1. Paragraph 5.7.2.2 will consider the extent to which national experiences with the implementation of the *acquis* are reflected in the DCFR. Paragraph 5.7.2.3 will end with some concluding remarks.

1361 R. Zimmerman, 'The Principles of European Contract law Contemporary manifestation of the old, and possible foundation for a new, European scholarship of private law', in: F. Faust, G. Thüsing (eds.), *Beyond borders: perspectives on international and comparative law*, Berlin: Carl Heymanns Verlag 2006, p. 145 points to the commentary of D. Busch et al. (eds.), *The Principles of European Contract Law and Dutch law: A Commentary*, Nijmegen: Ars Aequi Libri 2002.

1362 See for an overview of activities www.cilc.nl/?q=node/16. See also J.M Smits, 'Import and export of legal models: The Dutch experience', *Transnational Law & Contemporary Problems* 2003, p. 551.

5.7.2.1. Divergences between the DCFR, the *acquis*, and other soft laws

The previous chapter has pointed to several differences and similarities:

- The DCFR diverges from the *acquis* in several respects: in the definition of unfairness, the main terms of the contract, and the rule that an intransparent clause for that reason alone may be unfair. In these cases, the DCFR has – rightly so – not been followed.

- In some cases, in particular with regard to the rules on making STCs adequately available, rules should be included in the successor of the CESL, as is also the case under the DCFR.

A model rule might have been especially valuable for the Dutch legal order, considering the implementation of Directive 2000/31 and Directive 2006/123.[1363] Unfortunately, the DCFR also does not consider the question of whether STCs have been made sufficiently available if they have been deposited at courts or trade registers.

Dutch authors have pointed out that inconsistencies can also be seen in the *acquis* which could and should have been addressed by the DCFR. Knigge[1364] has pointed to inconsistencies between Brussels I and the Directive, not only with regard to the fairness of jurisdiction clauses and article 23 Brussels I, but also with regard to the *ex officio* obligation and article 24 Brussels I. Moreover, questions on jurisdiction may arise after the implementation of Directive 2013/11 on ADR. Article 13 requires traders to inform consumers of the ADR systems that the trader complies with, which seems to entail that if a dispute arises and parties turn to ADR, the consumer will have to make use of the ADR system of the trader, which can be a foreign ADR system. The trader, in turn, is not obliged or encouraged to take notice of, or participate in, foreign ADR systems. Even if Regulation Brussel I is not applicable to ADR disputes that take the form of arbitration,[1365] this solution does not seem consistent with the protection of consumers in Brussels I.

The DCFR does pay specific attention to jurisdiction clauses. Article II – 9: 409 on jurisdiction clauses provides that jurisdiction clauses are unfair if the clause is supplied by the business and confers exclusive jurisdiction arising under the contract to the court of the place where the business is domiciled. The Comments indicate that Brussels I concerns the procedural admissibility of a clause, while apparently, the Directive considers the substantial fairness of the clause, considering the drafting of the clause, other provisions in the contract and other relevant circumstances.

Yet the DCFR does not address article 24 Brussels I and further diverges from article 17 Brussels I that sets out circumstances in which a choice for jurisdiction in consumer cases is

1363 Comp. Y. Schaub, 'De informatieplichten van de dienstenrichtlijn (art. 6:230a-f BW)', *TvC* 2014, p. 21 who analyses the overlap between information duties from Directive 2001/31 on e-commerce, Directive 2011/83 on consumer rights, Directive 2005/29 and points to the overlap and inconsistencies between these duties.

1364 M.W. Knigge, 'Tegenstrijdige Europese regelgeving? De verhouding tussen de EEX-Verordening en de Richtlijn oneerlijke bedingen', *MvV* 2012, p. 95.

1365 MuchKomm/ZPO – EUGVo/Gottwald (2013), article 1, nr 3. Gottwald, at nr 24, traces the exception to the existence of the New York Convention which made additional rules on arbitration unnecessary, but the same cannot be said of binding advice.

permitted. Article 17 par. 1 sets out that this is the case if the choice is made in an agreement after the conflict has arisen – thus, STCs in consumer contracts, concluded before a dispute has arisen, are not permitted under this paragraph. Article 17 par. 2 further provides that a choice that allows the consumer to bring claims before courts other than the courts mentioned in this section, are valid, while par. 3 provides that jurisdiction clauses opting for domestic courts are permitted for domestic contracts, insofar as this is permitted under national law.

Therefore, although the explanation in the DCFR may offer some perspective on the inconsistency between Brussels I and Directive 93/13, it fails to address all relevant points. In contrast to article 17 Brussels I, article 84 sub e withdrawn CESL determined that clauses granting exclusive jurisdiction to the place where the trader is domiciled, unless that is also the place where the consumer is domiciled, were always unfair.

- It has been argued that with regard to the definition of STCs, following the DCFR is problematic and should be reconsidered.

Dutch experiences may, however, provide a different perspective. The definition of standard terms in article II – 1:109 DCFR seems not particularly problematic, considering the largely similar definition of article 6:231 BW, as well as article 2 sub d of the withdrawn Regulation for a CESL and article 7 of the withdrawn CESL.

However, the DCFR leaves considerable room for uncertainty. Would a future proposal for a 1993 Directive also refer to multiple contracts, differently from article 30 of the proposed Directive? If this is not the case, do inconsistencies arise between a successor of the CESL and a future reformed Directive? Other inconsistencies include the rules on making STCs adequately available.

Accordingly, the added value of the DCFR in these cases may be questioned as it does not offer a solution for or prompt debate on inconsistent rules, but merely adds another rule. This may limit the extent to which it may play a role for the European legislator and the CJEU, and it may more generally limit the extent to which the DCFR contributes to the accessibility and consistency of the law on STCs.

However, a closer look at recent decisions from the Hoge Raad indicates that differences in overlapping soft laws need not necessarily withhold national courts from referring to these sets of soft law. Rather than clinging to that set of soft law rules, the Hoge Raad, or rather A.G. Wissink,[1366] has apparently considered the DCFR as an additional possibility to discuss cases. Lower courts have also started to refer to the DCFR, although not in cases with regard on STCs.[1367]

Although the DCFR may, therefore, still be interesting for courts, the extent to which it contributes to the predictability, consistency and accessibility of the law remains limited.

1366 Comp. the conclusion of A.G. Wissink to HR 11 May 2012, *NJ* 2012, 318 and the conclusion of A.G. Wissink to HR 19 November 2010, *NJ* 2010, 623. Interestingly, A.G. Wissink, in note 9 to his conclusion to HR 16 September 2011, *NJ* 2012, 56, noted that the DCFR did not offer comparative material as it restricted itself, in article III – 3:712 DCFR to general rules on penalty clauses.

1367 Ktr. 's-Hertogenbosch 24 June 2010, *LJN* BN0636, Rb. Zutphen 3 November 2010, *LJN* BQ0980.

5.7.2.2. The DCFR and national practice

According to Miller,[1368] the DCFR will likely draw interest from national highest courts, and generate judicial debate, which in turn will foster indirect effect. In addition, the DCFR provides a framework for discussion of academics and courts. The German case study has demonstrated that so far, this has not become reality. In Dutch law, the DCFR has also not generated extensive judicial debate, and its ability to do so depends not only on the question whether academics and judges are familiar with the form that the DCFR has taken.

The DCFR could have increased its added value for Dutch actors by considering the following questions:

- The question of whether the avoidability of the contract obliges the judiciary to evaluate these clauses *ex officio*, or whether the Directive should be reformed.

The reform of the Directive should make clear that unfair clauses are void, which would clarify this issue much more effectively than simply – but correctly – maintaining that it is not essential to elaborate on the ineffectiveness of a clause and CJEU case law has made clear that clauses are to be evaluated *ex officio*.[1369]

- The definition of the main terms of the contract

This definition may be valuable because of the emphasis of the Hoge Raad on the legislative history of articles 6:231 et seq BW and the definition of the main terms in insurance contracts.[1370]

- As Dutch law is less well-developed than German law, it may be more interesting for the Dutch legislator to look at the DCFR as a possible model. This is especially the case in areas where a consistent approach has not been developed throughout the Union, such as the rules on the battle of forms.

Thus, article II – 4:209 DCFR stipulates that parties need to expressly reject the applicability of STCs, not by way of STCs, while article 6:225 par. 3 BW stipulates that referral to the second set of STCs shall not lead to the application of that second set of STCs if the second referral does not expressly reject the applicability of the first set of STCs. Arguably, the rule in the DCFR does not make clear which party needs to expressly reject the STCs of the other party, while Dutch law encourages the first user of STCs to reject the applicability of STCs of other parties, thereby forcing the counterparty to expressly reject these terms. However, Dutch law does not generally provide that the converging terms will be applicable.

1368 L. Miller, *The emergence of EU contract law: Exploring Europeanization*, Oxford: OUP 2011, p. 206.

1369 Ch. Von Bar et al. (eds.), *Principles, Definitions and Model Rules of European Private Law. Draft Common Frame of Reference, Outline Edition, Volume I*, München: Sellier 2009, p. 655.

1370 HR 23 April 2010, *NJ* 2010, 454, see the conclusion of the A.G. under par. 3.20–3.21, as well as Hof Amsterdam 14 October 2008, *NJF* 2008, 481.

Accordingly, the comparative notes remark that the law in this area is unsettled in various Member States,[1371] which may increase the inclination of national actors to consider the DCFR as a possible model for law reform. The added value of the DCFR may however, be limited if it does not indicate why it prefers a specific rule or if it does not provide a clear rule. If national law in contrast does elaborately explain why it has opted for a particular solution, national legislators might be more convinced by national law than by the DCFR, which may then act as a starting point for comparing the diverging solutions throughout the Union rather than an inspiration by itself.

→ Thus, the DCFR has failed to take into account national experiences in the implementation of the Directive as well as possible points for reform at the national level. Thereby, it has limited its added value as a toolbox for national actors and European actors in the reform of Directive 93/13 and national law. However, the lack of debate on the divergences between national laws and soft laws has not withheld national actors to consider the DCFR.

5.7.2.3. Conclusion on the use of the DCFR as an additional technique

In the development of the DCFR, actors have not sufficiently taken into account national law. However, the DCFR does provide a clearly added value by providing specific rules on STCs. The lack of explanation for the preference for a specific solution has not entailed that national actors have ignored the DCFR. The added value of the DCFR would increase if more interaction with relevant actors takes place, and if there is more clarity on the role of the DCFR and the relation between different sources of law.

5.7.3. Techniques in addition to blanket clauses

Various techniques have been suggested to improve the extent to which blanket clauses contribute to predictability and consistency, even though blanket clauses do not necessarily aim to increase these benchmarks. Should these techniques be developed or not?

Paragraph 5.7.3.1 will consider the development of comitology, and paragraph 5.7.3.2 will discuss the development of guidelines. Paragraph 5.7.3.3 will turn to the prejudicial procedure and paragraph 5.7.3.4 will consider the use of alternative regulation. Paragraph 5.7.3.5 will end with a conclusion.

5.7.3.1. Comitology

The development of comitology, in accordance with article 40 of the proposal for a Directive on consumer rights, will undermine rather than strengthen the predictability, consistency, accessibility and responsiveness of the law on STCs and should, therefore, be rejected.

1371 Ch. Von Bar et al. (eds), *Principles, Definitions and Model Rules of European Private Law. Draft Common Frame of Reference, Outline Edition, Volume I*, München: Sellier 2009, p. 333.

Notably, the proposal to use comitology aimed for a more flexible development of model lists. The use of comitology in this respect complements hierarchical decision-making,[1372] contrary to arguments that comitology as a new mode of governance is less hierarchically oriented. The WODC report advised against this option, but the Dutch legislator did not consider comitology. The use of comitology may not be unacceptable as such in the Dutch legal order because article 6: 239 BW is reminiscent of comitology.

The introduction of comitology in this area may be problematic for the following reasons:

1) The introduction of comitology might undermine the consistency of the law.

If model lists developed through comitology are not indicative but binding, this would oblige the national legislator to implement the model lists. The clauses on the European model list could diverge from national default law, which might lead to inconsistencies.

Also, the binding character of the model lists would make it difficult for the legislator to maintain existing lists, which would limit the extent to which these lists contribute to the predictable interpretation of article 6:233 sub a BW in a manner consistent with national default law.

2) The use of comitology may not necessarily contribute to responsiveness; this depends on the composition of committees.

Typically, experts and practitioners as well as legal servants may take place in comitology committees. Yet there is still a chance that relevant stakeholders are not included. The limited participation and uneven representation in European consultations indicate that the participation of actors with relevant experience in a representative manner is not self-evident.

Arguably, the possibility that model lists will be developed more one-sidedly in the interest of particular stakeholder groups may increase as relevant stakeholders are not included and representation is uneven, which is especially undesirable as the clauses in the model lists may subsequently affect national default law.

Krisch[1373] finds that higher adaptability is an advantage, but he also remarks that actors should 'show the required disposition for responding to argument and exchanging experiences and knowledge'. This has not been the case in this area of law.[1374]

3) The development of the model lists by a comitology committee could decrease the stable and predictable development of the law on STCs

In particular, comitology could lead to multiple amendments to the model lists, which might not be beneficial for the stable development of the law. The stable and predictable development of the

[1372] Comp. Ch.F. Sabel, J. Zeitlin, 'Learning from difference: The new architecture of experimentalist governance in the EU', *ELJ* 2008, p. 275–276.

[1373] N. Krisch, *Beyond constitutionalism: The pluralist structure of postnational law*, Oxford: OUP 2010, p. 81.

[1374] See previously par. 5.3.3.4.

model lists may be undermined further if the procedures through which a comitology committee would draft the rules are not sufficiently transparent.

4) The use of comitology could decrease the accessibility of the law on STCs.

The possibility that the model lists could be subject to multiple changes might prompt the legislator to implement the model lists outside of the BW. However, this would lead to fragmented implementation where the provisions of the model lists would be scattered over multiple laws, which would not benefit the accessibility of the law. The accessibility of the law on this matter may decrease more generally if it is left to committees that contract parties as well as legal practitioners may not be familiar with.

→ These possible difficulties in the implementation of the model lists under a maximum harmonisation Directive indicate that the introduction of comitology is more compatible with the development of Regulations. However, the development of Regulations and comitology would leave very little room to the national legislator. The potential problems of implementation of the model lists make the introduction of comitology an unattractive option.

5.7.3.2. Guidance

The development of Guidance by the European Commission is not likely to contribute to predictability and consistency, and may inhibit the responsiveness of the law on STCs. Consequently, this option should be rejected.

The experiences with Guidance at the national level show that it is unlikely to contribute to predictability and consistency. The development of Guidance on the *ex officio* evaluation of clauses at the national level[1375] has not been reflected in lower courts' decisions. Courts have not consistently decided in accordance with the Guidance.[1376] The guidance was not easily reconcilable with decisions of the Hoge Raad at the time of the publications of the guidelines, and this has very likely severely undermined the strength of the guidelines. Thus, national guidelines may likely not contribute to consistency and predictability if the Hoge Raad decides differently.

Guidance has also been criticised as not representative and in some cases, too strict.[1377] Koek en Van de Laarschot,[1378] however, point to the development of successful Guidance in other areas and the careful process through which this Guidance is developed.

For the use of European Guidance, the following potential problems should be considered:

1375 Available at www.rechtspraak.nl/Procedures/Landelijke-regelingen/Sector civiel recht/Documents/EindrapportLOVCKwerkgroepambtshalvetoetsing_17210.pdf.

1376 Comp. Ktr. Rotterdam 4 May 2012, *LJN* BX4196, Ktr. Alkmaar, 4 July 2011, *LJN* BU2932, Ktr. Alkmaar 22 November 2010, *LJN* BO7959, Rb. Groningen 31 March 2010, *LJN* BM1402.

1377 P.E.M. Messer- Dinnissen en J. Tromp, 'Bestuurders van en Raad voor de rechtspraak: houdt het bij raad aan de rechtspraak', *NJB* 2010, 1014.

1378 M. Koek, M. van de Laarschot, 'Kanttekeningen bij een vermeende uitglijer', *NJB* 2010, 1464.

1) Guidance have so far not been successful.

Particularly, the development of guidelines for Directive 2005/29 and additional alternatives from The Netherlands Authority for the Financial Markets[1379] have not been visible in the decisions of Dutch courts.

2) The development of Guidance will not help the responsive development of the law, for which article 3 Directive was initially inserted in the Directive.

Particularly, it may be doubted whether Guidance would be based on national case law and ADR, because it is highly unlikely that the Commission is sufficiently familiar with these national sources and insights.

3) Although the development of Guidance may be in accordance with defences of regulatory private law,[1380] it may be difficult to reconcile with the idea how the law develops on the basis of common principles.

If this is the case, it can be doubted whether the Commission can uniformly decide what behaviour is in accordance with good faith; this may also depend on national practice and surrounding national default law.

4) Questions on the status and the content of the Guidance arise.

On the one hand, if Guidance is not binding, the question arises what role it will play in the development of law by the judiciary – the experience with the model list in the Annex to the Directive indicates that national state actors may adopt restraint towards these non-binding measures. On the other hand, if Guidance has a clear binding status and clearly developed rules, they may not be politically feasible as they may limit the room left for national judges to decide in accordance with national practice and national legal views in justice, as reflected by national law.

→ Thus, although the use of Guidance has been suggested to improve the predictable and consistent interpretation of national laws implementing article 3 Directive, a preliminary question that should be addressed is to what extent Guidance will undermine or contribute to the responsive development of the law. The extent to which Guidance may contribute to the comprehensibility of the law on STCs also depends on their status and content.

5.7.3.3. The prejudicial procedure

The introduction of the prejudicial procedure is based on a 2007 report on the task of the Hoge Raad and inspired by the European prejudicial procedure as well as French

1379 Available at www.afm.nl/~/media/files/wetten-regels/leidraad/norm-misleiding.ashx. The case law on article 6: 193b BW does not indicate that the guidance developed in the area of unfair practices has been used.

1380 See previously par. 4.5.2.

procedures. The drafting of the law was preceded by a public consultation and advice from practitioners and the judiciary.[1381] The introduction of the prejudicial procedure is likely to contribute to the predictability and consistency of the law on STCs if questions are referred to the Hoge Raad.

The legislator expressly considered the need to prevent inconsistent decisions in the introduction of the prejudicial procedure.[1382] Will answers to questions on the inclusion, availability and evaluation of STCs also contribute more generally to the development of the law? The inconsistent decisions of lower courts on STCs indicate that referring prejudicial questions might improve the consistency and legal unity of Dutch decisions. However, as lower courts generally do not refer to one another's decisions, they may not be aware of inconsistency and, therefore, not refer questions to the Hoge Raad. Neither parties nor judges have consistently shown much interest in elaborately referring to relevant sources, perhaps also because it concerns cases that seem relatively straightforward with a limited financial interest. Currently, questions on the law on STCs have not yet been referred to the Hoge Raad.[1383]

In addition, not all questions will be referred to the Hoge Raad.

Questions likely not to be referred to the Hoge Raad are:

i) Questions on the interpretation of clauses.
These questions often concern decisions that are partially also questions of fact, and the wording of article 392 par. 1 Civil Procedure Code indicates that courts can refer questions of law to the Hoge Raad. The legislator has, however, indicated that this should also include these so-called mixed questions of law and fact.[1384]
ii) Decisions of lower courts based on an incorrect understanding of articles 6:236 and 237 BW in relation to article 6:233 BW may not fall within the scope of article 392 Civil Procedure Code.

Other questions such as the question when judges could and should mitigate penalty clauses in accordance with article 6:94 BW,[1385] or questions whether arbitration clauses in consumer cases are necessarily unfair,[1386] could arguably have been included.

Prejudicial questions may also be asked if new legislation is introduced.[1387] It may, however, be doubted whether the implementation of a future reformed Directive will lead to prejudicial questions, especially if such implementation does not give rise to considerable amendments. Yet if the reform of the 1993 Directive on unfair terms results in a maximum harmonisation Directive, this may well affect the interpretation of article 6:233 sub a BW, even though this need not result in a change in the wording of article 6:233 sub a BW. In particular, the question of whether, and if so, to what extent

1381 *Kamerstukken II*, 2010–2011, 32612, nr 3, p. 1.
1382 *Kamerstukken II*, 2010–2011, 32612, p. 4.
1383 Currently Rb. Amsterdam 4 December 2012, *LJN* BY6220 and Rb. 3 August 2012, *NJ* 2012, 663.
1384 *Kamerstukken II*, 2010–2011, 32612, p. 10.
1385 HR 24 March 2006, *NJ* 2007, 115.
1386 HR 21 September 2012, *RvdW* 2012, 1132.
1387 *Kamerstukken II*, 2010–2011, 32612, nr 3, p. 4.

the CJEU is competent to interpret the successor to current article 3 Directive, may arise.

In addition, questions may arise after the 2013 decision of the Hoge Raad.[1388] For example, questions may arise with regard to the obligation of the judge in cases where consumers do not appear, or the scope of the dispute in appeal.

Will the prejudicial procedure lead to more CJEU decisions? This will not necessarily be the case as the possibility to refer questions to the Hoge Raad does not automatically mean that the Hoge Raad, in turn, will refer questions that have been referred to it by the CJEU. Perhaps, such referral is not in accordance with the aim of the legislator to establish a relatively quick procedure to determine questions of law.

Thus, the prejudicial procedure may well improve the predictability and consistency of the law on STCs, if judges decide to refer questions to the Hoge Raad.

5.7.3.4. Alternative regulation

If courts refer to alternative regulation, this will likely contribute to the responsiveness of the law to national practices and parties' views in justice.

Self-regulation may contribute to the comprehensibility of the law on STCs in various ways:

1) Judges may take into account that STCs in consumer contracts have been collectively negotiated in their evaluation of the STCs under article 6: 233 sub a BW.

The Hoge Raad[1389] has stressed the importance of parties involved in collective negotiations in articles 6:231 et seq BW and indicated that the negotiations between representative parties is a circumstance that is relevant for assessing the fairness of clauses. Some decisions of lower courts, as well as ADR, already indicate that this is a circumstance that may be taken into account.[1390] This need not necessarily mean that judges should generally uphold collectively negotiated STCs – however, it is a relevant perspective and in accordance with predictability to enable users that have collectively negotiated STCs to rely on them. Yet it is also necessary to evaluate these clauses, if only because consumers subjected to these STCs have generally not had the opportunity to affect these clauses.[1391] Also, the evaluation of article 6:233 sub a BW is an individual assessment that should take relevant individual circumstances into account.

1388 HR 13 September 2013, *NJ* 2014, 274.

1389 HR 3 February 2012, *NJ* 2012, 261, par. 4.4.5.

1390 See for example Hof 's-Hertogenbosch 9 August 2011, *LJN* BR6638, Rb. Arnhem 30 December 2009, *RCR* 2010, 26, Ktr. 's-Gravenhage 5 August 2009, *NJF* 2009, 460, Hof; 's-Hertogenbosch 5 August 2003, comp. also Hof 's-Hertogenbosch 10 January 2006, *NJF* 2006, 261, for STCs agreed between an energy company and a small company, and differently Rb. Arnhem 5 November 2008,*LJN* BG4492. For more restraint see Rb. Amsterdam 24 March 2010, *TvA* 2011, 27.

1391 C.M.D.S. Pavillon, 'Private standards of fairness in European contract law', *ERCL* 2014, p. 112 points out that it is problematic to rely on customs alone, as Dutch courts sometimes do, as this does not prevent that standards developed by businesses, who have not taken into account consumers' interests, are decisive.

2) Judges may take into account codes of conduct that contradict clauses in the STCs.

This would also be in line with article 6 Directive 2005/29, and if consumers have relied on codes in entering into contracts, consumers could arguably justifiably have done so, in line with article 3:35 BW. It is not clear to what extent users of STCs actually do so, and whether courts would not already consider provisions in codes of conduct, in accordance with article 6 Directive 2005/29. Simultaneously, the CJEU[1392] has made clear that the inclusion of STCs as developed by professional organisations did not mean that those clauses did not fall within the scope of the Directive or did not have to be assessed.

Thus, courts have already recognised the added value of alternative regulation in the interpretation of blanket clauses.

5.7.3.5. Conclusion on the use of techniques in addition to blanket clauses

The extent to which article 6:233 sub a BW contributes to the predictability and consistency of the law has been severely undermined by the lack of interaction between courts. Particularly, the development of the prejudicial procedure and a more consistent use of alternative regulation in the interpretation may contribute to predictability and consistency. The use of alternative regulation also strengthens the responsive development of the law on STCs.

The suggestions in Dutch debate indicate that Dutch actors have more interest in new governance. The debate could offer starting points for the Dutch legislator to consider the desirability of new governance alongside the future revision of Directive 93/13. However, the development of comitology and Guidance are not likely to strengthen the law on STCs.

5.7.4. The development of collective negotiations

It is not clear whether the development of collective negotiations on STCs at the transnational level will contribute to the predictability and the responsiveness of the law on STCs.

There have been suggestions in Dutch literature to transpose the successful collective negotiations on STCs to the European level. This would increase the extent to which users of STCs take into account the interests of consumers, while it would also facilitate transnational trade.[1393] Possibly, organisations from different Member States where parties are familiar with collective negotiations, such as The Netherlands and Germany, may develop cross-border collective negotiations.

Transposing this model to the European level would entail the development of a European organisation as an equivalent to the the Social Economic Council ('*Sociaal*

1392 CJEU 15 February 2015 (Šiba v Arūnas Devėnas), C-537/13, [2015] ECR p. I-0, par. 29.
1393 A.G. Castermans, 'Towards a European contract law through social dialogue', *ERCL* 2011, p. 366.

Economische Raad').[1394] It can be doubted to what extent European institutions such as the European Economic and Social Council, currently provide a platform, and whether stakeholder groups are sufficiently organised and willing to develop collectively negotiated STCs at the European level. The question arises whether these stakeholder groups would represent national stakeholder groups throughout the Union, or whether it would be European stakeholder groups selected by the Commission.

However, collective negotiations still leave room for differences that may inhibit trade. If collective negotiations result in European STCs, they might still be interpreted differently throughout the Union. Additional difficulties would arise if STCs can set aside consumer protection laws throughout the Union. Possibly, introducing a European equivalent of three-quarter mandatory law ('*Tarifdispositives Gesetzesrecht*', or '*driekwart dwingend recht*') would provide a solution. It is, however, not clear whether there is political support for this form of mandatory law and collectively negotiated STCs would still be subject to judicial evaluation.

However, the success of this option depends on the capability and the willingness of private actors. Currently, it has not become apparent that there is much cooperation across borders between different stakeholder organisations, which would, however, be necessary. This depends on the capability and the willingness of private actors. The desirability and feasibility of this option further depends on the equal positions of parties and representativeness of parties and the inclusiveness of the process, which should be evaluated at the national level.

Thus, although cross-border collective negotiations would be an interesting development that could increase the responsive and predictable development of the law on STCs in cross-border trade, it need not necessarily be successful as clauses would still be evaluated differently in the Dutch and German legal order and the willingness and capacity of representative parties to enter into inclusive collective negotiations should also not be presumed.

5.7.5. *Conclusion on the use of additional and alternative techniques*

Which techniques in addition to or instead of currently used techniques are likely to contribute to the predictability, accessibility, consistency and responsiveness of the law on STCs?

Techniques that may be successful are the improved use of consultations, impact assessments, databases and networks, as well as the new Dutch prejudicial procedure and the use of alternative regulation in the evaluation of blanket clauses. Techniques discussed in the previous chapter, in particular, the study of the use of STCs, may also be beneficial.

[1394] This is an influential advisory organisation established to involve stakeholders in the decision-making process. It provides an independent framework for the Coordination Group on Negotiations for Self-regulation ('*Coordinatiegroep Zelfreguleringsoverleg*') for the collective negotiations on STCs, on which see further par. 8.5.1.2.

In contrast, notwithstanding arguments that these techniques facilitate the development of deliberation, it is not clear that the development of comitology procedures and the development of Guidance will strengthen the law on STCs. In contrast, it is more likely that these initiatives will be detrimental for the predictable, consistent, accessible and responsive development of the law on STCs through blanket clauses.

It is similarly not clear whether the development of collective bargaining and the development of the prejudicial procedure will strengthen comprehensibility. The potential of a successor of the CESL also depends on the initiative of private parties and lower courts.

Because of the differences between legal orders, additional or alternative techniques that may not work in some legal orders may still be interesting for other legal orders. The lack of success of article 6:214 BW can be explained by the success of overlapping self-regulation. In legal orders where similarly successful self-regulation is absent, initiatives such as article 6:214 BW may well be less unsuccessful, especially in legal orders where a need for more flexibility has been expressed, but where little self-regulation has developed, or where objections against self-regulation exist. Conversely, successful initiatives may not be similarly successful if they are transferred to other legal orders. Accordingly, the use of alternative regulation for the interpretation of blanket clauses may be problematic in legal orders where alternative regulation has hardly developed, or where important objections, such as objections to a potential a lack of private autonomy, in the German legal order also considered as *Fremdbestimmung*,[1395] have developed against this approach. Likewise, collective bargaining may not be as successful as in the Dutch legal order if this form of self-regulation is transferred to legal orders that limit the scope and effect of collectively negotiated rules, or that have little experience with collective bargaining.

The various suggestions for additional techniques may well overlap and reinforce one another. Particularly, the improved use of databases and networks may well support the improved use of consultations.

As European actors have preferred a hierarchical approach without combining top-down techniques with bottom-up techniques that have usually accompanied these top-down techniques, the suggestions in this chapter imply a shift towards a more bottom-up approach. If impact assessments become more critical, the possibility of developing bottom-up techniques before developing more top-down alternatives may be considered. Notably, the success of these options, and the success of bottom-up techniques in addition to top-down techniques, depends on the participation of non-state actors. However, parties in the area of STCs have shown considerable initiative.

5.8. Conclusion

Dutch law is not considered as a clear success, but nor has it been described as a failure. Interdependence between actors has clearly developed, more visibly than in the German legal order. Particularly, interdependence between the legislator and the courts has

1395 See further par. 7.1.

become more visible than in the German legal order as the restraint of courts has lessened the extent to which article 6:233 sub a BW limits the need for legislative intervention. Interdependence between national and European actors is also more outspoken than in the German legal order. The diminished ability of the BW to ensure predictable development of law became clearer as the legislator was obliged to amend article 6:238 BW in the newly introduced BW. Similarly, the decreased ability of codes to ensure the predictable development of the law as well as consistency has been compromised as multiple Directives resulted in multiple amendments and inconsistency between articles 6:230c and 6:234 BW. Additionally, the decreased ability of blanket clauses to ensure consistency and responsiveness have become clear as lower courts have ceased to consistently follow the Hoge Raad, and some courts have started following the CJEU instead. Notwithstanding increased interdependence, Dutch actors have not recognised interdependence in the use of national techniques, and they have not interacted accordingly. Can problems be traced to a lack of interaction between interdependent actors, in accordance with multilevel governance perspectives?

Arguably, the problems in the law on STCs can also be seen in the light of unpredictability and inconsistency that may more generally accompany recodification and the introduction of a new blanket clause. In comparison with German law, Dutch law was relatively abruptly introduced, rather than developed and finetuned through case law. A lack of interaction has aggravated the weaknesses in Dutch law. Particularly, the restraint of courts under article 6:233 sub a BW is problematic, and combined with a lack of interaction between lower courts, the Hoge Raad and the CJEU, it has led to inconsistency and unpredictability. In addition, the success of the Board in adjudicating consumer disputes beyond the courts has stood in the way of the visible development of the law. Additionally, in some areas, cases that require clarification, such as the obligation of courts to make STCs available in international cases, have not come before the Hoge Raad, which limits the extent to which the Hoge Raad can provide guidance.

Further, problems with regard to the development of the law on STCs that have become visible in the German legal order also become visible in the Dutch legal order. The restraint of the legislator and the courts in implementing and applying the Directive, and the restraint in referring cases to the CJEU is likely to undermine the revision of the Directive in line with the experiences with the Directive at the national level. Like in the German legal order, a circle of non-interaction may develop.

However, before the implementation of Directive 2013/11 on consumer ADR, the approach of the Dutch legislator in the implementation of the *acquis* seems more predictable than the strategy of the German legislator, who has not consistently implemented the private law *acquis* within the BGB. Unlike the German legislator, the Dutch legislator has not based its approach on the characterisation of Directives as *Sonderprivatrecht*, nor has the stable and consistent development of private law been considered in so many words. The implementation of Directive 93/13 in article 6:231 et seq BW, followed from the new structure of the BW, whereas the structure of the BGB indicates a more fragmented approach, which may also make the accessible implementation of the *acquis* more challenging for the German legislator. Simultaneously, it is likely that the implementation of Directive jeopardises the predictability, consistency and accessibility of the BW. While the Dutch legislator, like the German legislator, takes national law as a starting point in the European debate, the debate preceding the adoption of Directives shows shortcomings and Dutch representative non-state actors rarely participate in European debate.

Simultaneously, the coexistence of actors has led to a system of checks and balances, regulatory competition and mutual learning, but this has not consistently benefited the comprehensibility of the law.

The development of a limited system of checks and balances, though more visible in the Dutch than in the German legal order, has not contributed to better law. The narrow approach of Dutch actors has entailed that Dutch actors have maintained their approach. Despite the availability of comparative insights in the European debate, the Dutch legislator has not considered these insights to critically revise national law, which may also raise the question whether participation of foreign and international actors in national debate would prompt the Dutch legislator to take the interests of these actors into account in developing the law. However, the coexistence of national regimes, at least with regard to consumer contracts, is likely beneficial in terms of responsiveness.

Regulatory competition has not led to innovation. While English law inspired the Dutch legislator to develop a lenient regime towards international business contracts, there are gaps in the law that have not been addressed. The inclusion of a blanket clause implies an important role for case law, which is not beneficial in terms of accessibility for foreign and international parties, and the approach of the courts has further undermined the attractiveness of Dutch law.

Mutual learning has not consistently improved the law. German law served as a source of inspiration for the Dutch legislator, but it has not been transplanted into Dutch law. Rather, the Dutch legislator has developed the Dutch law on STCs in accordance with newly adopted surrounding national law and national problems. Yet problems have arisen with regard to Dutch rules that diverge from the German regime. However, as Dutch actors have adopted a narrow, national perspective and have not critically reflected on Dutch law or possibilities to enhance the law. Thus, opportunities to improve the law, in accordance with pluralist perspectives, have not been used.

Harmonisation has not stopped the legislator from amending the law, as the revisions of articles 6:236 and 237 BW indicate. The legislator has been inspired by the Annex to the Directive, as well as English and French law. The diminished role of the Hoge Raad entails that the amendment of the Dutch model lists, as inspired by comparative law, may well contribute to consistency and predictability more effectively than decisions from the Hoge Raad would have done. Harmonised law, which should have developed as a transplant, albeit an atypical one, in accordance with European actors' wishes, has been simultaneously rejected and integrated in Dutch law.

Dutch courts have shown less restraint in interacting with international and foreign actors in deciding cases under international regimes than German courts. However, courts have not done so consistently and predictably. The Hoge Raad has not provided guidelines for the use of foreign and international material, but if it did, one may ask whether lower courts would consistently follow these guidelines.

These problems accentuate the diminished ability of national actors to ensure the predictability, accessibility, consistency and responsiveness of the law through the development of national techniques. As Dutch state actors have not recognised interdependence, they have insufficiently considered the use of additional and alternative techniques that may mitigate problems. This is regrettable also because there is more room for experimentation in the Dutch legal order than in the German legal order. There are also more possibilities to compensate for shortcomings and solve problems. Dutch academics have suggested the use of alternative techniques, particularly expert committees and collective bargaining, to be used in the development of the law. Moreover, the Dutch legislator has introduced the prejudicial procedure that may enhance the predictable and consistent interpretation of blanket clauses, which has also benefited from the example of the European procedure and French law.

The changes suggested in this chapter are not only long-term changes. Courts should adopt a more active approach, and the law on the availability of STCs, especially in international cases, as well as the rules on unduly surprising clauses, should be reconsidered.

Chapter 6

MULTILEVEL GOVERNANCE AND PLURALIST PERSPECTIVES ON THE DEVELOPMENT OF THE LAW ON STCs AND EUROPEAN PRIVATE LAW

6.1. Introduction

The case studies have focussed on the development of the law on STCs in the German and Dutch legal order through codifications, blanket clauses and general principles. In the development of this area of law, interdependence has become apparent. Is the success of the German regime on STCs reflected in sufficient interaction between interdependent actors, in accordance with multilevel governance insights, and can the high quality of the German law on STCs also be attributed to the coexistence of actors, in accordance with pluralist perspectives? Conversely, can the problems in the Dutch law on STCs be traced to a lack of interaction between interdependent actors, in accordance with discourse on multilevel governance? Can its strong points also be attributed to the coexistence of actors, in accordance with pluralist arguments?

This chapter will consider the findings of the case studies in the light of multilevel governance and pluralist perspectives more generally and ask whether the coexistence of actors in the development of European private law is, theoretically, more generally problematic or beneficial.

Paragraph 6.2. will turn to multilevel governance perspectives and paragraph 6.3 will discuss pluralist perspectives. Paragraph 6.4. will draw a conclusion and sketch the outlay of the book, highlighting what questions will be considered in the light of the findings of the case studies.

6.2. Multilevel governance perspectives

The case studies have indicated that interdependence has developed and will likely become more visible as the aims of national and European actors diverge more clearly. In accordance with debate on multilevel governance more generally, actors are no longer able to independently safeguard the comprehensibility of the law through the use of national techniques.

The case studies support the view that the aims of European and national actors diverge, as national actors generally do not prioritise further harmonisation of national private law. The difference between European and German actors is most outspoken as German actors clearly and consistently target maintaining the quality of national law.

The aims of national and European state actors diverge especially if state actors do not perceive problems in the law, both in German and Dutch legal order. Notably, despite criticism at the national level, Dutch actors have not aimed to critically consider the quality of the law.

In the light of these diverging priorities, interdependence between European and national state and non-state actors may become more outspoken.[1396]

The diverging aims of national and European actors and interdependence between actors can be detected in the implementation of Directives. National legislators have adopted restraint in the implementation of Directives, in order to preserve the comprehensibility of the law on STCs. The BGH and the Hoge Raad followed this restraint, possibly to maintain the consistency and predictability of national law.[1397] Nevertheless, the predictable, stable development of Dutch law, exposed to repeated amendments, has been diminished, and national actors have also become less capable to independently ensure the consistent, responsive interpretation of blanket clauses.

The failed revision of Directive 93/13, as well as possible challenges to future measures[1398] can likewise be seen in the light of interdependent actors pursuing different aims. In addition, the case studies have demonstrated that European actors depend on national actors to revise the law in a sufficiently responsive manner. More generally, interdependence has been recognised at the European level. Cafaggi[1399] has argued that European actors have also begun to distinguish between actors at the national level, recognising the interdependence between national actors. The dependence of European actors on national judges has also become visible.[1400]

However, the ability of state actors to hinder the revision of the law, though substantial, may become limited. For example, non-state actors may also provide information to European decision-makers that enables them to revise the law accordingly. Non-state actors may alert the Commission of violations. Information may further be provided through other non-state actors' initiatives such as the DCFR or studies of the use of STCs in a cross-border context. Such initiatives, especially if they precede harmonisation developing a functional approach, are hardly appealing to national legislators. Yet national actors cannot stop European actors from exploring these decisions. These new modes of governance thus compensate the dependence of European actors on national actors and facilitate decision-making in a multi-level legal order. Yet for the adoption of proposals, support from national actors is still necessary, and if the European legislator maintains its approach to the revision of Directive 93/13, pursuing maximum harmonisation and comitology, this may eventually not benefit the quality of the law on STCs. So far, however, the European legislator has not explored possibilities that do not imply a top-down approach.

The different perspectives of national and European actors in addition raise the question whether "diagonal conflicts" arise.[1401] Yet the agreement on the problems that should be solved by

1396 F.W. Scharpf, *Governing in Europe: Effective and democratic?*, Oxford: OUP 1999, p. 191.

1397 See previously par. 4.3.2.3 and par. 5.3.3.3.

1398 Comp. J.J. Kuipers, 'The legal basis for an optional instrument', *ERPL* 2011, p. 545.

1399 F. Cafaggi, 'Introduction', in: F. Cafaggi (ed), *The Institutional Framework of European Private Law*, Oxford: OUP 2006, p. 17.

1400 H. Collins, 'Governance implications for the European Union of the changing character of private law', in: F. Cafaggi, H. Muir-Watt (eds.), *Making European private law: Governance implications*, Cheltenham: Elgar 2008, p. 272.

1401 Ch. Joerges, 'On the legitimacy of Europeanising private law: Considerations on a justice-making law for the EU multi-level system', *Electronic Journal of Comparative Law* 2003, available at www.ejcl.org/ejcl/73/art73-3.html, par. III.1.1.

harmonisation is not clear. From a European perspective, the existence of diagonal conflicts is a convincing analysis. For example, Directives aim to increase consumer confidence through harmonisation and accordingly frequently impose information duties on professional parties. Simultaneously, European measures rely on national contract law for the enforcement of these duties. In addition, the question when the consumer has received information from the professional, and the question when a contract has been formed, is a question generally answered by national contract laws. Whereas European actors are competent to develop information duties, competence with regard to general contract law remains at the national level. Thus, diagonal conflicts develop. However, from the national perspective, such conflicts are less clearly visible. As national private law need not directly pursue a specific aim, or solve a particular problem, it does not become immediately apparent how European actors have contributed towards pursuing these aims or addressing these problems. European actors do not seem to target the quality of private law regimes, and the perspective of German and Dutch actors seems to support the view that European actors may contribute to the quality of these regimes by not overly interfering with them. From a national perspective, problems may arise if transnational trade lessens the attractiveness of national regimes, and harmonisation may accordingly be promoted by national actors wishing to avoid a "race to the bottom".

Interdependence between courts in the multilevel legal order has become apparent especially in the Dutch legal order, as the role of the Hoge Raad in preserving the consistency of Dutch law has become compromised. The role of the BGH is less compromised as lower courts consistently follow the BGH. Notwithstanding the role of the BGH, however, German lower courts have referred questions to the CJEU. Both the BGH and the Hoge Raad have responded to these initiatives. Whereas the BGH has referred questions to the CJEU itself rather than leaving such questions to lower courts, the Hoge Raad has sought to take back control more directly in its 2013 decision.

Increased interdependence has also become visible between national actors whose aims do not diverge as visibly.

Interdependence between the national legislators and the courts in regulatory competition has become visible. Accordingly, the German rejection of regulatory competition may be compensated somewhat by the approach of national courts to international and foreign materials. In contrast, the Dutch attempt to make Dutch law attractive to international contract parties may be undermined by Dutch courts who have failed to consistently take into account foreign and international materials, while especially lower courts decide cases unpredictably and inconsistently.

Interdependence has also become visible between the legislators and courts in the development of the law through blanket clauses. Without an active approach of national courts, blanket clauses and codifications are less able to safeguard the stable development of the law, and the legislator may need to amend the law more frequently.

Interdependence has also developed between state and non-state actors. This is clearly visible in the Dutch legal order.

Dutch courts have taken a lenient approach towards clauses developed through collective negotiations. Furthermore, the Dutch experience with article 6:214 BW demonstrates that attempts to rein in self-regulation should not subsequently leave open more lenient routes for non-state actors, as non-state actors may reduce such initiatives to dead letters. This experience should be kept in mind when debating the development of additional or alternative techniques that rely upon non-state actors.

Yet the influence of non-state actors is limited: although non-state actors have developed sets of soft law, parties cannot opt to apply these sets of law to their contract under the Rome I Regulation,[1402] nor does international private law allow contract parties to avoid mandatory law, especially in consumer contracts. Also, non-state actors cannot independently push states towards regulatory competition. Interestingly, the German private initiative indicates that German actors remain focussed on legislation rather than alternative techniques that allow them to circumvent the German regime with regard to STCs. Ultimately, the extent to which non-state actors exercise influence depends on state actors' willingness to take non-state actors initiatives into account, and forms of alternative regulation successful (such as the VOB) or accepted (such as collectively negotiated STCs) in one legal order, may be unsuccessful or unacceptable in other legal orders. State actors may be especially inclined to take alternative regulation into account if non-state actors provide rules in highly complex areas or if they adequately reflect legitimate needs in (international) practice.

Despite the potential role of non-state actors, national state actors, especially in the German legal order, remain focussed on the development of private law through national techniques. Importantly, these techniques can hardly be replaced, but they have not been sufficiently amended or complemented with additional techniques.

At the European level, the use of additional and alternative techniques has similarly been overlooked, even though there is much more room for experimentation in the absence of a traditional, binding codification. Instead, top-down, hierarchical techniques have played a central role in the development of European private law. The suggestions for and the use of Regulations in the private law *acquis*, and the use of maximum harmonisation can be seen in this light.[1403] This preference may be institutionally embedded at the European level, perhaps because the conferral of competences takes the European institutions as a starting point and suggestions and initiatives take place within the existing framework of these institutions. The preference for top-down techniques is more generally echoed by non-state actors.[1404] However, hard law may not necessarily be successful.[1405] Actors' expectations about the extent to

1402 R. Michaels, 'Umdenken für die UNIDROIT-Prinzipien. Vom Rechtswahlstatut zum Allgemeinen Teil des Transnationalen Vertragsrechts', *RabelsZ* 2009, p. 871 adds that even if parties could choose existing sets of soft law to their contract, soft laws such as UNIDROIT, the PECL and the DCFR are still based on national laws.

1403 More generally, the European Commission, *European governance: A White Paper*, COM (2001) 428 final prefers a hierarchical approach.

1404 See, for example, M. Storme, 'The foundations of private law in a multilevel structure: Balancing, distribution of lawmaking power, and other constitutional issues', *ERPL* 2012, p. 249, this preference has also been signalled by P. Buck-Heeb, A. Dieckmann, *Selbstregulierung im Privatrecht*, Tübingen: Mohr Siebeck 2010, p. 230.

1405 Comp. also H.-J. Mertens, 'Nichtlegislatorische Rechtsvereinheitlichung durch transnationales Wirtschaftsrecht und Rechtsbegriff', *RabelsZ* 1992, p. 219. This, for example, becomes visible from the late implementation of Directives, the restraint of some national judges in referring to European law or the CJEU, or the creation of precontractual duties in, for example, the field of consumer credit, which makes it more difficult for consumers to determine the costs of online credit, see the 2011 consumer credit sweep at http://ec.europa.eu/consumers/enforcement/sweep/consumer_credits/index_en.htm.

which these hierarchical techniques contribute to benchmarks may be overly optimistic, especially if the existence of other actors is not taken into account. Expectations should be adjusted accordingly. The lack of attention for bottom-up instruments limits the extent to which harmonisation currently contributes to the comprehensibility of law.

From a European perspective, the study of STCs in cross-border trade is interesting. The improved use of consultations, impact assessments and networks could also contribute to better law. Further, in the Dutch legal order, the use of alternative regulation in the interpretation of blanket clauses could prove advantageous. In addition, if the DCFR pays more attention to inconsistent measures within the private law *acquis* and national experiences with the implementation of Directives, it could become a valuable source of inspiration for European and national actors in the revision of the *acquis*.

National actors may resist the development of techniques that will diminish the comprehensibility of national law, such as comitology. National actors will likewise resist techniques that will reduce the role of codifications, such as the use of Regulations, and techniques that may result in further harmonisation, such as the study of the use of STCs in cross-border trade. However, if sufficient Member States agree with the introduction of for example comitology, German and other national actors may find that they have lost control of the development of European law and they may also not stop the European legislator from exploring, for instance, the use of Regulations, the study of STCs, or the development of Guidance.

Despite increasing interdependence, neither German nor Dutch actors have considered the decreased ability of national techniques to ensure the comprehensibility of the law. Accordingly, they have not taken interdependence as a starting point in their interaction with other actors or in the development of the law through national techniques.

Especially in the German legal order, actors have adopted a defensive approach to preserve the high quality of the law on STCs, which may limit problems that may arise from interdependence. In the implementation of Directives, both legislators and judiciaries have adopted restraint.[1406] This minimalist approach is visible more broadly with regard to the implementation[1407] and the interpretation[1408] of the private law *acquis*. It has been argued that this restraint, including the restraint with regard to foreign

1406 Interestingly, courts in other Member States have also shown restraint in referring cases to the CJEU, see M. Kenny, 'The Law Commissions' 2012 Issues Paper on unfair terms: subverting the system of Europeanised private law?' *ERPL* 2013, p. 880.

1407 N. Reich, 'The implementation of Directive 93/13/EEC on unfair terms in consumer contracts in Germany', *ERPL* 1997, p. 172.

1408 B. Hess, 'Rechtsfragen des Vorabentscheidungsverfahrens', *RabelsZ* 2002, p. 479 notes that the restraint of the BGH is especially visible in the law on STCs, but also notes this inclination more widely, pointing out that the decision of the BVerfG 9 January 2001, *NJW* 2001, 1267 may not lead to a different approach. He contrasts this restraint with the approach of courts in civil procedure law. Interestingly, Dutch courts seem to have referred more questions to the CJEU on matters of intellectual property law and private international law than other areas of private law, although M.V. Polak, 'Verwijzen is zilver, zwijgen is goud?' in: A.G. Castermans et al (eds.), *Het zwijgen van de Hoge Raad, BWKJ 25*, Deventer: Kluwer 2009, p. 89 notes that some restraint is visible in the decisions of the Hoge Raad.

decisions, contributes to the nationalisation of international regimes.[1409] Possibly, in other areas, where German law has been less successfully developed, clashes may become more visible as German actors are less able to rely on a successful regime. The Dutch experience indicates that in these cases, a defensive approach might well undermine the quality of private law.[1410]

In other Member States, a more critical view on national law has been developed, and there has been more emphasis on the need to amend the law.[1411] The findings in chapters 4 and 5 indicate that harmonisation initiatives in areas that are considered successful, or not in need of improvement, may meet with a defensive approach from national actors. Nevertheless, in some of these areas, European initiatives have become visible.[1412]

A narrow perspective is also visible at the European level. The careful avoidance of potentially controversial terms, such as an optional instrument or a contract code, and especially criticism of seemingly structural shortcomings in the European legislative process in this area[1413] demonstrates that European actors are not particularly open for diverging national insights. In addition, the problems upon which European measures are based, particularly problems for the internal market or consumer protection, are not necessarily shared at the national level, remain rather vague and lack consistent, convincing empirical support.[1414] The approaches of European and national actors may unfortunately reinforce one another, which may further decrease the chance that the reform of the *acquis* will take into account relevant insights. As a result, the European legislative process may start resembling the 'Hayekian nightmare' as described by Sabel and Cohen:[1415] a 'pure bargaining democracy in which legislative decision-making is under no pressure to be deliberative, and hence under no pressure to explore improved solutions, or even to meet minimal conditions of coherence and efficiency. Outcomes will simply reflect the balance of political forces, with no obligation to consider how

1409 J. Basedow, 'Der Bundesgerichtshof, seine Rechtsanwälte und die Verantwortung für das europäische Privatrecht', in: G. Pfeiff er, J. Kummer, S. Scheuch (eds.), *Festschrift fur Hans Erich Brandner zum 70. Gerburtstag*, Köln: Schmidt 1996, p. 655.

1410 In contrast to the conclusion of N. Krisch, *Beyond constitutionalism: The pluralist structure of postnational law*, Oxford: OUP 2010, p. 248 that national actors may be more open to debate and changes if their views are less settled. However, even if the law is not as successful as the German law on STCs, the development of that particular area of law has likely shaped national actors' views, thereby making them less open for debate.

1411 Comp. the initiative in the UK to reform the law on unfair contract terms, see particularly the Law Commissions, 2012 Issues paper, Unfair terms in consumer contracts: A new approach, 25 July 2012, http://lawcommission.justice.gov.uk/docs/unfair_terms_in_consumer_contracts_issues.pdf.

1412 For example, Directive 2014/17 on mortgage credit.

1413 W. Doralt, 'Strukturelle Schwäche in der Europäisierung des Privatrechts', *RabelsZ* 2011, p. 260.

1414 See further on the shortcomings in the use of impact assessments below, par. 10.2.2.1.

1415 J. Cohen, Ch. Sabel, 'Directly-deliberative polyarchy', *ELJ* 1997, p. 325. Comp. N. Walker, 'The idea of constitutional pluralism', *MLR* 2002, p.357 who describes "strident fundamentalism", 'a refusal of dialogue with other sites or processes or with internal challenges to their authority'. Whereas actors are interested in interaction, they do not seem interested in dialogue that will be contrary to their interests.

legislative choices will cumulatively solve the problem.' Thus, bargaining, rather than deliberation has developed.[1416]

Have problems developed because of the severe shortcomings in the interaction between interdependent actors?

Interdependence, a lack of interaction and problems have become more visible in the Dutch case study. Particularly, a lack of clarity with regard to parties' obligations to make STCs sufficiently available in international cases has developed. Overlapping international, European and national sources have undermined accessibility, and courts have decided cases inconsistently and unpredictably. Inconsistent and unpredictable decisions in the interpretation of articles 6:233, 236 and 237 BW in consumer cases have similarly become visible. In this respect, the lack of interaction between Dutch lower courts, and the lack of referrals from the Hoge Raad to the CJEU as well as the willingness of Dutch courts to refer questions to the CJEU and follow CJEU decisions rather than Hoge Raad decisions has visibly contributed to problems.

Interestingly, similar shortcomings in the debate have resulted in less problems for German law. Particularly, restraint in the implementation of Directives, restraint in involving foreign and international actors in national democratic debate, and restraint with regard to referring questions to the CJEU have become visible. In German law, however, there is more clarity on the obligations of parties to make STCs available and no visible gaps in international cases. In contrast to Dutch law, international cases adjudicated under German law have been decided relatively responsively, in accordance with actors' preferences as reflected by foreign and international materials.

Yet on closer inspection, in the long term, problems have developed. German restraint has undermined the responsive development of the private law *acquis* and may lead to a circle of non-interaction. In addition, no consistent, predictable approach has been developed towards the implementation of Directives within or outside the BGB. Similarly, the responsive development of international regimes is diminished as German courts have exercised restraint in referring to foreign and international materials.

The lack of problems in German law, as opposed to the weaknesses in Dutch law, can be explained by the gradual and careful development of the German law on STCs that has formed the foundation for consistent, predictable and responsive law. The recodification, accompanied by the introduction of a new blanket clause in the BW, leaves more room for unpredictability and inconsistency, notwithstanding the inspiration from the successful AGBG. The introduction of article 6:233 BW did not codify case law – to the contrary, an argument against the use of a blanket clause was the case law of the Hoge Raad that was considered to prevent it from developing the law in this area.[1417] In contrast, even though the wide use of blanket clauses have been considered more

1416 Comp. F.W. Scharpf, 'The joint-decision trap: Lessons from German federalism and European integration', *Public Administration* 1988, p. 239, who has described the 'joint-decision trap'. As national actors have to make European decisions, and as (near) unanimous agreement is desired, sub-optimal policies – such as a private law *acquis* that continues to show shortcomings – remain. It appears that even in the absence of a formal need for unanimous agreement under article 114 TFEU, this problem remains.

1417 Parl. Gesch. NBW, Boek 6 (Inv. 3, 5 en 6), p. 1497, referring to HR 20 November 1981, *NJ* 1982, 517.

critically in the German legal order,[1418] German courts have consistently adopted a more active approach, even in the absence of a specific blanket clause to assess STCs, than Dutch courts.

In the German legal order, possibilities for ADR are less visible but they have developed.[1419] Notably, however, this has not undermined the amount of cases decided by courts, as more cases have been decided by German than by Dutch courts.

In the light of the interdependence between actors with regard to responsively developing Directive 93/13 and the private law *acquis* more generally, national actors should reconsider their defensive approach as it does not exactly discourage the European legislator or convince European actors that the unwillingness of national actors is not merely based on a preference for the *status quo*. Accordingly, even if a proposal closely resembles a national regime, national legislators should not adopt a minimum implementation approach, but make more effort to justify why national law is already in accordance with a Directive. A less defensive approach also means that harmonisation initiatives should prompt national legislators to critically consider the need for legislative changes, also if an apparently successful system has been established. Rejection based on a clear assessment of the disadvantages of a particular proposal, alongside alternative suggestions, or more detailed arguments setting out why harmonisation is undesirable, is more likely to have effect.

European actors should equally recognise the relevance of national views. Accordingly, the emphasis of the European legislator on the shortcomings of minimum harmonisation and the corresponding preference for maximum harmonisation should be reconsidered. EU actors' preference for maximum harmonisation overlooks the restraint of national actors in the application of national law implementing Directives. As Directives harmonise fragmented parts of private law, and as judges frequently do not refer questions to the CJEU and foreign decisions, the extent to which maximum harmonisation as such will strengthen the predictable and consistent interpretation of blanket clauses in the *acquis*, may be doubted.

A less defensive approach of both national and European actors would hopefully entail that both European and national actors carefully consider techniques that could be used to improve the functioning of the internal market, and take into account the combination of techniques. Rather than trying out techniques and subsequently abandoning them, a more consistent, and stable use of techniques would be developed as a result. In turn, more stability and consistency in the use of techniques could also make the development of the private law *acquis* a bit less unpredictable.

Thus, in accordance with multilevel governance insights, the lack of interaction between interdependent actors has undermined the quality of the law. Some of these

1418 Especially U. Diederichsen, *Die Flucht des Gesetzgebers aus der politischen Verantwortung im Zivilrecht*, Karlsruhe: Müller 1974, p. 29. In contrast, the use of blanket clauses in the Dutch legal order has generally received support, see especially T. Koopmans, 'Lof der onbestemdheid', *RM Themis* 1991, p. 209. See much more critically, however, J.M. Barendrecht, *Recht als model van rechtvaardigheid*, Deventer: Kluwer 1992.

1419 See the comparative oversight of the Study on the Use of Alternative Dispute Resolution of Civil Consulting of the Consumer Policy Evaluation Consortium, available at www.civic-consulting.de/reports/adr_study.pdf, p. 200 et seq.

problems have become immediately apparent, and some problems may become clearer in the long term. Some problems in Dutch law cannot be directly attributed to a lack of interaction between interdependent actors, but the lack of interaction has aggravated weaknesses. Generally, the lack of interaction and potential problems that can develop should be seen against the background of existing law. A less narrow perspective of both national and European actors should lead to better interaction, in the form of arguing rather than bargaining, which in turn should help to address problems.

6.3. Pluralist perspectives

The coexistence of actors may also be advantageous for European private law according to pluralist perspectives. Paragraph 6.3.1. will ask whether the case studies have demonstrated that the coexistence of actors enhances responsiveness. Paragraph 6.3.2. will turn to the question whether regulatory competition has enhanced the quality of the law on STCs and paragraph 6.3.3. will consider opportunities for learning. Paragraph 6.3.4. will consider criticism on the state-centric approach and paragraph 6.3.5. will end with a conclusion, asking whether the findings of the case study justify the conclusion that the coexistence of actors developing simultaneously applicable rules may be beneficial.

6.3.1. Responding to divergent preferences and the development of a system of checks and balances

The reallocation of competences from the national to the European level has not increased the responsiveness of the law.

The development of checks and balances is more visible in the Dutch legal order, where the CJEU has obliged the legislator to amend article 6:238 BW to implement Directive 93/13, and where the Hoge Raad has reconsidered its decisions on the *ex officio* obligation of judges to evaluate clauses under this Directive in the light of CJEU case law. The amendment of articles 6:231 ét seq BW prior to the CJEU decision is further in accordance with the development of a system of checks and balances.[1420] The role of the CJEU has also been beneficial as it has prompted a more active approach of Dutch lower courts, which has prompted further development of Dutch law under articles 6:233, 236 and 237 BW. Insofar as checks and balances at the European level have developed, resistance may however develop as it is not clear why European actors are well-placed to exercise control over national – especially German – actors with a well developed system, in domestic cases.

The case studies do not support the conclusion that the initiatives of European actors have led to the development of a system of checks and balances that prompt national or European actors to develop the law more in accordance with preferences of respectively foreign, international or national actors. Notably, the development of a system of checks and balances focussing on the comprehensibility of the law is more generally problematic.

1420 See previously par. 5.3.3.2.

European actors do not have sufficient competence to develop such a system of checks and balances. The division of competences between courts is not clear and both the Hoge Raad and the BGH have assumed competence to decide cases on the interpretation of provisions transposing article 3 Directive 93/13, rather than refer questions to the CJEU. The lack of clarity may stand in the way of the development of a system of checks and balances.

Furthermore, a sufficient enforcement system has not been developed at the European level. In the area of consumer law, parties in adjudication have not served as drivers for further integration by challenging national measures that they find contrary to EU law. In the case studies, very few decisions in cross-borders cases have become visible. Non-state actors, especially businesses faced with strict standards of consumer protection, may not be much inclined to challenge national measures, because more stringent national measures of consumer protection have been permitted under minimum harmonisation. Further, parties' financial interests do not outweigh the cost and time involved with challenging national law. Consumers may also not be motivated to challenge EU consumer protection measures, if they are sufficiently aware of this possibility to do so. Other procedures are not well suited to remedy the lack of responsiveness or the minimum implementation approach. Weiler[1421] has pointed out that the infringement procedure is not well suited to address small infractions: 'dedicating Community resources to infringements that do not raise an important principle or create a major economic impact is wasteful'.

Interestingly, in the case studies, the direct influence of primary law has not become apparent, notwithstanding the claim of European legislator that divergences in this area constitute obstacles to internal market, especially mandatory consumer protection law.

Are these weaknesses of the European enforcement system compensated by active lower courts? Arguably, it can be doubted whether the increased number of references by lower courts can be seen in the light of judicial empowerment. Weiler[1422] has argued that lower courts are empowered to subject statutes to scrutiny, which they had not been able to do before. Perhaps this development can be detected in more Europeanised areas of law, such as intellectual property law or private international law, but not in cases within the *acquis* which typically concern small domestic disputes. While Directive 93/13 does not similarly give lower courts the possibility to do so, it does enable – and oblige – Dutch lower courts to protect consumers more actively. Yet, in contract law matters, Dutch courts have only very rarely referred to the CJEU.[1423] Despite judicial empowerment, Dutch lower courts have not made wide and enthusiastic use of the possibility to refer questions to the CJEU. However, the questions referred to the CJEU have undermined the decisions of the Hoge Raad as well as the BGH, which have both resisted this development. More generally, lower courts are willing to follow the CJEU rather than national highest courts if they consider the decisions that highest court as

[1421] J.H.H. Weiler, 'The transformation of Europe', *Yale Law Journal* 1991, p. 2419–2420.

[1422] J.H.H. Weiler, 'The transformation of Europe', *Yale Law Journal* 1991, p. 2426.

[1423] Particularly, the Gerechtshof Arnhem-Leeuwarden referred questions with regard to Directive 1999/44 on consumer sales in *Faber v Autobedrijf Hazet Ochten BV*, case C-497/13.

incorrect, but they simultaneously adopt restraint towards applying European law for various practical reasons.[1424]

In contrast, the Directive 93/13 does not similarly empower German courts that already have the power to evaluate clauses *ex officio*. Theoretically, this may a reason why German lower courts have made less use of the possibility to refer questions to the CJEU or follow the CJEU rather than BGH. Although in other areas of law, German lower courts have more frequently referred questions on contract law matters to the CJEU, the number of questions in this field has similarly remained limited.[1425]

Consequently, because the development of a system of checks and balances shows sizeable gaps, it has largely not been advantageous to the comprehensibility of national law.

Further, European actors have not prompted national actors to take into account the interests of foreign and international actors. This is hardly surprising, because the development of Directive 93/13 was originally not prompted concerns of private parties engaged in international trade. Joerges[1426] notes that in the European legislative process, actors should not assume that their legal system is optimal and should be reflected in a European proposal. Instead, harmonisation, and proposals for harmonisation, should motivate national actors to reflect critically on their own legal system. Accordingly, in this rationalisation process, national actors should make explicit why their legal system should, for example, serve as an example for a European rule, or why legal systems should be respected even though barriers for the internal market develop. As Joerges recognises, the Directive has not been developed in accordance with this idea, as German actors debated the Directive within the context of German law. Similarly, the Dutch legislator was not willing to critically discuss a new recodification. Thus, the Dutch case makes clear that ill timing may severely undermine the interest in or, as it concerns newly adopted law, ability for critical reflection on one's own legal system. The lack of participation of actors from diverging jurisdictions in national debates on the implementation of Directive 93/13, which may prompt justification from national actors, further indicates the lack of critical reflection on actors' legal system. The failed attempt to reform the Directive has clearly also not prompted critical reflection, by German or by Dutch actors. Consequently, the development of the Directive has not enhanced the responsiveness of the law on STCs to the needs and preferences of international contract parties.

1424 T. Nowak et al., *National judges as European Union judges. Knowledge, experiences and attitudes of lower court judges in Germany and the Netherlands*, The Hague: Eleven 2011.

1425 For example, with regard to Directive 85/577 on distance selling, various questions were referred to the CJEU: the LG Bochum in *Schulte v Deutsche Bausparkasse Badenia AG*, case C-350/03, the Hanseatisches OLG Bremen in *Crailsheimer Volksbank eG v Klaus Conrads and others*, case C-229/04 and the OLG Stuttgart in *Hamilton v Volksbank Filder eG*, case C-412/06. With regard to Directive 90/314 on package travel, questions have been referred to the CJEU by LG Hamburg in *Blödel-Pawlik v HanseMerkur Reiseversicherung AG*, case 134/11 and LG Bonn in *Dillenkofer and others v Bundesrepublik Deutschland*, joined cases C-178/94, C-179/94, C-188/94, C-189/94 and C-190/94.

1426 Ch. Joerges, 'The Europeanisation process of private law as a rationalization process and as a contest of disciplines – an analysis of the Directive on unfair terms in consumer contracts', *ERPL* 1995, p. 185. Comp. N. Walker, 'The idea of constitutional pluralism', *MLR* 2002, p. 358 who finds that the assertion of metaconstitutional authority and demands for justification may be genuinely educational and transformative, free up debate, and lead to cross-fertilisation of ideas between states.

The coexistence of national regimes may however be beneficial in terms of responsiveness to national legal views on justice and national practice. The case studies have indicated that national law on STCs is closely intertwined with surrounding national law that reflects national legal views on justice and national practice. Both case studies indicate that courts interpret and apply harmonised law in accordance with their own legal traditions.[1427] Divergent preferences have become visible in German and Dutch law on STCs. German courts have consistently adopted a much stricter approach to the fairness of STCs in domestic business contracts than Dutch courts,[1428] and default law is more present as a benchmark for measuring the fairness of STCs in line with or contrary to these default rules in German law than in Dutch law. Pavillon[1429] indicates that French and English law similarly consider default rules as a standard for determining whether a clause is fair. Arguably, it follows that at least some remaining divergences can be seen in the light of the responsive development of the law on STCs. Even the Directive originally[1430] envisaged that continuing divergences were beneficial, in accordance with minimum harmonisation that allows for more stringent standards of consumer protection.

What does this mean for legal transplants? Because private law is developed within national legal systems, and reflects notions of distributive justice, practical uniformity will not be achieved. The close relationship between the law on STCs and national legal views on justice may limit further possibilities for harmonisation and the use of new techniques such as comitology.

That does not mean that harmonised provisions necessarily act as "legal irritants" in national law. Possibly, the development of legal irritants may take place especially if concepts that are imposed on national law are not familiar in that legal system, or more generally if, for example, national legislators introduce new concepts or blanket clauses – such as article 6:233 sub a BW – into national law. "Good faith" as such already existed in Dutch and German law, but in Dutch law, both integration and rejection of CJEU decisions have become visible.

The Dutch case study made clear that considerations in line with the *Richtigkeitsgewähr* played a role in the revision of national law.[1431] Notwithstanding harmonisation, ideas on justice, such as good faith, party autonomy and the *Richtigkeitsgewähr*, continue to play an important role in the development of national law. Rare instances in which principles underpinning harmonisation, such as consumer protection, may impose limits on the development of national law in accordance with one of these principles, such as the *Richtigkeitsgewähr*, have been decided in accordance with national ideas on justice.[1432] Simultaneously, even though similar principles underlie the national laws on

1427 H. Collins, 'Governance implications for the European Union of the changing character of private law', in: F. Cafaggi, H. Muir-Watt (eds.), *Making European private law: Governance implications*, Cheltenham: Elgar 2008, p. 272.

1428 See further above par. 4.4.3.3. and par. 5.4.3.5.

1429 C. Pavillon, 'Private standards of fairness in European contract law', *ERCL* 2014, p. 91.

1430 Consideration 62 in the preamble to Directive 2011/83 on consumer rights seems to take a different view.

1431 See par. 5.5.1.

1432 See BGH 15 April 2008, *BeckRS* 2008, 12098, see further par. 4.5.1.

STCs, the case studies show that this does not necessarily mean that Dutch law and German law will increasingly converge. Particularly, the view when a party is in such a weak bargaining position that it justifies the development of mandatory law may differ. Therefore, even if general principles underlying the German and Dutch law on STCs, as well as Directive 93/13, converge, and even if the serve as starting points for interaction, actors might still disagree on the future development of the law.

It may be concluded that in the multilevel legal order, harmonisation has not resulted in a system of checks and balances that aims to improve the predictability, consistency, accessibility and the responsiveness of the law. Harmonisation has similarly not motivated national actors to take into account the interests of foreign and international actors. Although national actors may have done so, this was not prompted by harmonisation. Conversely, Directive 93/13 was not prompted by concerns of foreign and international contract parties. The coexistence of national regimes may however be beneficial for the responsiveness of the law.

6.3.2. *Regulatory competition*

The case studies have shown that German state actors strongly oppose the possibility of a law market that would allow private actors to choose the rules most in accordance with their preferences. In German law, STCs are generally evaluated, as users of STCs may well impose their preferences on contract parties submitting to contract terms. Accordingly, the close relationship between the law on STCs, surrounding law and national legal views on justice may limit actors' interest in regulatory competition.[1433] Vogenauer[1434] points out that the law on STCs is the area *par excellence* where a "law market" is supposed to have developed. If regulatory competition has not developed in this area, is it likely to have developed in other areas?

Yet more generally, German state actors have supported initiatives for regulatory competition.[1435] On closer inspection, however, this initiative does not seem aimed at developing the best possible law, or the most attractive law. Instead, the initiative can be seen as a – somewhat defensive – response to the initiative to promote the English legal system.[1436] Therefore, German actors have not participated in regulatory competition to make the law more competitive. More generally, German law on STCs supports the view that regulatory competition does not necessarily result in an optimal set of laws. Despite the German legislator's refusal to engage in regulatory competition, its law on STCs has often been described as a "success story".

1433 G. Rühl, 'Regulatory competition in contract law: Empirical evidence and normative implications', *ERCL* 2013, p. 86.

1434 S. Vogenauer, 'Regulatory competition through choice of contract law and choice of forum: Theory and evidence', *ERPL* 2013, p. 13.

1435 As evidenced particularly by the initiative Law – made in Germany, see http://www.lawmadeingermany.de/.

1436 S. Vogenauer, 'Regulatory competition through choice of contract law and choice of forum: Theory and evidence', *ERPL* 2013, p. 30 et seq.

A different approach is visible in Dutch law that distinguishes between business contracts and consumer contracts. As businesses are not considered to need much protection, there is room for regulatory competition.

The idea of attracting international litigation motivated the Dutch legislator to develop a lenient regime for the evaluation of terms in international business contracts.[1437] Efforts to promote Dutch law are less visible, but they do exist.[1438] It has also been suggested to establish more specialised courts where parties could litigate in English.[1439] Simultaneously, this approach is also a defensive one: although the Dutch legislator does not think that businesses are in need of much protection, it is not willing to allow businesses in domestic contracts to opt out of national law Unfortunately, the approach of the Dutch legislator has not resulted in a "success story" even though important parts of the law were based on German law. Notwithstanding the success of the AGBG, the choice to model the law for national disputes on German law supports the view that regulatory competition did not involve modelling its new law on a regime often selected by international contract parties, but merely providing for a lenient regime. While the more lenient regime of Dutch law towards international business contracts was inspired by English law, this inspiration has merely resulted in exempting international business contracts from articles 6:231 et seq BW, which has left gaps and uncertainty. One may wonder whether this course was inspired by successful regimes, or whether a closer look at English or Swiss law would have yielded further, different insights.

Regulatory competition has also not fostered legal innovation. The Dutch legislator has continued to make use of blanket clauses, which obliges foreign and international actors opting into Dutch law to look at Dutch case law, which is likely not easily accessible to these parties. The Dutch legislator has not considered the role of alternative regulation or other techniques that may make Dutch law more accessible to foreign and international actors.

Especially the German case study does not support the argument that national actors feel "forced" to participate in regulatory competition.[1440] Possibly, this may be particular to contract law, as rules on taxation, insolvency and corporate law are considered to have a more significant impact on the investment climate.[1441] German and Dutch actors do not seem to feel compelled to clearly delineate between mandatory or super-mandatory law, regardless of their efforts to engage in regulatory competition, especially in a manner easily accessible to foreign and international parties.[1442] Cross-border trade also does not seem to have diminished territorial law-making to such an extent that contract parties do not try to pressure legislators to revise the law in accordance with their preferences.[1443]

The case studies indicate that successful attempts at regulatory competition depend on the involvement of multiple actors. However, the development of bargaining rather

1437 See previously par. 5.3.4.1. The reform of the French law of obligations has also been considered in this light, see C.M.D.S. Pavillon, 'Een nieuw contractenrecht voor Frankrijk', *NTBR* 2015, 11.

1438 See www.hollandfinancialcentre.com/item.php?id=71&language=EN.

1439 See for an overview C.J.M. Klaassen, 'Kroniek civiele rechtspleging', *NJB* 2015, 738.

1440 E.A. O'Hara, L.E. Ribstein, *The law market*, Oxford: OUP 2009, p. 217.

1441 As measured at www.doingbusiness.org/.

1442 See previously par. 4.4.3.3.1.1. and par. 5.4.3.1.

1443 As shown by the private initiative for regulatory competition, see further previously par. 4.3.3.1.3.

than deliberation[1444] does not enable regulatory co-opetition[1445] between European and national state actors. State actors do not sufficiently compete with one another in improving the law, nor do they sufficiently cooperate. However, the approach of German and Dutch courts further underlines the idea that successful regulatory competition depends on the involvement of multiple actors, including non-state actors. The German private initiative for the revision of the law on STCs, in line with regulatory competition, indicates the involvement of non-state actors in this respect. Interestingly, also, the private initiative for reform has prompted other stakeholders to argue for maintaining the law.[1446] In addition, the Dutch and German legislators and the courts have recognised the need for cooperation with non-state actors in drafting and interpreting the law in order to ensure the responsiveness of the law to the needs and preferences of non-state actors.

Notwithstanding the interaction between state and non-state actors regulatory competition has not addressed and likely will not address weaknesses in Dutch law. The question arises whether regulatory competition, if not inhibited by relations between the law and national legal views on justice, can be more generally beneficial for the comprehensibility of the law. The narrow view of national actors, focussing on preventing that national actors op out of domestic law, as well as the limited inspiration from internationally attractive regimes and the lack of legal innovation in areas where regulatory competition has been attempted, indicate otherwise.

6.3.3. *Opportunities for learning*

The case studies show that actors have recognised the value of comparative law and used opportunities for learning.

Thus, the Dutch legislator and the European legislator have benefited from the experience of German actors with the law on STCs. The Dutch legislator has further profited from comparative insights in amending articles 6:236 and 237 BW, as well as in the introduction of a prejudicial procedure. Courts have recognised the added value of foreign and international materials in international cases.

Notwithstanding these opportunities, they have not consistently improved the law on STCs that continues to show weaknesses. In areas where criticism has become apparent, the Dutch legislator does not seem aware of the need for revision or interested in improvement. In contrast, while German actors have taken into account the needs and preferences of national actors and generally value comparative research, German law has not been based on mutual learning. German lawmakers also do not seem keen to "learn" from the Dutch attitude towards regulatory competition, despite interest in regulatory competition more generally.[1447]

1444 See previously par. 4.3.2.4. and par. 6.2.

1445 D.C. Esty, D. Geradin, 'Regulatory co-opetition', *Journal of International Economic Law* 2000, p. 238.

1446 See www.markenverband.de/presse/archiv2012/pmverbaendeinitiativeagb_recht/pm_agb_recht_anlage.

1447 See www.lawmadeingermany.de/.

Arguably, once actors have developed the law, whether they made use of opportunities for learning or not, their willingness to make use of further opportunities, or to critically reflect on existing law decreases. Thus, state actors have developed a national approach that goes beyond methodological nationalism.

This is particularly visible in the failed reform of Directive 93/13, which did not prompt the Dutch legislator to critically reconsider its own law, although that was recommended. German actors were similarly unsupportive of amendments that contradicted German law. Interestingly, successful features of German law could be useful for diverging Dutch law, for example with regard to the availability of STCs.

Methodological nationalism has inhibited opportunities for mutual learning. It is visible in national suggestions for the further development of European private law through codification-like instruments such as the DCFR, blanket clauses and general principles. These techniques, once adopted in national law, may even be approached less critically in the European context. For example, in the drafting of the Dutch regime, it was also noted that case law in the law on STCs on the basis of good faith had little value as precedent as decisions on this basis differed depending on the circumstances of the contract, whilst the motivation to challenge STCs before the court was limited.[1448] Simultaneously, it was asked whether the inclusion of blanket clauses would effectively provide consumers with more protection.[1449] Typically, however, these questions were however not asked in the debate preceding the 1993 Directive.

Methodological nationalism is visible also in suggestions for experimentation, such as collective bargaining. Interestingly, however, the Dutch legislator has learned from EU and French experiences in the drafting of new initiatives such as the Dutch prejudicial procedure.

Notably, further opportunities for learning from the use of techniques exist. That does not mean that techniques that may work within one state will automatically be successful at the European level, an idea visible in the drafting of the DCFR. Possibly, however, if the need for reform is widely recognised or if problems in the law are immediately apparent, national actors may be more willing to learn from the experience of other actors. Conversely, ideas that have been reduced to dead letters in one state may prove interesting for other states. Thus, the possibility for collective STCs under article 6:214 BW[1450] may be interesting for legal orders where alternative regulation has not sufficiently developed or where alternative regulation is more controversial. In addition, while some legal orders may welcome, for example, collective bargaining, this approach need not necessarily be welcomed in other Member States. These differences indicate that there is no ideal combination of techniques, even for developing one area of law. An ideal combination of techniques may differ depending on the area of law, diverging national views and European perspectives.

1448 Parl. Gesch. NBW, Boek 6 (Inv. 3, 5 en 6), p. 1460.
1449 Parl. Gesch. NBW, Boek 6 (Inv. 3, 5 en 6), p. 1498.
1450 See previously in more detail par. 5.3.2.

Some of these techniques could enable or facilitate mutual learning and further deliberation, in accordance with pluralist arguments. Particularly, if the DCFR paid attention to national experiences with the *acquis* – which it does not – or if it paid more attention to inconsistencies within the *acquis*, it could further deliberation and mutual learning. Similarly, the study of STCs in cross-border trade can be a source of learning for European actors and prompt more deliberation between European and national actors.

The interaction between both German and Dutch actors with European actors and vice versa can be characterised as bargaining rather than arguing.[1451] In the absence of checks and balances aimed at preserving the predictability, consistency, accessibility, and responsiveness, and in the absence of contract parties as drivers of integration,[1452] the legal environment makes arguing more difficult than bargaining,[1453] especially if national actors realise that the consistent, predictable development of private law is at stake. In these cases, national actors will bargain to maintain their law rather than consider the various ways in which private law at the European level should be developed. As a result, actors have not shown interest in possibilities for further learning, and opportunities to improve the law have been missed.[1454] Perhaps, the environment may be more conducive to arguing rather than bargaining if national law is more clearly in need of improvement.

Yet mutual learning and further deliberation is not unequivocally beneficial. To the contrary, the case studies indicate that opportunities for mutual learning and more deliberation may have disadvantages. Accordingly, learning from foreign legislators' experiences with the implementation of Directives may be problematic as legislators develop initiatives for implementation at the same time, and the time for learning and debate is limited. Equally, especially lower courts may correctly prioritise quickly resolving small disputes – in accordance with standards of predictability, consistency, accessibility and responsiveness. In consumer cases, little financial interest may be at stake, and referring to foreign decisions or referring questions to the CJEU may not be in proportion to a relatively straightforward case. The criticism of CJEU decisions may also be a reason for judges to adopt restraint.[1455] If comparative law does not help actors to develop the law, for example if turning to comparative law undermines consistency, this may be a reason not to turn to comparative law. The availability of national familiar materials may form an additional reason to not also refer to less familiar materials such as foreign materials. Especially in the German legal order, an abundance of German materials is available. These reasons for restraint may also offer an explanation for the ad hoc manner of interaction.[1456]

1451 See more elaborately above, par. 6.2.

1452 See above par. 6.3.1.

1453 Comp. N. Krisch, *The pluralist structure of postnational law*, Oxford: OUP 2010, p. 234 who describes that a legal environment can push actors towards arguing.

1454 Comp. N. Walker, 'The idea of constitutional pluralism', *MLR* 2002, p.337 who states that benefits that may arise from constitutional pluralism are based on mutual recognition and respect.

1455 B. Hess, 'Rechtsfragen des Vorabentscheidungsverfahrens', *RabelsZ* 2002, p. 478.

1456 Comp. L. Miller, *The emergence of EU contract law: Exploring Europeanization*, Oxford: OUP 2011, p. 213.

It may be concluded that the success of the German regime and the strengths of the Dutch regime cannot consistently be attributed to mutual learning. Further, the German regime, while not based on comparative law insights, may still serve as a source of inspiration for other actors,[1457] including the Dutch and European legislator.

6.3.4. *Pluralist criticism of the state-centric approach*

To lawyers in the Dutch and German legal order, codifications remain central sources for locating private law. In this scenario, the role of state actors remains a central one. Both perspectives from multilevel governance and pluralist views have however recognised that the roles of state actors may change and, over time, become less prominent.

In accordance with multilevel governance perspectives, the involvement of more non-state actors, reinforced by ongoing Europeanisation, affects the role of non-state actors and the way in which European private law is developed. As non-state actors possess more expertise and more organisational resources, they can play a more important and influential role in legislative processes, both at the national and European level, and they may also suggest developing alternative regulation rather than legislation, thereby offering alternatives for legislation. This is also reflected in the – ultimately unsuccessful – European initiative to develop a platform for STCs used throughout the Union.[1458]

According to some pluralist views, the role of non-state actors in this area of law goes much further than reflected by the use of national techniques. Accordingly, De Sousa Santos[1459] has argued that a transnational legal space has been created, consisting of international commercial contracts, STCs and codes of conduct, and choices for ADR, especially for international businesses. In this view, non-state actors have become involved in the development of the law on STCs, and they have transformed from subjects of the law to actors who participate in the development of the law.[1460] As different legal spaces typically intersect, the transnational legal space frequently clashes with national law, as contractual agreements diverge from national law, businesses actively try to circumvent the applicability of national law and do not comply with national rules if they are applicable. The transnational legal order may however also mix with national legal orders or be integrated within national legal orders.

1457 R. Zimmerman, 'Schuldrechtsmodernisierung?' in: W. Ernst, R. Zimmerman (eds.), *Zivilrechtswissenschaft und Schuldrechtsreform – Zum Diskussionsentwurf des Bundesministeriums der Justiz*, Tübingen: Mohr Siebeck 2001, p. 22 and E.M. Meijers, 'Wijzigingen en aanvullingen van het Burgerlijk Wetboek na 1838', in: P. Scholten, E.M. Meijers (eds.), *Gedenkboek Burgerlijk Wetboek 1838–1938*, Zwolle: Tjeenk Willink 1938, p. 61.

1458 Communication from the Commission to the European Parliament and the Council, *A more coherent European contract law - An action plan*, COM (2003) 68, p. 21-23.

1459 B. de Sousa Santos, 'Law: A map of misreading. Toward a postmodern conception of law', *Journal of Law and Society* 1987, p. 293–294. Comp. L. Miller, *The emergence of EU contract law: Exploring Europeanization*, Oxford: OUP 2011, p. 162, who finds that transnational private regulation 'operates in complementarity with, but autonomously from, state law.' Comp. critically B.Z. Tamanaha, 'A non-essentialist view of legal pluralism', *Journal of Law and Society* 2000, p. 305.

1460 R. Michaels, 'Umdenken für die UNIDROIT-Prinzipien. Vom Rechtswahlstatut zum Allgemeinen Teil des Transnationalen Vertragsrechts', *RabelsZ* 2009, p. 868 describes this as "privatization".

Whether such a transnational space has in fact been developed falls beyond the scope of the case studies that focus on the development of the law on STCs through national techniques, which presupposes a central role for state actors. Yet multilevel governance and pluralist perspectives both raise questions about the central role of state actors. Accordingly, what other actors play a role in the development of private law more generally? If non-state actors have gained prominent roles in the development of the law, is this a reason to reconsider the prominent role of state actors or are there reasons that justify preserving the prominent role of state actors?

6.3.5. *Conclusion on pluralist perspectives*

Do case studies indicate that the coexistence of actors is beneficial, in accordance with pluralist insights?

Contrary to pluralist arguments, the reallocation of competences to the European level has not been beneficial in terms of responsiveness to the needs of foreign and international non-state actors. A system of checks and balances to safeguard the comprehensibility of the law has not been sufficiently developed. However, the coexistence of national regimes may be beneficial in terms of responsiveness to national legal views on justice.

The extent to which the law on STCs has benefited from mutual learning has been limited. Although especially Dutch and European actors have benefited from German experiences, opportunities for mutual learning have been limited, and the interaction between actors takes the form of bargaining rather than deliberation.

The case studies do not support arguments that regulatory competition is beneficial for the law on STCs. Regulatory competition has not prompted innovation, and state actors and non-state actors have not sufficiently cooperated, in line with the idea of regulatory co-opetition. Although German actors have rejected regulatory competition in this area, the German law on STCs is considered as a success story, and it has inspired other actors. Conversely, the approach of the Dutch legislator, in accordance with regulatory competition, has not resulted in a similarly successful regime and it has not visibly served as a source of inspiration for other actors. Regulatory competition has not resulted in harmonisation and neither harmonisation nor regulatory competition has prompted national actors to develop the law in accordance with the interests of foreign or international actors.

Notably, developing the law on STCs in accordance with pluralist arguments may also be detrimental. The development of comitology may well entail a lack of stability, and may disproportionally benefit strong actors with more expertise of and access to comitology processes.[1461] Similarly, regulatory competition, which can be stimulated through the development of optional instruments, may benefit especially strong parties with sufficient expertise and resources to compare the strengths and weaknesses of foreign law systems. These detriments may also be attributed to increasing

1461 Comp. N. Krisch, *Beyond constitutionalism: The pluralist structure of postnational law*, Oxford: OUP 2010, p. 257 who notes these detriments more generally in a pluralist legal order.

interdependence, in accordance with multilevel governance perspectives, if new techniques are developed in the light of increasing interdependence between state and non-state actors.

6.4. Conclusion and outlook

This chapter has asked whether the coexistence of actors in the development of European private law is more generally problematic or beneficial, in accordance with multilevel governance and pluralist perspectives.

Both multilevel governance and pluralist perspectives have recognised the increasing role of non-state actors. The case studies have focussed on the development of the law on STCs through national techniques, which leaves the question open what role non-state actors play. The role of non-state actors is important for the potential use of new governance or alternative techniques. As became apparent in the German case study, objections may arise against the development of new governance, while the Dutch legal order allows for more experimentation. However, in the Dutch legal order, the case study makes apparent that the role of non-state actors is not solely beneficial for European private law. This raises the question more generally what role state and non-state actors have played in the development of private law in respectively the German and Dutch legal order. Why have objections arisen against the role of non-state actors and can a consistent approach towards the role of non-state actors be discovered? These questions will be considered in chapter 7 and 8. In addition, the analysis of actors developing legally binding rules offers further insight in the question of whether a system of checks and balances has developed that is more likely to strengthen the comprehensibility of the law, for example through rationalisation, even though a sufficient system has not become visible for the law on STCs?

Interdependence and a need for more interaction between interdependent actors have become visible in the development of the law on STCs. In the Dutch legal order, problems in the development of the law on STCs through national techniques have become noticeable, while similar problems have not become visible in the German legal order. This difference may be explained against the background of existing successful law in the German legal order and newly introduced law in the Dutch legal order. Problems in the German legal order may eventually develop, as the responsive development and revision of the *acquis* is undermined, and if unpredictability arises in the implementation of Directives in the BGB. After chapters 7 and 8 have highlighted interdependence between state and non-state actors both at and beyond the national level in respectively the German and Dutch legal order as apparent in the constitutional frameworks, chapter 9 will accordingly turn to the development of the law through national techniques. Are the problems detected in the case studies visible more widely as national actors more generally fail to take interdependence as a starting point in the development of the law through national techniques, and interact accordingly? Similarly, have European actors taken interdependence as a starting point in developing the law through national techniques, in particular soft laws, blanket clauses and general principles, and how has that affected the comprehensibility of the law?

The coexistence of national regimes may benefit responsiveness and there is potential for further mutual learning. Some additional and alternative techniques may foster mutual learning and deliberation, but this has not generally become visible. In line with multilevel governance insights, these techniques may advance debate between interdependent actors. In accordance with pluralist perspectives, the development of new governance may facilitate more experimentation and mutual learning, but this is not always the case. Chapter 10 will analyse what techniques are already used in addition to national techniques and discuss whether their use could be improved. The case studies have not considered the use of Regulations instead of Directives, as well as the use of model laws and the OMC, as these initiatives may meet with considerable resistance from national state actors, regardless of their benefits and detriments at an abstract level. Chapter 10 will analyse the strengths and weaknesses of additional or alternative techniques. The chapter will also explore whether techniques, if they have not yet been widely used in the development of European private law, could potentially increase the comprehensibility of European private law. Regulatory competition has not strengthened the law on STCs. Is there further evidence that regulatory competition or regulatory co-opetition takes place in other areas of private law and do these competitive approaches benefit the law?

Chapter 7

ACTORS DEVELOPING PRIVATE LAW IN THE GERMAN LEGAL ORDER

7.1. Introduction

In the case studies, it has become clear that state actors still play a prominent role in the development of the law on STCs. Is this more generally the case, or do non-state actors also play an important part in the development of private law?. What actors develop private law in the German legal order, and what is the role of those actors in the German constitutional framework and the European framework?

'This book will defend that a framework to help determine the role of state and non-state actors can be deduced from German law. So far, no such framework has been defended as such for the development of European private law. Originally, private law discussion did not consider the development of alternative regulation in private law in the light of private autonomy ('*Privatautonomie*').'[1462]

'Literature on alternative regulation and later debate on self-regulation in private law did consider the development of binding rules in this light.'[1463]

'Despite a clearly delineated and defended framework, German law, literature and the various instances of alternative regulation make clear that such a framework could and should be construed.'

On the one hand, in the framework defended in this chapter, the role of especially non-state actors in the development of private law is based on the idea of private autonomy and self-determination ('*Selbstbestimmung*'), protected as a manifestation of the general freedom of action ('*allgemeine Handlungsfreiheit*') under article 2 *Grundgesetz* (GG), and the concept of '*Fremdbestimmung*', that has also been translated as 'hetero-determination',[1464] in Dutch: '*heteronomie*'.[1465]

1462 See S. Meder, *Ius non-scriptum – Traditionen privater Rechtssetzung*, Tübingen: Mohr Siebeck 2009, p. 2. Conversely, G. Bachmann, *Private Ordnung*, Tübingen: Mohr Siebeck 2006, p. 227 noted the hesitation in public law debate to engage in private law debate on this topic.

1463 P. Buck-Heeb, A. Dieckmann, *Selbstregulierung im Privatrecht*, Mohr Siebeck: Tübingen 2010.

1464 A. Colombi Ciacchi, 'Freedom of contract as freedom from unconscionable contracts', in: M. Kenny, J. Devenny, L. F. O'Mahoney (eds.), *Unconscionability in European private financial transactions*, Cambridge: CUP 2010, p. 12.

1465 This Dutch concept however seems to differ from *Fremdbestimmung*, as it has not been used generally to describe situations in which individuals become bound by rules they have not been able to influence.

Hetero-determination, or *Fremdbestimmung*, is the opposite of party autonomy. *Fremdbestimmung* arises if one is bound by rules one has not been able to influence. Legal persons can influence the rules that they are bound to by choosing to enter into a contract, by becoming a member of an association or by choosing to comply with self-regulation. One may indirectly influence legal rules one is bound by through the democratic process. In contrast, *Fremdbestimmung* refers to the situation where actors develop rules that bind other actors even though these actors have entered into a transaction with the rule-making actors, and even though they have not democratically elected the rule-making actors. Thus, *Fremdbestimmung* refers to being bound by non-democratically legitimised rules over which one has also not contracted.[1466]

The principles, upon which the framework as defended in this chapter, is based is closely intertwined with the GG, and it cannot simply be transposed or applied to other legal orders. Yet the concept of private autonomy is widely recognised, and the idea of *Fremdbestimmung* as such is recognised as problematic in other legal orders as well.[1467] Therefore, this chapter will consider private autonomy and *Fremdbestimmung* as analytical concepts to decide whether non-state actors should play a role in the development of private law is interesting for other legal orders.

The role of state actors and non-state actors under European law will also be considered.

The pluralist perspective gives rise to various questions. Firstly, the emphasis on the GG gives the impression that, in accordance with legal centralism, German law can be seen as an exclusive, unified, hierarchical ordering, with the GG as '*Grundnorm*'.[1468] Secondly, the chapter will consider various forms of alternative regulation, developed for specific areas of law. Do these forms of alternative regulation prompt reconsideration of the state-centric constitutional framework?

Furthermore, the description of the role of multiple actors involved in the development of European private law makes clear that interdependence has developed in accordance with the analysis of multilevel governance, as highlighted throughout this chapter. Interdependence might make it more complicated for actors to develop European private law in accordance with benchmarks of predictability, accessibility, consistency, and responsiveness, while it may also make it more complicated for actors to adequately identify the actor best suited or responsible for the development of European private law in accordance with these benchmarks.

This chapter will introduce the German constitutional framework, as defended in this book in paragraph 7.2, and contrast this framework with the role of actors under European law. Paragraph 7.3 will discuss the development of private law by state actors. Subsequently, paragraph 7.4 will consider the role of state actors and non-state actors in instances of co-regulation, and paragraph 7.5 will turn to the role of non-state actors. Paragraph 7.6 will end with conclusions.

Instead, '*heteronomie*' as a term has been used to describe situations where parties are not left a choice to contract with one another.

1466 See further on the idea of *Fremdbestimmung* par. 7.2.2.

1467 A. Colombi Ciacchi, 'Private autonomy as a fundamental right in the European Union', *ERCL* 2010, p. 303.

1468 As described and criticised by J. Griffiths, 'What is legal pluralism?', *Journal of Legal Pluralism* 1986, p. 3.

7.2. Central questions on the role of state actors and non-state actors

This paragraph will 'argue that a framework can de derived from the German legal order.

Paragraph 7.2.1 will discuss the traditional contrast between legislation ('*Rechtsnormen*') and contracts ('*Rechtsgeschäfte*') and go on to argue that in this basic model,[1469] alternative regulation is a hybrid. Paragraph 7.2.2 will discuss the development of alternative regulation and set out why the development of alternative regulation may be problematic, introducing the concept of *Fremdbestimmung* in more detail and contrasting it with private autonomy. Paragraph 7.2.3 will consider the development of legislation or alternative regulation that may affect constitutional rights. Paragraph 7.2.4 will turn to the role of state actors and non-state actors in the development of European legislation or alternative regulation and paragraph 7.2.6 will consider the development of European alternative regulation that affects constitutional rights. Paragraph 7.2.7 will compare the role of state actors and non-state actors in the German framework and European law.[1470] Paragraph 7.2.8 will end with a conclusion.

7.2.1. The distinction between law and juridical acts as a basis for binding rules

Traditionally,[1471] individuals can be bound by private autonomous juridical acts, which are legitimated by one's own free choice, in accordance with private autonomy, protected under article 2 GG. Alternatively, one can be bound by the law, which is democratically legitimated, in accordance with article 20 GG.[1472] Mendes[1473] finds that participation is commonly based on the idea that persons whose rights are affected should be able to defend their rights. Accordingly, in this perspective, individuals should have some influence on decisions that directly influence them. Consequently, if legal persons have bound themselves either on the basis of a juridical act, or if they are bound by democratically developed law, this is in accordance with principles of private autonomy and democracy, and hetero-determination should not develop. This distinction is not unfamiliar in other legal orders.[1474]

Correlated with this distinction is a central assumption that state actors may bind people because state actors develop rules in the public interest. Private parties may not

1469 This is a simplistic model that does not aim to describe reality in detail but rather to enable discussion of the basic principles involved. After par. 7.2 has introduced this model, this chapter will discuss the development of private law through traditional legislation and alternative regulation in more detail.

1470 This research will not separately consider the views of international actors on this point, as international law may be developed by a range of different actors that may adopt divergent approaches.

1471 See further P. Buck-Heeb, A. Dieckmann, *Selbstregulierung im Privatrecht*, Tübingen: Mohr Siebeck 2010, p. 262.

1472 Comp. H. Muir Watt, '"Party autonomy" in international contracts: from the makings of a myth to the requirements of global governance', *ERCL* 2010, p. 8, who distinguishes between state sovereignty and freedom of contract.

1473 J. Mendes, *Participation in EU rule-making: A rights-based approach*, Oxford: OUP 2011, p. 46–55. She provides a comparative overview of English, French, Italian, German, Spanish and Portuguese law.

1474 See further chapter 8 that discusses this distinction in the Dutch legal order.

bind other actors without their consent[1475] because they typically pursue their own interests that do not necessarily coincide with third parties' or public interests,[1476] while they are also not directly bound to constitutional rights.[1477]

At first sight, the assumption that state actors consistently act in accordance with the public interest seems confirmed by the case study that found that German state actors have consistently safeguarded the quality of the law on STCs.[1478] Further, this distinction is in accordance with the findings in the case study that revealed that the contributions of non-state actors to the legislative process in the failed revision of Directive 93/13 emphasised their own interests.[1479]

However, this distinction need not always be clear-cut. Between *Rechtsgeschäfte* and *Rechtsnormen*, alternative regulation has developed as a hybrid.[1480] Thus, rather than a contrast, the following vastly simplified model can be imagined:

Law

Hybrids

Juridical acts

1475 This idea is also reflected in article 1372 Italian Civil Code that stipulates that a contract has the force of law between parties. The provision allows to dissolve the obligations either on the basis of parties' mutual consent, or on the basis of the law. It is similarly visible in the revision of the English law on the privity of contract, particularly in the doctrine established in *Tweddle v Atkinson*, (1861) 1 B & S 393; 121 ER 762. In the revision of contract law, the Law Commission, *Privity of contract: Contracts for the benefit of third parties*, Report 242, available at http://lawcommission.justice.gov.uk, p. 6, par. 2.1. remarked that '[i]t would be an unwarranted infringement of a third party's liberty if contracting parties were able, as a matter of course, to impose burdens on a third party without his or her consent.' Privity of contract also reflects the other side of hetero-determination, namely the fact that if contracts are only binding on contract parties, this may hinder third parties if they want to invoke a contract to their benefit. If third parties are not able to invoke their rights under these contracts, this may decrease the effectiveness of those contracts as a regulatory technique, comp. F. Cafaggi, 'Self-regulation in European contract law', *EJLS* 2007, 1, par. II sub C.

1476 W. Schmidt-Rimpler, 'Grundfragen einer Erneuerung des Vertragsrechts', *AcP* 1941, p. 156, 159, 161, 164.

1477 This problem has for example also been recognised in English public law, see further C. Donnelly, 'The response of English public law to private actors in public governance', in: M. Ruffert (ed.), *The public-private law divide: Potential for transformation?*, Cambridge: CUP 2009, p. 169.

1478 See previously par. 4.6.1.

1479 See further previously par. 4.3.2.4.

1480 F. Cafaggi, 'Rethinking private regulation in European regulatory space', in: F. Cafaggi (ed.), *Reframing self-regulation in European private law*, Alphen aan den Rijn: KLI 2006, p. 10, describes the development of control mechanisms as "regulatory hybrids". Similarly H. Muir Watt, '"Party autonomy" in international contracts', *ERCL* 2010, p. 9, finds that alternative regulation that binds third parties should be developed transparently and actors should be accountable. H. Collins, *Regulating contracts*, Oxford: OUP 2002, p. 254, finds that intervention in parties' relationship may be justified by preventing an abuse of power, without however aiming to redistribute that power. Rather, the purpose is to control strong parties' exercise of power.

On the one end of the spectrum, people decide to contract with one another, and at the other end of the spectrum, people are bound by the law. Yet in this spectrum, hybrid forms have also developed. In these hybrids, private actors develop rules that are not only binding on themselves, but that may also become binding on third parties.

Various forms of alternative regulation beyond the case studies make clear that a sharp distinction between public and private actors pursuing the public and private interests may be problematic. Accordingly, private actors may develop *Rechtsnormen*, for example through collective labour agreements ('*Tarifverträge*', 'TVs') that contain *Rechtsnormen*, in accordance with article 1 par. 1 *Tarifvertragsgesetz* (TVG). Generally, agreements between works councils ('*Betriebsrate*') and employers ('*Betriebsvereinbarungen*,' 'BVs') are also considered *Rechtsnormen*. Further, guidelines on fair competition ('*Wettbewerbsrichtlinien*') may be taken into account in the interpretation of blanket clauses,[1481] as they reflect stakeholders' views on fair commercial practices. More generally, the view that private parties lack the perspective of the public interest can be questioned if various private parties cooperate to draft rules in the public, instead of their own interest, as is also recognised by state actors.[1482] A strict division between law and contracts has been considered outdated.[1483] Accordingly, Cohen and Sabel[1484] detect the development of many hybrids. Nevertheless, even if a sharp delineation is complicated and outdated, the distinction between public actors who pursue the public interest and non-state actors who pursue private interests confirm a state-centric view of the development of the law. If accurate, the distinction provides a convincing argument why public state actors should retain a central role, despite pluralist criticism.

This development indicates that multiple actors – specifically, state and non-state actors – coexist alongside one another and develop binding rules, in cooperation with another, in accordance with pluralist arguments. Does the development of hybrids indicate that the coexistence of state actors and non-state actors that apparently also pursue public interests is beneficial for European private law or have problems developed as state actors have retained a central role?

[1481] Köhler/Bornkamm/UWG/Köhler (2012), article 4 nr 10.45. Harte-Bavendamm/Henning-Bodewig/Gesetz gegen den unlauteren Wettbewerb/Schünemann (2009) article 3, nr 159 note that breach of these guidelines need not necessarily constitute an unfair commercial practice, and provide a further overview of *Richtlinien*.

[1482] Comp. for example U. Di Fabio, 'Selbstverpflichtungen der Wirtschaft – Grenzgänger zwischen Freiheit und Zwang', *JZ* 1997, p. 970.

[1483] G. Bachmann, *Private Ordnung, Grundlagen ziviler Regelsetzung*, Tübingen: Mohr Siebeck 2006, p. 120. K.-H. Ladeur, 'Methodology and European law – Can methodology change so as to cope with the multiplicity of law?', in: M. van Hoecke (ed.), *The epistemology and methodology of comparative law*, Oxford: Hart 2004, p. 95 with further references, who also finds that the distinction between public and private rule-making becomes less pertinent, necessitating the development of more procedural rules for the development of rules by private actors.

[1484] J. Cohen, Ch. Sabel, 'Directly-deliberative polyarchy', *ELJ* 1997, p. 314. Comp. similarly B.R. Weingast, 'The economic role of political institutions: Market preserving federalism and economic development', *Journal of Law, Economics and Organization* 1995, p. 6.

7.2.2. *Problems of* Fremdbestimmung

If private law is developed through hybrids, non-state actors may impose rules on third parties that are not based on the law, nor have parties consented to them.[1485] Problematically, non-state actors developing these hybrids have not been democratically elected, they are not bound to the GG and they may pursue their own interests rather than the public interest. The possibility that private actors pursue their own interests gives rise to concern with regard to one-sided rules or rules that pursue the interest of one group instead of the public interest are imposed on other actors.[1486] Moreover, rules developed in these hybrids may replace the rules that private actors would have consented to – which would logically be rules in the own interests of those parties – had hybrids not developed. In other words, hybrids may limit the private autonomy of parties:

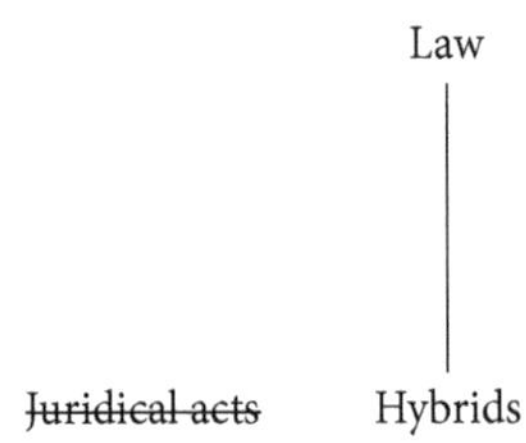

Consequently, *Fremdbestimmung* should theoretically not arise if parties are bound by either juridical acts,[1487] and *Fremdbestimmung* is less problematic if it arises from decisions by public actors that pursue the public interest and are bound by the GG, through the democratic process that parties have been able to influence. In contrast, in cases of alternative regulation, where private actors have developed rules that may become binding on other individuals, either through co-regulation or through reinforced self-regulation, *Fremdbestimmung* is problematic.

However, abandoning the development of hybrids is neither desirable nor realistic. Rather, *Fremdbestimmung* may be compensated by control mechanisms that subject alternative regulation to some control, depending on the extent to which alternative regulation imposes rules on third parties, and thereby limit non-state actors' roles.[1488] In addition, constitutional requirements should as far as possible be met.[1489] Control

1485 Comp. W. van Gerven, S. Lierman, *Beginselen van Belgisch privaatrecht. Algemeen deel, veertig jaar later*, Mechelen: Kluwer 2010, p. 306–307 who similarly link the development of additional safeguards of *democratic* legitimacy to the binding effect of privately developed rules that are reinforced by state actors.

1486 P. Buck-Heeb, A. Dieckmann, *Selbstregulierung im Privatrecht*, Tübingen: Mohr Siebeck 2010, p. 278.

1487 However, *Fremdbestimmung* may also arise if the bargaining process on which the contract should be based shows shortcomings; see further par. 7.4.1.

1488 See already, expressly, BVerfG 14 June 1983, *NJW* 1983, 1225, with further references: 'Der Gesetzgeber darf seine Normsetzungsbefugnis nicht in beliebigem Umfang außerstaatlichen Stellen überlassen, soll der Bürger nicht schrankenlos einer normsetzenden Gewalt nichtstaatlicher Einrichtungen ausgeliefert werden.'

1489 S. Augsberg, *Rechtsetzung zwischen Staat und Gesellschaft*, Berlin: Duncker & Humblot 2001, p. 84–85.

mechanisms may take various forms. For example, the development of alternative regulation may take place in carefully organised, extensive drafting processes. In these drafting processes, the participation of representative actors is increased, and drafters of alternative regulation should make clear how the interests and comments of these actors have been taken into account.[1490] *Fremdbestimmung* may also be an argument for judicial control over the content of alternative regulation. Thus, in this perspective, alternative regulation is developed within the framework of the law, while additional controls should compensate for potential *Fremdbestimmung*:

Law

Hybrids

Judiciary/participation

Individuals

As the drafting process of alternative regulation becomes more inclusive and transparent, judicial control may become less intense, if involved in alternative regulation have created rules that are not to the detriment or benefit of one group of stakeholders.[1491] These compensatory measures may, however, also decrease the flexibility of alternative regulation.

Therefore, even if, in this framework the German legal order adopts a state-centric approach the development of the law, insofar as the state retains the monopoly of recognising the binding force of rules and subject privately drafted rules to control if concerns of *Fremdbestimmung* justify such control, the potential of non-state actors to contribute to the development of the law is not neglected. However, the need to evaluate the initiatives of non-state actors is stressed. This emphasis is still based on the assumption that private parties pursue private rather than public interests.

1490 P. Buck-Heeb, A. Dieckmann, *Selbstreguliering im Privatrecht*, Tübingen: Mohr Siebeck 2010, p. 278. H. Collins, *Regulating contracts*, Oxford: OUP 2002, p. 252–253 finds that "procedural" requirements could and should be introduced. G. de Minico, 'A Hard look at self-regulation in the U.K.', *ELBR* 2006, p. 201, also notes the voluntary organisation of extensive drafting processes in English self-regulation. J. Black, 'Proceduralizing Regulation: Part I', *Oxford Journal of Legal Studies* 2000, p. 597 finds that 'procedures for participation' could be a valid remedy to the question of the democratization of rule-making.

1491 P. Buck-Heeb, A. Dieckmann, *Selbstreguliering im Privatrecht*, Tübingen: Mohr Siebeck 2010, p. 264, 279, 283, J. Köndgen, 'Privatisierung des Rechts', *AcP* 2006, p. 523.

7.2.3. *German alternative regulation and constitutional rights*

The question whether private law should be developed through traditional legislation or alternative regulation becomes especially important if these rules affect constitutional rights. The BVerfG[1492] has established that all matters directly affecting constitutional rights should be dealt with by formal laws (the *Wesentlichkeitsdoktrin*), which stands in the way of binding alternative regulation that interferes with third parties' constitutional rights. However, this doctrine does not mean that private actors may not develop alternative regulation. Notably, the development of alternative regulation may fall within the sphere of the freedom of association and private autonomy. Accordingly, the BVerfG[1493] has ruled that private autonomy entails that private parties may develop their own rules, and private autonomy in the sense of article 2 GG has been defended as the source of legitimation for self-regulation in private law.[1494] The *Wesentlichkeitsdoktrin* does not necessarily block private actors' involvement in the development of private law; on the contrary, state actors need to make use of the best suitable instrument when pursuing a specific aim (the *Effektivitätsgebot*), which may well entail including private actors.[1495] The BVerfG[1496] has considered the underlying reasons for the *Effektivitätsgebot*:

> 'Die Verleihung von Satzungsautonomie hat ihren guten Sinn darin, gesellschaftliche Kräfte zu aktivieren, den entsprechenden gesellschaftlichen Gruppen die Regelung solcher Angelegenheiten, die sie selbst betreffen und die sie in überschaubaren Bereichen am sachkundigsten beurteilen können, eigenverantwortlich zu überlassen, und dadurch den Abstand zwischen Normgeber und Normadressat zu verringern. Zugleich wird der Gesetzgeber davon entlastet, sachliche und örtliche Verschiedenheiten berücksichtigen zu müssen, die für ihn oft schwer erkennbar sind und auf deren Veränderungen er nicht rasch genug reagieren konnte.'

This reasoning clearly recognises the benefits of alternative regulation, and encourages the development of rules in accordance with divergent preferences. Thus, it does not seem that a central role of the state prevents non-state actors from developing rules in accordance with their preferences, although the GG impose limits on non-state actors' ability to do so. In other words, possible defaults in the drafting process that may lead to *Fremdbestimmung* should be compensated, for example, through control from the legislator or the judiciary.[1497]

1492 BverfG 9 May 1972, *NJW* 1972, 1504, par. C II 3.

1493 BVerfG 13 July 2004, *NJW* 2005, 45.

1494 P. Buck-Heeb, A. Dieckmann, *Selbstreguliering im Privatrecht*, Tübingen: Mohr Siebeck 2010, p. 257 et seq, earlier F. Kirchhof, *Private Rechtsetzung*, Berlin: Duncker & Humblot 1987, p. 511 et seq. Comp. however S. Meder, *Ius non scriptum – Traditionen privater Rechtssetzung*, Tübingen: Mohr Siebeck 2009, p. 2–4, 233–234, who argues that whereas autonomy can be associated with a competence to develop rules, private autonomy should be understood as private parties' ability to set their own rules within the limits set by the BGB.

1495 S. Augsberg, *Rechtsetzung zwischen Staat und Gesellschaft*, Berlin: Duncker & Humblot 2001, p. 87–88.

1496 BVerfG 9 May 1972, *NJW* 1972, 1504, C 2.

1497 S. Augsberg, *Rechtsetzung zwischen Staat und Gesellschaft*, Berlin: Duncker & Humblot 2001, p. 99.

The BVerfG[1498] has further established the scale step theory (‘*Stufentheorie*’), which provides that imposing intense limitations of constitutional rights is reserved for the legislator. The question whether private actors may interfere with third parties’ constitutional rights depends on the intensity of this interference and may only take place in the public interest. The legislator may not blindly delegate all his authority to non-state actors but needs to retain some level of control.

This perspective on alternative regulation seems in conformity with pluralist arguments. The involvement of non-state actors may be encouraged even if it does not directly benefit responsiveness, and even if it does not directly facilitate mutual learning or regulatory co-opetition. Rather, the development of alternative regulation can be beneficial in and of itself. This perspective is also in line with criticism of state-centric conceptions of the law, as the right of actors to develop their own rules, rather than being subjected to rules, is underlined. Not only the development of legislation through the democratic process can be valuable as it safeguards the exercise of constitutional rights – this is also the case for the development of alternative regulation. Does that mean that theoretically, private actors who pursue public interests and accordingly develop highly successful alternative regulation, should be able to reduce the role of the democratically elected legislator?

7.2.4. The role of actors under European law

The well-developed framework in the German legal order and its underlying principles offer a critical perspective on legislative practices of foreign and European actors. European law provides much less clarity on the role of actors, both state actors and non-state actors. European state actors play an important role in the development of the law as the largest part of the private law *acquis* consists of legislative measures and the CJEU has also played a prominent role in interpreting these measures. Rather, it is not clear how the tasks in developing European private law are allocated between the European and the national level. As European legislative competence is functional and may develop as problems for the internal market within the sense of article 114 TFEU arise, these competences are and will remain not strictly delineated.

The role of non-state actors is less clear – no coherent view can be detected at the European level. Although the principles of private autonomy and democracy have been recognised at the European level, the development of alternative regulation has not been problematised because of potential *Fremdbestimmung*. Instead, the European Commission has distinguished between legislation and alternative regulation, emphasising the principles of democratic legitimacy, subsidiarity and proportionality.[1499]

The European Commission[1500] considers the use of alternative regulation as a means to support the community method, i.e. the development of European legislation. Thus, the initiatives of non-state actors are subjected to European policy aims. Notably, alternative

1498 See more recently BVerfG 13 July 2004, *NJW* 2005, 45, par. C II 2 b.

1499 OJ 2003 C, 321/01, 31.12.2003, par. 2, 16.

1500 European Commission, *European governance, a white paper*, COM (2001) 428 final, p. 8.

regulation must be in accordance with European law and with the principles of transparency, representativeness, and of 'added value to the general interest',[1501] but it is not clear when these requirements are satisfied. Interestingly, the White Paper on Governance[1502] places the responsibility of complying with these principles on non-state actors.

7.2.5. The European view: alternative regulation and fundamental rights?

The Interinstitutional Agreement[1503] excludes the use of alternative regulation in cases where fundamental rights are at stake. Yet this apparent rejection is not in accordance with initiatives that may well affect constitutional rights – in particular the European social dialogue.[1504]

Possibly, however, the development of alternative regulation at the European level is more difficult from a political perspective, especially if Member States are critical of the possibility that rules developed beyond the legislative process at the European level may affect constitutional rights. The existence of successful national alternative regulation may be another reason to exclude additional European alternative regulation.

7.2.6. Comparison

Various similarities, but especially differences, have become visible between the role of actors under the German framework and under European law.

State actors play a primary role both in the German legal framework and in European law. However, beyond the prominent role of state actors, many differences become apparent between the role of actors in the development of European private law.

1) Whereas a framework can be construed at the national level, no similar framework has been developed for the European level.
2) At the European level, the development of alternative regulation, and, correspondingly, the role of non-state actors, has not been problematised because of *Fremdbestimmung*. Therefore, European law has also not consistently developed control mechanisms to limit the role of non-state actors. As a result, non-state actors at the European level may play a larger role than actors at the national level, if their initiatives pursue European policy aims.
3) Simultaneously, non-state actors have a smaller role under European law than under the German framework, as the GG protects the role of non-state actors. More particularly:
   a. The role of non-state actors in the German framework can be seen in the light of constitutional rights, whereas this view is not apparent at the European level. The German view is however, limited, as article 19 par. 3 GG stipulates that the

1501 OJ 2003 C, 321/01, 31.12.2003, par. 17.
1502 COM (2001) 428 final, p. 15.
1503 OJ 2003 C, 321/01, 31.12.2003.
1504 See further below, par. 7.4.2.1.

constitutional rights are applicable for domestic legal persons.[1505] Foreign businesses may invoke the provisions from international treaties.
In this respect, contrary to the findings in the case study,[1506] the existence of European and international norms has helped prevent that German actors do not sufficiently take into account the interests of non-nationals. It follows that in accordance with pluralist insights, the coexistence of actors should theoretically help responsiveness.[1507] However, the development of international treaties has not prompted German actors to reconsider this limitation in the GG, despite criticism.[1508]

b. Non-state actors have a smaller role under European law than under German law, as becomes apparent from the European definition of co-regulation: 'the mechanism whereby a community legislative act entrusts the attainment of the objectives defined by the legislative authority to parties which are recognised in the field'. This definition, as well as the rejection of alternative regulation in cases where fundamental rights are affected imply a top-down approach,[1509] which is difficult to reconcile with the German view that the drafting of alternative regulation can be an exercise of constitutional rights. In particular, the selection of representative actors by the European Commission is difficult to reconcile with the pursuit of constitutional rights.
c. At the European level, the development of alternative regulation is not considered as a goal in itself, but as a means to support European legislative interventions in terms of (democratic) legitimacy, effectiveness, and transparency.[1510]
d. The *Effektivitätsgebot* implies that non-state actors develop self-regulation or co-regulation. In contrast, the European legislator emphasises non-state actors' role in strengthening legislation.[1511]

1505 K. Vieweg, *Normsetzung und anwendung deutscher und internationaler Verbände*, Berlin: Duncker & Humblot 1990, p. 145 notes that this limitation gives the German legislator room to adequately deal with, for example, multinationals.

1506 See previously par. 4.6.2.

1507 Ch. Joerges, 'On the legitimacy of Europeanising private law: Considerations on a justice-making law for the EU multi-level system', *Electronic Journal of Comparative Law* 2003, par. III.1.2., available at www.ejcl.org/ejcl/73/art73-3.html.

1508 Maunz/Dürig, Grundgesetz-Kommentar/Remmert (Ergänzungslieferung 2012), article 19 par. 3, nr 19 et seq, who doubts, in nr 1, whether this limitation is compatible with European law.

1509 See, for example, Directive 97/7 on distance contracts, which provides, in consideration 18 in the preamble to the Directive, that its minimum rules could be supplemented by codes of practice. In its Recommendation (92/295/EC, OJ L 156/21 on codes of practice for the protection of consumers in respect of contracts negotiated at a distance), the European Commission recommended that trade associations of suppliers should adopt codes of practice and provided for a list of points to be adopted in the codes, and provided, in the annex, a number of points that these codes had to address.

1510 L.A.J. Senden, 'Soft law, self-regulation and co-regulation in European law: where do they meet?' *EJCL* vol. 9.1., 2005, p. 9.

1511 L.A.J. Senden, 'Soft law, self-regulation and co-regulation in European law: where do they meet?' *EJCL* vol. 9.1., 2005, p. 9.

7.2.7. *Conclusion on central questions*

The German framework benefits the consistency and the clarity of the law on the roles of actors. The German framework moreover values the development of alternative regulation, which should be beneficial to responsiveness.

However, the extent to which this framework fosters predictability, consistency and responsiveness may be limited as European law provides a different, less fully developed framework for the role of actors. Both the TFEU and the GG offer a state-centric conception of the development of the law. However, the German legal order simultaneously offers a constitutional reinforcement for the development of alternative regulation as a benefit in itself, apart from the advantages defended in pluralist debate. The German framework and the development of European law, combined with pluralist insights, give rise to the following questions that will be discussed in this chapter.

Firstly, do hybrids, especially if developed under European law, pose a threat to the development of private law in accordance with the GG and is this problematic for the comprehensibility of European private law?

Secondly, more generally, the development of private law seems focussed on national state actors, at least under the GG. Pluralist perspectives may defend that the development of European and international treaties prompts German actors to take the interests of foreign and international actors into account, even though article 19 GG was not amended. Is this visible in the development of private law in the German legal order more generally?

Thirdly, a central assumption underlying the framework is that public actors pursue public interests and private actors pursue their own interests. Is this assumption still visible in concerns of *Fremdbestimmung* and the corresponding development of control mechanisms?

This may be a reason to retain the central role of state actors. However, are there indications that private actors who pursue public interests and accordingly develop highly successful alternative regulation should be able to reduce the role of the democratically elected legislator or should control mechanisms be abandoned? Do state actors agree with this reasoning, and for what reasons?

7.3. State actors

This paragraph will analyse that role of actors in the development of private law. Paragraph 7.3.1 will discuss the role of German state actors. Paragraph 7.3.2 will consider the competences of European and international state actors.[1512] Paragraph 7.3.3 will end

[1512] This chapter has chosen to firstly consider German actors and subsequently turn to the role of European and international actors, even though national binding law may have to be set aside because of European law. However, international and European rules are much less developed than German private law and are considerably more fragmented than German law. Also, European law, when developed through Directives, cannot be invoked directly between private parties, but has to be implemented by the German legislator and the judiciary.

with a conclusion that points out the different role of state actors under the GG and the TFEU and draws attention to the interdependence between actors and the resulting need for interaction.

7.3.1. The national legislator and the judiciary

The legislator has played a central role in developing private law through codifications. *General* private law, codified in the *Bürgerlich Gesetzbuch* (BGB), is applicable for all citizens, while private law for particular groups of parties has been developed in separate statutes and codes (*Sonderprivatrecht*), such as the code on commercial law (*Handelsgesetzbuch*, or HGB), but also the act on the limited liability company (*Aktiengesetz* or AktG).[1513] However, the debate on the question whether the rules on STCs were *Sonderprivatrecht* or not shows that this distinction may not always be clear-cut.[1514] Therefore, although it provides an interesting starting point, the distinction between *Generalprivatrecht* and *Sonderprivatrecht* currently does not serve as a convincing basis for the predictable implementation of Directives in the BGB.[1515]

Notably, the introduction of the BGB did not entail that judges were reduced to mouthpieces of the law, nor did it limit the role of scholars.[1516] Instead, the inclusion of general principles and blanket clauses in the BGB has enabled the judiciary to develop private law without continuous interference from the legislator.[1517]

Although the BGH is the highest court to interpret private law, it should refer to the BVerG when the interpretation of private law touches upon the interpretation of the GG.[1518] Notably, the BVerfG only determines whether the GG has been interpreted correctly; it is not a higher instance that evaluates the correct interpretation of private law. The courts have taken an active approach in interpreting private law in accordance with the needs of practice, which has included *contra legem* interpretation.[1519] The active approach of the judiciary may mean that the BGH or the BVerfG establishes a rule, if the legislator, despite a constitutional obligation to do so, has steadfastly not provided rules to adequately cope with a specific problem.[1520]

Articles 3 and 20 par. 2 GG establish the limits of judiciary discretion. The BVerfG[1521] has made clear that the judge may not replace an existing legislative framework with his own model. The active approach of the judiciary has at times been subject to

1513 See further MunchKomm zum BGB/Säcker (2012), introduction, nr 1.

1514 See previously par. 4.3.1.

1515 See previously par. 4.3.1.3. and below par. 10.2.

1516 See critically J. Stürner, 'Der hundertste Geburtstag des BGB – nationale Kodifikation im Greisalter?' *JZ* 1996, p. 752.

1517 Staudinger Komm zum BGB/Coing/Honsell (2011) introduction, nr 30.

1518 BVerfG 15 January 1958, *NJW* 1958, 257, 257–258.

1519 R. Zimmerman, *The new German law of obligations, Historical and comparative perspectives*, Oxford: OUP 2005, p. 18–19, 30.

1520 See U. Diederichsen, *Die Flucht des Gesetzgebers aus der politische Verantwortung im Zivilrecht*, Karlsruhe: Müller 1974, p. 44–49.

1521 BVerfG 25 January 2011, *NJW* 2011, 836, par. B 4.

criticism,[1522] especially the reasoning in the decisions from the BVerfG in the area of private law.[1523]

7.3.2. *The development of private law beyond the national level*

This paragraph explores the role of the European legislator and judiciary and international actors. Paragraph 7.3.2.1 will consider the role of European actors and paragraph 7.3.2.2 will consider interdependence. Paragraph 7.3.2.3 will discuss the role of international actors.

7.3.2.1. European actors developing private law in the German legal order

This paragraph will consider the competence of European actors under respectively the TFEU and the GG, contrasting the German view with the European view that has become apparent from CJEU case law.

7.3.2.1.1. The competence of European actors under the TFEU

European actors play a prominent role as European law, once established, precedes national law, independently of national legislation.[1524] The Lisbon Treaty provides the European legislator with a wide range of legislative competences that also enable the European legislator to harmonise private law. In particular, article 81 TFEU, article 169 TFEU and article 352 TFEU, and most frequently, article 114 TFEU, have been used as legal bases.

Article 4 par. 2 TFEU makes clear that these competences are shared between the Union and its Member States. Therefore, national actors still play a role if harmonisation has been established. The reallocation of legislative competences to the European level, and the role of European and national actors, depends on the measure – a Directive leaves more room to Member States than a Regulation – and the degree of harmonisation pursued by that measure. The Directives in the private law *acquis* pursue both minimum and maximum harmonisation, and a suggestion for a Regulation pursuing optional harmonisation – the proposal for a Regulation on a CESL[1525] – has also been made and withdrawn. Also, the scope of a measure, which is often limited, is important for the reallocation of competences to the European level.

[1522] See for example MunchKomm zum BGB/Säcker (2012), introduction, nr 75. Staudinger Kommentar zum BGB/Coing/Honsell (2011), introduction, nr. 30.

[1523] In particular U. Diederichsen, 'Das Bundesverfassungsgericht als oberstes Zivilgericht – ein Lehrstück der juristischen Methodenlehre', *AcP* 1998, p. 171.

[1524] CJEU 15 July 1964 (Costa v E.N.E.L.), case 6–64, [1964] ECR, p. 585. CJEU 7 March 1985 (Van Gend & Loos NV v Inspecteur der Invoerrechten en Accijnzen), case 32/84, [1985], ECR, p. 779.

[1525] COM (2011) 635 final.

In the area of private international law, article 81 TFEU has served as a basis for a range of measures in cross-border cases.[1526] Article 169 TFEU has not served as an independent legal basis, but article 169 par. 2 sub a TFEU refers to article 114 TFEU and thereby permits the use of article 114 TFEU as a legal basis for advancing consumer protection. Article 352 TFEU provides the European legislator with a residual competence that requires unanimity.[1527] The majority of measures in the *acquis* are based on article 114 TFEU, promoting the internal market, consumer protection, or both. This is an ambiguously-worded competence, the limits of which are unclear.[1528] Because the TFEU only confers competences on the Union to intervene in cases where that promotes the aims of the Treaties, the approach of the European legislator is necessarily an instrumentalist approach.[1529]

The *acquis* in the area of private law mainly consists of Directives that leave the German legislator some leeway with regard to their implementation, mostly within the BGB.[1530]

The role of European actors may be increased by primary European law.[1531] The most visible influence in the area of private law on the basis of the Treaty has been the development of the Member States' liability for infringing Union law, as established in *Francovich*,[1532] *Brasserie du Pêcheur*,[1533] and *Dillenkofer*.[1534]

1526 Because of the reservations of Denmark (protocol 22 on the position of Denmark) and the United Kingdom and Ireland (protocol 21 on the position of the United Kingdom and Ireland in respect of the area of freedom, security and justice) to this part of the Treaty, measures adopted under this title do not bind these Member States.

1527 The BVerfG has maintained that it is competent to evaluate whether European measures have been established *ultra vires* as this could constitute a breach of the GG, see further below. Particularly, BVerfG 30 June 2009, *NJW* 2009, 2267 (Lisbon Treaty) set limits to the use of article 352 TFEU, as this residual legislative competence may lead to tensions with the principle of conferral. See critically J. Basedow, 'Ende des 28. Modells? – Das Bundesverfassungsgericht und das europäische Wirtschaftsprivatrecht', *EuZW* 2010, p. 41, who rightly points at successful measures under this article.

1528 See further E.A.G. van Schagen, 'More consistency and legal certainty in the private law *acquis*: A plea for better justification or harmonisation of private law', *MJ* 2012, p. 37.

1529 Comp. N. Jansen, R. Michaels, 'Private law and the state: comparative perceptions and historic observations', *RabelsZ* 2006, p. 10.

1530 See further on the approach of the legislator to the implementation of the *acquis* chapters 4 and 9.

1531 Either national legislation or case law: see for example the judgements of CJEU 24 January 1991 (Alsthom Atlantique SA v Compagnie de Construction), C-339/89, ECR 1991, p. I-107 and CJEU 13 October 1993 (CMC Motorradcenter GmbH v Pelin Baskiciogullari), C-93/93, ECR 1993, p. I-5009.

1532 CJEU 19 November 1991 (Francovich and Bonifaci and others v Italian Republic), joined cases C-6/90 and C-9/90, [1991] ECR p. I-5357.

1533 CJEU 5 March 1996 (Brasserie du Pêcheur SA v Bundesrepublik Deutschland), joined cases C-46/93 and C-48/93, [1996] ECR p. I-1029.

1534 CJEU 8 October 1996 (Dillenkofer and others v Bundesrepublik Deutschland), joined cases C-178/94, C-179/94, C-188/94, C-189/94 and C-190/94, [1996] ECR, p. I-4845.

Additionally, European law may, in some cases, affect contracts,[1535] including collective labour agreements and collective actions aimed at entering into a collective labour agreement.[1536]

Furthermore, the role of the European legislator increases as it enters into treaties, typically ratified through Regulations[1537] on the basis of article 216 TFEU and in accordance with the negotiations procedure prescribed under article 218 TFEU.[1538] The CJEU decision in AETR[1539] makes clear that the European legislator is competent to renegotiate on treaties that have been ratified by the European legislator if they are revised.[1540] It follows that if, for example, the Montréal Convention is to be revised, the competence to negotiate has been reallocated to the European legislator.

The ratification of treaties by the European legislator also means that the CJEU becomes competent to interpret treaties. This means that national courts should refer questions on these treaties to the CJEU. Arguably, in turn, the CJEU should refer to previous national interpretations of the Europeanised treaty in the interests of predictability and consistency, which may, however, be difficult if those decisions are not easily available or if the interpretations of courts in different Member States contradict one another.

Furthermore, where it concerns the interpretation of treaties that have also been ratified by third countries, it would be in the interest of consistency and predictability to refer to decisions on treaties in those third countries, provided that they are available.[1541] In some cases, competence to interpret treaties had already been referred to the CJEU, for example with regard to Regulation Brussels I.[1542]

1535 CJEU 22 January 1981 (Dansk Supermarked A/S v A/S Imerco), C-58/80, ECR [1981], p. 181, or CJEU 8 April 1976 (Defrenne 2), 43/758, ECR 1976, p. 455.

1536 CJEU 11 December 2007 (International Transport Workers' Federation and Finnish Seamen's Union v Viking Line ABP and OÜ Viking Line Eesti), C-438/05, [2007] ECR, p. I-10779 and CJEU 18 December 2007 (Laval un Partneri Ltd v Svenska Byggnadsarbetareförbundet), C-341/05, [2007] ECR, p. I-11767. Comp. also CJEU 18 July 2013 (Alemo-Herron and Others v Parkwood Leisure Ldt), C-426/11, [2013] ECR p. I-0, on article 16 Charter that covers freedom of contract, and the obligations of an employer in cases of transfer of undertakings under Directive 2001/23.

1537 See for an overview http://ec.europa.eu/world/agreements/default.home.do.

1538 See for the limits on this competence CJEU 28 March 1996, opinion 2/94, [1996] ECR p. I-1759 on the accession to the ECHR, in which the CJEU held that no provisions in the TFEU conferred competence on the Union to enact rules in the areas of human rights, while the residual competence – current article 352 TFEU – did not justify widening the scope of the Union's competence or result in amending the Treaty without the procedures indicated for such a change. This has not stopped the CJEU from referring to the ECHR (see CJEU 18 June 1991, (Tiléorassi AE, Omospondia, and Prossopikou v Pliroforissis, Kouvelas, Avdellas and others), C-260/89, ECR [1991], p. I-2925, par. 41). Article 218 par 6 sub a under ii TFEU now expressly refers to accession to the ECHR.

1539 CJEU 16 January 2003, (Cipra and Kvasnicka v Bezirkshauptmannschaft Mistelbach), C-439/01,[2003] ERC, p. I-745.

1540 For an overview of treaties entered into by the EU http://ec.europa.eu/world/agreements/default.home.do.

1541 This is however, not always the case: comp. CJEU 10 July 2008 (Emirates Airlines v Schenkel), C-173/07, [2008] ECR, p. I-5237, par. 43–46.

1542 Protocol of 3 June 1971 on the interpretation by the Court of Justice.

7.3.2.1.2. The competence of European actors under German constitutional law

German constitutional law on the reallocation of competences to the European level consistently emphasises the principle of democracy and the protection of constitutional rights, thereby putting restraints on the increasing role of European actors.

Under article 23 GG, Germany can reallocate competences to the European level, with permission from the *Bundesrat*. Article 23 GG stipulates that to realise European integration, Germany will work with the European Union as it similarly recognises principles of democracy, the *Rechtsstaat* and subsidiarity, as well as social and federal principles, in articles 1 and 2 TEU, while the European Union also provides protection of constitutional rights similar to the GG. Article 23 GG obliges German state actors to promote compliance to these standards.[1543] The protocol 1 to the TFEU on the role of national parliaments and protocol 2 to the TFEU subsidiarity and proportionality has enhanced the role of national parliaments which have gained the competence to lodge a complaint before the CJEU if they find that a European measure violates the principle of subsidiarity. Accordingly, par 1a has been inserted into article 23 GG.

The reallocation of legislative competence also increases the role of the CJEU. The BVerfG[1544] has emphasised that not referring questions to the CJEU when that is indicated by the highest courts, is contrary to article 101 par. 1 GG that stipulates that parties cannot be denied being heard by the competent judge according to the law. However, this doctrine has been applied strictly: if a case is decided apparently in accordance with a European measure, complaints are not upheld. This decision may constitute a breach of article 6 ECHR,[1545] and it may be difficult to reconcile with CJEU decisions under article 267 TFEU.[1546] Yet despite the restraint of the BVerfG, the roles of the CJEU and the ECHR increase as the BVerfG frequently refers to these courts.[1547] The insistence that the BVerfG[1548] remains competent to evaluate whether European measures breach the GG may also be difficult to reconcile with the primacy of European law. However, the *Honeywell* decision shows that the BVerfG exercises restraint in this matter.[1549]

For far-going reallocation of competences from the national to the European level that necessitate amendments to the Treaties, the GG provides restraints. Accordingly, article 79 par. 2 GG requires a two-third majority in both the *Bundestag* and the *Bundesrat*. Article 79 par. 3 GG prohibits amendments that affect states' roles in the federal state, states' participation in federal legislation, or the rights recognised in articles 1–20 GG. Thereby, the reallocation of competences to the European level is

1543 BT-Drucks. 12/6000, p. 20.
1544 BVerfG 9 January 2001, *NJW* 2001, 1267.
1545 Particularly in the light of ECHR 18 April 2014 (Dhahbi v Italy), case 17120/09.
1546 Similarly critically W. Roth, 'Verfassungsgerichtliche Kontrolle der Vorlagepflicht an den EuGH', *NVwZ* 2009, p. 345.
1547 See further R. Nickel, 'Zur Zukunft des Bundesverfassungsgerichts im Zeitalter der Europäisierung', *JZ* 2001, p. 625.
1548 BVerfG 12 October 1993, *NJW* 1993, 3047.
1549 BVerfG 6 July 2010, *NJW* 2010, 3422.

stipulated by national law. This is confirmed by BVerfG case law[1550] on article 79 par. 3 GG. The BVerfG has held that article 79 par. 3 GG entails that public tasks and acts of public authority should be sufficiently democratically legitimated by national parliaments, while the European Parliament additionally safeguards democratic legitimacy. With its decisions, the BVerfG distinguishes between democratic requirements at national and at transnational level and it has maintained competence to evaluate whether European measures are *ultra vires*. As integration continues, the democratic legitimation of the Union should increase, while democracy within the Member States should also be maintained.[1551] National democratic safeguards should prevent too much competence being reallocated to the European level. Specifically, legislation conferring competences to the transnational level should be sufficiently precise, respecting the principle of conferred competences and the lack of *Kompetenz-Kompetenz* at the European level.

The BVerfG further limited the reallocation of competences on central political questions in the sphere of personal development and social policy, including decisions fundamental for forming living conditions and fundamental decisions of cultural significance, in particular family law. It has been argued that private law constitutes law that is important for shaping one's living conditions,[1552] which would mean that the European legislator will not gain general legislative competence for private law and its role in this area would remain subject to constitutional limitations, leaving a central role for national legislators and courts. However, the assumption that contract law especially is essential for shaping one's living conditions has been challenged,[1553] and it is not clear whether the BVerfG will eventually set such a limitation.

7.3.2.2. The role of actors under the TFEU and the GG and interdependence

More actors – especially the European legislator and the CJEU – have become involved in the development of law, but neither the German legislator or the BVerfG nor the CJEU and the European legislator have based their decisions on the assumption that interdependence has developed and that more interaction is therefore necessary, notwithstanding the introduction of article 23 GG. Rather, although both national actors

1550 BVerfG 12 October 1993, *NJW* 1993, 3047, referring to BVerfG 29 May 1974, *NJW* 1974, 1697, BVerfG 22 October 1986, *NJW* 1987, 577, confirmed in BVerfG 30 June 2009, *NJW* 2009, 2267 and BVerfG 12 September 2009, *NJW* 2012, 3145.

1551 This perspective is reminiscent of N. Walker, 'The idea of constitutional pluralism', *MLR* 2002, p. 340-341. The European legal order is a developing legal order, and the ideas of polity and demos are mutually constitutive.

1552 The European legislator has emphasised this reasoning in various Directives, for example considerations 3, 4, 6, and 7 in the preamble to Directive 2008/48 on consumer credit. More elaborately H.-W. Micklitz, 'German Constitutional Court (Bundesverfassungsgericht BVerfG) 2 BvE 2/08, 30. 6. 2009 – Organstreit proceedings between members of the German Parliament and the Federal Government', *ERCL* 2011, p. 532.

1553 Comp. for example the alternative impact assessment for a Directive on consumer credit conducted by Oxera, *What is the impact of the proposed Consumer Credit Directive?*, April 2007, available at www.bba.org.uk.

and European actors have recognised the competences of other actors, they have interpreted other actors' roles in a limited manner while simultaneously reasserting their own competences under different frameworks – respectively the TFEU and the GG – and the perception of actors' roles from especially the CJEU and the BVerfG therefore contradict one another in the following respects:

1) The BVerfG bases the binding effect and the priority of European law upon article 23 GG. In contrast, the CJEU has held that the binding effect and the priority of European law follow from the European legal order.
2) Accordingly, the role of the BVerfG and the CJEU differ under these frameworks. The BVerfG plays a central role in safeguarding the GG and evaluates European measures with the GG. However, the TFEU reserves this competence to the CJEU, and thereby provides the CJEU with a more prominent role.

Thus, interdependence has developed: actors may undermine one another's decisions, especially because the views of the CJEU and the BVerfG on the roles of actors differ.

This interdependence becomes especially clear from the withdrawn proposal for a Regulation establishing a CESL on the basis of article 114 TFEU. This proposal may give rise not only to complaints to the CJEU, but also to the BVerfG. If the CJEU upholds such a measure, a subsequent complaint before the BVerfG would have opened up the possibility that the BVerfG will decide that the measure is *ultra vires*. In turn, under the TFEU, the German legislator is not competent to veto a measure under article 114 TFEU and a BVerfG decision holding that the CESL is *ultra vires* would not quash the CESL. As a result, an act would be adopted contrary to the GG, but under European law, the German legislator and judiciary would be bound to apply it. However, it seems unlikely that German actors would, in fact, act in a manner contrary to the GG, and this possibility may well make private parties hesitate to adopt the CESL.

German actors have, however, recognised interdependence. The BVerfG has exercised restraint in its evaluations of European measures, although it has not abandoned the possibility to do so. The German legislator has recognised the need to obtain approval for measures and amendments to the Treaty – such as the European Stability Mechanism – prior to approving amendments. Possibly, if it becomes clear that the use of article 114 TFEU for the successor of the a CESL is problematic under the GG as it breaches the principle of conferred powers, it is necessary to prevent the proposal being passed at the European level.

European actors have also recognised interdependence. The European Parliament, recognising the lack of support of a CESL from national parliaments, has accordingly organised an interparliamentary meeting in which suggestions for improvement were discussed.[1554] However, the debate at the European level still shows shortcomings.[1555]

1554 See www.europarl.europa.eu/committees/en/juri/events.html?id=workshops. Notably, the desirability of a CESL as such does not seem to have been discussed.

1555 Comp. W. Doralt, 'Strukturelle Schwächen in der Europäisierung des Privatrechts', *RabelsZ* 2011, p. 260.

Von Bogdandy and Schill[1556] note that constitutional courts generally limit themselves to protecting constitutional principles. They note that compared to other constitutional courts, the BVerfG has interpreted fundamental principles which justify limits to the exercise of European competences. At the European level, decision-makers need to take into account the possibility that European measures are constitutionally problematic at the national level, as recognised by national actors in European decision-making. Article 4 par. 2 TEU accordingly reflects the need to respect Member States' national identities. Thus, even though actors do not base their decisions on the assumption that interdependence has developed, mutual recognition and respect, emphasised in pluralist debate, can be detected.[1557]

7.3.2.3. The role of international actors

Article 59 par. 2 GG makes it clear that the competence of international actors to develop binding rules depends on the consent or cooperation of the bodies competent to legislate in that particular field. International law needs to be ratified and implemented in German law before it can become effective. Treaties that have been implemented in German law have the status of ordinary legislation, which theoretically may be altered or revoked by subsequent legislation.[1558]

Article 25 GG makes an exception for ius cogens, stipulating that ius cogens iare part of German law and may set aside legislation.[1559] Article 100 par. 2 GG makes clear that the BVerfG determines whether this is the case.

Importantly, the role of national actors to enter into treaties diminishes as the European legislator enters into treaties, which reallocates the competence to interpret and (re)negotiate on these treaties partially to the European level.[1560] The role of international actors becomes smaller if the European legislator, rather than ratifying a treaty, initiates harmonisation in areas previously harmonised through treaties. Importantly, the existence of international treaties is no impediment to the competence of the EU under article 114 TFEU.[1561]

Furthermore, international organisations have established model laws, legislative guides and recommendations. The extent to which these models and guides have been taken into account may also depend on the room left for model laws and recommendations under European law. For example, in the case of e-commerce, where Directive 2000/31 substantially differs from the UNIDROIT model law on e-commerce. In some cases, the

[1556] A. von Bogdandy, S. Schill, 'Overcoming absolute primacy: Respect for national identity under the Lisbon Treaty', *CMLRev* 2011, p. 20, 22–23.

[1557] N. Walker, 'The idea of constitutional pluralism', *MLR* 2002, p. 337, comp. A. Arnull, 'Judicial dialogue in the European Union', in: J. Dickson, P. Eleftheriadis (eds.), *Philosophical foundations of European Union law*, Oxford: OUP 2012, p. 113.

[1558] Comp. for example Graf, Bek'scher Online-Kommentar StPO/Valerius (2012) EMRK article 1, nr 2.

[1559] Maunz/Dürig, Grundgesetz-Kommentar/Herdegen, 65. Ergänzungslieferung 2012, article 25 GG, nr 1.

[1560] CJEU 16 January 2003, (Cipra and Kvasnicka v Bezirkshauptmannschaft Mistelbach), C-439/01,[2003] ERC, p. I-745.

[1561] CJEU 9 October 2001 (Netherlands v European Parliament and Council of the European Union), C-377/98, [2001], p. I-7079.

European legislator may also take international guidelines into account. For example, according to Micklitz,[1562] the OECD Guidelines on Unfair Commercial Practices that reiterate the necessity to coordinate the enforcement of consumer rights in cross-border cases and its International Consumer Protection Enforcement Network (ICPEN) has served as a basis for Regulation 2006/2004 that accordingly seeks to coordinate cross-border enforcement of the *acquis*. National agencies appointed or established on the basis of this Regulation may also address matters that do not fall within the scope of the *acquis*.

National legislators may well refrain drafting legislation in accordance with examples provided by treaties and international model laws that diverge from European measures. Conversely, if the European legislator uses a treaty or a model law as an example for European measures, this increases the role of international actors.

It follows that EU law may both inhibit and encourage mutual learning. Paradoxically, European law may deter national actors form developing the law in accordance with the needs and preferences of international actors not included in national democratic debate, if EU law diverges responsive international law. That does however not mean that in the absence of European measures, international materials would have prompted national actors to consider these interests.

More generally, one may ask whether the requirement that international measures are implemented in national law contributes to prompting national actors to consider national law critically in the light of international law. Possibly, if international law is directly applicable, this may leave less discretion to national legislators and more directly oblige actors to reconsider national rules that are contrary to international law.

7.3.3. *Conclusion on state actors*

State actors play a crucial role in the development of private law, both at the national and European level. However, the role of actors under the GG and the TFEU differs. Multiple actors have provided different rules of recognition on which the validity of private law depends,[1563] in accordance with constitutional pluralism.[1564] Mutual recognition and respect, based upon the recognition of fundamental constitutional principles, has been detected.[1565] Consequently, portraying the relation between European law and national law solely in terms of hierarchy is no longer convincing.[1566] This is in line with the conclusions in the case study, which noted that despite the supremacy of European law, national courts have to decide cases in line with the GG, also if they fall within the scope of the *acquis*.[1567]

1562 MunchKomm zur ZPO/Micklitz (2008), Introduction, nr. 46.

1563 Comp. N. Jansen, R. Michaels, 'Private law and the state: comparative perceptions and historic observations', *RabelsZ* 2006 p. 3.

1564 N. Walker, 'The idea of constitutional pluralism', *MLR* 2002, p. 317.

1565 See previously par. 7.3.2.2.

1566 L. Miller, *The emergence of EU contract law: Exploring Europeanization*, Oxford: OUP 2011, p. 192.

1567 See previously par. 4.4.1.2.

Thus, constitutional discourse takes place at multiple sites. What does this mean for the development of comprehensible European private law? As the European legislator starts developing parts of private law, this already does not take place in a predictable, consistent manner, despite the consistent, predictable German framework. Does the development of alternative regulation, either at the national or the European law, indicate that the predictability, consistency and accessibility of private law is diminished as the consistent German framework is undermined?

7.4. State actors and non-state actors: co-regulation

State actors and non-state have frequently encouraged and developed co-regulation.[1568] This paragraph will ask what role actors play in the development of alternative regulation.

Paragraph 7.4.1 will turn to the referral to self-regulation in legislation,[1569] and paragraph 7.4.2 will consider the development of collective labour agreements. Paragraph 7.4.3 will end with conclusions.

This paragraph will indicate in which instances non-state actors have developed co-regulation, and go on to describe non-state actors' roles and the role of state actors in limiting non-state actors' roles through the development of control mechanisms.

Non-state actors typically develop rules within the framework of the law as established by state actors. However, the role of non-state actors and the success of these initiatives is largely dependant upon non-state actors' initiatives – without such initiatives, state actors can provide all the frameworks they like, and they can encourage co-regulation, but to little avail.

7.4.1. Referral

This paragraph will consider instances of referral to private or non-democratically elected actors in legislation, what role non-state actors have played in these instances, and what role state actors have played in limiting the role of non-state actors through control mechanisms.

7.4.1.1. Instances of referral to privately drafted rules

The German legislator may refer to self-regulation in legislation ('*Verweisung*'). The legislator may either make use of *static* referral, to an entire set of self-regulation at a particular moment. Alternatively, *dynamic* referral allows for changes to be taken into account. Both the German and the European legislator have made use of dynamic referral.

1568 See previously for a definition of co-regulation and alternative regulation par. 1.1.

1569 Another technique is incorporation ('*Inkorporation*') that involves the inclusion of privately drafted rules into hard law, thereby strengthening the role of private actors and limiting the role of state actors to control and enforce these rules. Thus, existing self-regulation enters the legislative process and becomes hard law. S. Augsberg, *Rechtsetzung zwischen Staat und Gesellschaft*, Berlin: Duncker & Humblot 2001, p. 174–175 characterises *Inkorporation* as highly unusual, and this form will, therefore, not be discussed further.

Examples of dynamic referral at national level are:

- Article 310 par. 1 BGB for publicly tendered building contracts (VOB/B) drafted by various stakeholder groups and the state, exempting these clauses from judicial control.[1570]

- Article 362 HGB with regard to the duties of a company on the yearly accounts (*'Rechnungslegung'*).

The Ministry for Justice has contractually recognised the German Accounting Standards Committee (*'Deutsches Rechnungslegungs Standards Committee eV'*, DRSC) as a private committee in the sense of article 342 HGB to develop recommendations for the application of principles on the accounting standards for chains of businesses (*Konzern, concern*) in December 2011.[1571] Article 342 par. 2 HGB stipulates that compliance with these standards triggers an assumption (*'Vermutung der Richtigkeit'*) that the bookkeeping of that business is in accordance with principles of good bookkeeping (*'Grundsätzen ordnungsmäßiger Buchführung'*) in the meaning of article 238 HGB.[1572] In addition, the DRSC advises on the interpretation of article 315a HGB on firms that have to apply the standards developed by the IASB under Regulation 1606/2002.[1573]

- Article 161 AktG refers to the Corporate Governance Kodex that consists of three parts; one part describes positive law, the main part of the *Kodex* consists of recommendations and the last part consists of suggestions.[1574] Article 161 AktG obliges businesses to make public which recommendations in the *Kodex* they comply and which parts they do not comply with – and why.[1575]

Initially, one may get the impression that the *Kodex* is an example of co-regulation,[1576] where the legislator appoints a committee. The committee regularly checks whether amendments to the

1570 It has however, been doubted whether this exemption, if applied to consumer contracts, is in accordance with Directive 93/13. BGH 24 July 2008, *BeckRS* 2008, 15864 subjected VOB/B clauses in consumer contracts to evaluation under articles 307–309 BGB as it considered that consumers had not been involved in the drafting process of the VOB/B, while the exemption was also not in accordance with the aim of articles 305 et seq BGB.

1571 Available at www.drsc.de/docs/drsc/standardisierungsvertrag/111202_SV_BMJ-DRSC.pdf.

1572 See further on this central concept B.P. Paal, *Rechnungslegung und DRSC*, Baden baden: Nomos 2001, p. 42 et seq.

1573 See further www.drsc.de/service/ueber_uns/ziele/index_en.php#fachausschuesse.

1574 Deviations from the suggestions do not have to be made public or motivated. P. Buck-Heeb, A. Dieckmann, *Selbstreguliering im Privatrecht*, Mohr Siebeck: Tübingen 2010, p. 102, state that it has been argued that the amount of attention for the question whether the declarations in the sense of article 161 AktG has made businesses more careful of those declarations, which may undermine the effectiveness of those declarations.

1575 See for an overview of the declarations www.corporate-governance-code.de/ger/entsprechens erklaerung/index.html.

1576 As argued by W. Seidel, 'Der DGCK – ein private oder staatliche Regelung?' *ZIP* 2004, p. 285, who argues that the *Kodex* is not in conformity with the GG and thus invalid. M. Heintzen, 'Der Deutsche Corporate Governance Kodex aus der Sicht des deutschen Verfassungsrechts', *ZIP* 2004, p. 1933 also finds that the *Kodex* is non-binding state law, but in conformity with the GG.

Kodex are necessary, and may call for meetings if it finds that this is the case. The use of consultations in the drafting of the *Kodex* and the publication of the *Kodex* on the site of the ministry, after an evaluation of lawfulness by the ministry also point to co-regulation. However, it has been held the *Kodex* amounts to self-regulation as stakeholders themselves set rules for their behaviour,[1577] and it has accordingly been introduced as such.[1578]

An example of dynamic referral at the European level is:

- The role of the IASB that develops international accounting standards that, under Regulation 1606/2002, may be adopted by the European Commission in accordance with the regulatory comitology procedure set out in article 6 of the Regulation. The dynamic referral at the European level may limit the role of the DRSC.[1579] In addition, joint initiatives for the closer cooperation between the Financial Accounting Standards Board (FASB)[1580] have been developed.[1581]

Other forms of alternative regulation where competences to fill in the details of legislation are delegated to expert committees have been initiated at the European level. These forms are reminiscent of dynamic referral as competences to further develop rules are delegated to actors other than the legislature, including national civil servants and experts. These forms include:

- The comitology procedure involves the delegation of filling in technical details of European measures to expert committees by legislative acts that can be revoked, in accordance with article 290 TFEU.[1582] The competences of these committees may vary, depending on the sort of committee distinguished in Decision 1999/468 on comitology and Regulation 182/2011, introducing a regulatory procedure with scrutiny from the European Parliament.

The Commission may either be assisted by committees, composed of representatives of the Member States, with an advisory task, or by a management committee that may submit an opinion on the draft proposed by the Commission that is not binding, or a regulatory committee

1577 MunchKomm zum AktG/Semler (2003), article 161, nr. 29, comp. also Ringleb, 'Vorbemerkung', Ringleb et al (eds.), *Deutscher Corporate Governance Kodex*, 4th ed., 2010, II, nr. 14, as well as J. Köndgen, 'Privatisierung des Rechts', *AcP* 2006, 2006, p. 495.

1578 G. Cromme, 'Vorwort Deutscher Corporate Governance Kodex', 2002, available at www.corporate-governance-code.de/ger/download/DCG_vorwort_D200202.pdf.

1579 MunchKomm to AktG/Lutterman (2003), article 342 HGB, nr 70.

1580 See further www.fasb.org/home.

1581 See critically M. Dobler, S. Hettich, 'Geplante Änderungen der Rahmenkonzepte von IASB und FASB – Konzeption, Vergleich, Würdigung', *IRZ* 2007, p. 29.

1582 Article 291 TFEU stipulates that Member States shall implement European measures, but par. 2 provides that if uniform conditions for implementation are necessary, competence to implement legislation shall be delegated to the Commission, or to the council. Par. 3 makes clear that the European Parliament and the council in the ordinary legislative procedure shall determine the rules and mechanisms for Member States' control to which implementation measures by the Commission are subject.

that has further competences to consider the drafts of the Commission. If the draft regulation is not disapproved by the European Parliament or Council within three months, it will be adopted.

The CJEU[1583] has approved the use of comitology, requiring that the basic elements of the matter are decided in accordance with the applicable legislative procedure, while the delegation act should be sufficiently precise.

Article 40 in the Proposal for Consumer Rights Directive[1584] originally establishing an unfair contract terms committee, a regulatory comitology committee with scrutiny from the European Parliament.

- The Lamfalussy procedure[1585] involves the development of rules in the four-stage rulemaking process and non-state actors play an important role it this process.

The development of rules at four levels can be described as follows. Firstly, a broad, regulatory framework has been established in four Directives, i.e. Directive 2004/39 on markets in financial instruments, Directive 2003/6 on market abuse, Directive 2003/71 on the prospectus to be published when securities are offered to the public or admitted to trading and Directive 2004/109 on transparency requirements. At level 2, expert committees, the European Banking Committee (EBC), the European Insurance and Occupational Pensions Committee (EIOPC) and the European Securities Committee (ESC), that can also act as regulatory comitology committees, design more detailed, technical implementing measures, which are subsequently adopted by the Commission, which has, for example, resulted in Regulation 1287/2006 implementing Directive 2004/39. At level 3, expert committees the European Banking Authority (EBA), the European Insurance and Occupational Pensions Authority (EIOPA), and the European Securities and Markets Authority (ESMA) composed of members of national supervisory authorities, assist the Commission in the preparation of implementation measures and help to ensure the efficient cooperation of national supervisory bodies. Level 4 concerns the enforcement by the Commission of guidelines in national law.

- The development of Guidance on the implementation and application of Directive 2005/29 by the Commission.[1586] This guidance is not binding and appears not to have been considered – at least not expressly – by European courts.[1587]

Thus, in these forms of dynamic referral, both at the national and the European level, non-state actors play an important role and they may establish binding rules. Through referral, both German and European state actors have sought to benefit from the expertise

1583 CJEU 17 December 1970 (Einfuhr- und Vorratstelle für Getreide und Futtermittel v Köster and Berodt & Co), case 25–70, [1970] ECR, p. I-1161.

1584 COM (2008) 614 final.

1585 See http://ec.europa.eu/internal_market/securities/lamfalussy/index_en.htm.

1586 SEC (2009) 1666, specifically stating that the guidance is not binding on the Commission and that, although the guidelines aim to provide 'guidance on the key concepts and provisions of the Directive perceived to be problematic', the guidelines have 'no formal legal status' and ultimately, the CJEU is responsible for the interpretation of the Directive.

1587 A database on this Directive has been developed, see further https://webgate.ec.europa.eu/ucp/public/index.cfm?event=public.home.show.

and experience of non-state actors while also pursuing more flexible law that can be adapted more easily to with the needs of practice.

7.4.1.2. The role of non-state actors in instances of dynamic referral

In forms of static referral, the role of non-state actors is limited as subsequent changes in self-regulation do not affect the interpretation of hard law. This limitation has deterred legislators from using this form of referral, as it may not allow for sufficient flexibility. In cases of dynamic referral, private actors have a more prominent role, as they decide on further amendments. The role of the legislator decreases as the legislator does not control these amendments: this competence has been reallocated to non-state actors.[1588] In these cases, both the German and the European legislator have recognised that non-state actors are better placed to develop detailed rules, rather than the legislator. Non-state actors are more closely situated to practice and can therefore develop rules that adequately deal with it. In accordance with pluralist arguments, the coexistence of state and non-state actors becomes beneficial for the responsiveness of private law.

The attractiveness of this option for state actors should not be underestimated. Especially at the European level, the need to enhance the efficiency of decision-making and avoid very lengthy legislative procedures in rapidly developing fields has been emphasised.[1589]

Does the development of these hybrids pose a threat to more traditional legislation? Notably, referral eventually serves to strengthen legislation. German actors have emphasised that dynamic referral, and thereby the role of non-state actors, is limited, as private rules merely entail crystallising an ambiguous rule or concept,[1590] in which cases dynamic referral is allowed.[1591] Nevertheless, referral can not easily be reversed. Developing legislation after hybrids have been developed is likely complicated.

Furthermore, hybrids may undermine more traditional governance if the development of alternative regulation at the European level results in initiatives where European actors seek to circumvent the constraints of the legislative process.[1592]

1588 S. Augsberg, *Rechtsetzung zwischen Staat und Gesellschaft*, Berlin: Duncker & Humblot 2001, p. 176 stresses that referring to a privately-drafted rule does not mean that this rule subsequently becomes hard law, and does not have a similar effect to hard law; rather, its content may merely be relevant for the interpretation of a legislative provision.

1589 COM (91) 521 final.

1590 Accordingly, P. Buck-Heeb, A. Dieckmann, *Selbstreguliering im Privatrecht*, Tübingen: Mohr Siebeck 2010, p. 123 argue that theoretically, the DRSC does not directly establish binding rules; it merely provides a more precise interpretation of existing principles of good bookkeeping that have also been characterised as customary law.

1591 S. Augsberg, *Rechtsetzung zwischen Staat und Gesellschaft*, Berlin: Duncker & Humblot 2001, p. 178.

1592 H. Collins, *The European civil code. The way forward*, Cambridge: CUP 2008, p. 87.

7.4.1.3. The development of control mechanisms

The ability of non-state actors to establish binding rules may give rise to *Fremdbestimmung* which has led to calls for more control on the development of these rules in German literature.[1593] State actors need to retain some control over the development of alternative regulation. Consequently, have state actors sought to limit the role of non-state actors?

Potential *Fremdbestimmung* has prompted the development of control mechanisms. Accordingly, the contract between the Ministry and the DRSC stipulates, inter alia, the independence of the DRSC and the need for transparency in its decision-making. Further, in accordance with the need for participation of relevant stakeholders recognised in article 342 par. 1 HGB, the DRSC and its committees initiate consultations on drafts for standards.[1594] Furthermore, the effect of the recommendations is subject to subsequent approval and publication by the Ministry.

Similarly, the Ministry exercises control over the corporate governance *Kodex* as it appoints the committee drafting and amending the *Kodex* and as it subjects the *Kodex* to an evaluation of lawfulness before publishing it on the Ministry website.

Although problems of *Fremdbestimmung* have not been discussed as such, European state actors similarly to retain control over the development of alternative regulation. The involvement of European state actors has been emphasised as an important mechanism to retain some control over alternative regulation. Accordingly, the role of the IASB is subject to approval from the European Commission assisted by a regulatory comitology committee. The European Parliament may also be involved, especially as the European Parliament can participate in comitology procedures in article 5a Decision 1999/468/EC. In addition, the European Parliament may exercise control over the delegation of decision-making to the executive under article 290 TFEU. Further, the use of comitology has been limited to technical matters. Yet the proposal for a comitology committee in the proposal for a Directive on consumer rights and subsequent German resistance[1595] shows that European and national views on what matters are merely technical may well diverge.[1596]

[1593] Comp. R. Königsgruber, 'IASB und FASB zwischen Autonomie und Eingebunden-Sein', *IRZ* 2008, p. 245, who has noted that the reliance on private actors obliges private actors to justify the development of rules, but at times, it may also give private actors a possibility to limit the development of rules without sufficient justification. Also critically on the role of the IASB for example MunchKomm zum StGB/Sorgenfrei (2010), introduction to articles 331 et seq HGB, nr 35. Comp. on the comitology procedure. K.U. Schmolke, 'Die Einbeziehung des Komitologieverfahrens in den Lamfalussy-Prozess – Zur Forderung des Europäischen Parlaments nach mehr Entscheidungsteilhabe', *EuR* 2006, p. 439–440 and specifically on the Lamfalussy procedure M. Rötting, C. Lang, 'Das Lamfalussy-Verfahren im Umfeld der Neuordnung der europäischen Finanzaufsichtsstrukturen', *EuZW* 2012, p. 12, 13.

[1594] See further www.drsc.de/service/ueber_uns/arbeitsweise/index.php.

[1595] See the response of the Bundesministerium der Justiz to COM (2006) 744 final, http://ec.europa.eu/consumers/cons_int/safe_shop/acquis/responses/ms_bundesministerium.pdf, p. 17–18.

[1596] R.A.J. van Gestel, H.-W. Micklitz, 'European integration through standardization', *CMLRev* 2013, p. 151 point out that despite national concerns, the European Commission has not considered constitutional issues with private actors' involvement in the development of EU law.

Both German and European limitations may limit the flexibility of alternative regulation.[1597]

7.4.1.4. Comparison

Both German and European state actors have facilitated the development of co-regulation in the form of referral and collective labour agreements. Interestingly, both the European and the German legislator have made use of dynamic referral, despite German constitutional objections. Yet the role of state actors and non-state actors differs at the European and the national level. Especially the limitations on the role of non-state actors through the development of control mechanisms has logically been less developed at the European level, as the development of these mechanisms has not consistently been based on concerns over *Fremdbestimmung*. These different roles of actors may lead to problems from a German perspective, as non-state actors enjoy considerable discretion under European law that leads to *Fremdbestimmung*, for which German actors cannot compensate.

However, that does not mean that European procedures should be subject to national standards. This conclusion would overlook the distinction of the BVerfG between national and transnational democratic procedures.[1598] Accordingly, Joerges, Schepel and Vos[1599] rejected focusing on the lack of democratic legitimacy of private standard setting, pointing out that private standard setting '[draws] from a pool of relevant knowledge and expertise that lawmakers can only dream of'. They argue for an approach that would make private standard setting more publicly accountable, and defend 'deliberative supranationalism' that involves redesigning rulemaking processes so that rules developed in rulemaking processes derive their legitimacy from the debate in which they have been developed. Thus, the emphasis of Joerges, Schepel and Vos is not on inclusiveness and representation but on participation, which is reminiscent of the BVerfG distinction in its Lisbon judgment, stressing the quality of interaction between a limited number of actors. If new forms of governance lead to deliberation, this might prompt national actors to critically reflect on their own laws and to take into account the interests of European and foreign actors who are not included in more traditional decision-making processes.[1600]

1597 K.U. Schmolke, 'Die Einbeziehung des Komitologieverfahrens in den Lamfalussy-Prozess – Zur Forderung des Europäischen Parlaments nach mehr Entscheidungsteilhabe', *EuR* 2006, p. 446–447 traces the level of detail to the increased participation of stakeholders, the European Parliament, and the need for political compromise.

1598 Similarly, K.U. Schmolke, 'Die Einbeziehung des Komitologieverfahrens in den Lamfalussy-Prozess – Zur Forderung des Europäischen Parlaments nach mehr Entscheidungsteilhabe', *EuR* 2006, p. 443–444 has criticised the emphasis on European democratic procedures that are modelled after national democracies, noting that democratic control is useful especially in controversial matters where politically-organised minorities can influence majority decision-making. At the European level, Parliament cannot similarly be divided in politically organised minorities, and the decision-making at the European level also receives much less attention than national decision-making.

1599 Ch. Joerges, H. Schepel, E. Vos, *The problems with the involvement of non governmental actors in Europe's legislating process*, EUI/LAW 1999, p. 25–27, 50–53, 58–59.

1600 Nevertheless, as W. van Gerven, S. Lierman, *Beginselen van Belgisch privaatrecht. Algemeen Deel, veertig jaar later*, Mechelen: Kluwer 2010, p. 275–276 rightly point out, a lack of political and legal

7.4.2. *Collective agreements*

Collective labour agreements are an important technique in the development of employment contract law. This paragraph will firstly consider the use of TVs and European social dialogue and secondly, what role non-state actors play in these forms, and what role state actors have played in imposing limitations on the role of non-state actors through the development of control mechanisms.

7.4.2.1. *Tarifverträge* (TVs), *Betriebsvereinbarungen* (BVs) and framework agreements

This paragraph will respectively describe the use of TVs, BVs, and framework agreements developed within the European social dialogue.

- The development of TVs

The use of TVs is stipulated by the *Tarifvertragsgesetz* (TVG). Article 1 TVG makes clear that TVs establish rules for entering into labour contracts, the rights and duties in those contracts, and the termination of labour contracts (these rules are characterised as *Arbeitsverhältnisnormen*) as well as rules with regard to the company and its statutes (*Betriebsnormen*).[1601] Article 2 establishes that contract parties are unions, employers, and employers' organisations. A TV should not be too ambiguous, and parties may not leave it to the judge to decide parties' legal positions under a TV, but it may have a limited retroactive effect, taking into account the justified expectations of parties subject to the TVG.[1602] The *Arbeitsverhältnisnormen* in TVs are binding for contract parties and their members, which means that the TV does not have to be incorporated into individual contracts. The constitutional state based on justice and integrity ('*Rechtsstaat*') entails that unions should be democratically elected, especially as the decisions of unions and employers' organisations affect members' constitutional rights, and possibly the rights of third parties if TVs are declared generally binding.[1603] *Betriebsnormen* under article 3 par. 2 TVG have a binding effect on the employees of businesses that are party to the TV. *Betriebsnormen* concern provisions that realistically have to be applied uniformly, for example, throughout a company. This scope justifies its effect on third parties, as it would be ineffective to conclude these rules in individual contracts.[1604] According to article 4 TVG, individual contracts cannot set aside the rules in the TV, unless those contracts confer more rights on the employee or if the TV allows for deviations (the *Günstigkeitsprinzip*). Article 5 TVG establishes that TVs can be declared generally binding.

TVs must be in accordance with supranational laws, the GG, state constitutions, federal and state legislation, as well as official decisions ('*Verordnung*', *in Dutch: 'AMvB'*) and the statutes of public corporations.[1605] Mandatory provisions, which also include general principles underlying labour law and private law – such as the principle of good faith ('*Treu and Glauben*')[1606] – can

control on potentially binding privately developed rules may raise questions on fundamental matters such as democratic accountability and the independence of rule making actors.

1601 See for a definition BAG 17 June 1997, *NZA* 1998, 213, par. B 1 a.

1602 BAG 23 November 1994, AP TVG 1 Rückwirkung Nr. 12.

1603 Kommentar zum TVG/Wiedenmann (2007), introduction, nr 334–335.

1604 BAG 26 April 1990, AP GG Art. 9 Nr. 57, par. B V 2b.

1605 Kommentar zum TVG/Wiedenmann (2007), nr 350.

1606 Kommentar zum TVG/Wiedenmann (2007), nr, 350, 355.

be distinguished in mutually mandatory provisions ('*zweiseitig zwingend*') from which neither party can diverge, and partially mandatory ('*einseitig zwingend*') from which one party may diverge, usually to the advantage of the weaker party. Some mandatory provisions in the BGB, as well as other laws are *Tarifdispositives Gesetzesrecht*, which refers to mandatory rules from which parties to a TV may diverge, as it is assumed that TVs are negotiated between parties with an equal bargaining position.[1607] In contrast, parties to a BV or individual contracts may not depart from these rules. Similarly, case law ('*Tarifdispositives Richterrecht*') also leaves room for parties to TVs, but not for parties to BVs or individual contracts, to negotiate.[1608]

- The development of BVs

The use of BVs is stipulated by the *Betriebsverfassungsgesetz* (BetrVG). Work councils (*Betriebsrates*) may negotiate collectively with the employer on BVs within a company. BVs are limited to general rules, instead of specific, individual rules,[1609] with the exception of clauses on vacation and employee accommodation, in accordance with article 87 pars. 5 and 9 BetrVG.[1610] Some essential clauses are reserved for individual contracts.[1611] BVs are modelled on TVs, although they have a different basis.[1612] Importantly, the BAG has held that the *Betriebsrat* is assumed to be dependant of the employer and thus in an unequal position, which entails judicial control of BVs.[1613]

Article 77 par 4 BetrVG establishes that provisions in BVs that meet the requirements of article 77 par. 2 BetrVG have a direct mandatory effect on all the employees in a company entering into a BV, without having to be included in individual employment contracts.[1614] A central issue in the debate on BVs is the problem of *Fremdbestimmung* if private parties establish binding rules for employees, which are, not always to their benefit.[1615] It has been questioned whether the binding effect of BVs can in addition be justified on another basis. Notably, BVs are not negotiated by unions, but by the works councils, and the role of the work councils in establishing rules with a binding effect can therefore not be justified on the basis of a previous membership.[1616] Alternatively, the legitimation for the binding effect can be traced to the employment contract, as well as the democratic election of the works council in accordance with article 7 BetrVG. Thus, one may ask whether the competence of the council to enter into these agreements could also be

1607 Erfurter Kommentar zum Arbeitsrecht/Preis (2012), article 611, nr 207.

1608 Kommentar zum TVG/Wiedenmann (2007), introduction, nr 400 et seq.

1609 See critically Kommentar BetrVG/Richardi (2012), article 77, nr 95, as well as R. Waltermann, *Rechtsetzung durch Betriebsvereinbarung zwischen Privatautonomie und Tarifautonomie*, Tübingen: Mohr Siebeck 1996, p. 239–241.

1610 Erfurter Kommentar zum Arbeitsrecht/Kania (2012), article 87 no. 6.

1611 Kommentar BetrVG/Richardi (2012), article 77, nr 72, 86.

1612 See critically Kommentar BetrVG/Richardi (2012), article 77 nr 26–27, 69–70.

1613 See already BAG 30 January 1970, *NJW* 1970, 1620, par. B IV 3 b.

1614 P. Buck-Heeb, A. Dieckmann, *Selbstreguliering im Privatrecht*, Mohr Siebeck: Tübingen 2010, p. 204. Kommentar BetrVG/Richardi (2012), article 77, nr 296 argues that invalid BVs that are blocked by a TV in accordance with article 77 par. 3 BetrVG may become part of individual contracts.

1615 See for an overview on the extensive literature that this question has generated W. Linsenmaier, 'Normsetzung der Betriebsparteien und Individualrechte der Arbeitnehmer' *RdA* 2008, p. 2.

1616 H. Wiedemann, 'Normsetzung durch Vertrag', in: P. Hanau, F. Heither, J. Kühling (eds.), *Richterliches Arbeitsrecht, Festschrift für Thomas Dieterich*, München: Beck 1996, p. 680.

characterised in terms of an agency.[1617] Waltermann[1618] has convincingly argued that neither the contract for employment nor the possibility to elect members of the *Betriebsrat* can be seen as a sole basis for the competence of the *Betriebsrat.*

Although article 77 par. 3 BetrVG bars additional BVs, notwithstanding the *Günstigkeitsprinzip* in article 4 par. 3 TVG,[1619] which has also been accepted for BVs,[1620] parties to a TV may allow for complementary or even diverging BVs.[1621] If parties have not (expressly) allowed for additional BVs, the question whether a BV is allowed depends on the question of whether the TV seeks to provide an exhaustive arrangement of parties' rights and duties on a particular subject.[1622] In the light of these considerations, it can be doubted whether it is possible to extend the effect of TVs to non-member employees through additional BVs, thereby extending these agreements to parties who may not have had a chance to influence these agreements, increasing the chance of *Fremdbestimmung.*[1623]

- The development of framework agreements

At the European level, social dialogue finds it basis in article 155 TFEU. It is considered as an important medium to stimulate innovation and growth, as well as better governance by supporting the responsiveness of European measures.[1624] In contrast, it has been argued that article 155 TFEU merely sets a policy aim and cannot serve as a legal basis for European collective labour agreements.[1625] The European social dialogue may result in framework agreements, as an alternative to harmonisation. Notably, a framework agreement under article 155 TFEU can either be implemented in accordance with Member States practices, or it can, at the request of signatory parties, result in a Council Decision that is binding on the parties to whom it is addressed. Accordingly, the European Union Trade Confederation, in negotiation with the European Industry Federations, has established framework agreements on parental leave, part-time work and fixed-term contracts. Further sectoral agreements at the European level have also been established within this framework.[1626]

Smismans[1627] points out that so far, a refusal to enforce a framework agreement has not occurred. Notably, if the Commission does not accept the framework decision, an alternative

1617 See for example P. Kreutz, *Grenzen der Betriebsautonomie*, München: Beck 1979, p. 171–172.

1618 R. Waltermann, *Rechtsetzung durch Betriebsvereinbarung zwischen Privatautonomie und Tarifautonomie*, Tübingen: Mohr Siebeck 1996, p. 86 et seq, p. 205–206. W. Linsenmaier, 'Normsetzung der Betriebsparteien und Individualrechte der Arbeitnehmer' *RdA* 2008, p. 6 points out that there is no contractual basis for the agency between members of the works council and individual employees.

1619 Kommentar BetrVG/Richardi (2012), article 77, nr 241, Kommentar zum TVG/Wank (2007), article 5, nr 549.

1620 See, for example, BAG 7 November 1989, AP BetrVG 1972 §77 Nr. 46, par. C II 1.

1621 BAG 18 August 1987, *NZA* 1987, 779 par. II 3.

1622 BAG 17 December 1985, AP BetrVG 1972 §87 Tarifvorrang Nr. 5, in par. B II 3. See critically W. Däubler, 'Betriebsräte und Gewerkschaften', in: R. Anzinger, R. Wank (eds.), *Entwicklungen im Arbeitsrecht und Arbeitsschutzrecht. Festschrift für Otfried Wlotzke zum 70.* Geburtstag, München: Beck 1996, p. 273.

1623 See against this possibility Kommentar BetrVG/Richardi (2012), article 77, nr 289–290.

1624 COM (2002) 341 final.

1625 Grabitz/Hilf/Nettesheim, Das Recht der Europäischen Union/Benecke (48. Ergänzungslieferung 2012), article 155, nr 4.

1626 See www.etuc.org/r/2.

1627 S. Smismans, 'European social dialogue in the shadow of hierarchy', *Journal of Public Policy* 2008, p. 169.

agreement is not likely to be reached, and possible refusal or amendments may be a disincentive for parties negotiating on framework agreements. The question may arise whether provisions in such a Council Decision, as European law, put aside national mandatory law aiming to protect employees.

Article 153 par. 5 TFEU makes clear that framework agreements cannot concern the right to pay, the right to strike, the right to association or possible lock-outs. Also, framework agreements do not impose binding norms directly on their members' members – as individual employers and employees are not members of the parties negotiating framework agreements at the European level.

In addition, the European legislator has provided rules for European works councils or a procedure for Community-scale undertakings, but these councils do not have the right to bargain collectively. Directive 2009/38 aimed to provide rules for cross-border situation, reforming and repealing Directive 94/45, the application of which was problematic.[1628] The Directive further aimed to stimulate cross-border dialogue and accordingly consulted management and labour organisations in the reform of the 1994 Directive. As Müller and Platzer[1629] point out, the model of collective negotiations combined with works councils is reminiscent of both the German and the Dutch legal orders.

7.4.2.2. The role of non-state actors

What role do actors play in collective labour agreements at the national and European level?

Firstly, the role of non-state actors falls within the scope of article 9 par 3 GG.[1630] The BAG[1631] has held that the competence has been delegated from the state to unions and employers' organisations, which seems difficult to reconcile with article 9 par. 3 GG.[1632]

Arguably, the question of whether the competence of unions can be derived from constitutional rights may affect one's reasoning – it may, for example, have consequences for the scope of the competence of parties to alternative regulation: if parties exercise a constitutional right, this implies a broader competence than the exercise of a competence delegated by the state.[1633]

Regardless, the exercise of this right justifies a prominent role for private parties to develop binding rules that are not subsequently subject to democratic debate,[1634] which has been democratically sanctioned in the TVG. The role of non-state actors is, however,

1628 COM (2008) 419 final.

1629 T. Müller, H.-W. Platzer, 'European works councils', in: B. Keller, H.-W. Platzer (eds.), *Industrial relations and European integration*, Hampshire: Ashgate 2003, p. 58.

1630 BVerfG 18 November 1954, *NJW* 1954, 1881, par. A, and B, 2 b, BVerfG 24 May 1977, *NJW* 1977, 2255, par. B II 1 a. A. Söllner, 'Grenzen des Tarifvertrags', *NZA* 1996, p. 902 points out that the development of TVs is not seen against the background of private autonomy nor the freedom of association, as the TV is not an individual contract with a binding effect just for contract parties, but for third parties.

1631 BAG 15 January 1955, *NJW* 1955, 684, at 687.

1632 R. Waltermann, *Rechtsetzung durch Betriebsvereinbarung zwischen Privatautonomie und Tarifautonomie*, Tübingen: Mohr Siebeck 1996, p. 122 et seq notes that this theory can be traced to the more general idea of a monopoly for the state to establish *Rechtsnormen*.

1633 Kommentar zum TVG/Wiedemann (2007) article 1 nr 54, similarly G. Bachmann, *Private Ordnung*, Tübingen: Mohr Siebeck 2006, p. 127.

1634 H. Wiedemann, 'Normsetzung durch Vertrag', in: P. Hanau, F. Heither, J. Kühling (eds.), *Richterliches Arbeitsrecht, Festschrift fur Th omas Dieterich*, München: Beck 1996, p. 663.

limited as the exercise of private parties' constitutional rights does not justify *Fremdbestimmung*. If employees and employers subject themselves to rules developed in TVs through their membership of a union or employers' organisation, problems of *Fremdbestimmung* should theoretically not arise. Yet if he Minister declares TVs generally binding, this may lead to *Fremdbestimmung*.

Secondly, the role of non-state actors developing BVs is less prominent as the right to negotiate on BVs is not a constitutional right. The legislator is not constitutionally bound to prioritise TVs over BVs, but this priority follows from the better legitimation of TVs over BVs.[1635] Generally, BVs are considered to be more prone to *Fremdbestimmung* as BVs are negotiated by works councils and although these councils are democratically elected, employees cannot choose whether they will subject to the rules negotiated by the council.[1636]

The role of actors involved in the development of BVs is subject to more limitations, which has, however, not prevented BVs from playing an increasingly important role. This is also recognised by parties negotiating TVs who leave room for additional BVs. The question on what matters BVs may be established is controversial,[1637] and has given rise to the development of two competing theories, the *Vorrangtheorie*, followed by the BAG, and the *Zwei-Schranken-Theorie* that argues that the reservation in article 77 par. 3 BetrVG includes matters addressed by article 87 par. 1 BetrVG.[1638]

The BAG has held that, within the limits of article 77 par. 3 TVG, every matter addressed by article 1 TVG can be the subject of a BV.[1639] This is an *a contrario* interpretation of article 77 par. 3 BetrVG – if competences are not reserved to TVs, they can be dealt with through BVs. Notably, this is an extensive interpretation of parties' competence and one

1635 BVerfG 1 March 1979, *NJW* 1979, 699, par. C III 2 a.

1636 BAG 12 December 2006, AP BetrVG 1972 §77 Nr. 94, par. 21, 24, 25 has, however, held that the role of the democratically elected works councils safeguards that the interests of employees are taken into account, and are not compromised unfairly.

1637 See for example Kommentar BetrVG/Richardi (2012), article 77, nr 66–67, with an overview of recent case law and literature.

1638 See for example R. Waltermann, *Rechtsetzung durch Betriebsvereinbarung zwischen Privatautonomie und Tarifautonomie*, Tübingen: Mohr Siebeck 1996, p. 285 et seq.

1639 See already BAG 16 March 1956, *NJW* 1956, 1086, par. I. 1. BAG AP BetrVG 1972 §77 Nr. 21 (also available under *NZA* 1987, 639), par. B 4 bb, confirmed in BAG AP BetrVG 1972 §87 Lohngestaltung Nr. 51, par. C I 4. These decisions have been extensively motivated because of the controversy on this question and the following reasons can be deduced from these cases: Firstly, if article 77 par. 3 BetrVG would exclude BVs in issues addressed by article 87 par. 1 BetrVG, it would, according to the BAG, simultaneously exclude co-determination. Secondly, if no TV has been established, even though that is customary in the sense of article 77 par. 3 BetrVG, it is undesirable that article 77 par. 3 BetrVG would also block rights to co-determination, realised through BVs, which would leave employees without the protection of either a TV or a BV. Thirdly, the BAG points to the importance of the protection of employees, stating that if, in accordance with article 87 par. 1 BetrVG an issue is already stipulated by law or by TV, the possibility of the employer to decide independently on these issues will typically be limited and thus, the aim of mandatory co-determination – to limit the power of the employer – will already have been achieved. Somewhat confusingly, in contrast, the reasoning of the BAG in par. B 4 cc emphasises that the possibility of voluntary BVs in the absence of co-determination rights (in accordance with article 88 BetrVG) shows that co-determination rights should not be equated with BVs and that conversely, the reservation in article 77 par. 3 BetrVG with regard to BVs should not be equated with co-determination rights.

may ask how this interpretation sits with the question of *Fremdbestimmung* by parties to a BV.[1640] As a result, *Betriebsrate* and employers may establish a BV regardless of the existence of a TV. However, if there is no co-determination for the *Betriebsrat*, because a particular issue is left to voluntary BVs under article 88 BetrVG, TVs will have precedence.[1641]

Thirdly, at European level, the role of non-state actors is less prominent as constitutional rights do not play a similar role at the European level, although article 152 TFEU stipulates that the Union recognises the roles of social partners at the European level. However, the Commission has taken a top-down approach to the role of unions and employers' organisations, and exercises control over which non-state actors are involved in the development of framework agreements.[1642] Yet within the framework set by the Commission, parties are free to negotiate,[1643] and once parties have agreed, this agreement cannot be modified.

European free movement law may, in addition, limit the role of national unions.[1644] The question arises whether these restrictions will prompt parties negotiating TVs to take into account the interests of foreign businesses not involved in the negotiating process. Even if national parties do so, or even if they involve foreign businesses in negotiations, it need not mean that foreign businesses will be interested in complying with TVs rather than go below the levels of protection in TVs.

7.4.2.3. The development of control mechanisms

Both at the European and at the national level, state actors have imposed limits on the role of non-state actors to develop rules that may become binding on third parties. At the national level, the possibility that private actors may impose binding rules on third parties has led to the development of control mechanisms.

TVs are generally not subjected to judicial evaluation as they are established to the mutual benefit of both employer and employees and accordingly fall within the *Richtigkeitsgewähr*.[1645] This is also recognised in article 310 par. 4 BGB that exempts TVs from judicial control under articles 305–310 BGB.[1646] This exception gives private parties discretion with regard to the content of TVs, within the scope of mandatory laws.

[1640] Alternatively, it has been argued that the competence of *Betriebsrate* should be based on article 88 BetrVG, see for example Erfurter Kommentar zum BetrVG/Kania (2012), article 77, nr 36.

[1641] Erfurter Kommentar zu Arbeitsrecht/Kania (2012), article 77 nr 53.

[1642] COM (93) 600 final and COM (1998) 322 final.

[1643] COM (93) 600 final, par. 31.

[1644] CJEU 11 December 2007 (International Transport Workers' Federation and Finnish Seamen's Union v Viking Line ABP and OÜ Viking Line Eesti), C-438/05, [2007] ECR, p. I-10779, CJEU 18 December 2007 (Laval un Partneri Ltd v Svenska Byggnadsarbetareförbundet), C-341/05, [2007] ECR, p. I-11767.

[1645] W. Schmidt-Rimpler, 'Zum Vertragsproblem', in: F. Baur, L. Raiser (eds.), *Funktionswandel der Privatrechtsinstitutionen Festschrift für Ludwig Raiser*, Tübingen: Mohr Siebeck 1974, p. 13 has denied that TVs fall within the scope of the *Richtigkeitsgewähr*, as doubts with regard to the negative *Richtigkeitsgewähr* may arise.

[1646] P. Buck-Heeb, A. Dieckmann, *Selbstregulierung im Privatrecht*, Tübingen: Mohr Siebeck 2010, p. 202.

Yet *Fremdbestimmung* can arise when TVs are declared generally binding, a competence that is, however, reserved to state actors. Because possible *Fremdbestimmung* remains, various mechanisms should ensure that the declaration does not result in declaring the TV of a limited number of stakeholders binding, irrespective of the legitimate interests of others. These compensating mechanisms include:

1) It is only possible to declare TVs, or parts of TVs, generally binding when the public interest so requires.[1647] The Ministry may not suffice by merely sanctioning a TV, and a TV may not be declared generally binding because it is in the interest of the parties to a TV.
2) Article 5 par. 2 TVG stipulates that the interests of employees who are not members of a union and who have not had the opportunity to influence the TV should be taken into account in deciding whether to declare a TV generally binding or not, in accordance with the principle of democracy.[1648]
3) Unbound employees and employers subject to a generally binding TV may challenge the declaration before the court.[1649]
4) Parties to a TV who do not agree with the declaration – or the lack thereof – of their own TV or competing TVs may in addition turn to administrative courts, in accordance with article 40 *Verwaltungsgerichtsordnung*.[1650]
5) Parties' negotiating room has been limited by mandatory law.

The first four safeguards provide third parties with a possibility to influence rules that may be imposed upon them, thus limiting the role of negotiating parties to a TV as well as the discretion of the Ministry to declare TVs generally binding. The possibility for parties to resist or challenge declarations under article 5 TVG has contributed to the decreasing use of these declarations.[1651] As an alternative, the legislator has created the possibility to issue a *Verordnung* in the sense of article 80 GG in specific cases,[1652] instead of a declaration, which limits the possibility of parties to veto declarations in the sense of article 5 TVG.

1647 For example when non-bound employers seek to profit from not entering into a TV by offering lower salaries and benefits, which may undermine the positions of employers who have entered into a TV. This problem may be increased by Europeanisation. Comp. K.-S. Hohenstatt, N. Schramm, Tarifliche Mindestlöhne: Ihre Wirkungsweise und ihre Vermeidung am Beispiel des Tarifvertrags zum Post-Mindestlohn, *NZA* 2008, p. 435.

1648 E. Stalhacke, 'Die Allgemeinverbindlicherklärung von Tarifverträgen über das Arbeitszeitende im Verkauf', *NZA* 1988, p. 346.

1649 Kommentar zum TVG Löwisch/Rieble (2004), article 5 nr 141.

1650 BverwG 3 November 1988, *NJW* 1989, 1495.

1651 F.J. Düwell, 'Die gerichtliche Überprüfung der Allgemeinverbindlicherklärung von Tarifverträgen', *NZA-Beilage* 2011, p. 80. Kommentar zum TVG/Wank (2007) article 5, nr 10–11 holds that the generally binding TVs continue to play an important role in some branches in particular.

1652 See for example article 7 *Arbeitnehmer-Entsendegesetz*.

The role of parties to a BV is subject to further-going limitations in the form of judicial control as these agreements do not fall within the scope of the *Richtigkeitsgewähr*,[1653] although article 310 par. 4 BGB exempts BVs from judicial evaluation. The BAG[1654] has emphasised that the agreements entered into by the *Betriebsrat* must meet the requirements of proportionality, stating that the judicial control on BVs is stricter than TVs because, firstly, TVs are the result of the practice of a constitutionally-protected right, and secondly, the binding effect of TVs is legitimised with preceding membership.[1655] Richardi[1656] states that judicial control does not entail a control of the *content* of BVs and courts may not repair these agreements. Instead, courts evaluate whether parties to a BV have acted in accordance with the limits imposed by higher laws and TVs.

The role of non-state actors at the European level is also subject to limitations. Notably, the European Commission plays a central role in the selection of actors participating in the development of framework agreements, in accordance with the guidelines provided by the Commission.[1657] However, the CJEU exercises little control with regard to the requirement of representativeness:[1658]

> 'It is proper to stress the importance of the obligation incumbent on the Commission and the Council to verify the representativity of the signatories to [a framework agreement] (...) The participation of the two institutions in question has the effect (...) of endowing an agreement between management and labour with a Community foundation of a legislative character, without recourse to the classic procedures provided for under the Treaty for the preparation of legislation, which entail the participation of the European Parliament. As case-law makes clear, the participation of that institution in the Community legislative procedure reflects at Community level the fundamental democratic principle that people must share in the exercise of power through a representative assembly (...) the principle of democracy on which the Union is founded, requires – in the absence of the participation of the European Parliament in the legislative process – that the participation of the people be otherwise assured, in this instance through the parties representative of management and labour who concluded the agreement which is endowed by the Council.'

This test is a limited one, focusing on the assessment of the Council and the Commission. The Court does not question the criteria of representativeness established by the

1653 See already BAG 30 January 1970, *NJW* 1970, 1620, par. B IV 3 b. See critically H. Wiedemann, 'Normsetzung durch Vertrag', in: P. Hanau, F. Heither, J. Kühling (eds.), *Richterliches Arbeitsrecht, Festschrift fur Th omas Dieterich*, München: Beck 1996, p. 682, stating that the correctness of this assumption can just as well be doubted as the assumption of equality between parties to a TV. The reference to '*Recht und Billigkeit*' in article 75 par 1 BetrVG may be interpreted as an indication that there should be a test.

1654 BAG 12.12.2006, AP BetrVG 1972 §77 Nr. 94, par. 21, 24, 25.

1655 Accordingly, R. Richardi, *Kollektivgewalt und Individualwille bei der Gestaltung des Arbeitsverhältnisses*, München: Beck 1968, p. 313–314 qualifies the BV as '*Zwangsordnung*', a non-voluntary order.

1656 BetrVG/Richardi (2012) article 77 nr 124.

1657 COM (93) 600 final and COM (1998) 322 final.

1658 CJEU 17 June 1998 (UEAPME v Council of the European Union), T-135/96, ECR [1998], p. II-2335, par. 88–89.

Commission and Council.[1659] Consequently, actors that have been selected to participate in the development of framework agreements enjoy a wide range of discretion that is subject to few additional controls.

7.4.2.4. Comparison

The role of state actors and non-state actors diverges at the European and the national level. Even though the right of parties to bargain collectively has been recognised at the European level, and the development of framework agreements falls within this right, the role of non-state actors is simultaneously larger and smaller: if non-state actors participate in the development of framework agreements, their role will be considerably more influential than the role of parties involved in TVs and BVs that are subject to much more control mechanisms. Simultaneously, more collective agreements have been developed at national level.

The restrictions imposed by European law and the development of framework agreements may curtail the development of national collective agreements. Moreover, traditional notions of private autonomy and *Fremdbestimmung* become compromised as framework agreements are not subject to national control mechanisms, while European control mechanisms remain limited. Whittaker[1660] notes that collective contracts that are not in accordance with the individual notion of freedom of contract are likely to meet with resistance from national lawyers who find that the rights of weaker parties are limited through collectively-bargained contracts, which in the UAPME decision has clearly been the case.

7.4.3. Conclusion on state actors and non-state actors

State actors have enabled non-state actors to develop binding that have subsequently been reinforced by state actors. The inclusion of non-state actors through dynamic referral, for example the role of the IASB, and the development of the Lamfalussy procedure and comitology increases the chance that European law reflects the interests of non-national actors that are not sufficiently taken into account at the national level. However, on closer inspection, these interests are likely considered by the DRSC. Simultaneously, both German and European state actors have imposed limits on the role of non-state actors. German actors have developed a wide range of control mechanisms, often used in combination with one another: control of the substance of co-regulation such as the *Kodex*, conditions under which TVs can be declared generally binding, judicial control, for example over BVs; the appointment or control over actors developing co-regulation, such as the DRSC and the *Kodex*, the organisation of extensive decision-making processes, visible in the development of the *Kodex* and the DRSC, and the development of mandatory law, for TVs and BVs.

1659 Critically K. Armstrong, 'Rediscovering civil society: the European Union and the White Paper on Governance', *ELJ* 2002, p. 125–126 as well as Grabitz/Hilf/Nettesheim, Das Recht der Europäischen Union/Benecke (48. Ergänzungslieferung 2012), article 154, nr 10.

1660 S. Whittaker, 'On the development of European standard contract terms', *ERCL* 2006, p. 74.

The European legislator has sought to limit the role of non-state actors through much less varied control mechanisms: by imposing restraints on comitology and by the participation of state actors in the development of co-regulation. The European legislator has exercised restraint in controlling the substance of binding rules, because non-state actors may have considerable difficulty in reaching agreement on binding rules. The European legislator does not consider the organisation of extensive drafting processes as a way to compensate for *Fremdbestimmung*, if only because of the potential length of inclusive procedures. Quite the opposite: some decision-making processes preceding European co-regulation are the opposite of open and inclusive. Control over the substance of co-regulation is equally problematic considering the difficulties of parties at the European level to reach a consensus.

Differences have become apparent between the limitations of non-state actors' roles at the European and the national level. As a result, interdependence between European and German actors becomes visible. German actors are less able to influence the development of framework agreements and to determine the role of non-state actors. Notably, if fewer restrictions have been imposed on the role of non-state actors at the European level, potentially, more *Fremdbestimmung* may develop that German state actors cannot control.

In contrast, EU actors do have power to influence the role of non-state actors. Specifically, European law may impose restrictions on TVs, even if they are developed in accordance with the *Richtigkeitsgewähr*. These restrictions primarily concern the effect of TVs on foreign actors wishing to gain access to domestic markets. Thereby, the development of framework agreements that give rise to *Fremdbestimmung* and European restrictions on TVs may undermine traditional national techniques to develop private law in this area. Similarly, the introduction of international accounting standards at the European level may diminish the role of the DRSC, thereby circumventing the control mechanisms established at the national level. Consequently, insofar as forms of alternative regulation have been established to prevent that European legislative competences would expand, at the expense of national competences,[1661] this approach has clearly not been as successful as national actors would like.

Interdependece may simultaneously be the cause for the increasing visibility of non-state actors. Particularly, national and especially European state actors increasingly depend on the expertise of non-state actors, and the inclusion of non-state actors should strengthen the responsiveness of the law in this areas to the needs and preferences of practice, provided that all representative actors have bene included. That is not always the case.

If, in the development of European co-regulation, relevant actors are not included, this may inhibit the increased responsiveness of the law developed by national and transnational actors. A lack of responsiveness may also become visible if the development of framework agreements does not take place in an open and inclusive manner, which makes it difficult to verify that negotiations – rather than deliberation – has taken place

[1661] As argued by N. Krisch, *Beyond constitutionalism: The pluralist structure of postnational law*, Oxford: OUP 2010, p. 228.

in the development of framework agreements. It is not clear whether actors sufficiently representative of national actors have been included in the European social dialogue, or that their interests have been considered. This contradicts the ideal of 'directly-deliberative polyarchy',[1662] according to which interested parties directly participate and where local insights are shared in the decision-making process.

Furthermore, because European co-regulation has not been developed in procedures as thoroughly organised as procedures at the national level, and as European initiatives have overlooked national concerns, national actors may not feel particularly inclined to justify divergences in national initiatives, or pay more attention to the interests of international and foreign actors. It follows that the development of law by transnational actors need not prompt further justification from national actors, in conformity with pluralist arguments.

Conversely, it is not apparent that European actors take into account the interests of domestic parties. Foreign and international actors need not necessarily be interested in complying with or being included in TVs or BVs. Clearly, private actors may pursue private interests, for example by going below the level of protection in TVs, which may give these actors a competitive advantage over competitors complying with TVs or BVs. After the decisions in *UAPME*, *Viking* and *Laval*, international and foreign actors may have little interest in entering into national collective agreements, s national unions have less possibilities to pressure international employers.

Notwithstanding criticism on a state-centric perception of the law, the assumption that public actors pursue public interests and private actors pursue private interests remains valid. Although it has been argued in this overview that state actors are not the source of all binding rules, their orientation can be a good reason for the control of state actors on the development of binding rules.

7.5. Non-state actors

This paragraph will ask what role non-state actors play in the development of private law.

Non-state actors, including private parties, form a diverse group, who are generally not competent to establish binding rules. Instead, they may create rules through self-regulation.[1663] Generally, the success of self-regulation varies,[1664] and it is still considered critically, also in cases where successful self-regulation has been established:[1665]

[1662] J. Cohen, Ch. Sabel, 'Directly-deliberative polyarchy', *ELJ* 1997, p. 314.

[1663] It has been established previously that this research defines self-regulation as the making of rules and norms by both by contract parties or a group of persons or bodies binding contract parties or this group, including other private actors that choose to be bound by the rules made through self-regulation, see previously par 1.1.

[1664] See for an overview P. Buck-Heeb, A. Dieckmann, *Selbstregulierung im Privatrecht*, Tübingen: Mohr Siebeck 2010, p. 2.

[1665] M. Schmidhuber, *Verhaltenskodizes im nationalen und grenzüberschreitenden elektronischen Geschäftsverkehr, Zur Frage der Integration der Selbstregulierung durch Private in die staatliche Rechtsordnung*, Frankfurt am Main: Lang 2004, p. 23, 44.

> 'Deutlich wird (...) das die Selbstregulierung unter dauerndem Erfolgsdruck steht. Dabei gilt es darzutun, dass die schneller, beweglicher und wirksamer ist als seine gesetzliche Lösung. Schließlich wird die Praxis der Selbstregulierung sehr viel intensiver und argwöhnischer beobachtet als seine gesetzliche Regelung, so dass jeder Fall, bei dem sich Mängel des Systems zeigen, sofort als Beweis für das Versagen von Selbstregulierung herangezogen wird.'[1666]

However, increasing the chance of successful self-regulation by enabling private actors to establish binding rules meets with problems of *Fremdbestimmung*.

In addition, self-regulation may develop beyond the national level. Does the development of transnational self-regulation pose a threat to the German framework or does it prompt German actors to consider the interests of international actors?

Is the distinction between public and private actors visible in the development of self-regulation and should the role of state actors be diminished?

Notably, the German legal order distinguishes between various forms of self-regulation. Contractual self-regulation will be discussed in paragraph 7.5.1. Instances of contractual self-regulation need to be considered in the light of the *Richtigkeitsgewähr*. This theory considers the extent to which parties realise their own aims in accordance with private autonomy, and upholds or limits the effect of contracts accordingly. Other forms of self-regulation are the drafting of rules by organisations which can be enforced on the basis of the articles of association ('*Satzung*', in dutch: '*statuten*') of those organisations,[1667] analysed in paragraph 7.5.2, and self-regulation established by one-sided juridical acts, considered in paragraph 7.5.3. At first sight, this form of self-regulation may especially give rise to problems of enforcement as one-sided juridical acts are not binding.[1668] Paragraph 7.5.4 will end with a conclusion.

7.5.1. Contractual self-regulation

Paragraph 7.5.1.1 will consider the idea of the *Richtigkeitsgewähr* and the effect of individual contracts. Paragraph 7.5.1.2 will discuss collectively negotiated contracts. Paragraph 7.5.1.3 will turn to model contracts and paragraph 7.5.1.4 will discuss STCs. Paragraph 7.5.1.5 will end with a conclusion.

In discussing the instances of self-regulation and the roles of actors, the paragraph will look at the role of non-state actors that becomes apparent from these instances, the role of state actors in the reinforcement of self-regulation, and the subsequent role of state actors in the limitation of non-state actor roles.

1666 P. Buck-Heeb, A. Dieckmann, *Selbstregulierung im Privatrecht*, Tübingen: Mohr Siebeck 2010 p. 218.

1667 Self-regulation on the basis of articles of association has been considered as a separate category in German literature, see further below par. 7.2.5.6 and 7.2.5.7.

1668 See further below, par. 7.5.3.5.

7.5.1.1. The role of individual contract parties

What role do actors play in the development of rules in their contracts? Notably, not all contractual agreements are binding – this depends on the extent to which parties can realise their own aims through negotiating a contract. The view on the binding effects of contracts is in accordance with the principle of private autonomy and notions of *Fremdbestimmung*.

A central concept underlying the binding force of contracts is the concept of the *Richtigkeitsgewähr*[1669] defended by Schmidt-Rimpler:

> 'Der Vertrag ist ein *Mechanismus*, um ohne hoheitliche Gestaltung in *begrenztem* Rahmen eine richtige Regelung auch gegen unrichtigen Willen herbeizuführen, weil immer der durch die Unrichtigkeit Betroffene zustimmen muß.'[1670]

Linguistically, the *Richtigkeitsgewähr* refers to the safeguard ('*Gewähr*') of just and effective agreements ('*Richtigkeit*').[1671] That does not mean that the law as such assumes that all parties' negotiations are correct; merely, it respects the outcome of parties' negotiations as an expression of mutual party autonomy. Some authors[1672] have argued that it is more convincing to speak of *Richtigkeitschance* – the chance, rather than the warranty, that parties will come to just and effective agreements.

With its emphasis on parties' mutual autonomy, the *Richtigkeitsgewähr* explains why contracts should be binding on contact parties, and not on others. Although this question has been discussed extensively in contract theory, other legal orders have come up with diverging suggestions.[1673] The binding force of contracts has been justified on the basis of utilitarian principles, society's legal views on justice, and the mutual beneficiality of mutual executory promises,[1674] while other explanations base the binding force of contracts on party autonomy.[1675] The concept of *Richtigkeitsgewähr*, at first sight, is reminiscent of the consent of contract as bargain, visible in the English and U.S. legal

1669 This concept has, as such, not been studied in the Dutch legal order and also does not seem to have been studied in common law jurisdictions despite the emphasis on "contract as bargain". The concept may be more familiar in legal orders more influenced by the German legal order such as the Austrian legal order.

1670 W. Schmidt-Rimpler, 'Grundfragen einer Erneuerung des Vertragsrechts', *AcP* 1941, p. 156.

1671 W. Schmidt-Rimpler, 'Grundfragen einer Erneuerung des Vertragsrechts', *AcP* 1941, p. 132, defines *Richtig*, as, on the one hand, "just" as well as "effective", seen from the point of view of a legal order. Effectiveness may however, not contradict justice (p. 133). See critically L. Raiser, 'Vertragsfunktion und Vertragsfreiheit', in: E. von Caemmerer, E. Friesenhahn, R. Lange (eds.), *Hundert Jahre deutsches Rechtsleben, Festschrift zum hundertjährigen Bestehen des Deutschen Juristentages, I*, Karlsruhe: Muller 1960, p. 118.

1672 Roth/Schubert MunchKomm zum BGB 2012, art 242 nr 463, following M. Wolf, *Rechtsgeschäftliche Entscheidungsfreiheit und vertraglicher Interessenausgleich*, Tübingen: Mohr Siebeck 1970, p. 73–74.

1673 See for an overview of the most common theories and their defects R. Barnett, 'A consent theory of contract', *Columbia Law Review* 1986, p. 269.

1674 P.S. Atiyah, *Promises, morals, and the law*, Oxford: Clarendon 1982, p. 209 et seq.

1675 Ch. Fried, *Contract as promise: A theory of contractual obligation*, Cambridge, Mass: Harvard University Press 1981.

order, expressed, for example, in the requirement of consideration.[1676] Especially the emphasis on parties bargaining for consideration is reminiscent of the *Richtigkeitsgewähr*.[1677] However, differently from the German perspective, the process-based explanation of the requirement of consideration still requires that something of value in the eyes of the law is exchanged. This theory does not look critically enough at the quality of the bargaining process and the actors in that process. Therefore, this theory fails to explain why agreements between some parties (such as financial arrangements between family members) are not meant to be binding, whereas some business agreements that have not expressly been negotiated should be binding.[1678] In contrast, the *Richtigkeitsgewähr* has no trouble explaining cases in which negotiations will not necessarily lead to results that should be upheld.[1679] Furthermore, the process-based explanation of consideration overlooks implicit negotiations between parties. Of course the assumption that parties negotiate before entering into a contract may not always be realistic, yet even if parties are not inclined to negotiate everyday contracts, they may still choose with whom to do business, based on, for example, the pricing and quality of products offered for sale.

These justifications differ from the justification provided by the *Richtigkeitsgewähr* that should not, according to Schmidt-Rimpler,[1680] be traced to parties' wills, as those wills are not necessarily laudable. Consequently, the main basis of the *Richtigkeitsgewähr* is not the idea that contracts are a way for individual parties to realise *Selbstbestimmung*. Instead, the *Richtigkeitsgewähr* emphasises contract parties' negotiations with one another. Consequently, contracts will usually also contain an element of *Fremdbestimmung* for each party, as the result of the contract is a *compromise* between parties and the terms of the contract are influenced by *both* parties. If and insofar as both parties are able to establish their own rules through contracting with one another, there is *Selbstbestimmung* for both parties.[1681] The positive *Richtigkeitsgewähr* entails that negotiations lead to a contract where that is in both parties' interests, while the negative *Richtigkeitsgewähr* entails that if during negotiations parties find that a contract is not in their mutual interest, there will be no contract.[1682]

1676 This requirement entails that a party can only enforce a prominent as a contractually binding promise if the promisee must suffer a detriment or the promisor must obtain some benefit. In English law, consideration can be traced to *Pinnel's* case, (1603) 77 ER 237. In U.S. law, the requirement of consideration can be found in section 71 of the Restatement (Second) of Contracts.

1677 R. Barnett, 'A consent theory of contract', *Columbia Law Review* 1986, p. 287.

1678 R. Barnett, 'A consent theory of contract', *Columbia Law Review* 1986, p.289–290.

1679 Comp. W. Schmidt-Rimpler, 'Zum Vertragsproblem', in: F. Baur, L. Raiser (eds.), *Funktionswandel der Privatrechtsinstitutionen Festschrift fur Ludwig Raiser*, Tübingen: Mohr Siebeck 1974, p. 13–14, 17.

1680 W. Schmidt-Rimpler, 'Grundfragen einer Erneuerung des Vertragsrechts', *AcP* 1941, p. 157, 170–172 as well as W. Schmidt-Rimpler, 'Zum Problem der Geschäftsgrundlage', in: R. Dietz (ed.), *Festschrift für Hans Carl Nipperdey zum 60. Geburtstag*, München: Beck 1955, p. 8. See differently W. Flume, 'Rechtsgeschaft und Privatautonomie', in: E. von Caemmerer, E. Friesenhahn, R. Lange (eds.) *Hundert Jahre deutsches Rechtsleben, Festschrift zum hundertjährigen Bestehen des deutschen Juristentages, I*, Karlsruhe: Muller 1960, p. 141.

1681 W. Schmidt-Rimpler, 'Zum Vertragsproblem', in: F. Baur, L. Raiser (eds.), *Funktionswandel der Privatrechtsinstitutionen, Festschrift für Ludwig Raiser zum 70. Geburtstag*, Tübingen: Mohr Siebeck 1974, p. 20–22. The idea has been criticised as well, for example K. Adomeit, 'Die gestärte Vertragsparität – ein Trugbild', *NJW* 1994, p. 2468.

1682 W. Schmidt-Rimpler, 'Zum Vertragsproblem', in: F. Baur, L. Raiser (eds.), *Funktionswandel der Privatrechtsinstitutionen Festschrift fur Ludwig Raiser*, Tübingen: Mohr Siebeck 1974, p. 6.

Schmidt-Rimpler[1683] has emphasised that the idea of *Richtigkeitsgewähr* does not mean that contracts should be seen as a source of law.[1684] This argument can be traced to the distinction between *Rechtsnormen* and *Rechtsgeschäfte*, and the underlying assumption that private parties act mainly in their own interests. This line of reasoning also limits the effect of contracts: contracts that can be imposed upon third parties would bind third parties to rules that would be in the interest of contract parties but not necessarily of third parties, and problems of *Fremdbestimmung* would arise. Consequently, differing from other theories on the binding force of contract, the *Richtigkeitsgewähr*, and the *Fremdbestimmung* that arises in the absence of *Richtigkeitsgewähr*, also offer an explanation for limiting the binding force of contracts negotiated between parties.

Accordingly, the *Richtigkeitsgewähr* indicates that limits should be imposed on the role of private parties where negotiations between parties do not justify binding force, for example in cases of mistake, where the will of parties in negotiations is defective,[1685] or if parties do not have a choice of contract parties.[1686] Further, negotiations will not necessarily result in an outcome representing both parties' interests if parties are not in equal bargaining positions.[1687] Importantly, however, the *Richtigkeitsgewähr* itself will not indicate in which cases parties are unequal to such an extent that contracts between them should not be upheld – the decision to, for example, protect weaker parties by imposing limits on what parties can negotiate by establishing mandatory consumer protection, is the outcome of the political process.[1688]

Consequently, the *Richtigkeitsgewähr* need not be based on a formal view of contract parties' negotiations, nor does the law simply assume that because parties negotiate, the outcome needs to be respected. The law goes further and looks at the quality of the bargaining process. Therefore, differing from the justifications for the binding force of contracts in other legal orders,[1689] the justification of the binding force of contracts on contract parties remains the negotiation process between parties. The limitation of parties' negotiations, or the development of doctrines of mistake and duress, do not displace parties' *mutual* autonomy as a basis for the binding force of contracts.

1683 W. Schmidt-Rimpler, 'Grundfragen einer Erneuerung des Vertragsrechts', *AcP* 1941, p. 156, 159, 161, 164. Similarly W. Flume, 'Rechtsgeschaft und Privatautonomie', in: *Hundert Jahre deutsches Rechtsleben, Festschrift zum hundertjährigen Bestehen des deutschen Juristentages, I*, Karlsruhe: Müller 1960 p. 141–142. See differently F. Roschr, 'Vertragrechtstheorie mit Herrschaftsfunktion?' *ZRP* 1972, p. 111.

1684 C.F. von Savigny, *System des heutigen römischen Rechts, I*, Berlin: Veit 1840 p. 12.

1685 W. Schmidt-Rimpler, 'Grundfragen einer Erneuerung des Vertragsrechts', *AcP* 1941, p. 182, as well as W. Schmidt-Rimpler, 'Zum Problem derGeschäft sgrundlage', in: R. Dietz (ed.), *Festschrift fur Hans Carl Nipperdey zum 60. Geburtstag*, München: Beck 1955, p. 10.

1686 See further F. Bydlinski, 'Kontrahierungszwang', *AcP* 1980, p. 1.

1687 Comp. the criticism of L. Raiser, 'Vertragsfunktion und Vertragsfreiheit', in: E. von Caemmerer, E. Friesenhahn, R. Lange (eds.) *Hundert Jahre deutsches Rechtsleben, Festschrift zum hundertjahrigen Bestehen des deutschen Juristentages, I*, Karlsruhe: Muller 1960, p. 118. Differently U. Wackerbarth, 'Unternehmer, Verbraucher, und die Rechtfertigung der Inhaltskontrolle vorformulierter Verträge', *AcP* 2000, p. 57.

1688 Comp. prominently on this development C.-W. Canaris, 'Wandlungen des Schuldvertragsrechts – Tendenzen zu seiner "Marerialisierung"', *AcP* 2000, p. 273, 278.

1689 See for example P.S. Atiyah, *Promises, morals, and the law*, Oxford: Clarendon 1982, p. 215.

If contracts do not fall within the scope of the *Richtigkeitsgewähr*, the role of parties can be limited through various means. Potential *Fremdbestimmung* may be a reason for judicial control, for example the control of STCs.[1690] Alternatively the executive may encourage stakeholder organisations to provide guidelines and other instruments that improve weaker parties' bargaining positions.[1691] The problem of *Fremdbestimmung* may even trigger constitutional protection, for example, if the weaker party's lack of choice of contract parties leads to a breach of the right to free personal development in article 2 GG.[1692] In addition, the role of contract parties may be restricted by mandatory law.

Thus, the *Richtigkeitsgewähr* explains when contracts should not be binding, or when the binding force of contracts should be subject to control mechanisms – in other words, when the role of contract parties, or, more particularly, one contract party, should be limited. Other legal orders have not developed similar justifications that consistently explain the development of control mechanisms.

At the European level, the principle of freedom of contract has been recognised,[1693] specifically by the CJEU, in relation to article 16 Charter.[1694] The

1690 This option was rejected by W. Schmidt-Rimpler, 'Grundfragen einer Erneuerung des Vertragsrechts', *AcP* 1941, p. 157, 167. Arguably, judicial control does not "restore" private parties' autonomy. Instead, altering the contract puts the judge in the position of contract parties.

1691 For example, the Bundesministerium (BMELV) has advocated the development of such instruments, which has resulted in established protocols and checklists for negotiations with banks and finance companies. See www.bmelv.de/DE/Verbraucherschutz/Finanzen-Versicherung/finanzen-versicherung_node.html and www.vz-nrw.de/UNIQ134003479704955/link780871A.html.

1692 See for example BVerfG 27 August 2005, *NJW* 2006, 598, par. 2 b aa.

1693 The principle is also reflected in the free choice left to private parties in article 3 Regulation Rome I and various measures in consumer contract law emphasise consumers' freedom in choosing their contract parties across borders, see for example consideration 4 in the preamble to Directive 2008/48 on consumer credit, stating that divergences in contract law restrict consumers' freedom to make use of cross-border credit, consideration 3 in the preamble to Directive 90/314 on package travel, finding that harmonisation would enable consumers to compare package travel from tour operators in different Member States, or consideration 2 in the preamble to Directive 1999/44 on consumer sales that states that free movement entails that consumers should be free to purchase goods in another Member State on the basis of uniform rules. The principle is also reflected in EU soft law, see article II-1:102 DCFR, article 1:102 PECL and article 1.1. of the UNIDROIT Principles. Comp. G. Davies, 'Freedom of contract and the horizontal effect of free movement law', in: D. Leczykiewicz, S. Weatherill (eds.), *The involvement of EU law in private relationships*, Oxford: Hart 2013, p. 53 who considers restriction of free movement as a restriction upon parties' preferences to contract across borders.

1694 CJEU 18 July 2013 (Alemo-Herron and Others v Parkwood Leisure Ldt), C-426/11, [2013] ECR p. I-0, par. 31–32. The Explanations relating to the Charter of Fundamental Rights, O.J. 2007 C 303/17 specifically refers to freedom of contract with regard to article 16. Previously, see CJEU 10 July 1991 (Jean Neu and others v Secrétaire d'Ētat à l'Agriculture et à la Viticulture) joined Cases C-90 and 91/90, [1991] ECR I-3617, par. 13 stressed the freedom to choose who to do business with, alongside with freedom of trade and profession. CJEU 18 September 1992 (Automec v European Commission), T-24/90, [1992] ECR, p. II-2223, par. 50–52, held that it was not competent to order one party to enter into a contract with another party, as that would be contrary to the principle of freedom of contract, especially if there were other remedies to end infringement on competition law, freedom of contract must remain the rule. However, the court considered that national courts could order parties to enter into a contract, as a possible consequence of concluding a contract contrary to competition law. CJEU 5 October 1999 (Spain v Commission), C-240/97 [1999] ECR I-6571, par. 99 reiterated the principle of freedom of contract, holding that 'the right of parties to amend contracts concluded by them is based

CJEU[1695] has also recognised contracts as a source of binding obligations for parties. However, the role of actors entering into contracts falling under the scope of the private law *acquis* differs from the role of actors under German law as the European legislator has emphasised problems for the internal market and consumer protection rather than the quality of the negotiating process. Although the acquis stresses that in order to conclude a contract, parties need to agree, the way in which they come to their agreement has not been subject to further consideration. The *acquis* has, for example, not developed rules in the areas of mistake and other defects in consent. In addition, the view that private parties mainly pursue their own interests rather than the public interest has not been defended as such at European level.[1696]

At first sight, the emphasis at the European level on entering freely into transactions both domestically and transnationally may be difficult to reconcile with the development of EU mandatory law that limit parties' freedom of contract, both domestically and transnationally.[1697] These limitations have been defended in the light of market or economic failures[1698] and the CJEU[1699] has emphasised information requirements as a primary means of consumer protection, which may also ensure that consumers are aware of their rights and obligations under the contract, to enable them to enforce their rights and compare between competitors effectively.[1700]

Although the German case study[1701] doubted whether a more general principle of the protection of weaker parties can be deduced from Directive 93/13, a broader view of the *acquis* and the Charter does reveal a more general tendency to protect weaker parties. However, arguably, the intervention of the EU legislator and the CJEU in situations where parties are not in an equal bargaining position can theoretically also be defended in the light of controlling hetero-determination. The duty of sellers to provide sufficient

on the principle of contractual freedom and cannot, therefore, be limited in the absence of Community rules imposing specific restrictions in that regard.'

1695 CJEU 18 July 2007 (Société thermale d'Eugénie-les-Bains v Ministère de l'Économie, des Finances et de l'Industrie), C-277/05, [2007] ECR p. I-6428, par. 24.

1696 Comp. for example the notes to articles II- I: 101 et seq DCFR and the notes to these articles that do not discuss this principle.

1697 Comp. G. Alpa, 'Party autonomy and freedom of contract today', *ELBRev* 2010, p. 135.

1698 J. Basedow, 'Freedom of contract in the European Union', *ERPL* 2008, p. 904–905, 916.

1699 CJEU 7 March 1990 (GB-INNO-BM v Confédération du commerce luxembourgeois), C-362/88, [1990] p. 667, par. 18.

1700 CJEU 5 March 2002 (Axa Royale Belge SA v Ochoa and Stratégie Finance SPRL), C-386/00, [2002] ECR, p. I-2209, par. 24 and 29 makes clear that article 31 Directive 92/96 on life assurance should also enable to compare competitors in the internal market. O.O. Cherednychenko, 'Freedom of contract in the post-crisis era: Quo vadis?', *ERCL* 2014, p. 392, 394 finds that pre-crisis measures in financial law, such as MiFid I and Directive 2008/48 on consumer credit, can be analysed in this manner, but MiFiD II and Directive 2014/17 on mortgage credit rely less on information requirements to prevent financial decisions heavily detrimental to consumers' and financial stability more generally, and instead directly interfere with the context of financial contracts.

1701 See previously par. 4.5.4.

information can be construed as helping the consumers[1702] or employees[1703] to decide without interference of the stronger party that may attempt to impose his terms on the weaker party. This protection may also be extended to non-consumers.[1704] Reich[1705] traces the more general protection of weak parties as a form of protection against the abuse of contractual freedom by the stronger party.

The recognition of private autonomy and concerns about hetero-determination do not mean that the principles are well defined or that EU actors have consistently considered and balanced these principles. Rather, controlling hetero-determination should be seen in the light of the aim of the Treaties. This is also visible in the scope of the consumer *acquis*. Accordingly, the protection of consumers, and their substantive freedom of contract, has not been a reason for the Court to widen the scope of

1702 See for example in articles 4, 5, 6, 10 and 11 Directive 2008/48 on consumer credit or article in Directive 2014/17 on mortgage credit. In these cases, consumers may have difficulty in understanding their rights and obligations under the contract. Although Directive 93/13 does not impose an obligation upon professionals to inform consumers of their standard terms and conditions, this obligation can be found in other Directives, such as Article 22 Directive 2006/123 on services. According to consideration 2 in the preamble, the Directive aims to give consumer more choice by increasing transparency and information. Likewise, article 4 par. 2 sub b Directive 90/314 on package travel stipulates that the tour operator should provide consumers with the standard terms applicable to the contract. CJEU 27 June 2000 (Océano Grupo Editorial SA v Murciano Quintero and Salvat Editores SA v Sánchez Alcón Prades and others), joined cases C-240–244/98 [2000] ECR p. I-4941, par. 25, CJEU 26 October 2006 (Mostaza Claro v Centro Móvil Milenium SL), C-168/05, [2006] ECR p. I-10421, par. 25, CJEU 9 November 2010 (VB Pénzügyi Lízing Zrt. v Schneider), C-137/08, [2010] ECR, p. I-10847, par. 46, emphasised that Directive 93/13 is based on the idea of the unequal bargaining position between consumers and professional sellers and suppliers, which may result in the consumer's agreement to pre-drafted clauses that he is not able to influence. The ineffectiveness of unfair terms restores the balance between contract parties. Comp. in this sense also S. Grundmann, 'Information, party autonomy and economic agents in European contract law', *CMLRev* 2002, p. 273. Grundmann, at p. 276, considers the withdrawal period as an alternative "information right".

1703 CJEU 5 October 2004 (Pfeiffer et al v Deutsches Rotes Kreuz, Kreisverband Waldshut eV) joined cases C-397–403/01, [2004] ECR, p. I-8835, par. 82 reasoned that the employee is in a weaker bargaining position than the employer, and safeguards should be established to prevent that the employer can disregard the intentions of the employee or to impose a restriction of the employee's rights without his express agreement.

1704 For instance, consideration 28 in Directive 2011/7 on late payment targets the abuse of freedom of contract, particularly high fines and interest for late payment. Similarly, CJEU 20 September 2001 (Courage Ltd v Bernard Crehan and Bernard Crehan v Courage Ltd and Others),Case 453/99, [2001] ECR, p. I-6297, par. 33, referred to the unequal bargaining position of parties to an illegal contract, 'such as seriously to compromise or even eliminate his freedom to negotiate the terms of the contract', considering that this circumstance was to be ascertained by the national court, in evaluating whether the party to the illegal contract had suffered damages. CJEU 9 March 2006 (Werhof v Freeway Traffic Systems), C-499/04 [2006] ECR I-2397, par. 23–26 referred to the more general freedom of contract and the principle that contracts cannot bind third parties, which however did not prevent an employer who was not part of a collective labour agreement to be subjected to this agreement. The idea that not only consumers and employees but parties in a (considerably) weaker bargaining are protected has also been defended by V. Roppo, 'From consumer contracts to assymetric contracts: A trend in European contract law?', *ERCL* 2009, p. 304.

1705 N. Reich, *General principles of EU civil law*, Antwerp: Intersentia 2014, p. 41.

Directives.[1706] In contracts that do not fall within the scope of the *acquis*, between businesses, the CJEU[1707] has also not problematized hetero-determination as such. Specifically, in *Tilly Russ*, the CJEU considered that a jurisdiction clause between contract parties could be invoked against a third party who succeeds to all the rights and obligations of one of those contracts parties. This was confirmed in *Castelletti*[1708] and *Coreck*,[1709] where the Court held that it was not necessary to ensure whether the third party had accepted the jurisdiction clause in the original contract. The aims of the Treaties and the corresponding limitation of hetero-determination are also visible in article 102 TFEU that prohibits abuse of a dominant marketing position by imposing unfair terms on contract parties, or by making the conclusion of contracts dependent upon acceptance of additional obligations that do not have a connection with the main contract.

Consequently, principles of freedom of contract and the prevention of hetero-determination do not offer a reliable basis for assessing in what direction the private law *acquis* will develop. The prevention of hetero-determination at the EU level would also not necessarily lead to similar limitations to the binding effect of contracts, as the views on when negotiating processes are defective or absent may differ.

7.5.1.2. Collective contracts

What role have actors played in the development of private law through collectively-negotiated contracts?[1710] Firstly, instances of collective contracts will be considered, and secondly, the role of non-state actors in the development of collective contracts will be considered. Thirdly, the paragraph will ask what limitations are placed on the roles of non-state actors through the development of control mechanisms.

1706 CJEU 23 March 2000 (Berliner Kindl Brauerei AG v Andreas Siepert), C-208/98, [2000] ECR p. I-1741, par. 24. The Court distinguished its decision in CJEU 17 March 1998 (Bayerische Hypotheken- und Wechselbank AG v Dietzinger), C-45/96 [1998] ECR, p. I-1199 that also concerned a contract for guarantee which did fall within the scope of the Directive, even if it concerns a contract for the benefit of a third party, as the Directive is not limited with regard to the nature of the goods or services in the contract, only the private consumption of those goods or services and the capacity of one of the parties as a consumer contracting with a business.

1707 CJEU 19 June 1984 (Partenreederei Ms Tilly Russ and Ernest Russ v NV Haven- en Vervoerbedrijf NOVA and NV Goeminne Hout), Case 71/83, [1984] ECR p. 2417, par. 24.

1708 CJEU (16 March 1999 (Trasporti Castelletti Spedizioni Internazionali SpA v Hugo Trumpy SpA), C-159/97, [1999] ECR p. I-1636, par. 41.

1709 CJEU 9 November 2000 (Coreck Maritime GmbH v Handelsveen BV and others) Case C-387/98, [2000] ECR p. I-9362, par. 25.

1710 Collective contracts are frequently referred to as *Vereinbarungen*. This paragraph focuses on contracts that have been negotiated collectively by parties and that do not subsequently become directly binding on parties on the basis of law, such as TVs and BVs. Consequently, these collective contracts are considered self-regulation rather than co-regulation, and they differ from collective labour agreements that become *Rechtsnormen*.

7.5.1.2.1. The use of collective contracts

The German legislator has recognised the use of collective contracts in various areas.[1711] Prominent examples are

- Article 36 *Urhebergesetz* (UrhG) stipulates that associations of proprietors of intellectual property rights may negotiate with associations of users[1712] to determine the reasonable compensation in the meaning of article 32 UrhG, in accordance with the circumstances in that branch.[1713]
- Article 12 *Urheberrechtswahrnehmungsgesetz* (UhrWG) obliges copyright collectives ('*Verwertungsgesellschaft*') that manage copyrights in trust for owners of copyrighted works to enter into collective agreements with associations representing users with regard to the rights managed by the collective. In these cases, there is an obligation to enter into an agreement, unless this cannot be asked from the copyright collective as the association of users has too few members.
- Articles 558c and 558d BGB enable municipalities to establish simple (558c) or qualified (558d) *Mietspiegels*. These *Mietspiegels* enable municipalities, and possibly also stakeholders, to establish the height of rents in a municipality. Additionally, qualified *Mietspiegels* are established in accordance with scientific principles,[1714] which may improve the chance that a *Mietspiegel* adequately reflects the market for accommodation. This is important because article 558d par. 3 BGB stipulates that a qualified *Mietspiegel* will be assumed to reflect the height of rents normal in a particular area.

Like state actors, private parties have recognised the benefits of collective contracts. This may take various forms. Some of these contracts seem to be based on the idea that collective contracts may be in accordance with the *Richtigkeitsgewähr* more than individual contracts. Collective contracts in accordance with this idea are:

- Collective contracts such as insurance contracts negotiated between third parties to the collective contract – such as employers – on behalf of weaker parties – such as employees.
- Contracts concluded via platforms such as Groupon,[1715] that are in accordance with the idea that as the amount of consumers grows, groups of consumers can

[1711] Comp. G. Bachmann, *Private Ordnung*, Tübingen: Mohr Siebeck 2006, p. 33, who questions the use of *Vereinbarungen* by the legislator: firstly, whether the legislator is competent to give binding effect to these agreements, and secondly, whether the use of *Vereinbarungen* leads to problems with unfair competition.

[1712] See for an overview of agreements under article 36 UrhG Urheberrecht/Wantke/Grunert (2009) article 36 nr 31–34.

[1713] Under article 32 UrhG, the outcome of negotiations is considered reasonable in the sense of article 32 UrhG.

[1714] It is however, unclear what this additional requirement entails exactly – it has been held that this could entail representative random surveys, see MunchKomm zum BGB/Arzt (2012), article 558d BGB, nr 2.

[1715] This is a US-based platform, on which goods and services are offered, with a discount, per city, excluding applicability of the CISG and applying German law to its contracts. See further www.groupon.de/wie-funktioniert-groupon.

negotiate better terms for themselves than individual consumers, in accordance with the idea of *Richtigkeitsgewähr.* In these cases, the lack of the possibility to individually (re)negotiate the terms of the contracts offered to groups is compensated by the choice to opt in or opt out of the contract, if that is in the interests of potential contract parties.[1716] Interestingly, the forums for complaints for collective contracts such as Groupon indicate that complaints may in some cases lead to compensation.[1717]

In some collective contracts, it is not clear whether parties negotiate on behalf of, or in the interests of future contract parties, which may theoretically make a balanced collective contract to the benefit of all contract parties less likely. In these cases, the *Richtigkeitsgewähr* may be absent. This is the case when parties may choose to enter into agreements drafted as an alternative to a TV or a BV, for example, because these agreements are more flexible, or, possibly, to circumvent the inclusion of unions and works councils that have more expertise, experience and a stronger position when it comes to negotiating on employment matters. Agreements in accordance with these ideas include:

- Guidelines ('*Richtlinienverträge*') or recommendations that go beyond stipulating employment contracts and address a wide range of social issues.[1718]
- Agreements with businesses – especially hospitals – and unions ('*Gestellungsvertrag*') in order for their members to work for those hospitals. Although an employment contract is not established between the hospitals and the members, the hospital may have some duties similar to an employer, and members can elect and be elected for the works councils.[1719]

The European legislator has generally not made use of collective contracts, with the exception of framework agreements that are subsequently turned into law. Additionally, the Commission has frequently attempted to encourage dialogue between stakeholders

1716 However, the question arises, what happens if, despite the possibility to opt into group contracts, these contracts turn out to be to the disadvantage of either sellers or consumers. Comp. for example S. Iwersen, 'Ergo trickste auch bei Betriebsrenten', *Handelblatt* 27.7.2011, available at www.handelsblatt.com/unternehmen/versicherungen/skandal-versicherung-ergo-trickste-auch-bei-betriebsrenten-seite-all/4437306-all.html. Collective contracts concluded via platforms also show defects, for example if sellers do not recognise coupons or are booked because of the large amount of consumers responding to an offer, see Lena K., 'Groupon: Kursverluste nach Sperrfrist-Ende, weiterhin Probleme mit Deal-Qualität', *Finanzwelt-News* 4 June 2012, www.finanzwelt-news.de/groupon-kursverluste-sperrfrist-dealqualitaet/.

1717 Comp. the amount of resolved complaints at http://de.reclabox.com/firma/1168-Groupon-GmbH. There are also three complaints on http://verbraucherschutz.de/?s=groupon, including the reaction from Groupon.

1718 Kommentar zum TVG/Wiedenmann (2007) article 1 nr 20, 21.

1719 See further Münchener Handbuch zum Arbeitsrecht/Richardi (2009), article 340, Nichtärztliche Heilberufe und Heilhilfsberufe, nr 6 et seq.

at the European level,[1720] which has also been used in the drafting of legislation.[1721] A prominent example is:

The 2001 Recommendation[1722] that contained a substantive code of conduct on mortgage loans, which provides two standards form of information that is to be provided to the consumer. The information requirements are the result of negotiations between consumer organisations and European Credit Sector Associations under the supervision of the Commission.[1723]

The Commission has sought to facilitate dialogue between stakeholders at the European level, in order to improve the STCs used in travel package contracts. To evaluate the willingness of stakeholders, the Commission – not the BEUC – consulted the Consumer Committee[1724] while the European Confederation of Travel Agencies (ECTA) consulted its members, after which the Commission set up a group consisting of stakeholders and national experts.

7.5.1.2.2. The role of non-state actors

What role do non-state actors play in the development of collective contracts? In some cases, the national legislator has provided a framework for collective contracts, providing non-state actors with the possibility to negotiate agreements that are subsequently presumed to be in accordance with the law. This presumption provides negotiating parties with a prominent role that may give rise to *Fremdbestimmung*, thereby limiting the role of third parties subjected to these agreements. *Fremdbestimmung* is visible in collective contracts on intellectual property rights under article 32 UrhG, and *Mietspiegels*.

Fremdbestimmung may arise from the collective agreements on the use of intellectual property rights, which may bind members if parties negotiating on the contract have been authorised to negotiate on behalf of their members.[1725] Otherwise, the agreement on compensation will be considered reasonable, and parties cannot rebut this assumption, as article 32 par. 2 UrhG makes clear.[1726] Provisions negotiated under this article may also be held to be commonly used in a particular branch,[1727] which may

1720 See for example COM (2000) 248 final, p. 9–10 and more recently the European Parliament resolution of 20 May 2008 on EU Consumer Policy Strategy 2007–2013, A6–0155/2008, par. 6.7.

1721 See for example the dialogue between consumers and industry in the drafting of the proposal for a Directive on mortgages, COM (2011) 142 final, see further http://ec.europa.eu/internal_market/finservices-retail/credit/mortgage_en.htm.

1722 Recommendation OJ L 69/25, 10.03.2001.

1723 See the European Agreement on a voluntary code of conduct on pre-contractual agreements for home loans, and the register of signatories, available at http://ec.europa.eu/internal_market/finservices-retail/home-loans/code_en.htm.

1724 Currently, this is the European Consumer Consultative Group that consists of representatives of national and European consumer organisations as well as two associate members and two EEA observers, see further http://ec.europa.eu/consumers/empowerment/eccg_en.htm.

1725 Urheberrecht/Wantke/Grunert (2009) article 36 nr 18.

1726 Urheberrecht/Wantke/Grunert (2009) article 36 nr 2. See further S. Basse, *Gemeinsame Vergütungsregeln im Urhebervertragsrecht*, Berlin: Logos 2007.

1727 Urheberrecht/Wantke/Grunert (2009) article 36 nr 6.

affect the height of compensation in third parties' cases, especially if they do not agree on a specific price. In this respect, Hertin[1728] finds the lack of publicity problematic considering the normative character (*Normcharakter*) of these agreements. For the development of collective agreements under article 36 UrhG, the efficiency of the bargaining processes could be an assumption that justifies providing a framework for collective negotiations.

Simple *Mietspiegels* have also gained a considerable role in challenging the raise of rents that are contrary to the *Mietspiegel*.[1729] *Mietspiegels* are well-established and considered to be in the interests of both tenants and landlords.[1730] It seems as if the outcome of negotiations, as well as municipal decisions, is considered correct, reminiscent of the *Richtigkeitsgewähr*. Both for simple and qualified *Mietspiegels*, questions of *Fremdbestimmung* may also arise, because of the assumption under article 558d par. BGB, and the role of simple *Mietspiegels* in indicating the usual height of rents in a municipality. For qualified *Mietspiegels*, more questions of *Fremdbestimmung* may arise as the drafting of '*Mietspiegels*' is not infrequently left to third parties.[1731] Further, article 558a par. 2 BGB establishes that landlords will refer to *Mietspiegels* when establishing or raising the rent, even when they diverge from *Mietspiegel*, which may well trigger challenges from tenants. Although a *Mietspiegel* can thereby affect third parties' disputes, citizens cannot challenge a *Mietspiegel* before administrative courts; instead, civil courts are competent to evaluate the correctness of qualified *Mietspiegel*.[1732]

The role of non-state actors in other collective contracts depends on the question whether contracts fall within the scope of the *Richtigkeitsgewähr* or whether they give rise to *Fremdbestimmung*. Notably, various collective contracts are concluded on behalf of third parties by stronger parties, but they frequently lack binding force. Therefore, third parties are only bound if they opt into these contracts, which makes it more likely that these contracts fall within the scope of the *Richtigkeitsgewähr*. Notably, this provides stronger parties negotiating on the behalf of weaker parties with a considerable role, whereas it provides weaker parties with more possibilities to enter into contracts that they consider to their benefit.

For example, agreements drafted as an alternative to TVs (*Koalitionsvereinbarungen*) do not have a binding force similar to TVs.[1733] Similarly, collective contracts such as collective insurance contracts or Groupon contracts do not become binding on third parties, and in principle *Fremdbestimmung* need not arise if parties opt for those rules.

1728 P.W. Hertin, 'Urhebervertragsnovelle 2002: Up-Date von Urheberrechtsverträgen', *MMR* 2003, p. 17.

1729 MunchKomm zum BGB/Arzt (2012), article 558c BGB, nr 5, G. Bachmann, *Private Ordnung* p. 337.

1730 U.P. Börstinghaus, 'Der qualifizierte Mietspiegel – Die Geschichte einer „Verschlimmbesserung"', *NZM* 2000, p. 1088.

1731 U.P. Börstinghaus, C. Börstinghaus, 'Qualifizierte Mietspiegel in der Praxis – Eine empirische Untersuchung über Akzeptanz und praktische Umsetzung des neuen Rechtsinstruments', *NZM* 2003, p. 383.

1732 MunchKomm zum BGB/Arzt (2012), article 558c BGB, nr 3.

1733 See further on the use of collective agreements other than Tarifverträge U. Zachert, '"Jenseits des Tarifvertrags"? – Sonstige Kollektivvereinbarungen der Koalitionen', *NZA* 2006, p. 10.

The role of actors in European dialogues differs, as these dialogues have been organised by European state actors. As a result, non-state actors have less choice to enter into these dialogues; they must be invited. However, if non-state actors have been invited, their negotiations can have considerable influence, as the outcome of these negotiations has generally been used as a basis for legislation. So far, the European legislator considers collective negotiations as a suitable way to further responsive law-making.

However, if parties representative of national actors have not been sufficiently included in negotiations, the question arises whether collective agreements are also in line with national views and national practice.

7.5.1.2.3. Limitations to the role of non-state actors

How have state actors limited the role of non-state actors through collective contracts? At the national level, the possibility of *Fremdbestimmung* has prompted the development of control mechanisms that limit non-state actors' roles:

- For some collective contracts, especially collectively negotiated STCs, judicial evaluation may be exercised.
- Mandatory law may limit non-state actors' roles.

Accordingly, article 32 UrhG provides mandatory protection of weaker parties – artists – against users in article 36 UrhG that provides a framework for collective negotiation. Furthermore, article 32 par. 4 stipulates that parties to this agreement cannot diverge from the agreement to the detriment of the proprietor. Also, article 32a UrhG establishes the possibility to renegotiate if there is a clear imbalance ('*auffälliges Missverhältnis*') between the compensation and the benefit from the use of the intellectually protected works.[1734] Further, the emphasis on the representativeness, independence and competence (of potential contract parties) involved in negotiations under article 36 UrhG[1735] can also be seen in the light of the need to control *Fremdbestimmung*.[1736]

For collective contracts with, for example, consumers or policyholders, the legislator has recognised that the *Richtigkeitsgewähr* may be absent because of the unequal bargaining position between parties and has established mandatory protection for weaker parties. Accordingly, for insurance contracts, articles 6 and 7 Versicherungsvertragsgesetz establish information and advice duties for insurers.[1737] If contracts concluded via Groupon fall within the scope of articles 312b et seq BGB, which

1734 Urheberrecht/Wantke/Grunert (2009) article 32a nr 16 state that the question whether there is a clear imbalance is left to individual cases. See for an overview of case law nr 19.

1735 A clear imbalance under article 32a UrhG may be a reason against the competence of associations representing both the interests of users and proprietors, see Urheberrecht/Wantke/Grunert (2009) article 36 nr 14.

1736 It is however, unclear what these requirements entail exactly. According to Spindler/Schuster, Recht der elektronischen Medien/Wiebe (2011), UrhG article 36, nr 2, the requirements may not be interpreted too strictly, as parties may otherwise seek to evade these agreements.

1737 See further MunchKomm zum VVG/Armbrüster (2012) introduction to articles 6 and 7, nr 6 et seq.

implemented Directive 97/7 for distance contracts repealed by Directive 2011/83 on consumer rights, article 312c BGB establishing information duties is applicable. Additionally, if contracts are concluded solely via the internet, the information duties under articles 312b BGB may also become applicable. However, these duties do not become relevant because it concerns a collective contract that may give rise to *Fremdbestimmung* – if consumers opt into Groupon contracts, they enter into individual contracts. Instead, these information duties are triggered by the inequality of contract parties.

At the European level, the role of non-state actors is limited as state actors play a central role in the selection of negotiating parties. Also, the decision whether the outcome of negotiations will be used in legislation is reserved to the European legislator, who may also adopt Recommendations rather than binding rules.

7.5.1.2.4. Conclusion on collective contracts

State actors have recognised that non-state actors are more closely situated to practice and can therefore develop rules in accordance with the needs and preferences of practice. Non-state actors play a considerable role in the development of collective contracts, especially if the legislator has reinforced the outcome of parties' negotiations, which is likely to lead to *Fremdbestimmung*. Notably, this possibility has in turn given rise to control mechanisms that confine the role of contract parties. Contract parties may also play a considerable role at the European level, once they have been selected to participate in collective dialogues.

However, these instances differ from cases of referral; the legislator does not refer to a particular set of rules, but merely allows parties room to negotiate and recognises the results of these negotiations. The results of these negotiations must remain within the limits set by mandatory law and may be subject to judicial evaluation.

At the European level, not much self-regulation has developed. In cases where European actors have encouraged collective negotiations, this has served to strengthen the law.

7.5.1.3. Model contracts

This paragraph will ask what role contract parties play in the development of private law through model contracts. Firstly, the paragraph will turn to instances of model contracts, and discuss the role of non-state actors. Subsequently, limitations to the role of non-state actors through the development of control mechanisms will be considered.

The use of model contracts (*Formulare, Musterverträge, Standardverträge*) enables parties to draft (parts of) contracts in advance, and they are widely used.[1738] Beyond the

1738 Ulmer/Brandner/Hensen/AGB-Recht/Ulmer/Habersack (2011), article 305, nr 66 note that the use of model contracts is widespread in various branches, including insurance, tenant contracts for accommodation and motor vehicles, estate agents, tour operating, leasing, agency and dealership.

national level, stakeholders[1739] and international organisations[1740] have provided their members with model contracts.

The role of non-state actors through model contracts can be considerable, especially if model contracts are drafted by international organisations or stakeholder groups with many members using these models. In this way, drafters may influence the rights and obligations of many third parties. This does not mean that model contracts are binding, as parties must opt for the use of these models.

In these cases, notably, principles of private autonomy and the doctrine of the *Richtigkeitsgewähr* also offer a justification for the binding force of model contracts and limitations to the binding force of model contracts. Accordingly, the role of contract parties is limited as the use of predrafted model contracts, to be used in multiple contracts,[1741] limits the *Richtigkeitsgewähr*,[1742] which justifies judicial control under article 305–310 BGB.

This judicial control has been criticised. Firstly, as Coester-Waltjen[1743] has pointed out, *Fremdbestimmung* will not necessarily arise as predrafted agreements need not point to contracts favourable to the user of the model contract. Typically, notaries are considered neutral third parties,[1744] and it has been argued that subjecting these model contracts to judicial control may undermine the predictability of contracts drafted and approved by notaries.[1745] Alternatively, if, for example, a stakeholder organisation enables its members to do business with one another, it does not follow that a model is necessarily to the advantage of one of the contract parties. However, the current regime does not seem to distinguish between model contracts drafted by neutral third parties or by users themselves, to their own benefit, as it still concerns contracts that will, to

1739 For example, Orgalime provides its members with model contracts, see www.orgalime.org/publications/forms.htm or the model contracts of the Loan Market Association, see www.lma.eu.com/documents.aspx.

1740 Examples range from the ICC, (www.iccwbo.org/) the International Swap and Derivations Organisation (www2.isda.org/functional-areas/legal-and-documentation/protocols/), to the International Trade Centre, see www.intracen.org/, and the Association of International Petroleum Negotiators, see www.aipn.org/mcvisitors.aspx.

1741 MunchKomm/Basedow (2012), article 305, nr 13, 18–19, 21. For contracts between businesses and consumers, article 310 par. 3 sub 2 BGB stipulates that even if predrafted agreements are used only once, they will be subject to judicial control, insofar as the consumer could not influence the content of the model contract. H. Roth, 'Verbraucherschutz- Entwicklungen und Grenzen', in: E. Lorenz (ed.), *Karlsruher Forum 2011: Verbraucherschutz- Entwicklungen und Grenzen*, Karlsruhe: Versicherungswirtschaft 2012, p. 31 has pointed out that this rule has not resulted in a lot of decisions and is considered of little meaning.

1742 E. Schmidt, 'Die Verbandsklage nach dem AGB-Gesetz', *NJW* 1989, p. 1193.

1743 D. Coester-Waltjen, 'Die Inhaltskontrolle von Verträgen außerhalb des AGBG', *AcP* 1990, p. 20. Comp. MunchKomm/Basedow (2012), article 305, nr 22 et seq, who points out that it can be doubted whether model contracts fall under article 305 et seq BGB as they will typically not be imposed on one party by the other party. Critically also M. Habersack, 'Richtigkeitsgewähr notariell beurkundeter Verträge', *AcP* 1989, p. 419–421.

1744 See critically R. Stürner, 'Zur Gleichsetzung von Notarformularen und allgemeinen Geschäftsbedingungen einer Vertragspartei', *JZ* 1979, p. 758.

1745 Ulmer/Brander/Hensen, AGB-Recht/ Ulmer/Schäfer (2011), article 310, nr 82.

contract parties, appear to be correct without being negotiated.[1746] Thus, regardless of drafters' interests, their roles remain limited. Secondly, even if model contracts do benefit one contract party over the other,[1747] the question arises whether judicial control is still necessary in cases where a model contract has been explained to contract parties, in accordance with, for example, a notary's duty of care ('*Belehrungspflicht*') under article 17 *Beurkundungsgesetz*. Although explaining the consequences of model contracts may not simultaneously entail negotiating on these terms, the question arises whether this duty may, for example, cause a contract party to reconsider entering into an agreement. Thus, can neutral non-state actors not similarly mitigate *Fremdbestimmung*, or should this be left to state actors?

The European legislator is not similarly concerned with potential *Fremdbestimmung* and has not limited the role of non-state actors through judicial control. To the contrary, because the use of model contracts may facilitate cross-border trade, the European Union has encouraged the use of models in its Directives – both Directive 2008/48 on consumer credit and the proposal for a Directive on mortgages contain standardised information forms. Through the use of these forms, businesses may more easily fulfil their information duties to consumers. However, the role of non-state actors drafting model forms is subject to approval from the European legislator as the choice to include these forms remains with the European legislator.

Thus, the roles of contract parties through model contracts under German law and European law diverge. However, German law permits a larger role for private parties in several cases:

1) The involvement of state actors in model forms in Directives may be a reason to exempt these forms from judicial control, similar to the exemption of VOB/B clauses in article 310 BGB.
2) Model contracts may be exempt from judicial control if they reflect well-established customs in international trade or between parties, in accordance with articles 346 HGB and article 307 par. 3 BGB.
3) If both parties opt for well-established model contracts, contracts will not be subject to judicial evaluation as clauses have not been presented ('*gestellt*') by one of the parties to the contract in the sense of article 305 BGB.

Thus, contract parties drafting model contracts at the European level have a more prominent role than at the national level, but German law may well allow more room for contract parties if that does not lead to *Fremdbestimmung*.

[1746] Loosschelders/Olzen/Staudinger (2012) article 242, nr 477, as well as Munch Komm/Basedow (2012), article 310, nr 62–64.

[1747] For example if stakeholder organisations provide their members with model contracts to do business with parties from another branch. If models used by third parties employed by one party – for example, one contract parties' regular notary – that affects contract parties' legal position to the benefit of the contract party regularly employing the notary.

7.5.1.4. Standard contract terms ('Standard Terms and Conditions' – STCs)

What role do actors play in the development of private law through STCs? Firstly, the paragraph will consider instances of often used STCs. Secondly, the paragraph will sketch the role of non-state actors through STCs and thirdly, the limitations to the role of non-state actors through the development of control mechanisms will be discussed.

STCs are widely used:

- Several branch organisations have developed uniform STCs for their members.[1748]
- STCs in some specific contracts can be established by *Verordnung*.[1749]
- STCs may also be collectively negotiated. Even if STCs are negotiated collectively, this does not mean that they are negotiated by (representatives of) future contract parties, and consequently, they do not fall within the *Richtigkeitsgewähr*.[1750] Although collectively negotiated STCs may theoretically be less likely to overly benefit one contract party, they still fall under the definition of STCs as they are a part of contracts that are unlikely to be negotiated further between individual contract parties.
- Beyond the national level, actors have sought to provide their members with model STCs.[1751]

Contract parties drafting STCs may affect the rights and duties of both third parties and potential contract parties. Stakeholder groups and international organisations in particular, who provide their members with model STCs that can be used in contracts with third parties, affect the rights of these third parties. Also, the party drafting STCs may have a distinct advantage over the contract party faced with STCs, as the STCs of the party who drafted them, likely strengthening that party's legal position, form a starting point for negotiations.

STCs do not fall within the scope of the *Richtigkeitsgewähr*, but gives rise to problems of *Fremdbestimmung*. Specifically, *Fremdbestimmung* may arise as STCs will usually not be the result of negotiations.[1752] Parties entering into a contract may not understand STCs, but even if they do, they may not have the time to evaluate STCs and negotiate

1748 These STCs have to be reported to the German cartel office (*Bundeskartellamt*), see for an overview http://bundeskartellamt.eu/wEnglisch/img/pdf/AGB09.pdf). The guidelines established in the articles of association of the *Deutsche Börse* may be considered a special case, see P. Buck-Heeb, A. Dieckmann, *Selbstregulierung im Privatrecht*, Tübingen: Mohr Siebeck 2010, p. 114.

1749 For example for contracts for the supply of energy, under articles 11 par. 2 and 17 par. 3 Energy Section Act ('*Energiewirtschaftsgesetz*') and water, under article 243 Introductory Act to the BGB ('EGBGB').

1750 Ulmer/Brandner/Hensen/AGB-Recht/Ulmer/Habersack (2011), article 305, nr 59.

1751 Often mentioned examples include Orgalime, at the European level, and the ICC at the international level. UNCITRAL has endorsed various STCs developed by the ICC, see further www.uncitral.org/uncitral/en/other_organizations_texts.html.

1752 Contract parties have considerable discretion over individually negotiated terms that are not considered as STCs. Individual terms have precedence over STCs, in accordance with article 305b BGB. The main terms of the contracts will be important for contract parties and may well be individually negotiated, in which case these terms will fall within the *Richtigkeitsgewähr*, see Ulmer/Brandner/Hensen/AGB-Recht/Ulmer/Habersack (2011), article 305, nr 5.

terms that are to their detriment.[1753] Potential contract parties may also not have the time to compare the STCs of different potential contract parties. Consequently, the use of STCs is typically neither based on negotiations nor on the competition of different parties' STCs,[1754] which, in turn, may be a reason for users of STCs to draft STCs that benefit their legal position to the detriment of future contract parties.[1755] Potential *Fremdbestimmung* has prompted the German legislator and the judiciary to develop control mechanisms thats subject the role of users of STCs to limitations.

The lack of *Richtigkeitsgewähr* justifies judicial control over STCs under article 307 BGB. Articles 308 and 309 BGB respectively provide a list of grey and black clauses. Notably, STCs may be subjected to judicial control before a contract is concluded, for example, if STCs become a part of negotiations between parties, as article 305 BGB requires that STCs are presented, which does not require the conclusion of a contract. If STCs are unfair, they will be ineffective.

The Injunctions Act (*Unterlassensklagengesetz*, UklaG) provides organisations in the sense of articles 3 and 3a UklaG with the possibility of claiming an injunction under articles 1 and 2 UklaG. Article 7 UklaG stipulates that if a claim is upheld, this can also be published. Not many claims have been brought under these provisions, which can be traced to the well-established and more successful injunction under article 8 Act against Unfair Competition (*Gesetz gegen den unlauteren Wettbewerb*, UWG).[1756]

The European legislator has similarly subjected the role of businesses entering into contracts with consumers to restrictions. To protect consumers, judicial evaluation under Directive 93/13 on unfair contract terms has been established. Under the Directive, the role of stronger parties may be subject to more limitations than is the case under German law, as Member States may extend the regime of the Directive to the main terms of the contract.[1757] In contrast, German law theoretically leaves open the possibility for consumers to negotiate on STCs – which is not likely – that will accordingly fall within the *Richtigkeitsgewähr* and therefore, not be subject to judicial evaluation.

More generally, the use of STCs is not considered inherently problematic at the European level and contract parties are accordingly left considerable freedom under European law. Instead, the development of STCs that can be used across borders has been encouraged as uniform STCs may facilitate cross-border trade.[1758] However, the development of cross-border trade through these means has proven to be problematic.[1759]

1753 R. Zimmerman, *The new German law of obligations*, Oxford: OUP 2005, p. 176.

1754 Comp. P. Hommelhoff, K.-U. Wiedenmann, 'Allgemeine Geschäftsbedingungen gegenüber Kaufleuten und unausgehandelte Klauseln in Verbraucherverträgen', *ZIP* 1993, p. 566, who find that preformulating terms is, as such, not problematic. It only becomes problematic when terms are drafted for *multiple* contracts.

1755 Ulmer/Brandner/Hensen/AGB-Recht/Ulmer/Habersack (2011) introduction, nr 5.

1756 Ulmer/Brandner/Hensen/AGB-Recht/Ulmer/Habersack (2011) introduction, nr 72.

1757 CJEU 3 June 2010 (Caja de Ahorros), C-484/08, [2010] ECR, p. I-4785, par. 42–44.

1758 European Commission, *European Contract Law and the revision of the acquis: The way forward*, COM (2004) 651 final, p. 6–8.

1759 See further S. Whittaker, 'On the development of European standard contract terms', *ERCL* 2006, p. 60–61.

Thus, non-state actors may play a considerable role through the development of STCs, but both German and European actors have imposed considerable restraints on this role.

7.5.1.5. Conclusion on contractual self-regulation

Both under German law and European law, contract parties enjoy freedom of contract, and parties have considerable discretion to negotiate on the terms of their contracts. German and European actors have equally recognised possibilities to strengthen the position of weaker parties who enter into contracts, through information duties, withdrawal rights, and collective negotiations.

As German law has developed in accordance with the *Richtigkeitsgewähr*, German law has more consistently and frequently subjected the role of contract parties likely to impose their terms on either contract parties or third parties to limitations, both in individual contracts, collective contracts, model contracts, and STCs.

German actors have established various control mechanisms – mandatory law, judicial evaluation, participation of state actors in model contracts, model lists for unfair clauses and default law that may provide an indication of fairness. A control mechanism that does not limit the role of non-state actors as such is the development of collective enforcement mechanisms. However, the development of collective enforcement should, if frequently used, restrict the possibilities for users to draft collective STCs to the detriment of third parties while providing potentially interested parties with a way to influence STCs.

Simultaneously, the development of German contract law in conformity with the *Richtigkeitsgewähr* and the development of control mechanisms in cases where *Fremdbestimmung* may arise, indicates that German contract law reflects society's legal views on justice. Notwithstanding control mechanisms in cases where *Fremdbestimmung* may arise, the German legislator has recognised that contract parties are well placed to develop responsive rules, especially through collective contracts. The development of these contracts may become binding for third parties, within strict limits. However, negotiating parties have a less influential role than parties involved in dynamic referral.[1760]

European actors have similarly recognised the added value of collective negotiations and developed control mechanisms, but these mechanisms are not based on concerns of *Fremdbestimmung*. At first sight, European developments do not undermine the German framework. Few European collective contracts have been developed. However, if the results of negotiations influence European legislation, for example because European parties negotiate on a standard information form, this may affect the rights of third parties not privy to negotiations, and *Fremdbestimmung* may arise. In principle, for these cases, German actors may however not provide control mechanisms. Thereby, collective negotiations between non-state actors at the European level that result in binding agreements may undermine the German framework. However, national actors cannot do much to refrain national actors from participating in negotiations, in line

[1760] See previously above par. 7.4.1.

with the findings in the case study that national actors are less able to guide European actors away from options that may not be attractive to national actors.[1761] The negotiations are not transparent, and it is not apparent that these initiatives have prompted national actors to take more note of international and foreign actors' interests. The extent to which negotiations contribute to the responsiveness of the law, especially to national needs and preferences, may likewise be limited if not all representative actors are included in negotiations. This can be contrasted with model contracts and STCs recommended to parties interested in international trade. These forms of self-regulation are more likely to prompt contract parties to take into account the needs and preferences of foreign or international contract parties.

7.5.2. Self-regulation through articles of association

What role have organisations played in the development of private law through self-regulation based on articles of association?

Paragraphs 7.5.2.1–7.5.2.3 will describe the use of self-regulation based on article association, respectively internal codes of conduct, sports associations' codes, and professional conduct codes, insofar as they are based on organisations' articles of association.[1762] Paragraph 7.5.2.4 and 7.5.2.5 will also turn to the *Pressekodex* and *Werbekodex*. These codes have been developed through articles of association, but they are not binding on this basis. Nevertheless, these codes seem rather successful. Paragraph 7.5.2.6 will consider the role of non-state actors and paragraph 7.5.2.7 will address the limitations on the role of non-state actors through the development of control mechanisms. Paragraph 7.5.2.8 will compare the role of non-state actors and the limitation of non-state actors' roles and paragraph 7.5.2.9 will end with a conclusion.

7.5.2.1. Internally binding codes of conduct

Businesses may provide for an internal code of conduct in their articles of association. For limited liability companies (*'Aktiengesellschaft'*, in Dutch: *'naamloze vennootschap'*), article 77 par. 2 *Aktiengesetz* (AktG) enables the board of commissioners to establish a code of conduct for the business in its internal rules and regulation (*'Geschäftsordnung'*), in accordance with guideline 4.1.3 of the corporate governance *Kodex*. If the board chooses not to do so, the executive board can establish such rules. Notably, if the business chooses to comply with the corporate governance *Kodex* and issues a declaration in the meaning of article 161 AktG, this may require the implementation of the *Kodex* within contracts of employment of board members and the implementation of parts of the *Kodex* in the articles of association.[1763] If codes of conduct are based on articles of association, decisions from businesses inconsistent with this declaration may in some

[1761] See previously par. 4.7.1.

[1762] These codes do not include binding codes of conduct developed by sub-national actors representing, for example, professional organisations (*'Kammern'*) that have not been included in this chapter.

[1763] MunchKomm zum AktG/Semler (2003), article 161, nr 99.

cases be void.[1764] In addition, the question has arisen whether the *Kodex* that is valid within the company may be relevant for the interpretation of article 93 AktG that establishes a duty of care for the director, referring to the careful director ('*ordentliche und gewissenhaften Gesellschaftsleiter*').[1765] Furthermore, the question has arisen whether the guidelines in the *Kodex* can be used in the interpretation of blanket clauses such as article 116 AktG.[1766]

Thus, the development of codes has been encouraged. Alternatively, businesses may also take widely-developed codes such as the code on corporate social responsibility ('*Nachhaltigkeitskodex*')[1767] or the corporate governance *Kodex* as a starting point for these internal codes, but they are not obliged to do so. According to Ringleb,[1768] many businesses do not do so because of the need for frequent amendments to enable the *Kodex* to deal with developing business practices. In addition, businesses can establish best practices ('*Grundsätze ordnungsgemäßer Unternehmungsführung*').

7.5.2.2. Sports associations

Sports associations, considered as non-economical associations in the meaning of article 21 BGB, may impose and enforce various sorts of rules against members that can be divided in rules with regard to the association (for example requirements for membership or contributions), and sports' rules (such as rules on the composition or the constitution of teams) that are typically internally directed at members practicing a particular sport.

Typically, sports associations are members of continental and international organisations, while individuals, as a rule, are members of regional or local organisations. In accordance with the *Ein-Platz-Prinzip*, only one association per sport can become a member of the overarching organisation.[1769] Buck-Heeb and Dieckman[1770] explain the pyramid-like structure of sports organisations by pointing to the necessity to establish uniform rules for international competitions. Members of local or regional associations may be bound to the internationally established rules on the basis of the articles of association of their association, stipulating that the association and its members are bound to the rules established by the overarching organisation, which in turn stipulates that it is bound to the rules established by its overarching organisation.

1764 BGH 21 September 2009, 1270.

1765 P. Buck-Heeb, A. Dieckmann, *Selbstregulierung im Privatrecht*, Tübingen: Mohr Siebeck 2010, p. 102.

1766 P. Hommelhoff, A. Schwab, 'Regelungsquellen und Regelungsebenen der Corporate Governance', in: P. Hommelhoff, K.J. Hopt, A. Von Werder (eds.), *Handbuch Corporate Governance*, Köln: Schmidt 2009, 2nd ed., p. 79 point out this can only be the case if guidelines reflect established practice.

1767 See further below par. 7.5.3.1.

1768 H.-M. Ringleb, 'Die Umsetzung des Kodex in der Praxis', in: H.-M. Ringleb et al (eds.), *Deutscher Corporate Governance Kodex*, 4th ed., 2010, III, nr. 1543.

1769 See for example article 8 par. 2 of the articles of association of the German Soccer Association (*Deutscher Fussball-Bund*), available at www.dfb.de/uploads/media/02_Satzung_02.pdf, or article 9 par. 2 of the articles association of the German Tennis Association (*Deutscher Tennis Bund*, DTB), available at www.dtb-tennis.de/downloads/Satzung_2012.pdf.

1770 P. Buck-Heeb, A. Dieckmann, *Selbstregulierung im Privatrecht*, Tübingen: Mohr Siebeck 2010, p. 67.

7.5.2.3. Internally binding codes for professionals

Notably, the binding force and the scope of professional codes may vary. This paragraph will first turn to the guidelines for insolvency administrators and the professional rules for public auditors, which seem well-developed. Subsequently, the paragraph will turn to other codes, established in the financial sector, that seem less well-developed or that pose less clear sanctions for unprofessional behaviour. Well-developed codes are:

- The codes established by the Association of Professional Insolvency Administrators of Germany (*Verband Insolvenzverwalters Deutschlands e.V*, VID),[1771] after insolvency administration was recognised as an independent profession in the meaning of article 12 GG.[1772]

This self-regulation includes the Principles of Proper Insolvency Administration (*'Grundsätze ordnungsgemäßer Insolvenzverwaltung'*, GOI)[1773] as well as professional standards (*'Berufsgrundsätze'*).[1774] Article 4 of the articles of association[1775] requires that persons wishing to become a member must explicitly and in writing recognise the professional standards as well as the GOI. Thus, even if members would not be bound on the basis of the articles of association, they would be bound contractually, by their declaration. In addition, article 6 of the articles of association requires that members comply with the professional standards and the GOI, while articles 8 and 9 enable the VID to impose a reprimand or exclusion for breach of these duties, as well as exclusion from the VID, summed up in article 13. Furthermore, the VID refers to the recommendations of Prof. Uhlenbruck (*'Uhlenbruck-Kriterien'*)[1776] and the agreements on charts of accounts (*'Kontenrahmen'*, *SKR-InsO*).[1777] Frind[1778] states that the principles developed by the VID are directed internally, but he also finds that these principles have proved very useful for the interpretation of the Insolvency regulation (*Insolvenzverordnung*, InsO), even though these principles offer minimum standards only, which may lead to the petrification of these standards at only a minimum level. However, Frind also notes that the GOI and the *Berufsgrundsätze* can only be useful if they provide clear rules, which is not always the case.

1771 Insolvenzordnung/Braun (2012) article 56 nr 18 points to the possible overlap between the BRAO, when non-specialised lawyers act as insolvency administrators, and the GOI and the *Berufsgrundsätzen*.

1772 BverfG 3 August 2004, *NJW* 2004, 2725, par. B III 2 bb 2.

1773 Available at http://vid.de/images/stories/pdf_fuer_einzelseiten/grundstze_ordnungsgemaesser_insolvenzverwaltung_fassung_vom%2005.05.2012.pdf.

1774 Available at www.vid.de/images/stories/pdf_fuer_einzelseiten/vid-berufsgrundsaetze.pdf.

1775 Available at www.vid.de/images/stories/pdf_fuer_einzelseiten/vid-satzung_vom_5.5.2012.pdf.

1776 Available at http://vid.de/images/stories/pdf_fuer_einzelseiten/uhlenbruck-empfehlungen.pdf.

1777 See http://vid.de/de/qualitaet/kontenrahmen-qskr-insoq.html.

1778 F. Frind, 'Der Einfluss von Selbstregularien der Insolvenzverwalter-Zusammenschlüsse bei der Auswahl, Aufsicht über und der Entlassung von Insolvenzverwaltern', *NZI* 2011, p. 785–786.

- Uniform principles[1779] established by the Institute of Public Auditors in Germany (*Institut der Wirtschaftsprüfer in Deutschland e.V.*, IDW),[1780] in addition to self-regulation established by the *Wirtschaftprüferkammer.*

Article 4 pars. 8 and 9 of the articles of association establish that members have a duty to comply with these principles. Article 5 sub 4 makes clear that this breach can result in the exclusion of members, after a decision from the honorary council (*'Ehrengericht'*), in accordance with article 11 par. 3, which also enables the *Ehrengericht* to disapprove of behaviour. Criminal procedures for breach of professional duties can also lead to suspension and exclusion, in accordance with article 5 sub 5 of the articles of association.

Many organisations in the financial sector have also sought to establish codes of conduct, but these codes generally do not pose clear sanctions for breaching professional codes of conduct, or they impose sanctions that go barely beyond the minimum that is required. Codes established in this area are:

- The *Verhaltenskodex*[1781] as well as the DGFR (*'Deutsche Grundsätze für Finanz Research'*),[1782] established by the DVFA (*Deutsche Vereinigung für Finanzanalyse und Asset Management e.V.*).[1783]

Article 3 of the DVFA's articles of association stipulates that members have to recognise the professional rules (*'Standesrichtlinien'*). The articles of association of the DVFA enable the association to punish breaches of the rules by the *Ehrengericht*, which can impose fines up to € 5000 as well as exclusion from the association. Augsberg[1784] points out that previously, these rules have been criticised as confusing and as hardly going beyond the existing standards set by the law, which have led to reforms of the rules.

1779 Both the articles of association and the principles are available at www.idw.de/idw/portal/d589242/index.jsp.

1780 The IDW is also a member of several international organisations, which include the International Federation of Accountants (IFAC), the Fédération des Experts Comptables Européens (FEE). The IDW is also involved in the International Auditing and Assurance Standards Board (IAASB), and the International Ethics Standards Board for Accountants (IESBA). S. Augsberg, *Rechtsetzung zwischen Staat und Gesellschaft*, Berlin: Duncker & Humblot 2001, p. 238 notes that its activities at the international level, where harmonisation has been ongoing, may accelerate the compliance of the German profession with international standards.

1781 Available at www.dvfa.de/mitgliedschaft/dok/35293.php.

1782 In turn, these guidelines consist of the *Grundsätzen ordnungsmäßiger Finanz Research* (GoFR) and *Mindeststandards für Finanz Research* (MSFR). See further P. Buck-Heeb, A. Dieckmann, *Selbstregulierung im Privatrecht*, Tübingen: Mohr Siebeck 2010, p. 110.

1783 The DVFA is a member of the European Federation of Financial Analysts Societies (EFFAS, http://effas.net/) and the Association of Certified International Investment Analysts (ACIIA, www.aciia.org/pages/home.asp).

1784 S. Augsberg, *Rechtsetzung zwischen Staat und Gesellschaft*, Berlin: Duncker & Humblot 2001, p. 240.

- The professional rules on advice on financial planning drafted by the Financial Planning Standards Board Deutschland.

The articles of association enable an *Ehrengericht* to impose sanctions on the breach of those rules, from suspension of the certificate to a duty to follow courses and exclusion from the association. The preamble to the rules state that if the behaviour of a member has been sanctioned by the judiciary, the *Ehrengericht* will subsequently evaluate whether that behaviour was in accordance with the professional code of conduct. Somewhat confusingly, however, article 18.2 of the articles of association stipulate that state courts are only competent after the *Ehrengericht* has judged the case.[1785]

- The professional rules from the advisory committee of the BVFF (*Bundesverband für den Fachhandel Finanzdienstleistungen e.V.*),[1786] breach of which can be disciplined with exclusion.[1787]
- The code of ethics and the standards of professional conduct established by the German CFA Society can be traced to the CFA institute, the international organisation that it is a member of. Augsberg[1788] notes that as the rules come from a foreign party, members are not bound by the articles of association but from their own recognition of the code of conduct, which members have to reaffirm yearly, in writing.[1789]
- The code of conduct[1790] of the association for independent consultancy experts on remuneration (*Vereinigung unabhängiger Vergütungsberater*, VUVB), on the basis of article 2 of its articles of association.[1791] Although neither the code nor the articles of association impose sanctions for the breach of the code, the code aims to provide guidelines for compliance with article 4.2.2. of the corporate governance *Kodex*, which entails that businesses may issue a statement of compliance or non-compliance under article 161 AktG.[1792]
- The criteria established by the association and the International Centre for Franchising und Cooperation required by the German Franchise Association, Deutscher Franchise-Verband e.V. (DFV).[1793]
- The codes of conduct of the Resort Development Organisation (RDO).[1794] Its code of ethics provides that members may be excluded for breach of the code. However, the

1785 Available at www.fpsb.de/files/documents/Satzung_FPSB110617_formatiert1.pdf.
1786 See www.fifa.de/ – this website seems currently under construction (June 2012).
1787 P. Buck-Heeb, A. Dieckmann, *Selbstregulierung im Privatrecht*, Tübingen: Mohr Siebeck 2010, p. 111.
1788 S. Augsberg, *Rechtsetzung zwischen Staat und Gesellschaft*, Berlin: Duncker & Humblot 2001, p. 249.
1789 See www.gcfas.de/about/. Unfortunately, the code of conduct does not seem to be publicly available.
1790 Available at www.vuvb.de/assets/Uploads/Kodex-fuer-unabhaengige-Verguetungsberatung.pdf.
1791 Available at www.vuvb.de/assets/Uploads/Satzung.pdf. As the code has only been recently established, it can be doubted whether it may already be held to reflect established business practices.
1792 See further par. 7.4.1.1.
1793 See further www.franchiseverband.com/deutscher-franchise-verband-ev.html. The German Franchise Association is a member of the European Franchise Federation (EFF) has established a European code of ethics for franchising, available at www.eff-franchise.com/spip.php?rubrique13.
1794 See www.rdo.org/public_files/rdo_code_adr_scheme_09.pdf. The RDO used to be the Organisation for Timeshare in Europe (OTE).

duties imposed by the code are very general and do not go beyond the legal obligations. It does have a German chapter,[1795] but there do not seem to be German members.[1796]

- The Fractional and Shared Ownership[1797] Trade Association (FSOTA) apparently also requires that members comply with its code of conduct,[1798] the text of which currently does not seem to be publicly available. It is also unclear whether this association has German members.
- The codes of conduct from the federal association for German auctioneers (*Bundesverband deutschen Kunstversteigerer*, BDK) and the separate code for international trade in art,[1799] stating that its members recognise these codes as binding. Serious breaches of the code,[1800] if sufficiently proven, will be considered as breaches of decisions from the association under article 2 par. 7 of the articles of association, which may justify exclusion. At first sight, the codes do not seem to go far beyond what is already contractually, if not legally required.[1801]
- The code of conduct,[1802] of the federal association for German trade in art and antiquity (*Bundesverband des deutschen Kunst- und Antiquitätenhandelns e.V., BDKA*) partially overlaps with the code of conduct for international trade of the BDK. Although article 7 of the code stipulates that member associations will impose the code on their members, it is not clear whether the code is established on the basis of the articles of association of the BDKA and the code itself imposes no sanction on breaches of the code.

Thus, various codes on professional conduct have been established, but the strictness of these rules and their enforcement depends on the drafters of the codes. Accordingly, the code for insolvency administrators and auditors are stricter than codes for organisations in the financial sector, the timeshare business and art trade.

7.5.2.4. The Pressekodex

The *Pressekodex* has been drafted by the German Press Council (*Deutscher Presserat*) in 1972, after a two-year consultation period to ensure that the code was in accordance with the views of relevant stakeholders. It reflects professional ethical standards, which may be complemented and amended by guidelines.[1803] Article 9 of the articles of association[1804] makes clear that the *Presserat* is competent to decide on complaints in general, without a

1795 See www.rdo.org/Chapters/Germany.htm.
1796 See www.rdo.org/Members/Members-List.htm.
1797 Fractional and shared ownership is described as a direct interest in a luxury property (not only real estate, but also yachts, cars or jets) for periods of a year (based on rotation or fixed periods) fall within Directive 2008/122 on timeshare.
1798 See www.rdo.org/news-items/83.aspx.
1799 Both codes are available at http://service.kunstversteigerer.de/de/t/kodex/.
1800 For international trade, breaches also have to be durable.
1801 For example, article 3 states that separate property will be indicated as such.
1802 Available at www.bdka.de/de/id150.htm.
1803 See www.presserat.info/inhalt/der-pressekodex/pressekodex/richtlinien-zu-ziffer-1.html.
1804 Available at www.presserat.info/inhalt/der-presserat/statuten/satzung.html.

declaration of compliance, and article 10 par. 2 adds that members shall be bound to the *Pressekodex* and promote compliance with the *Kodex*. However, it can be doubted whether sanctions can be directly enforced on the basis of the *Presserat*'s articles of association. Notably, the federal associations in this area are members of the *Presserat*, but the publishing houses and journalists against whom the complaints can be directed are not. Indirectly, they are members of the state organisations and unions, which, in turn, are members of these federal associations that are members of the *Presserat*. However, the possibility of these federal organisations to enforce sanctions of the *Presserat* requires an explicit provision in the articles of association of those organisations,[1805] which is lacking.[1806] Dietrich[1807] finds that sanctions can also not be based on the obligation of loyalty of members towards the association ('*Treuepflicht*'). She finds that the obligation to print a reprimand can only be enforced if not doing so would make pursuing the aim of the association pointless, which will hardly be the case. Also, the aim of the federal associations should be distinguished from the aims of the *Presserat*, which means that members' duty to cooperate does not necessarily entail cooperation to publish a complaint. Article 10 of the articles of association of the *Presserat* seems to recognise the lack of possibilities to enforce sanctions on the basis of the articles of association by requiring a declaration of compliance by publishing houses in the area of the press that they comply with the code. It has been estimated that around 90% of relevant stakeholders have issued a declaration of compliance.[1808] Consequently, the declaration of compliance may entail a contractual duty of publishing houses to comply with the *Kodex*.

7.5.2.5. The Werbekodex

The German Advertising Standards Council (*Deutscher Werberat*), consisting of members of the German framework organisation for advertising branches (*Zentralverband der deutschen Werbewirtschaft*, ZAW), has developed a code of conduct[1809] that enables it to cope with undesirable practices and so-called grey areas before the legislator intervenes. The sanctions that can be imposed by the *Werberat* range from withdrawal or amendments to advertising or a public reprimand.[1810]

1805 MunchKomm zum BGB/Reuter, article 25, nr 44.

1806 Comp. the articles of association of the members of the Presserat: the Federation of German Newspaper Publishers, (*Bundesverband Deutscher Zeitungsverleger e.V.*, BDVZ, www.bdzv.de/ueber-den-bdzv/satzung/), the Organisation of German Magazine Publishers (*Verband Deutscher Zeitschriftenverleger*, VDZ, at www.vdz.de/ueber-den-vdz satzung/), the Association of German Journalists, (*Deutsche Journalisten Verband*, DJV, at www.djv.de/fileadmin/DJV/DJV/Satzung_2009-2010.pdf), and the German Journalists Union (*Deutsche Journalistinnen- und Journalisten-Union*, DJU, in Ver.di, at http://dju.verdi.de/ueber_die_dju/selbstdarstellung/geschaeftsordnung.

1807 N. Dietrich, *Der Deutsche Presserat*, Baden Baden: Nomos 2002, p. 55, 57–58.

1808 Spindler/Schuster, *Recht der elektronischen Medien* (2011), article 41 Bundesdatenschutzgesetz, nr 130.

1809 Available at www.werberat.de/.

1810 See www.werberat.de/content/Sanktionen.php.

Ruess[1811] points out that the *Werberat* does not involve determining whether advertising is in accordance with the law – for example whether it is misleading – but rather whether advertising is in accordance with generally accepted standards in society.[1812] This code is in accordance with article 2 of the articles of association of the ZAW. However, the ZAW is an overarching organisation, and the organisations that should comply with the code are not directly bound on the basis of their membership. It is unclear whether they are indirectly bound, or whether an express possibility to impose sanctions is included in the articles of association of organisations that they are a member of.[1813] According to the *Werberat*, compliance with its judgments is generally high,[1814] while it states that its standards are also stricter than those generally applied by the judiciary.[1815] Since 2010, the *Werberat* offers a confidential procedure in which businesses and agencies have the possibility to submit a commercial to the *Werberat* before it is made public.[1816]

7.5.2.6. The role of non-state actors

Generally, the role of non-state actors is prominent as the autonomy of associations ('*Vereinsautonomie*') is protected under article 9 GG and article 40 BGB,[1817] and it entails that members have the freedom to form associations in accordance with their preferences, within the confines of the law. Accordingly, organisations may bind their members through their articles of association. The *Vereinsautonomie* does not, however, justify the binding effects of rules established on the basis of the articles of association on non-members.[1818]

Moreover, codes may concern members' constitutional rights: the *Pressekodex* may affect the right to free speech under article 5 GG, and the freedom of profession under article 12 GG. Similarly, professional codes of conduct and sports' codes may affect members' rights under article 12 GG. These constitutional rights have prompted the German legislator to exercise restraint,[1819] which was maintained in the implementation

1811 P. Ruess, 'Das Recht der Werbung zwischen Staats- und Selbstkontrolle', in: C.-H. Witt (ed.), *Die Privatisierung des Privatrechts – rechtliche Gestaltung ohne staatlichen Zwang, Jahrbuch Junger Zivilrechtswissenschaftler 2002*, Stuttgart: Boorberg 2003, p. 217. See critically U. Di Fabio, 'Selbstverpflichtungen der Wirtschaft – Grenzgänger zwischen Freiheit und Zwang', *JZ* 1997, p. 971.

1812 The Werberat refers to the '*Werbemoral*': V. Nickel, 'Wie uberfluessig ist Werbemoral?' Report ZWA for the meeting of the Austrian Werberat 2011, at http://zaw.de/doc/Werbemoral_Wien.pdf.

1813 Unfortunately, the articles of association of the ZAW do not seem to be publicly available. Members of the ZAW also do not clearly and consistently provide for the enforcement of the code of conduct from the *Werberat* in their articles of association: see for an overview of members www.zaw.de/index.php?menuid=87.

1814 V. Nickel, Report ZWA for the meeting of the Austrian Werberat 2011, p. 10, as well as www.werberat.de/content/Durchsetzungsquote.php.

1815 V. Nickel, Report ZWA for the meeting of the Austrian Werberat 2011, p. 21.

1816 V. Nickel, Report ZWA for the meeting of the Austrian Werberat 2011, p. 22.

1817 MunchKomm zum BGB/Reuter (2012) article 40, nr 3.

1818 BVerfG 12 October 1995, *NJW* 1996, 1203. Comp. for Belgian law also W. van Gerven, S. Lierman, *Beginselen van Belgisch privaatrecht. Algemeen deel, veertig jaar later*, Mechelen: Kluwer 2010, p. 300, stating that professional codes may not limit the freedom of contract of third parties.

1819 N. Dietrich, *Der Deutsche Presserat*, Baden Baden: Nomos 2002, p. 10–12.

of Directive 95/46 on data protection, which in article 27 explicitly refers to self-regulation,[1820] Directive 2003/6 on market abuse,[1821] and Directive 2003/125.[1822]

The role of non-state actors depends on the content of the code, and the scope and influence of these rules. Whereas the scope of internally binding codes may be limited, especially if it concerns small businesses, the scope and influence of sports organisations' codes and professional codes may be considerable.

Sports associations are generally considered socially influential.[1823] The special expertise of sports associations provides these associations with a considerable amount of discretion in the evaluation of the behaviour of athletes that should be taken into account by the judiciary. Accordingly, sports associations' rules can be used for the interpretation of blanket clauses.[1824] Non-members who have not submitted to sports' rules may also be bound to sports' rules if they have implicitly agreed to sports' rules.[1825] Most states, including Germany, leave substantial room for a choice of law and forum in these matters. Consequently, sports matters are subject to the *lex sportiva* and supervised by international arbitration.[1826]

Typically, professional codes have a wide scope, affecting particular groups of professionals. Codes may also affect the view of third parties of a particular profession and accordingly affect rules for contracting with third parties. More generally, the rights of third parties may be influenced as professional behaviour is more clearly outlined. The public interest in the proper functioning professinals that act as public officials is clearly recognised in areas where *Kammern* have been established or where membership of a particular organisation, or adherence to a particular code, is not really optional.

The European legislator has left less room for private actors as it has shown less restraint in replacing self-regulation with legislation. Accordingly, the European legislator rejected self-regulation on market practices as it did not provide a viable alternative to traditional Directives.[1827] Particularly, the European legislator sought to

1820 The question whether Directives can be implemented through self-regulation is controversial; see further Spindler/Schuster, *Recht der elektronischen Medien* (2011), article 41 Bundesdatenschutzgesetz, nr 126–132.

1821 See for the position of the *Presserat* on the implementation of this Directive www.presserat.info/fileadmin/download/Stellungsnahme_AnSVG.pdf.

1822 Notably, article 34 par. 4 WpHG, which implements part of the Directive, stipulating that journalists are exempt from pars. 1, 2 and 5 if they are subject to self-regulation similar to these paragraphs and to article 34c WpHG, which should also include a clear enforcement mechanism.

1823 P. Buck-Heeb, A. Dieckmann, *Selbstregulierung im Privatrecht*, Tübingen: Mohr Siebeck 2010, p. 70.

1824 See for example BGH 11 January 1972, *NJW* 1972, 627.

1825 BGH 28 November 1994, *NJW* 1995, 583. This may also include audiences; see for example article t.82.3 of the FIE, www.britishfencing.com/uploads/files/book_t_23:04.pdf.

1826 Comp. MunchKomm zum BGB/Reuter (2012) article 25, nr 62 on possible problems if sports' rules diverge from national mandatory law.

1827 Institut für Europäisches Wirtschafts- und Verbraucherrecht, *Study on the feasibility for a general legislative framework on fair trading.* Executive summary, chapter VI, available at http://ec.europa.eu/consumers/rights/studies_reports_en.htm.

establish mandatory standards.[1828] Although a possibility for co-regulation was considered, it remains unclear to what extent the rules established by self-regulation have played a role in the drafting of Directive 2005/29.[1829]

The CJEU has clearly indicated that the use of self-regulation to implement Directives is problematic, because it has no binding effect.[1830] Accordingly, questions of sufficient enforcement have arisen with regard to the implementation of Directive 2003/125 through the additional guideline 7.4 for the coverage of money market reports of 24 March 2006.[1831] The normal sanctions of breach of the *Pressekodex* may entail a reprimand, which can be published, the disapproval of the *Presserat* or an instruction.[1832] Notably, the *Presserat* is not competent to impose compensation and cannot prohibit publication or order rectification.[1833] However, an upheld complaint – especially a published reprimand – may have further consequences for journalists violating professional ethics if associations at the state or regional level of which they are a member, or their employers, may take the decisions of the *Presserat* into account.[1834] In addition, the rules provided by the *Presserat* serve as a realisation of blanket clauses.[1835]

In conclusion, especially sports' organisations and organisations that provide strict professional rules have an influentual role. Further, the role of non-state actors at the national level is protected by constitutional rights. Within the constitutionally protected space, non-state actors are better placed than state actors develop rules. Non-state actors are also better placed to develop responsive rules. The emphasis of European actors on binding rules may undermine the room left for actors. So far, this pressure has been resisted.

[1828] T.W. Reader, 'Is self-regulation the best option for the advertising industry in the European Union? An argument for the harmonisation of advertising laws through the continued use of Directives, 16 *U. Pa. Int'l Bus. L.R.* 1995–1996, p. 210 points out that self-regulation is an inefficient method of harmonisation as Member States can simply ignore EU-wide self-regulatory standards at a national level. He suggests that the advertising industry should be involved in the drafting of Directives, and that self-regulation at a European level could be reinforced as Directives. See more cautiously B. Schmitz, 'Advertising and commercial communications – towards a coherent and effective EC policy', *JCP* 1993, p. 407–408.

[1829] Directive 2006/114 applies in business-to-business situations, and refers indirectly to misleading advertising towards consumers, whereas Directive 2005/29 and most codes of conduct target aggressive or misleading advertising towards consumers.

[1830] CJEU 19 October 1987 (Commission v The Netherlands), case 236/85, [1987] ECR, p. 3989.

[1831] T.M.J. Möllers, 'Effizienz als Maßstab des Kapitalmarktrechts', *AcP* 2008, p. 21, See affirmatively J.A. Kämmerer, R. Veil, 'Analyse von Finanzinstrumenten (§34b WpHG) und journalistische Selbstregulierung', *BKR* 2005, p. 383. P. Buck-Heeb, A. Dieckmann, *Selbstregulierung im Privatrecht*, Tübingen: Mohr Siebeck 2010, p. 106 note that an additional code of conduct, the *Kodex für anlegergerechte Kapitalmarktinformation*, does not play a prominent role for self-regulation for journalists.

[1832] See www.presserat.info/inhalt/beschwerde/anleitung.html.

[1833] See further on these issues Damm/Rehbock, *Widerruf, Unterlassung und Schadenersatz in den Medien*, 2008.

[1834] See in further detail on this question N. Dietrich, *Der Deutsche Presserat*, Baden Baden: Nomos 2002, p. 64 et seq.

[1835] N. Dietrich, *Der Deutsche Presserat*, Baden Baden: Nomos 2002 p. 96–97.

7.5.2.7. Limitations to non-state actors' roles

Articles of associations are a mixed form of self-regulation:[1836] on the one hand, the founders establish an organisation through a contract; on the other hand, once the organisation has been established, it is considered a legal person that can create rights and duties for other legal persons. Taupitz[1837] emphasises the difference between a contract and membership of an association. By becoming a member of an association, that member enters a community where rules have already been established ('*fertige Rechtsordnung*'). As articles of association impose rules on private parties that have typically not been an object of negotiations between parties, they may not fall within the scope of the *Richtigkeitsgewähr*, although this need not be absent in all cases.[1838]

The examples in the previous paragraphs have demonstrated that in some cases, professional organisations and sports organisations have developed rules aimed at fostering professional behaviour. This also seems to be the case for the *Pressekodex* and the *Werbekodex*. However, associations develop rules in accordance with their interests, which need not coincide with third parties' interests. If codes have binding force, *Fremdbestimmung* may develop.

The possibility of *Fremdbestimmung* does not necessarily give rise to control mechanisms as these mechanisms simultaneously limit parties' constitutional rights. Generally, judicial control may be difficult to reconcile with the *Vereinsautonomie*. Judicial control is an exception, which may only take place with regard to rules established by associations that are irreconcilable with general principles ('*Körperschaftlichen Prinzipien*'),[1839] or where organisations have a socially or economically influential role.[1840] The standard in article 242 BGB is taken as a starting point to evaluate whether the rules established by the association are unfairly to the advantage of the association.[1841]

Similarly, professional codes of conduct are developed against the background of article 12 GG and may simultaneously lead to *Fremdbestimmung*. It is unclear whether

1836 See further P. Buck-Heeb, A. Dieckmann, *Selbstregulierung im Privatrecht*, Tübingen: Mohr Siebeck 2010, p. 55 et seq. Confusingly, despite the use of articles of association that enable organisations to impose rules on their members, questions may still arise as to the basis of the binding effect of rules based on organisations' articles of association. See, for example, S. Augsberg, *Rechtsetzung zwischen Staat und Gesellschaft*, Berlin: Duncker & Humblot 2001, p. 245.

1837 J. Taupitz, *Die Standesordnungen der freien Berufe*, Berlin: De Gruyter 1991, p. 562.

1838 MunchKomm zum BGB/Reuter (2012) introduction to articles 21-54, nr. 120. Similarly L. Fastrich, *Richterliche Inhaltskontrolle im Privatrecht*, München: Beck 1992, p. 137 raises doubts whether subjection to the articles of association of a GmbH is subject to judicial control, despite previous legal counsel and form requirements. G. Bachmann, *Private Ordnung*, Tübingen: Mohr Siebeck 2006, p. 311-312 argues that problems of *Fremdbestimmung* may be resolved if members of associations have a right to cancel their membership, thereby avoiding being bound to a rule they did not negotiate and that is not in their interest.

1839 L. Fastrich, *Richterliche Inhaltskontrolle im Privatrecht*, München: Beck 1992, p. 138. This is, for example, the case where mandatory law does not safeguard that unfair burdens can be imposed on persons becoming members of, for example, *Publikumspersonsgesellschaften*, see BGH 14 April 1975, *NJW* 1975, 1318.

1840 Looschelders/Staudinger (2012) article 242 nr 480.

1841 BGH 24 October 1988, *NJW* 1989, 1724.

judicial evaluation would be problematic under article 12 GG. In the area of advertising, article 1 UWG provides a clear basis for judicial evaluation. However, when determining whether advertising is unfair in the sense of article 1 UWG, restraint should be adopted in limiting advertisers' freedom of speech by banning advertising.[1842]

However, self-regulation developed against the background of drafters' constitutional rights may simultaneously affect third parties' constitutional rights. Organisations must be careful that they do not infringe on third parties' rights to freely decide their profession, in accordance with the *Stufentheorie* established by the BVerfG. The controversy of self-regulation in areas affecting constitutional rights becomes clear when considering the area of advertising, where it has been argued that these issues should be dealt with by the law,[1843] especially as advertising may fall within the scope of article 5 GG.[1844]

German state actors have imposed limitations on the role of advertisers, but especially sports organisations.

In the area of advertising, the UWG and blanket clauses in the BGB may well contribute to limiting unfair or misleading advertising[1845] and courts have accordingly subjected advertising to judicial evaluation.[1846]

The role of sports associations have also been subjected to limitations:

1) Sports associations' rules with regard to the association (for example with regard to requirements for membership or contributions) are subject to judicial evaluation.[1847] Similarly, penalty clauses in employment contracts with athletes are subjected to evaluation under articles 305–310 BGB.[1848]
2) The binding effect of rules developed by transnational sports organisations is limited by objections to dynamic referral to these transnational organisations in the articles or association. Dynamic referral is not reconcilable with article 71 BGB[1849] that sets requirements for the amendments of articles of association, and as it entails an unacceptable delegation of members' decision-making to other institutions.[1850] Dynamic referral was previously much used,[1851] but associations have had to limit

[1842] BVerfG 12 December 2000, *NJW* 2001, 591, followed by BGH 6 December 2001, *NJW* 2002, 1200 which still banned the adverts from Benetton.

[1843] See in favour K.-H. Fezer, 'Diskriminierende Werbung – Das Menschenbild der Verfassung', *JZ* 1998, p. 265. See against P. Ruess, 'Das Recht der Werbung zwischen Staats- und Selbstkontrolle', in: C.-H. Witt (ed.), *Die Privatisierung des Privatrechts – rechtliche Gestaltung ohne staatlichen Zwang, Jahrbuch Junger Zivilrechtswissenschaft ler 2002*, Stuttgart: Boorberg 2003, p. 219.

[1844] See for example BVerfG 12 December 2000, *NJW* 2001, 591.

[1845] BVerfG 12 December 2000, *NJW* 2001, 591, par. 3 under b.

[1846] Less restraint has been adopted in the area of advertising, which also falls within the scope of article 5 GG, comp. BVerfG 12 December 2000, *NJW* 2001, 591. See further J. Kübler, F. Kübler, 'Werbefreiheit nach "Benetton"', M. Habersack et al. (eds.), *Festschrift für Peter Ulmer zum 70. Geburtstag am 2. Januar 2003*, Berlin: De Gruyter 2003, p. 918 et seq.

[1847] P. Buck-Heeb, A. Dieckmann, *Selbstregulierung im Privatrecht*, Tübingen: Mohr Siebeck 2010, p. 69.

[1848] MunchKomm zum BGB/Gottwald (2012), introduction to articles 336–345, nr 14.

[1849] BGH 28 November 1994, *NJW* 1995, 583.

[1850] G. Bachmann, *Private Ordnung*, Tübingen: Mohr Siebeck 2006 p. 309.

[1851] See K. Vieweg, *Normsetzung und anwendung deutscher und internationaler Verbande*, Berlin: Duncker & Humblot: 1990, p. 72, considering the permissibility of this practice at p. 346–347.

themselves to static referral, necessitating regular updates as articles of associations are revised. Heerman[1852] points out that this option may be problematic, especially as the number of sports supervised by an association continues. It is difficult for overarching organisations to respond adequately to developing practices and to ensure that the rules developed as a response to these practices are adequately implemented by local organisations, which is a requirements for their binding force on individual members.

3) Rules that may bind third parties who have implicitly agreed to these rules are subjected to judicial evaluation under article 242 BGB.[1853]

Notwithstanding the concerns with regard to *Fremdbestimmung* that may arise from self-regulation developed on the basis of articles of association, pluralist perspctives have argued for legal orders based on associations rather than the state. Krisch[1854] describes that the reasons for considering such a legal order as superior as leaves individuals with more freedom. Yet simultaneously, these perspectives assume that state actors safeguard *Vereinsautonomie.*

The concerns with regard to *Fremdbestimmung*, not only with regard to third parties but also with regard to members who enter a "ready-made" legal order show that this perspective should be adjusted. For one, it may be asked who would prevent *Fremdbestimmung* more generally? In addition, these pluralist perspectives should take into account that associations may well pursue their own rather than the public interest. Would associations sufficiently support the development and equal distribution of public goods? Further, the varying quality of the rules produced by associations does not support the view that a legal order based on associations is necessarily superior to a state-centered legal order.

European actors have shown less restraint in limiting the role of non-state actors, and consistent control mechanisms to limit the role the effects of self regulation based on articles of association have not developed because *Fremdbestimmung* has not consistently formed a concern. Simultaneously, the European legislator has sought to reinforce existing self-regulation.

7.5.2.8. Comparison

Various similarities but especially differences become apparent in the development of self-regulation on the basis of articles of association at the national and European level.

1852 G. Heerman, 'Die Geltung von Verbandssatzungen gegenüber mittelbaren Mitgliedern und Nichtmitgliedern', *NZG* 1999, p. 326, who also further analyses the different ways in which athletes can be bound to sports rules.

1853 K. Vieweg, *Normsetzung und anwendung deutscher und internationaler Verbände*, Berlin: Duncker & Humblot 1990, p. 326-327 has argued that these rules can also be characterised as STCs and should therefore be subject to judicial control under article 307 BGB. This characterisation does not seem convincing; it can be doubted whether sports' rules are included in an implicit contract by the behaviour of individuals under article 305 BGB.

1854 N. Krisch, *Beyond constitutionalism: The pluralist structure of postnational law*, Oxford: OUP 2010, p. 90 et seq.

Non-state actors have developed self-regulation both at the national level and beyond the national level, but self-regulation is much more developed at the national level. Perhaps, this development can be attributed to the development of this form of self-regulation within the law on articles of association, often company law. Possibly, as European forms of organisations are established, more self-regulation on the basis of articles of association will be established at the European level. It has not become apparent that the possibility of European self-regulation has prompted national actors to take more note of non-national interests, especially not if forms of self-regulation are nationally oriented. However, in the internationally developed *lex sportiva*, non-national interests have clearly been considered. Nevertheless, these rules have still been subjected to restraints.

The development of control mechanisms that limit potential *Fremdbestimmung* is less visible at the European level as this form of self-regulation is generally not recognised as a separate category that may give rise to *Fremdbestimmung*.

Also, the development of this form of self-regulation is not seen against the background of constitutional rights at the European level and the European legislator has shown less restraint in establishing legislation in areas where well-established, apparently successful self-regulation already exists. The CJEU[1855] has held that the fact that STCs have been recommended by a professional organisation does not exempt these STCs from evaluation under Directive 93/13.

7.5.2.9. Conclusion on self-regulation on the basis of articles of association

Especially at the national level, much self-regulation has been developed, and non-state actors may play an important role, depending on the content of codes and the scope and influence of the rules, which varies considerably. German actors have used various control mechanisms to limit potential *Fremdbestimmung*. Judicial evaluation has been used, while the extent to which actors can develop rules that interfere with constitutional rights has been limited and the possibility to make use of dynamic referral has been banned. Mandatory law has also been established.

Thus, though the expertise, resources and the constitutional rights of non-state actors justify their prominent role, the German framework remains state-centered. Alternative perspectives do not sufficiently address problems that could arise if the legal order was not state-centered but association-centered.

The role of non-state actors is subject to limitations established by both national and European state actors. However, European actors have not developed control mechanisms to limit the role of non-state actors, while they have shown less restraint in interfering in areas where self-regulation has already been established. Thus, German actors are less able to ensure that self-regulation that has been developed in the context of constitutional rights will not be replaced by legislation and interdependence has developed. The pressure to replace self-regulation by legislation indicates that the German framework may become compromised in the future.

[1855] CJEU 15 January 2015 (Šiba v Arūnas Devėnas), C-537/13 [2015] ECR p. I-0.

7.5.3. *One-sided juridical acts*

What role have non-state actors played in the development of private law through self-regulation based on non-binding one-sided juridical acts?

Paragraphs 7.5.3.1–7.5.3.4 will consider instances of various forms of voluntary self-regulation,[1856] ranging from instances of self-regulation sanctioned by the legislator (the *Nachhaltigkeitskodex* and the *BVI-Verhaltensregeln*), self-regulation that may or may not be binding on a contractual basis (the initiative to establish a simple payment account for everyone, '*Ein Girokonto für jedermann!*'), and codes of conduct that are one-sided juridical acts (codes and trustmarks for consumer sales). Paragraph 7.5.3.5 will discuss the roles of non-state actors, and paragraph 7.5.3.6 will consider limitations to the role of non-state actors through the development of control mechanisms. Paragraph 7.5.3.7 will provide a comparison and paragraph.5.3.8 will end with a conclusion.

7.5.3.1. Encouraging codes to complement hard law: corporate social responsibility

The German code on social corporate responsibility ('*Nachhaltigkeitskodex*')[1857] was developed by the council for sustainable development (*Rat für Nachhaltige Entwicklung*, RNE), which was appointed by the government to work on sustainability.[1858] Initially, the idea was to model the *Nachhaltigkeitskodex* after the corporate governance *Kodex*, including a provision similar to article 161 AktG, which would oblige businesses to make a declaration on their compliance with the code which subsequently could be a basis for liability. The code was developed in cooperation with relevant stakeholders,[1859] and it provides businesses with uniform standards on providing information with regard to sustainability, which should increase the credibility of businesses' statements in this regard. Interestingly, the RNE wishes to play a leading role in the development of codes in the area of sustainability at the European and international level, and has accordingly addressed international organisations and provided translations of the code.[1860] The RNE has collected declarations of compliance with the code,[1861] which was evaluated in 2013.[1862]

1856 Voluntary self-regulation has often been referred to as codes of conduct. Article 2 par. 1 sub 5 UWG implements the definition of a code of conduct from article 2 sub f Directive 2005/29 on unfair commercial practices. However, in German law there is some controversy with regard to this definition, see P. Buck-Heeb, A. Dieckmann, *Selbstregulierung im Privatrecht*, Tübingen: Mohr Siebeck 2010, p. 12.

1857 Available at www.nachhaltigkeitsrat.de/de/dokumente/?size=nxw.

1858 See further www.nachhaltigkeitsrat.de/de/der-rat/.

1859 See the overview at www.nachhaltigkeitsrat.de/deutscher-nachhaltigkeitskodex.

1860 RNE, *Der Deutsche Nachhaltigkeitskodex*, version of January 2012, p. 4.

1861 See the overview at www.nachhaltigkeitsrat.de/projekte/eigene-projekte/deutscher-nachhaltigkeitskodex/?subid=6690&cHash=41c117e7ec, see also the model declaration of compliance.

1862 RNE, *Der Deutsche Nachhaltigkeitskodex*, version of January 2012, p. 4.

7.5.3.2. Lack of interference because of self-regulation: the *BVI-Verhaltensregeln*

The BVI-Verhaltensregeln[1863] were drafted in 2002 and entered into force in 2003, drafted by the Bundesverband Investment und Asset Management e.V. (BVI). In 2005, an expert group developed the Corporate Governance-Kodex für Asset Management Gesellschaften, which has been merged in the *Verhaltensregeln*.[1864] Attempts to establish an independent expert commission to develop a code, taking into account the *Verhaltensregeln* while also expressing more strongly the interests of investors failed because of resistance of the BVI.[1865]

The BaFin[1866] has stated that in the interpretation of article 9 par 5 law on investments (*Investmentgesetz*, InvG), it will take the newly developed rules by the BVI as a starting point.[1867] An additional part of the code aims to reinforce the responsibility of professionals, beyond legal requirements. The competence of the BVI to establish codes of conduct has not been expressly established in the articles of association of the BVI,[1868] but article 3 par. 1 sub 4 of the articles of association stipulates that the BVI aims to provide information on private equity and asset management. The question arises whether the code can be seen in this light, and what this would mean for the effect of the code – may it impose binding rules on members under this article or not? In addition, the *Verhaltensregeln* do not provide for a sanction of the breach of the code. The articles of association similarly do not provide for the possibility to impose sanctions, although article 5 par. 1 sub 2 stipulates that members can be excluded from the BVI if they have acted against the interests of the BVI, and have not ceased their behaviour despite repeated warnings from the BVI. It can however be doubted whether breach of the *Verhaltensregeln* will necessarily amount to behaviour against the interests of the BVI. This would only be behaviour that breaches the code and that also damages the reputation of private equity and asset management to such an extent that pursuing the aim of the BVI becomes pointless. However, since July 2011, arbitration boards have been established for the settlement of disputes in consumer cases, which have been delegated to the Ombudsstelle für Investmentfonds des BVI, under article 134c par. 6 InvG and the *Investmentschlichtungstelleverordnung* established under this article.[1869]

1863 Available at www.bvi.de/de/bvi/leitlinien_standards/wohlverhaltensregeln/download/wohlverhaltens regeln.pdf.

1864 Schimansky/Bunte/Lwowski/*Bankrechts-Handbuch*/Köndgen/Schmiess (2011), article 113, nr 34.

1865 J. Köndgen, 'Privatisierung des Rechts,' *AcP* 2006, p. 498.

1866 Statement of 20 January 2010, WA 41 – Wp2136 – 2008/0009, www.bafin.de/SharedDocs/Veroeffentlichungen/DE/Auslegungsentscheidung/WA/ae_100120_wohlverhaltensregelnbvi.html?nn =2798666.

1867 Interestingly, the BVI characterises this use of the code as an '*Allgemeinverbindlichkeitserklärung*'.

1868 Available at www.bvi.de/de/bvi/download/bvi_satzung_2010.pdf.

1869 See for an overview of participating businesses www.ombudsstelle-investmentfonds.de/ombudsstelle Docs/verzeichnis_schlichtungsstellen.pdf.

7.5.3.3. Border cases: binding one-sided declarations?

The German Association of Creditors (*Deutsche Kreditwirtschaft*, DK, previously *Zentrale Kreditausschuss*),[1870] which represents associations for banks and other institutions extending credit, has established a recommendation to provide a simple payment account for everyone ('*ein Girokonto für Jedermann*').[1871]

It has been doubted whether the recommendation has any binding force, either externally or internally.[1872] It is unclear whether the articles of association of the DK contain the competence to establish a recommendation, and the recommendation itself establishes no sanction for acting against it. However, even if this recommendation was based on the articles of association, it would only be binding upon the members of the DK, which, in turn, are representatives of banks and other institutions providing credit.[1873]

The question arises whether the recommendation amounts to an offer in the sense of article 145 BGB, or a recognition of an obligation for the benefit of third parties ('*Schuldversprechen*' or '*Vertrag zugunsten Dritter*') in the sense of articles 780 and 328 BGB. There is some confusion on this question. The OLG Bremen[1874] followed by the LG Berlin,[1875] has held that the recommendation is made by the DK, which is not competent to enter into contracts, or to offer to do so, on behalf of its members.[1876] Moreover, it concerns a recommendation, which has been established to avoid a legal obligation to contract, and can thus not be held to constitute an offer, as there is no intention to be legally bound. Therefore, an average client could not interpret this recommendation as an offer. It was also held that the offer was too abstract to constitute a valid offer. In a 2008 decision,[1877] which was not followed in a subsequent decision in 2008,[1878] the LG Berlin held that without a simple payment account, participation in trade was not possible. Consequently, article 2 GG would entail an obligation to contract. Interestingly, a clear statement of compliance with the recommendation to a senate may also give a customer a direct claim for a simple payment account.[1879] Alternatively, Bachmann[1880] has held that in rare cases, non-compliance with the promise to provide all individuals

1870 See www.die-deutsche-kreditwirtschaft.de/dk/die-deutsche-kreditwirtschaft.html.

1871 Available at www.die-deutsche-kreditwirtschaft.de/die-deutsche-kreditwirtschaft/kontofuehrung/konto-fuer-jedermann/empfehlung.html.

1872 M. Geschwandtener, R. Bornemann, 'Girokonto für jedermann – Vertragsabschlussfreiheit, Selbstregulierung oder gesetzlicher Zwang?' *NJW* 2007, p. 1254 even consider the recommendation a 'Nullum'.

1873 Bericht der Bundesregierung zur Umsetzung der Empfehlungen des Zentralen Kreditausschusses zum Girokonto für jedermann, 27 December 2011, BT-Drucks. 17/8312, p. 3 notes that in some *Länder*, the articles of association have incorporated this aim.

1874 OLG Bremen 22 December 2005, *BKR* 2006, 294.

1875 LG Berlin 12 August 2008, *BeckRS* 2009, 06446.

1876 P. Buck-Heeb, A. Dieckmann, *Selbstregulierung im Privatrecht*, Tübingen: Mohr Siebeck 2010, p. 120.

1877 LG Berlin 8 May 2008, *BeckRS* 2008, 10013.

1878 LG Berlin 12 August 2008, *BeckRS* 2009, 06446.

1879 LG Berlin 24 April 2003, *BKR* 2004, 127.

1880 G. Bachmann, *Private Ordnung*, Tübingen: Mohr Siebeck 2006, p. 279.

with a bank account may lead to liability under article 242 BGB, if expectations have been created that the code would be complied with ('*Erwirkung*').[1881]

7.5.3.4. General declarations: consumer services

Trustmarks or certificates with regard to consumer services have been established.[1882] Various trustmarks, accompanied by quality standards, have been established in the area of consumer sales. Prominent trustmarks[1883] are

- The trustmark *Geprüfter online shop – Bundesverband des Deutschen versandhandlers*,[1884] established by the German e-commerce and distance selling trade association (*Bundesverband des Deutschen Versandhandlers*),[1885] in cooperation with EHI Retail Institute,[1886]
- The trust mark for online shopping[1887] established by S@fer Shopping,[1888]
- The trust mark for online shopping[1889] established by Trusted Shops.[1890]

Interestingly, Trusted Shops has established contracts with its participants, and the question arises whether these contracts can be qualified as contracts to the benefit of

1881 See further MunchKomm BGB Roth/Schubert (2012) article 242 nr 388.

1882 Interestingly, offerors of certificates and trustmarks claim that trustmarks and certificates play a central role in the decision-making of consumers as they increase consumer confidence, see the summary of research from TNS Infratest, *Online-Gütesiegel*, Berlin, 19 August 2005, available at www.trustedshops.de/shopbetreiber/pdf_download/tnsinfratest_studie.pdf, commissioned by D21. The complete study is unfortunately not available at the website of TNS Infratest (www.tns-infratest.com/). See also www.trustedshops.de/shopbetreiber/pdf_download/Studien-und-Umfragen.pdf.

1883 Other trustmarks have been found to lack, for example, regular monitoring or clear sanctions. These trustmarks include Chip/Xonio Online-Shop Zertifikat, for shops participating in price comparisons, see further www.chip.de/cxo/Die-Shop-Zertifizierung-2_10870164.html, and BoniCert, see for the requirements www.bonicert.de/files/BC-Quali_v2.0.pdf, as well as *Das Internetsiegel*, see for the requirements www.internetsiegel.net/Pruefungskriterien.pdf. Groupon Germany also offers participating businesses a trustmark, the Groupon Gütesiegel, which it awards to a limited number of businesses providing good services, see further www.groupon.de/internetsiegel. It is unclear how this trustmark is awarded, on what grounds, and whether companies in fact display the trustmark.

1884 See www.bvh.info/bvh/leistungen/guetesiegel/?no_cache=1&sword_list[0]=g%C3%BCtesiegel.

1885 See www.bvh.info/bvh/. The BVH is also an EMOTA member.

1886 See www.ehi.org/en/about-us.html. The quality standards of the EHI are available at www.shopinfo.net/haendler/kriterien/index.html.

1887 The requirements established by S@fer Shopping are available at www.safer-shopping.de/qualitaetskriterien.html.

1888 See www.safer-shopping.de/.

1889 See further www.trustedshops.de/guetesiegel/kaeuferschutz.html. The quality criteria that have to be met by members, as well as model STCs, are available at www.trustedshops.de/shopbetreiber/download.html. Breach of the standards prescribed by Trusted Shops can be sanctioned by a fine and by exclusion and publication of sanctions, in accordance with the contractual provisions between Trusted Shops and its members, see www.trustedshops.de/shopbetreiber/pdf_download/TS-Vertragsbedingungen.pdf. An overview of German trustmarks is also provided by the Global Business Dialogue on e-Society at www.gbd-e.org/ig/cc/TMorg_1212_EN_EU.pdf.

1890 See www.trustedshops.de/shopbetreiber/unternehmen.html.

third parties in the sense of article 328 BGB, which would also provide consumers with a direct remedy in cases of breach of this contract.[1891] Article 7 in this contract provides that if there is no direct contract between Trusted Shops and the consumer, but Trusted Shops is involved in the conclusion of the contract as an intermediary, it will ensure that the contract party of the consumer complies with articles 2–5 of his contract with Trusted Shops. In cases where Trusted Shops is not involved as an intermediary, the question arises whether the contract can be interpreted as a contract for the benefit of third parties, in accordance with article 328 par. 2 BGB, which stipulates that this should be derived from the circumstances and the aim of the contract. In this case, it seems that the aim of the contract is to increase consumers' trust in a particular seller by the use of a trust mark by ensuring correct behaviour towards consumers.

In turn, these trust marks have been recognised as meeting the requirements[1892] established by Initiative D21,[1893] a cooperation between selling associations. Although statements of compliance constitute a non-binding, one-sided juridical act, the associations recognised by D21 typically enforce compliance with these codes through contracts with members.[1894]

Initiatives have also been established at the European level:

- The Euro-Label, a European-wide internet trust mark, awarded to members who comply with the accompanying European code of conduct, developed by stakeholders with support from the European Commission, which does not, however, refer to D21 but to the EHI-Retail Institute.[1895]
- The European Trade Association representing e-commerce and mail-order (EMOTA), which has developed a European convention on cross-border mail order and distance selling[1896] that members are required to recognise. The BVH is a member of EMOTA.
- The Federation for direct selling in Europe (FEDSA)[1897] that has established codes of conduct both towards consumers and towards other direct sellers. It states that members are not directly bound by the codes; instead, the code is provided to (national) direct selling associations, which may, in turn, require members to comply with the code.

1891 MunchKomm zum BGB/Gottwald (2012) article 328 nr 3.

1892 See www.foehlisch.de/guetesiegel/docs/D21_Qualitaetskriterien_2011.pdf.

1893 See www.internet-guetesiegel.de/index.html.

1894 The EHI regularly monitors compliance with its standards. Breaches can be sanctioned by exclusion and withdrawal of the trustmark, see www.shopinfo.net/haendler/details-zur-pruefung/index.html. Similarly, breach of the standards established by S@fer Shopping results in withdrawal of the trustmark. Breach of the standards prescribed by Trusted Shops can be sanctioned by a fine and by exclusion and publication of sanctions, in accordance with the contractual provisions between Trusted Shops and its members, see www.trustedshops.de/shopbetreiber/pdf_download/TS-Vertragsbedingungen.pdf.

1895 Available at www.euro-label.com/en/about-us/index.html.

1896 Available at www.emota.eu/index.php?option=com_content&view=article&id=109&Itemid=91.

1897 See www.fedsa.be/main.html. The European organisation representing consumers, BEUC, also recognises a role of self-regulation in this field, see: http://ec.europa.eu/consumers/rights/docs/ds_resp_BEUC.pdf.

Thus, non-state actors have made liberal use of the possibilities to establish voluntary self-regulation.

7.5.3.5. The roles of non-state actors

Default law leaves non-state actors with a large amount of freedom to establish trustmarks if they choose, and to enter into contracts to ensure that codes of conduct are complied with. If private actors have sought to reinforce self-regulation on the basis of contracts, especially in the area of consumer sales, the binding effect of self-regulation should fall within the scope of the *Richtigkeitsgewähr.*

Notwithstanding this freedom, the role of non-state actors is at first sight rather limited as one-sided juridical acts are not binding. Bachmann[1898] points out that voluntary self-regulation (*'Freiwillige Selbstkontrolle'*) is often based on, for example, ethics and relies on informal sanctions administered out of court, such as naming and shaming on the one hand, and rewards in the form of trustmarks (*'Gütesiegel'*) on the other hand. It can be doubted whether businesses will be contractually bound to their statements of compliance with voluntary codes, as the statement is a juridical act without a contract partner. Notably, article 311 par. 1 BGB requires a contractual partner, which entails that one-sided declarations may often not have a binding effect (*'Konsensprinzip'*).[1899]

A statement of compliance may under some circumstances constitute an offer in the sense of article 145 BGB, or a recognition of an obligation for the benefit of third parties in the sense of articles 780 and 328 BGB – which may also result in an obligation enforceable by the consumer. This will also depend on whether actors intend to be legally bound. The answer to this question depends on various factors.[1900] Firstly, the question arises whether a code of conduct expressly targets a specific group, instead of addressing, for example, the legislator, in order to prevent legislative intervention. Secondly, if a code sets out clear rules, requires specific declarations of compliance or is clearly to the benefit of a clearly delineated group, this may more easily be assumed to have intended legal effect.

However, the impression that private actors playing a small role as self-regulation is not binding may be misleading. State actors have played an important role in reinforcing these codes in the following ways:

1) Both German and European state actors have frequently enhanced the role of non-state actors by encouraging and reinforcing non-binding self-regulation. German state actors have encouraged the development of self-regulation encouraging fair behaviour that goes beyond legal obligations, especially in areas where drafters' constitutional rights are at stake, in accordance with the *Effektivitätsgebot*.

[1898] G. Bachmann, *Private Ordnung*, Tübingen: Mohr Siebeck 2006 p. 35.

[1899] MunchKomm BGB/Emmerich (2012) article 311 nr 1. Of course, there are important exceptions to this rule, see further MunchKomm BGB/Emmerich (2012) article 311 nr. 21.

[1900] G. Bachmann, *Private Ordnung*, Tübingen: Mohr Siebeck 2006 p. 297.

2) The BVerfG[1901] has emphasised that privately drafted rules may serve to indicate that business practices are established. They do not necessarily establish a normative rule.
3) Codes of conduct can also gain binding force indirectly, if they are used in the interpretation of blanket clauses.[1902]
4) If businesses state that they comply with a code,[1903] article 3 par. 3 UWG that implements article 6 par. 2 Directive 2005/29 on unfair commercial practices stipulates that misleadingly giving a consumer the impression that one meets the requirements of a trust mark constitutes a tort.[1904]
5) Misleading statements of compliance may make the contract avoidable for mistakes or fraud.
6) Using a trust mark is not independently monitored by third parties for financial compensation, or which is not based on independent and public requirements, constitutes a misleading practice in the sense of article 5 UWG.[1905]

Thus, both national and European state actors clearly recognise the role of non-state actors and encourage self-regulation, within the legal framework.

7.5.3.6. Limitations to non-state actors' roles

The lack of success of self-regulation may give rise to two reactions.

Firstly, where binding force is lacking, which may also entail (and success) entails that *Fremdbestimmung* does not often arise, actors have sought to replace self-regulation with legislation.

The committee on financial affairs in the *Bundestag* has passed a motion emphasising the importance of the availability of a simple payment account to citizens, and has required the government to decide accordingly, at the European level. Simultaneously, the committee has called for a proposal for providing the alternative dispute resolution possibilities in disputes with regard to the refusal or termination of a bank account with binding force.[1906] Yet even if the available ADR systems gain binding force, this does not mean that banks will be obliged to choose to comply with the code, while they may also choose to not subject themselves to ADR. Geschwandtener and Bornemann[1907] have suggested a solution modelled after article 161 AktG, which would oblige banks to state compliance with the recommendation – this is different from article 161 AktG that does not, as such, oblige businesses to state compliance – but under this model, banks can also explain non-compliance.

1901 BverfGE 14 July 1987, *NJW* 1988, 191.
1902 BGB/Schulze (2012), article 276, nr 16, MunchKomm zum BGB/Grundmann (2012), article 276, nr 64.
1903 The Bundesverband Direktvertrieb Deutschland has based its code on the European code, see www.direktvertrieb.de/Verhaltensstandards.66.0.html. Other German members do however, not refer to the code, see http://corporate.vorwerk.com/en/home/.
1904 See further Köhler/Bornkamm/UWG/Bornkamm (2012), appendix to article 3 par. 3, nr 2.1 et seq.
1905 Köhler/Bornkamm/UWG/Bornkamm (2012), article 5, nr 2.165.
1906 Beschlussempfehlung und Bericht des Finanzausschusses, 25.5.2012, BT-Drucks. 17/9798.
1907 M. Geschwandtener, R. Bornemann, 'Girokonto für jedermann – Vertragsabschlussfreiheit, Selbstregulierung oder gesetzlicher Zwang?' *NJW* 2007, p. 1256.

Secondly, the lack of a binding effect and the critical approach to self-regulation has prompted state actors to reinforce self-regulation. In turn, *Fremdbestimmung* arising from reinforced self-regulation has been compensated in various ways, especially through the organisation of extensive drafting processes and through involving academics, who are considered more neutral than private actors, especially in the drafting of the *Nachhaltigkeitskodex*.

If the drafting process of a code has been transparent and representative, and independent actors have participated in the drafting of a code, the chance that compliance with this code is in the interest of a limited group of individuals decreases. In turn, this may be a reason for the judiciary to recognise or refer to privately drafted rules more easily: as the drafting process is of better quality, the problem of *Fremdbestimmung* may become smaller.[1908]

In some areas, the emphasis on *Fremdbestimmung* and compensating *Fremdbestimmung* are curiously absent. This is the case for the *BVI-Verhaltensregeln* that have been encouraged, and that are in accordance with Directive 2013/11 on ADR. The question arises whether these rules should be seen against the background of article 12 GG. Initiatives to revise the rules established by the BVI have already been established, but rejected. Although the *Effektivitätsgebot* does oblige German state actors to leave rulemaking to actors best placed to develop these rules, the current rules may arguably lead to *Fremdbestimmung*, especially as they have been reinforced by the judiciary. However, the judiciary also has the possibility to critically evaluate these rules before reinforcing them.

At the European level, state actors have exercised control over the participation of actors in the development of European initiatives, and state actors have participated in the drafting of self-regulation.

7.5.3.7. Comparison

Some similarities and differences have become visible in the development of self-regulation and the role of actors at the national and European level. Self-regulation has been encouraged and developed both at the national and the European level. Both European actors and national actors have subsequently reinforced self-regulation.

However, German actors have more critically looked at the independence of actors developing self-regulation and the drafting process, which may also be a way to limit potential *Fremdbestimmung* arising from the reinforcement of self-regulation. The examples in this paragraph demonstrate that making a distinction between actors may be justified. Some actors more clearly pursue their own interests – which may coincide with public interests – and some do not seem to prioritise their own interests as clearly. However, German control mechanisms allow for this distinction.

The European Commission has also exercised control over the drafting of self-regulation. However, this control is not based on concerns over potential *Fremdbestimmung*, but on the emphasis that self-regulation is a suitable means to support European policy aims, by supporting, for example, the development of legislation in

[1908] See similarly G. Bachmann, *Private Ordnung*, Tübingen: Mohr Siebeck 2006 p. 338.

accordance with some actors' needs and preferences. The use of self-regulation as a means to strengthen legislation has not led the European legislator to organise drafting processes that are as extensive and thorough as the drafting processes organised and encouraged by German state actors.

Overlapping self-regulation has developed at the national and European level, and national actors have adopted some sets of European self-regulation, which increases the chance that these rules are not contrary to foreign or international actors' interests, as these actors may well have been included.

The development of the *Nachhaltigkeitskodex* indicates that in some cases, national actors may actively seek to interact with foreign, European or international actors. These actors take into account previous experiences with self-regulation and seek to provide an innovative solution which in turn may appeal to other actors. Differently than the findings in the case studies,[1909] regulatory competition between non-state actors may lead to innovation and it may be beneficial as the German regime may become a potential source of inspiration for other actors. In accordance with the findings in the case studies,[1910] the cooperation between the German legislator, drafters and stakeholders supports the view that successful regulatory competition relies on sufficient cooperation between representative actors.

7.5.3.8. Conclusion on one-sided self-regulation

Non-state actors developing self-regulation on the basis of one-sided juridical acts may play an important role, and they may also affect the rights of third parties, if self-regulation is reinforced by state actors, which is frequently the case.

German state actors have subsequently developed control mechanisms, particularly the involvement of state actors, academics, and the organisation of extensive drafting processes, to remedy potential *Fremdbestimmung*. This development has, as such, not been mirrored by European state actors, though they have participated in the development of self-regulation. Possibly, this may result in the development of reinforced self-regulation in the form of models collectively negotiated between European non-state actors accompanying European legislative proposals or Recommendations that may give rise to *Fremdbestimmung*.

In these cases, German state actors are less able to independently prevent *Fremdbestimmung*. In other words, interdependence between German and European state actors has developed and these new forms of governance may undermine the German framework.

7.5.4. Conclusion on non-state actors

Non-state actors play an important role in the development of self-regulation, either on the basis of the basis of contracts, articles of association or one-sided juridical acts.

1909 See previously par. 4.6.2. and par. 5.6.2.

1910 See previously par. 5.6.2. as well as par. 6.3.2.

Legislators have provided private actors with ample opportunity to develop and enforce self-regulation. Although it did not become visible in the case studies, self-regulation has widely developed, on the basis of contracts, articles of association and one-sided acts.

Nevertheless, state actors have retained a central role. National state actors have limited the role of private actors that may not impose rules on third parties, especially not rules that interfere with third parties' rights. Contractual self-regulation has been enforced or limited in accordance with the idea of *Richtigkeitsgewähr* and the closely related notion of *Fremdbestimmung* that arises if contractual self-regulation does not fall under the scope of the *Richtigkeitsgewähr*.

Potential *Fremdbestimmung* has prompted German state actors to develop control mechanisms that mitigate the effect of binding self-regulation and that thereby limit non-state actors' role. Control mechanisms particularly frequently used are judicial control, the organisation of extensive drafting processes and mandatory law.

Although a distinction should be made between different kinds of non-state actors, the reasoning for retaining the role of state actors in controlling *Fremdbestimmung* sounds convincing. Alternative perspectives are not appealing, especially not when considering the differing quality of self-regulation. Yet the various forms of self-regulation also make clear that in some cases, non-state actors rather than state actors should develop rules, which has been recognised by state actors. This is the case if self-regulation seeks to promote behaviour that goes beyond behaviour that can be legally required of actors, or if it concerns rules developed in the context of fundamental rights. In these cases, developing control mechanisms may be difficult.

European actors developed less control mechanisms, not based on concerns with regard to *Fremdbestimmung* and use them less extensively, and less frequently in combination with one another. Especially the organisation of extensive drafting processes and the emphasis on the independence of actors is less visible, and less suited for the European level. To a limited extent, European actors have developed judicial control and mandatory law. Forms that are, however, much more present are the participation in the development of self-regulation, which is necessary as there is no (clearly visible) European *demos* that develops self-regulatory initiatives in a manner similar to the development of self-regulation at the national level within a legal framework. German state actors participate less intensely in the development of self-regulation developed in the context of constitutional rights, but this restraint is undermined as European actors seek to limit the role of non-state actors by (partially) replacing self-regulation by legislation.

The initiatives from European actors and the difference between actors' roles under German and European law make clear that interdependence has developed between European and national actors. On the one hand, European actors have demonstrated that they may not be aware of successful self-regulation, and accordingly have to rely on national actors to become familiar with relevant initiatives. This also means that European forms of self-regulation may not take into account the needs and preferences of relevant national actors, which will not be beneficial for responsiveness. The initiatives from EU state actors that overlook national concerns may in turn not prompt national actors to justify divergences or to increasingly consider non-national interests. Interestingly, forms of self-regulation at the European level have increased responsiveness, as national actors have adopted model contracts, STCs and codes of conducts recommended by transnational organisations.

On the other hand, national actors become less capable of independently subjecting non-state actors' roles to restrictions. Consequently, the consistency of the German framework has become undermined. However, this influence is not yet clearly visible as European self-regulation as encouraged by European actors has developed only to a limited extent, while other initiatives do not prevent German actors from subjecting self-regulation to control mechanisms.

7.6. Conclusion

This chapter has considered which actors develop private law in the German legal order, and what the role of those actors is in the German constitutional framework and the European framework. Paragraph 7.6.1. will compare the roles of actors under the German framework and the TFEU. Paragraph 7.6.2. will consider the development of coexisting claims to authority at the national and European level. Paragraph 7.6.3. will turn to the role of state actors in the light of pluralist criticism on state-centrism. Paragraph 7.6.4. will consider the development of private law in a pluralist legal order and paragraph 7.6.5. will conclude by asking for starting points for mutual recognition.

7.6.1. Differences between the roles of actors under German and European law

Differences between the German framework and European law have become apparent. Particularly, European and national state actors and non-state actors have different roles of actors under the GG and the TFEU. The following differences are important:

1) A coherent German framework for the role of European and national state actors, as well as non-state actors, can be construed, on the basis of principles of democracy, private autonomy and *Fremdbestimmung*.
   European law has not developed a similar framework, but takes a functional approach. The role of actors is accordingly less clearly delineated and more flexible than is the case under the German framework.
2) Under the GG, national actors retain a central role. Legislative intervention follows from the obligation of the legislator to protect constitutional rights (the '*Untermaßverbot*'),[1911] and a lack of intervention can, therefore, be problematic.[1912] The reallocation of competences to the European level should be in line with the GG.

[1911] See further Maunz/Dürig, Grundgesetz-Kommentar/Grzeszick (Ergänzungslieferung 2012), article 20, nr 126–127.

[1912] Bachmann, *Private Ordnung*, Tübingen: Mohr Siebeck 2006 p. 58, see more far-going K. Vieweg, *Normsetzung und anwendung deutscher und internationaler Verbande*, Berlin: Duncker & Humblot: 1990, p. 144.

In contrast, the CJEU has emphasised the hierarchy and the binding effect of European law independent of national law. Further, an *Untermaßverbot* at the European level would be difficult to reconcile with the principle of conferral of powers.

3) At the national level, non-state actors have a limited role in the development of legislation, but the role of non-state actors in the development of alternative regulation falls within the sphere of constitutional rights. To the contrary, non-state actors may play an essential role in the drafting of European legislation, while the development of alternative regulation is generally not considered in the light of fundamental rights. There is also no European equivalent of the *Wesentlichkeitsgebot*
4) In the private law *acquis*, the role of private parties has been less consistently limited than in German private law. German private law consistently bases parties' freedom and control mechanisms limiting non-state actors' influence on private parties' private autonomy thereby controlling constitutional rights, and *Fremdbestimmung.*

These differences also follow from the differences between the European Union and the national legal order. Accordingly, the Union does not have to meet the requirements of the representative democracy in the way that national legislators should; instead, the emphasis of the BVerfG has been on participative democracy, unfortunately without clarifying what this requirements entails. Similarly, subjecting comitology processes, as well as the Lamfalussy process, to national standards has been criticised. Further, developing drafting processes that are as extensive as the processes organised at the national level and consistent judicial control 'beyond the scope of the *acquis* is problematic at the European level.

Nevertheless, the development of stricter control mechanisms that take into account national concerns is desirable. Forms of alternative regulation encouraged by EU state actors such as framework agreements overlook national concerns, which provokes resistance and makes it unlikely that national actors will justify divergences between national initiatives or increasingly consider the interests of non-national actors. In contrast, successful forms of transnational self-regulation have indirectly ensured that the interests of foreign and international actors are taken into account, as German actors opt into these initiatives.

7.6.2. Coexisting claims to authority

In accordance with perspectives of multilevel governance and pluralist perspectives, the role of actors has been subject to change. This may entail a less central role for national state actors. Specifically, the roles of European, international and national state actors change as European actors become competent to enter into treaties and harmonise the law.

Both national and European actors have interpreted one another's roles in a limited manner. At first sight, European law takes precedence over national law, which theoretically entails that the roles of actors should be determined under European law. The decisions of the BVerfG however indicate that in the German legal order, the GG retains a central role. Theoretically, European acts may even be held *ultra vires* under the GG. However, the decisions of the BVerfG indicate restraint. German actors may similarly adopt restraint in subjecting European alternative regulation to limitations. At the European level, the room left for national identities has been expressly recognised in article 4 par. 2 TEU. Notably, European law has taken a functional approach and has not clearly outlined actors' roles. Because most of private law, including self-regulation, is still developed at the national level, the role of actors developing private law in Germany should, in principle, be determined in accordance with the principle of private autonomy and concerns of *Fremdbestimmung*. Thus, different claims to authority coexist at the national and the European level, and the role of actors under the GG and the TFEU may differ.

Although national courts and legislators continue to play an essential role in the application and enforcement of harmonised law, their obligations under the TFEU and the GG may lead to conflicts. Conflicts may arise, for example, if the CJEU approves of European measures that could subsequently be held *ultra vires* by the BVerfG. This may for example be the fate of an optional instrument based on article 114 TFEU. As a result, German state actors would be obliged, under European law, to enforce the optional instrument, while the GG prohibits them from doing so.

7.6.3. *The development of private law and state-centric perspectives*

According to pluralist criticism of state-centrism, the development of private law should not be considered in the state-centric manner demonstrated in the case studies and defended in this chapter. At first sight, the increasing role of non-state actors in the multilevel legal order makes this argument more, as the state in these instances is not source of rules developed by these actors, especially actors at the European or international level. National and European non-state actors may gain a more prominent role as they participate in the development of European alternative regulation or European legislation. Non-state actors might similarly become involved in the development of national law or alternative regulation, for example because of their expertise or because the development of alternative regulation is considered in the light of constitutional rights. Non-state actors at the national level such as the RNE may, moreover, seek to expand their influence beyond the national level. The initiatives of the RNE, as well as the experiences of the Deutscher Corporate Governance *Kodex* and the DRSC, show that regulatory competition and mutual learning may well lead to innovation, though this was not consistently the case in the case studies.[1913] Non-state actors can circumvent national constraints if they participate in the development of alternative regulation at the European level. It may be concluded that, national state actors are less able to limit non-state actors' roles to prevent or limit *Fremdbestimmung*.

Pluralist perspectives do not only recognise these developments, they welcome the decreasing role of state actors and argue that the central role of the state should be diminished further.

[1913] See previously par. 5.6.2., 6.3.2. and 6.3.3.

Nevertheless, the development of private law will likely continue to be considered in a state-centric manner. Yet the criticism of a state-centered conception of law depends on one's understanding of legal centralism.[1914] In Griffiths'[1915] definition of legal centralism, "law" seems to be defined as traditional "hard law", developed through the legislative process, in accordance with arguments that the state is the source of all binding rules.[1916] The development of hybrids clearly shows that non-state actors may have an important role in the development of *Rechtsnormen*[1917] state-centrism has been challenged as private law has been developed beyond the national level.[1918]

Importantly, state actors have a convincing reason to retain a central role, namely to prevent *Fremdbestimmung*. Accordingly, German state actors have imposed restraints on the roles of non-state actors if *Fremdbestimmung* develops, through mandatory law, participation from state actors, extensive drafting processes and judicial evaluation. More generally, the relation between national law and legal views on justice is a reason to maintain the role of state actors. Accordingly, the German case study found that the law on STCs is closely related to surrounding default that is relevant for evaluating clauses. Principles such as the *Richtigkeitsgewähr*, considered in the case study, play a role in German law more generally.

However, as European actors have become involved in the development of the law, the German framework has been compromised. Harmonisation through hard law takes place in a manner that is not predictable. Moreover, the development of alternative regulation at the European level may undermine national control mechanisms that prevent or limit *Fremdbestimmung*. Therefore, these new forms of governance may pose a threat to more traditional techniques of developing private law, and if national actors sought to prevent the expansion of European actors' competence by agreeing with the development of alternative regulation rather than legislation, this has not been as effective as national actors might have hoped.[1919]

Eventually, the development of European legislation may compromise the German framework as German actors are pressured to replace self-regulation with legislation. National actors may be more hard-pressed to guarantee non-state actors' roles, even if they are reinforced by constitutionally protected rights.

The decreased ability of actors under the GG to protect individuals against *Fremdbestimmung* is not beneficial for the comprehensibility of private law. It decreases

1914 B.Z. Tamanaha, 'A non-essentialist view of legal pluralism', *Journal of Law and Society* 2000, p. 298–299.

1915 J. Griffiths, 'What is legal pluralism?', *Journal of Legal Pluralism* 1986, p. 3.

1916 A prominent example is W. Flume, 'Rechtgeschäft und Privatautonomie', in: E. von Caemmerer (ed.), *Hundert Jahre Deutsches Rechtsleben, Festschrift zum hundertjährigen Bestehen des Deutschen Juristentages 1860–1960, Bd. I*, Verlag C.F. Karlsruhe: Müller 1960, p. 136 et seq.

1917 See previously par. 7.2.1.

1918 Particularly R. Michaels, N. Jansen, 'Private law and the state: Comparative perceptions and historical observations', *RabelsZ* 2007, p. 345 et seq rightly raise questions about the relation between private law and the state, as well as G. Teubner, 'Globale Zivilverfassungen: Alternativen zur staatszentrierten Verfassungstheorie', *ZaöRV* 2003, p. 1.

1919 As argued by N. Krisch, *Beyond constitutionalism: The pluralist structure of postnational law*, Oxford: OUP 2010, p. 228.

German actors' ability to compensate for *Fremdbestimmung* by, for example, organising extensive bargaining processes, which is advantageous in terms of responsiveness. Further, as actors at the European level do not develop rules in a transparent, inclusive manner, it may hinder predictability, responsiveness and accessibility, especially if rules are not subsequently transformed into law. Exercising control over rules that potentially bind parties may also be beneficial in terms of accessibility and predictability. As the German legislator is less able to guide the European legislator away from forms of new governance such as comitology, more potentially binding rules may be developed, and not in an accessible, predictable manner. To the contrary, comitology committees have been suggested to facilitate the amendment of the law, for the sake of flexibility. Furthermore, even if European rules are accessible, they may contradict national legal views on justice and not be developed consistently with overlapping national law. If forms of new governance clearly and consistently compromise principles of private autonomy and *Fremdbestimmung*, this may provoke resistance at the national level.[1920] In the long term, overlooking national objections may eventually undermine the use or extension of new governance techniques to private law, notwithstanding the potential of these techniques.

7.6.4. *The development of private law in the light of radical pluralist arguments*

The coexistence of competing claims to authority may undermine the German framework, which may in turn lessen the predictability, consistency, accessibility and responsiveness of private law. More generally, has the development of private law in accordance with pluralist perspectives become visible?

In a pluralist legal order, it has been argued that multiple claims to authority – for example in associations – coexist. Smits[1921] accordingly argues for a radical view of legal pluralism in which citizens can opt in or opt out of rules of communities, which can be produced by local communities, by states, or by international organisations, in accordance with public policy rules under international private law. In other "strong" versions of pluralism, multiple claims to authority coexist without an overarching hierarchical framework. This raises the question which bodies should have claims to authority.

What would be an optimal size of polities? This depends on the issue the polity seeks to address. Accordingly, what polity is best equipped to deal with, for example, problems of corporate social responsibility, or with agreements between employers or employees? Should rules be developed by actors that have the most expertise, or that are closest to the legal persons subjected to the rules developed by a polity? Krisch[1922] finds that an optimal

1920 S. Whittaker, 'On the development of European standard contract terms', *ERCL* 2006, p. 74.

1921 J.M. Smits, 'A radical view of legal pluralism', in: L. Niglia (ed.), *Pluralism and European private law*, Oxford: Hart 2013, p. 161.

1922 KriN. Krisch, *Beyond constitutionalism: The pluralist structure of postnational law*, Oxford: OUP 2010, p. 101. Comp. J. Cohen, Ch. Sabel, 'Directly-deliberative polyarchy', *ELJ* 1997, p. 315: 'an effective polity

polity is an optimal mix of deliberation, inclusion and strength of argument for pursuing specific goals. Thus, international regimes may be beneficial if many actors beyond the national level should be included. Accordingly, regimes seeking to promote corporate social responsibility should include as many actors as possible, which points to the involvement of international actors, while national actors are well placed to enforce these rules, and codes of conduct can be tailored to specific business practices. The German initiative on corporate social responsibility provides an interesting development in this respect. Interestingly, also, if alternative regulation seeks to promote behaviour that goes beyond legally required behaviour, non-state actors are better placed than state actors to develop rules to encourage such behaviour.

The development of various forms of alternative regulation in the German legal order underlines the increasing role of non-state actors more visibly than the case studies. Walker[1923] has found that non state actors '[carve] out a relatively autonomous space of political organisation in which the writ of the state runs increasingly faintly'. This is especially true for the development of the *lex sportiva*. The development of rules prescribing professional conduct for insolvency administrators and the professional rules for public auditors can also increasingly be characterised in this manner, even if they are developed within a clear constitutional and legal framework.

The development of rules through the Lamfalussy process also appears highly specialised, as does the development of rules through the comitology process. However, the development of rules through these latter two processes, even if it takes place relatively autonomously, takes place within the European legal framework, to support legislation. The framework has become more detailed as European state actors have sought to exercise more control over the development of these rules.[1924] In the Lamfalussy method and comitology, the development of regulatory private law rules is apparent; these rules are clearly market-oriented rather than based on the development of general principles. As the development of regulatory private law increases, this may in turn increase the development of private law through new modes of governance, and decrease the development of standards of behaviour between parties through more traditional private law techniques, in particular codes and blanket clauses.[1925]

Notwithstanding the decreased role of German state actors in the development of these rules, the rules developed by non-state actors are still subjected to limits by national state actors. Contrary to defences of strong pluralism, an overarching hierarchical framework may well prove beneficial, not only because of the varying quality of alternative regulation. The principle of private autonomy and concerns of

is one that balances responsibilities optimally among the arrangements that fall within those [social-political] boundaries'.

1923 N. Walker, 'The idea of constitutional pluralism', *MLR* 2002, p. 355.

1924 K.U. Schmolke, 'Die Einbeziehung des Komitologieverfahrens in den Lamfalussy-Prozess – Zur Forderung des Europäischen Parlaments nach mehr Entscheidungsteilhabe', *EuR* 2006, p. 446–447 traces the level of detail to the increased participation of stakeholders, the European Parliament, and the need for political compromise.

1925 Comp. O.O. Cherednychenko, 'Public supervision over private relationships: Towards European Supervision Private Law?', *ERPL* 2014, p. 37, 46 et seq, p. 57–58. She analyses Directive 2014/17 on mortgage credit, Directive 2008/48, Directive 2007/64 on payment services in this light.

Fremdbestimmung, underlying the development of the German framework present a convincing argument to maintain the development of rules within a constitutional framework. A framework may not only offer a consistent view on the roles of actors in the development of the law, but the state has an important task in preventing and correcting *Fremdbestimmung*. Accordingly, the binding force of the *lex sportiva* on the basis of articles of association is subjected to limits. Concerns of *Fremdbestimmung* have similarly led German state actors to limit the scope and binding force of other forms of alternative regulation. Thus, the central assumption underlying the distinction between state and non-state actors in the German legal order – that non-state actors need not necessarily pursue the public interest – remains visible. Some developments support this assumption – for example the *BVI-Verhaltensregeln* or weak codes of professional conduct in the financial sector. Simultaneously, German actors have recognised that in some cases, private actors are better placed to develop rules than public actors, specifically, if the development of rules falls within the sphere of constitutionally protected rights, or if actors develop rules that require behaviour that goes beyond legal standards, such as the *Werbekodex*. Other forms of self-regulation – for example codes of conduct in consumer sales, as well as the development of the *Nachhaltigkeitskodex* – indicate that the development of alternative regulation may not directly be developed only for private interests and they may be beneficial for private law. Consequently, in these areas, private actors may also be well-placed to develop rules. The German framework provides sufficiently diverse forms of strict and lenient control mechanisms to take differences between non-state actors into account. The diverging quality of rules developed through self-regulation does little to support the perspective that an association-centered legal order, rather than a state-centric legal order, would be superior.

This is also true for the European level, where a consistent view on the role of actors has not yet developed. Svilpaite[1926] notes that the development of the Interinstitutional Agreement on Better Lawmaking and the subsequent use of alternative regulation raise questions as to how the development of law can best be integrated within the European legal framework. The approach developed by the EU shows gaps as some well-established forms of alternative regulation do not meet the requirements set in the Interinstitutional Agreement on better law-making. In addition, in contrast to German actors, European actors have not recognised that private actors may be better placed than public actors to develop rules.

A more consistent perspective would be beneficial because, firstly, it would provide more clarity on the way in which the private law *acquis* will be developed, and how forms of new governance relate to the private law *acquis*. Secondly, more careful consideration of which actors are best suited to develop private law than visible in the case studies is desirable. In turn, such consideration may prompt more debate on the question of how European private law should be developed and facilitate deliberation.

That does not mean that a European framework will closely resemble national frameworks or that it will provide a sharp distinction between state and non-state actors

[1926] E. Svilpaite, *Self- and co-regulation instruments in the European legal framework*, August 2007, available at www.eu-newgov.org/database/DELIV/D04D69_Limits_of_self-regulation.pdf, p. 25 et seq.

or the competences of the Union and national competences. Further, a framework would be developed in line with the functional approach. This may for example justify a more instrumental approach of the role of non-state actors.

7.6.5. Mutual recognition and respect?

The differences between the GG and the TFEU may eventually lead to conflicts. However, principles of private autonomy and *Fremdbestimmung* could form a starting point for interaction between European and national actors. Between the CJEU and the BVerfG,[1927] the development of interaction on the basis of mutual recognition and respect has already been signalled. Possibly, private autonomy and *Fremdbestimmung* may provide starting points for further interaction, which should prevent that actors that become increasingly interdependent undermine one another's initiatives, in accordance with the discourse on multilevel governance.

The principle of private autonomy and concerns of *Fremdbestimmung* may form starting points as they are or should be recognised more widely at both the national and the European level. Firstly, at the European level, the principle of private autonomy has been recognised, as becomes clear from the DCFR and the withdrawn proposal for a CESL. Similarly, the opposite concept of *Fremdbestimmung* and the objections against *Fremdbestimmung* should be acknowledged at the European level.

Secondly, European actors have recognised the weaknesses of alternative regulation and have sought to improve alternative regulation accordingly. Criticism on comitology and the role of the IASB has prompted improvement, primarily in the form of more democratic control in increased participation by the European Parliament.

If actors at both levels expressly recognise principles of private autonomy and *Fremdbestimmung* in the development of European private law, this could lead to mutual respect. Specifically, European actors should exercise restraint in interfering with alternative regulation developed at the national level. Conversely, national actors should exercise restraint in subjecting initiatives developed at the both European level to scrutiny. As a starting point, state actors at both the national and the European should assume, when confronted with respectively national or European initiatives, that they have been developed in accordance with these principles of private autonomy and *Fremdbestimmung*.

[1927] See previously par. 7.3.2.2.

Chapter 8

ACTORS DEVELOPING PRIVATE LAW IN THE DUTCH LEGAL ORDER

8.1. Introduction

In the case studies, it has become clear that state actors still play a prominent role in the development of the law on STCs. The previous chapter concluded that notwithstanding this conclusion, a closer look at the development of private law in Germany reveals a more prominent role for non-state actors. In German law, convincing arguments to maintain the role of state actors have become visible.

This chapter asks which actors play a role in the development of private law in the Dutch legal order. In the Dutch legal order, a framework cannot yet be detected. If developed, what would a framework deduced from the Dutch legal order look like and is a central role of state actors similarly justified in the Dutch legal order?

This chapter consider a Dutch framework in paragraph 8.2. Paragraph 8.3 will discuss the development of private law by state actors. Subsequently, paragraph 8.4 will consider the role of state actors and non-state actors in instances of co-regulation, and paragraph 8.5 will turn to the role of non-state actors in the development of self-regulation. Paragraph 8.6 will end with a conclusion.

8.2. Central questions on the role of state actors and non-state actors

The legislator and the courts clearly have an important role in the development of Dutch private law, but they have also developed co-regulation, in cooperation with non-state actors, and encouraged the development of self-regulation. Nevertheless, the role of non-state actors is not clearly delineated. Thus, a framework to assess which role state actors and non-state actors should play in the development of private law is desirable. Giesen[1928] finds that guidelines would enhance the quality of alternative regulation. If alternative regulation is developed in sufficiently open and inclusive procedures, this may, in turn, increase the responsiveness of alternative regulation, and theoretically diminish the chance that contradictory sets of overlapping alternative regulation develop. Furthermore,

1928 I. Giesen 'Alternatieve regelgeving in privaatrechtelijke verhoudingen', in: W.J. Witteveen, I. Giesen, J.L. de Wijkerslooth, *Alternatieve regelgeving, Handelingen Nederlandse Juristen Vereniging*, Deventer: Kluwer 2007, p. 147.

a framework enables a more consistent, predictable approach to the development of alternative regulation. What would such a framework look like?

Paragraph 8.2.1 will consider the German constitutional framework, as the German framework has inspired the question whether a framework can, over time also be developed to assess the role of actors developing private law in the Dutch legal order. Because of the differences between the German and the Dutch legal order, the German framework cannot simply be transposed to the Dutch legal order. Therefore, this chapter will seek to explore the development of a framework based on principles underlying the German legal framework. Paragraph 8.2.2 will consider the contrast between legal norms and juridical acts and the role of state actors and non-state actors and paragraph 8.2.3 will consider the idea of alternative regulation as a hybrid form between legal norms and juridical acts that may lead to *Fremdbestimmung* and corresponding control mechanisms. Paragraph 8.2.4 will end with an argument for the development of a framework in the Dutch legal order.

8.2.1. The German constitutional framework as a starting point?

Although the notions underlying the German framework could serve as a starting point for a Dutch legal framework, in the German legal order, private autonomy and *Fremdbestimmung* have a constitutional connotation that may diverge from the connotation of private autonomy in the Dutch legal order. Unlike the German legal order, where private autonomy is protected under article 2 GG, the Dutch Constitution, the *Grondwet* (Gw) has not expressly recognised private autonomy as a constitutional right,[1929] and there has been very little theory on the idea of *Fremdbestimmung*, (in Dutch, '*heteronomie*').[1930] Thus, the prevention of *Fremdbestimmung* has not played as important a role in the Dutch legal order as in the German legal order. Further, the development of self-regulation is not necessarily an exercise of constitutional rights. Additionally, the Dutch legal order has not developed a doctrine equivalent to the *Wesentlichkeitsdoktrin*, while article 120 Gw stipulates more generally that the judiciary may not set aside legislation established in accordance with articles 81 et seq Gw. Thus, legislation, developed under this article, may not be set aside, even if it violates Dutch constitutionally protected rights. However, constitutional rights remain protected as the prohibition in article 120 Gw does not extend to the ECHR. As a result, the relation between the Dutch legislator and the courts differs from the relation between the German legislator and the courts. This may also entail a less critical approach towards the development of legislation, especially as the Gw does not include an equivalent of article 20 GG. Although articles 50 et seq Gw do refer to the representation of the Dutch people and elections, the Gw does not expressly refer to democratic principles. Interestingly, Kortmann[1931] finds that a prominent role of stakeholder groups, media,

[1929] Comp. however, A. Colombi Ciacchi, 'Private autonomy as a fundamental right in the European Union', *ERCL* 2010, p. 311–312, who points out that private autonomy has been defended by Dutch scholars.

[1930] One of the few extensive books is C.E. du Perron, *Overeenkomst en derden*, Deventer: Kluwer 1999.

[1931] C.A.J.M. Kortmann, *Constitutioneel recht*, Deventer: Kluwer 2008, p. 333.

and other interests that undermine the role of parliament are sociological problems rather than problems of positive constitutional law.

It follows from these differences that the role of actors and the relation between actors differs. Therefore, the German framework cannot simply be transposed towards the Dutch legal order. Particularly, a Dutch framework will have to take into account that the judiciary is not competent to set aside legislation. Meanwhile, the Gw imposes fewer restraints on the role of non-state actors in the legislative process. Simultaneously, non-state actors roles are not considered in the light of constitutional rights. The different role of non-state actors raises the question whether a Dutch framework should take the distinction between state actors who pursue the public interest and non-state actors who pursue their own interests as a starting point.

8.2.2. The distinction between legal norms and juridical acts

What would a Dutch framework look like? Importantly, a framework should be based on ideas generally recognised in the Dutch legal order. Notably, the distinction between legal norms and juridical acts is not unfamiliar in the Dutch legal order. State actors are the source of binding rules, for private law especially legislation in the sense of article 81 Gw.

This prominent role of state actors, especially the legislator, is recognised in article 6:1 BW that stipulates that the basis for legal obligations ('*verbintenis*') should follow from the law. In other words: state actors are competent to establish rules that can form the basis for obligations, but private parties cannot impose binding rules on third parties who have not consented to these rules. Previously, the traditional distinction between the law and juridical acts was more prominent in article 1269 Old BW, which stipulated that all obligations are based on the law or on contracts.[1932] Van Dunné[1933] finds that this distinction can be traced to Roman law.

It has been questioned whether article 6:1 BW establishes a closed system that only allows for an obligation on these bases, or whether this classification is more open and leaves room for obligation on other grounds, for example quasi-contract. The decisions of the Hoge Raad[1934] already indicate that neither article 6:1 BW nor article 1269 Old BW entails that the law has to precisely and exhaustively stipulate all sorts of obligations – the system of the law leaves room for discovering new obligations.[1935] Dutch law has accordingly been characterised as a partially open system, where article 6:1 BW leaves

1932 The distinction in article 1269 Old BW was criticised as it did not sufficiently recognise that contract was a basis for obligations insofar as the law permitted, Asser-Rutte I (1981), 6th ed. Zwolle, p. 53 et seq. The distinction between contracts and the law as a basis for obligations has instead been traced to the voluntariness of these obligations, see Ch. Fried, *Contract as promise: A theory of contractual obligation*, Cambridge Mass.: Harvard University Press 1981, p. 1–2. See critically on this distinction J.M. Smits, *Het vertrouwensbeginsel en de contractuele gebondenheid*, Arnhem: Gouda Quint 1995, p. 168 et seq.

1933 J.M. van Dunné, *Verbintenissenrecht: Onrechtmatige daad en overige verbintenissen*, Deventer: Kluwer 2004, 5th ed., p. 29.

1934 Particularly HR 30 January 1959, *NJ* 1959, 548.

1935 Parl. Gesch. NBW, Boek 6, p. 1438–1439.

the judiciary with sufficient room to establish obligations that are in accordance with the system of the law.

Nevertheless, obligations on parties require a specific justification.[1936] It is undesirable to abandon this requirement, which it enables parties to foresee on what basis they may be bound, which should mitigate inaccessibility as well as unpredictability that may arise from the development of rules by a large number of actors.

Thus, state actors retain a central role in the development of private law as they establish binding norms, but private law also leaves considerable freedom for parties to develop binding rules in relations between them.

This role of public actors may be traced to the view that public state actors pursue the public interest, which may not always be the case for private, non-state actors. Accordingly, a too prominent role of non-state actors and their initiatives may lead to corporatism, where groups of non-state actors, particularly stakeholders, pursue their own interests rather than the public interest.[1937] Thus, the competence of non-state actors to develop binding rules depends on state actors.

8.2.3. Alternative regulation as a hybrid between law and contract?

Even though legislation establishes binding rules and private parties cannot establish similarly binding rules, Dutch law often assumes that alternative regulation can become binding, at least for parties involved in alternative regulation.[1938] Accordingly, Van Driel[1939] has considered self-regulation as law, albeit in a particular societal circle. Interestingly, however, alternative regulation is therefore not generally seen as a hybrid form, embodying both elements of law, as it is binding on third parties, and contract, as it is based on negotiating parties' consent. Instead, the binding force of alternative regulation has been based on the consent of parties or the law.[1940] The emphasis in discussions on alternative regulation in private law is therefore not on potential *Fremdbestimmung*.

This perspective should be reconsidered. Rather than assuming that the binding force is sanctioned by the legislator or judiciary, or can be legitimised by consent, it is possible that that both these bases are absent. In other words, binding rules are developed beyond legislative procedures and they are also not based on consent of parties. This

[1936] For example J.M. Smits, *Bronnen van verbintenissen*, Deventer: Kluwer 2003, p. 23.

[1937] H.K. Lindahl, 'Zelfregulering: rechtsvorming, democratie en reflexieve identiteit', *RM Themis* 2006, p. 39.

[1938] I. Giesen, 'Alternatieve regelgeving in privaatrechtelijke verhoudingen', in: W.J. Witteveen, I. Giesen, J.L. de Wijkerslooth, *Alternatieve regelgeving, Handelingen Nederlandse Juristen Vereniging*, Deventer: Kluwer 2007, p. 93–95.

[1939] M. van Driel, *Zelfregulering: Hoog opspelen of thuisblijven*, Deventer: Kluwer 1989, p. 2.

[1940] I. Giesen, 'Alternatieve regelgeving in privaatrechtelijke verhoudingen', in: W.J. Witteveen, I. Giesen, J.L. de Wijkerslooth, *Alternatieve regelgeving, Handelingen Nederlandse Juristen Vereniging*, Deventer: Kluwer 2007, p. 95, who, at p. 100, also distinguishes between a third basis for the binding force of alternative regulation: reception of alternative regulation in the interpretation of blanket clauses or business practices that courts take into account.

possibility should be considered more attentively, even if *Fremdbestimmung* is not a problem expressly considered in the Gw.

The concept of *Fremdbestimmung* may offer a critical perspective on Dutch practice. *Fremdbestimmung* draws attention to potential problems that may become more urgent as the role of non-state actors increases. Specifically, as alternative regulation develops, there is more risk that parties are confronted with rules to which they have not consented, which, in turn, may undermine the predictability and accessibility of private law. In the multilevel legal order, the amount of possible sources to which parties may become bound is only likely to increase.

The lack of debate does not mean that no limits have been set to alternative regulation. As a general rule, non-state actors may not independently establish binding rules on third parties that have not consented to be bound.[1941] Thus, state actors retain some level of control over alternative regulation. The law remains a source for the binding force of alternative regulation.[1942] The need to safeguard the quality of alternative regulation has prompted actors to develop measures that are reminiscent of some of the German measures to prevent *Fremdbestimmung*, while the idea that actors will be bound by rules that they have not consented to by actors that have also not been democratically elected (i.e. *Fremdbestimmung*) hardly receives enthusiastic support. *Fremdbestimmung* makes clear in which cases the development of alternative regulation can become problematic and may also provide a starting point for the development of control mechanisms.

Thus, mechanisms reminiscent of German control mechanisms have been defended and established, and should be developed further. Particularly, Vranken[1943] has indicated that the support for self-regulation, as well as the representativeness of actors developing alternative regulation and the possibility to participate in drafting processes, is a starting point for benchmarks to evaluate the quality of alternative regulation. Giesen[1944] likewise suggests benchmarks similar to benchmarks for good law, adding that these requirements compensate the lack of democratic legitimation. Notably, the quality of alternative regulation should be evaluated by state actors who consequently retain an important role.

8.2.4. *Towards a framework for the role of actors developing private law in the Dutch legal order*

As the idea of *Fremdbestimmung* is recognised as problematic, this chapter will consider whether Dutch law, in particular instances of alternative regulation and limitations to the roles of actors, currently already offers starting points for the development of a framework based on private autonomy and *Fremdbestimmung*. Accordingly, this chapter

1941 Asser/Vranken 2005, p. 87.

1942 H.K. Lindahl, 'Zelfregulering: rechtsvorming, democratie en reflexieve identiteit', *RM Themis* 2006, p. 42.

1943 Asser/Vranken 2005, nr. 91.

1944 I. Giesen, 'Alternatieve regelgeving in privaatrechtelijke verhoudingen', in: W.J. Witteveen, I. Giesen, J.L. de Wijkerslooth, *Alternatieve regelgeving, Handelingen Nederlandse Juristen Vereniging*, Deventer: Kluwer 2007, p. 151–152.

will consider measures through which Dutch state actors have limited the role of non-state actors as the development of control mechanisms, i.e. mechanisms that control the extent to which alternative regulation leads to *Fremdbestimmung*. Notably, even if these mechanisms do not directly aim to compensate for *Fremdbestimmung*, they may still have that effect.

The development of a framework, in the face of the ongoing development of the *acquis*, combined with pluralist perspectives, gives rise to the following questions.

Firstly, as a framework has not been consistently developed, it is less likely that the development of European law undermines that framework. However, insofar as control mechanisms have already been developed, does the development of European law diminish these mechanisms and what does that mean for the comprehensibility of private law developed in the Dutch legal order?

Simultaneously, importantly, when developing a framework, the increasing role of European actors and the roles of actors under European law should be taken into account. While it is undesirable that the suggested framework diverges radically from European law, it should reflect Dutch legal views on justice. European law currently does not clearly outline the role of actors. Consequently, rather than taking the role of actors under European law as a starting point, the subsequent chapter will indicate the cases in which the suggested framework may be difficult to reconcile with European law. Possibly, these cases will largely converge with areas in which the German framework provides actors with a different role than European law.

Secondly, the development of private law is oriented towards legislation and case law developed by national state actors. Does the development of European law and international treaties prompt Dutch actors to take the interests of foreign and international actors into account?

Thirdly, the assumption that public actors pursue public interests and private actors pursue their own interests is not as clearly visible as in the German legal order. Can this assumption nevertheless be discovered in the Dutch legal order? Are there indications that the role of non-state actors should be critically considered or are there indications that private actors who pursue public interests and accordingly develop highly successful alternative regulation should be able to reduce the role of the democratically elected legislator or should control mechanisms be abandoned? Do state actors agree with this reasoning, and for what reasons?

8.3. State actors

This chapter will analyse the role of state actors in the development of private law. Paragraph 8.3.1 will turn to the role of national state actors, and paragraph 8.3.2 will discuss the role of European and international actors. Paragraph 8.3.3 will end with a conclusion.

8.3.1. *The legislator and the Hoge Raad*

In The Netherlands, the legislator has played a central role in the development of private law through the Burgerlijk Wetboek ('BW') as well as codes in other areas of law. Notably, a distinction between general private law and *Sonderprivatrecht* visible in the German legal order, has not, as such, been discussed in the Dutch legal order.

The BW leaves a considerable role for the judiciary. Notably, the relationship between the legislator and the Hoge Raad has been subject to debate,[1945] as well as the competence of the Hoge Raad to develop, rather than merely interpret, private law. Some authors[1946] object that the Gw does not provide the Hoge Raad with the competence to develop private law, while it is also contrary to the *trias politica*. Most authors[1947] do not dispute this role of the Hoge Raad – to the contrary, since the report *Versterking van de cassatierechtspraak*[1948] emphasising this role. The report has met with approval by the legislature[1949] and the Hoge Raad[1950] and has since become law, thereby providing the role of the Hoge Raad in the development of private law with a democratic basis.

8.3.2. *The development of private law beyond the state*

This paragraph asks what role European state actors and international actors play in the development of European private law. Paragraph 8.3.2.1 will consider the role of European actors and paragraph 8.3.2.2 will turn to the role of international actors. Paragraph 8.3.2.3 will end with a conclusion.

8.3.2.1. European actors

Paragraph 8.3.2.1.1 will consider the role of European actors under European law and paragraph 8.3.2.1.2 will consider the role of actors under Dutch constitutional law. Paragraph 8.3.2.1.3 will compare the role of actors under the TFEU and the Gw and interdependence between actors.

1945 See generally for the role of the Hoge Raad in the development of private law Asser/Scholten 1974, J.B.M. Vranken, *Mr. C. Asser's Handleiding tot de beoefening van het Nederlands burgerlijk recht. Algemeen deel. Deel II*, Zwolle: W.E.J. Tjeenk Willink 1995. (Hereafter, this volume will refer to this book in the following manner: Asser/Vranken 1995.) Comp. also Asser/Vranken 2005, and G.J. Wiarda, *Drie typen van rechtsvinding* (comments from T. Koopmans), Deventer: Tjeenk Willink 1999, 4th ed., p. 38–43.

1946 C.A.J.M. Kortmann, *Staatsrecht en raison d'Etat* (lecture Nijmegen), Deventer: Kluwer 2009, p. 11–12, C. Schutte, 'De rechtsvormende taak van de rechter? Een kritische noot', *AA* 2009, p. 676, P.P.T. Bovend'Eert, 'Wetgever, rechter en rechtsvorming. Partners in the business of law?' *RM Themis* 2009, p. 145.

1947 See for example A. Hammerstein, 'Rechtsvorming door de rechter is onvermijdelijk', *AA* 2009, p. 672.

1948 Commissie normstellende rol van de Hoge Raad, *Versterking van de cassatierechtspraak*, 2009, available at www.minjus.nl.

1949 *Kamerstukken II* 2007/08, 29 279, nr. 69 and 78.

1950 Hoge Raad der Nederlanden, Verslag 2007 en 2008, available at www.rechtspraak.nl/NR/rdonlyres/E4D94FD0-01D0-49A4-97F6-F1824C261971/0/08668HRjaarverslag2008_clickablePDF.pdf.

8.3.2.1.1. The role of European actors under the TFEU

European actors play a prominent role as European law as European law may precede national law.[1951] The private law *acquis* consists mostly of Directives and has been based primarily on article 114 TFEU.[1952] The private law *acquis* consists mostly of Directives that have generally been implemented in the BW. However, the role of European actors remains limited as the *acquis* only harmonises fragmented parts of private law and as various Directives pursue minimum harmonisation, leaving additional competence to the national legislator.

Further, European primary law may contain rules in the area of private law, particularly rules on non-contractual liability, as stipulated in article 340 TFEU. In addition, primary law, such as competition law, may affect contracts. Also, the role of the European legislator and the CJEU increases as the Union ratifies treaties.

8.3.2.1.2. The role of European actors under Dutch constitutional law

Dutch actors have not maintained that they remain competent to determine the role of European actors under the Gw. Quite the reverse – it has been argued that European law has binding effect apart from articles 93 and 94 Gw that stipulate that depending on their content, treaties such as the ECHR are directly binding and set aside national law.[1953] This has also been recognised by the Hoge Raad.[1954]

Thus, on the basis of European law, national private law may be challenged if, for example, it breaches free movement guaranteed in the Treaty.

8.3.2.1.3. The role of European actors under the Gw and the TFEU

Whereas the BVerfG has maintained a central role for the GG, this is not the case in the Dutch legal order. The Dutch view that European law is directly applicable in its own right and not on the basis of article 93 and 94 Gw is in accordance with CJEU decisions. Thus, European actors have an important role both under the TFEU and the Gw. The convergence between the TFEU and the Dutch view in this respect means that the Dutch judiciary is not competent to evaluate the reallocation of competences to the European level or the legality of European measures. Consequently, Dutch courts are less able to undermine CJEU decisions on the competence of the European legislator.

Consequently, interdependence has become less visible. The Hoge Raad does not have a similar need to exercise restraint in its decisions on the legality of European measures. This seems to be an exception rather than the rule among national highest courts

[1951] CJEU 15 July 1964 (Costa v E.N.E.L.), case 6-64, [1964] ECR, p. 585, CJEU 7 March 1985 (Van Gend & Loos NV v Inspecteur der Invoerrechten en Accijnzen), case 32/84, [1985], ECR, p. 779.

[1952] See previously par. 7.3.2.1.1.

[1953] See note 7 to article 93 Gw in Tekst & Commentaar Grondwet by Fleuren.

[1954] HR 2 November 2004, *NJ* 2005, 80. E.A. Alkema gives an overview of the debate in his note to this decision.

throughout the Union.[1955] It follows that the position of the Dutch legislator is less complicated than the position of the German legislator, because the Dutch legislator need not ensure that amendments to the treaties or proposed European measures are in accordance with the Gw, which is also not monitored as closely by the Hoge Raad as by the BVerfG. Nevertheless, interaction between national parliaments and the European Parliament to discuss proposed measures, especially if national parliaments have lodged a complaint that a measure is not in accordance with subsidiarity, seems useful for both actors at the national level and actors at the European level. In conformity with the principle of conferral, national actors retain national competences, including the competence to develop private law.

8.3.2.2. The role of international actors in the development of private law

International actors play an important role in the Dutch legal order on the basis of articles 93 and 94. Consequently, the role of the Dutch legislator, who does not have to implement treaties into Dutch law, is smaller than the German legislator. International instruments may however not set aside mandatory law that is applicable as *ordre public.*

The Dutch legislator has ratified various treaties in the area of private law.[1956] An important treaty and well-known example of treaties in the area of private law is the CISG. Other relevant treaties have been concluded on cultural heritage, international law on security interests,[1957] transport,[1958] and intellectual property.[1959] Prominent treaties in the area of international private law have since been ratified by the EU on the basis of articles 81 et seq TFEU.

In addition, international organisations have established model laws, legislative guides and recommendations. These sources are not directly binding and the extent to which national actors make use of these sources also depends on the extent to which European actors have chosen to use or disregard these sources.

8.3.2.3. Conclusion on the development of private law beyond the state

European actors have an important role in the development of private law. European actors may also influence the effect of international law in the Dutch legal order. International law may have direct effect in Dutch law. In contrast, European law requires that international law is implemented before it can become effective. As a result, as European actors increasingly enter into treaties, these treaties become effective after

1955 Accordingly, A. von Bogdandy, S. Schill, 'Overcoming absolute primacy: Respect for national identity under the Lisbon Treaty', *CLMRev* 2011, p. 1433-1434 provide an overview of national constitutional courts that have set limits, based on national constitutional law, to European competences.

1956 The site https://zoek.officielebekendmakingen.nl/zoeken/tractatenblad enables a search for currently ratified treaties.

1957 For example recently the UNIDROIT Convention on International Interests in Mobile Equipment.

1958 For example the Hague Rules (*Brussels cognossementsverdrag*).

1959 For example the 1962 Benelux Convention concerning Trademarks.

implementation into European law that has a direct effect, not on the basis of articles 93 and 94 Gw, but on the basis of European law.

Simultaneously, at first sight, competing claims to authority do not seem to have developed, as the Hoge Raad has not asserted the Gw as the source for claims to authority. That does however not mean that national actors have no claim to authority. A closer look at the Gw learns that private law should be codified. Article 4 TEU also recognises that competences not conferred upon the Union remain with its Member States. The Union does not have a general competence to harmonise or, more drastically, codify private law. It follows that competing claims to authority do exist. European law has been expressly based on European rather than national sources. Dutch law does not deny that claim, which at first sight seems characteristic of a hierarchical rather than a heterarchical relationship. On closer inspection, however, national competences have not been reallocated to the European level as such, nor is national law based on European rather than national claims to authority. National law is also not developed within the framework of European law.

8.3.3. *Conclusion on state actors*

State actors play a crucial role in the development of private law, both at the national and European level. The role of actors under the Gw and the TFEU differs, especially as the Dutch legislator is constitutionally bound to develop private law through a codification. In addition, the role of international actors is more prominent under the Gw than is the case under the TFEU, under which international measures have to be implemented in European law before they become binding. Yet as European actors have precedence on the basis of European law, under the Dutch framework, European law will precede international law. As a result, no conflict arises. Further, the role of European actors may also influence the role of international actors, as international law does not stand in the way of harmonisation.

Although the assertion of different rules of recognition is not as visible, national actors retain the claim to develop national private law and claims to authority coexist.

Because Dutch law recognises the direct effect and the supremacy of European law on the basis of European law, this may subject national law more directly to the influence of European law, without additional national constitutional limits, but this does not mean that the relationship between national and European actors is solely hierarchical. The competence of the Dutch legislator is based on national constitutional law and Dutch private law has to be codified in line with the Gw.[1960] This is also supported by the findings in the Dutch case study.[1961]

Accordingly, constitutional discourse takes place at multiple sites. What does this mean for the development of comprehensible European private law? The development of

[1960] Asser/Vranken 2005, nr. 140–143 notes that practitioners as well as scholars are often 'wired' to legal practice, and their reasoning is accordingly influenced. Comp. E.M.M. Meijers, *De taak der rechtswetenschap ten aanzien der vrije rechtspraak* (inaugural address Leiden), Haarlem: Tjeenk Willink 1910, p. 5 who finds that educating legal practice is the first task of legal academics.

[1961] See previously par. 5.6.1. and par. 6.2.

parts of private law by the European legislator does not take place in a predictable, consistent manner, notwithstanding the obligation for the Dutch legislator to develop private law through a codification. Does the development of European law diminish existing control mechanisms?

Conversely, do these developments benefit responsiveness, do they facilitate mutual learning or regulatory competition and are these developments likely to enhance the comprehensibility of European private law? Do potential benefits justify reconsidering the conclusions in the case studies that especially regulatory competition need not be beneficial for the comprehensibility of the law? Is there room for mutual recognition based on principles of private autonomy and *Fremdbestimmung*, as argued previously?[1962]

8.4. State actors and non-state actors: co-regulation

This paragraph will explore the role of state actors and non-state actors in the development of European private law.

Paragraph 8.4.1 will turn to the referral to private actors in legislation, and paragraph 8.4.2 will consider reinforced codes of conduct. Paragraph 8.4.3 will discuss the development of reinforced collective negotiations. Paragraph 8.4.4 will end with a conclusion.

This paragraph will not elaborately reconsider European instances of co-regulation that have already been considered in the previous chapter. Instead, this chapter will merely mention these instances and refer back to the previous chapter for further details. Only if Dutch actors have, for example, developed additional rules, will more attention be paid to already considered European forms of co-regulation.

8.4.1. Referral to private actors and new governance

What role do actors play if the legislator refers to self-regulation in legislation? Referral is rarely used by the Dutch legislator, but it is increasingly used by the European legislator.

Paragraph 8.4.1.1 will turn to instances of referral and paragraph 8.4.1.2 will ask what role non-state actors have played in these instances. Paragraph 8.4.1.3 will consider the lack of limitations on non-state actors' roles by the development of control mechanisms. Paragraph 8.4.1.4 will end with an argument to develop more control mechanisms on the basis of the principle of private autonomy and concerns of *Fremdbestimmung*.

8.4.1.1. Instances of referral

In the Dutch legal order, instances of referral are rare.

- A rare example of dynamic referral can be found in article 6:214 BW on the development of STCs by state and non-state actors, which has turned out to be a dead letter as STCs have been developed in collective negotiations between stakeholder groups.

[1962] See previously par. 7.6.5.

At the European level, referral to non-state actors is more commonly found:

- In Regulation 1606/2002, referral is made to the IASB.[1963]

Forms that are reminiscent of referral have also been developed at the European level:

- Comitology.[1964]

- The Lamfalussy process.[1965]

Directives adopted under this process have been implemented in Dutch administrative law, but they are also relevant for determining appropriate behaviour for financial institutions towards consumers, imposing information duties and duties to gather information about potential debtors ('know-your-client-principle') on creditors.[1966] In particular Cherednychenko[1967] has argued that as the maximum harmonisation approach in the MiFiD Directive leaves less room to develop diverging standards in contract law. The approach of the MiFiD Directive is visible in Directive 2008/48 that introduces the 'know-your-client principle'.

These harmonised rules have not withheld actors from developing codes of conduct in this field.[1968] Instead, existing initiatives, especially the Bureau on Credit Registration (*Bureau Krediet Registratie*, BKR),[1969] that manages a central credit information system, are in line with the principle of know-your-client. Despite these initiatives, a common standard for assessing the creditworthiness of consumers has not developed. The Netherlands Authority for the Financial Markets (*Autoriteit Financiële Markten*, AFM)[1970] has criticised the lacuna between the codes of conduct from the Dutch Banking Association (*Nederlandse Vereniging van Banken*, NVB) and the Association of Financing Companies (*Vereniging van Financieringsonder-*

1963 See more elaborately previously par. 7.4.1.1.

1964 See more elaborately previously par. 7.4.1.1.

1965 See more elaborately previously par. 7.4.1.1.

1966 Especially the Wet financieel toezicht. Comp. also the rules on supervision on stock exchange ('*Nadere Regeling Toezicht Effectenverkeer*') that establish a duty of care for credit institutions to gather information on the financial position and expertise of their clients.

1967 O.O. Cherednychenko, 'Zorgplichten bij financiële contracten: Is er nog een wezenlijke rol voor het contractenrecht weggelegd?', *Contracteren* 2007, p. 88. Comp. however HR 3 February 2012, *AA* 2012, p. 752, and the note of D. Busch with further references.

1968 These codes include including the Code of Conduct on Consumers' Credit ('*Gedragscode consumptief krediet*') of the NVB available at www.nvb.nl/scrivo/asset.php?id=290675, as well as its the Code of conduct on mortgage credit ('*Gedragscode Hypothecaire Financieringen*'), available at www.nvb.nl/scrivo/asset.php?id=106951, and the code of conduct on the granting of credit, developed by the Association of Financing Companies (*Vereniging van Financieringsondernemingen in Nederland*, VFN available at www.vfn.nl/index.php?p=30862.

1969 See for more information www.bkr.nl/OverBKR.aspx?pid=34.

1970 AFM, *Verantwoorde kredietverstrekking 2006*, available at www.afm.nl/marktpartijen/upl_documents/rapport_verantwoorde_kredietverstrekking_2006_120107.pdf.

nemingen in Nederland, VNF).[1971] In response, the NVB has suggested cooperation between interested parties.[1972]

The development of administrative law has, in addition, rendered the effect of some codes of conduct unclear. The Dutch association of insurers (*Verbond van Verzekeraars*) has decided to withdraw the code of conduct on the information provided by intermediaries (*'Gedragscode informatieverstrekking dienstverlening intermediair'*, GIDI) and the code of conduct on the return of commissions. They are considered outdated with the law on financial supervision (*Wet financieel toezicht*).[1973] Confusingly, associations and individual companies have adapted GIDI for their members and specific fields and still announce the applicability of this code of conduct.[1974] In addition, the code of conduct on the provision of information to consumers on the returns and the risks of life insurance and insurance on investments with profit sharing (*'Code rendement en risico'*),[1975] has been revised and integrated with the *Financiële bijsluiter*, a manual for complex financial products.

8.4.1.2. The role of non-state actors

As referral has barely taken place at the national level, the role of non-state actors in referral is limited, especially as article 6:214 BW is generally not used. In contrast, non-state actors at the European level can exercise considerable influence and develop binding rules.

8.4.1.3. Limitations on the role of non-state actors

At the national level, few control mechanisms have been developed, and the role of non-state actors is, therefore, subject to little restraints. The lack of control mechanisms is in accordance with the restraint of the legislator in establishing legislation, emphasising the capability of private actors to develop adequate rules. Accordingly, the legislator consistently considers whether, instead of legislation, alternative regulation can be established.[1976] This leaves a considerable role for non-state actors, despite the absence of an equivalent of the *Wesentlichkeitsgebot* an obligation to provide rules on matters that may affect consistutional rights.

1971 AFM Consultatiedocument toetskader hypothecaire kredietverlening, 2009, p. 24, available at www.afm.nl/marktpartijen/upl_documents/consultatiedocument_hypotheken.pdf.

1972 NVB – reactie AFM – Consultatie toetskader hypothecaire kredietverlening, available at www.nvb.nl/scrivo/asset.php?id=291762.

1973 See www.verbondvanverzekeraars.nl/sitewide/general/nieuws.aspx?action=view&nieuwsid=24.

1974 For example: www.rabohypotheekonline.nl/voorwaarden/gedragscode/. For the full text of GIDI, the bank refers to their brochure 'De Rabobank als bemiddelaar van uw verzekeringen' (www.rabobank.nl/images/2800_rabobank_als_bemiddelaar_29185695.pdf), which does not mention the GIDI. Other examples: Avéres Assurantiën (for conciliation for insurance and other financial services: see www.averes.nl/service/gidi), De Uitvaart Makelaar (for conciliation of insurances on funerals and cremations, see www.deuitvaartmakelaar.nl/gidi.pdf), Hypohome (specialised in advice on mortgages, see www.hypohome.nl/gidi-advieswijzer.htm).

1975 Available at www.verbondvanverzekeraars.nl/UserFiles/File/download/coderendementrisico2006.pdf.

1976 Aanwijzingen voor de regelgeving 7, 8.

Notwithstanding its usual restraint, the Dutch legislator has held that if the law refers to privately drafted rules, this will typically concern static, rather than dynamic referral, as privately drafted rules are not always sufficiently accessible.[1977] While this may be the reason for the scarcity of instances in which the Dutch legislator has made use of dynamic referral, this has not limited the role of non-state actors involved in dynamic referral at the European level. Even though the introduction of the Regulation has resulted in a reallocation of competence that has put the decision-making in this area out of Dutch democratic control, the Dutch legislator supported dynamic referral to the IASB.[1978]

Similarly, the Dutch government has not sought to limit the roles of non-state actors in comitology committees. In the consultation on the proposal for a Directive on consumer rights, the Dutch government, Dutch academics and Dutch stakeholders[1979] did not take a position on a possible comitology procedure. This is in line with the pragmatic approach towards the delegation of competences towards lower levels of government that does not show a particular emphasis on parliamentary involvement.[1980] However, this approach is not in line with more general criticism of alternative regulation.[1981]

8.4.1.4. A plea for a framework on the basis of private autonomy and *Fremdbestimmung*

A framework to determine the role of actors more consistently and predictably is desirable. Can starting points be found for the development of a future framework on the role of state actors and non-state actors in the development of private law?

Some starting points can be found in the criticism on the lenience of Dutch and European actors, pointing out that the prominent involvement of private actors may be detrimental to the quality of private law. Accordingly, Hijink[1982] finds that the current development of standards by the IASB undermines the stable development of the law, as well as sufficient accessibility of the law, while the development of binding law should in addition have a legal basis. The use of comitology has also been criticised as it might undermine democracy. It is also not a very transparent process;[1983] and it meets with similar criticism of skeleton legislation (*kaderwetgeving*) at a national

1977 Aanwijzingen voor de regelgeving 92.

1978 *Kamerstukken II*, 2001–2002, 28220, nr 3, comp. also Kamerstukken II, 2006–2007, 21501–07, nr 541.

1979 See the response available at http://ec.europa.eu/consumers/cons_int/safe_shop/acquis/responses/ms_netherlands.pdf. For an exception, see the WODC report on the consultation that rejects comitology, see par. 5.3.3.4.

1980 Comp. aanwijzingen voor de regelgeving 35.

1981 See especially T. Hartlief, 'Alternatieve regelgeving in privaatrechtelijke verhoudingen. Opmerkingen bij het preadvies van prof. mr. I. Giesen', *NJB* 2007, 21.

1982 J.B.S. Hijink, 'Naar een Europees jaarrekeningenrecht', *Ondernemingsrecht* 2012, 28.

1983 Comp. Ch.F. Sabel, J. Zeitlin, 'Learning from difference: The new architecture of experimentalist governance in the EU', *ELJ* 2008, p. 297 who note that some attempts have been made to increase transparency and accessibility in the Lamfalussy process, which has however increased complexity and increased the chance that influential stakeholders exercise too much influence in the decision-making process.

level.[1984] It follows that the proposed use of comitology in draft article 40 of the proposal for a Directive on consumer rights may also give rise to problems. The development of the black and grey list of unfair contract terms by private parties may result in situations where contract parties are confronted with rules that are contrary to national society's legal views on justice, especially as actors in comitology committees do not have sufficient insight in these views or in business practices. Consequently, the accessibility and the responsiveness of the law may be undermined. Generally, criticism on alternative regulation refers to potential corporatism and the question how alternative regulation fits with the traditional *trias politica*, especially with regard to the role of the judiciary, as well as the question whether alternative regulation will contribute to accessibility and predictability. A more critical approach towards the development of referral would also be in line with more general criticism of alternative regulation.

Private autonomy and *Fremdbestimmung* could provide a starting point for critically considering the desirability of extending the scope of existing alternative regulation such as dynamic referral to the IASB, comitology, the Lamfalussy process, and developing new forms of alternative regulation.

Notably, concepts of private autonomy and *Fremdbestimmung* do not stand in the way of the development of alternative regulation, but indicate the need to develop control mechanisms. The question of which mechanisms should be developed in turn depends on the question of how state actors want to mitigate potential *Fremdbestimmung* and when they consider that potential *Fremdbestimmung* has been sufficiently limited. Suggestions[1985] point towards ensuring the quality of the drafting process of alternative regulation, in accordance with the requirements of transparency, inclusiveness and responsiveness. Notably, these suggestions do not take national democratic procedures as a starting point; they are more in line with the suggestions of participative democracy.[1986]

The development of these control mechanisms may benefit responsiveness as actors affected by alternative regulation should be involved. This does not mean that calls for a more open process do not meet with problems. Control mechanisms for national alternative regulation may be developed at the national level, but Dutch actors are not competent to develop these mechanisms for European alternative regulation, and suggestions for these measures may not be met with sufficient political support at the European level. At most, Dutch state actors could promote more involvement of more representative actors in the development of comitology, while critically considering whether the development of new instances of comitology in the area of private law is desirable. In some areas, suggestions for wider participation may however be problematic. Especially in the Lamfalussy process and the development of international accounting standards, the level of expertise needed to decide rationally would make

1984 Comp. the Annual report of the Raad van State 2006, p. 57, available at www.raadvanstate.nl/publicaties/jaarverslagen/.

1985 See previously par. 8.2.3.

1986 BVerfG 30 June 2009, *NJW* 2009, 2267 (Lisbon Treaty), see previously par. 7.3.2.1.2.

wide participation difficult. However, other matters, such as the question of which clauses should be on a black or grey list, may well be discussed in a wider circle.

8.4.2. *Codes of conduct: the corporate governance code and the banking code*

Paragraph 8.4.2.1 will consider instances of co-regulation where state actors have reinforced codes of conduct developed by private actors and paragraph 8.4.2.2 will turn to the role of non-state actors in these instances. Paragraph 8.4.2.3 will discuss the limitations on non-state actors' roles through the development of control mechanisms.

8.4.2.1. Reinforced codes of conduct

In the Dutch legal order, reinforced codes have been established:

- The corporate governance code establishes norms for the relationships within a company. In turn, the behaviour of parties within companies influences various parties, especially parties contracting with these companies: employees, customers, and suppliers.

The establishment of the corporate governance code dates back to 1996, when stakeholders, pending the proposal for a law on protectionist constructions ('*beschermingsconstructies*'), established a committee to investigate corporate governance.[1987] This committee published its recommendations in 1997,[1988] and expressly stated that legislation on this subject was not required. Instead, self-regulation would be sufficient. However, after evaluation, compliance with these recommendations was judged as insufficient.[1989] Therefore, in 2003, stakeholders, cooperating with the Ministries of Economic Affairs and Finance established a committee to form a code of conduct for corporate governance that was published in the same year and entered into force in 2004.[1990] The government installed a Monitoring Committee on the Corporate Governance Code[1991] that reports to the government. Businesses cannot deviate from certain principles and best practices regulated in the Code, as parts of the Code can reflect Dutch accepted views on

1987 For more information on corporate governance code see J.M.M. Maeijer, F.J.P. van den Ingh. *Mr. C. Asser's handleiding tot de beoefening van het Nederlands burgerlijk recht. 2. Vertegenwoordiging en rechtspersoon. Deel III. De naamloze en de besloten vennootschap*, Deventer: Tjeenk Willink 2000, nr. 28–30, and the special issue of *Ondernemingsrecht* 2004–4.

1988 The text of the recommendations is available at www.commissiecorporategovernance.nl/Commissie%20Peters.

1989 See for the government reaction to the report *Kamerstukken II* 1998–1999, 25732, nr. 8. See for a critical reaction to the government's statement J.W. Winter, 'Oorlog en vrede', *Ondernemingsrecht* 1999, p. 203.

1990 The corporate governance code has been revised in 2008. Both versions are available at www.commissiecorporategovernance.nl/De_Corporate_Governance_Code_2003_%28de_Code_Tabaksblat%29. The government decided (Art. 2 Besluit 23 December 2004, Stb. 747) that the corporate governance code formed a Code in the sense of art. 2:391 par. 5 BW (expanded following Directive 2006/46, see *Stbl.* 2008, 550). See *Kamerstukken II* 2007–2008, 31508, nr. 3.

1991 *Strct.* 2004, 241, p. 11.

corporate governance and, thereby, form a source of law.[1992] The establishment of the corporate governance code fits with (newly developing) European standards.[1993]

- The new Dutch banking code from The Netherlands' Banking Association (*Nederlandse Vereniging van Banken*, NVB)[1994] that was adopted following a report from the Advisory Committee on the future of banks in The Netherlands[1995] sets standards for the supervisory board and the management board, risk management, audits, and remuneration. The Code explicitly aims to influence transactions between individuals: compliance with this Code is meant to improve the consumers' trust in banks, and to prevent (further) collapses. Also, the behaviour of banks directly influences its contracting parties, whether they are consumers, businesses or states.

Although state actors have not cooperated directly in creating the rules contained in the Code, the advisory committee expressly stated that the best practices in the first two chapters of the code were not meant as self-regulation and should be enforced by state legislation.[1996] The Ministry of Finance, in cooperation with stakeholders, has considered at what points and in what manner the Code can best be reinforced with hard law:[1997] possibly, the banking code could be appointed as a code of conduct in the sense of article 2:391 par. 5 BW that would oblige banks to account for compliance with these principles. Additionally, a monitoring committee will be established in cooperation with the Ministry of Finance. The banking code explicitly takes relevant national, European and international standards into account and can especially be seen in the light of the establishment of European supervisory bodies that also act as committees in the third level of the Lamfalussy process, supervising the enforcements of the Capital Requirements Directive.

The simultaneous initiatives at the national, European and international level after the credit crunch that preceded the establishment of these supervisory bodies[1998] have led to criticism on

1992 Comp. HR 21 February 2003, *NJ* 2003, 182, under 6.4.2, and HR 13 July 2007, *NJ* 2007, 434, under 4.4.

1993 European Commission, *Modernising company law and enhancing corporate governance in the European Union – a plan to move forward*, COM (2003) 284 final, and Decision of the Commission 15 October 2004, OJ 2004, L 321/53, resulting in Directive 2006/46, leading to the amendment of the decision of 23 December 2004, Stb. 747. See for more information J.N. Schutte-Veenstra, 'De toekomst van het Europese vennootschapsrecht', *Ondernemingsrecht* 2006, p. 577–580.

1994 Banking Code of 9 September 2009, available at the website of The Netherlands Bankers' Association, www.nvb.nl.

1995 Advisory Committee on the future of banks in The Netherlands, *Restoring trust*, 7 April 2009, available at www.nvb.nl.

1996 Advisory Committee on the future of banks in The Netherlands, *Restoring trust*, p. 9 and V.P.G. de Serière, '"Naar herstel van vertrouwen." Het rapport van de Adviescommissie Toekomst Banken', *Ondernemingsrecht* 2009, 83.

1997 Letter from the minister of finance to the *Tweede Kamer* (Parliament) 15 June 2009, FM/2009/1022 M, p. 3.

1998 These developments also include the report from the High-Level Group on Financial Supervision published on future financial regulation and supervision, available at http://ec.europa.eu/internal_market/finances/docs/de_larosiere_report_en.pdf, followed by a Communication on European financial supervision COM (2009) 252 final and EU legislative proposals, COM (2009) 576 final, COM (2009) 501 final, COM (2009) 502 final, COM (2009) 503 final. In addition the Committee of European Banking Supervisors (CEBS) published the Interim report on liquidity buffers & survival periods, 17 March 2009, and the Consultation paper on draft guidelines for liquidity buffers, 7 July 2009, CP28, both available at www.c-ebs.org/getdoc/ea5aa2f1-4395-4f06-9b0a-45c05df8ab86/CP28.aspx, and the

the uncoordinated multitude of approaches from various actors.[1999] Thereby, these initiatives could impair the accessibility of the law in this area. It follows that more restraint should be exercised by various actors, even in the light of uniform calls for the development of rules at various levels.

8.4.2.2. The role of non-state actors

The Dutch legislator has adopted restraint where private actors can provide rules themselves, which has also been visible in the development of the corporate governance code. Although the legislator has reinforced the corporate governance code, the code may also be binding if it reflects Dutch legal views on corporate governance. This prominent role can also be seen in the light of an increasing need for laws that can easily be amended. Consequently, non-state actors have played a prominent role in the development of reinforced codes of conduct. The reinforcement of initial voluntary self-regulation has increased the influence of private actors on potential third parties.

8.4.2.3. Limitations on the role of non-state actors

Interestingly, since the credit crunch, corporate governance has been described as 'one of the most important failures of the present crisis', leading to gaps in rules and norms, for example for the supervision on hedge funds.[2000] It is not clear whether this is due to the closed process in which corporate governance codes are developed, or whether the lack of compliance is something that cannot be remedied by the development of new rules.[2001] Generally, however, criticism on the prominent role of private actors seems rather rare.

Nevertheless, Dutch state actors have recognised the need for control mechanisms. In particular, the legislator[2002] has recognised the potential shortcomings of self-regulation and the risk of *Fremdbestimmung* if self-regulation is established in areas where stakeholders have unequal bargaining positions. Thus, unequal positions of stakeholders may be a reason to opt for legislation rather than alternative regulation. This is the case, according to the Dutch government, if participation requires a level of expertise that is unlikely to be found in weaker parties. Corporate governance may be one of those areas and safeguards reminiscent of German safeguards have accordingly been developed.

global plan for recovery and reform, statement from the G20 after the London summit, 2 April 2009, par. 13 et seq, available at www.londonsummit.gov.uk/resources/en/PDF/final-communique).

1999 G.T.M.J. Raaijmakers, 'De financiële markt en het ondernemingsrecht', *Ondernemingsrecht* 2009, 104.

2000 Report from the High-Level Group on Financial Supervision published on future financial regulation and supervision, par. 110 and 115, available at http://ec.europa.eu/internal_market/finances/docs/de_larosiere_report_en.pdf, and G. Kirkpatrick, 'The corporate governance lessons from the financial crisis', OECD Report, *Financial Market Trends* 2009-1.

2001 J. Winter, 'Corporate governance en wat het recht niet vermag', *AA* 2012, p. 416.

2002 *Kamerstukken II*, 2003-2004, 29752, nr 2, p. 18-19.

1) The need for transparency in the development of corporate governance standards, and the possibility for actors to participate through the use of consultations.

However, the question arises whether the consultation provided for sufficient time to respond, and whether actors participating in it were sufficiently representative. Interestingly, Van Solinge and Nowak[2003] criticised the lack of clarity on the question whether the corporate governance code, through the referral in article 3:291 par. 5 BW, became law.

2) Transparency on the compliance with the corporate governance code in annual accounts in article 3:291 par. 5 BW has been emphasised, while corporate governance codes simultaneously stipulated a larger role for shareholders.
3) The establishment of an adequately specialised judiciary.[2004]
4) The development of these codes takes place within the legal framework of book 2 BW and the proposals for the development of these rules within well-established structures such as the SER, which provides an independent platform for stakeholders.

The criticism on corporate governance codes has not withheld the development of the banking code, modelled on the corporate governance code, but previous experiences with the corporate governance codes may be a reason for the emphasis of the banking committee on the reinforcement of the code.

The development of these control mechanisms is not visible at the European level. However, the role of non-state actors is subject to some control as the European Commission exercises control over the actors participating in selected forums, particularly the European corporate governance forum.[2005]

8.4.3. *Collective bargaining*

Paragraph 8.4.3.1 will consider instances of reinforced collective bargaining and paragraph 8.4.3.2 will turn to the role of non-state actors in these instances. Paragraph 8.4.3.3 will consider limitations on non-state actors' roles through the development of control mechanisms. Paragraph 8.4.3.4 will end with a plea for a framework on the basis of principles of private autonomy and *Fremdbestimmung*.

8.4.3.1. Instances of collective bargaining

The reinforcement of collective bargaining, both in collective contracts on the conditions of employment (*'collectieve arbeidsovereenkomst'*, CAO) and collective settlements, is a well-established form of co-regulation. In collective bargaining, parties directly establish the rules in the agreement of the parties that they represent. These rules become binding when sanctioned by state actors (the ministry of social affairs and employment and the

2003 G.J. van Solinge, R. Nowak, 'Een krabbend anker', *WPNR* 6563 (2004).
2004 *Kamerstukken II*, 2003–2004, 29752, nr 2, p. 20–22.
2005 See further http://ec.europa.eu/internal_market/company/ecgforum/index_en.htm.

judiciary). This paragraph will first describe the development of CAOs and the development of agreements with works councils and go on to sketch collective settlements.

- A CAO is agreed between unions and employers' organisations or, for large companies, individual employers, and it stipulates the terms and conditions of employment (ranging from wages to fringe benefits).[2006]

Negotiations for CAOs take place within the framework of the *poldermodel*, established by the government and stakeholders in 1982 in the Wassenaar Agreement.[2007] Unions may, if they meet requirements of representativeness, require to be admitted to negotiations through the judiciary.[2008] If negotiations are unsuccessful, employees can try to reinforce their demands with a strike.[2009] In turn, employers can try to get an injunction against the strike. A CAO can be applicable within a specific branch, or for a specific company.[2010] These CAOs usually have a national scope, but their range can be limited to have a regional or a local scope. Provisions in the BW[2011] stipulate that in a CAO, parties can deviate from otherwise mandatory law. Apart from binding the contracting parties themselves, article 9 on the law for CAOs ('Wet CAO') stipulates that CAOs are also binding on the members of the unions that are a contracting party to the CAO. Article 12 and 13 Wet CAO stipulate that a clause contrary to a CAO within an individual labour contract between parties who are bound to the CAO (the individual employer and the employee who is a member to the union that is a contracting party to the CAO) is void and replaced by what the terms and conditions stipulated in the CAO. If issues are undecided in individual labour contracts, the terms and conditions in a CAO complement the individual contract. For employees who are not a member of one of the contracting unions, article 14 Wet CAO stipulates that the employer who is bound by the CAO is bound to comply with the CAO as regards contracts for employees who are not bound by the CAO. Article 10 Wet CAO stipulates that even if members cancel their membership, they remain bound to the CAO. However, the unbound employee cannot demand compliance with the CAO. The difference made between bound and unbound employees has been criticised, for example, because an employer may not know what employees are members of contracting unions. Article 14 Wet CAO is often evaded by incorporating the CAOs within all individual labour contracts with a bound employer.[2012] A collective agreement can be declared generally binding ('*algemeen verbindend*') for a sector under the Act of declaring CAOs binding or non-binding ('Wet AVV').[2013] It has been argued that this competence should be reallocated to the Association for Labour (*Stichting voor de*

2006 As defined in article 1 par. 1 of the Law on Collective agreements on terms of employment ('Wet CAO').

2007 The (Dutch) text of the agreement is available at www.parlement.com/9291000/modulesf/ggektig0.

2008 Rb. Amsterdam 20 January 1982, *NJ* 1984, 101.

2009 See L.A.J. Schut, *Internationale normen in het Nederlandse stakingsrecht*, The Hague: SDU 1996.

2010 The texts of CAOs for various branches are available via http://cao.startpagina.nl/.

2011 In articles 7:628 par. 7, 7:629a par. 7, 7:634 par. 3, 7:638 par. 2, 7:639 par. 2, 7:652 par. 6, 7:655 par. 2, 7:658b par. 7, 7:664, par. 1, sub c, 7:668a par. 5, 7:670 par. 13, and 7:672, par. 5, 7, 8 BW.

2012 G.J.J. Heerma van Voss, *Mr. C. Assers handleiding tot de beoefening van het Nederlands Burgerlijk Recht. 7 Bijzondere overeenkomsten. Deel V: Arbeidsovereenkomst, collectieve arbeidsovereenkomst en ondernemingsovereenkomst*, Deventer: Kluwer 2008, nr. 453. Hereafter, this volume will refer to this book in the following manner: Asser/Heerma van Voss 2008.

2013 See for an overview of the CAOs that have been declared generally binding http://cao.szw.nl/.

Arbeid) consisting of stakeholders,[2014] an advice that has however, not been acted upon. The suggestion was rejected by the majority of members of this organisation, who referred to the infringement of contractual freedom of parties bound to generally binding CAOs. If declared generally binding, a CAO may be considered hard law,[2015] and it is applicable to all individual contracts, also contracts with non-bound employees.

- Article 32 par. 1 Act on Works Council ('Wet op de Ondernemingsraden', WOR) stipulates that parties negotiating CAOs and public bodies can delegate competences to works councils. Article 27 WOR makes clear that works councils need to give permission for provisions with regard to secondary terms of employment. Employers may also extend the competence of works councils through additional agreements, including negotiations on employment contracts, which may, however, not set aside CAOs.[2016]

Differing from BVs, the agreements between the employer and works' councils are not directly binding for the employee, and only become binding when they have been incorporated in individual agreements or if CAOs stipulate that the agreements will be directly applicable.

- The collective settlement of claims the Dutch Class Action (Financial Settlement) Act ('WCAM') in 2005.

Previously, article 6:240 BW and article 3:305a BW[2017] already established a legal action for interests groups.[2018] Under the Act, parties first have to reach an agreement on the collective financial settlement before it can be submitted to the courts. Article 7:907 BW stipulates that the court can, on the joint request of parties, decide that the settlement becomes binding on an entire group of claimants, unless a claimant opts out of the settlement. In reaching a collective settlement, claimants can bring an action under article 3:305a BW to decide on points of law relevant for the collective settlement.[2019]

2014 Stichting van de Arbeid, *Advies inzake het beleid ten aanzien van het algemeen verbindend en het onverbindend verklaren van bepalingen van collectieve arbeidsovereenkomsten*, October 1989, p. 36–37.

2015 HR 31 May 2002, *NJ* 2003, 110 (Ziekenhuis De Heel); HR 14 February 2003, *NJ* 2003, 301 (Thuiszorg Centraal Twente). See for a CAO that was not declared generally binding but that was considered 'law' HR 20 October 2006, *NJ* 2006, 573.

2016 Asser/Heerma van Voss 2008, nr. 480.

2017 This provision excludes the possibility for a claim of damages.

2018 However, before this provision was enacted, in some cases a collective action was accepted: see for example HR 1 July 1983, *NJ* 1984, 360, HR 1 July 1983, *RvdW* 1983, 131.

2019 Well-known cases in which collective settlements have been reached include the agreement declared binding by the Amsterdam Court of Appeal 1 June 2006, *LJN* AX6440, agreement declared binding by the Amsterdam Court of Appeal 25 June 2007, *LJN* AZ7033, agreement declared binding by the Amsterdam Court of Appeal 29 May 2009, *LJN* BI5744, agreement declared binding by the Amsterdam Court of Appeal, 29 April 2009, *LJN* BI2717. Other case law on article 3:305a BW includes HR 5 June 2009, *RvdW* 2009, 565, HR 14 June 2002, *NJ* 2003, 689, and HR 7 November 1997, *NJ* 1998, 268. The *Consumentenbond* also assists Dutch consumers involved in foreign claims, see for examples A.J.C. Zwinkels, 'Productveiligheid en -aansprakelijkheid. Ervaringen van de Consumentenbond', *TvC* 1998, p. 316.

At the European level, possibilities for collective negotiations have also been developed in the European Social Dialogue and European law may affect CAOs.[2020]

In conclusion, various instances of collective bargaining can be found, especially at the national level.

8.4.3.2. The role of non-state actors: exercising fundamental rights?

The role of non-state actors is constitutionally protected, even though the freedom to collectively negotiate has not been recognised as such. However, article 8 Gw does recognise the freedom of association, and international treaties, especially article 11 ECHR and article 6 par. 4 European Social Charter that both have a direct effect,[2021] have respectively also recognised the right to association and the right to strike.

The constitutionally protected role of non-state actors has not withheld the Dutch legislator from pressuring the conclusion of agreements that are considered in the interest of the Dutch economy, as becomes apparent from the Wassenaar agreement,[2022] even though the freedom of contract of contract parties has been emphasised. Consequently, although collective bargaining is seen against the background of constitutional rights, it has also been considered as a means to develop employment contracts in a manner beneficial for the public interest. It follows that the role of non-state actors may be made subject to the public interest.

The possibility for mass settlement has generally not been considered within article 8 Gw or international provisions on the right to association. Articles 7:900 and seq BW take parties' freedom to contract as a starting point. The need to take into account party autonomy has been emphasised, although this has not expressly been recognised as a constitutional right. Nevertheless, private parties have been granted an important role in initiating and negotiating settlements, which was in accordance with previous case law as well as article 3:305a BW that already enabled stakeholder organisations to bring a collective claim.[2023]

8.4.3.3. Limitations on the role of non-state actors?

At the national level, debate has not, as such, focused on questions of *Fremdbestimmung*.[2024] In contrast, arguments for the retroactive effect and after effect of generally binding

[2020] CJEU 11 December 2007 (International Transport Workers' Federation and Finnish Seamen's Union v Viking Line ABP and OÜ Viking Line Eesti), C-438/05, [2007] ECR, p. I-10779 and CJEU 18 December 2007 (Laval un Partneri Ltd v Svenska Byggnadsarbetareförbundet), C-341/05, [2007] ECR, p. I-11767.

[2021] Other relevant international treaties include article 22 ICCPR, article 5 of the European Social Charter, and article 8 ICESC. The right to collective negotiations is recognised in article 6 European Social charter and the ILO Convention on the right to organise and collective bargaining 1949, C98.

[2022] See previously par. 8.4.3.1.

[2023] *Kamerstukken II*, 1991–1992, 22486, nr. 3.

[2024] Comp. however, C.E. du Perron, *Overeenkomst en derden*, Deventer: Kluwer 1999, p. 72, who characterises the binding force of CAOs as partially heteronomous, a source of obligations not dependant upon parties' wills, but on the law – and partially autonomous – a source of binding force as employees can prevent being bound by a CAO by cancelling their membership to a union. In his

CAOs have been made and recognised.[2025] Nevertheless, CAOs may meet with problems.[2026]

Different from the German legal order, the Dutch legal order does not generally assume that unions are in principle better capable of defending employees' rights, and CAOs do not fall within a Dutch equivalent of the *Richtigkeitsgewähr.* Mandatory law imposes some restraints on negotiating parties. Particularly, article 2 par. 5 Wet AVV prohibits some clauses in CAOs aimed at excluding or limiting the rights of employees.

If CAOs are declared generally binding, this may affect third parties' rights and obligations. Notwithstanding this influence, the decision to declare a CAO generally applicable is not open to appeal under article 8:2 Awb. However, articles 4 and 6 Wet AVV note that parties can object to declaring a CAO generally binding or non-binding prior to the declaration. Unless parties' objections are clearly unfounded, the decision-making process can only be continued once a reaction to the objections has been given.

It has been recognised that works' councils may be less independent than unions, but as the agreements between employers and works' councils are not directly binding, this will not generally lead to problems and the need to develop control mechanisms is not apparent.

For collective settlements, the Dutch legislator has acknowledged the need to guarantee third parties' access to the judiciary in accordance with article 17 Gw and article 6 ECHR and the need to compensate for potential *Fremdbestimmung*, by providing parties with a possibility to opt out of settlements once they have been established, in accordance with article 7:908 par. 3 BW. In addition, claimants may seek to influence the views of the judge by filing petitions.[2027] The possibilities for parties to challenge the declaration that a collective agreement will become generally binding has, however, been limited in article 1018 Civil Procedure Code.[2028]

Additionally, the Dutch legislator[2029] has sought to prevent an increasing amount of organisations seeking to represent claimants solely on a commercial basis. In that light, the legislator has approved the development of self-regulation, in particular the claim code that includes guidelines on the tasks, transparency and governance of these organisations on the basis of its articles of association.[2030] It is unclear why especially

analysis, however, the law as a source of binding obligations is considered as a breach of third parties' private autonomy, whereas in the German legal order, the democratic legitimacy of these rules is emphasised, and *Fremdbestimmung* is, in the German view, more likely to arise if a hybrid form between the law and contract, developed by private actors likely pursuing their own rather than the public interest, are the source of obligations.

2025 Asser/Heerma van Voss 2008, nr. 465.

2026 G.J.J. Heerma van Voss, 'Medezeggenschap van werknemers met betrekking tot arbeidsvoorwaarden', *RM Themis* 1999, p. 269.

2027 *Kamerstukken II*, 2003–2004, 29414, nr. 3, p. 4.

2028 Comp. the conclusion of P.G. C.L. de Vries Lentsch-Kostense par. 18–24 before HR 20 March 2015, *RvdW* 2015, 434 on the question why the WCAM is in accordance with article 6 ECHR and article 1 First Protocol to the ECHR. The Hoge Raad did not consider this question but rejected the complaint on the basis of article 81 Act on Judicial Organisation ('Wet op de Rechterlijke Organisatie').

2029 *Kamerstukken II*, 2011–2012, 33126, nr. 3.

2030 Available at www.consumentenbond.nl/morello-bestanden/716993/compljuniclaimcodecomm2011.pdf.

commercial organisations would choose to comply with this code. Further, it has been suggested to adopt a provision which enables the judge to reject claims if these claims are unlikely to be in the interests of claimants. A committee to monitor the enforcement of the code has been installed.

8.4.3.4. A plea for a future framework on the basis of principles of private autonomy and *Fremdbestimmung*

Can starting points be found for developing a future framework on the basis of principles of private autonomy and *Fremdbestimmung?*

Current control mechanisms, including mandatory law and opt-out possibilities, as well as suggestions for more control mechanisms could be seen in this light. Particularly, suggestions to evaluate the notion of representativeness of non-state actors in the negotiations of CAOs, in accordance with the Wet AVV, and in the negotiations on mass settlements in article 7:907 par. 3 sub f BW could provide a starting point to consider what role non-state actors should play, and if they play a prominent role, which requirements can be made of these actors?

Requirements of representativeness currently leave much room for discretion, of either the Minister declaring a CAO generally binding or non-binding, or for a judge declaring a mass settlement contract binding.[2031] Interestingly, the Dutch Association for the Judiciary[2032] has argued for additional measures to guarantee representativeness, which should prevent private actors seeking to represent victims in mass damages cases for commercial aims. Los[2033] notes that the standard of representativeness, as well as the process through which the settlement is achieved, is relevant for the reasonableness of the compensation in the settlement. Similarly, in the area of CAOs, more clarity on the question when requests for declaring a CAO generally binding would, in turn, increase predictability and enhance the chance that a consistent approach will be adopted towards declaring CAOs generally binding.

Questions of private autonomy and *Fremdbestimmung* may arise from proposals for reform. With regard to CAOs and works' councils, Heerma van Voss[2034] notes the differences between the role of Dutch and German works' councils and states that the direct effect of BVs should also be introduced in Dutch law, as that would be in accordance with the increasing use of agreements between works' council and employers. Notably, this would enhance the role of Dutch works' councils, which, in turn, raises the question whether considerations of *Fremdbestimmung* should similarly play a role in the Dutch

2031 R.R.A. Henkemans, 'De wetgevende taak van de rechter bij massaschade', in: N. van den Berg, R.R.A. Henkemans, A. Timmer (eds.), *Massaclaims, Class actions op z'n Nederlands*, Ars Aequi Libri: Nijmegen 2007, p. 40.

2032 Nederlandse Vereniging voor Rechtspraak, *Wetgevingsadvies Wijziging van de Wet collectieve afwikkeling massaschade*, 2011, p. 1–2.

2033 W.J.J. Los, 'Toepassing van de WCAM. Bespiegelingen over de rol en de taak van de rechter', in: W.J.J. Los et al., *Collectieve acties in het algemeen en de WCAM in het bijzonder*, The Hague: BJU 2013, p. 29.

2034 G.J.J. Heerma van Voss, 'Medezeggenschap van werknemers met betrekking tot arbeidsvoorwaarden', *RM Themis* 1999, p. 270–271.

legal order. The possibility that unions are more independent than works' councils may be a reason to establish control mechanisms compensating for a weaker bargaining position of works' councils.

This framework should not mean that the benefits of alternative regulation are overlooked. Accordingly, CAOs are generally considered in the interest of employees, and the introduction of mass settlements served to reduce the amount of procedures as well as predictability. The framework would, however, serve to critically consider the role of non-state actors in reinforced collective bargaining and consider points for improvement. The development of a framework may also prompt a more critical perspective on the role of non-state actors in the development of framework agreements.

Importantly, however, the development of a Dutch framework on the basis of notions of private autonomy and *Fremdbestimmung* may lead to problems if it leads to a more critical approach to European forms of alternative regulation. Yet such a framework may also be a starting point for a more consistent approach to the development of alternative regulation that may in turn prompt the European legislator to consider alternative regulation more carefully.

8.4.4. Conclusion on state actors and non-state actors

What is the role of state and non-state actors in the development of private law through co-regulation?

Generally, non-state actors are granted a central role in the development of co-regulation. At the national level, state actors allow a large role for non state actors.[2035] Non-state actors play a prominent role in the development of mass settlements, CAOs, the corporate governance code and the banking code. At the European level, non-state actors play a prominent role through referral and similar forms of new governance.

Dutch actors, like European state actors, have exercised restraint in imposing limits on the role of non-state actors. However, Dutch state actors have recognised that private actors do not necessarily pursue the public interest but also their own interests.

Dutch control mechanisms entail the development of platforms for negotiations between actors with unequal bargaining positions, mandatory law, opt-out possibilities, requirements of representativeness and inclusiveness and the development of additional self-regulation. Judicial control is not as visibly developed as in the German legal order. Interestingly, these control mechanisms are more diverse than mechanisms found in the German legal order, they have been established more on an ad hoc basis and not on the basis of pre-existing concerns over *Fremdbestimmung*. Accordingly, Dutch state actors have established control mechanisms, which seem relatively mild in comparison to German control mechanisms, and strict in comparison to European control mechanisms. Nevertheless, European law does not visibly undermine existing control mechanisms.

Comparisons between the role of non state actors at the national and the European level, in the previous chapter, show that the roles of non-state actors and state actors

[2035] M.-C. Menting, *Terra incognita: de functies van gedragscodes in het privaatrecht* (master thesis) Tilburg 2011, p. 94 et seq characterises the approach of the Dutch legislator as a passive, bottom-up approach.

under Dutch and European law do not differ as drastically as the role of actors under the GG and under European law, which makes the interdependence between actors at the national and European level less pronounced. That does, however, not mean that parties may not strengthen or weaken one another's initiatives.

In addition, coexisting claims to authority may become less pronounced if those claims do not come into conflict with one another. Yet Dutch law is oriented on Dutch state actors rather than European or international actors, or on the interests of these actors. The development of European law has not changed this, notwithstanding the direct effect of European law. The development of European or international actors has also not prompted national actors to coordinate the development of overlapping rules, which is especially visible in the development of the banking code, as various initiatives are developed alongside one another. These developments indicate that the development of European initiatives has not stopped the development of national initiatives, and it is not clear that EU initiatives have prompted Dutch actors to consider foreign and international interests. This does become clear in other areas, for example in the willingness of the Dutch legislator to allow for dynamic referral.

Interdependence has become visible between state and non-state actors. Both Dutch and European state actors have recognised the benefits of alternative regulation.

Even though control mechanisms have not been developed to prevent or mitigate *Fremdbestimmung* as such, ideas of private autonomy and *Fremdbestimmung* could form a suitable basis for developing a more consistent and, therefore, predictable approach to the development of alternative regulation and the role of state and non-state actors, which would also benefit the quality of European private law. Particularly, the predictability and accessibility of private law could be improved by developing a framework, as these mechanisms draw more attention to possible rules that parties may become bound by. Further, providing parties with an opportunity to influence rules that they will be subjected to is in accordance with legal views on justice.

Such a framework should not stand in the way of developing alternative regulation, but rather offer a critical perspective that may be a starting point for improving alternative regulation without, however, subjecting European forms of alternative regulation to national standards. The benefits of alternative regulation should not be overlooked.

The interdependence between actors leads to a corresponding need for interaction, both between state actors at the national and the European level and between state and non-state actors.

Sufficient interaction between actors is important if private autonomy and *Fremdbestimmung* are used as underlying principles to develop a framework to determine actors' roles. Sufficient interaction should prevent a framework being developed which undermines European initiatives. In turn, European initiatives should not ignore national objections to European forms of alternative regulation. Instead, these objections could prompt European actors to improve European alternative regulation.

8.5. Non-state actors

This paragraph will ask what role non-state actors have played in the development of private law through self-regulation, and ask how actors have approached these developments, and how that may affect the use of self-regulation in the development of private law in the Dutch legal order.

Private actors form a group that are not competent to establish binding rules. Instead, they may develop self-regulation.[2036]

The Dutch legal order generally distinguishes between contractual self-regulation, and a much wider category of non-contractual forms of self-regulation. Dutch law does not usually distinguish between self-regulation established on the basis of articles of association and one-sided juridical acts. Importantly, one-sided juridical acts are not necessarily non-binding. To the contrary, one-sided juridical acts may be binding under Dutch law, depending on the question whether actors making these declarations intend to be legally bound – thus constituting a juridical act by making a declaration – and whether actors have justifiably relied on them.[2037] Consequently, although there has been distinction between contractual and other forms of self-regulation, no such distinction is apparent between self-regulation based on articles of association and one-sided declarations.[2038] Instead, distinctions are made between, for example, self-regulation on technical matters, self-regulation targeted at affecting individuals' behaviour, such as codes of conduct, internal or external self-regulation, or one-sided and multilateral forms of self-regulation.[2039]

One of the reasons for making this distinction is that in cases where self-regulation is incorporated in a contract, enforcement is often not problematic, but for other forms of self-regulation, enforcement is a central problem.[2040] Yet this does not necessarily mean that one *cannot* make this distinction. Forms of self-regulation that would typically be associated with self-regulation based on articles of association typically fall under disciplinary rules ('*tuchtrecht*'), either voluntary or compulsory.[2041] Typically, voluntary disciplinary law (also referred to as '*vrijwillig verenigingstuchtrecht*') is not targeted at ensuring third parties' (for example, consumers') contention or the public interest but rather at maintaining a high level of standards within a specific group.[2042] This sort of *tuchtrecht*[2043] has been considered as a legal area *sui generis* that does not fall within private law, or criminal law, or administrative law, which might explain why it is not typically characterised as self-regulation or alternative regulation in private law.

2036 Self-regulation can be understood as the making of rules and norms by both contract parties or a group of persons or bodies binding contract parties or this group, and often, but not necessarily, other private actors that choose to be bound by the rules made through self-regulation. See previously chapter 1, footnote 3.

2037 Asser/Hartkamp & Sieburgh 2010, nr 125 et seq.

2038 See, for example, B. Baarsma et al, *Zelf doen? Inventarisatie van zelfreguleringsinstrumenten*, Report for the Ministry for Economic Affairs, 2003, available at www.debrancheorganisatie.nl/upload/File/Zelf%20doen.pdf.

2039 See for an overview I. Giesen, *Alternatieve regelgeving en privaatrecht*, Deventer: Kluwer 2007, p. 15–16.

2040 M.B.M. Loos, *De energieleveringsovereenkomst: algemene voorwaarden voor de levering van energie aan consumenten*, Deventer: Kluwer 1998, p. 8.

2041 "Compulsory self-regulation" in this sense includes self-regulation on free professions, such as lawyers and physicians.

2042 For example N.J.H. Huls, M.A. Kleiboer, 'Is er een toekomst voor wettelijk niet hiërarchisch tuchtrecht?' *AA* 2002, p. 72.

2043 Future referral to *tuchtrecht* will denote *vrijwillig verenigingstuchtrecht*.

This paragraph will accordingly distinguish between contractual self-regulation, self-regulation on the basis of articles of association and other forms of self-regulation. The question arises whether Dutch experiences demonstrate that self-regulation on the basis of articles of association should be treated like other forms of self-regulation. This would make the development of a pluralist association-centered legal order rather than state-centered legal order less complicated than is the case in the German legal order.

Accordingly, paragraph 8.5.1 will consider contractual self-regulation and paragraph 8.5.2 will consider self-regulation on the basis of articles of association. Paragraph 8.5.3 will consider self-regulation based on one-sided juridical acts and paragraph 8.5.4 will consider the usefulness of these categories in Dutch law. Paragraph 8.5.5 will end with a conclusion.

8.5.1. Contractual self-regulation

This paragraph will ask what role non-state actors play in the development of contractual self-regulation.

Paragraph 8.5.1.1 will consider the basis of the binding force of contracts under Dutch law and consider the role of actors. In the German legal order, the *Richtigkeitsgewähr* provides a basis for determining in which cases parties' agreements will be enforced and which limitations will be set on actors' roles.[2044] If an equivalent of the *Richtigkeitsgewähr* can be discovered, this may provide more clarity on the role of actors. Notably, however, even if a Dutch equivalent to the *Richtigkeitsgewähr* can be established, it is likely that the Dutch legal order will evaluate this matter differently from the German legal order, where *Fremdbestimmung* in the absence of *Richtigkeitsgewähr* can be seen against the background of article 2 GG. Paragraph 8.5.1.2 will turn to collective contracts, including collectively negotiated STCs, and paragraph 8.5.1.3 will consider model contracts. Paragraph 8.5.1.4 will turn to STCs, and paragraph 8.5.1.5 will end with a conclusion.

8.5.1.1. The role of contract parties

The Dutch legal order does not directly recognise the will of private actors as the source of obligations; rather, article 6:1 BW reiterates that obligations can only arise insofar as this follows from the law. Accordingly, article 3:33 BW stipulates that a juridical act requires an intention to establish a legal effect that has been made public. Article 3:35 BW stipulates that if parties have justifiably relied on the behaviour or statements of other parties, this may entail that the parties making the declaration or behaving in a way in accordance with an intention to be bound, are bound. It is not clear whether the

[2044] The effect on the role of actors can be twofold: on the one hand, the *Richtigkeitsgewähr* provides a basis for a large amount of discretion for contract parties. On the other hand, the absence of the *Richtigkeitsgewähr* may be a reason to subject contracts to judicial evaluation and other control mechanisms, depending on the question whether contracts are deemed to have been established in a process that sufficiently reflects the will of both parties and thus prevents *Fremdbestimmung*.

will of parties or the reliance of parties on that will is the source of obligation: article 3:35 BW both excludes the will as well as the declaration that differs from the will as the sole basis of parties' obligations.[2045] The discussion in literature has accordingly focused on the will and the reliance as the basis of obligations.[2046] Notably, articles 3:33 and 35 BW were not drafted to resolve dogmatic issues. Rather, they established a double basis for the binding force of contracts, parties' wills and parties' legitimate expectations, in accordance with previous case law.[2047]

This dual basis has been criticised by authors[2048] offering a correction on the combination of parties' wills and parties' justified expectations as a basis for the binding force of contracts, adding that the *causa*-principle, the legal cause for a contract, is also a principle underpinning the binding force of contracts.[2049]

Recently, the basis for the binding force of contracts has again been subject to debate. Nieuwenhuis[2050] explains contracting as *égoïsme à deux*, in line with the idea that parties negotiate a contract in their own interests. He emphasises that aside from their own interests, parties have to act in accordance with good faith, taking into account the justified interests of their contract party. Therefore, parties' duties of care protect the autonomy of one of the contract parties. Similarly, Hartkamp and Sieburgh[2051] note that the binding force of a contract is based on the party autonomy of *both* contract parties, in accordance with article 6:217 BW that stipulates that a contract is established by an offer that is accepted. Vranken[2052] agrees with the importance of duties of care. He finds that these duties are at the core of contract law.

2045 Asser/Hartkamp & Sieburgh 2010, nr 125.

2046 Asser/Hartkamp & Sieburgh 2010, nr 126 et seq.

2047 C.J. van Zeben, M.M. Olthof, J.W. du Pon, *Parlementaire geschiedenis van het nieuwe burgerlijk wetboek: parlementaire stukken systematisch gerangschikt en van noten voorzien. Boek 3 Vermogensrecht in het algemeen*, Deventer: Kluwer 1981, p. 164.

2048 J.H. Nieuwenhuis, *Drie beginselen van contractenrecht*, Deventer: Kluwer 1977. Comp. however S. Whittaker, K. Riesenhuber, 'Conceptions of contract', in: G. Danneman, S. Vogenauer (eds.), *The Common European Sales Law in context*, Oxford: OUP, p. 128, 129 who note that English law seems based on a dual conception of contract, on the one hand, contract as bargain, and on the other hand, agreement. However, 'English law has managed to continue quite happily for some century and a half with this central tension in its conception of contract'.

2049 The proposal for the revision of the French law of obligations, Ministère de la Justice, *Projet d'ordonannce du portant reforme du droit des contrats*, available at www.justice.gouv.fr/publication/j21_projet_ord_reforme_contrats_2015.pdf, proposes to delete the causa as a requirement for a binding contract. C.M.D.S. Pavillon, 'Een nieuw contractenrecht voor Frankrijk', *NTBR* 2015, 11 compares the French initiative to the Dutch recodification, finding that both in French and Dutch law, the separate, formal requirement of a valid cause was considered as difficult to reconcile with party autonomy, as this provides the courts with a starting point to judge the economic-social sense for a contract.

2050 J.H. Nieuwenhuis, *Paternalisme, fraternalisme, egoïsme* (valedictory address Leiden 2009), Leiden: Universiteit Leiden 2009, p. 4.

2051 Asser/Hartkamp & Sieburgh 2010, nr 41–42.

2052 J.B.M. Vranken, 'Over partijautonomie, contractsvrijheid en de grondslag van gebondenheid in het verbintenissenrecht', in: J.M. Barendrecht, M.A.B. Chao-Duivis, B.W.M. Nieskens-Isphording (eds.), *Beginselen van het contractenrecht*, Deventer: Tjeenk Willink, 2000, par. 15.

Accordingly, in a case where a consumer had traded in stock options and suffered a considerable loss, the Hoge Raad[2053] held that the bank, as a professional contract party with considerable expertise, had a far-going duty of care, which had not been fulfilled by the repeated warnings of the bank and the experience of the consumer with stock trading. In other words, the duty of care may mean that a bank should refuse to execute the orders from its client, to protect the consumer against his own rashness, while the bank had breached obligations flowing from administrative law that aim to protect consumers. The decision emphasises the weakness of consumers that prevents them from making a rational decision in their own interests, which necessitates that the bank takes his interests into account.

These arguments do not make the importance of the negotiation process explicit.

Arguably, the negotiating process preceding contracts and amendments to contracts offers an interesting addition to the current justification of the binding force of contracts. The idea of the negotiating process emphasises the wills of *both* parties in the contract, in accordance with Nieuwenhuis idea of *égoïsme à deux*. In the negotiation process, it is necessary for parties to be able to rely on one another's behaviour – consequently, parties should take into account the legitimate interests of (potential) contract parties. Simultaneously, if negotiations show defects, because parties cannot negotiate on the same level as their contract partner, parties must take into account the interests of that party – a conclusion that is in line with the duties of care recognised in contract law. If the will of parties shows defects, because of a mistake (article 6:228 BW), threat, deception, or the abuse of parties' vulnerable circumstances (article 3:44 BW), the contract will be avoidable. In both cases, the defects in the negotiation process – that can be traced to a defect in parties' wills – entail that one party is able to impose his terms on the other party, thus breaching the autonomy of that party.

The weak position of parties and the defective negotiation process between parties may be a reason for the legislator to develop mandatory rules, in order to prevent that situation where the stronger position of one party leads to unacceptable social or economical consequences,[2054] or, in German law, *Fremdbestimmung*. This conclusion, however, leaves open the question of when these consequences become unacceptable, a conclusion that will often be the result of political negotiations in the legislature.

The idea of taking the negotiation process as a starting point is also in accordance with the *causa* principle[2055] as the cause of the contract is inherent in negotiations.

2053 HR 26 June 1998, *NJ* 1998, 660.

2054 Comp. C.E. du Perron, *Overeenkomst en derden*, Deventer: Kluwer 1999, p. 16–17, who distinguishes between control over the conclusion of a contract – in the case of defects of will – and the control over the content of the contract – as is the case for STCs, see below par. 8.5.1.4. However, the unequal position of parties may influence the legal position of the buyer. Consequently, the control over the content of the contract is linked to the conclusion of the contract, which is also recognised in article 6:223 sub a BW that refers to circumstances during the formation of the contract in order to determine the fairness of STCs.

2055 Previously, articles 1356 and 1371 Old BW stipulated that contracts should have a permitted cause (*'geoorloofde oorzaak'*), without which it was invalid. Currently, the BW does not expressly require this. G.J. Scholten, 'De oorzaak van de verbintenis uit overeenkomst', *AA* 1985, p. 744 sets out that this principle can still be found throughout the BW.

In many everyday transactions, however, negotiations do not take place. Therefore, is a negotiation process an adequate and convincing explanation if negotiations are absent in everyday transactions? Importantly, the idea of negotiation processes is not based on an empirical assessment of how often actual negotiations take place – in Germany, *Richtigkeitsgewähr* is also present if parties, rather than factually negotiating, focus on the price and quality of products, and choose to contract with the party that has the best combination of both. In these cases, factual negotiations need not take place – rather, the negotiation process is implicit. Accordingly, Du Perron[2056] considers that the wills of parties, on which the binding force of contracts has been based, does not denote the factual free will, but the possibility to make choices, including the choice that parties eventually make.

This justification presupposes that the effect of the contract is limited to the contract parties involved in negotiations, in accordance with the more general rule that contract parties cannot bind third parties.[2057] Accordingly, the principle of the relativity of contract (*'relativiteitsbeginsel'*) has been traced to the principle of party autonomy.[2058] Article 1376 Old BW expressly stipulated that contracts are binding between parties and cannot be a source of obligations for third parties, either to their detriment or to their benefit, unless provided by article 1353 Old BW. In the drafting of the BW, the legislator has chosen not to include a similar provision, because it could stand in the way of the further development of the law. Even though the BW does not contain a similar provision, the law refers to the wills and the legitimate expectations of *parties*, which may bind a contract party to the contract – not a third party. Similarly, article 6:217 BW presupposes an offer and acceptance, and subsequent binding force, by parties. This principle is visible throughout the Union.[2059]

The principle of the relativity of contract has become subject to various exceptions.[2060] In these cases, binding effects of a contract on third parties should only be permitted where the reasonableness of doing so is clearly apparent.[2061] This reasonableness may well require that third parties have acted in a manner that justifies the obligation.

In Quint/Te Poel,[2062] the Hoge Raad recognised unjustified enrichment as a source of obligations, declining a narrow interpretation of article 1269 Old BW that stipulated that the law or contracts are the source of obligations. In this case, Te Poel, brother of the contract party of Quint, was

2056 C.E. Du Perron, *Overeenkomst en derden*, Deventer: Kluwer 1999, p. 16.

2057 Asser/Hartkamp & Sieburgh 2010, nr 514.

2058 C.E. du Perron, *Overeenkomst en derden*, Deventer: Kluwer 1999, p. 9.

2059 See for an overview the rights of third parties from contracts to their benefit Ch. Von Bar et al (eds.), *Principles, Definitions and Model Rules of European Private Law. Draft Common Frame of Reference, Outline Edition, Volume I*, München: Sellier 2009, notes to article II-9:301, p. 647–648.

2060 See for examples of these exceptions J.L.P. Cahen, *Overeenkomst en derden*, Deventer: Kluwer 2004.

2061 Parl. Gesch. NBW, Boek 6, p. 917–918. See for an overview of case law and literature C.E, du Perron, *Overeenkomst en derden*, Deventer: Kluwer 1999, p. 82–83, more recently, on the effect of exclusion clauses to the detriment of third parties S. van Gulick, 'Derdenwerking van exoneratiebedingen: een analyse van recente rechtspraak en enige opmerkingen over de ontwikkeling van dit leerstuk vanuit het bouwcontractenrecht', *WPNR* (7057) 2015.

2062 HR 30 January 1959, *NJ* 1959, 548.

enriched as Quint had contracted to build houses on land that turned out to belong to the brother of the contract party. The contract party became insolvent and his brother became the owner of the houses on the basis of accession. In cases such as these, the third party has a reason to foresee that an obligation will be imposed upon him. In this case, however, Quint had no claim on the basis of articles 658 and 1608 Old BW which obligated the contractor to check the public registers to verify questions of ownership of the land.

It follows that contract parties have considerable room to enter into contracts with one another, in accordance with principles of party autonomy and legitimate expectations. The negotiation process is an interesting additional explanation.

The role of contract parties may in some cases be more extensive than is the case under German law, in cases where contract parties are able to bind third parties. In German law, this may well meet with objections of *Fremdbestimmung*. That does not mean that Dutch law does not recognise the importance of parties' autonomy or is not concerned with *Fremdbestimmung*; rather, *Fremdbestimmung* may be justified if parties acted in a manner that justifies imposing obligations on them.

8.5.1.2. Collective contracts

This paragraph will consider instances of collective bargaining and ask what role actors play in the development of private law through collectively negotiated contracts.

- The collective negotiations on STCs in consumer contracts undoubtedly form the most prominent example of collective bargaining.[2063]

The STCs established within this framework generally are applicable in contracts for the sale of consumer goods.[2064] STCs established within this framework further include the STCs for mail-order businesses,[2065] the general banking conditions,[2066] the general conditions for individuals and the guarantees used by BOVAG (the representative organisation for the trade in personal transport),[2067] the travel terms and conditions used by the Dutch Association of Travel Agents and Tour Operators (*Algemene Nederlandse Vereniging van Reisondernemingen*, ANVR),[2068] standard contract terms used by energy producers, traders and retailers in The Netherlands (represented by EnergieNed),[2069] standard contract terms used by the Association for the Conciliation for real estate (representing Dutch real estate agents, *Vereniging voor de Bemiddeling van Onroerend Goed*, VBO),[2070] the relocation businesses (represented by the Cooperating Departments for Relocations and Furniture Transport, *Samenwerkende Vakafdelingen Verhuizen*

2063 Asser/Vranken 2005, nr. 88.
2064 Coördinatiegroep Zelfregulering, *Jaarverslag 2008*, CZ/352, 2009, (Annual Report 2008), see: www.ser.nl/~/media/Files/Internet/Publicaties/Overige/2000_2010/2009/CZjaarverslag2008.ashx.
2065 Available at www.thuiswinkel.org/bedrijven/thuiswinkel_waarborg/algemene_voorwaarden.html.
2066 Available at www.nvb.nl/scrivo/asset.php?id=291360.
2067 Available at www.bovag.nl/index.php?pageID=34.
2068 Available at www.anvr.travel/opreis.php?opreis_id=1282.
2069 Available at www.energiened.nl/_upload/bestellingen/publicaties/00000227.pdf.
2070 Available at www.vbo.nl/files/Consumentvoorwaarden%20juni%202007.pdf.

en Meubeltransport, SAVAM),[2071] the referential model for internet access,[2072] general conditions used in child care,[2073] and the general conditions used in the trade of non-food retail products, as agreed by the Central Branch Association for Living (*Centrale Brancheverening Wonen*, CBW).[2074]

- Various instances of collective bargaining, usually for specific groups of consumers and for specific contracts.

For instance, the *Vastelastenbond* states that it is an organisation of consumers that bargains collectively to gain advantageous contracts for electricity, insurance, internet and mobile phone subscriptions for its members.[2075] Other examples of collective bargaining are collective contracts with healthcare insurers, by employers,[2076] or unions.[2077] Further examples of collective bargaining are online collective bargaining platforms, where providers offer a platform for businesses to offer goods or services with considerable discounts, provided that enough people accept this offer, which ideally results in the promoting of these offers through social media. Examples of these platforms are Groupon[2078] and Groupdeal.[2079] Although the idea is that it is advantageous for both consumers and sellers to give big groups of consumers a reduction, the terms of these platforms that do not necessarily represent consumers, are not necessarily beneficial.[2080] Consumers have encountered problems.[2081]

At the European level, instances of collective bargaining have also been encouraged, for example in the area of mortgages[2082] and package travel.[2083]

2071 Available at www.erkendeverhuizers.nl/CMS5/upload/docs/alg_voorwaarden_Brochure.pdf.
2072 Available at www.ser.nl/nl/Taken/Zelfregulering/Consumentenvoorwaarden/Praktische%20Informatie/~/media/Files/Internet/Consumentenvoorwaarden/AV/cz_67%20pdf.ashx, used for example by Tele2, XS4All, KPN, and Telfort.
2073 Available at http://media.leidenuniv.nl/legacy/alg_vw_kinderopvang2005_1sept2005.pdf.
2074 Available at www.cbw-erkend.nl/websites/cbw_consumenten/docs/CBW-algemene-voorwaarden.pdf.
2075 See www.vastelastenbond.nl/over-de-vastelastenbond.html.
2076 Examples of these contracts with insurers: Tilburg university and CZ (www.uvt.nl/medewerkers/gezondheid/ziek/ziektekosten/collectieve-verzekering/), Leiden University and Zorg en Zekerheid (www.medewerkers.leidenuniv.nl/arbeidsvoorwaarden-personeelsbeleid/zorgverzekering/collectieve-zorgverzekering.html), Nijmegen university also offers its students a collective health care insurance (www.ru.nl/studenten/regelingen/collectieve/). The Netherlands Association for medium to small businesses (Midden- en Kleinbedrijf, MKB) provides information for collective health insurance at its website, see: www.mkbservicedesk.nl/479/hoe-regel-collectieve-zorgverzekering.htm.
2077 For example CNV (www.cnv.nl/ziekte-en-zorg/cnv-zorgverzekering/cnv-zorgverzekering/), or FNV (www.menzis.nl/web/Consumenten/Klantenservice/FormulierenEnDocumenten/VerzekeringAanvragen/AanvragenCollectieveZorgverzekeringFNV.htm).
2078 See further www.groupon.nl/how-does-groupon-work.
2079 See further www.groupdeal.nl/.
2080 The STCs of Groupdeal (www.groupdeal.nl/algemene-voorwaarden/) stipulate that in case of disputes, arbitration will be followed in Amsterdam, and if settlement is not possible, then the Amsterdam courts will be competent, which is hard to reconcile with CJEU case law, see previously par. 5.4.2.
2081 See for example www.jouwervaringen.nl/groupon/, as well as www.trosradar.nl/uitzending/archief/detail/aflevering/24-10-2011/groupon/.
2082 See previously par. 7.5.1.2.1.
2083 See previously par. 7.5.1.2.1.

Thus, private actors have recognised the added value of collective negotiations. The Dutch legislator has similarly recognised the added value of these negotiations and has not stood in the way of collective contracts more generally, that have also been entered into by state actors.[2084]

However, as parties in negotiations may not have an equal bargaining position, the question arises whether control mechanisms should not be developed. Accordingly, the collective negotiations on STCs take place within the framework of the Coordination Group on Negotiations for Self-regulation ('*Coördinatiegroep Zelfreguleringsoverleg*'),[2085] an independent organisation facilitating negotiations between branch organisations and consumer organisations.[2086] It may be concluded that negotiations are encouraged, but take place in an environment that allows for some overview and control. In other cases, collective contracts are not binding, but consumers can opt into collective contracts.

8.5.1.3. Model contracts

This paragraph will look at instances of model contracts and consider the role of actors in the development of private law through model contracts.

Both at the national and international level, instances of model contracts may be found:

- The use of a model contract provided by professional associations or sector associations to their members dates back a considerable time[2087]

2084 For example the collective contracts entered into by municipalities across The Netherlands, usually for inhabitants with an income below a threshold specified by the municipality, from smaller municipalities like Oisterwijk (www.oisterwijk.nl/smartsite6176.htm) or Wijchen (www.wijchen.nl/nl/zorg_en_ondersteuning/inkomensondersteuning/_/Collectieve_ziektekostenverzekering.html) to cities like Maastricht, (www.maastricht.nl/web/GemeenteLoket/Alle-producten-en-diensten/Productpagina.htm?dbid=793&typeofpage=79906), Rotterdam (www.monitor.nl/ziek.html?www.monitor.nl/s_1982_all_.htm), Groningen, (http://gemeente.groningen.nl/b-w-besluiten/12900), and Amstelveen, (www.amstelveen.nl/web/show?id=131238&langid=43&dbid=408&typeofpage=44744).

2085 The group is established on 15 March 1996, on the basis of article 2 and 43 Law on Business Organisation ('*Wet op de Bedrijfsorganisatie*').

2086 In view of the legislative framework in which both the drafting and the enforcement of STCs take place, the question arises whether or not STCs can be characterised as co-regulation, especially as collective negotiation is facilitated by the legislator (see for example Z.D. Laclé, A.C.M. Meuwese, *Self-regulation in The Netherlands*, NEWGOV Working paper 2006, p. 4, at www.eu-newgov.org/database/DELIV/DLTFIbD09d_Final_Chapters_on_self-regulation_The_Netherlands.pdf). Despite the legislative framework, STCs should not be characterised as co-regulation. The presence of a legislative framework (in this case especially article 6:231 et seq BW) does not necessarily imply that rules can be characterised as co-regulation. Moreover, STCs are part of contracts negotiated by parties and they are not hard law after the intervention of the legislator or the judiciary; they become binding through their incorporation in contracts. Furthermore, despite the framework in which STCs are negotiated, STCs are not formed in cooperation with state actors, and the enforcement is left to private actors.

2087 In 1936, the International Chamber of Commerce introduced standard trade definitions most commonly used in international sale, see www.iccwbo.org/incoterms/id3042/index.html, accessed 15 October 2009.

- Model contracts may also be established by collective bargaining.

For example, the model contract of sale (in the form of a deed) established by the consumers' association, the Dutch Association for home owners (*Vereniging Eigen Huis*) and the Dutch Association for Real Estate Agents (*Nederlandse Vereniging voor Makelaars en Vastgoed-deskundigen*).[2088]

- The International Chamber of Commerce (ICC) provides a number of often used models and terms and conditions, deviating from national non-mandatory rules.

Important models[2089] are for example the ICC Uniform Customs and Practices for Documentary Credits (endorsed by UNCITRAL[2090]), or Uniform Rules for Contract Guarantees. De Ly[2091] describes the legal nature of the Incoterms as controversial; there is debate as to whether the Incoterms should be seen as customary international law.

Van Erp[2092] has argued that model contracts do not fall within the definition of article 6:231 sub a BW and thus need not be subjected to judicial evaluation imposed on STCs, as this would undermine the use of model contracts aimed to further predictability. Notably, if terms in often used models are subjected to articles 6:233 et seq BW, parts of the model contracts should be declared ineffective. Yet model contracts may also contain guarantees that improve the consumer's position.[2093]

The freedom of contract parties to draft model contracts and the lack of judicial evaluation leave a prominent role for private actors, both at a national and international level. State actors have a less prominent role than is the case in the German legal order.

Similarly, at the European level, the use of model contracts is a well-established way to facilitate transactions across borders, and a large range of freedom is accordingly left to contract parties.

8.5.1.4. STCs

This paragraph will consider instances of STCs and ask what role actors play in the development of private law through STCs.

2088 There is debate as to whether the standard contract provides a guarantee for consumers: see for example C.M.H. Vlaanderen, 'Over (on) bekendheidsverklaringen en conformiteit in de NVM-koopakte', *WPNR* 6410 (2000), p. 514–519.

2089 See for a more complete overview of the various rules, models and codes the website of the ICC: www.iccwbo.org/.

2090 Resolution UNCITRAL on possible future work in e-commerce, Report of the UN Commission on International Trade law, 42nd session (29 June-17 July 2009), General Assembly, 64th session, Supplement no. 17, p. 70.

2091 F. de Ly, *International business law and lex mercatoria*, North Holland: The Hague 1992, p. 173–174. For example Asser/Scholten 1974, nr. 23 regards international self-regulation through – for example – the York-Antwerp rules as related to customary international law.

2092 J.H.M. van Erp, 'De NVM-koopakte: géén algemene voorwaarden', *WPNR* 6190 (1995).

2093 HR 23 December 2005, *NJ* 2010, 62 on which J.J. Dammingh, 'Non-conformiteit en de NVM-koopakte', *TvC* 2009, p. 120.

The use of STCs is widespread:

- The use of model STCs, provided by professional associations or sector associations to their members, dates back a considerable time.[2094]

- In several instances,[2095] the European Commission has unsuccessfully called for and announced developments of EU-wide STCs, including business-to-business (B2B) and business-to-government (B2G) contracts.

- International organisations have developed STCs. A prominent example is the ICC Hardship Clause 2003.

Van Beukering-Rosmuller[2096] argues that in this field, notwithstanding diverging national rules on hardship, self-regulation is seen as desirable as long-term contracts, in which there are large financial stakes, are vulnerable to unforeseen events such as war or natural calamities.

Both at the national and the international level, non-state actors play an important role in drafting STCs. The Dutch legislator has facilitated collectively negotiated STCs, and private actors accordingly play a prominent role in the drafting and negotiating of STCs.

However, various control mechanisms have been developed that limit contract parties' roles.

1. Articles 6:231 et seq BW, that also implement Directive 93/13, provide that STCs can be subjected to judicial evaluation

The legislator has expressly pointed to the lack of negotiations in the drafting of one-sided STCs, which formed a reason to provide legislation on STCs. The Dutch legislator has adopted an especially critical approach towards the use of STCs in consumer contracts, and is more lenient with regard to business contracts. Accordingly, article 6:235 BW provides that articles 6:233 and 234 BW are not applicable to large businesses. The Dutch legislator also adopts a lenient approach towards international business contracts, as article 6:247 BW stipulates that these contracts do not fall within the scope of articles 6:231 et seq BW. Clauses in international business contracts may still be subjected to judicial control under article 6:248 BW, but the Hoge Raad has generally exercised restraint in the evaluation of these clauses.[2097]

This control mechanism also provides stakeholders with the possibility to challenge the fairness of STCs. Article 6:240 BW gives interest groups an action in case of unfair contract terms.

2094 In 1936, the International Chamber of Commerce introduced standard trade definitions most commonly used in international sale, see www.iccwbo.org/incoterms/id3042/index.html, accessed 15 October 2009.

2095 European Commission, *Communication on European contract law*, COM (2001) 398 final, nr. 56; European Commission, *Action plan for a more coherent European contract law*, COM (2003) 68 final, nr. 84–88; European Commission, *European contract law and the revision of the acquis: The way forward*, COM (2004) 651 final, par. 2.2.

2096 E.J.M. van Beukering-Rosmuller, 'Imprévision en zelfregulering', *NTBR* 2006, par. 3.1.

2097 See further H. Schelhaas, 'Pacta sunt servanda bij commerciële contracten', *NTBR* 2008, 21.

This action can also be used preventively, for example, if a branch organisation provides unfair contract terms in the model standard contract terms it provides to its members.[2098] After the adoption of Directive 98/27 on injunctions for the protection of consumers' interests, foreign interest groups also have the possibility to challenge unfair contract terms through article 6:240 BW,[2099] and organisations like the Dutch Consumers' Association (*Consumentenbond*) or the consumers' authority (*Consumentenautoriteit*) should be able to start an action abroad. However, article 6:240 par. 4 BW limits this action: if a claimant has not given the other party the opportunity to negotiate on the standard terms and conditions, the claimant shall be inadmissible. This means that private actors have a considerable role in the drafting and the enforcement of STCs.

2. Two-sided STCs that have been negotiated collectively are considered less likely to be unfair, as becomes apparent from article 6:233 sub a BW that refers to the way in which the STCs have been drafted in the assessment of the fairness of terms. Thus, collective negotiations can be seen as a control mechanism that limits the chance of unfair STCs.[2100]

Consequently, although the role of contract parties is subjected to restrictions, especially in business-to-consumer contracts, control mechanisms also leave a considerable role for stakeholders challenging the fairness of STCs and parties involved in collective negotiations on STCs.

At the European level, the need to protect consumers from unfair contract terms has led to the introduction of the judicial evaluation of STCs under Directive 93/13 on unfair contract terms. The European legislator has encouraged stakeholders to challenge STCs and has also, through Directive 98/27 on injunctions for the protection of consumers' interests, obliged national actors to enable foreign stakeholders to challenge STCs. Further, parties to contracts that do not fall within the scope of Directive 93/13 have considerable room.

8.5.1.5. Conclusion on contractual self-regulation

Both the Dutch and the European legislator leave contract parties with considerable room. However, the Dutch legislator has provided for control mechanisms more consistently, through mandatory law. In the case study, Dutch law attached more weight to the protection of consumers in the law on STCs than the German legislator,[2101] but more generally, the Dutch legislator further recognises the added value of negotiations more clearly than the European legislator.

Even though German and Dutch law both recognise private autonomy, and seek to control *Fremdbestimmung*, the question when *Fremdbestimmung* arises may differ from state to state. This may mean that the coexistence of national actors is beneficial as

2098 HR 16 May 1997, *NJ* 2000, 1. This is in accordance with CJEU 26 April 2012 (Hatóság v Invitel Távközlési Zrt), C-472/10, [2012] ECR p. I-0, par. 37.

2099 For example Hof 's-Gravenhage 6 July 2004, *NJ* 2004, 483.

2100 See however critically C.M.D.S. Pavillon, 'Private standards of fairness in European contract law', *ERCL* 2014, p. 113 who points out that negotiated STCs can and do still diverge from legal standards.

2101 See previously par. 5.5.1.

divergent national regimes respond to divergent preferences, in accordance with pluralist arguments.[2102] Concerns of potential *Fremdbestimmung* that may arise in contracts where weak parties contract with strong parties may more generally motivate legislators and courts to adopt a defensive approach to harmonisation, especially harmonisation that limits consumer protection, and regulatory competition.

Notably, the dual basis of the binding force of contracts has led to criticism and does not provide a consistent, predictable view on the role of private parties in contractual self-regulation. The German perspective offers an interesting opportunity for further learning. If the negotiation process serves as an additional justification, this may provide more clarity, as this justification offers a consistent basis for upholding or not upholding contractual self-regulation. This additional justification is in accordance with the recognition of the added value of *collective* negotiations, and the emphasis of the lack of negotiations in the use of STCs.

This paragraph confirms the findings in the Dutch case study that harmonisation in this area did not make the Dutch legislator critically reconsider Dutch law or Dutch self-regulation, despite debate on this question.[2103] Consequently, the question whether model contracts also fall within the scope of article 6:231 et seq BW has not yet been answered. This also makes it less likely that initiatives from European state actors have prompted Dutch state actors to pay more attention to the interests of foreign and international parties. However, the development of prominent self-regulation at the international level may indirectly ensure that the interests of foreign and international level are taken into account, if Dutch parties for example use international model contracts or model STCs.

8.5.2. *Self-regulation on the basis of articles of association:* tuchtrecht

This paragraph asks what role private actors play in the development of private law through self-regulation based on articles of association, *tuchtrecht*.

Paragraphs 8.5.2.1 – 8.5.2.6 will consider instances of this sort of *tuchtrecht*, respectively internal self-regulation, sports' codes, self-regulation that has withheld the legislator from introducing legislation, and instances of other codes of conduct and self-regulation in the absence of mandatory law. Paragraph 8.5.2.7 will discuss the role of non-state actors, and paragraph 8.5.2.8 will turn to limitations on non-state actors' roles. Paragraph 8.5.2.9 will end with a conclusion.

8.5.2.1. Internally binding codes on the basis of articles of association

Organisations may impose rules internally, through rules ('*reglementen*'). Originally, the law did not stipulate these rules that were developed in practice.[2104] Internal rules may stipulate various matters. Articles of association may appoint relevant organs to develop rules.

2102 Comp. for example with regard to social justice R. Sefton-Green 'Social justice and the European identity in European contract law', *ERCL* 2006, p. 275.

2103 See previously par. 11.3.3.

2104 T.J. van der Ploeg, 'Reglementen bij verenigingen; een duik in troebel water', *WPNR* 5929 (1989).

8.5.2.2. Sports associations

The primary sports organisation in The Netherlands is the NOC*NSF. In its articles of association,[2105] it has stipulated that it is solely competent to nominate candidates for the Olympics, and it obliges its members to comply with the rules developed by the International Olympic Committee (IOC). However, the members of the NOC*NSF, the national associations for specific sports,[2106] have not systematically integrated this obligation in their articles of association. Instead, the degree to which members impose these rules and their rules on their members may vary. Consequently, the rules developed by the IOC are not necessarily binding on the basis of national sports associations' articles of association. Alternatively, rules imposed by the IOC may be enforced as associations provide their members with models for articles of associations, or on the basis of contracts.

8.5.2.3. The encouragement of self-regulation in a national and European context

The legislator[2107] has approved of the Advertising Code for Alcoholic Beverages (*'Reclamecode voor alcoholhoudende dranken'*, RvA), established by stakeholders organised in the Foundation for the Responsible Use of Alcohol (*Stichting verantwoord alcoholgebruik*, STIVA).[2108] The RvA is part of the Dutch Commercial Code (*'Nederlandse Reclame Code'*, NRC) that is supervised by the Dutch Foundation for Commercials Code (*Stichting Reclame Code*, SRC).[2109] Article 3.8 Mediawet obliges commercial broadcasting channels to participate with the NRC or a similar code supervised by the SRC. Compliance with the RvA is also monitored by the Foundation for Prevention of Alcohol related damage (*Stichting alcoholpreventie*, STAP)[2110] that criticises the use of self-regulation in this area.[2111] STAP participates in a European network, EUROCARE (Advocacy for the Prevention of Alcohol Related Harm in Europe) that promotes the

2105 Available at www.nocnsf.nl/statuten.

2106 See for an overview www.nocnsf.nl/cms/showpage.aspx?id=179&mid=99.

2107 *Kamerstukken II*, 2005–06, 29 894, 27 565, nr. 11, p. 3. STIVA has also published a report defending the effectiveness of self-regulation: STIVA, *Zelfregulering tegen het licht*, 2007, available at http://stiva.nl/Documenten.

2108 Available at http://stiva.nl/Documenten.

2109 The Dutch Commercials Code (*'Nederlandse Reclame Code'*) was formed in a cooperation between advertisers, advertising agencies and the media. Other codes of conduct approved by the SRC and part of the NRC are the Code email business recipients, the Code telemarketing, and the Code for the distribution of advertising leaflets without an address (*'Code verspreiding ongeadresseerd reclamedrukwerk'*). Codes not approved and supervised by the SRC are the Code Listbroking and Code streetmarketing, established by the Dutch Dialogue Marketing Association, and the DDMA privacy code, see www.ddma.nl/index.php?pag=4&sub=24. See further the website of the *Reclame Code Commissie*, www.reclamecode.nl/consument/default.asp?paginaID=1&hID=1.

2110 See www.alcoholpreventie.nl/info/?over.

2111 See for example STAP, *Alcoholreclame in Nederland: Zelf regelen of laten regelen?* Aanbevelingsrapport 2008, available at www.alcoholpreventie.nl/bestand/Aanbevelingenrapport.pdf.

dealing with the production, distribution, trade and consumption of alcohol at a European level.[2112]

While advertising in alcohol products is stipulated through self-regulation alone, the SRC supervises compliance with the NRC that generally prohibits misleading and comparative advertising. The establishment of the NRC has taken place within the framework provided by article 6:162 BW, and after the implementation of Directive 2005/29 on misleading and unfair commercial practices, article 6:193a BW. The effectiveness of the SRC has been criticised as not being able to provide sufficient protection for consumers: its competence is limited and it has no possibility to enforce its decisions.[2113]

The European Advertising Standards Alliance (EASA), in which the SCR participates, was established in 1992 to show that self-regulation in the advertising area was to be preferred over legislation.[2114] Apparently, the EASA has failed to convince the EU on this point.[2115] However, the adoption of legislation does not rule out self-regulation. Accordingly, the EASA, also a member of international organisations, continues to promote self-regulation, recommending codes of conducts developed at international level. In particular, the ICC Code on advertising and marketing clearly overlaps with the Directive on misleading and comparative advertising, as also noted by the Commission in the drafting of the Directive.[2116] The ICC code and the Directive converge at some points – for example, when banning the offers not sufficiently anticipating consumer demand. The code and the Directive also diverge. For example the ICC code does not take the well-informed, reasonably circumspect consumer as a starting point. Arguably, Directive 2006/114 that partially aims for maximum harmonisation, as well as Directive 2005/29 on unfair commercial practices that pursue maximum harmonisation, do not stand in the way of these developments. Both Directives expressly refer to self-regulation through the development of codes of conduct.

8.5.2.4. Encouraging self-regulation

Self-regulation has been encouraged in various instances, to complement legislation. Accordingly, the Dutch Bankers' Association (*Nederlandse Vereniging van Banken*, NVB), has established several self-regulatory instruments for the interaction between banks and their clients which are binding on their members. These codes specifically aim to complement legislation, for example, the privacy code of conduct ('*Gedragscode Verwerking Persoonsgegevens*'),[2117] and the Chinese walls code of conduct.[2118] The NVB

2112 See for more information www.eurocare.org/about_us.
2113 Asser/Hartkamp 2006, nr. 244.
2114 Www.easa-alliance.org/About-EASA/History/page.aspx/117 (accessed 31 May 2015).
2115 Most recently Directive 2006/114 concerning misleading and comparative advertising was adopted. Before that, legislation on advertising could be found in Directives 84/450/EC, as amended by Directive 1997/55/EC and Directive 2000/31/EC.
2116 COM (91) 147 final, p. 21.
2117 Available at www.nvb.nl/scrivo/asset.php?id=12355.
2118 Available at www.nvb.nl/scrivo/asset.php?id=11758.

is member of the European Banking Federation (EBF) that has issued very generally formulated guiding principles.[2119]

In insurance law, self-regulation also plays a prominent role. The legislator has explicitly chosen to refrain as much as possible from mandatory law, notwithstanding mandatory law in article 7: 925 et seq BW on contracts between insurers and consumers. Accordingly, codes on privacy (*'Gedragscode verwerking persoonsgegevens financiële instellingen'*),[2120] have been established, as well as the code of conduct on personal examinations (*'Gedragscode persoonlijk onderzoek'*).[2121] The code of conduct of informed renewal and contract periods for indemnity insurances to individuals (*'Gedragscode geïnformeerde verlenging en contractstermijnen particuliere schadeverzekeringen'*),[2122] is more precise. It came into effect on 1 January 2010 and was supposed to be evaluated in three years. The code of conduct on expertise on motor vehicles (*'Gedragsregels bij expertise motorrijtuigen'*) has been negotiated by the BOVAG, FOCWA, NIVRE/ NIAV.[2123] According to the HIV-code of conduct (*'HIV gedragscode'*)[2124] people with HIV may, under conditions, enter into life insurance contracts. According to The Netherlands HIV Association, the number of rejections for life insurance policies has decreased considerably since this advice.[2125]

In addition, compliance with the insurers' general code of conduct (*'Gedragscode verzekeraars'*)[2126] is a requirement for membership of the *Verbond voor Verzekeraars*. However, this code provides ambiguous, general rules that generally do not go beyond consumer protection legislation in this area, and which may, therefore, be of little added value in the interpretation of articles 7:925 et seq BW.

From January 2010, Adfiz, previously the Dutch Association representing independent financial and insurance agents and the Dutch Association for Insurance Agents will require its members to sign a code on independent advice (*'Code onafhankelijk advies'*).[2127]

8.5.2.5. Codes as conditions for membership: consumer sales

The Dutch home shopping association, (*Nederlandse Thuiswinkel Organisatie*)[2128] provides its members with a certificate, the *Thuiswinkel Waarborg*, and a code of conduct based on the European convention on cross-border mail order and distance selling.[2129] Interestingly, the EMOTA aims to add to international, European and national regulation

2119 Available at www.ebf-fbe.eu/index.php?page=guiding-principles.

2120 Available at www.verbondvanverzekeraars.nl/UserFiles/File/download/GVPFI.pdf.

2121 Available at www.verbondvanverzekeraars.nl/UserFiles/File/download/Bijlage1C.pdf.

2122 Available at www.verbondvanverzekeraars.nl/UserFiles/File/download/gedragscode_verl_en_contr_termijn_part_schadeverz_09.pdf.

2123 Available at www.verbondvanverzekeraars.nl/Publicaties.aspx?publicatieid=31.

2124 Available at www.verbondvanverzekeraars.nl/UserFiles/File/download/Bijlage1E.pdf.

2125 See www.hivnet.org/index.php?option=com_content&view=article&id=7987:hiv-als-verzekerbare-chronische-aandoening-erkend&catid=9:maatschappelijk-verzekering&Itemid=648.

2126 Available at www.verzekeraars.nl/UserFiles/Image/Gedragscode_Verzekeraars_juni2011.pdf.

2127 Available at www.denk.verzekeringstools.nl/downloads/adfiz/adfizcodevanonafhankelijkadvies.pdf.

2128 See www.thuiswinkel.org/consumenten/.

2129 Available at www.emota.eu/index.php?option=com_content&view=article&id=109&Itemid=91.

and thereby further the European internal market.[2130] The *Stichting Webshop Keurmerk*[2131] also provides its members with a trust mark for online shopping.

8.5.2.6. Codes as conditions for membership in the absence of mandatory law

Codes of conduct in the absence of sufficient legislation include codes in the area of franchising and debt collection.

The European Franchise Federation (EFF) has established a European code of ethics for franchising.[2132] It particularly requires its members, national organisations, to ensure that their members comply with its code. Accordingly, The Netherlands Franchise Association (*Nederlandse franchise vereniging*, NVF) requires its members to comply with this code.[2133] However, the code contains various ambiguous terms and does not seek to go beyond what is legally required. The code also does not contain enforcement mechanisms and despite the support of the NVF, there is insufficient support for the code in the franchising sector generally.[2134]

Additionally, self-regulation not established by stakeholders includes the UNIDROIT Model Franchise Disclosure Law and the ICC Model for International Franchising Contract. However, the Hoge Raad[2135] has not used soft law on franchising for interpreting the duties of a franchiser to provide information to the franchisee. In contrast, the district court Zutphen has since referred to the code of ethics.[2136]

Another example of self-regulation in the absence of mandatory law is self-regulation in the area of debt collection. The Dutch Association for Collecting Businesses (*Nederlandse Vereniging voor Incasso Ondernemingen*, NVI)[2137] has claimed a lack of specific regulation in the area of debt collection[2138] and provided a code of conduct that its members must comply with and a corresponding quality mark.[2139] At a European level, the NVI participates in the Federation of European National Collection Associations

2130 As stated on the website of EMOTA: www.emota.eu/index.php?option=com_content&view=article&id=109&Itemid=91.

2131 See http://biedmeerwebwinkels.nl/Page309/Webshop-Keurmerk.html.

2132 The text of this code is available at www.eff-franchise.com/spip.php?rubrique13.

2133 See www.nfv.nl/franchisegevers-vragen/#4.

2134 I.S.J. Houben, J. Sterk, J.A.J. Devilee, 'Codificatie of zelfregulering in de franchisesector?', *MvV* 2014, p. 2.

2135 HR 25 January 2002, *NJ* 2003, 31.

2136 Rb. Zutphen 27 August 2008, *LJN* BE9241. See, rather optimistically, and for further case law, A.J.J. van der Heiden, 'De invloed van door een franchisegever verstrekte prognoses voorafgaand aan het sluiten van een franchiseovereenkomst', *Contracteren* 2002, p. 93. However, the Rb. Noord-Nederland 29 November 2013, *NJF* 2014, 119, par. 5.15, has considered that the code does not contain legally enforceable obligations and Rb. Limburg, 26 February 2014, ECLI:NL:RBLIM:2014:2557 does not consider the code at all.

2137 See www.nvio.nl/de-organisatie. The NVI represents its members in negotiations with the government and consumer organisations and facilitates the exchange of information among its members.

2138 While claiming a lacuna in legislation on debt collection, the NVI has reacted very critically to legislative proposals ('*Wetsvoorstel incassokosten*') as too expensive and hindering the settlement out of court: NVI, *Belangen in balans*, Position paper 5 November 2009, available at: http://klanten.e-mark.nl/nvio/Position%20paper%20NVI%209%20november%202009.pdf.

2139 Available at www.nvio.nl/files/Gedragscode2.pdf.

(FENCA) that, apart from providing basic guidelines for contracts to its members, has established an overarching code of conduct for its members, against the background of members' existing codes of conducts.[2140] The FENCA requires its members to develop a code of conduct and the assurance that it is complied with.

8.5.2.7. The role of non-state actors

Non-state actors play a prominent role in the development of self-regulation on the basis of articles of association.

Notably, even though article 8 Gw recognises the right to association, the development of rules through articles of association has generally not been considered in this light. Nevertheless, state actors have left actors with considerable room to develop self-regulation and in the case of advertising for alcoholic products, insurance and banking, even abstained from legislation. Where legislation has been adopted, this has not stood in the way of self-regulation.

Accordingly, the law assumes that rules established in accordance with the articles of association are internally binding and decisions contrary to rules are avoidable under article 2:15 par. 1 sub c BW.

The compliance with codes of conduct differs across legal areas, but generally, compliance is not a complete failure. Thus, organisations manage to affect the behaviour of members in accordance with their codes. This does not mean that self-regulation generally is an immediate success – this also depends on the question of whether compliance with codes is compulsory or optional, whether codes provide sufficiently clear rules, and whether they provide clear sanctions on the breach of those rules. Various codes do not oblige members to comply with codes of conduct – although they encourage it – or they provide ambiguous rules without clear sanctions, or they do not supervise compliance.

Nevertheless, differently from the German legal order, self-regulation on the basis of articles of association is not recognised as a separate category of self-regulation in Dutch private law.

Moreover, the influence of codes can extend beyond organisations even if they are not directly binding.

For example, professional guidelines may be relevant for determining whether lawyers have behaved professionally.[2141] Similarly, third parties may, for example, complain about the lack of compliance with guidelines for experts as developed by the *Verbond van Verzekeraars*.[2142]

[2140] See www.fenca.org/uploads/FENCA%20Code%20of%20Conduct.pdf. Additionally, FENCA protects the interests of national member organisations and lobbies for European legislation. It provides basic rules and guidelines for contracts to its members.

[2141] Rb. 's-Gravenhage 10 July 2007, *NJF* 2007, 384, also Hof Amsterdam 24 May 2011, *LJN* BV2685, which has given rise to debate, see especially the theme issue of *WPNR* (6954). Although evaluating clauses in contracts between "liberal" professions (such as lawyers) and consumers is in line with CJEU 15 January 2015 (Šiba v Arūnas Devėnas), C-537/13 [2015} ECR p. I-0, it is not clear whether professional self-regulation may also play a role in the assessment of clauses. However, questions on the assessment of clauses and the role of professional self-regulation have so far not been referred to the CJEU.

[2142] A.Ch.H. Franken, 'Experts en hun gedragsregels', *AV & S* 2004, 4.

Thus, state actors have left non-state actors considerable freedom in the development of voluntary disciplinary law.

8.5.2.8. Limitations on the role of non-state actors

The membership of organisations has been characterised as a relationship that differs from a contractual relationship.[2143] Notwithstanding the special nature of membership, voluntary disciplinary law has generally not been a separately distinguished sort of self-regulation, and objections of *Fremdbestimmung* have generally not arisen. Accordingly, there is very little attention to the development of rules within organisations. Consequently, the adoption and amendment of rules is not stipulated in the law.[2144] Similarly, principal objections to the dynamic referral to the IOC in the articles of association of the NOC*NSF have not arisen.

8.5.2.9. Conclusion on *tuchtrecht*

A large variety of codes has been developed by associations. The binding force of these codes depends on the precision or the vagueness of the codes, the sanctions imposed on breaches of the codes and the enforcement of the codes against members. Codes may also serve to determine, for example, professional behaviour. The legislator has exercised restraint in replacing self-regulation with legislation, which has left non-state actors with much freedom to develop codes as they choose.

Codes on the basis of articles of association are not distinguished as a separate form of self-regulation and control mechanisms have accordingly not been developed. Therefore, the roles of non-state actors have not generally been subjected to restrictions. Notably, the development of internal rules of association may support the view that actors develop self-regulation without initially consulting the law or considering options for enforcement or other options under the surrounding legal framework. The lack of accessibility and the lack of academic attention for these internal rules makes it difficult to establish the extent and the scope of these internal rules. However, while actors have not taken the legal framework as a starting point in developing their rules, this does not mean that there is no such framework. A framework becomes especially relevant when the question arises how rules should be enforced. The development of self-regulation at the international level indicates that self-regulation can also be developed beyond the legal framework, which can nevertheless limit the scope and effect of such rules.

Notably, the willingness and capability of associations to develop rules differs, as also demonstrated by the varying success of self-regulation on the basis of *tuchtrecht*. Articles of association are not systematically recognised as a separate sort of self-regulation or as a means to enforce self-regulation, in addition to contractual rules used to enforce self-regulation. Even if, for example, sports associations' rules are developed on the basis of

[2143] Asser/Maeijer/Van Solinge/Nieuwe Weme 2005, nr 44.
[2144] Asser/Maeijer/Van Solinge/Nieuwe Weme 2005, nr 258.

articles of association, rules may not necessarily been integrated in members' articles of association.

8.5.3. *One-sided declarations*

Some forms of self-regulation are neither based on contracts nor based on articles of association. These codes may be the result of extensive negotiations, which are not especially one-sided. However, collectively negotiated self-regulation characteristically results in a code and one-sided recommendations or declarations of compliance.

Paragraphs 8.5.3.1 – 8.5.3.5 will consider instances of self-regulation. Respectively, codes in the area of consumer sales and energy supply, initiatives in the field of corporate social responsibility, the recommendations of the *Verbond van Verzekeraars* and basic payment services will be considered. Paragraph 8.5.3.6 will discuss the role of non-state actors and paragraph 8.5.3.7 will turn to the limitations to the roles of these actors. Paragraph 8.5.3.8 will end with a conclusion.

8.5.3.1. **Binding declarations: consumer sales**

Various initiatives for self-regulation have been developed in the area of consumer sales, especially online selling, both at the national and European level:

- The Electronic Commerce Platform in The Netherlands (ECP-EPN) has developed the model code of conduct on conducting business electronically.[2145] In turn, this code has been used as an example at international level.[2146]

This code overlaps with the self-regulation established by Thuiswinkel.org and Stichting Webshop Keurmerk. The model code provided by the ECP-EPN is a model code that clearly aims to provide members with tools to develop consistent self-regulation.[2147]

- In the *eConfidence* project,[2148] BEUC and UNICE, under the supervision of the European Commission, established the European Trustmark Requirements for e-commerce between businesses and consumers. The scheme set down standards for European trust marks in the EU with regard to several issues, including pre-contractual information, language, payment and security. However, it is unclear whether these requirements have been implemented.

2145 Available at www.ecp.nl/model-gedragscode-voor-elektronisch-zakendoen.

2146 See in particular Recommendation 32 of United Nations Centre for Trade Facilitation and Electronic Business (UN/CEFAC), March 2000, that claims that the OECD, ICC and the European Commission have also shown interest in this code.

2147 For example by Nieuwsbank, see www.nieuwsbank.nl/overnieuwsbank/gedragscode.htm.

2148 Available at http://legacy.quatro-project.org/files/file/unice-beuc/eConfidence.pdf.

- In the digital agenda for Europe, the Commission[2149] has announced that it will develop a Code of EU Online Rights and organise a European-wide platform on trust marks for stakeholders.

8.5.3.2. Binding declarations: contracts for the supply of energy

Because public utility companies use uniform STCs, collectively negotiated within the framework of the SER, the legislator has abstained from providing specific rules on contracts between public utility companies and consumers.[2150] Apart from these STCs, EnergieNed, representing public utility companies, in cooperation with consumer organisations, has established a code of conduct for consumers and providers of electricity, who can enter into a contract with EnergieNed that they will apply the code.[2151] If businesses apply the code, they need to develop protocols indicating how they ensure compliance with the code. Loos has suggested that the Civil Code should contain provisions on the contracts between consumers and public utility companies.[2152]

Several suppliers[2153] have committed themselves to the code and presented it expressly to consumers. However, problems with compliance have arisen.[2154]

8.5.3.3. Suggesting reinforced self-regulation: social corporate responsibility

The development of self-regulation in the area of social corporate responsibility recognises that states are less able to control the behaviour of parties beyond their territory and depend on information of third, non-state parties for enforcing correct behaviour. Businesses may also develop codes on corporate social responsibility themselves. Accordingly, such statements assert that businesses will not violate human rights or the environment, as is, for example, the case for Dutch multinationals such as Shell. This does, however, not necessarily mean that Shell can be held liable for environmental damage resulting from spills, which may not only be complicated under private international law,[2155] but which also requires, for example, ensuring the responsibility of Shell for damages arising, for example, from spills. The decisions[2156] on claims against

2149 COM (2010) 245 final/2, p. 13.

2150 Parl. Gesch. NBW, Boek 7, p. 33.

2151 See www.nma.nl/regulering/energie/elektriciteit/regelgeving/vrijwillige_afspraken/default.aspx.

2152 M. Loos, *De energieleveringsovereenkomst*, Deventer: Kluwer 1998, p. 247–280.

2153 See for an overview www.energie-nederland.nl/consument/. These suppliers include Nuon (www.nuon.nl/privacy-en-gebruiksvoorwaarden.jsp#Gedragscode), Essent (www.essent.nl/content/particulier/voorwaarden/algemene_voorwaarden/index.html), the NEM (www.nle.nl/Over_ons/Over_NLE/Gedragscode), Eneco (http://thuis.eneco.nl/klantenservice/informatie/voorwaarden/), Greenchoice (www.greenchoice.nl/thuis/klant-worden/voorwaarden), and Energie Direct (www.energiedirect.nl/algemenevoorwaarden).

2154 See the response of the Minister for Economic Affairs to questions of Parliament on 29 July 2009.

2155 Rb. 's-Gravenhage 30 January 2013, *LJN* BY9845, Rb. 's-Gravenhage 30 January 2013, *LJN* BY9850, Rb. 's-Gravenhage 30 January 2013, *LJN* BY9854.

2156 Rb. 's-Gravenhage 14 September 2011, *LJN* BU3538.

Shell have not referred to Shell's general statements, but evaluated the claim, based on non-contractual liability, under Nigerian law.

In 2001, to increase corporate social responsibility, the legislator proposed introducing a duty of transparency on Dutch multinationals.

The proposal[2157] aims to add a paragraph to article 3:291 BW that obliges companies to include, in their annual accounts, their compliance with social corporate responsibility. The proposal goes on to note that the correctness of the information provided by companies depends on the sense of responsibility of companies themselves, but adds that additional control by stakeholders, especially internationally operating NGOs, is desirable, while eventually, international guidelines may provide adequate starting points for evaluating whether companies' policies are in accordance with social corporate responsibility. However, despite the lenient approach to standards, the proposed article does make clear on what topics companies have to at least provide a report.

The proposal expressly rejects developing standards of social corporate responsibility in national law, as this may petrify the development of international rules. Accordingly, rather than passing the proposal, the Dutch government has supported and developed networks to support compliance with these guidelines.[2158] Further, curiously, the proposal considers that a legal standard may prevent that companies internalise this standard, which the legislator considers as the main incentive behind the dynamic development of standards. Accordingly, companies may decide for themselves according to which guidelines they measure their compliance to corporate social responsibility. The question, however, arises whether this will lead to guidelines that are more specific than a necessarily ambiguous legal standard.

The European Commission[2159] has announced a legislative proposal obliging companies to provide information. Article 1.14 Directive 2003/51 currently already stipulates that companies falling under this Directive must include non-financial aspects in their yearly accounts, which has been implemented in article 2:391 par. 1 BW. Yet unfortunately, the preamble makes clear that Member States can waive this obligation. At the European level, international rules have likewise served as a source of inspiration.[2160]

8.5.3.4. Codes of conduct on the basis of recommendations

Organisations may advise their members to comply with codes of conduct. Accordingly, members and cooperative organisations of the *Verbond van Verzekeraars* may recognise the code of conduct for expert organisations ('*Gedragscode expertiseorganisaties*'),[2161] as

2157 *Kamerstukken II*, 2000–2001, 27905, nr. 3.

2158 See further www.rijksoverheid.nl/onderwerpen/maatschappelijk-verantwoord-ondernemen/mvo-internationaal.

2159 COM (2011) 681 final, p. 11–12.

2160 COM (2011) 681 final.

2161 Available at www.verbondvanverzekeraars.nl/UserFiles/File/download/gedragscodeexpertiseorganisaties.pdf.

well as the protocol on fraud ('*Fraudeprotocol 1998*').[2162] Another example of non-binding codes of conduct adopted in the area of insurance contract law was the development of the *Verbond voor Verzekeraars*, the Insurers' Institute on Personal Injury (PIV),[2163] of the code of conduct on the treatment of personal injuries ('*Gedragscode behandeling letselschade*', GBL).[2164]

Some of the codes of conduct used by insurers are subject to criticism and support for these codes is doubted. An example of a problematic area can be found in the 2003 report on insurers' codes of conduct,[2165] which severely criticised the handling of personal injury claims and noted that the *Gedragscode verzekeraars* was often ignored by insurers, especially in cases with large financial stakes.

The GBL was developed in response to the report, but this code is not supported by the Dutch association for personal injury lawyers (*Vereniging van letselschadeadvocaten*, LSA). The LSA[2166] has pointed out that the professional code of conduct for lawyers ('*Gedragsregels 1992*') is not compatible with the GBL. According to the LSA, the GBL would oblige lawyers to aim for settlement, while that may not be in their clients' best interests, and lawyers can also not oblige clients to comply with the code. In addition, the LSA remarks that a duty to settle out of court may violate article 6 ECHR, and that the GBL differs from the previous code of conduct on the handling of personal injury in traffic (*Gedragscode bij de behandeling van personenschade in het verkeer*).

Since its establishment, very little has happened to develop the GBL.[2167] In his 2011 report, the Ombudsman concluded that the code has hardly facilitated the handling of disputes of personal injury, and most victims were unfamiliar with the code,[2168] despite the wide participation of interest groups in the drafting of the code.

2162 See for more information www.verbondvanverzekeraars.nl/page/render.aspx?id=607.

2163 See for more information www.stichtingpiv.nl/smartsite.dws?id=279445.

2164 Available at www.deletselschaderaad.nl/index.cfm?page=Richtlijnen. The compliance of this code is supervised by the Council for Personal Injuries (*de Letselschade Raad*, previously the *Nationaal Platform Personenschade*), representing stakeholders (insurers, experts, victims' representatives). There are guidelines dealing with specific situations, available at the website of the *Letselschade Raad*, www.deletselschaderaad.nl/index.cfm?page=Richtlijnen.

2165 Stichting Ombudsman, 'Onderhandelen met het mes op tafel, of een zoektocht naar redelijkheid', November 2003, summary available at www.deombudsman.nl/sites/default/files/docs/publicaties/Rapport_Onderhandelen_met_het_mes_op_tafel.pdf. Similarly W.C.T. Weterings, *Efficiëntere en effectievere afwikkeling van letselschadeclaims*, The Hague: BJU 2004, found serious problems in the handling of personal injury claims and made recommendations to facilitate negotiations between parties.

2166 LSA, Letter regarding decision of LSA 30 June 2005, available (in Dutch) at https://normering.rechten.uvt.nl/upload/111020051134796199977397.pdf.

2167 D.J. ten Boom, V.P. Reute, 'Gedragscode behandeling letselschade – commerciële of maatschappelijke business case?' available at www.stichtingpiv.nl/smartsite.dws?ch=TER&id=760550. Very critical on the Gedragscode behandeling letselschade (and on codes of conduct, certification and other self-regulation in general) from a bureau (non-lawyers) handling proceedings for personal injury victims (on a no cure no pay basis) G. Lijffijt, 'Pals Groep trekt eigen plan', *Assurantie Magazine* 6 March 2009, available at www.stichtingpiv.nl/smartsite.dws?ch=TER&id=759979. The compliance of the Code was severely criticised in an episode of the TV-program 'Radar' on 2 November 2009.

2168 Stichting De Ombudsman, *De Gedragscode Behandeling Letselschade: Een goed bewaard geheim?*, February 2011, at www.deombudsman.nl/sites/default/files/docs/publicaties/Stichting_De_Ombudsman_Rapport_Verbetering_afhandeling_letselschade.pdf.

8.5.3.5. Primary payment services: binding declarations?

In cooperation with the Ministry of Finance, debt counselling organisations, and the Salvation Army, the NVB has agreed on a covenant on basic payment services ('*Convenant inzake pakket primaire betaaldiensten*').[2169] The covenant aims to increase the access to basic payment accounts under strict conditions, outlined on a website.[2170]

According to the 2004 evaluation,[2171] the access to basic payment services had been improved, although some problems, for example, a lack of accessibility, were signalled. Notably, the legislator has adopted a proposal obliging banks to offer a basic payment account to all consumers. According to the draft,[2172] this initiative, largely based on the covenant, is necessary as not all banks – especially small banks – comply with the covenant. The obligation has since been established in article 4:71f on the law on financial supervision ('*Wet op het Financieel Toezicht*').

8.5.3.6. The role of non-state actors

The Dutch legislator has adopted considerable restraint in intervening in areas where non-state actors have established self-regulation.

In the area of social corporate responsibility especially, national state actors have a reduced role because they are less able to guarantee compliance with rules beyond their territory. The Dutch legislator has not sought to compensate for its diminishing role, and it does not see a particular need to intervene, even with regard to basic human rights. It is not apparent why these rights would not be internalised if they are imposed – presumably, businesses do recognise rules within the territory of states, and hopefully they have internalised some basic rules. Fortunately, the lack of initiative in this area has not been followed at the European level. The initiatives at the European level, and the initiative in the German legal order make clear that national and European state actors can exert influence, notwithstanding the limitation to the national or European territory.

In other areas, the role of national state actors is not as visibly reduced, and national law may provide starting points for enforcement. If declarations of compliance may be binding, drafters of codes may exert substantial influence over the behaviour of other private parties.

The question whether codes can be enforced by consumers depends on the question whether declarations of compliance are juridical acts that consumers can justifiably rely on under articles 3:33 and 35 BW. The main question that should be answered is whether declarations are meant to have a legal effect. If not, the declaration is merely a factual act, not a juridical act. The answer to the question whether a declaration is meant to have

2169 Available at www.nvb.nl/scrivo/asset.php?id=121608, see also the executive instruction ('*Uitvoeringsinstructie*') for this covenant, available at www.nvb.nl/scrivo/asset.php?id=121609.

2170 See www.basisbankrekening.nl/index.php?p=503067.

2171 Available at www.nvb.nl/pers_persberichten/rapportage-basis-bankdiensten.pdf.

2172 *Kamerstukken II*, 2010–2011, 32291, nr. 30.

legal effect depends on several circumstances. Nieuwenhuis[2173] rightly finds that societal interests may be an argument against the binding force of one-sided promises, for example, because it may inhibit parties from making promises, because there is no reciprocity, or because it concerns promises – for example, promises concerning marriage – that should not be enforceable.

Various other circumstances may be relevant as well. Particularly, the vagueness of a promise and a lack of further sanctions or publicity indicate that a declaration is not intended to have any legal effect. Especially if codes do not impose sanctions on breaching the rules, the question whether a consumer, as a third party, has a clear interest that is financially measurable, can be relevant. In its 2014 decision, the Hoge Raad[2174] has arguably demonstrated its willingness to consider privately developed rules, provided that parties have agreed on those rules. Menting[2175] highlights the Hoge Raad's referral to the content and the aim of privately drafted rules, which may not only refer to the specificity of rules, but also the existence of relevant legislation, the drafting of self-regulation in the interest of policyholders, as well as the obligatory nature of the code. Also, self-regulation based on an organisation's articles of association may be directed internally. However, they may also be directed externally, for example if self-regulation clearly addresses members as well as consumers.

Binding effects for these reasons can be defended in the following cases:

1. The code of conduct developed by Thuiswinkel.org aims to adopt consumer-friendly principles, as adequate consumer protection is recognised as essential for the interests of distance sellers across Europe. The code expressly aims to increase consumers' confidence, and a mere declaration that lacks binding force may not suffice. Also, the code is easily accessible online and provides sufficiently precise rules. It follows that businesses complying with this code seek to increase confidence, by binding themselves to standards, which may have a legal effect.
2. The code on the supply of energy specifically aims to increase consumers' confidence, and it provides sufficiently specific rules.

In other cases, the binding effect of declarations of compliance is less clear:

1. Insurance companies frequently do not communicate to victims that they comply with the code on personal injury claims,[2176] and in disputes, the code is generally not referred to. How can a declaration constitute a juridical act if it is, apparently, not aimed at the victims who

2173 Comp. J.H. Nieuwenhuis, 'Promises, promises', *NJB* 2001, 37. Similarly H.B. Krans in his note to HR 18 April 2014, *NJ* 2015, 20. Krans finds that if codes offer protection that goes beyond legal requirements, this may be a reason against enforcing these codes, as it may discourage parties from developing self-regulation.

2174 HR 18 April 2014, *NJ* 2015, 20.

2175 M. Menting, '(R)Evolutie in het privaatrecht? Enkele beschouwingen over de rol van private regelgeving en de invloed van het EVRM naar aanleiding van HR Achmea/Rijnberg', *NTBR* 2015, 16.

2176 Some companies, however, do refer to the code, see https://www.centraalbeheer.nl/SiteCollectionDocuments/Prive%20%28BDS%29/Productwijzer%20Rechtsbijstand%20in%20het%20verkeer_2011.pdf.

should be the main beneficiaries of the code? However, the code is publicly accessible and provides sufficiently specific rules. The declaration, although aimed at the *Letselschaderaad*, is arguably not solely internally directed, and as the Ombudsman rightly recognises, a code of conduct should not leave participants the option to simply ignore the code. Instead, the drafters of the code expressly aimed to facilitate disputes in this area, which raises the question of whether drafters can be bound to *settle* disputes.

2. The declarations of banks to provide basic payment accounts make clear that banks who participate consider this an obligation, and it is possible that future consumers have accordingly relied on this. However, the declaration as such does not constitute a binding offer; it is not precise enough, and subject to conditions. It may, in addition, be doubted whether banks can be obliged to enter into contracts with consumers who superficially meet criteria established within the covenant but who, for example, have outstanding debts that they cannot repay, who provide incorrect information, or who have been convicted for forgery or fraud.

Declarations of compliance may also be binding in the following cases:

1. If parties have relied on the declaration of compliance, in accordance with article 3:35 BW.[2177]

Accordingly, consumers may justifiably rely on the code of Thuiswinkel.org and the accompanying, well-known trust mark. Similarly, consumers may rely on the declarations of energy-suppliers.

2. If people have relied on businesses' declaration of compliance, non-compliance may constitute an unfair commercial practice.

Accordingly, breach of the code on the supply of energy breaches consumer protection law, which may prompt administrative fines.[2178] Possibly, breach of the codes of Thuiswinkel.org may also constitute unfair commercial practices.

3. Codes may play a role in the assessment of businesses' behaviour.

Accordingly, the district court Zutphen[2179] imposed additional damages for the way the insurer had handled the dispute on physical injury, contrary to the code. Likewise, the district court Leeuwarden[2180] took a code of conduct on text message services, recognised by the claimant, as a starting point for determining whether the consumer was liable. The Hoge Raad[2181] has confirmed the potential role of codes of conduct, ruling that an insurer who had conducted a personal

2177 Hof Amsterdam 22 July 1999, *NJ* 2001, 286.

2178 For example the 2011 fine of Greenchoice for misleading door-to-door selling (www.consumentenautoriteit.nl/nieuws/2011/consumentenautoriteit-beboet-greenchoice-misleidende-colportage), the 2010 fine for the Nederlandse Energie Maatschappij for misleading distance selling (www.consumentenautoriteit.nl/besluiten/sanctiebesluiten/besluit-zaak-nederlandse-energie-maatschappij).

2179 Rb. Zutphen 7 November 2007, *NJF* 2007, 545. Comp. also J.B.M. Vranken in his note to *NJ* 2008, 241.

2180 Rb. Leeuwarden 11 February 2009, *LJN* BH2709.

2181 HR 18 April 2014, *NJ* 2015, 20.

investigation had not conducted its investigation in accordance with its code of conduct on this matter, with which the stakeholder organisation intended to provide further interpretations on the way in which its members should balance their own interests against policyholders' interests, in accordance with existing legislation.[2182] The Hoge Raad also considered the content and the aim of the code.

Consequently, non-state actors drafting codes of conduct may exert substantial influence on businesses who seek to comply with the codes, but this depends on the willingness of these actors to formulate and publish sufficiently clearly worded codes. Compliance with these codes depends on the willingness of businesses to state their compliance and behave accordingly. State actors have, however, shown themselves willing to reinforce these statements.

The development of self-regulation has resulted in opportunities for learning which have been used. National initiatives have accordingly inspired international initiatives in consumer sales law. However, there is room for improvement. At the European level, European actors have apparently not made use of these opportunities. In addition, opportunities have not been used consistently in other areas. For social corporate responsibility, the legislator has not even recognised the possibility to take into account international standards, as German actors have done.

8.5.3.7. Limitations on the role of non-state actors?

The Dutch legislator has shown restraint even though problems with compliance with widely supported self-regulation have arisen. Similarly, control mechanisms to limit the role of non-state actors have generally not been developed. However, problems with enforcement have prompted the European legislator to establish rules on corporate social responsibility, while the Dutch legislator has intervened to provide vulnerable consumers with basic payment accounts. It is not clear why the legislator has exercised more restraint in other areas where problems with compliance have also arisen, especially with regard to personal injury claims, social corporate responsibility and codes on the supply of energy to consumers. The current approach to corporate social responsibility still emphasises the expectation that Dutch companies will act in accordance with international guidelines. Although compliance with these guidelines is a requirement for receiving subsidies, multinationals are not obliged to report their compliance with these standards, which may not always be in companies' immediate interests.[2183]

Other initiatives indicate that the legislator does seek to prevent problems that may arise from non-state actors' initiatives without, however, limiting non-state actors' roles. Accordingly, because the increasing use of trust marks may increase the chances of inaccessibility, the Ministry of Economics has provided an overview of reliable trust marks.[2184]

[2182] This was also relevant in HR 29 June 2007, *NJ* 2007, 639.

[2183] Letter of secretary of state of economic affairs 29 March 2012.

[2184] At www.consuwijzer.nl/keurmerken.

Notably, if codes are based on broad consensus, this may be a reason to take the rules developed through self-regulation into account, provided that parties have indicated that they seek to comply with self-regulation.[2185]

Interestingly, however, non-state actors have also developed initiatives reminiscent of German control mechanisms that are aimed at increasing the quality of alternative regulation in other areas. Accordingly, in the drafting of the insurers' code on personal injury claims, relevant actors widely participated, and third parties had opportunities to influence the code. This process did not lead to compliance with the code, nor have policyholders and consumers become more aware of it.

Likewise, in the area of social corporate responsibility, various stakeholders with considerable expertise in collective negotiations have been involved in various platforms that promote social corporate responsibility.[2186] Consequently, implementing social corporate responsibility is not wholly left to multinationals, but more independent organisations also play a role.

The European Commission has exercised less restraint than the Dutch legislator. Accordingly, it has suggested the EU code of online consumer rights that regrettably overlooks relevant Dutch initiatives. Even though the Commission does not, as such, reject alternative regulation or consider the possibility that private actors pursue private rather than public interests, the top-down approach of the European Commission has also led to a more decisive approach towards the development of social corporate responsibility that still leaves considerable room for non-state actors' and international actors' initiatives.

8.5.3.8. Conclusion on one-sided declarations

Because of the restraint of the Dutch legislator, both in intervening in areas where self-regulation has been established and in the development of control mechanisms, non-state actors play a substantial role. These non-state actors may primarily bind themselves to behave in accordance with self-regulation towards consumers, which has been reinforced by the courts. Interestingly, non-state actors have developed mechanisms that should improve the quality of self-regulation, instead of more straightforward control mechanisms that developed by state actors that limit the role of non-state actors. However, these mechanisms do not appear particularly successful.

The differences between German and Dutch law, even though based on principles of private autonomy, and recognising problems of *Fremdbestimmung*, also become visible in the divergences with regard to the binding force of one-sided juridical acts and codes of conduct in particular.

The lack of success of some forms of self-regulation in addition highlights the potential weaknesses of self-regulation, especially problems of enforcement and

2185 HR 2 March 2011, *NJ* 2001, 649.

2186 See for example www.idhsustainabletrade.com/organization. Comp. also the report of the SER, *Ontwikkeling door duurzaam ondernemen*, 2011, available at www.ser.nl/~/media/DB_Adviezen /2010_2019/2011/b30143.ashx.

insufficient accessibility, which has become apparent even if self-regulation has been developed in a transparent, inclusive process.

8.5.4. *Reconsidering the distinction between* tuchtrecht *and one-sided declarations in Dutch law*

This paragraph has made a distinction between contractual self-regulation, self-regulation based on *tuchtrecht*, and one-sided declarations. The distinction between these forms of self-regulation is not usually made, and the division in this chapter has made clear for which reasons: the distinction is not a sharp one, as various forms of self-regulation may overlap.

The development of self-regulation in the Dutch legal order shows that self-regulation can be developed through different means. Associations can be involved, but other actors may also be included, and enforcement of self-regulation through contractual and non-contractual liability is important. Notwithstanding successful forms of self-regulation, and even though some associations develop self-regulation without taking the existing legal framework as a starting point, it should not be assumed that all associations are equally willing to play a central role, in accordance with arguments for an association-centered rather than a state-centered legal order. Associations are not equally competent to consistently develop self-regulation of sufficient quality that other parties comply with.

Importantly, the differences between self-regulation established on the basis of articles of association and one-sided declarations do not entail a difference in the enforcement of self-regulation. The distinction between voluntary disciplinary law and one-sided declarations as such does not entail a difference in the binding force of codes.

In some instances, self-regulation developed by Thuiswinkel.org and Stichting Webshop Keurmerk are clearly successful, which certainly should not be seen apart from the careful scrutiny of potential members. Further, if self-regulation has been developed by associations with a large number of members, it is more likely that actors have recognised self-regulation. Furthermore, the enforcement of organisations of these rules is important for the influence of codes. A lack of enforcement in other areas – for example, with regard to the GBL – may be a reason to reconsider leaving compliance with this code to organisations that also represent the interests of a particular industry.

Yet codes developed on the basis of one-sided declarations may also become binding, if specific declarations, also aimed at consumers, are intended to have legal effect, or if consumers have justifiably relied on them. Declarations of compliance may also be relevant under Directive 2005/29 on unfair commercial practices. Notably, the possibility to enforce these declarations has not visibly inhibited initiatives in The Netherlands, as has been argued in both the Dutch and the German legal order.

8.5.5. *Conclusion on non-state actors*

A considerable amount of self-regulation has developed, especially at the national level, and non-state actors may exercise substantial influence. The Dutch legislator has shown restraint in intervening in unsuccessful self-regulation, but it is difficult to deduce a consistent approach to the role of non-state actors. Possibly, there may not be much political support to intervene in insurance contract law, which has only been adopted relatively recently. It may be doubted whether the restraint of the legislator in the area of insurances is in conformity with the more active approach defended by the legislator in areas where weaker parties are affected.

Arguably, the development of a framework should contribute to a more predictable and stable approach towards self-regulation. It would form a consistent starting point for the legislator to intervene in areas where self-regulation has not been sufficiently successful.

The European legislator adopts less restraint, despite the development of bottom-up initiatives at the European level.

Both under Dutch law and European law, non-state actors have a prominent role, but they have more liberty to establish self-regulation independently at the national level. State actors initiatives may both strengthen and weaken the position of non-state actors:

1. The weaknesses of self-regulation make self-regulation an unattractive option for implementing Directives, thereby diminishing the role of non-state actors.

The Dutch legislator found the level of self-regulation and supervision in the area of consumer credit high enough that, apart from the general provisions, specific legislation in the BW on contracts between banks and consumers were not considered necessary.[2187] Since Directive 2008/48 on consumer credit has been revised, specific legsilation has been developed.

2. The room left for non-state actors' initiatives in some new European instruments is not clear.

Self-regulation in the field of consumer sales is unlikely to be adopted for the implementation of a future revised Directive, especially if a future Directive pursues maximum harmonisation. It is also unclear what role self-regulation will play if parties choose to apply a future optional instrument to their contracts.[2188]

Simultaneously, interdependence between state actors and non-state actors has become visible:

1. State actors promoting particular policy aims through self-regulation have to take into account successful self-regulation.

The success of self-regulation encouraged at the European level may, among other things, depend on already existing successful initiatives, for example, in the case of consumer sales, where the

2187 W.H. van Boom, 'Algemene en bijzondere regelingen in het vermogensrecht', *RM Themis* 2003, p. 298. Comp. previously critically E.H. Hondius, 'De bankovereenkomst: Niets bijzonders? Bank en consument in het Nieuwe BW', in: A.G. Lubbers (ed.), *Om wille van de consument*, Zwolle: Tjeenk Willink 1990, p. 67.

2188 V. Mak, 'Volgens lokaal gebruik…' *NJB* 2013, p. 4 has argued for more accessibility of local codes of conduct and business practices, coordinated at the European level.

eConfidence project has apparently not been successful. This should be taken into account in the development of new initiatives, in particular, the EU Code of online consumer rights. Conversely, the absence of self-regulation at the national level will, however, not necessarily increase the chance that self-regulation at the European level is successful, as becomes clear in the area of franchising.

2. The initiatives of non-state actors may promote the aims of state actors.

Thus, the development of self-regulation in the area of consumer sales as well as advertising also emphasises the internal market, which may strengthen corresponding initiatives from European state actors. Nevertheless, opportunities for mutual learning have not been realised.

Interdependence has also become visible between state actors:

1. If national state actors do not take into account sets of self-regulation, this may undermine the encouragement of these sets of self-regulation at the European level.

The Hoge Raad's decision not to take into account soft law and self-regulation on franchising may withhold other courts from referring to the code.[2189]

2. Initiatives from actors at the European level may undermine the initiatives of national actors.

For instance, the development of European trust marks may make it more difficult to maintain an adequate overview of reliable trust marks. Although the European Commission may attempt to provide overviews of trust marks at the European level, consumers are more likely to be familiar with national initiatives.

The interdependence between both state and non-state actors underlines the need for adequate interaction between actors. If actors interact with one another, they may strengthen rather than undermine one another's initiatives.

International initiatives in consumer sales and advertising have inspired Dutch actors, and lower courts may take into account international materials, which makes it more likely that the interests of foreign and international parties have been taken into account. Simultaneously, initiatives of EU state actors that overlook relevant transnational and national initiatives are not likely to prompt national or non-state actors to pay more attention to the interests of foreign and international actors, especially for businesses that are primarily involved in domestic trade.

8.6. Conclusion

This chapter has considered which actors develop private law in the Dutch legal order, and what the role of those actors is under Dutch law and the European framework.

[2189] For example Ktr. Roermond 11 January 2012, *LJN* BV1313.

Paragraph 8.6.1. will compare the roles of actors under Dutch law and the TFEU, and compare the role of actors under the Gw and the TFEU with the German framework. Paragraph 8.6.2. will consider the development of coexisting claims to authority at the national and European level. Paragraph 8.6.3. will turn to the decreasing role of state actors in the light of pluralist criticism on state-centrism. Paragraph 8.6.4. will consider the development of private law in a radical pluralist legal order and paragraph 8.6.5. will conclude by asking for starting points for mutual recognition.

8.6.1. The role of actors under Dutch law, the TFEU and the GG

The roles of actors under the Gw and the TFEU both converge and diverge. The role of actors under Dutch law and European law shows a number of convergences, and differences from the German legal order:

1) The role of European actors

Both Dutch and European actors consider that the direct effect and the priority of European law is based on European law rather than the Gw. Consequently, the reallocation of competences to the national level is determined by the TFEU and the CJEU is recognised as the competent court to interpret European law, including actors' competence. In this respect, both Dutch and European law differ clearly from the GG and the BVerfG that emphasises the importance of the GG, also if it concerns the validity of European measures.

2) The role of non-state actors

Dutch and European actors generally do not consider the development of alternative regulation as the exercise of constitutional rights, but they have left considerable room, especially at the national level, for non-state actors.[2190]

In contrast, in the German legal order, private autonomy, protected by article 2 GG, the freedom of association in article 9 GG and the freedom of profession under article 12 GG leave private actors with a wide range of discretion to develop self-regulation. Thus, the role of private actors is both more controversial and constitutionally protected. The German legislator or judiciary may be constitutionally obliged to intervene if alternative regulation leads to *Fremdbestimmung*. This may complicate ensuring compliance with self-regulation – for example, problems with dynamic referral make additional measures to ensure compliance with international sports rules necessary. The German legislator seems unwilling to reinforce privately drafted rules with hard law, but rather imposes a duty on private actors to report their compliance with self-regulation, or expresses the expectation that compliance with privately developed rules will constitute good practice. Self-regulation may also be enforced on the basis of contracts, articles of association, or tort law, and instances in the German legal order that are not reinforced on a

[2190] M. Menting, J.B.M. Vranken, 'Gedragscodes in een meergelaagd privaatrecht in Europa en Nederland', in: M. Menting, J.B.M. Vranken, M.W. Scheltema, *Gedragscodes in internationaal, Europees en privaatrechtelijk perspectief, Preadviezen 2013 uitgebracht voor de Vereniging van Burgerlijk Recht*, Zutphen: Paris 2014, p. 40 find that the requirements for using self-regulation by Dutch and EU actors are not far apart.

contractual or other basis seem rare, but do exist – for example, the *Werbekodex*, or the initiative for basic payment accounts.

In the Dutch legal order, alternative regulation seems more easily reinforced with hard law, and subject to less control once it has been developed.

The controversy on the role of non-state actors also becomes clear from the potential problems surrounding the involvement of stakeholder groups in the development of *Sonderprivatrecht*, especially in highly specialised, rapidly developing areas in need of swift legislative intervention. The role of attorneys in the drafting of the financial market stabilising act (*'Finanzmarktstabilisierungsergänzungsgesetz'*) has given rise to the question of whether the involvement of private actors was in accordance with article 33 par. 4 GG that stipulates that the execution of legislative competences should be left to public services.[2191] More generally, the involvement of private actors in drafting legislation has been criticised, in accordance with the assumption that private actors mainly pursue their own, and not the public interest.[2192] Interestingly, Kloepfer[2193] expressly distinguishes the involvement of stakeholders from the involvement of academics. He considers that academics pursue the public interest, instead of particular aims, while their broad and systematic view makes their participation in the drafting of codifications, in his opinion, particularly useful.

The involvement of stakeholders in the Dutch legal order may have been criticised, but it is not constitutionally problematic.[2194] In the drafting of the BW, practitioners and other interested parties have been involved, but experts in particular have been given a central role in the drafting process.[2195] The involvement of legal experts and involved practice is currently an established practice, as shown in other important legislation on private law, for example, in the reform of insurance contract law,[2196] the attempt to reform insolvency law,[2197] the reform of arbitration law,[2198] and suggestions for an academic committee for patrimonial law.[2199] However, academic

2191 Comp. W. Wieland et al, *Privatisierung der Gesetzgebung durch die Erstellung von Gesetzentwürfen durch Rechtsanwaltskanzleien*, Kleine Anfrage 19.3.2012, BT-Drs.:17/9026. See further on constitutional problems J. Krüper, 'Lawfirm – legibus solutus?', *JZ* 2010, p. 655.

2192 S. Augsberg, *Rechtsetzung zwischen Staat und Gesellschaft*, Berlin: Duncker & Humblot 2001, p. 232, similarly J. Köndgen, 'Privatisierung des Rechts,' *AcP* 2006, p. 523.

2193 M. Kloepfer, 'Gesetzgebungsoutsourcing – Die Erstellung von Gesetzentwürfen durch Rechtsanwälte', *NJW* 2011, p. 134.

2194 W. van Gerven, S. Lierman, *Beginselen van Belgisch privaatrecht. Algemeen deel, veertig jaar later*, Mechelen: Kluwer 2010, p. 299 point out that in the Belgian legal order, concerns with regard to increasing corporatism and "pseudo-legislation" have been voiced.

2195 The research on the Dutch Civil Code was conducted initially by Prof. E.M.M. Meijers, later by Prof. J. Drion, Prof. J. Eggens en mr. F.J. de Jong, judge in the Hoge Raad, and adopted after extensive consultation among legal academics and legal practice. See further E.O.H.P. Florijn, *Ontstaan en ontwikkeling van het nieuwe Burgerlijk Wetboek*, Maastricht: UPM 1994.

2196 The draft bill was edited and revised by prof. T.J. Dorhout Mees, and, after an extensive consultation, commented upon by legal practitioners and involved parties such as insurers: Asser/Clausing & Wansink 2007, nr. 9.

2197 The draft bill was edited by the Commission on Insolvency law, chaired by prof. S.C.J.J. Kortmann. Comments are available at the website of the Ministry of Justice, www.justitie.nl/onderwerpen/wetgeving/insolventiewet/.

2198 The main initiator and author of the draft bill was Prof. A.J. van den Berg, see further H.J.Snijders, 'Algemene beschouwingen bij het Wetsvoorstel Modernisering Arbitragerecht', *Tijdschrift voor Arbitrage* 2013, 31.

2199 A.J. Verdaas, 'Wetgever, besteed meer aandacht aan ons vermogensrecht! Een oproep tot het instellen van een permanente Commissie vermogensrecht', *NTBR* 2010, 47.

experts are not expressly included in the development of alternative regulation because they are more neutral than stakeholders.

At the European level, the role of non-state actors is also less problematic than is the case under the German framework. The European view emphasises the added value of including private actors in the development of measures.[2200] In contrast to the German view, the possibility that private actors do not pursue the public interest but their own interests, and the possibility that legislation is drafted one-sidedly, has not been considered. Rather, the initiatives of private actors are seen in the light of European policy aims. Accordingly, the initiatives of non-state actors are typically reinforced, while these initiatives are subjected to relatively mild control mechanisms. For example, the initiatives of private actors may prompt legislative measures. This was, for example, the case in Directive 98/26 on settlement finality and Directive 2002/47 on financial collateral arrangements. The drafting of the Settlement Finality Directive was prompted by reports from the Bank for International Settlements[2201] that called for minimum standards for the operation and design for cross-border multi-currency netting systems, as well as enhancing the finality of transfers and settlements in domestic markets in order to limit risks and costs arising in cross-system settlements.[2202]

3) The role of state actors

In line with the findings in the case studies, both at the national level and the European level, state actors have played a central role in the development of private law either through the BW, the BGB and the GG, or the private law *acquis*.

In addition, many similarities between the roles of state actors at the national level can be found.

Both the German and the Dutch legislator have extensively considered comparative law in the drafting of the *Schuldrechtmodernisierungsgesetz* and the BW, and both codes make use of blanket clauses that leave considerable room for the judiciary. Academics have played an important role in the drafting of both the *Schuldrechtsmodernisierungsgesetz* and the BW. Neither the Dutch nor the German legislator has extensively considered European initiatives in the drafting of both the BGB and the BW.

2200 For example in Expert Groups, which may consist both of private actors as well as academics, provided that there is a 'balanced representation of relevant areas of interest', see the Communication from the President to the Commission, *Framework for Commission Expert Groups: Horizontal rules and public register*, C (2010) 7649 final, p. 3–4, on which see critically A. Pilniok, 'Struktur, Funktionen und Probleme der Expertengruppen der Europäischen Kommission: legitime Expertise oder unzulässige Einflussnahme?', *EuR* 2014, p. 62.

2201 Bank for International Settlements, *Report of the committee on interbank netting schemes of the central banks of the group of ten countries (Lamfalussy Report)*, Basle November 1990, p. 2–3, available at www.bis.org/publ/cpss04.pdf, Bank for International Settlements, *Delivery versus payment in securities settlement systems*, Basle September 1992, available at www.bis.org/publ/cpss06.pdf, Bank for International Settlements, *Cross-border securities settlements*, Basle March 1995, par. 1.4, available at www.bis.org/publ/cpss12.pdf?noframes=1. The Directive was established in close cooperation with experts and stakeholders: see COM (1996) 193 final.

2202 For example, transfers and settlements between domestic systems and international central securities depositories (ICSDs) that can make transfers and settlements within their own payment and securities systems.

Notwithstanding the central role of state actors at both the national and the European level, a clear distinction should be made between on the one hand the Dutch and German legislator, and on the other hand the European legislator.

Dutch and German actors play a central role through codifications. This central role is constitutionally indicated in the Dutch legal order, as article 107 Gw stipulates that private law shall be stipulated in the code. A German equivalent of this article cannot be found in the GG. Although parts of private law fall within the exclusive competence of the federal legislator,[2203] article 74 GG stipulates that the competence to establish private law is a shared one. However, it has been argued that principles such as legal unity and the stable development of the law without inconsistencies may entail codification rather than ad hoc legislation. Inconsistencies that are more likely to arise if private law is developed on an ad hoc basis rather than codification may meet with constitutional objections, as they may give rise to suspicions of arbitrariness.[2204] Regardless of an express codification provision in the constitution, many legal orders have developed a codification.

In contrast with both national legal orders, at the European level, legislative competence to establish a code is absent; instead, the legislative competence to develop private law follows from the TFEU which has led to the functional development of the private law *acquis*.[2205] Notwithstanding arguments for a European Civil Code, it may be doubted whether a codification at the European level would contribute to the quality of private law.[2206]

In line with the case studies, some further differences become apparent with regard to the role of Dutch and German courts, and the relation between the respectively the Dutch and German courts and the Dutch and German legislator.

These differences are in line with the more general development of constitutional review by the BVerfG and the CJEU, and the development of conflicting claims to authority by these courts.

The BVerfG should uphold the GG and set aside legislation, as well as judicial reasoning that is not in accordance with the GG. At the European level, the CJEU similarly may rule that European measures have been established *ultra vires*, but it has adopted considerably more restraint than the BVerfG in its decisions.[2207] The CJEU does not show a tendency to limit the Union's legislative competence in favour of Member States – quite the reverse![2208] In contrast, there is no separate constitutional court in the Dutch legal order. Instead, article 120 Gw stipulates that the judiciary

2203 For example intellectual property law, see article 73 par. 1 sub 9 GG.

2204 M. Lieb, 'Grundfragen einer Schuldrechtsreform', *AcP* 1983, p. 347.

2205 Comp. R. Zimmerman, 'Konturen einer Europäischen Vertragsrechts', *JZ* 1995, p. 491, who finds that a codification 'bedarf der ständigen Erprobung, Konkretisierung und Fortbildung in der Praxis und die geistigen Durchdringung durch die Wissenschaft.'

2206 See further chapter 9.

2207 Comp. O. Gerstenberg, 'From "democratic deficit" to "justice deficit"?', in: D. Kochenov, G. de Búrca (eds.), *Europe's justice deficit?*, Oxford: Hart 2015, p. 70, who points out that initially, the Court was considered as a specialised commercial court and not a constitutional court.

2208 See for example H. Unberath, A. Johnston, 'The double-headed approach of the CJEU concerning consumer protection', 44 *CMLRev* 2007, p. 1283. Comp. critically S. Weatherill, 'The limits of legislative harmonization ten years after Tobacco Advertising: how the Court's case law has become a drafting guide', *German Law Journal* 2011, p. 827.

shall not decide on the constitutionality of treaties or formal laws, that is, laws established by Parliament and the government under articles 81 Gw.

The BGH has adopted an active approach to the development of private law more generally, in line with German state actors' duty to uphold the GG, if necessary by intervening through legislation,[2209] or, if that is absent, through judicial decision-making.[2210] This is in line with the German case study that demonstrated that the German legislator has consciously refrained from amending the law on STCs, which has been facilitated by the active approach of German courts. The active approach of German courts may more generally mitigate problems arising from inflexible law. Koziol[2211] has argued that the development of rules that leave too little room for discretion or pragmatic solutions may be a reason for the increasing recourse of the German judiciary to blanket clauses. He doubts that these blanket clauses, in particular articles 242 and 826 BGB, are a sufficient basis for the rules that have been developed even though good faith, as such, is a very broad concept that does not necessarily clearly indicate how individual cases should be decided. Therefore, the prominent role of German courts may increase the responsiveness of private law but decrease predictability. For foreign parties, these developments may not be particularly accessible. In the case studies, it was already noted that the development of blanket clauses and the subsequent development of the law through case law on the basis of blanket clauses is not beneficial for regulatory competition. This is the case even if German courts take into account international and foreign materials and practices in the development of German private law, which strengthens the responsiveness of German law to international actors and should be beneficial for regulatory competition, even if regulatory competition has not been pursued by the legislator.[2212]

The inaccessibility of case law developed under blanket clauses for foreign actors has also been overlooked by the Dutch legislator in its pursuit of regulatory competition, as visible in the Dutch case study.[2213] The findings in the Dutch case study moreover underline the interdependence between the legislator and the court. Notwithstanding the ambition of the Dutch legislator to participate in regulatory competition, courts have not consistently taken into account the needs and preferences of foreign and international actors, as reflected in foreign and international materials. Yet this does not mean that Dutch courts have more generally adopted restraint in developing the law, as became visible in the Dutch case study. Contrary to the findings in the case studies, and notwithstanding its lack of competence to set aside legislation, the Hoge Raad has adopted an active approach towards the development of private law.

2209 This may also entail that the lack of legislative intervention may become subject to a constitutional complaint if a duty to intervene clearly follows from the GG; comp. Epping/Hillgruber/Bek'scher Online-Kommentar GG/Morgenthaler (2012), article 93, nr 60.

2210 MunchKomm zum BGB/Säcker (2012) nr 152. See for example BAG 29 March 1984, *NJW* 1984, 2374, par.III d 3 a.

2211 H. Koziol, 'Glanz und Elend der deutschen Zivilrechtsdogmatik', *AcP* 2012, p. 5–8.

2212 See previously par. 4.6.2.

2213 See previously par. 5.6.2.

The Hoge Raad has been characterised as an assistant legislator even before the amendments meant to strengthen its role in the development of the law were adopted.[2214] Yet although case law has prompted legislation,[2215] the Hoge Raad cannot oblige legislative intervention. Generally, the Hoge Raad exercises restraint, especially in cases where the law does not offer a clear indication what rule should be developed, and political considerations underpin the various possible options.[2216] In exceptional cases, when the legislator is aware that current law leads to an unacceptable situation – which was moreover, contrary to international law – the judiciary may provide rules.[2217] Giesen[2218] has signalled that in recent cases, the Hoge Raad's patience with the legislator seems to be wearing thin and a more active approach can be detected. In rare cases, the Hoge Raad has decided *contra legem*,[2219] although there is some disagreement on what decisions are *contra legem* – does the Hoge Raad decide *contra legem* if decisions go against the wording of legal provisions or if decisions go against the bearing of the law?[2220] The recent changes in the role of the Hoge Raad, which have been inspired by the previous House of Lords,[2221] highlight the role of the Hoge Raad in the development of law.

The active role of the Hoge Raad has also meant that judges have anticipated on the introduction of the BW, deciding cases on the basis of rules that not yet gone into force. In some cases, judges have also anticipated on Directives that had not yet gone into effect.[2222] In contrast, German judges have not anticipated the *Schuldrechtsreform*, especially because the decision of the legislator to reform the BGB, after years of silence, came as a surprise. The German judiciary has, however, anticipated Directives if they have not been timely implemented.[2223]

2214 J.M. Polak, M.V. Polak, 'Faux pas ou pas de deux?' *Netherlands International Law Review* 1986, p. 99. Comp. on the active role of the Hoge Raad and the consequences of changing its course recently F.M.J. Verstijlen, 'Hoe om te gaan met "omgaan"?', *TvI* 2015, 27, R.M. Wibier, 'De Hoge Raad op drift?', *WPNR* (7046) 2015.

2215 This is also the case in German law; see for examples D. Medicus, 'Entscheidungen des BGH als Marksteine für die Entwicklung des allgemeinen Zivilrechts', *NJW* 2000, p. 2926.

2216 HR 23 September 1988, *NJ* 1989, 740.

2217 HR 12 May 1999, *NJ* 2000, 170.

2218 I. Giesen, 'Wie hoedt het privaatrecht?', *NTBR* 2014, 26. In his note on HR 9 October 2009, *NJ* 2010, 387, J.B.M. Vranken, where the Hoge Raad underlined the pregorative of the legislator to decide on the compensation for emotional damages for bereaved, pleads for the development of rules through case law, in combination with expert soft law rules, which he characterises as "creeping legislation".

2219 Decisions that have been characterised as *contra legem* include for example HR 21 March 1986, *NJ* 1986, 585, where the Hoge Raad held, against the background of article 8 ECHR, that article 1:246 BW that stipulated that parental authority could only exist if parents were married did not stand in the way of joint parental authority of the parties who were not married. Comp. also HR 19 December 1975, *NJ* 1976, 537, where the Hoge Raad decided that article 1:150 BW that stipulates that divorce can be declared between spouses that have not been legally separated, in which case article 1:179 et seq BW are exclusively applicable does not stand in the way for declaring divorce in a case where one party had claimed for divorce, the decision on which had not yet become final while legal separation that was simultaneously claimed had been declared.

2220 G.J. Wiarda, *Drie typen van rechtsvinding* (comments from T. Koopmans), Deventer: Tjeenk Willink 1999, 4th ed., p. 39–40. Comp. the definition of T.J.M. Möllers, 'Doppelte Rechtsfortbildung contra legem? Zur Umgestaltung des Bürgerlichen Gesetzbuches durch den EuGH und nationale Gerichte', in: H. Schlosser (ed.), *Bürgerliches Gesetzbuch 1896–1996*, Heidelberg: Müller 1997, p. 154, 181.

2221 Commissie normstellende rol Hoge Raad, *Versterking van de cassatierechtspraak*, The Hague, February 2008.

2222 Ktr. Zaandam 2 April 2009, *NJF* 2009, 278. Comp. also Rb. Haarlem 25 June 2008, *IER* 2009, 6.

2223 BGH 24 May 1995, *NJW* 1995, 2034.

The role of the CJEU differs in various respects.

The CJEU is not concerned with developing private law within the framework of a code. Even where the Directives in the *acquis* show similarities – such as the use of similar blanket clauses or similar wording – this does not necessarily mean that the CJEU will provide consistent guidelines for the interpretation of these Directives, which also depends on the aim of Directives and the degree of harmonisation. Rather, the CJEU seeks to uphold and develop European law, in which it has played an active role.

Notwithstanding this active role, the CJEU cannot anticipate Directives – even if Directives still need to be implemented, a complaint before the CJEU requires that the Directive has already been adopted. In the case of Directives in the process of reform, the CJEU has not been known to anticipate future amendments. Doing so would be difficult to reconcile with the principle of conferred powers, especially as proposed amendments may be controversial. This also means that the CJEU, if it anticipated on proposal, runs the risk of anticipating a rule that will not become law. In exceptional cases, however, the CJEU[2224] has obliged Member States to set aside legislation even though the Directive obliging Member States to do so had not yet become effective.

Arguably, the different role of the CJEU should be a reason to show more restraint in the use of blanket clauses in the *acquis*, as it may well lead to inconsistencies within the *acquis*.[2225] Moreover, the question arises as to whether the CJEU has similar possibilities to mitigate inflexibility of the law or other potential problems.

Differences in the roles of international actors and non-state actors under Dutch, German, and European law are also visible.

1) The role of international actors

Whereas international law may have direct effect under articles 93 and 94 Gw, this is not the case for European law. German law likewise does not provide international law with direct effect, but requires implementation. Other approaches are visible in the European Union: although international law also has to be implemented in English law, the judiciary has adopted far more restraint in their evaluation of matters that fall under the prerogative of the Crown.[2226]

However, as long as international law does not interfere with European law, no conflicts need arise. If the European legislator harmonises law previously harmonised through treaties, the European background of that rule will likely precede the international background, unless European measures allow that treaties precede European law.

2224 CJEU 22 November 2005 (Mangold v Helm), C-144/04, [2005] ECR, p. I-9981.

2225 See further on the use of blanket clauses par. 9.4.

2226 Comp. *High Court (R. v Secretary of State for Foreign and Commonwealth Affairs, ex parte Rees-Mogg* (1994) 1 All ER 457 at 469, in accordance with Lord Denning MR from *Blackburn v. Attorney-General* (1971) 2 All ER 1380, the case in which Britain's decision to join the European Community was challenged: "The treaty-making power of this country rests not in the courts, but in the Crown; that is, Her Majesty acting on the advice of her Ministers. When her Ministers negotiate and sign a treaty, even a treaty of such paramount importance as this proposed one, they act on behalf of the country as a whole. They exercise the prerogative of the Crown. Their action in so doing cannot be challenged or questioned in these courts."

2) The restraint of the Dutch legislator in intervening in alternative regulation

In the absence of a Dutch equivalent of the *Untermaßverbot*, an obligation to legislate in order to protect constitutional rights, the Dutch legislator has shown restraint in intervening in alternative regulation, including instances where compliance with self-regulation is problematic. Notwithstanding the absence of the *Untermaßverbot*, Dutch state actors have retained a central role in the development of European private law, primarily through the BW.

At the European level, the lack of an equivalent of the *Untermaßverbot* has not withheld the European legislator from frequently intervening in private law.

3) The development of control mechanisms

Both actors at the national and the European level have recognised the need to exercise control over alternative regulation. The emphasis at the European level is on the increased involvement of state actors in the development of European law.

Dutch actors have adopted a more critical approach than European actors and developed more control mechanisms, especially in cases where parties in collective negotiations do not have an equal bargaining position. Thus, collective bargaining takes place in the framework of the SER, and the representativeness and inclusiveness of collective negotiations has also been evaluated. Further, drafting processes have been organised by both German and Dutch actors. These processes should minimise the chance that rules developed in self-regulation and co-regulation do not adequately reflect private actors' preferences. In the German legal order, the emphasis on involving neutral actors and the attention for the position of weak parties subject to *Fremdbestimmung* further diminishes the chances that alternative regulation reflects preferences of particular groups that have played an influential role in the development of alternative regulation. Some of the mechanisms in the Dutch legal order, such as the declaration that gives CAOs generally binding force, or that declares a mass settlement binding, however, leave a considerable amount of discretion to state actors. Interestingly, there have been suggestions to improve these mechanisms.

Frequently, also, in the Dutch legal order, control mechanisms have been developed to improve the quality of alternative regulation. In some cases, the lack of enforceability is seen as the main problem, which has led to the reinforcement of alternative regulation. Interestingly, control mechanisms may also entail more self-regulation.

Judicial control over alternative regulation has been developed by European actors – through Directive 93/13 – as well as Dutch and German actors. The German judiciary has played an important role in evaluating alternative regulation as it has developed an active approach in subjecting privately drafted rules to judicial evaluation to prevent *Fremdbestimmung*. The Dutch judiciary is arguably not similarly constitutionally bound to prevent *Fremdbestimmung*, and the Dutch judiciary has accordingly not developed a similar approach to evaluating contracts.

Consequently, judicial control in The Netherlands is not as often used as in Germany, and it is most visible in the control over the content of STCs. Thus, the findings in the case studies may not be representative for control mechanisms generally used in the Dutch legal order, even though the Dutch judiciary does have room to intervene in obligations as articles 6:2 and 6:248 BW stipulate that obligations also have consequences that follow from the law or from fairness. The judiciary may in addition set aside obligations if they would have consequences that are unacceptable from the perspective of fairness. In rare cases, the Hoge Raad has allowed fairness in the meaning of article 6:2 BW to play a central role in decisions: for example, the claim of a young widower who had murdered his elderly wife for the inheritance was denied on the basis of article 3:166 par. 3 and 6:2 BW.[2227]

In this respect, the role of the German and the Dutch courts clearly differs from the CJEU. Even though the private law *acquis* refers to good faith and fairness, the CJEU has insufficient insight into the factual background of cases to come to similar decisions, which will also depend on national law.

Overall, German actors have developed control mechanisms more consistently than either Dutch or European actors. The developments in particularly the Dutch legal order make clear that the development of alternative regulation and transnational trade may strengthen actors who already have sufficient expertise and organisation resources, further enpowering them to exert influence in decision-making, as argued by Krisch.[2228] Generally, powerful non-state actors may seek to influence the development of the law in accordance with their interests.[2229] The principle of *Fremdbestimmung* makes clear why this shift can be problematic. The lack of consistent safeguards in Dutch legal order and the lenient approach of Dutch state actors may lead to problems if the interests of non-state actors are hard to reconcile with the development of and compliance with self-regulation, as is the case in social corporate responsibility, corporate governance, and for energy suppliers and insurers developing codes of conduct. The lack of effective alternative regulation may especially be detrimental for consumers who have had no opportunity to influence the development of, for example, codes of conducts for insurers and energy suppliers, or foreign parties who cannot exert sufficient influence on multinationals that violate their human rights.

4) The Dutch approach to alternative regulation is more bottom-up

This becomes visible in the failure of the *standaardregeling*[2230] and the corresponding success of collectively negotiated STCs, as well as the development of the corporate governance codes and corporate social responsibility. It may in addition be wondered whether the dependence of state actors on non-state actors could be linked to far-reaching duties of care in private law.[2231] More generally, in line with the discourse on multilevel governance, the Dutch legislator[2232] has recognised the practical limitations of legislation, stressing the sometimes limited insight of the legislator in societal processes and the corresponding need for giving room to the development of alternative regulation rather than legislation.

The European legislator has adopted a top-down approach, and considers the initiatives of private actors in the light of European policy aims. Alternative regulation that has developed beyond the national level – for example, the EMOTA Convention – need not necessarily be taken into account by European actors.

2227 HR 7 December 1990, *NJ* 1991, 593.

2228 N. Krisch, *Beyond constitutionalism: The pluralist structure of postnational law*, Oxford: OUP 2010, p. 257.

2229 N. Krisch, *Beyond constitutionalism: The pluralist structure of postnational law*, Oxford: OUP 2010, p. 259–260.

2230 See previously par. 5.3.2.

2231 J.B.M. Vranken, 'Over partijautonomie, contractsvrijheid en de grondslag van gebondenheid in het verbintenissenrecht', in: J.M. Barendrecht, M.A.B. Chao-Duivis, B.W.M. Nieskens-Isphording (eds.), *Beginselen van het contractenrecht*, Deventer: Tjeenk Willink, 2000, par. 15.

2232 *Kamerstukken II*, 1990–1991, 22008, 1–2, p. 14.

The Dutch approach is also more bottom-up than the German approach, as evidenced by the active approach of German state actors towards the drafting of alternative regulation.

Less differences and potential conflicts between Dutch and European law arise than between German and European law, as the roles of actors under the Gw and the TFEU differ less clearly the role of actors under the GG and the TFEU.

However, resistance may arise if European initiatives do not take sufficient note of successful national initiatives, which may decrease the added value of European initiatives to private parties. This is the case if framework agreements limit private parties' room to develop CAOs. European initiatives may also limit the role of actors in successful self-regulation, for example, if Directive 93/13 stands in the way of collectively negotiated STCs or model contracts that go below the protection offered in the Directive. Further, European forms of alternative regulation, such as the dynamic referral to the IASB, as well as the development of comitology, have been criticised.[2233] However, differently from the case studies,[2234] in these areas, Dutch actors have been prompted to take into account the interests of non-national actors, and they may also feel pressured to justify divergences.

8.6.2. *Coexisting claims to authority*

The differences between the Gw and the TFEU are less pronounced than the differences between the GG and the TFEU. Dutch actors have not interpreted the role of European actors as narrowly as German actors. Consequently, coexisting claims to authority are less pronounced.

At first sight, direct conflicts between European and Dutch claims to authority are not likely to arise for several reasons. Firstly, Dutch law recognises the direct effect of European law based on European law. Secondly, the role of actors is not strictly delineated under Dutch law, and there is room for experimentation. Thirdly, Dutch state actors have adopted a *laissez-faire* approach, even in cases where alternative regulation shows shortcomings.

Yet on closer inspection, Dutch law is oriented on Dutch state actors rather than European or international actors, or on the interests of these actors, even though European and international law may have direct effect in the Dutch legal order. The development of private law continues to be developed mainly at the national level, in the BW, in accordance with the constitutional requirement for the national codification of private law.

8.6.3. *The development of private law and state-centric perspectives*

According to pluralist criticism of state-centrism, the development of private law should not be considered in a state-centric manner. At first sight, harmonisation and the development

2233 See previously par. 8.4.1.2. and 8.4.1.4.

2234 See previously par. 5.6.2.

of alternative regulation in the Dutch legal order support the view that the role of national state actors is decreasing and the role of non-state actors is increasing. Accordingly, Dutch state actors allow non-state actors more room to develop binding rules than German state actors. Furthermore, the Dutch legislator has permitted that self-regulation has been developed rather than legislation, and has exercised restraint to allow for self-regulation for contracts between banks and consumers, energy suppliers and consumers and insurers and consumers. Dutch courts have referred to self-regulation in their decisions. However, generally, national state actors have retained a central role in the development of European private law generally. Pluralist insights support these developments, arguing that the development of private law should not be considered in a state-centric manner.

The previous chapter argued that the prevention of *Fremdbestimmung* is a convincing reason to retain a central role for state actors. Accordingly, this chapter has argued for the development of a future framework on the basis of the principle of private autonomy and corresponding concerns of *Fremdbestimmung* in which national state actors retain a central role. The principles underlying the German framework and control mechanisms developed to mitigate potential *Fremdbestimmung* have generally been recognised in the Dutch legal order. Starting points include article 6:1 BW, the recognition of the added value of negotiations, and the development of mechanisms to mitigate one-sided rules or mechanisms to improve alternative regulation.

Firstly, article 6:1 BW reflects the idea that binding parties requires sufficient justification. Interestingly, although Dutch law is not a closed system, alternative regulation as such has not been recognised as a new category that should enable private parties to bind third parties. It is increasingly important, and in the multilevel legal order also increasingly difficult, for parties to be aware of rules by which they can be bound, which should prompt questions about how the law should deal with potential surprises.

Secondly, the emphasis on the autonomy of both parties, the idea of *égoïsme a deux* and especially the appreciation for collectively negotiated CAOs and STCs, shows that Dutch law recognises the added value of negotiations. Negotiated instruments are considered less one-sided than non-negotiated contracts and codes. Simultaneously, the importance of equal bargaining positions has been recognised as mandatory law protects weaker parties.

Thirdly, it has been recognised that in some cases, non-state actors may pursue their own interests rather than the public interest, although this is not a general assumption. Accordingly, control mechanisms limiting the role of non-state actors have been developed, particularly in the form of mandatory law, judicial control, and a controlled environment for collective negotiations. Arguments to ensure the representativeness of interest groups submitting mass claims have also been made.[2235] Criticism of the lenient Dutch approach to the referral to the IASB, which may jeopardise the stable development of the law,[2236] as well as criticism of so-called "skeleton legislation"[2237] indicate the need to consider the role of non-state actors more consistently.

2235 See previously par. 8.4.3.4.

2236 See previously par. 8.4.1.2.

2237 See previously par. 8.4.1.4.

Like German contract law, Dutch contract law has been based principles of private autonomy. The case study however made clear that a similarly close relation between general default contract law and general views on justice may not exist, as default law need not necessarily reflect legal views on justice. Accordingly, the Dutch legislator adopts a more lenient approach to STCs in domestic business contracts. This is in accordance with arguments that the needs of practice more generally should shape default law.[2238] However, legal views still play a role in default law,[2239] and are clearly visible in other areas of contract law, as reflected in article 3:12 BW that refers to Dutch legal views on justice ('*in Nederland levende rechtsovertuigingen*'), blanket clauses such as articles 6:2 and 248 BW and key provisions such as article 6:162 BW.[2240] The relation between the law and legal views on justice are clearly a reason to preserve the role of national actors.

However, in some areas, Dutch law might leave more room for regulatory competition than German law. The lenient approach to business contracts in the case study, and differences with regard to self-regulation on the basis of articles of association and one-sided declarations, as these rules are not considered in the light of *Fremdbestimmung*, give the impression that the Dutch legislator is less inclined to assume that *Fremdbestimmung* arises in business contracts.

Nevertheless, the need for a framework remains. A framework would arguably be better suited to the increasing role of non-state actors and the corresponding interdependence between state and non-state actors than the current *laissez-faire* approach. Particularly, this entails that the role of state actors with regard to privately developed rules should be reconsidered. State actors' discretion to take privately developed rules as a starting point or disregard them should be reconsidered. Obliging state actors to take into account alternative regulation would become especially apparent in hopefully lead to more predictability and consistency in case law on the binding force of self-regulation that has been recognised by private parties.[2241]

The development of a Dutch framework may contribute to the comprehensibility of European private law in various ways:

1) A framework may encourage state actors to intervene in the development of self-regulation and reconsider legislation. Especially if persistent problems with legislation or self-regulation arise, a framework may draw attention to the question of whether these rules are developed by the right actors. Should non-state actors continue to have room to develop self-regulation that is not complied with, or should state actors continue to play a central role in a particular area if the legislative process in that area consistently shows severe shortcomings[2242] that lead to factual *Fremdbestimmung*? If alternative regulation increasingly meets standards of participation, inclusion and transparency, and if it is sufficiently comprehensible and complied with, while the

2238 R. van Bijnen, *Aanvullend contractenrecht*, The Hague: BJU 2005.
2239 Asser/Scholten 1974, par. 6, M.A. Loth, *Dwingend en aanvullend recht*, Deventer: Kluwer 2009, p. 11–12.
2240 See generally A.S. Hartkamp, *Aard en opzet van het nieuwe vermogensrecht*, Deventer: Kluwer 2010, p. 55 et seq.
2241 See previously par. 8.5.3.6.
2242 See further on criticism on the legislative process par. 10.2.

legislative process seems unduly slow or non-state actors who are likely to pursue their own rather than the public interest, play too prominent a role, the question may arise why a matter should not be dealt with by alternative regulation rather than legislation.

2) A framework offers starting points for a more consistent approach to the role of actors and, correspondingly, for suggestions with regard to extending the use of new governance approaches, which would also benefit the predictable development of private law.
3) Developing a framework should entail the development of measures to ensure that self-regulation is drafted by representative actors. This may, in turn, lead to self-regulation that is responsive to business practices as well as other parties' interests, thereby striking an adequate balance between parties' interests.
4) As more self-regulation is developed in accordance with the principles of transparency, openness, inclusiveness and representativeness, this will increase the chance that parties are alert to relevant self-regulation, which, in turn, theoretically, would lessen problems of inaccessibility that are currently visible in the GBL.

Thus, a framework would consistently and predictably outline the role of actors, both state and non-state actors, based on the principles of private autonomy and *Fremdbestimmung*, indicating the development of control mechanisms if actors are likely to pursue their own interests and develop one-sided rules accordingly. Consequently, measures that help ensure transparency, representativeness and inclusiveness are more consistently developed. Possibly, the development of control mechanisms that give non-state actors a more prominent role such as the development of self-regulation in the area of collective settlement, may be critically reconsidered, especially if they do not prove sufficiently successful. Over time, as non-state actors gain a more prominent role, they gain more responsibility to develop alternative regulation in accordance with benchmarks of predictability, consistency, accessibility and responsiveness. In this scenario, the role of state actors gradually becomes a facilitative role. However, as alternative regulation is upheld and reinforced by state actors, these actors continue to play an important role in safeguarding the quality of alternative regulation and ensuring, through control mechanisms, ensuring that individuals are not subjected to rules without a proper basis.

The German framework and a Dutch framework need not stand in the way of the development of alternative regulation, nor does it stand in the way of regulatory competition or mutual learning.

Notwithstanding the more limited role of non-state actors in the German legal order, interesting instances of alternative regulation could also act as a source of inspiration for other actors. For example, the cooperation developed in the area of consumer sales by Trusted Shops may provide an interesting example of successful self-regulation for other legal orders. Similarly, the consistent analysis for upholding or not upholding contracts and the judicial control of STCs in accordance with the *Richtigkeitsgewähr* may provide particularly interesting starting points for other legal orders.

In the Dutch order, there is less resistance to new forms of governance developed at the European level that may be interesting for Dutch actors. In particular, the development of guidelines for the interpretation of blanket clauses and committees reminiscent of comitology committees have been suggested.[2243] Additionally, existing self-regulation may gain a European background. This is the case for the creditors' establishment of the BKR and the Association for the Guarantee of Travel Sums ('*Stichting Garantiefonds Reisgelden*', SGR),[2244] in the area of package travel.

At first sight, radically new forms of governance have not become apparent in the Dutch legal order. The Dutch legislator has made significantly less use of forms of dynamic referral than in Germany, even though dynamic referral has been more severely criticised in Germany. Similarly to the German legal order, much self-regulation has developed on the basis of contract. Interestingly, various similar non-state actors may play an important role in both the Dutch and German legal order, which has led to the development of alternative regulation in similar fields. Thus, professional organisations, unions and sports organisations are left with extensive room to develop alternative regulation. In addition, self-regulation in the area of consumer sales and advertising[2245] are well developed, while similar initiatives for increasing the access to basic payment accounts, corporate governance, and corporate social responsibility are visible. Especially in areas where similarities arise, it may be attractive for actors to look at corresponding developments. It has been argued that the success of self-regulation could also be sought in the level of expertise, the support within a sector, the extent to which that sector is organised, and the clarity of rules contained in self-regulation. Societal pressure may further accelerate the development of self-regulation.[2246] Van Driel[2247] stated that for the effectiveness of self-regulation, it is imperative that a branch is sufficiently organised and is both legally and *de facto* able to enforce self-regulation.

On the one hand, the bottom-up approach in the Dutch legal order has not enhanced alternative regulation. To the contrary, the German framework has strengthened

2243 Comp. C.M.D.S. Pavillon, *Open normen in het Europees consumentenrecht*, Deventer: Kluwer 2011, p. 521–523, as well as W.D.H. Asser, H.A. Groen, J.B.M. Vranken, I.N. Tzankova, *Uitgebalanceerd. Eindrapport fundamentele herbezinning Nederlands burgerlijk procesrecht*, The Hague: BJU 2006, p. 253–261.

2244 The SGR was established after a number of bankruptcies, on the initiative of the Ministry for Economic Affairs and stakeholders. The SGR provides a refund if travellers have contracted with a SGR member that subsequently becomes insolvent. For more information see L.J.H. Mölenberg, M.L.A.M.J. Olivers, R.R.J.A. Hallmans, 'De Stichting garantiefonds Reisgelden; gegarandeerd verzekerd?' *TvC* 1990, p. 346. The majority of travel agents are members of the SGR: by being a member, travel agents fulfil the conditions that were later made in article 7 Directive 90/314 on package travel: '[t]he organiser and/or retailer party to the contract shall provide sufficient evidence of security for the refund of money paid over and for the repatriation of the consumer in the event of insolvency.'

2245 However, whereas the development of the Dutch code has taken place within the framework of article 6:162 BW, the German code expressly rejects this approach and instead seeks to provide ethical rules. The development of ethical rules can be a clear reason to leave the development of these rules to private actors, as state actors are not well placed to enforce rules that go beyond what is legally required. The different characterisation of the Dutch and German code also has consequences for the development of the code. In the Dutch legal order, compliance with the code should be increased by the cooperation between the *Consumentenautoriteit* and the *Stichting Reclame Code*, available at https://www.reclamecode.nl/bijlagen/11-7-2011_13_46_12.PDF./.

2246 B. Baarsma et al, *Zelf doen? Inventarisatie van zelfreguleringsinstrumenten*, SEO Report 664, 2003, p. 30–31.

2247 M. van Driel, *Zelfregulering: Hoog opspelen of thuisblijven*, Deventer: Kluwer 1989, p. 75–76.

alternative regulation in the following respects. Firstly, the constitutional background in the German legal order may improve the stable development of private law, as legislative intervention in areas where alternative regulation was established is likely to be better motivated. This may also motivate state actors to anticipate problems with enforcement. Consequently, initial problems of enforcement were tackled more efficiently in the German legal order than in the Dutch legal order, for example with regard to the corporate governance code. Secondly, the supervision in the German legal order seems a better guarantee for ensuring the inclusiveness of alternative regulation as well as the accessibility. In contrast, the European approach towards alternative regulation, as visible in the development of framework agreements or the EU code for online consumer rights, may undermine responsiveness, consistency, and accessibility, as it may lead to multiple sets of alternative regulation, and the relations between them may not be directly visible. In the Dutch legal order, forms of alternative regulation have not led to more *deliberation* between relevant Dutch actors. Instead, interaction takes the form of collective negotiations, and these may not necessarily be open processes. Even in processes where interaction has developed, problems with compliance demonstrate that interaction has not served to make alternative regulation more accessible to directly interested parties; consumers are insufficiently aware of the GBL and of codes of conduct of energy suppliers. A more active approach could support further interaction more in line with deliberation. Thirdly, the more active approach of German state actors has benefited the responsiveness of alternative regulation, for example in the area of social corporate responsibility. This can be contrasted with the Dutch legal order where weak alternative regulation that does not cope well with problematic business practices may more easily continue to exist. Interestingly, it has been argued that the prominent inclusion of private actors may affect the development of legislation, if, for example, interdependence between state actors and non-state actors develops and the threat of legislative intervention decreases, or if well-organised non-state actors play a prominent role, which may make state actors less decisive.[2248] This may be an interesting explanation for the lack of intervention of the Dutch legislator in problematic forms of self-regulation.

On the other hand, because Dutch state actors have imposed less limitations on alternative regulation, there is more room for experimentation and mutual learning, which has benefited alternative regulation. Accordingly, a large amount of alternative regulation has developed in many areas, which may inspire foreign or international actors. Interesting Dutch examples are mass settlements on the basis of contractual settlements and the introduction of a national prejudicial procedure. Additionally, many codes of conduct have developed in the Dutch legal order. Some of these codes, especially in the area of consumer sales, may be interesting for foreign businesses, but the accessibility of these codes of conduct and trust marks depends on the question of whether the codes, trust marks and collectively negotiated STCs are sufficiently available to foreign businesses that may not have an extensive command of Dutch. Other codes of conduct are currently less known among Dutch consumers. However, if courts choose to bind businesses who have committed themselves to these codes, this could change, and

[2248] U. Di Fabio, 'Verlust der Steuerungskraft klassischer Rechtsquellen', *NZS* 1998, p. 450.

provide an interesting source of information to foreign or transnational actors. Collectively negotiated STCs are also well-established and relatively successful. However, the attractiveness of this option for other Member States also depends on the question of whether the use of collectively negotiated STCs is limited under Directive 93/13.

The development of regimes may also be the result of or lead to regulatory competition. However, the development of innovative rules in the absence of regulatory competition, such as the rules on collective redress, indicate that innovation may well develop in the absence of competition. These rules may prompt further competition, which provides actors with an extra incentive to develop innovative rules, including non-state actors. Ribstein and O'Hara[2249] have pointed out that the concept of the law market is not oriented towards legislation, but may also include alternative regulation, and competition may also take place between state and non-state actors. Regulatory competition may also develop between sets of alternative regulation, especially as non-state actors may be more internationally oriented than state actors. Whereas state law often takes national concepts as a starting point, non-state actors frequently emphasise the relevance of international developments – they may be members of international organisations,[2250] or codes may be modelled on international organisations,[2251] or they may find that representation at a transnational level may be useful as transnational rules are well suited to deal with transnational practices. In this context, non-state actors may seek take foreign and international developments into account, as was the case for the *Nachhaltigkeitskodex*[2252] and the corporate governance *Kodex*.[2253] The more international orientation of non-state actors is in accordance with the observation of Micklitz that convergence is more feasible in areas where private actors dominate.[2254]

Notwithstanding the central role of national state actors in a Dutch framework, it should take into account that in some cases, European actors and non-state actors are better placed to develop rules than national state actors. Thus, in accordance with pluralist insights that the reallocation of competences increases responsiveness, the existence of European actors may pressure actors to justify divergences or take into account the interests of non-national actors. However, so far, initiatives from European state actors have not prompted Dutch actors to reconsider Dutch self-regulation.

2249 E.A. O'Hara, L.E. Ribstein, *The law market*, Oxford: OUP 2009, p. 224.

2250 This is especially the case for sports associations.

2251 For example, the DRSC is modelled on successful international and foreign organisations, and may advise the Ministry with regard to legislative initiatives on accounting standards and a representation of Germany in international accounting organisations. See further MunchKomm zum HGB/Ebke/Paal, article 342, nr 3. W.D. Budde, E. Steubner, 'Normsetzungsbefugnis eines deutschen Standard Setting Body', *DStR* 1998, p. 1181 note that the development of article 342 HGB can be traced back to Directive 78/660.

2252 For example, internationally developed standards for reporting on sustainable development, such as the standards from the Global Reporting Initiative (GRI), have been taken as a starting point in the drafting of the *Nachhaltigkeitskodex* RNE, *Der Deutsche Nachhaltigkeitskodex*, version of January 2012, p. 3.

2253 Ringleb, 'Vorbemerkung', Ringleb et al (eds.), Deutscher Corporate Governance Kodex, 4th ed., 2010, VI, nr. 29 et seq.

2254 H.-W. Micklitz, 'Monistic ideology versus pluralistic reality: Towards a normative design for European private law', in: L. Niglia (ed.), *Pluralism and European private law*, Oxford: Hart 2013, p. 49.

Directive 93/13 did not prompt the Dutch legislator to reconsider collectively bargained STCs or model contracts. In contrast, initiatives from European and international non-state actors have inspired Dutch and European actors in the area of unfair advertising and consumer sales.

Thus, contrary to legal formalist views, a Dutch framework should facilitate the development of private law in many different forms, and the development of private law may include many different actors, which may provide opportunities for more responsiveness, and mutual learning.

8.6.4. The development of private law in the light of radical pluralist arguments

Despite the increasing role of non-state actors, national state actors retain a central role in the development of private law. The previous chapter has already argued that the development of "strong" versions of legal pluralism, without an overarching framework, is problematic. Accordingly, German actors have imposed limitations on the scope of forms of self-regulation developed in accordance with pluralist insights, for example the limitation of dynamic referral in the *lex sportiva*.[2255] Accordingly, this chapter has argued for a normative framework, which would be beneficial for private law.

However, this framework need not stand in the way of the development of alternative regulation. Eventually, it may form a starting point to critically consider why private law should be developed through legislation rather than alternative regulation, if the legislative process shows shortcomings. More generally, has the development of private law in accordance with pluralist perspectives become visible? Particularly, Akkermans[2256] has argued that, rather than considering law as being developed by the legislator and the courts, a new paradigm should be more in accordance with the large diversity of groups that contribute to private law and interact with one another. Thus, the development of private law in the traditional sense, through the legislator and the judiciary on the one hand, and the development of private law through self-regulation on the other hand should no longer be a primary distinction. However, in the framework defended in this and the previous chapter, the binding force and the scope of alternative regulation continues to depend on the approval of national or European state actors, and state actors therefore retain a central role. This is even the case in areas where non-state actors develop rules in a relatively autonomous space.[2257] The development of internal rules for associations can be seen in this light, as well as self-regulation for sports' organisations.

In a pluralist legal order, where multiple claims to authority coexist, which bodies should have claims to authority? At first sight, it seems likely that in the absence of consistent limitations and in accordance with Dutch actors' *laissez-faire* approach, successful alternative regulation by different bodies have developed, and claims to

2255 See previously par. 7.5.2.7.

2256 A.J. Akkermans, 'Beter recht door herziening van ons beeld van de herkomst van rechtsnormen', *NTBR* 2011, 72.

2257 N. Walker, 'The idea of constitutional pluralism', *MLR* 2002, p. 355.

authority over different matters accordingly coexist. However, where prominent self-regulation has developed, this has happened because the legislator has expressly decided to abstain from legislation. In areas where multiple, overlapping rules have developed, such as in franchise contracts, these have not consistently been taken into account by the courts. In consumer sales, multiple, overlapping codes do exist, but the rules in these codes do not drastically diverge and should be in line with mandatory law.

If an optimal polity is an optimal mix of deliberation, inclusion and strength of argument for pursuing specific goals,[2258] one may ask whether developing initiatives on collective redress, especially if it concerns cross-border matters, does not warrant more involvement of more international actors or European actors that have already developed rules on the competence of courts and the recognition of judicial decisions throughout the Union. Similarly, local actors are more likely to adequately identify consumers' wishes, and it seems that international and European non-state actors have succeeded in drafting forms of alternative regulation that are sufficiently attractive for businesses to adopt. This success justifies more involvement of these local and international actors in the development of European measures that aim to increase consumer confidence. From this perspective, in accordance with the conclusions in the case studies, it is not clear why the European legislator is well placed to provide rules for domestic consumer sales, especially not if measures are not prompted by concerns of businesses interested in trading throughout the Union.[2259]

In other cases, parties' expertise may be a reason to include them. Yet the Dutch experience with corporate governance code and with the GBL makes clear that even if non-state actors draft self-regulation, they do not necessarily comply with standards. In addition, even wide participation may not ensure that interested parties are familiar with the code. This lack of accessibility may in turn raise questions on the suitability of extensive drafting processes to prevent *Fremdbestimmung* and to foster responsiveness and familiarity with self-regulation, at least in the Dutch legal order. Additionally, the simultaneous initiatives of European and national actors in the development of the banking codes indicate that arguments for an optimal polity are considered differently. On the one hand, action at the European level may be lengthy, which is problematic if problems require immediate intervention. On the other hand, national measures may be more easily circumvented by multinational actors. Arguably, a combination of cooperation and competition, in accordance with arguments for regulatory co-opetition,[2260] would have been beneficial. The lack of a coordinated approach in this area has accordingly been criticised.[2261]

2258 N. Krisch, *Beyond constitutionalism: The pluralist structure of postnational law*, Oxford: OUP 2010, p. 101.

2259 See previously par. 4.3.2.1.

2260 D.C. Esty, D. Geradin, 'Regulatory co-opetition', *Journal of International Economic Law* 2000, p. 235.

2261 G.T.M.J. Raaijmakers, 'De financiële markt en het ondernemingsrecht', *Ondernemingsrecht* 2009, 104.

8.6.5. Starting points for mutual recognition

Currently, neither Dutch nor European actors have developed an approach towards the development of European private law as critically and consistently as German actors have. It has been argued that developing a more consistent approach at the European level would be beneficial.[2262] This chapter has argued for the development of a normative framework at the national level on the basis of private autonomy and *Fremdbestimmung*.

If European and Dutch actors simultaneously develop a more consistent and clear perspective on the role of actors, conflicts may become more outspoken, as already indicated in current criticism of European forms of alternative regulation. However, as the principle of private autonomy and concerns with regard to *Fremdbestimmung* have been recognised at both the European level and at the national level, they could provide a starting point for mutual respect, as currently visible in CJEU and BVerfG decisions.[2263] This means that Dutch actors should not subject European initiatives to additional scrutiny, unless they are clearly contrary to fundamental principles. However, in the absence of scrutiny of European measures by the CJEU, it does not seem likely that outspoken scrutiny will be developed. In turn, European actors should not undermine the developing Dutch framework. European measures should not undermine successful, well-established self-regulation.

[2262] See previously par. 7.6.4.
[2263] See previously par. 7.3.2.2.

Chapter 9

THE USE OF NATIONAL TECHNIQUES IN THE DEVELOPMENT OF EUROPEAN PRIVATE LAW

9.1. Introduction

The case studies[2264] found that the coexistence of actors had generally not benefited the quality of the law on STCs, contrary to pluralist arguments. However, the previous chapters have indicated that instances of innovation and mutual learning have developed, and regulatory competition may provide actors with an additional incentive to develop innovative rules. In addition, European initiatives – especially initiatives from non-state actors, and, otherwise, especially in already internationalised fields – have prompted actors to take into account the interests of non-national actors. It follows that in some cases, the coexistence of actors has proven beneficial. It has been argued that the development of a framework, based on the principle of private autonomy and concerns of *Fremdbestimmung* where national state actors retain a prominent role, will likely help to improve European private law.

According to pluralist perspectives, the coexistence of actors may also strengthen European private law developed through national techniques. However, the case studies[2265] indicated that the use of national techniques has not been amended to take into account interdependence. Especially in the Dutch case study, the lack of interaction between courts has led to inconsistency and unpredictability. Both in German and the Dutch legal order, the restraint of national and European actors has limited the responsive development of the *acquis*. More generally, national and European actors have adopted a narrow approach in the debate on the further development of European private law.[2266] This chapter asks whether these problems and the lack of benefits are visible more widely, or whether the coexistence of actors has benefited European private law developed through national techniques.

Paragraph 9.2 will discuss the use of codifications and paragraph 9.3 will turn to the use of soft laws. Subsequently, paragraph 9.4 will consider blanket clauses and paragraph 9.5 will analyse the use of general principles. Paragraph 9.6 will draw general conclusions.

2264 See previously par. 4.6.2. and 5.6.2.

2265 See previously par. 4.6.1. and 5.6.1.

2266 See previously par. 6.2.

9.2. The use of codifications in a multilevel legal order

Dutch and German actors have not taken interdependence as a starting point in their interaction with other actors or in the development of the law on STCs through codifications and problems of responsiveness, consistency and predictability have been signalled in the case studies.[2267] Is this approach of actors more widely visible and have problems more generally developed or has the coexistence of actors strengthened the comprehensibility of European private law, in accordance with pluralist perspectives?

This paragraph will focus on two instances where actors may be especially prompted to reconsider the development of private law through the BW and the BGB in the light of interdependence. Paragraph 9.2.1 will ask whether actors have considered decreased independence in the implementation of the private law *acquis* into codifications more generally, and the extent to which this influences the predictable, consistent, accessible and responsive development of European private law. Subsequently, paragraph 9.2.2 will ask whether actors have considered the decreased extent to which codifications to develop the law accessibly, consistently, precitably and responsively in private international law, an area of law that often has an inherent cross-border aspect. Paragraph 9.2.3 will end with a conclusion.

9.2.1. The implementation of the acquis *within codifications*

Why have the German and Dutch legislator emphasised the role of the codification in the ongoing development and implementation of the private law *acquis* and have legislators sufficiently recognised the capability of codifications to ensure the comprehensibility of private law in the light of the ongoing development of the private law *acquis*?

Both the German and the Dutch legislator have opted to implement the private law *acquis* into national codifications for the following reasons.

1) The implementation of Directives into the Civil Code furthers the accessibility of private law as the national Civil Code retains a prominent role for national private law.

Rösler[2268] adds that implementing the *acquis* into the Civil Code also enhances the visibility of consumer contract law and might lead to the simplification of private law. This argument is, however, not very convincing as implementation of consumer law within the Civil Code can simultaneously lead to problems of clarity and accessibility. The European background of many provisions implemented in the Civil Code is unclear, and parties may, therefore, overlook relevant CJEU case law.

2267 See previously par. 4.6.1. and 5.6.1.

2268 H. Rösler, 'Europeanisation of private law through Directives – determining factors and modalities of implementation', *European Journal of Law Reform* 2010, p. 316–317.

2) The development of specific laws alongside the Civil Code, which might lead to fragmented development of private law, and resulting inconsistencies, is prevented.[2269]

However, in the German legal order, the aim to retain the important role of the BGB[2270] may arguably be undermined by the simultaneous development of legislation implementing the private law *acquis*[2271] alongside the BGB.[2272] Yet the German experience with the AGBG[2273] indicates that the development of private law alongside the BGB need not necessarily result in inconsistencies.

Similarly, the decision of the Dutch legislator to implement Directive 2013/11 on consumer ADR and Directive 2008/52 on mediation outside the BW undermines a consistent approach towards the implementation of the *acquis*, despite the advice of the Raad van State,[2274] pointing out that this course weakens rather than strengthen accessibility, clarity and coherence.

Moreover, the implementation within the Civil Code does not effectively inhibit the fragmented and inconsistent development of private law; rather, the development of fragmented, specific laws at the national level is prevented. The development of private law by the European legislator and the CJEU takes place regardless of the rules within the national Civil Codes, or the subsequent implementation of those rules into the code, which may well lead to inconsistencies. The implementation of European concepts that are identical to the national concepts within the Civil Code may lead to the development of identical concepts with divergent meanings within one law.[2275] Arguably, if such concepts are to be introduced, implementation should preferably take place outside the Civil Code, or in a separate part of the code, as this could at least indicate that concepts in these laws, although identical to concepts in the Civil Code, may have to be interpreted differently, in accordance with European law.

Maybe experiences from other legislators will show that implementation within separate books of a code, or even separate legislation, may also ensure the interrelation between different provisions within the code.

3) The Dutch legislator[2276] holds that, by implementing the private law *acquis* within the Civil Code, it becomes clear which parts of simultaneously applicable private law should be reconciled with the *acquis*.

It can be doubted whether this implementation technique has been successful in this respect, as also became visible in the case studies. The rules on the unfairness of STCs and the effects of

2269 *Handelingen I*, 2004/05, 28 874, nr. 17, p. 759–760.

2270 R. Zimmerman, *The new German law of obligations*, Oxford: OUP, 2005, p. 226.

2271 Comp. for example the *Produkthaftungsgesetz* (Product Liability Act), or the *Wohnungseigentumsgesetz* (Act on the property of residences).

2272 R. Zimmerman, *The new German law of obligations*, Oxford: OUP 2005, p. 198.

2273 See previously par. 4.2. and 4.3.1.1.

2274 *Kamerstukken II*, 2013–2014, 33982, nr 4, p. 3–4. The Minister, in his response, rejected these arguments as he found that the provisions of the Directive concerned public rather than private law, and remarked that the close deadline for implementation of the Directive stood in the way of a drastic reconsideration of the proposal.

2275 W.-H. Roth, 'Europäischer Verbraucherschutz und BGB', *JZ* 2001, p. 482, speaks of *Begriffsinseln* as well as *Begriffsspaltungen* within the Civil Code.

2276 *Handelingen I*, 2004/05, 28 874, nr. 17, p. 760, similarly H. Rösler, 'Europeanisation of private law through Directives – determining factors and modalities of implementation', *European Journal of Law Reform* 2010, p. 317.

unfairness have been interpreted in conformity with the national principle of fairness in article 6:248 BW rather than in conformity with European rules.[2277] Similarly, German courts have shown restraint in referring questions on the interpretation of article 307 BGB to the CJEU as it concerns a central notion of German law.[2278] In addition, German case law on STCs developed on the basis of article 242 BGB, and the idea that STCs should be subjected to judicial evaluation is still based on the notion that the user of STCs may have misused the freedom of contract to impose rules to his advantage on his contract party, which is more generally contrary to good faith.[2279]

4) By implementing the *acquis* within the Civil Code, the coherence established by the Civil Code should be preserved

It may be doubted whether this is possible at all, because the EU legislator, in the ongoing harmonisation of private law, does not consider the coherence of private law at a national level.[2280] Also, implementing the *acquis* within the Civil Code may make the code vulnerable with regard to amendments as well as new harmonisation – as the *acquis* is reformed, the Civil Code will have to be amended as well, and as harmonisation of private law continues, the Civil Code will have to be increasingly adapted. Accordingly, Zimmerman,[2281] finds that incorporation did not improve the quality of the BGB, but instead brought with it the need for repeated amendments after the 2002 reform. The need to regularly amend the Civil Code in accordance with the *acquis*, the development of which may be hard to predict, may in that case also undermine the stable – and thereby predictable – development of private law.

The case studies already indicated that the question whether the private law *acquis* should be incorporated in the BGB or not should also be seen against the distinction between the BGB and *Sonderprivatrecht*.[2282] Whereas the BGB contains rules on general private law, *Sonderprivatrecht* seeks to develop rules targeted at a specific group such as consumers, usually from a political perspective. As the development of such special rules is considered to be less stable, keeping these rules outside the BGB may reduce the need to regularly amend the BGB – which is in accordance with the stable development of the BGB – and maintain the coherence of general private law. Thus, the choice whether to implement the *acquis* within the BGB also depends on the question whether one finds that the *acquis* provides rules of general private law or whether one finds that they pursue special aims. It is not clear on what basis this distinction is made – the incorporation of a large range of Directives in the area of consumer contract law indicates that the origin of Directives and their aims do not set them apart as *Sonderprivatrecht*.

On the one hand, the incorporation of Directives into the BGB may be defended as especially Directive 99/44 on consumer sales contains rules that are a central part of national contract laws. Zimmerman[2283] approves of the incorporation of consumer law into the BGB, as it concerns

2277 Comp. HR 14 June 2002, *NJ* 2003, 112.

2278 B. Heiderhoff, 'Die Berücksichtigung des Art. 3 Klauselrichtlinie bei der AGB-Kontrolle', *WM* 2003, p. 510.

2279 MunchKomm zum BGB/Wurmnest (2012), introduction to article 307, nr 11.

2280 W.H. van Boom, 'Algemene en bijzondere regelingen in het vermogensrecht', *RM Themis* 2003, p. 299–300.

2281 R. Zimmerman, *The new German law of obligations*, Oxford: OUP 2005, p. 201.

2282 See, par. 4.3.1.1.

2283 R. Zimmerman, *The new German law of obligations*, Oxford: OUP 2005, p. 224. Zimmerman noted that German academics were uncharacteristically divided on the *Schuldrechtsmodernisierung*. See for a different option for example W. Ernst, B. Gsell, 'Kaufrechtslinie und BGB', *ZIP* 2000, p. 1410. See especially critically W. Flume, 'Vom Beruf unserer Zeit zur Gesetzgebung', *ZIP* 2000, p. 1427 (on the implementation of Directive 97/7).

general contract law, and pursues an end similar to general contract law, i.e. protecting parties' substantive freedom of choice when they enter into a contract. These rules may, therefore, be seen in the light of more general questions of private autonomy and *Fremdbestimmung* underpinning the BGB.[2284] In particular, Zimmerman[2285] finds that consumer contract law should not be based on 'loosely defined social concerns'.

On the other hand, the idea that consumer contract law established by the EU pursues general aims of contract law in a manner comparable to German private law is not self-evident. Rather, looking at the Directives reveals that the *acquis* hardly seems to be based on maintaining the balance between parties – instead, it seems to be based on loosely defined economic concerns, while the question of whether general principles underpin the private law *acquis* is subject to debate, in line with the findings in the case studies.[2286] In particular, private autonomy and concerns of *Fremdbestimmung* were not discussed during the drafting of the Directive.

National legislators are well aware of the need to deal with ongoing harmonisation. Retaining the BGB and the BW is an important consideration in the implementation of the *acquis*. The implementation of the *acquis* within these codes further facilitates the interpretation of the *acquis* in accordance with national law, even if the European legislator adopts detailed measures to harmonise private law that are subsequently interpreted by the CJEU[2287] as also visible in the case studies.[2288] The aims of codifications are stressed without considering whether the development of the *acquis* makes it more difficult to achieve these aims. Further, the reasons for implementing the *acquis* within or outside of codifications are not based on a clear, consistent strategy. In other words, national legislators adopt a defensive approach in the implementation of the *acquis* in codifications. As a result, problems of predictability, consistency and responsiveness are likely to develop more widely.

9.2.2. *The use of codifications in areas of private law with a cross-border aspect*

Has the development of international private law been a reason for legislators to critically consider the extent to which codifications contribute to consistency, accessibility and predictability?

National legislators[2289] are inclined to preserve codification even in areas that have an inherently transnational character and that have become increasingly harmonised, as is the case for international private law.

2284 See previously par. 7.5.1.1.

2285 R. Zimmerman, *The new German law of obligations*, Oxford: OUP 2005, p. 225.

2286 See par. 4.5.2.

2287 Comp. M. Delmas-Marty, *Ordering pluralism, A conceptual framework for understanding the transnational world*, Oxford: Hart 2009, p. 56 who emphasises the need for supervision bodies to prevent that international and European law become renationalised.

2288 See par. 4.3., 4.4., and 5.3. and 5.4.

2289 S. Symeonides, 'Codification and flexibility in private international law', *General reports to the XVIIIth Congress of the International Academy of Comparative Law/ Rapports*, 2011, p. 5–10, with an extensive

The German legislator initially opted for codification in the EGBGB. The German legislator codified private international law in articles 3 et seq EGBGB in 1986, as BVerfG case law necessitated the reform of private international law.[2290] Originally, there was debate as to whether the development of private international law should be left to international law, which was an argument against the inclusion of private international law in the BGB.[2291] Kropholler[2292] held that international law had improved the quality of German private international law, but also found that as internationalisation increased, the codification would increasingly be overshadowed and replaced by relevant treaties. If international law was applicable, Kropholler, therefore, preferred referral to international law to incorporation. The 1986 reform did not abolish private international law outside of the EGBGB that existed in separate laws, treaties and customary law.[2293]

However, the German legislator has reconsidered its approach. Whereas, in the 1986 reform, future EU initiatives were a reason for the German legislator to abstain from providing rules in the area of non-contractual obligations,[2294] the German legislator took a more active approach in the 1999 reform. The German legislator did provide rules for non-contractual obligations, notwithstanding simultaneous developments at the European level, apparently in an attempt to influence the future Regulation.[2295] It is not apparent that the development of harmonisation has prompted the German legislator to revise the law in accordance with the needs and preferences of foreign and international actors.

After Regulations Rome I and II, the German legislator abandoned overlapping national private international law.[2296] The German legislator did retain articles 40–42 EGBGB on non-contractual obligations as Regulation Rome II did not provide a sufficiently comprehensive regime to justify abolishing these provisions. However, the scope of articles 40–42 EGBGB was considerably reduced by the Regulation.[2297]

Further, the difficulties in maintaining coherence at the national level when private international law is developed at the European or international level have been considered, and the legislative approach to future European initiatives has also been considered. This consideration may be beneficial for private international law as it has provided the European legislator with a set of rules that it may take as an example in drafting European initiatives.

overview of the number of codifications of international private law, detects an international tendency for the codification of international private law.

2290 See further Max Planck Institute für ausländisches und internationales Privatrecht, 'Kodifikation des deutschen Internationalen Privatrechts. Stellungnahme des Max-Planck-Instituts für ausländisches und internationales Privatrecht zum Regierungsentwurf von 1983', *RabelsZ* 1983, p. 595.

2291 O. Hartwieg, 'Der Gesetzgeber des EGBGB zwischen den Fronten heutiger Kollisionrechts-Theorien', *RabelsZ* 1978, p. 431.

2292 J. Kropholler, 'Der Einfluß der Haager Übereinkommen auf die deutsche IPR-Kodifikation', *RabelsZ* 1993, p. 222.

2293 Schulze/BGB/Dörner (2012), introduction to articles 3–6 EGBGB, nr 9–10.

2294 MunchKomm zum BGB/Junker (2010), introduction to article 38 EGBGB, nr 2.

2295 Comp. A. Spickhoff, 'Die Restkodifikation des Internationalen Privatrechts: Außervertragliches Schuld- und Sachenrecht ', *NJW* 1999, p. 2214–2215, who notes that the 1999 reform took place in the light of European developments.

2296 BT-Drucks. 16/12104. It concerns in particular articles 27–37 EGBGB.

2297 MunchKomm zum BGB/Junker (2010), introduction to article 38 EGBGB, nr 38.

The development of legislation prior to harmonisation is reminiscent of the influence of the German law on STCs on Directive 93/13, which more generally has limited unpredictability and inconsistency that may arise after harmonisation.[2298] Similarly, the consistency and stable development of German private international law may benefit from the German legislator's initiative.

The introduction of the law in the German legal order provided an opportunity to experiment with these rules, which should make visible in which respects these rules were successful or problematic. Accordingly, problematic rules will be adapted and successful rules will be adopted. The European legislator has realised an opportunity for learning, which should benefit the development of the law in this area.[2299] Notably, the BGB does not stand in the way for opportunities for mutual learning, contrary to pluralist arguments.

In contrast, the Dutch legislator has not sought to influence European initiatives by reforming the law. Accordingly, in 2001, the Dutch legislator developed private international law on non-contractual obligations, without referring to simultaneous European developments.[2300] These rules were abandoned after Regulation Rome II was established, and the Dutch legislator extended the rules of the Regulation to cover areas falling outside its scope.[2301]

Further, the Dutch legislator did not critically consider the possibility that the aims of codifications can be undermined by European or international initiatives. Instead the Dutch legislator has emphasised the benefits of codification in the drafting of book 10. Particularly, the Dutch legislator maintains that the development of a code benefits accessibility.[2302] In the view of the Dutch legislator, the chance that national provisions may gain a European background[2303] and ongoing harmonisation strengthens the need for a national codification of international private law.

However, relevant questions for the capability of codifications to independently achieve accessibility, as well as predictability, consistency and responsiveness have not been sufficiently recognised. Specifically, the question to what extent the national legislator can still offer a framework for international private law in the light of international and European initiatives, has been debated in the Dutch legal order when Book 10 of the BW

2298 See previously par. 4.3.2.1.

2299 This opportunity for learning contradicts that the observation of L. Miller, *The emergence of EU contract law: Exploring Europeanization*, Oxford: OUP 2011, p. 196, that actors should pay attention to the form of contract law instruments which may facilitate or hinder "the free movement of ideas", and that 'rigid codes' may stand in the way of mutual learning.

2300 *Kamerstukken II*, 26608, 2000–2001, nr. 3.

2301 *Kamerstukken II*, 2009–2010, 32137, nr 3, p. 87.

2302 Similarly, M.V. Polak, 'Oppassen – inpassen – aanpassen. Taken en bevoegdheden van wetgever en rechter bij de receptie van internationaal en communautair IPR in de Nederlandse rechtsorde', in: C.A. Joustra, M.V. Polak, *Internationaal, communautair en nationaal IPR (Mededelingen van de vereniging voor Internationaal Recht 2002)*, The Hague: Asser Press 2002, p. 95–96 argues that especially considering the fragmented nature of harmonised private international law, it might be beneficial for legal practice to oversee the rules in private international law in a particular subject, rather than categorising the different rules of private international law in accordance with the different actors issuing that particular set of rules.

2303 *Kamerstukken II*, 2009/10, 32 137, nr. 3, p. 4.

came into effect in 2012.[2304] Codification cannot prevent the development of private international law alongside the code, which may necessitate further amendments to the code,[2305] which may undermine the predictable development of private law in the code. Codification does also not ensure the consistent development of international private law at the European level. Additionally, as the territorial scope of codifications is limited to the territory of a state, it may be asked whether codifications are particularly suitable to deal with cross-border issues such as international private law.[2306] Also, importantly, the aim of Book 10 to improve accessibility has already been undermined by the development of various Directives[2307] that contain international private law provisions, which have been implemented in the various parts of the Civil Code[2308] and other laws.[2309] This is unlike the German approach, where article 46b EGBGB provides an overview of areas where particular conflict rules, following from Directives, apply.[2310]

It may be concluded that the Dutch legislator has not sufficiently recognised interdependence, which has necessitated amendments in recently reformed laws, and the accessibility, predictability and consistency of private international law may be diminished.

9.2.3. *Conclusion on the use of codifications*

Have Dutch and German actors more generally failed to take interdependence as a starting point in their interaction with other actors or in the development of the law

2304 H.U. Jessurun d'Oliveira, 'Is een codificatie van het Nederlandse IPR nog zinvol? Oftewel, geloven we nog in Boek 10?' *NTBR* 2005, p. 428, A.V.M. Struycken, 'Veelheid van rechtsbronnen: één IPR?' *AA* 1996, p. 68, remarks that the existence of multiple sources of international private law makes the codification of IPR more difficult ('De veelsoortigheid van rechtsbronnen is een gegeven dat de codificatie van het IPR bemoeilijkt.'), see also V. van den Eeckhout, 'Codificatie van het Nederlands ipr of het vastleggen van een nationaal navigatiesysteem voor internationale vliegroutes', *NTER* 2011, p. 10.

2305 Comp. for example the adaptation of article 6 par. 2 Directive 93/13 on unfair terms in consumer contracts, article 12 par. 2 Directive 97/7 on distance contracts, repealed by Directive 2011/83 on consumer rights, or article 9 Directive 94/47 on timeshare, modified by article 12 par. 2 Directive 2008/122 on timeshare.

2306 Other objections that have been made is that codifications do not leave sufficient room for the flexible, judicial development of international private law, while flexibility is necessary in international private law. However, the Dutch codification shows quite clearly that codifications may leave sufficient room for judicial development, at least at a national level. Whether this would also be true for codifications at another level may be doubted. Comp. also S. Symeonides, 'Codification and flexibility in private international law', *General reports to the XVIIIth congress of the International Academy of Comparative Law/ Rapports*, 2011.

2307 For example article 12 Directive 93/7 on the return of cultural objects, article 9 Directive 2002/47 on financial collateral arrangements, article 12 Directive 2002/65, or article 22 par 4 Directive 2008/48.

2308 See for example article 7:73, implementing article 22 par. 4 Directive 2008/48 on consumer credit, article 7:50i par. 3, implementing article 12 par. 2 Directive 2008/122 on timeshare. See critically on this approach V. Heutger, 'De toekomst van richtlijn 87/102 betreffende consumentenovereenkomsten', in: A.S. Hartkamp, C.H. Sieburgh, L.A.D. Keus (eds.), *De invloed van het Europese recht op het Nederlandse privaatrecht II*, Deventer: Kluwer 2007, p. 95.

2309 See for example article 1012 Civil Procedure Code, implementing article 12 Directive 93/7 on the return of cultural objects.

2310 See further MunchKomm zum BGB/Martiny (2012), article 46b EGBGB, nr 4 et seq.

through respectively the BW and the BGB, and if so, have problems in terms of predictability, consistency and responsiveness become visible more widely?

Firstly, neither the German and Dutch legislator's choice for the incorporation of the *acquis* within respectively the BGB and BW has been based on interaction with other actors; instead, in both legal orders, maintaining codifications played a large role. Interestingly, the approach of the German legislator can be contrasted with its previous approach towards the implementation of the *acquis* in separate legislation. This change makes clear that even if the German legislator initially did not insist on incorporation, the harmonisation of central areas of private law makes it unattractive for legislators to implement the *acquis* outside the code. The Dutch legislator was much more focused on retaining its codification that had just been established as the *acquis* began to develop. However, even if this had not been the case, one may ask whether the codification principle in 107 Gw does not limit the Dutch legislator's choices in the implementation of the *acquis*. If measures cover central areas of contract, tort or – less likely – property law, can the Dutch legislator still implement these measures outside of the BGB? For both legislators, retaining the code has been a decisive reason to implement the *acquis* within the codification, notwithstanding the diminished ability of codes to ensure predictability, consistency, accessibility and responsiveness.

However, legislators in other legal orders do not necessarily share that opinion. If codes already distinguish between consumer codes and general codifications, implementation outside of the general code is more consistent with the existing approach to consumer law.[2311] In short, the choice how to implement the *acquis* depends not only on the abstract strengths and weaknesses of a codification in the multilevel legal order. Instead, the choice to implement the *acquis* is predetermined by the way in which private law has developed within a legal order, and legislators will therefore primarily focus on their own legal order. This may explain why legislators seem especially interested in learning from actors with similar backgrounds, as became visible in the German case study.[2312] This reasoning supports the comparison of "path-dependency" in the development of private law.[2313]

Nevertheless, interaction with European actors and other legislators is valuable as it may indicate whether legislators need to take further harmonisation initiatives into account. Alternatively, the experience of other actors with many separate laws, or with older codifications may indicate whether the development of separate legislation is necessarily problematic – depending on the approach of the judiciary and the existence of adequate handbooks – and in which ways the private law *acquis* can be implemented within codifications.

2311 Comp. L. Miller, *The emergence of EU contract law: Exploring Europeanization*, Oxford: OUP 2011, p. 94–96 who describes the debate in the French implementation of Directive 1999/44 on consumer sales. Miller describes the two possible choices: limiting the implementation to the Code de la consommation and extending the implementation to the Code Civil. This latter option would eventually entail that the distinction between these regimes would disappear.

2312 See par. 4.3.1.2. Particularly, the drafters of the comparative report noted that The Netherlands and Switzerland had comparative codifications.

2313 Comp. C.-H. Ladeur, 'Methodology and European law – can methodology change so as to cope with the multiplicity of the law?', in: M. van Hoecke (ed.) *Epistemology and methodology of comparative law*, Oxford: Hart 2004, p. 98.

Secondly, the approach of the German and Dutch legislator towards the codification of private international law differs. The German legislator is more inclined to interact with especially European actors, defending German law as a blueprint for European law, as also became visible in the case study.[2314] This approach is also particularly visible in its 1999 initiative on private international law in non-contractual obligations. Notably, the 1999 initiative provided a set of rules that could serve as an example, which increases the chance that developments at the European level that are undesirable in the German view – in particular, inconsistencies between European rules and national law – are prevented or amended. Yet as more legislators opt for this approach, the influence of individual proposals may decline. In other words, as more national actors defend their laws as blueprints for European law, their individual influence may diminish, depending on the quality of the blueprint. Importantly, however, this approach does allow for thorough debate based on various options, which may contribute to the eventual outcome of the debate, provided that actors are willing to accept compromises.

Arguably, this has benefited the stable development of German private international law that did no have to be amended as often as Dutch law. The Regulation also showed less inconsistencies with German law, but whether this will remain the case depends on the future development of the Regulation by the CJEU.

The Dutch legislator has not similarly considered its approach to codification in the light of European and international initiatives, and has had to amend newly established law. Nevertheless, it is not apparent that Dutch law is less comprehensible than German law. Although it has taken a less active approach than the German legislator, the Dutch legislator does not fail to interact and it is hardly the only legislator to establish a code on private international law. Book 10 BW arguably is more accessible than German private international law, but the EGBGB provides a better overview of diverging rules following from the private law *acquis*. Yet as considerable parts of book 10 directly refer to Regulation Rome I, the Dutch approach is less likely than German law to lead to inconsistencies between remaining private international law and harmonised private international law. The choice of the Dutch legislator to extend the scope of Rome II rather than maintain national provisions may further decrease the chance of future inconsistencies, unless future European initiatives develop that differ from Rome II.

In other areas, both the German[2315] and the Dutch[2316] legislator have anticipated Directives. In these cases, the Union may benefit from national experiences in the case of anticipated implementation. If implementation precedes harmonisation, this may make visible how a Directive or Regulation works in practice.

2314 See previously par. 4.3.2.1.

2315 The German legislator anticipated the doorstep selling Directive. See further P. Gilles, 'Das Gesetz über den Widerruf von Haustürgeschäften und ähnlichen Geschäften – Anmerkungen zum jüngsten Verbraucherschutzsondergesetz im Zivilrecht unter Berücksichtigung seines rechtspolitischen Gesamtkontextes', *NJW* 1986, p. 1135–1136.

2316 Originally, the Dutch legislator anticipated European initiatives for more stringent professional rules of conduct for auditors, in particular the suggestion for mandatory rotation of auditors, see COM (2011) 779/3 p. 8. This has however, been postponed. Comp. the letter from the Minister of Finance of 7 December 2012, nr FM/2012/1856 M and *Kamerstukken I*, 2011–2012, 33025, nr J, stating that European legislation should only be anticipated if this is urgently necessary.

More generally, the development of the *acquis* and harmonisation of private international law make clear that increasing the accessibility, consistency and the predictable development of private law within the framework provided by the code becomes more complicated in the multilevel legal order where multiple actors – not just the legislator involved in codification – develop binding private law.

These difficulties do not mean that codifications may not still contribute to the accessibility, consistency and predictability, as well as private law's responsiveness to both practice and society's views on justice, especially because large parts of private law are still developed at the national level. Further, it has become clear that private law has also benefited from the coexistence of actors. However, problems of predictability have become visible more widely, not only with regard to the implementation of the *acquis* in the BGB but also with regard to the development of the *acquis*. As the implementation of the *acquis* within Civil Codes facilitates the nationalist interpretation and further development of the *acquis*, and as national actors have maintained a defensive approach, problems with regard to the responsive development of the *acquis* may remain.

Ensuring the comprehensibility of European private law through codifications will eventually require an approach of national legislators that is more attuned to the increasing interdependence between European and national actors. If legislative competence is transferred to the European level, legislators should adopt a more active approach to harmonisation, in order to become aware of future initiatives for harmonisation and the corresponding need to adapt codes. They may also defend successful national law as a blueprint for European law. In addition, national state actors, if they participate in European legislative procedures, need to contribute to a consistent development of the *acquis*, as this will lessen the chance that they will subsequently have to implement inconsistent European measures.[2317] European state actors should be equally aware of the need to develop the law in a more consistent manner. If national legislators adopt this approach, codifications may still improve accessibility. It is, therefore, not surprising that the use of codification continues to be widespread and is also adopted by new European Member States. Thus, any hopes that civil law jurisdictions will come to consider codification as superfluous and outmoded may, fortunately, continue to be disappointed.[2318]

9.3. The use of soft laws

At the European level, various sets of soft law have developed that partially overlap.

This is especially the case for contract law, where soft law rules have been developed in the PECL, which has also been used as a basis in the development of the DCFR. Notably, a revised version of the PECL[2319] as well as the UNIDROIT Principles have been drafted. Furthermore, there is also the

2317 Comp. J.M. Smits, 'The complexity of transnational law: coherence and fragmentation of private law', *ERPL* 2012, p. 153.

2318 T. Weir, 'Difficulties in transposing Directives', *ZEuP* 2004, p. 614.

2319 Association de Henri Capitant des Amis de la Culture Juridique Française, Société de Législation Comparé (ed.), *European contract law – Materials for a Common Frame of reference: Terminology, Guiding Principles, Model Rules*, München: Sellier 2008.

Draft for a European contract code, drafted by Prof. Gandolfi,[2320] which shows considerable overlap with the PECL. The aims of these sets of soft law seem to overlap as well: they are to function as a toolbox, an optional regime that parties can apply to their contract, or they are to be used for the further development of private law at a European level, as well as academic debate and education on transnational or comparative European contract law. Other projects such as the Trento common core project,[2321] and the Ius commune casebooks[2322] may serve these aims as well.

The case studies found that Dutch and German actors have not taken interdependence as a starting point in the development of the law on STCs through national techniques, and problems of responsiveness, consistency and predictability have been signalled in the case studies.[2323] Yet if instruments based on a successful, prominent national technique, namely codification, have been developed at the European level, does that mean that European actors have taken interdependence as a starting point in the drafting of soft laws, and interacted accordingly? The case studies indicate that the DCFR has not sufficiently taken into account parts of the *acquis* and national experiences, which may limit the extent to which the DCFR will contribute to the predictability, consistency, accessibility and responsiveness of the law on STCs.[2324] If this is more generally the case, has this undermined the comprehensibility of private law developed through soft laws?

This paragraph will pay particular attention to the DCFR because of its role in the reform of the private law *acquis* and the development of a successor of the withdrawn proposal for a CESL.

Paragraph 9.3.1 asks whether actors have taken interdependence as a starting point in the development of the DCFR as a set of soft law rules. Paragraph 9.3.2 will consider whether will ask whether drafters of soft laws have sufficiently discussed other sets of soft law, which should enable actors to benefit from one another's experiences and paragraph 9.3.3 will consider the development of the DCFR alongside the *acquis*. Paragraph 9.3.4 will end with a conclusion.

9.3.1. *Soft laws modelled on national codifications*

This paragraph asks whether the drafters have taken interdependence as a starting point in the drafting of the DCFR as a set of soft law rules, and how the approach of these actors has affected the extent to which the DCFR can contribute to the comprehensibility of private law.

Concerns about interdependence are not visible in the choice for a codification-like instrument. The difficulties that traditional codifications already have in safeguarding the predictability, consistency and responsiveness of private law indicate that soft laws may face even more difficulties in upholding predictability, consistency, accessibility and responsiveness. Nevertheless, the choice to model soft laws on successful codifications does not seem to have been given much thought. Instead, the choice of the drafters of soft

2320 G. Gandolfi, *Code européen des contracts/Avant-projet, Livre premier*, Milan: Giuffrè 2001.
2321 See further www.common-core.org/index.php?option=com_content&view=article&id=46&Itemid=34.
2322 See further www.casebooks.eu/casebooks/overview/.
2323 See previously par. 4.6.1. and 5.6.1.
2324 See previously pat. 4.7.2. and 5.7.2.

law is in line with the widespread use of codifications throughout the European Union, and arguments for codification at the European level.[2325] The drafters of the DCFR, which was intended as an instrument to support the European legislator, felt that a codification was a drafting technique that had proven successful beyond other techniques.[2326] The impression arises that the drafters have assumed that the use of codification will significantly contribute to predictability, consistency and accessibility.[2327] Even though the DCFR can be seen as a new mode of governance to improve European private law,[2328] the drafters adopted a more traditional private law approach: instead of considering questions on governance, they went straight to discussing matters of substantive private law. This is also reflected in the top-down drafting process of the DCFR.[2329] Even if the approach of the DCFR cannot be characterised as "regulatory private law", oriented at market-building,[2330] it is difficult to reconcile with the praise of the DCFR as an instrument that '[moves] away from the powerful nineteenth century image of national private law'.[2331] It has been argued[2332] that the use of the DCFR, as well as other new modes of governance[2333] may instead facilitate a top-down approach as these forms of governance make European actors less dependent on national actors to gather information on the implementation of the *acquis*.

This national approach towards drafting soft law is not specific to the DCFR, but is visible in other sets of soft laws as well. Similar to the DCFR, the soft law rules at both the European and the international level typically take a rather national approach to private law – which is especially visible in the Gandolfi code, which is inspired by the Italian Civil Code and a draft for an English contract Code.[2334] The UNIDROIT Principles have also been characterised in this manner. Michaels[2335] even characterises the UNIDROIT

2325 See for example the Resolution of the European Parliament of 6 May 1994, OJ C 205/518.

2326 C. von Bar, 'Coverage and structure of the Academic Frame of Reference', *ERCL* 2007, p. 354. Comp. also Staudinger Komm zum BGB/Coing, Honsell, (2011), introduction, nr.48, where the DCFR is characterised as a Civil Code, with the remarks that the EU legislator severely misjudges the importance of a European codification, and where the English style of provisions in the DCFR is criticised.

2327 Comp. M.W. Hesselink, 'The Common Frame of Reference as a source of European private law', *Tulane Law Review* 2009, p. 923: 'The DCFR will prove to be irresistible. It has all the characteristics of a civil code which are familiar to lawyers in Continental Europe and which intrigue English common lawyers.'

2328 As defended by L. Miller, *The emergence of EU contract law: Exploring Europeanization*, Oxford: OUP 2011, p. 172.

2329 Comp. rather suspiciously on this point H.-W. Micklitz, 'The visible hand of European regulatory private law. The transformation of European private law from autonomy to functionalism in competition and regulation', *EUI Working Paper* 2008, p. 29.

2330 The characterisation of regulatory private law has been defended more generally by H.-W. Micklitz, 'Monolistic ideology or pluralistic reality', in L. Niglia (ed.), *Pluralism and European private law*, Oxford: Hart 2013, p. 38–39. see further previously par. 4.5.2.

2331 L. Miller, *The emergence of EU contract law: Exploring Europeanization*, Oxford: OUP 2011, p. 172.

2332 See previously par. 6.2.

2333 Specifically, the development of studies on the use of STCs in cross-border cases, see previously par. 4.7.4.

2334 R. Zimmerman, '"Wissenschaftliches Recht" am Beispiel (vor allem) des europäischen Vertragsrechts', in C. Bumke, A. Röthel (eds.), *Privates Recht*, Tübingen: Mohr Siebeck 2012, p. 31.

2335 R. Michaels, 'Umdenken für die UNIDROIT-Prinzipien. Vom Rechtswahlstatut zum Allgemeinen Teil des Transnationalen Vertragsrechts', *RabelsZ* 2009, p. 873–874.

Principles as a codification that seeks to make private international law superfluous by providing a set of rules summarising the similarities between private laws:

> 'Ein Hauptziel für die Formulierung der PICC war ja gerade, die angebliche Unsicherheit des Kollisionsrechts zu überwinden (...) Das Ziel der PICC is nicht, die Zahl der Vertragsrechtsordnungen zu erhöhen (was für echte Rechtswahlfreiheit gut wäre), sondern vielmehr, die bestehenden Vertragsrechtsordnungen auf einem gemeinsamen Kern zusammenzuführen.'

Not only the form of soft law sets in the form of codifications, even if they are not especially focused on a particular national code,[2336] can be seen in the light of methodological nationalism, but also their use of black letter rules in the form of model rules and definitions, which seek to discover similarities between divergent law in a manner reminiscent of the discovery of general principles.[2337] Notably, this does not mean that sets of soft law reflect the common law of Europe: although parts of soft law do seek to discover common elements, other parts may be intended as an innovation.[2338]

Miller[2339] has rightly criticised this practice in the light of methodological nationalism. In a multilevel legal order, harmonisation of private law through general rules leaves considerable room for diversity at the national level, as also became clear in the case studies. Miller[2340] and Pavillon[2341] have both demonstrated that such diversity is visible in the interpretation of national law implementing respectively Directive 1999/44 on consumer sales and Directive 93/13 on unfair contract terms, as well as Directive 2005/29 on unfair commercial practices. Against this background, the DCFR could still contribute to the comprehensibility of private law, not by providing black letter rules, but by serving as a source of inspiration, considering the national experiences with the *acquis* and divergences from the *acquis* and other sets of soft law, as was also argued in the case studies.[2342] Nevertheless, this approach may also have its benefits: legislators familiar with codifications may choose to make use of soft law drafted in this form rather than projects on comparative private law.[2343]

The question, however, arises whether soft laws contribute to the benchmarks of predictability, consistency, accessibility and responsiveness in a manner similar to national codifications. In particular, the ongoing development of binding private law

2336 Comp. also HKK/Schmoeckels nr 81, who points out that initially soft laws did not aim for a system of the law of obligations but were, instead, limited to contract law.

2337 See further below, par. 9.5.2.1.

2338 Comp. for example with regard to the PECL J.M. Smits, 'The Principles of European Contract law and the harmonisation of private law in Europe', in: A. Vaquer (ed.), *La tercera parte de los principios de derecho contractual Europeo*, Valencia: Tirant 2005, p. 575–576. Comp. R. Michaels, 'Privatautonomie und Privatkodifikation', *RabelsZ* 1998, p. 622, who points out that the national origin of the rules in soft law does not mean that these rules are of the best quality.

2339 L. Miller, *The emergence of EU contract law: Exploring Europeanization*, Oxford: OUP 2011, p. 168.

2340 L. Miller, *The emergence of EU contract law: Exploring Europeanization*, Oxford: OUP 2011, p. 90–103.

2341 C.M.D.S. Pavillon, *Open normen in het Europees consumentenrecht*, Deventer: Kluwer 2011, p. 479 et seq.

2342 See previously par. 4.7.2.4.

2343 R. Michaels, 'Umdenken für die UNIDROIT-Prinzipien. Vom Rechtswahlstatut zum Allgemeinen Teil des Transnationalen Vertragsrechts', *RabelsZ* 2009, p. 879.

alongside the DCFR not only seems possible, but likely, which necessitates that the DCFR takes the existence of other sources of *binding* private law alongside the DCFR as a starting point. Notably, this characteristic may make effectively pursuing the accessibility of private law in the DCFR especially difficult. Moreover, the DCFR needs to take as a starting point that it depends upon other actors for its success: in order for the DCFR to become successful, it needs to be consistently used by other actors, such as the European legislator and judiciary, which, in turn, may be an incentive for other actors, at the national level, to refer to it. If European actors perceive that the DCFR has a clearly added value, for example, because it facilitates the use of consistent terminology within the *acquis*, because it provides insights in national problems that are important in the reform of the *acquis*, or because it draws attention to the need to clarify the relation between overlapping European measures, this makes it more likely that European actors will consistently refer to the DCFR. In addition, as national judiciaries are starting to refer to the PECL,[2344] the added value of the DCFR to the PECL should also be clear for these actors, providing them with an incentive to start referring to the DCFR rather than the PECL.

It may be concluded that the drafters of the DCFR did not take interdependence as a starting point in the drafting of the DCFR, which makes it less likely that the DCFR sufficiently considers and discusses the *acquis*, national experiences with the *acquis*, as well as other sets of soft law. The drafters also did not sufficiently recognise that the success of soft law instruments depends on the use of soft law made by other actors, which, in turn, depends on the added value of those instruments for other actors. Because drafters have not recognised this interdependence, and have insufficiently discussed the divergences between the DCFR, the *acquis*, and national experiences with the *acquis*, the added value of the DCFR to European private law, and to the quality of the *acquis*, may remain limited.

9.3.2. *Overlapping sets of soft law*

The case study found that the DCFR does not adequately discuss divergences from and between the different sets of soft laws with regard to the law on STCs. This paragraph will ask more generally whether drafters of soft laws have sufficiently discussed other sets of soft law. Does the discussion enable actors to benefit from one another's experience in developing private law predictably, consistently, accessibly, and responsively?

Typically, sets of soft law such as the DCFR, the PECL, the Gandolfi code and the UNIDROIT Principles are based on comparative research, and presuppose the coexistence of national private laws. In contrast, they subsequently do not, equally typically, make clear how they relate to the *acquis* or to one another, which may be especially interesting when divergences become apparent.[2345] This may, in particular, diminish the consistency and accessibility of private law in the following ways:

2344 D. Busch, 'The Principles of European Contract Law before the Supreme Court of The Netherlands', *ZEuP* 2008, p. 549.

2345 The Gandolfi code provides an interesting exception. E.H. Hondius, 'Towards a European Ius Commune: The current situation in other fields of private law', in: K. Boele-Woelki (ed.), *Perspectives for the unification and harmonisation of family law in Europe*, Antwerp: Intersentia 2003, p. 126 points

Firstly, the coexistence of various sets of soft laws gives rise to doubts with regard to the added value of multiple sets of soft law, especially considering the overlap between the different sets of soft law rules. Vogenauer[2346] has questioned whether the aims pursued by the DCFR could not also be fulfilled by the UNIDROIT principles, asking whether there is a need for another set of soft law rules, next to the UNIDROIT Principles and the PECL. Notably, these instruments also already may provide starting points for a "common language" for further discussion and learning in the debate on European private law,[2347] and the added value of the DCFR in this respect is not immediately apparent.[2348] The question arises whether soft law sets in fields where soft law has not already been established would be more successful. Accordingly, the DCFR rules on specific contracts, such as service contracts, franchise contracts, and distribution contracts have more added value.[2349] Possibly, the rules of the DCFR on these contracts can draw attention to measures aimed at specific goods or services throughout the Union that affect matters of contract and tort law. This would be useful, as service contracts are important to the internal market and the European legislator increasingly develops a regulatory approach to foster the internal market for services.[2350] Unfortunately, the DCFR does not do so. Instead, he DCFR focusses on comparing the national rules on services contracts throughout the Union. It does not consider Directive 2006/123 on services or even measures aimed at specific services, such as transport for consumers for example stipulated in Regulation 261/2004.

Alternatively, the development of regulatory competition, between different sets of soft law, or between the drafters of soft law and state actors, could provide an interesting source for innovation.[2351] Competition could and should prompt drafters of soft laws to make clearer why a particular set of soft law is better suited to be used as a source of inspiration for lawmakers or as an optional set of rules for contract parties.[2352] However,

out that the Gandolfi code initiates debate with the PECL and the ideas brought forward by the colleagues of Prof. Gandolfi.

2346 S. Vogenauer, 'Common Frame of Reference and UNIDROIT Principles of International Commercial Contracts: Coexistence, competition, or overkill of soft law?' *ERCL* 2010, p. 143.

2347 M.W. Hesselink, 'The Principles of European Contract Law: some choices made by the Lando Commission', in: M.W. Hesselink, G, de Vries (eds.), *Principles of European Contract Law, Preadviezen uitgebracht voor de Vereniging voor Burgerlijk Recht*, Deventer: Kluwer 2001, p. 13 finds that establishing neutral language that could be used in debate, whether on comparative law or on the unification of private laws, is one of the most important benefits of the PECL.

2348 This is for example suggested by L. Miller, *The emergence of EU contract law: Exploring Europeanization*, Oxford: OUP 2011, p. 205–206.

2349 Comp. M.B.M. Loos, 'Scope and application of the Optional instrument', in: D. Voinot, J. Sénéchal (eds.), *Vers un droit européen des contrats spéciaux / Towards a European Law of Specific Contracts*, Gent: Larcier 2011, p. 122.

2350 Comp. H.-W. Micklitz, 'Regulatory strategies in services contracts law', *EUI Working Paper* 2008/06.

2351 In line with the suggestion of E.A. O'Hara, L.E. Ribstein, *The law market*, Oxford: OUP 2009, p. 224.

2352 Interestingly, in the drafting of the UNIDROIT Principles, representatives of interested international organisations and arbitration centres or association were invited to observe the working groups, and decisions on the UNIDROIT principles are easily accessible in the UNILEX database, available at www.unilex.info/. Possibly, combined with the international scope of the principles, the UNIDROIT principles could have a competitive advantage, which however did not become visible in the drafting of the DCFR on the basis of the PECL.

such competition has hardly developed. Interestingly, the drafting groups of soft laws show considerable overlap – especially between the Commission of European contract law and the Study Group on a European Civil Code, which considers itself the successor of the Commission of European contract law,[2353] while the chairman of this group, Prof. Lando, also participated in the drafting of the UNIDROIT rules. Bonell[2354] has argued that the PECL, as a *European* set of soft law, may serve as a source of inspiration for the European legislator, but they are not expected to act as a source of inspiration beyond the Union, and in that respect, competition between the PECL and UNIDROIT will hardly develop. Currently, theoretically some extent of competition may be detected between state actors and drafters of soft laws, insofar as soft laws aim to provide an optional regime for contract parties, which may be attractive especially in cases of arbitration.[2355] This has however not prompted drafters of soft law to argue in which respects their rules are of better quality than specific state laws.

Secondly, questions of accessibility arise. Would the area of European contract law not be easier to overview if there were one set of soft law rules, or if the various soft law rules indicated how they relate to one another? Zimmerman[2356] remarks that, although the coexistence of different sets of soft law may initially inhibit accessibility, comparison between the different sets reveals similarities and reflects current comparative law research. Differences between the sets of soft law can mainly be found in the details and may be overcome by further discussion. Yet the differences between the different sets of soft law rules, as well as a lack of coordination, may give rise to confusion. This becomes apparent when considering, for example, the question how the DCFR, the revised versions of the PECL, as well as the since withdrawn CESL and the reformed Directives in the *acquis* relate to one another. It is a bit rash to conclude that the PECL has no further meaning now that it has served, along with other sources, as a basis for the DCFR.[2357] Nevertheless, it also does not seem completely illogical if the focus shifts to the DCFR and especially a future Optional Instrument, rather than the PECL.[2358] On the

2353 Two thirds of the members of the Commission for European contract law also participate in the Study Group, consider for example the joint response of the Commission on European contract law and the Study Group to the Communication on European contract law, COM (2001) 398 final, available at http://ec.europa.eu/consumers/archive/policy/developments/contract_law/comments/5.23.pdf.

2354 M.J. Bonell, 'The UNIDROIT Principles of International Commercial Contracts and the Principles of European Contract Law: Similar rules for the same purposes', *ULR* 1996, p. 642.

2355 Comp. further J.C. Wichard, "Die Anwendung der UNIDROIT-Prinzipien für internationale Handelsverträge durch Schiedsgerichte und staatliche Gerichte', *RabelsZ* 1996, p. 269.

2356 R. Zimmerman, '"Wissenschaftliches Recht" am Beispiel (vor allem) des europäischen Vertragsrechts, in C. Bumke, A. Röthel (eds.), *Privates Recht*, Tübingen: Mohr Siebeck 2012, p. 55–56: 'In der Regel dürfte sich dabei ein weitreichendes Maß an Übereinstimmung zeigen, das den gegenwärtigen Stand der rechtsvergleichenden Diskussion widerspiegelt. Die nach wie vor bestehenden Detailunterschiede sind präzise herauszuarbeiten und argumentativ zu überwinden.'

2357 R. Zimmerman, 'Textstufen in der modernen Entwicklung des europäischen privatrechts', *EuZW* 2009, p. 319.

2358 Comp. K. Riesenhuber, 'A competitive approach to EU contract law', *ERCL* 2011, p. 119. According to C.M.D.S. Pavillon, 'Een nieuw contractenrecht voor Frankrijk', *NTBR* 2015, 11, the revision of the French law of obligations has also been inspired by EU instruments, including the DCFR, but also the PECL and the Unidroit principles, as well as the since withdrawn proposal for a CESL.

other hand, practitioners and courts may be more aware of the PECL than of more recent initiatives, and in cases outside of the scope of the *acquis*, they may not find it problematic that the PECL are not also based on the private law *acquis*.[2359] Practitioners and courts may also refer to the UNIDROIT Principles.[2360] However, A.G.s' opinions preceding CJEU decisions[2361] as well as national legislators[2362] and courts[2363] have also started to refer to the DCFR.

Thus, although overlapping black letter rules in soft laws currently do provide examples for actors developing the law, they do not, typically, discuss divergences and similarities, or their relations with one another. Interaction between the drafters of different sets of soft law might have formed a starting point for discussion, clarifying why

2359 Comp. D. Busch, 'The Principles of European Contract Law before the Supreme Court of The Netherlands', *ZEuP* 2008, p. 549. See for the application of the PECL before the Spanish courts C. Vendrell Cervantes, 'The application of the Principles of European Contract Law by Spanish Courts', *ZEuP* 2008, p. 534.

2360 Comp. for example also *Proforce Recruit Limited, The Rugby Group Limited* (2006), EWCA Civ 69 (n. 57) *per* Arden LJ, at par. 57, who referred to the UNIDROIT Principles.

2361 Some references even date from before the publication of the revised edition of the DCFR, including the opinion of A.G. Trstenjak of 11 June 2008 before case C-275/07 (Commission of the European Communities v Italian Republic), [2009] ECR p. I-2005, note 48 and 55; opinion of A.G. Trstenjak of 18 February 2009 before case C-489/07 (Messner v Kruger), [2009] ECR p. I-7315, par. 85, 94, note 74, 75 and 79. After the publication of the DCFR, references have continued to be made, see opinion of A-G Trstenjak 7 May 2009 before case C-227/08 (Martin Martin v EDP Editors SL), [2009] ECR p. I-11939, par. 51, note 40; the opinion of A.G. Trstenjak of 8 September 2009 (E Friz GmbH v Von der Heyden), [2010] ECR p. I- 2927, note 62, 65, and 72; opinion of A.G. Trstenjak of 24 March 2010 before case C-540/08 (Mediaprint Zeitungs- und Zeitschriftenverlag GmbH & Co. KG v 'Österreich'-Zeitungsverlag GmbH), [2010] ECR p. I-10909, note 7; opinion of A- Trstenjak of 6 July 2010 before case C-137/08 (VB Pénzügyi Lízing Zrt. v Schneider), [2010] ECR p. I-10847, note 54; opinion of A-G Cruz Villalon of 15 November 2012 before case C-113/11 P (European Commission v Systran SA and Systran Luxembourg SA), [2013] ECR p. I-0, note 24; opinion of A-G Kokott of 24 October 2013 before case C-396/12, (Van der Ham and Van der Ham-Reijersen van Buuren v College van Gedeputeerde Staten van Zuid-Holland), note 39; opinion of A.G. Kokott of 30 January 2014 before case C-557/12 (KONE AG and others v OBB-Infrastruktur BB), note 24.

2362 Particularly the Scottish Law Commission, see for example Scottish Law Commission, *Review of contract law, Discussion paper 157 on third party rights in contract*, March 2014, available at www.scotlawcom.gov.uk/files/8013/9592/4224/DP_TSO.pdf. Coincidentally, Prof. MacQueen, who was also a member of the Study Group for a European Civil Code, has been appointed as a Commissioner in the Scottish Law Commission and he leads the project "Contract law in the light of the Draft Common Frame of Reference (DCFR)", see www.scotlawcom.gov.uk/law-reform/law-reform-projects/contract-law-light-draft-common-frame-reference-dcf/.

2363 See for example the conclusion of A.G. Wissink before HR 19 November 2010, NJ 2010, 623, note 12 and 19; conclusion of A-G Wissink before HR 8 July 2011, *NJ* 2012, 684, par. 2.31.3, note 17; conclusion of A.G. Langemeijer before HR 24 February 2012, *NJ* 2012, 144, par. 2.18; conclusion of A.G. Wuisman before HR 27 April 2012, *NJ* 2012, 239, par. 3.10.2, 3.12.14, note 22; conclusion of A.G. Wissink before HR 1 June 2012, *RvdW* 2012, 765, par. 3.19; conclusion of A.G. Rank-Berenschot before HR 2 November 2012, *NJ* 2014, 332, par. 2.35–2.36; conclusion of A-G Wissink before HR 21 February 2014, *NJ* 2014, 265, note 31; conclusion of A.G. Wissink before HR 14 June 2014, *NJ* 2014, 406, note 75; conclusion of P-G. De Vriesch-Lents Kostensche before HR 10 October 2014, *NJ* 2015, 70, par. 11, conclusion of A.G. Leus before HR 17 October 2014, *RvdW* 2014/1166, note 5 and 8. Notably, in his conclusion before HR 16 September 2011, *NJ* 2012, 56, A.G. Wissink, note 9, remarked that the DCFR did not offer comparative insights as it only covered certain types of penalty clauses.

rules in sets of soft law diverge, providing the European legislator with multiple soft laws and discussion on which rules in sets of soft law might serve as a source of inspiration for European legislation. Accordingly, European actors may be more inclined to make use of these sources if they make clear how they relate to the *acquis* and other measures, which may improve accessibility. In turn, such use may be a reason for national actors to consider several sets of soft laws more consistently and thoroughly.

9.3.3. Soft laws and the private law acquis

The case studies[2364] found that the drafters of the DCFR have diverged from Directive 93/13, without sufficient discussion, which has diminished the potential of the DCFR as a source of mutual learning. In the light of these findings, this paragraph will ask whether drafters of soft laws and drafters of the private law *acquis* have sufficiently discussed one another's initiatives and how that has affected the potential for mutual learning.

The drafters of soft law have not consistently referred to the private law *acquis*.[2365] Early sets of soft law, in particular the PECL, were developed before or during the development of the private law *acquis*, which was a reason for not including the *acquis*. Yet more modern versions have also not consistently referred to the private law *acquis*. In particular, the DCFR has taken the original version of the PECL,[2366] which did not take into account the private law *acquis*, as a starting point.[2367] Even though it was initially suggested that the drafting of the DCFR and the development of Directive 2011/83 on consumer rights would be closely intertwined,[2368] it was not clear which, if any, coordination took place between the drafting of the DCFR and the simultaneous reform of the *acquis*.[2369]

This course may be increasingly problematic. Not taking into account the private law *acquis* and relevant case law may be particularly problematic if soft law is to play a role in the further development of the private law *acquis*, in which case a lack of

2364 See previously par. 4.7.2.1. and 5.7.2.1.

2365 See further for example H.-W. Micklitz, 'The Principles of European Contract Law and the protection of the weaker party', *Journal of Consumer Policy* 2004, p. 339.

2366 R. Zimmerman, 'Europäisches Privatrecht – Irrungen, Wirtungen', in: Professorinnen und Professoren der Bucerius Law School (eds.), *Begegnungen im Recht, Ringvorlesung der Bucerius Law School zu Ehren von Karsten Schmidt anlässlich seines 70. Geburtstags*, Tübingen: Mohr Siebeck 2011, p. 330, notes that the drafters of the PECL and UNIDROIT may also have chosen to not include the *acquis* because of unhappiness with the quality of the private law *acquis*. M.W. Hesselink, 'The Principles of European Contract Law: Some choices made by the Lando Commission', in: M.W. Hesselink, G. de Vries (eds.), *Principles of European Contract Law, Preadviezen uitgebracht voor de Vereniging van Burgerlijk Recht*, Deventer: Kluwer 2001 p. 11, states that the improvement of fragmented and inconsistent state of the *acquis* was also considered by the drafters of the PECL.

2367 R. Zimmerman, 'Textstufen in der modernen Entwicklung des europäischen Privatrecht', *Europäisches Zeitschrift für Wirtschaftsrecht* 2009, p. 321.

2368 European Commission, *First annual progress report on European contract law and the acquis review*, COM (2005) 456, final p. 4.

2369 Ch. Twigg-Flesner, D. Metcalfe, 'The proposed consumer rights Directive – less haste, more thought?' *ERCL* 2011, p. 369–370.

interaction may increase the chance of inconsistencies, inhibit the predictable development of the private law *acquis* and give rise to confusion.[2370]

These potential problems become clear from various questions that can be raised from the future development of the DCFR and the private law *acquis*. Firstly, the drafters have occasionally diverged from existing European law,[2371] which may lead one to wonder whether the DCFR will be used as source of inspiration in the continuing reform of the consumer *acquis*, as well as the interpretation of the *acquis* more generally. The failure of the European legislator to consistently take the DCFR as a starting point in the (re)formation of the *acquis*[2372] indicates otherwise and may be a reason for national legislators and judiciaries not to refer to the DCFR in the implementation and interpretation of the *acquis*, as such referral may lead to the incorrect implementation of European law. As a result, opportunities for learning have not been realised. Similarly, one may wonder to what extent the DCFR will play a role in the further development of the amended proposal for a CESL, which stipulates in article 1 that it will be developed autonomously, in accordance with the (few) principles underlying it and its aim to advance the internal market. Hesselink[2373] states that the DCFR could still serve as a source of inspiration for the amendment of the withdrawn proposal.[2374]

Secondly, after the reform of the *acquis* that limited the level of consumer protection, reconsideration of the DCFR, which at various points provided a wider protection than the old, more protective, Directives would seem a desirable exercise if the DCFR is still to fulfil a function as toolbox in the further development of the private law *acquis*. After all, it may be doubted whether actors would make use of a toolbox that provides for a level of protection inconsistent with the *acquis*.[2375] More generally, inclusion of the consumer law *acquis* in the DCFR may also provide an opportunity to take the criticism of the DCFR into account, and discuss the role of the different sets of soft law, thereby increasing potential for mutual learning.

The consequences of such a reconsideration of the DCFR are however not clear. Possibly, a re-examination might not lead to the provision of different rules, if the revised DCFR is to be used as a toolbox. At most, a critical examination could indicate a need for reform – yet it may not be desirable to initiate more reform after the *acquis* has already

2370 W. Devroe, 'Impact van door het Europees Hof van Justitie ontwikkelde algemene beginselen op privaatrechtelijke verhoudingen', in: A.S. Hartkamp, C.H. Sieburgh, L.A.D. Keus (eds.), De *invloed van het Europese recht op het Nederlandse privaatrecht I*, Deventer: Kluwer 2007, p. 188.

2371 See for example the comparison of R. Zimmerman, N. Jansen, 'Contract formation and mistake in European contract law: A genetic comparison of transnational model rules', *OJLS* 2011, p. 1. Comp. also the various comparisons in G. Danneman, S. Vogenauer (eds.), *The Common European Sales Law in context*, Oxford: OUP 2013.

2372 Comp. M.W. Hesselink, 'The consumer rights Directive and the CFR: two worlds apart?' *ERCL* 2009, p. 290–303.

2373 M.W. Hesselink, 'The consumer rights Directive and the DCFR: two worlds apart?' *ERCL* 2009, p. 297–302.

2374 Notably, as an exception, the DCFR has been considered in the reform of some Directives, see for example consideration 28 in the preamble of Directive 2011/7 combating late payment.

2375 However, that does not mean that lowering the level of consumer protection would be a good move. Rather, ideally, it would prompt a reconsideration of especially full targeted harmonisation, comp. M.W. Hesselink, 'The consumer rights Directive and the DCFR: two worlds apart?' *ERCL* 2009, p. 297.

been reformed, as ongoing reform may limit not only the accessibility of the *acquis*, but also the predictable and consistent development of the private law *acquis*. In addition, *if* the DCFR should reflect the consumer law *acquis* more, when should that take place – before the reform of Directive 90/314 has been finished? On the one hand, if the review of Directives takes a long time, they may benefit from a revised DCFR. On the other hand, the review of Directives may also be held up by the revision process. Unfortunately, it is difficult to predict how long the reform of Directives will take.

It may be concluded that drafters especially of the DCFR have not sufficiently discussed the divergences between the *acquis*. In addition, actors have not made clear how the rules in soft law will be used in the development of the private law *acquis* and how soft laws will cope with changes in the private law *acquis*. Consequently, the role of the DCFR in the reform of the *acquis* is not clear, and mutual learning has generally not been realised. As a result, the predictable development of the private law *acquis* is undermined, and the chance of inconsistencies has been increased, especially if the European legislator uses the DCFR inconsistently.

9.3.4. Conclusion on the use of soft laws

State actors have not taken interdependence as a starting point in the development of codifications, but codification-like instruments have also been developed at the European level. This paragraph has asked, in the light of the case studies,[2376] whether the DCFR has more generally failed to discuss the *acquis* and national experiences with the *acquis*, as well as other sets of soft law, and how this has affected the value of the DCFR as a source for mutual learning.

Firstly, the choice for soft law in the form of a codification has not been given much thought, which indicates that the drafters did not take interdependence as a starting point in the drafting of the DCFR. This is especially unfortunate for the DCFR as a set of soft law, alongside which *binding* private law is developed.

Secondly, the lack of interaction and debate on the different provisions are a missed opportunity to provide the European legislator – for whom the DCFR was drafted – with a more elaborately discussed set of rules that can serve as an inspiration for the development of the *acquis*. It also diminishes the value of the DCFR as a source of inspiration for national actors, in addition to other sets of soft laws. Regulatory competition does not seem to have developed between drafters of soft laws. Possibly, the participation of stakeholders in the drafting of the DCFR could have provided more insights in the needs and preferences of these actors, for example by considering these needs and preferences in the comments. This might, for example, have been useful for regulatory competition, but also for identifying problems in the *acquis* and problems for the internal market. In turn, more clarity on the needs and preferences of these actors could prompt national actors to pay more attention to needs and preferences, especially if they are representative for international trade. Nevertheless, particularly those interested in or already familiar with codifications, have started considering the DCFR.

2376 See previously par. 4.7.2. and 5.7.2.

Possibly, drafters, if they had wished to maintain the codification technique, could have considered the additional use of techniques to compensate for potential weaknesses arising from the use of codification, especially techniques that might have a chance to successfully further the consistent, accessible, and predictable development of the *acquis*, for example, the development of databases and networks.[2377]

Thirdly, it is not clear how the DCFR relates to the *acquis*, how it would cope with developments and changes in the *acquis* and how it would be used in the reform in the *acquis*. This has given rise to confusion on the development of the *acquis* and the role of the DCFR, which decreases the chance that European private law will develop in s stable, consistent and accessible manner through the development of soft law.

9.4. The use of blanket clauses in a multilevel legal order

The case studies found that Dutch and German actors have not taken interdependence as a starting point in the development of the law on STCs through blanket clauses, and problems of responsiveness, consistency and predictability have been signalled in the case studies.[2378] Is this approach visible more widely in the development of the law through blanket clauses by both national and European actors, and how has that affected the extent to which blanket clauses improve the predictability, consistency, accessibility and responsiveness of European private law?

Paragraph 9.4.1 will consider the reasoning of the European and national legislators for using blanket clauses in the private law *acquis*, and paragraph 9.4.2 will consider the interaction between courts in the interpretation of blanket clauses in the private law *acquis*. Paragraph 9.4.3 will end with a conclusion.

9.4.1. *Reasons for the use of blanket clauses in the* acquis

This paragraph will ask for what reasons legislators at the national and European level have used blanket clauses (‘*open normen*’, ‘*Generalklauseln*’) and consider whether, in this reasoning, legislators have sufficiently considered the coexistence of actors, and how this has affected the quality of European private law.

National legislators frequently use blanket clauses to provide for some leeway in national laws, and allow the national judiciary some room for reaching a just outcome in individual cases.[2379] In this way, the use of blanket clauses should strengthen the responsiveness of private law, both to practice and to society’s legal views on justice.

2377 See previously par. 4.7.1., 5.7.1. and below par. 10.2.3. and 10.2.4. Especially the use of databases on case law and literature on further legislative or judicial development could provide a valuable source of information, showing, for example, when the DCFR was or was not followed, or how a particular term has been interpreted.

2378 See previously par. 4.6.1. and 5.6.1.

2379 A.S. Hartkamp, ‘Judicial discretion under the New Civil Code of The Netherlands’, *American Journal of Comparative Law* 1992, p. 569, W.-H. Roth, ‘Generalklauseln im Europäischen Privatrecht’, in: J. Basedow, K.J. Hopt, H. Kötz (eds.), *Festschrift für Ulrich Drobnig zum siebzigsten Geburtstag*, Tübingen: Mohr Siebeck, 1998, p. 140 on the functions of blanket clauses.

At the European level, the use of blanket clauses has been hard to avoid, if the private law *acquis* is to deal adequately with future developments.[2380] Further, the use of blanket clauses in the *acquis* may allow judges to reach a just outcome, as demonstrated in the case studies.[2381] More generally, references to similar concepts, for example the "equitable" payment of indemnity to commercial agents in Directive 86/653 on self-employed commercial agents have been based on German law.[2382] Later proposals that refer to good faith, for example in article 2 of the withdrawn Regulation establishing a CESL, are similarly based on comparative law.[2383] Accordingly, European blanket clauses should also contribute to the responsiveness of private law to society's legal views on justice.

Yet simultaneously, blanket clauses in the *acquis* may set harmonised standards, aimed at providing access to markets for foreign and international actors.[2384] Even when derived from comparative law, blanket clauses may over time be interpreted in this manner, and new modes of governance, such as comitology or guidance, may assist the predictable and consistent development of blanket clauses which facilitates market access.[2385] Accordingly, measures in financial services, such as Directive 2008/48 on consumer credit, Directive 2014/17 on mortgage credit and Directive 2007/64 on payment services have been characterised in this manner.[2386]

Several difficulties however, become apparent in the use of blanket clauses at the European level. Firstly, the inclusion of blanket clauses may entail that the CJEU is competent to interpret – but not apply – these blanket clauses. Mak[2387] notes that the CJEU is not meant to balance the interest of parties to a dispute, and 'lacks sufficient insight in the social and economic make-up of individual Member States to assess which

2380 See T.C. Hartley, 'Five forms of uncertainty in European Community Law', *Cambridge Law Journal* 1996, p. 265.

2381 See previously par. 4.5.2. See particularly in this light consideration 16 in the preamble to Directive 93/13 on unfair contract terms holds that the assessment of the fairness of contract terms in consumer contracts 'must be supplemented by a means of making an overall evaluation of the different interests involved; (...) this constitutes the requirement of good faith'.

2382 European Commission, *Report on the application of article 17 of Council Directive on the coordination of the laws of the Member states relating to self-employed commercial agents*, COM (96) 364 final, p. 2.

2383 Comp. the publication of the Expert Group, *A European contract law for consumers and businesses: Publication of the results of the feasibility study carried out by the Expert Group on European contract law for stakeholders' and legal practitioners' feedback*, available at http://ec.europa.eu/justice/contract/files/feasibility_study_final.pdf, p. 5.

2384 H.-W. Micklitz, 'Monolistic ideology or pluralistic reality', in L. Niglia (ed.), *Pluralism and European private law*, Oxford: Hart 2013, p. 38–39. See further previously par. 4.5.2.

2385 Ch. Joerges, 'The Europeanisation process of private law as a rationalization process and as a contest of disciplines – an analysis of the Directive on unfair terms in consumer contracts', *ERPL* 1995, p. 182.

2386 Comp. O.O. Cherednychenko, 'Public supervision over private relationships: Towards European Supervision Private Law?', *ERPL* 2014, p. 37.

2387 V. Mak, 'Harmonisation through "Directive-related" and "cross-Directive" interpretation: The role of the CJEU in the development in European consumer law', *ZeuP* 2010, p. 141, similarly Ch. Schmid, 'The CJEU as a constitutional and a private law court: A methodological comparison', *ZERP Diskussionspaper* 2006, p.12, comp. also H. Collins, *The European Civil Code: the way forward*, Cambridge: CUP 2008, p. 51–61.

outcome would be appropriate in individual cases'. Wissink[2388] points out that the interpretation of blanket clauses may depend upon factual circumstances, which might, in combination with the increased workload of the CJEU, be a reason for the CJEU to give some leeway to national judges. Roth[2389] holds that the duty to act in good faith may, for example, concern the limitation of the exercise of rights under national law. In those cases, it is especially necessary to take national private laws into account. It follows that the inclusion of blanket clauses in the *acquis* and the potential corresponding competence of the CJEU may not be a good way to contribute to the responsiveness of the private law *acquis*.

Secondly, it can be questioned to what extent European blanket clauses allow for responsiveness to practice. On the contrary, it seems as if blanket clauses, especially when combined with maximum harmonisation, may lead to outdated law, as it may severely limit the ability of other actors than the European legislator to respond to developing legal practices. The flexibility provided by national blanket clauses is also difficult to attain at the European level, especially if Union law strives for maximum harmonisation. At the European level, the development and adaptation of the private law *acquis* takes place at a rather slow pace, if only because of the necessity to reach political consensus between 27 Member States. Consequently, maximum harmonisation petrifies parts of national private law, leaving further development to the European level.

Thirdly, it may be asked whether legislators have sufficiently taken into account the weaknesses of blanket clauses if they are used in a multilevel legal order. Particularly, the use of blanket clauses, especially identical blanket clauses with dfferent meaning at the national and European level, also entails disadvantages in the form of inconsistencies, both at the national level and the European level. This is also recognised at the European level, where the wording of those blanket clauses places before the legislator a difficult choice: whether to use new terms or to use ones that are identical to national blanket clauses that already have a particular meaning in national private laws. Dannemann, Ferreri and Graziadei[2390] point out that to some extent, the use of existing terms, including blanket clauses, is inevitable. Inventing new terms at a European level may also cause misunderstanding, lead to multiple, diverging interpretations of the same concept, and undermine harmonisation as well as predictability. They point out that the *Joint practical guide of the European Parliament, the Council and the Commission for persons involved in the drafting of legislation within the Community institutions*[2391] recommends a restrictive use of terms that carry a specific meaning in national laws, which is visible in some of the private law *acquis* – for example Directive 1999/44 referring to 'guarantee'

2388 W.H. Wissink, *Richtlijnconforme interpretatie van burgerlijk recht*, Deventer: Kluwer 2001, p. 372. Comp. M. Schillig, *Konkretisierungskompetenz und Konkretisierungsmethoden im Europäischen Privatrecht*, Berlin: De Gruyter 2009, p. 155–156. See also S. Whittaker, 'Assessing the fairness of contract terms: The parties' essential bargain, its regulatory context and the significance of the requirement of good faith', *ZEuP* 2004, p. 75.

2389 W.-H. Roth, 'Generalklauseln im Europäischen Privatrecht', in: J. Basedow, K.J. Hopt, H. Kötz (eds.), *Festschrift für Ulrich Drobnig zum siebzigsten Geburtstag*, Tübingen: Mohr Siebeck, 1998, p. 140.

2390 G. Dannemann, S. Ferreri, M. Graziadei, 'Language and terminology', in: Ch. Twigg-Flesner (ed.), *The Cambridge companion to European Union private law*, Cambridge: CUP 2010, p. 78–79.

2391 Point 5 of the Guide, available at http://eur-lex.europa.eu/en/techleg/pdf/en.pdf.

instead of 'warranty'. However, in some cases, the private law *acquis* still makes use of concepts also known in national laws, such as good faith.

Unfortunately, this may result in the insertion of a blanket clause into national law that already exists in national private law, but that has to be interpreted differently. Consequently, two seemingly identical concepts with divergent interpretations coexist – one concept in national general contract law and one original European concept that has to be implemented in national law. Roth[2392] has pointed out that this is especially problematic if a European blanket clause is implemented within a Civil Code, as this practice may lead to existence of isolated islands of concepts within Civil Codes ('*Begriffsinseln*') as well as instances where identical concepts within the Civil Code have a divergent meaning ('*Begriffsspaltungen*').

Fourthly, the use of blanket clauses may lead to inconsistencies within the private law *acquis*. Notably, the interpretation of identical or similar blanket clauses in the private law *acquis* may well diverge.

Fifthly, inconsistencies within the private law *acquis* may also arise from the divergent interpretation of blanket clauses at the European level. Pavillon[2393] convincingly argues that the interpretation of unfair contract terms may diverge from the interpretation of unfair commercial practices, pointing out that, for example, a contract term that is unfair under Directive 93/13 may not constitute an unfair commercial practice in the sense of Directive 2005/29 if the seller has drafted transparent terms and complied with his information duties. Conversely, as Pavillon points out, a contract term that is not necessarily unfair may constitute an unfair commercial practice if it is ambiguously drafted and the seller has not complied with information duties. The interpretation of these concepts may also diverge because the degree of harmonisation and the aim that Directives pursue differ.[2394] The importance of a coherent interpretation of the consumer law *acquis* has recently been emphasised by A.G. Trstenjak in her advice before *Pereničová and Perenič v SOS*.[2395] A.G. Trstenjak emphasised the importance of a coherent interpretation of unfair contracts terms in the sense of Directive 93/13 on unfair contract terms and unfair commercial practices in the sense of Directive 2005/29 on unfair commercial practices in the consumer law *acquis*.

The divergent interpretation of blanket clauses and key concepts in the *acquis* is visible more generally throughout the *acquis*.[2396] Although the differences in interpretation do not benefit the consistency and predictability of Union law, divergent

2392 W.-H. Roth, 'Europäischer Verbraucherschutz und BGB', *JZ* 2001, p. 482.

2393 C.M.D.S. Pavillon, *Open normen in het Europees consumentenrecht*, Deventer: Kluwer 2011, p. 516–517.

2394 C.M.D.S. Pavillon, *Open normen in het Europees consumentenrecht*, Deventer: Kluwer 2011, p. 518.

2395 Conclusion of A.G. Trstenjak of 29 November 2011 in case C-453/10 (Pereničová and Perenič v SOS), par. 90–92. Notably, the A.G. refers to a coherent interpretation, but mainly refers to the importance of preventing contradictory – thus inconsistent – judgments.

2396 See for example W. van Gerven, 'The CJEU case law as a means for the unification of private law?' In: A.S. Hartkamp, E.H. Hondius (eds.), *Towards a European Civil Code?*, Nijmegen: Ars Aequi Libri 2004, p. 118–120, P. Rott, 'What is the role of the CJEU in EC private law? – a comment on the CJEU judgments in Océano Grupo, Freiburger Kommunalbauten, Leitner and Veedfald', 1 *Hanse LR* 2005, p. 14 notes that the CJEU 'has not developed a clear line between cases where it exercised deference and cases where it made a final decision'.

interpretation follows logically from the character of Union law, which develops private law for varying purposes. Notably, the coexistence of divergent aims is not necessarily problematic from the perspective of Union law.

Unfortunately, it does not appear as if legislators have foreseen the difficulties that may arise from the use of blanket clauses, especially problems from European blanket clauses that closely resemble blanket clauses that play a central role in national private law. If the *acquis* itself develops inconsistent blanket clauses or if blanket clauses are interpreted divergently throughout the Union, this likely also inhibits the extent to which these blanket clauses facilitate market access. As also became visible in the case studies, the development of private law on the basis of blanket clauses may entail that actors interested in cross-border trade have to assess their legal position in accordance with case law developed mainly for domestic (consumer) contracts, in another Member State.[2397] The development of new governance has not prevented these problems. Accordingly, the development of guidance for the interpretation of unfair commercial practices under Directive 2005/29 has apparently not prevented the development of inconsistencies.

Thus, while the use of blanket clauses may be hard to avoid, the difficulties outlined in this paragraph demonstrate that blanket clauses should not simply be transferred to the European level. Instead, the European legislator should carefully consider the use of blanket clauses in the *acquis*. Depending on the aim of the European legislator, the use of additional or alternative techniques to either foster responsiveness or predictability and consistency throughout the Union should be considered. Such considerations have however not become apparent as blanket clauses have been based on comparative law.

9.4.2. *Interaction between courts in the interpretation of blanket clauses*

The case studies[2398] found that courts, following the restraint of the legislator in the implementation of the Directive, adopted restraint in interacting with the CJEU in the interpretation of harmonised law, instead developing harmonised law in accordance with national law. Is this approach visible more widely in the development of the law through blanket clauses by both national and European actors, and how has that affected the extent to which blanket clauses improve the predictability, consistency, accessibility and responsiveness of European private law?

Similar blanket clauses have been used in the BGB, BW and the private law *acquis*. However, the lack of clarity on the allocation of competences to interpret blanket clauses and the restraint of national actors more generally indicates that neither the CJEU nor national courts have sufficiently taken into account interdependence.

Firstly, especially the CJEU needs to clarify the allocation of competences to interpret blanket clauses in the private law *acquis*.

[2397] As previously argued by K.P. Berger, 'Für eine Reform des AGB-Rechts im Unternehmerverkehr', *NJW* 2010, p. 466, see par. 4.3.3.1.3.

[2398] See previously par. 4.6.1 and 5.6.1.

The question of which courts are competent to interpret the blanket clauses in the private law *acquis* has given rise to debate. Roth[2399] holds that blanket clauses intend to leave discretion to national legislators, in conformity with the general character of a Directive that is binding with regard to the results to be achieved, but not the techniques. Alternatively, Schillig,[2400] Remien,[2401] Micklitz,[2402] and Wolff[2403] find that the competence of the CJEU depends on the aim and the degree of harmonisation that a Directive pursues, as well as relevant national private law. Yet another view is taken by Basedow,[2404] who points out that blanket clauses are concepts of Union law and, therefore, need to be interpreted autonomously by the CJEU, even if these clauses are incorporated in minimum harmonisation Directives. Yet it can be doubted whether the autonomous interpretation of blanket clauses at the European level would contribute to responsiveness.

Unfortunately, CJEU case law does not take a consistent approach to the interpretation of blanket clauses in the private law *acquis*, as rightly criticised by Schmid[2405] and Collins.[2406] Consequently, an answer to questions on the general competence of the CJEU to interpret blanket clauses cannot be deduced from CJEU case law.

In turn, the lack of clarity on this point may undermine the consistent interpretation of blanket clauses throughout the *acquis* to national legal views on justice, as national courts assume that they have remained competent to interpret blanket clauses that have not changed on the surface, but that have gained a European background. A general competence of the CJEU could inhibit the responsiveness of the private law *acquis*, and have consequences for the interpretation of the law that parties have not foreseen, thus limiting predictability. Also, national courts are less able to preserve the consistent development of national law if they are not competent to interpret blanket clauses.

2399 W.-H. Roth, 'Generalklauseln im Europäischen Privatrecht', in: J. Basedow, K.J. Hopt, H. Kötz (eds.), *Festschrift für Ulrich Drobnig zum siebzigsten Geburtstag*, Tübingen: Mohr Siebeck, 1998, p. 141. Comp. also C.-W. Canaris, 'Der EuGH als zukünftige privatrechtliche Superrevisionsinstanz?' *EuZW* 1994, p. 417.

2400 M. Schillig, *Konkretisierungskompetenz und Konkretisierungsmethoden im Europäischen Privatrecht*, Berlin: De Gruyter 2009, p. 226 et seq, K. Gutman, *The constitutionality of European contract law*, Leuven 2010, p. 81, also refers to the approach adopted by Directives. She notes that the Court cannot remedy ongoing divergence of national private law if Directives pursue minimum harmonisation.

2401 O. Remien, 'Die Vorlagepflicht bei Auslegung unbestimmter Rechtsbegriffe', *RabelsZ* 2002, p. 528–529.

2402 H.-W. Micklitz, 'The targeted full harmonisation approach: looking behind the curtain', in: G. Howells, R. Schulze (eds.), *Modernising and harmonising consumer contract law*, München: Sellier 2009, p. 59–60.

2403 I. Wolff, *Die Verteilung der Konkretisierungskompetenz für Generalklauseln in privatrechtsgestaltenden Richtlinien*, Baden Baden: Nomos 2002, p. 61–62, and specifically on several Directives in the private law *acquis* p. 201–250. Wolff, at p. 179 et seq argues that, considering the principle of proportionality, there is an assumption that the national judiciary retains some competence in the harmonisation of blanket clauses in the *acquis*.

2404 J. Basedow, 'Der Bundesgerichtshof, seine Rechtsanwälte und die Verantwortung für das europäische Privatrecht', in: G. Pfeiffer, J. Kummer, S. Scheuch (eds.), *Festschrift für Hans Erich Brandner zum 70. Geburtstag*, Köln: Schmidt 1996, p. 675. See also for a uniform interpretation by the CJEU M.W. Hesselink, 'Case: CJEU- Freiburger Kommunalbauten v Hofstetter', *ERCL* 2006, p. 374–375, and I. Klauer, 'General clauses in European private law and "stricter" national standards', *ERPL* 2000, p. 187.

2405 Ch. Schmid, 'The CJEU as a constitutional and a private law court: a methodological comparison', *ZERP Diskussionspaper* 2006, p. 15–16.

2406 H. Collins, *The European Civil Code: The way forward*, Cambridge: CUP 2008, p. 60.

Secondly, national actors need to consider the interpretation of European blanket clauses in accordance with European law more generally. Currently, national legislators appear to have overlooked the possibility that the use of blanket clauses at the European level also means that these blanket clauses should be interpreted in accordance with European law.[2407] Further, there are indications that blanket clauses in the *acquis*, especially if they closely resemble national blanket clauses, may become nationalised if the national judiciary interprets European blanket clauses in conformity with national law. Wissink[2408] holds that the interpretation of implementation law is affected by national law, and warns that judges should not just assume that the interpretation of European law and national law will converge. This sort of interpretation would undermine harmonisation.[2409]

As courts have not sufficiently recognised interdependence, courts at the European and the national level have not sufficiently interacted with one another, in accordance with the findings of the case studies.[2410] This is unfortunate, because the CJEU depends on national courts to refer relevant cases to the CJEU. Currently, it may take some time before questions on the interpretation of blanket clauses come before the CJEU, because national judges may show some restraint in referring questions on the interpretation of blanket clauses to it.[2411] The German case study[2412] however indicates that even if national courts and the CJEU do not sufficiently interact, problems with regard to unpredictability and inconsistency need not directly develop at the national level. Rather, the lack of interaction may inhibit the responsive and predictable development of the *acquis*.

Regardless of the question of whether this is desirable, *if* blanket clauses in the *acquis* are to be interpreted in a similar manner throughout the Union, this also necessitates interaction between national courts. The Hoge Raad[2413] and the BGH[2414] do not generally

2407 Comp. T. Ritter, 'Europarechtsneutralität mitgliedstaatlicher Generalklauseln?', *NJW* 2012, p. 1549.

2408 M.H. Wissink, *Richtlijnconforme interpretatie in het burgerlijk recht*, Deventer: Kluwer 2001, 372–374, referring to HR 10 January 1992, *NJ* 1992, 576, par. 4.4 where the Hoge Raad holds that the law on self-employed commercial agents has remained the same after the implementation of Directive 86/653.

2409 P. Rott, 'What is the role of the CJEU in EC private law? – a comment on the CJEU judgments in Océano Grupo, Freiburger Kommunalbauten, Leitner and Veedfald', 1 *Hanse LR* 2005, p. 6 notes that, notwithstanding the principle of autonomous interpretation and consistent interpretation, national courts may tend to strive for application of Directives that is consistent with 'pre-harmonisation' case law.

2410 See previously par. 4.6.2. and 5.6.2.

2411 L. Niglia, 'The non-Europeanisation of private law', *ERPL* 2001, p. 575, even finds that national courts do not take note of the private law *acquis* when ruling on private law. See on the practice of the Hoge Raad with regard to international private law M.V. Polak, 'Spreken is zilver, zwijgen is goud', in: A.G. Castermans et al (eds.), *Het zwijgen van de Hoge Raad*, *BWKJ* 25, Deventer: Kluwer 2009, p. 89. See on the practice of the German BGH, J. Basedow 'Der Europäische Gerichtshof und die Klauselrichtlinie 93/13 – Der verweigerte Dialog', in: G. Müller et al. (eds.), *Festschrift für Günter Hirsch zum 65. Geburtstag*, München: Beck 2008, p. 51.

2412 See previously par. 4.6.2.

2413 J.M. Smits, E.A.G. van Schagen, 'De Hoge Raad als Europese rechter: Mag het een ietsje meer zijn?', in: A.G. Castermans et al (eds.), *Het zwijgen van de Hoge Raad*, *BWKJ 25*, Deventer: Kluwer 2009, p. 79–87.

2414 H. Kötz, 'Das Bundesgerichtshof und die Rechtsvergleichung', in: A. Heldrich, K. Hopt (eds.), *50 Jahre Bundesgerichtshof, Festgabe aus der Wissenschaft, Band III, Handels- und Wirtschaftsrecht, Europäisches und Internationales Recht*, München: Beck 2000, p. 831.

seem to have made it a practice to refer to foreign decisions in the interpretation of harmonised private law. This restraint may be motivated by convincing concerns of consistency and predictability. In addition, the use of foreign decisions may not be predictable and accessible to parties.

In addition, if national courts do not sufficiently interact with one another, unpredictability and inconsistency may arise.[2415] As a result, blanket clauses may leave actors acting contrary to good faith, better off than actors violating a more clearly delineated rule forbidding specific behaviour.[2416] The Law Commissions[2417] have pointed out that ambiguous terms leave room for argument on the duties of contract parties, which may not necessarily be beneficial for the weaker party without expertise or sufficient resources to argue why a professional's behaviour is contrary to, for example, good faith.

It can be concluded that courts in the interpretation of blanket clauses in the private law *acquis* do not sufficiently interact with one another, which may inhibit the responsive and predictable development of the *acquis*.

9.4.3. *Conclusion on the use of blanket clauses*

This paragraph has asked whether actors have more widely failed to take interdependence as a starting point in the development of European private law through blanket clauses, and whether problems detected in the case studies have become visible more widely.

Firstly, both the national and European legislator have aimed to increase the responsiveness of private law in the use of blanket clauses. Simultaneously, the European legislator has sought to facilitate access to domestic markets. Unfortunately, actors seem to have been insufficiently aware of potential problems that can arise from the use of blanket clauses, which may in turn diminish the extent to which blanket clauses and additional new modes of governance build the internal market.

Secondly, both at the national and European level, courts have shown restraint in interacting with one another, which has not contributed to the predictability and responsiveness to national legal views on justice of the private law *acquis*. The lack of referral to foreign law further indicates that opportunities for mutual learning may not have been realised. The case studies however indicated that courts may have good reasons for their restraint.[2418]

2415 See previously par. 5.4.4.

2416 E.S. van Nimwegen, 'Handhaving door de Consumentenautoriteit: een goed samenspel met het Burgerlijk Wetboek en Europese regelgeving?', *Contracteren* 2010, p. 57.

2417 English law Commission Law Commission, the Scottish Law Commission, *An optional Common European Sales Law: Advantages and problems, Advice to the UK Government*, 10 November 2011, available at www.justice.gov.uk/lawcommission/docs/Common_European_Sales_Law_Advice.pdf, p. viii, x.

2418 See previously par. 4.6.2, 5.6.2 and 6.3.3.

9.5. The use of general principles

In the case studies, it became apparent that the development of the law on STCs at the national level has taken place on the basis of general principles, but European law develops differently.[2419] Although general principles,[2420] especially principles of good faith and consumer protection, may provide a starting point for interaction between actors, this was not the case for the law on STCs. This paragraph asks whether this approach is more widely visible or whether general principles have been used as a starting point for interaction. If this is the case, however, a closer inspection of the weaknesses of general principles makes clear that the use of general principles may give rise to potential problems that justify carefully considering the use of general principles.

It may be counter-intuitive to consider the *use* of general principles, as this may denote the use of ideas on justice. However, general principles are used in the reasoning of the courts, or in the development of codes on the basis of not only abstract ideas on justice, but also general rules or concepts deduced from specific rules. Furthermore, especially at the European level, the idea of using private law, including ideas of justice, to promote the aims of the Treaties, is less unfamiliar than may the case at the national level.

Paragraph 9.5.1 will consider whether general principles contribute to the interaction between actors in the multilevel legal order by providing a starting point for discussion. Paragraph 9.5.2 will turn to the weaknesses that become apparent when considering the use of general principles. Paragraph 9.5.3 will end with a conclusion.

9.5.1. *Interaction on the basis of general principles?*

Has the extent to which national law may develop on the basis of general principles been compromised more generally as European law develops differently? If not, have principles served as a starting point for interaction?

Traditionally, general principles may contribute to a more comprehensible private law in various ways. General principles are characteristically primarily used to improve the coherence of private law, either filling in lacunae in the law, as a weighty argument in the interpretation of law, or in the evaluation of laws,[2421] which may enhance the consistent development of law. Moreover, deducing general principles from private law

2419 See par. 4.5.2.

2420 Previously, in par. 4.5.1, it was submitted that the use of general principles is not necessarily based on interaction, but instead, on converging basic ideas on justice that may allow for multiple outcomes. Accordingly, this volume considers general principles as ideas on justice, such as legal equality, in accordance with the definition of the Study Group on Social Justice in European Private Law, 'Social justice in European contract law: a manifesto', *ELJ* 2004, p. 656.

2421 Comp. A.S. Hartkamp, 'De algemene beginselen van het Unierecht en het privaatrecht', *WPNR* 6901 (2011), more recently, on the distinction between rights and principles in the EU Charter J.E. Emaus, 'Rechten, beginselen en horizontale directe werking van de grondrechten uit het EU-Handvest ', *NTBR* 2015, 10. Comp. in this light also CJEU 30 April 2014 (Barclays Bank SA v Sánchez García and Chacón Barrera), C-280/13, [2014] ECR p. I-0, par. 43–44 and D. Gudmundsdóttir, 'A renewed emphasis on the Charter's distinction between rights and principles: Is a doctrine of judicial restraint more appropriate?', *CMLRev* 2015, p.691–693, who considers that according to the Charter, principles do not give rise to justiciable claims.

may provide starting points to determine the future development of private law, which may contribute to the predictable development of private law. Furthermore, principles can play an important role in furthering the responsiveness of European private law to society's ideas on justice.

In the German case study,[2422] it became clear that guiding principles underpinning the German law on STCs continued to play an important role in German law, despite harmonisation in this area.

Arguably, the added value of general principles in the multilevel legal order is especially their role in providing starting points for debate.[2423] According to Mak,[2424] by recognising general principles instead of imposing one solution, the CJEU could provide some leeway for states in the implementation of the *acquis* and increase the acceptability of the *acquis* in states. In this view, general ideas on justice (for example, equality) are common to Member States and the Union, but further interpretation and application of these principles are left to the national level. Such leeway may also prevent private law from eventually becoming outdated, as national judges are given some room for coping with new developments in practice. Similarly, Reich[2425] finds that general principles may serve as a means of coordinating national and European rules.

Accordingly, the relation between the BVerfG and the CJEU can be seen in this light.[2426] Even though both courts emphasise, respectively, the GG and the TFEU as their source of authority, both courts respect fundamental principles, such as requirements of democracy, rule of law and fundamental rights, either guaranteed in the GG or the Charter. From this perspective, general principles allow for mutual recognition and respect.

Similarly, the CJEU recognised principles common to Member States, leaving leeway to national courts to develop the law in accordance with these principles.[2427] National courts

2422 See previously par. 4.8.

2423 In this sense V. Mak, 'A shift of focus: systematisation in European private law through EU law', *ELJ* 2011, p. 417: '[Principles] are anchor points, able to ensure the observance of fundamental values and a coherent development of the legal system, while leaving room for further development according to the needs of society.' Similarly V. Trstenjak, E. Beysen, 'European consumer protection law: *Curia simper dabit remedium*?' *CMLR* 2011, p. 116.

2424 C. Mak, 'Hedgehogs in Luxembourg?' A Dworkinian reading of the CJEU's case law on principles of private law and a reply of the fox', *ERPL* 2012, p. 340.

2425 N. Reich, 'Pluralism and private law in the European Union', in: L. Niglia (ed.), *Pluralism and European private law*, Oxford: Hart 2013, p. 74–75.

2426 See previously par. 7.3.2.2.

2427 See for example CJEU 3 December 1974 (van Binsbergen v Bestuur van de Bedrijfsvereniging voor de Metaalnijverheid), [1974], p. 1299, par. 12–14. Comp. CJEU 20 September 2001 (Courage Ltd v Crehan), C-453/99, [2001] ECR, p. I-6297, where the Court held that European law stands in the way of a national rule barring a party to a contract contrary to article 101 TFEU from claiming damages for loss caused by performance of the illegal contract on the sole ground that the claimant is a party to that contract. Yet the Court did allow a national rule that prevented parties from relying on their own illegal conduct to obtain damages where it is established that that party bears significant responsibility for the distortion of competition. Preventing parties from relying on their own illegal conduct is, as the Court noted, a principle recognised in many – but not all – legal systems throughout the Union. More recently CJEU 10 April 2008 (Hamilton v Volksbank Filder), C-412/06, [2008] ECR, p. I-2383, par. 42 and CJEU 3 September 2009 (Messner v Firma Stefan Krüger), C-489/07, [2009] ECR, p. I-7315, par. 26.

have likewise recognised the added value of general principles in soft laws,[2428] although restraint in referring to these principles is also visible in, for example, the Dutch legal order.[2429] More generally, courts do not seem to have made excessive use of principles reflected in soft laws as an inspiration for the interpretation of European private law.[2430]

European actors have more generally recognised the role of general principles. The European legislator, in article 340 TFEU, already recognised that the contractual liability of the Union is determined by common principles. Already in *AM&S v Commission*,[2431] the CJEU recognised the relevance of principles common to Member States and has since then repeatedly referred to common principles in some of its leading cases. Accordingly, in *Francovich*,[2432] the CJEU referred to the principle of equal treatment, ruling that equal treatment did not stand in the way of a Directive aimed to protect employees from insolvency.

Although principles play an important role in the development of European law, it is not developed on the basis of principles similar to the development of national law. Rather, European law emphasises, for example, equal access to markets.[2433] This approach can be detected in *Colemann v Attridge law*,[2434] in which the CJEU reiterated the objectives of Directive 2000/78 as seeking to establish a 'level playing field as regards employment and occupation', stressing the free movement of citizens throughout the Union. In *Raccanelli*,[2435] the CJEU considered the prohibition of discrimination on the basis of nationality and stressed the freedom movement of workers under (then) article 39 EC. Decisions that can have profound impact on national labour law, such as *Viking*[2436] and *Laval*,[2437] can also be seen in the light of equal market access.

However, principles have not consistently formed a starting point for interaction in the development of European private law. In addition, national courts continue to adopt restraint in interacting with European actors in the development of harmonised law[2438] and they have generally not considered general principles as starting points for interaction

2428 See above, par. 9.3.2. on the use of soft law made by national courts.

2429 See for examples J.M. Smits, E.A.G. van Schagen, 'De Hoge Raad als Europese rechter: Mag het ietsje meer zijn?' in: A.G. Castermans et al (eds.), *Het zwijgen van de Hoge Raad*, *BWKJ* 25, Deventer: Kluwer 2009, p. 84.

2430 G. Danneman, S. Vogenauer (eds.), *The Common European Sales Law in context*, Oxford: OUP 2013.

2431 CJEU 18 May 1982 (AM & S v Commission), C 155/79, [1982] ECR, p. I-1575, par. 18.

2432 CJEU 9 November 1995 (Francovich v Italian Republic), C- 479/93, [1995], p. I-3843, par. 23.

2433 Comp. N.C.R. Reich, *General principles of EU civil law*, Antwerp: Intersentia 2014, p. 73, who characterises the 'constitutional approach' to non-discrimination as a feature necessarily supporting the position of EU citizens.

2434 CJEU 17 July 2008 (Colemann v Attridge law et al), C-303/06, [2008] ECR, p. I-5603, par. 47.

2435 CJEU 17 July 2008 (Raccanelli v Max-Planck-Gesellschaft zur Förderung der Wissenschaften eV), C-94/07, [2008] ECR, p. I-5939.

2436 CJEU 11 December 2007 (International Transport Workers' Federation and Finnish Seamen's Union v Viking Line ABP and OÜ Viking Line Eesti), C-438/05, [2007] ECR, p. I-10779.

2437 CJEU 18 December 2007 (Laval un Partneri Ltd v Svenska Byggnadsarbetareförbundet, Svenska Byggnadsarbetareförbundets avdelning 1, Byggettan and Svenska Elektrikerförbundet), C-341/05, [2007] ECR p. I-11767.

2438 See previously par. 9.4.2.

with European actors. Instead, referral to general principles is used in the context of developing national law coherently.[2439]

In conclusion, general principles can form a starting point for interaction, as visible in CJEU decisions. The use of general principles in this manner fosters the consistent development of law throughout the Union while it simultaneously leaves room for discretion at the national level, which may facilitate the responsive development of the law. Simultaneously, general principles oblige national actors to justify impediments to free movement throughout the Union, and national law may accordingly have to be amended, which may not always be predictable. General principles may also, by prompting national actors to justify their actions, provide a starting point for revision and mutual learning. In time, this should theoretically improve the responsiveness of European private law to the needs of foreign and international actors.

9.5.2. *Weaknesses arising from the use of general principles?*

Although the development of the law on the basis of general principles may foster coherence, as well as responsiveness and consistency, while also creating opportunities for mutual learning, the use of general principles may give rise to problems that justify carefully assessing the benefits and detriments of general principles before promoting their increased use.

This paragraph will subsequently discuss unpredictability in paragraph 9.5.2.1. Subsequently, paragraph 9.5.2.2 will address problems of inaccessibility. Paragraph 9.5.2.3 will end with a conclusion.

9.5.2.1. The discovery of general principles and predictability

This paragraph will discuss the unpredictability that may arise from the discovery of general principles by the judiciary, turning firstly to the reallocation of competences that may arise from the use of general principles and secondly to the weaknesses of the inductive process.

1) The use of general principles gives the impression that law is discovered. Because it does not entail the development of new law, the discovery of principles is not subject to principles of conferral of competence, even though principles may profoundly affect the further development of European private law as well as the allocation of competences between the Union of its Member States.[2440]

Devroe[2441] points out that although formally, the Court merely discovers an already existing principle, the recognition of that principle enables the Court to evaluate whether private law is in

2439 See previously par. 2.6.2.

2440 S. Weatherill, 'The "principles of civil law" as a basis for interpreting the legislative *acquis*', *ERCL* 2010, p. 77.

2441 W. Devroe, 'Impact van door het Europees Hof van Justitie ontwikkelde algemene beginselen op privaatrechtelijke verhoudingen', in: A.S. Hartkamp, C.H. Sieburgh, L.A.D. Keus (eds.), De *invloed van het Europese recht op het Nederlandse privaatrecht I*, Deventer: Kluwer 2007, p. 134–135.

conformity with these principles. Referring to CJEU decisions such as *Francovich*,[2442] Devroe further argues that the Court may even, by using general principles, extend the scope of existing European law.

Furthermore, the emphasis on the discovery of general principles suggests that the discovery of such principles takes place in a neutral, objective manner. This can, however, be doubted,[2443] especially if general principles denote society's ideas on justice, which may differ throughout the Union.

2) Finding general principles of private law typically takes place through inductive reasoning, which has been defined as: 'the process of inferring a general law or principle from the observation of particular instances'.[2444]

A well-known example of inductive reasoning is the conclusion that all swans are white because of all the separate instances (swans a, b, c, d, e, f, etc) that are white. The weakness in this form of reasoning lies in the assumption that from the separate instances, a more general conclusion logically follows, while that may not necessarily be the case. Consequently, objections can be made against such discovery of general principles. Accordingly, Collins[2445] points out that generalisation of the repetitively used withdrawal periods in the consumer *acquis* to general contract law, on the basis that the use of withdrawal periods can be explained by the principle of self-determination,[2446] may not be without risk, because the European legislator may have consciously limited the use of withdrawal periods to specific fields.

Although the fragmented nature of the *acquis* may make the problems of inductive reasoning more apparent, this weakness in the discovery of general principles is not particular to the *acquis*. At a national level, Scholten[2447] considers that finding general principles on which specific rules are based may not necessarily lead to the conclusion that some rules can be also be applied in situations that fall outside of the scope of the rule. Lord Goff[2448] warns against a number of pitfalls that can occur in the search of legal principles, including the temptation of elegance: just because a solution is simple and elegant does not necessarily mean that it is accurate, that it allows for exceptions and further qualifications, or that it adequately reflects a complex area of law.

Accordingly, Metzger[2449] notes that the inductive process may entail that general principles do not have absolute effect. Instead, principles should be seen as ideas that add a dimension of

2442 CJEU 19 November 1991 (Francovich and others v Italian Republic), joined cases C-6/90 and C-9/90, ECR [1991], p. I-5357, par. 32–36.

2443 S. Weatherill, 'The "principles of civil law" as a basis for interpreting the legislative *acquis*', *ERCL* 2010, p. 74–85, A. Metzger, 'Allgemeine Rechtsgrundsätze im europäischen Privatrecht: Ansätze für eine einheitliche Techniquenlehre im europäischen Mehrebenensystem', *Rechtstheorie* 2009, p. 325.

2444 Comp. the definition of the Oxford English Dictionary that defines 'induction' as '[t]he process of inferring a general law principle from the observation of particular instances'. J. Vickers, 'The problem of induction', *Stanford Encyclopedia of Philosophy*, accessible at http://plato.stanford.edu/entries/induction-problem/ points out that this definition is not completely correct, as inductive reasoning is generally considered to include more instances of reasoning than the one stated in the OED.

2445 H. Collins, 'The alchemy of deriving general principles of contract law from European legislation: in search of the philosopher's stone', *ERCL* 2006, p. 221.

2446 As defended by K. Riesenhuber, 'System and principles of EC contract law', *ERCL* 2005, p. 297.

2447 Asser/Scholten 1974, p. 45–46.

2448 Lord Goff, 'The search for principle', *Maccabean lectures on Jurisprudence, Proceedings of the British Academy* 1984, p. 174–177.

2449 A. Metzger, *Extra legem, intra ius: Allgemeine Rechtsgrundsätze im Europäischen Privatrecht*, Tübingen: Mohr Siebeck 2009, p. 60–61, p. 546, A. Metzger, 'Allgemeine Rechtsgrundsätze im europäischen

weight to an argument ('*Abwägungsgebote*') – they may play a role in the arguments that have a dimension of weight for actors developing private law. Alternatively, principles, in Metzger's view, may be seen as rules that are probably binding, as the inductive reasoning process may not be suitable for definite conclusions – findings based on inductive reasoning may instead be valid until there is an atypical instance (the black swan) that disproves the finding.

3) It may difficult to predict which general principles may be discovered.

Devroe[2450] rightly points out that a similarity of national laws may not necessarily point to the existence of a general principle in European law. But if private laws show great similarities and a general principle is not recognised, is there an additional requirement for the recognition of general principles? Metzger[2451] finds that the recognition of general principles may depend on either extra-legal elements such as the views of justice in society, or the political aims of the Union. This answer does not improve the predictability or accessibility of private law, as courts frequently only briefly refer to general principles without giving an insight into the premises upon which the courts' inductive conclusions are based.[2452] Confusingly, however, general principles can be recognised in the absence of the similarity of laws, and it seems as if the similarity between private laws is not a strict requirement.

The lack of predictability on the recognition of principles becomes apparent from the drafting of the DCFR. Initially, the interim outline edition[2453] sought to introduce a number of fundamental principles, including justice, solidarity, legal certainty and efficiency. These principles were severely criticised,[2454] because the restrictions in the interim draft of party autonomy went too far, because the rules of non-discrimination were ineffective, and because private law in general did not aim to further distributive justice. Accordingly, the later 2009 outline edition[2455] had substantively altered the principles underlying European private law, to freedom, security, justice and efficiency, unfortunately without explaining why the drafters had chosen to alter their approach and what elements of the general principles suggested in the 2008 edition were still adhered to.[2456]

Privatrecht: Ansätze für eine einheitliche Methodenlehre im europäischen Mehrebenensystem', *Rechtstheorie* 2009, p. 315, p. 317–318.

2450 W. Devroe, 'Impact van door het Europees Hof van Justitie ontwikkelde algemene beginselen op privaatrechtelijke verhoudingen', in: A.S. Hartkamp, C.H. Sieburgh, L.A.D. Keus (eds.), De *invloed van het Europese recht op het Nederlandse privaatrecht I*, Deventer: Kluwer 2007, p. 136, similarly V. Mak, 'A shift of focus: systematisation in European private law through EU law', *ELJ* 2011, p. 422.

2451 A. Metzger, *Extra legem, intra ius: Allgemeine Rechtsgrundsätze im Europäischen Privatrecht*, Tübingen: Mohr Siebeck 2009, p. 219, p. 466.

2452 A. Metzger, *Extra legem, intra ius: Allgemeine Rechtsgrundsätze im Europäischen Privatrecht*, Tübingen: Mohr Siebeck 2009, p. 546, as well as A. Metzger, 'Allgemeine Rechtsgrundsätze im europäischen Privatrecht: Ansätze für eine einheitliche Methodenlehre im europäischen Mehrebenensystem', *Rechtstheorie* 2009, p. 323.

2453 C. von Bar et al. (eds.), *Principles, Definitions and Model Rules of European Private Law. Draft Common Frame of Reference, Full edition* 2008, available at http://ec.europa.eu/justice/contract/files/european-private-law_en.pdf, München: Sellier 2008, par. 22.

2454 H. Eidenmüller, 'Party autonomy, distributive justice and the conclusion of contracts in the DCFR', *ERCL* 2009, p. 109.

2455 C. von Bar et al. (eds.), *Draft Common Frame of Reference, Outline Edition*, München: Sellier 2009.

2456 See critically M.W. Hesselink, 'If you don't like our principles we have others', in: R. Brownsword et al. (eds.), *The foundations of European private law*, Oxford: Hart 2008, p. 59.

4) Even the use of clearly recognised principles may still may still result in unpredictability,[2457] because general principles do not single out one particular rule or conclusion.[2458] Typically, various conflicting principles play a role in the development of national private law and the adjudication of disputes. In the absence of an established hierarchy between principles, the outcome in individual cases is not predetermined by these general principles.[2459] Instead, the choice for a specific outcome is influenced in the preferences of the legislator, the judge or the academic.[2460]

For example, article 6:2 BW stipulates that contracting parties have to comply, in their behaviour towards one another, with the principle of fairness ('*redelijkheid en billijkheid*'), but that duty still leaves open how contract parties' rights and duties arising from contracts are affected in individual cases, where the consequences of choices between, for example, predictability and fairness become clear.[2461] Similarly, if the CJEU concludes that a general principle of civil law exists – for example, the principle that 'full performance of a contract results, as a general rule, from discharge of the mutual obligations under the contract or from termination of that contract',[2462] it is difficult to predict whether this principle will play a role in areas that fall beyond the scope of the Directive.[2463] Consequently, a decision based on principles may still give rise to questions of how private law will be developed in individual cases.

Nevertheless, in individual cases, principles may have far-reaching impact on the development of European private law.[2464] A well-known example of far-reaching and unexpected development on the basis of the principle of legal equality is the CJEU ruling in *Mangold*[2465] that set aside provisions of legislation on the termination of contract of employment that parties had relied on.

2457 Comp. Lord Goff, 'The future of the common law', *International and Comparative Law Quarterly* 1997, p. 753: 'Continental lawyers love to proclaim some great principle, and then knock it into shape afterwards. Instead, the boring British want to find out first whether, and if so, how these great ideas are going to work in practice.'

2458 Lord Goff, 'In search for principle', *Maccabean lectures on Jurisprudence, Proceedings of the British Academy* 1984, p. 174–177 has pointed out that even if legal principles are established, one may still not know a complete answer to a particular problem, especially as the law is continually developing.

2459 R. Dworkin, *Taking rights seriously*, London: Duckworth 1977, p. 25–26.

2460 Accordingly, K.P. Purnhagen, 'Principles of European private or civil law? A reminder of the symbiotic relationship between the CJEU and the DCFR in a pluralistic European private law', *ELJ* 2012, p. 848, points to the relevance of the question which actor has the competence to find principles.

2461 See for example HR 28 April 2000, *NJ* 2000, 430.

2462 CJEU 10 April 2008, (Hamilton v Volksbank Filder eG), C-412/06, ECR [2008], p. I-2383, par. 42.

2463 S. Weatherill, 'The "principles of civil law" as a basis for interpreting the legislative *acquis*', *ERCL* 2010, p. 77.

2464 W. Devroe, 'Impact van door het Europees Hof van Justitie ontwikkelde algemene beginselen op privaatrechtelijke verhoudingen', in: A.S. Hartkamp, C.H. Sieburgh, L.A.D. Keus (eds.), De *invloed van het Europese recht op het Nederlandse privaatrecht I*, Deventer: Kluwer 2007, p. 133, considers the use of general principles as one of the most powerful tools of lawyers in European law.

2465 CJEU 22 November 2005 (Mangold v Helm), C-144/04, [2005] ECR, p. I-9981, par. 59–65, 74. In this decision, the Court established that in the European legal order, a general principle of legal equality prohibiting discrimination on the basis of age existed, on which Directive 2000/78 was based. This principle could set aside German law stipulating that although objective reasons needed to be given for the conclusion of fixed term employment contracts, these objective reasons were not required if the employee was, at the time of conclusion of the employment contract, 52 years or older. Although the court considered that this exception, which was made in order to reduce the unemployment of people

Therefore, general principles may profoundly affect the development of the law, but both the recognition of principles and the further development of the law on the basis of principles may undermine the predictable development of private law.

9.5.2.2. The discovery and the use of general principles: problems of accessibility

Problems of inaccessibility may arise especially as general principles do not necessarily have to be written. General principles introduce an *unwritten* source of private law, alongside other sources of private law, which does not benefit accessibility.[2466] Admittedly, private parties can look at case law and use decisions of the judiciary as a starting point to discover general principles. However, case law can only offer a starting point, which, moreover, may be subject to change. Furthermore, courts need not make explicit what premises they base general principles. Metzger[2467] rightly points out that especially national civil law courts as well as the CJEU frequently do not make all of the premises on which they base the recognition of a general principle explicit. Especially if extra-legal elements, such as moral or political points of view play a role in the recognition of general principles, these may not always be found in either statutes or case law. Yet for private parties these underlying ideas on justice, and their consequences in individual cases, may not always be self-evident.

However, simultaneously, the development of private law on the basis of general principles may also increase accessibility as it contributes to the development of private law in accordance with society's legal views on justice, which, in turn, should facilitate the understanding of private law for parties not familiar with private law.

9.5.2.3. Conclusion on the weaknesses arising from the use of general principles

The development of private law on the basis of general principles may undermine predictability, because of the way in which principles are discovered as well as the application of principles in individual cases and their effect on the outcome of disputes. Further, general principles are an unwritten source of law that may undermine the accessibility of the law. At first sight, the development of national law in this manner reinforces criticism on arguments that focus *solely* on democratic legitimacy.[2468] As became apparent in the German case study, they may form a starting point for case law that may subsequently be codified.[2469] The development of

over the age of 52 in Germany, was legitimate, it was not proportional to the aim it pursued, also considering that the age of workers was the only criterion for the exception, notwithstanding other relevant circumstances. Both the recognition of this principle and the effects in this case are not entirely uncontroversial. For example, A.S. Hartkamp, 'The general principles of EU law and private law', *RabelsZ* 2011, p. 246 calls the recognition of this principle 'unconvincing'.

2466 Comp. the view that principles may also be used to introduce society's views into private law – thus, principles introduce an interaction between private law and society: J.H. Nieuwenhuis, *Drie beginselen van contractenrecht*, Deventer: Kluwer 1979, p. 41–42.

2467 A. Metzger, *Extra legem, intra ius: Allgemeine Rechtsgrundsatze im Europaischen Privatrecht*, Tübingen: Mohr Siebeck 2009, p. 219, 412, 466, 546.

2468 See previously par. 1.8.

2469 See previously par. 4.5.1.

the law on STCs, though sanctioned by the German legislator that established a thorough set of rules generally considered successful, had developed before the legislative process that resulted in the AGBG. This supports the argument that private law need not exclusively be developed and designed by legislators; instead, business practices and subsequent decisions have sparked the development of case law later sanctioned and improved by the legislator.

As the development of the law on the basis of general principles may also increase responsiveness, which, in turn, is advantageous for accessibility, actors involved in the development of private law should take into account these potential problems and seek to alleviate them, by making the recognition of principles more insightful and by mitigating the effect that principles may have on the outcome of individual cases. Alternatively, literature could seek to provide more insight in underlying ideas – although if the premises of courts are not made explicit, the insight provided by literature may necessarily have to rely upon some amount of guesswork.

9.5.3. *Conclusion on the use of principles*

In the light of the case studies,[2470] that found that general principles were not used as a starting point for interaction between national and European actors in the law on STCs, this paragraph has asked whether this approach is more widely visible or whether general principles have been used as a starting point for interaction. If so, what problems may arise from the use of general principles?

Actors have recognised that principles may serve as a useful starting point for developing harmonised law and for debate. However, actors have not consistently adopted this approach. Both the national courts and the CJEU have not consistently referred to principles common to the Member States. While this approach has not directly led to problems in terms of predictability, consistency, accessibility and responsiveness, opportunities to increasingly use general principles in this manner may not only create opportunities for learning, but also allow for consistency and responsiveness in the development of harmonised private law.

The use of general principles may also undermine the predictable development of private law, particularly because of a lack of clarity with regard to the recognition and further application of principles. A more careful use of general principles that is aimed at interaction may lessen current problems of unpredictability as well as inaccessibility. These weaknesses should, therefore, not stand in the way of a more prominent role of general principles in the development of European private law as a starting point for interaction.

9.6. Conclusion

From the previous chapters, it has become clear that national state actors retain a central role in the development of private law. Accordingly, large parts of private law continue to

[2470] Par. 4.5.5. and 5.5.4.

be developed through national techniques, and self-regulation is frequently developed within the framework of these techniques. The attention of national state actors, national practitioners and scholars seems to be concentrated on national law and national issues.[2471] The implementation of the *acquis* within codifications further shows that national legislators have sought to retain the central role of the BW and the BGB and blanket clauses within these codes, based on general principles. In this regard, comparisons with path-dependency have been made.[2472] Path-dependency has not only developed with regard to the development of material rules, but also with regard to the use of national techniques. Abandoning the use of codifications, blanket clauses and general principles is difficult, if not impossible to imagine. Even if it would be attempted, despite constitutional restraints, it entails adjusting the infrastructure in which private law is developed. As long as practice appears largely satisfied with use of national techniques, such drastic change is not likely.

However, some change is desirable as actors have not taken interdependence as a starting point in the development of the private law through codifications, soft laws, blanket clauses, and general principles, in accordance with the findings in the case studies.[2473] Problems have arisen, as the *acquis*, and interdependence alongside it, has developed. Particularly, since German and Dutch actors have not sufficiently taken interdependence into account in the development of codifications, they have failed to develop a consistent, predictable approach to the implementation of the *acquis*. As a result, national experiences with implemented measures are not considered in the revision of EU measures and the Dutch legislator has had to amend newly adopted law, which was also visible in the case studies.[2474] Soft laws do not sufficiently enable the European legislator to consider national experiences with the *acquis* in the revision of the *acquis*, which undermines responsiveness. Problems have also become visible in the use of blanket clauses and general principles. These techniques seem particularly suited to ensure responsiveness at the national level, but they are also used by the European legislator who has similarly sought to develop the law responsively. Yet the discovery of general principles is not very predictable, and general principles have not consistently served as a starting point for between either legislators or courts. In addition, so far, the

2471 Asser/Vranken 2005, nr. 140–143 notes that practitioners as well as scholars are often 'wired' to legal practice, and their reasoning is accordingly influenced. Comp. E.M.M. Meijers, *De taak der rechtswetenschap ten aanzien der vrije rechtspraak* (inaugural address Leiden), Haarlem: Tjeenk Willink 1910, p. 5 who finds that educating legal practice is the first task of legal academics and comp. S. Prechal, R.H. van Ooik, J.H. Jans, K.J.M. Mortelmans, *Europeanisation of the law: Consequences for the Dutch judiciary*, Report of October 2005, available at www.rechtspraak.nl/Organisatie/Raad-Voor-De-Rechtspraak/WetenschapsOnderzoek/Overzichtonderzoeksprojecten/Europeanisering/Pages/default.aspx, p. 49–50. S. Ferreri, 'General report: Sources of transnational law', *ERPL* 2012, p. 9–11, p. 29, p. 40 also finds that both practitioners and judges in many legal orders adopt a somewhat conservative approach to both foreign law and international law, and instead, seem to focus on national law and national issues.

2472 C.-H. Ladeur, 'Methodology and European law – can methodology change so as to cope with the multiplicity of the law?', in: M. van Hoecke (ed.) *Epistemology and methodology of comparative law*, Oxford: Hart 2004, p. 98.

2473 See previously par. 4.6.2. and par. 5.6.2.

2474 See previously par. 5.3.3.2.

simultaneous use of blanket clauses by national and European actors has led to problems of unpredictability and inconsistency within the *acquis* and within codifications. These problems have been aggravated as the European legislator has simultaneously developed a regulatory approach. Accordingly, European actors stress the need for further harmonisation and new modes of governance to mitigate unpredictability and inconsistency. Unfortunately, this approach may limit the extent to which blanket clauses contribute to the responsiveness and the consistency of national private law.[2475] Meanwhile, the use of maximum harmonisation and new modes of governance under Directive 2005/29 on unfair commercial practices has not prevented that inconsistencies have developed.

In accordance with the debate on multilevel governance more generally, actors are no longer able to independently safeguard the comprehensibility of the law through the use of national techniques. Nevertheless, the use of national techniques has not been adapted. Interdependence has not – yet – consistently resulted in the development or expansion of new modes of governance adapting the use of national techniques, even though this has been defended in the Dutch legal order. Specifically, Krans[2476] has suggested establishing expert committees to facilitate implementation, and Verdaas has proposed an expert committee to discuss amendments to the BW more generally.[2477]

Some explanations for this approach can be considered. The diminished ability of national techniques to contribute to the comprehensibility of European private law may not be an attractive idea for national legislators. Accordingly, if less interaction takes place, the limitations to national techniques are not as apparent. Further, if the initiatives of European actors undermine the quality of private law, national actors may avoid much interaction with these actors, in order to maintain the quality of private law. In that case, the lack of interaction between actors may not be directly problematic for private parties in terms of predictability, accessibility, consistency and responsiveness, as has become visible in the case studies.[2478] Yet the lack of interaction in itself indicates problems. Because of incnsistency in the *acquis* or unpredictability, national legislators may be reluctant to actively implement Directives and courts may be hesitant to refer questions to the CJEU that may result in answers that are difficult to reconcile with surrounding national law. Restraint may also be motivated by the need to ensure quick decisions in relatively straightforward cases.

Avoiding interaction does not mean that European actors will cease to develop the law and a lack of interaction will only enhance the chance that the *acquis* will disturb national law. Consequently, while no interaction – for example, between national courts and the CJEU – may be beneficial for private parties in the short term, it is not a long term solution that can, moreover, be undermined as some highest courts[2479] have actively

2475 This is especially the case for comitology, see previously par. 5.7.3.1.

2476 H.B. Krans, 'De druk van de ketel', *NTBR* 2014, 15, p. 133–134.

2477 A.J. Verdaas, 'Wetgever, besteed meer aandacht aan ons vermogensrecht! Een oproep tot het instellen van een permanente Commissie vermogensrecht', *NTBR* 2010, 47.

2478 See previously par. 4.6.2. and par. 5.6.2.

2479 Particularly, to date, Spanish courts have referred many questions on Directive 93/13: (Océano Grupo Editorial SA v Murciano Quintero), joined cases C-240/98 to C-244/98; (Mostaza Claro v Centro Móvil

started referring questions to the CJEU. Eventually, keeping silent and ignoring the role of the European legislator and the unclear role of the CJEU, where possible, is not going to improve the quality of private law.

The advantages of more interaction can be seen in the German development of private international law. The European legislator has been able to learn from newly adopted German law, and the German legislator successfully sought to limit inconsistencies between German and European law. In contrast, the Dutch legislator did not similarly anticipate harmonisation, and more frequent amendments proved necessary to Dutch than to German law. The anticipation of harmonisation has also been detected in other areas and should be developed further.

The benefits of more interaction between actors in the development of European private law through soft law have also been considered. Although competition has not developed between various sets of soft law, more debate in the development of overlapping sets of soft law could make clear why drafters prefer different rules, which would enable European and national actors to consider these arguments in the development of private law. Arguments that general principles can serve as anchor points further indicate that more interaction may enhance the responsive development of law at the national level.

Changes in the development of private law may however be hindered as the aims of European and national actors increasingly diverge. On the one hand, national actors retain a focus on national law and national issues. A national approach to the development of private law is similarly visible at the European level, especially with regard to the development of the DCFR and the drafting of blanket clauses in the *acquis*. Typically, the use of national techniques may also lead one to compare the use of those techniques at the European level with the use of techniques at the national level. If the European use of a national technique is not as successful as at the national level, does that mean that the use of that technique is problematic?

Milenium SL); C-168/05 (Asturcom Telecomunicaciones SL v Rodríguez Nogueira); C-40/08 (Caja de Ahorros y Monte de Piedad de Madrid v Asociación de Usuarios de Servicios Bancarios); C-484/08 (Banco Español de Crédito SA v Calderón Camino); C-618/10 (Aziz v Caixa d´Estalvis de Catalunya, Tarragona i Manresa (Catalunyacaixa)); C-415/11 (Asociación de Consumidores Independientes de Castilla y León v Anuntis Segundamano España SL); C-413/12 (Banco Popular Español SA v Teodolinda Rivas Quichimbo); joined cases C-537/12 and C-116/13 (Barclays Bank SA v Sánchez García and Alejandro Chacón Barrera); C-280/13 (Sánchez Morcillo and Carmen Abril García v Banco Bilbao Vizcaya Argentaria SA, C-169/14; Constructora Principado SA v Ignacio Menéndez Álvarez), C-226/12; (Unicaja Banco SA v Hidalgo Rueda and Others, Caixabank SA v María Rueda Ledesma and Mesa Mesa, Labella Crespo and Others, Galán Luna and Galán Luna), joined cases C-482/13, C-484/13, C-485/13, C-487/13. H.-W. Micklitz, N. Reich, 'The Court and the Sleeping Beauty: The revival of the unfair contract terms Directive', *CMLRev* 2014, p. 805–806 point out that the CJEU has acted as a court of last resort in various cases on Directive 93/13, when national actors offer no recourse. They speculate on the possible causes for the surge of case law, including the financial crisis, but remark that further socio-legal research is needed. Comp. in this light also J. Stuyck, 'The Court of Justice and the unfair commercial practice directive', *CMLRev* 2015, p. 749–750 who considers the relatively high number of cases on Directive 2005/29 on unfair commercial practices before the CJEU, pointing out that these cases come from a small group of Member States. These are different from the Supreme Courts in the Member States who have referred questions on Directive 93/13.

On the other hand, European actors increasingly adopt a regulatory approach. Interdependence may become more visible, especially if Member States hinder the revision of the *acquis* and the introduction of maximum harmonisation and new modes of governance, in the private law *acquis*. This may prompt EU actors to increasingly investigate the development of alternative techniques, despite resistance of national actors.

The case studies have indicated that the introduction of new modes of governance such as comitology, and other new techniques that would also foster mutual learning,[2480] may be problematic. The question whether these new modes for governance are interesting for other areas of private law should therefore be more generally considered.

[2480] L. Miller, *The emergence of EU contract law: Exploring Europeanization*, Oxford: OUP 2011, p. 196.

Chapter 10

THE USE OF ADDITIONAL AND ALTERNATIVE TECHNIQUES

10.1. Introduction

The previous chapter has analysed the use of national techniques in the multilevel legal order. In accordance with the findings in the case studies,[2481] actors did not take interdependence as a starting point in the development of European private law through national techniques. Accordingly, it has been argued that European actors, rather than emphasising top-down techniques, should develop a combination of top-down and bottom-up techniques, and some areas of law have already been characterised as a hybrid of top-down and bottom-up approaches.[2482] The case studies[2483] indicated that some additional techniques may contribute to the comprehensibility of the law on STCs, and some techniques could foster deliberation, mutual learning and increase the predictability, consistency, accessibility and responsiveness of European private law.[2484] However, suggestions for the use of additional and alternative techniques may meet with resistance from national actors, in accordance with the normative frameworks defended in chapters 7 and 8.

The case studies[2485] have argued for more interaction between actors. Techniques in addition to or instead of currently used techniques may facilitate more interaction between interdependent actors, in accordance with multilevel governance insights. In the light of some pluralist arguments for the development of new governance, such as comitology,[2486] this chapter will ask whether the use of additional and alternative techniques more generally are likely to foster deliberation and mutual learning. If techniques have already been widely used, this chapter will consider the use of these techniques and possible improvement. With regard to techniques that have not yet been widely used in the development of European private law, this chapter will consider their strengths and weaknesses and their potential to strengthen European private law.

2481 See previously par. 4.6.2. and 5.6.2.

2482 Especially J. Basedow, 'The state's private law and the economy – commercial law as an amalgam of public and private rule-making', *American Journal of Comparative Law* 2008, p. 703, considering the circumstances under which state law or privately drafted rules may be developed.

2483 See previously par. 4.7.7. and 5.7.5.

2484 See previously par. 6.3.2.

2485 See previously par. 4.7.7. and par. 5.7.5.

2486 See previously par. 3.4. and 6.3.2 and above par. 9.6.

This chapter does not aim to provide a comprehensive overview of techniques that could be used in addition to or instead of currently used techniques.[2487] Instead, the chapter will focus on the use of techniques that seem particularly suitable to cope with the problems detected in the use of codifications, blanket clauses and general principles. Notably, this will include techniques that have been not been considered, rejected or doubted in the case studies, such as the use of Regulations, the use of model laws, the OMC, the development of optional regimes and comitology. While these techniques may not be likely to improve the law on STCs, they may well be interesting for other areas of private law. For example, the use of Regulations and comitology may be more interesting for areas of private law that are not developed within codes or that concern technical matters.

This chapter will consider the use of additional and alternative techniques in the order in which they have also been considered in the case studies.[2488] Accordingly, paragraph 10.2 will consider additional techniques that are typically used to support the legislative process. Paragraph 10.3 will consider additional techniques that more particularly aim to strengthen the extent to which blanket clauses support predictability, consistency and responsiveness. Paragraph 10.4 will consider whether more attention for STCs will enhance the predictable development of the private law *acquis*, which could help actors to maintain the predictable development of private law. Paragraph 10.5 will ask whether the use of the OMC could contribute to the responsiveness of legislation. From paragraph 10.6, the chapter will pay attention to alternative techniques. Accordingly, paragraph 10.6 will discuss the use of Regulations and paragraph 10.7 will turn to the development of optional regimes. Paragraph 10.8. will address the development of techniques inspired by the U.S. legal order and paragraph 10.9. will draw attention to arguments to develop collective bargaining at the European level. Paragraph 10.10. will end with a conclusion.

10.2. Additional techniques supporting the legislative process

Weaknesses in the use of codifications and blanket clauses may be traced to defects in the legislative process. Shortcomings in this process have been detected in the Dutch legal order, where the long period of reforms and tendencies to overlook relevant comments have been criticised.[2489] Similarly, in contrast to the German case

[2487] Particularly, the use of the Lamfalussy method, the use of education as a "technique" and general academic research will not be considered. As explained in the introduction to the case studies in par. 3.5, the Lamfalussy method seems confined to financial law, and the effects of education are difficult to assess, while it should also not be considered solely as a technique. Similarly, the use of academic research in general is not merely a technique, and separately considering academic research shows too much overlap with the development of databases and soft laws, as well as the study of STCs.

[2488] Additional techniques that are least disruptive will be considered first, and alternative techniques that are more disruptive shall be considered subsequently, as also explained in par. 4.7.

[2489] H.M. Vletter- van Dort, 'Horen, zien en luisteren', *Ondernemingsrecht* 2011, 73 has signalled a tendency for government officials to ignore advice on legislative proposals that they find inconvenient. Eventually, this trend might result in legislation ignoring the needs and preference of legal practice. Redactie WPNR, 'Onvrede over wetgevingsproces', *WPNR* 6868 (2010) (the editorial board of a prominent Dutch journal) has also expressed dissatisfaction with the reform of Dutch company law, as well as other projects, including the reform of the law on the community of property, as well as the introduction of title 7.13 on

study,[2490] where the legislator appeared relatively successful in maintaining the relatively stable development of the law on STCs despite harmonisation, the blunders in the legislative process and the frequent amendments of the BGB in the implementation of the *acquis* have been criticised.[2491] At the European level, the lack of openness and debate has been criticised.[2492] The reasoning in courts does not show similar shortcomings, but courts have not sought to compensate, insofar as possible, for weaknesses in the implementation of Directives by referring to foreign courts and the CJEU.[2493] Both in the

trading partnerships. Comp. also critically on the reform of insolvency law F.M.J. Verstijlen, 'Alles (te) rustig aan het wetgevingsfront', *TvI* 2011, 12, N.E.D. Faber, R.G.J. Nowak, 'Hoezo wetgevingskwaliteit?' *NJB* 2001, 12. Reforms in insolvency law have since taken place – comp. for example, the inclusion of article 22*bis* Invorderingswet on the position of the tax collector in insolvencies.

2490 See previously par. 4.2.

2491 J. Huber, 'Das Gesetz zur Beschleunigung fälliger Zahlungen', *JZ* 2000, p. 966 has criticised the approach of the German legislator towards late payments. More drastic criticism has been voiced by W. Flume, 'Vom Beruf unserer Zeit zur Gesetzgebung', *ZIP* 2000, p. 1427, on the implementation of Directive 97/7 on distance contracts and in particular the introduction of articles 13 and 14 BGB introducing a definition of respectively consumers and entrepreneurs. Similarly, H.H. Seiler, 'Bewahrung von Kodifikationen in der Gegenwart am Beispiel des BGB', in: O. Behrends, W. Sellert (eds), *Der Kodifikationsgedanke und das Modell des Bürgerlichen Gesetzbuches*, Göttingen: Van den Hoek & Ruprecht 2000, p. 109–110 has criticised the regulatory frenzy ('*Regelwut*'), which he traces to the need to involve a large amount of committees in a process without an actor who clearly has final responsibility for a product – in this case a provision in the BGB. Further, Seiler points to the increased emphasis of policy aims and the need to realise this through speedy legislation, which, in his opinion, leads to *Wegwerfgesetze*. R. Zimmerman, 'Characteristic aspects of German legal culture', in: J. Zekoll, M. Reimann (eds.), *Introduction to German law*, The Hague: KLI 2005, p. 17 has criticised German legislative practices, referring to 'blunders' that 'have given rise to doubts whether the German legislature is still capable today of legislating in an academically sound and responsible manner.'

2492 W. Doralt, 'Strukturelle Schwächen in der Europäisierung des Privatrechts', *RabelsZ* 2011, p. 280. refers to the withdrawal of a critical member of the Expert Group studying the possible uses of the DCFR (Prof. S. Whittaker), and notes that the relatively rapid withdrawal does not give the impression that many opportunities for debate arise within the Expert Group. See also R. Zimmerman, 'Europäisches Privatrecht – Irrungen, Wirtungen', in: Professorinnen und Professoren der Bucerius Law School (eds.), *Begegnungen im Recht, Ringvorlesung der Bucerius Law School zu Ehren von Karsten Schmidt anlasslich seines 70. Geburtstags*, Tübingen: Mohr Siebeck 2011, p. 333 and K. Riesenhuber, 'A competitive approach to EU contract law', *ERCL* 2011, p. 119–121 who notes that the time pressure in the drafting of the DCFR may have severely curtailed opportunities for wide consultation and responses from a wide range of stakeholders and experts.

2493 More interaction between courts has been defended especially strongly by M. Lutter, 'Die Auslegung angeglichenen rechts', *JZ* 1992, p. 604, but also by H. Kötz, 'Der Bundesgerichtshof und die Rechtsvergleichung', in: C.-W. Canaris et al (eds.), *50 Jahre Bundesgerichtshof, Festgabe aus der Wissenschaft, II*, München: Beck 2000, p. 835, and, more recently, J. Brinkhof, *De Europese uitdaging voor rechtspraak, rechtswetenschap en onderwijs* (valedictory address Utrecht), Amsterdam: DeLex 2010, p. 10. J.B.M. Vranken, 'Taken van de Hoge Raad en zijn parket in 2025', in: I. Giesen, A.M. Hol, (eds.), *De Hoge Raad in 2025: Contouren van de toekomstige cassatierechtspraak*, The Hague: BJU 2011, par. 2.5. has likewise emphasised the need for interaction between the judiciaries, as they are increasingly confronted with cross-border cases, and O. Remien, 'Einheit, Mehrstufigkeit und Flexibilität', *RabelsZ* 1998, p. 633 has supported the idea of interaction between the CJEU and national courts, suggesting that national courts referring a question to the CJEU may provide insight in questions of national law, while other states and experts may provide expertise on other national laws with regard to the question.

German[2494] and Dutch[2495] legal order, courts have exercised restraint in referring to the CJEU and referring to foreign law. This restraint may, however, also be traced to the restraint of parties to adjudication in relying on comparative law arguments, especially where comparative law is not directly relevant or not to the benefit of parties' position.

These shortcomings do not mean that the legislative process cannot lead to successful initiatives, which are also visible, such as the BW,[2496] as well as the Community trademark.[2497] In these cases, it seems as if the democratic process does guarantee open and transparent debate and it therefore has a clear added value over private law that is formed by actors that do not similarly allow for open and transparent debate.

Interestingly, the shortcomings visible in the legislative processes coincide with comments for more debate.[2498] Various additional techniques may improve debate, which can be a step towards deliberation.[2499]

Paragraph 10.2.1 will turn to consultations and paragraph 10.2.2 will discuss impact assessments. Paragraph 10.2.3 will consider databases and paragraph 10.2.4 will address the use of networks. Paragraph 10.2.5 will end with a conclusion.

2494 For the BGH, restraint has been deduced from the relatively limited amount of cases in which the BGH has referred to foreign courts by M. Siems, 'The adjudication of the German Federal Supreme Court, 2007, *Oxford University Comparative Law Forum*, 4, available at ouclf.iuscomp.org. That does not mean that comparative law reasoning cannot be found in prominent cases; comp. the examples in E. Kramer, 'Konvergenz und Internationalisierung der juristischen Methode', in: Ch.J. Meier-Schatz (ed.), *Die Zukunft des Rechts*, Basel/Geneva/München: Helbing & Lichtenhahn 1998, p. 83.

2495 V. van den Eeckhout, 'The application of foreign law by judicial and non-judicial authorities – The Netherlands', via www.ssrn.com, p. 6 indicates that national courts seem to prefer to apply national law rather than foreign law, in order to avoid difficulties with regard to establishing the content of foreign law. The Hoge Raad provides an exception to this point as A.G.s may include comparative private law in their conclusions, but the extent to which the Hoge Raad does so has been criticised by J.M. Smits, E.A.G. van Schagen, 'De Hoge Raad als Europese rechter: Mag het ietsje meer zijn?' in: A.G. Castermans et al (eds.), *Het zwijgen van de Hoge Raad, BWKJ 25*, Deventer: Kluwer 2009, p. 79.

2496 W. van Gerven, S. Lierman, *Algemeen Deel, Veertig jaar later*, Mechelen: Kluwer 2010, p. 192 however consider the Dutch codification, especially the involvement of Parliament, as well as the emphasis on comparative law in the drafting of the code, as 'atypical', and doubt whether Parliaments, especially Parliaments that focus more on their responsibility to exercise political control on the executive rather than its role in the legislative process, can still have a decisive say in the drafting of codifications.

2497 Regulation 207/2009 on a Community Trademark.

2498 L.A.J. Senden, 'De lidstaten en de kwaliteit van Europese wetgeving: geen consumenten, maar co-actoren', *SEW* 2006, p. 57 has argued that problems with regard to European legislation and a lack of interaction between actors should not be seen in isolation: if a Directive, because of its detailed nature, leaves no room for discretion to the national legislator that has to implement it into national law – which seems frequently the case in European private law – the national legislator has fewer possibilities to cope with fragmentation in national private laws, and may choose to copy-paste the Directive into national law, a phenomenon not unfamiliar in European private law. W. van Gerven, S. Lierman, *Algemeen deel. Veertig jaar later*, Mechelen: Kluwer 2010, p. 146 have held that in order to achieve convergence, cooperation of both state actors – legislators and judges – as well as non-state actors – including legal practice and academics – is necessary. Although the added value of comparative law insights in the drafting of legislation is familiar in private law, the added value of these insights have recently been recognised more generally by W. Voermans et al, *Legislative processes in transition*, Leiden/The Hague: WODC 2012, available at www.wodc.nl.

2499 This chapter does not argue that deliberation is a *de facto* mode of communication in the development of European private law.

10.2.1. *Consultations*

To what extent can consultations contribute to more interaction between actors in the development of codifications and blanket clauses in the legislative process?

Paragraph 10.2.1.1 will summarise current consultation practices and paragraph 10.2.1.2 will discuss shortcomings in the use of consultations. Paragraph 10.2.1.3 will ask how the use of consultations can be improved and paragraph 10.2.1.4 will end with a conclusion.

10.2.1.1. The current use of consultations

Consultations are used widely by Dutch, German and European actors. In the German legal order, more emphasis has been put on the participation of academics. In particular, proposals from committees of academics, commissioned by the legislator, may produce a first academic draft ('*Referententwurf*'), which generally starts debate, sometimes in the form of preliminary reports, which may lead to a proposal of the legislator ('*Regierungsentwurf*'). These proposals will be discussed by the committees, during which stakeholders and experts may also be heard. In addition, academics may discuss the proposal, insofar it is amended, further. Comments are frequently taken into account. In this procedure, both the academic draft and the legislative proposal are circulated by way of generating debate and feedback.

Similarly, in the Dutch legal order, a committee of academics, commissioned by the legislator, may issue a first draft, which will generally trigger debate. The draft may lead to a legislative proposal that may subject to further debate and which is advised upon by the *Raad van State*. Announcements in journals may further prompt debate and online consultations can be opened for submissions. Consultations usually last around one or two months.[2500] The Dutch legislator has not developed standard consultation procedures. The way in which parties are consulted may differ among departments, and they take place on an ad hoc basis. The inclination of some departments to contact parties that they are already familiar with may benefit repeat players.[2501] Unfortunately, doubts have arisen whether submissions to consultations are generally sufficiently to be taken into account by Parliament.[2502] Although some legislative initiatives have been developed in the context of regulatory competition, it has not become a habit to consult foreign parties; instead, referral to comparative law is widespread.

[2500] P. Popelier et al., *Consulteren over ontwerpregelgeving: alibi voor vrijblijvendheid of prikkel tot actie? Een inventarisatie van de Nederlandse consultatiepraktijk*, Antwerp: University of Antwerp, Tilburg University, WODC 2007 available at www.wodc.nl, p. 114.

[2501] P. Popelier et al., *Consulteren over ontwerpregelgeving: alibi voor vrijblijvendheid of prikkel tot actie? Een inventarisatie van de Nederlandse consultatiepraktijk*, Antwerp: University of Antwerp, Tilburg University, WODC 2007 available at www.wodc.nl, p. 114.

[2502] T. Cardoso Ribeiro, *Naar een zichtbaar effectieve wisselwerking tussen beleid en uitvoering*, The Hague 28 March 2007, available at www.eerstekamer.nl.

In accordance with the findings in the case studies,[2503] neither the German nor the Dutch legislator has made it a habit to include foreign or European actors in consultations. European and foreign actors are not involved in the drafting process of legislation developed in the light of regulatory competition nor are they involved in the implementation of Directives. There are varous explanations for this lack of involvement of European and international actors. Notably, national consultations may not be similarly accessible to foreign and European actors. Further, when implementing European law national legislators may prefer simply informing the Commission of implementation afterwards, as is already generally required. In particular, the possibility that implementation becomes subject to an extra instance of control within the national democratic process may be considered as intrusive and, therefore, problematic. Additionally, the resources of European actors may be limited and participation in consultative procedures throughout the Union may, therefore, be problematic.

Notwithstanding harmonisation and regulatory competition, the lack of participation of foreign and international actors in national consultations limits the chance that national actors are sufficiently aware of the needs and preferences of these actors to develop the law responsively to their interests. Accordingly, national legislators, in pursuing regulatory competition, have limited the extent to which national actors opted out of national law.[2504]

Likewise, the European Commission frequently uses Green Papers in the development of the private law *acquis*, initiating consultations that discuss possible future action.[2505] These consultations proved to be starting points for especially academic debate on the future of the private law *acquis*, and they have played an important role in the debate on the future of European contract law.[2506] Senden[2507] has, however, remarked that the Commission is generally not under a duty to take the outcomes of consultations into account.

Thus, consultations aim to generate interaction between relevant actors and, thereby, contribute to the quality of legislation.

2503 See previously par. 4.3.2. and 5.3.3.

2504 See previously par. 6.3.3.

2505 See for example the Communication from the Commission to the Council and the European Parliament on European contract law, COM (2001) 398 final, the Communication from the Commission to the European Parliament and the Council, *European contract law and the revision of the acquis: the way forward*, COM (2004) 651 final, European Commission, *Green Paper on the Review of the consumer acquis*, COM (2006) 744 final, and the European Commission, *Green Paper on policy options for progress towards a European contract law for businesses and consumers*, COM (2010) 348 final.

2506 See, for example, the February issue of the European Review of Contract Law 2011, or the collection of essays on the Green Paper on policy options for progress towards a European contract law for businesses and consumers, COM (2010) 348 final, M.W. Hesselink et al. (eds.), *Het Groenboek Europees contractenrecht: naar een optioneel instrument?*, The Hague: BJU 2011.

2507 L.A.J. Senden, 'De lidstaten en de kwaliteit van Europese wetgeving: geen consumenten, maar co-actoren', *SEW* 2006, p. 55.

10.2.1.2. Shortcomings in the use of consultations

Various shortcomings may be detected in the use of consultations by both national legislators and the European Commission.

1) Both the German and the Dutch legislator generally consult national stakeholders on the implementation of Directives. However, during this stage, the choice for a Directive has already been made, and amendments cannot be made to provisions in the Directive that national stakeholders or experts perceive as particularly problematic.

2) In European consultations, future action is already determined when consultations are initiated, which guarantees that future action is not based on the responses to consultations.

The clearest example is the 2010 Green Paper on policy options towards progress towards a European contract law, discussing various possible uses for a final CFR. It may be doubted what weight is given to the preferences of stakeholders for the different options sketched in the Green Paper. Although the consultation lasted from July 2010 to February 2011, the Expert Group working on a feasibility study[2508] that would be used to decide which parts of the DCFR were to be used for a Common Frame of Reference, was already appointed in April 2010.[2509] Although the Green Paper duly stated that the Expert Group would study the feasibility of an instrument of European contract law,[2510] and that further action by the Commission in 2012 would depend on the evaluation of the responses to the Green Paper,[2511] the Commission seemed to favour the fourth option set out in the Green Paper, the optional instrument of a European contract code, in the form of a Regulation, and pointed out significant disadvantages associated with the other six options.[2512] This preference was also expressed by the European Parliament.[2513] In the Digital Agenda for Europe,[2514] the Commission indicates that one of the actions to be

2508 Comp. the criticism of E. Clive, 'European contract law feasibility study', *European private law news*, 11 May 2011 available at www.law.ed.ac.uk/epln/blogentry.aspx?blogentryref=8658 (consulted 26 August 2011): ' "Feasibility study" is a nice, neutral, non-committal name which did not, however, feature in the group discussions at all and which is not very accurate because this text is not a study about the feasibility of anything. The only doubt about feasibility within the expert group was whether a text could be produced within the limited time available. The text could be used as a partial basis for discussions about what might be feasible politically, but that is something different.'

2509 Commission Decision of 26 April 2010, OJ L 105, 27.4.2010, p. 109.

2510 European Commission, *Green Paper on policy options for progress towards a European contract law for businesses and consumers*, COM (2010) 348 final, p. 4.

2511 European Commission, *Green Paper on policy options for progress towards a European contract law for businesses and consumers*, COM (2010) 348 final, p. 2.

2512 Comp. also V. Reding, 'Warum Europa ein optionales Europäisches Vertragsrecht benötigt', *ZEuP* 2011, p. 1.

2513 Resolution P7_TA-PROV(2009)0090 of the European Parliament of 25 November 2009 on the Communication from the Commission to the European Parliament and the Council – An area of freedom, security and justice serving the citizen – Stockholm programme, par. 99–100.

2514 Communication from the Commission to the European Parliament, the Council, the European Economic and Social Committee and the Committee and the regions, *A digital agenda for Europe*,

undertaken is the development of an optional instrument of European contract law. Accordingly, the Expert Group has worked 'on the assumption of an optional instrument'.[2515] The clearly expressed preference of the Commission for a particular option may have limited the amount of responses.[2516]

3) Consultations at the European level have narrowed debate.

Consultations typically do not discuss all possible options, but focus on a limited number of options that are the focus of subsequent debate. Consequently, other options are overlooked. For example, the 2007 Green Paper on the review of the consumer *acquis*[2517] discusses the degree of harmonisation, proposing either full harmonisation, minimum harmonisation, or minimum harmonisation combined with a mutual recognition clause, while not discussing other options, such as optional harmonisation that gives businesses the option to apply either to national or European law, or partial harmonisation that establishes two sets of rules, without leaving businesses involved in cross-border trade with the option to apply national laws to their contracts.[2518] These latter two degrees of harmonisation are aimed at harmonising the law for cross-border trade, and not the law applicable to domestic trade.[2519]

Furthermore, the 2007 Green Paper proposes the different degrees of harmonisation as opposites, overlooking the possibility to combine minimum and maximum harmonisation, as is, for example, the case in Directive 2006/114 on misleading and comparative advertising. Typically, the options suggested in consultations in European private law include options that are not feasible or not likely to contribute to solving the problem signalled in the consultation. A clear example of this is the 2001 Green Paper on European contract law, which proposes four options to improve the private law *acquis*. The first option, no European action, is not likely to improve the

COM (2010) 245 final, p. 13. See similarly Communication from the Commission, *Europe 2020, a strategy for smart, sustainable and inclusive growth*, COM (2010) 2020 final, p. 21.

2515 Expert Group on a Common Frame of Reference in European contract law, *Synthesis of the fourth meeting*, 1–2 September 2010, available at http://ec.europa.eu/justice/policies/consumer/docs/cfr_report_10_09_01_02_en.pdf, p. 1.

2516 G. Howells, 'European contract law reform and European consumer law – two related but distinct regimes', *ERCL* 2011, p. 175: 'one might even portray the present consultation as rather cosmetic given the emphasis placed in day-to-day discussions on the Optional Instrument. Indeed there is a danger that the Commission may not receive as full a range of responses as otherwise might have been the case for many commentators may believe the only realistic option on the Commission's agenda is the Optional Instrument. Subtly the debate has been manipulated implicitly to assume there will be an Optional Instrument and so the focus debate is on its nature, scope and content and relationship with private international law.' See also K. Riesenhuber, 'A competitive approach to EU contract law', *ERCL* 2011, p. 124–125. Similarly R. Zimmerman, 'Europäisches Privatrecht – Irrungen, Wirtungen', in: Professorinnen und Professoren der Bucerius Law School (eds.), *Begegnungen im Recht, Ringvorlesung der Bucerius Law School zu Ehren von Karsten Schmidt anlasslich seines 70. Geburtstags*, Tübingen: Mohr Siebeck 2011, p. 345–346, who finds the consultation 'einem leeren Legitimationsritual'.

2517 COM (2006) 744 final, par. 4.5.

2518 See on the different options P.J. Slot, 'Harmonisation', *ELR* 1996, p. 383–384.

2519 D. Curtin, 'Emerging institutional parameters and organised difference in the European Union', in: B. de Witte, D. Hanf, E. de Vos (eds.), *The many faces of differentiation in EU law*, Antwerp: Intersentia 2001, p. 363–364, remarks that optional harmonisation has been used predominantly to further the free movement of goods, and should be seen within that context. Nevertheless, she recognises that partial harmonisation, which has also been used to adopt measures under article 114 TFEU, could perhaps be successfully used in other areas.

private law *acquis*, while the fourth option, comprehensive legislation at a European level, is not politically feasible. Unsurprisingly, a considerable majority of the consulted parties preferred the remaining options 2 and 3.[2520]

Green Papers may also steer towards an option preferred by the Commission. Accordingly, the outcome of consultations are affected by the questioning techniques used in consultations. Rutgers and Sufton-Green[2521] find that the 2007 Green Paper on the reform of the consumer law *acquis* suggests several courses of action, one of which is the drafting of an optional instrument. Subsequent questions concern the horizontal instrument, and other options are not discussed. In this manner, the questioning style of the Green Papers, already favouring a particular course of action, is not structured in a way most suitable to receive suggestions on what particular grounds private law could or should be harmonised.

4) Not all relevant parties are consulted.

This means that respondents who may have valuable insights into the use of a particular technique or who may suggest alternative techniques are not consulted.[2522] Accordingly, neither the Dutch consumers' association (*Consumentenbond*) nor the German consumer protection association (*Deutscher Verbraucherschutzverein*) separately participated in the consultation preceding Directive 2011/83 on consumer rights.[2523]

Consultations are currently used in a way that does not aim at generating the maximum amount of input. Accordingly, both Senden[2524] and Zimmerman[2525] have doubted the added value of especially European consultations.

10.2.1.3. Improving the use of consultations

The use of consultations may be improved if shortcomings currently visible in the private law *acquis* are remedied. Additional measures may further enhance the quality of consultations:

2520 Comp. the Commission's summary of the reactions to the communication on European contract law, available at http://ec.europa.eu/consumers/cons_int/safe_shop/fair_bus_pract/cont_law/comments/summaries/sum_en.pdf.

2521 J.W. Rutgers, R. Sufton-Green, 'Revising the consumer *acquis*: (Half) opening the doors of the Trojan Horse', *ERPL* 2008, p. 431.

2522 Comp. also L. Miller, *The emergence of EU contract law: Exploring Europeanization*, Oxford: OUP 2011, p. 195 who finds that the inclusion of "competing voices" enhances the decision-making process.

2523 See the responses at http://ec.europa.eu/consumers/rights/responses_green_paper_acquis_en.htm. The Consumentenbond is a member of BEUC and may have contributed to the BEUC response to the consultation, but this is not apparent from the response as such. Interestingly, Thuiswinkel.org which has established a successful trust mark, has criticised withdrawal and refund obligations (see www.thuiswinkel.org/thuiswinkel.org-wants-to-get-rid-of-two-consumer-rights).

2524 L.A.J. Senden, 'De lidstaten en de kwaliteit van Europese wetgeving: geen consumenten, maar co-actoren', *SEW* 2006, p. 55.

2525 R. Zimmerman, 'Europäisches Privatrecht – Irrungen, Wirtungen', in: Professorinnen und Professoren der Bucerius Law School (eds.), *Begegnungen im Recht, Ringvorlesung der Bucerius Law School zu Ehren von Karsten Schmidt anlasslich seines 70. Geburtstags*, Tübingen: Mohr Siebeck 2011, p. 345–346.

1) Organising consultations in addition to European consultations preceding the drafting of Directives.

Neither the Dutch nor the German legislator has chosen to organise consultations in addition to European consultations. In Germany, however, European consultations are sometimes announced in legal journals.[2526] In the Dutch legal order, the legislator may organise closed consultations prior to its reaction to European initiatives, in particular obtaining advice from the Commission for Consumer Affairs (*Commissie voor Consumentenaangelegenheden*, CCA).[2527] However, the CCA has not participated in the debate at the European level. The German approach seems somewhat more successful when comparing the participation of German and Dutch actors in the debate at the European level.[2528] A valuable example is set by the English legislator, who generally initiates consultations on European proposals. As was argued in the Dutch case study,[2529] more participation in European consultations should result in more than brief responses.

More participation of legal practitioners and the judiciary from the national level may be beneficial as these actors are presumably well-placed to signal problems arising in legal practice. However, the question arises as to why practitioners and judges would have an interest in the development of foreign private law or the development of private law at the European or international level. Perhaps practitioners in areas of private law with an inherent cross-border aspect, such as international private law or intellectual property law have more interest in the development of private law at a European or international level than practitioners in more nationally developed areas. In these areas, the size of polities is more clearly international rather than local.

2) Establishing an obligation for the Commission to account how the outcomes of a consultation have been taken into account.

This obligation should be included in the Interinstitutional Agreement on better law-making, which currently states that the Commission will take into account the results from consultations.[2530]

2526 Comp. for example the announcement on the consultation on the doorstep selling Directive, *EuZW* 2007, p. 748, or the announcement of the consultation on collective enforcement, *NZG* 2011, p. 295.

2527 Comp. the CCA advice on unfair commercial practices, *Oneerlijke handelspraktijken op consumententerrein in de EU*, 13 April 2004, Report 04/06, available at www.ser.nl/nl/publicaties/adviezen/2000–2007/2004/b22670.aspx or the report on consumer rights, *Consumentenrechten in de interne markt*, 17 June 2009, 09/05, available at www.ser.nl/~/media/DB_Adviezen/2000_2009/2009/b27871.ashx. It is not the only organisation that may be consulted. Alternatively, the Expert Centre on European Law (Expertisecentrum Europees Recht) has provided a 2008 report on the CFR, available at www.minbuza.nl/ecer/icer/zoeken-in-icer-adviezen/2008/2008--rapport-common-frame-of-reference.html.

2528 Comp. the responses to COM (2006) 744 final, at http://ec.europa.eu/consumers/rights/responses_green_paper_acquis_en.htm, where clearly, (much) more German than Dutch stakeholders participated, or, similarly, the participation in the reform of Directive 94/47 on timeshare, available at http://ec.europa.eu/consumers/cons_int/safe_shop/timeshare/consultation2006_en.htm, as well as the participation in the consultation on an optional instrument, COM (2010) 348, available at http://ec.europa.eu/justice/newsroom/contract/opinion/100701_en.htm.

2529 See previously par. 5.7.1.

2530 OJ C 321/1, 31 December 2003, par. 12.

3) Invite members of the European Parliament to participate in national consultations.

Members of the European Parliament may be well placed to participate in national consultations, because of their expertise on European matters and their national political experiences. Participation of actors with both a national and a European background may prevent incorrect implementation and maybe increase the chance that an implementation law is judged as best practice and may serve as inspiration to other actors.

4) Encouraging national Parliaments to participate in European consultations.

The Protocol on the role of national Parliaments and the Protocol on the application of the principle of subsidiarity and proportionality to the TFEU may provide national Parliaments with a possibility to engage more actively in the development of the consumer law *acquis*. Notably, national Parliaments have already delivered opinions on recent initiatives in European private law, especially the withdrawn proposal for a Regulation establishing the CESL.[2531] It will be interesting to see whether some national Parliaments in particular, provide frequent opinions, and to look at the possibilities to encourage less active national Parliaments to adopt an active approach as well.

5) Using separate consultations on future action and legislative proposals.

Sandstorm[2532] has argued that consultations should include drafts of proposed legislation, as this may provide an opportunity for consulted parties to address all relevant points. This argument does, however, raise the question whether it would not be useful to distinguish the course of action to be adopted first, and to subsequently consult on a specific legislative proposal that includes the draft proposal. Green Papers in European private law now seek to answer both questions in one consultation.

6) Promoting the better circulation of consultations.

It would be interesting to gain insight in the way that, for example, Green Papers are circulated.[2533] The promotion tactics exercised at the European level may not be as successful as national practices. Consequently, national legal practitioners may not be aware of the consultations issued by the Commission. Possibly, successful national practices to spread policy documents could be taken as a starting point to reach more national legal practitioners.

2531 See for an overview of the reaction of Parliaments www.ipex.eu/IPEXL-WEB/dossier/dossier.do?code=COD&year=2011&number=0284&appLng=EN.

2532 G. Sandström, 'Knocking EU law into shape', *CLMR* 2003, p. 1310.

2533 L. Senden, *Soft law in European Community law*, Oxford: Hart 2004, p. 126 notes that one of the weaknesses of the Green Papers is that they do not provide insight into the ways in which they are circulated, stating: 'one may wonder whether Green Papers that are silent on this particular aspect are notified to interested parties at all'.

7) Providing more opportunities for responses to consultations.

In this regard, the initiative to extend the minimum period of consultations from 8 to 12 weeks[2534] should be welcomed. The introduction of an alert service[2535] should, in addition, ensure that actors who sign up for that service will be made aware of subsequent consultations in their field.

These measures would significantly increase the chance that relevant actors become aware of consultations. Remedying the shortcomings in the current use of consultations and improvements, some of which have already been made, may also make it more likely that actors will subsequently respond to consultations.

10.2.1.4. Conclusion on the use of consultations

The shortcomings in the current use of consultations have not helped bringing the separate debates on private law at the national and the European level closer. In particular, the lack of interaction between European and national actors may help to maintain the separation between national and European debate, which, in turn, makes it more likely that actors will continue to overlook increasing interdependence and overlook national experiences in the revision of the *acquis*. Perhaps, if consultations encourage European and national actors to interact more and take into account one another's responses, this will benefit the use of codifications and blanket clauses in the multilevel legal order. Specifically, if European actors become aware of national experiences and problems in the implementation and application of Directives, this may prompt European actors to provide more clarity on the meaning of concepts used in Directives and encourage national actors to compare strategies to the implementation of Directives under reform. More awareness of problems at the national level should also prompt European actors to reconsider the use of blanket clauses in the private law *acquis*, as well as the need for responsiveness at the national level, and provide more clarity on the allocation of competences between the CJEU and national courts. If national actors interact more with European actors, this may make national actors more aware of future initiatives for harmonisation, or they may lobby for more clarity on future European measures. National actors may also anticipate the development of the *acquis*.

The suggestions for improvement make the interdependence between actors apparent. Notably, national actors may compensate for shortcomings in European consultations, and European actors should rely more on national actors to ensure that relevant actors are consulted. However, the efforts of national actors have little added value if European actors do not take actors′ responses into account. Simultaneously, European actors may compensate for shortcomings in national consultation practices and suggest improvement. The participation of European actors may in addition prompt national

2534 European Commission, 'Have a bigger say in European policy-making: Commission extends public consultations to twelve weeks and creates new alert service', *Press Release European Commission* 3 January 2012, http://europa.eu/rapid/pressReleasesAction.do?reference=IP/12/1&format=HTML&aged=0&language=EN&guiLanguage=en.

2535 See http://europa.eu/transparency-register/index_en.htm.

actors to justify divergences or to take the interests of international and foreign actors more clearly into account.

10.2.2. *Impact assessments*

Dutch and German actors have not subjected private law initiatives to impact assessments, but European actors have started using impact assessments. As the use of impact assessments is relatively new, their use should still be developed further.[2536] According to the Commission,[2537] impact assessments are not meant to replace political decision-making. Instead, they are aimed to further decision-making based on 'transparent, comprehensive and balanced evidence'.[2538] Notably, however, impact assessments are not binding and do not diminish the discretion of the Commission to initiate harmonisation.[2539] To what extent can impact assessments contribute to the predictability and responsiveness of the private law *acquis*?

Paragraph 10.2.2.1 will discuss the shortcomings in the current use of impact assessments and paragraph 10.2.2.2 will turn to starting points to improve the use of impact assessments. Paragraph 10.2.2.3 will end with a conclusion.

10.2.2.1. Shortcomings in the use of impact assessments

Various serious shortcomings are currently visible in the use of impact assessments in the private law *acquis*:

1) Impact assessments assess the impact of the options suggested in consultations, even though these options are hardly exhaustive. Consequently, problems signalled in impact assessments may be dealt with in other ways that have not been assessed.

For example, impact assessments, before the withdrawn proposal for a Regulation establishing a CESL did not include optional harmonisation in their analysis.[2540] Also, impact assessments have

[2536] A.C.M. Meuwese, *Impact assessment in EU lawmaking*, Zutphen: Wöhrmann Print Services 2008, p 11.

[2537] European Commission, *Communication from the Commission on impact assessment*, COM (2002) 276 final, p. 3.

[2538] European Commission, *Impact assessment guidelines*, 15 January 2009, SEC (2009) 92, p. 4.

[2539] Comp. CJEU 13 May 1997 (Federal Republic of Germany v European Parliament and Council), C-233/94, [1997] ECR, p. I-2405, par. 56. A.C.M. Meuwese, *Impact assessment in EU lawmaking*, Zutphen: Wöhrmann Print Services 2008, p. 160–162 finds that CJEU 7 September 2006 (Spain v Council), C-310/04, [2006] ECR p. I-7285 could be a sign that the CJEU will take more note of impact assessments. However, as Meuwese also points out, this concerns a case in which an impact assessment had not been made, which led the Advocate General and the Court to doubt whether the Commission could have made proper use of its discretion as it was not sufficiently familiar with all relevant facts. If an impact assessment has been conducted, the CJEU may continue to exercise restraint – it is not clear whether shortcomings in impact assessments discussed below will prompt a more critical approach.

[2540] The European Economic and Social Committee, 'The 28th regime – an alternative allowing less lawmaking at Community level', OJ 2011, C 21/26, 21.2.2011, par. 1.14 has suggested to include this option in future impact assessments.

insufficiently considered alternative means to improve consumer confidence. If consumers think they are more likely to become a victim of fraud when entering into cross-border contracts, especially via the Internet, a service like Paypal might further consumer confidence, as it guarantees consumers a refund if, for example, they have not received the product they bought or if the product is not in accordance with the contract.[2541] Similarly, Van Boom[2542] points out that increasing consumer confidence may be more effectively pursued by other techniques, such as inserting standard clauses in often used contracts.

Even if stakeholders suggest alternative measures, these have not been considered in impact assessments. Accordingly, the suggestion of stakeholders to introduce professional licensing requirements in timeshare matters was not assessed. The reasoning for this choice is interesting:[2543]

> 'The minimum intervention priority induced the elimination of the sub-option of professional licensing requirements in the proposal for a revised Directive, despite the merits of this sub-option, and strong support from numerous Member States and stakeholders. When weighing the benefits for consumers of introducing the licensing requirements sub-option, and the additional regulatory burden it would impose on the industry, it was concluded that, on balance, the benefits did not, at this stage, justify this measure.

It can, however, be doubted whether this minimum requirement principle – which in the form of the principles of subsidiarity and proportionality should not be taken as a starting point for only one option and which does not seem to have led to reconsideration of the maximum harmonisation approach – justifies the exclusion of professional licensing. Arguably, licensing may well be suitable to achieve the objective pursued by the European Union, especially limiting the amount of rogue traders, which, in time, may contribute to consumer confidence. One may also ask whether impact assessments are not meant to analyse the benefits and disadvantages of a particular option. Apparently, however, it is also possible to reject an option without such an analysis. In addition, the report appears to contradict itself by stating that the option to introduce licensing requirements receives strong support, while previously admitting that there were few responses from stakeholders on this point. However, an explanation for the small amount of responses may also be that the consultation never asked for this possibility.[2544]

2541 See for the full terms and conditions (in Dutch) https://cms.paypal.com/nl/cgi-bin/?&cmd=_render-content&content_ID=ua/UserAgreement_full#13.%20PayPal%20Buyer%20Protection.

2542 W.H. van Boom, 'The Draft Directive on consumer rights: Choices made and arguments used', *Journal of Contemporary European Research* 2009, p. 462.

2543 Commission staff working document, *Accompanying document to the proposal for a Directive of the European Parliament and of the Council on the protection of consumers in respect of certain aspects of timeshare, long-term holiday products, resale and exchange, Impact assessment*, SEC (2007) 743 final, p. 37.

2544 Comp. the consultation document, available http://ec.europa.eu/consumers/rights/travel_en.htm #time.

2) Impact assessments are based on controversial assumptions that are, however, essential for the outcome of the assessment.

Accordingly, impact assessments generally assume that divergences between private laws pose an obstacle to the internal market,[2545] overlooking that this assumption is quite controversial.[2546] This assumption is also difficult to reconcile with the *Tobacco Advertising*,[2547] where the CJEU held that the existence of divergences and the abstract risk of obstacles to the internal market do not by themselves justify harmonisation. In addition, impact assessments do not make use of insights that draw into doubt that divergences between private laws always present an obstacle to cross-border trade, or present the most pressing obstacle to cross-border trade.[2548]

Notably, previous legislation was also not based on impact assessments. For example, in the proposal for Directive 97/7 on distance selling,[2549] the Commission relies on data provided by stakeholders and seems to assume, rather than investigate, that divergences of national laws provide an obstacle to the internal market: 'It is the Commission's job to avoid such

2545 See for example recently European Commission, *Commission staff working paper, Impact Assessment accompanying the document Proposal for a Regulation of the European Parliament and of the Council on a Common European Sales Law*, SEC (2011) 1165 final, p. 10, the Commission Staff Working Document, *Accompanying document to the proposal for a Directive of the European Parliament and Council on the protection of consumers in respect of certain aspects of timeshare, long-term holiday products, resale and exchange, Impact Assessment*, SEC (2007) 743 final, p. 24. See, somewhat more extensively, the Commission Staff Working Paper, *Extended Impact Assessment on the Directive of the European Parliament and of the Council concerning unfair business-to-consumer commercial practices in the internal market*, SEC (2003) 724 final, p. 5–8.

2546 See on this question for example M. Schillig, *Konkretisierungskompetenz und Konkretisierungsmethoden im Europäischen Privatrecht*, Berlin: De Gruyter 2009, p. 294, Study Group on Social Justice in European Private Law, 'Social justice in European contract law: A Manifesto', *ELJ* 2004, p. 656, E. McKendrick, 'Harmonisation of European contract law: The state we are in', in: S. Vogenauer, S. Weatherill (eds.), *The harmonisation of European contract law*, Oxford: Hart 2006, p. 21, O. Remien, Denationalisierung des Privatrechts in der Europäischen Union?', *Zeitschrift für Rechtsvergleichung* 1995, p. 129–130, H. Beale, 'Finding the remaining traps instead of unifying contract law', in: S. Grundmann, J. Stuyck (eds.), *An academic Green Paper on European contract law*, The Hague: KLI 2002, p. 67–72, H. Collins, 'Transaction costs and subsidiarity in European contract law', in: S. Grundmann, J. Stuyck (eds.), *An academic Green Paper on European contract law*, The Hague: KLI 2002, p. 270–271, G. Wagner, 'The virtues of diversity in European private law', in: J.M. Smits (ed.), *The need for a European contract law*, Groningen: Europa Law Publishing 2005, p. 17–18.

2547 CJEU 5 October 2000 (Federal Republic of Germany v European Parliament and Council of the European Union), C-376/98, ECR [2000], p. I-8419, par. 84.

2548 J.M. Smits, 'Diversity of contract law and the European internal market', in: J.M. Smits (ed.), *The need for a European contract law*, Groningen: Europa Law Publishing 2005, p. 169–170. Smits, at p. 171, also points out that the effect of uniform law on contracting is scarce. Similarly, E.-M. Kieninger *Wettbewerb der Privatrechtsordnungen im Europäischen Binnenmarkt*, Tübingen: Mohr Siebeck 2002, p. 86–87 remarks that the choice to start business in a particular market may be influenced more by factors like a potential market for a product, availability of employees, infrastructure, or tax law than diverging private laws.

2549 European Commission, *Proposal for a Directive on distance selling*, COM (92) 11 final, p. 3–5. Although the Commission refers to 'recent study' (p. 5) and 'detailed study' (p. 7) it does not become clear what the subject of these studies was or by whom it was performed, which makes it difficult to retrieve these studies. I can find no impact assessment empirically underpinning the arguments of the Commission that fragmentation of laws hinders the internal market.

fragmentation.'[2550] An impact assessment on the impact of divergent private laws on the internal market is long overdue.

3) Impact assessments are superficial and do not sufficiently take into account elements that are relevant for the outcome of the assessment.

A good example is the impact assessment accompanying the since withdrawn CESL, which does not compare the impact of alternative optional instruments that would, for example, also deal with complex contracts containing elements of manufacturing, finance, and transport. The limitation of the CESL to sales contracts and the exclusion of mixed contracts in article 5, 6 and article 2 (m) withdrawn Regulation means that parties to often used complex contracts would have been less likely to opt for the CESL, as it would only have covered the sales part of the contract and not the parts of the contract relating to, for example, manufacture, transport, finance and installation.[2551] Arguably, inserting such provisions into an optional instrument may significantly enhance the added value and the success of an optional instrument to parties to complex contracts. Consequently, the impact assessment fails to point out which content of an optional instrument is most likely to generate optimal impact for the internal market.

Frequently, impact assessments also overlook other relevant factors that may affect the success of a new or reformed Directive. In particular, impact assessment do not pay sufficient attention to the possibility that parties upon whom rights are conferred – in particular, consumers – are sufficiently aware of these rights and enforce these rights. Generally, the possibility that a party *can* enforce his rights may serve as an additional incentive for other parties to meet their obligations under private law – thus, the *possibility* of enforcement may have a preventive function in itself.[2552] Yet characteristically, the enforcement of private law depends on private parties. Therefore, if private parties do not enforce their rights, this may lead to a lack of case law and literature discussing this case law, and a lack of information of the development and application of rules in legal practice.[2553] Consequently, rules that do not respond to the needs of legal practice, or society's views on justice, or rules that are circumvented because they give rise to problems of unpredictability and inconsistency, or rules that are not accessible, may continue to exist because of a lack of information on these problems. Arguably, this may be a reason to exercise some caution in the conclusions of impact assessments: possibly, the failure of a rule to visibly advance the internal market may not necessarily be due to, for example, minimum harmonisation, but also because parties have not enforced their rights, which, in turn, can be due to multiple reasons: consumers were already satisfied with the service provided by sellers, or they were unaware of

2550 European Commission, *Proposal for a Directive on distance selling*, COM (92) 11 final, p 11.

2551 Comp. the response of the British Exporters Association to the Feasibility Study, available at http://ec.europa.eu/justice/contract/expert-group/index_en.htm, p. 2, under 8.

2552 H.J. Snijders, C.J.M. Klaassen, G.J. Meijer, *Nederlands burgerlijk procesrecht*, Deventer: Kluwer 2007, 4th ed., par. 11, rightly note that the preventive effect may also be a disadvantage, especially if it has a greater effect on a party with less financial resources and expertise than the party he contracts with.

2553 Notably. a large amount of case law does not necessarily mean that a particular rule is problematic – rather, especially blanket clauses need to be interpreted taking into account all the relevant circumstances in individual cases, while a lack of case law need not necessarily mean that a provision is not of importance to legal practice, see for Dutch law recently A.S. Hartkamp, 'Het nieuwe BW – ontwikkelingen sinds 1992', *AA* 2012, p. 49, referring to the interpretation of article 6:162 par. 2 BW as well as the supplementary function of good faith in article 6:248 BW in HR 12 January 2001, *NJ* 2001, 253 and HR 12 December 2003, *NJ* 2004, 117.

their rights. Alternatively, they may suffer only limited damage that does not outweigh litigation costs.[2554]

Because of these shortcomings, impact assessments currently do not contribute to evidence-based interaction between actors, which should be one of the important advantages associated with impact assessments.[2555] Instead, impact assessments may undermine debate, as they generally support harmonisation rather than debate on the desirability of harmonisation, or debate on the possible ways to address problems for the internal market. Impact Assessment Reports frequently present rather exact transaction costs and percentages[2556] that provide a false sense of exactness which may inhibit further debate.

10.2.2.2. Improving the use of impact assessments

Despite shortcomings in the use of impact assessments, the European Commission has not critically considered the use of impact assessments in the development of the private law *acquis*.[2557] Nevertheless, the use of impact assessments can be improved if shortcomings are addressed and if measures for improved impact assessments are taken:

1) Impact assessments should accompany general consultations on future action and precede legislative proposals.

Thus, impact assessments are able to critically evaluate the need for proposed legislation, critically test assumptions, and go beyond the options suggested in consultation documents.

[2554] See further W.H. van Boom, *Efficacious enforcement in contract and tort*, The Hague: BJU 2006, who has identified various features of contract law that may stand in the way of the effective enforcement of contract and tort law, which may be particularly problematic if these rules pursue a specific aim.

[2555] W.H. van Boom, 'The Draft Directive on consumer rights: Choices made and arguments used', *Journal of Contemporary European Research* 2009, p. 460.

[2556] See for example SEC (2008) 2544. These predictions seem rather perilous to begin with and moreover, have already been challenged by stakeholders, see Oxera, *What is the impact of the proposed Consumer Credit Directive?*, April 2007, available at www.oxera.com/cmsDocuments/Oxera%20report%20on%20CCD%20April%202007.pdf (study commissioned by APACS, the British Bankers' Association, the Consumer Credit Association and the Finance & Leasing Organisation.) See for example also the claim of Open Plus that the new Directive will impose around € 10 billion on retailers, see www.openplus.co.uk/news/new-eu-law-will-cost-e-retail-consumers-10-billion/.

[2557] The House of Lords European Union Committee, *Impact Assessments in the EU: room for improvement?* available at www.parliament.the-stationery-office.co.uk/pa/ld200910/ldselect/ldeucom/61/6106.htm, 2009–10, par. 66 has pointed out that early drafts of impact assessments and draft Directives are not generally available, which makes it more difficult to estimate the influence of these documents on one another during the drafting process.

2) Actors participating in European consultations should take impact assessments into account.

More attention on impact assessments may pressure European actors to improve the use of impact assessments. The Roadmap service[2558] should contribute to the awareness of actors of planned impact assessments as well as facilitate an overview of the wide range of European initiatives.

3) National actors should consider carrying out separate impact assessments.

Senden[2559] has suggested that impact assessments should also be held at the national level. Arguably, national impact assessments will enable a clearer view on the impact of the reform of contract law on national markets, which may lead to a more evidence-based debate.

10.2.2.3. Conclusion on the use of impact assessments

This paragraph has considered whether the use of impact assessments strengthens the legislative processes, which, in turn, could benefit the use of blanket clauses. Impact assessments currently hinder rather than help interaction between actors. The shortcomings in impact assessments are unfortunate, as impact assessments are a suitable means of drawing attention to the question which techniques should be used in the development of private law. Perhaps a more critical approach to the use of techniques would have encouraged both national and European actors to use blanket clauses more sparingly. If the use of impact assessments is improved, they may more clearly help actors to pay more attention to the use of techniques. Possibly, the outcome of more critical impact assessments may be considered with more interest in the Dutch legal order, as the Dutch legislator is more inclined to leave room for the bottom-up development of private law than German actors.[2560] More critical and thorough impact assessments would, hopefully, lead to more specific guidelines when differences in national private laws could pose barriers to the internal market, indicating in what areas of law the Union is likely to pursue harmonisation, thereby furthering the predictability of harmonisation and limiting the arbitrariness of harmonisation.[2561]

10.2.3. Networks

Networks are frequently well-developed in nation states and accordingly facilitate interaction between various actors involved in the development of private law. Networks may be used to create discussion outside of the legislative process, but their role in

2558 See http://ec.europa.eu/governance/impact/planned_ia/planned_ia_en.htm.

2559 L.A.J. Senden, 'General Report, The quality of European legislation and its implementation and application in the national legal order', in: E.M.H. Hirsch Ballin, L.A.J. Senden (eds.), *Co-actorship in the development of European law-making'*, The Hague: Asser Press 2005, p. 157.

2560 See previously par. 8.6.1.

2561 J.M. Smits, 'European private law: A plea for a spontaneous legal order', in: D.M. Curtin, J.M. Smits (eds.), *European integration and the law*, Antwerp: Intersentia 2006, par. 6.

facilitating debate in the legislative process can be essential and often, actors simply rely on networks in the development of private law. In the multilevel legal order, networks are not as well-developed, while there is more need for interaction between actors as interdependence develops further. How can the use of networks contribute to the legislative process, in particular the extent to which codifications and blanket clauses contribute to the comprehensibility of European private law?

Paragraph 10.2.3.1 will consider the use of current networks and paragraph 10.2.3.2 will discuss shortcomings in the use of networks. Paragraph 10.2.3.3 will turn to the improved use of networks and paragraph 10.2.3.4 will end with a conclusion.

10.2.3.1. The current use of networks

Generally, the scope and function of networks differ widely from one another. Initiatives may range from cross-border cooperation between specific institutes,[2562] to well-established national networks.[2563] At the European level, different forms of networks have also developed, ranging from SECOLA,[2564] to, for example, the Network of the Presidents of the Supreme Judicial Courts of the European Union.[2565] Both European and national state actors have recognised the added value of networks in the development of private law. Generally, networks facilitate targeting actors with relevant expertise and experience who could contribute to the quality of private law.

10.2.3.2. Current shortcomings in the use of networks

What shortcomings are currently visible in the use of networks?

1) Generally, networks have failed to sufficiently facilitate and interest members in entering into debate across borders and across levels.

Parties involved in national legal practice or research and education do not necessarily also participate in networks at the European level. Consequently, a separation exists between the debate on national private law on the one hand, where discussion takes place between national actors, through well-established national networks, and literature, taking national statutory and

2562 For example, the Deutsch-Russische Juristenvereinigung e.V. (DRJV), or cooperation between universities in different legal orders.

2563 For example, the Dutch Lawyers' Society (*Nederlandse Juristen Vereniging)* see http://njv.nl/), as well as the Dutch Society on Private Law (*Nederlandse Vereniging voor Burgerlijk Recht*, see www.verenigingvoorburgerlijkrecht.nl/), The Netherlands Comparative law Association (*Nederlandse Vereniging voor Rechtsvergelijking*), see www.ejcl.org/general/nvvrhome.html), the Council for the Judiciary (*Raad voor de Rechtspraak*), see www.rechtspraak.nl/Organisatie/Raad-Voor-De-Rechtspraak/OverDeRvdr/Pages/default.aspx), and the Dutch Bar (*Orde van Advocaten*), see www.advocatenorde.nl/consumenten/). See for Germany for example the German Jurist Association ('*Deutscher Juristentag*'), see http://www.djt.de/ and the German Bar Association ('*Deutscher Anwaltsverein*'), see http://anwaltverein.de/de/

2564 See further www.secola.org/.

2565 See further www.rpcsjue.org/.

case law as a starting point. European law generally takes a less prominent position.[2566] On the other hand, debate on European private law, which includes the development of the private law *acquis*, the desirability of further harmonisation, and the interaction between European and national private law, takes European law and questions whether national private laws diverge as a starting point, where prominent European stakeholders may play an important role.[2567] Grundmann and Stuyck[2568] state that:

> 'The attendees [of the 2001 SECOLA conference] (...) represent the academic circles with a strong interest in the Europeanisation of private law. These circles, however, encompass probably not more than 10–20 per cent of private law scholars in the Member States (...) Therefore, the reservations which have been made against more intensive unification or in favour of maintaining elements of flexibility and diversity by a large majority even in this forum in Leuven have to be taken very seriously. It is not impossible that the majority view in legal academia in general could go in a direction more or less opposite or less favourable to any more harmonisation or unification.'

More generally, Schepel and Wesseling[2569] have emphasised the 'homogeneity of the European legal community'. Further, Armstrong[2570] has noted the emphasis of the Commission on including especially transnational actors in civil society in the White Paper on European governance, in order to support European legislation.

The separation may explain why, in the law on STCs,[2571] European networks have not, for example, prompted Dutch actors to critically reconsider national law.

2) Stakeholders who can easily organise themselves may participate more prominently in networks than weaker stakeholders. Thus, the formation of networks does not necessarily encourage *inclusive* debate.

[2566] Comp. S. Prechal, R.H. van Ooik, J.H. Jans, K.J.M. Mortelmans, 'Europeanisation of the law: Consequences for the Dutch judiciary', Report of October 2005, available at www.rechtspraak.nl/Organisatie/Raad-Voor-De-Rechtspraak/WetenschapsOnderzoek/Overzichtonderzoeksprojecten/Europeanisering/Pages/default.aspx, p. 49–50.

[2567] For example, the drafting of the Optional Instrument (see for the members of the stakeholder group http://ec.europa.eu/justice/contract/stakeholder-meeting/index_en.htm), Directive 2011/83 on consumer rights (see for the members of the stakeholder group http://ec.europa.eu/consumers/rights/cons_acquis_en.htm). Comp. also the members of the Round Table on Travel Contracts, on the review of Directive 90/314 on package travel (see for the members of the group http://ec.europa.eu/consumers/cons_int/safe_shop/pack_trav/pack_trav03_en.pdf).

[2568] Comp. the observation of S. Grundmann, J. Stuyck, 'An academic Green Paper on European contract law – Scope, common ground and debated issues', in: S. Grundmann, J. Stuyck, (eds.), *An academic Green Paper on European contract law*, The Hague: KLI 2002, p. 7–8.

[2569] H. Schepel, R. Wesseling, 'The legal community: Judges, lawyers, officials and clerks in the writing of Europe', *ELJ* 1997, p. 165.

[2570] K. Armstrong, 'Rediscovering civil society: the European Union and the White paper on Governance', *ELJ* 2002, p. 116.

[2571] See previously par. 4.7.1. and par. 5.7.1.

3) European actors take European networks as a starting point instead of turning to national networks.

As also argued in the case studies,[2572] European networks should not be used as an alternative to various national networks, but as a supplement to national networks, and make use of the contacts established in these national networks. Arguably, national state actors are best placed to involve actors in debates on European legal reform.[2573] State actors may also be better placed than actors at the European or international level to recognise important actors and well-established, representative stakeholder groups at the national level.

The development of multiple networks which apparently overlap may lead to confusion. This becomes apparent in Directive 2013/11 on ADR in consumer disputes,[2574] which envisages an important role for the European Consumer Centres-network, and also notes that ADR organisations should be encouraged to join FIN-NET with regard to ADR in financial services. However, the existence of the European Extra-Judicial network may also create some confusion, as the division of tasks between the EEJ-net and the ECC-net, as well as the relationship between these two networks, is not clear. This confusion also makes it more difficult for national state actors to keep track of developments in these areas.

Consequently, shortcomings in the debate in European private law can also be traced to shortcomings in the use of networks.

10.2.3.3. Improvements in the use of networks

The use of networks can be improved in various ways:

1) Networks should be more open to wider participation.

Networks may not be open to participation by all relevant actors, which may limit the extent to which these networks encourage inclusive, accessible and transparent debate. Important national networks may require members to have a law degree from a university in that particular Member State,[2575] and discussions in networks are held in the language of the Member State, which may limit the extent to which foreign actors can participate in the debate in Member States. In some cases, cross-border networks have developed.[2576]

2572 See previously par. 5.7.1.

2573 Comp. the European Union Select Committee, *Correspondence with Ministers November 2007 to April 2008*, Review of the consumer *acquis*, accessed at www.parliament.the-stationery-office.co.uk/pa/ld200910/ldselect/ldeucom/29/29250.htm#note133.

2574 COM (2011) 793 final.

2575 This is the case for the Dutch Jurists' Association (*Nederlandse Juristen Vereniging*), see http://njv.nl/lidmaatschap/lid-worden/. The German Law Association (*Deutscher Juristentag*) provides that foreign lawyers can become members if they are recommended by members, see www.djt.de/recht-mitgestalten/mitglied-werden/.

2576 For example the Anglo-German Law Society, www.aglawsoc.org/ or the Association for comparative legal studies in Belgium and The Nederlands ('*Vereniging voor de vergelijkende studie van het recht van België en Nederland*').

2) Actors should be made aware of relevant networks

Miller[2577] has argued that especially the European Law Institute should play a central role in coordinating the development of private law at the national and European level. Zimmerman[2578] argues that networks such as the European Law Institute[2579] should provide an overview of existing networks. In this way, a European Law Institute could contribute to keeping an overview of the different existing networks, forging contacts when the work of such networks could further debate in European private law, while making use of the memberships and contacts established in existing networks, instead of potentially creating confusion by replacing one network with another while actors may already be familiar with one network.

10.2.3.4. Conclusion on the use of networks

Currently, the use of networks in the multilevel legal order does not facilitate debate on private law to the extent that they facilitate debate within Member States. Networks currently do not make actors involved in legislative process more aware of other actors also developing private law. Suggestions for improvement encourage actors to look at foreign and European networks, while European actors should pay more attention to prominent national networks. However, the success of networks depends on the participation by relevant actors, and attempts to establish networks may not necessarily be successful, while it may take up considerable resources. Even if all relevant actors are participating in a network, this may not, necessarily, point towards a specific outcome.

10.2.4. Databases

The use of databases is important in facilitating evidence-based interaction between actors. Therefore, paragraph 10.2.4.1 will consider the current use of databases, and paragraph 10.2.4.2 will consider shortcomings in the use of databases. Paragraph 10.2.4.3 will consider improvements in the use of databases and paragraph 10.2.4.4 will end with a conclusion.

10.2.4.1. The current use of databases

Databases are widely used in national legal orders as well as the European legal order. They provide actors with the necessary information to participate in debate based on adequate knowledge of the law. National databases provide one with information about relevant national and European legislation and (most) case law. At the European level, databases have been established within various European networks: from the well-known EU consumer law *acquis* database[2580] to the less well-known and accessible

[2577] L. Miller, *The emergence of EU contract law: Exploring Europeanization*, Oxford: OUP 2011, p. 207–208.

[2578] R. Zimmerman, 'Reflections on a European Law Institute – based on the proceedings of the Florence Conference', *ZEuP* 2010, p. 721.

[2579] See further www.europeanlawinstitute.eu/eli/index.php.

[2580] Available at www.eu-consumer-law.org/.

search engine of national case law established by the Network of the Presidents of the Supreme Judicial Courts of the European Union.[2581] Thus, the scope and content of these databases varies: from widely available information on the implementation of the *acquis*, to information shared between courts.

10.2.4.2. Shortcomings in the use of databases

Currently, databases are not used optimally within the multilevel legal order:

1) Few databases on national decisions on the private law *acquis* have been established and the success of databases that do exist varies and is difficult to assess.

Whereas the CLABB-database was not well-known and abandoned after some years, the EU consumer law *acquis* database was used as a starting point to evaluate which Directives would be included in the review of the consumer *acquis*.

2) Databases on the implementation of the *acquis* are established in addition to well-established national databases.

Accordingly, the European legislator has similarly recognised the added value of more information on the interpretation of the private law *acquis*, considering its proposal to collect information on the application of the withdrawn Regulation by both national courts and the CJEU in article 14 par. 2 Regulation for a CESL. Databases have also been established with regard to Directive 2005/29[2582] and in private international law.[2583]

Typically, national databases that are most often used do not provide one with information on foreign statutory law or case law implementing the private law *acquis*. Actors who are familiar with these databases will not seek to rely on other databases without a clear incentive to do so. Including decisions on the implementation of the *acquis* in national databases may increase the chance that actors will become more aware of these decisions.

It is, however, important to realise why databases are established. For some actors, databases that are interesting for other actors may have little added value. For example, a database on the implementation of the *acquis* may have limited value for Member States. Generally, Member States simultaneously have to draft implementation legislation. By the time the database contains information on these implementation laws, most Member States will already have implemented the *acquis*, and, therefore, will not make use of a database providing information on the implementation of a Directive throughout the Union.[2584]

[2581] See www.reseau-presidents.eu/rpcsjue/?lang=en

[2582] See https://webgate.ec.europa.eu/ucp/public/index.cfm?event=public.home.show.

[2583] See http://ec.europa.eu/civiljustice/jure/login_en.cfm.

[2584] L.A.J. Senden, 'General Report, The quality of European legislation and its implementation and application in the national legal order', in: E.M.H. Hirsch Ballin, L.A.J. Senden (eds.), *Co-actorship in the development of European law-making*, The Hague: Asser Press 2005, p. 128–129.

10.2.4.3. Improving the use of databases

The use of databases can be improved in various ways:

1) Rather than establishing separate and possibly overlapping databases, the European legislator should consider the use of national databases to make actors more aware of European and foreign decisions.

The development of overlapping databases – as well as networks – alongside one another may give rise to confusion. Similar to networks, it may be, therefore, worthwhile to take existing, well-established networks – insofar as they exist throughout the Union – and databases as starting points in the collection of information. European actors may also make actors more aware of well-established databases in various legal orders.

2) More use could be made of national databases in the development of transnational private law

Databases on national case law or national laws could underpin the development of model rules found in the different sets of soft law as well as debates on the question whether and how a model rule (detailed or otherwise) could be distilled from these cases.[2585]

3) Foreign databases should be made more accessible.

In accordance with the findings in the case studies,[2586] national actors should make databases more accessible to foreign actors. The Dutch case study found that accessibility may be facilitated by the Dutch Centre of International Legal Cooperation (CILC). Particularly, the availability of the database in multiple languages may further its successful use. Doralt[2587] points out that not all lawyers have a good command of more than one foreign language and that translations of national case law, or summaries, could for that reason be valuable.

Weatherill[2588] finds that merely mentioning foreign decisions may not be as interesting as also providing information of the contents of a decision, previous decisions, and its relevance for legal practice. Furthermore, users should be able to overview the information offered in databases, to avoid an information overload.

2585 J.M. Smits, 'A European law on unjustified enrichment? A critical view on the law of restitution in the Draft Common Frame of Reference', in: A. Vaquer (ed.), *European private law beyond the Common Frame of Reference*, Groningen: ELP 2008, p. 7, W. Doralt, 'Strukturelle Schwächen in der Europäisierung des Privatrechts', *RabelsZ* 2011, p. 268–269.

2586 See previously par. 4.7.1. and 5.7.1.

2587 W. Doralt, 'The Optional European Contract Law and why success or failure may depend on scope rather than substance', *Max Planck Private Law Research Paper* 2011, p. 6.

2588 S. Weatherill, 'Can there be common interpretation of European private law?', *Georgia Journal of International and Comparative Law* 2002, p. 164.

10.2.4.4. Conclusion on the use of databases

The current use of databases does not sufficiently support interaction between actors at different levels in a manner similar to nation states and can be improved. Rather than establishing new, overlapping databases, European actors should make more use of well-established databases in Member States, and the accessibility of these databases to foreign actors should be improved. In turn, wider accessibility may make actors more aware of the relevant initiatives of other actors.

10.2.5. Conclusion on the techniques used to strengthen the legislative process

Techniques such as impact assessments, consultations, databases and networks may foster deliberation between interdependent actors and mutual learning, in accordance with pluralist arguments. However, typically, the legislative process and the techniques that support this process show shortcomings and are currently not designed in a way that maximises interaction and mutual learning between interdependent actors in the multilevel legal order. The shortcomings in the techniques discussed in this paragraph lead to problems not only in nation states, but also in the multilevel legal order. Problems of predictability, consistency, and responsiveness in the private law *acquis* could also be seen in this light. If shortcomings in legislative processes remain, the extent to which other actors may learn from law developed through these defective processes is decreased. As a result, the chance that the coexistence of actors leads to benefits such as mutual learning, experimentation and regulatory competition lessens. Similarly, the chance that the existence of European actors prompts national actors to take more note of the interests of foreign and international actors, or to critically consider divergent law in the light of free movement, diminishes.

The use of consultations and impact assessments is closely intertwined, and problems in the use of one of these techniques may undermine the quality of legislation in the area of private law.

1) This has already become clear from incomplete assessments based on the options presented in preceding consultations.

2) In addition, shortcomings in the use of consultations and impact assessments may facilitate *ad hoc* legislation, which may undermine the stable development as well as the responsiveness of European private law.[2589]

For example, the reform of Dutch insolvency law was defended as a necessary modernisation that would ensure that insolvency law was in accordance with legal practice, and further accessibility, and could even prevent the bankruptcy of businesses that had less chance under the old insolvency law.[2590] Instead, the government eventually found that a far-reaching reform of insolvency law

[2589] Comp. W. van Gerven, S. Lierman, *Algemeen Deel. Veertig jaar later*, Mechelen: Kluwer 2010, p. 184, on Belgian legislative practices.

[2590] Comp. the interview with Prof. B. Kortmann, presiding over the expert committee drafting the legislative proposal: L. Cornelisse, 'Nieuwe insolventiewet kan bedrijven redden', Interview

was undesirable in times of recession, and existing insolvency law was maintained to improve predictability.[2591] That does not mean that insolvency law is not amended; instead, a legislative programme targeting specific aspects of insolvency law was announced.[2592] If impact assessments underpin legislative proposals, would this ensure that either reforming or postponing reforming laws is based on more than assertions?

Failed suggestions for reform suggest that impact assessments or other empirical support for legislation do not stand in the way of *ad hoc* legislation or the delay or cancellation of well-established projects. For example, the proposal to allow for the compensation of emotional harm from the death or injury of a loved one in Dutch law[2593] was rejected[2594] despite empirical support for the legislative proposal.[2595]

3) Defects in the use of consultations make it less likely that the law is developed in a responsive manner. This can be aggravated by shortcomings in the use of impact assessments, which decrease the chance that the development of private law is based on a demonstrable need for the development of private law in a specific way in practice.

A defective use of both consultations and impact assessments will not serve to further debate, and makes it more likely that legal reform is not based on views from legal practice, experts, and stakeholders. Ignoring expert advice may undermine the quality of private law, especially if it leads to inconsistencies between national private laws and private law at the European level. In turn, national private law that is, for example, inconsistent, easily outdated, largely circumvented in practice, or unpredictable, may affect the interpretation of Directives.

Interestingly, there are indications that Dutch private law judges in courts of first instance and appeal courts only rarely apply European law in private law cases, also due to a lack of familiarity with European law.[2596] Accordingly, Niglia[2597] traces the lack of enforcement to the limited involvement of national scholars and judges in the drafting of the private law *acquis*.

The use of networks and databases does not show similarly serious shortcomings, but neither do they compensate for the shortcomings in consultations in impact assessments.

The success of suggestions for improvement for the additional techniques depends on the participation of both national and European actors, as well as non-state actors.

11 November 2010, available at www.sconline.nl/artikelen/details/2010/11-november/11/Nieuwe-insolventiewet-kan-bedrijven-redden.html.

2591 *Kamerstukken II*, 2010–2011, 1014, Aanhangsel.

2592 *Kamerstukken II*, 2012–2013, 29911, nr. 74.

2593 *Kamerstukken II*, 2002–2003, 28 781, nr. 3, p. 4, referring to HR 8 September 2000, *NJ* 2001, 734, and HR 22 February 2002, *NJ* 2002, 240.

2594 *Handelingen I*, 2009–2010, 28781, nr. 23.

2595 The rejection refers to A.J. Akkermans et al, *Slachtoffers en aansprakelijkheid: Een onderzoek naar behoeften, verwachtingen en ervaringen van slachtoffers en hun naasten met betrekking tot het civiele aansprakelijkheidsrecht, Deel II*, Amsterdam: WODC 2008, available at http://wodc.nl/onderzoeksdatabase/affectieschade.aspx.

2596 Hague Institute for the Internationalisation of Law, *Research project: National judges as European Union judges, results and recommendations*, summary available at www.hiil.org/research/main-themes/highest-courts/research-project-national-judges-as-european-union-judges/results-and-recommendations/.

2597 L. Niglia, 'The non-Europeanisation of private law', *ERPL* 2001, p. 595.

Therefore, actors have become interdependent in improving European private law. Interdependence also becomes visible when shortcomings are visible in the legislative process at one level.

1) Delay in the legislative process at the European or national level may in turn affect the legislative process at, respectively, the national or the European level.

Lengthy legislative procedures at the European level may inhibit the reform of national private law as harmonisation on an issue is forthcoming. Alternatively, national legislators may speed up reform, in order for reformed law to act as a model for European measures, or the national legislature may choose to anticipate harmonisation or quickly implement harmonised law, trying to compensate for a lengthy legislative procedure at the European level. If this is not the case, the delay in legislative procedures may also add up, leading to a lengthy legislative procedure at the European level, as well as a lengthy (and probably late) implementation into national law.

2) Shortcomings in the European legislative process frequently entail ignoring insights from practice, which decreases the chance that harmonised private law will be responsive. Importantly, this lack of responsiveness may subsequently spread to national law if European measures pursue maximum harmonisation.

In other words, the use of techniques commonly used in addition to the legislative process is flawed and if actors seek to improve European private law by enhancing the use of these techniques, the success of these attempts may depend on other actors. If the use of these techniques is improved they may foster mutual learning and deliberation, in accordance with pluralist arguments. The improved use of techniques supporting the legislative process may in turn strengthen harmonisation, and it may support regulatory competition.

This requires that in the multilevel legal order, debate should not merely resemble the debate in nation states; there should be more and better interaction than is the case in nation states, between more actors.

In particular, interaction between actors from different levels should be encouraged. National legal practitioners and academics should be involved more in the debate at a European level. Also, national Parliaments should already be involved in the drafting of the private law *acquis* at an early stage.[2598] Accordingly, national Parliaments are well-placed to initiate debate on the reform of the *acquis* at the national level.[2599] Additionally, national state actors should more closely interact with European actors, for example, with regard to the question of what role soft laws should play in the reform of the private law *acquis*. European actors should also be more involved in developments at the national and the international level.

[2598] In this sense L.A.J. Senden, 'De lidstaten en de kwaliteit van Europese wetgeving: geen consumenten, maar co-actoren', *SEW* 2006, p. 56.

[2599] See for example the select European Union committee that collected evidence on the *Green Paper on the Review of the consumer acquis* COM (2006) 744 final and the response of the UK government to the Green Paper. See for a summary of responses from stakeholders www.parliament.the-stationery-office.co.uk/pa/ld200910/ldselect/ldeucom/29/29250.htm#note133.

The debate could be strengthened if advisory organs to legislators also pay attention to comparative law and developments by other states or developments at a European and the international level.[2600] National advisory organs could also participate in the drafting of European law.[2601] At the European level, Sandström[2602] has pointed to the possible role of the Council Legal Service in this respect, and suggested a European Council on legislation.

Regrettably, the shortcomings in the use of these techniques that became visible in the case studies[2603] may stand in the way of using these techniques as a means for mutual learning and more deliberation. The potential for improvement may be limited if European or national actors are not interested in improvement. As became visible in the case studies,[2604] national and European actors have bargained rather than deliberated in the development of European private law and focussed on, respectively, maintaining national law and further harmonising the law. If the responses to consultations or the outcomes of impact assessments are not in line with the preferences of national or European state actors, will this prompt more deliberation or will actors be pressured to develop private law responsively to stakeholders' needs and preferences or the needs of the internal market?

However, the approach of actors has not stood in the way of some instances of anticipation[2605] and mutual learning,[2606] and some Member States seem to be more willing to amend the law, especially if there is sufficient agreement that the law needs to be improved.[2607] It has also been argued[2608] that the defensive approach of national actors should be replaced by clear assessments of the disadvantages of a particular proposal, alongside alternative suggestions, or more detailed arguments setting out why harmonisation is undesirable. This approach is likely to have more effect than the defensive approach that so far has not exactly discouraged the European legislator from pursuing further harmonisation. In turn, European actors need to pay more attention to national experiences and initiatives in order to develop the *acquis* more responsively.

2600 M. Scheltema, *Het recht van de toekomst* (inaugural address Utrecht), Deventer: Kluwer 2005, p. 8. Possibly, the Association of the Councils of State and Supreme Administrative Jurisdictions of the European Union could provide a forum for such exchanges – see further www.juradmin.eu/en/home_en.html.

2601 Comp. L.A.J. Senden, 'General Report, the quality of European legislation and its implementation and application in the national legal order', in: E.M.H. Hirsch Ballin, L.A.J. Senden (eds.), *Co-actorship in the development of European law-making'*, The Hague: Asser Press 2005, p. 124.

2602 G. Sandström, 'Knocking EU law into shape', *CMLRev* 2003, p. 1311–1312.

2603 Particularly, in the German case study, in par. 4.7.1. it was pointed out that judges are not likely to consider databases on foreign decisions because of the abundant amount of national materials that are available. Considering arguments derived from foreign law, especially divergent foreign law, may also give rise to problems of inconsistency with national law and unresponsiveness to national legal views on justice.

2604 See previously par. 4.6.3. and 5.6.3.

2605 See previously par. 9.2.2. and 9.2.3.

2606 See previously par. 6.3.2.

2607 See previously par. 6.2.

2608 See previously par. 6.2.

If achieved, the improvements recommended in this paragraph may be a step towards deliberation, but deliberation, which aims at achieving consensus, may well turn out to be cumbersome and lengthy.[2609] The length of this process is not only affected by the number of participants, but also by the number of points that parties have to agree upon. Thus, the wider the scope of harmonisation initiatives, the more difficult it will be to achieve consensus and the lengthier the process. However, the current shortcomings in the legislative process have also led to problems that include slow, cumbersome and inefficient processes.

Until these improvements have been realised, the shortcomings in the legislative process, both at the national and the European level may give rise to the question what this means for democratic legitimacy, in accordance with Smits'[2610] argument that even if law is developed through the legislative process, rules may still lack legitimacy.

The approach of national and European actors, combined with the problems in the *acquis*, may give rise to questions with regard to the normative frameworks defended in chapters 7 and 8. According to the German framework,[2611] state actors develop rules in the public interest, but the approach of national and European actors make clear that public interests may differ, and even if they do not differ, public actors' idea of how to best protect these interests may still differ. Importantly, the public interest need not necessarily be focussed on the development of comprehensible European private law, but, especially at the European level, on policy aims such as consumer protection or the internal market. If state actors routinely overlook the needs and preferences of actors affected by legislation, does de facto *Fremdbestimmung* not arise? If this is the case, and if non state actors more convincingly pursue the development of a more comprehensible European private law, and if potential *Fremdbestimmung* is sufficiently compensated, should non-state actors not play a more important role? Accordingly, Verdaas[2612] prefers non-democratically legitimated experts that actively develop private law comprehensibly, rather than an inactive, but democratically legitimated legislator.

10.3. Additional techniques beyond the legislative process: blanket clauses

The use of blanket clauses may give rise to unpredictability, and suggestions for the use of additional techniques to compensate for these problems can be found both at the European and the national level. At both levels, the importance of coordination between different actors has been emphasised. This paragraph asks which techniques used in addition to currently used techniques could contribute to the predictability and consistency of private law developed through blanket clauses.

Paragraph 10.3.1 will discuss the suggestions for guidance on the interpretation of blanket clauses and paragraph 10.3.2 will consider the development of comitology

2609 F.W. Scharpf, 'European governance: common concerns vs the challenge of diversity', *Jean Monnet Working Paper* 6/01, p. 6.

2610 J.M. Smits, 'Democracy and (European) private law: A functional approach', *EJLS* 2009, p. 34.

2611 See previously par. 7.2.1.

2612 A.J. Verdaas, 'Wetgever, besteed meer aandacht aan ons vermogensrecht! Een oproep tot het instellen van een permanente Commissie vermogensrecht', *NTBR* 2010, 47, par. 39.

procedures and reminiscent national procedures. Paragraph 10.3.3 will address the use of alternative regulation and paragraph 10.3.4 will end with a conclusion.

10.3.1. Guidance on the interpretation of blanket clauses

The Dutch case study[2613] found that the development of Guidance for the interpretation of article 3 Directive 93/13 is not likely to contribute to predictability and consistency, and may even diminish responsiveness. The question arises whether this is more generally the case or whether guidelines are likely to contribute to a more comprehensible law, as well as mutual learning and deliberation.

The development of Guidance has been suggested for both the European and the national level. For the European level, Pavillon[2614] finds that there should be more information on the interpretation of harmonised law throughout the Union, in order for judges to be able to refer to it. To this end, she suggests the development of Guidance by the European Commission, which should be available in the different languages spoken in the EU, as well as being easily accessible, and based on a database collecting decisions on the interpretation of blanket clauses.[2615] Accordingly, Guidance on the interpretation of Directive 2005/29 on unfair commercial practices has been developed.[2616] It appears, however, that Dutch courts have not referred to the Guidance in private law disputes.

Guidance has also been developed at the national level, for example in the English legal order.[2617] In the German legal order, Guidance has also developed, but their scope has been subject to limitations. Although Guidance can help courts in their decision, they should not be binding, nor should they be mechanically followed. However, some rules, such as the *Düsseldorfer Tabelle*, are *de facto* consistently followed.[2618]

In the Dutch legal order, a particularly prominent example of Guidance has been developed by the *Kring van Kantonrechters*,[2619] a committee of judges competent to deal with simple cases.[2620] This committee has developed a widely followed formula for calculating compensation (the '*Kantonrechtersformule*') for employees who have been

2613 See previously par. 5.7.3.2.

2614 C.M.D.S. Pavillon, *Open normen in het Europees consumentenrecht*, Deventer: Kluwer 2011, p. 521–523.

2615 Available at https://webgate.ec.europa.eu/ucp/public/index.cfm?event=public.home.show.

2616 See for example the Guidance on the interpretation of Directive 2005/25 on unfair commercial practices.

2617 The European Parliament in its resolution of 13 January 2009, on the transposition, implementation and enforcement of Directive 2005/29/EC concerning unfair business-to-consumer commercial practices in the internal market and Directive 2006/114/EC concerning misleading and comparative advertising (2008/2114(INI)), par. 23 refers to the UK Guidance "Consumer Protection from Unfair Trading Regulations: a basic guide for business", available at www.oft.gov.uk/shared_oft/business_leaflets/cpregs/oft979.pdf, as an example of 'best practice'.

2618 See for further references J.J.J. Sillen, 'Tussen dogmatiek en pragmatisme: binding aan rechtersregelingen in Nederland en Duitsland', *AA* 2014, p. 572–573.

2619 See further www.rechtspraak.nl/Procedures/Landelijke-regelingen/Sector-kantonrecht/Aanbevelingen-van-de-kring-van-kantonrechters/Pages/Kantonrechtersformule.aspx.

2620 Although this is a well-known, prominent example, it is hardly the only set of rules developed through the cooperation of judges. See for an overview www.rechtspraak.nl/Procedures/Landelijke-regelingen/Pages/default.aspx.

dismissed, and this formula has strengthened predictability and consistency in this area of law.

Asser, Groen, Vranken and Tzankova,[2621] in their 2006 report on the reform of Dutch civil procedure law, state that alongside a new codification, Guidance on the interpretation of the new codification should be developed, in addition to case law and literature that will develop on a new codification. In their opinion, such Guidance will considerably accelerate the understanding and application of reformed law in legal practice, which may otherwise be a lengthy process in which a lack of clarity exists on the meaning of reformed law. The additional ways in which Guidance is offered should be seen in combination with one another, and include setting up a helpdesk dealing with questions on the new law, the answers to which should be made available to legal practice. However, eventually, Guidance was not adopted.

The success of Guidance in the German and Dutch legal order makes clear that Guidance can contribute to the predictability and consistency of the law. The lack of attention for Guidance in private law disputes in the area of unfair commercial practices and the rejection of this suggestion in civil procedure law make clear that the success of Guidance may be limited to technical, non-controversial matters, such as the calculation of damages or alimony, at least in the Dutch and German legal order. In addition, the case studies indicate that the success of Guidance is limited if it contradicts case law of higher courts.[2622] Arguably, the potential of European Guidance to contribute to the comprehensibility of European private law or mutual learning is subject to similar limitations.

10.3.2. Suggestions for comitology procedures

The Dutch case study[2623] found that comitology developed to amend a binding European model list would weaken rather than strengthen the predictability, consistency, accessibility and responsiveness of the law on STCs. Yet for areas not developed within codes, and for technical matters, comitology may still be attractive, in accordance with pluralist arguments according to which comitology should foster deliberation.[2624] and in line with arguments for comitology at the European and the national level. Accordingly, Pavillon[2625] points to article 40 proposal for a Directive on consumer rights, which initially suggested establishing a comitology committee for further developing black and grey lists. Yet it was insufficiently clear what sort of comitology committee would be established, and whether the suggestion that the black and grey lists are a merely technical issue that can be dealt with through comitology is convincing.

2621 W.D.H. Asser, H.A. Groen, J.B.M. Vranken, I.N. Tzankova, *Uitgebalanceerd. Eindrapport fundamentele herbezinning Nederlands burgerlijk procesrecht*, The Hague: BJU 2006, p. 253–261.

2622 Particularly, the Guidance on the *ex officio* application of the law on STCs, see previously par. 5.7.3.2.

2623 See previously par. 5.7.3.1.

2624 See previously par. 7.4.1.4.

2625 C.M.D.S. Pavillon, *Open normen in het Europees consumentenrecht*, Deventer: Kluwer 2011, p. 524–525.

The suggestion for comitology committees is in line with other suggestions for accelerating procedures to amend European law rather than using blanket clauses, to enhance the flexibility of European law.[2626] Alternatively, arguably, minimum harmonisation should leave national state actors with sufficient competence to respond to developing practices, and society's legal views on justice. Thus, minimum harmonisation takes the coexistence of actors as a starting point and allows for the legal experimentation by Member States, which in turn may provide a source of inspiration for other Member States as well as European actors.[2627]

Proposals for procedures reminiscent of comitology have also been made at the national level. The 2006 Dutch report has suggested establishing a committee with limited competences to provide rules on the interpretation of blanket clauses, as well as benchmark figures and other ambiguous provisions in codifications. Such a committee should ideally consist of legal practitioners as well as scholars.[2628] However, this suggestion has met with objections by the advisory committee[2629] that suggested that periodical meetings between judges had proven sufficiently effective. In its strategic agenda for 2008–2011, the judiciary emphasised these meetings more generally as a means to increase coordination to enhance legal unity.[2630] These periodical judicial meetings did not meet with objections that would arise from providing an advisory committee with rule-making competences. The committee also pointed out that questions on the relation between the helpdesk and the courts could arise. These periodical meetings,[2631] which aimed to foster legal unity, did however not prevent problems of inconsistency and unpredictability in the Dutch case study.[2632]

Differently than the European proposal, the Dutch suggestion did not concern the amendment of the Dutch black and grey lists. Instead, the suggestion in the 2006 report should be seen in the context of possible recodification of civil procedure law, which considered ways to provide clarity on the interpretation of blanket clauses. The European suggestion, however, was also aimed at promoting flexibility. At the national level, there was less need for flexibility, and more need to guarantee the predictable and consistent development of the law in the event of recodification.

The success of the *Kantonrechtersformule* indicates that comitology may successfully contribute to the predictability and consistency of law. The meetings of the *Kring van Kantonrechters* are likely to foster deliberation and mutual learning, but the meetings are not public. Theoretically, the formula may lead to *Fremdbestimmung* as the rights and duties of parties are decided in accordance with the formula. The Hoge Raad has more generally decided that some sets of rules developed by judges can become binding,[2633]

2626 E. Terryn, 'The Green Paper on the review of the consumer *acquis*', *TvC* 2007, p. 108.

2627 E. Terryn, 'The Green Paper on the review of the consumer *acquis*', *TvC* 2007, p. 108.

2628 For other legal orders, different composition of committees may be suggested.

2629 Adviescommissie voor het burgerlijk procesrecht, advice to the Minister, 29 December 2003, 16, p. 16.

2630 Raad van de Rechtspraak, *Agenda van de Rechtspraak 2008–2011, Onafhankelijk en betrokken*, available at www.rechtspraak.nl/Organisatie/Publicaties-En-Brochures/Agenda-voor-de-Rechtspraak/Documents/Strategischeagenda20082011DEF.pdf, p. 24.

2631 As reported in the annual reports of courts, available at www.rechtspraak.nl.

2632 See previously par. 5.4.

2633 HR 28 June 1996. *NJ* 1997, 495.

because of principles of consistency and predictability.[2634] However, the formula was developed by state actors, who do not necessarily pursue a specific interest, and the rules developed by judges frequently benefit the comprehensibility of law.

Initiatives reminiscent of comitology may meet with criticism not only in the Dutch legal order,[2635] but also in the German legal order. Sillen[2636] points out that in the German legal order, article 97 GG emphasises judicial independence. Consequently, the development of rules by committees of experts or even the development of rules by committees of judges, may be problematic. However, as general rules developed by judges, as well as other case law may strengthen legal unity, courts may take into account the decisions of other courts and guidance.

Notably, the scope of comitology, and of national rules developed, seems to be limited. National rules should help judges decide consistently on the amount of damages, and not on the interpretation of crucial rules. More generally, the German concerns make clear that a German initiative may have limited value as it may not be binding, and there are hardly guarantees that in the absence of binding force, German judges will voluntarily turn to rules developed by committees. The objections to the binding force of rules developed by judges, as well as more general concerns of *Fremdbestimmung*, make clear that comitology and the development of guidance, will likely be resisted in the German legal order, especially for the interpretation of crucial blanket clauses.

10.3.3. The use of alternative regulation in the interpretation of blanket clauses

The Dutch case study[2637] found that the use of alternative regulation in the interpretation of blanket clauses could be beneficial in terms of responsiveness. Collecting information on alternative regulation throughout the Union may also be defended as a source of mutual learning and as a means to increase accessibility and predictability in cross-border trade.[2638] Taking into account national alternative regulation would also allow for differentiation in the interpretation of blanket clauses in EU measures.[2639] However, German objections based on potential *Fremdbestimmung*[2640] make clear that alternative regulation, if used, should be limited to actors who have recognised alternative regulation,

2634 K. Teuben, *Rechtersregelingen in het (burgerlijk) procesrecht*, Deventer: Kluwer 2004, p. 115–116.

2635 P.P.T. Bovend'Eert, 'De rechter als wetgever: uniforme rechtstoepassing in rechtersregelingen vanuit staatsrechtelijk perspectief', *Regelmaat* 2010, p. 17, considers the various points of criticism that relate to the lack of democratic legitimacy, inconsistency of judicial rule-making with newly adopted legislation. He more generally considers the compatibility of judicial rule-making with constitutional principles, particularly the separation of powers, as well as legal impediments to general rules developed by the courts.

2636 J.J.J. Sillen, 'Tussen dogmatiek en pragmatisme: binding aan rechtersregelingen in Nederland en Duitsland', *AA* 2014, p. 570–572.

2637 See previously par. 5.7.3.4.

2638 V. Mak, 'According to custom ...? The role of 'Trade Usage' in the Proposed Common European Sales Law (CESL)', *ERCL* 2014, p. 64.

2639 V. Mak, 'Scharnierpunt tussen Europees en nationaal consumentenrecht', *MvV* 2011, p. 185.

2640 See previously par. 7.5.3.6.

or in cases where one-sided declarations should be binding,[2641] which may differ throughout the Union.[2642]

Possibly, consistently looking to both surrounding private law and well-established self-regulation and co-regulation may increase responsiveness and make clearer to foreign private parties what standards of behaviour are expected from businesses, *if* those standards are freely and fully available to those foreign private parties. However, if self- and co-regulation bind third parties, it is essential that foreign parties that are affected by those rules are aware of these rules and consent to them; this means not only publicly providing these rules, but also making them available in multiple languages. Subsequently, more sharply delineated rules could be evaluated by the judiciary.

Perhaps, comparing self-regulation in different Member States, and collecting information on codes of conduct in different Member States would make self-regulation more accessible to foreign contract parties. Additionally, actors may be made more aware of relevant self-regulation through databases and through network organisations that promote self-regulation, while the members of these organisations also widely develop self-regulation, such as the European Advertising Standards Alliance.

However, this presupposes that such codes of conduct exist, and that they are also generally acceptable in other Member States. Difficulties may also arise if self-regulation is interpreted differently in different Member States, or if relevant national mandatory private laws diverge.

Pavillon[2643] argues against the use of national default law or alternative regulation as a decisive means to clarify or differentiate in the interpretation of European concepts. She points out that putting too much weight on national viewpoints may undermine harmonisation. Yet if measures pursue minimum harmonisation, this arguably leaves room for courts to take national viewpoints into account, provided that the level of consumer protection does not go below the standard set by the Directives, or violates the fundamental freedoms set out in the TFEU. In contrast, if measures pursue full or targeted full harmonisation, it is less likely that judges can take national points of view into account. In those cases, however, perhaps cross-border self-regulation – such as the EMOTA Convention – may be used to interpret blanket clauses.

However, alternative regulation currently does not undermine harmonisation as becomes visible in Dutch case law. Giesen[2644] has pointed out that Dutch courts occasionally refer to alternative regulation without adopting a consistent approach to the use of alternative regulation, and the use of alternative regulation does not lead to a specific outcome. Vranken,[2645] on the other hand, holds that the Hoge Raad does take alternative regulation into account, but often does not do so explicitly, and this is the reason for the criticism of unpredictability in the interpretation of ambiguous concepts.

2641 See previously par. 8.5.3.6.
2642 See previously par. 8.5.
2643 C.M.D.S. Pavillon, *Open normen in het Europees consumentenrecht*, Deventer: Kluwer 2011, p. 520.
2644 I. Giesen, 'De omgang met en handhaving van "meervoudigheid van maatschappelijke normstelsels"', *WPNR* 6772 (2008).
2645 J.B.M. Vranken, 'Taken van de Hoge Raad en zijn parket in 2025', in: I. Giesen, A.M. Hol (eds.), *De Hoge Raad in 2025: Contouren van de toekomstige cassatierechtspraak*, The Hague: BJU 2011, par. 2.2.

Therefore, Vranken suggests that the Hoge Raad should explicitly leave room for filling in blanket clauses.

10.3.4. The introduction of the prejudicial procedure in Dutch law

According to the Dutch case study,[2646] the introduction of the prejudicial procedure is likely to contribute to the predictability and consistency of the law on STCs, provided that questions are referred to the Hoge Raad. This may also be the case more generally as the introduction of the prejudicial procedure in collective procedures in Dutch law should, in combination with the cassation in the public interest (*'cassatie in het belang der wet'*) stimulate the development of case law by the highest courts on issues that do not frequently come before higher courts.[2647] Generally, this procedure should enable the courts to refer questions at the request of parties or *ex officio*[2648] on questions of law arising from cases where mass damages may arise, thus contributing to the responsiveness of private law to legal practice. Article 392 par. 1 sub b Dutch Civil Procedure Code also enables courts to refer questions for cases where the answer to the question is of direct interest for the adjudication of multiple similar cases where a similar question arises. In other words, questions should reflect a more general public interest. The standard established in article 392 Dutch Civil Procedure Code indicates that referral should not be done lightly, and the legislator did not expect that this new procedure would give rise to a considerable additional number of cases before the Hoge Raad; the legislator estimated that ten prejudicial questions per year would be decided.[2649] Van Kampen and Giesen[2650] note that the willingness of judges to ask prejudicial questions may also depend on the line developed by the Hoge Raad in the area where these questions should be asked.

The extent to which prejudicial questions will contribute to the relatively quick adjudication of cases will depend on the stage of proceedings in which a question is referred.[2651] Initially, courts with a single member could not refer prejudicial questions

[2646] See previously par. 5.7.3.3.

[2647] See further M.M. Stolp, J.F. de Groot, 'Een nieuwe procesvorm: Het stellen van prejudiciële vragen aan de Hoge Raad (art. 392–394 nieuw Rv)', *MvV* 2012, p. 165.

[2648] The legislator has argued that this is not contrary to party autonomy as it concerns claims that they have brought before the courts, against which there is no appeal (article 392 par. 3 Dutch Civil Procedure Code). Similarly, the rejection of referring questions to the Hoge Raad is also not open to appeal. However, interested parties (including parties in the case) have the opportunity to express their views under articles 392 par. 2 and 393 par. 2 and 4 Dutch Civil Procedure Code. Notably, parties – and third parties – have to bear the costs of the prejudicial procedure. It is not clear whether the judge should also refer questions to the Hoge Raad if both parties express that they are not interested in doing so; comp. *Kamerstukken II*, 2010–2011, 32612, nr 3, p. 14.

[2649] *Kamerstukken II*, 2010–2011, 32612, nr 3, p. 4.

[2650] S.S. van Kampen, I. Giesen, 'Prejudiciële vragen aan de Hoge Raad, valkuilen voor de Hoge Raad', *TCR* 2013, p. 1.

[2651] R.P.J.L. Tjittes, R. Meijer, 'Franse en Europese lessen voor een prejudiciële procedure bij de Hoge Raad', *RM Themis* 2009, p. 165 point out that if prejudicial questions are brought and answered in an early stage of proceedings where all facts have not yet been established, it may also be important that judges bringing the question can later deviate from the Hoge Raad's judgment, especially if facts turn out to lie

to the Hoge Raad, which also includes cantonial courts. This would have considerably limited the extent to which the introduction of the prejudicial procedure could have contributed to predictable and consistent decisions in consumer law, as article 93 sub d Dutch Civil Procedure Code provides that consumer cases[2652] are decided by cantonial courts which are typically composed of one judge. It concerns an experiment, which, in accordance with article IV Act on prejudicial questions, will be evaluated in five years. The initiative has been inspired by the European prejudicial procedure as well as French procedures. The drafting of the law was preceded by a public consultation and advice from practitioners and the judiciary.[2653]

Arguably, the successful introduction of a national prejudicial procedure in the Dutch legal order may encourage the Hoge Raad to submit more questions to the CJEU, especially if it concerns cases that would otherwise not have reached the Hoge Raad. However, although the procedure enables the Hoge Raad to refer questions, that does not necessarily mean it will in fact do so, especially if referring questions undermines the intention of the legislator to establish a relatively quick procedure to establish more clarity in the law.

10.3.5. Conclusion on the use of techniques in addition to blanket clauses

The case studies found that in the Dutch legal order,[2654] the introduction of alternative regulation and the prejudicial procedure could contribute to consistency, predictability, and the responsiveness of the law, while this was less clear in the German legal order. The Dutch case study[2655] found that the use of Guidance and comitology would be less likely to strengthen European private law. In the German case study,[2656] an immediate need to improve the predictability and consistency of blanket clauses such as article 307 BGB has not become immediately apparent. However, this may be different for other areas of law. Although the added value of guidance and prejudicial procedures may not become sufficiently clear for the law on STCs, blanket clauses have been subject to criticism in the past more generally.[2657] However, that has not resulted in the development of additional techniques. Instead, a more traditional approach becomes apparent: by establishing a general part, and a coherent system, the legislator has provided guidelines to the interpretation of blanket clauses.[2658] The amount of case law subsequently contributes to

differently than the judge in the first or second instance realised. According to N. Frenk, A.M. Wolffram-van Doorn, 'Het voorontwerp prejudiciële vragen aan de Hoge Raad', *RM Themis* 2009, p. 162–163, judges may in those cases deviate from the answer of the Hoge Raad.

2652 Cases on employment contracts and contracts for accommodation are also decided by cantonial courts.

2653 *Kamerstukken II*, 2010–2011, 32612, nr 3, p. 1.

2654 See previously par. 5.7.3.3 and 5.7.3.4.

2655 See previously par. 5.7.3.1. and 5.7.3.2.

2656 See previously par. 4.6.1.

2657 Especially J.W. Hedemann, *Die Flucht in Generalklauseln*, Tübingen: Mohr Siebeck 1933.

2658 HKK/Schmoeckel, Allgemeiner Teil des BGB, introduction, nrs 35, 41. It is unclear, however, how general provisions may provide *specific* guidance on the interpretation of blanket clauses in individual cases.

the predictability and consistency of newly drafted blanket clauses. Although judicial Guidance has been developed, it is not formally binding.

There is more attention for additional techniques in the Dutch legal order. Interestingly, suggestions for the use of Guidance and suggestions reminiscent of comitology committees can be found both at the national and European level. Both the suggestions of Asser, Groen, Vranken and Tzankova[2659] as well as Pavillon[2660] indicate that ideally, Guidance and practice directions should be based on debate between all relevant actors, and they set out various techniques to be used alongside one another. The suggestions of Pavillon make clear that the clarification of blanket clauses in the private law *acquis* could be achieved by using additional techniques that contribute to the harmonised interpretation of those provisions throughout the Union.

Yet a more harmonised interpretation and application of blanket clauses might not leave sufficient room for responsiveness, especially if blanket clauses in the private law *acquis* may not be interpreted in accordance with national alternative regulation, or if blanket clauses have to be interpreted in line with binding European model lists rather than default law. In addition, national experiences indicate that the development of comitology and Guidance beyond small, technical matters may meet with resistance, at least from Dutch and German actors.

Importantly, objections may arise against additional techniques in the German legal order as these techniques may lead to *Fremdbestimmung*. However, if committees consist of academics and members of the judiciary, this is likely less problematic than committees where stakeholder groups or practitioners play a prominent role if stakeholders and practitioners pursue their own rather than the public interest. Further, the transparency of the drafting processes, and opportunity for debate, are also relevant, as it may provide actors affected by these rules with a chance to influence these rules. Yet even if such committees were accepted, their role in developing, for example, black and grey lists would be limited, as these lists are considered as clearly political, and development of these lists should therefore be subject to democratic scrutiny. Consequently, Guidance and rules developed by expert committees would still have to be subjected to democratic debate, depending on the political content of these rules.

10.4. Additional techniques beyond the legislative process: Standard Terms and Conditions (STCs)

This paragraph will ask will ask how STCs could be used as an additional technique, and how that could improve European private law.

Paragraph 10.4.1 will consider the use of STCs and paragraph 10.4.2 will consider how STCs may contribute to the predictable and responsive development of the private law *acquis*. Paragraph 10.4.3 will end with a conclusion.

2659 W.D.H. Asser, H.A. Groen, J.B.M. Vranken, I.N. Tzankova, *Uitgebalanceerd. Eindrapport fundamentele herbezinning Nederlands burgerlijk procesrecht*, The Hague: BJU 2006, p. 259.

2660 C.M.D.S. Pavillon, *Open normen in het Europees consumentenrecht*, Deventer: Kluwer 2011, p. 529.

10.4.1. *The current use of STCs*

STCs have frequently been recognised as an important element in trade.[2661] A number of often used clauses identified by McKendrick[2662] include: clauses to ensure that the standard terms are applicable to contracts, retention of title clauses – also recognised by the Commission[2663] – hardship clauses, clauses limiting or excluding liability, price escalation clauses, clauses on the payment of interest, clauses on arbitration and choice of law and clauses with regard to assignment. In addition, the International Contracts Working Group has analysed the use of a number of often used clauses in international commercial practice, also discussing the use of confidentiality clauses, penalty clauses and termination clauses.[2664]

10.4.2. *Improving the predictability and responsiveness of private law*

STCs can contribute to a more predictable development of the *acquis* in the following ways:

1) In the German case study,[2665] it has already been argued that STCs could be studied to determine which divergences of private laws may pose an obstacle to cross-border trade.

Mandatory private law especially may block the application of foreign STCs. In addition, the private law *acquis*, especially Directive 86/653 on self-employed commercial agents and Regulations in the field of international private law, may affect the validity of STCs.[2666] Also, the use of cross-border STCs may be affected by surrounding national default contract law. If these default rules are identified, the question arises whether these divergences should subsequently be harmonised. Notably, private parties, if made aware of these divergences, could thereafter provide for specific rules in their contracts that diverge from these default rules. Notwithstanding these possibilities, harmonisation in this area has already been proposed.

2661 R.P.J.L. Tjittes, 'Uitleg van schriftelijke contracten', *RM Themis* 2005, p. 2 even states that these clauses can be considered as more adequately reflecting principles of contract law in the European Union than soft law rules such as the DCFR, PECL and the UNIDROIT Principles.

2662 E. McKendrick, *The creation of a European law of contracts – the role of standard form contracts and principles of interpretation*, Deventer: Kluwer 2004, p. 5.

2663 See for example European Commission, *Proposal for a European parliament and Council Directive combating late payment in commercial transactions*, COM (1998) 126 final, p. 8.

2664 M. Fontaine, F. de Ly, *Drafting international contracts: An analysis of contracts clauses*, Leiden/Boston: Nijhoff 2009.

2665 Par. 4.7.4.

2666 U. Bernitz, 'The Commission's Communications and standard contract terms', in: S. Vogenauer, S. Weatherill (eds.), *The harmonisation of European contract law*, Oxford: Hart 2006, p. 186.

2) The development of STCs that could be used throughout the Union could contribute to predictability.

In its 2003 Action Plan, the Commission suggested promoting the use of STCs throughout the Union.[2667] Subsequently, the 2004 Communication[2668] on the revision of the *acquis* suggested that private parties develop standard terms and conditions that could subsequently be used throughout the Union, claiming that 'there are a number of examples of EU-wide STC being used successfully', unfortunately without elaborating which standard terms are defended as such.[2669] The Commission emphasised the role of private parties and the use of a website by way of a platform to promote the exchange of information and the consideration of the possibility that mandatory law could be an obstacle.

However, in later policy papers, this idea has disappeared. In its first annual report on European contract law and the *acquis* review,[2670] the Commission states that providing a website to promote the exchange of information is problematic for a number of reasons:

i) European-wide STCs would have to meet the requirements of the national private law extending the most extensive control over STCs, which may make them less attractive for actors involved in cross-border trade in states with less extensive constraints.
ii) EU-wide STCs would only be used in specific sectors instead of several sectors. The complexity of this initiative should not be underestimated. If the development of these sets is not coordinated, fragmentation and inconsistencies may arise.
iii) The necessity of keeping STCs up to date with changing legislation and case law may be problematic, and require considerable time and money. Parties that have invested in up-to-date standard contract terms may not be inclined to make the results of their investment freely available.
iv) Providing a platform for STCs while not checking the compatibility of these terms with contract law and competition law constraints undermines the value of that exchange.
v) Whittaker[2671] points out that problems might arise with regard to the question in what languages European STCs should be provided, and the lack of autonomous interpretation of these terms throughout the Union, as the CJEU would not have competence to interpret these terms.
vi) Both McKendrick[2672] and Whittaker[2673] point out that European STCs would still be interpreted differently throughout the Union, even in the absence of mandatory law restrictions, as judges adopt a different approach to the interpretation of contracts, and make use of different sources for the interpretation of contracts.

2667 Communication from the Commission to the European Parliament and the Council, *A more coherent European contract law: an action plan*, COM (2003) 68 final, p. 21 et seq.

2668 Communication from the Commission to the European Parliament and the Council, *European contract law and the revision of the acquis: the way forward*, COM (2004) 651 final, par. 2.2.1, 2.2.2.

2669 These might include the standard terms and conditions developed by Orgalime and the terms and conditions developed by the Chartered Institute of Purchasing and Supply. See further http://ec.europa.eu/internal_market/contractlaw/2004workshop_summary_en.htm.

2670 European Commission, *First annual report on European contract law and the acquis review*, COM (2005) 456, par. 41.

2671 S. Whittaker, 'On the development of European standard contract terms', *ERCL* 2006, p. 60–61.

2672 E. McKendrick, *The creation of a European law of contracts – the role of standard form contracts and principles of interpretation*, Deventer: Kluwer 2004, p. 27–43.

2673 S. Whittaker, 'On the development of European standard contract terms', *ERCL* 2006, p.66–67.

These potential problems may also be arise if STCs are collectively negotiated, as suggested in the Dutch case study.[2674] However, these objections may be diminished if STCs are negotiated collectively between parties from two Member States.

In addition to the disadvantages recognised by the Commission, this option may not be feasible politically. An important added value of a European set of STCs would be the applicability of STCs throughout the Union, regardless of diverging mandatory law. However, this possibility would entail radical changes of national mandatory laws, and quite probably it is much less feasible than traditional harmonisation.

Nevertheless, the idea has reappeared in the Commission's 2011 Communication preceding the since withdrawn CESL[2675] as a possible "flanking measure", alongside specialised training and publicly accessible databases.[2676]

3) Actors may also collect and provide information of often used clauses and, thereby, improve parties' ability to adequately assess their legal position in cross-border contracts. Increasing parties' awareness of the risks in the use of STCs may enable them to cope with these difficulties more easily, especially if STCs are interpreted in accordance with national default law.

Of course, gathering information on STCs in itself does little to overcome divergences in national private laws, and this might lessen the attractiveness of this course of action for the European legislator.[2677]

Collecting information, and making it available to private parties, if possible in multiple languages, may take place through various ways that may also be pursued in combination with one another – through establishing databases on boilerplate clauses, case law and legislation, and academic research and publications on often used clauses may well provide a suitable starting point. However, the success of such an enterprise being made possible also depends on the use that private parties make of this information, and the awareness of private parties that such information *is* provided.

4) Studying STCs may also contribute to the responsiveness of the law

According to Montaine and De Ly,[2678] the study of international legal practice may add an insight on practices, such as the use of letters of intent that are currently ignored in traditional debates on

2674 See previously par. 5.7.4.

2675 COM (2011) 636, p. 11.

2676 Comp. L. Bernstein, 'An (un)common frame of reference: An American perspective on the jurisprudence of the CESL', *CMLRev* 2013, p. 185 who points out that traders will want to strictly enforce successful STCs, which may motivate them to opt for English law, or arbitration, which would undermine the success of the CESL. However, a lack of pan-European STCs so far may indicate that there is no common agreement on good commercial practices and clauses throughout the EU.

2677 Comp. also S. Whittaker, 'On the development of European standard contract terms', *ERCL* 2006, p. 54, who points out that contracts generally seek to provide contract parties with predictability with regard to their legal position and its rights and duties towards other contract parties, and asserts that this primary aim of contracts should not be distracted by an implicit aim to further convergence of private laws throughout the Union.

2678 M. Fontaine, F. de Ly, *Drafting international contracts: An analysis of contracts clauses*, Leiden/Boston: Nijhoff 2009, p. 621.

private law. Montaine and De Ly[2679] also point out that studying international legal practice may provide more insight in creative drafting processes and enable rules to adequately cope with these practices, thus contributing to the responsiveness of private law to legal practice. For example, instead of concentrating upon the question whether an offer and an acceptance lead to a contract, it is also possible to look at the international practice of letters of intent, heads of agreement and memorandum of understanding and question what legal consequences these different kinds of letters have for private parties, or give guidelines as to whether and which parts of such letters or agreements could be binding.[2680]

10.4.3. Conclusion on the use of STCs

STCs can contribute to the predictable and responsive development of the private law *acquis*. In accordance with the findings in the German case study,[2681] studying STCs to identify divergences that hinder cross-border trade may benefit predictability, while it also enhances insight in cross-border businesses. If the European legislator supports its proposals with studies that clearly show barriers to international trade, this may make potential problems more convincing and, hopefully, support deliberation. This functional approach may however increase fragmentation at the national level as proposals might target various areas of private laws simultaneously. For example, divergences in property law may be found to pose a barrier to the cross-border use of the title of retention clauses,[2682] but the effectiveness of the retention of title clauses may also depend on insolvency law and civil procedural law.

In addition, sharing information on STCs may increase the predictability for parties involved in cross-border trade. International organisations with members throughout the Union may be well positioned to facilitate sharing, which should enhance mutual learning. Chapters 7 and 8 indicate that, for example, EMOTA, as well as the EASA and the ICC may be well placed to initiate mutual learning among members.

STCs can be used in combination with various other techniques. Accordingly, *if* harmonisation in these different areas is considered desirable, as well as feasible, impact assessments and consultations could contribute to finding techniques to deal with fragmentation and inconsistencies in the *acquis* and national private laws that may arise after harmonisation – or other actions. European-wide STCs could be developed more easily under an optional instrument that provides a framework for drafting and interpreting STCs. Also, soft laws could be used to clarify the meaning of often used terms in so-called boilerplate clauses.[2683]

2679 M. Fontaine, F. de Ly, *Drafting international contracts: An analysis of contracts clauses*, Leiden/Boston: Nijhoff 2009, p. 634–635.

2680 See on this question G. Cordero Moss, 'The function of letters of intent and their recognition in modern legal systems', in: R. Schulze (ed.), *New features in European contract law*, München: Sellier 2007, p. 139.

2681 See previously par. 4.7.4.

2682 Despite article 9 Directive 2011/7 on combating late payment, which merely establishes that these clauses should be recognised.

2683 E. McKendrick, *The creation of a European law of contracts – The role of standard form contracts and principles of interpretation*, Deventer: Kluwer 2004, p. 43–44 suggests that predictability in cross-border trade could be enhanced if there is agreement on a common meaning of often used terms, in the

10.5. Additional techniques beyond the legislative process: The Open Method of Coordination (OMC)

This paragraph will ask whether the use of OMC may contribute to the development of European private law that is more predictable, consistent, accessible or responsive.

Paragraph 10.5.1 will describe the OMC and paragraph 10.5.2 will ask in what ways the use of OMC can contribute to a more comprehensible European private law. Paragraph 10.5.3 will address the drawbacks of OMC and paragraph 10.5.4 will end with a conclusion.

10.5.1. A closer look at the OMC

Typically, the OMC has primarily been used in social policy areas where the Union has little or no legislative competences.[2684] Accordingly, article 5 par. 3 TFEU recognises that coordination may take place with regard to Member States' social policies.[2685] Rather than emphasising harmonisation, the OMC focuses on the development of policies, and may stress other softer methods than legislation, such as the use of databases, networks, or model laws.[2686]

The OMC emphasises cooperation between actors, to establish common goals, and exchange best practices.[2687] Four stages can be distinguished in OMC: firstly, common aims are established, as well as schedules to achieve these aims. Subsequently, benchmarks and indications to identify and compare best practices are developed, and actors establish policies to achieve the common aims. Finally, periodical reviews and evaluation are established.[2688]

DCFR. The 2004 Communication of the Commission Communication from the Commission to the European Parliament and the Council, *European contract law and the revision of the acquis: the way forward*, COM (2004) 651 final, par. 2.1.2 states that a CFR could be used as 'a body of standard contract terms to be made available to legal practitioners'. S. Whittaker, 'On the development of European standard contract terms', *ERCL* 2006, p. 57 however, rightly notes that the idea of developing STCs, which necessarily would be sector-specific, does not agree with the DCFR as a non-sector specific instrument, and accordingly, the idea of the DCFR containing STCs has been abandoned. Additionally, as the DCFR may at points diverge from the private law *acquis*, the question arises to what extent the DCFR is suitable to be used as such as a dictionary in transnational commercial contracts.

2684 E. Szyszczak, 'Experimental governance: the Open Method of Coordination', *ELJ* 2006, p. 488.

2685 Comp. also articles 23 TFEU (with regard to diplomatic assistance to Union citizens in third countries), articles 67 and 73 TFEU (with regard to a high level of security in the area of freedom, security, and justice), article 85 TFEU (on Eurojust), articles 119 TFEU (with regard to a economic policy), article 150 TFEU (with regard to an Employment Committee), article 156 TFEU (on social policies), article 171 TFEU (with regard to trans-European networks of energy, transport and energy infrastructures), 173 TFEU (industry), article 181 TFEU (research and technical development activities), articles 210 and 214 TFEU (humanitarian aid).

2686 See further on the use of model laws below par. 10.6.3.3.

2687 Comp. the Presidency Conclusions of the Lisbon European Council, www.europarl.europa.eu/summits/lis1_en.htm, 23–24 March 2000, par. 37, European Commission, *European governance. A White Paper*, COM (2001) 428 final, p. 21–22.

2688 Presidency Conclusions of the Lisbon European Council, www.europarl.europa.eu/summits/lis1_en.htm, 23–24 March 2000, par. 37.

The Commission plays an active coordinating role, which implies a top-down approach towards OMC. De la Rosa[2689] also signals the prominent role of both the Commission and the Council in the OMC. According to the European Council, the OMC does not only involve state actors. Instead, it includes the Union, Member States, sub-national actors, the social partners and civil society.[2690] Possibly, if the OMC is used in a way that includes relevant (affected) actors, this could stimulate debate between those actors on the basis of, for example, exchanged best practices or similar problems. Senden[2691] notes that the OMC should not be considered as one instrument that necessarily embodies all the characteristics summed up above and is generally based upon soft techniques such as benchmarks and peer pressure.

For European private law, the use of the OMC entails that the Union may encourage Member States to coordinate their policies, in the interest of the internal market or the freedoms established in the Treaties.[2692] The OMC may also serve to align the aims of national and European state actors. As argued previously,[2693] the aims of European and national state actors diverge: whereas the European legislator targets further harmonisation, Member States seek to maintain their own laws. Through the OMC, an environment can be created in which these divergent preferences are reconsidered or transformed.[2694] Reich[2695] has suggested the OMC to assess fundamental matters of contract law and clarify whether divergences between contracts laws hinder the internal market. As Borrás and Greve[2696] point out, the OMC generally emphasises a common aim, rather than the means to achieve that aim, which provides Member States with a considerable amount of leeway to take measures to achieve common aims, and takes away the need for detailed rules and mechanisms at a European level.

The OMC could be used in addition to existing harmonisation measures. If actors are not willing to participate in the OMC, this could prompt the use of less voluntary methods. The OMC could also serve as a first step towards future harmonisation initiatives. Typically, the use of OMC does not confer competences from the national to

2689 S. de la Rosa, 'The Open Method of Coordination in new Member States – the perspectives for its use as a tool of soft law', *ELJ* 2005, p. 627–628.

2690 Presidency Conclusions of the Lisbon European Council, www.europarl.europa.eu/summits/lis1_en.htm, 23–24 March 2000, par. 38.

2691 L.A.J. Senden, 'Reguleringsintensiteit en regelgevingsinstrumentarium in het Europees Gemeenschapsrecht. Over de relatie tussen wetgeving, soft law en de open methode van coördinatie', *SEW* 2008, p. 50.

2692 L.A.J. Senden, 'Reguleringsintensiteit en regelgevingsinstrumentarium in het Europees Gemeenschapsrecht. Over de relatie tussen wetgeving, soft law en de open methode van coördinatie', *SEW* 2008, p.54. The European Commission, *European governance, A White Paper*, COM (2001) 428 final, p. 21–22 has clearly considered OMC as a complementary technique, to support, not replace, the traditional method of harmonisation.

2693 See previously par. 6.2.

2694 Comp. Ch.F. Sabel, J. Zeitlin, 'Experimentalist governance in the European Union', in: J. Zeitlin, Ch.F. Sabel (eds.), *Experimentalist governance in the European Union: Towards a new architecture*, Oxford: OUP 2010, p. 2.

2695 N.C.R. Reich, 'A European contract law: Ghost or host for European integration?', *Wisconsin International Law Journal* 2006, p. 468.

2696 S. Borrás, B. Greve, 'Concluding remarks: New method or just cheap talk?' *JEPP* 2004, p. 332.

the European level.[2697] Yet if the OMC can be used as a starting point for harmonisation, it may simultaneously strengthen competence creep.[2698]

10.5.2. Improving the responsiveness of European private law?

The OMC could contribute to the quality of European private law in various ways:

1) The OMC could stimulate regulatory competition.

The OMC has already been mentioned in the Lisbon conclusions with regard to the reform of company law.[2699] Similarly, in other areas, such as corporate governance or collective redress, regulatory competition and further convergence could be improved.

2) The OMC could improve interaction between actors.

Van Gerven[2700] has suggested the use of an 'Open Method of Convergence', rather than the Open Method of Coordination that focuses on the coordination of national policies. The Open Method of Convergence entails that convergence would not only be the result of harmonisation efforts from the European Union, but also from comparative law research and databases, education throughout the EU on a firm comparative and European law basis and a better coordinated implementation of the *acquis*, based on voluntary participation by not only Member States but also non-state actors. Reich[2701] similarly finds that the development of the DCFR should move to OMC, remarking that 'the Commission lacks convincing ideas in this direction, but one should never abandon hope.'

3) The OMC could improve participation in alternative regulation.

For example, the Commission has suggested that the OMC could stimulate the involvement of relevant stakeholders to social dialogue, which could, for example, affect the participation of relevant stakeholders to consultations preceding framework agreements.[2702] Although increasing the amount of responses to consultations may be useful and provide more insight into the views

[2697] V. Hatzopoulos, 'Why the Open Method of Coordination is bad for you: a letter to the EU', *ELJ*, p. 318–319.

[2698] E. Szyszczak, 'Experimental governance: The Open Method of Coordination', *ELJ* 2006, p. 501. Comp. also J. Scott, D.M. Trubek, 'Mind the gap: law and new approaches to governance in the European Union', *ELJ* 2002, p. 7. Comp. Ph. Syrpis, 'Legitimising European governance: Taking subsidiarity seriously within the Open Method of Coordination', *EUI Working Paper* 2002, p. 28, who is critical of the OMC insofar as actors increasingly set specific goals at the European level even if the benefit of those aims is not clear.

[2699] See European Council, Conclusions of the Presidency of the meeting of 23 and 24 March 2000, available at www.europarl.europa.eu/summits/lis1_en.htm#b, par. 14–15.

[2700] W. van Gerven, 'The Open Method of Convergence', *Juridica International* 2008, p. 40.

[2701] N.C.R. Reich, 'A European contract law: Ghost or host for European integration?', *Wisconsin International Law Journal* 2006, p.469–470.

[2702] European Commission, *The European social dialogue, a force for innovation and change*, COM (2002) 341 final, p. 14.

and needs of stakeholders, depending on their responses, this need in itself not increase the influence of consulted parties.

Thus, the OMC can contribute to the responsiveness of private law as it emphasises interaction between actors, which increases the chance that state actors will become aware of other actors developing private law as well as the needs and preferences of non-state actors.

10.5.3. Drawbacks

The following potential drawbacks of the OMC should not be overlooked:

1) A lack of openness and transparency.[2703]

Szyszczak[2704] has even stated that 'the approach of the OMC runs counter to the principles of good governance that have emerged (transparency, accountability, democratic input). He has pointed to '[t]he lack of transparency and the failure to engage with the (more) democratic institutions of the EU'. However, part of this lack of transparency is also due to the technicality of some subjects.[2705] The Study Group on Social Justice[2706] has criticised the use of technical language and the evasion of political choices. Arguably, a lack of open debate is not specific to the OMC, but if the OMC is to be used, the use of technical terms is problematic. For example, it may entail that groups with considerable amounts of expertise, financial and organisational resources may gain privileged access to the debate on European private law. Problems with regard to participation in the development of European private law are already visible.[2707] These problems do not need to be reinforced by the OMC, especially as it fails to stimulate participation.[2708]

Accordingly, the Open Method of Convergence emphasises the participation by expert actors, while less attention is given to the role, expectations, and preferences of, for example, contract parties. It is not clear how open the process would be to actors that are affected by this strategy, but who have insufficient knowledge of private law to participate in debate. Unfortunately, it can be doubted whether affected actors who have not been included in the use of the OMC, have an action to secure access to the OMC.[2709]

2703 V. Hatzopoulos, 'Why the Open Method of Coordination is bad for you: A letter to the EU', *ELJ* 2007, p. 325.

2704 E. Szyszczak, 'Experimental governance: The Open Method of Coordination', *ELJ* 2006, p. 495.

2705 Comp. S. Borrás, B. Greve, 'Concluding remarks: New method or just cheap talk?' *JEPP* 2004, p. 333 point out that the OMC covers multiple policy areas: 'The more [OMC] grows, the less people will be able to read, understand and digest what is happening in the OMC process.'

2706 Study Group on Social Justice in European Private Law, 'Social justice in European contract law: a manifesto', *ELJ* 2004, p. 653.

2707 Comp. also the shortcomings in the use of networks, par. 10.2.3.2.

2708 S. de la Rosa, 'The Open Method of Coordination in new Member States – the perspectives for its use as a tool of soft law', *ELJ* 2005, p. 623, C. de la Porte, P. Nanz, 'The OMC – a deliberative-democratic mode of governance? The cases of employment and pensions', *JEPP* 2004, p. 267.

2709 V. Hatzopoulos, 'Why the Open Method of Coordination is bad for you: a letter to the EU', *ELJ*, p. 326.

2) A lack of success in increasing debate.

The success of the OMC in increasing participation is subject to debate. Trubek and Trubek[2710] point out that while the Commission has evaluated the OMC in the area of the European Employment Strategy rather positively,[2711] other evaluations have been more critical, and note the lack of agreement of the success of this particularly well-developed area in which the OMC is used. Szyszczak[2712] points out that positive evaluations of the OMC come from within, especially the Commission.

3) The success of the OMC depends on the willingness of both state actors and non-state actors at the different levels to participate in this method.

It is not encouraging, in this respect, that in areas where coordination, particularly regulatory competition, has been encouraged, shortcomings in national legislative processes remain.[2713] Notably, Hatzopoulos,[2714] presenting an overview of empirical research on the use of the OMC, notes that the OMC has limited direct effect. However, if the OMC is used in addition to existing harmonisation techniques, this may improve the effect of the OMC.

Because of these shortcomings, the extent to which the OMC improves the responsiveness of private law may be severely undermined.

10.5.4. *Conclusion on the use of the OMC*

Will the OMC contribute to a more responsive European private law? The OMC might support the development of regulatory competition, and an environment in which actors' divergent preferences are reconsidered and transformed seems an attractive idea. However, the success of this possibility should not be assumed. Instead, use of the OMC may reinforce shortcomings already visible in the debate in European private law.

2710 D.M. Trubek, L.G. Trubek, 'Hard and soft law in the construction of social Europe: The role of the Open Method of Co-ordination', *ELJ* 2005, p. 350–351.

2711 Comp. the indeed rather positive evaluation of the European Employment Strategy, one of the well-established areas for the OMC with a Treaty basis: European Commission, *Taking stock of five years of the European Employment Strategy*, COM (2002) 416 final.

2712 E. Szyszczak, 'Experimental governance: The Open Method of Coordination', *ELJ* 2006, p. 496. Accordingly, Ph. Syrpis, 'Legitimising European governance: Taking subsidiarity seriously within the Open Method of Coordination', *EUI Working Paper* 2002, p. 38 is decidedly less optimistic on the European Employment Strategy.

2713 Attempts to encourage regulatory competition in this area has apparently not prompted the Dutch legislator to take into account criticism if that is inconvenient, as criticised by H.M. Vletter- van Dort, 'Horen, zien en luisteren', *Ondernemingsrecht* 2011, 73. See for further criticism par. 10.2.

2714 V. Hatzopoulos, 'Why the Open Method of Coordination is bad for you: A letter to the EU', *ELJ*, p. 309. Comp. also C. de la Porte, 'Is the Open Method of Coordination appropriate for organising activities at European level in sensitive policy areas?', *ELJ* 2002, p. 56, finds that the diverse social models may also be relevant for the success of the OMC in these areas.

10.6. Implementation problems and strategies: Regulations instead of Directives

Will the use of Regulations rather than Directives improve the consistent and accessible development of European private law?

An important objection against this option is the political feasibility. Particularly, national state actors may oppose this option in central areas of law such as the law on STCs[2715] or sales law, as the development of Regulations rather than Directives means that parts of private law will be developed outside national codes. However, for other areas of private law, such as private international law[2716] or passenger rights law,[2717] similar objections may not arise.

The use of Directives allows Member States a margin of appreciation that enables them to preserve a coherent set of national rules. Coherent national law increases the accessibility of private law for private parties at a national level.[2718] Johnston and Unberath[2719] emphasise that Directives provide for more flexibility in the legislative process. However, this benefit is not achieved.[2720] Directives, especially if they aim for maximum harmonisation, frequently contain rather detailed provisions, and the CJEU has provided strict standards for implementation in *Commission v The Netherlands*,[2721] and *Commission v Sweden*.[2722]

The use of Directives also entails disadvantages that have become visible in the implementation of the *acquis* in the BGB and the BW. Member States have adopted different strategies in the implementation of the *acquis*, which has not helped the consistency of the *acquis* throughout the Union, nor is implemented law visible as such, which may inhibit accessibility, as the European background of a rule, and the corresponding need for harmonised interpretation, are not visible.

The use of Regulations would remedy some of these weaknesses:

1) The use of Regulations, instead of Directives, would remedy the lack of accessibility and, moreover, have direct effect, which is in line with the aim of some of the measures in the *acquis* aiming to further consumer protection.[2723]

2715 As became clear in the debate on the *Schuldrechtsreform*, see previously par. 4.3.1.3 and par. 4.7.

2716 For example, Regulation 2001/44 on jurisdiction and recognition and enforcement of judgments in civil matters, Regulation 864/2007 on the law applicable to non-contractual obligations, or Regulation 593/2008 on the law applicable to contractual obligations.

2717 For example, Regulation 2061/2004 establishing common rules on compensation and assistance to passengers in the event of denied boarding and of cancellation or long delay of flights.

2718 COM (2008) 614 final, p. 8.

2719 A. Johnston, H. Unberath, 'Law at, to or from the centre?' in: F. Cafaggi (ed.), *The institutional framework of European private law*, Oxford: OUP 2006, p. 150–151.

2720 Comp. also Ch. Twigg-Flesner, D. Metcalfe, 'The proposed consumer rights Directive – less haste, more thought?', *ERCL* 2011, p. 374.

2721 CJEU 10 May 2001 (Commission v The Netherlands), C-144/99, [2001] ECR, p. I-3541, par. 17–18.

2722 CJEU 7 May 2002 (Commission v Sweden), C-478/99, ECR [2002], p. I-4147, par. 21–23.

2723 See for example N. Reich, 'A European contract law, or an EU contract law Regulation for consumers?', *Journal of Consumer Policy* 2005, p. 399.

2) If the European legislator aims for maximum harmonisation, this may be achieved more easily through Regulations.[2724]
3) The use of Regulations rather than Directives may simplify the legislative process and relieve the legislative burden of Member States.[2725]

Accordingly, the Commission has recognised the benefits of Regulations.[2726] In the 2010 Green Paper on progress towards a European contract law,[2727] the Commission favoured the use of a Regulation, emphasising that this choice would advance the internal market.

However, do the disadvantages arising from the use of Regulations entail that the European legislator should continue to use Directives rather than Regulations? These disadvantages are:

1) The development of Regulations would entail the development of more sources that may be simultaneously applicable, which is not likely to increase the accessibility of European private law.

2) The use of Regulations may mean that parties remain unaware of these rules and do not sufficiently rely on them, while implementation of the private law *acquis* in codifications increases the chance that private parties will consider these rules.

However, as argued in the case studies,[2728] the lack of awareness may be mitigated if consumers are already well aware of their rights, as is the case for the German law on STCs.

3) The use of Regulations may raise questions with regard to minimum harmonisation. It is not clear whether the use of Regulations stands in the way of minimum harmonisation. This may inhibit the predictable development of private law.

On the one hand, minimum harmonisation is hard to reconcile with the ruling in *Variola v Amministrazione italiana delle Finanze*,[2729] where the Court decided that the effect of a Regulation does not depend on national laws. Member States may not obstruct this direct effect, and 'strict compliance with this obligation is an indispensable condition of simultaneous and uniform application of Community regulations throughout the Community'. Moreover, 'Member States are under an obligation not to introduce any measure which might affect the jurisdiction of the

2724 W.H. van Boom, 'The Draft Directive on consumer rights: choices made & arguments used', *Journal for Contemporary European Research* 2009, p. 457.

2725 A. Johnston, H. Unberath, 'Law at, to or from the centre?', in: F. Cafaggi (ed.), *The institutional framework of European private law*, Oxford: OUP 2006, p. 189–190, who for that reason suggest that in the review of the consumer *acquis*, the choice between Directives and Regulations should be discussed.

2726 European Commission, *Communication of the Commission, a Europe of results – applying Community law*, COM (2007), 502 final, footnote 12.

2727 European Commission, *Green paper on policy options for progress towards a European contract law for businesses and consumers*, COM (2010) 348 final, p. 9–10.

2728 See previously par. 4.7.

2729 CJEU 10 October 1973 (Variola S.p.A. v Amministrazione italiana delle Finanze), 34–73, ECR [1973], p. I-981, par. 9–11.

Court to pronounce on any question involving the interpretation of Community law or the validity of an Act of the institutions of the Community, which means that no procedure is permissible whereby the Community nature of a legal rule in concealed from those subject to it.' Arguably, if Member States would introduce more stringent rules, they oblige consumers and businesses to also inform themselves of national law, which may undermine accessibility and clarity, and raise questions on the competence with regard to the interpretation of provisions in the Regulation and national law.

On the other hand, if Regulations are adopted under article 114 TFEU, minimum harmonisation as such is not precluded.[2730] Furthermore, article 169 TFEU, which expressly allows for minimum, harmonisation is not limited to Directives, but speaks of measures, which include Regulations adopted under article 114 TFEU or measures which support consumer protection measures by Member States.[2731]

If Regulations stand in the way of more stringent consumer protection, or more generally, the interpretation of the law in accordance of overlapping national default law that is closely intertwined with that area of law – for example the close interrelation between the German law on STCs and default law – this may severely inhibit consistency with national private law and the responsiveness of harmonised law to national legal views on justice, as reflected in notions of *Richtigkeitsgewähr.* In addition, if a Regulation entails that national judges can no longer turn to national, well-established case law or surrounding case law, this may lessen the predictability of national decisions.

→ Thus, the use of Regulations may be beneficial for the consistency of the *acquis* throughout the Union, but it may simultaneously inhibit the consistent development of private law at the national level. In addition, if Regulations stand in the way of minimum harmonisation and recourse to national sources in developing harmonised law, this may inhibit the responsiveness of harmonised law, as well as predictability. Also, the use of Regulations clarifies the European background of a rule, which may contribute to accessibility, but the use of Regulations may simultaneously inhibit accessibility as it leads to the development of more potentially overlapping sources, while parties may not be sufficiently aware of the existence and the relevance of Regulations. Therefore, Regulations would hinder rather than help consistency and accessibility, and they should not be used as an alternative to contribute to these benchmarks.

10.7. Optional regimes

This paragraph will ask whether the use of optional regimes rather than traditional harmonisation may contribute to a more comprehensible European private law.

2730 K. Gutman, *The constitutionality of European contract law,* Leuven 2010, p. 39. See also S.A. de Vries, *Tensions within the internal market – the functioning of the internal market and the development of horizontal and flanking policies*, Groningen: Europa Law Publishing 2006, p. 255, I. Wolff, *Die Verteilung der Konkretisierungskompetenz für Generalklauseln in privatrechtsgestaltenden Richtlinien*, Baden Baden: Nomos 2002, p. 156–157, S. Weatherill, 'Measures of consumer protection as impediments to export of goods', *ECRL* 2009, p. 153.

2731 Comp. N. Reich, 'A European contract law, or an EU contract law Regulation for consumers?' *JCP* 2005, p. 400.

Paragraph 10.7.1 will consider optional regimes more closely and paragraph 10.7.2 will ask how optional regimes may contribute to the comprehensibility of European private law. Paragraph 10.7.3 will turn to more general questions that should be addressed by actors drafting optional regimes. Paragraph 10.7.4 will end with a conclusion.

10.7.1. A closer look at optional regimes

The German case study[2732] pointed out that in accordance with pluralist arguments,[2733] the development of the since withdrawn CESL could have provided opportunities for mutual learning, and it might have stimulated the development of regulatory competition. Yet it is not clear whether future optional instruments may contribute to the predictability, consistency, accessibility and responsiveness of the law on STCs; this depends on its success, as well as the extent to which it addresses questions of overlap with national law and questions with regard to the interpretation of ambiguous terms in it, especially in the absence of clear sources to interpret these terms.

Optional regimes can be developed in various ways. European sets of rules have been established under article 352 TFEU.[2734] However, the use of article 352 TFEU may well be complicated further by the BVerfG Lisbon decision.[2735] In addition, sets of soft law such as the PECL can be developed, although opting for these sets of soft law as applicable law is not permitted under Rome I. Other options to establish optional regimes, which were not sufficiently considered in the drafting of a possible CESL, include enhanced cooperation, under which Member States enter into treaties in the sense of article 329 TFEU. So far, this possibility has led to the development of a regime in divorce law.[2736] Also, a German-French optional regime on matrimonial property law has been established through a bilateral treaty.[2737] Alternatively, optional regimes on sales law in the EU may also be realised if the EU had the competence to accede to the CISG. Optional regimes may entail opt-in as well as opt-out rules.[2738] Presently, article 6 CISG makes clear that the CISG establishes an opt-out system that allows for derogation by contract parties. In contrast, article 3 of the withdrawn proposal for a Regulation establishing a CESL makes clear that parties can opt for the future optional instrument.

Optional harmonisation has been established under article 114 TFEU[2739] although it has been doubted whether the proposed Regulation for a CESL can be based on this

2732 See previously par. 4.7.5.

2733 L. Miller, *The emergence of EU contract law: Exploring Europeanization*, Oxford: OUP 2011, p. 171.

2734 For example Regulation 1435/2003 on the Statute for a European Cooperative Society.

2735 BVerfG 30 June 2009, *NJW* 2009, 2267.

2736 See Council Decision 2010/405/EU, 12 July 2010, OJ L 189/12, of 22 July 2010.

2737 See further S. Braun, 'Die Wahl-Zugewinngemeinschaft: Ein neuer Güterstand im deutschen (und französischen) Recht', *MittBayNot* 2012, p. 89.

2738 G. Bachmann, 'Optionsmodelle im Privatrecht', *JZ* 2008, p. 11 distinguishes between strict and lenient options.

2739 Before the withdrawn proposal for a Regulation establishing a CESL, COM (2011) 635 final, optional harmonisation was primarily used under article 114 TFEU to further the free movement of goods.

article. Nevertheless, future initiatives in the area of insurance law were announced.[2740] Eventually, the extent to which optional instruments contribute to comprehensibility depends on the adoption of optionally harmonised rules by private parties. The scope of optionally harmonised rules may also play an important role in the subsequent success of those rules.[2741] Notably, the success of various optional instruments in this respect varies. Fauvarque-Cosson and Behar-Touchais[2742] outline that while the European trademark and the European patent appear well used, other initiatives, such as the small payment procedure, and European cooperative societies are not. The question arises whether, if optional harmonisation is not sufficiently successful, the European legislator will turn towards more hierarchical approaches, perhaps by transforming measures pursuing optional harmonisation into measures pursuing partial harmonisation, i.e. mandatory harmonisation for cross-border transactions.

The development of optional regimes gives rise to a number of questions that should more generally be considered:

1) What level of consumer protection would be considered satisfactory in optional harmonisation measures?[2743]
2) Can optional harmonisation effectively be pursued by Directives, or does a choice for optional harmonisation also entail a choice for Regulations?
3) Is the possible future use of optional harmonisation a reason to abandon the fragmented approach visible in the private law *acquis*?

Developing optional harmonisation necessitates more thought about these questions as they are important for the further development of the private law *acquis*.

2740 EU Justice Commissioner Viviane Reding meets with leaders of Europe's insurance industry, Press release MEMO/11/624, 21 September 2011, available at http://europa.eu/rapid/press-release_MEMO-11-624_en.htm.

2741 Comp. A.G. Castermans, 'Multiple choice: Nationaal recht in het DCFR', in: M.W. Hesselink et al (eds.), *Het Groenboek Europees contractenrecht: naar een optioneel instrument?*, The Hague: BJU 2011, p. 33. See also W. Doralt, 'The Optional European Contract law and why success or failure may depend on scope rather than substance', *Max Planck Private Law Research Paper* 2011, p. 13–15, as well as J. Kleinschmidt, 'Stellvertretung, IPR und ein optionales Instrument für ein europäisches Vertragsrecht', *RabelsZ* 2011, p. 538. Comp. also E.A.G. van Schagen, 'The proposal for a Common European Sales Law: How its drafting process might affect the optional instrument's added value and its success', in: A.L.M. Keirse, M.B.M. Loos (red.), *Alternative ways to a ius commune*, Intersentia 2012, p. 85.

2742 B. Fauvarque-Cosson, M. Behar-Touchais, *Implementation of optional instruments throughout the Union*, Study January 2012, available at www.europarl.europa.eu/RegData/etudes/etudes/join/2012/462425/IPOL-JURI_ET%282012%29462425_EN.pdf.

2743 Previously, in par. 4.7.5, it was argued that while businesses might not necessarily oppose a high level of consumer protection, a low standard of consumer protection might prove problematic. Comp. O. Bar-Gill, O. Ben-Shahar, 'Regulatory techniques in consumer protection: A critique of European consumer contract law', *CMLRev* 2013, p. 125 who suggest an initial low level of consumer protection to motivate sellers to opt in. Once sellers have opted in, and are reluctant to abandon the use of an optional instrument, additional consumer protection could be established.

10.7.2. *How can optional regimes contribute to more comprehensible European private law?*

Smits[2744] describes three benefits of optional harmonisation:

1) Optional harmonisation allows private parties to opt for either harmonised, national or international rules if that is in their own interests, which should increase the law's ability to respond to divergent preferences.
2) The development of optional rules could give rise to regulatory competition that should be beneficial for European private law in the long term.
3) Optional harmonisation could also provide an attractive alternative to full harmonisation of national private laws, establishing a level playing field that parties can opt into if they choose, while leaving Member States with the discretion to develop national rules in accordance with the needs and preferences of their own legal order. Therefore, petrification and lack of responsiveness that may follow from maximum harmonisation can be avoided while divergences of harmonised law throughout the Union are prevented as well.

10.7.3. *Drawbacks*

Importantly, the development of optional regimes also shows detriments that should not be overlooked:

1) Developing optional regimes in addition to national, as well as other harmonised rules and international rules may inhibit the accessibility of European private law.

Both Cartwright[2745] and Mak[2746] have pointed to possible confusion that may arise when multiple instruments apply simultaneously – especially if those sources of law provide for different levels of consumer protection. This could, for example, be the case if an optional instrument, the consumer law *acquis*, as well as national consumer contract law, apply simultaneously, while also setting divergent levels of consumer protection.

In addition, as also became apparent in the German case study,[2747] questions on the simultaneous application of national law and optional instruments may arise. Further, as optional instruments have to be interpreted autonomously, the adoption of optional instruments may give rise to unpredictability.

2744 J.M. Smits, 'Optional law: a plea for multiple choice in private law', *MJ* 2010, p. 350–351.
2745 J. Cartwright, '"Choice is good". Really?', *ERCL* 2011, p. 344.
2746 V. Mak, 'Hoe meer keus, hoe beter?', *TvC* 2010, p. 250.
2747 Previously par. 4.7.5.

2) The choice of parties for optional regimes is not necessarily a rational one, which may limit the extent to which private actors prompt legislators to participate in regulatory competition.

Arguably, a choice for an optional instrument does not have to be founded upon the superior quality of the instrument. Instead, the choice may also be traced to parties who are not aware that an optionally harmonised rule can be applied to the contract. Similarly, a choice against an optional instrument does not have to be based upon disapproval of the instrument, but based on, for example, model contracts that habitually opt out of optional instruments. Likewise, a choice not to apply an optional instrument may be based on model contracts that do not contain an opt-in clause, or, generally, an unwillingness to try out new law rather than familiar law systems.[2748] Cognitive limitations and biases may also limit the extent to which parties opt for an instrument that they are not familiar with.[2749] Notably, these flawed choices undermine the idea of regulatory competition, as parties do not always base their decisions on the quality of optional instruments. Thus, even if legislators design an optional instrument that exists alongside national laws, competition will not *necessarily* result in better law. The case studies[2750] demonstrated that legislators may also enter into regulatory competition to prevent that national contract parties opt out of national law.

Despite shortcomings in the theory that private parties make rational choices between different legal regimes, legislators still choose to participate in regulatory competition.

Notably, in the drafting of optional harmonisation measures, actors will have to take possible problems with accessibility into account. Actors should not assume that parties will choose an optional instrument because of its superior quality, and recognise that problems of inconsistency and unpredictability may withhold actors from opting for an optional instrument.

10.7.4. *Conclusion on the use of optional regimes*

This paragraph has asked whether the use of optional regimes rather than traditional harmonisation will contribute to a more comprehensible European private law.

The development of optional regimes may mean that the ability of private law to respond to varying preferences improves, and it provides an attractive alternative to previously pursued maximum harmonisation. In addition, the development of optional regimes may stimulate regulatory competition.

2748 E.A. Posner, 'The questionable basis of the Common European Sales Law: The role of an optional instrument in jurisdictional competition', *CMLRev* 2013, p. 271–272, who also points out that '[c] reating the CESL is a bit like creating a new language like Esperanto and inviting everyone to learn it.' Similarly, S. Augenhofer, 'A European Civil law – for whom and what should it include? Reflections on the scope and application of a future European legal instrument', *ERCL* 2011, p. 211 and J. Cartwright, '"Choice is good". Really?', *ERCL* 2011, p. 34, 7 who points out that businesses may be unwilling to act as "guinea pigs".

2749 G. Low, 'The (ir)relevance of harmonization and legal diversity to European contract law: A perspective from psychology', *ERPL* 2010, p. 298–302.

2750 See previously par. 4.3.3.1.1 and par. 5.3.4.1.

The success of optional regimes varies and depends on the question of whether drafters of these regimes sufficiently consider crucial questions. Further, the development of optional regimes may undermine the accessibility of European private law as it leads to multiple overlapping sets of regimes. In addition, regulatory competition need not necessarily lead to better law.

It is submitted that these potential drawbacks are not sufficient reason to abandon the development of optional regimes, provided that drafters sufficiently take into account parties' preferences as well as the relation between optional regimes and other sources of private law.

10.8. American inspiration

Could techniques inspired by the U.S. legal order, especially the U.S. Restatements and model laws, contribute to the comprehensibility of European private law?

In particular, Restatements, similar to the DCFR, or model laws, could replace currently used techniques at the European level. This would, however, entail a significant change from the private law *acquis*.

Paragraph 10.8.1 will consider the DCFR, which has been compared to Restatements in the European legal order and paragraph 10.8.2 will ask whether current experiences with it support the further use of these instruments. Paragraph 10.8.3 will consider whether model laws should be used if harmonisation is not feasible. Paragraph 10.8.4 will end with a conclusion.

10.8.1. The use of Restatements in the European legal order

Various similarities are visible between the U.S. Restatements and the DCFR, which were inspired by the U.S. Restatements:

1) The DCFR claims to restate existing law in black letter rules, accompanied by comparative notes.[2751]

Gutman[2752] states that the aim of Restatements was not purely to 'restate' existing laws. Instead, Restatements should also consider 'situations not yet discussed by the courts or dealt with by the legislatures', as well as reflecting what the law should be if the law was not clear, and suggest changes. Consequently, Gutman describes the Restatements as 'theoretical hybrids' between descriptions of what the law is and what it should be.[2753]

2751 H. Schulte-Nölke, 'Arbeiten an einem europäischen Vertragrecht – Fakten und populäre Irrtümer', *NJW* 2009, p. 2162, H. Schulte-Nölke, 'Restatement – nicht Kodifikation', in: O. Remien (ed.), *Schuldrechtsmodernisierung und Europäisches Vertragsrecht: Zwischenbilanz und Perspektiven – Würzburger Tagung vom 27. und 28. 10. 2006*, Tübingen: Mohr Siebeck 2008, p. 26.

2752 K. Gutman, *The constitutionality of European contract law*, Leuven 2010, p. 136.

2753 See similarly, with interesting examples in the area of product liability, J. Zekoll, 'Das American Law Institute – ein Vorbild für Europa?' in: R. Zimmerman (ed.), *Globalisierung und Entstaatlichung des Rechts, Teilband II, Nichtstaatliches Privatrecht: Geltung und Genese*, Tübingen: Mohr Siebeck 2008,

2) Both the DCFR and the Restatements seek to establish systematisation.

Gutman[2754] holds that although the Restatements were not drafted in the form of a code, they are reminiscent of codes as they did intend to provide a *systematic* description of the law.

3) Both the Restatements and the DCFR seek to establish a common terminology.[2755]

Hyland[2756] holds that a European codification should mainly seek to establish a common terminology and a structure that furthers debate, and should, therefore, be based on soft law such as the PECL and the UNIDROIT Principles. Accordingly, these sets of soft law already have been described as Restatements.[2757]

Notwithstanding some similarities, the assertion that the DCFR was a Restatement has been doubted by various authors who point to divergences between the DCFR and the American Restatements:

1) The DCFR has resulted in the since withdrawn proposal for a Regulation for a CESL,[2758] but the Restatements are expressly aimed at the judiciary and they are not meant to be adopted as laws throughout the United States.[2759]

2) Rather than restating a black-letter rule of a complicated area of law, the DCFR seeks to formulate black-letter rules that are, as such, arguably not a re*statement* of existing law.

Notably, the Study Group on a European Civil Code took the PECL (formulated by the Commission on European Contract Law, the predecessor of the Study Group) as a starting point to drafting the

p.113–115. N. Jansen, *The making of legal authority,* Oxford: OUP 2010, p. 56–57 notes that the choice between purely describing or also prompting changes in the law was a source of debate and Restatements have both been criticised for purely describing the law and deviating too much from existing law.

2754 K. Gutman, *The constitutionality of European contract law,* Leuven 2010, p. 139. Comp. in the same sense C.U. Schmid, 'Legitimitätsbedingungen eines Europäischen Zivilgesetzbuchs', *JZ* 2001, p. 680, and C.U. Schmid, 'Ways out of the maquis communautaire, On simplification and consolidation and the need for a Restatement of European primary law', *EUI Working Paper* 1999, par. V.2: 'a legal text resembling a codification'.

2755 K. Gutman, *The constitutionality of European contract law,* Leuven 2010, p. 140–141.

2756 R. Hyland, 'The American experience: Restatements, the UCC, uniform laws and transnational coordination', in: A.S. Hartkamp, E.H. Hondius (eds.) *Towards a European Civil Code,* Nijmegen: Ars Aequi Libri 2004, p. 70–71.

2757 For example, by R. Goode, 'International Restatements of contract and English contract law', *Uniform Law Review* 1997, p. 231. C.U. Schmid, 'Ways out of the maquis communautaire, On simplification and consolidation and the need for a Restatement of European primary law', *EUI Working Paper* 1999, par. V.3 notes that Restatements should be made available in multiple languages, which should considerably further deliberation.

2758 COM (2011) 635 final.

2759 R. Hyland, 'The American experience: Restatements, the UCC, uniform laws and transnational coordination', in: A.S. Hartkamp, E.H. Hondius (eds.) *Towards a European Civil Code,* Nijmegen: Ars Aequi Libri 2004, p. 59. J. Zekoll, 'Das American Law Institute – ein Vorbild für Europa?' in: R. Zimmerman (ed.), *Globalisierung und Entstaatlichung des Rechts, Teilband II, Nichtstaatliches*

DCFR. The Commission recognised that the PECL did not serve to restate the law, but rather served as a starting point for a European Civil Code. As such, the Commission held that there is no common law in Europe that could be restated. Therefore the PECL were not based on an already existing black-letter rule common to the Member States, but on comparative law.[2760]

Schmid,[2761] moreover, points out that a Restatement restating existing law would necessarily include not only the *acquis*, but also, for example, CJEU case law on general principles of European law. Jansen and Zimmerman[2762] point out that especially for areas other than contract law, the argument that common rules – in the form of black-letter rules, no less – can be found, overlooks the differences between national laws. Consequently, the DCFR contains rules that differ from national laws and such deviations should be justified more explicitly.

3) Whereas the Restatements focus on separate areas of law, the DCFR provides a systematisation of private law as such.[2763]

Is the DCFR a European equivalent of the Restatements? While the DCFR certainly differs from the Restatements as it does not restate the law, it adequately demonstrates what a European equivalent would look like.

The fact that the DCFR does not restate the law as such is not surprising, because of the differences between the U.S. and the European legal order.[2764] The *acquis* is fragmented and there is currently no common law in the European legal order that is similar to a common law that can be deduced from the U.S. legal order. Moreover, it is unfortunate that the DCFR has been developed in spite of existing instruments – which

Privatrecht: Geltung und Genese, Tübingen: Mohr Siebeck 2008, p. 112 however, remarks that questions on the aim of the Restatements may receive multiple answers ('die Frage nach dem Zweck der *Restatements* [wird] bis zum heutigen Tage nicht einheitlich beantwortet').

2760 The Commission on European contract law, *Introduction to the Principles of European Contract Law*, available at http://frontpage.cbs.dk/law/commission_on_european_contract_law/survey_pecl.htm, expressly held that '[t]he Principles have, therefore, been established by a more radical process. No single legal system has been their basis. The Commission has paid attention to all the systems of the Member States, but not every of them has had influence on every issue dealt with. The rules of the legal systems outside of the Communities have also been considered. So have the American Restatement on the Law of Contracts and the existing conventions, such as The United Nations Convention on Contracts for the International Sales of Goods (CISG). Some of the Principles reflect ideas which have not yet materialised in the law of any state.'

2761 C.U. Schmid, 'Legitimitätsbedingungen eines Europäischen Zivilgesetzbuchs', *JZ* 2001, p. 682.

2762 N. Jansen, R. Zimmerman, 'Was ist und wozu der DCFR?', *NJW* 2009, p. 3403.

2763 N. Jansen, R. Zimmerman, 'Was ist und wozu der DCFR?', *NJW* 2009, p. 3405, speak of 'systematisch verhärtern', also N. Jansen, *The making of legal authority*, Oxford: OUP 2010, p. 53.

2764 Comp. for example, M. Reimann, 'American private law and European legal unification – can the United States be a model?', *MJ* 1996, p. 217, emphasising that U.S. private law may not be as uniform as European observers assume, while M. Reimann, 'Towards a European Civil Code: why continental jurists should consult their transatlantic colleagues', *Tulane Law Review* 1998–1999, p. 1337, stresses that European lawyers should look to the U.S. experience in codification as the U.S. legal order shows some important similarities with the European legal order, including the coexistence of common and civil law jurisdiction within a legal order. K. Gutman, *The constitutionality of European contract law*, Leuven 2010, p. 502–504, also points to differences between the U.S. and EU legal order when considering using "American techniques" as a source of inspiration, and argues that the European legislator has a set of different techniques at its disposal that may be better suited for the EU legal order.

it does not adequately take into account – rather than being developed in close coordination with other instruments, as is the case for the Restatements. In this respect, the DCFR should take more note of the Restatements. The DCFR could also take the more transparent debate on the Restatements as an example.

In contrast to the Restatements, the DCFR is not primarily directed at the judiciary. A recommendation to a European judiciary would be difficult as no hierarchical judiciary has been established to interpret and apply European law. Instead, national courts are also tasked with applying European law. However, the majority of judicial decisions relate to national law, and courts correspondingly make use of sources on national private law rather than European private law.

In conclusion, the DCFR resembles a European Restatement in some respects that is, however, in clear need of improvement.

10.8.2. Experiences with the DCFR and the Restatements

Do the experiences with the DCFR indicate that European Restatements should be used further or should their use be reconsidered?

Experiences so far do not indicate success. Interestingly, Jansen[2765] finds that one of the reasons that Restatements are so much more prominent in the U.S. legal order than the PECL and the DCFR may be that the Restatements were drafted as a response to a widely agreed crisis in American private law and, thereby, responded to a need for legal practice. The higher responsiveness of the Restatements enhances the chances that they are subsequently widely accepted and used in legal practice. In contrast, as Jansen points out, the PECL especially was not developed in response to a need expressed by legal practice,[2766] which considerably diminishes the chances for its subsequent use and acceptance by legal practice and judges. Accordingly, Jansen finds it unlikely that actors will turn to European texts as primary sources or reflections of private law, unless European texts are cearly useful to national texts for legal practice. This would be the case if the harmonisation of national private laws continues to the point that it replaces national private law as the primary source for private law. In that scenario, the relevance of national texts as sources of private law is severely diminished, and consequently, a European text would have a clearly added value that is also apparent to legal practice.

Currently, Nilsen[2767] remarks that in contrast with Restatements, the DCFR, as well other soft law principles, do not serve to improve accessibility. On the contrary, they are an irritant at the national level where there is no immediate need for soft law principles.

2765 N, Jansen, *The making of legal authority*, Oxford: OUP 2010, p. 66, p. 51.

2766 Also H. Schulte-Nölke, '"Restatements" in Europe and the US: Some comparative lessons', in: R. Brownsword et al. (eds.), *The foundations of European private law*, Oxford: Hart 2011, p. 29 notes that 'there is neither need nor justification for the making of legal authority by way of private restatements in Europe'.

2767 N. Jansen, 'Dogmatising non-legislative codification. Non legislative texts in European legal discourse', in: R. Brownsword, H.-W. Micklitz, L. Niglia (eds.), *The foundations of European private law*, Oxford: Hart 2011, p. 36.

Notably, the criticism of the DCFR with regard to the confusion on the relation between the DCFR and the private law *acquis* and other soft laws indicates that the drafters of the DCFR should take more note of the development of the U.S. Restatements against the background of other measures. Particularly, the UCC and the uniform and model laws (established by the National Conference of Commissioners on Uniform State Laws (the NCCUSL), the Restatements (developed by the American Law Institute (ALI)), and the federal common law,[2768] as well as the division of competences between the federal and the state level in the U.S., should be considered in combination with one another. Accordingly, Gutman[2769] describes the development of the different techniques in the U.S. legal system as 'inextricably intertwined', and emphasises the influence of constitutional questions in the use of these techniques. Furthermore, when comparing the drafting of the DCFR and the development of Restatements, the transparency in the U.S. debate sets a good example for the drafting of the DCFR.[2770]

Therefore, the extent to which the DCFR or other European Restatements currently contribute to the benchmarks of predictability, accessibility, consistency and responsiveness is limited.

10.8.3. The use of model laws

Besides the American Restatements, the question arises of whether the use of model laws[2771] can be a source of inspiration for actors in the European legal order.

U.S. model laws allow for amendments and are generally used in more controversial areas of private law. In the European legal order, examples of such areas are property or insolvency laws. Gutman[2772] compares the use of model laws with non-binding recommendations. Other instruments reminiscent of model laws have also been used in the European legal order:

1) Soft laws as well as international conventions frequently use model rules, and legislators can use these rules as a source of inspiration when drafting legislation. However, this does not entail adopting a model law but merely looking at the European level for incidental ideas.

2768 See for a comparison between U.S. and EU 'federal common law' K. Lenaerts, K. Gutman, '"Federal common law" in the European Union', *American Journal of Comparative Law* 2006, p. 1.

2769 K. Gutman, *The constitutionality of European contract law*, Leuven 2010, p. 102, 165.

2770 Comp. J. Zekoll, 'Das American Law Institute – ein Vorbild für Europa?' in: R. Zimmerman (ed.), *Globalisierung und Entstaatlichung des Rechts, Teilband II, Nichtstaatliches Privatrecht: Geltung und Genese*, Tübingen: Mohr Siebeck 2008, p. 118–119, see in the same sense C.U. Schmid, 'Legitimitätsbedingungen eines Europäischen Zivilgesetzbuchs', *JZ* 2001, p. 681.

2771 This does not include uniform laws, the most prominent example of which is the Uniform Commercial Code. K. Gutman, *The constitutionality of European contract law*, Leuven 2010, p. 502 emphasises the American understanding of uniform laws – which are intended to be implemented without amendments by state legislators. Uniform laws are particularly resorted to if convergence of state laws are considered desirable. Therefore, uniform laws resemble current harmonisation initiatives and are, therefore, not considered as an alternative technique.

2772 K. Gutman, *The constitutionality of European contract law*, Leuven 2010, p. 503.

2) Divergent private laws throughout the Union may also inspire legislators. Admittedly though, possible inspiration takes place in the absence of a uniform model rule.
3) Model laws drafted by international organisations such as UNCITRAL, as well as the legislative guides used in areas are less likely to be harmonised such as insolvency law.

Consequently, the use of model laws is not limited to the U.S. legal system. Yet their use in the European legal order may give rise to questions:

1) Are these instruments likely to be used in areas that show an overlap with the private law *acquis*, especially if model laws are not attuned to the *acquis*?

For example, the UNCITRAL model law on cross-border insolvencies coexists with Regulation 1346/2000 on insolvency proceedings, and the UNCITRAL model laws have mostly been adopted by states outside the Union. Notably, the Regulation contains rules for jurisdiction issues, applicable law and provisions on the effects of the initiation of insolvency proceedings on the rights of third parties, and the law applicable for a number of specified contract parties, as well as the recognition of insolvency proceedings. The contents of the model law on the recognition of insolvencies overlaps with some of these provisions, but the model laws also provides rules on cross-border cooperation for cross-border insolvencies. Notably however, in the postponed revision of Dutch insolvency law, the expert committee did not only take into account the Regulation, but also considered the model law for insolvencies involving states outside the Union that fall beyond the scope of the Regulation.[2773]

2) Will the promotion by UNCITRAL of uniformity through model laws inspire the European legislator?

Several reactions are possible. If further harmonisation is not feasible, the Union may recommend its Member States to adopt the model laws provided by prominent international organisations. Alternatively, the Union may attempt to establish harmonisation in areas covered by model laws, as was the case in e-commerce. In 1996, UNCITRAL provided states with a model law on e-commerce. This prompted the Union[2774] to consider EU initiatives in this field in order to ensure a prominent role in international negotiations, which led to the adoption of Directive 2000/31 on e-commerce. In contrast, outside the European Union most states have adopted laws based on the UNCITRAL model law.[2775] In these cases the harmonisation of laws at a European level may considerably diminish the influence of model laws.[2776]

2773 Commissie insolventierecht, *Voorontwerp Insolventiewet*, 2007, p. 4 (t).

2774 European Commission, *Proposal for a European Parliament and Council Directive on certain legal aspects of electronic commerce in the internal market*, COM (1998) 586 final, p. 3.

2775 UNCITRAL, *Promoting confidence in electronic commerce: legal issues on international use of electronic authentication and signature methods*, Vienna 2009, available at www.cnudci.org/pdf/english/texts/electcom/08-55698_Ebook.pdf, par. 87.

2776 See critically C. Hultmark Ramberg, 'The e-commerce directive and the formation of contract in a comparative perspective', *Global Jurist Advances* 2001-2, who criticises Directive 2000/31 for overlooking relevant international developments such as the UNCITRAL model law.

3) If a model law is successfully used throughout the Union, will this bar the Commission's competence to initiate harmonisation in that particular field?

If a model law has been followed throughout the Union, it is more difficult to argue that divergences in private laws give rise to barriers to the internal market. Yet in the *Biotechnology* case,[2777] the CJEU ruled that obscurities or divergences in the interpretation of an international convention could give rise to barriers to the internal market, enabling the Commission to initiate harmonisation that would ensure an autonomous interpretation of the rules in the convention throughout the Union. Thus, the Commission may initially try to recommend states to take model laws as starting points when they are revising areas of private law.

If a model law is especially successful, and states are able to observe the application of model laws in practice, they may be less likely to object. However, if states find they prefer a larger say in the harmonisation of private law in particular areas – if they prefer harmonisation at all – this is a reason to opt for harmonisation, as states may have less influence in the drafting of model laws by international organisations.

Is the use of model laws likely to contribute to the benchmarks of predictability, accessibility, consistency and responsiveness?

The success of model laws depends on the use of model laws by the European legislator. The use made of model laws by states may be affected if harmonisation measures diverge from model laws and do not leave room for the national legislator to take model laws into account. Model laws are, however, more likely to be successful than Recommendations and soft laws, as states and the European legislator may observe more easily how model laws are used in practice. The adoption of model laws by third states may encourage both national legislators and the European Commission to take these model laws into account, while their use does not necessarily bar harmonisation. Therefore, model laws may present an interesting alternative for the use of Recommendations and soft laws.

10.8.4. Conclusion on American inspiration

Is the use of European equivalents of the Restatements and model laws likely to contribute to the predictability, consistency, accessibility and responsiveness of European private law?

The European equivalent of the U.S. Restatements, in the form of the DCFR, is not likely to be as successful, not only because of weaknesses in the drafting process in the DCFR that is not similarly visible in the U.S. legal order, but also because of the differences between the European and the U.S. legal order.

However, the use of international model laws may present an interesting alternative to harmonisation, particularly in areas less likely to be subject to harmonisation. They also offer opportunities for mutual learning, as states can observe how model laws function within legal orders. They should be considered more prominently in improved

[2777] CJEU 9 October 2001 (Kingdom of The Netherlands v European Parliament and Council of the European Union), C-377/98, ECR [2001], p. I-7079, par. 19–20.

consultations and impact assessments, provided that successful relevant model laws exist. Model laws may also be used as an additional technique that may precede harmonisation.

10.9. Collective bargaining

This paragraph will ask whether the use of collective bargaining can contribute to a more comprehensible European private law.

Paragraph 10.9.1 will address the various possible ways in which collective bargaining can be used. Paragraph 10.9.2 will identify potential problems. Paragraph 10.9.3 will end with a conclusion.

10.9.1. Suggestions for collective bargaining[2778]

Collins[2779] has suggested the formation of autonomous agreements through collective bargaining under article 155 TFEU. Under article 155 TFEU, framework agreements have been considered as an alternative to traditional harmonisation in social policy areas.[2780] Collins[2781] points out that the participation of private parties ensures responsiveness, reflecting business needs and practices, and leads to a more balanced result than one-sided self-regulation.

This idea is not entirely novel, considering the attempt of the Economic Commission for Europe (ECE) that provided standard forms of contracts and general conditions of sale to facilitate international commercial contracting.[2782] However, these initiatives had to compete with prominently used international models provided by the ICC. The outcome of collective negotiations in this form may set aside national mandatory law, which may, theoretically, make these agreements more attractive than widely used models provided by the ICC.

If national actors seek to initiate collective agreements with actors at the European level, for example, as they need to bargain with multinational organisations to adequately

2778 The suggestion in this paragraph differs from the previous suggestion to establish a 'European Self regulatory consultation system' by A.G. Castermans, 'Towards a European contract law through social dialogue', *ERCL* 2011, p. 366, as this form of self-regulation does not lead to framework agreements that can be transformed into binding law under article 155 TFEU. See previously for this suggestion par. 5.7.4. Comp. also J. Cartwright et al., 'Grensoverschrijdend contracteren? Dat lossen we zelf wel op', *NJB* 2011, p. 1250.

2779 H. Collins, 'The freedom to circulate documents: regulating contracts in Europe', *ELJ* 2004, p. 798–802. D. Schiek, 'Autonomous collective agreements as a regulatory device in European labour law: how to read article 139', *Industrial Law Journal* 2005, p. 26 similarly argues that the 'European social dialogue' established under article 155 TFEU can be considered as an example for other areas of contract law. Similarly G. Guéry, 'European collective bargaining and the Maastricht Treaty', *International Labour Review* 1992, p. 583–584.

2780 See previously par. 7.4.2.1.

2781 H. Collins, 'The freedom to circulate documents: regulating contracts in Europe', *ELJ* 2004, p. 798–802.

2782 UNCITRAL Report of the Secretary-General, 23 September 1966, Sixth Committee, doc.no. A/6396, par. 67, referring to the ECE General Conditions of Sale and Standard Forms of Contract.

protect the interests of their members at a national level, European collective bargaining may have a clear added value for national actors. For example, Schiek[2783] points to the initiative shown by various national unions to engage in collective negotiations with a transnational business established under Regulation 2157/2001.

Could collective bargaining at a European level also be undertaken for a limited amount of Member States, so that actors in Member States that are familiar with collective bargaining for business-to-consumer transactions can enter into transnational framework agreements? This would enable other actors and other Member States to observe collective bargaining in a cross-border context on a limited scale, which would create opportunities for mutual learning. Also, it would be easier to achieve a consensus on framework agreements if fewer parties who, moreover, have similar backgrounds, are involved in framework agreements.

However, it may be doubted whether the Commission wants a two-speed Europe – or several-speeds Europe – where businesses from states not participating in the framework agreements should not have access to states participating in framework agreements without being bound to those agreements.[2784]

10.9.2. The need for inclusive and representative negotiations between equal parties

Collective negotiations should be inclusive and negotiations should take place between sufficiently representative parties with equal bargaining power. Collins[2785] also points to the need to ensure the representativeness of the stakeholder organisations involved in the drafting process. Similarly, Schiek[2786] stresses the need for the representativeness of stakeholder organisations participating in collective bargaining.[2787] If this is not the case, agreements may become binding on parties who have had no chance to influence the process, which may severely limit the responsiveness of the outcomes of collective negotiations to society's – and contract parties' – views on justice.

In particular, problems of *Fremdbestimmung* may arise, and consequently the outcomes of collective bargaining should, but could not, be subject to judicial evaluation

2783 D. Schiek, 'Autonomous collective agreements as a regulatory device in European labour law: how to read article 139', *Industrial Law Journal* 2005, p. 24.

2784 H. Cullen, E. Campbell, 'The future of social policy-making in the European Union', in: P. Craig, C. Harlow (eds.), *Lawmaking in the European Union*, The Hague: KLI 1998, p. 275.

2785 H. Collins, 'The freedom to circulate documents: regulating contracts in Europe', *ELJ* 2004, p. 798–802.

2786 D. Schiek, 'Autonomous collective agreements as a regulatory device in European labour law: How to read article 139', *Industrial Law Journal* 2005, p. 26.

2787 K. Armstrong, 'Rediscovering civil society: the European Union and the White Paper on Governance', *ELJ* 2002, p. 123 however, argues that a distinction should be made between the different sorts of stakeholders participating in the 'social dialogue', that consists of actors having to implement policies later agreed upon, actors whose interests are directly affected by the outcome of the process, as well as actors that represent a public interest while they are not directly affected by the outcome of the process. These actors, Armstrong argues, act in their own interest rather than 'public' interests.

in the German legal order.[2788] Whittaker[2789] has questioned whether collective agreements violate the freedom of contract.

Accordingly, Member States frequently impose requirements with regard to representativeness. Insofar as they exist, these national requirements may be taken as a starting point to ensure the inclusiveness of European collective bargaining. In addition, collective bargaining at the European level may involve European stakeholder organisations representing these representative national stakeholder organisations. A lack of representativeness can be grounds for challenging the validity of Decisions. However, the CJEU[2790] has adopted considerable restraint in assessing the representativeness of parties admitting to collective bargaining. Furthermore, restrictions found in mandatory national law and the consumer law *acquis,* as well as competition law, should be taken into account.

10.9.3. Conclusion on the use of collective bargaining

Will collective bargaining, as an alternative to traditional harmonisation, contribute to the predictability, consistency, accessibility and responsiveness of European private law?

Extending framework agreements to consumer contract law may provide interesting alternatives that could be considered in more thorough impact assessments, especially if collective negotiations are also possible between actors from a limited number of Member States. This option would, on the one hand, allow for more experimentation. On the other hand, it would also lead to a two-tier Europe which is politically problematic and may lead to free riders. Also, current safeguards to ensure the inclusiveness of framework agreements are not satisfactory and should be improved.

However, the success of framework agreements could be undermined as the scope of framework agreements is likely limited and the success of this alternative depends on initiatives from private parties. The amount of initiative shown by stakeholders must not be overestimated or taken for granted,[2791] and initiatives from stakeholders may not necessarily result in an agreement. The Commission[2792] has suggested that the Open Method of Coordination (OMC) could be used to stimulate the involvement of relevant stakeholders, which has led to the adoption of frameworks of action.[2793] However,

2788 In instances where STCs had not become binding under article 155 TFEU, clauses were ineffective despite the recommendation of stakeholder organisations, see BGH 25 October 1995, *NJW* 1996, 389.

2789 S. Whittaker, 'On the development of European standard contract terms', *ERCL* 2006, p. 74.

2790 CJEU 17 June 1998 (UEAPME v Council of the European Union), T-135/96, ECR [1998], p. II-2335, par. 88–89. See further previously par. 7.4.2.3.

2791 Comp. H. Cullen, E. Campbell, 'The future of social policy-making in the European Union', in: P. Craig, C. Harlow (eds.), *Lawmaking in the European Union*, The Hague: KLI 1998, p. 274–275.

2792 European Commission, *The European social dialogue, a force for innovation and change*, COM (2002) 341 final, p. 14.

2793 For example, the Framework agreement on gender equality.

Smismans[2794] has argued that collective negotiations usually take place 'in the shadow of hierarchy', i.e. under the threat of legislative intervention.

10.10. Conclusion

Is the use of additional and alternative techniques more generally likely to foster deliberation and mutual learning? In addition, if techniques have already been widely used, can their improved use strengthen deliberation, mutual learning, and the predictability, consistency, accessibility and responsiveness of European private law?

The problems in the case studies[2795] and the weaknesses in the use of codifications, soft laws, blanket clauses and general principles can be linked to criticism of the legislative process and arguments for more debate in European private law. Specifically, the use of consultations and impact assessments show serious shortcomings that are not remedied by other actors or techniques. Improving the use of consultations, European impact assessments, databases and networks will likely foster deliberation, mutual learning and may be beneficial for regulatory competition. It may be particularly interesting for the Dutch legal order, where the interaction between the government and Parliament has been criticised more generally, as the negotiation processes at the national and the European level are separated and insufficiently coordinated. Once proposals have been negotiated at the European Parliament, they are not elaborately discussed in Parliament, with the exception of more fundamental matters.[2796] National democratic scrutiny seems to be better organised in Germany, as well as other Member States.[2797] These improvements may be a first step to deliberation. Improving the legislative process in turn makes it more likely that legislators will benefit from the involvement of other actors in the development of European private law, in accordance with pluralist arguments.

Generally, it is difficult to predict whether techniques that have not yet been widely used will promote deliberation, mutual learning, and comprehensibility. Arguably, the case studies[2798] and this chapter[2799] made clear that the suitability of additional and

2794 S. Smismans, 'European social dialogue in the shadow of hierarchy', *Journal of Public Policy* 2008, p. 161.

2795 See previously par 4.6.2. and par. 5.6.2. Although problems have private parties have not directly become visible in the German legal order, the lack of attention for the decreased ability of national techniques may lead to unpredictability, for example with regard to the implementation of the *acquis*, in the long term.

2796 W. Voermans, 'De Nederlandse wetgever in de communautaire toekomst', in: P. Koorn, L.H.M. Loeber (eds.), *De betekenis van de Europese Conventie voor de wetgevingspraktijk, Preadviezen voor de Vereniging voor wetgeving en wetgevingsbeleid*, The Hague: SDU 2004, p. 84–85.

2797 In particular the United Kingdom, where the European Scrutiny Committee scrutinises European proposals; see for a wider comparison B. van Mourik, *Parlementaire controle op Europese besluitvorming. Een rechtsvergelijkend onderzoek naar mandaatsystemen en parlementaire behandelingsvoorbehouden*, Nijmegen: Wolf Legal Publishers 2012.

2798 See previously par. 4.7 and par. 5.7.

2799 For example, the development of Guidance and comitology may be problematic for central areas of law but national experiences (on which see further par. 10.3.1 and par. 10.3.2) may help to make the amount

alternative techniques not only depends on the area of law, but also on the way in which private law has developed. This does not mean that parties cannot look at the use of additional or alternative techniques in other legal orders. The use of impact assessments in the English legal order, the use of collective bargaining in the Dutch legal order and the use of lower regulation in the implementation of the *acquis* in the German legal order may serve as sources of inspiration for actors in other legal orders. Which techniques that have not been widely used may foster deliberation, mutual learning, and comprehensibility?

1) The use of techniques in addition to blanket clauses will enhance the extent to which blanket clauses contribute to predictability, consistency, and responsiveness.

In the Dutch legal order, the newly-introduced prejudicial procedure could advance predictability and consistency. The responsiveness of private law may be enhanced if courts consistently consider well-established and accepted alternative regulation in the interpretation of blanket clauses. The use of Guidance and comitology – the acceptability of which may also depend on the composition of committees – may increase consistency and predictability, but may be limited to small, technical areas.

2) The study of STCs may enhance the responsiveness of the *acquis*.

Studying STCs likely will improve debate as studies may more convincingly make clear whether divergences are problematic for the internal market. Subsequent harmonisation may be more clearly in accordance with the need of parties involved in cross-border trade. If the study of STCs subsequently leads to harmonisation, theoretically, they may also prompt national actors to take into account interests of other actors and improve the law to avoid harmonisation. Studying STCs may make it easier to identify potential areas for harmonisation, which may, unfortunately, simultaneously inhibit the consistent development of national private law. The exchange of information on STCs may also contribute to predictability for private parties.

3) The development of collective bargaining, especially between experienced actors, may increase predictability for businesses relying on collectively negotiated clauses in cross border trade. State actors and non-state actors may consider these sets of STCs as a source of inspiration, as they may provide insight on the needs and preferences of actors involved in cross-border trade and set an example for actors in various sectors interested in cross-border trade.

4) Theoretically, despite criticism on the OMC, the use of the OMC could contribute to deliberation and regulatory competition, which could make actors more aware of areas of private law in need of improvement. In turn, reforming outdated areas of private law may contribute to the responsiveness of private law.

of damages awarded in specific cases more predictable. The development of Regulations may also meet with objections of national actors for central areas of private law, as such initiatives may undermine the central role of codifications, see previously par. 10.6. In areas where the law is not codified, less objections against the use of Regulations may develop.

5) Optional regimes could facilitate the consistent and predictable development of private law within national codifications and enhance the capacity of law to respond to divergent preferences

6) Model laws could enhance the consistent development of private law throughout the Union, as model laws encourage convergence and states interested in adopting (parts of) successful model laws have the opportunity to see how model laws are applied in practice, which is beneficial for predictability.

The emphasis of this chapter has been on potentially successful additional and alternative techniques that are often bottom-up techniques. The use of these techniques implies a shift towards the use of soft and bottom-up techniques.

Arguably, although soft or bottom-up techniques may form a valuable addition to currently used techniques, they are not defended solely a means to support the existing preferences for hierarchical techniques. German law rightly emphasises that the development of alternative regulation can have value in itself, as an exercise of constitutional rights.[2800] Even if the development of alternative regulation does not have a similar constitutional background, the ability of actors to develop and enforce their own rules is in accordance with the widely recognised principle of private autonomy and, therefore, has value in and of itself. Pluralist perspectives further lay out arguments for this approach, especially more responsiveness and opportunities for mutual learning.

Currently, the preference for the use of traditional techniques has meant that techniques such as, for example, impact assessments, but also the use of model laws have been overlooked and that the strengths and weaknesses of various alternative techniques may not have been sufficiently or thoroughly considered. The perspective of national actors makes it less probable that the use of techniques in the multilevel legal order is subject to debate. This not only means that the use of national techniques is not the result of careful consideration, it also means that the possible development of alternative regulation is currently overlooked and that successful national techniques are transferred to the European level, as visible especially in the use of blanket clauses at the European level, without taking into account potential detriments and an increasingly regulatory approach at the European level.[2801] Transferring successful national techniques to the European level may be problematic because these techniques are typically not used in isolation from other techniques, but in combination with one another. As a result, if a technique is transferred to the European level, it is not clear how this technique will function without the use of additional techniques.

The similarly uncritical approach of the European legislator to the use of techniques is especially unfortunate because the European legislator pursues a specific aim, and consequently, one would expect more focus on the question of how to achieve that aim. It follows that debate should focus more on the use of techniques. This means that actors should reconsider simply transferring successful national techniques to the European

2800 See previously par. 7.2.3.
2801 See previously par. 9.4.1.

level, and consider alternatives to traditionally used techniques. Interaction may entail that actors become better acquainted with alternative approaches from other actors and benefit from experiences in other legal orders. Possibly, this may make actors more aware of strengths or shortcomings in the techniques they use and provide them with a more critical perspective on the use of techniques.

Notably, the choice for optimal techniques is not a definitive choice, but may also change over time, as the roles of actors change. In order to better assess the use of techniques, and the strengths and weaknesses of techniques, the way in which actors interact with each other should be adjusted.

This does not mean that additional or alternative bottom-up techniques will necessarily be more successful than traditional legislation,[2802] but legislation is not necessarily more successful than alternative regulation. To the contrary, especially if the legislative process consistently shows severe shortcomings – which is currently not the case – and does not show improvement, formally democratically developed rules may *de facto* lead to *Fremdbestimmung*. The current shortcomings in the legislative process already make the need to use additional and alternative techniques more visible and attractive. As the legislative process becomes more flawed, the distinction between the development of private law by democratically elected state actors and non-state actors becomes smaller and the preference for democratically elected state actors over non-democratically elected state actors also becomes less convincing. Accordingly, Scheltema[2803] finds that the development of private law by the legislator is not necessarily preferable to the development of private law through case law. Should the judiciary, therefore, play a more important role in providing guidelines for the interpretation of blanket clauses, and should the judiciary more generally play a more active role in the multilevel legal order? Should soft laws be a more prominent source in the interpretation of blanket clauses?[2804]

Unfortunately, the strengths of bottom-up techniques may be overlooked as the current use of bottom-up techniques does not remedy problems apparent in the use of techniques. Bottom up techniques have various weaknesses that should be more carefully considered. Particularly, the following drawbacks of bottom-up techniques that may reinforce problems in the legislative process should not be overlooked:

2802 Comp. J. Köndgen, 'Privatisierung des Rechts', *AcP* 2006, p. 507–508, who, referring to the *Enron* and *Worldcom* cases, states that positive (criminal) law has failed rather than self-regulation. He emphasises that self-regulation is not intended to have preventive effect – instead, it can help the judiciary by indicating what behaviour can be expected from, for example, a particular profession. However, it seems that behaviour has not been in accordance with such rules, despite the involvement of relevant actors. This may form an indication against the argument that involvement of interested parties – such as professions – will strengthen compliance. Similar conclusions may also be drawn for corporate governance codes, see previously par. 8.4.2.3.

2803 M. Scheltema, *Het recht van de toekomst* (inaugural address Utrecht), Deventer: Kluwer 2005, p. 9.

2804 Comp. R. Michaels, 'Umdenken für die UNIDROIT Prinzipien. Vom Rechtswahlstatut zum Algemeinen Teil des transnationalen Vertragsrecht', *RabelsZ* 2009, p. 885.

1) The development of bottom-up development takes time and its success depends on the initiatives from private parties.

Notably, the development of bottom-up techniques also depends on the awareness of private actors of the possibilities to develop such initiatives. As long as (many of) those initiatives do not seem to be progressing rapidly, bottom-up techniques take a long time to develop.

2) Some bottom-up initiatives do not adequately ensure representativeness and inclusiveness.

Presently, the development of the DCFR has resulted in debate with a, in comparison to national codifications, relatively limited number of highly qualified participants. It seems that in debate on European private law, prominent European stakeholders may play an important role.[2805] Armstrong[2806] points out that collective negotiation processes at the European level typically only include actors at the European level who, moreover, *negotiate* to achieve an agreement, whilst pursuing their own interests. The suggestions for comitology and an Open Method of Convergence also presuppose the inclusion of a limited number of highly qualified participants. Notably, this small number of highly qualified participants may be beneficial for stimulating the exchange of rational arguments based on sufficient expertise. Notwithstanding the desirability of this exchange, however, the lack of participation from practitioners specialised in national law considerably weakens the debate in European private law, as it seems cut off from at least part of practice which, in many areas, is still predominantly national. Consequently, it is not likely that practice will develop many initiatives even if additional or alternative techniques provide room for actors to do so.

[2805] For example, the drafting of the Optional Instrument (see for the members of the stakeholder group http://ec.europa.eu/justice/contract/stakeholder-meeting/index_en.htm), Directive 2011/83 on consumer rights (see for the members of the stakeholder group http://ec.europa.eu/consumers/rights/cons_acquis_en.htm). Comp. also the members of the Round Table on Travel Contracts, on the review of Directive 90/314 on package travel (see for the members of the group http://ec.europa.eu/consumers/cons_int/safe_shop/pack_trav/pack_trav03_en.pdf) Comp. S. Grundmann, J. Stuyck, 'An academic Green Paper on European contract law – scope, common ground and debated issues', in: S. Grundmann, J. Stuyck, (eds.), *An academic Green Paper on European contract law*, The Hague: KLI 2002, p. 7–8.

[2806] K. Armstrong, 'Rediscovering civil society: the European Union and the White Paper on Governance', *ELJ* 2002, p. 123–124.

Chapter 11

CONCLUSIONS

11.1. Introduction

This volume has asked whether the coexistence of actors in the development of European private law is beneficial or problematic. First, paragraph 11.2 will summarise the questions raised by this book. Paragraph 11.3. will discuss the role of actors. The paragraph will first turn to criticism on state-centeredness, and go on to discuss the role of actors under the GG, TFEU, and a Dutch framework. Paragraph 11.4. will turn to multilevel governance insights. The findings in the case studies will be considered, and subsequently, it will be debated whether these findings can be generalised. Paragraph 11.5. will discuss pluralist insights. The paragraph will first debate the findings in the case studies and go on to consider whether the coexistence of actors has proven beneficial more generally for European private law. Paragraph 11.6. will end with the conclusions.

11.2. Multilevel governance and pluralist insights

The book has been inspired by multilevel governance and pluralist perspectives that emphasise the coexistence and interdependence of actors. Both multilevel governance and pluralist perspectives recognise that multiple state actors have become involved in the development of European private law. Non-state actors also play an increasingly important role as the development of private law more and more involves cross-border matters and requires more expertise and organisational resources that state actors may not possess. In addition, the increasing development of alternative regulation typically presupposes the involvement of non-state actors.

Both multilevel governance and pluralist perspective recognise that interdependence has developed between both state actors from different levels and state actors and non-state actors. These actors therefore need to take into account one another's initiatives.

Multilevel governance and pluralist perspectives further both recognise that the roles of actors are subject to change.[2807] The role of national state actors changes as competences are reallocated to the European level. The increasing complexity of problems may prompt

[2807] See par. 1.4.

actors at the European and at the national level to delegate tasks to non-state actors with considerable expertise, such as the IASB.[2808]

Pluralist criticism on the state-centric approach of the development of European private law give rise to questions on the role of actors in the development of European private law. While the case studies focussed on national techniques, subsequent chapters considered the role of actors in the development of private law in respectively the German and Dutch legal order more generally.

In accordance with multilevel governance perspectives,[2809] the lack of interaction between interdependent actors simultaneously involved in the development of European private law may be problematic. Specifically, national actors are no longer able to independently safeguard the comprehensibility of private law through codifications, blanket clauses and general principles, the use of which has been closely interrelated with notions of predictability, consistency, accessibility and responsiveness. Therefore, national actors have to recognise interdependence and interact with other actors accordingly. As actors have to interact with more non-state actors and state actors from different levels, with whom they may not be as familiar with as state actors from the same level, interdependence may entail higher standards for the process through which private law is developed, in particular, for the interaction between actors. The case studies found that actors have not sufficiently recognised interdependence. Instead, both national and European actors have adopted a narrow, defensive perspective in the debate on European private law. Accordingly, national and European actors have not sufficiently considered the use of additional and alternative techniques. This perspective is visible more generally in the implementation of the *acquis* into the BGB and the BW, the insertion of blanket clauses in the *acquis* and in the development of soft law. Simultaneously, a different approach has become visible in the development of international private law, as well as in the anticipation of Directives. In some cases, general principles have also been used as a starting point for interaction.

In contrast, pluralist perspectives[2810] underline that the involvement of multiple actors in the development of European private law may be beneficial. The coexistence of actors at the European and national level may benefit responsiveness as the law is increasingly developed in accordance with the needs and preferences of both national and transnational actors. This is not the case in areas of law that concern small, domestic disputes, such as disputes in consumer cases, but in other areas, more drivers for integration may exist. Alternatively, the coexistence of national actors may be beneficial as various state actors develop private law reflecting divergent legal views on justice. If the law is closely intertwined with legal views on justice, or with national practices, this impedes further harmonisation as well as regulatory competition as was concluded in the case studies. Contrary to pluralist perspectives, mutual learning and regulatory competition have not consistently benefited the law. However, opportunities

2808 See par. 7.4.1.1.
2809 See par. 1.5.
2810 See par. 1.6.

for mutual learning and experimentation that will strengthen European private law may still develop.

11.3. The state-centric approach to the development of European private law

The case studies have focussed on the development of the law on STCs through national techniques, in which state actors have played a central role. More generally, a preference for a hierarchical approach towards the development of European private law has become visible, combined with the preference to use techniques that have also been successful at the national level[2811] or hierarchical modes of new governance.[2812] The hierarchical approach is also visible in initiatives from non-state actors, both in the German case study[2813] and in the development of soft laws.[2814] However, hierarchical initiatives are not necessarily successful,[2815] which is regrettably often overlooked.

Pluralist insights have criticised the state-centric, hierarchical approach towards the development of the law. Pluralist arguments further criticise the assumption that the development of the law is best left to actors at one (either the national or the European) level or even one state actor (such as the legislator or the judiciary). This raises the question which actors are more generally involved in the development of private law, beyond national techniques, and what actors should develop private law?

The framework that can be discovered in Germany offers starting points for answers to these questions, which will be considered in paragraph 11.3.1. Paragraph 11.3.2. will contrast the German approach to the European approach and paragraph 11.3.3. will turn to the Dutch approach, where no framework can yet be construed, although starting points for such a framework can be found, as a middle road. Paragraph 11.3.4. will end with a conclusion.

11.3.1. A principled approach: the German framework

In the German legal order, a framework for assessing the role of especially private actors can be discovered.[2816] This framework is based on principles of democracy, private autonomy ('*Privatautonomie*') and concerns of *Fremdbestimmung. Fremdbestimmung* arises if actors are bound without their consent, by rules that are also not based on the law.[2817] This framework can be sketched as follows:

- Originally, two sources of binding rules were recognised: legal norms or private autonomous juridical acts. However, hybrids have developed. Private actors increasingly have the possibility

[2811] For example, the development of codification-like instruments, such as the DCFR, see par. 9.3.1., and some blanket clauses, see par. 9.4.1.
[2812] See par. 7.4.1.1.
[2813] See par. 4.3.3.1.3.
[2814] See par. 9.3.1.
[2815] See par. 10.10.
[2816] See further par. 7.2.
[2817] See further par. 7.2.2.

to participate in the development of rules that may have binding effect on third parties. As a result, parties become bound, not based on the law or their consent.
- This development coincides with the increased number of actors developing private law in the multilevel legal order, which in turn increases the chance that individuals are confronted with rules not based on the law or their consent.[2818]
- As such, the development of binding rules by private actors need not necessarily be problematic. In some cases, privately drafted rules reflect well-established practices, such as the development of collective labour agreements. Yet privately drafted rules are not necessarily drafted in the public interest. It is also possible that rules – such as STCs – have been drafted by private actors with particular interests, so that rules insufficiently take into account the legitimate interests of parties subsequently subjected to these rules.
- This situation can be mitigated in various ways. If processes where rules are drafted are sufficiently transparent, and open to the participation of relevant actors, representative of stakeholder groups, this may help to prevent rules being drafted solely in the interests of one group of actors. Rules may also be developed in collective negotiations processes, or processes may be supervised by state actors. Alternatively, privately drafted rules can be subject to judicial control.
- In other words, as privately drafted rules become more binding and, therefore, more like state rules, they are subjected to standards that are also imposed on state rules. These control mechanisms may overlap, yet they are also flexible, depending on the binding force of rules and their one-sidedness.

This framework cannot simply be transposed to other legal orders, as it is closely interrelated with the GG. However, private autonomy and *Fremdbestimmung* may be used as starting points to critically consider which actors should be involved in the development of private law.

Pluralist perspectives are critical of the argument that the state is the source of all binding rules. Nevertheless, the German framework makes clear that state actors have retained an important role in the development of private law, but it also offers a convincing justification for that role: protecting individuals against *Fremdbestimmung*. This is the case even in areas where actors have developed a relatively autonomous space, such as the *lex sportiva*: the scope of these rules have been limited by restrictions on dynamic referral.[2819] This framework is accordingly not limited to the development of traditional "hard law", nor does it stand in the way of alternative regulation. To the contrary, German actors have clearly recognised cases where non-state actors rather than state actors should develop rules, for example if the development of alternative regulation falls within the scope of constitutional rights. Many instances of alternative regulation can accordingly be considered in the light of free speech, protected under article 5 GG,[2820] the freedom of association protected by article 9 GG,[2821] or the freedom of profession, protected by article 12 GG.[2822] Likewise, a role of non-state actors has been

2818 Notably, privately drafted rules are often also less accessible to private parties, which may increase the chance of surprises.
2819 See previously par. 7.5.2.2. and 7.5.2.7.
2820 See previously par. 7.5.2.4 and 7.5.2.5.
2821 See previously par. 7.4.2.2. and 7.5.2.6.
2822 See previously par. 7.5.2.3., par. 7.5.2.4.

recognised if self-regulation promotes behaviour that goes beyond what is legally required.[2823]

11.3.2. *An instrumental approach: the European view*

The German framework can be contrasted especially with the European view. Not only is the European view considerably less developed, it is also more instrumental.[2824] This approach follows from the attribution of competences to the European legislator. The role of actors in the development of European private law depends on the extent to which those actors can contribute to European policy aims.

As European actors seek to enhance the functioning of the internal market, it is logical to consult the parties faced with obstacles to the internal market, and non-state actors may have more interest in European, as well as foreign and international, initiatives than state actors.[2825] However, in the case studies, European initiatives were not prompted by the concerns of transnational actors. More generally, it may be asked why the European legislator rather than national or local actors should develop rules of consumer contract law.[2826] These developments can be conrasted with cases where EU initiatives were clearly prompted by transnational actors.[2827] New governance initiatives such as the Lamfalussy method have also been designed in a way that leaves much room for expert actors involved at the European level.[2828]

European actors have recognised the need for representativeness and inclusiveness in the development of initiatives.[2829] Like German state actors, the European legislator has recognised the need for judicial control of STCs in consumer contracts,[2830] as well as the unequal bargaining position between businesses and consumers, which has prompted the European legislator to establish information duties and withdrawal periods – that have, however, not been uniformly introduced, but rather for specific contracts, or in specific situations, and also to improve the internal market. Notably, however, these control mechanisms have not been developed because STCs or other initiatives are considered as alternative regulation, the effects of which should be controlled.[2831]

Although European actors cannot rely on a civil society in the way that national actors can, the European legislator has actively sought to involve civil society in the development of binding rules.[2832] Yet a closer look reveals that frequently, European civil society is largely made up of carefully selected actors and repeat players. Relevant actors

2823 See previously par. 7.5.2.5. Possibly, the declarations with regard to consumer services, discussed in par. 7.5.3.4. can also be seen in this light.

2824 See par. 7.2.4.

2825 See par. 8.6.1.

2826 See par. 8.6.4.

2827 The involvement of the IASB in European law may be seen in this light, see par. 7.4.1.1.

2828 See par. 7.4.1.1.

2829 See par. 7.4.2.3.

2830 See par. 7.5.1.4.

2831 See par. 7.5.1.5 and 7.5.4.

2832 See pars. 7.5.1.2., 7.5.3.4., 7.5.4., 8.5.3.7. For European consultations, see pars. 4.3.2.4. and 5.3.3.4.and 10.2.1.2.

at the national level are frequently not included, either in European consultations or in the development of European alternative regulation. Also, reaching agreement between state actors and non-state actors and between non-state actors in the development of alternative regulation is notoriously difficult, which may discourage state actors from undermining the effect of alternative regulation by applying control mechanisms to alternative regulation.[2833] Therefore, ensuring representativeness and inclusiveness at the European level is problematic.

How does the instrumental approach of the European Commission affect the role of non-state actors at the national level?[2834]

- European law may decrease the role of well-established national actors, especially unions, while equivalent European initiatives such as framework agreements, are encouraged.
- This development is also visible in other fields, such as the law on STCs and accounting standards, where the European Union encourages the development of further alternative regulation to help achieve European policy aims, without considering the need for restraint because of potential *Fremdbestimmung*, and overshadowing national initiatives where control mechanisms are better developed and applied.
- Control mechanisms at the European level are exercised with restraint, which, from the perspective of *Fremdbestimmung* and private autonomy, is especially problematic if alternative regulation leads to the development of binding rules on third parties that may not have been subjected to adequate control mechanisms at the European level.
- The impression arises that the European legislator is not opposed to alternative regulation as such,[2835] but finds that potential divergences may give rise to barriers to the internal market. Therefore, the European legislator prefers European alternative regulation to national alternative regulation, even without well-established control mechanisms, and notwithstanding the success of some well-established national initiatives.

In contrast to German state actors, European actors have not clearly recognised cases in which non-state actors rather than state actors should develop rules.

11.3.3. The middle road: the Dutch approach

The Dutch legal system provides a middle road between European law and the German framework although a Dutch framework cannot yet be construed.

2833 Particularly visible in the lenient evaluation of framework agreements, see par. 7.4.2.3.
2834 See on these questions pars. 7.4.3., 7.5.4. and 8.5.5.
2835 This becomes visible in the encouragement of Dutch initiatives in consumer credit or package travel, see par. 8.6.3. Notably, simultaneously, overlapping self-regulation may inhibit accessibility, see further par. 8.5.5.

Dutch actors have adopted a pragmatic approach to the development of alternative regulation.[2836] Accordingly, collectively negotiated STCs in consumer contracts, collective labour agreements, corporate governance initiatives and mass settlements have been developed.

Simultaneously, control mechanisms have been developed: collective negotiations take place between parties in equal bargaining positions, within a platform established by state actors,[2837] and the judiciary evaluates the representativeness of parties involved in alternative regulation.[2838] As enforcement is considered an important problem that may explain the lack of success of alternative regulation in a particular area,[2839] this may also be considered as a solution for problems arising in areas where alternative regulation has been developed. More alternative regulation may also be an option.[2840]

Dutch actors have not considered the development of alternative regulation as an exercise of constitutional rights, with the exception of collective labour agreements.[2841] This consideration has, however, not withheld the Dutch legislator to adopt a pragmatic approach to the development of these agreements, which indicates that a principled approach need not necessarily exclude a pragmatic approach.[2842] Yet the German perspective and the principles on which that perspective is based are not unfamiliar within the Dutch legal order.[2843]

In the Dutch legal order, more experimentation has taken place, perhaps because of the more pragmatic approach towards the role of private actors, but perhaps also because the Dutch legislator adopts a more bottom-up approach than both German and European actors. The Dutch approach has led to innovative alternative regulation but also to weak alternative regulation. Meanwhile, the German framework has allowed for innovative alternative regulation as well.[2844]

These different developments from German, European and Dutch actors make clear that the view on the role of private actors and possible problems of *Fremdbestimmung* are essential for the development of control mechanisms.[2845]

Arguably, the German perspective may offer useful insights on the roles of actors that may help Dutch actors to develop a more consistent and predictable approach towards the role of private actors.[2846] Specifically, the German approach may draw attention to the development of alternative regulation in the light of constitutional rights. Further, the German approach may prompt Dutch actors to consider the possibility that private actors need not necessarily pursue the public interest, which may be a reason to develop

2836 See par. 8.4.4.
2837 Particularly CAOs, see par. 8.4.3.3. and collectively negotiated STCs, see par. 8.5.1.2.
2838 Particularly mass settlements and CAOs, see par. 8.4.3.3.
2839 Particularly corporate governance codes, see par. 8.4.2.1., as well as primary payment services, par. 8.5.3.5.
2840 Particularly for mass settlements, see par. 8.4.3.3.
2841 See par. 8.4.3.2.
2842 See par. 8.4.3.1.
2843 See par. 8.6.3.
2844 See par. 8.6.3.
2845 See par. 8.6.3.
2846 See par. 8.6.1.

more control mechanisms in some areas, such as corporate governance or corporate social responsibility. The assumption that private actors pursue private rather than the public interest is, however, too general.

The development of a Dutch framework need not stand in the way of the development of alternative regulation. Under this framework, the development of rules by non-state actors or the judiciary rather than the legislator may be indicated, especially if the legislative process shows consistent, severe shortcomings.[2847]

The European approach may benefit from German and Dutch insights.[2848] In some cases, overlooking relevant national initiatives decreases the relevance of European initiatives, when businesses and consumers already familiar with well-established self-regulation are not aware of European initiatives.

11.3.4. *A coherent approach?*

The principles underlying the German framework offer a useful starting point for a more critical approach towards the role of actors, which may be useful considering the lack of attention for the question by whom private law ought to be developed. Yet despite the development of frameworks based on principles of private autonomy and *Fremdbestimmung* the roles of actors may still differ throughout the Union.

- Even if views on the role of actors are based on principles of private autonomy, the views of when parties' autonomy is actually at stake, if *Fremdbestimmung* arises, whether it should be controlled or which mechanisms are best suited to remedy potential breaches, may differ.[2849]
- Actors' roles are subject to change. For example, as actors organise themselves better and are more willing to make transparent how they develop self-regulation, alternative regulation may be indicated rather than legislation, especially if legislation shows severe and persistent shortcomings. More European integration might justify a more prominent role of European non-state actors. Conversely, if alternative regulation turns out to be problematic, the legislator or the courts may intervene.
- The comparison between the Dutch, German and European approach has revealed differences with regard to the role of actors in the development of private law that have not affected the use of techniques, indicating that differences in the relation between the legislature and judiciary need not necessarily lead to a radically different use of techniques.[2850]

2847 See par. 8.6.3. and more generally, par. 10.10.
2848 See par. 8.6.3.
2849 See pars. 7.5.1.1. and 8.5.1.1.
2850 See par. 8.6.1.

11.4. Multilevel governance insights: restraint in deliberation

The case studies make clear that in the development of the law on STCs, interdependent actors have exercised restraint in interacting with one another. The lack of interaction and shortcomings in interaction need not necessarily directly lead to problems, but it may aggravate existing weaknesses in the law and lead to problems in the longer term.

- The German case study made clear that the German legislator has participated actively in the drafting of Directive 93/13 on unfair contract terms. The German and Dutch case study both show that national legislators have simultaneously exercised restraint in the implementation of the Directive into national private law.
- Both German and Dutch courts follow the legislator's restraint.[2851] A reason for this restraint may be the efficient and just settlement of disputes, which may be overlooked in European debate, where actors directly concerned with settling disputes do not sufficiently participate.[2852] Generally, this restraint is exercised by both higher and lower courts. However, both the Dutch and German case study indicate that the role of highest courts, and restraint exercised by these courts, may be undermined if their decisions are not easily reconcilable with CJEU decisions and lower courts refer to these decisions or the CJEU.[2853] The role of highest courts may also be undermined if the highest courts of other Member States actively refer many questions to the CJEU.[2854]
- In the implementation and interpretation of article 3 Directive 93/13, German and Dutch state actors have similarly adopted restraint – in both legal orders, judges have emphasised the competence of the national judiciary in the evaluation of cases in accordance with harmonised blanket clauses that are closely interrelated with central national blanket clauses.[2855]
- European actors have exercised restraint in the revision of Directive 93/13. Although in the drafting of the Directive, European actors did consider and follow up on German criticism, the failed attempt to revise the Directive makes clear that the European legislator pursues further harmonisation.[2856]
- In the case studies, the legislators and courts adopted a national approach to European initiatives that goes beyond methodological nationalism.[2857]

Although interdependence has developed, actors have not sufficiently interacted with one another. In accordance with insights from multilevel governance, this should lead to problems. Accordingly, actors' restraint has aggravated unpredictability and

2851 See pars. 4.3.2.3. and 5.3.3.3.
2852 See the case studies, par. 4.3.2.4. and 5.3.3.4. and more generally par. 10.2.1.2.
2853 See pars. 4.4.1.2., 5.4.1.2. and 5.4.2.2.
2854 See par. 9.6.
2855 HR 21 September 2012, *RvdW* 2012, 1132, BGH 14 July 2004, *BeckRS* 2004, 7903.
2856 See par. 4.3.2.1., par. 4.3.2.4., par. 5.3.3.1., par. 5.3.3.4 and more generally par. 6.2 and par. 10.2.1.
2857 See par. 4.6.2.

inconsistency that are more generally associated with recodification and the introduction of new blanket clauses.

- In the Dutch legal order, inconsistencies have arisen because lower courts do not sufficiently take into account decisions of other lower courts and the Hoge Raad, as well as the CJEU. Both German[2858] and Dutch lower courts[2859] have referred to the CJEU despite previous case law from the BGH and the Hoge Raad, which indicates the need for a more active approach of the BGH and the Hoge Raad. Accordingly, the BGH[2860] has referred a question to the CJEU and the Hoge Raad[2861] has elaborated on the obligation of Dutch courts to evaluate clauses of their own motion. Although lower courts have referred questions to the CJEU directly, the amount of cases from Dutch and German lower courts remains limited. Consequently, German and Dutch courts have not focussed on the enforcement of Directives, and higher courts have resisted the development of the *acquis* in a manner that conflicts with national law.[2862]
- The restraint of the Dutch judiciary has also lessened the extent to which blanket clauses can reduce the need for legal reform, in the interest of the stable development of the law, as visible in the German case study.[2863]
- In the Dutch legal order, problems have also arisen with regard to the correct application and interpretation of overlapping international law and the *acquis*.[2864]

In contrast, in the German legal order, restraint has not directly resulted in problems in the law on STCs for private parties. A possible explanation for more directly visible problems in the Dutch legal order and less visible problems in the German legal order, despite similar restraint of national actors, is the existence of carefully developed, successful national law in the German legal order that has influenced Directive 93/13, whereas the Dutch regime had just been introduced when Directive 93/13 was adopted.[2865] However, upon closer inspection, problems have become visible:

- The restraint of national actors prevents that problems and relevant questions on the implementation of Directives become visible at the European level. Consequently, revision of these measures will overlook these questions and concerns, which may lead to a circle both in the Dutch and German legal order: because of a lack of

2858 OLG Oldenburg 14 December 2010, *BeckRS* 2011, 8627.
2859 Hof Amsterdam 8 March 2011, *NJF* 2011, 242 (Case C-488/11).
2860 BGH 9 February 2011, *NJW* 2011, 1392.
2861 HR 13 September *2013*, *NJ* 2014, 274.
2862 See par. 6.3.1.
2863 See par. 4.2.
2864 See further par. 5.3.4.2.
2865 See par. 5.8.

responsiveness, national actors will continue to exercise restraint, and relevant questions will, therefore, not be addressed at the European level, etc.[2866]

- The lack of participation of sufficient and representative actors in European initiatives[2867] increases the chance that the needs of national actors are overlooked, as well as their views on justice.[2868]
- The distinction between *Sonderprivatrecht* and general private law offers insufficient clarity on the future implementation of the *acquis*,[2869] but it offers interesting starting points for debate on the implementation of Directives.
- The restraint of the courts makes it less likely that incorrect implementation is compensated by the judiciary.[2870]
- The BGH[2871] has decided on overlapping international law and the *acquis* rather than the CJEU. Thus, while German courts consistently follow the BGH, there is less clarity on the relation between different Directives as well as the *acquis* and international sources, and the chance of inconsistent decisions on simultaneously applicable sources of rules throughout the Union increases.

The findings in the case studies are more generally valid for the development of European private law.

- Actors have more generally adopted a national approach to the development of European private law. This is even visible in instances where actors have adopted an active approach to the development of the *acquis*. Accordingly, the use of national blueprints for the development of the *acquis*[2872] can be seen in this manner, as well as suggestions – also defended in this book – to consider the development of successful self-regulation at the European level.[2873] The development of soft laws can similarly be seen in the light of methodological nationalism.[2874]
- Interaction has not prompted actors to reconsider the use of national techniques.[2875] Instead, actors have attempted to transpose successful national techniques – such as codifications and blanket clauses – to the European level, which has resulted in unpredictability, inconsistency and a lack of responsiveness.[2876]

2866 See pars. 4.6.1. and 5.6.1.

2867 See par. 4.3.2.1, par. 4.3.2.4., par. 5.3.3.1. and par. 5.3.3.4 and more generally par. 10.2.1.2. and 10.2.2.1.

2868 The lack of referral to national practice in the DCFR can be seen in this light; see pars. 10.7.2.2. and 11.7.2.2.

2869 See par. 4.3.1.4.

2870 See pars. 4.3.2.3. and 5.3.3.3.

2871 Comp. BGH 28 March 1996, *NJW* 1996, 1819, which is however, in accordance with CJEU 14 December 1976 (Colzani/Rüwa), Case 24–76, [1976] ECR, p. 1831. Also, BGH 31 October 2001, *NJW* 2002, 370, which has however, been followed by Dutch courts, see par. 11.3.4.2.2. The decisions in BGH 1 February 2005, *NJW* 2005, 1774 and BGH 5 December 2006, *NJW* 2007, 997, consistent with BGH 20 January 1983, *NJW* 1983, 1322, are also problematic.

2872 See par. 9.2.3.

2873 See par. 5.7.4. and more generally par. 10.9.

2874 See par. 9.3.1.

2875 See par. 9.6.

2876 See par. 9.6.

- The restraint at the national level makes it highly unlikely that national state actors will signal problems for the internal market and suggest harmonisation.
- The distinction between general and special private law can more generally be criticised as a basis for the choice to implement Directives within or outside the BGB.[2877]
- The implementation of the *acquis* in the German and Dutch codes should be seen against the background of efforts of national legislators to maintain the predictable, accessible and consistent development of national law.[2878] Therefore, the amendments to national laws are frequently kept to a minimum in the German and Dutch legal order, which also makes the European background of harmonised rules less clear for private parties and practitioners.
- Despite restraint in the implementation of Directives, the German legislative process has been criticised as numerous amendments have been introduced in the BGB in the implementation of the *acquis*.[2879]
- The restraint of European actors is visible in the lack of debate in the development and revision of the *acquis*, especially at the national level in the Dutch legal order. Rather than considering debate as something that can contribute to the quality of the *acquis*, the debate is organised and limited to the choices preselected by European actors,[2880] as becomes especially visible from the shortcomings in the use of consultations[2881] and impact assessments.[2882]
- Actors should more critically consider the use of techniques in the multilevel legal order, not only paying more attention to possible bottom-up techniques, but also to the combination of techniques.[2883] Notably, techniques – for example, codifications – are not used in isolation from other techniques, but alongside blanket clauses, based on general principles, studied in commentaries, developed in case law collected in databases, and further discussed in legal journals and networks. At the national level, the use of top-down techniques is often combined with bottom-up techniques, but the success of bottom-up techniques typically depends on the initiatives of non-state actors.[2884]

Shortcomings at the national and European level should not be considered separately from one another. Shortcomings at both levels decrease the chance that shortcomings in the democratic process at one level are compensated at another level. Instead, shortcomings may reinforce one another.

2877 See par. 9.2.1.
2878 See par. 9.2.1.
2879 See par. 10.2.
2880 See par. 6.2.
2881 See further par. 8.2.1.2.
2882 See further par. 8.2.2.1.
2883 See par. 7.6.
2884 See further par. 8.7.

11.5. Benefits arising from the coexistence of actors in the multilevel legal order

According to pluralist insights, the coexistence of actors may be beneficial for various reasons. Paragraph 11.5.1. will consider the development of a system of checks and balances and paragraph 11.5.2. will turn to the coexistence of national actors. Paragraph 11.5.3. will discuss the development of regulatory competition and paragraph 11.5.4. will analyse opportunities for mutual learning. Paragraph 11.5.5. will conclude by exploring opportunities for improvement.

11.5.1. Checks and balances for European private law

The case studies[2885] make clear that a system of checks and balances has not contributed to the comprehensibility of European private law. Accordingly, harmonisation has not prompted German and Dutch actors to reform national law, even if national law, especially Dutch law, shows deficiencies.[2886] Although the CJEU has prompted Dutch courts to take a more active approach to unfair clauses,[2887] this in turn has not prompted Dutch lower courts to refer many questions to the CJEU[2888] or to ensure consistency in Dutch case law. This restraint is more generally exercised, also because the BGB[2889] and the BW[2890] have been reformed relatively recently – if the law is generally regarded as problematic, national state actors may perhaps be more open to suggestions for reform.

The development of a system of checks and balances is more generally not geared towards the comprehensibility of European private law, and checks and balances may not be effective as a sufficient enforcement system has not been developed at the European level. The restraint of national state actors makes it unlikely they will alert European actors to infractions, the infringement procedure is not cost-effective, and parties in adjudication in relatively small, domestic disputes have not served as drivers for further integration.[2891]

In other areas, European initiatives have been driven by the concerns of transnational actors, making it more likely that EU initiatives prompt actors to take more note of international concerns, for example in financial law.[2892] As European actors increasingly adopt a regulatory approach, in more areas of private law, there will likely be more emphasis on the development of modes of new governance such as comitology and Guidance.[2893] Over time, these developments may put pressure on national actors to reconsider their approach to traditional legislation and pay more attention to the development of new governance at the European level.

2885 See par. 4.6.2. and 5.6.2.
2886 See par. 5.3.3.4 and 9.2.2.
2887 See par. 5.4.1.3.
2888 See par. 6.3.1.
2889 See par. 4.3.2.4. Notably, the reform did not entail amendment of the law on STCs, see par. 4.3.1.3.
2890 See par. 5.3.3.1. and 5.3.3.2.
2891 See par. 6.3.1.
2892 See par. 7.4.1.1.
2893 See par. 9.4.1.

This is not consistently the case, as is visible in the simultaneous development of banking codes by Dutch and European actors.[2894] Moreover, if EU initiatives simultaneously overlook national concerns, and diminish the scope of carefully developed national alternative regulation, they are more likely to provoke resistance than justification, especially in the German legal order that adopts a more principle-based approach than the Dutch legal order.[2895] More attractive alternatives can be found in the initiatives from transnational non-state actors, such as the ICC or EMOTA, which may indirectly ensure that the interests of foreign and international actors are taken into account.[2896]

11.5.2. The coexistence of national actors

The case studies[2897] demonstrate that the coexistence of actors may be beneficial in other ways. It became clear that the coexistence of national actors may be beneficial for responsiveness to national legal views on justice, as both German and Dutch law on STCs reflect society's ideas on justice. The relation between law and legal views on justice as well as national practice influences the way in which the law responds to legal transplants and the interest of the legislator and the courts in further harmonisation and regulatory competition. Interestingly, Dutch law on STCs in consumer contracts reflects society's legal views on justice, but the legislator has made clear that there is less need to protect businesses[2898] and has accordingly pursued regulatory competition.[2899]

In this respect, the importance of general default law in the evaluation of clauses, which reflects legal views on justice, may more generally indicate a relation between legal views on justice and national practice, and national law.[2900] The importance of private autonomy, the *Richtigkeitsgewähr* and *Fremdbestimmung* in Dutch and German contract law indicate that contract law more generally reflects legal views on justice.[2901] The differences between Dutch and German law suggest that the views on private autonomy and *Fremdbestimmung* may differ. Therefore, the coexistence of these diverging national regimes more generally benefits responsiveness. The question arises whether a lack of harmonisation in areas such as property law can similarly be traced to the relation between national property laws and national practice and legal views on justice.

2894 See par. 8.4.2.
2895 See par. 7.4.3.
2896 See previously par. 7.5.1.5. and par. 8.5.1.5.
2897 See par. 4.6.2. and 5.6.2.
2898 As reflected in articles 6:235, 236, 237 and 247 BW that limit the scope of the Dutch regime. This is also reflected in Dutch case law, see par. 6.4.3.5. See more generally par. 8.6.3.
2899 See par. 5.3.4.1.
2900 See par. 6.3.1.
2901 See par. 8.5.1.5. and 8.5.3.8.

11.5.3. *Regulatory competition*

The case studies further made clear that actors have recognised the potential of regulatory competition. Regulatory competition has however not consistently strengthened the law.

- The Dutch legislator has recognised the potential of regulatory competition.[2902] However, Dutch law shows more weaknesses than German law, even though German legislator has rejected regulatory competition in this area.[2903]
- In accordance with the idea of regulatory co-opetition, the role of other actors than national legislators is relevant. The lack of predictability and consistency in the decisions of Dutch courts may undermine the legislator's attempts at regulatory competition,[2904] whereas German case law may help the attractiveness of German law in international trade, which is, however, less visible than legislation.[2905]
- Regulatory competition has also been encouraged at the European level, for example, in the area of company law.[2906] In line with ideas of regulatory co-opetition, the success of encouraging regulatory competition depends also on both national and European actors. European initiatives for regulatory competition may be undermined if lengthy national legislative procedures overlook relevant initiatives from European actors, which renders the proposals at the national level ineffective.[2907]
- More generally, although national actors do not seem to feel forced to enter into regulatory competition in areas where they principally object to it, the development of regulatory competition in German law is defensive, and aims to prevent that German actors opt out of German law. This is also visible in the approach of the Dutch legislator that prohibits parties in domestic transactions to opt out of Dutch law. The Dutch approach has not led to innovative rules,[2908] but that does not mean this can never be the case.
- Regulatory competition may also take place between non-state actors involved in the development of alternative regulation.[2909] The German initiative on corporate social responsibility shows that the idea of international success provides actors with an additional reason to develop innovative rules.
- Innovation has also become visible in areas where regulatory competition is not as clear, for example in the German law on STCs, the area of mass settlements, the new prejudicial procedure and collectively negotiated STCs.

2902 See par. 5.3.4.1.
2903 See par. 4.3.3.1.1.
2904 See par. 9.3.3.7.
2905 See par. 9.3.3.3.
2906 See par. 10.5.2.
2907 For example, the postponed Dutch reform of company law can be seen in this light. See further par. 10.2.
2908 See par. 6.3.2.
2909 See par. 8.6. and 10.5.2.

More generally, regulatory competition may be inhibited or discouraged in fields where weaker parties may be subjected to the preferences of stronger private parties, such as consumer law or employment law.

11.5.4. Mutual learning

In the case studies, actors have recognised the potential of mutual learning, but this has not consistently benefited the law.

- The German and Dutch legislator have recognised the added value of comparative insights in codifying the law.[2910] However, the German legislator did not base the law on STCs on comparative insights, even when paying specific attention to insights from legal orders that were comparable to the German legal order. In addition, even though Dutch law was inspired by German law, it shows more shortcomings than German law.[2911]
- German and Dutch courts have recognised the added value of foreign and international materials in international cases, and both German and Dutch courts evaluate clauses in international contracts more leniently than clauses in domestic cases. However, Dutch courts have not adopted a predictable approach to foreign and international materials, and German courts exercise restraint in referring to these materials when deciding cases under international regimes.[2912]
- European actors have also recognised that actors at the national level with well-established regimes may provide valuable feedback for harmonisation initiatives, for example, in the area of unfair terms.[2913] However, the restraint of German courts and the preference of the European legislator for full harmonisation indicates that the European legislator is not similarly aware of or interested in national experiences in the revision of the Directive.

More generally, however, opportunities for mutual learning have been realised.

- National legislators have generally recognised the use of comparative law in the drafting of codifications.[2914] Interesting new initiatives such as the Dutch prejudicial procedure have also carefully taken into account insights from comparative law as well as relevant European initiatives.[2915]

2910 See pars. 4.3.1.2. and 5.3.1.
2911 See par. 5.2.
2912 See par. 6.3.3.
2913 Accordingly, the European legislator took into account German feedback of the 1990 draft for a Directive on unfair terms in consumer contracts, see further par. 10.3.2.1.
2914 See pars. 4.3.1.2. and 5.3.1.
2915 See par. 10.3.4 even if actors involved in the drafting of legislation have extensively taken into account comparative law, the needs and preferences of legal practice and relevant European developments, this does not mean that problems will not arise. The legislator may, for political reasons, choose not to develop the law in this manner.

- The interest of European actors in national initiatives may prompt national actors to anticipate harmonisation initiatives or the implementation of Directives that are not politically controversial.[2916]
- National actors may actively engage in the drafting of Directives in the hopes that measures will not diverge too much from national law, as became apparent in the German case study[2917] and the harmonisaiton of private international law.[2918] Opportunities for experimentation are created if national actors go further and revise the law before the European legislator initiates harmonisation. The introduction of national law, if it serves as a source of inspiration for the European legislator, may improve European law by enabling European actors to learn from national experiences.

11.5.5. Further opportunities for mutual learning

Both in the case studies and more generally, opportunities for further learning and possibilities for improvement have been considered.

- More interaction in the implementation of Directives may prompt national actors to consider national law more critically, and if necessary, reform outdated or unsatisfactory national law.[2919]
- More interaction would allow actors to learn more from one another. The Dutch bottom-up approach may offer insights gained from more experimentation for actors from other legal orders and at other levels.[2920] Particularly, the insight that the involvement of non-state actors in the development of binding rules may not necessarily motivate more compliance, as became apparent for the Dutch corporate governance code and the Dutch code on personal injury claims, should be carefully considered. Yet even though some initiatives, in particular, the development of Dutch law on collective redress, appear to be successful, constitutional considerations, in particular, the right to access to a judge and *Fremdbestimmung*, withhold German actors from copying these initiatives. Simultaneously, the more lenient approach of Dutch actors may be beneficial for regulatory competition between forms of alternative regulation, for example in the area of advertising or consumer sales. In addition, considering codes of conduct in disputes with regard to contracts for energy supply involving suppliers who have expressly recognised these codes, especially if the courts declare these codes binding on suppliers, may strengthen responsiveness and the experience may be interesting for other actors.

  Initiatives that are successful in some legal orders, such as the VOB in Germany, may not be successful in other legal orders, as visible in dead letter article 6:214 BW and

2916 See further par. 9.2.3.

2917 See par. 4.3.2.1.

2918 See par. 9.2.2.

2919 For example by following the WODC report on the attempted reform of Directive 93/13, which however, did not happen, see par.5.3.3.4.

2920 See pars. 6.2. and 6.4.2.

the rejection of comitology procedures in Germany. Conversely, these initiatives may inspire other actors where alternative regulation is less accepted.[2921]

- More interaction may make national actors more aware of potential inconsistencies in the *acquis* as they develop.[2922]
- More interaction might make European actors more aware of national experiences and problems in the *acquis*, enabling European actors to improve Directives and prevent future inaccessibility, inconsistency and unpredictability.[2923] Accordingly, if actors involved in the drafting of the DCFR take into account national experiences in the implementation of Directives, this could significantly contribute to the responsiveness of reformed Directives and contribute to the consistent development of the law.[2924]
- Further study on STCs in cross-border trade may reveal instances where divergences between national law, but also between the different interpretation of identical clauses may compromise the predictability of the law for foreign and international actors.
- More communication, either from more clarity at the European level or from more lobbying at the national level, may make clearer why the European Union seeks to initiate harmonisation in a particular area, which may make these initiatives less unpredictable.[2925]
- More and better interaction between courts at the national and the European level would lead to more clarity on the allocation of competences between national and European courts in the interpretation of blanket clauses.[2926]
- If judges are more consistently enabled to take into account relevant self-regulation in the interpretation of blanket clauses if actors have committed themselves to particular codes with sufficiently precise norms and sanctions,[2927] this would enhance responsiveness
- More interaction between Dutch courts would contribute to more consistent and therefore more predictable decisions.[2928]
- Consistently publishing decisions in ADR procedures would increase the predictability of decisions in these procedures for private parties and the consistency of these decisions with European and national consumer contract law,[2929] and could provide more insight in domestic consumer cases that should be taken into account in the revision of the consumer *acquis*.
- The increased use of general principles as a starting point of interaction would benefit the consistent and responsive development of harmonised law.[2930]

2921 See par. 10.10.
2922 See par. 5.6.1.
2923 See par. 10.2.1.4.
2924 See pars. 4.7.2. and 5.7.2.
2925 See par. 10.2.1.4.
2926 See pars. 4.4.1., 5.4.1.3. and 9.4.2.
2927 Particularly, in the Dutch legal order, this may enhance the effectiveness of the GBL, as well as the code of conduct on energy contracts. See further par. 8.5.3.6.
2928 See pars. 5.3.4.2.1., 5.3.4.2.2., 5.4.1.4., 5.4.2.2.
2929 See par. 5.6.3.
2930 See par. 9.5.1.

- The argument for a framework in the Dutch legal order in this book has been inspired by principles in German private law, in particular principles of private autonomy and concerns of *Fremdbestimmung*.

The national approach, visible in the case studies and more generally in the development of European private law, may stand in the way of mutual learning as comparative law or European law do not prompt actors to critically reconsider their laws[2931] and opportunities to improve the law through minimum harmonisation, or new modes of governance, for example in reinforcing codes of conduct as a means to further consumer protection throughout the Union,[2932] or through the use of model laws, are overlooked.[2933] Better impact assessments should draw more attention to these opportunities.[2934]

This book has suggested more and better interaction, in accordance with the suggestion for deliberation. Deliberation requires a further step: reconsidering the national approach both at the national and the European level. Actors should not focus on their own laws and interests, as is currently the case, but rather on the question how private law can be improved in terms of predictability, consistency, accessibility, and responsiveness. National actors should reconsider their defensive approach, which has so far not discouraged European actors. Instead, national state actors should explain carefully if and why European initiatives will not contribute to more comprehensible European private law. European actors should pay more attention to the need to preserve the predictability, accessibility, consistency, and responsiveness of private law from the perspective of national actors, to remedy the odd difference in emphasis on the quality of European private law, which was especially visible between German and European actors.[2935] This also means that the European legislator should exercise restraint and not pursue harmonisation for the sake of harmonisation.

Considering the debate on the reform of the *acquis* and the approach of actors in this debate, it may be doubted whether deliberation is likely to develop.[2936]

Various points of improvement are possible at the national level.[2937] Actors should adopt a more active approach to European initiatives, which entails:

- National actors should generally pay more attention for possible inconsistencies that may arise in the *acquis*.
- National actors should compete with one another in trying to convince the European legislator to use successful national law as a blueprint for European initiatives.[2938]

2931 See pars. 5.6.2., 6.2, and 6.3.3.
2932 See par. 8.6.3.
2933 See pars. 10.8.4., 10.10.
2934 See par. 10.2.2.
2935 See par. 4.6.1. and par. 6.2.
2936 See par. 6.2.
2937 See par. 4.6.3, par. 5.6.3, par. 6.3.3.
2938 See par. 9.2.3.

- National legislators should consider national law more critically in the light of European proposals, rather than assuming that national law is already in accordance with the Directive – initiatives for harmonisation should also be considered as an opportunity to consider whether reform is necessary.
- National legislators should also increasingly and actively involve foreign and European actors – in particular Members of the European Parliament – in the reform of the law and especially in the implementation of Directives.
- National legislators should adopt a more consistent and predictable approach to the implementation of future initiatives. Notably, an optimal approach also depends on national developments, and therefore, the use of Directives – including Directives that pursue maximum harmonisation – will generally result in fragmented approaches to harmonisation. Nevertheless, taking into account the approach of foreign legislators to the implementation of Directive may still be beneficial.
- Highest courts should more actively questions to the CJEU. Highest courts should also exercise less restraint in referring to foreign courts and international materials and develop a consistent approach to avoid unpredictability and inconsistencies with national law. In the Dutch legal order, lower courts need to take more notice of one another's decisions as well as decisions from the CJEU and the Hoge Raad.
- National actors should encourage more involvement in European legislative processes by non-state actors, possibly by issuing separate consultations, as currently visible in the English legal order, or alert national actors to consultations in prominent national networks and legal journals.

At the European level:

- The European legislator should take responses to consultations into account and indicate more clearly how responses are taken into account.[2939]
- Actors should improve the use of impact assessments.[2940]
- European actors should rely more on well-established national networks and databases rather than establishing multiple overlapping European databases.[2941]
- The improved use of consultations and impact assessments in turn entails that the European legislator considers possibilities such as the study of STCs in cross-border cases, the development of Regulations and optional regimes, the possibility to consider national and EU alternative regulation in the interpretation of blanket clauses, and collective bargaining. More use of model laws may particularly offer opportunities for mutual learning.
- Non-state actors – especially involved in the drafting of soft law – should take into account the *acquis*, overlapping sets of soft law, and national experiences in the

[2939] See par. 10.2.1.3.

[2940] See pars. 10.2.1.3. and 10.2.2.3.

[2941] See pars. 10.2.3.3. and 10.2.4.3.

implementation of the *acquis*, if it is to serve as a toolbox for European and national state actors.[2942]
- The CJEU, as well as national courts, should make more explicit when it recognises general principles and what principles effect general principles may have. More generally, general principles should serve as a starting point for interaction between courts.[2943]

These improvements should not be seen in isolation from one another. Rather, improvements and shortcomings at one level may compensate or reinforce shortcomings from actors at other levels.

11.6. Problematic or beneficial coexistence?

In accordance with insights from multilevel governance, actors have become less capable to independently ensure the predictability, consistency, accessibility and responsiveness of European private law through national techniques. Codifications are less able to contribute to the stable development of private law by constraining legislative over-enthusiasm as the aim of the European legislator to advance the internal market may prompt initiatives for harmonisation that inherently remain difficult to predict. The capability of highest national courts to maintain a course diverging from CJEU case law is undermined by lower national courts and foreign courts. As the European legislator increasingly adopts a regulatory approach, the development of new governance initiatives such as Guidance or binding model lists may diminish the extent to which blanket clauses can be interpreted in line with national practice and national default law that reflects national legal views on justice. Meanwhile, converging principles may continue to play an important role in national and European law. Although European law is market-oriented and may over time limit the development of particular rules, it does not prevent that general principles continue to play a role in the development of national law. Instead, it may leave national and European actors with leeway to develop European private law responsively and consistently.

If actors do not sufficiently recognise interdependence and interact accordingly, weaknesses in the law may be aggravated and problems may develop. This became especially visible in the Dutch legal order, where newly introduced law had to be amended repeatedly, while the lack of interaction between courts led to inconsistency and unpredictability. However, problems are not necessarily immediately visible. Instead, unpredictability may develop over a longer period, as national legislators do not take a predictable approach to the implementation of the *acquis*. A lack of predictability may also develop as national courts are reluctant to refer questions to the CJEU on the interpretation of ambiguous terms or blanket clauses, especially if blanket clauses play a central role in national private law, or if courts come across questions on the interpretation of harmonised law in small, domestic cases that are relatively straightforward. Problems

2942 See par. 4.7.2. and 5.7.2.

2943 See par. 9.5.2.

of inconsistency and unpredictability in European measures may in turn motivate national legislators and courts to adopt restraint in the implementation and application of the *acquis*, and a circle of non-interaction may develop as national experiences are not considered at the European level and subsequently not considered in the revision of the *acquis*. This may eventually diminish the responsive development of the *acquis*.

In accordance with pluralist arguments, the coexistence of actors has proven beneficial for various reasons. In highly internationalised areas of law, the development of European law may reflect concerns of transnational actors, which is beneficial for responsiveness to the needs and preferences of foreign and international actors. However, these initiatives simultaneously ignore fundamental objections, for example with regard to one-sided legislation, that are most clearly visible in the German legal order. These initiatives may therefore provoke resistance rather than justification. Non-state actors' initiatives that do not ignore these fundamental concerns have proven more successful.

Simultaneously, the case studies and the role of private autonomy, the *Richtigkeitsgewähr* and *Fremdbestimmung* in national contract law support the conclusion that general national private law may reflect national legal views on justice and the coexistence of national regimes strengthens responsiveness to national practice and national legal views on justice.

The relationship between legal views on justice and national law may stand in the way of regulatory competition. The success of regulatory competition does not only depend on the cooperation between relevant national and European state and non-state actors, in line with ideas of regulatory co-opetition. It also depends on whether actors have adopted a defensive approach or whether they strive to develop the best possible rules, as visible in initiatives of non-state actors. As such, regulatory competition provides actors with an extra incentive to develop innovative rules, but innovation has also developed through experimentation and mutual learning, in the absence of competition. Although mutual learning does not have to result in optimal results, as reflected in the Dutch law on STCs, it has led to interesting initiatives, such as the new Dutch prejudicial procedure. In this respect, the Dutch regime with its bottom-up approach to alternative regulation has allowed for more experimentation than the German legal order, and accordingly, successful instances of alternative regulation, such as the law on mass settlements and collectively negotiated STCs have been developed. Simultaneously, the German framework has also not stood in the way of successful instances of self-regulation, but the more top-down approach in the German legal order means that fewer instances of weak alternative regulation, such as the code on the compensation for personal injuries or social corporate responsibility, or codes of conduct for energy suppliers, were allowed to continue unsuccessfully, as has been permitted in the Dutch legal order.

Further opportunities for learning remain, not only with regard to interesting new forms of alternative regulation but also with regard to the development of a more consistent approach to the role of state and non-state actors in the development of European private law, based on principles of private autonomy and concerns of *Fremdbestimmung*. Preventing *Fremdbestimmung* offers a convincing justification for the important role of state actors, but the frameworks defended in this book do not stand in the way of a more prominent role of non-state actors. Both under the German framework and under Dutch law, there are arguments to leave the development of rules to non-state rather than state actors.

The use of additional and alternative techniques in the development of European private law should help to foster deliberation between interdependent actors, which should create more opportunities for mutual learning, which can be beneficial for European private law. However, as both national and European actors have adopted a national approach to the development of European law, they have refused to critically consider national law and they have overlooked these possibilities. As the role of state and non-state actors continues to change, a more consistent approach to the role of state and non-state actors and the correspondent development of additional and alternative techniques has become necessary. In this respect, national and European actors should adopt an approach in accordance with principles of private autonomy and concerns of *Fremdbestimmung*, based on mutual respect.

BIBLIOGRAPHY

K. Adomeit, 'Die gestärte Vertragsparität – ein Trugbild', *NJW* 1994, p. 2468.

A.J. Akkermans, 'Beter recht door herziening van ons beeld van de herkomst van rechtsnormen', *NTBR* 2011, 72.

A.J. Akkermans et al, *Slachtoffers en aansprakelijkheid: Een onderzoek naar behoeften, verwachtingen en ervaringen van slachtoffers en hun naasten met betrekking tot het civiele aansprakelijkheidsrecht, Deel II*, WODC: Amsterdam 2008, available at http://wodc.nl/onderzoeksdatabase/affectieschade.aspx.

B. Akkermans, E. Ramaekers, 'Free movement of goods and property law', *ELJ* 2013, p. 237.

G. Alpa, 'Party autonomy and freedom of contract today', *ELBRev* 2010, p. 135.

G. Alpa, 'European Community resolutions and the codification of "private law"', *ERPL* 2000, p. 328.

A.G.F. Ancery, 'Toetsing van oneerlijke bedingen: de fictieve toetsing op de kaart?', *MvV* 2014, 104.

A.G.F. Ancery, *Ambtshalve toepassing van EU recht*, Deventer: Kluwer 2012.

A.G.F. Ancery, C.M.D.S. Pavillon, 'Processuele aspecten van reflexwerking van consumentenrecht', *WPNR* (7026) 2014.

Aristotle, *Nichomean Ethics*, through http://classics.mit.edu/Aristotle/nicomachaen.html, Book V.

Aristotle, *Politics*, Book 3, section 1280a, available at www.perseus.tufts.edu.

K. Armstrong, 'Rediscovering civil society: The European Union and the White Paper on Governance', *ELJ* 2002, p. 116.

A. Arnull, 'Judicial dialogue in the European Union', in: J. Dickson, P. Eleftheriadis (eds.), *Philosophical foundations of European Union law*, Oxford: OUP 2012, p. 113.

W.D.H. Asser, H.A. Groen, J.B.M. Vranken, I.N. Tzankova, *Uitgebalanceerd. Eindrapport fundamentele herbezinning Nederlands burgerlijk procesrecht*, The Hague: BJU 2006.

Association de Henri Capitant des Amis de la Culture Juridique Française, Société de Législation Comparé (ed.), *European contract law – Materials for a Common Frame of reference: Terminology,Guiding Principles, Model Rules*, München: Sellier 2008.

P.S. Atiyah, 'Pragmatism and theory in English law', *Hamlyn Lectures* 1987.

P.S. Atiyah, 'Common law and statute law', *MLR* 1985, p. 5.

P.S. Atiyah, *Promises, morals, and the law*, Oxford: Clarendon 1982.

S. Augenhofer, 'A European Civil law – for whom and what should it include? Reflections on the scope and application of a future European legal instrument', *ERCL* 2011, p. 211.

S. Augsberg, *Rechtsetzung zwischen Staat und Gesellschaft*, Berlin: Duncker & Humblot 2001.

J. Austin, *The providence of jurisprudence determined*, London: Murray 1861.
M. Avbelj, J. Komárek (eds.), *Four visions of constitutional pluralism*, EUI Working Paper 2008/21
B. Baarsma et al, *Zelf doen? Inventarisatie van zelfreguleringsinstrumenten*, SEO Report 664, 2003.
I. Bache, M. V. Flinders, 'Themes and issues in multilevel governance', in: I. Bache, M. V. Flinders (eds), *Multilevel governance*, Oxford: OUP 2004, p. 3.
G. Bachmann, 'Optionsmodelle im Privatrecht', *JZ* 2008, p. 11.
G. Bachmann, *Private Ordnung, Grundlagen ziviler Regelsetzung*, Tübingen: Mohr Siebeck 2006.
F. Bacon, *Treatise on universal justice or the foundations of equity*, by aphorisms, from: *The works of Francis Bacon*, 1889, Yale, aphorism 8.
K.U. Bahnsen, 'AGB-Kontrolle bei den Allgemeinen Deutschen Spediteurbedingungen', *Transportrecht* 2010, p. 19.
K. Baier, *Europäische Verbraucherverträge und missbräuchliche Klauseln, die Umsetzung der Richtlinie 93 /13 /EWG über missbräuchliche Klauseln in Verbraucherverträgen in Deutschland, Italien, England und Frankreich*, Hamburg: Kovač 2004.
H.J. Bakker, R.H.C. Jongeneel, 'Een rechtlijnige richtlijn', *TvC* 1992, p. 7.
J.M. Barendrecht, *Recht als model van rechtvaardigheid*, Deventer: Kluwer 1992.
R. Barnett, 'A consent theory of contract', *Columbia Law Review* 1986, p. 269.
J. Basedow, 'Ende des 28. Modells? – Das Bundesverfassungsgericht und das europäische Wirtschaftsprivatrecht', *EuZW* 2010, p. 41.
J. Basedow 'Der Europäische Gerichtshof und die Klauselrichtlinie 93/13 – Der verweigerte Dialog', in: G. Müller et al. (eds.), *Festschrift für Günter Hirsch zum 65. Geburtstag*, München: Beck 2008, p. 51.
J. Basedow, 'The state's private law and the economy – commercial law as an amalgam of public and private rulemaking', *American Journal of Comparative Law* 2008, p. 703.
J. Basedow, 'Freedom of contract in the European Union', *ERPL* 2008, p. 904–905, 916.
J. Basedow, 'Der Bundesgerichtshof, seine Rechtsanwälte und die Verantwortung für das europäische Privatrecht', in: G. Pfeiffer, J. Kummer, S. Scheuch (eds.), *Festschrift für Hans Erich Brandner zum 70. Geburtstag*, Köln: Schmidt 1996, p. 675.
S. Basse, *Gemeinsame Vergütungsregeln im Urhebervertragsrecht*, Berlin: Logos 2007.
E. Bauw, 'Ruim baan voor de consument. Achtergronden en gevolgen van de verhoging van de competentiegrens van de kantonrechter', *TvC* 2010, p. 256.
H. Beale, 'Finding the remaining traps instead of unifying contract law', in: S. Grundmann, J. Stuyck (eds.), *An academic Green Paper on European contract law*, The Hague: KLI 2002, p. 67.
F. Becker, 'Die Reichweite der AGB-Inhaltskontrolle im unternehmerischen Geschäftsverkehr', *JZ* 2010, p. 1098.
J. Bentham, *Principles of the Civil Code*, in: J. Bowring (ed.), *The Works of Jeremy Bentham, vol. 1 (Principles of Morals and Legislation, Fragment on Government, Civil Code, Penal Law)*, Chapter XIVV, available at http://oll.libertyfund.org/index.php?option=com_staticxt&staticfile=show.php?person=172&Itemid=99999999.
K.P. Berger, 'Für eine Reform des AGB-Rechts im Unternehmerverkehr', *NJW* 2010, p. 466.
K.P. Berger, *The creeping codification of the lex mercatoria*, Alphen aan den Rijn: KLI 2010, p. 124
K.P. Berger, 'Abschied von Privatautonomie im unternehmerischen Geschäftsverkehr?', *ZIP* 2006, p. 2149.

K.P. Berger, 'Die Einbeziehung von AGB in internationalen Kaufverträge', in: K.P. Berger, N. Horn (eds.), *Zivil- und Wirtschaftsrecht im europäischen und globalen Kontext, Festschrift für Norbert Horn zum 70. Geburtstag*, Berlin: De Gruyter 2006, p. 4.

P.S. Berman, 'Global legal pluralism', *Southern California Law Review* 2007, p. 1155.

U. Bernitz, 'The Commission's Communications and standard contract terms', in: S. Vogenauer, S. Weatherill (eds.), *The harmonisation of European contract law*, Oxford: Hart 2006, p. 186.

L. Bernstein, 'An (un)common frame of reference: An American perspective on the jurisprudence of the CESL', *CMLRev* 2013, p. 169.

Ch.E. Bethlem, 'Beslechting van consumentengeschillen: hoe alternatief zijn de alternatieven?', *TvC* 2006, p. 1.

Lord Bingham of Cornhill, 'The rule of law', *Sir David Williams Lecture*, Cambridge 2006, p. 6.

P. Birks, The need for the Institutes in England, *Zeitschrift der Savigny-Stiftung für Rechtsgeschichte, Romanistische Abteilung* 1991, p. 711.

B. Bix, *Jurisprudence: Theory and context*, Durham: Carolina Academic Press 2006, 4th ed.

J. Black, 'Proceduralizing Regulation: Part I', *Oxford Journal of Legal Studies* 2000, p. 597.

U. Blaurock, 'Wirtschaft und Rechtsordnung', U. Blaurock, N. Goldschmidt, A. Hollerbach (eds.), *Das selbstgeschaffene Recht der Wirtschaft. Zum Gedenken an Hans Großmann-Doerth (1894–1944)*, Tübingen: Mohr Siebeck 2005, p. 70.

A.R. Bloembergen, 'De eenheid van het recht', in: A.R. Bloembergen, *Bloembergens werk*, Deventer: Kluwer 1992, p. 559.

S. Borrás, B. Greve, 'Concluding remarks: New method or just cheap talk?', *JEPP* 2004, p. 332.

U.P. Börstinghaus, C. Börstinghaus, 'Qualifizierte Mietspiegel in der Praxis – Eine empirische Untersuchung über Akzeptanz und praktische Umsetzung des neuen Rechtsinstruments', *NZM* 2003, p. 383.

U.P. Börstinghaus, 'Der qualifizierte Mietspiegel – Die Geschichte einer „Verschlimmbesserung"', *NZM* 2000, p. 1088.

P.P.T. Bovend'Eert, 'De rechter als wetgever: uniforme rechtstoepassing in rechtersregelingen vanuit staatsrechtelijk perspectief', *Regelmaat* 2010, p. 17.

P.P.T. Bovend'Eert, 'Wetgever, rechter en rechtsvorming. Partners in the business of law?', *RM Themis* 2009, p. 145.

H.E. Brandner, 'Wege und Zielvorstellungen auf dem Gebiet der Allgemeinen Geschäftsbedingungen', *JZ* 1973, p. 613.

H.E. Brandner, P. Ulmer, 'EG-Richtlinie über mißbräuchliche Klauseln in Verbraucherverträgen. Kritische Bemerkungen zum Vorschlag der EG-Kommission', *BB* 1991, p. 701.

H.E. Brandner, 'Die Rechtsprechung der BGH-Senate zum AGB-Gesetz', in: H. Heinrichs, W. Löwe, P. Ulmer (eds.), *Zehn Jahre AGB-Gesetz*, Köln: Kommunikationsforum Recht 1987, p. 50.

S. Braun, 'Die Wahl-Zugewinngemeinschaft: Ein neuer Güterstand im deutschen (und französischen) Recht', *MittBayNot* 2012, p. 89.

J. Brinkhof, *De Europese uitdaging voor rechtspraak, rechtswetenschap en onderwijs* (valedictory address Utrecht), Amsterdam: DeLex 2010.

C.J.H. Brunner, *De normen van het privaatrecht* (lecture Groningen), Deventer: Kluwer 1996.

P. Buck-Heeb, A. Dieckmann, *Selbstregulierung im Privatrecht*, Tübingen: Mohr Siebeck 2010.

W.D. Budde, E. Steubner, 'Normsetzungsbefugnis eines deutschen Standard Setting Body', *DStR* 1998, p. 1181.

Bundesminister der Justiz, 'Einleitung', in: Bundesminister der Justiz (ed.), *Vorschläge und Gutachten zur Überarbeitung des Schuldrecht*, Vol. I, Köln: Bundesanzeiger 1981, p. I.

D. Busch, 'The Principles of European Contract Law before the Supreme Court of The Netherlands', *ZEuP* 2008, p. 549.

D. Busch et al, (eds.) *The Principles of European Contract Law and Dutch law: A Commentary*, Nijmegen: Ars Aequi Libri 2002.

F. Bydlinski, 'Kontrahierungszwang', *AcP* 1980, p. 1.

F. Cafaggi, 'Self-regulation in European contract law', *EJLS* 2007, 1.

F. Cafaggi, 'Rethinking private regulation in European regulatory space', in: F. Cafaggi (ed.), *Reframing self-regulation in European private law*, Alphen aan den Rijn: KLI 2006, p. 10.

F. Cafaggi, 'Introduction' in F. Cafaggi (ed.), *The institutional framework of European private law*, Oxford: OUP 2006, p. 16–17.

F. Cafaggi, H. Muir-Watt, 'Introduction', in: F. Cafaggi, H. Muir-Watt (eds.), *Making European private law: Governance design*, Cheltenham: Elgar 2008, p. 5.

C.-W. Canaris, 'Wandlungen des Schuldvertragsrechts – Tendenzen zu seiner "Marerialisierung"', *AcP* 2000, p. 273.

C.-W. Canaris, 'Der EuGH als zukünftige privatrechtliche Superrevisionsinstanz?', *EuZW* 1994, p. 417.

C.-W. Canaris, *Systemdenken und Systembegriff in Jurisprudenz*, Berlin: Duncker und Humblot 1983, 2nd ed.

T. Cardoso Ribeiro, *Naar een zichtbaar effectieve wisselwerking tussen beleid en uitvoering*, The Hague 28 March 2007, available at www.eerstekamer.nl.

J. Cartwright, '"Choice is good". Really?', *ERCL* 2011, p. 344.

J. Cartwright et al., 'Grensoverschrijdend contracteren? Dat lossen we zelf wel op', *NJB* 2011, p. 1250.

D. Caruso, 'Private law in the age of state-making and globalization', *New York Journal of International Law and Politics* 2006, p. 3.

A.G. Castermans, 'Multiple choice: Nationaal recht in het DCFR', in: M.W. Hesselink et al (eds.), *Het Groenboek Europees contractenrecht: naar een optioneel instrument?*, The Hague: BJU 2011, p. 33.

A.G. Castermans, 'Towards a European contract law through social dialogue', *ERCL* 2011, p. 366.

C. Cauffman, M. Faure, T. Hartlief, *Harmonisatie van het contractenrecht in Europa: consequenties voor Nederland*, Advice 26 March 2009, WODC.

M.D. Chalmers, 'Codification of mercantile law', *LQR* 1903, p. 14.

O.O. Cherednychenko, 'Freedom of contract in the post-crisis era: Quo vadis?', *ERCL* 2014, p. 392.

O.O. Cherednychenko, 'Public supervision over private relationships: Towards European Supervision Private Law?', *ERPL* 2014, p. 37.

O.O. Cherednychenko, *Fundamental rights, contract law and the protection of the weaker party: a comparative analysis of the constitutionalisation of contract Law, with emphasis on risky financial transactions*, München: Sellier 2007.

O.O. Cherednychenko, 'Zorgplichten bij financiële contracten: Is er nog een wezenlijke rol voor het contractenrecht weggelegd?', *Contracteren* 2007, p. 88.

D. Coester-Waltjen, 'Die Inhaltskontrolle von Verträgen außerhalb des AGBG', *AcP* 1990, p. 20.

J. Cohen, C. Sabel, 'Directly-deliberative polyarchy', *ELJ* 1997, p. 313.

H. Collins, 'Governance implications for the European Union of the changing character of private law', in: F. Cafaggi, H. Muir-Watt (eds.), *Making European private law: Governance design*, Cheltenham: Elgar 2008, p. 270

H. Collins, *The European Civil Code. The Way Forward*, Cambridge: Cambridge University Press 2008.

H. Collins, 'The alchemy of deriving general principles of contract law from European legislation: In search of the philosopher's stone', *ERCL* 2006, p. 221.

H. Collins, 'The freedom to circulate documents: regulating contracts in Europe', *ELJ* 2004, p. 798.

H. Collins, 'Transaction costs and subsidiarity in European contract law', in: S. Grundmann, J. Stuyck (eds.), *An academic Green Paper on European contract law*, The Hague: KLI 2002, p. 269.

H. Collins, 'European private law and the cultural identity of states', *ERPL* 1995, p. 362.

A. Colombi Ciacchi, 'Freedom of contract as freedom from unconscionable contracts', in: M. Kenny, J. Devenny, L.F. O'Mahoney (eds.), *Unconscionability in European private financial transactions*, Cambridge: CUP 2010, p. 12.

A. Colombi Ciacchi, 'Private autonomy as a fundamental right in the European Union', *ERCL* 2010, p. 303.

Commissie voor Consumentenaangelegenheden, *Advies inzake het vraagstuk van de toepassing van standaardvoorwaarden bij transacties met de consument*, The Hague: SER 1978.

Commissie voor Consumentenaangelegenheden, *Oneerlijke bedingen in consumentenovereenkomsten*, advice 91/11, 30 May 1991, The Hague: SER 1991.

Commissie voor Consumentenaangelegenheden, *Consumentenrechten in de interne markt*, advice 09/05, 17 June 2009, available at www.ser.nl/~/media/DB_Adviezen/2000_2009/2009/b27871.ashx

G. Cordero Moss, 'The function of letters of intent and their recognition in modern legal systems', in: R. Schulze (ed.), *New features in European contract law*, München: Sellier 2007, p. 139.

E. Clive, 'European contract law feasibility study', *European private law news*, 11 May 2011, available at www.law.ed.ac.uk/cpln/blogentry.aspx?blogentryref=8658.

G. Cromme, 'Vorwort Deutscher Corporate Governance Kodex', 2002, available at www.corporate-governance-code.de/ger/download/DCG_vorwort_D200202.pdf.

H. Cullen, E. Campbell, 'The future of social policy-making in the European Union', in: P. Craig, C. Harlow (eds.), *Lawmaking in the European Union*, The Hague: KLI 1998, p. 275.

D. Curtin, 'Emerging institutional parameters and organised difference in the European Union', in: B. de Witte, D. Hanf, E. de Vos (eds.), *The many faces of differentiation in EU law*, Antwerp: Intersentia 2001, p. 347.

R. Damm, 'Verbraucherrechtliche Sondergesetzgebung und Privatrechtssystem', *JZ* 1978, p. 175–176.

J.J. Dammingh, 'Non-conformiteit en de NVM-koopakte', *TvC* 2009–3, p. 120.

G. Danneman, S. Ferreri, M. Graziadei, 'Language and terminology', in: Ch. Twigg-Flessner (ed.), *Cambridge companion to European Union private law*, Cambridge: CUP 2010, p. 70.

G. Danneman, S. Vogenauer (eds.), *The Common European Sales Law in context*, Oxford: OUP 2013.

B. Dauner-Lieb, C. Axer, 'Quo vadis AGB-Kontrolle im unternehmerischen Geschäftsverkehr?', *ZIP* 2010, p. 309.

G. Davies, 'Freedom of contract and the horizontal effect of free movement law', in: D. Leczykiewicz, S. Weatherill (eds.), *The involvement of EU law in private relationships*, Oxford: Hart 2013, p. 53.

C. de la Porte, P. Nanz, 'The OMC – a deliberative-democratic mode of governance? The cases of employment and pensions', *JEPP* 2004, p. 270–271.

S. de la Rosa, 'The Open Method of Coordination in new Member States – the perspectives for its use as a tool of soft law', *ELJ* 2005, p. 627.

F. de Ly, 'Het wetsvoorstel Modernisering van het arbitragerecht en de internationale arbitrage', TvA 2013, 38.

F. de Ly, *International business law and lex mercatoria*, North Holland: The Hague 1992.

G. de Minico, 'A Hard look at self-regulation in the U.K.', *ELBR* 2006, p. 201.

V.P.G. de Serière, '"Naar herstel van vertrouwen." Het rapport van de Adviescommissie Toekomst Banken', *Ondernemingsrecht* 2009, 83.

B. de Sousa Santos, 'Law: A map of misreading. Toward a postmodern conception of law', *Journal of Law and Society* 1987, p. 298,

G.P.J. de Vries, 'Paal en perk aan bedingen ter stilzwijgende verlenging van consumentenovereenkomsten, maar hoe?', *TvC* 2007, p. 122.

S.A. de Vries, *Tensions within the internal market – the functioning of the internal market and the development of horizontal and flanking policies*, Groningen: Europa Law Publishing 2006.

L. Del Duca, 'Developing global transnational harmonization procedures for the twenty-first century: The accelerating pace of common and civil law convergence', 42 *Texas International Law Journal* 2006–2007, p. 658.

M. Delmas-Marty, *Ordering pluralism, A conceptual framework for understanding the transnational world*, Oxford: Hart 2009

W. Devroe, 'Impact van door het Europees Hof van Justitie ontwikkelde algemene beginselen op privaatrechtelijke verhoudingen', in: A.S. Hartkamp, C.H. Sieburgh, L.A.D. Keus (eds.), *De invloed van het Europese recht op het Nederlandse privaatrecht I*, Deventer: Kluwer 2007, p. 188.

U. Di Fabio, *Das Recht offener Staaten*, Tübingen: Mohr Siebeck 1998.

U. Di Fabio, 'Verlust der Steuerungskraft klassischer Rechtsquellen', *NZS* 1998, p. 450.

U. Di Fabio, 'Selbstverpflichtungen der Wirtschaft – Grenzgänger zwischen Freiheit und Zwang', *JZ* 1997, p. 970.

A. Diamond, 'Codification of the law of contract', *MLR* 1968, p. 861.

Sir John Davies, preface to *Le Pimer Report des Cases en Ireland*, 1615

U. Diederichsen, 'Das Bundesverfassungsgericht als oberstes Zivilgericht – ein Lehrstück der juristischen Methodenlehre', *AcP* 1998, p. 171.

U. Diederichsen, *Die Flucht des Gesetzgebers aus der politische Verantwortung im Zivilrecht*, Karlsruhe: Müller 1974.

N. Dietrich, *Der Deutsche Presserat*, Baden Baden: Nomos 2002.

M. Dobler, S. Hettich, 'Geplante Änderungen der Rahmenkonzepte von IASB und FASB – Konzeption, Vergleich, Würdigung', *IRZ* 2007, p. 29.

C. Donnelly, 'The response of English public law to private actors in public governance', in: M. Ruffert (ed.), *The public-private law divide: Potential for transformation?*, Cambridge: CUP 2009, p. 169.

W. Doralt, 'Strukturelle Schwächen in der Europäisierung des Privatrechts', *RabelsZ* 2011, p. 260.

W. Doralt, 'The Optional European Contract Law and why success or failure may depend on scope rather than substance', *Max Planck Private Law Research Paper* 2011.

H. Dörner, 'Die Integration des Verbraucherrechts in das BGB', in: R. Schulze, H. Schulte-Nölke (eds.), *Die Schuldrechtsreform vor dem Hintergrund des Gemeinschaftsrechts*, Tübingen: Mohr Siebeck 2001, p. 178.

C.E. Drion, 'Een pamflet voor het fundamenteel op de schop nemen van onze regelgeving over algemene voorwaarden', *Contracteren* 2007, p. 3.

H. Drion, 'Het rechtszekerheidsargument', in: H. Drion et al., (eds.), *De hanteerbaarheid van het recht*, Zwolle: Tjeenk Willink 1981, p. 1.

C.E. du Perron, *Overeenkomst en derden*, Deventer: Kluwer 1999.

F.J. Düwell, 'Die gerichtliche Überprüfung der Allgemeinverbindlicherklärung von Tarifverträgen', *NZA-Beilage* 2011, p. 80.

R. Dworkin, *Law's empire*, Cambridge, Mass.: Harvard University Press 1986.

R. Dworkin, *Taking rights seriously*, London: Duckworth 1977.

H. Eidenmüller, 'Recht als Produkt', *JZ* 2009, p. 641

H. Eidenmüller, 'Party autonomy, distributive justice and the conclusion of contracts in the DCFR', *ERCL* 2009, p. 109.

H. Eidenmüller et al, 'Towards a revision of the consumer-*acquis*', *CMLR* 2011, p. 1077.

Ph. Eijlander, 'Possibilities and constraints in the use of self-regulation and co-regulation in legislative policy: Experiences in The Netherlands – Lessons to be learned for the EU?', *EJCL* 2005, p. 3.

J.E. Emaus, 'Rechten, beginselen en horizontale directe werking van de grondrechten uit het EU-Handvest ', *NTBR* 2015, 10.

H.A. Engelhard, 'Zu den Aufgaben einer Kommission für die Überarbeitung des Schuldrechts', *NJW* 1984, p. 1201.

W. Ernst, 'Zum Kommissionsentwurf für eine Schuldrechtsreform', *NJW* 1994, p. 2179.

W. Ernst, B. Gsell, 'Kaufrechtslinie und BGB', *ZIP* 2000, p. 1410.

J. Esser, 'Gesetzesrationalität im Kodifikationszeitalter und heute', in: H.-J. Vogel, J. Esser, *Recht und Staat im Geschichte und Gegenwart, 100 Jahre oberste deutsche Justizbehörde*, Tübingen: Mohr Siebeck 1977, p. 13.

J. Esser, *Grundsatz und Norm in der richterlichen Fortbildung des Privatrechts*, Tübingen: Mohr Siebeck 1956, reprinted 1990.

D.C. Esty, D. Geradin, 'Regulatory co-opetition', *Journal of International Economic Law* 2000, p. 235.

European Commission, 'Have a bigger say in European policy-making: Commission extends public consultations to twelve weeks and creates new alert service', Press Release European Commission 3 January 2012, http://europa.eu/rapid/pressReleasesAction.do?reference=IP/12/1&format=HTML&aged=0&language=EN&guiLanguage=en.

European Commission, *Green Paper on policy options for progress towards a European contract law for businesses and consumers*, COM (2010) 348 final.

European Commission, *Communication of the Commission, a Europe of results – applying Community law*, COM (2007), 502 final.

European Commission, *Green Paper on the Review of the consumer acquis*, COM (2006) 744 final.

European Commission, *First annual progress report on European contract law and the acquis review*, COM (2005) 456, final.

European Commission, *European Contract Law and the revision of the acquis: the way forward*, COM (2004) 651 final.
European Commission, *Modernising company law and enhancing corporate governance in the European Union – a plan to move forward*, COM (2003) 284 final.
European Commission, *A more coherent European contract law. An Action Plan*, COM (2003) 68 final.
European Commission, *Taking stock of five years of the European Employment Strategy*, COM (2002) 416 final.
European Commission, *The European social dialogue, a force for innovation and change*, COM (2002) 341 final.
European Commission, *Communication from the Commission on impact assessment*, COM (2002) 276 final.
European Commission, *European governance, a white paper*, COM (2001) 428 final.
European Commission, *Communication from the Commission to the Council and the European Parliament on European contract law*, COM (2001) 398 final.
European Commission, *Report on the application of article 17 of Council Directive on the coordination of the laws of the Member states relating to self-employed commercial agents*, COM (96) 364 final.
Expert Group, *A European contract law for consumers and businesses: Publication of the results of the feasibility study carried out by the Expert Group on European contract law for stakeholders' and legal practitioners' feedback*, available at http://ec.europa.eu/justice/contract/_les/feasibility_study_final.pdf.
N.E.D. Faber, R.G.J. Nowak, 'Hoezo wetgevingskwaliteit?', *NJB* 2001, 12.
L. Fastrich, *Richterliche Inhaltskontrolle im Privatrecht*, München: Beck 1992.
B. Fauvarque-Cosson, 'EU contract law through and beyond pluralism', in: L. Niglia (ed.), *Pluralism and European private law*, Oxford: Hart 2013, p. 95.
B. Fauvarque-Cosson, M. Behar-Touchais, *Implementation of optional instruments throughout the Union*, Study January 2012, available at www.europarl.europa.eu/RegData/etudes/etudes/join/2012/462425/IPOL-JURI_ET%282012%29462425_EN.pdf.
S. Ferreri, 'General report: Sources of transnational law', *ERPL* 2012, p. 9.
K.-H. Fezer, 'Diskriminierende Werbung – Das Menschenbild der Verfassung', *JZ* 1998, p. 265.
W. Fikentscher, *Methoden des Rechts in vergleichenden Darstellung, Teil IV: Dogmatischer Teil, Anhang*, Tübingen: Mohr Siebeck 1977.
E.O.H.P. Florijn, *Ontstaan en ontwikkeling van het nieuwe Burgerlijk Wetboek*, Maastricht: UPM 1994.
W. Flume, 'Vom Beruf unserer Zeit zur Gesetzgebung', *ZIP* 2000, p. 1427.
W. Flume, 'Rechtsgeschaft und Privatautonomie', in: E. von Caemmerer, E. Friesenhahn, R. Lange (eds.), *Hundert Jahre deutsches Rechtsleben, Festschrift zum hundertjährigen Bestehen des deutschen Juristentages, I*, Karlsruhe: Muller 1960, p. 101, 136.
M. Fontaine, F. de Ly, *Drafting international contracts: An analysis of contracts clauses*, Leiden/Boston: Nijhoff 2009.
A.D.M. Forte, 'If it ain't broke, don't fix it: On not codifying commercial law', in: H.L. MacQueen (ed.), *Scots law into the 21st century*, Edinburgh: Sweet & Maxwell 1996, p. 93–94.
A.Ch.H. Franken, 'Experts en hun gedragsregels', *AV & S* 2004, 4.

N. Frenk, 'Ambtshalve toetsing van dwingend Europees consumentenrecht: gevolgen van het arrest van het Europese Hof van Justitie van 27 juni 2000 voor het Burgerlijk Wetboek', *WPNR* 6431 (2001).

N. Frenk, A.M. Wolffram-van Doorn, 'Het voorontwerp prejudiciële vragen aan de Hoge Raad', *RM Themis* 2009, 162.

K. Frey, 'Wie ändert sich das AGB-Gesetz?', *ZIP* 1993, p. 579.

B.S. Frey, R. Eichenberger, *The New Democratic Federalism for Europe. Functional, Overlapping, and Competing Jurisdictions*, Cheltenham: Elgar 1999.

Ch. Fried, *Contract as promise: A theory of contractual obligation*, Cambridge, Mass.: Harvard University Press 1981.

F. Frind, 'Der Einfluss von Selbstregularien der Insolvenzverwalter-Zusammenschlüsse bei der Auswahl, Aufsicht über und der Entlassung von Insolvenzverwaltern', *NZI* 2011, p. 785.

L.L. Fuller, *The morality of law*, London: Yale University Press 1973, 9th ed.

G. Gandolfi, *Code européen des contracts/Avant-projet, Livre premier*, Milan: Giuffrè 2001.

O. Gerstenberg, 'From "democratic deficit" to "justice deficit"?', in: D. Kochenov, G. de Búrca (eds.), *Europe's justice deficit?*, Oxford: Hart 2015, p. 70.

O. Gerstenberg, 'Private law and the new European constitutional settlement', *ELJ* 2004, p. 766.

M. Geschwandtener, R. Bornemann, 'Girokonto für jedermann – Vertragsabschlussfreiheit, Selbstregulierung oder gesetzlicher Zwang?', *NJW* 2007, p. 1254.

Gesellschaft für Rechtsvergleichung, *Richterliche Kontrolle von AGB*, Frankfurt am Main: Metzner 1968.

I. Giesen, 'Wie hoedt het privaatrecht?', *NTBR* 2014, 26.

I. Giesen, 'De omgang met en handhaving van "meervoudigheid van maatschappelijke normstelsels"', *WPNR* 6772 (2008).

I. Giesen, 'Alternatieve regelgeving in privaatrechtelijke verhoudingen', in: *Alternatieve regelgeving, Handelingen Nederlandse Juristen Vereniging* 2007-I, Deventer: Kluwer 2007, p. 67.

I. Giesen, H.N. Schelhaas, 'Samenwerking bij rechtsvorming', *AA* 2006, p. 159.

P. Gilles, 'Das Gesetz über den Widerruf von Haustürgeschäften und ähnlichen Geschäften – Anmerkungen zum jüngsten Verbraucherschutzsondergesetz im Zivilrecht unter Berücksichtigung seines rechtspolitischen Gesamtkontextes', *NJW* 1986, p. 1135.

Lord Goff of Chievely, 'The future of the common law', *International and Comparative Law Quarterly* 1997, p. 753.

Lord Goff of Chievely, 'The search for principle', *Maccabean lecture on Jurisprudence, Proceedings of the British Academy* 1984.

J. Gordley, *Foundations of private law*, Oxford: OUP 2006.

E. Gottschalck, 'Neues zur Abgrenzung zwischen AGB und Individualabrede', *NJW* 2005, p. 2493.

R. Goode, 'International Restatements of contract and English contract law', *Uniform Law Review* 1997, p. 231.

M. Góra, Z. Mach (eds.), *Collective identity and democracy, The impact of EU enlargement*, RECON Report 12, Oslo: October 2010, available at www.reconproject.eu/main.php/RECONReport1210.pdf?fileitem=4472889.

F. Graf von Westphalen, 'AGB-Recht im Jahre 2004', *NJW* 2005, p. 1987.

F. Graf von Westphalen, 'Das Verbot von Nr. 1b des Anhangs zur EG-Klauselrichtlinie 93/13/EWG', *ZGS* 2004, p. 467.

F. Graf von Westphalen, 'AGB-Recht ins BGB – Eine erste "Bestandsaufnahme"', *NJW* 2002, p. 18.

F. Graf von Westphalen, '30 Jahre AGB-Recht - Eine Erfolgsbilanz', *ZIP* 2007, p. 149.

F. Gras, *De sociale werkelijkheid van het standaard-kontrakt: een rechtssociologisch onderzoek*, Amsterdam: Kobra 1979.

J. Griffiths, 'What is legal pluralism?', *Journal of Legal Pluralism* 1986, p. 1.

H. Großmann-Doerth, 'Selbstgeschaffenes Recht der Wirtschaft und staatliches Recht', reprinted in U. Blaurock, N. Goldschmidt, A. Hollerbach (eds.), *Das selbstgeschaffene Recht der Wirtschaft. Zum Gedenken an Hans Großmann-Doerth (1894-1944)*, Tübingen: Mohr Siebeck 2005, p. 77.

S. Grundmann (ed.) *Constitutional values in private law*, Alphen aan den Rijn: KLI 2008.

S. Grundmann,'Information, party autonomy and economic agents in European contract law', *CMLRev* 2002, p. 273.

S. Grundmann, J. Stuyck, 'An academic Green Paper on European contract law - Scope, common ground and debated issues', in: S. Grundmann, J. Stuyck, (eds.), *An academic Green Paper on European contract law*, The Hague: KLI 2002, p. 7–8.

D. Gudmundsdóttir, 'A renewed emphasis on the Charter's distinction between rights and principles: Is a doctrine of judicial restraint more appropriate?', *CMLRev* 2015, p.691–693.

G. Guéry, 'European collective bargaining and the Maastricht Treaty', *International Labour Review* 1992, p. 583.

M. Günes, T. Ackermann, 'Die Indizwirkung der §§308 und 309 BGB im unternehmerischen Geschäftsverkehr', *ZGS* 2010, p. 400.

K. Gutman, *The constitutionality of European contract law*, Leuven 2010.

O.A. Haazen, 'Precedent in The Netherlands', in: E.H. Hondius (ed.), *Precedent and the law*, Brussels: Bruylant 2007, p. 250.

J. Habermas, *Between facts and norms*, (translated by W. Rehg) Cambridge, Mass.: MIT 1996.

M. Habersack, 'Richtigkeitsgewähr notariell beurkundeter Verträge', *AcP* 1989, p. 419.

A. Hammerstein, 'Rechtsvorming door de rechter is onvermijdelijk', *AA* 2009, p. 672.

H.L.A. Hart, *The concept of law*, Oxford: OUP 1961.

H.L.A. Hart, 'Book review', *Harvard Law Review* 1964–1965, p. 1286.

H.L.A. Hart, 'Positivism and the separation of law and morals', *Harvard Law Review* 1958, p. 594.

A.S. Hartkamp, 'Het nieuwe BW - ontwikkelingen sinds 1992', *AA* 2012, p. 49.

A.S. Hartkamp, 'De algemene beginselen van het Unierecht en het privaatrecht', *WPNR* 6901 (2011).

A.S. Hartkamp, 'The general principles of EU law and private law', *RabelsZ* 2011, p. 246.

A.S. Hartkamp, *Aard en opzet van het nieuw vermogensrecht*, Deventer: Kluwer 2010

A.S. Hartkamp, 'Judicial discretion under the New Civil Code of The Netherlands', *American Journal of Comparative Law* 1992, p. 569.

T.C. Hartley, 'Five forms of uncertainty in European Community Law', *Cambridge Law Journal* 1996, p. 265.

T. Hartlief, 'Alternatieve regelgeving in privaatrechtelijke verhoudingen. Opmerkingen bij het preadvies van prof. mr. I. Giesen', *NJB* 2007–21.

O. Hartwieg, 'Der Gesetzgeber des EGBGB zwischen den Fronten heutiger Kollisionrechts-Theorien', *RabelsZ* 1978, p. 431.

V. Hatzopoulos, 'Why the Open Method of Coordination is bad for you: A letter to the EU', *ELJ*, p. 318.

J.W. Hedemann, *Die Flucht in Generalklauseln*, Tübingen: Mohr Siebeck 1933.

G.J.J. Heerma van Voss, 'Medezeggenschap van werknemers met betrekking tot arbeidsvoorwaarden', *RM Themis* 1999, p. 269.
G. Heerman, 'Die Geltung von Verbandssatzungen gegenüber mittelbaren Mitgliedern und Nichtmitgliedern', *NZG* 1999, p. 326.
B. Heiderhoff, 'Die Berücksichtigung des Art. 3 Klauselrichtlinie bei der AGB-Kontrolle', *WM* 2003, p. 510.
H. Heinrichs, 'Das Gesetz zur Änderung des AGB-Gesetzes Umsetzung der EG-Richtlinie über mißbräuchliche Klauseln in Verbraucherverträgen durch den Bundesgesetzgeber', *NJW* 1996, p. 2196.
H. Heinrichs, 'Umsetzung der EG-Richtlinie über mißbräuchliche Klauseln in Verbraucherverträgen durch Auslegung Erweiterung des Anwendungsbereichs der Inhaltskontrolle', *NJW* 1995, p. 153.
M. Heintzen, 'Der Deutsche Corporate Governance Kodex aus der Sicht des deutschen Verfassungsrechts', *ZIP* 2004, p. 1933.
R.R.A. Henkemans, 'De wetgevende taak van de rechter bij massaschade', in: N. van den Berg, R.R.A. Henkemans, A. Timmer (eds.), *Massaclaims, Class actions op z'n Nederlands*, Nijmegen: Ars Aequi Libri 2007, p. 40.
H.-D. Hensen, 'Zur Entstehung des AGB-Gesetzes', in: A. Heldrich, P. Schlechtriem, E. Schmidt (eds.), *Recht im Spannungsfeld von Theorie und Praxis, Festschrift für Helmut Heinrichs zum 70. Geburtstag*, München: Beck 1998, p. 76.
P.W. Hertin, 'Urhebervertragsnovelle 2002: Up-Date von Urheberrechtsverträgen', *MMR* 2003, p. 17.
B. Hess, 'Rechtsfragen des Vorabentscheidungsverfahrens', *RabelsZ* 2002, p. 479.
M.W. Hesselink, 'Democratic contract law', *ERCL* 2015, p. 81.
M.W. Hesselink, 'The case for a common European Sales Law in an age of rising nationalism', *ERCL* 2012, p. 342.
M.W. Hesselink, 'An optional instrument on European contract law: could it increase legal certainty and foster cross-border trade?', in: M.W. Hesselink et al. (eds.), *Het Groenboek Europees contractenrecht: Naar een optioneel instrument?*, The Hague: BJU 2011, p. 9–23.
M.W. Hesselink, 'The Common Frame of Reference as a source of European private law', *Tulane Law Review* 2009, p. 923.
M.W. Hesselink, 'The Consumer Rights Directive and the CFR – Two worlds apart?', *ERCL* 2009, p. 290.
M.W. Hesselink, 'If you don't like our principles we have others', in: R. Brownsword et al. (eds.), *The foundations of European private law*, Oxford: Hart 2008, p. 59.
M.W. Hesselink, 'Case: CJEU- Freiburger Kommunalbauten v Hofstetter', *ERCL* 2006, p. 374.
M.W. Hesselink, 'Who has a stake in European contract law?', *ERCL* 2005, p. 295.
M.W. Hesselink, 'The Principles of European Contract Law: Some choices made by the Lando Commission', in: M.W. Hesselink, G. de Vries (eds.), *Principles of European Contract Law, Preadviezen uitgebracht voor de Vereniging van Burgerlijk Recht*, Deventer: Kluwer 2001, p. 9.
M.W. Hesselink, *De redelijkheid en billijkheid in het Europese privaatrecht*, Deventer: Kluwer 1999.

V. Heutger, 'De toekomst van richtlijn 87/102 betreffende consumentenovereenkomsten', in: A.S. Hartkamp, C.H. Sieburgh, L.A.D. Keus (eds.), *De invloed van het Europese recht op het Nederlandse privaatrecht II*, Deventer: Kluwer 2007, p. 95.

High-Level Group on Financial Supervision, *Report on future financial regulation and supervision*, available at http://ec.europa.eu/internal_market/finances/docs/de_larosiere_report_en.pdf.

J.B.S. Hijink, 'Naar een Europees jaarrekeningenrecht', *Ondernemingsrecht* 2012, 28.

E.M.H. Hirsch Ballin, 'Reflections on co-actorship', in: E.M.H. Hirsch Ballin, L.A.J. Senden (eds.), *Co-actorship in the development of European lawmaking*', The Hague: Asser Press 2005, p. 14.

K.-S. Hohenstatt, N. Schramm, 'Tarifliche Mindestlöhne: Ihre Wirkungsweise und ihre Vermeidung am Beispiel des Tarifvertrags zum Post-Mindestlohn', *NZA* 2008, p. 435.

P. Hommelhoff, A. Schwab, 'Regelungsquellen und Regelungsebenen der Corporate Governance', in: P. Hommelhoff, K.J. Hopt, A. Von Werder (eds.), *Handbuch Corporate Governance*, Köln: Schmidt 2009, 2nd ed., p. 79.

P. Hommelhoff, K.-U. Wiedenmann, 'Allgemeine Geschäftsbedingungen gegenüber Kaufleuten und unausgehandelte Klauseln in Verbraucherverträgen', *ZIP* 1993, p. 562.

P. Hommelhoff, 'Zivilrecht unter dem Einfluß europäischer Rechtsangleichung', *AcP* 1992, p. 90.

E.H. Hondius, *Sense and nonsense in the law. Towards clarity and plain meaning* (inaugural address Utrecht) 2007.

E.H. Hondius, 'Towards a European Ius Commune: The current situation in other fields of private law', in: K. Boele-Woelki (ed.), *Perspectives for the unification and harmonisation of family law in Europe*, Antwerp: Intersentia 2003, p. 126.

E.H. Hondius, 'Tien jaar Nieuw Burgerlijk Wetboek: De regeling van de algemene voorwaarden', *WPNR* 6472 (2002).

E.H. Hondius, 'Non-implementation of the Directive on unfair contract terms: The Dutch case', *ERPL* 1997, p. 195.

E.H. Hondius, 'Naar een wettelijke regeling van algemene voorwaarden', in: *Handelingen der Nederlandse Juristen-Vereniging*, volume 109, issue 1, Zwolle: Tjeenk Willink 1979, p. 91–290.

E.H. Hondius, 'Standaardregelingen in de bouw', in: E.H. Hondius, A.G.J. van Wassenaer, *Van standaardvoorwaarden naar standaardregeling?, Preadviezen voor de Vereniging van Bouwrecht*, Deventer: Kluwer 1993, p. 10–11.

E.H. Hondius, 'Het Nieuw Burgerlijk Wetboek en de gewone burger: de algemene voorwaarden', *Rechtshulp* 1991, p. 4.

E.H. Hondius, 'De bankovereenkomst: Niets bijzonders? Bank en consument in het Nieuwe BW', in: A.G. Lubbers (ed.), *Om wille van de consument*, Zwolle: Tjeenk Willink 1990, p. 67.

E.H. Hondius, *Standaardvoorwaarden. Rechtsvergelijkende beschouwingen over de standaardisering van kontraktsbedingen en overheidstoezicht daarop*, Deventer: Kluwer 1978.

L. Hooghe, G. Marks, 'Unravelling the central state, but how? Types of multilevel governance', *American Political Science Review* 2003, p. 233.

I.S.J. Houben, 'Sectorspecifieke wetgeving en algemene voorwaarden', *NbBW* 2004, p. 107.

I.S.J. Houben, J. Sterk, J.A.J. Devilee, 'Codificatie of zelfregulering in de franchisesector?', *MvV* 2014, p. 2.

G. Howells, 'European contract law reform and European consumer law – Two related but distinct regimes', *ERCL* 2011, p. 175.

J. Huber, 'Das Gesetz zur Beschleunigung fälliger Zahlungen', *JZ* 2000, p. 966.

N.J.H. Huls, M.A. Kleiboer, 'Is er een toekomst voor wettelijk niet hiërarchisch tuchtrecht?', *AA* 2002, p. 72.

C. Hultmark Ramberg, 'The e-commerce directive and the formation of contract in a comparative perspective', *Global Jurist Advances* 2001–2.

R. Hyland, 'The American experience: Restatements, the UCC, uniform laws and transnational coordination', in: A.S. Hartkamp, E.H. Hondius (eds.) *Towards a European Civil Code*, 2004, p. 70.

J. Hijma, *Algemene voorwaarden*, Deventer: Kluwer 2010.

J. Hijma, 'Richtlijn 93/13/EEG betreffende oneerlijke bedingen in consumentenovereenkomsten', in: S.C.J.J. Kortmann et al. (eds.), *Onderneming en 5 jaar Nieuw Burgerlijk Recht*, Deventer: Tjeenk Willink 1997, p. 425.

Institut für Europäisches Wirtschafts- und Verbraucherrecht, *Study on the feasibility for a general legislative framework on fair trading*, November 2000, available at http://ec.europa.eu/consumers/rights/studies_reports_en.htm.

S. Iwersen, 'Ergo trickste auch bei Betriebsrenten', *Handelblatt* 27.7.2011, available at www.handelsblatt.com/unternehmen/versicherungen/skandal-versicherung-ergo-trickste-auch-bei-betriebsrenten-scite-all/4437306-all.html.

W.A. Jacobs, *ADR en consument, Een rechtsvergelijkende studie naar de mogelijkheden van alternatieve geschiloplossing*, Deventer: Kluwer 1998.

N. Jansen, Legal pluralism in Europe', in: L. Niglia (ed.), *Pluralism and European private law*, Oxford: Hart 2013, p. 109.

N. Jansen, 'Dogmatising non-legislative codification. Non legislative texts in European legal discourse', in: R. Brownsword, H.-W. Micklitz, L. Niglia (eds.), *The foundations of European private law*, Oxford: Hart 2011, p. 31.

N. Jansen, *The Making of Legal Authority, Non legislative codifications in historical and comparative perspective*, Oxford: OUP, 2010.

N. Jansen, 'Klauselkontrolle im Europäischen Privatrecht. Ein Beitrag zur Revision des Verbraucheracquis', *ZeuP* 2010, p. 69.

N. Jansen, R. Michaels, 'Private Law and the State: Comparative Perceptions and Historic Observations', *RabelsZ* 2006, p. 3.

N. Jansen, R. Zimmerman, 'Was ist und wozu der DCFR?', *NJW* 2009, p. 3403.

Ch. Joerges, 'On the legitimacy of Europeanising private law: Considerations on a justice-making law for the EU multilevel system', vol 7.3 *EJCL*.

Ch. Joerges, H. Schepel, E. Vos, *The problems with the involvement of non governmental actors in Europe's legislating process*, EUI/LAW 1999.

Ch. Joerges, 'The Europeanisation process of private law as a rationalization process and as a contest of disciplines – an analysis of the Directive on unfair terms in consumer contracts', *ERPL* 1995, p. 184.

A. Johnston, H. Unberath, 'Law at, to or from the centre?', in: F. Cafaggi (ed.), *The institutional framework of European private law*, Oxford: OUP 2006, p. 150–151.

R.H.C. Jongeneel, 'Reactie', *WPNR* 6217 (1996).

R.H.C. Jongeneel, 'Een richtlijn die weinig schade aanricht', *TvC* 1993, p. 118.

R.H.C. Jongeneel, *Algemene voorwaarden en het AGB-Gesetz*, Deventer: Kluwer 1991.
R.H.C. Jongeneel, 'Vallen door een ander dan partijen opgestelde algemene voorwaarden onder afd. 6.5.3.?', *WPNR* 6027 (1991).
Lena K., 'Groupon: Kursverluste nach Sperrfrist-Ende, weiterhin Probleme mit Deal-Qualität', *Finanzwelt-News* 4 June 2012, www.finanzwelt-news.de/groupon-kursverluste-sperrfrist-dealqualitaet/.
R.A. Kagan, 'On "responsive law"', in: R.A. Kagan, M. Krygier, K. Winston (eds.), *Legality and community, On the Intellectual Legacy of Philip Selznick*, Berkeley: Rowman & Littlefield/ Berkeley Public Policy Press 2002.
J.A. Kämmerer, R. Veil, 'Analyse von Finanzinstrumenten (§34b WpHG) und journalistische Selbstregulierung', *BKR* 2005, p. 383.
S. Kaufhold, 'AGB-Anschein trotz Verhandlungsbestätigung – Ist der Individualvertrag im Unternehmerverkehr noch zu retten?', *NJW* 2014, p. 3488.
M. Kenny, 'The Law Commissions' 2012 Issues Paper on unfair terms: subverting the system of "Europeanized" private law?', *ERPL* 2013, p. 880.
E.-M. Kieninger, 'Vollharmonisierung des Rechts der AGB', *RabelsZ* 2009, p. 793
E.-M. Kieninger *Wettbewerb der Privatrechtsordnungen im Europäischen Binnenmarkt*, Tübingen: Mohr Siebeck 2002.
F. Kirchhof, *Private Rechtsetzung*, Berlin: Duncker & Humblot 1987.
G. Kirkpatrick, 'The corporate governance lessons from the financial crisis', *OECD Report, Financial Market Trends* 2009–1.
C.J.M. Klaassen, 'Kroniek civiele rechtspleging', *NJB* 2015, 738.
C.J.M. Klaassen, 'Verzekeringsgeschillen en ADR. Enkele observaties over geschilbeslechting in "een kleine wereld"', *AV & S* 2014, 22.
I. Klauer, 'General clauses in European private law and "stricter" national standards', *ERPL* 2000, p. 187.
J. Kleinschmidt, 'Stellvertretung, IPR und ein optionales Instrument für ein europäisches Vertragsrecht', *RabelsZ* 2011, p. 538.
M. Kloepfer, 'Gesetzgebungsoutsourcing – Die Erstellung von Gesetzentwürfen durch Rechtsanwälte', *NJW* 2011, p. 134.
M.W. Knigge, 'Tegenstrijdige Europese regelgeving? De verhouding tussen de EEX-Verordening en de Richtlijn oneerlijke bedingen', *MvV* 2012, p. 95.
R. Koch, 'Das AGB-Recht im unternehmerischen Verkehr: Zu viel des Guten oder Bewegung in die richtige Richtung?', *BB* 2010, p. 1813.
D. Kochenov, 'The ought of justice', in: D. Kochenov, G. de Búrca, A. Williams (eds.), *Europe's justice deficit?*, Oxford: Hart 2015, p. 22.
M. Koek, M. van de Laarschot, 'Kanttekeningen bij een vermeende uitglijer', *NJB* 2010, 1464.
J. Köndgen, 'Privatisierung des Rechts, *Private governance* zwischen Deregulierung und Rekonstitutionalisierung', *AcP* 2006, p. 477.
J. Köndgen, 'Josef Esser – Methodologie zwischen Theorie und Praxis', *JZ* 2001, p. 808.
R. Königsgruber, 'IASB und FASB zwischen Autonomie und Eingebunden-Sein', *IRZ* 2008, p. 245.
T. Koopmans, 'Lof der onbestemdheid', *RM Themis* 1991, p. 209.
C.A.J.M. Kortmann, *Staatsrecht en raison d'Etat* (lecture Nijmegen), Deventer: Kluwer 2009.
C.A.J.M. Kortmann, *Constitutioneel recht*, Deventer: Kluwer 2008.
S.C.J.J. Kortmann, N.E.D. Faber, 'Het moet niet veel gekker worden!', *WPNR* 6531 (2003).

H. Kötz, 'Der Bundesgerichtshof und die Rechtsvergleichung', in: C.-W. Canaris et al. (eds.), *50 Jahre Bundesgerichtshof. Festgabe aus der Wissenschaft, II*, München: Beck 2000, p. 825.
H. Kötz, *Welche gesetzgeberischen Massnahmen empfehlen sich zum Schutze des Endverbrauchers gegenüber Allgemeine Geschäftsbedingungen und Formularverträgen: dargestellt an Beispielen aus dem Kaufs- und Werkvertrags- sowie dem Maklerrecht, Gutachten für den 50. Deutschen Juristentag*, München: Beck 1974, Volume I, A.
H. Koziol, 'Glanz und Elend der deutschen Zivilrechtsdogmatik', *AcP* 2012, p. 1.
E. Kramer, 'Konvergenz und Internationalisierung der juristischen Methode', in: Ch.J. Meier-Schatz (ed.), *Die Zukunft des Rechts*, Basel/Geneva/München: Helbing & Lichtenhahn 1998, p. 71.
H.B. Krans, 'De druk van de ketel', *NTBR* 2014, 15, p. 133–134.
P. Kreutz, *Grenzen der Betriebsautonomie*, München: Beck 1979.
N. Krisch, *Beyond constitutionalism: The pluralist structure of postnational law*, Oxford: OUP 2010.
A. Kronman, 'Contract law and distributive justice', *Yale Law Journal* 1980, p. 472.
J. Kropholler, 'Der Einfluß der Haager Übereinkommen auf die deutsche IPR-Kodifikation', *RabelsZ* 1993, p. 222.
S.A. Kruisinga, 'Reactie op T.H.M. van Wechem en H.J.M. Spanjaard', *Contracteren* 2010, p. 110.
S. Kruisinga, 'De battle of forms in internationaal perspectief: een eerlijke strijd?', *Contracteren* 2005, p. 5.
J. Krüper, 'Lawfirm – legibus solutus?', *JZ* 2010, p. 655.
J. Kübler, F. Kübler, 'Werbefreiheit nach "Benetton"', in: M. Habersack et al. (eds.), *Festschrift für Peter Ulmer zum 70. Geburtstag am 2. Januar 2003*, Berlin: De Gruyter 2003, p. 918.
T. Kuhn, 'Überschießende Umsetzung bei mindest- or vollharmonisierenden Richtlinien: Einheitliche oder gespaltene Anwendung?', *EuR* 2015, p. 226.
Z.D. Laclé, A.C.M. Meuwese, *Self-regulation in The Netherlands*, NEWGOV Working paper 2006, available at www.eu-newgov.org/database/DELIV/DLTFIbD09d_Final_Chapters_on_self-regulation_The_Netherlands.pdf.
K.-H. Ladeur, 'Methodology and European law – Can methodology change so as to cop with the multiplicity of the law?', in: M. van Hoecke (ed.), *Epistemology and methodology of law*, Oxford: Hart 2004, p. 89.
H.-G. Landfernmann, 'Überarbeitung des deutschen Schuldrechts', *RabelsZ* 1981, p. 127.
K. Larenz, *Methodenlehre der Rechtswissenschaft*, Berlin: Springer 1991, 6th ed.
Law Commission, *Unfair terms in consumer contracts: A new approach*, 25 July 2012, http://lawcommission.justice.gov.uk/docs/unfair_terms_in_consumer_contracts_issues.pdf.
Law Commission, *An optional Common European Sales Law: Advantages and problems, Advice to the UK Government*, 10 November 2011, available at www.justice.gov.uk/lawcommission/docs/Common_European_Sales_Law_Advice.pdf.
Law Commission, *Privity of contract: Contracts for the benefit of third parties*, Report 242, available at http://lawcommission.justice.gov.uk.
K. Lenaerts, 'Constitutionalism and the many faces of federalism', *American Journal of Comparative Law* 1990, p. 205–206.
K. Lenaerts, K. Gutman, '"Federal common law" in the European Union', *American Journal of Comparative Law* 2006, p. 1.
M. Lieb, 'Grundfragen einer Schuldrechtsreform', *AcP* 1983, p. 347.

M. Lieb, 'Sonderprivatrecht für Ungleichgewichtslagen?', *AcP* 1978, p. 197.
H.K. Lindahl, 'Zelfregulering: rechtsvorming, democratie en reflexieve identiteit', *RM Themis* 2006, p. 39.
W. Linsenmaier, 'Normsetzung der Betriebsparteien und Individualrechte der Arbeitnehmer', *RdA* 2008, p. 2.
M.B.M. Loos, 'Scope and application of the Optional instrument', in: D. Voinot, J. Sénéchal (eds.), *Vers un droit européen des contrats spéciaux / Towards a European Law of Specific Contracts*, Gent: Larcier 2011, p. 117.
M.B.M. Loos, 'Individuele handhaving van het consumentenrecht', in: M.B.M. Loos, W.H. van Boom (eds.), *Handhaving van het consumentenrecht, preadviezen uitgebracht voor de Vereniging voor Burgerlijk Recht* 2009, Deventer: Kluwer 2010 p. 103.
M.B.M. Loos, 'Verboden exoneraties in energieleveringsovereenkomsten en vernietiging van met de wet strijdige bindende adviezen', *TvC* 2006, p. 1.
M.B.M. Loos, *Algemene voorwaarden*, The Hague: BJU 2001.
M.B.M. Loos, *De energieleveringsovereenkomst: algemene voorwaarden voor de levering van energie aan consumenten*, Deventer: Kluwer 1998.
M.B.M. Loos, J.A. Luzak, 'Ontwikkelingen betreffende het voorstel voor een Richtlijn consumentenrechten: de positie van de Raad en het Europees Parlement', *NTER* 2011, p. 168.
D. Looschelders, 'Diskriminierung und Schutz vor Diskriminierung im Privatrecht', *JZ* 2012, p. 105.
S. Lorenz, 'Der geplante Verbraucherschutz in Europa ist trügerisch', *FAZ* 14 July 2009.
W. Lorenz, 'On the "calling" of our time for civil legislation', in: A. Harmathy, A. Nemeth (eds.), *Questions of civil law codification*, Budapest: Hungarian Academy of Sciences 1990, p. 128.
W.J.J. Los, 'Toepassing van de WCAM. Bespiegelingen over de rol en de taak van de rechter', in: W.J.J. Los et al., *Collectieve acties in het algemeen en de WCAM in het bijzonder*, The Hague: BJU 2013, p. 29.
M.A. Loth, *Dwingend en aanvullend recht*, Deventer: Kluwer 2009.
G. Low, 'The (ir)relevance of harmonization and legal diversity to European contract law: A perspective from psychology', *ERPL* 2010, p. 298.
M. Lutter, 'Die Auslegung angeglichenen rechts', *JZ* 1992, p. 604
G. Lijffijt, 'Pals Groep trekt eigen plan', *Assurantie Magazine* 6 March 2009, available at www.stichtingpiv.nl/smartsite.dws?ch=TER&id=759979.
N. MacCormick, *Rhetoric and the rule of law*, Oxford: OUP 2005.
N. MacCormick, 'Democracy, subsidiarity, and citizenship in the 'European Commonwealth'', *Law and Philosophy* 1997, p. 339–340.
C.P.B. Mahé, 'Pleidooi voor de herziening van de Nederlandse battle of forms-regeling', *VrA* 2006, p. 5.
J. Maidl, *Ausländische AGB im deutschen Recht*, München: Beck 2000.
G. Majone, 'Europe's "democratic deficit": A question of standards', *ELJ* 1998, p. 5.
C. Mak, 'Hedgehogs in Luxembourg?' A Dworkinian reading of the CJEU's case law on principles of private law and a reply of the fox', *ERPL* 2012, p. 323.
C. Mak, *Fundamental rights in European contract law*, Alphen aan den Rijn: KLI 2008.
V. Mak, 'According to custom ...? The role of 'Trade Usage' in the Proposed Common European Sales Law (CESL)', *ERCL* 2014, p. 64.

V. Mak, 'Volgens lokaal gebruik…', *NJB* 2013, p. 4.

V. Mak, 'A shift of focus: Systematisation in European private law through EU law', *ELJ* 2011, p. 417.

V. Mak, 'Scharnierpunt tussen Europees en nationaal consumentenrecht', *MvV* 2011, p. 185.

V. Mak, 'Harmonisation through "Directive-related" and "cross-Directive" interpretation: The role of the CJEU in the development in European consumer law', *ZeuP* 2010, p. 129.

V. Mak, 'Hoe meer keus, hoe beter?', *TvC* 2010, p. 250.

G. Marks, 'Structural policy and multilevel governance in the EC', in: A. Cafruny, G. Rosenthal (eds.), *The state of the European Community Vol. 2: The Maastricht debates and beyond*, Boulder: Rienner 1993, p. 392.

G. Marks, L. Hooghe, 'Contrasting visions of multi-level governance', in: I. Bache, M. Flinders (eds.), *Multi-level governance*, Oxford: OUP 2004, p. 19

Max Planck Institute für ausländisches und internationales Privatrecht, 'Kodifikation des deutschen Internationalen Privatrechts. Stellungnahme des Max-Planck-Instituts für ausländisches und internationales Privatrecht zum Regierungsentwurf von 1983', *RabelsZ* 1983, p. 595.

Max Planck Institut für ausländisches und internationales Privatrecht, 'Rechtsvergleichung', in: Bundesminister der Justiz (ed.), *Vorschläge und Gutachten zur Überarbeitung des Schuldrecht*, Vol. I, Köln: Bundesanzeiger 1981, p. 67–68.

E. McKendrick, 'Harmonisation of European contract law: The state we are in', in: S. Vogenauer, S. Weatherill (eds.), *The harmonisation of European contract law*, Oxford: Hart 2006, p. 21.

E. McKendrick, *The creation of a European law of contracts – The role of standard form contracts and principles of interpretation*, Deventer: Kluwer 2004.

S. Meder, *Ius non scriptum – Traditionen privater Rechtssetzung*, Tübingen: Mohr Siebeck 2009.

D. Medicus, 'Entscheidungen des BGH als Marksteine für die Entwicklung des allgemeinen Zivilrechts', *NJW* 2000, p. 2926.

E.M. Meijers, *Ontwerp voor een Nieuw Burgerlijk Wetboek, Boek 6*, completed by J. Drion, G. de Grooth, and F.J. de Jong, The Hague: Staatsdrukkerij 1961.

E.M. Meijers, 'Wijzigingen en aanvullingen van het Burgerlijk Wetboek na 1838', in: P. Scholten, E.M. Meijers (eds.), *Gedenkboek Burgerlijk Wetboek 1838–1938*, Zwolle: Tjeenk Willink 1938, p. 61.

E.M. Meijers, 'Het feillooze deel van ons Burgerlijk Wetboek', in: E.M. Meijers, *Verzamelde privaatrechtelijke opstellen, Eerste deel*, Leiden: Universitaire Pers Leiden: Leiden 1954, p. 98.

E.M. Meijers, 'Voor- en nadelen van het samenstellen van een nieuw burgerlijk wetboek', in: E.M. Meijers, *Verzamelde privaatrechtelijke opstellen, Eerste deel*, Leiden: Universitaire Pers Leiden 1954, p. 173.

E.M. Meijers, *De taak der rechtswetenschap ten aanzien der vrijen rechtspraak* (inaugural address Leiden), Haarlem: Tjeenk Willink 1910

P. Memelink, *De verkeersopvatting*, The Hague: BJU 2009.

J. Mendes, *Participation in EU rule-making: A rights-based approach*, Oxford: OUP 2011, p. 46–55.

A.J. Menéndez, 'Whose justice? Which Europe?', in: D. Kochenov, G. de Búrca, A. Williams (eds.), *Europe's justice deficit?*, Oxford: Hart 2015, p. 137.

M. Menting, '(R)Evolutie in het privaatrecht? Enkele beschouwingen over de rol van private regelgeving en de invloed van het EVRM naar aanleiding van HR Achmea/Rijnberg', *NTBR* 2015, 16.

M.-C. Menting, *Terra incognita: de functies van gedragscodes in het privaatrecht* (master thesis) Tilburg 2011.
M. Menting, J.B.M. Vranken, 'Gedragscodes in een meergelaagd privaatrecht in Europa en Nederland', in: M. Menting, J.B.M. Vranken, M.W. Scheltema, *Gedragscodes in internationaal, Europees en privaatrechtelijk perspectief, Preadviezen 2013 uitgebracht voor de Vereniging van Burgerlijk Recht*, Zutphen: Paris 2014, p. 40.
S.E. Merry, ' Legal pluralism', *Law and Society Review* 1988, p. 883–886.
H.-J. Mertens, 'Nichtlegislatorische Rechtsvereinheitlichung durch transnationales Wirtschaftsrecht und Rechtsbegriff', *RabelsZ* 1992, p. 219.
P.E.M. Messer-Dinnissen en J. Tromp, 'Bestuurders van en Raad voor de rechtspraak: houdt het bij raad aan de rechtspraak', *NJB* 2010, 1014.
A. Metzger, *Extra legem, intra ius: Allgemeine Rechtsgrundsätze im Europäischen Privatrecht*, Tübingen: Mohr Siebeck 2009.
A. Metzger, 'Allgemeine Rechtsgrundsätze im europäischen Privatrecht: Ansätze für eine einheitliche Techniquenlehre im europäischen Mehrebenensystem', *Rechtstheorie* 2009, p. 325.
A.C.M. Meuwese, *Impact assessment in EU lawmaking*, Zutphen: Wöhrmann Print Services 2008.
R. Michaels, 'Why we have no theory of European private law pluralism', in L. Niglia (ed.), *Pluralism and European private law*, Oxford: Hart 2013, p. 139.
R. Michaels, 'Of islands and the ocean', in: R. Brownsword et al. (eds.), *The foundations of European private law*, Oxford: Hart 2011, p. 142–143.
R. Michaels, 'Umdenken für die UNIDROIT-Prinzipien. Vom Rechtswahlstatut zum Allgemeinen Teil des Transnationalen Vertragsrechts', *RabelsZ* 2009, p. 873.
R. Michaels, N. Jansen, 'Private law and the state: Comparative perceptions and historical observations', *RabelsZ* 2007, p. 345.
R. Michaels, N. Jansen, 'Private law beyond the state? Europeanization, Globalization, Privatization', *American Journal of Comparative Law* 2006, p. 843.
R. Michaels, 'Privatautonomie und Privatkodifikation', *RabelsZ* 1998, p. 622.
H.-W. Micklitz, 'Monistic ideology versus pluralistic reality', in: L. Niglia (ed.), *Pluralism and European private law*, Oxford: Hart 2013, p. 47
H.-W. Micklitz, 'German Constitutional Court (Bundesverfassungsgericht BVerfG) 2 BvE 2/08, 30. 6. 2009 – Organstreit proceedings between members of the German Parliament and the Federal Government', *ERCL* 2011, p. 532.
H.-W. Micklitz, 'The targeted full harmonisation approach: Looking behind the curtain', in: G. Howells, R. Schulze (eds.), *Modernising and harmonising consumer contract law*, München: Sellier 2009, p. 59.
H.-W. Micklitz, 'The visible hand of European regulatory private law. The transformation of European private law from autonomy to functionalism in competition and regulation', *EUI Working Paper* 2008.
H.-W. Micklitz, 'Regulatory strategies in services contracts law', *EUI Working Paper* 2008/06.
H.-W. Micklitz, 'The concept of competitive contract law', *Penn State International Law Review* 2005, p. 572.
H.-W. Micklitz, 'The Principles of European Contract Law and the protection of the weaker party', *Journal of Consumer Policy* 2004, p. 339.

H.-W. Micklitz, N. Reich, 'The Court and the Sleeping Beauty: The revival of the unfair contract terms Directive', *CMLRev* 2014, p. 806.

H.-W. Micklitz, N. Reich, 'Der Kommissionsvorschlag vom 8. 10. 2008 für eine Richtlinie über „Rechte der Verbraucher", oder: „der Beginn des Endes einer Ära ..."', *EUzW* 2009, p. 279.

L. Miller, *The emergence of EU contract law: Exploring Europeanization*, Oxford: OUP 2011.

L.J.H. Mölenberg, M.L.A.M.J. Olivers, R.R.J.A. Hallmans, 'De Stichting Garantiefonds Reisgelden; gegarandeerd verzekerd?', *TvC* 1990, p. 346.

Ch. Möllers, 'European governance, meaning and value of a concept', *CMLR* 2006, p. 313.

T.M.J. Möllers, 'Effizienz als Maßstab des Kapitalmarktrechts', *AcP* 2008, p. 21.

T.J.M. Möllers, 'Doppelte Rechtsfortbildung contra legem? Zur Umgestaltung des Bürgerlichen Gesetzbuches durch den EuGH und nationale Gerichte', in: H. Schlosser (ed.), *Bürgerliches Gesetzbuch 1896–1996*, Heidelberg: Müller 1997, p. 154.

F. Möslein, K. Riesenhuber, 'Contract governance – a draft research agenda', *ERCL* 2009, p. 251

Montesquieu, *Over de geest van de wetten*, Amsterdam: Boom 2006 (translation J. Holierhoek).

L. Moral Soriano, 'A modest notion of coherence in legal reasoning. A model for the European Court of Justice', *Ratio Juris* 2003, p. 302.

F. Möslein, K. Riesenhuber, 'Contract governance – A draft research agenda', *ERCL* 2009, p. 251.

J. de Mot, G. de Geest, 'De toekomst van het Europees privaatrecht na het Groenboek', *NJB* 2002, 18.

H. Muir Watt, '"Party autonomy" in international contracts', *ERCL* 2010, p. 9.

T. Müller, H.-W. Platzer, 'European works councils', in: B. Keller, H.-W. Platzer (eds.), *Industrial relations and European integration*, Hamphshire: Ashgate 2003.

J. Neyer, 'Justice, not democracy: The legitimacy of the European Union', *CMLS* 2010, p. 908.

J. Neyer, 'Discourse and order in the EU: A deliberative approach to multilevel governance', *JCMS* 2003, p. 689.

V. Nickel, 'Wie uberfluessig ist Werbemoral?', Report ZWA for the meeting of the Austrian Werberat 2011, at http://zaw.de/doc/Werbemoral_Wien.pdf.

R. Nickel, 'Zur Zukunft des Bundesverfassungsgerichts im Zeitalter der Europäisierung', *JZ* 2001, p. 625.

J.H. Nieuwenhuis, *Paternalisme, fraternalisme, egoïsme* (valedictory address Leiden 2009) Leiden: Universiteit Leiden 2009.

J.H. Nieuwenhuis, *Confrontatie & compromis*, Deventer: Kluwer 2007.

J.H. Nieuwenhuis, 'Promises, promises', *NJB* 2001, 37.

J.H. Nieuwenhuis, *Drie beginselen van contractenrecht*, Deventer: Kluwer 1977.

L. Niglia, 'The double life of pluralism in Europe: Between constitutionalism and private law – Arguments for a post-formalism paradigm', in: L. Niglia (ed.), *Pluralism and European private law*, Oxford: Hart 2013, p. 17–18.

L. Niglia, 'The non-Europeanisation of private law', *ERPL* 2001, p. 575.

P. Nonet, P. Selznick, *Law & society in transition*, New Brunswick: Transaction Publishers 2001.

T. Nowak et al., *National judges as European Union judges. Knowledge, experiences and attitudes of lower court judges in Germany and the Netherlands*, The Hague: Eleven 2011.

P. Oestmann, 'Rechtsvielfalt', in: N. Jansen, P. Oestmann (eds.), *Gewohnheit, Gebot, Gesetz*, Tübingen: Mohr Siebeck 2011, p. 99.

H.U. Jessurun d'Oliveira, 'Is een codificatie van het Nederlandse IPR nog zinvol? Oftewel, geloven we nog in Boek 10?', *NTBR* 2005, p. 428.

V. Ostrom, C.M. Tiebout, R. Warren, 'The organization of government in metropolitan areas: A theoretical inquiry', *American Political Science Review* 1961, p. 831

Oxera, *What is the impact of the proposed Consumer Credit Directive?*, April 2007, available at www.bba.org.uk.

B.P. Paal, *Rechnungslegung und DRSC*, Baden Baden: Nomos 2001.

C.M.D.S. Pavillon, 'Een nieuw contractenrecht voor Frankrijk', *NTBR* 2015, 11.

C.M.D.S. Pavillon, 'Private standards of fairness in European contract law', *ERCL* 2014, p. 91.

C.M.D.S. Pavillon, *Open normen in het Europees consumentenrecht, De oneerlijkheidsnorm in vergelijkend perspectief*, Deventer: Kluwer 2011.

C.M.D.S. Pavillon, 'Beter consumentenrecht: Naar een scherpere consumentvriendelijke onredelijk bezwarend-norm', *NTBR* 2011, 63.

C.M.D.S. Pavillon, 'De wisselende betekenis van de Richtlijn oneerlijke bedingen in de Nederlandse rechtspraak: een overzicht', *VrA* 2006, p. 43.

L.D. Pels Rijcken, 'Rechtszekerheid, Assepoester van rechtsvindingstheorieën', in: P. Abas et al (eds.), *Non sine causa*, Zwolle: Tjeenk Willink 1979, p. 310.

T. Pfeiffer, 'Europäisch-autonome Auslegung der Klauselrichtlinie am Beispiel der Hauptleistungsklauseln', *NJW* 2014, p. 3069–3070.

Th. Pfeiffer, 'Die Integration von Nebengesetzen in das BGB', in: W. Ernst, R. Zimmerman (eds.), *Zivilrechtswissenschaft und Schuldrechtsreform – Zum Diskussionsentwurf des Bundesministeriums der Justiz*, Tübingen: Mohr Siebeck p. 481.

Th. Pfeiffer, 'Die Reichweite der Inhaltskontrolle nach Art. 4 Abs. 2 RL 93/13/EWG und §8 AGBG im Kontext der "Schuldrechtsmodernisierung"', *VuR* 2001, p. 95.

Th. Pfeiffer, B. Schinkels, 'Schuldrechtsmodernisierung und AGB-Gesetz', in: H.-W. Micklitz et al. (eds.), *Schuldrechtsreform und Verbraucherschutz*, Baden Baden: Nomos 2001, p. 133.

A. Pilniok, 'Struktur, Funktionen und Probleme der Expertengruppen der Europäischen Kommission: legitime Expertise oder unzulässige Einflussnahme?', *EuR* 2014, p. 62.

B. Pilz, 'Incoterms und UN-, Kaufrecht', in: K.-H. Thume (ed.), *Transport- und Vertriebsrecht 2000, Festschrift fur Prof.Dr. Rolf Herber*, Luchterhand: Neuwied 2000, p. 21.

M.V. Polak, 'Spreken is zilver, zwijgen is goud', in: A.G. Castermans et al (eds.), *Het zwijgen van de Hoge Raad, BWKJ* 25, Deventer: Kluwer 2009, p. 89.

M.V. Polak, 'Oppassen – inpassen – aanpassen. Taken en bevoegdheden van wetgever en rechter bij de receptie van internationaal en communautair IPR in de Nederlandse rechtsorde', in: C.A. Joustra, M.V. Polak, *Internationaal, communautair en nationaal IPR (Mededelingen van de Vereniging voor Internationaal Recht 2002)*, The Hague: Asser Press 2002, p. 95.

J.M. Polak, M.V. Polak, 'Faux pas ou pas de deux?', *Netherlands International Law Review* 1986, p. 99.

P. Popelier et al., *Consulteren over ontwerpregelgeving: alibi voor vrijblijvendheid of prikkel tot actie? Een inventarisatie van de Nederlandse consultatiepraktijk*, Antwerp: University of Antwerp, Tilburg University, WODC 2007 available at www.wodc.nl.

P. Popelier, *Rechtszekerheid als beginsel voor behoorlijke regelgeving*, Antwerp: Intersentia 1997.

E.A. Posner, 'The questionable basis of the Common European Sales Law: The role of an optional instrument in jurisdictional competition', *CMLRev* 2013, p. 272–275.

S. Prechal, R.H. van Ooik, J.H. Jans, K.J.M. Mortelmans, 'Europeanisation of the law: Consequences for the Dutch judiciary, Report of October 2005, available at www.rechtspraak.nl/

Organisatie/Raad-Voor-De-Rechtspraak/WetenschapsOnderzoek/Overzichtonderzoeksprojecten/Europeanisering/Pages/default.aspx.
U. Preis, 'Persönlicher Anwendungsbereich der Sonderprivatrechte', *ZHR* 1994, p. 603.
K.P. Purnhagen, 'Principles of European private or civil law? A reminder of the symbiotic relationship between the CJEU and the DCFR in a pluralistic European private law', *ELJ* 2012, p. 844.
G.T.M.J. Raaijmakers, 'De financiële markt en het ondernemingsrecht', *Ondernemingsrecht* 2009, 104.
G. Radbruch, 'Statutory lawlessness and *supra*-statutory law (1946)', *OJLS* 2006, p. 1.
G. Radbruch, *Rechtsphilosophie, Gestamtausgabe Band 2* (ed. and rev. A. Kaufmann), Heidelberg: Müller 1993.
L. Raiser, 'Vertragsfunktion und Vertragsfreiheit', in: E. von Caemmerer, E. Friesenhahn, R. Lange (eds.), *Hundert Jahre deutsches Rechtsleben, Festschrift zum hundertjährigen Bestehen des Deutschen Juristentages, I*, Karlsruhe: Müller 1960, p. 118.
L. Raiser, *Das Recht der Allgemeinen Geschäftsbedingungen*, Hamburg: Hanseat 1935.
J. Rawls, *A theory of justice*, Cambridge, Mass.: Harvard University Press 1999, p. 3.
T.W. Reader, 'Is self-regulation the best option for the advertising industry in the European Union? An argument for the harmonization of advertising laws through the continued use of Directives, 16 *U. Pa. Int'l Bus. L.R.* 1995-1996, p. 210.
Redactie WPNR, 'Onvrede over wetgevingsproces', *WPNR* 6868 (2010).
V. Reding, 'Warum Europa ein optionales Europäisches Vertragsrecht benötigt', *ZEuP* 2011, p. 1.
N. Reich, *General principles of EU civil law*, Antwerp: Intersentia 2014.
N. Reich, 'A "Trojan Horse" in the access to justice – Party autonomy and consumer arbitration in conflict in the ADR-Directive 20133/11/EU?', *ERCL* 2014, p. 272–274.
N. Reich, 'Pluralism and private law in the Union: Some thoughts on the impact of the non-discrimination principle on private autonomy', in: L. Niglia (ed.), *Pluralism and European private law*, Oxford: Hart 2013, p. 74.
N. Reich, 'A European contract law: Ghost or host for European integration?', *Wisconsin International Law Journal* 2006, p. 468.
N. Reich, 'A European contract law, or an EU contract law Regulation for consumers?', *Journal of Consumer Policy* 2005, p. 399.
N. Reich, 'The implementation of Directive 93/13/EEC on unfair terms in consumer contracts in Germany', *ERPL* 1997, p. 168.
N. Reich, 'Zivilrechtstheorie, Sozialwissenschaften und Verbraucherschutz', *ZRP* 1974, p. 187.
M. Reimann, 'Towards a European Civil Code: Why continental jurists should consult their transatlantic colleagues', *Tulane Law Review* 1998–1999, p. 1337.
M. Reimann, 'American private law and European legal unification – Can the United States be a model?', *MJ* 1996, p. 217.
O. Remien, 'Die Vorlagepflicht bei Auslegung unbestimmter Rechtsbegriffe', *RabelsZ* 2002, p. 528.
O. Remien, 'Einheit, Mehrstufigkeit und Flexibilität', *RabelsZ* 1998, p. 633.
O. Remien, 'Denationalisierung des Privatrechts in der Europäischen Union?', *Zeitschrift für Rechtsvergleichung* 1995, p. 129–130.
M. Rheinstein (ed.), *Max Weber on law in economy and society*, London: OUP 1969, 3rd print.
L.E. Ribstein, E. O'Hara, *The law market*, Oxford: OUP 2009

R. Richardi, *Kollektivgewalt und Individualwille bei der Gestaltung des Arbeitsverhältnisses*, München: Beck 1968.
K. Riesenhuber, 'A competitive approach to EU contract law', *ERCL* 2011, p. 119.
K. Riesenhuber, 'System and principles of EC contract law', *ERCL* 2005, p. 297.
K. Riesenhuber, *System und Prinzipien des Europäischen Privatrechts*, Berlin: De Gruyter 2003.
H.-M. Ringleb, 'Die Umsetzung des Kodex in der Praxis', in: H.-M. Ringleb et al (eds.), *Deutscher Corporate Governance Kodex*, 4th ed., 2010, III, no. 1543.
T. Ritter, 'Europarechtsneutralität mitgliedstaatlicher Generalklauseln?', *NJW* 2012, p. 1549.
V. Roppo, 'From consumer contracts to assymetric contracts – A trend in European contract law?', *ERCL* 2009, p. 304.
F. Roschr, 'Vertragrechtstheorie mit Herrschaftsfunktion?', *ZRP* 1972, p. 111.
J. Rosenau, *Along the domestic-foreign frontier: Exploring governance in a turbulent world*, Cambridge: CUP 1997.
H. Rösler, 'Europeanisation of private law through Directives – Determining factors and modalities of implementation', *European Journal of Law Reform* 2010, p. 316.
H. Roth, 'Verbraucherschutz – Entwicklungen und Grenzen', in: E. Lorenz (ed.), *Karlsruher Forum 2011: Verbraucherschutz – Entwicklungen und Grenzen*, Karlsruhe: Versicherungswirtschaft 2012, p. 31.
W.-H. Roth, 'Verfassungsgerichtliche Kontrolle der Vorlagepflicht an den EuGH', *NVwZ* 2009, p. 345.
W.H. Roth, 'Transposing "pointillist" EC guidelines into national systematic codes – Problems and consequences', *ERPL* 2002, p. 761.
W.-H. Roth, 'Europäischer Verbraucherschutz und BGB', *JZ* 2001, p. 482.
W.-H. Roth, 'Generalklauseln im Europäischen Privatrecht', in: J. Basedow, K.J. Hopt, H. Kötz (eds.), *Festschrift für Ulrich Drobnig zum siebzigsten Geburtstag*, Tübingen: Mohr Siebeck, 1998, p. 140.
A. Röthel, *Normkonkretisierung im Privatrecht*, Tübingen: Mohr Siebeck 2004
P. Rott, 'What is the role of the CJEU in EC private law? – A comment on the CJEU judgments in Océano Grupo, Freiburger Kommunalbauten, Leitner and Veedfald', 1 *Hanse LR* 2005, p. 14.
M. Rötting, C. Lang, 'Das Lamfalussy-Verfahren im Umfeld der Neuordnung der europäischen Finanzaufsichtsstrukturen', *EuZW* 2012, p. 12.
P. Ruess, 'Das Recht der Werbung zwischen Staats- und Selbstkontrolle', in: C.-H. Witt (ed.), *Die Privatisierung des Privatrechts – rechtliche Gestaltung ohne staatlichen Zwang, Jahrbuch Junger Zivilrechtswissenschaftler 2002*, Stuttgart: Boorberg 2003, p. 209.
J.G. Ruggie, 'Territoriality and Beyond: Problematizing Modernity in International Relations', *International Organization* 1993, p. 139
G. Rühl, 'Regulatory competition in contract law: Empirical evidence and normative implications', *ERCL* 2013, p. 61.
J.W. Rutgers, 'An Optional Instrument and social dumping revisited', *ERCL* 2011, p. 350.
J.W. Rutgers, 'An optional instrument and social dumping', *ERCL* 2006, p. 199
J.W. Rutgers, R. Sufton-Green, 'Revising the consumer *acquis*: (Half) opening the doors of the Trojan Horse', *ERPL* 2008, p. 431.
G.J. Rijken, 'De Wet algemene voorwaarden na één jaar: een trieste tussenbalans', *NJB* 1994, p. 643.

Ch.F. Sabel, J. Zeitlin, 'Experimentalist governance in the European Union', in: J. Zeitlin, Ch.F. Sabel (eds.), *Experimentalist governance in the European Union: Towards a new architecture*, Oxford: OUP 2010, p. 2.

Ch.F. Sabel, J. Zeitlin, 'Learning from difference: The new architecture of experimentalist governance in the EU', *ELJ* 2008, p. 272.

M. Safjan, *Why a European Law Institute?*, Speech held at the ELI Founding Congress, Paris 1 June 2011, text available at www.europeanlawinstitute.eu/fileadmin/user_upload/p_eli/_17__Marek_Safjan.pdf.

G. Sandström, 'Knocking EU law into shape', *CLMR* 2003, p. 1310.

W. Seidel, 'Der DGCK - ein private oder staatliche Regelung?', *ZIP* 2004, p. 285.

F.W. Scharpf, 'The joint-decision trap: Lessons from German federalism and European integration', *Public Administration* 1988, p. 239.

F.W. Scharpf, *Governing in Europe: Effective and democratic?*, Oxford: OUP 1999.

F.W. Scharpf, 'European governance: Common concerns vs the challenge of diversity', *Jean Monnet Working Paper* 6/01.

H.N. Schelhaas, *Algemene voorwaarden in handelstransacties*, Deventer: Kluwer 2011.

H.N. Schelhaas, 'Pacta sunt servanda bij commerciële contracten', *NTBR* 2008, 21.

M. Scheltema, *Het recht van de toekomst* (inaugural address Utrecht), Deventer: Kluwer 2005.

H. Schepel, R. Wesseling, 'The legal community: Judges, lawyers, officials and clerks in the writing of Europe', *ELJ* 1997, p. 165.

D. Schiek, 'Autonomous collective agreements as a regulatory device in European labour law: How to read article 139', *Industrial Law Journal* 2005, p. 26.

D. Schiek, 'Freedom of contract and a non-discrimination principle - Irreconcilable antonyms?', in: T. Loene, P.R. Rodrigues (eds.), *Non-discrimination law: Comparative perspectives*, The Hague: KLI 1999, p. 86.

M. Schillig, 'Directive 93/13 and the "price term exemption": a comparative analysis in the light of the "market for lemons" rationale', *ICLQ* 2011,p. 947.

M. Schillig, *Konkretisierungskompetenz und Konkretisierungsmethoden im Europäischen Privatrecht*, Berlin: De Gruyter 2009.

P. Schlechtriem, 'Battle of Forms in International Contract Law, Evaluation of approaches in German law, UNIDROIT Principles, European Principles, CISG; UCC approaches under consideration', www.cisg.law.pace.edu/cisg/biblio/schlechtriem5.html.

C.U. Schmid, 'The CJEU as a constitutional and a private law court: A methodological comparison', *ZERP Diskussionspaper* 2006.

C.U. Schmid, 'Legitimitätsbedingungen eines Europäischen Zivilgesetzbuchs', *JZ* 2001, p. 680.

C.U. Schmid, 'Ways out of the maquis communautaire, On simplification and consolidation and the need for a Restatement of European primary law', *EUI Working Paper* 1999.

M. Schmidhuber, *Verhaltenskodizes im nationalen und grenzüberschreitenden elektronischen Geschäftsverkehr, Zur Frage der Integration der Selbstregulierung durch Private in die staatliche Rechtsordnung*, Frankfurt am Main: Lang 2004

M. Schmidt, *Konkretisierung von Generalklauseln im Europäischen Privatrecht*, Berlin: De Gruyter 2010.

E. Schmidt, 'Die Verbandsklage nach dem AGB-Gesetz', *NJW* 1989, p. 1193.

M. Schmidt-Kessel, 'Einbeziehung von Allgemeinen Geschäftsbedingungen unter UN-Kaufrecht', *NJW* 2002, p. 3445.

J. Schmidt-Räntsch, 'Reintegration der Verbraucherschutzgesetze durch den Entwurf eines Schuldrechtsmodernisierungsgesetzes', in: R. Schulze, H. Schulte-Nölke (eds.), *Die Schuldrechtsreform vor dem Hintergrund des Gemeinschaftsrechts*, Tübingen: Mohr Siebeck 2001, p. 169.

J. Schmidt-Salzer, 'Transformation der EG-Richtlinie über mißbräuchliche Klauseln in Verbraucherverträgen in deutsches Recht und AGB-Gesetz', *BB* 1995, p. 735.

W. Schmidt-Rimpler, 'Zum Vertragsproblem', in: F. Baur, L. Raiser (eds.), *Funktionswandel der Privatrechtsinstitutionen. Festschrift für Ludwig Raiser*, Tübingen: Mohr Siebeck 1974, p. 20.

W. Schmidt-Rimpler, 'Zum Problem der Geschäftsgrundlage', in: R. Dietz (ed.), *Festschrift für Hans Carl Nipperdey zum 60. Geburtstag*, München: Beck 1955, p. 8.

W. Schmidt-Rimpler, 'Grundfragen einer Erneuerung des Vertragsrechts', *AcP* 1941, p. 156.

B. Schmitz, 'Advertising and commercial Communications – Towards a coherent and effective EC policy', *JCP* 1993, p. 407.

H. Schmoeckel, '100 Jahre BGB: Erbe und Aufgabe', *NJW* 1996, p. 1697.

K.U. Schmolke, 'Die Einbeziehung des Komitologieverfahrens in den Lamfalussy-Prozess – Zur Forderung des Europäischen Parlaments nach mehr Entscheidungsteilhabe', *EuR* 2006, p. 439.

G.J. Scholten, 'De oorzaak van de verbintenis uit overeenkomst', *AA* 1985, p. 744.

H. Schulte-Nölke, 'No market for lemons', *ERPL* 2015, p. 195.

H. Schulte-Nölke, 'Arbeiten an einem europäischen Vertragrecht – Fakten und populäre Irrtümer', *NJW* 2009, p. 2162.

H. Schulte-Nölke, 'Restatement- nicht Kodifikation', in: O. Remien (ed.), *Schuldrechtsmodernisierung und Europäisches Vertragsrecht: 'Zwischenbilanz und Perspektiven – Würzburger Tagung vom 27. und 28. 10. 2006'*, Tübingen: Mohr Siebeck 2008, p. 26.

W.B. Schünemann, 'Wandlungen des Vertragsrechts', *NJW* 1982, p. 2033

L.A.J. Schut, *Internationale normen in het Nederlandse stakingsrecht*, The Hague: SDU 1996.

C. Schutte, 'De rechtsvormende taak van de rechter? Een kritische noot', *AA* 2009, p. 676.

C. Scott, 'Analysing regulatory space: fragmented resources and institutional design', *PL* 2001, p. 329.

J. Scott, D. Trubek, 'Mind the gap: Law and new approaches to governance', *ELJ* 2002, p. 1.

Scottish Law Commission, *Review of contract law, Discussion paper 157 on third party rights in contract*, March 2014, available at www.scotlawcom.gov.uk/files/8013/9592/4224/DP_TSO.pdf.

R. Sefton-Green 'Social justice and the European identity in European contract law', *ERCL* 2006, p. 275.

H.H. Seiler, 'Bewahrung von Kodifikationen in der Gegenwart am Beispiel des BGB', in: O. Behrends, W. Sellert (eds), *Der Kodifikationsgedanke und das Modell des Bürgerlichen Gesetzbuches*, Göttingen: Van den Hoek & Ruprecht 2000, p. 109.

P. Selznick, *Law, society, and industrial justice*, New York: Russell Sage Foundation 1969.

L.A.J. Senden, Reguleringsintensiteit en regelgevingsinstrumentarium in het Europees Gemeenschapsrecht. Over de relatie tussen wetgeving, soft law en de open methode van coördinatie', *SEW* 2008, p. 50.

L.A.J. Senden, 'De lidstaten en de kwaliteit van Europese wetgeving: geen consumenten, maar co-actoren', *SEW* 2006, p. 47.

L.A.J. Senden, 'Soft law, self-regulation and co-regulation in European law: Where do they meet?', *EJCL* vol. 9.1., 2005, p. 9.

L.A.J. Senden, 'General Report, The quality of European legislation and its implementation and application in the national legal order', in: E.M.H. Hirsch Ballin, L.A.J. Senden (eds.), *Co-actorship in the development of European lawmaking'*, The Hague: Asser Press 2005, p. 157.

L.A.J. Senden, *Soft law in European Community law*, Portland: Hart 2004.

C.H. Sieburgh, 'Legitimiteit van de confrontatie van Europees recht en burgerlijk recht van nationale origine', in: W.J.M. Voermans, M.J. Borgers, C.H. Sieburgh, *Controverses rondom legitimiteit en legitimatie, Preadvies Nederlandse Juristen Vereniging 2010*, Deventer: Kluwer 2011, p. 190.

C. Sieburgh, *Tertium datur. De niet uitgesloten derde in het burgerlijk recht*, (inaugural address Nijmegen) Deventer: Kluwer 2004.

M. Siems, 'The adjudication of the German Federal Supreme Court, 2007, *Oxford University Comparative Law Forum*, 4, at ouclf.iuscomp.org.

J.J.J. Sillen, 'Tussen dogmatiek en pragmatisme: binding aan rechtersregelingen in Nederland en Duitsland', *AA* 2014, p. 572–573.

P.J. Slot, 'Harmonisation', *ELR* 1996, p. 383–384.

S. Smismans, 'European social dialogue in the shadow of hierarchy', *Journal of Public Policy* 2008, p. 169.

J.M. Smits, 'A radical view of legal pluralism', in: L. Niglia (ed.), *Pluralism in Europe*, Oxford: Hart 2013, p. 161.

J.M. Smits, 'The complexity of transnational law: Coherence and fragmentation of private law', *ERPL* 2012, p. 153.

J.M. Smits, 'Democracy and (European) private law – A functional approach', in: M. Faure, A. van der Walt (eds.), *Globalization and private law: The way forward*, Cheltenham: Elgar 2010, p. 26.

J.M. Smits, 'Optional law: A plea for multiple choice in private law', *MJ* 2010, p. 350.

J.M. Smits, 'Contractenrecht als meergelaagde rechtsorde: Uitdagingen voor de komende tien jaar', *Contracteren* 2009, p. 112.

J.M. Smits, 'A European law on unjustified enrichment? A critical view on the law of restitution in the Draft Common Frame of Reference', in: A. Vaquer (ed.), *European private law beyond the Common Frame of Reference*, Groningen: ELP 2008, p. 7.

J.M. Smits, 'The Draft Common Frame of Reference, methodological nationalism and the way forward', *ERCL* 2008, p. 270.

J.M. Smits, 'European private law: A plea for a spontaneous legal order', in: D.M. Curtin et al (eds.), *European integration and law*, Antwerp: Intersentia 2006, p. 55.

J.M. Smits, 'Diversity of contract law and the European internal market', in: J.M. Smits (ed.), *The need for a European contract law*, Groningen: ELP 2005, p. 169.

J.M. Smits, 'The Principles of European Contract law and the harmonisation of private law in Europe', in: A. Vaquer (ed.), *La tercera parte de los principios de derecho contractual Europeo*, Valencia: Tirant 2005, p. 575.

J.M. Smits, 'Constitutionalisering van het vermogensrecht', in: J.M. Smits, P.H.M. Gerver, D.A. Lubach, *Preadviezen uitgebracht door de Nederlandse Vereniging van Rechtsvergelijking*, Deventer: Kluwer 2003, p. 1.

J.M Smits, 'Import and export of legal models: The Dutch experience', *Transnational Law & Contemporary Problems* 2003, p. 551.

J.M. Smits, *Bronnen van verbintenissen*, Deventer: Kluwer 2003.

J.M. Smits, *Het vertrouwensbeginsel en de contractuele gebondenheid*, Arnhem: Gouda Quint 1995.

J.M. Smits, E.A.G. van Schagen, 'De Hoge Raad als Europese rechter: Mag het ietsje meer zijn?', in: A.G. Castermans et al. (eds.), *Het zwijgen van de Hoge Raad, BWKJ* 25, Deventer: Kluwer 2009, p. 84.

H.J.Snijders, 'Algemene beschouwingen bij het Wetsvoorstel Modernisering Arbitragerecht', *Tijdschrift voor Arbitrage* 2013, 31.

H.J. Snijders, 'Arbitrage en/of bindend advies bij de SGC', *TvC* 2011, p. 3.

H.J. Snijders, C.J.M. Klaassen, G.J. Meijer, *Nederlands burgerlijk procesrecht*, Deventer: Kluwer 2007, 4th ed.

A. Söllner, 'Grenzen des Tarifvertrags', *NZA* 1996, p. 902.

A. Spickhoff, 'Die Restkodifikation des Internationalen Privatrechts: Außervertragliches Schuld- und Sachenrecht ', *NJW* 1999, p. 2214.

J. Spier, 'Nogmaals het wetsontwerp algemene voorwaarden', *Kwartaalbericht Nieuw BW* 1985, p. 7.

J. Spier, 'Het wetsontwerp algemene voorwaarden: voor de praktijk funest', *Kwartaalbericht Nieuw BW* 1984, p. 130.

E. Stalhacke, 'Die Allgemeinverbindlicherklärung von Tarifverträgen über das Arbeitszeitende im Verkauf', *NZA* 1988, p. 346.

A. Staudinger, 'Zur Novellierung des Produkthaftungsgesetzes', *NJW* 2001, p. 275.

M.M. Stolp, J.F. de Groot, 'Een nieuwe procesvorm: Het stellen van prejudiciële vragen aan de Hoge Raad (art. 392-394 nieuw Rv)', *MvV* 2012, p. 165.

M. Storme, 'There is nothing like European private law twenty years later', *ERPL* 2012, p. 1.

M. Storme, 'The foundations of private law in a multilevel structure: Balancing, distribution of lawmaking power, and other constitutional issues', *ERPL* 2012, p. 249.

A.V.M. Struycken, 'Veelheid van rechtsbronnen: één IPR?', *AA* 1996, p. 68.

Study Group on Social Justice in European Private Law, 'Social justice in European contract law: A manifesto', *ELJ* 2004, p. 656.

J. Stürner, 'Der hundertste Geburtstag des BGB – nationale Kodifikation im Greisalter?', *JZ* 1996, p. 752.

R. Stürner, 'Empfiehlt sich die von der Schuldrechtskommission vorgeschlagene Neuregelung des allgemeinen Leistungsstörungsrechts, der Mängelhaftung bei Kauf- und Werkvertrag und des Rechts der Verjährung? – Versuch einer Themenpräsentation', *NJW*-Beilage 1994, p. 1.

R. Stürner, 'Zur Gleichsetzung von Notarformularen und allgemeinen Geschäftsbedingungen einer Vertragspartei', *JZ* 1979, p. 758.

J. Stuyck, 'The Court of Justice and the unfair commercial practice directive', *CMLRev* 2015, p. 749-750.

V.J.A. Süto, *Nieuw Vermogensrecht en rechtsvergelijking – reconstructie van een wetgevingsproces (1947-1961)*, The Hague: BJU 2004.

E. Svilpaite, *Self- and co-regulation instruments in the European legal framework*, August 2007, available at www.eu-newgov.org/database/DELIV/D04D69_Limits_of_self-regulation.pdf.

S. Symeonides, 'Codification and flexibility in private international law', *General reports to the XVIIIth Congress of the International Academy of Comparative Law/ Rapports*, 2011.

Ph. Syrpis, 'Legitimising European governance: Taking subsidiarity seriously within the Open Method of Coordination', *EUI Working Paper* 2002.

E. Szyszczak, 'Experimental governance: the Open Method of Coordination', *ELJ* 2006, p. 488.

B. Tamanaha, *The perils of pervasive legal instrumentalism*, Nijmegen: Wolf Legal Publishers 2006.

B.Z. Tamanaha, 'A non-essentialist view of legal pluralism', *Journal of Law and Society* 2000, p. 398.

J. Taupitz, *Die Standesordnungen der freien Berufe*, Berlin: De Gruyter 1991.

D.J. ten Boom, V.P. Reute, 'Gedragscode behandeling letselschade – commerciële of maatschappelijke business case?', available at www.stichtingpiv.nl/smartsite.dws?ch=TER&id=760550.

E. Terryn, 'The Green Paper on the review of the consumer *acquis*', *TvC* 2007, p. 108.

K. Teuben, *Rechtersregelingen in het (burgerlijk) procesrecht*, Deventer: Kluwer 2004.

G. Teubner, 'Globale Zivilverfassungen: Alternativen zur staatszentrierten Verfassungstheorie', *ZaöRV* 2003, p. 1.

G. Teubner, 'Legal Irritants: Good faith in British law or how unifying law ends up in new divergencies', *MLR* 1998, p. 11.

G. Teubner, 'Rethinking legal pluralism', *Cardozo Law Review* 1992, p. 1448.

G. Teubner, 'Substantive and reflexive elements in modern law', *Law & Society Review* 1983, p. 275.

W. Tilman, 'Das AGB-Gesetz und die Einheit des Privatrechts', *ZHR* 1978, p. 54.

R.P.J.L. Tjittes, 'Uitleg van schriftelijke contracten', *RM Themis* 2005, p. 1.

R.P.J.L. Tjittes, R. Meijer, 'Franse en Europese lessen voor een prejudiciële procedure bij de Hoge Raad', *RM Themis* 2009, p. 165.

TNS Infratest, *Online-Gütesiegel, Summary*, Berlin, 19 August 2005, available at www.trustedshops.de/shopbetreiber/pdf_download/tnsinfratest_studie.pdf.

K. Tonner, M. Tamm, 'Der Vorschlag einer Richtlinie über die Rechte der Verbraucher', *JZ* 2009, p. 277.

A. Torres Perez, *Conflict of rights in the European Union, A theory of supranational adjudication*, Oxford: OUP 2009, p. 67.

V. Triebel, S. Balthasar, 'Auslegung englischer Vertragstexte unter deutschem Vertragsstatut – Fallstricke des Art. 32 I Nr. 1 EGBGB', *NJW* 2004, p. 2193.

V. Trstenjak, E. Beysen, 'European consumer protection law: *Curia simper dabit remedium*?', *CMLR* 2011, p. 116.

V. Trstenjak, 'Die Auslegung privatrechtlicher Richtlinien durch den EuGH: Ein Rechtsprechungsbericht under Berücksichtigung des Common Frame of Reference', *ZEuP* 2007, p. 145.

D.M. Trubek, L.G. Trubek, 'Hard and soft law in the construction of social Europe: The role of the Open Method of Co-ordination', *ELJ* 2005, p. 350.

Ch. Twigg-Flesner, D. Metcalfe, 'The proposed consumer rights Directive – less haste, more thought?', *ERCL* 2011, p. 369.

K. Uffmann, 'Informationspflichten und ergänzende Auslegung bei Preisanpassung in Energielieferverträgen', *NJW* 2015, p. 1216.

P. Ulmer, 'Das AGB-Gesetz: Ein eigenständiges Kodifikationswerk', *JZ* 2001, p. 492.

P. Ulmer, 'Der AGB-Gesetz nach der Umsetzung der EG-Richtlinie über mißbräuchliche Klauseln in Verbraucherverträgen', in: P. Ulmer, U. Hübner, *Das Recht der Allgemeinen Geschäftsbedingungen nach der Umsetzung der EG-Richtlinie über mißbräuchliche Klauseln in Verbraucherverträgen, Karlsruher Forum 1997*, Karlsruhe: Versicherungswirtschaft 1998, p. 9.

P. Ulmer, 'Zur Anpassung des AGB-Gesetzes über mißbräuchliche Klauseln', *EuZW* 1993, p. 344.

P. Ulmer, 'Zehn Jahre AGB-Gesetz – Rückblick und Ausblick', in: H. Heinrichs, W. Löwe, P. Ulmer (eds.), *Zehn Jahre AGB-Gesetz*, Köln: Kommunikationsforum Recht 1987, p. 5.

H. Unberath, A. Johnston, 'The double-headed approach of the CJEU concerning consumer protection', 44 *CMLRev* 2007, p. 1283.

L. van Almelo (ed.), *Onze Grondwet: de rechtsstaat en de grondrechten verklaard voor nieuwe Nederlandse burgers*, The Hague: VNG 2003.

E.J.M. van Beukering-Rosmuller, 'Imprévision en zelfregulering', *NTBR* 2006, 2.

R. van Bijnen, *Aanvullend contractenrecht*, The Hague: BJU 2005.

W.H. van Boom, 'The Draft Directive on consumer rights: Choices made and arguments used', *Journal of Contemporary European Research* 2009, p. 457.

W.H. van Boom, *Efficacious enforcement in contract and tort*, The Hague: BJU 2006.

W.H. van Boom, 'Algemene en bijzondere regelingen in het vermogensrecht', *RM Themis* 2003, p. 298.

W.H. van Boom, S.D. Lindenbergh (eds.), *Politiek privaatrecht*, The Hague: BJU 2013.

R. van Caenegem, *Judges, legislators, and professors*, Cambridge: CUP 1987.

P.A.J. van den Berg, *Codificatie en staatsvorming. De politieke en politiek-theoretische actergronden van de codificatie van het privaatrecht in Pruisen, de Donaumonarchie, Frankrijk en Nederland, 1450–1811*, Groningen: Wolters-Noordhoff 1996

V. van den Eeckhout, 'Codificatie van het Nederlands ipr of het vastleggen van een nationaal navigatiesysteem voor internationale vliegroutes', *NTER* 2011, p. 10.

V. van den Eeckhout, 'The application of foreign law by judicial and non-judicial authorities – The Netherlands', via www.ssrn.com.

A.J.J. van der Heiden, 'De invloed van door een franchisegever verstrekte prognoses voorafgaand aan het sluiten van een franchiseovereenkomst', *Contracteren* 2002, p. 93.

T.J. van der Ploeg, 'Reglementen bij verenigingen; een duik in troebel water', *WPNR* 5929 (1989).

M. van Driel, *Zelfregulering: Hoog opspelen of thuisblijven*, Deventer: Kluwer 1989.

J.M. van Dunné, *Verbintenissenrecht: Onrechtmatige daad en overige verbintenissen*, Deventer: Kluwer 2004, 5th ed.

J.H.M. van Erp, 'De NVM-koopakte: géén algemene voorwaarden', *WPNR* 6190 (1995).

J.H.M. van Erp, 'Van onredelijk bezwarend naar oneerlijk, of: van Nederzwart en Nedergrijs naar Euroblauw', *WPNR* 6079 (1993).

W. van Gerven, S. Lierman, *Algemeen Deel, Veertig jaar later*, Mechelen: Kluwer 2010.

W. van Gerven, 'The CJEU case law as a means for the unification of private law?', in: A.S. Hartkamp, E.H. Hondius (eds.), *Towards a European Civil Code?*, Alphen aan den Rijn: KLI 2004, p. 118.

W. van Gerven, 'The Open Method of Convergence', *Juridica International* 2008, p. 40.

W. van Gerven, 'Codifying European private law? Yes, if ...!', *ELR* 2002, p. 174.

R.A.J. van Gestel, H.-W. Micklitz, 'European integration through standardization', *CMLRev* 2013, p. 151.

S. van Gulick, 'Derdenwerking van exoneratiebedingen: een analyse van recente rechtspraak en enige opmerkingen over de ontwikkeling van dit leerstuk vanuit het bouwcontractenrecht', *WPNR* (7057) 2015.

S.S. van Kampen, I. Giesen, 'Prejudiciële vragen aan de Hoge Raad, valkuilen voor de Hoge Raad', *TCR* 2013, p. 1.

E.S. van Nimwegen, 'Handhaving door de Consumentenautoriteit: een goed samenspel met het Burgerlijk Wetboek en Europese regelgeving?', *Contracteren* 2010, p. 57.

E.A.G. van Schagen, 'The proposal for a Common European Sales Law: How its drafting process might affect the optional instrument's added value and its success', in: A.L.M. Keirse, M.B.M. Loos (red.), *Alternative ways to a ius commune*, Antwerp: Intersentia 2012, p. 85–109.

E.A.G. van Schagen, 'More consistency and legal certainty in the private law *acquis*: A plea for better justification or harmonisation of private law', *MJ* 2012, p. 37.

E.A.G. van Schagen, 'The Draft Common Frame of Reference and multilevel governance', *Edinburgh Student Law Review* 2010, p. 74.

G.J. van Solinge, R. Nowak, 'Een krabbend anker', *WPNR* 6563 (2004).

T.H.M. van Wechem, *De toepasselijkheid van algemene voorwaarden*, Deventer: Kluwer 2007.

T.H.M. van Wechem, J.H.M. Spanjaard, 'De toepasselijkheid van algemene voorwaarden onder het Weens Koopverdrag: Nieuwe trend in de Nederlandse (lagere) rechtspraak?', *Contracteren* 2010, p. 35.

T.H.M. van Wechem, J.H.M. Spanjaard, S.A. Kruisinga, 'Een bespreking van CISG Advisory Council opinion no 13 inclusion of standard contract terms under the CISG', *NTHR* 2013, p. 267.

B. van Zelst, *The politics of European Sales Law*, Alphen aan den Rijn: KLI 2008.

C. Vendrell Cervantes, 'The application of the Principles of European Contract Law by Spanish Courts', *ZEuP* 2008, p. 534.

A.J. Verdaas, 'Wetgever, besteed meer aandacht aan ons vermogensrecht! Een oproep tot het instellen van een permanente Commissie vermogensrecht', *NTBR* 2010, 47.

A.J. Verheij, 'Wie is verantwoordelijk voor hanteerbaar privaatrecht?', in A.L.M. Keirse et al. (eds.), *Beter Burgerlijk Recht*, Deventer: Kluwer 2012, p. 179.

F.M.J. Verstijlen, 'Hoe om te gaan met "omgaan"?, *TvI* 2015/27.

F.M.J. Verstijlen, 'Alles (te) rustig aan het wetgevingsfront', *TvI* 2011, 12.

J. Vickers, 'The problem of induction', *Stanford Encyclopedia of Philosophy*, accessible at http://plato.stanford.edu/entries/induction-problem/.

K. Vieweg, *Normsetzung und -anwendung deutscher und internationaler Verbände*, Berlin: Duncker & Humblot 1990.

C.M.H. Vlaanderen, 'Over (on)bekendheidsverklaringen en conformiteit in de NVM-koopakte', *WPNR* 6410 (2000).

H.M. Vletter- van Dort, 'Horen, zien en luisteren', *Ondernemingsrecht* 2011, 73.

S. Vogenauer, 'Common Frame of Reference and UNIDROIT Principles of International Commercial Contracts: Coexistence, competition, or overkill of soft law?', *ERCL* 2010, p. 143.

S. Vogenauer, 'Regulatory competition through choice of contract law and choice of forum in Europe: Theory and evidence', *ERPL* 2013, p. 6.

J.E. Vollebregt, 'Wetsonwerp algemene voorwaarden', *NJB* 1984, p. 813.

Ch. von Bar, 'Coverage and structure of the Academic Frame of Reference', *ERCL* 2007, p. 354.

Ch. Von Bar et al (eds.), *Principles, Definitions and Model Rules of European Private Law. Draft Common Frame of Reference, Outline Edition*, München: Sellier 2009, p. 83.

Ch. Von Bar et al (eds.), *Principles, Definitions and Model Rules of European Private Law. Draft Common Frame of Reference, Outline Edition, Volume I*, München: Sellier 2009.

Ch. Von Bar et al (eds.), *Principles, Definitions and Model Rules of European Private Law. Draft Common Frame of Reference, Full edition* 2008, available at http://ec.europa.eu/justice/contract/files/european-private-law_en.pdf.

A. von Bogdandy, S. Schill, 'Overcoming absolute primacy: Respect for national identity under the Lisbon Treaty', *CLMRev* 2011, p. 1433.

E. Von Hippel, 'Der Schutz des Verbrauchers vor unlauteren Allgemeinen Geschäftsbedingungen in den EG-Staaten', *RabelsZ* 1977, p. 244.

C.F. von Savigny, *System des heutigen römischen Rechts, I*, Berlin: Veit 1840.

J.B.M. Vranken, 'Taken van de Hoge Raad en zijn parket in 2025', in: I. Giesen, A.M. Hol, (eds.), *De Hoge Raad in 2025: Contouren van de toekomstige cassatierechtspraak*, The Hague: BJU 2011, p. 29.

J.B.M. Vranken, 'Niets in het recht is blijvend, behalve verandering', *WPNR* 6560 (2004).

J.B.M. Vranken, 'Over partijautonomie, contractsvrijheid en de grondslag van gebondenheid in het verbintenissenrecht', in: J.M. Barendrecht, M.A.B. Chao-Duivis, B.W.M. Nieskens-Isphording (eds.), *Beginselen van het contractenrecht*, Deventer: Tjeenk Willink, 2000.

J.B.M. Vranken, 'Vertrouwen en rechtszekerheid in het overeenkomstenrecht', in: *Vertrouwensbeginsel en rechtszekerheid in Nederland*, Deventer: Tjeenk Willink 1997, p. 1.

J.B.M. Vranken, 'De hercodificatie van het verbintenissenrecht in de Bondsrepubliek Duitsland', *NJB* 1985, p. 769.

H. Vuye, 'Communautaire pacificatie in België: is de grens bereikt?', *AA* 2008, p. 797.

H. Vuye, 'België: Een staat in hervorming of in ontbinding', *AA* 2008, p. 719.

U. Wackerbarth, 'Unternehmer, Verbraucher, und die Rechtfertigung der Inhaltskontrolle vorformulierter Verträge', *AcP* 2000, p. 57.

G. Wagner, 'The virtues of diversity in European private law', in: J.M. Smits (ed.), *The need for a European contract law*, Groningen: ELP 2005, p. 17.

J. Waldon, 'Positivism and legality: Hart's equivocal response to Fuller', *New York University Law Review* 2008, p. 1135.

N. Walker, 'The idea of constitutional pluralism', *MLR* 2002, p. 317.

J.H. Wansink, 'Het KIFID en vervalbedingen: Verval van recht of recht in verval?', *AV & S* 2011, 17.

R. Waltermann, *Rechtsetzung durch Betriebsvereinbarung zwischen Privatautonomie und Tarifautonomie*, Tübingen: Mohr Siebeck 1996.

A. Watson, 'Legal Transplants and European Private Law', *Electronic Journal of Comparative Law* 2000, available at www.ejcl.org/ejcl/44/44-2.html.

A. Watson, *Legal transplants*, Edinburgh: Scottish Acdemic Press 1974

S. Weatherill, 'The limits of legislative harmonization ten years after Tobacco Advertising: How the Court's case law has become a drafting guide', *German Law Journal* 2011, p. 827.

S. Weatherill, 'The "principles of civil law" as a basis for interpreting the legislative *acquis*', *ERCL* 2010, p. 77.

S. Weatherill, 'Measures of consumer protection as impediments to export of goods', *ECRL* 2009, p. 153.

S. Weatherill, 'Can there be common interpretation of European private law?', *Georgia Journal of International and Comparative Law* 2002, p. 164.

J.H.H. Weiler, 'The transformation of Europe', *Yale Law Journal* 1991, p.2403.

B.R. Weingast, 'The economic role of political institutions: Market preserving federalism and economic development', *Journal of Law, Economics and Organization* 1995, p. 6

T. Weir, 'Difficulties in transposing Directives', *ZEuP* 2004, p. 614.

B. Wessels, 'Collectief actierecht komt moeizaam tot bloei', *WPNR* 6249 (1996).

B. Wessels, 'Reflexies bij reflexwerking'. *WPNR* 6240 (1996).

B. Wessels, 'Drie vuistregels voor de uitleg van algemene voorwaarden', *WPNR* 6239 (1996).

H.P. Westermann, 'Verbraucherschutz', in: Bundesminister der Justiz (ed.), *Gutachten und Vorschläge zur Überarbeitung des Schuldrechts*, Vol. III, Köln: Bundesanzeiger 1983, p. 74.

W.C.T. Weterings, *Efficiëntere en effectievere afwikkeling van letselschadeclaims*, The Hague: BJU 2004.

S. Whittaker, 'The Optional Instrument of European contract law and freedom of contract', *ERCL* 2011, p. 387.

S. Whittaker, 'On the development of European standard contract terms', *ERCL* 2006, p. 54.

S. Whittaker, 'Assessing the fairness of contract terms: The parties' "essential bargain", its regulatory context and the significance of the requirement of good faith ', *ZEuP* 2004, p. 75.

S. Whittaker, K. Riesenhuber, 'Conceptions of contract', in: G. Danneman, S. Vogenauer (eds.), *The Common European Sales Law in context*, Oxford: OUP 2013, p. 123.

G.J. Wiarda, *Drie typen van rechtsvinding* (comments from T. Koopmans), Deventer: Tjeenk Willink 1999, 4th ed.

R.M. Wibier, 'De Hoge Raad op drift?', *WPNR* (7046) 2015.

J.C. Wichard, "Die Anwendung der UNIDROIT-Prinzipien für internationale Handelsverträge durch Schiedsgerichte und staatliche Gerichte', *RabelsZ* 1996, p. 269.

F. Wieacker, 'Aufstieg, Blute und Krisis der Kodifikationsidee', in: G. Boehmer (ed.), *Festschrift für Gustav Boehmer*, Bonn: Roerscheid 1954, p. 34.

H. Wiedemann, 'Normsetzung durch Vertrag', in: P. Hanau, F. Heither, J. Kühling (eds.), *Richterliches Arbeitsrecht, Festschrift für Thomas Dieterich*, München: Beck 1999, p. 661.

H. Wiedemann, 'Rechtssicherheit - ein absoluter Wert?' in: G. Paulus, U. Diederichsen, C.-W. Canaris (eds.), *Festschrift für Karl Larenz zum 70. Geburtstag*, München: Beck 1973, p. 199.

W. Wilburg, *The development of a flexible system in the area of private law* (inaugural address Graz, 1950), Vienna: Manzsches Verlag- und Universitätsbuchhandlung 2000, (translation from H. Hausmaninger).

T. Wilhelmsson, 'Private law in Europe: harmonised or fragmented Europeanisation?', *ERPL* 2002, p. 77.

J.W. Winter, 'Corporate governance en wat het recht niet vermag', *AA* 2012, p. 416.

J.W. Winter, 'Oorlog en vrede', *Ondernemingsrecht* 1999, p. 203.

L.J. Wintgens, 'Zeker weten? Enkele rechtsfilosofische en rechtstheoretische opmerkingen over rechtszekerheid', *RW* 1993–94, p. 1077.

W.H. Wissink, *Richtlijnconforme interpretatie van burgerlijk recht*, Deventer: Kluwer 2001.

W.J. Witteveen, 'Laws of lawmaking', in: W.J. Witteveen, W. Van der Burg (eds.) *Rediscovering Fuller*, Amsterdam: Amsterdam University Press 1999, p. 328.

S. Whittaker, 'On the development of European standard contract terms', *ERCL* 2006, p. 60.

A. Wolf, 'Die Überarbeitung des Schuldrechts', *AcP* 1982, p. 80.

M. Wolf, 'Vertragsfreiheit und Vertragsrecht im Lichte des AGB-Rechtsprechung des BGH', in: C.-W. Canaris et al (eds.), *50 Jahre Bundesgerichtshof, Festgabe aus der Wissenschaft, I*, München: Beck p. 123.

M. Wolf, 'Auslegung und Inhaltskontrolle von AGB im internationalen kaufmännischen Verkehr', *ZHR* 1989, p. 312.

M. Wolf, *Rechtsgeschäftliche Entscheidungsfreiheit und vertraglicher Interessenausgleich*, Tübingen: Mohr Siebeck 1970.

I. Wolff, *Die Verteilung der Konkretisierungskompetenz für Generalklauseln in privatrechtsgestaltenden Richtlinien*, Baden Baden: Nomos 2002.

P.T.J. Wolters, 'De strikken van de redelijkheid en billijkheid', *WPNR* (7045) 2015.

S. Worthington, 'The unique charm of the common law', *ERPL* 2011, p. 348.

Lord Wright, 'Precedents', *Cambridge Law Journal* 1944, p. 133.

L. Zabel, 'Die Anforderungen an Preisanpassungsklauseln in Gas- und Fernwärmelieferverträgen', *KommJur* 2011, p. 269.

U. Zachert, '"Jenseits des Tarifvertrags"? - Sonstige Kollektivvereinbarungen der Koalitionen', *NZA* 2006, p. 10.

J. Zekoll, 'Das American Law Institute - ein Vorbild für Europa?', in: R. Zimmerman (ed.), *Globalisierung und Entstaatlichung des Rechts, Teilband II, Nichtstaatliches Privatrecht: Geltung und Genese*, Tübingen: Mohr Siebeck 2008, p.113.

R. Zimmerman, '"Wissenschaftliches Recht" am Beispiel (vor allem) des europäischen Vertragsrechts', in C. Bumke, A. Röthel (eds.), *Privates Recht*, Tübingen: Mohr Siebeck 2012, p. 21.

R. Zimmerman, 'Europäisches Privatrecht - Irrungen, Wirtungen', in: Professorinnen und Professoren der Bucerius Law School (eds.), *Begegnungen im Recht, Ringvorlesung der Bucerius Law School zu Ehren von Karsten Schmidt anlässlich seines 70. Geburtstags*, Tübingen: Mohr Siebeck 2011, p. 321.

R. Zimmerman, 'Reflections on a European Law Institute - based on the proceedings of the Florence Conference', *ZEuP* 2010, p. 721.

R. Zimmerman, 'The current state of European private law', *American Journal of Comparative Law* 2009, p. 479

R. Zimmerman, 'Textstufen in der modernen Entwicklung des europäischen privatrechts', *EuZW* 2009, p. 319.

R. Zimmerman, 'The Principles of European Contract law Contemporary manifestation of the old, and possible foundation for a new, European scholarship of private law', in: F. Faust, G. Thüsing (eds.), *Beyond borders: perspectives on international and comparative law*, Berlin: Carl Heymanns Verlag 2006, p. 145.

R. Zimmerman, *The new German law of obligations, Historical and comparative perspectives*, Oxford: OUP 2005.

R. Zimmerman, 'Characteristic aspects of German legal culture', in: J. Zekoll, M. Reimann (eds.), *Introduction to German law*, The Hague: KLI 2005, p. 17.

R. Zimmerman, 'Schuldrechtsreform?', in W. Ernst, R. Zimmerman (eds.), *Zivilrechtswissenschaft und Schuldrechtsreform*, Tübingen: Mohr Siebeck 2001, p. 15–16.

R. Zimmerman, 'Codification: History and present significance of an idea', *ERPL* 1995, p. 114.

R. Zimmerman, 'Konturen einer Europäischen Vertragsrechts', *JZ* 1995, p. 491.
R. Zimmerman, 'Das Römisch-Kanonische Ius commune als Grundlage europäischer Rechtseinheit', *JZ* 1992, p. 8.
R. Zimmerman, N. Jansen, 'Contract formation and mistake in European contract law: A genetic comparison of transnational model rules', *OJLS* 2011, p. 1.
R. Zimmerman, N. Jansen, '"A European Civil Code in all but name": Discussing the nature and purposes of the Draft Common Frame of Reference', *CLJ* 2010, p. 98.
W.J. Zwalve, 'Regelgeving in het vermogensrecht', *RM Themis* 2009, p. 20.
A.J.C. Zwinkels, 'Productveiligheid en -aansprakelijkheid. Ervaringen van de Consumentenbond', *TvC* 1998, p. 316.

IUS COMMUNE EUROPAEUM

A peer-reviewed book series in which the common foundations of the legal systems of the Member States of the European Union are the central focus.

The *Ius Commune Europaeum* series includes horizontal comparative legal studies as well as studies on the effect of treaties within the national legal systems. All the classic fields of law are covered. The books are published in various European languages under the auspices of METRO, the Institute for Transnational Legal Research at Maastricht University.

Recently published:
Volume 130: *Legal Aid in the Low Countries*, B. Hubeau and A. Terlouw (eds.)
Volume 131: *State Aid and Public Procurement in the European Union*, S. Schoenmaekers, W. Devroe and N. Philipsen (eds.)
Volume 132: *Property Law Perspectives III*, A. Apers, S. Bouly et al. (eds.)
Volume 133: *Multi-Party Redress Mechanisms in Europe: Squeaking Mice?*, V. Harsági and C.H. van Rhee (eds.)
Volume 134: *Europe at the Edge of Pluralism*, D. Gozdecka and M. Kmak
Volume 135: *Cooperative Agreements between Public Authorities. The Influence of CJEU Case Law on National Legal Systems*, K. Wauters
Volume 136: *Common Core, PECL and DCFR: Could They Change Shipping and Transport Law?*, W. Verheyen, F.G.M. Smeele and M.A.I.H. Hoeks
Volume 137: *Who does What? On the Allocation of Competences in European Private Law*, B. Akkermans, J. Hage, N. Kornet and J.M. Smits
Volume 138: *The Nature of Mutual Recognition in European Law*. W. van Ballegooij
Volume 139: *Evidence in Contemporary Civil Procedure. Fundamental Issues in a Comparative Perspective*, C.H. van Rhee and A. Uzelac (eds.)
Volume 140: *The effect of D&O insurance on managerial risk taking*, Max Gaber
Volume 141: *Information and Notification Duties*, Ilse Samoy and Marco B. Loos
Volume 142: *The Application of the Theory of Efficient Breach in Contract Law. A Comparative Law and Economics Perspective*, Wenqing Liao
Volume 143: *A European Legal Framework for Nuclear Liability. Rethinking Current Approaches*, Tobias Heldt

www.ingramcontent.com/pod-product-compliance
Ingram Content Group UK Ltd.
Pitfield, Milton Keynes, MK11 3LW, UK
UKHW051924100926
8556IPUK00022B/1363

9 781780 683676